Psychology's Roots

The first laboratory dedicated to the new science of psychology was founded by Wilhelm Wundt at the University of Leipzig in Germany in 1879. But psychology's roots go back further than that. Philosophers and scientists have long been interested in understanding how the mind works. Early schools of thought like structuralism and functionalism developed into contemporary perspectives, each distinguished by different areas of emphasis, and prompting different kinds of questions.

BIOPSYCHOSOCIAL PERSPECTIVE
Examine the biological, psychological, and sociocultural factors influencing behavior.

HUMANISTIC PERSPECTIVE
Maintain an optimistic focus on human behavior; believe that each person is a master of his own fate.

 Carl Rogers 1902–1987

Abraham Maslow 1908–1970

SOCIOCULTURAL PERSPECTIVE

 Mamie Phipps Clark 1917–1983

 Lev Vygotsky 1896–1934

Understand behavior by examining influences of other people and the larger culture.

What biological, psychological, and social factors influence the way I manage my allergy to tree pollen?

PSYCHOANALYTIC PERSPECTIVE

 Sigmund Freud 1856–1939

Interested in abnormal functioning and unconscious thought; personality is shaped by unconscious conflict.

Will tending to and nurturing this tree help me reach my fullest potential?

How do cultures differ in their attitudes toward nature?

Charles Darwin 1809–1882

EVOLUTIONARY PERSPECTIVE
Use knowledge about evolutionary forces to understand behavior.

How do your feelings about the size of this tree relate to your unconscious aggression toward your father?

BEHAVIORAL PERSPECTIVE

 B. F. Skinner 1904–1990

Ivan Pavlov 1849–1936

John Watson 1878–1958

Interested in studying only behavior that can be observed and measured.

COGNITIVE PERSPECTIVE

 George Miller 1920–2012

Renewed focus on mental processes, including physiological explanations.

Is my fear of heights inherited? Could it have contributed to my survival?

Is spending time relaxing under this tree reinforced? If yes, I will come back again.

How am I able to remember where this tree is in the forest?

STRUCTURALISM

 Edward Titchener 1867–1927

Used reports of subjective experience (introspection) to describe the structure of the mind.

 Margaret Floy Washburn 1871–1939

BIOLOGICAL PERSPECTIVE
Use knowledge about underlying physiology to explain behavior and mental processes.

FUNCTIONALISM

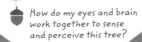 Mary Whiton Calkins 1863–1930

William James 1842–1910

Interested in how the mind functions to help us adapt and survive.

How do my eyes and brain work together to sense and perceive this tree?

Describe in detail each element of this tree, including color, shape, size, etc.

 Wilhelm Wundt (1832–1920), "Father of Psychology," founded the first laboratory dedicated to psychology.

How does resting under this tree promote my long-term survival?

PHILOSOPHICAL AND SCIENTIFIC ROOTS

 Plato 427–347 BCE

 Aristotle 384–322 BCE

 Descartes 1596–1650

 Gustav Fechner 1801–1887

Ancient and modern philosophers and scientists explored the connection between mind and body.

Does this tree exist in the physical world or only in my mind?

PSYCHOLOGY

Second Edition

PSYCHOLOGY

Deborah M. Licht
Pikes Peak Community College
Colorado

Misty G. Hull
Pikes Peak Community College
Colorado

Coco Ballantyne

· A PARTNERSHIP BETWEEN ·
worth publishers
Macmillan Learning
SCIENTIFIC
AMERICAN.

worth publishers
Macmillan Learning
New York

Vice President, Social Sciences and High School: Charles Linsmeier

Executive Acquisitions Editor: Daniel McDonough

Assistant Editor: Kimberly Morgan-Smith

Developmental Editors: Burrston House, Mimi Melek

Senior Marketing Manager: Lindsay Johnson

Executive Media Editor: Noel Hohnstine

Media Editors: Anthony Casciano, Lauren Samuelson

Media Editorial Assistant: Nik Toner

Media Producer: Eve Conte

Director, Content Management Enhancement: Tracey Kuehn

Managing Editor, Sciences and Social Sciences: Lisa Kinne

Senior Production Supervisor: Sarah Segal

Senior Project Editor: Elizabeth Geller

Director of Design, Content Management: Diana Blume

Art Manager: Matthew McAdams

Senior Photo Editor: Cecilia Varas

Photo Researcher: Jacqui Wong

Cover and Text Designer: Blake Logan

Layout Designer: Sheridan Sellers

Infographic Designer: DeMarinis Design LLC

Infographic Illustrator: Anne DeMarinis

Illustrations: Todd Buck, Evelyn Pence, Eli Ensor

Printing and Binding: LSC Communications

Cover Photo: Emily Weiss Photography

Cover Illustrations on Book Pages: Evelyn Pence

Icon of Figures around Table (cover and text): Browndogstudios/Getty Images

Library of Congress Control Number: 2016959422

Paperback:

ISBN-13: 978-1-4641-9949-3

ISBN-10: 1-4641-9949-3

Loose-leaf:

ISBN-13: 978-1-319-06702-1

ISBN-10: 1-319-06702-6

Worth Publishers

One New York Plaza

Suite 4500

New York, NY 10004-1562

www.macmillanlearning.com

To the instructors and students across the country whose feedback guided the revision of this book. Your insights and support have been invaluable.

about the authors

Edee Chesire.

Steve Hull.

Kevin Luker.

Deborah Licht Deborah Licht is a professor of psychology at Pikes Peak Community College in Colorado Springs, Colorado. She received a BS in psychology from Wright State University, Dayton, Ohio; a MS in clinical psychology from the University of Dayton; and a PhD in psychology (experimental psychopathology) from Harvard University. She has over two decades of teaching and research experience in a variety of settings, ranging from a small private university in the Midwest to a large public university in Copenhagen, Denmark. Deborah has taught introductory psychology, psychology of the workplace, abnormal psychology, the history of psychology, child development, and elementary statistics, in traditional, online, and hybrid courses. Working with community college students for over a decade has been very inspiring to Deborah; the great majority of students who attend community colleges often must overcome many challenges in pursuit of their dreams. Deborah continues to be interested in research on causal beliefs, particularly in relation to how college students think about their successes and failures as they pursue their degrees.

Misty Hull Misty Hull is a professor of psychology at Pikes Peak Community College in Colorado Springs, Colorado. She has taught a range of psychology courses at Pikes Peak Community College, including introductory psychology, human sexuality, and social psychology in a variety of delivery formats (traditional, online, and hybrid). Her love of teaching comes through in her dedication to mentoring new and part-time faculty in the teaching of psychology. She received her BS in human development and family studies from Texas Tech University in Lubbock, Texas, and an MA in professional counseling at Colorado Christian University in Lakewood, Colorado. Misty has held a variety of administrative roles at Pikes Peak Community College, including as interim associate dean and coordinator of the Student Crisis Counseling Office. In addition, she served as the state psychology discipline chair of the Colorado Community College System from 2002 to 2010. One of her many professional interests is research on the impact of student persistence in higher education.

Coco Ballantyne Coco Ballantyne is a New York–based journalist and science writer with a special interest in psychology. Before collaborating with Misty Hull and Deborah Licht on *Scientific American: Psychology* and *Scientific American: Presenting Psychology*, Coco worked as a reporter for *Scientific American* online, covering the health, medicine, and neuroscience beats. She has also written for *Discover* magazine and *Nature Medicine*. Coco earned an MS from the Columbia University School of Journalism, where she received a Horgan Prize for Excellence in Critical Science Writing. Prior to her journalistic career, Coco worked as a teacher and tutor, helping high school and college students prepare for standardized tests such as the SAT, GRE, and MCAT. She also worked as a physics and math teacher at Eastside College Preparatory School in East Palo Alto, California, and as a Human Biology course associate at Stanford University, where she earned a BA in human biology.

brief contents

contents

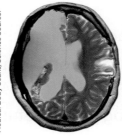

Patrick Foto/Getty Images.

Garo/Phanie/Superstock.

Kiko Jimenez/Shutterstock.

Thomas Deerinck, NCMIR/
Science Source.

Medical Body Scans/
Science Source.

CHAPTER 8 human development 327

Mel Yates/Getty Images.

CHAPTER 9 motivation and emotion 377

Jump Run Productions/Getty Images.

BSIP SA/Alamy.

James Whitlow Delano/Redux.

Philip Lee Harvey/Getty Images.

Ascent Xmedia/Getty Images.

CHAPTER 14 treatment of psychological disorders   577

CHAPTER 15 social psychology   619

preface

This is *your* book

When we set out to write the first edition of *Scientific American: Psychology,* our goal was to combine practical, classroom experience with the best science writing—to create an innovative introductory psychology textbook that students would truly want to read. The first edition was more successful than we had ever imagined; it was rewarding to discover that both instructors and students embraced our approach. While the positive feedback has been encouraging, we realize that our work is just beginning. There are always opportunities to learn and grow, and to better serve our readers.

The first edition of *Scientific American: Psychology* has been formally reviewed by over 1,000 instructors and students around the country. Drawing from their feedback, our own experience in the classroom, and extensive research by the publisher, we have refined and updated our product to meet your needs. The pedagogy has been fine-tuned, the research updated, and new high-interest case studies and examples integrated throughout. We have also improved and expanded the technology for delivering and reinforcing our content. It is our pleasure to present you with this fresh and enhanced edition of *Scientific American: Psychology.*

We get it: the challenges of teaching intro psych students

We are instructors, so we understand the joys and difficulties associated with teaching introductory psychology. Many of today's students are struggling to balance school, family, and careers; reading their textbook may not be a top priority. Just getting students to come to class prepared and ready to learn can be a major challenge. With this in mind, we have worked to remove as many barriers as possible, creating a textbook experience that maximizes reading interest and efficiency without compromising depth and breadth of content. The second edition of *Scientific American: Psychology* is designed to engage the hardest-to-reach students, but also stimulate those who need to be challenged.

It's all about solving problems: 10 challenges we address

What are the greatest obstacles to student learning? For years we have been discussing this question with our colleagues, and for years the publisher has been researching it. This book was created to address the issues identified as most troublesome in the introductory psychology classroom. Let's take a look at how we tackle them.

1. Creating relevance and student engagement

Students learn and remember material better when they see how it applies to personal experience, world events, and cultural phenomena. We draw students in by exploring topical issues such as sports-related head injuries and global warming, often by way of *Integrated Thematic Features*. These features, all of which explore key themes in psychology, are seamlessly incorporated into the running text (not relegated to "boxes" that your students will skip over). We use small labels to identify the features so that they are recognized, but not set apart. *Scientific American: Psychology,* Second Edition, includes the following integrated thematic features:

 ACROSS THE WORLD Focuses on cross-cultural studies, highlighting salient findings on behavior variation across cultures.

 CONTROVERSIES Examines debates over contemporary research and provocative issues in the psychological community.

 DIDN'T SEE THAT COMING Presents unexpected, high-interest, and newsworthy developments related to the chapter's focus.

 NATURE AND NURTURE Explores studies on twins, genetics, heritability, and other topics related to the complex dynamic between nature and nurture.

 SOCIAL MEDIA AND PSYCHOLOGY Highlights contemporary research exploring how social media applications, such as Facebook, Instagram, and Twitter, impact behaviors, thoughts, and emotions.

 THINK IT THROUGH Challenges students to hone their critical thinking skills by evaluating the strengths and limitations of research.

 THINK POSITIVE (new feature) Shines the spotlight on psychology's more uplifting findings, offering information intended to help students increase their happiness and well-being.

Integrated thematic features are just one way to increase relevance and student engagement; we also appreciate the impact of visual content. The chapter narratives are interspersed with thought-provoking photos, figures, and 52 full-page *Infographics* that primarily focus on presenting the hardest-to-teach topics in an engaging and relevant context—a direct response to our research with students.

Another source of variety (and thus engagement) is our new *In Class: Collaborate and Report* feature, which prompts students to apply material and generate new ideas in small groups. This feature was created in response to instructors' requests for more active learning exercises and recent research confirming the impact of this type of learning tool on concept understanding and retention. In our own classrooms, we have noted that the use of these "learning by doing" tools is very effective and has become increasingly popular.

Another key ticket to student engagement, and perhaps in this regard the most defining feature of our text, is the *Integrated Story* and how we utilize it. Every chapter contains one or two stories of real people whose experiences help us understand and apply psychology to real life—but, very importantly, note that our pedagogical use of this resource is unique. Unlike the isolated case studies and opening vignettes commonly seen in other textbooks, our stories are written in a journalistic style and *woven throughout* the chapters, offering memorable examples that reinforce important concepts at key intervals. And when we say journalistic style, we really mean it. The majority of the chapter stories are based on direct interviews with subjects—not simply background information gathered from secondary sources. The questions used in the interviews were designed to gather information that reinforces chapter concepts.

The profile subjects featured in the stories were carefully researched and selected to represent people from all walks of life, providing a diverse mosaic of gender, culture, race, age, nationality, and occupation. Students will read about identical twins separated at birth and reunited in middle age, an Olympic athlete and devoted humanitarian, the "dog whisperer" Cesar Millan, and many other fascinating people. Our goal is for every student to see aspects of him- or herself in the stories presented in this book, and to convey our strong sense of optimism and hope. Most chapters feature ordinary people who encounter difficult circumstances but persevere and grow nonetheless.

An Introduction to Learning

BEFORE HE WAS THE DOG WHISPERER   December 23, 1990: Cesar Millan had made up his mind; it was time to leave Mexico and start a new life in America. He was 21 years old, spoke no English, and had exactly $100 in his pocket. Since the age of 13, Cesar had dreamed of becoming the greatest dog trainer in the world. Now he was ready to pursue that goal, even if it meant saying goodbye to everything he knew and cherished—his family, his homeland, and his culture (Millan & Peltier, 2006).

From his home in Mazatlan, Cesar traveled to the dangerous border city of Tijuana, where he spent two weeks sleeping in the back of a nightclub. After three unsuccessful attempts crossing the border on his own, Cesar met a human smuggler, or "coyote," who said he would get him into the United States for a fee of—you guessed it—$100. Trudging over muddy terrain, darting across a busy freeway, and hiding in

Every chapter features a custom *Online Video Profile* associated with its integrated story. The video profiles are *free* to all students and include segments titled "In Their Own Words" and "You Asked, They Answered," which tell the subject's story and engage students on a personal level. Assessable versions may be found in LaunchPad and incorporate thoughtful questions that tighten the link between the video and the chapter content, creating a more relevant and memorable learning experience.

Cesar, in His Own Words

http://qrs.ly/ae5a5au

2. Demonstrating psychology is a science

In the first few pages of Chapter 1, we establish that psychology is rigorous science, detailing the steps of the scientific method and emphasizing the importance of critical thinking. We continue to drive home this essential message throughout the book, dispelling common psychological myths and encouraging students to evaluate research claims presented in our *Controversies* and *Think It Through* features, which address topics as diverse as polygraphs ("lie detectors") and pheromones.

Our partnership with the highly respected publication *Scientific American* tacitly reinforces the notion that psychology is a science. Equally important, it provides us with the opportunity to feature the work of leading science journalists. Every chapter includes a *From the Pages of Scientific American* feature that relates impactful research in the field.

from the pages of SCIENTIFIC AMERICAN

Fake Weed, Real Crisis

Synthetic cannabinoids are cheap, widespread, hard to track and highly toxic.

When powerful street drugs collectively known as synthetic pot are smoked, the resulting high mimics the effects of marijuana. Yet these man-made cannabinoids are not marijuana at all. The drugs, more commonly called spice, fake weed or K2, are made up of any number of dried, shredded plants sprayed with chemicals that live in a murky legality zone. They are highly dangerous—and their use is on the rise.

Synthetic pot, which first hit the market in the early 2000s, has especially caught the attention of public health officials in the past couple of years, stemming from a surge in hospitalizations and violent episodes. Although the drugs act on the same brain pathway as weed's active ingredient, they can trigger harsher reactions, including heart attacks, strokes, kidney damage and delusions. Between June and early August usage of these drugs led to roughly 2,300 emergency room visits in New York State alone. Nationwide more than 6,000 incidents involving spice have been reported to U.S. poison-control centers this year—about double the number of calls in 2013.

3. Helping students see the "big picture"

To help students see that topics in different chapters are conceptually linked, we have strategically placed *Connections* features in the margins. Considerably more detailed than typical cross-references, these brief summaries complement what many instructors do in the classroom—point out the relationships between topics currently being presented and material previously covered. Many students won't automatically make a connection between perception and memory, or see how transference might relate to obedience, but the Connections spell it out without requiring them to return to the original discussion of the linked topic. And our *Test Bank* includes assessment questions directly related to these links.

clocks, known as the *suprachiasmatic nucleus (SCN)*, actually consists of two clusters, each no bigger than an ant, totaling around 20,000 neurons (Bedrosian, Fonken, & Nelson, 2016; Forger & Peskin, 2003; Wright, 2002). The SCN plays a role in our circadian rhythm by communicating with other areas of the hypothalamus, which regulates daily patterns of hunger and temperature, and the reticular formation, which regulates alertness and sleepiness (**INFOGRAPHIC 4.1** on the next page).

Although tucked away in the recesses of the brain, the SCN knows the difference between day and night by receiving signals from a special type of light-sensing cells in the eye, called *retinal ganglion cells*. One way the SCN keeps you on schedule is by indirectly communicating with the pineal gland, a part of the endocrine system, to regulate the release of *melatonin*, a hormone that promotes sleep (Bedrosian et al.,

CONNECTIONS

In **Chapter 3,** we described how light enters the eye and is directed to the retina. The rods and cones in the retina are photoreceptors, which absorb light energy and turn it into electrical and chemical signals. Here, we see how light-sensing cells relay information to the SCN.

4. Teaching and mastering the toughest concepts

We understand that difficult concepts require multiple examples underscoring connections with everyday life; we also know that students benefit from expanded assessment opportunities. But sometimes more examples and intensive assessment are not enough; in order for things to really "click," a student must see the information presented in a new light. This is the purpose of the 50-plus Infographics interspersed throughout the chapters. Patterned after the visual features in *Scientific American*, these full-page visual presentations combine concepts and/or data into a single storyboard format. The majority illuminate concepts identified through research as the most challenging for instructors to teach and students to master. Examples include communication within neurons, positive and negative reinforcement and punishment, and critical thinking. Some of the most enthusiastic feedback from our student reviewers cited these Infographics. Assessable versions are available through LaunchPad.

5. Illustrating real-world applications

Any time we see an opportunity to apply psychological findings to students' lives, we seize upon it. In addition to pointing out applications through traditional avenues (photo captions, tables, figures, and so on), we have created certain features that compel students to make these connections on their own.

All chapters contain four or five In Class: Collaborate and Report features that offer quick, engaging activities to generate active class participation and stimulate discussions. By performing these active learning exercises, students learn from each other and cooperate as a team. Research continues to shed light on the benefits of such experiences.

Also appearing throughout the chapters are *Try This* exercises, which ask students to apply key concepts by performing simple

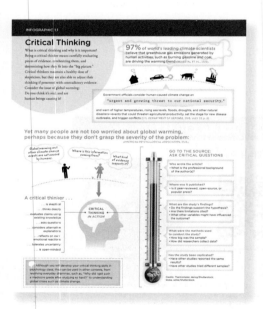

In Class: Collaborate and Report

Consider how language influences thinking. In your group, **A)** discuss the implications of using terms like spokes*man*, *man*kind, and *man*made. **B)** What other potential biases can you identify in English words and phrases? **C)** How can we counter their influences?

try this ↓

Holding your book at arm's length, close your right eye and stare at the orange with your left eye. Slowly bring the book closer to your face. The apple on the left will disappear when light from that picture falls on your blind spot.

activities. These are typically fast, easy-to-do, and designed to reinforce chapter content.

Your Scientific World is yet another new application-based feature in this edition. In these online immersive learning activities students are placed in a role-playing scenario requiring them to think critically and apply their knowledge of psychological science to solve a real world problem. In Chapter 5, for example, students take on the role of a dog owner, using the principles of learning to train a dog to be a therapy animal. Animations, videos, and assessments keep the student engaged throughout the activity. Instructors can assign and assess Your Scientific World activities through LaunchPad.

6. Keeping it positive

Many students enter the course thinking that psychology is all about abnormal and maladaptive patterns of human behavior. We think it is extremely important to address this belief. In our new *Think Positive* feature, we have highlighted the many ways psychological findings can guide us in a positive direction, helping us become healthier, happier people. Our integrated stories center on people who remain optimistic, hardworking, and kind to others—no matter how hard life gets. Throughout the text, we emphasize what is positive about psychology and the world we live in.

7. Emphasizing gender and cultural diversity

Our integrated stories, photos, in-text examples, and numerous application exercises have been carefully selected to provide exposure to a broad array of linguistic, cultural, and socioeconomic experiences. (Download full lists of the gender and cultural coverage integrated throughout the book at the *Scientific American: Psychology* page at macmillanlearning.com) We also devised a specific feature dedicated to exploring the impact of culture on human thoughts, emotions, and behavior. The thirteen *Across the World* pieces appearing throughout the text examine phenomena such as acculturative stress, individualism versus collectivism, and culture-specific symptoms of mental disorders.

THINK POSITIVE

Saifa the Self-Actualizer

According to Maslow, mentally healthy people are able to satisfy their self-focused needs and direct their attention toward helping others and making the world a better place (D'Souza & Gurin, 2016). Saifa began to move in this direction early in life, volunteering at the Gay Men's Health Crisis, an organization devoted to preventing HIV/AIDS and supporting families impacted by the epidemic. (This work was motivated by personal experience; Saifa lost his own father to AIDS.) He continued on this path as a young adult, working with women in prison, conducting HIV research at the University of California at San Francisco (UCSF), and helping lesbian, gay, bisexual, and transgender (LGBT) high school

HEALTHY PEOPLE HELP THEMSELVES BY HELPING OTHERS

ACROSS THE WORLD

Death in Different Cultures

What does death mean to you? Some of us believe death marks the beginning of a peaceful afterlife. Others see it as a crossing over from one life to another. Still others believe death is like turning off the lights; once you're gone, it's all over.

Views of death are very much related to religion and culture. A common belief among Indian Hindus, for example, is that one should spend a lifetime preparing for a "good death" (*su-mrtyu*). Often this means dying in old age, after conflicts have been put to rest, family matters settled, and farewells said. To prepare a loved one for a good death, relatives place the person on the floor at home (or on the banks of the Ganges River, if possible) and give her water from the hallowed Ganges. If these and other rituals are not carried out, the dead person's soul may become trapped and the family suffers the consequences: nightmares, infertility, and other forms of misfortune (Firth, 2005). In Korea and Taiwan, where practices of Confucianism are strongly held, family members show great respect, taking care of parents at the end of their lives: "In Korea and Taiwan, dying and death is perceived not as a personal issue, but rather as a family issue" (Cheng et al., 2015,

DEALING WITH DEATH IN DIFFERENT WAYS

THINK IT THROUGH

Is There a "Sixth Sense"?

ESP, psychic powers, the sixth sense—call it what you will, there is no compelling scientific evidence to support its existence (Farha, 2007; Rouder & Morey, 2011). Nevertheless, a handful of respected researchers have published research suggesting it exists. In 2011 Cornell University's Daryl Bem set off a firestorm of controversy with a journal article offering evidence for ESP. The article, which reported nine experiments involving some 1,000 participants, suggested that human beings have the ability to predict the future (Bem, 2011). Other psychologists pointed out flaws in Bem's statistical analysis (Wagenmakers, Wetzels, Borsboom, & van der Maas, 2011), which Bem then defended (Bem, Utts, & Johnson, 2011). The research was further called into question in 2012, when a team of scientists tried to replicate Bem's results using his same methodology and failed (Ritchie, Wiseman, & French, 2012).

THERE IS NO SCIENTIFIC EVIDENCE TO SUPPORT ITS EXISTENCE

8. Dispelling myths

Many students have trouble distinguishing between pseudoscience and actual science. We begin to chip away at this problem in Chapter 1, offering evidence to refute a series of commonsense myths, and continue to tackle it as opportunities arise, often by way of the Controversies and Think It Through features. For example, Chapter 1 addresses common misconceptions about global warming and "false balances" in the media, while Chapter 4 evaluates common myths about sleep and hypnosis, such as "drinking alcohol before bed helps you sleep better" and "people can be hypnotized without consent."

9. Testing works: More opportunities for assessment

As instructors, we keenly understand the value of both formative and summative assessment. We've read the research and we have seen it play out in the classroom: Students learn better when they are active participants in the process and are given ample opportunities to be tested on the material. But testing needn't be restricted to high-stakes exams and stressful pop quizzes. We have built assessment into the learning rubric of *Scientific American: Psychology*, Second Edition, by using end-of-section *Show What You Know* and end-of-chapter *Test Prep* questions that reward students for reading carefully, thinking critically, and applying concepts. Answers to the questions in both features are provided at the back of the book, in Appendix C.

---

show what you know

1. You want to learn how to play basketball, so you watch videos of Seth Curry executing plays. If your game improves as a result, this would be considered an example of:
   a. observational learning.   c. prosocial behavior.
   b. association.   d. your cognitive map.

2. Bandura's Bobo doll study shows us that observational learning results in a wide variety of learned behaviors. Describe several types of behaviors you have learned by observing others.

3. Although Skinner believed that reinforcement is the cause of learning, there is robust evidence that reinforcement is not always necessary. This comes from experiments studying:
   a. positive reinforcement.   c. latent learning.
   b. negative reinforcement.   d. stimulus generalization.

✓ CHECK YOUR ANSWERS IN APPENDIX C.

---

test prep *are you ready?*

1. One basic form of learning occurs during the process of _____, which is evident when an organism does not respond as strongly or as often to an event following multiple exposures to it.
   a. insight
   b. habituation
   c. classical conditioning
   d. operant conditioning

2. Even turtles can learn through operant conditioning, as evidenced by their:
   a. innate urge to get food.
   b. reaction to an unconditioned stimulus.
   c. ability to learn through positive reinforcement.
   d. reactions to predators

3. The behaviors learned with classical conditioning are _____, whereas those learned with operant conditioning are _____.
   a. involuntary; voluntary
   b. voluntary; involuntary
   c. voluntary; innate
   d. involuntary; innate

4. Every time you open the pantry where dog food is stored, your dog starts to salivate. His reaction is a(n):
   a. unconditioned response.
   b. conditioned response.
   c. stimulus discrimination.
   d. reaction based on observational learning.

5. Your first love wore a musky-scented perfume, and your heart raced every time he or she appeared. Even now when you smell that scent, your heart speeds up, suggesting the scent is a(n)
   a. unconditioned stimulus.
   b. conditioned stimulus.
   c. conditioned response.
   d. unconditioned response.

6. Avoiding foods that induce sickness has _____. This taste aversion helps organisms survive.
   a. adaptive value
   b. stimulus generalization
   c. stimulus discrimination
   d. higher order conditioning

7. Little Albert was a baby who originally had no fear of rats. In an experiment conducted by Watson and Rayner, he was classically conditioned to fear white rats through the pairing of a loud noise with exposure to a rat. His resulting fear is an example of a(n):
   a. unconditioned stimulus.
   b. operant conditioning.
   c. conditioned emotional response.
   d. biological preparedness.

11. A child is reprimanded for misbehaving, but then she seems to misbehave even more! This indicates that reprimanding her was:
    a. negative punishment.
    b. positive reinforcement.
    c. positive punishment.
    d. an unconditioned response.

12. In Bandura's Bobo doll study, children who saw an adult attacking and shouting at the doll_____.
    a. were more likely to display aggressive behavior
    b. were less likely to display aggressive behavior
    c. did not play with the Bobo doll at all
    d. began to cry when they saw the adult acting aggressively

13. According to research, there is a strong association between physical aggression and exposure to violent music, video games, and TV. However, this association between media portrayals and violent behaviors does not mean a _____ exists. There could be other factors like parenting involved.
    a. cause-and-effect relationship
    b. prosocial relationship
    c. neutral stimulus
    d. conditioned emotional response

14. Rats allowed to explore a maze, without getting reinforcers until the 11th day of the experiment, subsequently behaved in the maze as if they had been given reinforcers throughout the entire experiment. Their behavior is evidence of:
    a. latent learning.
    b. observational learning.
    c. classical conditioning.
    d. operant conditioning.

15. Wolfgang Köhler's research on chimpanzees suggests that animals are capable of thinking through a problem before taking action, and having a sudden coming together of awareness of a situation, leading to a solution. This is called:
    a. observational learning.
    b. insight.
    c. modeling.
    d. higher order conditioning.

16. What is the difference between stimulus generalization and stimulus discrimination?

17. Give an example showing how you have used shaping and partial reinforcement to change your behavior. Which schedule of reinforcement do you think you were using?

In addition to the Show What You Know and Test Prep, there are ample assessment opportunities beyond the book. The comprehensive Test Bank, created specifically for this textbook, includes more than 4,000 questions, each of which is keyed to a specific learning objective, page and section reference, and APA learning goal. Question types include multiple-choice, true/false, and essay prompts. Through LaunchPad, instructors can access and assign assessments, edit questions, add new questions, format assessments, and more. Instructors can also download the Test Bank in Diploma format for use off-line.

10. Creating interactive, technology-based learning in partnership with the authors

We recognize that a student's learning experience does not end with the printed text. Accordingly, our authorship extends beyond the pages of the book and into the digital space. As instructors with experience teaching traditional, online, and hybrid courses, we will continue to develop a text that marries the printed page with the online space, using multimedia to create a seamless online experience for students. The digital authorship of *Scientific American: Psychology*, Second Edition, is not an afterthought. We have carefully aligned each activity with the goals and outcomes of the American Psychological Association (APA). Looking closely at the foundational indicators, we strive to provide digital content that encourages students to think critically about psychological science.

LaunchPad offers Worth's acclaimed online content curated in collaboration with the text authors themselves and organized for easy assignability. LaunchPad includes a full e-Book, LearningCurve quizzing (see below), student self-assessment, simulations, videos, instructor resources, and an easy-to-use gradebook. It also includes Video Profile Assessments—versions of the text's Online Video Profiles that contain questions to help students connect the book's stories to core content. Infographic Assessments within the e-Book turn the printed Infographics into mini-quizzes.

LaunchPad is a breakthrough user interface distinguished by its powerful simplicity. We are also able to offer integration with LMS providers such as Canvas and Black-Board. Learn more and request access at launchpadworks.com

LearningCurve quizzing combines adaptive question selection, personalized study plans, and state-of-the-art question analysis reports. With thousands of questions written by authors Deborah Licht and Misty Hull, LearningCurve provides a unique learning experience (as opposed to a generic set of questions intended for use with any introductory psychology textbook)—offering a game-like feel that keeps students engaged in the material while helping them master concepts.

In a Nutshell

This book represents our most complete and sincere effort to tear down barriers for instructors teaching psychology and students learning psychology. When we say barriers, we mean *all* that we perceive and the research reveals. Removing those barriers involves listening to you and your students, devising creative solutions, generating evidence-based pedagogical tools, and creating state-of-the-art learning resources. We are confident that, collectively, the solutions and integrated approach to the 10 challenges addressed above represent a unique, enhanced tool that will stimulate more student interest and result in increased learning. As stated earlier, we could never accomplish this without the valuable feedback of people like you. This text is the product of collaborations and conversations with students and faculty across the country, and it always will be.

What's New, Chapter by Chapter

It's a given that every chapter contains ample research updates, fresh examples, and new photos, but there are also several chapter-specific changes:

Chapter 1: Introduction to the Science of Psychology

- New Integrated Story of Sharon Poset and Debbie Mehlman, identical twins separated at birth and reunited at age 45
- New Online Video Profile to accompany the story of Sharon and Debbie
- Expanded treatment of twin research and the nature and nurture theme
- New critical thinking Infographic using the example of global warming
- New Think It Through feature on "twin telepathy"
- New From the Pages of *Scientific American* feature exploring genetic influences on cooperative and selfish behavior
- More examples of descriptive research, particularly case studies
- New Across the World feature examining happiness in different countries
- New table detailing some of the guidelines for ethical treatment of animals in research
- New Think Positive feature introducing the importance of positive psychology
- Five new In Class: Collaborate and Report features

Chapter 2: Biology and Behavior

- Refined coverage of neural communication
- New table detailing the surprising effects of key neurotransmitters
- Updated information on the gender gap in math, science, and engineering
- New table describing the functions of various regions in the cortex
- New table describing the functions of various brain regions below the cortex
- New From the Pages of *Scientific American* feature examining how sugar affects brain health
- New table presenting the potential brain benefits of certain foods
- New Think Positive feature on neuroplasticity
- Five new In Class: Collaborate and Report features

Chapter 3: Sensation and Perception

- New table presenting the various theories used to explain pitch perception
- New Controversies feature on the debatable existence of "human pheromones"
- New table offering practical guidance for protecting the senses
- New Think It Through feature exploring perceptions of the color red
- New perceptual illusions Infographic
- Enhanced coverage of color constancy
- New Think Positive feature about viewing disability as a gift
- Five new In Class: Collaborate and Report features

Chapter 4: Consciousness

- New Integrated Story of Dr. Divya Chander, a neuroscientist and anesthesiologist who studies consciousness
- New table outlining strategies for effective multitasking

- New Didn't See That Coming feature examining how screen time in the evening affects sleep
- Realigned coverage of the sleep stages
- New From the Pages of *Scientific American* feature reporting on the synthetic marijuana trend
- Four new In Class: Collaborate and Report features

Chapter 5: Learning

- New Integrated Story of the "dog whisperer" Cesar Millan; examines how learning processes have played a role in his life and work
- New Online Video Profile to accompany the story of Cesar Millan
- New Infographic explaining four partial reinforcement schedules
- New From the Pages of *Scientific American* feature exploring how the use of delayed feedback affects learning
- New Nature and Nurture feature exploring how genes and environment impact one's ability to learn
- New Think Positive feature about finding one's place and learning niche in society
- Four new In Class: Collaborate and Report features

Chapter 6: Memory

- New table detailing the relationship between sleep and memory
- New Try This exercise illustrating encoding failure—uses altered versions of the Apple logo as opposed to the traditionally utilized coins
- New From the Pages of *Scientific American* feature about first memories
- New Nature and Nurture feature exploring the causes of Alzheimer's disease
- Discussion of chronic traumatic encephalopathy (CTE), a neurodegenerative disease caused by repetitive head trauma
- New Infographic exploring the causes and symptoms of CTE
- Four new In Class: Collaborate and Report features

Chapter 7: Cognition, Language, and Intelligence

- New Integrated Story of former NFL linebacker Harry Carson, who suffers from language difficulties that appear to be linked to repeated head injuries sustained on the football field
- Discussion of CTE research, both its history and recent developments
- New Nature and Nurture feature proposing that each case of CTE is a unique interplay between genes and environment
- Enhanced coverage of heuristics
- Five new In Class: Collaborate and Report features

Chapter 8: Human Development

- New Integrated Story about the multigenerational family of Ericka Harley of Generation Hope, a nonprofit organization that supports teen parents as they strive to attain college degrees

- New Online Video Profile to accompany the story of Ericka and her family
- New table illustrating newborn reflexes (photos included)
- New table providing a streamlined presentation of Kohlberg's stages of moral development
- New Think Positive feature about resilience in the face of hardship
- Four new In Class: Collaborate and Report features

Chapter 9: Motivation and Emotion

- New From the Pages of *Scientific American* feature exploring how multitasking while eating can diminish the experience of taste, and thus promote overeating
- Updated coverage of social media, and its role in satisfying needs
- New Think Positive feature about maximizing happiness by taking advantage of what Mihaly Csikszentmihalyi calls "flow"
- Coverage of Barbara Fredrickson's broaden-and-build model of positive emotions
- Four new In Class: Collaborate and Report features

Chapter 10: Sexuality and Gender

- New From the Pages of *Scientific American* feature examining how frequency of sex may affect happiness
- Expanded treatment of intersex development and "trans" experiences
- Updated treatment of homosexuality and the sexual orientation continuum
- Four new In Class: Collaborate and Report features

Chapter 11: Personality

- New Integrated Story about the personality development of intersex activist Sean Saifa Wall
- New Online Video Profile to accompany the story of Saifa
- Augmented coverage of temperament and personality
- New Think Positive feature on self-actualization
- Four new In Class: Collaborate and Report features

Chapter 12: Stress and Health

- New Integrated Story examining the stressors facing veteran police officer Christy Sheppard
- New Online Video Profile to accompany the story of Christy
- New From the Pages of *Scientific American* feature about how "performance anxiety" can be channeled in a positive way
- New Infographic on health psychology and the biopsychosocial perspective
- New Across the World feature on "blue zones," regions of the world where people enjoy exceptional health and longevity
- New table describing the characteristics of people living in the so-called blue zones
- New Think It Through feature describing how later school start times are associated with better health outcomes for teenagers
- Expanded coverage of strategies for healthy living, including a discussion of the role and importance of nutrition

- New Think Positive feature about using mindfulness meditation to reduce stress
- Four new In Class: Collaborate and Report features

Chapter 13: Psychological Disorders

- Enhanced discussion of the cultural variation related to psychological disorders
- New From the Pages of *Scientific American* feature exploring the psychological roots of nail biting and other "body-focused repetitive behaviors"
- Discussion of autism spectrum disorder—its symptoms and hypothesized causes
- Updated coverage of eating disorders (content discussed in Chapter 9 of the prior edition)
- Four new In Class: Collaborate and Report features

Chapter 14: Treatment of Psychological Disorders

- Expanded discussion of psychological disorders among jail and prison inmates
- New From the Pages of *Scientific American* feature illuminating the negative and potentially life-threatening side effects experienced by teens who take antidepressants
- Updated discussion on the efficacy of self-help groups
- New table describing the variables that affect psychotherapy outcomes
- New table providing the names and treatment targets of medications for psychological disorders
- More detailed examination of the role that social media should, or should not, play in therapy
- Four new In Class: Collaborate and Report features

Chapter 15: Social Psychology

- New From the Pages of *Scientific American* feature describing how yoga practice might help reduce aggressive impulses among the incarcerated
- Updated discussion of the role that social media plays in romantic relationships
- New Think Positive feature addressing the ways that knowledge of social psychology, and psychology in general, can have a positive impact on everyday life
- Five new In Class: Collaborate and Report features

Instructor's Resources

Instructor's Resource Manual

Written and compiled by experienced instructors of introductory psychology, the *Instructor's Resource Manual* is the perfect tool for busy instructors who want to make the introductory psychology course more engaging for their students. This manual includes chapter objectives; chapter summaries; lecture, discussion, and classroom activity suggestions organized by section; multimedia suggestions from Worth's rich video and student media offerings; plus tips for embracing new classroom technologies and teaching online.

Video Anthology

Instead of searching the entirety of Worth's vast video collection, users can now access a "best of" collection that showcases 250 videos by topic from the following:

- Video Tool Kit for Introductory Psychology (including 30 new videos co-produced by *Nature* and *Scientific American*)
- Digital Media Archives, Volumes 1 and 2
- *Scientific American Frontiers Teaching Modules,* Third Edition

Interactive Presentation Slides for Introductory Psychology

This series of "next-generation" PowerPoint® lectures gives instructors a dynamic but easy-to-use way to engage students during classroom presentations. Each lecture provides opportunities for discussion and interaction, and includes a wide array of embedded video clips and animations.

Enhanced Course Management Solutions and Single Sign-On

Blackboard, Angel, Desire2Learn, Moodle, Sakai, and more.

Course packs offer a completely integrated solution that you can easily customize and adapt to meet your teaching goals and objectives. Examples of instructor content now included in our enhanced solutions are the complete Test Bank, the complete Instructor's Resources, a variety of PowerPoint® slides, and much more. Course packs are available at www.macmillanlearning.com/lms. For information about arranging single sign-on/grade-sync between your department's course management system and LaunchPad, inquire with your local sales representative.

Alignment with APA Learning Guidelines 2.0

Alignment with APA Learning Guidelines 2.0

GOAL 1: KNOWLEDGE BASE IN PSYCHOLOGY

AMERICAN PSYCHOLOGICAL ASSOCIATION LEARNING OUTCOMES

1.1 Describe key concepts, principles, and overarching themes in psychology

1.2 Develop a working knowledge of psychology's content domains

1.3 Describe applications of psychology

Scientific American: Psychology, 2e, Learning Objectives/Content

CHAPTER 1: LO 1–LO 11

CHAPTER 2: LO 1–LO 16

CHAPTER 3: LO 1–LO 15

CHAPTER 4: LO 1–LO 12

CHAPTER 5: LO 1–LO 15

CHAPTER 6: LO 1–LO 15

CHAPTER 7: LO 1 –LO 13

CHAPTER 8: LO 1–LO 19

CHAPTER 9: LO 1–LO 14

CHAPTER 10: LO 1–LO 11

CHAPTER 11: LO 1–LO 15

CHAPTER 12: LO 1–LO 12

CHAPTER 13: LO 1–LO 12

CHAPTER 14: LO 1–LO 12

CHAPTER 15: LO 1–LO 12

APPENDIX A: Introduction to Statistics

APPENDIX B: Careers in Psychology

INTEGRATED THEMATIC FEATURES in each chapter

CONNECTIONS in Chapters 2–15 and Appendix A

INFOGRAPHICS in each chapter

TRY THIS application activities in Chapters 1–3, 5–7, 9–10, 12, 14–15 and Appendix A: Introduction to Statistics

IN CLASS: COLLABORATE AND REPORT activities in each chapter

LAUNCHPAD RESOURCES

LEARNINGCURVE

INSTRUCTOR'S RESOURCE MANUAL

GOAL 2: SCIENTIFIC INQUIRY AND CRITICAL THINKING

AMERICAN PSYCHOLOGICAL ASSOCIATION LEARNING OUTCOMES

2.1 Use scientific reasoning to interpret psychological phenomena

2.2 Demonstrate psychology information literacy

2.3 Engage in innovative and integrative thinking and problem solving

2.4 Interpret, design, and conduct basic psychological research

2.5 Incorporate sociocultural factors in scientific inquiry

Scientific American: Psychology, 2e, **Learning Objectives/Substantive Content**

Inside front cover: Infographic: How to Read a Scientific Article

CHAPTER 1: LO 5–LO 11; *Think It Through:* Does Twin Telepathy Exist?; *Think It Through:* Psychology in the Media; *Didn't See That Coming:* SpongeBob on the Brain; *Across the World:* The Happiest Places on the Planet; *From the Pages of Scientific American:* Are People Inclined to Act Cooperatively or Selfishly? Is Such Behavior Genetic?; Infographic 1.1: Critical Thinking; Infographic 1.2: The Scientific Method; Infographic 1.3: The Correlation Coefficient: What's in a Number?; Infographic 1.4: The Experimental Method

CHAPTER 2: LO 1, 2, & 10; *Think It Through:* Where's My Morning Antagonist?; *Social Media and Psychology:* Facebook in the Brain; *From the Pages of Scientific American:* Sugar May Harm Brain Health; Infographic 2.1: Ways to Study the Living Brain

CHAPTER 3: LO 6, 11, & 15; *Controversies:* Sexy Smells?; *Didn't See That Coming:* The Scent of Money; *Think It Through:* Red and Hot Go Hand-in-Hand; *Think It Through:* Is There a Sixth Sense?; *From the Pages of Scientific American:* Brain Freeze Explained; Infographic 3.4: Gestalt Organizing Principles: The Whole Is Greater

CHAPTER 4: *Didn't See That Coming:* Are Screens Ruining Your Rhythm?; *Think It Through:* 9 Sleep Myths; *From the Pages of Scientific American:* Fake Weed, Real Crisis; *Social Media and Psychology:* Can't Get Enough; *Controversies:* False Claims About Hypnosis

CHAPTER 5: LO 14; *Think It Through:* Rescuing Animals with Classical Conditioning; *Think It Through:* Chickens Can't Play Baseball; *Social Media and Psychology:* Contagious Behaviors; *Controversies:* Spotlight on Spanking; *From the Pages of Scientific American:* Wait for It; Infographic 5.1: Learning Through Classical Conditioning; Infographic 5.2: Learning Through Operant Conditioning; Infographic 5.3: Partial Reinforcement; Infographic 5.4: Learning: Punishment and Reinforcement

CHAPTER 6: *Social Media and Psychology:* Multitasking and Memory; *Didn't See That Coming*: Google Brain; *Controversies:* The Debate over Repressed Childhood Memories; *Nature and Nurture:* Why Alzheimer's?; *From the Pages of Scientific American:* What's Your First Memory?; Infographic 6.1: Study Smarter: Methods of Improving Your Memory; Infographic 6.3: Chronic Traumatic Encephalopathy

CHAPTER 7: LO 8, 10, & 12; *Think It Through:* Fearing the Friendly Skies; *Across the World:* Problem Solving in Different Cultures; *Didn't See That Coming:* The Perks of Being Bilingual; *Think It Through:* Language Without Sound; *Controversies:* Do Animals Use Language, Too?; *From the Pages of Scientific American:* Laughter Leads to Insight; Infographic 7.1: Concepts and Prototypes; Infographic 7.2: Problem Solving; Infographic 7.4: How Smart Are Intelligence Tests?

CHAPTER 8: LO 18; *Nature and Nurture:* Genie the "Feral Child"; *From the Pages of Scientific American:* Join a Club, Stay

Sharp; Infographic 8.1: Research Methods in Developmental Psychology; Infographic 8.3: Piaget's Theory of Cognitive Development

CHAPTER 9: LO 3, 5, 7, 10, 11, & 14; *Controversies:* Problems with Polygraphs; *From the Pages of Scientific American:* Food Tastes Bland While Multitasking; *Think Positive:* Going with the Flow; Infographic 9.2: Mechanisms in Hunger Regulation; Infographic 9.4: The Anatomy of Fear

CHAPTER 10: LO 11; *Nature and Nurture:* The Case of Bruce Reimer; *Didn't See That Coming:* Great Ape Sex; *Think It Through:* Sext You Later; *From the Pages of Scientific American:* Keeping Up with the Joneses

CHAPTER 11: *Nature and Nurture:* The Funny Thing About Personality; *Controversies:* How Birth Order May—or May Not—Affect Your Personality; *From the Pages of Scientific American:* Open Mind, Longer Life; Infographic 11.1: Ego Defense Mechanisms; Infographic 11.2: The Social-Cognitive Perspective on Personality; Infographic 11.3: Examining the Unconscious: Projective Personality Tests

CHAPTER 12: LO 2 & 3; *Think It Through:* Waking Up Is Hard to Do; *From the Pages of Scientific American:* Performance Anxiety; Infographic 12.1: Stressed Out; Infographic 12.2: Physiological Responses to Stress; Infographic 12.3: Health Psychology; Infographic 12.4: The Process of Coping

CHAPTER 13: LO 9; *Think It Through:* The Insanity Plea; *Think It Through:* On Being Sane in Insane Places; *Nature and Nurture:* Four Sisters; *From the Pages of Scientific American:* Nail Biting May Arise from Perfectionism

CHAPTER 14: LO 9; *Didn't See That Coming:* Virtual Reality Exposure Therapy; *From the Pages of Scientific American:* The Hidden Harm of Antidepressants

CHAPTER 15: LO 10; *Nature and Nurture:* Why the Attitude?; *Think it Through:* Something Doesn't Feel Right; *Controversies:* The Stanford "Prison"; *From the Pages of Scientific American:* Prisoner's Escape

APPENDIX A: Introduction to Statistics

DIVERSE CHARACTER profiles integrated throughout each chapter

INTEGRATIVE CONNECTIONS found in Chapters 2–15 and Appendix A

TRY THIS application activities in Chapters 1–3, 5–7, 9–10, 12, 14–15, and Appendix A: Introduction to Statistics.

IN CLASS: COLLABORATE AND REPORT activities in each chapter

LAUNCHPAD RESOURCES

LEARNINGCURVE

INSTRUCTOR'S RESOURCE MANUAL

GOAL 3: ETHICAL AND SOCIAL RESPONSIBILITY IN A DIVERSE WORLD

AMERICAN PSYCHOLOGICAL ASSOCIATION LEARNING OUTCOMES

3.1 Apply ethical standards to evaluate psychological science and practice

3.2 Build and enhance interpersonal relationships

3.3 Adopt values that build community at local, national, and global levels

....

Scientific American: Psychology, 2e, Learning Objectives/Substantive Content

CHAPTER 1: LO 11; *Across the World:* The Happiest Places on the Planet; *From the Pages of Scientific American:* Are People Inclined to Act Cooperatively or Selfishly? Is Such Behavior Genetic?; *Think Positive:* Introducing Positive Psychology; Infographic 1.1: Critical Thinking

CHAPTER 2: *Social Media and Psychology:* Facebook in the Brain; *Think Positive:* The Versatile Brain

CHAPTER 3: *Think Positive:* Can a Disability Be a Gift?

CHAPTER 5: *Social Media and Psychology:* Contagious Behaviors; *Think Positive:* You Are a Valuable Member of the Pack

CHAPTER 7: *Across the World:* Problem Solving in Different Cultures

CHAPTER 8: *Across the World:* Death in Different Cultures; *Social Media and Psychology:* The Social Networking Teen Machine; *Think Positive:* Resilient in the Face of Hardship

CHAPTER 9: *Across the World:* Can You Feel the Culture?; *Social Media and Psychology:* Network Needs

CHAPTER 10: *Across the World:* Homosexuality and Culture; *Across the World:* What They Are Doing in Bed . . . or Elsewhere

CHAPTER 11: *Across the World:* Culture of Personality; *Social Media and Psychology:* It's Written All Over Your Facebook; *Think Positive:* Saifa the Self-Actualizer

CHAPTER 12: *Across the World:* The Stress of Starting Anew; *Across the World:* The "Blue Zones"

CHAPTER 13: *Across the World:* The Many Faces of Social Anxiety; *Across the World:* A Cross-Cultural Look at Eating Disorders

CHAPTER 14: LO 9; *Across the World:* Know Thy Client; *Social Media and Psychology:* Therapist or Friend?

CHAPTER 15: LO 5, 8, 11 & 12; *Across the World:* Slackers of the West; *Social Media and Psychology:* Relationships Online; *Think Positive:* Making Psychology Work for You; Infographic 15.3: Thinking About Other People: Discrimination, Stereotype, and Prejudice

DIVERSE CHARACTER profiles integrated throughout each chapter

IN CLASS: COLLABORATE AND REPORT activities in each chapter

GOAL 4: COMMUNICATION

AMERICAN PSYCHOLOGICAL ASSOCIATION LEARNING OUTCOMES

4.1 Demonstrate effective writing for different purposes

4.2 Exhibit effective presentation skills for different purposes

4.3 Interact effectively with others

....

Scientific American: Psychology, 2e, Learning Objectives/Substantive Content

Inside front cover: Infographic: How to Read a Scientific Article

CHAPTER 7: LO 9 & 10; Infographic 7.3: The Building Blocks of Language

CHAPTER 8: LO 8 & 9; *Social Media and Psychology:* The Social Networking Teen Machine; *From the Pages of Scientific American:* Join a Club, Stay Sharp

CHAPTER 9: LO 12; *Social Media and Psychology:* Network Needs; *Across the World:* Can You Feel the Culture?

CHAPTER 11: LO 6 & 7; *Nature and Nurture:* The Funny Thing About Personality; *Social Media and Psychology:* It's Written All Over Your Facebook

CHAPTER 14: LO 8 & 9; *Across the World:* Know Thy Client; *Social Media and Psychology:* Therapist or Friend?

CHAPTER 15: LO 3, 6 & 12; *Social Media and Psychology:* Relationships Online; *Think Positive:* Making Psychology Work for You

SHOW WHAT YOU KNOW and **TEST PREP: ARE YOU READY?** assessment questions in each chapter

IN CLASS: COLLABORATE AND REPORT activities in each chapter

TEST BANK essay questions

LAUNCHPAD RESOURCES

LEARNINGCURVE

INSTRUCTOR'S RESOURCE MANUAL

GOAL 5: PROFESSIONAL DEVELOPMENT

AMERICAN PSYCHOLOGICAL ASSOCIATION LEARNING OUTCOMES

5.1 Apply psychological content and skills to career goals

5.2 Exhibit self-efficacy and self-regulation

5.3 Refine project-management skills

5.4 Enhance teamwork capacity

5.5 Develop meaningful professional direction for life after graduation

Scientific American: Psychology, 2e, Learning Objectives/Substantive Content

CHAPTER 1: LO 1; Infographic 1.1: Critical Thinking

CHAPTER 2: *Think It Through:* Where's My Morning Antagonist? *Didn't See that Coming:* The Scent of Money

CHAPTER 4: *Think It Through:* 9 Sleep Myths

CHAPTER 5: *Social Media and Psychology:* Contagious Behaviors; *Think Positive:* You Are a Valuable Member of the Pack

CHAPTER 6: LO 6; *Social Media and Psychology:* Multitasking and Memory; *Didn't See That Coming:* Google Brain; Infographic 6.1: Study Smarter: Methods of Improving Your Memory

CHAPTER 7: LO 5, 6, & 7; *From the Pages of Scientific American:* Laughter Leads to Insight; *Didn't See That Coming:* The Perks of Being Bilingual; Infographic 7.2: Problem Solving; Infographic 7.3: The Building Blocks of Language

CHAPTER 8: *Social Media and Psychology:* The Social Networking Teen Machine; *From the Pages of Scientific American:* Join a Club, Stay Sharp

CHAPTER 9: LO 1, 7, & 9; *Social Media and Psychology:* Network Needs; *Think Positive:* Going with the Flow

CHAPTER 11: LO 6 & 7; *Across the World:* Culture of Personality; *From the Pages of Scientific American:* Open Mind, Longer Life; Social Media and Psychology: It's Written

All Over Your Facebook; Infographic 11.1 Ego Defense Mechanisms

CHAPTER 12: LO 7, 9, 11, & 12; *Across the World:* The Stress of Starting Anew; *From the Pages of Scientific American:* Performance Anxiety; *Think Positive:* Right Here, Right Now; Infographic 12.1: Stressed Out; Infographic 12.3: Health Psychology; Infographic 12.4: The Process of Coping

CHAPTER 14: LO 11 & 12; *Didn't See That Coming:* Virtual Reality Exposure Therapy; *Across the World:* Know Thy Client; *Social Media and Psychology:* Therapist or Friend?

CHAPTER 15: LO 2, 6, 8, 10 & 12; *Across the World:* Slackers of the West; *From the Pages of Scientific American:* Prisoner's Escape; *Think Positive:* Making Psychology Work for You

APPENDIX B: Careers in Psychology

IN CLASS: COLLABORATE AND REPORT activities in each chapter

LAUNCHPAD RESOURCES

LEARNINGCURVE

INSTRUCTOR'S RESOURCE MANUAL

Psychology Content on the MCAT

The Medical College Admission Test (MCAT) began to include psychology on its exam in 2015. The requirements stipulate that 25% of the test will include questions pertaining to the "Psychological, Social, and Biological Foundations of Behavior." Many of these topics are covered during the introductory psychology course, so we've made a useful chart that aligns the psychology topics to be covered on the MCAT with the location of that material in the book. This chart is available for download from the *Scientific American: Psychology* page at worthpublishers.com.

Acknowledgments

Seven years ago, the three authors came together to discuss the possibility of creating a bold new psychology textbook. We dreamed of creating an introductory text that would bring relevance and student engagement to a whole new level. We believe that dream has now materialized, but it would not have been possible without the hard work and talent of reviewers, focus group attendees, students, interview subjects, contributors, and editors.

The early years were arduous, but we had many champions in our corner: a special thanks to Erik Gilg and Jim Strandberg. Catherine Woods, you have been with us from the beginning, and we are thankful for your ongoing support and oversight. Rachel Losh, you picked up this project and ran with it in all the right directions. We miss your hands-on involvement, but we know you continue to support this project with your exciting work on personalized learning technology.

Executive Acquisitions Editor Daniel McDonough, you jumped into the mix with wonderful enthusiasm, and you have proven yourself to be a loyal, conscientious, and forward-thinking team leader. Thank you, Dan, for appreciating our hard work, advocating on our behalf, and communicating with us in a refreshingly direct manner. Assistant Editor Kimberly Morgan-Smith, it was clear from the beginning that you were excited to join the team and invested in the project. You juggled many responsibilities, and you did it with grace. We could always count on you to get the job done with professionalism.

Brad Rivenburgh, Glenn and Meg Turner of Burrston House, you came to this project just when we were in great need of your extensive publishing experience and vast fund of research knowledge. Thank you for your indefatigable efforts assembling panels of reviewers, and distilling their feedback into practical suggestions for us to consider. The student and instructor focus groups you have organized are essential to the ongoing success of the project. Meg, your work reaching out to schools and connecting with instructors is critical; we understand how much energy and persistence it requires, and we cannot thank you enough. Glenn, what would we do without your wisdom and guidance? Your edits have been invaluable!! (double exclamation mark intended). Brad, your attention to detail and your ability to manage so many tasks simultaneously is remarkable.

Mimi Melek, Anne DeMarinis, and Dawn Albertson, thank you for making the infographics come to life so elegantly.

Senior Photo Editor Cecilia Varas and photo researcher Jacqui Wong, you have outdone yourself with this second edition! We know the work was demanding and difficult, but you have assembled a set of phenomenal photos for this book. Your efforts are so appreciated.

Producing a high-quality college textbook is a formidable task, but we had the experts in our corner: Senior Project Editor Liz Geller. Thank you, Liz, being an excellent project manager. You run a tight ship, and your dedication to producing a top-quality product is obvious. Director, Content Management Enhancement, Tracey Kuehn, you made the transition from development to production smooth and manageable—and perhaps more importantly, you kept us sane during that first production experience. Copy editor Patti Brecht, we are grateful for your help keeping track of all those citations, and answering innumerable questions about hyphens, semicolons, capital letters, and other copy issues. Senior Design Manager Blake Logan, you have done a remarkable job presenting densely packed information in a clear and stimulating visual format. And Layout Designer Sheridan Sellers, thank you for your heroic work arranging all the elements of the book into a cohesive and beautiful unit on a very tight schedule.

To all the managers, designers, illustrators, editors, and other team members with whom we did not have direct contact, please know that we are thoroughly impressed with your work; we

feel lucky to have had you on our team. A huge thanks to Senior Production Supervisor Sarah Segal, Managing Editor Lisa Kinne, Art Manager Matt McAdams, illustrators Todd Buck, Evelyn Pence, and Eli Ensor, and Market Development Assistant Stephanie Ellis.

Peter Levin, John Philp, and Barbara Parks of Splash Studios, your videos give us goose bumps, and some of them move us to tears. Thank you for conveying the chapter stories in a way that was real, yet respectful to the interview subjects. No one could have done it better.

Noel Hohnstine, Mimi Melek, Anthony Casciano, and Lauren Samuelson, you have provided essential support in the development and refinement of our supplements and online learning activities. Thanks to your expertise and tireless efforts, students can take full advantage of all that LaunchPad has to offer.

Marketing guru Lindsay Johnson, thank you for helping us bond with the sales team and ensuring that real college students read this book! Without you, our work would be pointless.

We have benefited in countless ways from an exceptional group of academic reviewers. Some have been our greatest champions, and others our sharpest critics. We needed both. We are grateful for the hundreds of hours you spent examining this text, writing thoughtful critiques, and offering bright ideas—many of which we have incorporated into our text. This is your book, too.

Mary Beth Ahlum, *Nebraska Wesleyan University*

Maya Aloni, *Western Connecticut State University*

Winifred Armstead-Hannah, *City College of Chicago, Richard R. Daley College*

Sandra Arntz, *Carroll University*

Christopher Arra, *Northern Virginia Community College*

Shaki Asgari, *Iona College*

Sherry Ash, *San Jacinto College Community College*

Diane Ashe, *Valencia College, West*

Sheryl Attig, *Tri-County Technical College*

Nani Azman, *University of Hawaii, Maui College*

Rosenna Bakari, *Des Moines Area Community College*

Michelle Bannoura, *Hudson Valley Community College*

Michael E. Barber, *Sante Fe College*

Nazira Barry, *Miami Dade College, Wolfson*

Holly Beard, *Midlands Technical College*

Michael Behar, *Suffolk Community College*

Patrick Bennett, *Indiana State University*

Garrett L. Berman, *Roger Williams University*

Leslie Berntsen, *University of Southern California*

John Bickford, *University of Massachusetts, Amherst*

David Biek, *Middle Georgia State College*

Andrew Blair, *Palm Beach State College*

Marilyn Bonem, *Eastern Michigan University*

Leanne Boucher, *Nova Southeastern University*

Saundra Boyd, *Houston Community College*

Amy A. Bradshaw, *Embry-Riddle Aeronautical University*

Karen Brakke, *Spelman College*

Nicole Brandt, *Columbus State Community College*

Jennifer Branscome, *Valdosta State College*

Deborah Briihl, *Valdosta State College*

Lauren Brown, *Mott Community College*

Amy Buckingham, *Red Rocks Community College*

Michael Butchko, *University of Nebraska, Lincoln*

Michelle A. Butler, *U.S. Air Force Academy*

Robin Campbell, *Eastern Florida State College*

Judith Caprio, *Rhode Island College*

Jessica Carpenter, *Elgin Community College*

Gabriela Carrasco, *University of North Alabama*

Jenel Cavazos, *University of Oklahoma*

Sharon Chacon, *Northeast Wisconsin Technical College*

Daniel Chadborn, *Southeastern Louisiana University*

Sherri Chandler, *Muskegon Community College*

Gabriela Chavira, *California State University–Northridge*

Regina Chopp, *University of Southern California*

Diana Ciesko, *Valencia College–East*

Shirley Clay, *Northeast Texas Community College*

Deborah Conway, *Community College of Allegheny County, South Campus*

Barbara Corbisier, *Blinn College*

Kristie Coredell-McNulty, *Angelo State University*

Cheryl Cotten, *Wor-Wic Community College*

Lauren Coursey, *The University of Texas at Arlington*

Baine B. Craft, *Seattle Pacific University*

Margaret Davidson, *Rockwall–Heath High School*

Scott Debb, *Norfolk State University*

Amber DeBono, *Winston-Salem State University*

Deanna DeGidio, *Northern Valley Community College*

David Devonis, *Graceland University*

Rebekah Phillips DeZalia, *Coastal Carolina Community College*

Amanda di Bartolomeo, *University of California, Los Angeles*

Matthew D. Diggs, *Collin College*

Evelyn Doody, *College of Southern Nevada*

Karen Trotty Douglas, *Alamo Colleges, San Antonio College*

Kimberly Duff, *Cerritos College*

Dawn Eaton, *San Jacinto Community College*

Jeanne Edman, *Consumnes River College*

Mitchell Estaphan, *Bristol Community College*

Roel Evangelista, *Community College of Baltimore–Essex*

Frank Eyetsemitan, *Roger Williams University*

Kelvin Faison, *Pasco Hernando Community College*

Robert Fauber, *Temple University*

Dan Fawaz, *Georgia Perimeter College–Clarkston*

Celeste Favela, *El Paso Community College*

Christina Feeley, *Farmingdale State College*

Christopher Ferguson, *Stetson University*

Jason Fernandez, *Lone Star College*

Frank M. Ferraro III, *Nebraska Wesleyan University*

Stephen Fox, *University of Hawaii–Maui College*

Lisa Fozio-Thielk, *Waubonsee Community College*

Susan Frantz, *Highline Community College*

Anne Marie Freeman, *Rockingham Community College*

Jeanette Gassaway, *Ohio University–Chillicothe*

Bernard Gee, *Western Connecticut State University*

Rachel Gentry, *Ball State University*

Sherry Ginn, *Rowan–Cabarrus Community College*

Kimberly Glackin, *Metropolitan Community College*

Jennifer Gonder, *Farmingdale State College*

Jeffery Gray, *Charleston Southern University*

Gladys Green, *State College of Florida*

Jerry Green, *Tarrant County College, Northwest*

Christine Grela, *McHenry County College*

Angela Griffin, *Midlands Technical College*

Bettye P. Griffin, *West Hills Community College District*

Donnell Griffin, *Davidson County Community College*

Justin Hackett, *California University of Pennsylvania*

Lynn Haller, *Morehead State University*

Julie Hanauer, *Suffolk County Community College*

Keith Happaney, *Lehman College*

Christine Harrington, *Middlesex County College*

Carol Kozak Hawk, *Austin Community College*

Cathy Hawkins, *North Hennepin Community College*

Rickye Heffner, *University of Toledo*

Byron Heidenreich, *Illinois State University*

Bryan Hendricks, *University of Wisconsin, Madison*

Jennifer Higa-King, *Honolulu Community College*

Mia Holland, *Bridgewater State University*

Debra Hollister, *Valencia College–Lake Nona*

Amy Holmes, *Davidson County Community College*

Karen Y. Holmes, *Norfolk State University*

Laura Holt, *Trinity College*

Nancy Honeycutt, *Alamance Community College*

Mary Susan Horton, *Mesa Community College*

Vivian Hsu, *Rutgers University*

Christopher Hubbell, *Rensselaer Polytechnic Institute*

Ken Hudson, *Florida Community College*

Mayte Insua-Auais, *Miami Dade College–North*

Judy Jankowski, *Grand Rapids Community College*

Joan Jensen, *Central Piedmont Community College*

Catherine Jockell, *University of Houston*

Barry Johnson, *Davidson County Community College*

Jessica Jolly, *Gloucester County College*

Judith Josephs, *Salem State University*

Diana Joy, *Community College of Denver*

Nora Kametani, *Nunez Community College*

Katrina Kardiasmenos, *Bowie State University*

Carolyn Kaufman, *Columbus State Community College*

Luanna Kea, *Midlands Technical College*

Kevin Keating, *Broward College*

Zelida Keo-Trang, *Saddleback College*

Lynnel Kiely, *City Colleges of Chicago, Harold Washington College*

Yuthika Kim, *Oklahoma City Community College*

Norman Kinney, *Southeast Missouri State University*

Cheri Kittrell, *State College of Florida*

Nicole Korzetz, *Lee College*

Michelle LaBrie, *College of the Canyons*

Monica Lackups, *Eastern Michigan University*

Cindy Lahar, *York County Community College*

Elizabeth Laurer, *Owens Community College*

Jennifer Lee, *Cabrillo College*

Juliet Lee, *Cape Fear Community College*

Kris Leppien-Christensen, *Saddleback College*

Christine Lofgren, *University of California–Irvine*

Pamela Joan Marek, *Kennesaw State University*

Alexander Marvin, *Seminole State College of Florida*

Kirsten Matthews, *Harper College*

Brent Mattingly, *Ashland University*

Cindy Matyi, *Ohio University, Chillicothe Campus*

Ashley Maynard, *University of Hawaii*

Dan McConnell, *University of Central Florida*

Cheryl McGill, *Florence-Darlington Technical College*

Lisa Moeller, *Devry University*

Thurla Moore, *Tallahassee Community College*

Kristie Morris, *SUNY Rockland Community College*

Julie Morrison, *Glendale Community College*

Elizabeth Moseley, *Cleveland State Community College*

Paige Muellerleile, *Marshall University*

Ronald Mulson, *Hudson Valley Community College*

Robin Musselman, *Lehigh Carbon Community College*

Margaret Nauta, *Illinois State University*

Roderick Neal, *Patrick Henry Community College*

Ronn Newby, *Des Moines Area Community College*

John L. Oliver, *Florida Community College*

Sophia Ogunlana, *Prince George's Community College*

Jennifer Ounjian, *Contra Costa College*

William Oye, *Diablo Valley College*

Karl Oyster, *Tidewater Community College*

Joanna Palmer, *Baker College of Flint*

Carol Pandey, *Los Angeles Pierce College*

Jan Pascal, *Johnson County Community College*

Melissa Patton, *Eastern Florida State College, Cocoa*

Linda Perrotti, *University of Texas at Arlington*

Michaela Porubanova, *Farmingdale State College*

Kristin Price, *Owens Community College*

Judy Quon, *California State University–Long Beach*

Marianna Rader, *Rockingham Community College*

Barbara Radigan, *Community College of Allegheny County*

Elena Reigadas, *Los Angeles Harbor College*

Tanya Renner, *Kapi'olani Community College*

Nan Rice, *Springfield Tech Community College*

Danielle Richards, *College of Southern Nevada*

Sharon Richards, *Tri-County Technical College*

Edrica Richardson, *Broward College*

Vicki Ritts, *St. Louis Community College, Meramec*

Michelle Robinson, *Saddleback College*

Jennifer Rosales, *El Paso Community College*

Fredric E. Rose, *Palomar College*

Karen Saenz, *Houston Community College*

Ronald Arthur Salazar, *San Juan College*

Carol Schachat, *Orange Coast College*

Derek Schorsch, *Valencia College*

Clint Selman, *Tyler College*

Rebecca E. Shepherd, *College of the Canyons*

Melinda Shoemaker, *Broward College–North*

Maria Shpurik, *Florida International University*

Joan Siebert, *Community College of Allegheny County*

Debra Silverman, *Keiser University*

Theresa Simantirakis, *Wright College*

Valerie A. Simon, *Wayne State University*

Karyn Skaar, *Northeast Texas Community College*

Peggy Skinner, *South Plains College*

Deidre Slavik, *Northwestern Arkansas College*

Don Smith, *Everett Community College*

Jerry Snead, *Coastal Carolina Community College*

Jonathan Sparks, *Vance-Granville Community College*

Jason Spiegelman, *Community College of Baltimore County–Catonsville*

Susan Nash Spooner, *McLennan Community College*

Chris Stanley, *Winston-Salem State University*

Betsy Stern, *Milwaukee Area Technical College*

Lara Tedrow, *Tidewater Community College*

Jennifer Thompson-Watson, City *Colleges of Chicago, Kennedy–King College*

David Tom, *Columbus State Community College*

Carole Toney, *Polk State College*

Elizabeth Tuckwiller, *George Washington University*

Chantal Tusher, *Georgia State University*

Mary Ann Valentino, *Fresno City College*

Jennifer M. Verive, *Western Nevada College*

Jeff Wachsmuth, *Napa Valley College*

Linda Walsh, *University of Northern Iowa*

David Wasieleski, *Valdosta State University*

Martha Weaver, *Eastfield College*

Melissa B. Weston, *El Centro College*

Tanya Whipple, *Missouri State University*

Brian Wiley, *Florida State College*

Shannon Williams, *Prince George's Community College*

Janis Wilson Seeley, *Luzerne County Community College*

Dana Wood, *George College*

Ric Wynn, *County College of Morris*

Clare Zaborowshi, *San Jacinto College Community College*

Valerie Zurawski, *St. John's University*

Thank you to the following student reviewers who provided valuable feedback and contributed questions for our video interviews:

Nicole Adamcyzk, *Suffolk County Community College*

Hilary Allen, *Waubonsee Community College*

Wes Armstrong, *Georgia Perimeter College*

Michael Baker, *Suffolk County Community College*

Michael Blackburn, *Valencia College*

Rebecca Blackburn, *Valencia College*

Zandi Bosua, *Suffolk County Community College*

Michael Burt, *Valencia College*

Joseph Calabrese, *Waubonsee Community College*

Paul Calzada, *College of Southern Nevada*

Tracy Cleary, *Valencia College*

James Ferguson, *Suffolk County Community College*

Amanda Flood, *Suffolk County Community College*

Marie Forestal, *Valencia College*

Casey Frisque, *Northeast Wisconsin Technical College*

Jordana Gaines, *Suffolk County Community College*

Chris Henderson, *Georgia Perimeter College*

Daisy Hidalgo, *Valencia College*

Matthew Hirschland, *Georgia Perimeter College*

Eric Hollenback, *Waubonsee Community College*

Michael Hollenback, *Waubonsee Community College*

Meridith Hollister, *Valencia College*

Zane Howard, *Georgia Perimeter College*

Caitlyn Ingram, *Suffolk County Community College*

Carole Keef, *Valencia College*

Zoe Kiefer, *Waubonsee Community College*

Donya Kobari, *Georgia Perimeter College*

Emily Kolk, *Suffolk County Community College*

Deanna Krane, *Suffolk County Community College*

Kayla Krasnee, *Suffolk County Community College*

Amanda Landolt, *Northeast Wisconsin Technical College*

Joline Ledbetter, *College of Southern Nevada*

Adam R. Leicht, *Georgia Perimeter College*

Amanda Meyer, *Waubonsee Community College*

Justin Oge, *Tarrant County College–Northwest*

Melissa Ortiz, *Suffolk County Community College*

Kimberly Peterson, *Suffolk County Community College*

Jacob Rodgers, *Tarrant County College–Northwest*

Jared Rodgers, *Tarrant County College–Northwest*

Chloe Rodriguez, *Tarrant County College–Northwest*

Sarah Rogers, *Suffolk County Community College*

Carolina Rosales, *Waubonsee Community College*

Amber Roth, *Georgia Perimeter College*

Danika Sanders, *College of Southern Nevada*

Olivia Schlabra, *Georgia Perimeter College*

Whitney Schmidt, *Tarrant County College–Northwest*

Cheyenne Sharpe, *Tarrant County College–Northwest*

Monica Sheehan, *Tarrant County College–Northwest*

Lydia Simone, *College of Southern Nevada*

Analiese Smith, *Tarrant County College–Northwest*

Deb Stipp, *Ivy Technical Community College*

Melanie Tabak, *Kent State University*

Victoria Vallance, *Suffolk County Community College*

Katherine Weinmann, *Tarrant County College–Northwest*

Stephanie Willes, *College of Southern Nevada*

Courtney Williams, *Tarrant County College–Northwest*

Lauren Wissing, *Tidewater Community College*

Owen Wood, *Tarrant County College–Northwest*

Sarah Woolf, *Tarrant County College–Northwest*

The following instructors graciously attended our focus groups. Their feedback both informed and influenced many key aspects of the text, as well as the resources that accompany it.

Anora Ackerson, *Kalamazoo Valley Community College*

Judith Addelston, *Valencia College*

Winifred Armstead-Hannah, *City Colleges of Chicago, Richard R. Daley College*

Diana Aria, *County College of Morris*

Marina Baratian, *Eastern Florida State College*

Nazira Barry, *Miami College, Dade, Wolfson*

Shirley Bass Wright, *St. Phillip's College*

Sonia Bell, *Prince George's Community College*

Mark Berg, *Stockton College*

Christopher Beverly, *St. Johns River State College*

Andrew Blair, *Palm Beach State College*

Marilyn Bonem, *Eastern Michigan University*

Leanne Boucher, *Nova Southeastern University*

Lauren Brewer, *Stephen F. Austin State University*

Winfield Brown, *Florence-Darlington Technical College*

Alison Buchanan, *Henry Ford Community College*

Jessica Cail, *Pepperdine University*

Anthony Carboni, *St. Johns River State College*

Christie Cathey, *Missouri State University*

Shakiera Causey, *Guilford Technical Community College*

Svetlana Chesser, *University of Tennessee at Chattanooga*

Ruby Christian-Brougham, *Los Angeles Valley College*

Benjamin Clark, *Florida State College at Jacksonville*

Julia Cohen, *Los Angeles Pierce College*

Kyle Conlon, *Stephen F. Austin State University*

Bonnie Dennis, *Virginia Western Community College*

Dianne DeSousa, *Prairie State Community College*

Peggy Dombrowski, *Harrisburg Area Community College*

AnnMarie Donohue, *Montgomery County Community College*

Emily Dunlap, *Chattanooga State University College*

Deniss Edwards, *San Jacinto Community College*

Susan Edwards, *Mott Community College*

Jason Fernandez, *San Jacinto Community College*

Urminda Firlan, *Kalamazoo Valley Community College*

Ricardo Frazer, *Atlanta Metropolitan State College*

Amanda Frei, *University of Phoenix*

Diana Fuller, *Georgia Perimeter College*

Sherry Ginn, *Rowan–Cabarrus Community College*

Deborah Greenspan, *Montgomery County Community College*

Marlene Groomes, *Miami Dade–Homestead*

Monique Guishard, *Bronx Community College*

Janice Hartgrove-Freille, *Lone Star College– North Harris*

James Haugh, *Rowan University*

John Haworth, *Chattanooga State Community College*

Julie Hernandez, *Rock Valley College*

Sallie Herrin, *Rowan–Cabarrus Community College*

Debra Hollister, *Valencia College–Lake Nona*

Nancy Honeycutt, *Alamance Community College*

Ray Huebschmann, *Georgia Perimeter College*

Kathleen Hughes-DeSousa, *Pasco Hernando Community College*

Susan Johnson, *Cypress College*

Paul Johnson, *Oakton Community College*

Lynda Karlis, *Macomb Community College– Center Campus*

Ken Kikuchi, *College of Lake County*

Andrew Kim, *Citrus College*

Cheri Kittrell, *State College of Florida*

Sharon Kline, *Eastern Florida State College*

Rachel Laimon, *Mott Community College*

Samuel Lamb, *Tidewater Community College, Virginia Beach*

Marika Lamoreaux, *Georgia State University*

Irv Lichtman, *Houston Community College*

David Christopher Ludden, Jr., *Georgia Gwinnett College*

Sabine Maetzke, *Florida Southwestern State College*

Deborah Maher, *Orange Coast College*

Jeni Maijala, *University of Phoenix*

Richard Manley, *Antelope Valley College*

Randy Martinez, *Cypress College*

Myssie Mathis, *Cape Fear Community College*

Dan McConnell, *University of Central Florida*

Yvonne McCoy, *Tarrant County College*

Cheryl McGill, *Florence–Darlington Technical College*

David McGrevy, *Palomar Community College*

Russ McGuff, *Tallahassee Community College*

Emily McSpadden, *Bronx Community College*

William Mellan, *Hillsborough Community College–Plant City*

Charles Miron, *Community College of Baltimore County–Catonsville*

Paulina Multhaupt, *Macomb Community College–Center Campus*

Sonia Nieves, *Broward Community College– South Campus*

James O'Brien, *Tidewater Community College, Virginia Beach*

Marco O'Brien, *Milwaukee Area Technical College*

Laura Ochoa, *Bergen Community College*

Belinda Ann Oliver, *Clark Atlanta University*

Denise Orme, *Golden West College*

Enrique Otero, *North Lake College*

Jennifer Pemberton, *Community College of Baltimore County– Catonsville*

Kathleen Peters, *Eastern Florida State College*

Diane Plummer, *Clark Atlanta University*

Debbie Podwika, *Kankakee Community College*

James Previte, *Antelope Valley College*

Christopher Raye, *Santa Fe College*

Alan Richey, *Wilkes Community College*

MaryLou Robins, *San Jacinto Community College*

Martin Rosenman, *Morehouse College*

Debra Rowe, *Oakland Community College– Royal Oak*

Claire Rubman, *Suffolk County Community College*

Carlos Sandoval, *Cypress College*

Spring Schaefer, *Delta College*

Alex Schwartz, *Santa Monica College*

Angi Semegon, *Flagler College*

Maria Shpurik, *Florida International University*

Cyd Skinner, *Northampton Community College*

Cindy Sledge, *Lone Star College– CyFair*

Morgan Slusher, *Community College of Baltimore County–Essex*

Steven Smith, *California State University, Fullerton*

Wallace Smith, *Union County College*

Jason Spiegelman, *Community College of Baltimore County–Catonsville*

Eli Stav, *Broward Community College–North Campus*

Cari Stevenson, *Kankakee Community College*

Krishna Stilianos, *Oakland Community College–Highland Lakes*

William Suits, *Seminole State College of Florida*

Shawn Talbot, *Kellogg Community College*

Anita Tam, Greenville *Technical College*

Anne Taylor-Spitzer, *Antelope Valley College*

Khia Thomas, *Broward Community College–North Campus*

Chris Thomas, *Florence–Darlington Technical College*

Jennifer Thompson-Watson, *City Colleges of Chicago, Kennedy–King College*

Angela Tiru, *Naugatuck Valley Community College*

Katherine Trotter, *Chattanooga State Community College*

Donna Vandergrift, *Rowan College at Burlington County*

Lora Vasiliauskas, *Virginia Western Community College*

Rebekah Wanic, *Grossmont College*

Linda Weldon, *Community College of Baltimore County–Essex*

Rhonda Whitten, *Tri-County Technical College*

Katherine Wickes, *Blinn College*

Glenda Williams, *Lone Star College–North Harris*

Steve Withrow, *Guilford Technical Community College*

Dreama Witt, *Guilford Technical Community College*

Brandy Young, *Cypress College*

There is one "unofficial" reviewer whose contributions cannot be quantified. Working behind the scenes from start to finish, reading every line of this text alongside us was Dr. Eve Van Rennes. Dr. Van Rennes, thank you for your intelligent critiques and unwavering support.

It goes without saying that this project would not have been the same without the hard work and dedication of our author team. Every sentence in this textbook has been a group effort: We have written and reviewed everything together. Our minds work differently and we have distinct skill sets, but we recognize and appreciate those in each other. Writing this book has been an arduous task (who knew three women could live on just a few hours of sleep every night?), but we have encouraged and supported each other along the way. We are more than a work team—we are lifelong friends.

We should acknowledge that none of us would have written these words if it hadn't been for our parents and grandparents, who made our education their top priority.

Last, but certainly not least, we would like to thank the extraordinary people whose life stories are woven throughout these chapters. We selected you because your stories touched and inspired us. Learning about your lives has helped us become more thoughtful and compassionate people. We believe you will have the same effect on college students across the country.

A special thanks to Ericka Harley and her intelligent, kind, and beautiful daughter Aa'Niyah, who provided us with the cover photo. We smile every time we see Niyah's face.

Deborah M. Licht
Misty G. Hull
Coco Ballantyne

GRANT ROONEY PREMIUM/Alamy Stock Photo.

leungchopan/Shutterstock.

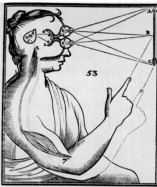
National Library of Medicine.

CHAPTER OUTLINE AND LEARNING OBJECTIVES

Presenting Psychology

LO 1 Define psychology and describe its scope.

LO 2 Summarize the goals of psychology.

Roots, Schools, and Perspectives of Psychology

LO 3 Identify the people who helped establish psychology as a discipline, and describe their contributions.

LO 4 List and summarize the major perspectives in psychology.

Science and Psychology

LO 5 Evaluate pseudopsychology and its relationship to critical thinking.

The Scientific Method

LO 6 Describe how psychologists use the scientific method.

Research Basics

LO 7 Distinguish between a random sample and a representative sample.

Descriptive Research

LO 8 Recognize the forms of descriptive research.

LO 9 Describe the correlational method and identify its limitations.

Experimental Research

LO 10 Explain how the experimental method can establish cause and effect.

Research Ethics

LO 11 Identify measures psychologists take to support ethical treatment of their research participants.

10 HAPPIEST COUNTRIES IN THE WORLD

Macmillan Learning.

Macmillan Learning.

1 introduction to the science of psychology

Presenting Psychology

HALF OF ME MISSING Sharon Poset had a happy childhood in Delanco, New Jersey. Her mother made perfect birthday cakes and sewed pretty dresses, and her father was kind, gentle, and made her feel safe. Sharon knew she was adopted, and she was comfortable with this truth. In fact, she considered her adoption an important part of who she was, and would often tell people about it. But even though Sharon felt secure in herself, something seemed missing. She was, in her own words, "pathologically lonely," despite the fact that she had two younger siblings. "[It] felt like there was a half of you, or like your right side, your left side, just was missing all the time," Sharon recalls. "And I just thought everybody felt that way, and I couldn't understand why my brother and sister weren't lonely that way too."

If only Sharon had known that her "missing half" was just 20 miles away, growing up in another New Jersey town—an identical twin named Debbie. The girls had been separated a week after birth and adopted by different families. Debbie didn't know she was adopted, but she too felt "pathologically lonely." When she was a little girl, toy stores were selling a doll called Patti Playpal. The doll was life-size, and Debbie wished she had magical powers to bring it to life. She longed for a playmate her own age and size, a little girl just like herself.

Sharon and Debbie went through childhood and adolescence oblivious to the other's existence. Both went away to college, and married shortly after graduation. They hoped that marrying wonderful men would cure them

Separated at Birth
Sharon Poset (left) and Debbie Mehlman were born in the county hospital of Mount Holly, New Jersey, on Saturday, March 22, 1952. Their birth mother gave them up for adoption because she had gotten pregnant out of wedlock. One week later, the girls were sent home to different families. Courtesy Sharon Poset (left) and Debbie Mehlman (right).

Do They Look Alike?
Sharon (left) and Debbie pose for photos in (top to bottom) kindergarten, middle school, and high school. Raised by different families and separated by a distance of 20 miles, the twins grew up unaware of each other's existence. Courtesy Sharon Poset (left) and Debbie Mehlman (right).

Sharon and Debbie, in Their Own Words

http://qrs.ly/pt4brgp

Photo: Macmillan Learning.

of their loneliness, but wedding bells did not fix the problem. Even after having children they loved and cherished—a son for Sharon and a daughter for Debbie—their loneliness persisted. They tried filling the void with pets; Sharon went for breeds like Dobermans and boxers, while Debbie opted for fluffy poodles, keeshonds, and sheepdogs. But none of these animals provided the type of companionship they craved.

What would happen if Sharon and Debbie met? Would finding her "missing half" make each woman feel complete? ●

Welcome to the Fascinating World of Psychology

Imagine you could observe the reunion of Sharon and Debbie. What kinds of characteristics would you notice? You may be struck by their physical similarities: ocean blue eyes, apple cheeks, fine reddish hair, and broad smiles. But perhaps you would be more intrigued by their common *psychological* characteristics, that is, those related to their behavior and mental processes: attitudes, beliefs, personality traits, sense of humor, the way they cross their eyes when exasperated.

Psychologists have long been fascinated by identical twins, particularly those raised in separate homes. At conception, identical twins share 100% of their genes (the units of heredity passed from parents to children), so they are equivalent in their **nature,** or inherited biological factors (Abdellaoui et al., 2015; McRae, Visscher, Montgomery, & Martin, 2015). But being raised in separate households means they differ in their **nurture;** that is, they are subject to distinct sets of environmental forces. Thus, the similarities observed between these twins are likely to be influenced by their common nature, while differences are apt to be linked to their unique upbringing and life experiences, or nurture. For example, identical twins—even those raised apart—tend to be very close on measures of intelligence (Bouchard, Lykken, McGue, Segal, & Tellegen, 1990; Shakeshaft et al., 2015). This suggests that genes (nature) can play a major role in determining intellectual ability.

Twin research is not just important to twins; it has implications for all of us. Suppose one identical twin develops cancer but his twin does not. That means that something in the environment likely set off the disease process. If we can figure out what the trigger is, then we can all benefit from that knowledge (Segal, 1999; Winerman, 2015).

Studies of identical twins and fraternal twins (who, like non-twin siblings, share approximately 50% of their genes) have helped psychologists untangle the roles of nature and nurture for a variety of topics, including intelligence (Chapter 7), sexual orientation (Chapter 10), and aspects of personality (Chapter 11). We will continue this exploration of nature and nurture later in this chapter, and throughout the book, but first let's establish a basic understanding of psychology, the science.

What Is Psychology?

LO 1 **Define psychology and describe its scope.**

Psychology is the scientific study of behavior and mental processes. Smiling, hugging, and laughing are observable behaviors you might expect Sharon and Debbie to display upon meeting; all of these activities are potential research topics in psychology. And

Note: Quotations attributed to Sharon Poset, Debbie Mehlman, and Dr. Nancy L. Segal are personal communications.

TABLE 1.1 MENTAL HEALTH PROFESSIONALS

Degree	Occupation	Training	Focus	Prescribes Medications
Medical Doctor, MD	Psychiatrist	Medical school and residency training in psychiatry	Treatment of psychological disorders; may include research focus	Yes
Doctor of Philosophy, PhD	Clinical or Counseling Psychologist	Graduate school; includes dissertation and internship	Research-oriented and clinical practice	Varies by state
Doctor of Psychology, PsyD	Clinical or Counseling Psychologist	Graduate school; includes internship; may include dissertation	Focus on professional practice	Varies by state
Master's Degree, MA or MS	Mental Health Counselor	Graduate school; includes internship	Focus on professional practice	No

Mental health professionals come from a variety of backgrounds. Here, we present a handful of these, including general information on training, focus, and whether the training includes licensing to prescribe medication for psychological disorders.

although the twins' thoughts are not observable, they are valid topics of psychological research as well.

Psychologists are scientists who work in a variety of subfields, all of which include the study of behavior and underlying mental processes. People often associate psychology with therapy, and many psychologists do provide therapy. These *counseling* and *clinical psychologists* might also conduct research on the causes and treatments of psychological disorders (**TABLE 1.1**; Chapters 13 and 14). Clinical practice is just one slice of the gigantic psychology pie. There are psychologists who spend their days observing rats in laboratories or assessing the capabilities of children in schools. Psychologists may also be found poring over brain scans in major medical centers, spying on monkeys in the Brazilian rainforest, and offering expert testimony in legal cases (**FIGURE 1.1**; see Appendix B for more on careers in psychology).

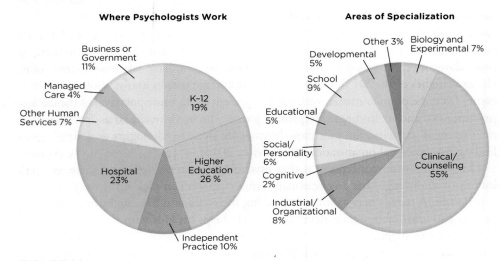

FIGURE 1.1
Fields of Psychology
The pie charts above show the primary place of work for full-time doctorate-level psychologists working in 2014 and their areas of specialty. As you can see, psychologists work in diverse contexts and specialize in many subfields. In the photo at right, a clinical psychologist counsels a displaced flood survivor in a Thai refugee camp. Information from APA Center for Workforce Studies (2015) and U.S. Bureau of Labor Statistics (2014). Photo: Boris Roessler/dpa/Landov.

nature The inherited biological factors that shape behaviors, personality, and other characteristics.

nurture The environmental factors that shape behaviors, personality, and other characteristics.

psychology The scientific study of behavior and mental processes.

psychologists Scientists who study behavior and mental processes.

Psychology is a broad field that includes many perspectives and subfields. The American Psychological Association (APA), one of psychology's major professional organizations, has over 50 divisions representing various subdisciplines and areas of interest (APA, n.d.-a). The Association for Psychological Science (APS), another major professional organization in the field, offers a list on its website of over 100 different societies, organizations, and agencies that are considered to have some affiliation with the discipline of psychology (APS, n.d.). In fact, each of the chapters in this textbook covers a broad subtopic that represents a subfield of psychology.

In Class: Collaborate and Report

Psychology is the scientific study of behavior and mental processes. In your group, **A)** generate a list of diverse behaviors; **B)** generate a list of subfields and careers in psychology; **C)** try to match the items in the two lists.

BASIC AND APPLIED RESEARCH Psychologists conduct two major types of research. Basic research, which often occurs in university laboratories, focuses on collecting data to support (or refute) theories. The goal of basic research is not to find solutions to specific problems, but rather to gather knowledge for the sake of knowledge. Suppose a researcher is curious about how cognitive abilities (thinking and other mental activities) develop from adolescence to young adulthood. She conducts a twin study, and her findings suggest a link between genetic similarity and some cognitive abilities (Friedman et al., 2016). This basic research may pave the way for applied research—for example, a study investigating how interventions such as after-school reading programs can influence cognitive ability, despite genetic predispositions. Applied research focuses on changing behaviors and outcomes, and often leads to real-world applications, such as specific behavioral interventions for children with autism, innovative keyboard layouts that improve typing performance, or methods for helping students study more successfully. This type of research is often conducted in natural settings outside the laboratory. Although applied research may incorporate findings from basic research, its goals are more practical.

MISCONCEPTIONS ABOUT PSYCHOLOGY Looking at Figure 1.1, you may have been surprised to learn about the variety of occupations available to psychologists. If so, you are not alone; many people assume that all psychologists provide therapy, when in fact they perform numerous roles in the workforce. There are also various misconceptions about psychology topics, even among students who have taken some psychology classes (Hughes et al., 2015). Most of what the average person knows about psychology comes from the popular media, which fail to present an accurate portrayal of the field, its practitioners, and its findings. Frequently, guests who are introduced as "psychologists" or "therapists" by television talk show hosts really aren't psychologists as defined by the leading psychological organizations (Stanovich, 2013).

One common misconception is that psychology is simply common sense, or a collection of knowledge that any reasonably smart person can pick up through everyday experiences. A parent may assume that raising three children has taught him everything he needs to know about child development. He helps his kids with homework because common sense suggests it will increase their success in school. What he doesn't know (and what psychology research will tell him) is that giving help doesn't always benefit children: "Even when math-anxious parents have good intentions, their homework help may backfire, decreasing children's math learning and increasing their math anxiety across the school year" (Maloney, Ramirez, Gunderson, Levine, & Beilock, 2015, p. 6).

As the above example illustrates, common sense and popular wisdom are not always correct (Lilienfeld, 2012). Common sense is an important ability that helps us survive

FIGURE 1.2

What Is This?

Throughout this book, you will find parenthetical notes like the one highlighted below. These citations tell you the source of research or findings being discussed, in this case an article published by researchers Maloney, Ramirez, Gunderson, Levine, and Beilock in 2015. Information provided in this brief citation allows you to locate the full reference in the alphabetized reference list at the back of the textbook: Look for Maloney, Ramirez, Gunderson, Levine, & Beilock (2015) on page R-36. That way, if you want to know more about a topic, you can look up the source and read the original article or book. There are many systems and formats for citing sources, but this textbook uses the APA style established by the American Psychological Association (APA, 2010b). The infographic **How To Read A Scientific Article** (on the inside front cover of this text) guides you through the process of finding and reading an article, skills that will help you in psychology and many other classes.

TABLE 1.2 DISPELLED: SIX "COMMONSENSE" MYTHS

Myth	Reality
People only use 10% of their brains.	Neuroscientists consider this claim to be absurd; the reality is that we use essentially all of our brains (Boyd, 2008, February 7; Howard-Jones, 2014).
Most older people live sad and solitary lives.	Many people become happier with age (Lilienfeld, Lynn, Ruscio, & Beyerstein, 2010). In fact, one study suggests that the average 83-year-old is just as content as the average 26-year-old (Fischer, 2009).
Once you're married and have kids, your sex life goes down the tubes.	According to the National Survey of Sexual Health and Behavior (Center for Sexual Health Promotion, 2010), men and women in their late twenties and early thirties are having more sex than people in other age groups.
After birth, your brain no longer generates new neurons.	Neurons in certain areas of the brain are replenished during adulthood (Eriksson et al., 1998; Ernst & Frisén, 2015).
Sugar makes kids hyper and inattentive.	This is a common belief among educators across the world, but not one supported by solid scientific data (Howard-Jones, 2014; Vreeman & Carroll, 2008).
People have distinct "learning styles." For example, "visual learners" absorb information better when it is presented in ways they can see (graphs, animations, etc.).	Although we all have different skill sets and areas of interest, there is no compelling evidence that we possess specific learning styles (Riener, 2010/2011).

Here are a few examples of commonsense wisdom that have been debunked by psychological research.

Photo: Jesse Cowan/Getty Images.

and adapt, but it should not take the place of scientific findings. As you learn more about how humans think and remember, you will start to see that we are prone to making errors (Chapters 6 and 7). **TABLE 1.2** identifies some commonsense myths that have been dispelled through research. Have you fallen for any of them?

The false notion that psychology is common sense, and that psychological findings are obvious and predictable, may stem partly from *hindsight bias,* or the feeling that "I knew it all along." Many people shrug their shoulders and say, "I could have told you that," when they learn about psychology research findings. Although the outcome of a study may seem obvious in retrospect, that doesn't mean they could have predicted it beforehand. Examples of hindsight bias abound in everyday life. Suppose your instructor returns an exam, and you are surprised at one of the questions you got wrong. Now that you're staring at the correct answer, it seems so obvious (*I knew the answer was "evolution"!*). But if you really knew it all along, why did you choose the wrong answer (Tauer, 2009)? You may be expressing hindsight bias when you make this assertion. If so, you're in good company. Even practicing physicians fall victim to hindsight bias. When doctors hear about the details of an autopsy and then learn of the deceased person's diagnosis, for example, they often believe they could have easily predicted it (Arkes, 2013). In both of these situations, hindsight bias can get in the way of learning. How do you learn from your mistakes if you can't correctly identify the gaps in your knowledge (Arkes, 2013; Tauer, 2009)?

PSYCHOLOGY IS A SCIENCE   Unlike common sense, psychology is a rigorous discipline based on meticulous and methodical observation, as well as data analysis. Like chemistry and biology, psychology is a *science*, a systematic approach to gathering knowledge through careful observation and experimentation. It requires sharing results (see the infographic **How To Read a Scientific Article** on the inside front cover) and doing so in a manner that permits others to duplicate and therefore verify work. This chapter is dedicated to helping you understand the science of psychology.

The Goals of Psychology

LO 2   **Summarize the goals of psychology.**

What exactly do those who study behavior and mental processes hope to accomplish? The answer to this question varies according to subfield, but there are four main goals: to describe, explain, predict, and control behavior. These goals lay the foundation for the scientific approach used in psychology. Let's take a closer look at each one, keeping in mind that the order presented doesn't necessarily indicate their importance.

DESCRIBE   One goal is simply to describe or report what is observed. Imagine a psychologist who wants to *describe* differences in children's food preferences. What kind of study would she conduct? First, she would need access to a group of parents and caregivers who are willing to keep track of their children's food intake. Once the participants have been assembled, she might request permission to perform tests evaluating the children's moods, social adjustment, and physical health. She would likely want to monitor the children over time, conducting more assessments at a later date. Eventually, she would present her observations in a scientific article published in a respected journal, and use her findings to help plan future research.

EXPLAIN   Another goal is to organize and make sense of what researchers have observed. If the psychologist noticed an interesting pattern of food preferences among the children, she might develop a preliminary explanation for this finding. Suppose the children enjoyed the same kinds of food as their siblings; then the psychologist might look for factors that could influence their likes and dislikes. Searching the scientific literature for clues, she might come across studies suggesting that food preferences are established early in life (Shutts, Kinzler, & DeJesus, 2013). If she learned that food preferences were associated with shared home environments, this could help *explain* why siblings had similar tastes, although she still would have to conduct a controlled experiment to identify a causal relationship between these two variables.

PREDICT   Yet another goal is to predict behaviors or outcomes on the basis of observed patterns. If the researcher noted a link between the children's food choices and those of their siblings, then she could *predict* that the preferences of other close family members (such as first cousins) might lead to the same outcome: similar eating patterns. Jeremiah loves green beans, and so do his cousins. However, she would still have to untangle the effects of nature and nurture, so she might decide to study pairs of identical and fraternal twins. If there was greater similarity between the identical twins than the fraternal twins, she could assume that the greater degree of shared genetics (in the identical twins) played a role in determining food preferences (Pallister et al., 2015).

CONTROL   One more goal of psychology is to use research findings to shape, modify, and control behavior. Here, we are referring to how we can *apply* the findings of psychological research to change and direct (*control*) behaviors in a beneficial way. Perhaps the researcher could use her findings to help public health experts design programs to

Why So Picky?
One of the goals of psychology is to *predict* behavior. Suppose a researcher discovers that siblings have similar food preferences. This leads her to predict that other close relatives, such as cousins, share food likes and dislikes as well. Even if this prediction is correct, how would the researcher determine the relative influences of heredity (nature) and environment (nurture)? She could design a study comparing the food preferences of identical and fraternal twin pairs. If the identical twins, who share nearly 100% of their genes, have more similar tastes than the fraternal twins, who share about 50% of their genes, heredity is probably a factor (Pallister et al., 2015). David Malan/ Getty Images.

TABLE 1.3 STUDY SMART

Technique	What to Do
Survey	Skim the material to determine what may be useful to you: review questions, learning objectives, chapter summaries. Identify main ideas and concepts.
Question	Note any questions that arise after your survey. Create an outline to help organize your study based on the questions you generate.
Read	Read through your chapter and take notes on its content.
Recall	Go over the material you have read in your mind. Identify key points and crucial processes. Discuss how other material supports the key points and processes.
Review	Reread the material, and include additional information to enhance your notes. "Teach" it to someone else.
Individualize the process	Break down the reading into small sections you can read, recall, and review effectively.
Space your study	Build in breaks and spread the study sessions over time.
Minimize distractions	Focus on the task at hand; multitasking while studying diverts attention, resulting in more time spent learning the material.
Test frequently	Test yourself frequently. Low-stakes feedback provides an opportunity to learn the material and retain it longer.
Sleep	Get enough rest. Good sleep helps us learn new material and retain it.

Listed here are some practical tips for remembering information you learn in your classes. This advice is largely based on research presented in Chapter 6. Information from Al Firdaus (2012); Roediger, Putnam, & Smith (2011); Rohrer & Taylor (2006).

encourage healthier eating choices among kids (Pallister et al., 2015). Psychological research can be applied to your life, too. See **TABLE 1.3** for some evidence-based tips on remembering information for your classes.

The distinction among the four goals is not always clear, and researchers may not address all of them in the same study. What's more, their order is not universal— sometimes researchers make predictions before trying to explain a behavior.

You have now learned the definition, scope, and goals of psychology. You will soon explore the ins and outs of psychological research: how psychologists use a scientific approach, the many types of studies they carry out, and the ethical standards for acceptable conduct that guide them through the process. But let's start with some history, meeting the people whose philosophies, insights, and research findings molded psychology into the vibrant science it is today.

 **show what you know**

1. Psychology is the scientific study of _____ and _____.

2. A researcher is asked to devise a plan to help improve food choices of elementary schoolchildren. Based on his research findings, he creates posters for the school cafeterias that he believes will modify the children's food selections. This attempt to change behaviors falls under which of the main goals of psychology?

   a. describe   c. predict
   b. explain   d. control

3. How is common sense different from the findings of psychology? If one of your friends says, "I could have told you that!" when you describe the results of various studies on food preferences, how would you respond?

   ✔ CHECK YOUR ANSWERS IN APPENDIX C.

Roots, Schools, and Perspectives of Psychology

The field of psychology is almost 140 years old, very young compared to other scientific disciplines, but its core questions are as old as humanity itself. Read the works of the ancient Greeks, and you will see that they asked some of the same questions as modern psychologists—*What is the connection between the body and mind? How do we obtain knowledge? Where does knowledge reside?* Making your way through this book, you will discover that many of these questions are still under investigation.

Philosophy and Physiology

LO 3 Identify the people who helped establish psychology as a discipline, and describe their contributions.

The roots of psychology lie in disciplines as diverse as philosophy and physiology. In ancient Greece, the great philosopher Plato (427–347 BCE) believed that truth and knowledge exist in the soul before birth; that is, humans are born with some degree of innate or inborn knowledge. Plato raised an important issue psychologists still contemplate: the contribution of *nature* in the human capacity for cognition.

Aristotle (384–322 BCE) was one of Plato's renowned students. Unlike his mentor, Aristotle believed that we know reality through our perceptions, and we learn through our sensory experiences. This approach is now commonly referred to as *empiricism,* and it is how scientists acquire knowledge through their observations and experiments (Schultz & Schultz, 2016). Aristotle has been credited with laying the foundation for a scientific approach to answering questions, including those pertaining to psychological concepts such as emotion, sensation, and perception (Slife, 1990; Thorne & Henley, 2005). He believed knowledge is the result of experience, and thus paved the way for scientists to study the world through their observations.

This notion that experience, or *nurture,* plays an all-important role in how we acquire knowledge contradicts Plato's belief that it is inborn. Aristotle therefore provided

Nature and Nurture
Both nature and nurture influence the development of living things. Would you believe that these trees belong to the same species? Both are Jeffrey pines (*Pinus jeffreyi*), but they have been exposed to dramatically different environmental pressures. Jeffrey pines typically reach 80 to 130 feet. The tree on the left appears to be growing in fertile soil in a thriving forest, whereas the one on the right has virtually sprung from a slab of rock on an 8,122-foot peak in Yosemite National Park (St. John, 2003, August 19). A testament to the power of nurture.
Left: Bob Gibbons/Science Source. Right: Kent and Donna Dannen/Science Source.

the opposing position in the discussion of nature and nurture, a central theme in the field of psychology. Today, psychologists agree that nature and nurture are both important, and current research explores the relative contributions of each through studies of heredity and environmental factors.

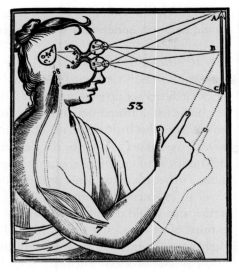

If Aristotle placed great confidence in human perception, French philosopher René Descartes (day-KART; 1596–1650) practically discounted it. Famous for saying, "I think, therefore, I am," Descartes believed that most everything else was uncertain, including what he saw with his own eyes. He proposed that the body is like a tangible machine, whereas the mind has no physical substance. The body and mind interact as two separate entities, a view known as *dualism,* and Descartes (and many others) wondered how they were connected. How can the mind direct our hand to answer a phone call, or how can the touch of a loved one create a sensation our mind can interpret? The nature of the mind and body are different, yet these entities are connected, according to Descartes. Descartes' work allowed for a more scientific approach to examining thoughts, emotions, and other topics previously considered beyond the scope of study.

About 200 years later, another scientist experienced a "flash of insight" about the mind–body connection. It was October 22, 1850, when German physicist Gustav Theodor Fechner (1801–1887) suddenly realized that he could "solve" the mind–body conundrum, that is, figure out how they connect. Fechner reasoned that by studying the physical ability to sense stimuli, we are simultaneously conducting experiments on the mind. In other words, we can understand how the mind and body work together by studying sensation. Fechner's efforts laid the groundwork for research on sensation and perception (Benjamin, 2007; Robinson, 2010).

Psychology Is Born

Thus far, the only people in our presentation of psychology's history have been philosophers and a physicist. You might ask where all the psychologists were during the time of Descartes and Fechner. The answer is simple: It wasn't until the 19th century that psychology emerged as a scientific discipline. In 1879 Wilhelm Wundt (VILL-helm Vundt) (1832–1920) founded the first psychology laboratory, at the University of Leipzig in Germany, and for this he generally is considered the "father of psychology." Equipped with its own laboratory, research team, and meticulous accounts of experiments, psychology finally became a discipline in its own right.

The overall aim of Wundt's early experiments was to measure psychological processes through **introspection,** a method used to examine one's own conscious activities. For Wundt, introspection involved effortful reflection on the sensations, feelings, and images experienced in response to a stimulus, followed by reports that were *objective,* meaning free of opinions, beliefs, expectations, and values. In order to ensure reliable data, Wundt required all his participants to complete 10,000 "introspective observations" prior to starting data collection. His participants were asked to make quantitative judgments about physical stimuli—how strong they were, how long they

Descartes and Dualism
French philosopher René Descartes proposed that the eye and other body parts work like machines. The mind, he suggested, is separate and intangible. But as you will discover in this textbook, many activities of the mind have been traced back to physical interactions among nerve cells. National Library of Medicine.

Wundt Measures the Mind
In 1861 Wilhelm Wundt conducted an experiment on reaction time, which was a turning point in the field of psychology. Using a pendulum that hit a bell upon reaching its outer limits, Wundt demonstrated a 10th of a second delay between hearing the bell and noting the position of the pendulum (and vice versa), and it was during that very brief period that a mental process occurred. Finally, activities of the mind could be measured (Thorne & Henley, 2005). The Drs. Nicolas and Dorothy Cummings Center for the History of Psychology, The University of Akron.

introspection The examination of one's own conscious activities.

The next time your cell phone vibrates, take the opportunity to engage in some introspection. Grab the cell phone and hold it in your hands (try to resist answering the call). Pay attention to what you experience as you wait for the vibrations to stop. Then put down the phone and consider your experience. Report on your sensations (the color, shape, and texture of the phone) and feelings (anxiety, excitement, frustration), but make your observations *objective*.

Breaking Ground
Margaret Floy Washburn is perhaps most famous for becoming the first woman psychologist to earn a PhD, but her scholarly contributions must not be underestimated. Her book *The Animal Mind: A Textbook of Comparative Psychology* (1908), which drew on her extensive research with animals, had an enduring impact on the field (APA, 2013b; Washburn, 2010). Macmillan Learning.

structuralism An early school of psychology that used introspection to determine the structure and most basic elements of the mind.

functionalism An early school of psychology that focused on the function of thought processes, feelings, and behaviors and how they help us adapt to the environment.

lasted, and so on (Boring, 1953; Schultz & Schultz, 2016). The Try This to the left should help you understand Wundt's method of introspection.

STRUCTURALISM Edward Titchener (TITCH-e-ner) (1867–1927), who was a student of Wundt, developed the school of psychology known as **structuralism.** In 1893 Titchener set up a laboratory at Cornell University in Ithaca, New York, where he conducted introspection experiments aimed at determining the structure and "atoms" (or most basic elements) of the mind. Titchener's participants, also very well-trained, were asked to describe the elements of their current consciousness. In contrast to Wundt's focus on *objective,* quantitative, or measurable, reports of conscious experiences, Titchener's participants provided detailed reports of their *subjective* (unique or personal) experiences (Hothersall, 2004). So instead of providing labels for objects, participants would describe them; an egg would be referred to as a "white orb with a textured outer layer," but not an "egg." The school of structuralism did not last past Titchener's lifetime, and even most of his contemporaries regarded structuralism as outdated. Nevertheless, Titchener helped to demonstrate that psychological studies could be conducted through observation and measurement.

FUNCTIONALISM In the late 1870s, William James (1842–1910) offered the first psychology classes in the United States, at Harvard University, where he was granted $300 for laboratory and classroom demonstration equipment (Croce, 2010). James had little interest in pursuing the experimental psychology practiced by Wundt and other Europeans; instead, he was inspired by the work of English naturalist Charles Darwin (1809–1882), as it supported the notion that human consciousness serves a purpose (Schultz & Schultz, 2016). Studying the elements of introspection was not a worthwhile endeavor, James believed, because consciousness is an ever-changing "stream" of thoughts that helps us adapt. Consciousness cannot be studied by looking for fixed or static elements (like the "atoms" of the mind), because they don't exist, or so he reasoned. But James believed consciousness does serve a function, and it is important to study the purpose of thought processes, feelings, and behaviors, and how they help us adapt to the environment. This focus on purpose and adaptation in psychological research is the overarching theme of the school of **functionalism.**

Students often confuse "functionalism" with "structuralism," perhaps because the terms sound similar, but they are very different. The focus of structuralism was to uncover the *structure* of the mind, whereas functionalism aimed to identify the adaptive *function* of thoughts, feelings, and behaviors. Although it didn't endure as a separate field of psychology, functionalism has continued to influence educational psychology, research on emotion, comparative studies of animal behavior, and other areas of psychology (Benjamin, 2007).

HERE COME THE WOMEN Like most sciences, psychology began as a "boys' club," with men earning the degrees, teaching the classes, and running the labs. There were, however, women as competent and inquiring as their male counterparts who beat down the club doors long before women were formally invited. One of William James' students, Mary Whiton Calkins (1863–1930), completed all the requirements for a PhD at Harvard, but was not allowed to graduate from the then all-male college because she was a woman. Nonetheless, she persevered with her work and established her own laboratory at Wellesley College, eventually becoming the first female president of the APA. If you are wondering, the first woman to earn a PhD in psychology was Margaret Floy Washburn (1871–1939), a student of Titchener's. Her degree, which was granted in 1894, came from Cornell University, which—unlike Harvard—allowed women to earn doctorates at the time.

Mamie Phipps Clark (1917–1983) was the first Black woman to be awarded a PhD in psychology from Columbia University. Her work, which she conducted with her husband Kenneth Bancroft Clark, examined the impact of prejudice and discrimination on child development. In particular, she explored how race recognition impacts a child's self-esteem (Pickren & Burchett, 2014). Her husband held a faculty position at City University of New York, but she was never allowed to teach there. Instead, she found a job analyzing research data and eventually became executive director of the Northside Center for Child Development in upper Manhattan (Pickren & Burchett, 2014).

Thanks to trailblazers such as Calkins, Washburn, and Clark, the field of psychology is no longer dominated by men. In fact, about three quarters of students earning master's degrees and PhDs in psychology are women, a statistic that suggests more men are needed in various subfields (Cynkar, 2007; Willyard, 2011). The situation remains lopsided in the job market as well; between 2012 and 2013, the psychology workforce showed an increase of almost 9% for women and a decrease of around 10% for men (APA, 2015a).

Psychology's Perspectives

LO 4   **List and summarize the major perspectives in psychology.**

Some of the early schools of psychology had a lasting impact and others seemed to fade. Nevertheless, they all contributed to the growth of the young science. The infographic **Psychology's Roots** (see inside front cover) illustrates how these schools developed into perspectives that continue to shed light on the complex nature of human behavior.

PSYCHOANALYTIC   Toward the end of the 19th century, while many early psychologists were investigating the "normal" functioning of the mind (in experimental psychology), Sigmund Freud (1856–1939), an Austrian neurologist, focused much of his attention on the "abnormal" aspects. Freud believed that behavior and personality are influenced by conflicts between one's inner desires (such as sexual and aggressive impulses) and the expectations of society—clashes primarily occurring unconsciously or outside of awareness (Gay, 1988). This **psychoanalytic perspective** suggests that personality development is heavily influenced by processes of which we are unaware, and these processes become apparent early in life, and result from interactions with caregivers (Chapter 11). Freud also pioneered *psychoanalysis,* a new approach to psychotherapy, or "talk therapy" (Chapter 14). The psychoanalytic perspective is used as an explanatory tool in many of psychology's subfields.

BEHAVIORAL   As Freud worked on his new theories of the unconscious mind, a Russian physiologist named Ivan Pavlov (1849–1936) was busy studying canine digestion. During the course of his research, Pavlov got sidetracked by an intriguing phenomenon. The dogs he was studying were salivating in response to sights and sounds associated with food, such as the footsteps of a lab assistant coming to feed them. The type of learning that led to this response eventually became known as *classical conditioning* (Chapter 5). Building on Pavlov's conditioning experiments, American psychologist John B. Watson (1878–1958) established **behaviorism,** which viewed psychology as the scientific study of behaviors that could be seen and/or measured. Consciousness, sensations, feelings, and the unconscious were not suitable topics of study, according to Watson.

For the Children
The work of Mamie Phipps Clark raised awareness about the unique psychological issues affecting African American and other minority children. She and her husband founded Harlem's Northside Center for Child Development, an organization that continues to provide psychological and educational support to children in the community. Macmillan Learning.

Freud Takes Off
Psychology's most famous icon boards his first airplane in 1928, years after psychoanalysis had gotten off the ground in Europe and America. Freudian ideas are still alive and well, though people often overestimate their importance in psychology. About 90% of American Psychological Association members do not practice psychoanalysis, and most science-minded psychologists have distanced themselves from Freudian notions because they are not supported by solid experimental data (Stanovich, 2013; Hobson, 2006, April/May). ASSOCIATED PRESS.

psychoanalytic perspective An approach developed by Freud suggesting that behavior and personality are shaped by unconscious conflicts.

behaviorism The scientific study of observable behavior.

Carrying on the behaviorist approach to psychology, American psychologist B. F. Skinner (1904–1990) studied the relationship between behaviors and their consequences. Skinner's research focused on *operant conditioning,* a type of learning that occurs when behaviors are rewarded or punished (Chapter 5). Skinner acknowledged that mental processes such as memory and emotion might exist, but he did not believe such topics should be studied in psychology. To ensure that psychology was a science, he insisted on studying behaviors that could be observed and documented.

The **behavioral perspective** promoted by Watson and Skinner suggests that behaviors and personality are primarily determined by learning. People tend to repeat behaviors that lead to desirable consequences, and discontinue behaviors with undesirable consequences. According to this view, personalities are largely shaped by forces in the environment—that is, *nurture.* But twin studies suggest that *nature* also plays a pivotal role; the genes we inherit from our parents can have an important influence on the people we become (Polderman et al., 2015). You will witness the power of nature in the story of Sharon and Debbie.

HUMANISTIC   American psychologists Carl Rogers (1902–1987) and Abraham Maslow (1908–1970) took psychology in yet another direction. These founders of **humanistic psychology** were critical of psychoanalysis and behaviorism, and the presumed lack of control people have over their lives. The humanistic perspective suggests that human nature is essentially positive, and that people are naturally inclined to grow and change for the better (Chapter 11) (Maslow, 1943; Rogers, 1961). Humanism challenged the thinking and practice of researchers and clinicians who had been "raised" on Watson and Skinner. Reflecting on the history of psychology, we cannot help but notice that new developments are often reactions to what came before. The rise of the humanistic perspective was, in some ways, a rebellion against the rigidity of psychoanalysis and behaviorism.

COGNITIVE   During the two-decade prime of *behaviorism* (1930–1950), many psychologists only studied observable behavior. Yet prior to behaviorism, psychologists had emphasized the study of thoughts and emotions. The situation eventually came full-circle in the 1950s, when a new force in psychology brought these unobservable elements back into focus. This renewed interest in examining mental processes played an important role in the development of *cognitive psychology* (Wertheimer, 2012), and the work of another American, memory researcher George Miller (1920–2012), was an important catalyst for this cognitive revolution (Chapter 6). The **cognitive perspective** examines mental activities that direct behavior, focusing on processes such as thinking, memory, and language. The *cognitive neuroscience* perspective, in particular, explores the physiological underpinnings of mental processes, searching for connections between behavior and the human nervous system, especially the brain. With the development of brain-scanning technologies, cognitive neuroscience has flourished, interfacing with fields such as medicine, computer science, and psychology.

EVOLUTIONARY   According to the **evolutionary perspective,** behaviors and mental processes are shaped by the forces of evolution. This perspective is based on Charles Darwin's theory of evolution by natural selection. Darwin observed great variability in the characteristics of humans and other organisms. He believed these traits were shaped by **natural selection,** the process through which inherited traits in a given population either increase in frequency because they are adaptive or decrease in frequency because they are maladaptive. Humans have many adaptive traits and behaviors that appear to have evolved through natural selection. David Buss, currently a professor of psychology at the University of Texas at Austin, is one of the founders of evolutionary

behavioral perspective An approach suggesting that behavior is primarily learned through associations, reinforcers, and observation.

humanistic psychology An approach suggesting that human nature is by and large positive, and the human direction is toward growth.

cognitive perspective An approach examining the mental processes that direct behavior.

evolutionary perspective An approach that uses knowledge about evolutionary forces, such as natural selection, to understand behavior.

natural selection The process through which inherited traits in a given population either increase in frequency because they are adaptive or decrease in frequency because they are maladaptive.

biological perspective An approach that uses knowledge about underlying physiology to explain behavior and mental processes.

sociocultural perspective An approach examining how social interactions and culture influence behavior and mental processes.

biopsychosocial perspective Explains behavior through the interaction of biological, psychological, and sociocultural factors.

psychology. He and others have used the evolutionary perspective to explain a variety of personality traits, intelligence, and behaviors like risk-taking (Buss & Penke, 2015; Schultz & Schultz, 2016).

BIOLOGICAL   The **biological perspective** uses knowledge about underlying physiology to explain behavior and mental processes. Psychologists who take this approach explore how biological factors, such as hormones, genes, and brain activities, are involved in behavior and cognition. Researchers study a diverse array of biological factors in relation to twins—everything from the genetic basis of physical fitness to the influence of hormones on the structure of children's brains (Brouwer et al., 2015; Schutte, Nederend, Hudziak, de Geus, & Bartels, 2016). Chapter 2 provides a foundation for understanding this perspective as well as the field of *neuroscience,* which refers to the study of the brain and nervous system.

SOCIOCULTURAL   The **sociocultural perspective** emphasizes the importance of social interactions and culture, including the roles we play. Russian psychologist Lev Vygotsky (1896–1934) proposed that we must examine how social and cultural factors influence the cognitive development of children (Chapter 8). With this realization, researchers such as Mamie Phipps Clark have studied how prejudice, segregation, and discrimination impact the development of the self (Pickren & Burchett, 2014).

In the past, researchers often assumed that the findings of their studies were applicable to people of all ethnic and cultural backgrounds. Then in the 1980s, cross-cultural research began to uncover differences that called into question the presumed universal nature of these findings. New studies revealed that Western research participants are not always representative of people from other cultures. Even being a part of a group within a culture can influence behavior and mental processes; thus, we need to take into account these various settings and subcultures.

BIOPSYCHOSOCIAL   Many psychologists use the **biopsychosocial perspective;** in other words, they examine the biological, psychological, and sociocultural factors influencing behavior (Beauchamp & Anderson, 2010). The biopsychosocial perspective suggests that these factors are highly interactive: It's not just the convergence of factors that matters, but the way they interact. This perspective is used by scientists in many fields, from psychologists studying the mental health of men (McDermott, Schwartz, & Rislin, 2016) to physicians treating patients with sickle-cell disease (Crosby, Quinn, & Kalinyak, 2015).

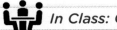
In Class: Collaborate and Report

A) Identify a movie or television show that is familiar to all members of your group. **B)** Pick a scene that shows a character exhibiting inappropriate or risky behavior. **C)** Try to explain the behavior using at least two of the perspectives of psychology.

COMBINING THE PERSPECTIVES   You can see that the field of psychology abounds with diversity. With so many perspectives (**TABLE 1.4** on the next page), how do we know which one is the most accurate and effective in achieving psychology's goals? Human behavior is complex and requires an integrated or eclectic approach—using the findings of multiple perspectives—to explain its origins. In some cases, creating a theoretical *model* helps clarify a complex set of

May the Biggest Beak Win
In a population of finches, some have little beaks that can only crack open small, soft seeds; others have big beaks that can open big seeds; and still others fall somewhere in between. During times of food scarcity (such as a drought), the big-beaked birds are more likely to survive and reproduce because they have a greater variety of seeds to choose from. Looking at the finch population during this period, you will see more birds being born with bigger beaks. It's natural selection right before your eyes (Grant, 1991). David Hosking/Science Source.

Culture Matters
A group of Flower Hmong women shop for fabric in Vietnam. In many Asian markets, the customer is expected to bargain with the seller. How does this compare to shopping in the United States, where prices are preestablished? When it comes to studying human thoughts and behavior, understanding cultural context is key. GRANT ROONEY PREMIUM/Alamy Stock Photo.

TABLE 1.4 CURRENT PERSPECTIVES IN PSYCHOLOGY

Perspective	Main Idea	Questions Psychologists Ask
Psychoanalytic	Underlying conflicts influence behavior.	How do unconscious conflicts affect behavior?
Behavioral	Behavior is learned primarily through associations, reinforcers, and observation.	How does learning shape behavior?
Humanistic	Humans are naturally inclined to grow in a positive direction.	How do choice and self-determination influence behavior?
Cognitive	Behavior is driven by cognitive processes.	How do thinking, memory, and language direct behavior?
Evolutionary	Humans have evolved characteristics that promote survival and adaptation to the environment.	How does natural selection advance our behavioral predispositions?
Biological	Behavior and mental processes arise from physiological activity.	How do biological factors, such as hormones, genes, anatomy, and brain structures, influence behavior and mental processes?
Sociocultural	Other people, as well as the broader cultural context, influence behavior and mental processes.	How do culture and environment shape our behavior and attitudes?
Biopsychosocial	Behavior and mental processes are shaped by an interaction of biological, psychological, and sociocultural factors.	How do the interactions of biology, psychology, and culture influence behavior and mental processes?

Psychologists draw on a variety of theories in their research and practice. Listed here are the dominant theoretical perspectives, all of which reappear many times in this textbook. Human behaviors are often best understood when viewed through more than one lens.

observations. Models often enable us to form mental pictures of what we seek to understand. Many psychologists pick and choose among the various models and perspectives to explain and understand a given phenomenon. Remember this integrated approach as you learn more about Sharon and Debbie. What biological, psychological, social, and cultural factors could be used to explain their behaviors? How did these factors and others combine to form their overall experience?

 WHAT? I HAVE A TWIN?! Sharon and Debbie went through 45 years of life with no knowledge of each other. Then one day in 1997, Debbie's mother phoned with an important message: She was coming to visit, and she wanted to talk to Debbie alone, without her husband and daughter present. *What could this be about?* Debbie wondered. *Maybe she wants to talk with me about the family finances.* When her mother dropped the news about the adoption, Debbie was floored. So was her younger sister, who learned that weekend that she too was adopted. Debbie's sister ended up hiring a private investigator who found Debbie's birth mother and ultimately tracked down Sharon. It didn't take long for Sharon to pick up the phone and call Debbie.

"Mom, your *sister* is on the phone," Debbie's daughter said in a soft, sweet tone. "I couldn't understand why she was saying it like that," recalls Debbie, who assumed it was her other (non-biological) sister calling. Debbie picked up the phone and heard a familiar voice on the line; it sounded exactly like her own, only with a Southern accent. "It was like Scarlett O'Hara was calling!" she laughs. The phone

You Asked, Sharon and Debbie Answer

http://qrs.ly/ko5a57i

Do you regret not sharing the first 45 years together?

scan this ➔

conversation lasted 2 hours, and it would have gone on longer if Debbie hadn't had a class to attend that evening.

Four days later, Sharon was on an airplane, traveling through an ice storm to meet Debbie in Harford, Connecticut. When Sharon stepped off the plane, the first thing Debbie noticed was her outfit: *Why didn't she wear nicer clothes?* she wondered. Sharon saw that Debbie was all "duded up" with matching clothes and perfectly coiffed hair, and thought, *what a stick in the mud!* As Debbie puts it, "We were like so under-impressed with one another!"

But first impressions soon dissipated when the twins began talking. It was as if they were looking in the mirror, because they sounded and looked alike, swirling their hands around their faces just the same way. One of the twins made a joke about having "unibrows" (eyebrows that join in the middle) and they erupted in cackles. Their laughter even sounded identical. Studying Debbie's face, Sharon saw her own eyes, cheekbones, laugh lines. "That's my face, but on somebody else," she recalls saying. "Don't look at me. I can't take it anymore!" And they just kept laughing. ●

Reunited
When Sharon and Debbie first met at age 45, there were no tears, just laughter. Everyone who witnessed their reunion at the Hartford airport, including the camera crew from the local news station, was awed and amused by how much the twins looked and acted alike.
Courtesy Debbie Mehlman and Sharon Poset.

  show what you know

1. Wilhelm Wundt's research efforts all involved _____, which is the examination of one's own conscious activities.
   a. functionalism
   b. structuralism
   c. reaction time
   d. introspection

2. Your psychology instructor is adamant that psychologists should only study observable behaviors. She acknowledges consciousness exists, but insists it cannot be observed or documented, and therefore should not be a topic for psychological research. Which of the following perspectives is she using?
   a. psychoanalytic
   b. behavioral
   c. humanistic
   d. cognitive

3. We have presented eight perspectives in this section. Describe how two of them are similar. Pick two other perspectives and explain how they differ.

✓ CHECK YOUR ANSWERS IN APPENDIX C.

Science and Psychology

PEAS IN A POD Sharon stayed at Debbie's house for the whole weekend. Before the visit, both twins worried they would have nothing more to discuss. *What more could we have in common?* they wondered. Once together, the twins could not get enough of each other. They visited Debbie's synagogue, met her friends at work, and chattered late into the night, waking up Debbie's husband with their laughter. It was the beginning of the relationship that would finally make each twin feel complete.

As Sharon and Debbie got to know each other, they discovered all sorts of common interests, habits, and traits. Both suffer from migraines, enjoy Motown music, and prefer hot tea over coffee. They are always running late, and set their watches 7 or 8 minutes ahead of time as a corrective measure. In terms of intellectual ability, both are avid readers but they struggle with math (in fact, their IQ scores are just 3 points apart). Sharon and Debbie married similar men, had one child, and spent much of their careers helping people with disabilities. It drives them crazy to hear people coughing, chewing, or blowing air out their noses, and they *hate* the feeling of bumping their heads on cabinet doors and other objects. Sharon was raised as a Christian, Debbie was brought up Jewish, and they are both passionate about their faith. Neither understood why their siblings, who grew up in the same household and attended the same church/synagogue, never took to religion in the same way. At one point, Sharon and Debbie entertained the idea of one

You Asked, Sharon and Debbie Answer

http://qrs.ly/xb5a57n

What is the most amazing similarity that you have discovered in each other?

scan this →

A Twin Thing?
When Sharon and Debbie first met, they took out photos of their families to break the ice. Sharon pointed out her favorite picture of her son (top), and Debbie shared her favorite shot of her daughter; the similarities between these photos were uncanny. At that moment, the twins looked at each other and thought, *There is really something to this twin thing!* Courtesy of Sharon Poset (top) and Debbie Mehlman (bottom).

of them converting (Sharon to Judaism or Debbie to Christianity), but they decided against it. Ultimately, each twin respected the other for abiding by her conviction. And, thanks to their "weird sense of humor," they were able to get over "the whole religion thing."

Now that Sharon and Debbie have known each other for 19 years, they are extremely close—more than best friends. "We're always thinking of each other," says Debbie, who wishes she had a "mini me" of Sharon to carry around in her pocket all day. "We could be locked in a closet for the weekend, and we would have the best time ever," Sharon says. Although Sharon lives in Birmingham, Alabama, and Debbie lives in West Hartford, Connecticut, they talk and text frequently, and visit as often as possible. When the twins are together, all they need to do is make eye contact and they know what the other is thinking. It's as if they have some sort of "twin telepathy," or ability to communicate without words or body language. ●

THINK IT THROUGH
Does Twin Telepathy Exist?

Some people believe that identical twins can communicate on a supernatural level, reading each other's thoughts and emotions. They attempt to support their conviction with gripping anecdotal evidence: "Daisy and Denise finish each other's sentences; they feel the same emotions; one time, Daisy broke her leg at soccer practice, and Denise had this eerie feeling her twin was in trouble even before she heard about the incident." Many twins believe they have communicated with each other through *telepathy*, reporting they were able to know what was happening to their twin, without any form of "normal" communication occurring. Twins recall suffering from an injury or illness, and their twin responding in kind (for example, one twin fainted when the other twin was getting anesthetized for an operation). Twins also report remarkable coincidences such as giving birth on the same day or buying the same presents for each other (Brusewitz, Cherkas, Harris, & Parker, 2013).

"I JUST KNOW MY TWIN IS IN TROUBLE."

Sounds like these twins are really in tune with each other, but does that mean they have telepathic powers? Look at the research, and you will find no compelling objective support for the existence of these types of psychic powers (Farha, 2007; Rouder & Morey, 2011). And Dr. Nancy L. Segal, professor of psychology at California State University, Fullerton, agrees there is no scientific evidence to suggest that twin telepathy exists. One of the world's leading twin researchers, Dr. Segal has studied hundreds of identical twins, triplets, and quadruplets (including Sharon and Debbie), and witnessed the remarkable communication that can occur between them. How does Dr. Segal explain it?

"Identical twins have the same genes, and they respond to the world in many of the same ways," Dr. Segal explains. "They process information in many similar ways, and they think a lot alike about most topics." So when twins finish each other's sentences, they are probably just thinking along parallel lines. Likewise, when twins select similar outfits or choose the same types of friends, they are expressing "tastes and preferences [that are] grounded in their similar biological makeup."

If twin telepathy doesn't exist, then why do some twins report that they can "sense" when their twin is in trouble? Like Sharon and Debbie, many twins spend a lot of time thinking about each other. "If you call your twin 10 times a day and think about your twin constantly, one of those times your twin will be in trouble," Dr. Segal says. "We only hear about the hits; we never hear about the misses."

What does Dr. Segal mean by "hits" and "misses"? "Hits" refer to the isolated events that support the notion of twin telepathy (the one time Twin #1 correctly guessed Twin #2 was in trouble). "Misses" are the many occasions that Twin #1 suspects Twin #2 was in danger, when in fact Twin #2 is perfectly fine. We don't tend to hear about those "misses," because they aren't very interesting, and they don't support the titillating idea that twins are telepathic. Paying attention to pieces of evidence that validate our beliefs, and ignoring those that contradict them, demonstrate a lack of *critical thinking*.

Critical Thinking

LO 5 Evaluate pseudopsychology and its relationship to critical thinking.

Critical thinking is the process of weighing various pieces of evidence, synthesizing them (putting them together), and determining how each contributes to the bigger picture. Critical thinking requires one to consider the source of information and the quality of evidence before deciding if it is valid. But critical thinking goes far beyond verifying the facts (Davies, 2015; Yanchar, Slife, & Warne, 2008). The process involves thinking beyond definitions, focusing on underlying concepts and applications, and being open-minded and skeptical at the same time. Psychology is driven by critical thinking—disciplined thinking that is clear, rational, and accepting of new ideas. **INFOGRAPHIC I.I** on the next page shows how critical thinking is useful for tackling problems that may seem unrelated to psychology.

In your everyday life, you will encounter many examples of belief systems that present themselves as "psychological science" but lack critical thinking. They fall into the category of **pseudopsychology,** an approach to explaining and predicting behavior and events that appears to be psychology but is not supported by objective evidence. One familiar example is *astrology,* which uses a chart of the heavens called a *horoscope* to "predict" everything from the weather to romantic relationships. These predictions, however, have no scientific basis. Surprisingly, many people have difficulty distinguishing between pseudosciences, like astrology, and true sciences, even after earning a college degree (Impey, Buxner, & Antonellis, 2012; Schmaltz & Lilienfeld, 2014).

How then does astrology often seem to be accurate in its descriptions and predictions? Consider this excerpt from a monthly Gemini horoscope: "You could meet a lot of fascinating people and make many new friends as autumn begins. You could also take up a creative new interest or hobby" (Horoscope.com, 2014). If you really think about it, this statement could apply to just about any human being on the planet. We all are capable of starting new activities and meeting "fascinating people" (Isn't every person "fascinating" in his or her own way?). How could you possibly prove such a statement wrong? You couldn't. That's why astrology is not science. A telltale feature of a pseudopsychology, like any pseudoscience, is its tendency to make assertions so broad and vague that they cannot be refuted (Stanovich, 2013).

Why can't we use pseudopsychology to help predict and explain behaviors? Because there is no solid evidence for its effectiveness, no scientific support for its findings. Critical thinking is absent from the "pseudotheories" used to explain the pseudosciences (Rasmussen, 2007; Stemwedel, 2011, October 4).

The American Psychological Association (APA) views critical thinking as an essential skill for all undergraduate psychology majors. To achieve APA's goal of Scientific Inquiry and Critical Thinking, students must be able to think critically about psychological claims, determine whether a source is objective and credible, and distinguish between real science and pseudoscience (APA, 2013a).

"What's nice about working in this place is we don't have to finish any of our experiments."

S. Harris/Cartoonstock.

critical thinking The process of weighing various pieces of evidence, synthesizing them, and determining the contributions of each; disciplined thinking that is clear, rational, open-minded, and informed by evidence.

pseudopsychology An approach to explaining and predicting behavior and events that appears to be psychology, but has no empirical or objective evidence to support it.

Critical Thinking

What is critical thinking and why is it important? Being a critical thinker means carefully evaluating pieces of evidence, synthesizing them, and determining how they fit into the "big picture." Critical thinkers maintain a healthy dose of skepticism, but they are also able to adjust their thinking if presented with contradictory evidence. Consider the issue of global warming: Do you think it's real, and are human beings causing it?

97% of world's leading climate scientists believe that greenhouse gas emissions generated by human activities, such as burning gasoline and coal, are driving the warming trend (BENESTAD ET AL., 2016).

Government officials consider human-caused climate change an

"urgent and growing threat to our national security,"

and warn of higher temperatures, rising sea levels, floods, droughts, and other natural disasters—events that could threaten agricultural productivity, set the stage for new disease outbreaks, and trigger conflicts (U.S. DEPARTMENT OF DEFENSE, 2015, JULY 23, p. 3).

Yet many people are not too worried about global warming, perhaps because they don't grasp the severity of the problem:

(AMERICAN PSYCHOLOGICAL ASSOCIATION, 2015d).

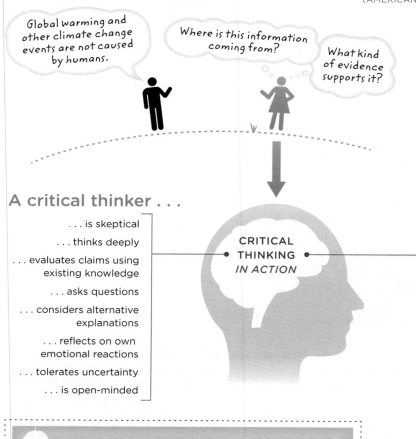

Global warming and other climate change events are not caused by humans.

Where is this information coming from?

What kind of evidence supports it?

A critical thinker . . .

. . . is skeptical

. . . thinks deeply

. . . evaluates claims using existing knowledge

. . . asks questions

. . . considers alternative explanations

. . . reflects on own emotional reactions

. . . tolerates uncertainty

. . . is open-minded

CRITICAL THINKING *IN ACTION*

Although you will develop your critical thinking skills in psychology class, they can be used in other contexts, from resolving everyday dilemmas, such as, "Why did I get such a mediocre grade after studying so hard?" to understanding global crises such as climate change.

GO TO THE SOURCE: ASK CRITICAL QUESTIONS

Who wrote the article?
• What is the professional background of the author(s)?

Where was it published?
• Is it peer-reviewed, open-source, or popular press?

What are the study's findings?
• Do the findings support the hypothesis?
• Are there limitations cited?
• What other variables might have influenced the outcome?

What were the methods used to conduct the study?
• How big was the sample?
• How did researchers collect data?

Has the study been replicated?
• Have other studies reported the same results?
• Have other studies tried different samples?

Credits: Thermometer, dencg/Shutterstock; Globe, adike/Shutterstock.

Critical thinking is an invaluable skill, whether you are a psychologist planning an experiment or a student trying to earn a good grade in psychology class. Has anyone ever told you that choosing "C" on a multiple-choice question is your best bet when you don't know the answer? There is little research showing this is the best strategy (Skinner, 2009). Accepting this type of advice without thinking critically can be a barrier to developing better strategies. Next time you're offered a tempting bit of folk wisdom, think before you bite: Does objective evidence exist to support this claim? Can it be used to predict future events?

 show what you know

1. An instructor in the psychology department assigns a project requiring students to read several journal articles on a controversial topic. They are then required to weigh various pieces of evidence from the articles, synthesize the information, and determine how the various findings contribute to understanding the topic. This process is known as:

   a. pseudotheory.
   b. critical thinking.
   c. hindsight bias.
   d. applied research.

2. _____ is an approach to explaining and predicting events that appears to be psychology but is not supported by empirical, objective evidence.

3. How would you explain to someone that astrology is a pseudopsychology?

✓ CHECK YOUR ANSWERS IN APPENDIX C.

The Scientific Method

LO 6 Describe how psychologists use the scientific method.

Critical thinking is an important component of the **scientific method,** the process scientists use to conduct research (see **INFOGRAPHIC 1.2** on page 22). The goal of the scientific method is to provide *empirical evidence,* or data from systematic observations or experiments. This evidence is often used to support or refute a **hypothesis** (hi-POTH-uh-sis), which is a statement that tests a prediction about the outcome of a study. An **experiment** is a controlled procedure involving scientific observations and/or manipulations by the researcher to influence participants' thinking, emotions, or behaviors. In the scientific method, an observation must be objective, or outside the influence of personal opinion and preconceived notions. Humans are prone to errors in thinking, but the scientific method helps to minimize their impact.

Suppose a researcher is studying the core characteristics of how identical twins like Sharon and Debbie think, act, and feel. He could get a good sense of this by talking with them for several hours, but his impressions may differ from that of another researcher doing the same thing. A more objective approach would be to administer an objective *personality* test with a standard set of questions (true/false, multiple choice, circle the number) and an automated scoring system. The results of such a test do not depend on the researchers' biases or expectations, and will be the same no matter who administers it.

Now let's take a look at the five basic steps of the scientific method.

STEP 1: DEVELOP A QUESTION The scientific method typically begins when a researcher observes something interesting in the environment and comes up with a research question. Twin researcher Dr. Nancy L. Segal got the idea for her first twin study at a child's birthday party. She noticed a pair of fraternal twins working on a puzzle together, fighting over it like mad, and wondered, *would identical twins cooperate better?* Her curiosity also stemmed from years of studying behavioral genetics and evolutionary theory—the work of scientists who had come before her. Reading books and articles written by scientists is an excellent way to generate ideas for new studies. (Refer to the infographic "How to Read a Scientific Article" on the inside front cover

scientific method The process scientists use to conduct research, which includes a continuing cycle of exploration, critical thinking, and systematic observation.

hypothesis A statement that can be used to test a prediction.

experiment A controlled procedure that involves careful examination through the use of scientific observation and/or manipulation of variables (measurable characteristics).

to review how best to find and read an article; learning these skills will help you in psychology and many other classes.)

In Class: Collaborate and Report

In your group, **A)** brainstorm areas of research that might involve twins. **B)** Connect to an online database through your college, public library, or Google Scholar. **C)** Search for journal articles, refining your search with appropriate key terms. **D)** Using APA style, create a reference list including at least two of the articles your team found.

STEP 2: DEVELOP A HYPOTHESIS   Once a research question has been developed, the next step in the scientific method is to formulate a hypothesis, the statement used to test predictions about a study's outcome. The data collected by the experimenter will either support or refute the hypothesis. Dr. Segal's hypothesis was essentially the following: *When given a joint task, identical twins will cooperate more and compete less than fraternal twins.* Hypotheses can be difficult to generate for studies on new and unexplored topics, because researchers may not have fully developed expectations for the outcome; in these situations, a general prediction may take the place of a formal hypothesis. Researchers often turn to their favorite perspective(s) to guide the development of their hypotheses. What perspective do you think influenced Dr. Segal's hypothesis?

While developing research questions and hypotheses, researchers should always be on the lookout for information that could offer explanations for the phenomenon they are studying. Dr. Segal based her hypothesis on behavioral genetics and evolutionary theory. **Theories** synthesize observations in order to explain phenomena, and they can be used to make predictions that can then be tested through research. Many people believe scientific theories are nothing more than unverified guesses or hunches, but they are mistaken (Stanovich, 2013). A theory is a well-established body of principles that often rests on a sturdy foundation of scientific evidence. Evolution is a prime example of a theory that has been mistaken for an ongoing scientific controversy. Thanks to inaccurate portrayals in the media, many people have come to believe that evolution is an active area of "debate," when in reality it is a theory embraced by the overwhelming majority of scientists, including psychologists.

STEP 3: DESIGN STUDY AND COLLECT DATA   Once a hypothesis has been developed, the researcher designs an experiment to test it and then collects the data. Dr. Segal's study involved videotaping sets of identical and fraternal twin children working on a puzzle together. She included only those twins who had very similar IQs. As she explains, "I wanted the kids to be more or less matched in ability, because I didn't want the smarter kid taking over the whole activity." Once the instructions were given ("Complete the puzzle together"), the children were free to solve the puzzle as they wished (Segal, 1984, p. 94). Later, looking at the videos, Dr. Segal and her colleagues rated the children using all sorts of "indices of cooperative behavior." For example, the researchers looked to see if the twins were equally involved, how often they handed each other pieces, whether they physically leaned on one another, pushed or hit. They even tallied up the number of facial expressions each twin displayed (for example, sadness, surprise, and pride).

Researchers must establish **operational definitions** that specify the precise manner in which the characteristics of interest are defined and measured. A good operational definition helps others understand how to perform an observation or take a measurement. In the example above, Dr. Segal may have operationally defined *cooperative behavior* based on how often twins handed each other puzzle pieces, how long they spent leaning on one another, or the number of times they smiled.

It's in the Data
Neurologist Richard D. King uses neuroimaging technologies to study brain changes associated with neurodegenerative diseases, such as Alzheimer's. His research involves complex data analysis (King et al., 2009). Cheryl Diaz Meyer/Newscom/Tribune News Service/DALLAS/TX/USA.

theory Synthesizes observations in order to explain phenomena and guide predictions to be tested through research.

operational definition The precise manner in which a variable of interest is defined and measured.

Gathering data must be done in a very controlled fashion to ensure there are no errors, which could arise from recording problems or from unknown environmental factors. We will address the basics of data collection later in the chapter.

STEP 4: ANALYZE THE DATA   The researcher now has data that need to be analyzed, or organized in a meaningful way. As you can see from **FIGURE 1.3**, rows and columns of numbers are just that, numbers. In order to make sense of the "raw" data, one must use statistical methods. *Descriptive statistics* are used to organize and present data, often through tables, graphs, and charts. *Inferential statistics,* on the other hand, go beyond simply describing the data set, allowing researchers to make inferences and determine the probability of events occurring in the future (for a more in-depth look at statistics, see Appendix A).

Once the data have been analyzed, the researcher must ask several questions: Did the results support the hypothesis? Were the predictions met? In Dr. Segal's case, the results supported her hypothesis: "The identicals were more cooperative on almost every index that I used," she says. "My conclusion was that yes, identical genes do underlie greater cooperation between partners."

Next, the researcher evaluates her hypothesis, rethinks her theories, and possibly designs a new study. This procedure is an important part of the scientific method because it enables us to think critically about our findings. If these ideas are worth pursuing, the researcher could develop a new hypothesis and embark on a study to test it. You can see the cyclical nature of the scientific method illustrated in Infographic 1.2.

STEP 5: PUBLISH THE FINDINGS   Once the data have been analyzed and the hypothesis tested, it's time to share findings with other researchers who might be able to build on the work. This typically involves writing a scientific article and submitting it to a scholarly, peer-reviewed journal. Journal editors send these submitted manuscripts to subject-matter experts, or peer reviewers, who carefully read them and make recommendations for publishing, revising, or rejecting the articles altogether.

The peer-review process is notoriously meticulous, and it helps provide us with more certainty that findings from research can be trusted. This approach is not foolproof, of course. There have been cases of fabricated data slipping past the scrutiny of peer reviewers. In some cases, these oversights have had serious consequences for the general public. Case in point: the widespread confusion over the safety of routine childhood vaccines.

In the late 1990s, researchers published a study suggesting that vaccination against infectious diseases caused autism (Wakefield et al., 1998). The findings sparked panic among parents, some of whom shunned the shots, putting their children at risk for life-threatening infections such as the measles. The study turned out to be fraudulent and the reported findings were deceptive, but it took 12 years for journal editors to retract the article (Editors of *The Lancet,* 2010). One reason for this long delay was that researchers had to investigate all the accusations of wrongdoing and data fabrication (Godlee, Smith, & Marcovitch, 2011). The investigation included interviews with the parents of the children discussed in the study, which ultimately led to the conclusion that the information in the published account was inaccurate (Deer, 2011).

Since the publication of that flawed research, several high-quality studies have found no credible support for the autism-vaccine hypothesis (Honda, Shimizu, & Rutter, 2005; Jain et al., 2015; Madsen et al., 2002). Still, the publicity given to the original article continues to cast a shadow: Many parents continue to refuse vaccines for their children, with serious consequences. Measles outbreaks involving unvaccinated children have occurred in various parts of the United States in recent years (Chen, 2014, June 26; Palmer, 2015, January 26).

Variable	Record Number	Columns	Format
FAMILYID	1	3–7	Numeric
FROMWHO	1	9–12	Numeric
WHICHATT	1	14–17	Numeric
INT_T_	1	19–24	Numeric
INT_S_	1	26–31	Numeric
CON_T_	1	33–38	Numeric
CON_S_	1	40–46	Numeric
PERS	1	48–52	Numeric
GLOB	1	54–58	Numeric
STA_C_	1	60–64	Numeric
STA_O_	1	66–70	Numeric
BARR	1	72–76	Numeric
BREW	2	1–5	Numeric

FIGURE 1.3
Raw Data
The information in this figure comes from a data file. Until the researcher analyzes the data, these numbers will have little meaning.

Misguided Marchers?
Actors Jenny McCarthy and Jim Carrey (pictured here with his daughter, left) lead a rally calling for changes in childhood vaccines. Studies suggest that routine vaccinations are safe, but some parents believe they trigger autism, a misconception stemming from a widely publicized but problematic study published in a peer-reviewed journal. CD1/Newscom/WENN/Carrie Devorah.

The Scientific Method

Psychologists use the scientific method to conduct research. The scientific method allows researchers to collect empirical (objective) evidence by following a sequence of carefully executed steps. In this infographic, you can trace the steps taken in an actual research project performed by two psychologists who were interested in the effect of "counting your blessings" (Emmons & McCullough, 2003). Notice that the process is cyclical in nature. Answering one research question often leads researchers to develop additional questions, and the process begins again.

The researchers see an article suggesting happiness is related to greater overall health. The researchers think about their own study and wonder:

ASK NEW QUESTIONS

Does counting your blessings also lead to better overall health?

To develop a question, a researcher will:
• observe the world around him;
• identify a personally interesting topic;
• review scientific literature on this topic.

To develop a hypothesis (a testable prediction), a researcher will:
• look for existing theories about the topic;
• establish operational definitions to specify variables being studied.

STEP 1: DEVELOP A QUESTION

Grandma always says, "Count your blessings." Why? What is the impact of a grateful outlook?

STEP 2: DEVELOP A HYPOTHESIS

HYPOTHESIS:
People who think about positive events in their lives will report greater psychological well-being than people who think about negative events.

STEP 5: PUBLISH THE FINDINGS

A researcher writes a description of the study and submits it to an academic journal, where it will be peer-reviewed and if approved, published for other researchers to read and use in their own research.

The researchers write an article titled, "Counting blessings versus burdens: An experimental investigation of gratitude and subjective well-being in daily life." It is published in the *Journal of Personality and Social Psychology.*

Group 1 participants reported significantly greater well-being than other groups. Researchers conclude that people who count their blessings feel better about their lives as a whole.

STEP 4: ANALYZE THE DATA

1 2 3 Researchers randomly assign participants to three groups. Every week, Group 1 participants list five things they are grateful for; Group 2 participants list five things that bother them; and Group 3 participants list any five things that happened. All three groups are surveyed weekly to determine their psychological well-being.

STEP 3: DESIGN STUDY & COLLECT DATA

A researcher organizes and analyzes the data and determines whether the hypothesis is supported.

A researcher plans a well-controlled study. Data are collected when the study is performed.
• A design can be experimental or descriptive.
• Data are collected using controlled measurement techniques.

The peer-review process serves as a safeguard against fraud and inaccuracies, but it is not always successful, and problematic findings make their way into peer-reviewed journals. About once a day an article is retracted, the result of plagiarism, data meddling, and other forms of inappropriate behavior, and retractions occur more often in top journals than in lower-profile ones (Marcus & Oransky, 2015, May 22).

Publishing an article is a crucial step in the scientific process because it allows other researchers to **replicate** an experiment, which might mean repeating it with other participants or altering some of the procedures. This repetition is necessary to ensure that the initial findings were not just a fluke or the result of a poorly designed experiment. The more a study is replicated and produces similar findings, the more confidence we can have in those findings.

In the case of Wakefield's fraudulent autism study, other researchers tried to replicate the research for over 10 years, but could never establish a relationship between autism and vaccines (Godlee et al., 2011). This fact alone made the Wakefield findings highly suspect.

ASK NEW QUESTIONS Most studies generate more questions than they answer, and here lies the beauty of the scientific process. The results of one scientific study raise a host of new questions, and those questions lead to new hypotheses, new studies, and yet another collection of questions. This continuing cycle of exploration uses critical thinking at every step.

 show what you know

1. We all hold opinions about various issues and events in our environments, but how are those opinions different from theories?

2. A researcher identifies affection between partners by counting the number of times they gaze into each other's eyes while in the laboratory waiting room. The cutoff for those who would be considered very affectionate partners is gazing more than 10 times in 1 hour. The researcher has created a(n) _____ of affection.
   a. theory
   b. hypothesis
   c. replication
   d. operational definition

3. A _____ synthesizes observations to try to explain phenomena, and we can use it to help make predictions.
   a. theory
   b. hypothesis
   c. descriptive statistic
   d. peer-reviewed journal

   ✓ CHECK YOUR ANSWERS IN APPENDIX C.

Research Basics

SHARON AND DEBBIE'S RESEARCH ADVENTURE

Three months after meeting, Sharon and Debbie became participants in the monumental Minnesota Study of Twins Reared Apart (MISTRA). The study, led by Dr. Thomas J. Bouchard, Jr., spanned two decades and included 137 sets of twins (identical and fraternal) that had been separated at a young age and raised in different families (Segal, 2012). This unique population provided researchers with what they referred to as the "simplest and most powerful method for disentangling the influence of environmental and genetic factors on human characteristics" (Bouchard et al., 1990, p. 223)—that is, an excellent way to study how nature and nurture interact to produce the people we are. The MISTRA produced a wealth of data about many physical and psychological characteristics. For example, the researchers reported that the genes we inherit from our parents have a strong influence on our intelligence (Bouchard et al., 1990). But personality, they concluded, results from a more balanced interplay of nature and nurture: "Our analyses indicate that, on average, about 50% of measured personality diversity can be attributed to genetic diversity" (Tellegen et al., 1988, p. 1035). As you will read in later chapters, some of these early findings have been supported, while others have been called into question by more recent studies.

You Asked, Sharon and Debbie Answer

http://qrs.ly/u25a57s

Did differences in your upbringing account for differences in your personalities?

scan this ➜

replicate To repeat an experiment, generally with a new sample and/or other changes to the procedures, the goal of which is to provide further support for the findings of the first study.

Minnesota Twin Study
Dr. Nancy L. Segal stands between twins Tim Carpenter (left) and Bill Henry, who participated in the historic Minnesota Study of Twins Reared Apart (MISTRA). This 20-year research endeavor included 81 monozygotic (identical) and 56 dizygotic (fraternal) twin pairs (Segal, 2012). Courtesy of Dr. Nancy Segal, Set: Morning Live, Boston, MA 1985.

Participating in the Minnesota twin study was an eye-opening experience for Sharon and Debbie. Not only did they learn what it means to participate in research; they realized the extent to which they think alike and respond to situations in the same way. During their one-week stay in Minnesota, the twins were submitted to a battery of medical and psychological tests—dental exams, lung function tests, questionnaires about job satisfaction, sleeping patterns, sexual behaviors, and many other assessments. In all, each twin answered approximately 15,000 questions (Segal, 2012). As Sharon and Debbie filled in bubbles and checked boxes, they began to wonder if all the surveys and inventories were really just a front for studying something else. Maybe the researchers were administering tests they never intended to evaluate, and their real goal was to observe how the twins responded to the test situation—through their facial expressions, body language, and comments. Both twins developed this suspicion independently, before mentioning anything to the other. Then one night, they got back to their motel room, turned on the water so no one could hear them talking, and began checking the room for cameras, bugs, and one-way mirrors (the twins agree that a life of espionage would have suited them quite well!). Their detective work produced no evidence that someone was spying on them. As it turns out, the researchers were simply investigating the factors, or *variables,* they claimed to be studying. ●

Research on twins has provided psychologists with a wealth of information on psychological traits. Let's see how one expert uses twin research to explain the origins of selfishness.

from the pages of
SCIENTIFIC AMERICAN

Are People Inclined to Act Cooperatively or Selfishly? Is Such Behavior Genetic?

The jury is still out on whether we are fundamentally generous or greedy and whether these tendencies are shaped by our genes or environment.

Some evidence points to humans being innately cooperative. Studies show that in the first year of life, infants exhibit empathy toward others in distress. At later stages in life, we routinely work together to reach goals and help out in times of need.

Yet instances of selfish behavior also abound in society. One recent study used a version of the classic Prisoner's Dilemma, which can test people's willingness to set aside selfish interests to reach a greater good. After modeling different strategies and outcomes, the researchers found that being selfish was more advantageous than cooperating. The benefit may be short-lived, however. Another study showed that players who cooperated did better in the long run.

It seems that human nature supports both prosocial and selfish traits. Genetic studies have made some progress toward identifying their biological roots. By comparing identical twins, who share nearly 100 percent of their genes, and fraternal twins, who share about half, researchers have found overwhelming evidence for genetic effects on behaviors such as sharing and empathy. In these twin studies, identical and fraternal twins are placed in hypothetical scenarios and asked, for example, to split a sum of money with a peer. Such studies often also rely on careful psychological assessments and DNA analysis.

Other work highlights specific genes as key players. My colleagues and I recently identified a gene linked to altruistic behavior and found that a particular variant of it was associated with more selfish behavior in preschoolers.

As for how we might have acquired a genetic blueprint for collaboration, evolutionary scientists offer several explanations. Cooperative behavior may have evolved first among relatives to promote the continuation of their genetic line. As communities diversified, such mutual support could have broadened to include individuals not linked by blood. Another possibility is that humans cooperate to gain some advantage, such as a boost in reputation. Finally, a hotly debated idea is that evolutionary processes take place at the group level. Groups of highly cooperative individuals have higher chances of survival because they can work together to reach goals that are unattainable to less cooperative groups.

Yet almost no behavior is entirely genetic, even among identical twins. Culture, school, and parenting are important determinants of cooperation. Thus, the degree to which we act cooperatively or selfishly is unique to each individual and hinges on a variety of genetic and environmental influences. **Ariel Knafo. Reproduced with permission. Copyright © 2014 Scientific American, a division of Nature America, Inc. All rights reserved.**

Variables

Virtually every psychology study includes **variables,** which are measurable characteristics that vary, or change, over time or across people. In chemistry, a variable might be temperature, mass, or volume. In psychological experiments, researchers study a variety of characteristics relating to humans and other organisms. Examples of variables include personality characteristics (shyness or friendliness), cognitive characteristics (memory), number of siblings in a family, gender, and socioeconomic status. The Minnesota twin study examined a vast quantity of variables, among them cholesterol. Sharon and Debbie expected their cholesterol levels to be quite different because Sharon, a self-proclaimed couch potato, contends that Debbie is an "exercise-aholic." At the time of the test, Debbie was also on a macrobiotic diet, so she seemed to be "the healthier twin." When the results of the blood test came back, the twins were shocked: Their cholesterol levels were the same!

Often researchers are interested in exploring relationships between variables. In many experiments, the goal is to see how changing one variable affects another. A researcher might be interested in finding out how changes in cholesterol levels are linked to cognitive performance: Do people with high cholesterol face a greater risk of developing dementia? Researchers have studied this very topic, and there does seem to be a link (Wendell, Waldstein, & Zonderman, 2014). Once the variables for a study are chosen, the researcher must create operational definitions with precise descriptions and manners of measurement.

Population and Sample

LO 7   Distinguish between a random sample and a representative sample.

How do researchers decide who should participate in their studies? It depends on the **population,** or overall group, the researcher wants to examine. If the population is large (all college students in the United States, for example), then the researcher selects a subset of that population called a **sample.**

There are many methods for choosing a sample. One way is to pick a **random sample,** that is, theoretically any member of the designated population has an equal chance of being selected to participate in the study. A researcher forming a random sample of high school seniors might try to gain access to SAT or ACT databases and then randomly select students from lists compiled by those test companies. Or if your doctor orders a blood test, the lab doesn't remove all of your blood to run these tests; rather, it takes a small sample. What is true within a *representative sample* will likely be true of the whole.

Think about the problems that may occur if a sample is not random. Suppose a researcher is trying to assess attitudes about undocumented workers living in the United States, but the only place she recruits participants is Nevada, the state with the highest population percentage of undocumented immigrants (Pew Research Center, 2016, November 3). How might this bias her findings? Nevada residents do not constitute a **representative sample,** or group of people with characteristics similar to those of the population of interest (in this case, the entire U.S. population).

It is important for researchers to choose representative samples, because this allows them to generalize their findings, or apply information from a sample to the population at large. Let's say that 44% of the respondents in the study on attitudes toward undocumented workers believe current immigration laws are acceptable. If the

Why Do People Do Good Deeds?
Volunteers sweep the grounds of the Shwedagon Pagoda in Yangon, Myanmar. Research suggests both nature and nurture have a hand in determining how selfless—or selfish—we are (Knafo, 2014, September/October). Chris Mellor/ Getty Images.

variables Measurable characteristics that can vary over time or across people.

population All members of an identified group about which a researcher is interested.

sample A subset of a population chosen for inclusion in an experiment.

random sample A subset of the population chosen through a procedure that ensures all members of the population have an equal chance of being selected to participate in the study.

representative sample A subgroup of a population selected so that its members have characteristics similar to those of the population of interest.

Representative Sample?
People gather on the National Mall in Washington, D.C., to advocate for immigration reform. If a researcher aims to understand American attitudes about immigration, she would be foolish to limit her study to a single state, because immigrant populations vary significantly across the country (Pew Research Center, 2014, November 18). Douglas Graham/Roll Call/Getty Images.

sample was similar enough to the overall U.S. population, then the researcher may be able to infer that this finding from the sample is representative: "Approximately 44% of people in the United States believe that current immigration laws are acceptable."

In Class: Collaborate and Report

A) Compare representative samples to random samples. **B)** In your group, discuss why it is so important to have a representative sample, and **C)** what can happen when a sample is not representative of the population. **D)** Generate a list of characteristics that a researcher should consider when designing a study on the attitudes of monozygotic and dizygotic twins. In other words, pinpoint the variables that should be measured to ensure the sample is representative.

The topics we have touched on thus far—variables, operational definitions, and samples—apply to psychology research in general. You will see how these concepts are relevant to studies presented in the upcoming sections when we explore the two major categories of research design: descriptive and experimental.

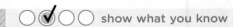 **show what you know**

1. A researcher is interested in studying college students' attitudes about banning supersized sodas. She randomly selects a group of students from across the nation, trying to pick a _____ that will closely reflect the characteristics of college students in the United States.
   a. variable
   b. debriefing
   c. representative sample
   d. representative population

2. Psychology studies focus on _____, which are characteristics that vary or change over time or across people.

3. If a researcher was interested in studying the relationship between GPA and hours of study, how might he pick a random sample from your college?

   √ CHECK YOUR ANSWERS IN APPENDIX C.

Descriptive Research

LO 8 Recognize the forms of descriptive research.

Talking on the phone with both Sharon and Debbie can be a bit confusing. Because their voices sound so much alike, you find yourself falling behind in the conversation and wondering *who just said that?* When you try to catch up, Sharon and Debbie are already 10 steps ahead, laughing about a new topic. Their communication is so effortless, their chemistry so perfect, it's easy for an outsider to get lost. But after a while, you start getting a sense of each twin, as they have slightly different styles of conveying information. Both women are open and direct, but Sharon tends to "spill it out"; she says what's on her mind. Debbie seems slightly more reserved, a bit more deliberate about choosing her words.

Given that these women started life genetically identical, you begin to wonder about the sources of their differences. When did these disparities emerge, and what environmental factors shaped them? It would be fascinating to travel back in time and observe Sharon and Debbie as little girls playing with friends, interacting with family, and studying at school. If only time travel were possible, there would be endless opportunities for a psychologist to use *descriptive research methods* to study their differing childhoods. **Descriptive research** is a type of investigation psychologists use to explore a phenomenon. It is primarily concerned with describing, and is useful for studying new or unexplored topics when researchers might not have specific expectations about outcomes. But there are some things descriptive research cannot achieve. This method provides clues about the causes of behaviors, but it *cannot* reveal cause-and-effect relationships, a point we will revisit later in the chapter. But first, let's explore four descriptive research methods.

Naturalistic Observation

One form of descriptive research is **naturalistic observation,** which involves studying participants in their natural environments using systematic observation. And when we say "natural environments," we don't necessarily mean the "wild." It could be an office, a home, or even a preschool. In one naturalistic study, researchers explored the interactions that occurred when parents dropped off their children at preschool. One variable of interest was the length of time it took parents to leave the children at school. The researchers found that the longer parents or caregivers took to leave, the less time the children played with their peers and the more likely they were to stand by and watch other kids playing. The researchers also noted that women were somewhat more likely than men to hold the children and physically pick them up during drop-off. These drop-off interactions seemed to get in the way of children "settling into" the classroom (Grady, Ale, & Morris, 2012).

The most important feature of naturalistic observation is that researchers do not disturb the participants or their environment. Why? Imagine you were a participant in the naturalistic observation of families dropping off preschoolers. Researchers have been deployed throughout your child's preschool, and every time you walk through the doors, you feel as if you're under surveillance. Parking your car, you spot a researcher peeping at you from behind a tree; at the front office, you catch another one videotaping you. It would be extremely difficult for most people to behave naturally under these circumstances. It is important for researchers to be unobtrusive so participants don't change their normal behaviors.

NATURALLY, IT'S A CHALLENGE As with any type of research, naturalistic observation centers around variables, and those variables must be pinned down with operational definitions. Let's say a researcher wants to study aggression in identical twins reared apart—an intriguing topic given that both genes and environment seem to set the stage for aggressive behavior in children (Lacourse et al., 2014). The researcher might try to find pairs of identical twin children who have been adopted by different families (an unlikely opportunity, we should note). These twins are therefore equivalent in nature, but differ in nurture. At the beginning of the study, the researcher would need to operationally define aggression, including detailed descriptions of specific behaviors that illustrate it. Then she might create a checklist of aggressive behaviors like shouting and pushing, and a coding system to help keep track of them.

Naturalistic observation allows psychologists to observe participants going about their business in their normal environments, without the disruptions of artificial laboratory settings. Some problems arise with this arrangement, however. Natural environments are cluttered with a variety of unwanted variables, and removing them can alter the natural state of affairs the researchers are striving to maintain. And because the variables in natural environments are so hard to control, researchers may have trouble replicating findings. Suppose the researcher opted to study the behavior of the identical twin children playing at the park. In this natural setting, she would not be able to control how many children are at the playground, the ages of the kids present, or the type of adult supervision occurring.

OBSERVER BIAS How can we be sure observers will do a good job recording behaviors? A researcher who is a mother to four boisterous children (and thus might

Please Wash Your Hands
According to one study, male college students are less conscientious about hand-washing in the restroom than female college students. Even after a reminder was placed in the restroom, only 35% of men washed their hands, compared to 97% of women (Johnson, Sholcosky, Gabello, Ragni, & Ogonosky, 2003). Researchers in this study took great care to look as though they were regular people who just happened to be using the restroom themselves. Do you think more men would have washed their hands if they knew they were being observed? Jutta Klee/Getty Images.

descriptive research Research methods that describe and explore behaviors, but with findings that cannot definitively state cause-and-effect relationships.

naturalistic observation A type of descriptive research that studies participants in their natural environment through systematic observation.

"Twinsters"
The film *Twinsters* tells the story of Samantha Futerman and Anais Bordier, identical twins who were separated at birth and reunited with the help of YouTube and Facebook. The twins were born in South Korea and adopted by families from different cultures (Anais was raised in France, Samantha in the United States). The rare circumstances of their situation make them wonderful candidates for a case study. Dr. Nancy L. Segal and her colleague Franchesca Cortez studied Anais and Samantha and found both "striking similarities and intriguing differences" between them (Segal & Cortez, 2014, p. 97). Rex Features via AP Images.

observer bias Errors in the recording of observations, the result of a researcher's value system, expectations, or attitudes.

case study A type of descriptive research that closely examines an individual or small group.

survey method A type of descriptive research that uses questionnaires or interviews to gather data.

be familiar with typical displays of childhood aggression) may not rate behaviors in the same way as someone who has no experience with kids. One way to avoid such problems is to include multiple observers and then determine how similarly they record the behaviors. If the observers don't execute this task in the same way, there may be **observer bias,** which refers to errors introduced as a result of an observer's value system, expectations, and attitudes.

Case Study

Another type of descriptive research method is the **case study,** a detailed examination of an individual or small group. Case studies typically involve collecting a vast amount of data on one person or group, often using multiple avenues to gather information. The process might include in-depth interviews with the person being studied and her friends, family, and coworkers, and questionnaires about medical history, career, and mental health.

The goal of a case study is to provide a wealth of information from a variety of resources. Unlike naturalistic observation, where the researcher assumes the role of detached spectator, the case study may require complete immersion in the participant's environment. How do you think this might impact the researcher's observations and the conclusions of the study?

One of the most fascinating case studies in the history of twin research is that of the "Jim Twins." Identical twins Jim Springer and Jim Lewis were separated shortly after birth and reunited at age 39. When the Jims finally met, they discovered some jaw-dropping similarities: Both were named "James" by their adoptive parents and gravitated toward math and carpentry as kids. Each man had a dog named "Toy," a first wife named "Linda," and a second wife named "Betty." They even smoked the same cigarettes (Salems), drove the same blue Chevy, and traveled to the same vacation spot in Florida (Leo, 1987, January 12; Rawson, 1979, May 7; Segal, 2012). The Jim Twins captivated the interest of Dr. Bouchard, lead researcher of the Minnesota twin study. According to Dr. Segal, who worked with Dr. Bouchard for many years, the reunion of the Jims "was ultimately responsible for the launch of MISTRA" (Segal, 2012, p. 10). See **TABLE 1.5** on page 29 for other examples of classic case studies, many of which we will examine in later chapters.

No matter how colorful or thought-provoking a case study may be, it cannot be used to support or refute a hypothesis (Stanovich, 2013). Hypothesis testing involves drawing comparisons between different conditions (Stanovich, 2013), and this is not possible with a case study. Like naturalistic observation, this method is useful for furthering the development of theories, but it cannot identify the causes of behaviors and events. Case studies can help guide the design of studies on relatively underexplored topics (Stanovich, 2013), such as the health and behavior of an astronaut on a space mission compared to his identical twin back on Earth (Gushanas, 2015, April 14). But as knowledge advances and researchers become more concerned with testing hypotheses, the case study grows increasingly irrelevant.

Case studies are isolated examples, so be wary of using them to make generalizations. Suppose you are trying to examine how parent–child interactions at home might relate to preschoolers' transitions during morning drop-off. What would happen if you limited your research to a case study of a family with two working parents and 10 children? The dynamics of this family may not be representative of those in other families. We should not make sweeping or definitive statements based on our observations of a single person or group.

TABLE 1.5 CLASSIC CASE STUDIES IN PSYCHOLOGY

Case Study	Description	Outcome
Phineas Gage	A railroad worker who survived after an iron rod blasted through his skull	Suggested that the frontal lobes play a role in personality
H.M.	A man who suffered from profound memory loss following brain surgery	Showed how brain damage can be linked to memory loss
Little Albert	An 11-month-old who was conditioned to fear rats	Revealed the ability to classically condition fear in humans
The Genain Quadruplets	Identical quadruplet sisters who all developed schizophrenia	Demonstrated that genetic factors are involved in schizophrenia
"Rat Man"	A man with obsessive thoughts, including a punishment involving rats	Exemplified a case study on which Sigmund Freud based his theories
Lorenz's Geese	Goslings that became attached to Konrad Lorenz	Documented the imprinting phenomenon

Summarized here are some of the most colorful case studies in the history of psychology. These classic case studies have provided psychologists with valuable insights into human behaviors, and you will read about many of them in the chapters to come.

Survey Method

One of the fastest ways to collect descriptive data is the **survey method,** which relies on questionnaires or interviews. A survey is basically a series of questions that can be administered on paper, in face-to-face interviews, via telephone, or through a few mouse clicks. Your college might send out surveys to gauge student attitudes about new online classes and e-books (possible questions on a college survey might include, "How often do you encounter technical difficulties with your online courses?" or "How would you rate your overall satisfaction with an assigned e-book?"). The benefit of the survey method is that one can gather data from numerous people in a short period of time. Surveys can be used alone or in conjunction with other research methods.

WORDING AND HONESTY   Like any research design, the survey method has its limitations. The wording of surveys can lead to biases in responses. A question with a positive or negative spin may sway a participant's response one way or the other: Do you prefer a half-full glass of soda or a half-empty glass of soda? **FIGURE I.4** on the next page shows how the wording of a survey can influence participant responses.

More importantly, participants in studies using the survey method are not always forthright in their responses, particularly when they have to admit to things they are uncomfortable discussing face-to-face. In short, people lie. In one study, psychologists asked thousands of American women if they had ever cheated on their husbands. When a researcher questioned them in person, 1% of the wives admitted cheating; but when asked through a computer-based questionnaire, 6% confessed their infidelity (Whisman & Snyder, 2007). Gender and the threat of getting caught may influence one's tendency to lie. In another study, male and female college students were

"87% of the 56% who completed more than 23% of the survey thought it was a waste of time."

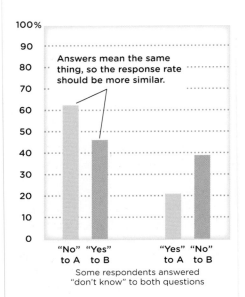

"No" "Yes"
to A to B

"Yes" "No"
to A to B

Some respondents answered "don't know" to both questions

FIGURE 1.4
It Depends How You Ask
In a classic study, researchers asked two versions of the same question:

(A) Do you think the United States should allow public speeches against democracy?

(B) Do you think the United States should forbid public speeches against democracy?

Answering "no" to Question A *should* be the same as answering "yes" to Question B. However, far more respondents answered "no" to Question A than answered "yes" to Question B. According to the researchers, "the 'forbid' phrasing makes the implied threat to civil liberties more apparent" than the "not allow" phrasing does (Rugg, 1941, p. 91). And that's something fewer people were willing to support.

Synonyms

correlation coefficient Pearson's correlation coefficient

correlational method A type of descriptive research examining the relationships among variables.

correlation An association or relationship between two (or more) variables.

correlation coefficient The statistical measure (symbolized as *r*) that indicates the strength and direction of the relationship between two variables.

asked questions about cheating in relationships. When it appeared their responses were being analyzed by a lie detector, men and women were equally likely to provide honest answers about their cheating behaviors. But when they believed their self-reports were anonymous, the men were more likely to be honest than the women (Fisher & Brunell, 2014). People often exhibit a desire not to reveal attitudes or behaviors that are embarrassing or deal with sensitive topics, and it is not always easy to determine if this bias toward *social desirability* has influenced self-reports (Moshagen, Hilbig, Erdfelder, & Moritz, 2014; Tourangeau & Yan, 2007). This may lead to an inaccurate representation of participants' attitudes and beliefs.

SKIMMING THE SURFACE Another disadvantage of the survey method is that it tends to skim the surface of people's beliefs or attitudes, failing to tap into the complex issues underlying responses. Ask 1,000 people if they *intend* to exercise regularly, and you might get more than a few affirmative responses. But *yes* might mean something quite different from one person to the next ("Yes, it crosses my mind, but I can never go through with it" versus "Yes, I have a specific plan, and I have been able to follow through"). To obtain more precise responses, researchers often ask people to respond to statements using a scale that indicates the degree to which they agree or disagree (for example, a 5-point scale ranging from *strongly agree* to *strongly disagree*), or the degree to which they have had an experience (for example, a 5-point scale ranging from *never* to *almost always*).

REPRESENTATIVE SAMPLES AND SURVEYS The representativeness of survey samples can also be called into question. Some surveys fail to achieve representative samples because their *response rates* fall short of ideal. If a researcher sends out 100 surveys to potential participants and only 20 people return them, how can we be sure that the answers of those 20 responders reflect those of the entire group? Without a representative sample, we cannot generalize the survey findings.

Correlational Method

LO 9 Describe the correlational method and identify its limitations.

The final form of descriptive research we will cover is the **correlational method,** which examines relationships among variables and assists researchers in making predictions. When researchers collect data on many variables, it can be useful to determine if these variables are related to each other in some way. A **correlation** is a relationship or link between variables (**INFOGRAPHIC 1.3**). For example, there is probably a correlation between the amount of time Sharon and Debbie spend interacting, and the amount of knowledge they possess about one another. The more they talk on the phone and visit, the more they learn about each other's lives. This is an example of a positive correlation. As one variable increases, so does the other. A negative correlation, on the other hand, means that as one variable goes up, the other goes down (this is an inverse or negative relationship). A good example would be the number of hours Sharon and Debbie talk and text on their cell phones during the day, and the amount of battery power remaining on their phones. As phone usage increases, battery power goes down. You have probably noticed correlations between variables in your own life. Increase the hours you devote to studying, and you will likely see your grades go up (a positive correlation). The more you hold a baby, the less she cries (a negative correlation).

CORRELATION COEFFICIENT Some variables are tightly linked, others weakly associated, and still others not related at all. Lucky for researchers, there is one number that indicates a correlation's strength and direction (positive or negative): a statistical measure called the **correlation coefficient,** which is symbolized as *r*. Correlation coefficients

The Correlation Coefficient: What's in a Number?

A correlation indicates a relationship between two variables, such as the amount of time you spend studying and the grade you get on a test. This relationship is often indicated using a correlation coefficient, symbolized as *r*. To interpret the relationship using a correlation coefficient (*r*), ask yourself two questions:

(1) What is the *direction* of the relationship?

(2) What is the *strength* of the relationship?

A *scatterplot* helps us see what the relationship looks like.

And remember, a correlation between two variables does not necessarily mean that one variable caused the change in the other variable.

$$r = +.73$$

↕ What Is the **Direction** of the Correlation?

- *positive* (+) correlation
  as one variable increases, the other also increases

- *negative* (–) correlation
  as one variable increases, the other decreases (an inverse relationship)

Example: +.73 is a positive number, showing a **positive correlation**. As hours spent studying increase, test grades also increase.

BEWARE
of the
potential
Third Variable

Correlation does not indicate that one variable *causes* a change in the other. A **third variable** may have influenced the results.

Example: Although time spent studying and exam grades are strongly and positively correlated, attendance is another variable. Students who attend classes regularly tend to spend more hours studying. Likewise, students who attend classes regularly know what to expect on the test and are therefore likely to get better grades.

⚫—⚫ What Is the **Strength** of the Correlation?

strength ranges from +1.00 to –1.00

- a value close to +1.00 or –1.00 is a **strong** correlation

- a value close to 0.00 is a **weak** correlation

Example: +.73 is close to 1.00. This shows a **strong correlation** between hours spent studying and test grades.

👁 What does the Correlation **look** like?

Using a scatterplot, we can express the relationship between two variables. One variable is labeled on the horizontal axis, and the second variable is labeled on the vertical axis. Each dot represents one participant's scores on the two variables. Notice how the shape of the graph changes depending on the direction and strength of the relationship between the variables.

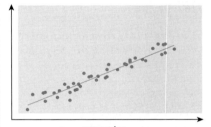

example:
+.73 (strong positive correlation)

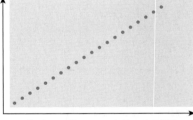

perfect positive correlation (+1.00)

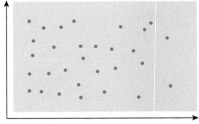

no relationship (.00)

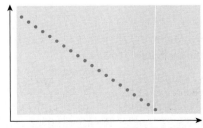

perfect negative correlation (–1.00)

Salary Isn't Everything
Working as a research assistant can be highly satisfying, even though you might not bring home a huge paycheck (Griswold, 2013, December 27). Research suggests that the correlation between salary and job satisfaction is very weak, with a correlation coefficient (*r*) of .14 (Judge, Piccolo, Podsakoff, Shaw, & Rich, 2010). LL28/Getty Images.

Synonyms
third variable Third factor

third variable An unaccounted for characteristic of participants or the environment that explains changes in the variables of interest.

range from +1.00 to –1.00, with positive numbers indicating a positive relationship between variables and negative numbers indicating an inverse relationship between variables. The closer *r* is to +1.00 or to –1.00, the stronger the relationship. The closer *r* is to .00, the weaker the relationship. When the correlation coefficient is very close to zero, there may be no relationship at all between the variables. For example, consider the variables of shoe size and intelligence. Are people with bigger (or smaller) feet more intelligent? Probably not. There would be no link between these two variables, so the correlation coefficient between them (the *r* value) is around zero. Take a look at Infographic 1.3 to see how correlation coefficients are portrayed on graphs called *scatterplots*.

THIRD VARIABLE   Even if there is a very strong correlation between two variables, this does not indicate a causal link exists between them. No matter how high the *r* value is or how logical the relationship seems, it does not *prove* a cause-and-effect connection. Researchers consistently report a positive relationship between exposure to violence in media and aggressive behavior, and it's easy to jump to the conclusion that the exposure causes the aggression (Bushman et al., 2016). It is also important to consider that some other variable may be influencing both exposure to media violence and aggressive behavior. What additional variables might "cause" increases or decreases in aggression? One possibility is parenting behaviors; limiting the content and amount of exposure children have to violent media is associated with a decrease in aggressive behavior (Bushman et al., 2016). When parents actively discuss the portrayal of media violence with their children, aggression tends to decrease as well (Coyne, 2016). Parenting style therefore would be considered a **third variable,** some unaccounted for characteristic of the participants or their environment that explains the changes in the two other variables (parent involvement influences both exposure to violence and aggressive behaviors). When you observe strong links between variables, consider other factors that could be related to both.

Now let's consider the direction of the relationship between variables. With a positive correlation between exposure to violent media and aggressive behavior, you might have assumed that exposure leads to aggression. The more violent video games a child plays, the more aggressive he is. But could it be that aggressive children are more likely to be attracted to violent video games in the first place? If this is the case, then aggressive tendencies influence the amount of time spent using violent media, not the other way around. The direction of the relationship (*directionality*) matters. And in the case of exposure to violent media and aggressive behaviors, the causal direction can go both ways (Coyne, 2016).

Remember, correlational and other descriptive methods can't identify the causes of behaviors. But this type of research *can* provide clues to what underlies behaviors, and thus it serves as a valuable tool when other types of experiments are unethical or impossible to conduct (in the previous example, researchers couldn't ethically manipulate real-world variables like exposure to violence). Moreover, descriptive research can produce fascinating results. In some cases, these results may even guide important government decisions; just consider the following example.

ACROSS THE WORLD
The Happiest Places on the Planet

Where in the world do the happiest people reside, and what is their secret to contentment? According to the *World Happiness Report,* published by the United Nations Sustainable Development Solutions Network (SDSN), Earth's happiest people live in Switzerland (**FIGURE 1.5**). The runners up are Iceland, Denmark, and Norway, while the United States claims 15th place on the list of 158 countries. The unhappiest spots include several nations in sub-Saharan Africa, as well as Afghanistan and Syria.

AND THE WINNER IS . . . SWITZERLAND!

10 HAPPIEST COUNTRIES IN THE WORLD

FIGURE 1.5

Happiness Hotspots
Highlighted on this map are the 10 happiest countries in the world. Five of them—Denmark, Iceland, Norway, Finland, and Sweden—are Nordic countries. Why do you think people in this Northern European region are so content? (Information from Helliwell et al., 2016.)

On average, the women of the world are just a bit happier than the men (Helliwell, Layard, & Sachs, 2015).

Why are some populations happier than others? According to the report, most of the variation in happiness can be attributed to a handful of factors, and the three most critical are these: (1) "Gross Domestic Product (GDP) per capita" (a measure of economic prosperity), (2) "social support" or having people to lean on when times get tough, and (3) "healthy years of life expectancy," meaning how long you can expect to enjoy good health (Helliwell et al., 2015, p. 6). Thus, it seems that financial security, caring relationships, and health are very important variables in the happiness equation.

The *World Happiness Report* is a great example of descriptive research, but what is the point of studying happiness around the globe? The concept of happiness is closely associated with that of *sustainable development,* or development that "meets the needs of the present without compromising the ability of future generations to meet their own needs" (Helliwell et al., 2015; United Nations, General Assembly, 1987, August 4, p. 54). Sustainable development is about making economic progress, but also protecting the environment and the social needs of citizens. When these goals are balanced, human happiness and well-being are likely to increase. Some governments are beginning to appreciate this relationship, and now use happiness data in making policy decisions (Helliwell et al., 2015). 🌐➡

 show what you know

1. _____ is primarily useful for studying new or unexplored topics.
   a. An operational definition
   b. Observer bias
   c. Descriptive research
   d. A correlation

2. A researcher was interested in studying the behaviors of parents dropping off children at preschool. He gave teachers a stopwatch to measure how long it took a caregiver to enter and leave the classroom, and a checklist to record the subsequent behaviors of the children. This approach to collecting data is referred to as:
   a. naturalistic observation.
   b. representative sampling.
   c. informed consent.
   d. applied research.

3. Describe the strengths and weaknesses of the correlational method.

4. The more time students spend studying, the higher their grades will be. This is an example of a _____.

✓ CHECK YOUR ANSWERS IN APPENDIX C.

Fountain of Youth?
Everyone knows that exercise is good for the body, but did you know it's also good for the brain? Being physically active can reduce your risk of cognitive decline, especially if you are genetically predisposed to developing Alzheimer's disease (Reas, 2014). Keren Su/Getty Images.

Experimental Research

Debbie and Sharon are now in their sixties. Both are physically and mentally healthy, and they intend to stay that way for decades to come. Debbie keeps her body and mind fit by exercising at least 4–5 times a week, a regimen that includes zumba, body combat, and boot camp classes. She takes calcium supplements and doesn't eat sugar, dairy, gluten, or processed foods. Sharon cares for her 2-year-old grandson, which keeps her very active, both physically and mentally.

Staying active and eating a healthy diet are critical for women in Sharon and Debbie's age group, who are at risk for developing osteoporosis, a disease characterized by frail, brittle bones. Vitamin D is of particular importance for bone health, but its benefits appear to be broader. For example, studies suggest vitamin D is essential for maintaining a strong immune system and perhaps even optimal cognitive performance for some people (Assmann et al., 2015; Christakos et al., 2013; Lee, O'Keefe, Bell, Hensrud, & Holick, 2008; Przybelski & Binkley, 2007).

Suppose you are interested in researching how vitamin D supplements affect cognitive abilities, such as problem solving and memory among women in their sixties. How could you isolate the effects of vitamin D when so many other factors can affect cognitive function, such as intelligence, education, age, diet, and overall physical health? There is a research method that allows you to monitor these other possible sources of interference: the *experimental method.* Performing research in a controlled laboratory environment using this type of method has huge benefits; you have greater control over who participates in the study, freedom to manipulate variables, and the ability to draw comparisons between groups that differ only with respect to your target variables.

Experimental Method

LO 10 Explain how the experimental method can establish cause and effect.

At last, we arrive at the type of research method we have been alluding to all along, a design that uncovers causes of behaviors and events. Unlike the descriptive studies discussed earlier, the **experimental method** can tell us about cause and effect, because it aims to ensure that every variable except those being manipulated by the researcher is held constant, or controlled (**INFOGRAPHIC 1.4** on page 36). To identify a particular cause of an outcome, we assign research participants to two or more groups, and with the exception of some sort of manipulation or treatment done by the experimenter, these groups are equivalent. If, following the manipulation or treatment, the groups differ on a measure of interest, we can say with confidence that the experimental manipulation caused that change. Thus researchers can observe the variable of interest without interference from other variables.

If you are having trouble understanding what it means to control variables, consider this analogy: You are outside a football stadium, desperately trying to follow a friend lost in a swarm of people. Everyone is moving in different directions, making it exceedingly difficult to pinpoint your friend's location and direction of movement. But what if everyone in the crowd except your friend froze for a moment in time? Would it be easier to observe him now that he is the only one moving? This is similar to what researchers try to do with variables—hold everything steady except the variables they are examining.

Returning to your population of older women, let's examine how you might design a simple research study using the experimental method to investigate the cognitive effects of a vitamin D supplement. Your hypothesis is that participants who are given vitamin D supplements for a certain amount of time will perform better on cognitive tasks than participants given a sugar pill. In order to conduct this study the right way, we must gather a group of women who are very similar in age, educational background,

experimental method A type of research that manipulates a variable of interest (independent variable) to uncover cause-and-effect relationships.

random assignment The process of appointing study participants to the experimental or control groups, ensuring that every person has an equal chance of being assigned to either.

experimental group The members of an experiment who are exposed to the treatment variable or manipulation by the researcher; represents the treatment group.

control group The participants in an experiment who are not exposed to the treatment variable; this is the comparison group.

independent variable (IV) In the experimental method, the variable manipulated by the researcher to determine its effect on the dependent variable.

dependent variable (DV) In the experimental method, the characteristic or response that is measured to determine the effect of the researcher's manipulation.

physical health, and other variables that might affect their cognitive performance. You would also want to make sure none of them have taken vitamin D supplements prior to the study, and that their exposure to the sun is roughly the same. (Exposure to the sun enables the body to produce vitamin D.) Before doing this, you would obtain permission from an ethics committee and informed consent from the participants—more on this to come. Next you would divide the women into two groups—one receives vitamin D supplements and the other gets a sugar pill—and compare their performance on various mental tasks after a designated amount of time has passed. If the group receiving the vitamin D performs better, then you can attribute the difference to vitamin D. Although this may sound fairly straightforward, there are still a few more things you need to know.

RANDOM ASSIGNMENT   Assigning participants to groups is a crucial step of the experimental method. Fail to divide participants in the correct way and your whole study is compromised. For this reason, researchers use **random assignment** to ensure that participants have an equal chance of being assigned to any of the groups. Randomly choosing which treatment the participants receive reduces the possibility of some participant characteristics influencing the findings. You may have noticed some similarities between random assignment and the "random sample" introduced earlier in the chapter. But here's the difference: Random sampling is used at the onset of a study to gather participants from a larger population. Random assignment comes into play later, when you are assigning participants to different groups. You can flip a coin, roll dice, or use a computer to generate numbers, but the goal of random assignment is always the same: to ensure that the groups are roughly equal on all characteristics. If the groups are lopsided with respect to some variable, the results may be affected. Getting back to your study on vitamin D and cognition, imagine that you assigned all the highly educated participants to one group and the less educated participants to the other. Might educational experience influence the results of a cognitive test? Perhaps. Random assignment helps reduce some of the interference resulting from these types of characteristics.

EXPERIMENTAL AND CONTROL GROUPS   Let's assume you did use random assignment to divvy your participants into two groups. One will receive the treatment (a daily dose of vitamin D), and the other will receive no treatment at all (the participants will, however, be handed a sugar pill that looks identical to the vitamin D supplement). Those who get the treatment (the real vitamin D supplements) comprise the **experimental group,** and those who get the sugar pill (fake treatment) are the **control group.** (We explain the need for the fake treatment in a moment.)

INDEPENDENT AND DEPENDENT VARIABLES   Let's restate a point we made earlier in the section, this time using our new vocabulary terms: The only difference between the experimental and control groups should be the variable the researchers are manipulating—in this case, vitamin D intake. The different treatments the two groups receive is called the **independent variable (IV),** because it is the one variable the researchers are deliberately changing (in this case, some participants get vitamin D, others a sugar pill). In the experimental method, an independent variable is that which the researcher is manipulating, and due to the complex nature of human behavior, often more than one independent variable may be used. The **dependent variable (DV)** is the characteristic or response the researchers are trying to observe or measure. In the hypothetical study, the dependent variable is the participants' performance on cognitive tests. Just remember, the independent variable is what is manipulated and the dependent variable is what is being measured as a result of that manipulation. In other words, researchers are trying to determine whether the dependent variable (in this case, performance on cognitive tests) "depends" on the treatment (either vitamin D or the sugar pill).

"Well. I guess we're the control group."

Cartoonstock.

Synonyms

experimental group treatment group
independent variable explanatory variable
dependent variable response variable

The Experimental Method: Are You in Control?

The experimental method is the type of research that can tell us about causes and effects. It is different from descriptive studies in that key aspects of the experiment—participants, variables, and study implementation—are tightly controlled. The experiment typically includes at least two groups—an experimental group and a control group. This allows the researcher to isolate the effects of manipulating a single variable, called the independent variable.

Imagine you want to know if laws that ban texting while driving are worthwhile. Does texting really *cause* more accidents? Perhaps texting is merely correlated with higher accident rates in certain populations, such as college students, because college students are both more likely to text and more likely to have accidents. In order to find out, you have to perform an experiment.

VARIABLES

INDEPENDENT VARIABLE

The variable that researchers deliberately manipulate.

Example: The independent variable is texting while driving.

- **Experimental group** drives through obstacle course while texting.
- **Control group** drives through obstacle course without texting.

DEPENDENT VARIABLE

The variable measured as an outcome of manipulation of the independent variable.

Example: The dependent variable is the number of accidents (objects hit in obstacle course).

EXTRANEOUS VARIABLE

An unforeseen factor or characteristic that could interfere with the outcome.

Example: Some participants have more driving experience than others. Without controlling the amount of driving experience, we can't be certain the independent variable caused more accidents.

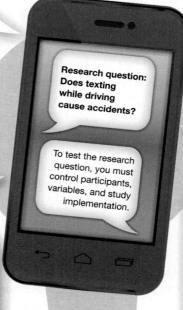

Research question: Does texting while driving cause accidents?

To test the research question, you must control participants, variables, and study implementation.

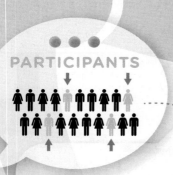

PARTICIPANTS

REPRESENTATIVE SAMPLE

Subset of the population chosen to reflect population of interest.

Example: Participants must be college students. Other groups might be affected differently by the independent variable.

RANDOM SAMPLE

Method used to ensure participants do not introduce unexpected bias.

Example: Researchers recruit participants by randomly selecting students from the college directory.

STUDY IMPLEMENTATION

RANDOM ASSIGNMENT

Process by which researcher randomly assigns participants to experimental or control group.

Example: Experimenter flips coin to determine participant's group.

EXPERIMENTER BIAS

Researchers' expectations and unintentional behaviors can unwittingly change the outcome of a study.

Example: Without thinking, researcher says "good luck" to one group. This might unintentionally cause them to try harder.

Researchers control for these effects by using a **double-blind study** in which neither researcher nor participant knows what group participants are assigned to.

EXTRANEOUS VARIABLES   When planning their experiments, researchers must take steps to ensure that **extraneous variables** are not allowed to interfere with their measures. Extraneous variables are characteristics of the environment or participants that potentially interfere with the outcome of the research. While conducting your study of vitamin D supplements, you discover that three of the participants have been working a night shift and sleeping during the day. If these individuals came directly from work, their exhaustion would affect their performance on the cognitive tasks. Unfortunately, you failed to consider this very important variable in your research design, making it an extraneous variable. Researchers have to carefully contemplate the different kinds of variables that might influence the dependent variable.

There is a specific type of extraneous variable that can *confound* the results of an experiment. **Confounding variables** are a type of extraneous variable that changes in sync with the independent variable, making it very difficult to discern which variable—the independent variable or the confounding variable—is causing changes in the dependent variable. Imagine you house the participants in your study in a very nice lab setting, but because the lab can only hold half the participants at a time, you decide to wait and collect data from the control group later in the year. At that point, your lab assistant has gone on maternity leave, so you need to hire a new lab assistant, a young man who will administer the sugar pills to the control group. When the data are collected on cognitive performance, you can't be sure whether differences between groups on test scores result from the vitamin D pills, or some other variables. Perhaps only the male lab assistant wore a white coat, which influenced participants' perceptions of authority, or maybe the time of year affected the participants' vitamin D levels (a result of seasonal differences in exposure to sunlight). These other variables (gender of lab assistant and time of year) could be confounding variables.

The good news is that there are numerous ways of eliminating the influence of an extraneous variable. This is called *controlling* a variable. As we mentioned earlier, random assignment to the treatment and control groups can help to lessen the impact of such variables. In this example, that means ensuring both groups have approximately the same number of participants who are working the night shift. Or, if you wanted to control the impact of exhaustion on the outcome of your study, you could just remove these participants from your sample and not include their information in your statistical analyses.

If you succeed in holding all variables constant except the independent variable, then you can make a statement about cause and effect. Let's say your study does uncover cognitive differences between the experimental and control groups. It is relatively safe to attribute that disparity to the independent variable. In other words, you can presume that the vitamin D caused the superior performance of the experimental group.

DOUBLE-BLIND STUDY   Deception can sometimes be useful in scientific research. One way researchers use deception is by conducting a *single-blind study* in which participants do not know what treatment they are receiving. An even stronger experimental design is a **double-blind study,** an experiment in which neither the participants nor the researchers working directly with those participants know who is getting the real treatment and who is getting the pretend treatment. In our example, neither the person administering the pills nor the participants would know who was receiving the vitamin D supplement and who was receiving the sugar pill. Keeping participants in the dark is relatively easy; just make sure the treatment and sugar pill look the same from the outside (see how the vitamin D and sugar pill look identical in the photo above right). Blinding the researchers is a little trickier but can be accomplished with the help of clever assistants who make it appear that all participants are getting the same treatment.

THINKING IS BELIEVING   There are some very compelling reasons for making a study double-blind. Prior research tells us that the expectations of participants can

Looks Real
One of these pills contains an active ingredient; the other is a placebo. In placebo-controlled drug trials, researchers give some participants drugs and others placebos. People taking the placebos often experience effects that are similar to those reported by the participants taking the actual drug. Cordelia Molloy/Science Source.

extraneous variable A characteristic of participants or the environment that could unexpectedly influence the outcome of a study.

confounding variable A type of extraneous variable that changes in sync with the independent variable, making it difficult to discern which one is causing changes in the dependent variable.

double-blind study Type of study in which neither the researchers who are administering the independent variable nor the participants know what type of treatment is being given.

TABLE 1.6   RESEARCH METHODS: ADVANTAGES AND DRAWBACKS

Research Method	Advantages	Disadvantages
Naturalistic Observation	Good for new research questions; can study phenomena in their naturally occurring environment.	Very little control; increased experimenter bias; cannot determine cause and effect.
Correlational	Shows whether two variables are related; useful when experimental method is not possible.	Directionality and third-variable problems; cannot determine cause and effect.
Experimental	Can determine cause and effect; increased control over variables.	Results may not generalize beyond lab setting; potential for extraneous variables.

How does a researcher choose which method to use? It depends on the research question. Here we compare the pros and cons of three research methods.

Cartoonstock.

"Good morning. Here's your placebo—I mean medicine... well, I'm fired."

Synonyms

experimenter bias experimenter effect, researcher expectancy effect

placebo An inert substance given to members of the control group; the fake treatment that has no benefit, but is administered as if it does.

experimenter bias Researchers' expectations that influence the outcome of a study.

influence results. If someone hands you a sugar pill but tells you it is real medicine, you might end up feeling better simply because this is what you expect will happen when you believe you are being treated. Apparently, thinking is believing. When people are given a fake pill or other inactive "treatment" known as a **placebo** (pluh-SEE-bo), they often get better even though the contents of the pill are inert. The *placebo effect* has been shown to ease pain, anxiety, depression, and the symptoms of Parkinson's disease. And although placebos are not able to shrink the size of tumors, they can help with some of the side effects of treatment, such as pain, fatigue, and nausea (Kaptchuk & Miller, 2015). Researchers believe that the placebo effect arises through both conscious expectations and unconscious associations between treatment cues and healing. One's expectation influences the placebo's actual effect.

EXPERIMENTER BIAS   We've discussed the rationale for keeping participants in the dark, but why is it necessary to keep the researchers clueless as well? Researchers' expectations can influence the outcome of a study, a phenomenon known as **experimenter bias.** A researcher may unwittingly color a study's outcome through subtle verbal and/or nonverbal communication with the participants, conveying hopes or beliefs about the experiment's results (Nichols & Edlund, 2015). A statement by the researcher like "I really have high hopes for this medicine" might influence participants' reactions to the treatment. The researcher's value system may also impact the results in barely noticeable but very important ways. Beliefs and attitudes can shape the way a researcher frames questions, tests hypotheses, or interprets findings (Rosenthal, 2002).

Congratulations! You have now learned the nuts and bolts of the experimental method, one of psychology's greatest myth-debunking, knowledge-gathering tools (Infographic 1.4). This method gives us more control over variables than any other type of study we have discussed; it also stands out in its ability to establish cause and effect. However, like any scientific approach, the experimental method is not without its flaws. Laboratory settings are inherently unnatural and therefore cannot always paint an accurate picture of behaviors that would occur in a natural setting. Remember, when people know they are being observed, their behavior changes. Other weaknesses of the experimental method include cost (it's expensive to maintain a laboratory) and time (collecting data in a laboratory setting can be much slower than, say, sending out a survey). **TABLE 1.6** gives an overview of some of the advantages and disadvantages of the research methods we have described.

Now it's time to test our understanding of the experimental method with the help of a sprightly yellow square named SpongeBob.

DIDN'T SEE THAT COMING
SpongeBob on the Brain

 A little television won't hurt a child, will it? Kids' programs are interspersed with lessons on colors, words, and numbers, and only run for periods of 20 to 30 minutes. It seems reasonable to assume that little snippets of TV can't possibly have any measurable effect.

TURNING YOUNG BRAINS TO "SPONGE"?

When it comes to the rapidly developing juvenile brain, however, it's probably not safe to assume anything. Consider the following controlled experiment examining the cognitive changes observed in preschool children after just 9 minutes of exposure to a talking yellow sponge zipping across a television screen.

The research participants were 60 four-year-olds, most of whom came from White, upper-middle-class households. Researchers randomly assigned the children to one of three conditions: watching the extremely fast-paced cartoon *SpongeBob SquarePants,* viewing an educational program, or drawing with crayons and markers. Following 9 minutes of the assigned activities, the children took a series of four commonly used tests to assess their executive function—the collection of brain processes involved in self-control, decision making, problem solving, and other higher-level functions. The results were shocking: Children in the SpongeBob group performed considerably worse than those in the other groups (Lillard & Peterson, 2011). Just 9 minutes of SpongeBob produced a temporary lapse in cognitive function.

How do we know that this was not the result of a different variable, such as some children's preexisting attentional issues or television-watching habits at home? Those factors were accounted for in the study. In the experimental method, researchers hold nearly all variables constant except the one they want to manipulate—the 9-minute activity, in this case. This is the independent variable (IV). That way, the researchers can be somewhat confident that changes in the IV are driving changes in the dependent variable (DV)—performance on the cognitive tests.

What aspect of the cartoon caused these effects? The researchers hypothesized it had something to do with the show's "fantastical events and fast pacing" (Lillard & Peterson, 2011, p. 648), and a subsequent study suggests that the fantastical content may be the problem. Shows that are highly fantastical, or involve "physically impossible events" (think cartoon characters that magically change shape, disappear in poofs of smoke, or fly with capes), seem to compromise short-term executive function in a way that non-fantastical shows do not. The negative impact of fantasy is even apparent with slow-paced programs like *Little Einsteins* and "educational" shows, such as *Martha Speaks* (Lillard, Drell, Richey, Boguszewski, & Smith, 2015). Researchers have yet to determine how fantastical television affects the developing brain, but further studies are in the works. And as we noted earlier, the replication of findings is a key component of the scientific method. Stay tuned. 👁!

Sponge Brain
No one expects cartoons to make kids smarter, but can they hurt them? One study suggests that preschool children watching just 9 minutes of the high-energy, ultra-stimulating kids' show *SpongeBob SquarePants* experience a temporary dip in cognitive function.
HANDOUT/KRT/Newscom.

⭕✔⭕⭕ show what you know

1. The experimental method can provide findings on the _____ of variables.
   a. experimenter bias
   b. confounding
   c. random assignment
   d. cause-and-effect relationship

2. A researcher studying the impact of vitamin D on cognitive functioning gave supplements to the experimental group and a placebo to the control group. After 2 months, she tested the participants' cognitive functioning, which is a measure of the _____ variable.

3. A study of preschool children looked at the impact of watching fast-paced cartoons on executive functioning. Half of the children were assigned to watch *SpongeBob SquarePants* in a room alone. The other half were assigned to draw for the same amount of time while sitting at a table with other children. The researcher mistakenly introduced a confounding variable, which in this case was:
   a. whether the child watched the cartoon or not.
   b. whether the child was alone or with others.
   c. whether the child was drawing or not.
   d. that both groups spent the same amount of time in their activity.

4. Describe a double-blind study and explain why it requires deception.

✔ CHECK YOUR ANSWERS IN APPENDIX C.

Research Ethics

Shady Research?

In the 1960s, researchers Peter Neubauer and Viola Bernhard launched an ethically dubious twin study in New York City. Their research focused on identical twins and triplets who had been given up for adoption and intentionally placed in separate homes. It was no secret a study was occurring, because the researchers periodically observed the children in their homes, interviewed the mothers, and administered tests. But neither the children nor the adoptive parents were told about the existence of the twin/triplet siblings being raised by other families (Perlman & Segal, 2005). Do you think this approach was fair to the adopted children and their families?

LO 11 Identify measures psychologists take to support ethical treatment of their research participants.

Conducting psychological research carries an enormous ethical responsibility. Psychologists do not examine dinosaur fossils or atomic particles. They study humans and other living creatures who experience pain, fear, and other complex feelings, and it is their professional duty to treat them with dignity and respect.

Like most other professionals, psychologists have established specific guidelines to help ensure ethical behavior in their field. Professional organizations such as the American Psychological Association (APA), the Association for Psychological Science (APS), and the British Psychological Society (BPS) provide written guidelines their members agree to follow. These guidelines attempt to ensure the ethical treatment of research participants, both human and animal. (Keep in mind that notions of "ethical treatment" are highly variable; not everyone agrees with the codes established by these organizations.) The guidelines encourage psychologists to do no harm; safeguard the welfare of humans and animals in their research (see **TABLE 1.7**); know their responsibilities to society and community; maintain accuracy in research, teaching, and practice; and respect human dignity, to name a few examples (APA, 2010a).

WHOSE WORDS ARE THESE? One important way that psychologists share information is through scientific journal articles. Along with this sharing comes an ethical responsibility to give credit where credit is due. Let's take a look at how APA style supports the fair use of other people's work.

 In Class: Collaborate and Report

In your group, discuss the meaning of fair use and explain how it differs from plagiarism. **A)** Pick any short paragraph in this chapter and copy it, word-for-word, at the top of a piece of paper. **B)** Copy the paragraph again, but this time include quotation marks at its beginning and end, and use APA style to cite the authors' last names, year of publication, and page number from the textbook. **C)** Finally, paraphrase the content of the paragraph in your own words, and use APA style to cite the authors' last names and year of publication. **D)** Which of the paragraphs would be plagiarism and which would be fair use? Discuss with your group why it is important to cite other people's work and how the APA guidelines make it obvious to whom the words belong.

CONFIDENTIALITY An important component of ethical treatment is confidentiality. Researchers must take steps to protect research data from misuse or theft. Psychologists who offer therapy services are obligated to keep client and therapy session information confidential; in fact, they are required to safeguard this information in their offices. Confidentiality enables clients to speak freely about deeply personal issues. It ensures

A Lofty Responsibility
Researchers study a newborn baby responding to smells such as curry and garlic. Certain flavors are familiar to babies because they were exposed to them in utero (through their mothers' diets). Conducting research on infants and other minors involves additional ethical considerations, and informed consent must be obtained from parents or legal guardians. Thierry Berrod, Mona Lisa Production/Science Source.

TABLE 1.7 ETHICAL USE OF ANIMALS IN RESEARCH

Guiding Principles	Ethical Conduct
Approving the use of animals	• Before any nonhuman animal can be used in research, the Institutional Animal Care and Use Committee (IACUC) must approve the research methods as humane.
Housing animals	• Researchers must meet standards that "exceed current regulations." • The housing conditions will be inspected twice a year. • Their conditions must be "humane and healthful" and must be approved by the IACUC.
Obtaining animals	• Animals must be obtained legally. • During transport, the animals must have access to food, water, ventilation, space. • No undue stress should be placed on the animal(s).
Experimenting on animals	• The animals' welfare must be part of the design of the experiment.
Animals in the classroom	• Can be very useful in the classroom, but needs approval by the IACUC. • Psychologists should determine if the animal is necessary, or if there are "non-animal alternatives."

The American Psychological Association (APA) provides guidelines for the ethical use of animals in research. The principles listed here are not exhaustive, and good judgment should be used. Information from American Psychological Association (2012a).

that research participants feel protected when they share sensitive information (about sexual or controversial matters, for example), because they may rest assured researchers will keep it safe.

INFORMED CONSENT AND DEBRIEFING   Ethical treatment also involves sharing information. Researchers have a duty to tell participants as much as they can about a study's purpose and procedures; they do this through *informed consent* and *debriefing*.

Suppose a researcher has chosen a population of interest and identified her sample. Before enlisting these people as participants and collecting data, she must make certain that they are comfortable with their involvement. Through **informed consent,** participants acknowledge that they understand what their participation will entail, including any possible harm that could result. For example, Sharon, Debbie, and all the twins who participated in the Minnesota twin study gave informed consent before undergoing any tests or examinations. As Dr. Segal recalls in her book *Born Together—Reared Apart,* "We first reviewed the week-long schedule with the twins as part of the informed consent procedure. We encouraged them to complete all the medical and psychological tests we administered, but we assured them that they were free to decline any activity they preferred not to do" (Segal, 2012, p. 55). Informed consent is a participant's way of saying, "I understand my role in this study, and I am okay with it." It's also the researcher's way of ensuring that participants know what they are getting into.

Following a study, there is a second step of disclosure called **debriefing.** In a debriefing session, researchers provide participants with useful information about the study; in some cases, this means revealing any deception or manipulation used—information that couldn't be shared beforehand. Remember that deception is a key part of the double-blind study (neither participants nor researchers know which group is getting the treatment and which is receiving the placebo). Other types of psychological research require deception as well. Reading this book, you will learn about experiments in which participants were initially unaware of the study's

informed consent Acknowledgement from study participants that they understand what their participation will entail.

debriefing Sharing information with participants after their involvement in a study has ended, including the purpose of the research and any deception used.

Binkie Brouhaha
In 2012 researchers published a study showing a correlation between pacifier use in boys and lower levels of emotional intelligence later in life. The findings of this study could easily be interpreted as "pacifier use stunts emotional development," but this is a reckless conclusion. Think of all the other variables that might affect emotional development: parenting style, exposure to television, nutrition, interactions with siblings. Need we go on? leungchopan/ Shutterstock.

Synonyms

Institutional Review Board (IRB)
reviewing committee, Animal Welfare Committee, Independent Ethics Committee, Ethical Review Board

False Balance in the Media
If 97% of climate scientists agree that humans are causing global warming, and only 3% disagree, why do news outlets often present this issue as a "debate" between two individuals? By giving equal attention to the two viewpoints, the media promote the misconception that scientists are split 50-50 on the issue. We call this "false balance."

Institutional Review Board (IRB) A committee that reviews research proposals to protect the rights and welfare of all participants.

purpose. In some cases, researchers purposely lied to participants, either because it was part of the manipulation, or because they needed to conceal the study's objective until the debriefing phase. It is important to note that no one is or should ever be forced to become a research participant. Involvement is completely voluntary, and participants can drop out at any time. And remember, all experiments on humans and animals must be approved by an **Institutional Review Board (IRB)** to ensure the highest degree of ethical standards.

THINK IT THROUGH
Psychology in the Media

As you venture deeper into the study of psychology, you may find yourself becoming increasingly skeptical of media reports on psychological research. We encourage a healthy dose of skepticism. Although many news stories on scientific findings are accurate and balanced, others are flawed and overhyped. Look at these headlines about a 2012 study on the psychological impact of pacifier, or "binkie," use:

"Pacifier Use Can Lead to Emotional Problems in Boys, Study Finds"
(Fox News, 2012, September 19)

"UW Study Says Boys' Pacifier Use Limits Social Development"
(Seely, 2012, September 19).

It sounds as if pacifiers are *causing* emotional problems in males. We must have a cause-and-effect relationship, right? Wrong. The following is a rough description of the research, which is actually a combination of three studies described in one article. In a study of elementary schoolchildren, researchers found that boys (but not girls) who had used pacifiers during infancy were more likely to have trouble mimicking the facial expressions of others. (Mirroring facial expressions is believed to promote *empathy*, or the ability to put oneself in someone else's shoes, and pacifiers could potentially interrupt the development of this skill by blocking muscles around the mouth.) Additional studies of college students linked pacifier use during infancy to lower levels of empathy and emotional intelligence, but only in males (Niedenthal et al., 2012).

Provocative as these findings may be, they do not allow us to conclude that pacifiers cause emotional impairments. Isn't it possible that the reverse is true? Infants

Scientists debate whether humans are causing global warming

with emotional problems are more likely to be given pacifiers (thus, the emotional problems are leading to the pacifier use)? The authors explicitly highlight this problem: "The studies do not allow us to draw causal conclusions, as the children were not randomly assigned to pacifier use" (Niedenthal et al., 2012, p. 392). And while the researchers did control for some variables such as the mother's education and the child's anxiety level, it is impossible to control for every third variable that might influence emotional health. Can you think of any other factors that could impact the results?

The take-home message: If a news report claims that *X causes Y*, don't automatically assume that the media have it right. The only way to really understand the results and limitations of a psychological study is to read it for yourself.

 **show what you know**

1. _____ is the process through which research participants acknowledge their understanding of their role in a study.
   a. Informed consent
   b. Research ethics
   c. Debriefing
   d. Positive psychology

2. Following a study involving a double-blind procedure with a treatment and a placebo, a researcher met with each participant individually to discuss important information about the study. This is known as:
   a. informed consent.
   b. debriefing.
   c. deception.
   d. naturalistic observation.

3. In the study about pacifier use, newspapers and websites ran headlines that were somewhat misleading with regard to the findings. How would you write a headline for an article on the findings of this study so that it draws readers in but still represents the findings fairly?

✓ CHECK YOUR ANSWERS IN APPENDIX C.

"LET'S ENJOY IT" People sometimes ask Sharon and Debbie if they are sad that they spent the first 45 years of life apart. The twins don't spend much time thinking about what "could have been." They feel blessed to have met when they did and believe their relationship is stronger as a result. "We're very competitive," Debbie says. "I don't think we would have really gotten along as well [if we had grown up together]." Both twins believe, though, that it would have been nicer had they been there for each other during the early years of parenting. The infant stage was especially difficult for both mothers, full of ear infections and projectile vomit. "I think it would have been helpful for both of us to have each other during those times. But you can't dwell on that," Debbie says. "We were 45 when we met, and we don't know how much longer we have," says Debbie. "It's like a miracle. Let's enjoy it."

For Sharon, meeting Debbie came at a perfect time: "It was like God's hand came down, and he lifted me up." Sharon's son had just left home to participate in the civil service program AmeriCorps, and she missed him terribly. "When I was at my lowest, wow did I get a surprise!" Sharon says, "It's just been a wonderful adventure not just to have Debbie, but to go to so many places together. . . . We've done things that we never would have been able to do on our own." When the twins are together, their courage appears to multiply, and good things seem to happen to them. "It can only get better," Sharon says. "So we didn't celebrate our twelfth birthday together. Big whoop." ●

Family × 2
After the twins reunited at age 45, they introduced one another to their relatives. As Debbie says, "It was like getting this family that you've always wanted to have." Sharon's son and Debbie's daughter, who are 5 years apart and genetically as close as real siblings, developed a special bond.
Courtesy Debbie Mehlman and Sharon Poset.

TABLE 1.8	RECURRING THEMES	
Theme	**Definition**	**What to Look For**
Nature and Nurture	The relative weight of heredity and environment in relation to behaviors, personality characteristics, and so on	Adaptation, heredity, environment, genes, instincts, reflexes, upbringing, peers, parents
Culture	The relative importance of cultural influences on behaviors, personality characteristics, and so on	Diversity, ethnicity, ethnic groups, cultural context, cross-cultural factors, ethnocentrism
Gender	The relative importance of one's gender as it relates to behaviors, personality characteristics, and so on	Gender bias, gender differences, social roles, masculinity, femininity, gender roles
Positive Psychology	The focus on positive aspects of human beings, as opposed to the more traditional focus on abnormality and maladaptive behavior	Strengths, optimal behavior, happiness, well-being, achievement, self-confidence, human potential

Throughout this textbook, you will come across four important themes: nature and nurture, culture, gender, and positive psychology.

THINK POSITIVE

Introducing Positive Psychology

Sharon and Debbie are wonderful examples of people who opt to see the brighter side of life. Instead of lamenting the fact that they spent decades apart, they rejoice in being united, and anticipate good things to come. As Debbie explains, they even look forward to rolling their wheelchairs through a nursing home and telling people the same stories day after day.

HAPPINESS, CREATIVITY, LOVE, AND ALL THAT IS BEST ABOUT PEOPLE

The twin's viewpoint is somewhat analogous to the *positive psychology* movement in the study of human behaviors and mental processes. **Positive psychology** is a relatively new approach that studies the positive aspects of human nature—happiness, creativity, love, and all that is best about people (Seligman & Csikszentmihalyi, 2000). Historically, psychologists have tended to focus on the abnormal and maladaptive patterns of human behavior. Positive psychology does not deny the existence of these darker elements; it just directs the spotlight elsewhere. Positive psychologists explore the upside of subjective experiences, traits, and institutions. They generally believe that humans "strive to lead meaningful, happy, and good lives" (Donaldson, Dollwet, & Rao, 2015, p. 185). In this sense, positive psychology is similar to the humanistic perspective. In fact, the early work of the humanists helped set the stage for the current field of positive psychology (Friedman, 2014; Robbins, 2008). Many studies have focused on well-being and optimal functioning (Donaldson et al., 2015), producing results with immediate relevance to everyday life. For example, early evidence suggests that people who have a positive outlook tend to flourish and have better mental health than their less optimistic peers (Catalino & Fredrickson, 2011).

In this book, we feature the stories of people like Sharon and Debbie, underscoring the importance of nature and nurture, culture, and gender, and highlighting what's best about human nature (**TABLE 1.8**). Each chapter introduces you to one or more individuals who have faced challenges with courage and optimism, keeping their heads high when all hope seemed to be lost. Learning about these men and women has been a humbling experience for the authors. Their stories inspire us to be more thoughtful, compassionate, and fearless in our lives. We hope they move you in the same way. Welcome to *Scientific American: Psychology!*

"It Can Only Get Better"
Sharon (left) and Debbie, now 64, have known each other for nearly two decades. They are grateful for each other and look forward to many happy years together. As Sharon says, "It can only get better." Macmillan Learning.

positive psychology An approach that focuses on the positive aspects of human beings, seeking to understand their strengths and uncover the roots of happiness, creativity, humor, and so on.

summary of concepts

LO 1 Define psychology and describe its scope. (p. 2)

Psychology is the scientific study of behavior and mental processes. Psychologists are scientists who work in a variety of fields. They conduct two major types of research: basic and applied. Basic research focuses on collecting data to support or refute theories, gathering knowledge for the sake of knowledge. Applied research focuses on changing behaviors and outcomes, often leading to real-world applications.

LO 2 Summarize the goals of psychology. (p. 6)

The goals of psychology are to describe, predict, explain, and control behavior. These goals lay the foundation for the scientific approach and the research designs used to carry out experiments.

LO 3 Identify the people who helped establish psychology as a discipline, and describe their contributions. (p. 8)

The roots of psychology lie in disciplines such as philosophy and physiology. The early philosophers established the foundation for some of the longstanding discussions in psychology (nature and nurture). In 1879 psychology was officially founded when Wilhelm Wundt created the first psychology laboratory, located in Leipzig, Germany. Edward Titchener established structuralism to study the elements of the mind. In the late 1870s, William James offered the first psychology class in the United States, at Harvard, and his work helped to establish the early school of psychology known as functionalism.

LO 4 List and summarize the major perspectives in psychology. (p. 11)

Psychologists use different perspectives to understand and study issues and topics in the field. Each perspective provides a different vantage point for uncovering the complex nature of human behavior. The psychoanalytic perspective looks at the unconscious conflicts at the root of personality development. The behavioral perspective examines human behavior as learned primarily through associations, reinforcers, and observation. The humanistic perspective focuses on the positive and growth aspects of human nature. The cognitive perspective considers the mental processes that direct behavior. The evolutionary perspective examines heritable traits that increase or decrease in frequency across generations. The biological perspective identifies the physiological basis of behavior. The sociocultural perspective looks at the social and cultural influences that impact behavior. The biopsychosocial perspective explains human behavior in terms of biological, psychological, and sociocultural factors.

LO 5 Evaluate pseudopsychology and its relationship to critical thinking. (p. 17)

Pseudopsychology is any approach to explaining and predicting behavior and events that appears to be psychology but is not supported by empirical, objective evidence. Critical thinking, on the other hand, is the process of weighing various pieces of evidence, synthesizing them, and determining how each contributes to the bigger picture. Critical thinking is absent from the "pseudotheories" used to explain the pseudopsychologies.

LO 6 Describe how psychologists use the scientific method. (p. 19)

Psychologists use the scientific method to provide empirical evidence based on systematic observation or experiments. The scientific method includes five basic steps: develop a question, formulate a hypothesis, collect data, analyze the data, and publish the findings. The scientific method is a continuing cycle of exploration that uses critical thinking at each step in the process, and asks new questions along the way.

LO 7 Distinguish between a random sample and a representative sample. (p. 25)

A population includes all members of a group a researcher wants to study. If the population is large, then the researcher will select a subgroup, called a sample. A random sample is a subset of the population chosen through a procedure that ensures all members have an equal chance of being selected. Random sampling increases the likelihood of achieving a representative sample, or subgroup, whose characteristics are similar to the population of interest.

LO 8 Recognize the forms of descriptive research. (p. 26)

Descriptive research is a type of investigation used to explore and describe a phenomenon. It is especially useful for studying new or unexplored topics when researchers might not have specific expectations about outcomes. Descriptive research methods include naturalistic observation, case studies, the survey method, and the correlational method.

LO 9 Describe the correlational method and identify its limitations. (p. 30)

The correlational method is a type of descriptive research that examines relationships, or correlations, between variables. Variables can be positively correlated (as one variable goes up, the other goes up), negatively correlated (as one variable goes up, the other goes down), or not at all related. The correlation coefficient (r) is a statistical measure indicating the strength and direction of the correlation between variables; r values range from +1.00 to –1.00, with positive numbers indicating the relationship is positive and negative numbers indicating it is negative (the inverse). The closer r is to +1.00 or –1.00, the stronger the relationship. The correlational method is useful for illuminating links between variables, and it helps researchers make predictions, but it cannot determine cause and effect. Even if variables X and Y are strongly correlated, we cannot assume that changes in X are driving changes in Y (or vice versa); there may be some third variable influencing both X and Y.

LO 10 Explain how the experimental method can establish cause and effect. (p. 34)

The experimental method is a type of research that incorporates independent and dependent variables to uncover cause-and-effect relationships. A well-designed experiment holds everything constant, except for the variables being manipulated by the researcher. If following the manipulation the groups of participants differ on the measure of interest, we can say with confidence that the experimental manipulation caused such a change.

LO 11 Identify measures psychologists take to support ethical treatment of their research participants. (p. 40)

Researchers must abide by guidelines to ensure the ethical treatment of research participants. These guidelines encourage psychologists to do no harm; safeguard the welfare of humans and animals in their research; know their responsibilities to society and community; maintain accuracy in research, teaching, and practice; and respect human dignity.

key terms

test prep *are you ready?*

1. Experts at a large university were asked to devise and evaluate a campaign to reduce binge drinking. Using findings from prior research, they created a program to curb binge drinking among students.. This is an example of:
   a. basic research.
   b. applied research.
   c. naturalistic observation.
   d. case studies.

2. _____ is a collection of knowledge that any reasonably smart person can pick up through casual observations of everyday experiences.
   a. Common sense
   b. Hindsight bias
   c. Psychology
   d. Psychomythology

3. The Greek philosopher Plato believed that truth and knowledge exist in the soul before birth and that humans have innate knowledge. This position supports:
   a. empiricism.
   b. the nurture side of the nature–nurture issue.
   c. the nature side of the nature–nurture issue.
   d. dualism.

4. Inspired by the work of Charles Darwin, William James proposed that the purpose of thought processes, feelings, and behaviors is to adapt to the environment, which is an important concept of:
   a. introspection.
   b. behaviorism.
   c. structuralism.
   d. functionalism.

5. _____ suggests that human nature is by and large positive.
   a. Natural selection
   b. Psychoanalysis
   c. Structuralism
   d. Humanistic psychology

6. Psychology is driven by _____, but pseudopsychology is not.
   a. unverified guesses
   b. critical thinking
   c. lessons learned
   d. folk wisdom

7. The goal of _____ is to provide empirical evidence or data based on systematic observation or experimentation.
   a. operational definitions
   b. critical thinking
   c. the scientific method
   d. a hypothesis

8. _____ allow us to make inferences and determine the probability of certain events occurring.
   a. Inferential statistics
   b. Descriptive statistics
   c. Operational definitions
   d. Theories

9. A psychologist studying identical twins was interested in their leadership qualities and educational backgrounds. These characteristics are generally referred to as:
   a. operational definitions.
   b. hypotheses.
   c. variables.
   d. empiricism.

10. One way to pick a random sample is to make sure every member of the population has:
    a. no extraneous variables.
    b. no confounding variables.
    c. an equal chance of having a characteristic in common.
    d. an equal chance of being picked to participate.

11. Descriptive research is invaluable to psychologists at the beginning stages of a study. Some forms of descriptive research can provide information on:
    a. cause-and-effect relationships.
    b. random assignment.
    c. relationships among variables.
    d. experimenter bias.

12. A researcher interested in learning more about the effect of separating identical twins shortly after birth might use the "Jim Twins" as a(n) _____, which is a type of descriptive research invaluable for studying rare events.
    a. experiment
    b. case study
    c. naturalistic observation
    d. correlational study

13. The _____ variable is what the researcher manipulates, and the _____ variable is the response the researcher measures.
    a. confounding; extraneous
    b. extraneous; confounding
    c. dependent; independent
    d. independent; dependent

14. With a(n) _____ study, neither the researchers nor the participants know who is getting the treatment or who is receiving the placebo.
    a. double-blind
    b. experimental
    c. correlational
    d. blind

15. A researcher forming a _____ of high school seniors might use a comprehensive database of all seniors in the United States to select participants, as all members of the population theoretically would have an equal chance of being selected to participate in the study.
    a. control group
    b. experimental group
    c. random assignment
    d. random sample

16. Describe the goals of psychology and give an example of each.

17. A researcher is planning to conduct a study on aggression and exposure to media violence. What can she do to ensure the ethical treatment of the children in her study?

18. Use the major perspectives of psychology to explain the similarities between the "Jim Twins."

19. Find an article in the popular media that presents variables as having cause-and-effect relationships, but that is really a correlational study.

20. Reread the feature on the SpongeBob study. How does it establish a cause-and-effect relationship between watching the cartoon and changes in cognitive function? If you were to replicate the study, what would you do to change or improve it?

✓ CHECK YOUR ANSWERS IN APPENDIX C.

YOUR SW

YOUR SCIENTIFIC WORLD
Apply psychology to the real world!
Go to LaunchPad for access.

Corbis Wire/Corbis.

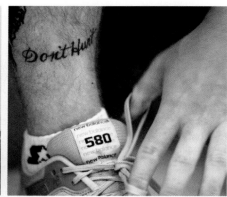

A.J. Wolfe/The Commercial Appeal/Zuma Press.

Laura Burns.

CHAPTER OUTLINE AND LEARNING OBJECTIVES

Introducing the Brain

LO 1 Define neuroscience and biological psychology and explain their contributions to our understanding of behavior.

LO 2 Compare and contrast tools scientists use to study the brain.

Neurons and Neural Communication

LO 3 Label the parts of a neuron and describe an action potential.

LO 4 Illustrate how neurons communicate with each other.

LO 5 Describe specific neurotransmitters and summarize how their activity affects human behavior.

The Supporting Systems

LO 6 Explain how the central and peripheral nervous systems connect.

LO 7 Describe the organization and function of the peripheral nervous system.

LO 8 Summarize how the endocrine system influences behavior and physiological processes.

The Hemispheres

LO 9 Describe the two brain hemispheres and how they communicate.

LO 10 Define lateralization and explain what the split-brain experiments reveal about the right and left hemispheres.

LO 11 Identify areas in the brain responsible for language production and comprehension.

The Amazing Brain

LO 12 Define neuroplasticity and recognize when it is evident in the brain.

LO 13 Identify the lobes of the cortex and explain their functions.

LO 14 Describe the association areas and identify their functions.

Digging Below the Cortex

LO 15 Distinguish the structures and functions of the limbic system.

LO 16 Distinguish the structures and functions of the brainstem and cerebellum.

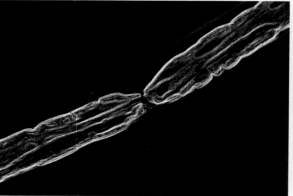

Jean-Claude Revy, ISM/Phototake.

William Johnson.

Medical Body Scans/Science Source.

2 biology and behavior

Introducing the Brain

IN THE LINE OF FIRE   It was November 9, 2004, and U.S. Marine Brandon Burns was surrounded on all sides by gunfire. The enemy was everywhere, in the buildings, streets, and alleyways of Fallujah. "I was in the deepest part of the city [and] there was chaos," remembers Brandon. At age 19, Brandon was on the front lines in the Iraq War, fighting in the battle of Fallujah.

"I was on top of the Humvee automatic grenade launcher shooting round after round," Brandon recalls. Suddenly, there was darkness. A bullet from an enemy sniper had pierced Brandon's helmet and skull, and ricocheted through the back left side of his brain. Bleeding and unconscious, Brandon was rushed from Fallujah to Baghdad. Medics had to resuscitate him on five separate occasions during that ambulance ride. Brandon explains, "Five times I died."

From Baghdad, Brandon was transferred to a hospital in Germany. Doctors concluded that some parts of his brain were no longer viable. "They removed part of my skull and dug out the injured part of my brain," and now, Brandon says, "one third of my brain is gone." ●

Ready for Duty
Brandon Burns poses for a photo at the Marine Corps Recruit Depot in Parris Island, South Carolina, in the fall of 2003. The following year, he was shot by an enemy sniper in the battle of Fallujah.
Laura Burns.

Note: Quotations attributed to Brandon Burns, Laura Burns, and Christina Santhouse are personal communications.

A Complex Communication Network

Imagine that you lost a sizable chunk of your brain. How would it impact your life? Would you be the same person as before? Your brain houses your thoughts, emotions, and personality, and orchestrates your behavior. It files away all your memories and dark secrets, and is involved in your every move, from the beat of your heart to the blink of your eye.

Scientists suspect the human brain is "the most complex entity in the known universe" (Huang & Luo, 2015, p. 42). This squishy, pinkish organ is definitely the most important component of your *nervous system*—a communication network that conveys messages throughout your body, using electrical and chemical processes. In this chapter, you will learn all about the human nervous system, which includes the brain, spinal cord, and nerves.

The brain is home to somewhere between 86 and 100 billion nerve cells (Herculano-Houzel, 2012; Huang & Luo, 2015). And since a typical nerve cell can communicate with thousands of others, the total number of links among them has been estimated by some to be about 100 trillion (10^{14}) (Huang & Luo, 2015). This intricate, ever-adapting web of connections gives us the power to think and feel in ways that are different from—and vastly more complex than—the thinking and feeling capacities of most other organisms.

Consider the many tasks your brain is juggling at this very moment. As you scan the words on this page, your brain helps control the tiny muscles moving your eyes back and forth as well as the larger muscles in your neck and torso that keep you sitting upright. Light-sensitive cells in the back of your eyes relay signals, using electricity and chemicals, to various brain regions that transform the black marks on this page into words, sentences, and ideas for you to remember. And all the while, your brain is processing sounds and smells, and working with other nerve cells in your body to make sure your heart keeps pumping, your lungs keep breathing, and your glands and organs keep releasing hormones properly.

The Last Frontier: From Bumps to Brain Scans

LO 1　Define neuroscience and biological psychology and explain their contributions to our understanding of behavior.

Brandon's injury resulted in a significant loss of his brain tissue. Remarkably, not only did he survive, but he can still talk about what occurred, think about the events, and feel emotions associated with the experience. How exactly does his brain orchestrate all these complex functions, especially after severe trauma? And how does a noninjured brain carry out these processes? Scientists have developed a decent understanding of how individual brain cells communicate with each other, but they have yet to provide definitive answers to "big questions" involving the brain and other parts of the nervous system such as: How do we think? What is consciousness? Why do we need to sleep? This is why the brain may be regarded as the "last frontier of scientific inquiry" (Huang & Lo, 2015, p. 44). **Neuroscience,** the study of the brain and nervous system, draws upon disciplines as diverse as medicine, engineering, computer science, and our personal favorite—psychology. The subfield of psychology concerned with understanding how the brain and other biological systems influence human behavior is called **biological psychology,** which brings us to the goal of this chapter: to examine how biology influences our behavior.

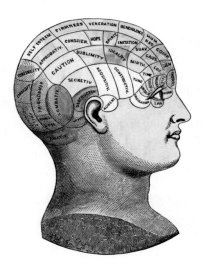

All in Your Head

Are you a secretive person? How high is your self-esteem? The answers to these questions lie on the surface of the skull, or so claimed 19th-century phrenologists, such as the one depicted in this 1886 illustration (right). The phrenological map (left) shows the locations of brain "organs" thought to be responsible for various psychological traits. Left: North Wind Picture Archives/The Image Works. Right: Image Asset Management Ltd./Superstock.

LO 2 **Compare and contrast tools scientists use to study the brain.**

Brandon underwent many brain scans before and after his surgeries, which allowed doctors to get a detailed look inside his head without lifting a scalpel. But had Brandon lived in a different era, brain scans would not have been an option.

Before there were technologies to study the brain, people could only speculate about what was going on beneath the skull of a living person. One theory was that bumps on the skull revealed characteristics about an individual. Judging the topography of a person's head was a core part of **phrenology,** the now discredited **brain "science"** that achieved enormous popularity at the beginning of the 19th century through its founder, German neuroanatomist Franz Joseph Gall (1757–1828). Another early (but more scientific) way of studying the brain was through *ablation,* a technique used by French physiologist Pierre Flourens (1794–1867) to explore the functions of different brain regions (Pearce, 2009). This technique involved destroying parts of a living animal's brain and then determining whether some functioning was lost thereafter. Despite the limitations of their methodologies, the work of Gall and Flourens advanced the idea that areas of the brain might have particular functions (Wickens, 2015). In other words, specific regions of the brain are in charge of certain activities: There is a *localization* of function.

Brain research has come a long way since the days of Gall and Flourens. The last century, and particularly the last few decades, have witnessed an explosion of technologies for studying the nervous system (see **INFOGRAPHIC 2.1**). Such advances have made it possible to observe the brain as it sleeps, reads a book, or even tells lies (Horikawa, Tamaki, Miyawaki, & Kamitani, 2013; Hsu, Jacobs, Altmann, & Conrad, 2015; Jiang et al., 2015). With emerging technologies such as *optogenetics,* researchers can manipulate the activity of individual brain cells (Max-Planck-Gesellschaft, 2015).

With this overview, we are now ready to begin our chapter-long "learning tour" of the nervous system. Our journey begins in the microscopic world of nerve cells, or **neurons.** Neurons are specialized cells that communicate with each other through electrical and chemical signals. They are the building blocks of the brain, spinal cord, and nerves. When large numbers of these building blocks are lost or damaged, as occurred in Brandon's injury, the consequences can be severe.

CONNECTIONS

If phrenology were practiced today, we would consider it a pseudoscience, or an activity that resembles science but is not supported by objective evidence. See **Chapter 1** to read more on critical thinking.

Admissible in Court?

A growing number of attorneys are submitting brain scans as legal evidence in court (Stix, 2014, May/June). In a criminal case, for example, a defense attorney might use a brain scan to demonstrate her client has a psychological disturbance. But many judges are reluctant to accept this type of evidence; they believe neuroscience needs more time to mature (Davis, 2015, October 20). AP Photo/ The Paduca Sun, John Wright.

Ways to Study the Living Brain

In the past, scientists were limited in their ability to study the brain. Most of what they learned came from performing surgeries, often on cadavers. Today, imaging and recording technologies enable us to investigate the structure and function of the living brain. CAT and MRI techniques provide static pictures of brain structures, while functional imaging and recording techniques allow us to see the relationship between brain activity and specific mental functions. Functional techniques can also be used to diagnose injuries and diseases earlier than techniques that look at structure.

New technologies are continually being developed, allowing us to study the brain in ways we couldn't imagine just a few years ago.

Looking at Brain STRUCTURE

COMPUTERIZED AXIAL TOMOGRAPHY — CAT

Using X-rays, a scanner creates multiple cross-sectional images of the brain. Here, we see the brain from the top at the level of the ventricles, which form the butterfly-shaped dark spaces in the center.

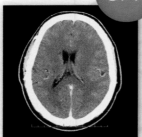

MAGNETIC RESONANCE IMAGING — MRI

An MRI machine's powerful magnets create a magnetic field that passes through the brain. A computer analyzes the electromagnetic response, creating cross-sectional images similar to those produced by CAT, but with superior detail.

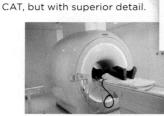

What's Next?
Making Connections

The intricate pathways of myelinated axons in the brain can't be seen in the imaging techniques shown here. But new technologies like diffusion spectrum imaging (DSI), which tracks the diffusion of water molecules through brain tissue, are being used to map neural connections. The resulting images show a complex information superhighway, with different colors indicating directions of travel.

Watching Brain FUNCTION

EEG — ELECTROENCEPHALOGRAM

Electrodes placed on the scalp record electrical activity from the cortical area directly below. When the recorded traces are lined up, as in the computer readout seen here, we can see the scope of functional responses across the lobes.

PET — POSITRON EMISSION TOMOGRAPHY

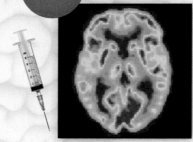

A radioactively labeled substance called a tracer is injected into the bloodstream and tracked while the participant performs a task. A computer then creates 3-D images showing degrees of brain activity. Areas with the most activity appear in red.

fMRI — FUNCTIONAL MAGNETIC RESONANCE IMAGING

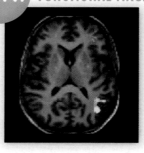

The flow of oxygen-rich blood increases to areas of the brain that are active during a task. fMRI uses powerful magnets to track changes in blood-oxygen levels. Like PET, this produces measurements of activity throughout the brain.

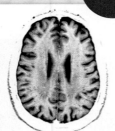

CAT: Southern Illinois University/Science Source. MRI (brain): Living Art Enterprises, LLC/Science Source. MRI (person in MRI machine): Arno Massee/Science Source. EEG: Science Source. Woman with EEG electrodes: AJPhoto/Science Source. PET scan: National Institute on Aging/Science Source. Syringe: istockphoto/thinkstock. DSI scan: Laboratory of Neuro Imaging at UCLA and Martinos Center for Biomedical Imaging at MGH, Consortium of the Human Connectome Project. fMRI: ISM/Phototake. Background image of brain: PASIEKA/SCIENCE PHOTO LIBRARY.

○✓○○ show what you know

1. A researcher studying the impact of Brandon's brain injury might work in the field of _____, or the study of the brain and nervous system.

2. Match the technology with its characteristic:

   a. Positron emission tomography

   b. Electroencephalogram

   c. Magnetic resonance imaging

   d. Computerized axial tomography

   e. Functional magnetic resonance imaging

   _____ using X-rays creates cross-sectional images

   _____ records electrical activity from cortical area

   _____ tracks changes of radioactive substances

   _____ tracks changes in blood-oxygen levels

   _____ with magnet creates cross-sectional images

3. In the next section, you will learn much more about neurons, which are often referred to as the "building blocks" of the nervous system. What building blocks are you familiar with in other fields of study?

✓ CHECK YOUR ANSWERS IN APPENDIX C.

Neurons and Neural Communication

THE AWAKENING   Two weeks after the shooting, Brandon finally awoke from his coma. He could not move or feel the right side of his body, and he had lost the ability to use language. There were so many things he wanted to say to his family, but when he opened his mouth, the only sound that came out was "ugh." Weeks went by before Brandon uttered his first word: "no." That was all he could say for months, even when he was dying to say "yes."

Apart from the paralysis to his right side and his difficulty with language, Brandon's other faculties appeared to be intact. He could remember people, places, and objects, and he reported no trouble hearing, smelling, or tasting. Although Brandon was not as outgoing and self-assured as before, he hadn't changed much overall.

Why did the trauma to Brandon's brain cause deficits in language, but not memory? Why was the right side of his body paralyzed, while the left side worked fine? Our discussion of the brain's organization later in this chapter will clear up these mysteries for you. But first, let's find out how neurons in the brain and body communicate, for this biological process underlies your every behavior, thought, and emotion. ●

Just the Basics

LO 3   Label the parts of a neuron and describe an action potential.

THE STRUCTURE OF A TYPICAL NEURON   A typical neuron has three basic parts: a cell body, dendrites, and an axon (**FIGURE 2.1** on the next page). The **cell body** of a neuron contains the standard components found in most human cells, including structures that nourish the cell and a nucleus containing DNA. Extending from the cell body are many **dendrites** (DEN-drites), which are tiny, branchlike fibers. Generally projecting in the opposite direction from the dendrites is a single **axon,** which is a long, skinny, tube-like extension of the cell body, with branches ending in _terminal buds_. Many axons are surrounded by a **myelin sheath** (MY-el-in sheeth), a fatty substance that provides insulation for the activities occurring within. In such cases the axon is not entirely enclosed, but rather, covered in segments of myelin. The breaks between the myelin segments are called _nodes of Ranvier_. The **synapse** (SIN-aps) is the tiny gap between a terminal bud of one axon and a dendrite of a neighboring neuron (see image on p. 58). Just for perspective, the synaptic gap is only about 0.000127 millimeters (1.27×10^{-4}) wide, whereas a single sheet of printer paper is 0.1 millimeter thick (the equivalent of about 788 synaptic gaps combined).

One-Handed
Brandon ties his shoelaces with his left hand. His traumatic brain injury occurred on the left side of his brain, causing paralysis and loss of sensation on the right side of his body. Photo by A.J. Wolfe/The Commercial Appeal/Zuma Press.

Synonyms

cell body soma

terminal buds axon buds, synaptic knobs, terminal buttons

synapse synaptic cleft, synaptic gap

cell body The region of the neuron that includes structures that nourish the cell, and a nucleus containing DNA.

dendrites Tiny, branchlike fibers extending from the cell body that receive messages from other neurons and send information in the direction of the cell body.

axon Skinny tube-like structure of a neuron that extends from the cell body, and which sends messages to other neurons through its terminal buds.

myelin sheath Fatty substance that insulates the axon and speeds the transmission of neural messages.

synapse Tiny gap between a terminal bud of one axon and a dendrite of a neighboring neuron; junction between neurons where communication occurs.

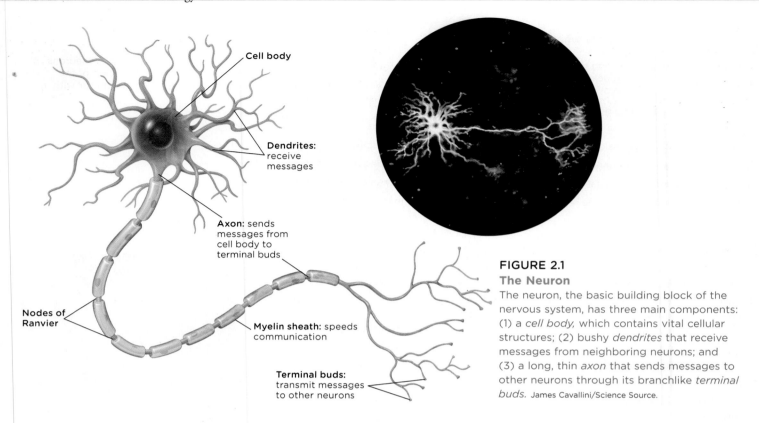

Cell body

Dendrites: receive messages

Axon: sends messages from cell body to terminal buds

Nodes of Ranvier

Myelin sheath: speeds communication

Terminal buds: transmit messages to other neurons

FIGURE 2.1
The Neuron
The neuron, the basic building block of the nervous system, has three main components: (1) a *cell body,* which contains vital cellular structures; (2) bushy *dendrites* that receive messages from neighboring neurons; and (3) a long, thin *axon* that sends messages to other neurons through its branchlike *terminal buds.* James Cavallini/Science Source.

Glia to the Rescue
A scanning electron micrograph shows neurons (green) and glia (orange). Glial cells serve as the "glue" of the nervous system, providing cohesion and support for the neurons. Thomas Deerinck, NCMIR/Science Source.

HOLDING IT TOGETHER: GLIAL CELLS Neurons transmit information up and down the body all day and night, and they need a little support and nurturing to get the job done. This is where the **glial cells** (GLEE-ul) come into play. By some estimates, glial cells outnumber neurons by approximately 50 to 1 (Yuhas & Jabr, 2012, June 13), holding neurons together and maintaining the structure of the nervous system. (*Glia* means "glue" in Greek.) Others estimate that the number of glial cells and neurons are approximately the same (Herculano-Houzel, 2012). More research is needed to clear up this controversy.

For many years, scientists believed that glial cells simply kept things together, but we now know they do much more (Hoogland & Parpura, 2015; Ndubaku & de Bellard, 2008). For example, glial cells come to the rescue if the brain is injured. When Brandon was shot in the head, glial cells called *microglia* worked to defend his brain from infection and inflammation (d'Avila et al., 2012; Streit, 2000). Another class of glial cells called *astrocytes* began to restore the barrier between his brain and blood (Burda, Bernstein, & Sofroniew, 2016; Gruber, 2009). Astrocytes support communication between neurons as well (Araque & Navarrete, 2010; Martín, Bajo-Grañeras, Moratalla, Perea, & Araque, 2015). Yet another type of glial cells, *Schwann cells,* produce the myelin that envelops axons.

Processes Inside the Neuron

Neurons have properties that allow them to communicate with other cells. But what information do they convey? In essence, the message is simple: "I have been activated." Neurons are activated in response to other neurons, which can be stimulated by receptors attached to your skin, muscles, and other organs; the communication among groups of neurons underlies your every sensation, thought, emotion, and behavior.

A neuron is surrounded by and is filled with fluid containing particles (ions) that have an electrical charge (INFOGRAPHIC 2.2 on the next page). The neuron's charge is determined by the electrical characteristics of the ions. Some ions have a negative charge; others are positively charged. The difference in the "sum" of the positive and negative charges inside and outside of the neuron determines the degree to which the neuron has a positive or negative charge overall. Although humans can't detect the overall charge, its impact is undeniable.

Two processes direct the flow of positive (+) and negative (−) ions into and out of the cell. *Diffusion* is the natural tendency of ions to spread out or disperse, and *electrostatic pressure* causes similarly charged ions to spread apart and oppositely charged ions to move toward each other (like magnets). The concentrations or accumulations of positively and negatively charged ions inside and outside of the cell determine the activity or potential difference (voltage) between the inside and outside of most neurons. Imagine a long building, with people standing inside and outside, all of them holding either a positive or negative sign. If we were to count up the total number of positives inside and outside the building, and do the same for the negatives, we could determine the overall difference. This summation of negatives and positives produces the voltage difference in a neuron.

A neuron is encased in a membrane that is *selectively permeable,* allowing only some of the ions to pass in and out of its channels. The membrane is impermeable to positive sodium ions and negative protein ions (it does not allow these ions to enter or exit). Positive sodium ions approach the membrane from the outside, and negative protein ions approach the membrane from the inside; they move because the opposite charges are attracted to each other (like the opposite poles of magnets). If you're having trouble imagining this, consider that the membrane plays the same role as a gate at the top of a hydroelectric dam. The dam holds back the water until the gate opens. This water has the potential to do work (the higher the dam holding back the water, the more work the water can do). We call this ability to do work the potential energy of the water relative to the river below. The difference between the negative and positive charges being held back by the membrane produces a similar ability to do work, which is called the potential energy between the inside and the outside of the neuron. And the passage of ions through the membrane plays an important role in how neurons transmit information.

Let's start by considering the inside of the cell. Here's what is going on when the neuron is not active: The negative protein ions are only on the inside of the cell, but they are attracted to the excess positive charge outside and move toward the membrane. Because the protein ions (−) are too big to get through the membrane, the inside of the neuron is negatively charged (Infographic 2.2). Although there are some positive potassium ions inside the neuron, the concentration of sodium ions (+) outside the cell is much greater than that inside. As a result, sodium ions on the outside are attracted to the membrane (because of diffusion and electrostatic pressure). An electrical potential is created by the difference in charge between the outside and the inside of the neuron, which is its *resting potential.* Like the water at the top of the dam, it has the potential to produce energy.

RESTING POTENTIAL   The **resting potential** represents the *electrical potential* of a cell "at rest." The solutions on either side of the membrane wall come into equilibrium with a slightly more negative charge inside. In the resting state, the voltage inside the cell is about −70 millivolts (mV) compared to the voltage on the outside. (Think of a resting neuron like a battery. The voltage of one AA battery is 1,500 mV.) But what does this have to do with neurons transmitting information? Let's look at what happens when a neuron stops "resting" and goes into "action" (Infographic 2.2).

ACTION POTENTIAL   Although the sodium ions (+) are being pulled toward the membrane, they cannot move into the cell, unless the neuron is stimulated by neighboring cells. When this happens, a signal instructs the channels, or gates, in the cell

glial cells Cells that support, nourish, and protect neurons; some produce myelin that covers axons.

resting potential The electrical potential of a cell "at rest"; the state of a cell when it is not activated.

Communication Within Neurons

Neural communication involves different processes *within* and *between* neurons. In this infographic, we follow the electrical action that conveys messages *within* the neuron, from one end to the other.

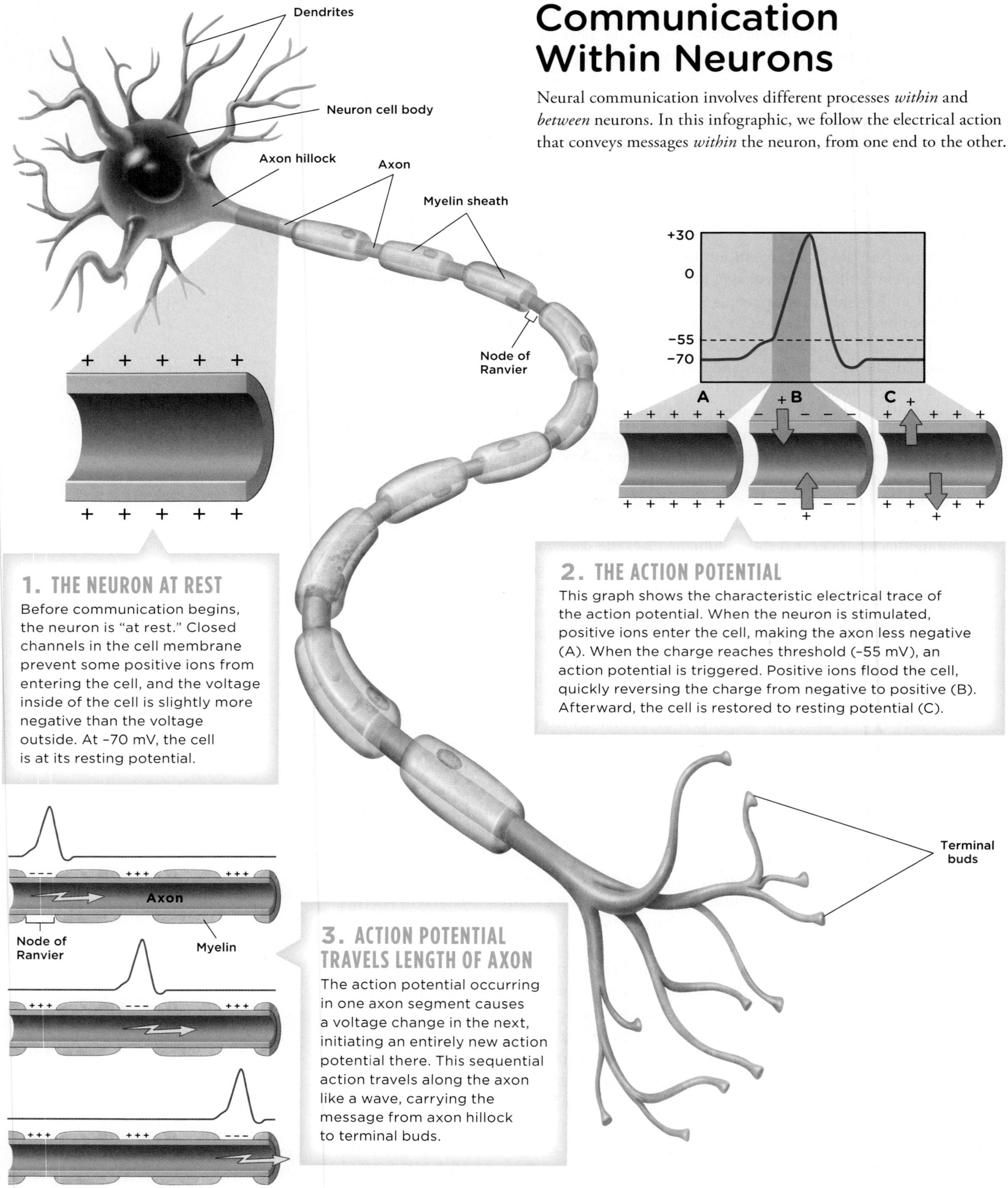

Dendrites

Neuron cell body

Axon hillock

Axon

Myelin sheath

Node of Ranvier

+ + + + +

+ + + + +

A   + B   C +

+ + + + +   − − − − −   + + + +

+ + + +   − − − −   + + + +
                +   +

1. THE NEURON AT REST

Before communication begins, the neuron is "at rest." Closed channels in the cell membrane prevent some positive ions from entering the cell, and the voltage inside of the cell is slightly more negative than the voltage outside. At –70 mV, the cell is at its resting potential.

2. THE ACTION POTENTIAL

This graph shows the characteristic electrical trace of the action potential. When the neuron is stimulated, positive ions enter the cell, making the axon less negative (A). When the charge reaches threshold (–55 mV), an action potential is triggered. Positive ions flood the cell, quickly reversing the charge from negative to positive (B). Afterward, the cell is restored to resting potential (C).

+30

0

−55

−70

Axon

Node of Ranvier

Myelin

+ + +   − − −   + + +

+ + +   + + +   − − −

Terminal buds

3. ACTION POTENTIAL TRAVELS LENGTH OF AXON

The action potential occurring in one axon segment causes a voltage change in the next, initiating an entirely new action potential there. This sequential action travels along the axon like a wave, carrying the message from axon hillock to terminal buds.

membrane to open up. The channels in the dendrites open, freeing the sodium ions (+) to enter the cell and move into the cell body, to finally reach the beginning of the axon, known as the *axon hillock.*

The influx of sodium ions (+) at the axon hillock raises the internal cell voltage of the first segment of the axon from a resting voltage of –70 mV to the *threshold potential* of –55 mV (relative to the outside of the cell). This change in voltage causes sodium gates to open in that first segment of the axon, and the sodium ions (+) flood into the cell. The voltage inside that section rises rapidly, increasing from –55 mV to +30 mV, and then the sodium gates immediately close. This produces a spike in voltage, as the charge inside the cell becomes more positive than that outside of the cell. This is the **action potential,** or the change in electrical energy that passes through the axon of a neuron.

What happens after this sudden jump in voltage? Resting potential is reestablished in order to return the neuron to its "natural" state. Here's how: Because the ions are no longer at equilibrium, a sodium/potassium pump in the membrane restores their original values by pumping the excess sodium ions (+) back outside the cell and the potassium ions (+) back in. In other words, the neuron must "reset," forcing the solutions inside and outside this segment of the axon to return to balance so that it is ready to do more work.

MOVING DOWN THE AXON　Now let's talk about how the action potential travels along the axon. The firing of the first segment of the axon produces excess sodium ions on the inside of the cell, which diffuse to the next segment within the axon. This causes the voltage of this second segment to reach the threshold potential (–55 mV), which leads to a spike of voltage there (+30 mV). Meanwhile, the first segment of the axon returns to its resting potential, preventing the voltage spike from traveling back in that direction. This process repeats through each segment of the axon, like a row of dominoes tumbling down. Every time an axon segment fires, the positive sodium ions flood in from the outside of the cell, while the prior segment returns to its resting potential, all along the length of the axon to its end. Each action potential takes about 1 millisecond to complete, and a typical neuron can fire several hundred times per second. It's hard to comprehend, but the action potentials constantly occurring in billions of neurons are the basis for all of our thoughts, feelings, and behaviors.

EXCITATORY AND INHIBITORY SIGNALS　What triggers a neuron to fire an action potential? The message begins at the dendrites. Neighboring neurons deliver chemical messages, prompting channels in the dendrites to open up and allow the sodium ions into the cell. If enough sending neurons signal the receiving neuron to pass along the message, their combined signal becomes *excitatory* and the neuron fires. However, not all neighboring neurons send an excitatory signal. Some deliver an *inhibitory* signal, instructing the neuron not to fire. For an action potential to occur, excitatory signals must exceed inhibitory signals, and the difference between them has to meet the threshold potential of –55 mV. If enough positively charged ions enter the cell, the potential of the neuron reaches its threshold, or trigger point, and the cell "fires." Let's return to the top of the dam—imagine that thousands of people are yelling at the person in charge of the gate, some shouting "Open it!" and others screaming "Don't open it!" If enough people are in favor, the gatekeeper will open the gate.

ALL-OR-NONE　Action potentials are **all-or-none:** They either happen or they don't, and their strength remains the same regardless of the conditions. So how does a neuron convey the strength of a stimulus? By (1) firing more often and (2) delivering its message to more neurons. Consider a loud scream and a quiet whisper. The loud scream is a stronger stimulus, so it causes more *sensory neurons* to fire than the quiet whisper. The loud scream also prompts each neuron to fire more often. Thus, there is no such thing as a partial action potential, or a strong or weak action potential.

Synonyms
threshold potential stimulus threshold
action potential spike potential

action potential The spike in voltage that passes through the axon of a neuron, the purpose of which is to convey information.

all-or-none A neuron either fires or does not fire; action potentials are always the same strength.

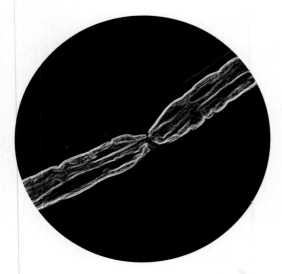

ROLE OF MYELIN SHEATH The firing of a neuron is facilitated by the myelin sheath, which insulates and protects the tiny voltage changes occurring inside the axon. Myelin is a good insulator, but the axon is not covered with myelin at the nodes of Ranvier (you can see this in the photograph to the left). The action potential appears to "jump" from node to node, as opposed to traversing the entire axon in one continuous movement, and this accelerates the transmission of the signal. The speed of the action potential in an unmyelinated axon is approximately 1.1 to 4.5 miles per hour (mph), while that in a myelinated neuron is about 157 to 268 mph (Susuki, 2010). Unmyelinated axons have slower transmission speeds because the signal must make its way down the entire length of the axon. Imagine you are in a loud, crowded room (unmyelinated) versus a quiet room (myelinated). How quickly would you be able to understand, and then respond to important directions given in the quiet room? Very quickly we assume. It would take much longer in the loud, crowded room. Myelination damage from diseases such as multiple sclerosis can lead to many symptoms, including fatigue, trouble with vision, and cognitive disabilities (Calabrese et al., 2015; Su, Banker, Bourdette, & Forte, 2009).

So Fast
Action potentials may travel as fast as 268 miles per hour through a myelinated axon (Susuki, 2010). Myelin is a protein that envelops and insulates the axon, facilitating faster transmission. The action potential "skips" over the segments of myelin, hopping from one node of Ranvier to the next (see small space in the center), instead of traversing the entire length of the axon. Jean-Claude Revy, ISM/Phototake.

Communication Between Neurons

 LO 4 Illustrate how neurons communicate with each other.

Neurons communicate with each other via chemicals called **neurotransmitters.** (**INFOGRAPHIC 2.3** illustrates communication between neurons in detail.) An action potential moves down the axon, eventually reaching the terminal buds. The voltage change associated with the action potential causes *vesicles* (small fluid-filled sacs) in the terminal buds to unload neurotransmitters into the synaptic gap. The majority of these neurotransmitters drift across the synaptic gap and come into contact with **receptor sites** of the receiving neuron's dendrites. Just as it takes the right key to unlock a door, the neurotransmitter must fit a corresponding receptor site to convey its message. Because there are a variety of neurotransmitters, a variety of receptor sites also exist.

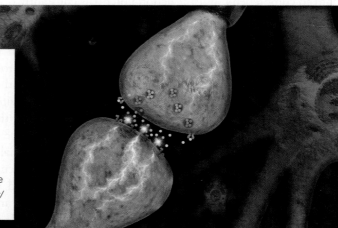

The Synapse
The terminal bud of a sending neuron (top) interacts with a dendrite of a receiving neuron by releasing chemical messengers (neurotransmitters) into the synapse. Once the neurotransmitters migrate across the gap and latch onto the dendrite's receptor sites, the message has been conveyed. Carol and Mike Werner/ Science Source.

neurotransmitters Chemical messengers that neurons use to communicate at the synapse.

receptor sites Locations on the receiving neuron's dendrites where neurotransmitters attach.

reuptake Process by which neurotransmitters are reabsorbed by the sending terminal bud.

When the neurotransmitters latch onto the receptors of the receiving neuron's dendrites, gates in the receiving neuron's membrane fly open, ushering in positively charged particles and thus restarting the cycle of the action potential (if the threshold is met).

What happens to the neurotransmitters once they have conveyed their message? Neurotransmitters that latch onto receptors may be reabsorbed by the sending terminal bud in a process known as **reuptake.** Those that are not reabsorbed may drift out of the synaptic gap through diffusion. This is how the synapse is cleared of neurotransmitters, in preparation for the next release of chemical messengers.

Communication Between Neurons

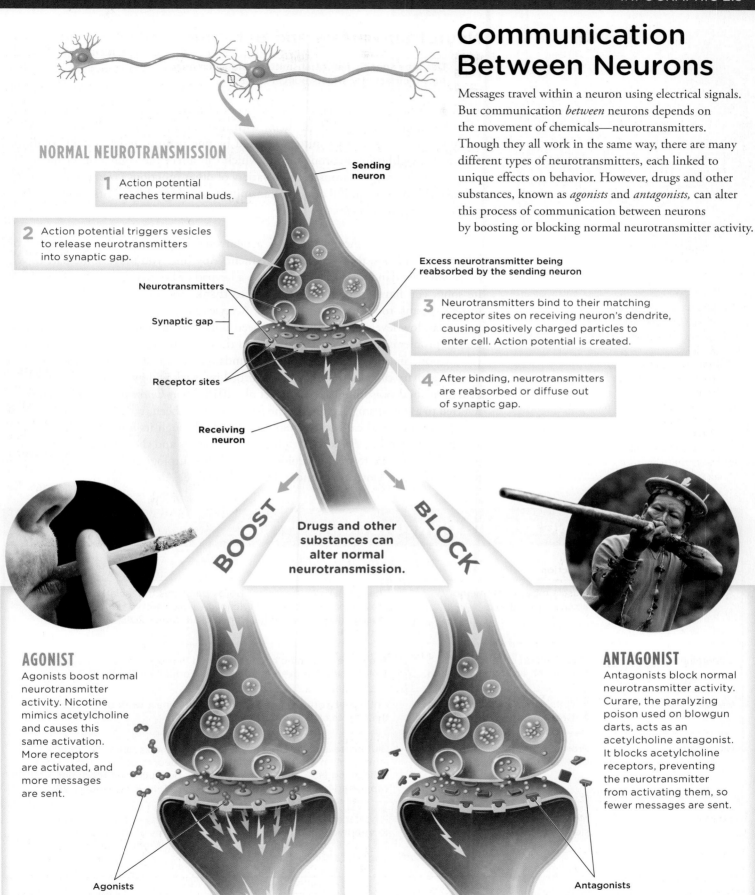

Messages travel within a neuron using electrical signals. But communication *between* neurons depends on the movement of chemicals—neurotransmitters. Though they all work in the same way, there are many different types of neurotransmitters, each linked to unique effects on behavior. However, drugs and other substances, known as *agonists* and *antagonists,* can alter this process of communication between neurons by boosting or blocking normal neurotransmitter activity.

NORMAL NEUROTRANSMISSION

1 Action potential reaches terminal buds.

2 Action potential triggers vesicles to release neurotransmitters into synaptic gap.

Neurotransmitters

Synaptic gap

Receptor sites

Receiving neuron

Sending neuron

Excess neurotransmitter being reabsorbed by the sending neuron

3 Neurotransmitters bind to their matching receptor sites on receiving neuron's dendrite, causing positively charged particles to enter cell. Action potential is created.

4 After binding, neurotransmitters are reabsorbed or diffuse out of synaptic gap.

BOOST

BLOCK

Drugs and other substances can alter normal neurotransmission.

AGONIST

Agonists boost normal neurotransmitter activity. Nicotine mimics acetylcholine and causes this same activation. More receptors are activated, and more messages are sent.

Agonists

ANTAGONIST

Antagonists block normal neurotransmitter activity. Curare, the paralyzing poison used on blowgun darts, acts as an acetylcholine antagonist. It blocks acetylcholine receptors, preventing the neurotransmitter from activating them, so fewer messages are sent.

Antagonists

Neurotransmitters and Behavior

LO 5 Describe specific neurotransmitters and summarize how their activity affects human behavior.

As mentioned, there are many different types of neurotransmitters. Researchers have identified approximately 100 of them, with many more yet to be discovered. We already know that neurotransmitters secreted by one neuron under certain conditions can cause neighboring neurons to fire, which can affect the regulation of mood, appetite, muscles, organs, arousal, and a variety of other functions (**TABLE 2.1**). Here, we will describe only a handful of neurotransmitters, starting with the first neurotransmitter discovered, *acetylcholine.*

ACETYLCHOLINE Acetylcholine is a neurotransmitter that relays messages from neurons to muscles, thus enabling movement. Any time you move some part of your body, whether dancing your fingers across a keypad or bouncing your head to a favorite song, you have, in part, acetylcholine to thank. Too much acetylcholine leads to muscle spasms; too little causes paralysis. Acetylcholine is also involved in memory. In particular, low levels in the brain have been linked to Alzheimer's disease, which can lead to problems of memory, language, and thinking (Bishara, Sauer, & Taylor, 2015; Johannsson, Snaedal, Johannesson, Gudmundsson, & Johnsen, 2015). Normal acetylcholine activity can also be seriously disturbed by black widow spider and snake bites, as well as food poisoning (Duregotti et al., 2015). *Botulinum neurotoxin,* commonly referred to as botulism, is a food-borne poison that has been transformed into a tool for treating various medical and cosmetic conditions through its impact on acetylcholine activity (for example, *Botox* for treating muscle spasms and the muscle activity leading to wrinkles). Its use to treat neurological and non-neurological disorders has led some to refer to it as a "potential wonder drug" (Gooriah & Ahmed, 2015).

TABLE 2.1   SURPRISING EFFECTS OF NEUROTRANSMITTERS

Neurotransmitter	Function	Did You Know?
Acetylcholine	Muscle movement, memory, arousal, attention	The anti-wrinkle treatment Botox paralyzes the facial muscles by preventing activity of acetylcholine, which would normally enable muscle movement (Sinha, Hurakadli, & Yadav, 2015; Ghose, 2014, August 18).
Dopamine	Coordination of muscle movement, attention, pleasure	The same dopamine circuits involved in drug addiction may also be implicated in overeating and food addiction (Baik, 2013).
GABA	Inhibits communication between neurons	Antianxiety drugs, such as Valium and Xanax, work by enhancing the effects of GABA (Drexler et al., 2013).
Glutamate	Promotes communication between neurons	Glutamate is a close chemical relative to the savory food additive monosodium glutamate, or MSG. Some people believe that consuming MSG causes brain damage, but such claims are not supported by solid scientific data (Hamzelou, 2015, January 26).
Serotonin	Mood, appetite aggression, sleep	Physical exercise may boost serotonin activity in the brain, leading to improved mood and decreased symptoms of depression (Heijnen Hommel, Kibele, & Colzato, 2015; Wipfli, Landers, Nagoshi, & Ringenbach, 2011).

Every thought, behavior, and emotion you have ever experienced can be traced to neurotransmitter activity in the nervous system. Read this table to discover some unexpected effects of common neurotransmitters.

GLUTAMATE AND GABA Much of the communication within the nervous system involves two neurotransmitters: *glutamate* and *GABA* (short for gamma-aminobutyric acid). Glutamate is an excitatory neurotransmitter, so its main job is to kick neurons into action (make them fire), whereas GABA is inhibitory (it puts the brakes on firing). Glutamate plays a central role in learning and memory (André, Güntürkün, & Manahan-Vaughan, 2015; Mukherjee & Manahan-Vaughan, 2013); its overactivity is associated with strokes (Campos et al., 2011; Khanna, Briggs, & Rink, 2015); and its underactivity is theorized to be involved in some of the symptoms of schizophrenia (Catts, Lai, Weickert, Weickert, & Catts, 2016; Javitt & Sweet, 2015).

As an inhibitory neurotransmitter, GABA plays a role in controlling sleep and wakefulness (Vanini, Lydic, & Baghdoyan, 2012) as well as behaviors associated with fear and anxiety (Botta et al., 2015; Füzesi & Bains, 2015). The long-term use of alcohol can decrease the production of GABA, as well as the responsiveness of GABA receptors. This means that with continued exposure, a person needs more alcohol to get the same experience, which can lead to a variety of withdrawal symptoms after the person quits or reduces drinking (Sachdeva, Choudhary, & Chandra, 2015).

NOREPINEPHRINE *Norepinephrine* has a variety of effects in the nervous system, but one of its most important functions is to help prepare the body for stressful situations. Think about Brandon being surrounded by gunfire in the battle of Fallujah. Norepinephrine was working to enable Brandon's nervous system to initiate action to promote his survival. In the brain, norepinephrine is involved in regulating arousal and sleep (Mitchell & Weinshenker, 2010; Moore & Depue, 2016). Norepinephrine plays an important role in maintaining attention, but in some situations, high levels could lead to overarousal and hypervigilance, which could dramatically interfere with thinking and attention (Moore & Depue, 2016).

SEROTONIN *Serotonin* plays a key role in controlling appetite, aggression, and mood, and also regulates sleep and breathing. Abnormally low serotonin activity is thought to drive depression (Moore & Depue, 2016). Antidepressants called serotonin reuptake inhibitors (SSRIs), including Prozac and Zoloft, boost the effects of this "feel good" neurotransmitter (Chapter 14). Normally, neurotransmitters that do not connect with receptor sites can be reabsorbed by the sending terminal bud in the reuptake process. SSRIs work to prevent this reabsorption. The longer the serotonin is available in the synapse, the more time it has to attach to a receptor and exert its effects.

DOPAMINE The neurotransmitter *dopamine* plays a role in the abuse of some substances, in particular, stimulants like cocaine and amphetamines (Nutt, Lingford-Hughes, Erritzoe, & Stokes, 2015). Repeated use of some drugs overstimulates and impairs functioning of the neurons in the brain's reward circuit, theoretically making it more difficult to enjoy non-drug-related activities. Dopamine also plays a key role in attention, learning through reinforcement, and regulating body movements. Deterioration of neurons that produce dopamine is linked to Parkinson's disease, an incurable disorder that causes trembling of the hands, arms, legs, and face, and difficulty with movement, coordination, and balance. People have various responses to medications that increase dopamine activity, which complicates the treatment of Parkinson's disease. But researchers are working hard to understand these individual differences occurring at the level of the neuron (Herz et al., 2015; Michely et al., 2015).

ENDORPHINS *Endorphins* are a group of naturally produced opioids (drugs that minimize perception of pain; Chapter 4) that regulate the secretion of other neurotransmitters. The term endorphin is derived from the words "endogenous," meaning it is created within, and "morphine." Released in response to pain, endorphins block pain

Synonyms
norepinephrine noradrenaline

receptor sites. Brisk exercise increases their production, reducing the experience of pain and elevating mood.

Agonists and Antagonists

Drugs and other substances influence behavior by interfering at the level of the synapse (Chapters 4 and 14). Certain substances act like neurotransmitters, while others block neurotransmitter action. *Agonists* increase the normal activity of a neurotransmitter (whether its signal is excitatory or inhibitory) and *antagonists* diminish the effects of a neurotransmitter or block its release (Infographic 2.3). For example, nicotine and muscarine (found in poisonous mushrooms) increase the secretion of acetylcholine, causing sweating, pupil constriction, nausea, and respiratory distress. Because these substances amplify the normal activity of acetylcholine, they are agonists. On the other hand, the popular anti-wrinkle treatment Botox is an antagonist because it blocks the release of acetylcholine, paralyzing the facial muscles so they can no longer wrinkle the overlying skin (Michaels, Csank, Ryb, Eko, & Rubin, 2012).

THINK IT THROUGH
Where's My Morning Antagonist?

CAFFEINE MANIPULATES YOUR NERVOUS SYSTEM....

Did you jump-start your day with a cup of coffee, an energy drink, or a cup of tea? Caffeine perks you up at the crack of dawn or jolts you from a midafternoon daze by manipulating your nervous system. One way caffeine works is by blocking the receptors for a neurotransmitter called *adenosine;* it is an adenosine antagonist. When adenosine latches onto receptors, it slows down their activity (making them less likely to fire), and this tends to make you feel drowsy. Caffeine resembles adenosine enough that it can dock onto the same receptors ("posing" as adenosine). With caffeine occupying its receptors, adenosine can no longer exert its calming effect (Julien, Advokat, & Comaty, 2011; Landolt, 2015). The result: More neurons fire and you feel full of energy. The effects of caffeine do not stop at the brain. As anyone who has enjoyed a double latte or a Red Bull can testify, caffeine kicks the body into high gear, and researchers have found that it even enhances stamina in endurance exercise (Hodgson, Randell, & Jeukendrup, 2013). For those of us who have to stay awake overnight and then not get enough sleep during the day, a few cups of strong coffee seem to do the trick. Even after several days of reduced sleep, reaction time, attentiveness, and reasoning skills can be maintained with the right dose of caffeine (Kamimori et al., 2015).

What are the health consequences of regular caffeine consumption? When used in moderation, caffeine may boost your ability to form long-term memories (Borota et al., 2014). Drinking coffee, in particular, has been associated with a lower risk of type 2 diabetes, Parkinson's disease, and stroke among women, but these effects may be attributed to other compounds found in coffee—not necessarily the caffeine (Ding, Bhupathiraju, Chen, van Dam, & Hu, 2014; Lee et al., 2013; Lopez-Garcia et al., 2009). High caffeine consumption may have a protective effect against multiple sclerosis (MS)—people who drink a lot of coffee are less likely to be diagnosed with MS (Hedström et al., 2016; Wijnands & Kingwell, 2016). Caffeinated sports drinks may enhance performance during short bursts of exercise, but these products contain ingredients that have not been well studied, and they are generally not good for rehydrating (Mora-Rodriguez & Pallarés, 2014).

In the short term, caffeine consumption can "prolong the time to fall asleep, enhance nighttime wakefulness, and reduce depth of sleep" (Landolt, 2015, p. 1289). Also note that continued use of caffeine can lead to irritability, exhaustion,

iStockphoto/thinkstock/Getty Images.

and headaches if you reduce your consumption (Chawla, 2013; Chapter 4). For some people (pregnant women, children, and those with certain health conditions), caffeine use should be limited or avoided entirely (Medline Plus, 2013).

Caffeine is not only in our drinks, but may also be in cold medicine, lotions, shampoos, and breath mints (James, 2014). With caffeine in so many products, sometimes it's hard to keep track of how much we are consuming. Additionally, researchers have found that adults with jobs tend to consume more caffeine than those without jobs (Drewnowski & Rehm, 2016). Why do you think working people consume more caffeine than non-working people? Given the potential benefits and consequences of caffeine, should you change your caffeine habits?

In Class: Collaborate and Report

Discuss the following scenario as a group: You need to stay up late preparing for an exam, so you head to the local coffee shop. **A)** How does the caffeine in your drink affect the adenosine receptors in your neurons? **B)** How does this translate to you staying awake?
C) What are the potential problems with using this method to burn the midnight oil?
D) Can you think of an analogy (not associated with drugs) that helps you remember the difference between agonists and antagonists?

Now sit back, relax, and sip on a beverage, caffeinated or not. It's time to examine the nervous system running through your arms, legs, fingers, toes—and everywhere else.

◯✓◯◯ show what you know

1. Many axons are surrounded by a _____, which is a fatty substance that insulates the axon.

2. When Brandon was injured, _____ played an important role in his recovery by defending against infection and inflammation of the brain, as well as holding neurons together and maintaining the structure of the nervous system.
   a. glial cells
   b. dendrites
   c. action potentials
   d. sodium ions

3. _____ are released into the _____ when an action potential reaches the terminal buds.
   a. Sodium ions; synaptic gap
   b. Neurotransmitters; synaptic gap
   c. Potassium ions; cell membrane
   d. Neurotransmitters; sodium gates

4. Describe how three neurotransmitters impact your daily behavior.

✓ CHECK YOUR ANSWERS IN APPENDIX C.

The Supporting Systems

Like any complex system, the brain needs a supporting infrastructure to carry out its directives and relay essential information from the outside world. Running up and down your spine and branching throughout your body are neurons that provide connections between your brain and the rest of you. The **central nervous system (CNS)** is made up of the brain and spinal cord. The **peripheral nervous system (PNS)** includes all the neurons that are not in the central nervous system and is divided into two branches: the *somatic nervous system* and the *autonomic nervous system*. The peripheral nervous system provides the communication pathway between the central nervous system and the rest of the body. **FIGURE 2.2** (on the next page) gives an overview of the entire nervous system.

The Spinal Cord and Simple Reflexes

Brandon suffered a devastating brain injury that temporarily immobilized half of his body. The paralysis could have affected his entire body if the bullet had pierced his **spinal cord.** This bundle of neurons allows communication between the brain and the peripheral nervous system, which connects with the body's muscles, glands, and organs. The spinal cord has two major responsibilities: (1) receiving information from the body and sending it to the brain; and (2) taking information from the brain

central nervous system (CNS) A major component of the human nervous system that includes the brain and spinal cord.

peripheral nervous system (PNS) The part of the nervous system that connects the central nervous system to the rest of the body.

spinal cord The bundle of neurons that allows communication between the brain and the peripheral nervous system.

FIGURE 2.2

Overview of the Nervous System

The nervous system is made up of the central nervous system (CNS), which includes the brain and spinal cord, and the peripheral nervous system (PNS), which connects the central nervous system to the rest of the body. Photo: moodboard/Alamy.

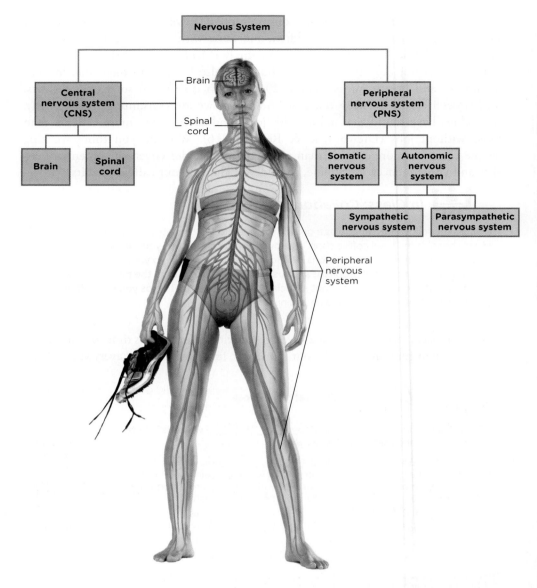

Synonyms

sensory neurons afferent neurons

motor neurons efferent neurons

interneurons association neurons, relay neurons

sensory neurons Neurons that receive information from the sensory systems and convey it to the brain for further processing.

motor neurons Neurons that transmit information from the central nervous system to the muscles and glands.

interneurons Neurons that reside exclusively in the brain and spinal cord; act as a bridge connecting sensory and motor neurons.

reflex arc An automatic response to a sensory stimulus, such as the "knee-jerk" reaction; a simple pathway of communication from sensory neurons through interneurons in the spinal cord back out through motor neurons.

and delivering it throughout the body. If this pathway is blocked, commands from the brain cannot reach the muscles responsible for making you walk, talk, and pour yourself a glass of orange juice. Likewise, the skin and other parts of the body have no pathway for communicating sensory information to the brain, like "Ooh, that burner is hot," or "Oh, this massage feels good."

LO 6 Explain how the central and peripheral nervous systems connect.

TYPES OF NEURONS How do the brain and spinal cord, which make up the *central nervous system,* communicate with the rest of the body through the *peripheral nervous system?* In essence, there are three types of neurons participating in this back-and-forth chatter. **Sensory neurons** receive information about the environment from the sensory systems and convey this information to the brain for processing. **Motor neurons** carry information from the central nervous system to various parts of the body, causing muscles to contract and glands to release chemicals. **Interneurons,** which reside exclusively in the brain and spinal cord, act as bridges connecting sensory and motor neurons. By assembling and processing sensory input from multiple neurons, interneurons facilitate the nervous system's most complex operations, from solving equations to creating life-long memories. They are also involved in a relatively simple operation, the reflex.

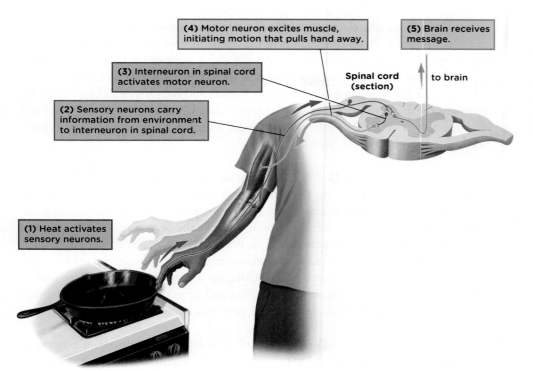

(4) Motor neuron excites muscle, initiating motion that pulls hand away.

(5) Brain receives message.

(3) Interneuron in spinal cord activates motor neuron.

Spinal cord (section)

to brain

(2) Sensory neurons carry information from environment to interneuron in spinal cord.

(1) Heat activates sensory neurons.

FIGURE 2.3
The Spinal Cord and Reflex Arc
Without any input from the brain, neurons in the spinal cord are capable of carrying out a simple reflex. While this reflex is occurring, sensory neurons also send messages to the brain, letting it know what has happened.

THE REFLEX ARC Have you ever touched a burning hot pan? You probably withdrew your hand before you even had a chance to think about it. This ultrafast response to a painful stimulus is known as a reflex (**FIGURE 2.3**). Touching the hot pan activates a pathway of communication that goes from your sensory neurons through interneurons in your spinal cord and right back out through motor neurons, without initially involving the brain.

This type of pain reflex includes a number of steps: (1) Your hand touches the hot pan, activating sensory receptors, which cause the sensory neurons to carry a signal from your hand to the spinal cord. (2) In the spinal cord, the signal from the sensory neurons is received by interneurons. (3) The interneurons quickly activate motor neurons and instruct them to respond. (4) The motor neurons then command your muscles to contract, causing your hand to withdraw quickly. A sensory neuron has a rendezvous with an interneuron in the spinal cord, which then commands a motor neuron to react—no brain required. We refer to this process, in which a stimulus causes an involuntary response, as a **reflex arc.**

Eventually, your brain does process the event; otherwise, you would have no clue it happened. You become consciously aware of your reaction *after* it has occurred (*My hand just pulled back; that pan was hot!*). Although many sensory and motor neurons are involved in this reaction, it happens very quickly, hopefully in time to reduce injury in cases when the reflex arc involves pain. Think about touching a flame or something sharp. You want to be able to respond, without waiting for information to get to the brain or for the brain to instruct motor neurons to move your muscles.

try this ↓

Test your knowledge of the reflex arc using Brandon as an example. As you recall, Brandon's brain injury led to paralysis on the right side of his body. What do you think would happen if a doctor tapped on his right knee—would he experience a reflex?

✓ CHECK YOUR ANSWERS IN APPENDIX C.

What Lies Beyond: The Peripheral Nervous System

LO 7   Describe the organization and function of the peripheral nervous system.

The peripheral nervous system (PNS) includes all the neurons that are not in the central nervous system. These neurons are bundled together in collections called

nerves, which act like electrical cables carrying signals from place to place. Nerves of the peripheral nervous system inform the central nervous system about the body's environment—both the exterior (for example, sights, sounds, and tastes) and the interior (for example, heart rate, blood pressure, and temperature). The central nervous system, in turn, makes sense of all this information and then responds by dispatching orders to the muscles, glands, and other tissues through the nerves of the peripheral nervous system. The PNS has two functional branches: the *somatic nervous system* and the *autonomic nervous system.*

THE SOMATIC NERVOUS SYSTEM   The **somatic nervous system** includes sensory nerves and motor nerves. (*Somatic* means "related to the body.") The sensory nerves gather information from sensory receptors and send it to the central nervous system. The motor nerves receive information from the central nervous system and relay it to the muscles, instructing them to initiate *voluntary* muscle activity (which results in movement). The somatic nervous system controls the skeletal muscles that give rise to voluntary movements, like picking up a pencil or climbing into bed. It also receives sensory information from the skin and other tissues, providing the brain with constant feedback about temperature, pressure, pain, and other stimuli.

THE AUTONOMIC NERVOUS SYSTEM   Meanwhile, the **autonomic nervous system** (au-te-NOM-ic) is working behind the scenes, regulating *involuntary* activity, such as the pumping of the heart, the expansion and contraction of blood vessels, and digestion. Most of the activities supervised by the somatic nervous system are voluntary (within your conscious control and awareness), whereas processes directed by the autonomic nervous system tend to be involuntary (automatic) and outside of your awareness. Just remember: Autonomic controls the automatic.

The autonomic nervous system has two divisions involved in our physiological responses to stressful or crisis situations (**FIGURE 2.4**). The **sympathetic nervous system** initiates what is often referred to as the "fight-or-flight" response, the way the body prepares to deal with a crisis. When faced with a stressful situation, the sympathetic nervous system preps the body for action by increasing heart rate and respiration, and by slowing digestion and other maintenance functions. Earlier, we mentioned that caffeine makes you feel physically energized. This is because it activates the fight-or-flight response (Corti et al., 2002).

The fight-or-flight response would certainly come in handy if fleeing predators was part of your day-to-day life (as it may have been for our primitive ancestors), but you probably are not chased by wild animals very often. You may, however, notice your heart racing and your breathing rate increase during other types of anxiety-producing situations—going on a first date, taking a test, or speaking in front of an audience. For these effects, you have your sympathetic nervous system to thank (Chapter 12).

The **parasympathetic nervous system,** on the other hand, oversees the "rest-and-digest" process, which basically works to bring the body back to a noncrisis mode. When a crisis has ended, the parasympathetic system reverses the activity initiated by the sympathetic system (for example, by lowering heart rate and respiration, and increasing digestion). The two systems work together, balancing the activities of these primarily involuntary processes. Sometimes they even have a common goal. For example, parasympathetic stimulation increases blood flow to the penis to create an erection, but it is the sympathetic system that causes ejaculation (Reynard, Brewster, & Biers, 2013). The parasympathetic and sympathetic systems allow us to fight if we need to, flee when necessary, and calm down when danger has passed.

nerves Bundles of neurons that carry information to and from the central nervous system; provide communication between the central nervous system and the muscles, glands, and sensory receptors.

somatic nervous system The branch of the peripheral nervous system that includes sensory nerves and motor nerves; gathers information from sensory receptors and controls the skeletal muscles responsible for voluntary movement.

autonomic nervous system The branch of the peripheral nervous system that controls involuntary processes within the body, such as contractions in the digestive tract and activity of glands.

sympathetic nervous system The division of the autonomic nervous system that mobilizes the "fight-or-flight" response to stressful or crisis situations.

parasympathetic nervous system The division of the autonomic nervous system that orchestrates the "rest-and-digest" response to bring the body back to a noncrisis mode.

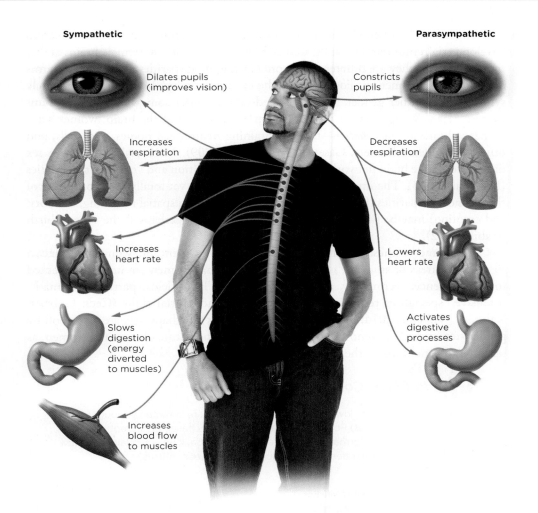

Sympathetic

Dilates pupils (improves vision)

Increases respiration

Increases heart rate

Slows digestion (energy diverted to muscles)

Increases blood flow to muscles

Parasympathetic

Constricts pupils

Decreases respiration

Lowers heart rate

Activates digestive processes

FIGURE 2.4

The Sympathetic and Parasympathetic Nervous Systems

The autonomic nervous system has two divisions, the sympathetic and parasympathetic nervous systems. In a stressful situation, the sympathetic nervous system initiates the "fight-or-flight" response. The parasympathetic nervous system calms the body when the stressful situation has subsided. Photo: PhotoObjects.net/Thinkstock/Getty Images.

HER BRAIN, HIS BRAIN Fighting and running like mad are not the only ways we respond to stress. Many women have an inclination to "tend and befriend" in response to a threatening situation—that is, they direct energy toward nurturing offspring and forging social bonds (Taylor et al., 2000). Men, too, exhibit this response. In one small study, men placed in a stressful situation were more likely to show increased trust of others; and those others tended to reciprocate the trust (von Dawans, Fischbacher, Kirschbaum, Fehr, & Heinrichs, 2012). While serving in Iraq, Brandon likely experienced this increase of trust with his fellow soldiers.

Women are not "inherently superior" at providing support under threatening circumstances, but they are more adept at comforting others when they are stressed themselves. Giving sensitive support tends to be difficult for many men when they feel stressed, and when those needing support express emotion. If distress is communicated in a matter-of-fact way, however, men respond effectively (Bodenmann et al., 2015).

Women are generally more likely to "tend and befriend" in coping with stress (Taylor & Master, 2011), but are there other gender disparities related to the nervous system? Some people think males

Tend and Befriend

Women at the Kopila Valley Women's Center in Surkhet, Nepal, support each other in their educational and career goals. Many of the women have endured extreme poverty, abuse, and other hardships, but working together gives them strength (BlinkNow, n.d.). During times of stress, women are inclined to "tend and befriend," or direct their energy toward nurturing offspring and developing social relationships. Courtesy of BlinkNow Foundation.

CONNECTIONS

In **Chapter 1,** we presented the nature–nurture issue and its importance in the field of psychology. Here, we can see this theme in relation to the gender imbalance in the tend-and-befriend response to stress. Researchers continue to evaluate the relative influence of nature and nurture in the development of gender differences in behavior patterns.

and females are "hardwired" differently; others believe they are socially conditioned to develop certain interests and skills. Research shows that male and female brains are far more alike than they are different, but some intriguing disparities exist, both in terms of anatomy and function. For example, the cerebral hemispheres are not completely symmetric for either gender, and males and females differ somewhat in these asymmetries (Tian, Wang, Yan, & He, 2011). In various areas of the brain, women have higher volumes of *gray matter*—tissue containing neuron cell bodies, glial cells, and other components (Luders, Gaser, Narr, & Toga, 2009). MRI analyses point to sex differences in the brain networks involved in social cognition and visual-spatial abilities (Feis et al., 2013). The implications for behavior are not yet totally clear, but some of these gender disparities (for example, in regions involved in spatial reasoning, memory, and emotion) may be present very early in development, perhaps at the time of birth (Cahill, 2012).

Could some of these differences help explain why men and women are drawn to different areas of study? It is a well-known fact that women are underrepresented in some science, technology, and mathematics (STEM) fields, particularly "math-intensive" specialties requiring high-level math and spatial skills (Ceci, Ginther, Kahn, & Williams, 2014; Halpern, 2014; FIGURE 2.5). Perhaps they are turned off by gender stereotypes, or commonly held beliefs about the nature of men and women, as opposed to something in their biology?

In Class: Collaborate and Report

In your group discuss the following: **A)** What occupations are commonly thought to be more suitable for women? **B)** For men? **C)** Are these beliefs based on stereotypes or scientific evidence? Use information from the textbook to back up your claims. **D)** How might such beliefs about gender impact education and career choices?

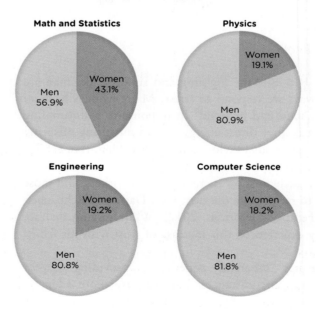

FIGURE 2.5
Bachelor's Degrees Awarded in the United States
Women earn the majority (57.3%) of all bachelor's degrees awarded in the United States. But when it comes to degrees awarded in science, math, and engineering, the numbers look very different. Why do so many fewer women receive degrees in STEM fields? Information from the National Science Foundation, 2015.

The Endocrine System and Its Slowpoke Messengers

Imagine that you are 19-year-old Brandon Burns fighting in the battle of Fallujah, one of the bloodiest battles of the Iraq War. The sound of gunfire rings through the air. Bullets zip past your helmet. People are dying around you. Your life could end at any moment. Unless you have been in a similar situation, it would be difficult to fathom how you would feel. But one thing seems certain: You would be extremely stressed.

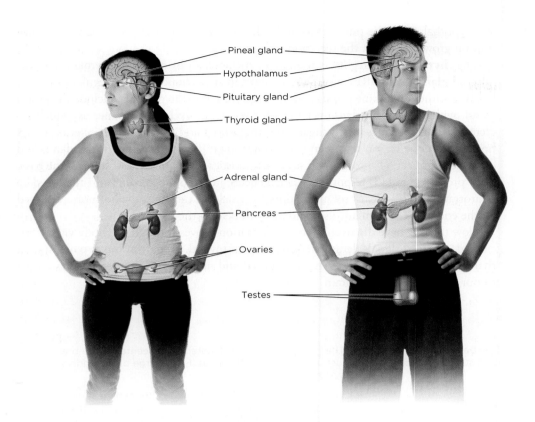

Pineal gland
Hypothalamus
Pituitary gland
Thyroid gland
Adrenal gland
Pancreas
Ovaries
Testes

FIGURE 2.6
The Endocrine System
This system of glands communicates within the body by secreting hormones directly into the bloodstream. Photos: (left, face) Hemera/Thinkstock/Getty Images; (left, body) © Yuri Arcurs/Alamy; (right) Asiaselects/Getty Images.

When faced with imminent danger, the sympathetic nervous system responds almost instantaneously. Activity in the brain triggers the release of neurotransmitters that cause increases in heart rate, breathing rate, and metabolism—changes that will come in handy if you need to flee or defend yourself. But the nervous system does not act alone. The *endocrine system* is also hard at work, releasing stress hormones, such as *cortisol,* which prompt similar physiological changes.

LO 8 Summarize how the endocrine system influences behavior and physiological processes.

The **endocrine system** (EN-doe-krin) is a communication system that uses glands, rather than neurons, to send messages (**FIGURE 2.6**). These messages are conveyed by **hormones,** chemicals released into the bloodstream. There are many types of hormones; some promote aggression and mood swings; others influence growth, alertness, cognition, and appetite. Like neurotransmitters, hormones are chemical messengers that affect many processes and behaviors. In fact, some chemicals, such as norepinephrine, can act as both neurotransmitters and hormones depending on where they are released. Neurotransmitters are unloaded into the synapse, whereas hormones are secreted into the bloodstream by endocrine glands stationed around the body. These glands collectively belong to the endocrine system.

When neurotransmitters are released into a synaptic gap, their effects can be almost instantaneous. Hormones usually make long voyages to far-away targets by way of the bloodstream, creating a relatively delayed but usually longer-lasting impact. A neural impulse can travel over 250 mph, much faster than messages sent via hormones, which take minutes (if not longer) to arrive where they are going. However, the messages sent via hormones are more widely spread because they are disseminated through the bloodstream.

If the endocrine system had a chief executive officer, it would be the **pituitary gland,** a gland about the size of a pencil eraser located in the center of the brain, just under the *hypothalamus* (a structure of the brain we will explore later). Controlled by

endocrine system The communication system that uses glands to convey messages by releasing hormones into the bloodstream.

hormones Chemical messengers released into the bloodstream that influence mood, cognition, appetite, and many other processes and behaviors.

pituitary gland The pea-sized gland located in the center of the brain just under the hypothalamus; known as the master gland.

the hypothalamus, the pituitary gland influences all the other glands, as well as promoting growth through the secretion of hormones.

The **thyroid gland** regulates the rate of metabolism by secreting thyroxin, and the **adrenal glands** (uh-DREEN-ul) are involved in stress responses and regulation of salt balance. Other endocrine glands and organs directed by the pituitary include the pineal gland, which secretes melatonin (controls sleep–wake cycles); the pancreas, which secretes insulin (regulates blood sugar); and the ovaries and testes, whose secretion of sex hormones is one reason that men and women are different. Together, these glands and organs can impact: (1) growth and sex characteristics, (2) regulation of some of the basic body processes, and (3) responses to emergencies. Just as our behaviors are influenced by neurotransmitters we can't see and action potentials we can't feel, the hormones secreted by the endocrine system are also hard at work behind the scenes.

Now that we have discovered how information moves through the body via electrical and chemical signals, let's turn our attention toward the part of the nervous system that integrates this activity, creating a unified and meaningful experience. Let's return to our exploration of the brain.

○◉○○ **show what you know**

1. _____ carry information from the central nervous system to activate various parts of the body, such as muscles and glands.
   a. Interneurons
   b. Dendrites
   c. Sensory neurons
   d. Motor neurons

2. When a stimulus causes an involuntary response, we refer to it as a reflex; the simple communication pathway goes from sensory neurons through interneurons in the _____ and back out through motor neurons.
   a. brain
   b. spinal cord
   c. axon hillock
   d. nodes of Ranvier

3. The _____ gland, located in the center of the brain, just under the hypothalamus, is in charge of the endocrine system.

4. When confronted with a potentially threatening situation, the sympathetic nervous system sometimes prepares for "fight or flight" and/or "tend and befriend." How would you explain these two very different responses using the evolutionary perspective?

✓ CHECK YOUR ANSWERS IN APPENDIX C.

The Hemispheres

Jack Hollingsworth/
Getty Images.

THE GIRL WITH HALF A BRAIN   As Brandon Burns began his long journey to recovery, a 17-year-old girl in Bristol, Pennsylvania, was enjoying a particularly successful senior year of high school. Christina Santhouse was an honor roll student for the fourth year in a row, and she had been named captain of the varsity bowling team. But these accomplishments did not come so easily. It took Christina twice as much time as classmates to do homework assignments because her brain needed extra time to process information. She had to invent a new bowling technique because the left side of her body was partially paralyzed, and she was constantly aware of being "different" from the other kids at school. Christina wasn't simply *different* from her classmates, however. She was *extraordinary* because she managed to do everything they did (and more) with nearly half of her brain missing.

Christina's remarkable story began when she was 7 years old. She was a vibrant, healthy child who loved soccer and playing outside with her friends. Barring an occasional ear infection, she basically never got sick—that is, until the day she suffered her first seizure. It was the summer of 1995 and Christina's family was vacationing on the Jersey Shore. While playing in a swimming pool with her cousins, Christina hopped onto the deck to chase a ball and noticed that something wasn't quite right. She looked down and saw her left ankle twitching uncontrollably. Her life was about to change dramatically.

thyroid gland Endocrine gland that regulates metabolic rate by secreting thyroxin.

adrenal glands Endocrine glands involved in the stress response and the regulation of salt balance.

cerebrum The largest part of the brain, includes virtually all parts of the brain except brainstem structures; has two distinct hemispheres.

corpus callosum The thick band of nerve fibers connecting the right and left cerebral hemispheres; principal structure for information shared between the two hemispheres.

As the days and weeks wore on, the tremors in Christina's ankle moved up her left side and eventually spread throughout her body. In time, she was having seizures every 3 to 5 minutes. Doctors suspected she had Rasmussen's encephalitis, a rare disease that causes severe swelling in one side of the brain, impairing movement and thinking and causing seizures that come as often as every few minutes (National Institute of Neurological Disorders and Stroke, 2011b).

Christina and her mother decided to seek treatment at The Johns Hopkins Hospital in Baltimore, the premiere center for treating children with seizure disorders. They met with Dr. John Freeman, a pediatric neurologist and an expert in *hemispherectomy,* a surgery to remove nearly half of the brain. A rare and last-resort operation, the hemispherectomy is only performed on patients suffering from severe seizures that can't be controlled in other ways. After examining Christina, Dr. Freeman made the same diagnosis—Rasmussen's encephalitis—and indicated that the seizures would get worse, and they would get worse fast. He recommended a hemispherectomy and told Christina (and her mother) to let him know when she had reached her limit with the seizures. Then they would go ahead with the operation.

Why did Dr. Freeman recommend this drastic surgery to remove nearly half of Christina's brain? And what side of the brain did he suggest removing? Before addressing these important questions, we need to develop a general sense of the brain's geography. ●

Right Brain, Left Brain: The Two Hemispheres

LO 9 Describe the two brain hemispheres and how they communicate.

If you look at a photo or an illustration of the brain, you will see a walnut-shaped wrinkled structure—this is the **cerebrum** (Latin for "brain"), the largest and most conspicuous part of the brain. The cerebrum includes virtually all parts of the brain except the brainstem structures, which you will learn about later. Like a walnut, the cerebrum has two distinct halves, or *hemispheres.* Looking at the brain from above, you can see a deep groove running from the front of the head to the back, dividing it into the right cerebral hemisphere and the left cerebral hemisphere. Although the hemispheres look like mirror images of one another, with similar structures on the left and right, they do not have identical jobs nor are they perfectly symmetrical. The two hemispheres are linked by a bundle of nerve fibers known as the **corpus callosum** (KOR-pus kuh-LOW-sum). Through the corpus callosum, the left and right sides of the brain communicate and work together to process information. Generally speaking, the right hemisphere controls the left side of the body, and the left hemisphere controls the right. This explains why Brandon, who was shot on the *left* side of his head, suffered paralysis and loss of sensation on the *right* half of his body. Christina's situation is roughly the opposite. Rasmussen's encephalitis struck the *right* side of her brain, which explains why her *left* ankle started twitching at the pool and why all of her subsequent seizures affected the left side of her body. This is why Dr. Freeman recommended the removal of her right hemisphere.

 CHRISTINA MAKES THE DECISION Within 2 months, Christina's seizures were occurring every 3 minutes, hundreds of times a day. She was unable to play soccer or go outside during school recess, and she sat on a beanbag chair in class so she wouldn't hurt herself when overcome with a seizure. "I couldn't do anything anymore," Christina says. "I wasn't enjoying my life."

Staying Strong
Christina Santhouse relaxes with her mother at Johns Hopkins, where she had a dramatic brain surgery known as a hemispherectomy. Prior to the operation, Christina experienced hundreds of seizures a day. William Johnson.

Christina, in Her Own Words
http://qrs.ly/c65a583

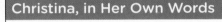

Photo: Macmillan Learning.

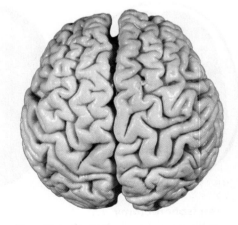

Two Hemispheres
The cerebrum looks like a walnut with its two wrinkled halves. Regions of the left and right hemispheres specialize in different activities, but the two sides of the brain are constantly communicating and collaborating. Science Source.

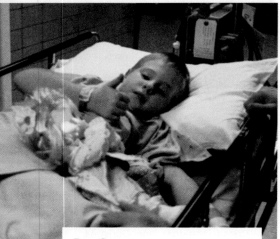

Pre-Op
Christina is wheeled into the operating room for her 14-hour hemispherectomy. She had a seizure in the elevator on the way to the surgery. William Johnson.

You Asked, Christina Answers

http://qrs.ly/jz5a587

How does your condition affect your confidence and social life?

scan this →

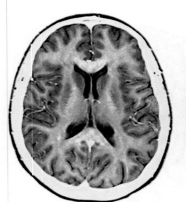

Hemispherectomy
On the left is an MRI scan of a brain with both hemispheres intact. The scan on the right shows the brain of a person who has undergone a hemispherectomy. The green area, once occupied by the removed hemisphere, is now filled with cerebrospinal fluid. Medical Body Scans/Science Source.

In February 1996 the doctors at Johns Hopkins removed the right hemisphere of Christina's brain. The operation lasted some 14 hours. When Christina emerged from the marathon surgery, her head was pounding with pain. "I remember screaming and asking for medicine," she recalls. The migraines persisted for months but eventually tapered off, and ultimately the surgery served its purpose: Christina no longer experienced debilitating seizures. ●

The Split-Brain Operation

LO 10 Define lateralization and explain what the split-brain experiments reveal about the right and left hemispheres.

Removing nearly half of a brain may sound barbaric, but hemispherectomies have proven to be effective for eliminating seizures, with success rates from multiple studies ranging from 54% to 90% (Lew, 2014). In a study of the 111 children who had hemispherectomies at Johns Hopkins between 1975 and 2001, 65% no longer suffered seizures, 21% experienced infrequent, "non-handicapping" seizures, and the remaining 14% still had seizures described as "troublesome" (Kossoff et al., 2003). A similar study from the Cleveland Clinic found that 83% of hemispherectomy patients could walk independently nearly 13 years after surgery. Meanwhile, 70% possessed good spoken language skills, and 42% were able to read satisfactorily (Moosa et al., 2013).

Hemispherectomies are exceptionally rare, used only when seizures occur many times a day, cannot be tempered with drugs, and stem from problems in one hemisphere (Choi, 2007, May 24; Neligan, 2014). Another less extreme, last-resort surgery for drug-resistant seizures is the **split-brain operation,** which essentially disconnects the right and left hemispheres. Normally, the two hemispheres communicate through the corpus callosum. But this same band of nerve fibers can also serve as a passageway for the electrical storms responsible for seizures. With the split-brain operation, the corpus callosum is severed so that these storms can no longer pass freely between the hemispheres (Wolman, 2012, March 15).

STUDYING THE SPLIT BRAIN In addition to helping many patients with severe, drug-resistant epilepsy (Abou-Khalil, 2010), the consequences of split-brain operations have provided researchers with an excellent opportunity to explore the specialization of the hemispheres. Before we start to look at this research, you need to understand how visual information is processed. Each eye receives visual sensations, but that information is sent to the opposite hemisphere, and shared between the hemispheres via the corpus callosum. Specifically, information presented in the right visual field is processed in the left hemisphere, and information presented in the left visual field is processed in the right hemisphere.

Equipped with this knowledge, American neuropsychologist Roger Sperry and his student Michael Gazzaniga conducted ground-breaking research on epilepsy patients who had undergone split-brain operations to alleviate their seizures. Not only did Sperry and Gazzaniga's "split-brain" participants experience fewer seizures, they had surprisingly normal cognitive abilities and showed no obvious changes in "temperament, personality, or general intelligence" as a result of their surgeries (Gazzaniga, 1967, p. 24). But under certain circumstances, the researchers observed, they behaved as though they had two separate brains (Gazzaniga, 1967, 1998, 2005; FIGURE 2.7).

Because the hemispheres are disconnected through the surgery, researchers can study each hemisphere separately to explore its unique capabilities (or specializations). Imagine that researchers flashed an image (let's say an apple) on the right side of a screen, ensuring that it would be processed by the brain's *left* hemisphere. The

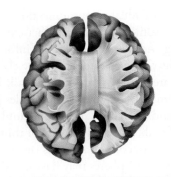

FIGURE 2.7
The Split-Brain Experiment

The image to the left shows a top view of the corpus callosum, the bundle of neurons linking the right and left hemispheres. When the corpus callosum is severed, we can see clear functional differences between the two sides of the brain. Studies of people who have undergone this procedure are known as "split-brain" experiments. An example of this type of experiment is shown below.

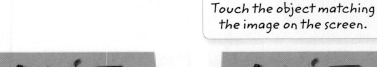

Touch the object matching the image on the screen.

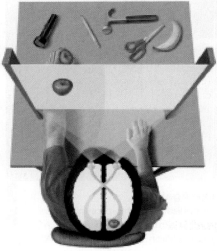

I see an apple.

I don't see anything.

Information presented to right visual field is processed in left hemisphere where language processing occurs. Participant can speak the answer.

Information presented to left visual field is processed in right hemisphere. Participant can't use language to say what he was shown.

The participant can touch the correct object even if he can't say what has been projected in his left visual field. The participant uses his left hand, which is controlled by the right hemisphere, where the visual information has been processed.

split-brain participant could articulate what she had seen (*I saw an apple*). If, however, the apple appeared on the left side of the screen (processed by the *right* hemisphere), she would claim she saw nothing. But when asked to identify the image in a non-verbal way (pointing or touching with her left hand), she could do this without a problem (Gazzaniga, 1967, 1998).

LATERALIZATION The split-brain experiments offered an elegant demonstration of **lateralization,** the tendency for the left and right hemispheres to excel in certain activities. When images are flashed in the right visual field, the information is sent to the left side of the brain, which excels in language processing. This explains why the split-brain participants were able to articulate the image they had seen on the right side of the screen. Images appearing in the left visual field are sent to the right side of the brain, which excels at visual-spatial tasks but is generally not responsible for processing language. Thus, the participants were tongue-tied when asked to report what they had seen on the left side of the screen. They could, however, reach out and point to it using their left hand, which is controlled by the right hemisphere (Gazzaniga, 1998; Gazzaniga, Bogen, & Sperry, 1965).

The split-brain studies revealed that the left hemisphere plays a crucial role in language processing and the right hemisphere in managing visual-spatial tasks. These are only generalizations, however. While there are clear differences in the way the hemispheres process information (and the speed at which they do it), they can also process

Synonyms

split-brain operation callosotomy

split-brain operation A rare procedure used to disconnect the right and left hemispheres by cutting the corpus callosum.

lateralization The idea that each cerebral hemisphere processes certain types of information and excels in certain activities.

the same types of information. In a split-brain individual, communication between the hemispheres is limited. This is *not* the case for someone with an intact corpus callosum. The hemispheres are constantly integrating and sharing all types of information (Lilienfeld, Lynn, Ruscio, & Beyerstein, 2011). Next time you hear someone claim that some people are more "left-brained" and others are more "right-brained," ask him to identify the research that backs up such a claim. Similarly, beware of catchy sales pitches for products designed to increase your "logical and analytical" left-brain thinking or to help you tap into your "creative" right brain (Staub, 2016). This way of thinking is oversimplified. Keep this in mind while reading the upcoming sections on specialization in the left and right sides of the brain. The two hemispheres may have certain areas of expertise, but they work as a team to create your experience of the world.

The Special Roles of the Left and the Right

Armed with this new knowledge of the split-brain experiments, let's return our focus to Brandon. Brandon's injury occurred on the left side of his brain, devastating his ability to use language. Before the battle of Fallujah, he had breezed through Western novels at breakneck speeds. After his injury, even the simplest sentence baffled him. Words on a page looked like nothing more than black lines and curls. Brandon remembers, "It was like a puzzle that I couldn't figure out."

HANDEDNESS AND LANGUAGE DOMINANCE Brandon's difficulties with language are fairly typical for someone with a brain injury to the left hemisphere, because regions on the left side of the brain tend to predominate in language. This is not true for everyone, however. The left hemisphere handles language processing in around 95% to 99% of people who are right-handed, but only in about 70% of those who are left-handed (Corballis, 2014). Using brain scan technology, one group of researchers determined participants' predominant side for language processing. They found that around 27% of strongly left-handed participants and 4% of strongly right-handed participants had language dominance in the *right* hemisphere (Knecht et al., 2000). What does this suggest? The left hemisphere controls language in most but not all people, though it doesn't always correspond to right- or left-handedness.

LO 11 Identify areas in the brain responsible for language production and comprehension.

Speak Again
Brandon works on his pronunciation in front of a mirror during a speech therapy session at the Memphis VA hospital. You can see the extent of his injury on the left side of his head. Upon awaking from his coma, Brandon could not articulate a single word. Today, he can hold his own in complex conversations. Photo by A.J. Wolfe/The Commercial Appeal/Zuma Press.

FIGURE 2.8
Language Areas of the Brain
For most people, the left hemisphere controls language. Broca's area plays a critical role in language production, and Wernicke's area in language comprehension.

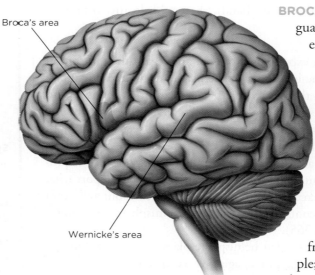

Broca's area

Wernicke's area

Broca's area A region of the cortex that is critical for speech production.

Wernicke's area A region of the cortex that plays a pivotal role in language comprehension.

BROCA'S AREA Evidence for the "language on the left" notion appeared as early as 1861, when a French surgeon by the name of Pierre Paul Broca (1824–1880) encountered two patients who had, for all practical purposes, lost the ability to talk. One of the patients could only say the word "tan," and the other had an oral vocabulary of five words. When Broca later performed autopsies on the men, he found that both had sustained damage to the same area on the side of the left frontal lobe (right around the temple; **FIGURE 2.8**). Over the years, Broca identified several other speech-impaired patients with damage to the same area, a region now called **Broca's area** (BRO-kuz) (Greenblatt, Dagi, & Epstein, 1997; Martin & Allen, 2012), which is involved in speech production. However, some researchers propose that other parts of the brain may also be involved in generating speech (Tate, Herbet, Moritz-Gasser, Tate, & Duffau, 2014).

WERNICKE'S AREA Around the same time Broca was doing his research, a German doctor named Karl Wernicke (1848–1905) pinpointed a different place in the left hemisphere that seemed to control speech comprehension. Wernicke noticed that patients suffering damage to a small tract of tissue in the left temporal lobe, now called **Wernicke's area** (VAIR-nick-uhz), struggled to make sense of what others were saying. Wernicke's area is the brain's headquarters for language comprehension.

Broca's and Wernicke's work, along with other early findings, highlighted the left hemisphere's critical role in language. Scientists initially suspected that Broca's area was responsible for speech creation and Wernicke's area for comprehension, but it is now clear the use of language is far more complicated (Berwick, Friederici, Chomsky, & Bolhuis, 2013). These areas may perform additional functions, such as processing music and interpreting hand gestures (Schlaug, 2015; Xu, Gannon, Emmorey, Smith, & Braun, 2009), and they cooperate with multiple brain regions to allow us to produce and understand language (Tate et al., 2014). Furthermore, some speech processing appears to occur in the right hemisphere.

THE ROLE OF THE RIGHT We know that the left hemisphere tends to dominate in language processing, but where does the right hemisphere excel? Research suggests that the right hemisphere surpasses the left when it comes to identifying mirror images and spatial relationships, and mentally rotating images (Gazzaniga, 2005). The right side of the brain also appears to specialize in understanding abstract and humorous use of language (Coulson & Van Petten, 2007), and is somewhat better at following conversations that change topic (Dapretto, Lee, & Caplan, 2005). This hemisphere also plays a key role in recognizing faces and processing information about the faces of people who are chewing or exhibiting emotional expressions (De Winter et al., 2015; Kanwisher, McDermott, & Chun, 1997; Rossion, 2014). And while the left hemisphere seems to focus on creating hypotheses and exploring causality, the right hemisphere appears more involved in evaluating hypotheses, and rejecting those that lack supporting evidence (Marinsek, Turner, Gazzaniga, & Miller, 2014).

Enjoying Life
Christina, as a teenager, walking her dog. The left side of her body is partially paralyzed, but her gait is quite natural. She wears a device on her left leg that activates her nerves, causing her muscles to contract at the appropriate time. William Johnson.

 In Class: Collaborate and Report

In your groups, discuss the following: **A)** How is a split-brain operation different from a hemispherectomy? **B)** If you were faced with a hypothetical decision to undergo a hemispherectomy, which half of your brain would you choose to have removed and why? **c)** What associated functions might you lose as a result?

 show what you know

1. The left hemisphere excels in language and the right hemisphere excels in visual-spatial tasks. This specialization of the two hemispheres is known as:
   a. split-brain.
   b. callosotomy.
   c. hemispherectomy.
   d. lateralization.

2. A man involved in a car accident suffered severe brain trauma. As he recovered, it became clear he was having difficulty producing speech, even though he could understand what people were saying. It is very likely he had suffered damage to the left frontal lobe in a part of the brain referred to as:
   a. Wernicke's area.
   b. Broca's area.
   c. the visual field.
   d. the corpus callosum.

3. How do the two brain hemispheres communicate? How does this change after a split-brain operation?

✓ CHECK YOUR ANSWERS IN APPENDIX C.

Brain Games
Christina's dramatic recovery was facilitated by physical, occupational, vision, and speech therapy. "The more therapy," says Christina, "the better chance of recovery." William Johnson.

You Asked, Christina Answers

http://qrs.ly/cl5a58g

What kind of therapy did you have and for how long?

scan this ➜

CONNECTIONS

In **Chapter 1** we described the guidelines psychologists use to ensure the ethical treatment of humans and animals. In order to conduct the experiment described here, the researchers had to get pre-approval from an ethics board. The board determined that the proposed research necessitated the surgery on the newborn opossums and they would be treated humanely.

neuroplasticity The brain's ability to heal, grow new connections, and reorganize in order to adapt to the environment.

neurogenesis The generation of new neurons in the brain.

stem cells Cells responsible for producing new neurons.

cerebral cortex The wrinkled outermost layer of the cerebrum, responsible for higher mental functions, such as decision making, language, and processing visual information.

frontal lobes The area of the cortex that organizes information among the other lobes of the brain and is responsible for cognitive functions, such as thinking, perception, and impulse control.

The Amazing Brain

CHRISTINA WAKES UP When Christina was wheeled out of surgery, her mother approached, grabbed hold of her right hand, and asked her to squeeze. Christina squeezed, demonstrating that she could understand and respond to language. Remember, she still had her left hemisphere.

Losing the right side of her brain did come at a cost, however. We know that Christina suffers partial paralysis on the left side of her body; this makes sense, because the right hemisphere controls movement and sensation on the left. We also know that it took Christina extra time to do her schoolwork. But if you ask Christina whether she has significant difficulty with any of the "right-brain" tasks described earlier, her answer will be no.

In addition to making the honor roll and leading the bowling team, Christina managed to get her driver's license (even though some of her doctors said she never would), and graduate from high school and college. These accomplishments are the result of Christina's steadfast determination, but also a testament to the brain's amazing ability to heal and regenerate. ●

Neuroplasticity

LO 12 Define neuroplasticity and recognize when it is evident in the brain.

The brain undergoes constant alteration in response to experiences, and is capable of some degree of physical adaptation and repair. Its ability to heal, grow new connections, and make do with what is available is a characteristic we refer to as **neuroplasticity.** New connections are constantly forming between neurons, and unused ones are fading away. Vast networks of neurons have the ability to reorganize in order to adapt to the environment and an organism's ever-changing needs, a quality particularly evident in the young. After brain injuries, younger children have better outcomes than do adults; their brains show more plasticity (Johnston, 2009).

In one study, researchers removed the eyes of newborn opossums and found that brain tissues normally destined to become visual processing centers took a developmental turn. Instead, they became areas that specialized in processing other types of sensory stimuli, such as sounds and touch (Karlen, Kahn, & Krubitzer, 2006). The same appears to happen in humans. Brain scans reveal that when visually impaired individuals learn to read Braille early in life, a region of the brain that normally specializes in handling visual information becomes activated, suggesting it is used instead for processing touch sensations (Burton, 2003; Lazzouni & Lepore, 2014; Liu et al., 2007).

Remarkably, this plasticity is evident even with the loss of an entire hemisphere. Researchers report that the younger the patient is when she has a hemispherectomy, the better her chances are for recovery. In fact, even with the loss of an entire left hemisphere (the primary location for language processing), speech is less severely impacted (though some impact is inevitable) in young patients. The younger the person undergoing the procedure, the less disability is evident in speech, although factors such as language delays prior to surgery and ongoing seizures after surgery can impact further language development (Choi, 2008, March; Moosa et al., 2013).

Stem Cells

Scientists once thought that people were born with all the neurons they would ever have. Brain cells might die, but no new ones would crop up to replace them. Thanks to research beginning in the 1990s, that dismal notion has been turned on its head. In the last few decades, studies with animals and humans have shown that some areas of the brain are constantly generating new neurons, a process known as **neurogenesis,** which might be tied to learning and creating new memories (Eriksson et al., 1998; Gould, Beylin, Tanapat, Reeves, & Shors, 1999; Jessberger & Gage, 2014; Reynolds & Weiss, 1992). According to one estimate, a brain structure called the hippocampus produces around 700 new neurons per day (Spalding et al., 2013).

The cells responsible for churning out new neurons are known as **stem cells,** and they are quite a hot topic in biomedical research. Scientists hope to harness these little cell factories to repair tissue that has been damaged or destroyed. Imagine that you could use stem cells to bring back all the neurons that Brandon lost from his injury or replace those that Christina lost to surgery. Cultivating new brain tissue is just one potential application of stem cell science. These cellular cure-alls might also be used to alleviate the symptoms of Parkinson's disease, or replenish neurons of the spine, enabling people with spinal cord injuries to regain movement. Both have already been accomplished in mice (Keirstead et al., 2005; Wernig et al., 2008). Although embryonic stem cells can be used for such purposes, some stem cells can be found in tissues of the adult body, such as the brain and bone marrow. There has been great hope that "adult-born neurons" might be used to repair injured brain tissue, but a growing body of evidence suggests it is beyond their capability (Lois & Kelsch, 2014).

The Cortex: A Peek Beneath the Skull

Imagine you were one of the surgeons performing Christina's hemispherectomy. What exactly would you see when you peeled away the scalp and cut an opening into the skull? Before seeing the brain, you would come upon a layer of three thin membranes, the *meninges,* which envelop and protect the brain and spinal cord. Perhaps you have heard of meningitis, a potentially life-threatening condition in which the meninges become inflamed as a result of an infection. The meninges are bathed in a clear watery substance called cerebrospinal fluid, which offers additional cushioning and helps in the transport of nutrients and waste in and out of the brain and the spinal cord. Once you peeled back the meninges, you would behold the pink cerebrum.

As Christina's surgeon, your main task would be to remove part of the cerebrum's outermost layer, the **cerebral cortex** (suh-REE-brul). The cerebral cortex processes information and is the layer of cells surrounding nearly all the other brain structures. You'll remember our earlier comment that the cerebrum looks like a wrinkled walnut. This is because the cortex is scrunched up and folded onto itself to fit inside a small space (the skull). This outermost section of the brain is also the part that is "newest," or most recently evolved compared to the "older" structures closer to its core. We know this because researchers have compared the brains of humans with those of other primates. The structures we share with our primate relatives are considered more primitive, or less evolved, than the structures that are unique to humans.

LO 13	Identify the lobes of the cortex and explain their functions.

The cortex overlying each hemisphere is separated into different sections, or lobes (**INFOGRAPHIC 2.4** on the following page). The major function of the **frontal lobes** is to organize information from the other lobes. The frontal lobes also direct higher-level cognitive functions, such as thinking, perception, and impulse control.

Baby Beethoven
For millions of Chinese children, learning to play an instrument like the violin or piano begins early. Children with musical training outperform their untrained peers on tests of IQ and language skills (Schellenberg, 2011; Schellenberg & Winner, 2011). Is this because music lessons make children smarter, perhaps by stimulating positive changes in the brain? Or is it because smart children are more likely to take lessons? Researchers are still trying to get to the bottom of this conundrum. Sinopix/REX/Shutterstock.

Cure All?
Because stem cells can differentiate into any type of cell in the body, they have great therapeutic potential. The cells pictured here are derived from a human embryo, but stem cells also reside in various adult tissues such as the brain and bone marrow. Professor Miodrag Stojkovic/Science Source.

Getting into the Brain

Finding Personality in the Brain

In 1848 an accidental blast drove a 3-foot iron bar through the head of railroad worker Phineas Gage. He survived, but his personality was markedly changed. Previously described as having a "well-balanced" mind, post-injury Gage was prone to angry outbursts and profanity (Harlow, 1868, 1869, as cited in Macmillan, 2000).

Phineas Gage holding the iron bar that injured him.

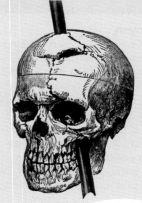

Using measurements from his fractured skull, scientists have been able to estimate where the damage occurred (Ratiu, Talos, Haker, Lieberman, & Everett, 2004; Van Horn et al., 2012). Cases like this have helped psychologists understand the role of different structures in the brain.

Getting TO the Brain

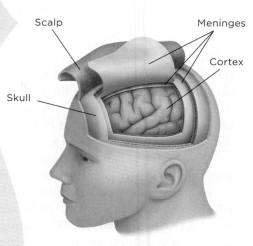

Scalp
Meninges
Cortex
Skull

In order to study the brain, we must get to it first. Peel away the scalp and cut away the bony skull, and you will find still more layers of protection. Three thin membranes—the meninges—provide a barrier to both physical injury and infection. Bypass them, and the outermost layer of the brain, the cortex, is revealed.

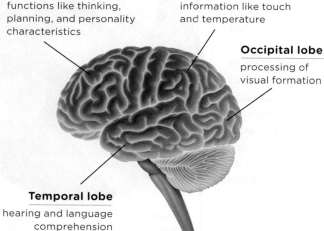

Frontal lobe
higher-level cognitive functions like thinking, planning, and personality characteristics

Parietal lobe
integration of sensory information like touch and temperature

Occipital lobe
processing of visual formation

Temporal lobe
hearing and language comprehension

Motor cortex
commands the body's movements

Somatosensory cortex
receives sensory information from the body

Wernicke's area
language comprehension

Broca's area
language production

Lobes of the Brain
This drawing shows the left hemisphere of the brain. Each hemisphere is divided into lobes, which are known for the major functions found there.

Specialized Areas of the Brain
Unlike the lobes, which are associated with many functions, some areas of the brain have one specialized function.

The **parietal lobes** (puh-RYE-uh-tul) receive and process sensory information like touch, pressure, temperature, and spatial orientation. Visual information goes to the **occipital lobes** (ok-SIP-i-tul) for processing, and hearing and language comprehension are largely handled by the **temporal lobes**. We'll have more to say about the lobes as we discuss each in turn below (**TABLE 2.2**, on page 82).

The Lobes: Up Close and Personal

Prior to her hemispherectomy, Christina was extroverted, easygoing, and full of energy. "I had absolutely no worries," she says, recalling her pre-Rasmussen's days. After her operation, Christina became more introverted and passive. She felt more emotionally unsettled. "You go into surgery one person," she says, "and you come out another."

The transformation of Christina's personality may be a result of many factors, including the stress of dealing with a serious disease, undergoing a major surgery, and readjusting to life with disabilities. But it could also have something to do with the fact that she lost a considerable amount of brain tissue, including her right frontal lobe. Networks of neurons in the frontal lobes are involved in processing emotions, making plans, controlling impulses, and carrying out a vast array of mental tasks that each person does in a unique way (Williams, Suchy, & Kraybill, 2010). The frontal lobes play a key role in the development of personality and many of its characteristics (Forbes et al., 2014; Stuss & Alexander, 2000). A striking illustration of this phenomenon involves an unlucky railroad foreman, Phineas Gage.

PHINEAS GAGE AND THE FRONTAL LOBES The year was 1848, and Phineas Gage was working on the railroad. An accidental explosion sent a 3-foot iron tamping rod clear through his frontal lobe (Infographic 2.4). The rod, about as thick as a broom handle, drove straight into Gage's left cheek, through his brain, and out the top of his skull (Macmillan, 2000). What's peculiar about Gage's accident (besides the fact that he was walking and talking just hours later) is the extreme transformation it caused. Before the accident, Gage was a well-balanced, diligent worker whom his supervisors referred to as their "most efficient and capable foreman" (Harlow, 1848, as cited in Neylan, 1999, p. 280). After the accident, he was unreliable, unpleasant, and downright vulgar. His character was so altered that people acquainted with him before and after the accident claimed he was "no longer Gage" (Harlow, 1848, as cited in Neylan, 1999, p. 280). However, there is evidence that Gage recovered to some degree, illustrating again the remarkable neuroplasticity of the brain (Griggs, 2015a). He spent almost 8 years working as a horse caretaker and stagecoach driver after the accident (Harlow, 1868, 1869, as cited in Macmillan, 2000).

Modern scientists have revisited Gage's case, using measurements from his fractured skull and brain-imaging data to estimate exactly where the damage occurred. Their studies suggest that the metal rod caused destruction in both the left and right frontal lobes (Damasio, Grabowski, Frank, Galaburda, & Damasio, 1994), although later researchers now believe the rod did not pierce the right hemisphere (Ratiu et al., 2004; Van Horn et al., 2012). The only good thing about Gage's horrible accident, it seems, is that it illuminated the importance of the frontal lobes in defining personality characteristics.

DOGS, CARTOONS, AND THE MOTOR CORTEX Toward the rear of the frontal lobes is a strip of the brain known as the **motor cortex,** which works with other areas to plan and execute voluntary movements (Infographic 2.4). Evidence for this region's involvement in muscle movement first came from a study of dogs by Germans Gustav Fritsch (1838–1927) and Edvard Hitzig (1838–1907). Working from a makeshift lab, the two doctors discovered they could make the animals move by electrically stimulating their brains (Gross, 2007). A mild shock to the right side of the cortex might cause

parietal lobes The area of the cortex that receives and processes sensory information such as touch, pressure, temperature, and spatial orientation.

occipital lobes The area of the cortex in the back of the head that processes visual information.

temporal lobes The area of the cortex that processes auditory stimuli and language.

motor cortex A band of tissue toward the rear of the frontal lobes that works with other brain regions to plan and execute voluntary movements.

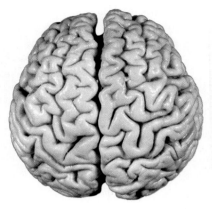

Superbrain

A photo of Einstein's brain shows what researchers have referred to as his "extraordinary prefrontal cortex" (Falk, Lepore, & Noe, 2013, p. 1304). The irregularities in Einstein's parietal lobes may explain some of his spectacular mathematical and visual-spatial abilities (Witelson et al., 1999; Falk et al., 2013). Could it be that Einstein's mathematical activities caused changes to his parietal lobes? National Museum of Health and Medicine, Otis Archives.

CONNECTIONS

In **Chapter 1** we discussed the importance of having a sample size large enough to give us reliable findings, and the potential problems with using case studies for making generalizations about the population. Here, the use of Einstein as a single participant to compare to the control group could be problematic on both counts.

Synonyms

association areas intrinsic processing areas

somatosensory cortex A band of tissue running parallel to the motor cortex that receives and integrates sensory information from all over the body.

association areas Regions of the cortex that integrate information from all over the brain, allowing us to learn, think in abstract terms, and carry out other intellectual tasks.

a twitch in the left forepaw or the left side of the face, whereas stimulating the left would spur movement on the right (Finger, 2001).

North American neurosurgeon Wilder Penfield (1891–1976) conducted research with humans in which he used a method similar to that of Fritsch and Hitzig to create a map showing which points along the motor cortex corresponded to the various parts of the body (Penfield & Boldrey, 1937). Penfield's map is often represented by the "homunculus" (huh-MUN-kyuh-lus; Latin for "little man") cartoon, a distorted image of a human being with huge lips and hands and a tiny torso (**FIGURE 2.9**). The size of each body part in the figure roughly reflects the amount of cortex devoted to it, which explains why parts requiring extremely fine-tuned motor control (the mouth and hands) are gigantic in comparison to other body parts.

ALBERT EINSTEIN AND THE PARIETAL LOBES   Directly behind the frontal lobes on the crown of your head are the parietal lobes (Infographic 2.4). The parietal lobes help orient the body in space, are involved in tactile processing (for example, interpreting sensations related to touch, such as pain and pressure), and may play a role in mathematical reasoning associated with spatial cognition (Desco et al., 2011; Grabner et al., 2007; Wolpert, Goodbody, & Husain, 1998). A study published in 1999 • compared the brain of Albert Einstein to a control group of 35 brain specimens from men who had donated their bodies for use in research. Prior to their deaths, these men had normal cognitive functioning, average intelligence, and no mental health issues.

The researchers reported that Einstein's brain did not weigh more than the average brain of the control group, but a region of his parietal lobe believed to be important for visual–spatial processing was 15% larger than those of the control group. They proposed that the differences in that specific region of the parietal lobe in Einstein's brain may have been linked to his "exceptional intellect" in areas of visual-spatial cognition and mathematical thinking (Witelson, Kigar, & Harvey, 1999). Of course, the link between the size of Einstein's parietal region and his "exceptional intellect" is correlational, so we should be cautious in our interpretations. We are also left to wonder how Einstein's experiences (nurture) molded the structure of his brain; for example, his long history playing the violin may have contributed to a "large 'knob'-shaped fold" in the part of his cortex responsible for movement of his left hand (Chen, Chen, Zeng, Zhou, & Hou, 2014).

PENFIELD AND THE SOMATOSENSORY CORTEX   The parietal lobes are home to the **somatosensory cortex,** a strip of brain running parallel to the motor cortex, which receives and integrates sensory information from all over the body (pain and temperature, for example). Penfield, the neurosurgeon who created the homunculus for the motor cortex, mapped the somatosensory cortex in the same way (Penfield & Boldrey, 1937; Figure 2.9). As you might expect, the most sensitive areas of the body, like the face and tongue, are oversized on the homunculus, whereas areas less sensitive to stimulation, such as the forearm and the calf, are smaller.

THE TEMPORAL LOBES AND THE AUDITORY CORTEX   Below the parietal lobes, on the sides of your head, are the temporal lobes, which process auditory stimuli, recognize visual objects, especially faces, and play a key role in language comprehension and memory (Hickok & Poeppel, 2000; Infographic 2.4). The temporal lobes are home to the *auditory cortex,* which receives information from the ears and allows us to "hear" sounds. In particular, researchers have supported the notion, based on studies of primate vocalizations, that the ability to recognize language has evolved over time and is processed within the temporal lobes (Scott, Blank, Rosen, & Wise, 2000; Squire, Stark, & Clark, 2004).

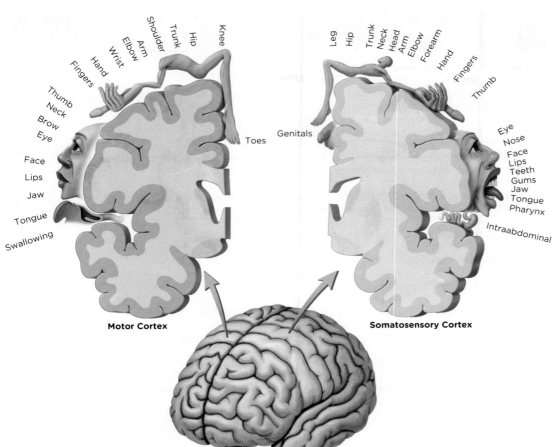

Motor Cortex

Somatosensory Cortex

FIGURE 2.9
The Motor and Somatosensory Cortex
This illustration shows how areas on the motor and somatosensory cortex correspond to the various regions of the body. Parts of the body that are shown larger, such as the face and hands, indicate areas of greater motor control or sensitivity. The size of each body part reflects the amount of cortex allocated to it.

THE OCCIPITAL LOBES AND THE PRIMARY VISUAL CORTEX
Visual information is initially processed in the occipital lobes, in the lower back of the head (Infographic 2.4). If you have ever suffered a severe blow to the rear of your head, you may remember "seeing stars," probably because activity in the occipital lobes was disrupted (hopefully only for a few seconds). It is here, where the optic nerve connects to the *primary visual cortex,* that visual information is received, interpreted, and processed (for example, about color, shape, and motion). (See Chapter 3 for more on the visual process.) Even for a person with healthy eyes, if this area were damaged, severe visual impairment could occur. At the same time, the individual would still be able to "see" vivid *mental* images (Bridge, Harrold, Holmes, Stokes, & Kennard, 2012).

___

LO 14 Describe the association areas and identify their functions.

___

THE ASSOCIATION AREAS In addition to the specialized functions of the different lobes described above, the cortex contains **association areas** whose role is to integrate information from all over the brain. The association areas are located in all four lobes; however, they are much harder to pinpoint than the motor and sensory areas. The association areas allow us to learn (just as you're doing now), to have abstract thoughts (for example, 2 + 2 = 4), and to carry out complex behaviors like texting and tweeting. The language-processing hubs we learned about earlier, *Broca's area* and *Wernicke's area,* are association areas that play a role in the production and

Seeing Stars
If you have ever been struck or fallen on the back of the head, you may recall perceiving bright blobs or dots floating by. The occipital lobes at the rear of the brain are home to the visual processing centers. Repeated blows to the head may lead to the development of chronic traumatic encephalopathy (CTE). For more on CTE, see Chapters 6 and 7. Toshifumi Kitamura/Getty Images.

TABLE 2.2 REGIONS OF THE CORTEX

Structure	Function and Importance
Association areas	Integrate information from all over the brain; allow us to learn, have abstract thoughts, and carry out complex behaviors.
Broca's area	Involved in speech production; helps us generate speech.
Corpus callosum	Connects the hemispheres; allows the left and right sides of the brain to communicate and work together to process information.
Frontal lobes	Organize information among the other lobes of the brain; responsible for higher-level cognitive functions, such as thinking, perception, and impulse control.
Left cerebral hemisphere	Controls the right side of the body; excels in language processing.
Motor cortex	Plans and executes voluntary movements; allows us to move our body.
Occipital lobes	Process visual information; help us see.
Parietal lobes	Receive and process sensory information; orient the body in space.
Primary visual cortex	Receives and interprets visual information; allows us to "see" vivid mental images.
Right cerebral hemisphere	Controls the left side of the body; excels in visual-spatial tasks.
Somatosensory cortex	Receives and integrates sensory information from the body; for example, helps us determine if the touch we feel is pleasurable or painful.
Temporal lobes	Comprehension of hearing and language; process auditory stimuli; recognize visual objects; key role in language comprehension and memory.
Wernick's area	Controls language comprehension; enables us to make sense of what is being said.

The cortex, or outermost layer of the brain, can be divided into functionally significant areas. Read this table to learn about the areas of the cortex and their importance.

comprehension of speech. In humans, the vast majority of the cortical surface is dedicated to the association areas (Table 2.2).

SOCIAL MEDIA AND PSYCHOLOGY
Facebook in the Brain

A major theme of this chapter is localization of function, the idea that certain areas of the brain tend to specialize in performing certain tasks. When we say "tasks," we mean just about any activity you can imagine, from riding a bicycle to managing friend networks on Facebook.

The average number of Facebook "friends" is 338, but the friend tally varies significantly from one person to the next, ranging from zero to 5,000, the maximum allowed by Facebook (Facebook Help Center, 2015; Pew Research Center, 2014, February 3). What does a Facebook friend number reveal about a person—job networking skills, offline popularity, time wasted at work? According to one preliminary study, friend volume may reflect something about the brain of the user.

FACEBOOK FRIENDS: A GRAY MATTER

Using MRI technology, researchers studied the brain structures of a sample of Facebook users. They discovered a correlation between the number of Facebook friends and the density of gray matter in areas of the brain important for social interaction. One of those regions, the *superior temporal sulcus,* is thought to be important for detecting socially meaningful movements such as hand gestures and eye shifts. Another, known as the *entorhinal cortex,* appears to play a key role in matching faces to names, a critical skill for Facebookers (Kanai, Bahrami, Roylance, & Rees, 2012). As anyone with a few hundred friends can testify, keeping track of all those names and faces can be challenging.

We should point out that this study is correlational. So it cannot reveal whether the number of friends causes changes in brain structure, or the characteristics of the brain structures determine the number of friends. Perhaps some other variable is responsible for both. This single study needs replication, but it has generated intriguing questions for researchers to tackle in the future. While there remain many unknowns, one thing seems certain: Social media provides psychologists with a whole new laboratory for studying the brain and social behavior. There is no shortage of data: "Each day, people send one billion posts to Facebook, tweet 400 million messages through Twitter, upload 12 years' worth of videos to YouTube, and make 300,000 edits to Wikipedia" (Mesh, Tamir, & Heekeren, 2015, p. 771).

 In Class: Collaborate and Report

This section introduced the lobes of the cortex and their associated functions. In your group, come up with two to three memory strategies, such as a rhyme, to remember the lobes of the cortex and their functions.

 show what you know

1. The brain is constantly undergoing alterations in response to experiences and is capable of a certain degree of physical adaptation and repair. This ability is known as:
   a. neuroplasticity.
   b. phrenology.
   c. ablation.
   d. lateralization.

2. The major function of the _____ is to organize information among the other lobes of the brain.
   a. parietal lobes
   b. frontal lobes
   c. corpus callosum
   d. temporal lobes

3. The _____ are regions of the cortex that integrate information from all over the brain, allowing us to learn, have abstract thoughts, and carry out complex behaviors.

4. Briefly describe the lobes of the cortex and their associated functions.

✓ CHECK YOUR ANSWERS IN APPENDIX C.

Digging Below the Cortex

Now that we have surveyed the brain's outer terrain, identifying some of the hotspots for language and other higher cognitive functions, let's dig deeper and examine some of its older structures (**TABLE 2.4**, on page 88).

Drama Central: The Limbic System

LO 15 Distinguish the structures and functions of the limbic system.

Buried beneath the cortex is the **limbic system,** a group of interconnected structures that plays an important role in our experiences of emotion, motivation, and memory. It also fuels our most basic drives, such as hunger, sex, and aggression. The limbic system includes the *thalamus, hypothalamus, amygdala,* and *hippocampus* (**FIGURE 2.10,** on the next page).

THALAMUS Seated at the center of the limbic system is the **thalamus** (THAL-uh-muss), whose job is to process and relay sensory information to the appropriate parts of the cortex (visual information to the visual cortex, and so on). The great majority of the data picked up by all the sensory systems, except olfaction (sense of smell), pass

limbic system A collection of structures that regulates emotions and basic drives like hunger, and aids in the creation of memories.

thalamus A structure in the limbic system that processes and relays sensory information to the appropriate areas of the cortex.

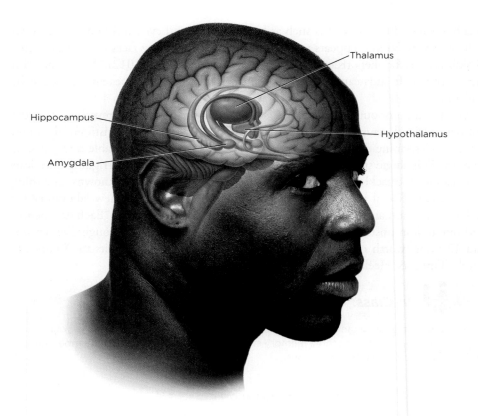

through the thalamus before moving on to the cortex for processing (Kay & Sherman, 2007). You might think of the thalamus as an air traffic control tower guiding incoming aircraft; when pilots communicate with the tower, the controllers direct the route to take and assign the runway to use.

HYPOTHALAMUS Just below the thalamus is the **hypothalamus** (hi-po-THAL-uh-muss; *hypo* means "under" in Greek), which keeps the body's systems in a steady state, making sure variables like blood pressure, body temperature, and fluid/electrolyte balance remain within a healthy range. The hypothalamus is also involved in regulating sleep–wake cycles (Xu et al., 2015; Saper, Scammell, & Lu, 2005), sexual arousal, and appetite (Hurley & Johnson, 2014). For example, neurons from the digestive system send signals to the hypothalamus ("stomach is empty"), which then sends signals to higher regions of the brain ("it's time to eat"). But deciding what and when to eat does not always come down to being hungry or full. Other brain areas are involved in eating decisions and can override the hypothalamus, driving you to polish off the french fries or scarf down that chocolate bar even when you are not that hungry.

AMYGDALA Another structure of the limbic system is the **amygdala** (uh-MIG-duh-la), which processes aggression and basic emotions such as fear, and the memories associated with them (Janak & Tye, 2015; Kluver & Bucy, 1939). Having spent many months in a war zone, Brandon encountered more than his fair share of fear-provoking near-death experiences. On one occasion, he was riding at nearly 60 mph in a Humvee that spun out of control and almost flipped over. "My heart was beating faster than ever before," Brandon recalls. In dangerous situations like this, the amygdala is activated and the nervous system orchestrates a whole-body response (racing heart, sweaty palms, and the like), as well as an emotional reaction (fear).

War zones are filled with situations that are obviously life-threatening, but sometimes the brain has to determine whether a real threat exists. In such cases, the amygdala shares information with areas in the frontal lobes to make this assessment

hypothalamus A small structure located below the thalamus that maintains a constant internal environment within a healthy range; helps regulate sleep–wake cycles, sexual behavior, and appetite.

amygdala A pair of almond-shaped structures in the limbic system that processes aggression and basic emotions such as fear, as well as associated memories.

hippocampus A pair of structures located in the limbic system; primarily responsible for creating new memories.

(Likhtik, Stujenske, Topiwala, Harris, & Gordon, 2014). Once a situation is deemed safe, the frontal lobes give the amygdala an "all clear" signal and fear diminishes. Like many parts of the nervous system, the structure of the amygdala has divisions that seem to play different roles; in assessing the threat of a situation, some structures come into play immediately (reflexive behavior occurs), while others react slightly later as attention is focused on the threat (voluntary behavior results). The speed of our fear reactions depends on these types of "dual routes" (de Gelder, Hortensius, & Tamietto, 2012; also see Chapter 9). The amygdala also helps us to perceive and experience a wide range of positive emotions, with processing speed depending on the intensity of the emotion (Bonnet et al., 2015).

HIPPOCAMPUS The largest structure in the limbic system is a pair of C-shaped structures called the hippocampus. The **hippocampus** is primarily responsible for processing and forming new memories from experiences, but it is not where memories are permanently stored (Eichenbaum, 2004). Given its key role in memory, it may come as no surprise that the hippocampus is one of the brain areas affected by Alzheimer's disease (Henneman et al., 2009; Hsu et al., 2015). On the brighter side of things, the hippocampus is also one of the few places in the brain known to generate new neurons throughout life (Eriksson et al., 1998; Tate et al., 2014). Given the special role of the hippocampus, you would be wise to take good care of it—but how? One simple way might be changing your diet.

Sugar May Harm Brain Health

High levels of blood glucose are linked to memory impairments.

from the pages of
SCIENTIFIC AMERICAN

A poor diet can eat away at brain health. Now a study in *Neurology* helps elucidate why. It suggests that eating a lot of sugar or other carbohydrates can be hazardous to both brain structure and function.

Diabetes, which is characterized by chronically high levels of blood glucose, has been linked to an elevated risk of dementia and a smaller hippocampus, a brain region critical for memory. The new study sought to identify whether glucose had an effect on memory even in people without the disease because having it could induce other brain changes that confound the data. In the experiment, researchers at the Charité University Medical Center in Berlin evaluated both short- and long-term glucose markers in 141 healthy, nondiabetic older adults. The participants performed a memory test and underwent imaging to assess the structure of their hippocampus.

Higher levels on both glucose measures were associated with worse memory, as well as a smaller hippocampus and compromised hippocampal structure. The researchers also found that the structural changes partially accounted for the statistical link between glucose and memory. According to study co-author Agnes Flöel, a neurologist at Charité, the results "provide further evidence that glucose might directly contribute to hippocampal atrophy," but she cautions that their data cannot establish a causal relation between sugar and brain health.

These findings indicate that even in the absence of diabetes or glucose intolerance, higher blood sugar may harm the brain and disrupt memory function. Future research will need to characterize how glucose exerts these effects and whether dietary or lifestyle interventions might reverse such pathological changes.

Now that we've delivered the bad news about sugar and carbs, let's talk about foods that are good for your brain. Research suggests that the brain benefits from a diet that is highly plant-based, or rich in fruits, vegetables, nuts, whole grains, and legumes (such as peas, lentils, and beans), and low in saturated fat and red meat. This "Mediterranean diet," which also features olive oil and fish, has been correlated with lower rates of cognitive deterioration and decreased Alzheimer's risk (Lourida et al., 2013). For specific foods linked to better brain health, see **TABLE 2.3**, on the next page.

TABLE 2.3 FOOD FOR THOUGHT?

Food	Potential Benefits
Walnuts	Walnuts contain chemical compounds called *polyphenols* that may reduce inflammation, boost communication between neurons, and promote neurogenesis (Poulose, Miller, & Shukitt-Hale, 2014). Eating walnuts has been associated with enhanced verbal reasoning, and better learning, recall, and processing speed (Arab & Ang, 2015; Pribis et al., 2012).
Berries	Berries abound with polyphenols and other nutrients that reduce inflammation and limit the activity of free radicals driving age-related diseases (Nile & Park, 2014). Eating blueberries and strawberries has been linked to better memory and cognitive function in older people (Devore, Kang, Breteler, & Grodstein, 2012; Krikorian et al., 2010; Pribis & Shukitt-Hale, 2014).
Cocoa (unprocessed cocoa powder, not chocolate candy)	Cocoa beans are packed with polyphenols called *flavonoids,* which promote the development of new blood vessels and neurons in areas of the brain important to memory and learning (Nehlig, 2012). Cocoa flavonoids appear to boost performance of the *dentate gyrus* (part of the hippocampus), and improve memory (Brickman et al., 2014; Yuhas, 2013, March/April).
Oily fish	Oily fish, such as salmon, lake trout, sardines, and albacore tuna, are packed with *omega-3 fatty acids,* which may play "an important role in maintaining brain structure and function with advancing age" (Pottala et al., 2014, p. 435). High intake of omega-3 fatty acids has been linked to larger brain volume and gains in cognitive function (Pottala et al., 2014; Witte et al., 2014).
Broccoli	Broccoli is an excellent source of vitamin K, choline, and folic acid, all of which appear to have a positive impact on cognition (Ferland, 2012; Poly et al., 2011; Presse et al., 2013).

Here are just a handful of the many foods that may promote brain health. If you have an allergy or any other medical condition, check with your doctor before adding new foods to your diet.

Deeper Yet: The Brainstem and Cerebellum

The brain is made up of structures responsible for processes as complex as rebuilding a car's engine or selecting the right classes for a degree program. Yet delving deeper in the brain, we find structures that control more primitive functions.

LO 16 **Distinguish the structures and functions of the brainstem and cerebellum.**

COMPONENTS OF THE BRAINSTEM The brain's ancient core consists of a stalk-like trio of structures called the *brainstem* (**FIGURE 2.11**). The brainstem, which includes the midbrain, pons, and medulla, extends from the spinal cord to the **forebrain,** which is the largest part of the brain and includes the cerebral cortex and the limbic system.

The top portion of the brainstem is known as the **midbrain,** and although there is some disagreement among researchers about which brain structures belong to the midbrain, most agree it plays a role in levels of arousal. The midbrain is also home to neurons that help generate movement patterns in response to sensory input (Stein, Stanford, & Rowland, 2009). For example, if someone shouted "Look out!," neurons in your midbrain would play a role when you flinch. Also located in the midbrain is part of the **reticular formation,** an intricate web of neurons that is responsible for levels of arousal—whether you are awake, dozing off, or somewhere in between. The reticular formation is also involved in your ability to attend selectively to important incoming information by sifting through sensory data on its way to the cortex, picking out what's relevant and ignoring the rest. Imagine how overwhelmed you would feel by all the sights, sounds, tastes, smells, and physical sensations in your environment if you didn't have a reticular formation to help you discriminate between information that is important (the sound of a honking car horn) and that which is trivial (the sound of a dog barking in the distance).

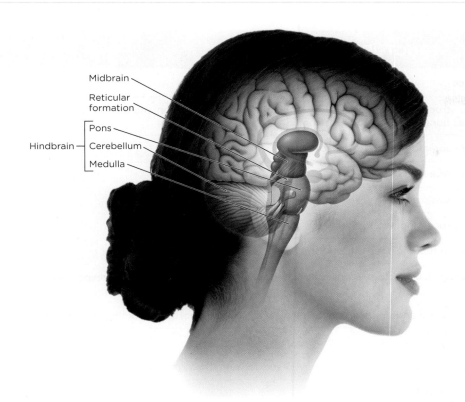

Midbrain
Reticular formation
Pons
Hindbrain — Cerebellum
Medulla

FIGURE 2.11
The Brainstem and Cerebellum
Located beneath the structures of the limbic system, the brainstem includes the midbrain, pons, and medulla. These structures are involved in arousal, movement, and life-sustaining processes. The cerebellum is important for muscle coordination and balance and, when paired with the pons and medulla, makes up the hindbrain. Photo: Onoky/Corbis.

The **hindbrain** includes areas of the brain responsible for fundamental life-sustaining processes. The **pons,** which helps regulate sleep–wake cycles and coordinates movement between the right and left sides of the body, is an important structure of the hindbrain. The pons sits atop the **medulla** (muh-DUL-uh), a structure that oversees some of the body's most vital functions, including breathing and heart rate maintenance (Broadbelt, Paterson, Rivera, Trachtenberg, & Kinney, 2010).

CEREBELLUM   Behind the brainstem, just above the nape of the neck, sits the orange-sized **cerebellum** (sehr-uh-BELL-um). (Latin for "little brain," the cerebellum looks like a mini-version of the whole brain.) Centuries ago, scientists found that removing parts of the cerebellum from animals caused them to stagger, fall, and act clumsy. Although the cerebellum is best known for its importance in muscle coordination and balance, researchers are exploring how this "little brain" influences higher cognitive processes in the "big brain," such as abstract reasoning and language production (Mariën et al., 2014; Fine, Ionita, & Lohr, 2002). People with damaged cerebellums struggle with certain fine distinctions, such as telling the difference between words that sound somewhat alike (for example, "pause" versus "paws") or producing emotional reactions that are appropriate for a given situation (Bower & Parsons, 2003, July 14; Lupo et al., 2015).

In Class: Collaborate and Report

Now that you are almost finished reading this chapter, you probably realize how hard your brain works 24/7, often in ways beyond your awareness. In your group, **A)** choose an important activity that you would like to examine (for example, giving a presentation in class, going on a first date) and discuss how specific structures of the **B)** limbic system, **C)** brainstem, and **D)** cerebellum may be involved.

Hooray! We have finally completed our tour of the nervous system. We started on the micro level, exploring communication in and between neurons, and then worked our way through the macro structures of the brain, spinal cord, and peripheral

Synonyms

reticular formation reticular activating system

forebrain Largest part of the brain; includes the cerebral cortex and the limbic system.

midbrain The part of the brainstem involved in levels of arousal; responsible for generating movement patterns in response to sensory input.

reticular formation A network of neurons running through the midbrain that controls levels of arousal and quickly analyzes sensory information on its way to the cortex.

hindbrain Includes areas of the brain responsible for fundamental life-sustaining processes.

pons A hindbrain structure that helps regulate sleep–wake cycles and coordinate movement between the right and left sides of the body.

medulla A structure that oversees vital functions, including breathing, digestion, and heart rate.

cerebellum Structure located behind the brainstem that is responsible for muscle coordination and balance; Latin for "little brain."

TABLE 2.4 BELOW THE CORTEX: STRUCTURES TO KNOW

Structure	Function and Importance
Limbic system	Group of interconnected structures that play a role in our experiences of emotion, motivation, and memory; fuels basic drives, such as hunger, sex, and aggression.
Thalamus	Processes and relays sensory information to the cortex.
Hypothalamus	Keeps the body's systems in a steady state.
Amygdala	Processes aggression and basic emotions like fear, and the memories associated with them.
Hippocampus	Primarily responsible for processing and forming new memories from experiences.
Forebrain	The largest part of the brain that includes the cerebral cortex and the limbic system.
Midbrain	Plays a role in levels of arousal; home to neurons that help generate movement patterns in response to sensory input.
Reticular formation	Responsible for levels of arousal and our ability to selectively attend to important incoming sensory data.
Hindbrain	Responsible for fundamental life-sustaining processes.
Pons	Helps regulate sleep–wake cycles and coordinates movement between the right and left sides of the body.
Medulla	Oversees functions such as breathing and heart rate.
Cerebellum	Involved in muscle coordination and balance.

Tucked below the cortex are brain structures with a variety of different functions. Make sure you are familiar with these key regions.

nervous system. As you delve into topics covered in other chapters, remember that communication between neurons underlies every psychological phenomenon. Do not hesitate to revisit this chapter throughout the course; this is your biological foundation.

○ ✓ ○ ○ show what you know

1. The _____ is a group of interconnected structures that process emotions, memories, and basic drives.
   a. left hemisphere
   b. limbic system
   c. corpus callosum
   d. superior temporal sulcus

2. The specific brain structure that processes aggression and basic emotions like fear, and the memories associated with them, is the _____.

3. The primary role of the thalamus is to:
   a. relay sensory information.
   b. keep the body's systems in a steady state.
   c. generate movement patterns in response to sensory input.
   d. regulate sleep–wake cycles.

4. The structure located behind the brainstem that is responsible for muscle coordination and balance is the _____.

✓ CHECK YOUR ANSWERS IN APPENDIX C.

WHERE ARE THEY NOW? You may be wondering what became of Brandon Burns and Christina Santhouse. Three years after returning from Iraq, Brandon married a young woman named Laura who has witnessed his dramatic recovery. When Laura first met Brandon, he had a lot of trouble communicating his thoughts. His sentences were choppy; he often omitted words and spoke in a flat and emotionless tone. "His speech was very delayed, very slow," Laura recalls.

Life Is Good
Three years after his traumatic brain injury, Brandon celebrated his marriage to Laura. The couple now has three children. Laura Burns.

Hard at Work
With her master's degree in speech–language pathology, Christina now works full time in Pennsylvania's public school system. Bucks County Courier Times/Calkins Media, Inc.

Now he is able to use more humor and emotion, articulate his thoughts in lengthy, complex sentences; read a book; and write for his website. Much of Brandon's time is spent caring for his sons, 7-year-old Porter and 5-year-old Morgan, and his 3-year-old daughter MacCrea Iona. He also works in a church ministry and in that capacity has traveled to numerous countries, including Haiti, Kenya, and Honduras.

As for Christina, she continues to reach for the stars—and grab them. After studying speech–language pathology at Misericordia University in Dallas, Pennsylvania, for 5 years (and making the dean's list nearly every semester), Christina graduated with both a bachelor's and a master's degree. But those years were not smooth sailing. Christina remembers the department chairman telling her that she wouldn't be able to handle the rigors of the program. According to Christina, on graduation day, that same chairman presented her with the department's Outstanding Achievement Award. "People often don't expect too much from people with disabilities," she says.

Today, Christina works as a full-time speech–language pathologist in Pennsylvania's public school system, helping elementary schoolchildren overcome their difficulties with stuttering, articulation, and other speech problems. She is also a member of the local school district's Brain STEPS team, which supports students who are transitioning back into school following brain injuries. "Hopefully, I have opened some doors for other people with disabilities," Christina offers. "There were never doors open for me; I've had to bang them down." ●

THINK POSITIVE

The Versatile Brain

Brandon and Christina provide breathtaking illustrations of neuroplasticity—the brain's ability to heal, grow new connections, and make do with what is available. These amazing changes can occur under a variety of circumstances—after a stroke, in the face of blindness, and even adapting to motherhood (Convento, Russo, Zigiotto, & Bolognini, 2016; Hasson, Andric, Atilgan, & Collignon, 2016; Kim, Strathearn, & Swain, 2016). Your brain

YOUR BRAIN CAN CHANGE, TOO

can change, too. Every time you acquire knowledge or learn a new skill, whether it's cooking Pad Thai or plucking out melodies on a guitar, new networks of communication are sprouting between your neurons (Barss, Pearcey, & Zehr, 2016; Vaquero et al., 2016). Expose yourself to new information and activities, and your brain will continue to develop and adapt. There is no limit to the amount you can learn!

The stories of Brandon and Christina also highlight the importance of maintaining hope, even in the face of stress and daunting obstacles (Abel, Hayes, Henley, & Kuyken, 2016; Brady et al., 2016). There were many times Brandon and Christina could have lost hope and wallowed in self-pity, but instead they decided to fight. So, too, did the neuropsychologists, physical therapists, occupational therapists, speech pathologists, and other professionals who assisted in their rehabilitation. The recoveries of Brandon and Christina bear testimony to the awesome tenacity of the human spirit. 👍

You Asked, Christina Answers

http://qrs.ly/j25a58m

Which medical professional had the biggest impact on your recovery?

scan this ➡

Improve your grade! Use 📚 **LearningCurve** macmillan learning adaptive quizzing to create your personalized study plan, which will direct you to the resources that will help you most in 📚 **LaunchPad** macmillan learning

---

2 summary of concepts

LO 1 Define neuroscience and biological psychology and explain their contributions to our understanding of behavior. (p. 50)

Neuroscience is the study of the nervous system and the brain, and it overlaps with a variety of disciplines and research areas. Biological psychology is a subfield of psychology focusing on how the brain and other biological systems influence behavior. These disciplines help us discover connections between behavior and the nervous system (particularly the brain) as well as physiological explanations for mental processes.

LO 2 Compare and contrast tools scientists use to study the brain. (p. 50)

Researchers use a variety of technologies to study the brain. An electroencephalogram (EEG) detects electrical impulses in the brain. Computerized axial tomography (CAT) uses X-rays to create many cross-sectional images of the brain. Magnetic resonance imaging (MRI) uses magnets to produce more detailed cross-sectional images; both MRI and CAT scans only reveal the structure of the brain. Positron emission tomography (PET) uses radioactivity to track glucose consumption to construct a map of the brain. Functional magnetic resonance imaging (fMRI) captures changes in brain activity by tracking patterns of blood flow.

LO 3 Label the parts of a neuron and describe an action potential. (p. 53)

A typical neuron has three basic parts: a cell body, dendrites, and an axon. The dendrites receive messages from

other neurons, and branches at the end of the axon send messages to neighboring neurons. These messages are electrical and chemical in nature. An action potential is the electrical signal that moves down the axon, causing a neuron to send chemical messages across the synapse. Action potentials are all-or-none, meaning they either fire or do not fire.

LO 4 Illustrate how neurons communicate with each other. (p. 58)

Neurons communicate with each other via chemicals called neurotransmitters. An action potential moves down the axon to the terminal buds, where the command to release neurotransmitters is conveyed. Most of the neurotransmitters released into the synapse drift across the gap and come into contact with receptor sites of the receiving neuron's dendrites.

LO 5 Describe specific neurotransmitters and summarize how their activity affects human behavior. (p. 60)

Neurotransmitters are chemical messengers that neurons use to communicate. There are many types of neurotransmitters, including acetylcholine, glutamate, GABA, norepinephrine, serotonin, dopamine, and endorphins, and each has its own type of receptor site. Neurotransmitters can influence mood, cognition, behavior, and many other processes.

LO 6 Explain how the central and peripheral nervous systems connect. (p. 64)

The brain and spinal cord make up the central nervous system (CNS), which communicates with the rest of the body through the peripheral nervous system (PNS). There are three types of neurons participating in this back-and-forth communication: motor neurons carry information from the CNS to various parts of the body such as muscles and glands; sensory neurons relay data from the sensory systems (for example, eyes and ears) to the CNS for processing; and interneurons, which reside exclusively in the CNS, act as bridges connecting sensory and motor neurons. Interneurons mediate the nervous system's most complex operations, including sensory processing, memory, thoughts, and emotions.

LO 7 Describe the organization and function of the peripheral nervous system. (p. 65)

The peripheral nervous system is divided into two branches: the somatic nervous system and the autonomic nervous system. The somatic nervous system controls the skeletal muscles that enable voluntary movement. The autonomic nervous system regulates the body's involuntary processes and has two divisions: the sympathetic nervous system, which initiates the fight-or-flight response, and the parasympathetic nervous system, which oversees the rest-and-digest processes.

LO 8 Summarize how the endocrine system influences behavior and physiological processes. (p. 69)

Closely connected with the nervous system, the endocrine system uses glands to send messages throughout the body. These messages are conveyed by hormones—chemicals released into the bloodstream that can cause aggression and mood swings, and influence growth and alertness, among other things.

LO 9 Describe the two brain hemispheres and how they communicate. (p. 71)

The cerebrum includes virtually all parts of the brain except for the primitive brainstem structures. It is divided into two hemispheres: the right cerebral hemisphere and the left cerebral hemisphere. The left hemisphere controls most of the movement and sensation on the right side of the body. The right hemisphere controls most of the movement and sensation on the left side of the body. Connecting the two hemispheres is the corpus callosum, a band of fibers that enables them to communicate.

LO 10 Define lateralization and explain what the split-brain experiments reveal about the right and left hemispheres. (p. 72)

Researchers have gleaned valuable knowledge about the brain hemispheres from experiments on split-brain patients —people whose hemispheres have been surgically disconnected. Under certain experimental conditions, split-brain individuals act as if they have two separate brains. By observing the brain hemispheres operating independent of one another, researchers have discovered that each hemisphere excels in certain activities, a phenomenon known as lateralization. Generally, the left hemisphere excels in language and the right hemisphere excels in visual-spatial tasks.

LO 11 Identify areas in the brain responsible for language production and comprehension. (p. 74)

Several areas in the brain are responsible for language processing. Broca's area is primarily responsible for speech production, and Wernicke's area is primarily responsible for language comprehension.

LO 12 Define neuroplasticity and recognize when it is evident in the brain. (p. 76)

Neuroplasticity is the ability of the brain to form new connections between neurons and adapt to changing circumstances. Networks of neurons, particularly in the young, can reorganize to adapt to the environment and an organism's ever-changing needs.

LO 13 Identify the lobes of the cortex and explain their functions. (p. 77)

The outermost layer of the cerebrum is the cerebral cortex. The cortex is separated into different sections called lobes. The major function of the frontal lobes is to organize information among the other lobes of the brain. The frontal lobes are also responsible for higher-level cognitive functions, such as thinking and personality. The parietal lobes receive and process sensory information such as touch, pressure, temperature, and spatial orientation. Visual information goes to the occipital lobes for processing. The temporal lobes are primarily responsible for hearing and language comprehension.

LO 14 Describe the association areas and identify their functions. (p. 81)

The association areas in the lobes integrate information from all over the brain, allowing us to learn, have abstract thoughts, and carry out complex behaviors.

LO 15 Distinguish the structures and functions of the limbic system. (p. 83)

The limbic system is a group of interconnected structures that play an important role in our emotions and memories. The limbic system includes the hippocampus, amygdala, thalamus, and hypothalamus. In addition to processing emotions and memories, the limbic system fuels the most basic drives, such as hunger, sex, and aggression.

LO 16 Distinguish the structures and functions of the brainstem and cerebellum. (p. 86)

The brain's ancient core consists of a stalklike trio of structures called the brainstem, which includes the midbrain, pons, and medulla. The brainstem extends from the spinal cord to the forebrain, which is the largest part of the brain that includes the cerebral cortex and the limbic system. Located at the top of the brainstem is the midbrain, which appears to play a role in levels of arousal. The hindbrain includes areas responsible for fundamental life-sustaining processes. Behind the brainstem is the cerebellum, which is responsible for muscle coordination and balance.

key terms

action potential, p. 57
adrenal glands, p. 70
all-or-none, p. 57
amygdala, p. 84
association areas, p. 81
autonomic nervous system, p. 66
axon, p. 53
biological psychology, p. 50
Broca's area, p. 75
cell body, p. 53
central nervous system (CNS), p. 63
cerebellum, p. 87
cerebral cortex, p. 77
cerebrum, p. 71
corpus callosum, p. 71

dendrites, p. 53
endocrine system, p. 69
forebrain, p. 86
frontal lobes, p. 77
glial cells, p. 54
hindbrain, p. 87
hippocampus, p. 85
hormones, p. 69
hypothalamus, p. 84
interneurons, p. 64
lateralization, p. 73
limbic system, p. 83
medulla, p. 87
midbrain, p. 86
motor cortex, p. 79
motor neurons, p. 64
myelin sheath, p. 53

nerves, p. 66
neurogenesis, p. 77
neurons, p. 51
neuroplasticity, p. 76
neuroscience, p. 50
neurotransmitters, p. 58
occipital lobes, p. 79
parasympathetic nervous system, p. 66
parietal lobes, p. 79
peripheral nervous system (PNS), p. 63
phrenology, p. 51
pituitary gland, p. 69
pons, p. 87
receptor sites, p. 58
reflex arc, p. 65

resting potential, p. 55
reticular formation, p. 86
reuptake, p. 58
sensory neurons, p. 64
somatic nervous system, p. 66
somatosensory cortex, p. 80
spinal cord, p. 63
split-brain operation, p. 72
stem cells, p. 77
sympathetic nervous system, p. 66
synapse, p. 53
temporal lobes, p. 79
thalamus, p. 83
thyroid gland, p. 70
Wernicke's area, p. 75

test prep *are you ready?*

1. _____ communicate with each other through electrical and chemical signals.
   - a. Neurotransmitters
   - b. The hemispheres
   - c. Neurons
   - d. Hormones

2. When positive ions at the axon hillock raise the internal cell voltage of the first segment of an axon from its resting voltage to its threshold potential, the neuron becomes activated. This spike in voltage causes _____ to occur.
   - a. an action potential
   - b. reuptake
   - c. a reflex arc
   - d. lateralization

3. Your friend has been diagnosed with multiple sclerosis. Her doctors explain that the disease is associated with damage to the _____ covering the axons in her nervous system.
   - a. myelin sheath
   - b. reticular formation
   - c. glutamate
   - d. neurotransmitters

4. Match the neurotransmitter with its primary role(s).
   - _____ 1. acetylcholine
   - _____ 2. glutamate
   - _____ 3. endorphins
   - _____ 4. serotonin
   - a. reduction of pain
   - b. learning, memory
   - c. movement
   - d. mood, aggression, appetite

5. A neuroscientist studying the brain and the spinal cord would describe her general area of interest as the:
   - a. central nervous system.
   - b. peripheral nervous system.
   - c. autonomic nervous system.
   - d. neurons.

6. A serious diving accident can result in damage to the _____, which is responsible for receiving information from the body and sending it to the brain, and for transmitting information from the brain to the body.
   - a. corpus callosum
   - b. spinal cord
   - c. reflex arc
   - d. somatic nervous system

7. Beep! You have a text. That sound is received by your auditory system and information is sent via sensory neurons to your brain. Here, we can see how the _____ provides a communication link between the central nervous system and the rest of the body.
   - a. endocrine system
   - b. cerebrum
   - c. corpus callosum
   - d. peripheral nervous system

8. After Brandon returned from a frightening situation in a war zone, his parasympathetic nervous system reacted with a:
   - a. "fight-and-rest" response.
   - b. "fight-or-flight" response.
   - c. "tend-and-befriend" process.
   - d. "rest-and-digest" process.

9. Lately, your friend has been prone to mood swings and aggressive behavior. The doctor has pinpointed a problem in his _____, which is a communication system that uses _____ to convey messages via hormones.
   a. endocrine system; action potentials
   b. endocrine system; glands
   c. central nervous system; glands
   d. central nervous system; peripheral nervous system

10. Which of the following statements is correct regarding the function of the right hemisphere in comparison to the left hemisphere?
    a. The right hemisphere is less competent handling visual tasks.
    b. The right hemisphere is more competent handling visual tasks.
    c. The left hemisphere is more competent judging if lines are oriented similarly.
    d. The right hemisphere is more competent with speech production.

11. Although Gall's phrenology has been discredited as a true brain "science," Gall's major contribution to the field of psychology is the idea that:
    a. locations in the brain are responsible for certain activities.
    b. the left hemisphere is responsible for activity on the right side of the body.
    c. the left hemisphere is responsible for language production.
    d. stem cells can be used to repair tissue that has been damaged.

12. Broca's area is involved in speech production, and_____ is critical for language comprehension.
    a. the corpus callosum
    b. the right hemisphere
    c. the parietal lobe
    d. Wernicke's area

13. Match the structures with their principal functions.
    _____ 1. association areas
    _____ 2. temporal lobes
    _____ 3. meninges
    _____ 4. occipital lobes
    _____ 5. parietal lobes
    a. three thin membranes protect brain
    b. integration of information from all over brain
    c. hearing and language comprehension
    d. receive sensory information, such as touch
    e. process visual information

14. The limbic system is a group of interconnected structures in the brain. Match the structures below with their principle functions:
    _____ 1. amygdala
    _____ 2. hippocampus
    _____ 3. hypothalamus
    _____ 4. thalamus
    a. responsible for making new memories
    b. processes basic emotions
    c. relays sensory information
    d. keeps body systems in a steady state

15. The _____ is located in the midbrain and is responsible for levels of arousal and your ability to selectively attend to important stimuli.
    a. cerebellum
    b. thalamus
    c. hippocampus
    d. reticular formation

16. What is neuroplasticity? Give an example of when it is evident.

17. The "knee-jerk" reaction that occurs when a doctor taps your knee with a rubber hammer provides a good example of a reflex arc. Describe this involuntary reaction and then draw your own diagram to show the reflex arc associated with it.

18. Compare and contrast the body's two major chemical messengers.

19. The research conducted by Sperry and Gazzaniga examined the effects of surgeries that severed the corpus callosum. Describe what these split-brain experiments tell us about the lateralization of the hemispheres of the brain and how they communicate.

20. We described a handful of tools scientists use to study the brain. Compare their functions and limitations.

✓ CHECK YOUR ANSWERS IN APPENDIX C.

YOUR SCIENTIFIC WORLD
Apply psychology to the real world!
Go to LaunchPad for access.

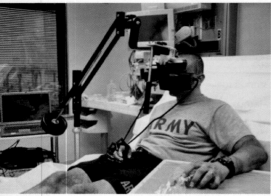

Steve Elliot, U. S. Army Photo.

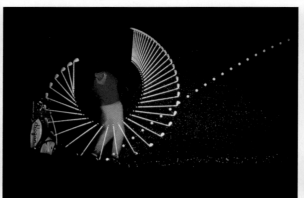

Vandystadt/Michael Hans/Science Source.

Patrick Foto/Getty Images.

CHAPTER OUTLINE AND LEARNING OBJECTIVES

An Introduction to Sensation and Perception

LO 1 Define sensation and perception and explain how they are different.

LO 2 Define transduction and explain how it relates to sensation.

LO 3 Describe and differentiate between absolute thresholds and difference thresholds.

Vision

LO 4 Summarize the properties of light and color, and describe the structure and function of the eye.

LO 5 Describe the functions of rods and cones.

LO 6 Compare and contrast the theories of color vision.

Hearing

LO 7 Summarize how sound waves are converted into the sensation of hearing.

LO 8 Illustrate how we sense different pitches of sound.

Smell, Taste, Touch: The Chemical and Skin Senses

LO 9 Describe the process of olfaction.

LO 10 Discuss the structures involved in taste and describe how they work.

LO 11 Explain how the biopsychosocial perspective helps us understand pain.

LO 12 Illustrate how we sense the position and movement of our bodies.

Perception

LO 13 Identify the principles of perceptual organization.

LO 14 Describe some of the visual cues used in depth perception.

LO 15 Define extrasensory perception and explain why psychologists dismiss claims of its legitimacy.

Mark Richards/Photo Edit.

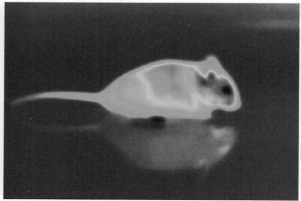

Julius Lab at UCSF.

AP Photo/The Canadian Press. Frank Gunn.

3 sensation and perception

Bobbie Osborne/
Getty Images

An Introduction to Sensation and Perception

GOOD MORNING, TRIPLETS Long before the sun rises, Liz Allen is awake, making sure that her 13-year-old triplets Emma, Zoe, and Sophie make it to school on time. First she walks into the bedroom of Emma and Zoe.

The floor may be sprinkled with toys if Emma has been awake in the night. She likes to climb inside the storage box in her room and toss out its contents. Zoe is a better sleeper, but she, too, might be up for several hours at a time. "They're pretty active at night," explains Liz. When sleeping, Emma and Zoe are almost certain to be found cuddled lengthwise, feet-to-head.

Gently shaking the girls, Liz says, "Wake up. Let's get ready," but she needn't utter a word. She "speaks" to Emma and Zoe by moving her hands, and they "listen" by feeling her fingers dance through the motions of sign language. Emma and Zoe are completely blind and deaf. During the day, the triplets use *cochlear implants,* electronic devices that provide them with some degree of hearing. But these implants only enable a hearinglike experience; they do not "fix" deafness (UCSF Medical Center, n.d.). The third triplet, Sophie, is easier to rouse; she is deaf but possesses some limited vision. Flipping the light switch is enough to get her started on her morning routine.

Welcome to the world of Emma, Zoe, and Sophie. They are, as far as we know, the world's only deaf and blind triplets. ●

Note: Quotations attributed to Liz Allen are personal communications.

The Triplets
The Dunn sisters, Sophie (left), Zoe, and Emma (front), are the world's only deaf and blind triplets. Emma and Zoe can see nothing, while Sophie has very limited vision even when donning corrective lenses. All three girls wear cochlear implants, devices that simulate the sensation of hearing. Worldwide Features/Barcroft Media/Landov.

The Basics

LO 1 Define sensation and perception and explain how they are different.

Have you ever wondered what it is like to be blind and deaf? Most people depend on sights and sounds for virtually every daily activity, from buttering toast to answering the phone. Thanks to our eyes and ears, we can tell the difference between blue sky and dark rain clouds, the chirp of a bird and the honk of a car horn. Sights and sounds provide a foundation for many of our thoughts and memories. When we think about people, we "see" their faces and "hear" their voices in our minds.

How does a deaf-blind person function in the world? We humans are adaptive creatures; when faced with disabilities, we make the best of what we have. Emma, Zoe, and Sophie have come to rely on their other senses—touch, smell, and taste—to compensate for what they cannot see or hear. Instead of rising to an alarm clock or the sunlight streaming through their window, Emma and Zoe feel their mother nudging them and signing "Wake up" and "Let's get ready" into their hands. They recognize Mom by touch and smell, and they find their way around new places by running their fingers along the edges and contours of objects and walls. "You would think . . . that they are missing out on a lot," Liz says, "but they don't miss much."

SENSATION VERSUS PERCEPTION The subject of this chapter is sensation and perception, the absorbing and deciphering of information from the environment. **Sensation** is the process by which receptors in our sensory organs (located in the eyes, ears, nose, mouth, skin, and other tissues) receive and detect stimuli. **Perception** is the process through which information about these stimuli is organized, interpreted, and transformed into something meaningful. Sensation is seeing a red burner on the stove; perception is thinking *hot*. Sensation is hearing a loud, shrill tone; perception is recognizing it as the warning sound of a fire alarm. Sensation and perception work together to provide a coherent experience of the world around and inside you, and they often occur without your effort or awareness.

Psychologists frequently characterize the processing of sensory information as *bottom-up* or *top-down*. **Bottom-up processing** occurs when the brain collects basic information about incoming stimuli and prepares it for further interpretation. **Top-down processing** generally involves the next step, using past experiences and knowledge to understand and pay attention to sensory information. Bottom-up processing is what cameras and video recorders do best—collect data without any expectations. Top-down processing is where humans excel. For example, if your cell phone signal momentarily breaks up, you can't hear every word the other person is saying. Thanks to top-down processing, you can often fill in the gaps and make sense of what you are hearing. Using both types of processing, the brain constructs a representation of the world based on what we have learned and experienced in the past. This representation is not always accurate, however. Both bottom-up and top-down processing can lead us astray in our interpretations of ambiguous figures, and the resulting errors may have serious consequences. Just think what might happen if a doctor failed to detect a hemorrhage (bleed) on a patient's brain scan, or mistook a normal anatomical variation for a breast mass. Sometimes radiologists have to base difficult diagnostic decisions on ambiguous X-ray images (Buckle, Udawatta, & Straus, 2013).

Now it's time to learn how your sensory systems collect information from inside and outside your body and transform it into your impressions of the world. How are beams of light turned into an image of a fiery orange sunrise, and chemical sensations converted into the taste of a sweet strawberry? It all begins with transduction.

Liz, in Her Own Words
http://qrs.ly/g65a59a

Sensory Blending
Singer-songwriter Pharrell Williams says he sees colors when he listens to music (NPR, 2013, December 31). Williams is describing *synesthesia,* a "rare experience where one property of a stimulus evokes a second experience not associated with the first" (Banissy, Jonas, & Kadosh, 2014, para. 1). With synesthesia, the senses seem to blend; for example, the word "Tuesday" might taste like bacon, or the letter Y may smell like pine trees.
Kevin Winter/WireImage/Getty Images.

| LO 2 | Define transduction and explain how it relates to sensation. |

TRANSDUCTION Sensation begins when your sensory systems receive input from the internal and external environment. Each sensory system is designed to respond to stimuli of a certain kind. Light waves and sound waves accost your eyes and ears, heat waves bathe your skin, molecules of different chemical compositions float into your nostrils and descend upon your taste buds, and physical objects press against your body. But none of these stimuli can have an impact on your brain unless they are translated into a language it understands: electrical and chemical signals. This is the job of the specialized sensory cells located in the back of your eyes, the caverns of your ears and nose, the spongy surface of your tongue and within your skin, muscle, and other tissues. The process of transforming stimuli into the electrical and chemical signals of neurons is called **transduction,** and it is the first step of sensation. The neural signals are then processed by the central nervous system, resulting in what we consciously experience as *sensations* (*seeing* a person's face or *smelling* smoke).

For sensations to be useful, we must assign meaning to them: "That face belongs to my girlfriend," or "I smell smoke; there must be a fire." And even though we may describe sensation and perception as two distinct events, there is no physical boundary in the brain marking the end of sensation and the beginning of perception. The processing of stimuli into sensations and perceptions happens quickly and automatically.

How do these concepts figure into *psychology,* the scientific study of behavior and mental processes? Sensation and perception are the starting points for every psychological process you can imagine, from learning psychology concepts to creating pinboards on Pinterest. Psychologists continue to discover the many ways that sensation and perception affect our thoughts, emotions, and behaviors. How? Through careful and systematic observation of behavior.

Studying Sensation

Liz began to suspect that her triplets had vision and hearing impairments when she noticed irregularities in their behavior. When Zoe lost her hearing, for example, she became frustrated with one of her favorite toys—a cube that made music when she pushed its buttons. Liz's careful observation of her daughter's behavior prompted her to consult a specialist. Eventually, it became clear that there was a problem with the *sensory* receptors in Zoe's ears, but Liz initially noticed a *behavioral* change.

SENSATION: IT'S VARIABLE Studying sensation means studying human beings, who are complex and variable. Not everyone is born with the same collection of stimulus-detecting equipment. Some people have eyes that see 20/20; others have been wearing glasses since they were toddlers. There is even variation within a given individual. The ability to detect faint stimuli, for instance, depends on your state of mind and body (such as how preoccupied, bored, or stressed you happen to be, or whether you've had your morning cup of coffee).

Such fluctuations in sensing ability can have profound consequences. Think about the enormous responsibility taken on by lifeguards, for example. These men and women are expected to prevent drownings and injuries at beaches and pools, yet they must contend with visual challenges like glare, interpret ambiguous behaviors (*are those joyous yelps or terrified screams?*), and maintain constant attention even when they are hot, bored, or experiencing strong emotions (Lanagan-Leitzel, 2012; Lanagan-Leitzel, Skow, & Moore, 2015). Their attention is divided because their brains are juggling multiple tasks. Research suggests that only around 2% of people might be able to multitask flawlessly, and it appears this may be due, in part,

CONNECTIONS

In **Chapter 2,** we described how neurons work together to shape our experiences. Information moves through the body via electrical and chemical processes, including action potentials traveling along the neuron's axon and neurotransmitters released at the synapse. Here, we see how this activity ultimately is translated into sensation and perception.

CONNECTIONS

As discussed in **Chapter 2,** the brain and the spinal cord make up the central nervous system. The peripheral nervous system includes the somatic and autonomic branches of the nervous system.

Synonyms

bottom-up processing data-based processing

top-down processing knowledge-based processing

sensation The process by which sensory organs in the eyes, ears, nose, mouth, skin, and other tissues receive and detect stimuli.

perception The organization and interpretation of sensory stimuli by the brain.

bottom-up processing Taking basic information about incoming sensory stimuli and processing it for further interpretation.

top-down processing Drawing on past experiences and knowledge to understand and interpret sensory information.

transduction The process of transforming stimuli into neural signals.

to their ability to efficiently handle "cognitive overload" (Medeiros-Ward, Watson, & Strayer, 2015).

The rest of us are limited in our ability to attend to the environment, especially when focusing on more than one demanding task (Medeiros-Ward et al., 2015; Watson & Strayer, 2010). With handheld technology imminently available, the challenge to resist the urge to multitask is growing more and more difficult. In some situations, the safety of ourselves and others might hinge on the ability to resist multitasking. Some experts suggest we approach texting and driving as we have drinking and driving. One company is actually developing a *textalyzer* that would enable law enforcement officials to determine if someone has been texting and driving, just as a *breathalyzer* can detect alcohol (Richtel, 2016, April 27). There's no doubt about it—multitasking while driving is dangerous!

LO 3 Describe and differentiate between absolute thresholds and difference thresholds.

ABSOLUTE THRESHOLDS Our sensory systems are prone to interferences from outside and within, making it challenging for psychologists to develop measures of sensory abilities. Researchers can determine various types of sensory thresholds, which are the lowest levels of stimulation people can detect. Of particular interest to psychologists are **absolute thresholds,** defined as the weakest stimuli that can be detected 50% of the time. The absolute threshold commonly cited for vision, for instance, is the equivalent of being able to see the flame of one candle, in the dark of night, 30 miles away 50% of the time (Galanter, 1962). But, remember, the state of a person's body and mind can influence his ability to sense a faint stimulus: although absolute thresholds have been established for the general population (**FIGURE 3.1;** Galanter, 1962), these thresholds are not necessarily absolute for a particular person over time. Absolute thresholds are important, but there is more to sensation than noting the presence of a stimulus. Sometimes it's critical to detect changes in stimuli.

SENSORY ADAPTATION Have you ever put on deodorant or cologne and wondered if its scent was too strong, but within a few minutes you no longer notice it? Or perhaps you have jumped into an ice-cold swimming pool, and after 30 minutes you are oblivious to the frigid temperature. Our sensory receptors become less sensitive to constant stimuli through a process called **sensory adaptation,** a natural reduction in

FIGURE 3.1
Absolute Thresholds
Absolute thresholds are the weakest stimuli that can be detected 50% of the time. Listed here are absolute thresholds for each of the five senses. Information from Galanter, 1962.

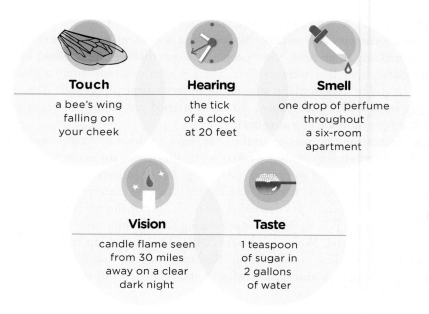

Touch	Hearing	Smell
a bee's wing falling on your cheek	the tick of a clock at 20 feet	one drop of perfume throughout a six-room apartment

Vision	Taste
candle flame seen from 30 miles away on a clear dark night	1 teaspoon of sugar in 2 gallons of water

absolute thresholds The weakest stimuli that can be detected 50% of the time.

sensory adaptation The process through which sensory receptors become less sensitive to constant stimuli.

awareness of unchanging conditions. This allows us to focus instead on changes in our environment—a skill that has proven invaluable for survival.

DIFFERENCE THRESHOLDS Suppose a friend asks you to turn down the volume of your music. How much does the sound level need to drop in order for her to notice? There is a certain *change in volume* that will catch her attention, but what is it, and does that value also apply to increases in sound level? Early psychologists asked similar questions; they wanted to know *how different* sounds and other stimuli must be in order for someone to notice their difference. Through careful experimentation, they established various **difference thresholds,** or the minimum differences between two stimuli noticed 50% of the time.

Let's say you are blindfolded, holding 20 sheets of paper weighing 100 grams, and somebody places a strip of paper on top (the strip weighs 0.5 grams, which means you're adding 0.5% of the weight of the stack of paper). Do you think you'd notice the added weight of that strip? Probably not. But if someone added an entire sheet (which weighs 5 grams, or 5% of the stack's weight), then you would almost definitely notice the change, right? Somewhere in between that strip of paper and the full sheet of paper is the difference threshold.

According to German physiologist Ernst Heinrich Weber (1795–1878), difference thresholds are determined by ratios, not absolute numbers. In fact, the *just noticeable difference* for weight is 2%; that is, the proportion of added weight needed for you to feel the difference 50% of the time. Getting back to our 100-gram stack of paper, we only need to add around half a sheet of paper weighing 2 grams (which is a ratio of 2/100, or a 2% difference) for you to notice someone has added to your burden. If we started with 200 grams and added 2 grams, you would not feel the difference; we would need to add 4 grams for you to really notice the change (4/200 is equivalent to 2/100 or 2%). What if you were holding 500 grams (or 100 pages) of paper? How much would need to be added for you to detect the difference in weight*? **Weber's law** states that *ratios,* not raw number values, determine these difference thresholds, and each sense has its own constant Weber ratio. To determine if there is a difference between two stimuli, at least 50% of the time, the intensity of two lights must differ by 8%, the weight of objects lifted must differ by 2%, the intensity of sounds must differ by 4%, the taste of salt must differ by 8%, and electric shocks must differ by 1% (Poulton, 1967; Teghtsoonian, 1971). You can explore these just noticeable differences together in class.

In Class: Collaborate and Report

Team up with classmates to design an experiment to verify the accuracy of one of the constant ratios listed above. **A)** Choose the constant you will be studying (e.g., the weight of an object). **B)** Decide what stimuli you will use (e.g., sheets of paper). **C)** Write the procedure for conducting your study (e.g., "We will use a scale to measure out the weight of a single piece of paper"). **D)** Provide an example for: two stimuli that would *not* be noticeably different (include the ratio of their difference), two stimuli that would be just noticeably different (include the ratio of their difference), and two stimuli that would be definitely noticeably different (include the ratio of their difference).

Difference thresholds vary slightly from person to person because each of us has a unique sensory toolkit. But do people experience similar thresholds across different cultures? In one study, researchers compared participants' ability to detect changes to pictures (for example, their brightness and color) of flowers, balloons, rabbits, and

---

**Answer:* 2% of 500 grams is 10 grams.

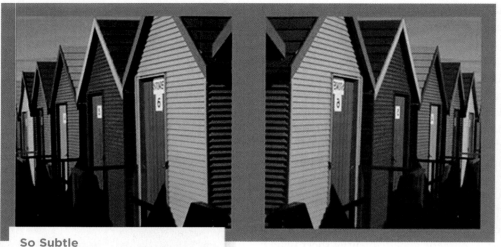

other objects (see photo to the left). The just noticeable difference was the same for the Chinese and Dutch participants "for most images" (Qin, Ge, Yin, Xia, & Heynderickx, 2010, p. 25). The implication is that this aspect of sensation and perception might not be influenced by cultural factors.

So Subtle
Participants from China and the Netherlands were asked to choose the less colorful image. Can you tell there's a difference in brightness? The difference threshold, or just noticeable difference, is the minimum difference between two stimuli noticed 50% of the time.
Republished with permission of Qin, S., Ge, S., Yin, H., Xia, J., & Heynderickx, I. From Displays, 31, 25-34 (2010); permission conveyed through Copyright Clearance Center, Inc.

CONNECTIONS

In **Chapter 1,** we discussed critical thinking. The claim that subliminal advertising can make us buy unwanted items is an example of "misinformation" about human behavior. With critical thinking, we determine if there is scientific evidence to support a claim, including those conveyed in urban myths.

You Are in Control: Subliminal Influences

The absolute and difference thresholds discussed above pertain to stimuli that we can detect at least 50% of the time. What about stimuli below these thresholds? Do *subliminal* stimuli, which are well beneath our absolute thresholds (such as light too dim to see and sounds too faint to hear), have an impact on us? Perhaps you have heard of "subliminal advertising," or stealthy attempts by marketers to woo you into buying products. Here's an example: You're in a theater and suddenly the words "Buy Popcorn!" flash across the screen, but only for a few milliseconds. Your sensory receptors may detect this fleeting stimulus, but it's so brief that you don't notice it. According to urban myth, subliminal marketing can make you run out and buy popcorn, soft drinks, or whatever products happen to be advertised. The truth is that subliminal marketing cannot affect behavior in this way. Subliminal messages cannot manipulate you to purchase something you had not planned on buying, or to quit smoking, for example (Karremans, Stroebe, & Claus, 2006). This is especially true if you have been warned of a subliminal message (Verwijmeren, Karremans, Bernritter, Stroebe, & Wigboldus, 2013). But there may be some personality characteristics involved. After being exposed to subliminal flashes of the words "Red Bull," participants who were classified as sensation seekers (also known as "adrenaline junkies") were more likely than nonsensation seekers to report they would drink Red Bull if they had to stay up late (Bustin, Jones, Hansenne, & Quoidbach, 2015). But remember, you have conscious authority over the purchases and life choices you make.

That being said, the brain does register information presented at an unconscious or nonconscious level. Neuroimaging studies suggest that neural activity is triggered by the "subliminal presentation" of stimuli (Axelrod, Bar, Rees, & Yovel, 2014; Kouider & Dehaene, 2007). These subliminal messages may be able to influence fleeting moods through *priming,* which occurs when memories are awakened by cues in the environment (Chapter 6). Priming occurs without our awareness. One study found that if you expose people to ugly scenes (for example, pictures of dead bodies or buckets of snakes) for several milliseconds (thus "priming" them), they will rate a neutral picture of a woman's face as less likable than when exposed to feel-good subliminal images (such as pictures of kittens and bridal couples) (Krosnick, Betz, Jussim, & Lynn, 1992). Researchers have also found that subliminally exposing people to images of happy faces leads them to rate cartoons as funnier than people subliminally exposed to images of angry faces. Interestingly, this only occurs if participants were able to react with their own facial expressions (some participants were asked to hold a pen in their mouths so they couldn't move their faces; Foroni & Semin, 2011). As you will read throughout the textbook, we are often unaware of how events and people in our environments, experienced initially as sensations and perceptions, influence us in an untold number of ways.

Thus far, we have focused on the stimulus itself. But what about other environmental factors, such as background stimuli competing for the observer's attention, or internal factors like the observer's state of mind—how do these variables affect our sensing capacity?

SIGNAL DETECTION THEORY As previously noted, our ability to detect weak stimuli in the environment is based on many factors, including the intensity of the stimulus, the presence of interfering stimuli, and our psychological state (how alert we are, for example). The theory that draws all these facets together is called **signal detection theory.** It is based on the idea that "noise" from our internal and external environments can interfere with our ability to detect weak signals. Imagine you are participating in an experiment exploring the detection of weak stimuli, and you are told to push a button when you see a light flash. The strength of the flashes will range from clearly noticeable to undetectable. You sometimes press the button, but it turns out no light flash occurred: a false alarm. Other times you press the button and are correct: a hit. How many hits and false alarms you get depends on many internal factors, including how tired you are, when you last ate, your expectations about the importance of success, your motivation, and so on. It also depends on external variables, such as the light level in the room and the dust in the air.

Signal detection theory is useful in a variety of real-world situations. In one study, researchers applied the theory to explain how nurses respond and make decisions about patient safety—how background noises influence their ability to hear patient alarm monitors, for example. One of the issues raised by this study was the impact of "missed signals," that is, medical errors resulting from interference with the nurses' ability to detect and interpret patient signs and symptoms (Despins, Scott-Cawiezell, & Rouder, 2010).

In situations like this, the ability to sense and perceive may have life or death implications. But how exactly do our senses collect and process information? Let's start by exploring the sense that is generally considered most dominant: vision.

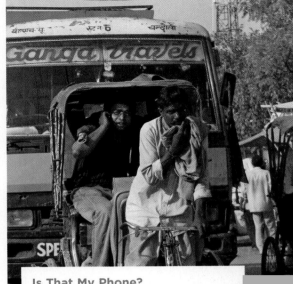

Is That My Phone?
It's difficult to detect the sound of a cell phone ringing in a noisy, chaotic environment. Is that why people are willing to pay for a unique ring tone? Signal detection theory explains how internal factors, such as emotional state, and external factors, like competing sights and sounds (or the intensity of the stimulus), influence our ability to detect weak signals in the environment. Paul Springett C/Alamy.

 show what you know

1. _____ makes the information received by the sensory receptors more meaningful by drawing from experience to organize and interpret sensory data.
   a. Perception
   b. Transduction
   c. Sensation
   d. Signal detection

2. Transduction is the process of transforming stimuli into neural signals. Identify some stimuli in your current surroundings that are being transformed into neural signals you experience as sensations.

3. A woman standing next to you at the supermarket has some very strong-smelling cheese in her basket. You notice the odor immediately, but within a matter of minutes you can barely detect it. This reduced sensitivity to a constant smell results from the process of:
   a. sensation.
   b. transduction.
   c. perception.
   d. sensory adaptation.

4. Weber's law states that ratios, not raw number values, determine _____, the minimum differences between two stimuli noticed 50% of the time.

✓ CHECK YOUR ANSWERS IN APPENDIX C.

Vision

THE EYES OF THE TRIPLETS When Liz became pregnant with triplets, she was busy caring for her firstborn child, 3-year-old Sarah. Her marriage wasn't working. In fact, she and her husband had already begun to contemplate divorce. It could not have been a worse time for Liz to discover she was going to have not one, not two, but three babies.

Many triplets are fraternal, meaning they come from three distinct egg–sperm combinations, each with its own genetic makeup. Liz was pregnant with *identical* triplets, which results when one fertilized egg splits three ways. The babies were born more than 3 months early by emergency cesarean delivery due to grave concerns about Zoe's fetal heartbeat. Each baby weighed less than 2 pounds. Liz was

signal detection theory A theory explaining how internal and external factors influence our ability to detect weak signals in the environment.

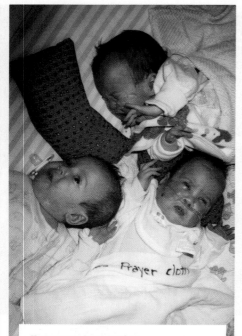

Extreme Preemies
Emma, Zoe, and Sophie were born over 3 months early, long before fetal development had run its course. Premature infants are at risk for serious complications, including respiratory distress, heart irregularities, and vision problems (March of Dimes, 2013). Worldwide Features/Barcroft Media/Landov.

well aware of the health dangers associated with prematurity (breathing problems, brain bleeds, visual impairment, and so on), but she could only hope for the best.

After spending their first months of life in the hospital, hooked to feeding tubes, breathing tubes, and IVs, the triplets finally came home—Sophie first, Emma second, and finally Zoe. But 2 days after Emma arrived home, Liz realized that something was wrong. Emma's eyes weren't "tracking," or following moving objects. Liz took Emma to a specialist, who said she was blind. Soon it became clear that Zoe and Sophie also had vision problems.

What happened to the triplets' eyes? To understand how the girls lost their vision, we must first learn how the eye turns light into electrical and chemical impulses for the brain to interpret. ●

Light and Color

LO 4　Summarize the properties of light and color, and describe the structure and function of the eye.

When you look at a stop sign, would you believe you are sensing light waves bouncing off the stop sign and into your eyes? The eyes do not sense faces, objects, or scenery. They detect light. Remember, if you don't have light, you don't have sight. But what exactly *is* light? Light is an electromagnetic energy wave, composed of fluctuating electric and magnetic fields zooming from place to place at a very fast rate. And when we say "fast," we mean from Atlanta to Los Angeles in a tenth of a second. Electromagnetic energy waves are everywhere all the time, zipping past your head, and bouncing off your nose. As you can see in **FIGURE 3.2,** light that is visible to humans falls along a spectrum, or range, of electromagnetic energy.

WAVELENGTH　The various types of electromagnetic energy can be distinguished by their **wavelength,** which is the distance from one wave hump to the next (like the distance between the crests of waves rolling in the ocean; Figure 3.2). Gamma waves have short wavelengths and are located on the far left of the spectrum. At the opposite extreme (far right of the spectrum) are the long radio waves. The light humans can see falls in the middle of the spectrum, measuring between 400 and 700 nanometers

FIGURE 3.2
Visible Light and the Electromagnetic Spectrum
Only a small part of the electromagnetic spectrum can be detected by the human visual system. Visible light wavelengths range from approximately 400 to 700 nanometers. We use electromagnetic energy for a variety of purposes, from warming our dinners to carrying on digital conversations. Radioactive symbol, Thinkstock/ Getty Images; X-Ray hand, AJ Photo/Science Source; Marines, Lance Cpl. Tucker S. Wolf. U. S. Marine Corps; Hand holding phone, © Rob Bartee/Alamy; Radio tower, TERADAT SANTIVIVUT/Getty Images.

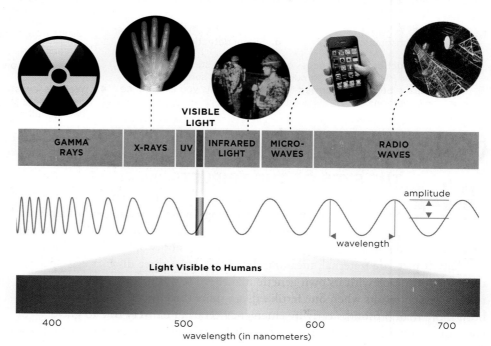

(nm) or billionths of a meter (Brown & Wald, 1964). Wavelength also plays an important role in determining the colors humans and animals can detect.

THE COLORS WE SEE Although dogs can only see the world in blues, yellows, and grays (Coren, 2008, October 20; Kasparson, Badridze, & Maximov, 2013), primates, including humans, can detect a wider spectrum of colors, including reds and oranges. This ability to see reds and oranges may be an adaptation to spot ripe fruits against the green backdrop of tree leaves, and facilitate memorization and recognition of objects (Hofmann & Palczewski, 2015; Melin et al., 2014). Other creatures can see "colors" that we can't. Snakes can detect infrared waves radiating off the bodies of their prey, and birds evaluate potential mates by sensing ultraviolet (UV) waves reflected by their feathers (Bennett, Cuthill, Partridge, & Maier, 1996; Gracheva et al., 2010; Lind & Delhey, 2015).

FEATURES OF COLOR The colors you see result from light reflecting off of objects and reaching your eyes. Every color can be described according to three factors: hue, brightness, and saturation. The first factor, **hue,** is what we commonly refer to as "color" (blue jeans have a blue hue). Hue is determined by the wavelength reflecting off of an object: Violet has the shortest wavelength in the visible spectrum (400 nm), and red has the longest (700 nm). The *brightness* of a color represents a continuum from intense to dim. Brightness depends on wave height, or **amplitude,** the distance from midpoint to peak (or from midpoint to trough; Figure 3.2). Just remember, the taller the height, the brighter the light. **Saturation,** or color purity, is determined by uniformity of wavelength. Saturated colors are made up of same-size wavelengths. Objects we see as pure violet, for instance, are reflecting only 400-nm light waves. We can "pollute" the violet light by mixing it with other wavelengths and the result will be a less saturated, pale lavender.

Most colors in the environment are not pure. The pigments in Kerry Washington's red lipstick probably reflect a mixture of waves in the 600–700 nm range, rather than pure 700-nm red. Combinations of these three basic features—hue, brightness, and saturation—can produce an infinite number of colors; our eyes are just not sensitive enough to tell them all apart. Findings vary, but some researchers estimate that humans can detect approximately 2.3 million colors (Linhares, Pinto, & Nascimento, 2008; Masaoka, Berns, Fairchild, & Moghareh Abed, 2013).

PERCEPTION OF COLORS And now, the 2.3 million-dollar question: Most of us agree that stop signs are red and most taxicabs are yellow, but can we be sure that one person's *perception* of color is identical to another's? Is it possible that your "red" may be someone else's "yellow"? Without getting inside the mind of another person and perceiving the world as he does, this question is very difficult to answer. The colors we perceive do not actually exist in the world around us. Rather, they are the product of (1) the properties of the object and the wavelengths of light it reflects, and (2) the brain's interpretation of that light. When any of these factors change, so too do the colors we see.

I "See" You

This is what you might perceive if you were a snake searching for dinner in the dark. The western diamondback rattlesnake has facial sensors that detect infrared radiation from warm-blooded prey. Scientists have yet to determine exactly how the heat waves are transduced into neural signals, but the process depends on specialized channels in nerve fibers of the snake's face (Gracheva et al., 2010). Julius Lab at UCSF.

Red Hot

Kerry Washington sported intensely red lipstick at the Daily Front Row's 2015 Annual Fashion Los Angeles Awards. Her lipstick may appear to be a pure red, but the color is most likely a blend of various red wavelengths. Most colors we encounter in the real world are a mix of different wavelengths. Jon Kopaloff/FilmMagic/Getty Images.

---

try this ↓

Find a strong flashlight and a bright, saturated object with a yellow hue. Wait until it is dark outside. Now put the object on a table right in front of you and look at it with a dim light shining overhead. Next, shine the flashlight directly onto the yellow object and notice how your perception of the color changes. Finally, turn off all the lights in the room and notice again how your perception of the color changes.

---

wavelength The distance between wave peaks (or troughs).

hue The color of an object, determined by the wavelength of light it reflects.

amplitude The height of a wave; distance from midpoint to peak, or from midpoint to trough.

saturation Color purity.

Your three perceptions of this same yellow object will be very different—not because the object itself has changed, but rather because the light shining upon it (and thus, the light it reflects) has changed. Color perception results from factors outside the body (the type of light in the environment) and the brain's interpretation of that light (neural activity). The eyes take light energy and transform it into neural code for the brain to interpret. The exquisite specificity of this code allows us to distinguish between electric blue and cobalt, lime green and chartreuse. All this is made possible by the eye's remarkable biology.

You Won't Believe Your Eyes

The human eye is nothing short of an engineering marvel (**INFOGRAPHIC 3.1**). When you look in the mirror, you see only a fraction of each ping-pong-sized eyeball; the rest is hidden inside your head. Let's explore this biological wonder, starting from the outside and working our way toward the brain.

THE CORNEA The surface of the eye looks wet and glassy. This clear outer layer over the colored portion of the eye is called the **cornea,** and it has two important jobs: (1) shielding the eye from damage by dust, bacteria, or even a poke, and (2) focusing incoming light waves. About 65–75% of the focusing ability of the eye comes from the cornea, which is why imperfections in its shape can lead to blurred vision (National Eye Institute, n.d.-a).

THE IRIS AND PUPIL Directly behind the cornea is the donut-shaped **iris.** When you say someone has velvety brown eyes, you are really talking about the color of her irises. The black hole in the center of the iris is called the *pupil.* In dim lighting, the muscles of the iris relax, widening the pupil to allow more light inside the eye. In bright sunlight, the iris muscles squeeze, constricting the pupil to limit the amount of light. Interestingly, the pupils also constrict when people look at photographs of the sun (Binda, Pereverzeva, & Murray, 2013).

THE LENS AND ACCOMMODATION Behind the pupil is the lens, a tough, transparent structure that is similar in size and shape to an "M&M's candy" (Mayo Clinic, 2014, October 17). Like the cornea, the lens specializes in focusing incoming light, but it can also change shape in order to adjust to objects near and far, a process called **accommodation.** If you take your eyes off this page and look across the room, faraway objects immediately come into focus because your lens changes shape. As we age, the lens begins to stiffen, impairing our ability to focus up-close, like on the words you are reading right now. You can tell if a person has this condition, called *presbyopia,* when she strains to read a book or holds a restaurant menu at arm's length. Most people develop some degree of presbyopia between 40 and 65 years of age (Mayo Clinic, 2014, October 17).

The Retina

After passing through the cornea, pupil, and lens, light waves travel through the eyeball's jellylike filling and land on the **retina,** a carpet of neurons covering the back wall of the eye. This part of the eye was the source of the triplets' visual impairments. Emma, Zoe, and Sophie all suffered from retinopathy of prematurity (ROP), a condition in which blood vessels in the retina grow incorrectly (Hartnett, 2015). The last 3 months of pregnancy are critical for fetal eye development, when webs of blood vessels rapidly branch from the center of the retina outward, delivering crucial oxygen

Sexy Pupils
When looking at someone she finds attractive, a woman's pupils dilate—especially during the most fertile time of her monthly cycle. For men, there is a strong link between their genital arousal and the dilation of their pupils (Laeng & Falkenberg, 2007; Rieger et al., 2015). Stephanie Zieber/Shutterstock.

cornea The clear, outer layer of the eye that shields it from damage and focuses incoming light waves.

iris The muscle responsible for changing the size of the pupil.

accommodation The process by which the lens changes shape in order to focus on objects near and far.

retina The layer of the eye containing photoreceptor cells, which transduce light energy into neural activity.

Seeing

"Seeing" involves more than simply looking at an object. Vision is a complex process in which light waves entering the eye are directed toward the retina, where they are transduced into messages the brain can understand. Flaws in the clear outer layer of the eye, the cornea, are primarily to blame for so many people (about a third of the American population) needing glasses or contact lenses (National Eye Institute, n.d.-a). LASIK eye surgery, a popular alternative to corrective lenses, uses a laser to reshape the cornea so that it can focus light properly.

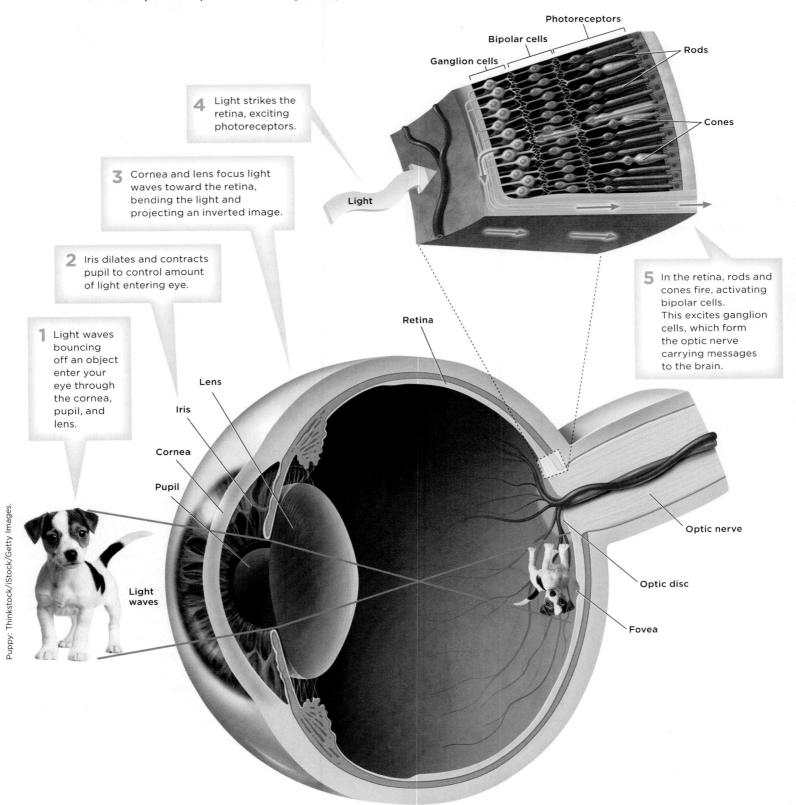

4 Light strikes the retina, exciting photoreceptors.

3 Cornea and lens focus light waves toward the retina, bending the light and projecting an inverted image.

2 Iris dilates and contracts pupil to control amount of light entering eye.

1 Light waves bouncing off an object enter your eye through the cornea, pupil, and lens.

5 In the retina, rods and cones fire, activating bipolar cells. This excites ganglion cells, which form the optic nerve carrying messages to the brain.

Ganglion cells · Bipolar cells · Photoreceptors · Rods · Cones

Light

Retina · Lens · Iris · Cornea · Pupil · Light waves

Optic nerve · Optic disc · Fovea

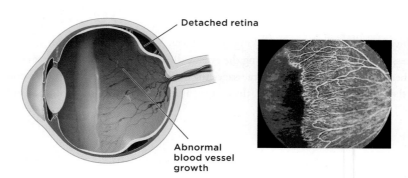

Detached retina

Abnormal
blood vessel
growth

FIGURE 3.3
Retinopathy of Prematurity (ROP)
ROP is a condition characterized by
irregular blood vessel growth in the eye.
If a baby is born before 31 weeks, blood
vessels serving the retina may fail to
develop properly. Scar tissue may also pull
the retina away from its normal position
in the back of the eye (National Eye
Institute, n.d.-b). The triplets all suffered
vision loss from ROP. The photo at right
shows incomplete blood vessel growth
characteristic of the condition. The vessels
in yellow stop before they reach the front
of the eye. Photo: BSIP/Getty Images.

and nutrients to the developing tissue. After the triplets' very early birth, these vessels
began to branch abnormally, eventually pulling the retina from the back of the eye
(**FIGURE 3.3**).

The retina is responsible for the *transduction* of light energy into neural activity;
that is, sensing light and relaying a message to the brain. Without the retina, vision
is impossible.

LO 5 Describe the functions of rods and cones.

CONNECTIONS

In **Chapter 2,** we noted that neurons are
activated in response to sensations. In
the case of vision, sensation begins when
photoreceptors in the retina transduce
light into neural signals. This causes a
chain reaction in neurons of the visual
pathway, which convey the message to
the brain.

PHOTORECEPTORS AND OTHER NEURONS The retina is home to mil-
lions of specialized neurons called **photoreceptors,** which absorb light energy and
turn it into electrical and chemical signals for the brain to process. Two types of
photoreceptors are located in the retina: *rods* and *cones,* which get their names
from their characteristic shapes. **Rods** are extremely sensitive, firing in response
to even a single *photon,* the smallest possible packet of light, although the absolute threshold for people to detect light through their rods is at minimum
50 photons (Hofmann & Palczewski, 2015; Rieke & Baylor, 1998). If rods were all we
had, the world would look something like an old black-and-white movie. **Cones** enable
us to enjoy a visual experience more akin to HDTV (except for those of us with *color
deficiencies,* discussed later). In addition to providing color vision, cones allow us to see
fine details, such as the small print on the back of a gift card.

Rods and cones are just the first step in a complex neural signaling cascade
that ultimately leads to a visual experience in the brain
(see Infographic 3.1). Near the rods and cones are
bipolar cells, another specialized type of neuron,
located approximately in the middle of the
retina. When a rod or cone is stimulated by
light energy, it conveys its signal to nearby
bipolar cells. These, in turn, convey their
signal to *ganglion cells,* yet another type
of neuron, located toward the front of
the retina. Axons of the ganglion cells
bundle together in the **optic nerve,**
which is like an electrical cable (one
extending from each eye) hooking the
retina to the brain. The optic nerve exits
the retina at the *optic disc,* causing a **blind
spot,** since this area lacks rods and cones.
You can find your blind spot by following the
instructions in Try This.

Rods and Cones
You can see why the light-
sensing neurons in the back
of the eye are called rods
(tan) and cones (green).
Rods outnumber cones by
a factor of 20 and are found
everywhere in the retina except
the centrally located fovea.
This is where the color-sensing
cones are concentrated. Steve
Gschmeissner/Science Source.

THE FOVEA The retina in each eye is home to approximately 120 million rods and 6 million cones (Amesbury & Schallhorn, 2003; Luo & da Cruz, 2014). Rods are found everywhere in the retina, except in the optic disc (mentioned earlier) and a tiny central spot called the *fovea.* Cones are packed most densely in the fovea, but are also sprinkled through the rest of the retina. When you need to study something in precise detail (like the tiny serial number on the bottom of a laptop), hold it under a bright light and stare at it straight-on. The cones in the fovea excel at sensing detail and operate best in ample light. If, however, you want to get a look at something in dim light, focus your gaze slightly to its side, stimulating the super-light-sensitive rods outside the fovea.

Dark and Light Adaptation

The eye has an amazing ability to adjust to drastic fluctuations in light levels. This process starts with the pupil, which rapidly shrinks and expands in response to light changes, and then continues with the rods and cones, which need more time to adjust to changes in lighting. When you walk into a dark movie theater, you can barely see an inch in front of your face. After a few minutes, your eyes start to adjust to the dark in a process called **dark adaptation,** which takes about 8 minutes for cones and 30 minutes for rods (Hecht & Mandelbaum, 1938; Klaver, Wolfs, Vingerling, Hoffman, & de Jong, 1998; Wolfe & Ali, 2015). Cones respond more quickly, so they are more useful in the first few minutes of dark adaptation. Then the rods kick into action, allowing you to make out silhouettes of objects and people. Why are these photoreceptors so sluggish in their responses to darkness? To restore their sensitivity to light, rods and cones must undergo a chemical change associated with protein molecules, and this takes time (Caruso, 2007, August 13; Ludel, 1978).

When you leave the dark theater and return to the blinding light of day, the eyes also adjust. With **light adaptation,** the pupil constricts to reduce the amount of light flooding the retina, and the rods and cones become less sensitive to light. Light adaptation occurs relatively quickly, lasting at most 10 minutes (Ludel, 1978).

Is That Oprah Winfrey Over There?

Let's stop for a moment and examine how information flows through the visual pathway (Infographic 3.1). Suppose you are looking at Oprah Winfrey's face. Remember, you're actually seeing the light that her face reflects. Normally, light rays bouncing off Oprah would continue moving along a straight-line path, but they encounter the bulging curvature of the cornea covering your pupil, which bends them. (The light is further bent by the lens, but to a lesser extent.) Rays entering the top of the cornea bend downward and those striking the base bend upward. The result is an inverted, or flip-flopped, projection on your retina. It's like your eye is a movie theater, the retina is its screen, and the feature film being played is *Your World, Turned Upside Down* (Kornheiser, 1976; Ramachandran & Rogers-Ramachandran, 2008; Stratton, 1896, August). The neurons of the retina respond to the stimulus; signals are sent from the photoreceptor cells to the bipolar cells, which then signal the ganglion cells that bundle into the optic nerves.

photoreceptors Specialized cells in the retina that absorb light energy and turn it into electrical and chemical signals for the brain to process.

rods Photoreceptors that enable us to see in dim lighting; not sensitive to color, but useful for night vision.

cones Photoreceptors that enable us to sense color and minute details.

optic nerve The bundle of axons from ganglion cells leading to the visual cortex.

blind spot A hole in the visual field caused by the optic disc (the location where the optic nerve exits the retina).

dark adaptation Ability of the eyes to adjust to dark after exposure to bright light.

light adaptation Ability of the eyes to adjust to light after being in the dark.

CONNECTIONS

In **Chapter 2,** we explained how interneurons of the central nervous system (the brain and spinal cord) receive and process signals from sensory neurons.

All Together It Makes White

When red, blue, and green light wavelengths are combined in equal proportions, they produce white light. This may seem counterintuitive, because most of us have learned that mixing different-colored paints yields brown (not white). The rules of light mixing differ from those of paints and other pigmented substances. ©2009 Richard Megna-Fundamental Photographs.

feature detectors Neurons in the visual cortex specialized in detecting specific features of the visual experience, such as angles, lines, and movements.

trichromatic theory The perception of color is the result of three types of cones, each sensitive to wavelengths in the red, green, and blue spectrums.

afterimage An image that appears to linger in the visual field after its stimulus, or source, is removed.

The optic nerves (one from each eye) intersect at a place in the brain called the *optic chiasm* (see Infographic 4.1 on page 152). From there, information coming from each eye is split, with about half traveling to the same-side thalamus and half going to the opposite-side thalamus. **Interneurons** then shuttle the data to the *visual cortex,* located in the occipital lobes in the back of your head. Neurons in the visual cortex called **feature detectors** specialize in detecting specific features of your visual experience, such as angles, lines, and movements. How these features are pieced together into a unified visual experience (*I see Oprah!*) is complex. Hubel and Wiesel (1979, September) proposed that visual processing begins in the visual cortex, where teams of cells respond to specifically oriented lines (as opposed to just pixel-like spots of light), and then continues in other parts of the cortex, where information from both eyes is integrated. Scientists have now identified at least 30 different areas in the brains of humans and other primates that play a role in visual processing (Ramachandran & Rogers-Ramachandran, 2009).

What Color Do You See?

Although we have discussed various features of color, we have not yet explained how waves of electromagnetic energy result in our perception of colors. How does the brain know red from maroon, green from turquoise, yellow from amber? Two main theories explain human color vision—the *trichromatic theory* and the *opponent-process theory*—and you need to understand both because they address different aspects of the phenomenon.

LO 6 **Compare and contrast the theories of color vision.**

THE TRICHROMATIC THEORY Proposed in the 1800s by an English physician–scientist, Thomas Young (1773–1829), and then expanded upon decades later by Hermann von Helmholtz (1821–1894), a Prussian physicist, the **trichromatic theory** (try-kroh-MAT-ic) suggests that we have three types of cones. Red cones are excited by electromagnetic energy with wavelengths in the red range (about 620–700 nm); green cones fire in response to electromagnetic energy with wavelengths in the green realm (500–575 nm); and blue cones are activated by electromagnetic energy with wavelengths corresponding to blues (about 450–490 nm; Mollon, 1982). The primary colors of light are also red, green, and blue, and when mixed together in equal proportions, they appear as white light (see the photograph to the left).

So how is it that we can detect millions of colors when our cones are only sensitive to red, green, and blue? According to the trichromatic theory, the brain identifies a precise hue by calculating patterns of excitement among the three cone populations. When you look at a yellow banana, for example, both the red and green cones fire, but not the blue ones. The brain interprets this pattern of red and green activation as "yellow." And because white light is actually a mixture of all the wavelengths in the visible spectrum, it excites all three cone types, creating a sensation of "white" in the mind's eye. Thus, the brain makes its color calculations based on the relative activity of the three cone types.

COLOR DEFICIENCY AND COLOR BLINDNESS Loss or damage to one or more of the cone types leads to *color deficiency,* more commonly known as "color blindness." These terms are often used interchangeably, but true color blindness is extremely rare. Sometimes color blindness is accompanied by extreme sensitivity to light and poor vision for detail, both resulting from deficient or missing cones (Kohl, Jägle, & Wissinger, 2013; Tränkner et al., 2004). Most people with color deficiencies have trouble distinguishing between red and green because they are missing the red or green receptors, or have a deficient amount of them, but they can see other colors very well. If you can't see the number shown in the Ishihara color plate at right, then you may have a red–green deficiency (Wong, 2011). This condition affects about 8% of men and 0.4% of women of European ancestry. And although estimates for other groups are variable, some research suggests that about 4–7% of men of Chinese and Japanese ancestry and 6–7% of African American men have difficulty distinguishing red and green (Birch, 2012; Deeb, 2005).

In Class: Collaborate and Report

In 2015 the New York Jets and the Buffalo Bills met to play their regularly scheduled game. The Jets wore uniforms that were completely green, and the Bills wore completely red uniforms. This created confusion for some people watching the game. In your groups, use the trichromatic theory to explain why distinguishing between the teams was difficult for people with red-green color blindness (see the photos below). **A)** Write a definition of the trichromatic theory in your own words. **B)** Summarize your group's explanation. **C)** Describe other situations when people with red-green color blindness might have difficulty.

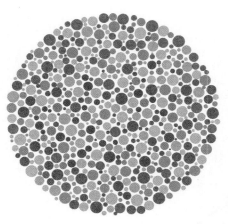

See It?
If you cannot make out the number 45 in this Ishihara color plate, then you might have a red–green color deficiency, the most common variation of "color blindness." Red–green deficiency results from a problem with the red or green cones. Science & Society Picture Library/Getty Images.

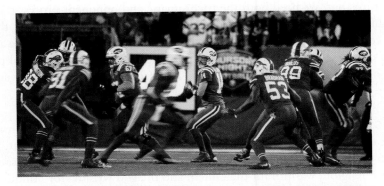

Carlos M. Saavedra/Sports Illustrated.

Ample research backs up the trichromatic theory, but there are some color-related phenomena it cannot explain. A prime example is the *afterimage effect.* An **afterimage** is an *image* that appears to linger in your visual field *after* its stimulus, or source, is gone.

try this ⬇
Fix your eyes on the black cross in the center of the image to the left. After 30 seconds, shift your gaze to the blank white area at the far left. What colors do you see now? Jacquelyn S. Wong/ViewFinder Exis, LLC.

OPPONENT-PROCESS THEORY German physiologist Ewald Hering (1834–1918) realized that the trichromatic theory could not explain the afterimage effect and thus developed the **opponent-process theory** of color vision. Hering proposed that in addition to the color-sensitive cones, a special group of neurons responds to opponent colors—pairs of colors such as red–green and blue–yellow that cannot be perceived simultaneously (there is no such thing as reddish-green or bluish-yellow light). For example, one neuron in an opponent pair fires when you look at red, but is inactive when you see green. Meanwhile, the other neuron gets excited by green but turned off by red. If you spend enough time staring at the red and blue picture in the Try This on the previous page, the neurons excited by these colors become exhausted and stop responding. When you shift your gaze to the white surface (white reflects all colors), the opponent neurons fire in response to the green and yellow, and you end up seeing a green and yellow afterimage. Research has provided strong support for the opponent-process theory, identifying particular types of neurons in a region of the thalamus (DeValois & DeValois, 1975; Jameson & Hurvich, 1989).

As it turns out, we need both the trichromatic and opponent-process theories to clarify different aspects of color vision. Color perception occurs both in the light-sensing cones in the retina and in the opponent cells serving the brain. The ability to perceive color is not based on processing at a single point along the visual pathway, or even one area of the brain (Rentzeperis, Nikolaev, Kiper, & van Leeuwen, 2014; Solomon & Lennie, 2007).

COLORS AND CULTURE Our perceptions of color can be explained by many psychological and sociocultural factors. For example, blue is the most popular "favorite color" in the world, but it carries different meanings for various groups: sanctity in the Jewish religion, warmth for the Dutch, and the god Krishna for Hindus (Akcay, Dalgin, & Bhatnagar, 2011; Sable & Akcay, 2011; Taylor, Clifford, & Franklin, 2013). Thus learning shapes the cultural meanings of color (Sable & Akcay, 2011). If a color is repeatedly presented in a certain context (black clothes at a funeral, pink clothes on a girl baby), mental associations begin to take hold (black is for grieving; pink is for girls). This type of learning may also explain how gender-specific color preferences evolve (Sorokowski, Sorokowska, & Witzel, 2014).

Perception of color may vary significantly across cultures, and even between individuals, but the early stages of sensation are virtually the same for everyone with normal vision. The fact that the complex visual system works so well for so many people is really quite remarkable. Equally intricate is the auditory system. Next we'll discover how hearing works—and how easily it can be dismantled—using the triplets as our example.

show what you know

1. Hue is determined by the _____ of the light reflecting off an object.

2. Cells in the retina that absorb light energy and turn it into electrical and chemical signals are called:
   a. opponent-processing.
   b. photoreceptors.
   c. fovea.
   d. feature detectors.

3. Explain the two major theories of color vision.

4. It's dark in your house, and you are struggling to see what time it is without turning on the light. You notice that if you turn your gaze slightly to the side of your watch, you can make out the large numbers. The ability to see them is due to your:
   a. presbyopia.
   b. optic disk.
   c. cones.
   d. rods.

✓ CHECK YOUR ANSWERS IN APPENDIX C.

Hearing

THE EARS OF THE TRIPLETS Taking care of three blind infants and a preschooler was no easy task, but Liz was strong, stubborn, and determined to see her girls thrive. They were beginning to reach the major developmental milestones of babyhood—walking and talking—when, at 20 months, everything fell apart.

It started with Zoe who out of the blue stopped playing with her favorite toy, the cube that made different sounds when she pushed on its sides. Zoe would push the buttons over and over, then burst into tears. Eventually, Zoe and her sisters stopped responding to Liz's voice. Hearing had been the main portal connecting the triplets to the outside world. It allowed them to communicate their needs to Liz, babble among themselves, and take pleasure in music. But now that door had closed, too.

It was also during this period that the triplets began to act as if they had some kind of stomach illness—refusing to eat, vomiting during car rides, curling up in the fetal position, and banging their heads against the floor. These behaviors did not stem from a simple stomachache, but something much more troubling: vertigo, a dizzying sensation of spinning or whirling.

Both conditions—the deafness and the vertigo—arose from deterioration of the *inner ear,* home to the delicate structures responsible for hearing and balance. The damage was caused by antibiotics the triplets had received in the hospital. The drugs may have saved the girls' lives, but they had a devastating side effect: ototoxicity, or "ear poisoning." ●

Toddling Triplets
Liz sits with her firstborn Sarah (left back), and the triplets (left to right) Sophie, Emma, and Zoe. The triplets were about 12 months old when this photo was taken. Worldwide Features/Barcroft Media/Landov.

Listen, Hear

LO 7 Summarize how sound waves are converted into the sensation of hearing.

The wind howling. A baby crying. Rain pelting the roof of a car. These sounds are perceived so differently, yet they all begin with the same type of stimulus: a sound wave moving through the environment. When we use our sense of hearing, or **audition,** we are detecting sound waves that enter our ears. Sound waves are rhythmic molecular vibrations traveling through air or other materials, like water, metal, or wood.

SOUND WAVES Every sound wave begins with a vibration. That could mean a pulsating loudspeaker, a quivering guitar string, or vocal chords fluttering in your throat. When an object vibrates, it sends a pressure disturbance through the molecules of the surrounding medium (usually air). Imagine a very quiet environment, such as the inside of a parked car, where the air molecules are fairly evenly distributed. Now turn on the radio, and the membrane of the amplified speaker immediately bulges outward, pushing air molecules out of its way. This creates a zone where the particles are tightly packed and the pressure is high; the particles directly in front of the speaker will hit the particles right in front of them, and so on throughout the interior of your car. As the speaker retracts, or pulls back, it gives the air particles ample room to move, creating a zone where particles are spread out and pressure is low. As the speaker rhythmically pushes back and forth, it sends *cycles* of high-pressure waves (with particles "bunched up") and low-pressure waves (with particles "spread out") rippling through the air (Ludel, 1978). It's important to note that molecules are not being transmitted when you speak to a friend across the room, for example; air particles from your mouth do not travel to his ears, only the sound wave does.

Now that we have established what sound waves are—alternating zones of high and low pressure moving through the environment—let's address the immense variation in

opponent-process theory Perception of color derives from a special group of neurons that respond to opponent colors (red-green, blue-yellow).

audition The sense of hearing.

Spine-Chilling Scream
Harry Potter (Daniel Radcliffe) lets out a ghastly scream in the film *Harry Potter and the Order of the Phoenix.* Why is the sound of a scream so terrifying? Unlike normal speech, whose volume remains relatively constant over time, the loudness of a scream rises and falls at a very fast rate. This rapid variation in volume excites the brain's fear pathways—an adaptive response because screams often indicate the presence of danger (Arnal, Flinker, Kleinschmidt, Giraud, & Poeppel, 2015; Williams, 2015, July 16).
Warner Bros./Courtesy Everett Collection.

ANT Photo Library/
Science Source.

Synonyms

loudness volume

pitch The degree to which a sound is high or low, determined by the frequency of its sound wave.

frequency The number of sound waves passing a given point per unit of time; higher frequency is perceived as higher pitch, and lower frequency is perceived as lower pitch.

sound quality. Why are some noises loud and others soft, some shrill like a siren and others deep like a bullfrog? Sounds can be differentiated by three main qualities that we perceive: *loudness, pitch,* and *timbre.*

LOUDNESS Loudness is determined by the amplitude, or height, of a sound wave. A kitten purring generates low-amplitude sound waves; a NASCAR engine generates high-amplitude sound waves. Just remember: The taller the mound, the louder the sound. The intensity of a sound stimulus is measured in decibels (dB), with 0 dB being the absolute threshold for human hearing; normal conversation is around 60 dB. Noises at 140 dB can be instantly detrimental to hearing (Liberman, 2015). But you needn't stand next to a 140-dB jet engine to sustain hearing loss. Prolonged exposure to moderately loud sounds such as gas-powered lawn mowers and music at concerts or clubs can also cause damage. We will discuss how exposure to loud sounds and other events can lead to hearing loss later in this section.

PITCH The **pitch** of a sound describes how high or low it is. An example of a high-pitched sound is a flute at its highest notes; a low-pitched sound is a tuba at its lowest notes. Pitch is based on wave **frequency.** We measure frequency with a unit called the *hertz* (Hz), which indicates the number of wave peaks passing a given point in 1 second. If you are hearing a 200-Hz sound wave, then theoretically 200 waves enter your ear per second. A higher-pitched sound will have a higher frequency of waves; the time between the "bunched up" particles and the "spread out" particles will be less than that for a lower-pitched sound. Humans can detect frequencies ranging from about 20 Hz to 20,000 Hz, but we tend to lose the higher frequencies as we get older. For comparison, bats have an exquisite sense of hearing, and can detect sound frequencies from 2,000 Hz to 110,000 Hz, well beyond the range of human hearing. Beluga whales can sense frequencies from about 100 Hz to 123,000 Hz and mice from 1,000 Hz to 91,000 Hz (Strain, 2003). And just remember, faster peaks mean higher squeaks; waves moving slow make pitch sound low.

When Emma, Zoe, and Sophie began to go deaf, they lost their ability to hear high frequencies first, which means they stopped hearing high-pitched sounds, like female voices. It pains Liz to reminisce about this period because she wonders how her babies felt when it seemed like their mom had stopped talking to them.

TIMBRE How is it possible that two sounds with similar loudness and pitch (Beyoncé and Ariana Grande belting the same note at the same volume) can sound so different to us? The answer to this question lies in their *timbre* (TAM-ber; Patil, Pressnitzer, Shamma, & Elhilali, 2012). Most everyday sounds—people's voices, traffic noises, humming air conditioners—consist of various wave frequencies. A sound typically has one dominant frequency, which we perceive as pitch. Let's say Beyoncé hits a middle C note, which has a frequency of 282 Hz. As she hits that note, her vocal chords also produce softer accompanying frequencies, which may be higher or lower than 282 Hz. These additional frequencies, and the way they fluctuate across time, are referred to as timbre (Patil et al., 2012). Timbre allows us to distinguish the voice of Beyoncé from that of Ariana Grande, or any person, singing the same note at the same volume.

All Ears

We have outlined the basic properties of sound. Now let's learn how the ears transform sound waves into the language of the brain. As you will see, your ears are extraordinarily efficient at what they do—transducing the physical motion of sound waves into the electrical and chemical signals of the nervous system (**INFOGRAPHIC 3.2**).

Can You Hear Me Now?

Side effects of lifesaving drugs given to the triplets as newborns eventually led to deterioration of the inner ear, home of the delicate structures where vibrations are converted to electrical and chemical signals that the brain understands as sound. Without this conversion, sound waves may enter the ear, but we do not "hear." Hearing is a process in which stimuli (sound waves) are mechanically converted to vibrations that are transduced to neural messages. If one part of this complicated system is compromised, hearing loss results.

1 The pinna funnels sound waves into the auditory canal, focusing them toward the eardrum.

2 Vibrations of the eardrum cause hammer to push anvil, which moves stirrup, which presses on oval window, amplifying waves.

3 Pressure on oval window causes fluid in cochlea to vibrate.

4 Vibrating fluid in cochlea bends hair cells on basilar membrane, triggering action potentials in the auditory nerve.

5 Auditory nerve carries signals to auditory cortex in brain, where sounds are given meaning.

Pinna

Auditory canal

Ear drum

Hammer

Anvil

Stirrup

Oval window

Cochlea

To auditory cortex in brain

Hair cells

Basilar membrane

Oval window

Cochlea

INNER EAR

MIDDLE EAR

OUTER EAR

Decibels and Damage

The intensity of a sound stimulus is measured in decibels (dB). The absolute threshold for human hearing—the softest sound a human can hear—is described as 0 dB. Loud noises, such as the 140 dB produced by a jet engine, cause immediate damage leading to hearing loss. Chronic exposure to moderately loud noise, such as traffic or an MP3 player near maximum volume, can also cause damage (Keith, Michaud, & Chiu, 2008).

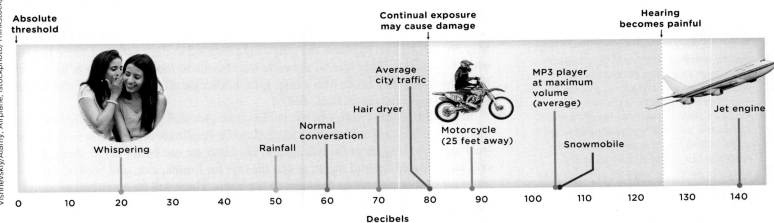

Absolute threshold

Continual exposure may cause damage

Hearing becomes painful

Whispering

Rainfall

Normal conversation

Hair dryer

Average city traffic

Motorcycle (25 feet away)

MP3 player at maximum volume (average)

Snowmobile

Jet engine

0   10   20   30   40   50   60   70   80   90   100   110   120   130   140

Decibels

FROM SOUND WAVE TO BONE MOVEMENTS What exactly happens when a sound wave reaches your ear? First it is ushered inside by the ear's funnel-like structure. Then it sweeps down the auditory canal, a tunnel leading to a delicate membrane called the eardrum, which separates the outer ear from the middle ear. The impact of the sound wave bouncing against the eardrum sets off a chain reaction through the three tiny bones in the middle ear: the hammer, anvil, and stirrup. The chain reaction of these tiny bones moving each other amplifies the sound wave, turning it into a physical motion with great strength. The hammer pushes the anvil; the anvil moves the stirrup; and the stirrup presses on a membrane called the *oval window* leading to the ear's deepest cavern, the inner ear. It is in this cavern that transduction occurs.

FROM BONE MOVEMENT TO MOVING FLUID The primary component of the inner ear is the **cochlea** (KOHK-lee-uh), a snail-shaped structure filled with liquid. The entire length of the cochlea is lined with the *basilar membrane,* which contains about 16,000 hair cells. These hair cells are the receptor cells for sound waves. Recall that the sound waves enter your ear from the outside world, causing the eardrum to vibrate, which sets off a chain reaction in the middle ear bones. When the last bone in this chain (the stirrup) pushes on the oval window, the fluid inside the cochlea vibrates, causing the hair cells to bend. Below the base of the hair cells are dendrites of neurons whose axons form the *auditory nerve* (Ludel, 1978). If a vibration is strong enough in the cochlear fluid, the bending of the hair cells causes the nearby nerve cells to fire. Signals from the auditory nerve pass through various processing hubs in the brain, including the thalamus, and eventually wind up in the auditory cortex, where sounds are given meaning. Let's summarize this process: (1) Sound waves hit the eardrum, (2) the tiny bones in the middle ear begin to vibrate, (3) this causes the fluid in the cochlea to vibrate, (4) the hair cells bend in response, initiating a neural cascade that eventually leads to the sensation of sound.

COCHLEAR IMPLANTS The cochlea is an extremely delicate structure. If the hair cells are damaged or destroyed, they will not regrow like blades of grass (at least in humans and other mammals). So when Emma, Zoe, and Sophie lost their hearing around age 2, there was no magical drug or surgical procedure that could restore their hearing. Hope arrived about a year later, when the triplets were outfitted with cochlear implants, electronic devices that help those who are deaf or hard-of-hearing (**FIGURE 3.4**). These "bionic ears," as they are sometimes called, pick up sound waves from the environment with a microphone and turn them into electrical impulses that stimulate the auditory nerve, much as the cochlea would do were it functioning properly. From there, the auditory nerve transmits electrical signals to the brain, where they are "heard," or interpreted as human voices, hip-hop beats, and dog barks.

Cochlear implants have enabled many people to understand language and appreciate music, but "hearing" with a cochlear implant is not exactly the same as hearing with two ears. Voices may sound computerized or Mickey Mouse–like (Oakley, 2012, May 30). Liz had no idea how the girls would respond to their first experience hearing with the implants. They reacted the same way they do to most everything in life—each in her own way. Zoe broke into a huge grin; Emma sat still, just listening; and Sophie started crying (Hudson & Paul, 2007).

You might be wondering why the triplets were provided with cochlear implants, not *hearing aids*. Hearing aids work by increasing the amplitude of incoming sound waves (making them louder) so the hair cells in the inner ear can better detect them. If hair cells are damaged beyond repair, as was the case for Emma, Zoe, and Sophie, then the inner ear cannot pass along messages to the brain. There will be no sensation of hearing, no matter how much you turn up the volume.

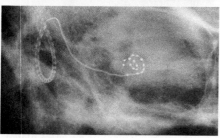

FIGURE 3.4
Cochlear Implants
Cochlear implants enable hearing by circumventing damaged parts of the inner ear. An external microphone gathers sound, which is organized by a speech processor. Internally, an implanted receiver converts this signal into electrical impulses that directly stimulate the auditory nerve. The X-ray on the bottom shows the cochlear implant's electrode array coiling into the cochlea, directly reaching nerve fibers leading to the auditory nerve. Top: Debbie Noda/Modesto Bee/ZUMA Press/Newscom. Bottom: © ISM/Phototake—All rights reserved.

Processing Pitch in the Brain

We know how sound waves are transformed into auditory sensations, but there are many types of sounds. How does the brain know the difference between the yap of a Chihuahua and the deep bark of a Rottweiler, or the whine of a dentist's drill and the rumble of thunder? In other words, how do we distinguish between sound waves of high and low frequencies? There are two complementary theories that explain how the brain processes pitch.

LO 8 Illustrate how we sense different pitches of sound.

PLACE THEORY According to **place theory,** the location of neural activity along the cochlea allows us to sense the different pitches of high-frequency sounds. Hair cells toward the oval-window end of the basilar membrane vibrate more when exposed to higher-frequency sounds. Hair cells toward the opposite end of the basilar membrane vibrate more in response to lower-frequency sounds. The brain determines the pitch of high-frequency sounds by judging where along the basilar membrane neural signals originate. Place theory works well for explaining higher-pitch sounds, but not so well for lower-pitch sounds—specifically those with frequencies below 4,000 Hz. This is because lower-frequency sounds produce vibrations that are more dispersed along the basilar membrane, with less precise locations of movement.

FREQUENCY THEORY To understand how humans perceive lower pitches, we can use the **frequency theory,** which suggests it is not where along the cochlea hair cells are vibrating, but how frequently they are firing (the number of neural impulses per second). The entire basilar membrane vibrates at the same frequency as a sound wave, causing the hair cells to be activated at that frequency, too. The nearby neurons fire at the same rate as the vibrations, sending signals through the auditory nerve at this rate. If the sound wave has a frequency of 200 Hz, then the basilar membrane vibrates at 200 Hz, and the neurons in the auditory nerve fire at this rate as well.

Neurons, however, can only fire so fast, the maximum rate being about 1,000 times per second. How does the frequency theory explain how we hear sounds higher than 1,000 Hz? According to the **volley principle,** neurons can "work" together so that their combined firing exceeds 1,000 times per second. Imagine a hockey team practicing for a tournament. The coach challenges the players to fire shots on the goal at the fastest rate possible. The team members get together and decide to work in small groups, alternating shots on the goal. The first group skates and shoots, and as they skate away and return to the back of the line, the next group takes their shots. Each time a group is finished shooting on the goal, the next group is ready to shoot. Groups of neurons work in a similar way, firing together in *volleys;* as one group finishes firing and is "recovering," the next group fires. The frequency of the combined firing of all neuron groups results in one's perception of pitch. TABLE 3.1 (page 116) draws all of this together.

We have now examined what occurs in a hearing system working at an optimal level. But many of us have auditory functioning that is far from perfect.

I Can't Hear You

In the United States, nearly half of people over age 65 and a quarter of those between 55 and 64 have hearing problems (Mayo Clinic, 2015, September 3). At the onset of hearing loss, high frequencies become hard to hear, making it difficult to understand certain consonant sounds such as the "th" in thumb (American Speech-Language-Hearing Association, 2015). Everyone experiences some degree of hearing loss as they age, primarily resulting from normal wear and tear of the delicate hair

CONNECTIONS

In **Chapter 2,** we described how neurons must recover after they fire so that each neuron can return to its resting potential. It is during this period that they cannot fire, that is, they are "recovering."

cochlea Fluid-filled, snail-shaped organ of the inner ear lined with the basilar membrane.

place theory States that pitch corresponds to the location of the vibrating hair cells along the cochlea.

frequency theory States that pitch is determined by the vibrating frequency of the sound wave, basilar membrane, and associated neural impulses.

volley principle States that the perception of pitches between 400 Hz and 4,000 Hz is made possible by neurons working together to fire in volleys.

TABLE 3.1 HUMAN PERCEPTION OF PITCH

Structure	Frequency Theory	Volley Principle	Place Theory
20–400 Hz	x		
400–4,000 Hz		x	
1,000–4,000 Hz		x	x
4,000–20,000 Hz			x

Human beings can hear sounds ranging in frequency from 20 to 20,000 Hz. The frequency theory explains how we perceive sounds from 20 to 400 Hz; the volley principle from 400 to 4,000 Hz; and the place theory from 4,000 to 20,000 Hz. At times, both place theory and the volley principle can be used to explain perceptions of sounds between 1,000 and 4,000 Hz.

Not Too Loud

Next time you use your earbuds, remember that long-term exposure to loud music can cause hearing damage. A sound needn't be earsplitting to harm your delicate auditory system. Hangon Media Works Private Limited/Alamy.

cells. Damage to the hair cells or the auditory nerve leads to *sensorineural deafness*. In contrast, *conduction hearing impairment* results from damage to the eardrum or the middle-ear bones that transmit sound waves to the cochlea.

But it's not just older adults who ought to be concerned. One large study found that about 20%, or 1 in 5, of American teenagers suffer from some degree of hearing loss (Shargorodsky, Curhan, Curhan, & Eavey, 2010). Worldwide, some 1.1 billion young people are considered to be at risk of damage to their hearing because of their "unsafe listening practices" (World Health Organization [WHO], 2015, p. 1). Exposure to loud sounds, such as music played at a high volume through earbuds, may contribute (Infographic 3.2 on page 113). Keep in mind (and remind your friends) that hearing loss often occurs gradually and goes unnoticed for some time. But the damage is permanent, and its impact on communication and relationships can be life-changing (Portnuff, 2016).

As you know from the triplets' story, certain medications can also harm the fragile structures of the ear, as can ear infections, tumors, and trauma. Some babies (between 1 and 6 of every 1,000) are born with severe to profound hearing loss, with the potential to delay speech, social, and emotional development if it goes undetected (Cunningham & Cox, 2003; Williams, Alam, & Gaffney, 2015). How do those babies adjust to their hearing deficit? How does anyone with a sensory weakness cope? They find ways to compensate, and often that means fine-tuning other sensory systems. Case in point: Zoe and her exquisite sense of smell.

 **show what you know**

1. The pitch of a sound is based on the _____ of its waves.
   a. frequency
   b. timbre
   c. amplitude
   d. purity

2. When a sound wave hits the eardrum, it causes vibrations in the bones of the middle ear, making the fluid in the cochlea vibrate. Hair cells on the basilar membrane bend in response to the motion, causing nerve cells to fire. This process is known as:
   a. the volley principle.
   b. transduction.
   c. the frequency theory.
   d. audition.

3. A researcher studying the location of neural activity in the cochlea finds that hair cells nearest the oval window vibrate more to high-frequency sounds. This supports the _____ theory of pitch perception.

✓ CHECK YOUR ANSWERS IN APPENDIX C.

Smell, Taste, Touch:
The Chemical and Skin Senses

THE SCENT OF A MOTHER One day when Zoe was walking in the park with a friend, Liz decided to pay her an unexpected visit. As soon as her mom came within 15 feet, Zoe turned off the trail and made a beeline toward her with outstretched arms. She knew her mother had arrived because she could smell her, and she could do it while strolling through the breezy outdoors and eating a potent-smelling orange. Zoe was so confident in her sense of smell, explains Liz, "[that] she was willing to walk off the path into the grass to unknown territory, positive that's where I was." Either Zoe's sense of smell is extraordinarily sharp, or she has learned to use it more effectively than the average person. Do you think your nose could accomplish the same? ●

At Play
Zoe rocks on a spring rider at the playground. The triplets spend much of their time outdoors—at the playground, the park, and the swimming pool. Worldwide Features/Barcroft Media/Landov.

Smell: Nosing Around

LO 9 Describe the process of olfaction.

Many people take **olfaction** (ohl-FAK-shun)—the sense of smell—for granted. But such individuals might think twice if they actually understood how losing olfaction would affect their lives. People with the rare condition of *anosmia* are unable to perceive odors. They cannot smell smoke in a burning building or a gas leak from a stove. They cannot tell whether the fish they are about to eat is spoiled. Nor can they savor the complex palates of pesto, curry, chocolate, coffee, or prime rib. Because, without smell, food doesn't taste as good.

A CHEMICAL SENSE Olfaction and taste are called chemical senses because they involve sensing chemicals in the environment. For olfaction, those chemicals are odor molecules dispersed through the air. For taste, they are flavor molecules surfing on waves of saliva. Odor molecules, which are emitted by a variety of sources (for example, spices, fruits, flowers, bacteria, and skin), make their way into the nose by hitchhiking on currents of air flowing into the nostrils or through the mouth. About 3 inches into the nostrils is a patch of tissue called the *olfactory epithelium*. Around the size of a typical postage stamp, the olfactory epithelium is home to millions of olfactory receptor neurons that provide tiny docking sites, or receptors, for odor molecules (much as a lock acts as a docking site for a key; **FIGURE 3.5** on the next page). When enough odor molecules attach to an olfactory receptor neuron, it fires, causing an action potential; this is how *transduction* occurs in the chemical sense of olfaction.

OLFACTION IN THE BRAIN Olfactory receptor neurons project into a part of the brain called the *olfactory bulb,* where they converge in clusters called *glomeruli* (Figure 3.5). From there, signals are passed along to higher brain centers, including the hippocampus, amygdala, and olfactory cortex (Firestein, 2001; Seubert, Freiherr, Djordjevic, & Lundström, 2013). The other sensory systems relay information through the thalamus before it goes to higher brain centers. But the wiring of the olfactory system is unique; olfaction is on a fast track to the limbic system, where emotions like fear and anger are processed.

Humans have about 350 different *types* of odor receptors, and some researchers estimate that we theoretically could distinguish over 1 trillion smells (Bushdid, Magnasco, Vosshall, & Keller, 2014). Each receptor type recognizes several odors, and each odor activates several receptors; a given scent creates a telltale pattern of neural activity

CONNECTIONS

In **Chapter 2,** we introduced the concept of neuroplasticity, which refers to the ability of the brain to heal, grow new connections, and make do with what's available. Here, we suggest that Zoe's heavy reliance on other senses is made possible by the plasticity of her nervous system.

CONNECTIONS

In **Chapter 2,** we discussed the properties that allow neurons to communicate. When enough sending neurons signal a receiving neuron to pass along its message, their combined signal becomes excitatory and the neuron fires. Similarly, if enough odor molecules bind to an olfactory receptor neuron, an action potential occurs.

olfaction The sense of smell.

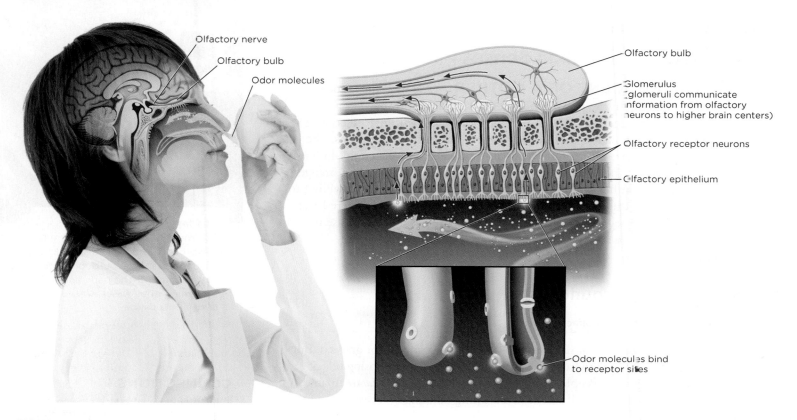

FIGURE 3.5
Olfaction
When enough odor molecules attach to an olfactory receptor neuron, it fires, sending a message to the olfactory bulb in the brain. From there, the signal is sent to higher brain centers. Photo: Collage Photography/Veer.

that the brain recognizes as lemon, garlic, or smelly feet. The types of receptors and the degree to which they are activated enable the brain to identify the odor (Firestein, 2001). Not surprisingly, we are much better at picking up on faint human odor "footprints" (the unique scents of people) than smells coming from inanimate objects (Pazzaglia, 2015).

Scents have a powerful influence on behaviors and mental processes. Minutes after birth, babies use the scent of their mother's breast to guide them toward the nipple, and they quickly learn to discriminate Mom's milk from someone else's. Within two days, they can recognize the odors of their mother's axillary areas (armpits) (Makin & Porter, 1989; Marin, Rapisardi, & Tani, 2015; Porter & Winberg, 1999). For adults, scents can trigger emotions (both positive and negative) and measurable physiological reactions (Kadohisa, 2013). Odors of burning and vomit bring about disgust (Glass, Lingg, & Heuberger, 2015), while the scent of rose oil seems to dampen the body's stress response, perhaps by interfering with activity in the hypothalamic–pituitary–adrenal (HPA) system (Chapter 12; Fukada, Kano, Miyoshi, Komaki, & Watanabe, 2012).

DIDN'T SEE THAT COMING
The Scent of Money

DOES THIS MARKETING STRATEGY SMELL?

Next time you pass by an upscale hotel, walk into the lobby and perk up your nose. You may catch wind of lavender, white tea, or citrus. Hotel chains are among the many commercial establishments now using "scent marketing" to allure customers. Abercrombie & Fitch uses a specialized scent delivery system to ensure its Fierce scent is dispersed evenly throughout the store. A bank in Florida is considering how it could use scented checkbook covers and pens (Smiley, 2014). Sony Style uses hints of orange, vanilla, and cedar; and Las Vegas casinos such as the Mirage have been piping odors through their gambling halls since the 1990s, apparently in an attempt to drive up customer satisfaction and boost revenues (Rosenblum, 2010; Vlahos, 2007, September 9). But what does the science say?

Some research suggests that ambient odors can sway customer perceptions of stores and products. In one study, clothing store shoppers were more satisfied with their experience and spent more money when ambient scents were "gender congruent." Men reacted more positively when the store smelled "masculine" (like rose maroc) as opposed to "feminine" (vanilla), and women reacted more positively when the store smelled feminine (Spangenberg, Sprott, Grohmann, & Tracy, 2006). Another study found that diffusing an orange essence through the waiting room of a dental office reduced patients' anxiety and lightened their moods (Lehrner, Eckersberger, Walla, Pötsch, & Deecke, 2000). Similarly, the use of a lavender scent in a plastic surgeon's waiting room seemed to reduce patients' anxiety before their appointments (Fenko & Loock, 2014). Researchers are still trying to determine the extent to which aromas and other sensory stimuli affect sales revenues, but it's probably safe to say that no aroma, no matter how luscious and enticing, will force you to squander your hard-earned cash. 👁️!

Scent of a Woman
Model Allyssa Bishop is one of the many women who have embraced their colorfully dyed armpit hair. Some people think it's beautiful; others find it gross (Newman, 2015, July 14). Hair or no hair, the armpits are thought to be a potential source of pheromones—chemical signals that can trigger hormonal changes and other effects in members of the same species. JEREMY KORESKI/The New York Times.

The relationship between olfaction and sexual behavior has long intrigued researchers, and evidence suggests that scent plays an important role in romantic attraction (Gangestad & Haselton, 2015; Griskevicius, Haselton, & Ackerman, 2015; Pazzaglia, 2015). Some researchers even suspect that humans, like animals, communicate via odor molecules called *pheromones* (Tan & Goldman, 2015; Wyatt, 2015).

CONTROVERSIES

Sexy Smells?

➡️⬅️ Animals of all different kinds use pheromones to communicate with members of the same species. Rats, for example, release pheromones to mark territory and warn other rats of danger, and female elephants invite males to mate by secreting a pheromone in their urine (Tirindelli, Dibattista, Pifferi, & Menini, 2009).

Humans may unconsciously communicate through pheromones released into the air by glands in the armpits, breasts, lips, and other parts of the body (Wyatt, 2015). Early studies found that women living in close quarters, such as college dormitories, became synchronized in their menstrual cycles (McClintock, 1971), perhaps because they were exchanging signals via pheromones released in their armpit sweat (Stern & McClintock, 1998). More recently, researchers found that smelling female armpit and genital secretions affects male testosterone levels (Cerda-Molina, Hernández-López, de la O, Chavira-Ramírez, & Mondragón-Ceballos, 2013; Miller & Maner, 2010). In one study, college men sniffed T-shirts recently worn by women in different phases of their menstrual cycles. The guys who smelled shirts of women in their most fertile phase (around the time of ovulation) experienced higher levels of testosterone than those who sniffed shirts worn by women in the non-fertile phase, or shirts that had been worn by no one. What's more, the men preferred the odors of ovulating women (Miller & Maner, 2010). These results suggest that something in the women's armpit secretions—perhaps a pheromone—may trigger hormonal changes in men, making them more inclined to pursue sexual relationships with women ripe for reproduction.

THEIR ARMPITS SMELLED ENTICING. . . .

CONNECTIONS

In **Chapter 2,** we described testosterone as a hormone that promotes sexual and aggressive behaviors, among other things. Here, we see how the sensation of smell may be linked to the production of this hormone.

Such findings have sparked great excitement in the media and popular culture. (Perhaps you have heard of "pheromone parties," where people try to find the perfect mates by smelling their sweaty T-shirts.) Yet experts do not agree which chemicals are the best human pheromone candidates, and how those substances should be investigated (Liberles, 2015; Wyatt, 2015). Until researchers start using "rigorous methods already proven successful in pheromone research on other species" (Wyatt, 2015, para. 1), it may be impossible to determine whether human pheromones exist. In the meantime, be wary of advertisements for perfumes and colognes packing sex-magnet "pheromones." There is no evidence that applying these chemicals to your body will make you more attractive than you already are. ➜ ⬅

👥 In Class: Collaborate and Report

The study by Miller and Maner (2010) used the experimental method to explore the effect of pheromones. In your group, identify **A)** the hypothesis, independent variable, dependent variable, and control group in the study. **B)** Use the evolutionary perspective to explain how communication through pheromones might be advantageous to the survival of our species. **C)** Discuss how you may have been influenced by pheromones.

RECEPTOR REPLENISHMENT Have you ever been brought back in time by a smell—the sweet scent of your grandmother's fresh-baked cookies or the musky scent of your father's aftershave? Earlier we described how the wiring of the olfactory system differs from that of other senses. Rather than passing through the thalamus on its way to higher brain areas, smell information is conveyed directly to the limbic system, where emotions and emotional memories are processed. This may be the reason that odor-induced memories are "more emotional, [and] associated with stronger feelings of being brought back in time" (Larsson & Willander, 2009, p. 318). There is another reason smell is special. Olfactory receptor neurons are one of the few types of neurons that regenerate. Once an olfactory receptor neuron is born, it does its job for a minimum of 30 days, then dies and is replaced (Brann & Firestein, 2014; Schiffman, 1997). This process slows with age, impairing odor sensitivity (Doty & Kamath, 2014; Larsson, Finkel, & Pedersen, 2000). If it weren't for this continual replenishment of olfactory neurons, we wouldn't smell much of anything. Olfactory neurons are in direct contact with the environment, so they are constantly under assault by bacteria, dirt, and noxious chemicals. Some toxins—like the fumes and dust at New York City's World Trade Center site after the terrorist attacks in 2001—can even cause long-term damage to the olfactory system. Many workers involved in the clean-up effort following 9/11 may be permanently impaired in their ability to smell (Dalton et al., 2010, May 18).

Taste: Just Eat It

Eating is as much an olfactory experience as it is a taste experience. Just think back to the last time your nose was clogged from a really bad cold. How did your meals taste? When you chew, odors from food float up into your nose, creating a flavor that you perceive as "taste," when it's actually smell. If this mouth–nose connection is blocked, there is no difference between apples and onions, Sprite and Coke, or wine and cooled coffee (Herz, 2007). Don't believe us? Then do the Try This experiment to the left.

LO 10 Discuss the structures involved in taste and describe how they work.

TASTY CHEMICALS If the nose is so crucial for flavor appreciation, then what role does the mouth play? Receptors in the mouth are sensitive to five basic but very important tastes: *sweet, salty, sour, bitter,* and *umami.* You are likely familiar with all these tastes, except perhaps umami, which is a savory taste found in seaweed, aged cheeses,

try this ⬇

Tie on a blindfold, squeeze your nostrils, and ask a friend to hand you a wedge of apple and a wedge of onion, both on toothpicks so that you can't feel their texture. Now bite into both. Without your nose, you probably can't tell the difference (Rosenblum, 2010).

gustation The sense of taste.

protein-rich foods, mushrooms, and monosodium glutamate (MSG; Chandrashekar, Hoon, Ryba, & Zuker, 2006; Singh, Hummel, Gerber, Landis, & Iannilli, 2015). We call the ability to detect these stimuli our sense of taste, or **gustation** (guh-STAY-shun; FIGURE 3.6).

Stick out your tongue, and what do you see in the mirror? All those little bumps are called *papillae,* and they are home to some 5,000 to 10,000 taste buds (Society for Neuroscience, 2012). Jutting from each of these buds are 50 to 100 taste receptor cells, and it is onto these cells that food molecules bind (similar to the lock-and-key mechanism of an odor molecule binding to a receptor in the nose). These taste receptor cells are found in the taste buds in the tongue's papillae, the roof of the mouth, and the lining of the cheeks.

As you bite into a juicy orange and begin to chew, chemicals from the orange (sour acid and sweet sugar) are released into your saliva, where they dissolve and bathe the taste buds throughout your mouth. The chemicals find their way to matching receptors and latch on, sparking action potentials in sensory neurons, another example of *transduction.* Signals are sent through sensory neurons to the thalamus, and then on to higher brain centers for processing.

Receptors for taste are constantly being replenished, but their life span is only about 8 to 12 days (Feng, Huang, & Wang, 2013). If they didn't regenerate, you would be in trouble every time you burned your tongue sipping hot coffee or soup. Even so, by age 20, you have already lost half of the taste receptors you had at birth. And as the years go by, their turnover rate gets slower and slower, making it harder to appreciate the basic taste sensations, although not necessarily reducing eating pleasure or appetite (Arganini & Sinesio, 2015; Feng et al., 2013; Kaneda et al., 2000). Drinking alcohol and smoking worsen the problem by impairing the ability of receptors to receive taste molecules. Losing taste is unfortunate, and it may take away from life's simple pleasures, but it's probably not going to kill you—at least not if you are a modern human. We can't be so sure about our primitive ancestors.

EVOLUTION AND TASTE The ability to taste has been essential to the survival of our species. Tastes push us toward foods we need and away from those that could harm

A Sixth Taste?
Scientists have long suspected there was a sixth taste in addition to the five already identified (sweet, salty, sour, bitter, and umami). Now there is strong evidence that this sixth taste exists: Researchers call it *oleogustus,* or "the unique taste of fat" (Running, Craig, & Mattes, 2015, p. 1). Cheng Ping-hung/agefotostock.

CONNECTIONS

In **Chapter 2,** we explained that sensory neurons receive information from the sensory systems and send it to the brain. With gustation, the sensory neurons send information about taste. Once processed in the brain, information is sent back through motor neurons signaling you to take another bite!

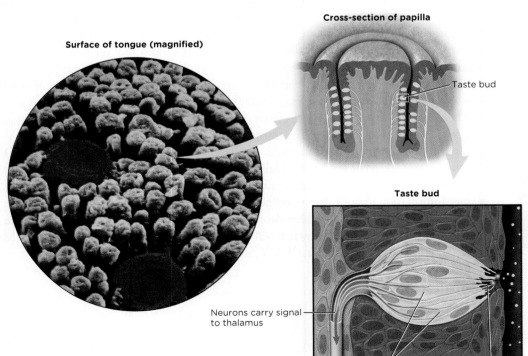

Surface of tongue (magnified)

Cross-section of papilla

Taste bud

Taste bud

Neurons carry signal to thalamus

Taste receptor cells   Receptor sites

FIGURE 3.6
Tasting
Taste buds located in the papillae are made up of receptor cells that communicate signals to the brain when stimulated by chemicals from food and other substances. Photo: Omikron/Science Source.

us. We gravitate toward sweet, calorie-rich foods for their life-sustaining energy—an adaptive trait if you are a primitive human foraging in trees and bushes, not so adaptive if you are a modern human looking for something to eat at the food court in your local shopping mall. We are also drawn to salty foods, which tend to contain valuable minerals, and to umami, which signals the presence of proteins essential for cellular health and growth. Bitter and sour tastes we tend to avoid, on the other hand. This also gives us an evolutionary edge because poisonous plants or rancid foods are often bitter or sour. Some people, known as "supertasters," are extremely sensitive to bitterness and other tastes and thus are "picky eaters," although food preferences are influenced by families and culture (Catanzaro, Chesbro, & Velkey, 2013; Hayes & Keast, 2011; Rupp, 2014, September 30). It is interesting to note that our *absolute threshold* for bitter is lower than the threshold for sweet. Can you see how this is advantageous?

Every person experiences taste in a unique way. You like cilantro; your friend thinks it tastes like bath soap. Taste preferences may begin developing before birth, as flavors consumed by a pregnant woman pass into amniotic fluid and are swallowed by the fetus. For example, babies who were exposed to carrot or garlic flavors in the womb (through their mothers' consumption of carrot juice or garlic pills) seem more tolerant of those flavors in their food and breast milk (Mennella, Coren, Jagnow, & Beauchamp, 2001; Underwood, 2014). It's not clear how these early-established taste preferences impact lifelong eating choices, but understanding how they develop could be useful for encouraging healthy habits in children (Underwood, 2014).

We have made some major headway in this chapter, examining four of the sensory systems: vision, hearing, smell, and taste. Now it is time to get a feel for a fifth sense. Are you ready for tingling, tickling, and titillating touch?

Touch: Feel the Magic

If you were introduced to Zoe, she would probably explore your face for about 20 seconds, and then return to whatever she was doing. Emma would likely spend more time getting to know you. She might give you a hug, put her cheek against yours, and carefully examine your head with her fingers. Emma pores over things, paying close attention to detail. Zoe moves fast and focuses on the goal. At the dinner table, Emma is neat and tidy, and does not like to get food on her hands and face. Zoe loves to dig in and make a mess. These two girls, who have nearly identical genes, experience the world of touch in dramatically different ways. But both rely on touch receptors within the body's main touch organ—the skin.

Take a moment to appreciate your vast *epidermis,* the outer layer of your skin. Weighing around 6 pounds on the average adult, the skin is the body's biggest organ and the barrier that protects our insides from cruel elements of the environment (bacteria, viruses, and physical objects) and distinguishes us from others (fingerprints, birthmarks). It also shields us from the cold, sweats to cool us down, and makes vitamin D (Bikle, 2004; Grigalavicius, Moan, Dahlback, & Juzeniene, 2015). And perhaps most importantly, skin is a data collector. Every moment of the day, receptors in our skin gather information about the environment. Among them are *thermoreceptors* that sense hot or cold, *Pacinian corpuscles* that detect vibrations, and *Meissner's corpuscles* sensitive to the slightest touch, like a snowflake landing on your nose (Bandell, Macpherson, & Patapoutian, 2007; Zimmerman, Bai, & Ginty, 2014; **FIGURE 3.7**).

Pain: It Hurts

Not all touch sensations are as pleasant as the tickle of a snowflake. Touch receptors can also communicate signals that are interpreted as pain. *Nociceptive pain* is caused by heat, cold, chemicals, and pressure. *Nociceptors* that respond to these stimuli are primarily housed in the skin, but they also are found in muscles and internal organs.

Feeling Her World
Zoe approaches eating in a very tactile way, digging in and feeling the food on her skin. While Zoe cannot see or hear, her senses of smell, taste, and touch are extremely fine-tuned.
Worldwide Features/Barcroft Media/Landov.

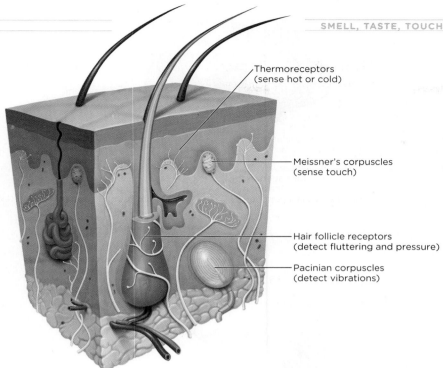

Thermoreceptors
(sense hot or cold)

Meissner's corpuscles
(sense touch)

Hair follicle receptors
(detect fluttering and pressure)

Pacinian corpuscles
(detect vibrations)

FIGURE 3.7
Touch
The sensation of touch begins with
our skin, which houses a variety of
receptors including those shown here.

Speaking of pain, have you ever experienced a brief, piercing headache immediately after gulping down ice cream? What is this brain freeze, and why does it happen?

Brain Freeze Explained

Cold drinks cause a major artery in the skull to dilate.

Ice cream headache is a familiar summertime sensation, but the pain's source has been mysterious until now. A team led by Jorge Serrador of Harvard Medical School produced brain scans of "second-by-second changes" in blood flow while subjects sipped iced water through a straw pressed against the roof of the mouth, which caused the brain's major artery to widen. "Blood flow changes actually preceded the pain" that subjects reported, Serrador says. As the vessel narrowed again, the discomfort ebbed. He suspects that the influx of blood is meant to protect the brain from extreme cold and that increased pressure inside the skull could cause the pain. Serrador presented the results at Experimental Biology 2012 in April in San Diego. **Stephani Sutherland. Reproduced with permission. Copyright © 2012 Scientific American, a division of Nature America, Inc. All rights reserved.**

from the pages of
SCIENTIFIC AMERICAN

TWO PATHWAYS FOR PAIN Pain is unpleasant, but it serves an important purpose —protecting you from harm. The "ouch" that results from the stub of a toe or the prick of a needle tells you to stop what you're doing and tend to your wounds. Thanks to the elaborate system of nerves running up and down our bodies, we are able to experience unpleasant, yet very necessary, sensations of pain. *Fast nerve fibers,* made up of large, myelinated neurons, are responsible for conveying information about pain occurring in the skin and muscles, generally experienced as a stinging feeling in a specific location. If you stub your toe, your first perception is a painful sting where the impact occurred. *Slow nerve fibers,* made up of smaller, unmyelinated neurons, are responsible for conveying information about pain throughout the body. Pain conveyed by the slow nerve fibers is more like a dull ache, not necessarily concentrated in a specific region. The diffuse aching sensation that follows the initial sting of the stubbed toe results from activity in the slow nerve fibers. As the names suggest, **fast nerve fibers** convey information quickly (at a speed of 30–110 meters/second) and slow nerve fibers convey information more slowly (8–40 meters/second; Puce & Carey, 2010). Where do they send this information?

CONNECTIONS

In **Chapter 2,** we explained how a myelin sheath insulates the axon and speeds the transmission of neural messages. The myelin covering the fast nerve fibers allows them to convey pain information more rapidly than the slow, unmyelinated nerve fibers.

FIGURE 3.8

Fast and Slow Pain Pathways

When you stub your toe, two kinds of pain messages can be communicated to your brain. Your first perception of pain may be a sharp, clear feeling where the impact occurred. The message quickly travels through your spinal cord to your brain, signaling arousal and alerting you to react. Slow nerve fibers also travel through your spinal cord to carry messages about the pain that lingers after the initial injury, often generating an emotional response.

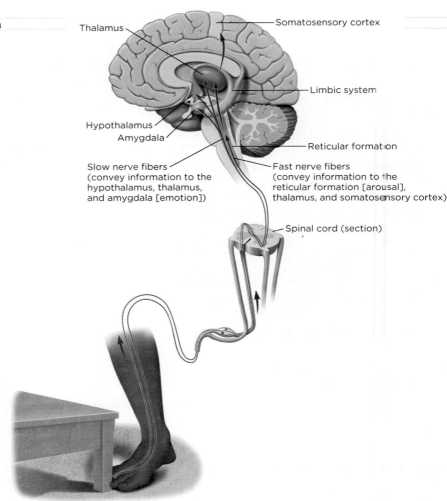

Thalamus — Somatosensory cortex

Limbic system

Hypothalamus
Amygdala

Reticular formation

Slow nerve fibers
(convey information to the
hypothalamus, thalamus,
and amygdala [emotion])

Fast nerve fibers
(convey information to the
reticular formation [arousal],
thalamus, and somatosensory cortex)

Spinal cord (section)

CONNECTIONS

In **Chapter 2,** we discussed the pain reflex, which occurs when we automatically respond to painful stimuli before becoming conscious of it. Here, we describe the process by which pain is brought into our conscious awareness.

gate-control theory Suggests that the perception of pain will either increase or decrease through the interaction of biopsychosocial factors; signals are sent to open or close "gates" that control the neurological pathways for pain.

The axons of these fast and slow sensory nerve fibers band together as nerves on their way to the spinal cord and up to the brain (**FIGURE 3.8**). The bundled fast nerve fibers make their way to the reticular formation in the brainstem, alerting it that something important has happened. The information then goes to the thalamus and on to the somatosensory cortex, where sensory information from the skin is processed further (for example, indicating where it hurts most). The bundled slow nerve fibers start out in the same direction, toward the brain, with processing occurring in the brainstem, hypothalamus, thalamus, and limbic system. In the midbrain and amygdala, for example, emotional reactions to the pain are processed (Gatchel, Peng, Peters, Fuchs, & Turk, 2007). As with other neurons, the transmission of information, in this case about pain, occurs through electrical and chemical activities. *Substance P* and glutamate are two important neurotransmitters that work together to increase the firing of the pain fibers at the injury location.

Understanding the mechanisms of pain at the neural level is important, but biology alone cannot explain how we perceive pain and why people experience it so differently. How can the same flu shot cause great pain in one person but mere discomfort in another? And why does one person's sensitivity to pain sometimes fluctuate over time?

LO 11 Explain how the biopsychosocial perspective helps us understand pain.

As with most complex topics in psychology, pain is best understood using a multilevel method, such as the biopsychosocial perspective. Chronic pain, for example, can be explained by biological factors (the neurological pathways involved), psychological factors (distress, cognition), and social factors (immediate environment, relationships; Gatchel et al., 2007). Prior experiences, environmental factors, and cultural expectations influence how the pain is processed (Gatchell, Haggard, Thomas, & Howard, 2013; Gatchell & Maddrey, 2004).

Researchers studying pain once searched for a direct path from pain receptors to specific locations in the brain, but this simple relationship does not exist (Melzack, 2008). Instead, there is a complex interaction between neurological pathways and psychological and social factors.

GATE CONTROL The most influential theory of pain perception is the **gate-control theory,** which proposes that *gates* are involved in the shuttling of information between the brain and the rest of the body. According to gate-control theory, a person's perception of pain can increase or decrease depending on how the brain interprets pain signals, and this depends on the interaction of a variety of biopsychosocial factors (Melzack & Wall, 1965). After receiving and then interpreting pain information, the brain sends a signal back down through the spinal cord, instructing the "gates" in the neurological pain pathways to open or close. Depending on the situation and psychological and social factors, the gates may open to increase the experience of pain, or close to decrease it. In situations where it's important to keep going in spite of an injury (athletes in competitions, soldiers in danger), the gates might be instructed to close. But when feeling intense pain has value (during an illness, when your body needs to rest), the gates may be instructed to remain open.

Signals to shut the gates do not always come from the brain (Melzack, 1993, 2008). The pain receptors in the body can also send messages to open and close the neurological gates from the bottom up, depending on which type of fiber is active. If the small unmyelinated fibers (slow) are active, the gates are more likely to open, sending the pain message up the spinal cord to the brain. If the large myelinated fibers (fast) are active, the gates are more likely to close, inhibiting pain messages from being passed on. This information may be useful if you stub your toe. To ease the pain, try rubbing the injured area, which stimulates the pressure receptors of the large fibers. This activity closes the gates, interfering with the pain message that would otherwise be sent to the brain.

It is clear that everyone experiences pain in a unique way. But are there factors that predispose a person to be more or less sensitive to pain?

THE PSYCHOLOGY OF PAIN Pain sensitivity can ebb and flow for an individual, with psychological factors exerting a powerful effect (Gatchel et al., 2007; Gatchel, Haggard, Thomas, & Howard, 2013; Raichle, Hanley, Jensen, & Cardenas, 2007). Negative feelings such as fear and anxiety can amplify pain, whereas laughter and distraction can soften it, by redirecting your attention. Certain types of stressors (for example, running in a marathon, or giving birth) trigger the release of endorphins. Endorphins reduce pain by blocking the transmission of pain signals to the brain and spinal cord,

CONNECTIONS

In **Chapter 2,** we reported that endorphins are naturally produced opioids that regulate the secretion of other neurotransmitters.

Escape the Pain

The last thing you want to look at while undergoing an unpleasant or painful medical procedure is the ceiling tiles in your hospital room. Being immersed in a virtual winter scene, complete with snowmen and penguins, can help take one's mind off the pain (Li, Montaño, Chen, & Gold, 2011). Army Sergeant Oscar Liberato (left) gets lost in the virtual reality video game SnowWorld (right) as he undergoes a painful procedure. Left: Steve Elliot, U. S. Army Photo; Right: Hunter Hoffman.

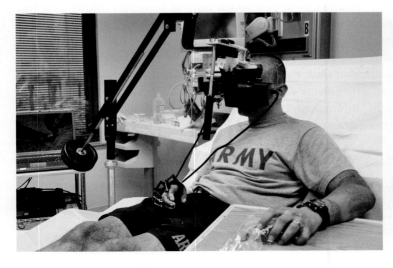

possibly through the inhibition of substance P, a neurotransmitter in the spinal cord and brain (Rosenkranz, 2007).

As you can see, pain is a complex psychological phenomenon, dependent on many factors beyond the initial stimulus—so complex that a stimulus may not even be necessary. Can you imagine feeling a piercing burn or a stabbing cramp in a leg that you don't even have?

PHANTOM LIMB PAIN   Sometimes people who have had an arm or leg amputated feel like they are experiencing intense pain in the limb they have lost. Phantom limb pain occurs in 50–80% of amputees, who may report burning, tingling, intense pain, cramping, and other sensations that seem to come from the missing limb (Ramachandran & Brang, 2009; Ramchandran & Hauser, 2010; Rosenblum, 2010). Researchers are still trying to determine what causes phantom limb pain, but they have proposed a variety of plausible mechanisms, ranging from changes in the structure of neurons to reorganization of the brain in relation to sensations felt in different locations of the body (Flor, Nikolajsen, & Jensen, 2006). When the brain doesn't receive normal signals from the limb, conflicting messages are sent to the brain from nerve cells and these messages seem to be interpreted as pain, although the link between reorganization and pain has not been definitively established (Makin, Scholz, Slater, Johansen-Berg, & Tracey, 2015).

Kinesthesia: Your Body in Space

LO 12   Illustrate how we sense the position and movement of our bodies.

You may have thought "touch" was the fifth and final sense, but there is more to sensation and perception than the traditional five categories. Closely related to touch is the sense of **kinesthesia** (kin-ehs-THEE-zhuh), which provides feedback about body position and movement. Kinesthesia endows us with the coordination we need to walk gracefully, dance the Cupid Shuffle, and put on our clothes without looking in the mirror. This knowledge of body location and orientation is made possible by specialized nerve endings called **proprioceptors** (PRO-pree-oh-sep-turz), which are primarily located in the muscles and joints. Proprioceptors monitor changes in the position of body parts and the tension in muscles. When proprioception is impaired, our ability to perform physical tasks like holding a book or opening a door is compromised.

You may recall from earlier in the chapter that Emma, Zoe, and Sophie began to curl up in the fetal position and vomit while riding in the car during the same period that they lost their hearing. This was because they were losing their **vestibular sense** (veh-STIB-u-ler), which helps the body maintain balance as it deals with the effects of gravity, movement, and position. Astronauts often become nauseated during their first days in space because their vestibular systems are confused. The vestibular system comprises fluid-filled organs in the inner ear: the *semicircular canals* and the nearby *vestibular sacs*. When the head tilts, fluid moves the hairlike receptors in these structures, causing neurons to fire (transduction once again), initiating a signal that travels to the cerebellum. Motion sickness, which many people experience on boats and roller coasters, can be caused by conflicting information coming from the eyes and vestibular system. This explanation derives from *sensory conflict theory* (Lackner, 2014; Johnson, 2005).

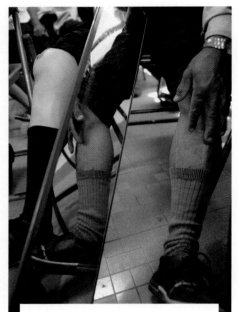

Mirror Therapy
A person suffering from phantom limb pain undergoes mirror therapy. The reflection of a leg in the mirror seems to take on the identity of the one that is missing, which may help the patient resolve his pain. Research suggests that mirror therapy can reduce phantom limb pain in some people, perhaps because it triggers changes in the brain (Foell, Bekrater-Bodman, Diers, & Flor, 2014). TANG CHHIN SOTHY/AFP/ Getty Images.

Walk the Wire
Without his sense of kinesthesia, stuntman Nik Wallenda never would have crossed the Niagara Falls on an 1,800-foot tightrope. Kinesthesia enables us to know our body position and movement.
AP Photo/The Canadian Press, Frank Gunn.

 In Class: Collaborate and Report

Before moving on to the topic of perception, take a moment to appreciate the sensory systems that allow you to know and adapt to the surrounding world. In your group, discuss **A)** how you would function without vision, hearing, smell, taste, and touch, and **B)** what steps you can take to preserve them (**TABLE 3.2**).

TABLE 3.2 PROTECTING YOUR SENSES

Sense	Simple Steps to Guard Against Damage
Vision	Don't smoke. Wear sunglasses and a hat in the sun. Both smoking and sun exposure heighten your risk of developing cataracts and other eye diseases. Put on protective eye gear when doing work or playing sports that could endanger your eyes (mowing the lawn or playing baseball, for example); 90% of eye injuries can be avoided by wearing the right eye gear (American Academy of Ophthalmology, 2014a, b, & c).
Hearing	Listen to iPods and other media players at or below half volume. Wear earplugs or earmuffs when using leaf-blowers, power tools, and other loud devices (American Speech-Language-Hearing Association, 2015). If the sound level seems too high at your workplace, talk to your employer; you are legally entitled to a working environment that is safe for your ears (Occupational Safety & Health Administration, n.d.).
Smell	Two of the leading causes of olfactory loss are head trauma and upper respiratory infections like the common cold and sinus infections (Keller & Malaspina, 2013; Temmel et al., 2002). Avoid head injuries by buckling your seatbelt, wearing a bike helmet, and using protective headgear for contact sports. Minimize your exposure to respiratory viruses with regular hand washing.
Taste	Don't smoke. Nicotine may change the structure and function of the tongue's papillae, which could explain why most smokers have decreased sensitivity to taste (Pavlos et al., 2009). Smoking also impairs olfaction (Katotomichelakis et al., 2007), and therefore dampens the appreciation of flavors.
Touch	Touch receptors are located in the skin and throughout the body, so protecting your sense of touch means taking good care of your body in general. Spinal cord or brain injuries can lead to widespread loss of sensation, so take commonsense precautions like buckling your seatbelt and wearing protective headgear for biking, football, construction work, and so on.

Here are just a few tips for protecting your senses. These measures should be considered in addition to regular medical checkups, such as annual eye exams.

 show what you know

1. The chemical sense called _____ provides the sensation of smell.
2. Chemicals from food are released in saliva, where they dissolve and bathe the taste buds. The chemicals find matching receptors and latch on, sparking action potentials. This is an example of:
   a. olfaction.
   b. transduction.
   c. sensory adaptation.
   d. thermoreceptors.
3. List five things you are currently doing that involve the use of kinesthesia.
4. Maya notices that her severe back pain seems to diminish when friends visit and she is laughing and enjoying their company. This illustrates _____, which suggests a variety of biopsychosocial factors can interact to amplify or diminish pain perception.
   a. the theory of evolution
   b. an absolute threshold
   c. the gate-control theory
   d. proprioception

✓ CHECK YOUR ANSWERS IN APPENDIX C.

Perception

We have learned how the sensory systems absorb information and transform it into the electrical and chemical language of neurons. Now let's look more closely at the next step: *perception,* which draws from experience to organize and interpret sensory information, turning sensory data into something meaningful.

To illustrate the importance of perception, let's turn our attention to the color red. You "see" red when your visual system takes light waves in the red range (with wavelengths approximately 700 nm) and transduces the energy into electrical and chemical messages that eventually reach the brain. But "seeing" red is just the beginning of the visual experience. What does red mean to us?

kinesthesia Sensory system that conveys information about body position and movement.

proprioceptors Specialized nerve endings primarily located in the muscles and joints that provide information about body location and orientation.

vestibular sense The sense of balance and equilibrium.

THINK IT THROUGH
Red and Hot Go Hand-in-Hand

Would you believe that athletes wearing red uniforms are more likely to win competitions than those dressed in blue and other colors (Attrill, Gresty, Hill, & Barton, 2008; Hill & Barton, 2005)? Wearing red may intimidate rivals, who tend to perceive red competitors as more dominant and threatening; likewise, players dressed in red may feel an increased sense of their own "relative dominance and threat." These responses may have an evolutionary basis, as red is associated with aggression and dominance in other primate species (Feltman & Elliot, 2011). Red seems to have a similar influence in non-athletic competitions. In an online poker game, for instance, players competing against an opponent with red chips (as opposed to blue or white) are more likely to perceive him as intimidating and give up (Ten Velden, Baas, Shalvi, Preenen, & De Dreu, 2012). Similarly, people taking cognitive tests—even those in China, where red is associated with luck—seem to perform at a lower level when exposed to red stimuli, such as red-colored words (Shi, Zhang, & Jiang, 2014).

> **THE RED TEAM WAS INTIMIDATING....**

While red may cause people to back down in competitive situations, it seems to "activate approach behavior" in romantic settings, at least among men (Elliot & Niesta, 2008; Gnambs, Appel, & Oeberst, 2015, para. 5; Guéguen, 2012). Men are more likely to approach a woman at a bar if she is wearing red lipstick (as opposed to pink, brown, or no lipstick at all). They also tend to leave bigger tips for waitresses wearing red T-shirts (Guéguen, 2012; Guéguen & Jacob; 2012). Apparently, women wearing red are perceived as more "sexually receptive," or available for mating, which tends to encourage male attention and make other women feel threatened (Pazda, Elliot, & Greitemeyer, 2012; Pazda, Prokop, & Elliot, 2014). Now that you've read this, in what situations would you want to wear red? And when would you avoid it?

As you can see, there is more to seeing red than detecting wavelengths of light. The signals that begin in the eye eventually reach the brain, where memories, thoughts, and emotions shape our perceptual experience. And perceptions are rife with bias and, often, inaccuracies. Perhaps the most important lesson you will learn in this section is that *perception is far from foolproof.* We don't see, hear, smell, taste, or feel the world exactly as it is, but as our brains judge it to be.

Illusions: Did You See That?

What you see is not always what you get. Consider this experiment: Researchers asked a group of undergraduates studying *oenology* (the study of wine) to sample two beverages. One was a white wine, and the other was the exact same white wine—colored red with flavorless dye. When it came time to evaluate the aromas, the students used the standard white-wine adjectives (for example, honey and apple) to describe the white wine, and this came as no surprise. When asked to describe the "red wine," which was really the same white wine, the tasters used the standard red-wine adjectives (for example, raspberry and peppery; Morrot, Brochet, & Dubourdieu, 2001). It appeared as if they had been tricked by their eyes! What they *saw* was red wine, so what they *perceived* were red wine aromas, even though they did not actually smell red wine aromas. *Perception* is essential to our functioning, but as the wine-tasting example illustrates, it is sometimes misleading.

Illusions reveal distortions in perceptual processes. An **illusion** is a perception that is incongruent with actual sensory data, conveying an inaccurate representation of reality (INFOGRAPHIC 3.3). When perception is working "incorrectly," we can examine top-down processing, which draws upon past experience to make sense of incoming information (Carbon, 2014). If a clock stops ticking, you can open it up

Is Red a Winning Color?
Manchester United soccer players embrace in celebration after a goal. Their red jerseys may seem inconsequential, but some research suggests otherwise. Researchers who analyzed decades of performance data from teams in the English Football League concluded that red-jersey teams may have an edge: "Across all league divisions, red teams had the best home record, with significant differences in both percentage of maximum points achieved and mean position in the home league table" (Attrill, Gresty, Hill, & Barton, 2008, p. 577). Laurence Griffiths/Getty Images.

illusion A perception that is inconsistent with sensory data.

Perceptual Illusions

What we see, hear, taste, touch, smell, and feel may seem very real, but perceptions are not always accurate representations of reality. The brain's perceptual systems are prone to errors and distortions. Studying illusions, like those shown here, we can detect and better understand the brain's misinterpretations of visual input.

Moon illusion

Have you ever noticed that the moon can appear much larger when it's on the horizon versus high in the sky? Don't let perceptual errors trump logic: you know the moon does not change size! Researchers have yet to agree upon a definitive explanation for this illusion, but many suspect it has something to do with the surrounding environment (Weidner et al., 2014). Seeing the moon along with trees and other objects at different distances may influence our perception of the moon's size.

Ponzo illusion

Which of the two red bars is longer? Neither! They are identical. When you see two lines converging in the distance, your brain perceives them as getting farther away. Line A appears farther away. It seems longer because the images of the two lines projected onto the retina are the same size, but we interpret the farther line as being bigger. The Ponzo illusion demonstrates how we judge an object's size based on its context.

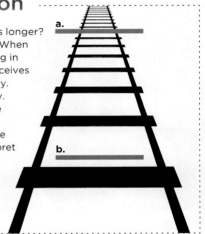

Ames Room illusion

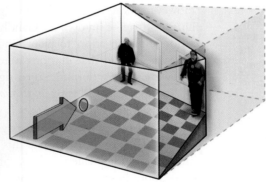

Would you believe that the two people in this room (left) are approximately the same height? The woman on the right appears about twice as big, because the room isn't rectangular! The Ames room is actually trapezoidal (see diagram on the right), but, as the image on the left shows, this is not apparent when it is viewed through a peephole with one eye.

the Shepard Tables illusion

Look carefully at these two tables. Is one longer than the other? If you compare their measurements with your fingers or a piece of paper, you will see that both the length and width are identical.

The brain sees table (a) and thinks the back edge is farther away than table (b), and thus table (a) appears narrower and longer than table (b).

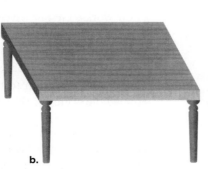

FIGURE 3.9
The Müller–Lyer Illusion
Which line looks longer? All are, in fact, the same length. Visual depth cues cause you to perceive that (b) and (d) are longer because they appear farther away.

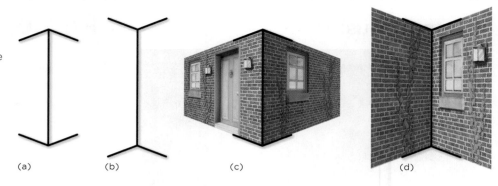

(a)   (b)   (c)   (d)

LOL :-)
When your friend texts you a smiley face, bottom-up processing enables you to see two dots, a hyphen, and a parenthesis. But how does your brain understand the collective meaning of these symbols? Through top-down processing, you draw on past experience to make sense of the new information presented to you. Hero Images/Getty Images.

See It Move
The golf club and golf ball seem to be moving because their images appear in rapid succession. Stroboscopic motion is an example of a visual illusion. Vandystadt/Michael Hans/Science Source.

gestalt The natural tendency for the brain to organize stimuli into a whole, rather than perceiving the parts and pieces.

to see what's wrong and understand how it works. Illusions serve a similar purpose. Let's examine one.

Look at the Müller–Lyer illusion in **FIGURE 3.9.** Lines (b) and (d) appear to be longer, but in fact all four lines (a–d) are equal in length. Why does this illusion occur? Our experiences looking at buildings tell us that the corner presented in line (c) is nearer because it is jutting toward us. The corner presented in line (d) seems to be farther away because it is jutting away. Two objects that are the same size but different distances from the eye will not project identical images on the retina; the farther object will project a smaller image. People living in "carpentered worlds" (that is, surrounded by structures constructed with corners, angles, and straight lines, as opposed to living in more "traditional" settings) are more likely to be tricked by this illusion because of their experience seeing manufactured structures. People in more traditional settings, without all the hard edges and straight lines, are less likely to fall prey to such an illusion (Segall, Campbell, & Herskovits, 1968). However, more recent research suggests that the "processing mechanisms" involved in illusions may be hardwired (Gandhi, Kalia, Ganesh, & Sinha, 2015). In what started as a humanitarian effort to help blind children in India, neuroscientist Pawan Sinha and colleagues found that illusions were perceived by children and adolescents immediately following surgery to restore their sight (Chatterjee, 2015).

Another visual illusion is *stroboscopic motion*, the appearance of motion produced when a sequence of still images is shown in rapid succession. (Think of drawing stick figures on the edges of book pages and then flipping the pages to see your figure "move.") The brain interprets this as movement. Even infants appear to perceive this kind of motion (Valenza, Leo, Gava, & Simion, 2006). Although illusions provide clues about how perception works, they cannot explain everything. Let's take a look at principles of perceptual organization, which provide universal guidelines on how we perceive our surroundings.

Perceptual Organization

LO 13 Identify the principles of perceptual organization.

Many turn to the Gestalt (guh-SHTAHLT) psychologists to understand how perception works. Gestalt psychologists, who were active in Germany in the late 1800s and early 1900s, became interested in perception after observing illusions of motion. They wondered how stationary objects could be perceived as moving and thus attempted to explain how the human mind organizes stimuli in the environment. Observing the tendency for perception to be organized and complete, Gestalt psychologists realized that the whole is greater than the sum of its parts. As a result, they concluded that the brain naturally organizes stimuli in their entirety rather than perceiving the parts and pieces. In other words, "the whole is entirely different from a mere sum; it is prior to its parts" (Wertheimer, 2014, p. 131). **Gestalt** means "whole" or "form" in German. The Gestalt psychologists, and others who followed, studied the principles that explain how the brain perceives objects in the environment as wholes or groups (**INFOGRAPHIC 3.4**).

Gestalt Organizing Principles: The Whole is Greater

The Gestalt psychologists identified principles that explain how the brain naturally organizes sensory information into meaningful wholes rather than distinct parts and pieces. These principles help you navigate the world by allowing you to see, for example, that the path you are walking on continues on the other side of an intersection. Gestalt principles also help you make sense of the information presented in your textbooks. Let's look at how this works.

figure-ground

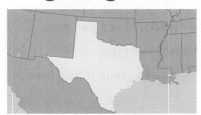

We tend to perceive visual stimuli as figures existing on a background. On this map, one area becomes the focus, while the rest functions as background context.

Some stimuli, such as this classic figure ground vase, are *reversible figures*. You see something different depending on whether you focus on the yellow or the black portion.

LAW OF proximity

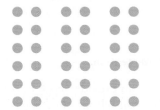

We tend to perceive objects that are near each other as a unit. This set of dots is perceived as three groups rather than six separate columns or 36 individual dots.

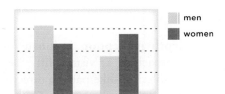

men
women

Proximity helps us read graphs like this one. We understand that bars close together should be compared.

LAW OF similarity

We see objects as a group if they share features such as color or shape. In this example, we perceive eight vertical columns rather than four rows of alternating squares and dots.

Canada
U.S.
Mexico

0   5   10   15   20   25

Similarity helps us read color-coded charts and graphs. We understand the graph above as having horizontal bars because we naturally group the similarly colored icons.

LAW OF connectedness

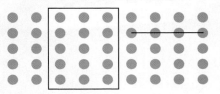

We tend to see objects as a group if there is something that connects them. In this group of dots, the ones enclosed in or connected by lines appear related even though all dots are the same.

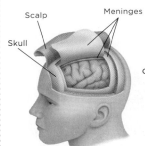

Scalp
Meninges
Skull

In a textbook figure, connectedness helps us understand what is being labeled.

LAW OF closure

We tend to fill in incomplete parts of a line or figure. In this example, we perceive a circle even when the line is broken.

Closure allows us to read letters and images that are interrupted. We can read this letter even though it is made up of unconnected lines.

LAW OF continuity

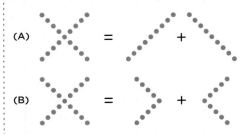

(A)
(B)

We perceive groups where objects appear to be going in the same direction. In this example, we perceive the figure as made up of two continuous lines that intersect (A) rather than two angles that are brought together (B).

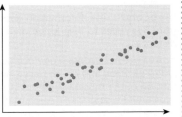

Continuity helps us read graphs like this scatterplot, where we perceive the overall pattern.

One central idea illuminated by the Gestalt psychologists is the **figure-ground** principle (Fowlkes, Martin, & Malik, 2007). As you focus your attention on a figure (for example, the vase in Infographic 3.4), all other features drop into the background. If, however, you direct your gaze onto the faces, the vase falls into the background with everything else. The figure and ground continually change as you shift your focus. Other gestalt organizational principles include the following:

- **Proximity**—Objects close to each other are perceived as a group.
- **Similarity**—Objects similar in shape or color are perceived as a group.
- **Connectedness**—Objects that are connected are perceived as a group.
- **Closure**—Gaps tend to be filled in if something isn't complete.
- **Continuity**—Parts tend to be perceived as members of a group if they head in the same direction.

Although these organizational principles have been demonstrated for vision, it is important to note that they apply to the other senses as well. Imagine a mother who can discern her child's voice amid the clamor of a busy playground: Her child's voice is the figure and the other noises are the ground.

Depth Perception

LO 14 Describe some of the visual cues used in depth perception.

One other thing about figure-ground cues is that they can provide depth information (Burge, Fowlkes, & Banks, 2010). That same mother can tell the slide extends from the front of the jungle gym, thanks to her brain's ability to pick up on cues about depth. How can a two-dimensional image projected on the retina be perceived in three dimensions? There appear to be inborn abilities and learned cues for perceiving depth and distance. Let's start by examining one inborn ability to recognize depth and its potential for danger. Watch out, baby!

VISUAL CLIFF In order to determine whether **depth perception** is innate or learned, researchers studied the behavior of babies approaching a "visual cliff" (see photo above left), a flat glass surface with a checkered tablecloth-like pattern directly underneath that gives the illusion of a drop-off (Gibson & Walk, 1960). The researchers placed infants ages 6 to 14 months at the edge of the glass. At the other end of the glass were the babies' mothers, coaxing them to crawl over. For the most part, the children refused to move toward what they perceived to be a drop-off, suggesting that the perception of depth was innate. Without ever having explored the edge of an actual abyss, these infants seemed instinctively to know it should be avoided. Interestingly, the original research included a series of studies with a variety of non-human animals, starting with rats, and then one-day-old chicks, newborn kids and lambs—and all of them avoided the visual cliff (Rodkey, 2015).

BINOCULAR CUES Some cues for perceiving depth are the result of information gathered by both eyes. **Binocular cues** provide information from the right and left eyes to help judge depth and distance. For example, **convergence** is the brain's interpretation of the tension (or lack thereof) in the eye muscles that direct where both eyes focus. If an object is close, there is more muscular tension (as the muscles turn our eyes inward toward our nose), and the object is perceived as near. This perception of distance is based on experience; throughout life, we have learned that the more muscular tension, the closer an object. Let's take a moment and feel that tension.

Whoa, Baby
A baby appears distressed when he encounters the visual cliff, a supportive glass surface positioned over a drop-off, or "cliff." Most babies will not proceed, even when coaxed by a trusted caregiver. This finding suggests that depth perception is already in place by the time a child is crawling (Gibson & Walk, 1960). Mark Richards/Photo Edit.

Synonyms

retinal disparity binocular disparity

figure-ground A central principle of Gestalt psychology, involving the shifting of focus; as attention is focused on one object, all other features drop or recede into the background.

depth perception The ability to perceive three-dimensional objects and judge distances.

binocular cues Information gathered from both eyes to help judge depth and distance.

convergence A binocular cue used to judge distance and depth based on the tension of the muscles that direct where the eyes are focusing.

retinal disparity A binocular cue that uses the difference between the images the two eyes see to determine the distance of objects.

monocular cues Depth and distance cues that require the use of only one eye.

try this ↓

Point your finger up to the ceiling at arm's length with both eyes open. Now slowly bring your finger close to your nose. Can you feel tension and strain in your eye muscles? Your brain uses this type of convergence cue to determine distance.

Another binocular cue is **retinal disparity,** which is the difference between the images seen by the right and left eyes. The greater the difference, the closer the object. The more similar the two images, the farther the object. With experience, our brains begin using these image disparities to judge distance. The following Try This provides an example of retinal disparity.

try this ↓

Hold your index finger about 4 inches in front of your face pointing up to the ceiling. Quickly open your right eye as you are closing your left eye, alternating this activity for a few seconds; it should appear as if your finger is jumping back and forth. Now do the same thing, but this time with your finger out at arm's length. The image does not seem to be jumping as much.

MONOCULAR CUES Judgments about depth and distance can also be informed by **monocular cues,** which do not necessitate the use of both eyes. An artist who paints pictures can transform a white canvas into a three-dimensional perceptual experience by using techniques that take advantage of monocular cues. The monocular cues include (but are not limited to) the following:

- **Relative Size**—If two objects are similar in actual size, but one is farther away, it appears to be smaller. We interpret the larger object as being closer.

- **Linear Perspective**—When two lines start off parallel, then come together, where they converge appears farther away than where they are parallel.

- **Interposition**—When one object is in front of another, it partially blocks the view of the other object, and this partially blocked object appears more distant.

- **Texture Gradient**—When objects are closer, it is easier to see their texture. As they get farther away, the texture becomes less visible. The more apparent the texture, the closer the object appears.

Monocular Cues
You can gauge the distance and depth in this photo with at least four types of monocular cues: (1) People who are farther away look smaller (relative size). (2) The two sides of the street start out parallel but converge as distance increases (linear perspective). (3) The trees in the front block those that are behind (interposition). (4) Textures are more apparent for closer objects (texture gradient). Corbis Wire/Corbis.

Motion Parallax
As you walk along a busy street, nearby objects appear to move by faster than objects faraway. This monocular cue, known as motion parallax, also helps with depth perception when you are sitting still and objects in the environment are moving around you (for example, cars driving past at different distances). Martin Botvidsson/Getty Images.

Your Perceptual Toolkit

All these perceptual skills are great—if you are standing still—but the world is constantly moving. How do our perceptual systems adapt to changes? We possess the ability to perceive objects as having stable properties, although our environments are always changing. **Perceptual constancy** refers to the tendency to perceive objects as maintaining their shape, size, and color even when the angle, lighting, and distance change. A door is shaped like a rectangle, but when it opens, the image projected on our retina is not a rectangle. Yet, we still perceive the door as having a rectangular shape. This is called **shape constancy,** and sometimes it can be misleading. When people are shown pictures of windows from a variety of perspectives, and then asked to match those images with outlines of shapes, they often have a difficult time choosing an outline that matches the angle of the window. More often than not, shape constancy takes over and participants pick shapes that look more like rectangles than the actual shape of the window images they saw (Cohen & Jones, 2008). Interestingly, artists don't seem to be any better at making these types of matches than non-artists (Ostrofsky, Kozbelt, & Seidel, 2012).

As you gaze on cars and trucks from the window of an airplane, they may look like bugs scurrying around, but you know some are as big as elephants because your perceptual toolkit also includes **size constancy.** Through experience, we get to know the size of everyday objects and perceive them accordingly, regardless of whether they are far or near. Similarly, **color constancy** allows us to see the world in stable colors, even when the sensory data arriving at our photoreceptors change. A bright red backpack appears bright red outside in the sunshine or inside a house. The light waves bouncing off of the backpack have changed, but your understanding of the color has not been altered.

Once a Rectangle, Always a Rectangle
How do you know that all these doors are the same size and shape? The images projected onto your retina suggest that the opened doors are narrower, nonrectangular shapes. Your brain, however, knows from experience that all the opened doors are identical rectangles. This phenomenon is referred to as shape constancy. Image Source/Getty Images.

Although examples of these organizational tendencies occur with robust regularity, some of these perceptual skills are not necessarily universal. Some studies suggest that children *learn* to perceive size constancy. For example, their ability to estimate the size of distant objects improves by around 9 years old, in step with cognitive development, such as their reasoning abilities (Granrud, 2009; Kavšek & Granrud, 2012).

Learning also plays a role in the phenomenon of **perceptual set**—the tendency to perceive stimuli in a specific manner based on past experiences and expectations. If someone handed you a picture of two women and said, "This is a mother with her daughter," you would be more likely to rate them as looking alike than if you had been given the exact same picture and told, "These women are unrelated." Indeed, research shows that people who believe they are looking at parent–child pairs are more likely to rate the pairs as similar than those who believe the members of the pairs are not related (even though they are looking at the same adult–child pairs; Oda, Matsumoto-Oda, & Kurashima, 2005). In short, we tend to see what we are looking for.

Perceptual sets are molded by the context of the moment. If you hear the word "sects" in a TV news report about feuding religious groups, you are unlikely to think the reporter is saying "sex" even though "sects" and "sex" sound the same. Similarly, if you see a baby swaddled in a blue blanket, you are probably more likely to assume it's a boy than a girl. Studies show that expectancies about male or female infants influence viewers' perceptions of gender (Stern & Karraker, 1989). These expectancies apply to crying babies as well—higher-pitched cries are assumed to be those of female infants, even though there are no measurable sex differences in the pitch of their cries. In a recent study, adults not only wrongly assumed they could attribute "sex and gender-related traits to crying babies," they were often misguided in their "assessment of the babies' discomfort" (Reby, Levréro, Gustafsson, & Mathevon, 2016, p. 7). Finally, simply labeling infants as *premature* or *full-term* will shape people's attitudes about them (Porter, Stern, & Zak-Place, 2009).

What Color Is the Dress?

In the winter of 2015, millions of social media users hotly debated this seemingly simple question. Why people had conflicting perceptions is still an open question, but it might have something to do with *color constancy,* the tendency for the brain to perceive objects as having the same color, even in different lighting conditions. In essence, the brain takes the lighting into account when determining the color of an object. If you thought the dress was blue and black, your brain got it right. If you perceived white and gold, your brain may have been working under the assumption that the dress was illuminated by bluish light from the sky (as opposed to the yellowish sun), and therefore it removed this blue light from its color calculation, leading to a perception of white and gold (Lafer-Sousa, Hermann, & Conway, 2015; Macknik, Martinez-Conde, & Conway, 2015).

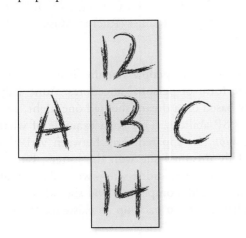

Letters or Numbers?
Look in the green square. What do you see? That depends on whether you viewed the symbol as belonging to a row of letters (A B C) or a column of numbers (12 13 14). Perceptions are shaped by the context in which a stimulus occurs, and our expectations about that stimulus.

perceptual constancy The tendency to perceive objects in our environment as stable in terms of shape, size, and color, regardless of changes in the sensory data received.

shape constancy An object is perceived as maintaining its shape, regardless of the image projected on the retina.

size constancy An object is perceived as maintaining its size, regardless of the image projected on the retina.

color constancy Objects are perceived as maintaining their color, even with changing sensory data.

perceptual set The tendency to perceive stimuli in a specific manner based on past experiences and expectations.

Although our perceptual sets may not always lead to the right conclusions, they do help us organize the vast amount of information flooding our senses. But can perception exist in the absence of sensation? Some would say "yes." Have you ever *felt* your phone vibrating in your pocket only to find out that there was no call, message, or notification? Phantom Phone Signals (PPS) are very common, especially among avid cell phone users (Tanis, Buekeboom, Hartmann, & Vermeulen, 2015). In one study, researchers found as many as 96% of medical interns fell prey to phantom phone vibrations (Lin, Lin, Li, Huang, & Chen, 2013). Researchers also noted a correlation between severe phantom vibrations/ringing and anxiety and depression, suggesting these phantom signals may be good predictors of stress and burnout (Chen, Wu, Chang, & Lin, 2014; Lin, Chen, Li, & Lin, 2013).

Extrasensory Perception: Where's the Evidence?

LO 15 **Define extrasensory perception and explain why psychologists dismiss claims of its legitimacy.**

Have you ever had a dream that actually came to pass? Perhaps you have heard of psychics who claim they can read people's "auras" and decipher their thoughts. **Extrasensory perception (ESP)** is this purported ability to obtain information about the world without any sensory stimuli. And when we say "no sensory input," we are not referring to sights, sounds, smells, tastes, and feelings occurring subliminally, or below absolute thresholds. We mean absolutely no measurable sensory data. The study of these kinds of phenomena is called **parapsychology.**

THINK IT THROUGH
Is There a "Sixth Sense"?

ESP, psychic powers, the sixth sense—call it what you will, there is no compelling scientific evidence to support its existence (Farha, 2007; Rouder & Morey, 2011). Nevertheless, a handful of respected researchers have published research suggesting it exists. In 2011 Cornell University's Daryl Bem set off a firestorm of controversy with a journal article offering evidence for ESP. The article, which reported nine experiments involving some 1,000 participants, suggested that human beings have the ability to predict the future (Bem, 2011). Other psychologists pointed out flaws in Bem's statistical analysis (Wagenmakers, Wetzels, Borsboom, & van der Maas, 2011), which Bem then defended (Bem, Utts, & Johnson 2011). The research was further called into question in 2012, when a team of scientists tried to replicate Bem's results using his same methodology and failed (Ritchie, Wiseman, & French, 2012).

THERE IS NO SCIENTIFIC EVIDENCE TO SUPPORT ITS EXISTENCE

The importance of replicating experiments was discussed in **Chapter 1.** The more a study is replicated and produces similar findings, the more confident we can be in it; replication is a key step in the scientific method. If similar results cannot be reproduced using the same methods, then the original findings may have resulted from chance or experimenter bias.

CONNECTIONS

Despite ESP's lack of scientific credibility, many people remain firm believers. Most often, their "evidence" comes in the form of personal anecdotes. Aunt Tilly predicted she was going to win the lottery based on a dream she had one night, and when she did win, it was "proof" of her ESP abilities. This is an example of what psychologists might call an *illusory correlation,* an apparent link between variables that are not closely related at all. Aunt Tilly dreamed she won the lottery, but so did 1,000 other people around the country, and they didn't win—what about that evidence? Although some may find the idea of ESP compelling, you should be very skeptical about it, because there are no reliable data to back up its existence (Farha, 2007; Rouder & Morey, 2011).

THINK POSITIVE
Can a Disability Be a Gift?

More interesting than ESP, we would argue, are the remarkable (and real) stories of people who thrive despite difficulties with sensation and perception. One example is Claudia Gordon, who is (to our knowledge) the first deaf African American woman to earn a law degree, or *Juris Doctor.* Gordon spent her early childhood in Jamaica, where deaf people were not integrated into mainstream

"I THOUGHT I WAS THE ONLY DEAF PERSON IN THE WORLD."

society. After a few years of staying home from school and suffering from social isolation, Gordon moved to New York where she began to shine academically (DeafPeople.com, n.d.). Eventually, she served as a public engagement advisor for the disability community in the Obama administration (National Association of the Deaf, 2013).

People sometimes view sensory disabilities such as deafness as medical problems. But many Deaf individuals don't feel their deafness needs curing (Ringo, 2013, August 9). According to this view, deafness is a "difference" rather than a "disability," and Deaf people belong to a minority culture that has a unique language, literature, art, and educational system (Denworth, 2014, April 25; Padden & Humphries, 1988; Swanson, 1997). Some individuals view their deafness as a gift and would choose to remain deaf even if given the opportunity to acquire normal hearing (Sparrow, 2005). For them, their "disability" is a fundamental part of their identity as well as a source of pride. "Deaf pride" spokesperson Mark Drolsbaugh has come to be proud of his deafness, in spite of his struggle to understand mainstream schoolteachers, the ridicule of his peers, and speech specialists' attempts over the years to "correct" him. "I am no longer ashamed of my deafness, I am proud of it," Drolsbaugh writes, "I am proud of who I am, proud of what I've overcome, and proud of my culture" (Drolsbaugh, 1996, para. 3). 👍

MOVING FORWARD Are you wondering what became of Emma, Zoe, and Sophie? When the triplets were about 5 years old, Liz and her husband got a divorce, and Liz faced the daunting task of caring for four young children. Today, Sarah is a high school graduate, Emma and Zoe study at the prestigious Texas School for the Blind and Visually Impaired, and Sophie is holding her own in the public school system. Liz operates her own business and recently wed her true love from two decades past.

Inspiring Leader
When Claudia Gordon lost the ability to hear at 8 years old, she thought she was "the only deaf person in the world" (Baggetto, 2010, para. 5). Gordon eventually became a leader in the deaf community and in society at large, serving in the Obama administration as public engagement advisor for the disability community. SourceAmerica.

In It Together
Liz and her eldest daughter Sarah (back left) relax with the triplets: Zoe (front left), Emma (front right), and Sophie (back right). Zoe and Emma currently attend the Texas School for the Blind and Visually Impaired, while Sophie goes to school in the local district. Worldwide Features/Barcroft Media/Landov.

With the love and support of family, Emma and Zoe have made significant strides in their social and linguistic skills. Both can communicate with about 50 signs, but they understand many more and are building their vocabulary all the time. As for Sophie, having limited vision has enabled her to take classes alongside sighted children. ●

extrasensory perception (ESP) The purported ability to obtain information about the world without any sensory stimuli.
parapsychology The study of extrasensory perception.

○✓○○ **show what you know**

1. _____ means the "whole" or "form" in German.

2. One binocular cue called _____ is based on the brain's interpretation of the tension in muscles of the eyes.
   a. convergence
   b. retinal disparity
   c. interposition
   d. relative size

3. Using what you have learned so far in the textbook, how would you try to convince a friend that extrasensory perception does not exist?

4. Have you ever noticed how the shape of a door seems to change as it opens and closes, yet you know its actual shape remains the same? The term _____ refers to the fact that even though sensory stimuli may change, we know objects do not change their shape, size, or color.
   a. perceptual set
   b. perceptual constancy
   c. convergence
   d. texture gradient

✓ CHECK YOUR ANSWERS IN APPENDIX C.

Improve your grade! Use 🔷 **LearningCurve** macmillan learning adaptive quizzing to create your personalized study plan, which will direct you to the resources that will help you most in 🔷 **LaunchPad** macmillan learning

3 summary of concepts

LO 1 Define sensation and perception and explain how they are different. (p. 96)

Sensation is the manner in which physical stimuli are received and detected. Perception is the process of giving meaning to sensations. Bottom-up processing describes how the brain takes in basic sensory information and processes this incoming stimuli. Top-down processing uses past experiences and knowledge in order to understand sensory information.

LO 2 Define transduction and explain how it relates to sensation. (p. 97)

Sensory organs receive stimuli from the environment (for example, sound waves, light energy). Transduction is the transformation of stimuli into electrical and chemical signals. The neural signals are then processed by the central nervous system, resulting in what we consciously experience as sensations.

LO 3 Describe and differentiate between absolute thresholds and difference thresholds. (p. 98)

One of the important goals of studying sensation and perception is to determine absolute thresholds, the weakest stimuli that can be detected 50% of the time. Difference thresholds indicate the minimum difference between two stimuli noticed 50% of the time. According to Weber's law, certain ratios determine these difference thresholds. The ability to detect weak signals in the environment is based on many factors.

LO 4 Summarize the properties of light and color, and describe the structure and function of the eye. (p. 102)

The eyes do not sense faces, objects, or scenery; they detect light, which is a form of electromagnetic energy. The light we see (visible light) comprises one small portion of the electromagnetic spectrum, which also includes gamma rays, X-rays, ultraviolet light, infrared light, microwaves, and radio waves. The color, or hue, of visible light is determined by its wavelength. Apart from their hue, colors can be characterized by brightness (intensity) and saturation (purity). When light first enters the eye, it passes through a glassy outer layer known as the cornea. Then it travels through a hole called the pupil, followed by the lens. Both the cornea and the lens focus the incoming light waves, and the lens can change shape in order to adjust to objects near and far. Finally, the light travels through the eye's jellylike center and reaches the retina, where it is transduced into neural activity.

LO 5 Describe the functions of rods and cones. (p. 106)

Rods are photoreceptors in the retina that are extremely sensitive to light and enable us to see in dim lighting. Rods do not provide the sensation of color. Cones, also in the retina, are responsible for our sensation of color and our ability to see the details of objects. Cones are not used when ambient light is low. Cones are concentrated in the fovea.

LO 6 Compare and contrast the theories of color vision. (p. 108)

The trichromatic theory of color vision suggests there are three types of cones, each sensitive to particular wavelengths in the red, green, and blue spectrums. The three types of cones fire in response to different electromagnetic wavelengths. The opponent-process theory of color vision suggests that in addition to the color-sensitive cones, we also have neurons that respond differently to opponent colors. These colors cannot be viewed simultaneously (for example, red–green, blue–yellow).

LO 7 Summarize how sound waves are converted into the sensation of hearing. (p. 111)

Audition is the term used for the sense of hearing. When we hear, we are sensing sound waves, which are rhythmic vibrations of molecules traveling through a variety of forms of matter (including air). The cochlea is a fluid-filled, snail-shaped organ of the inner ear. When the oval window vibrates, it causes the fluid in the cochlea to move. The cochlea is lined with the basilar membrane, which contains hair cells. When the fluid moves, the hair cells lining the basilar membrane bend in response. The hair cells cause the nerve cells nearby to fire, sending neural messages through the auditory nerve to the auditory cortex via the thalamus.

LO 8 Illustrate how we sense different pitches of sound. (p. 115)

Place theory suggests that the location of neural activity along the cochlea allows us to sense different pitches of high-frequency sounds. With a high-frequency sound, vibrations occur closer to the end of the basilar membrane near the oval window. Frequency theory suggests that the frequency of the neural impulses determines the experience of pitch. The entire basilar membrane vibrates at the same rate as the sound wave; the neural impulses occur at this same rate. The frequency theory explains how we perceive the pitch of sounds from 20 Hz to 400 Hz. The volley principle explains our perception of the different pitches between 400 Hz and 4,000 Hz. And, the place theory explains our perception of pitches from 4,000 Hz to 20,000 Hz.

LO 9 Describe the process of olfaction. (p. 117)

The chemical sense referred to as olfaction provides the sensation of smell. Molecules from odor-emitting objects in our environments make their way into our nostrils up through the nose or mouth. The olfactory epithelium is home to millions of olfactory receptor neurons, which provide receptors for odor molecules. When enough odor molecules bind to the receptor neuron, a signal is sent to the brain.

LO 10 Discuss the structures involved in taste and describe how they work. (p. 120)

Gustation is the sense of taste. The receptor cells for taste are located in the taste buds, which are embedded in the papillae on the tongue, as well as in the roof of the mouth and inside the mouth on the cheeks. Each taste bud contains 50 to 100 taste receptor cells; taste molecules bind onto these cells. Taste is essential to the survival of species. Tastes push organisms toward needed foods and away from harmful ones.

LO 11 Explain how the biopsychosocial perspective helps us understand pain. (p. 124)

The biopsychosocial perspective explains the perception of pain by exploring biological, psychological, and social factors. This multilevel method examines how these factors play a role in the experience of pain. According to the gate-control theory, a person's perception of pain can increase or decrease depending on how the brain interprets pain signals. Neural activity makes its way to the brain, where it is processed. The brain is capable of blocking pain by sending a message through the interneurons to "close the gate" so the pain won't be felt.

LO 12 Illustrate how we sense the position and movement of our bodies. (p. 126)

Kinesthesia is the sense of position and movement of the body. We know how our body parts are oriented in space because of specialized nerve endings called proprioceptors, which are primarily located in the muscles and joints. Our proprioceptors monitor changes in the position of body parts and the tension in our muscles. The vestibular sense helps us deal with the effects of gravity, movement, and body position to keep us balanced.

LO 13 Identify the principles of perceptual organization. (p. 130)

Gestalt psychologists sought to explain how the human mind organizes stimuli from the environment. They realized the whole is greater than the sum of its parts, meaning the brain naturally organizes stimuli as a whole rather than parts and pieces. Gestalt indicates a tendency for human perception to be organized and complete. The organizational principles include: proximity, similarity, connectedness, closure, and continuity.

LO 14 Describe some of the visual cues used in depth perception. (p. 132)

Depth perception appears partially to be an innate ability. Children in the visual cliff experiment, for example, refuse to move toward what they perceive to be a drop-off. Binocular cues use information gathered from both eyes to help judge depth and distance. Monocular cues can be used by either eye alone and also help judge depth and distance.

LO 15 Define extrasensory perception and explain why psychologists dismiss claims of its legitimacy. (p. 136)

Extrasensory perception (ESP) is the purported ability to obtain information about the world without any sensory stimuli. The study of these kinds of phenomena is called parapsychology. There is no scientific evidence to back up claims of ESP and other parapsychology phenomena.

key terms

absolute thresholds, p. 98
accommodation, p. 104
afterimage, p. 109
amplitude, p. 103
audition, p. 111
binocular cues, p. 132
blind spot, p. 106
bottom-up processing, p. 96
cochlea, p. 114
color constancy, p. 134
cones, p. 106
convergence, p. 132
cornea, p. 104
dark adaptation, p. 107
depth perception, p. 132
difference threshold, p. 99

extrasensory perception (ESP), p. 136
feature detectors, p. 108
figure-ground, p. 132
frequency, p. 112
frequency theory, p. 115
gate-control theory, p. 125
gestalt, p. 130
gustation, p. 121
hue, p. 103
illusion, p. 128
iris, p. 104
kinesthesia, p. 126
light adaptation, p. 107
monocular cues, p. 133

olfaction, p. 117
opponent-process theory, p. 110
optic nerve, p. 106
parapsychology, p. 136
perception, p. 96
perceptual constancy, p. 134
perceptual set, p. 135
photoreceptors, p. 106
pitch, p. 112
place theory, p. 115
proprioceptors, p. 126
retina, p. 104
retinal disparity, p. 133
rods, p. 106

saturation, p. 103
sensation, p. 96
sensory adaptation, p. 98
shape constancy, p. 134
signal detection theory, p. 101
size constancy, p. 134
top-down processing, p. 96
transduction, p. 97
trichromatic theory, p. 108
vestibular sense, p. 126
volley principle, p. 115
wavelength, p. 102
Weber's law, p. 99

test prep *are you ready?*

1. Stimuli are detected through the process called:
   a. perception.
   b. bottom-up processing.
   c. sensation.
   d. top-down processing.

2. You're listening to music on your iPod. The sound waves transmitted through the earbuds lead to vibrations in the fluid in your cochlea. This activity causes the hair cells to bend, which causes nearby nerve cells to fire. This process of transforming stimuli into electrical and chemical signals of neurons is:
   a. transduction.
   b. perception.
   c. top-down processing.
   d. convergence.

3. According to signal detection theory, our ability to detect weak stimuli in the environment is based on many factors, including which of the following?
   a. characteristics of the experimenter
   b. fatigue and motivation
   c. false alarms
   d. hits

4. While rollerblading outside, you get something in your eye. As the day goes on, your eye still feels irritated. It is possible you've scratched your _____, which is the transparent outer layer, the function of which is to protect the eye and bend light to help focus light waves.
   a. lens
   b. retina
   c. iris
   d. cornea

5. The various types of electromagnetic energy can be distinguished by their _____, which also play[s] an important role in determining the colors humans can detect.
   a. binocular cues
   b. wavelength
   c. interposition
   d. feature detectors

6. In color vision, the opponent-process theory was developed to explain the _____, which could not be explained by the _____ theory.

a. afterimage effect;
   trichromatic
b. blind spot; place

c. feature detectors;
   trichromatic
d. color deficiencies;
   frequency

a. tension of the muscles
   focusing the eyes
b. relative size of two
   similar objects

c. two lines initially some
   distance apart coming
   together
d. interposition

7. A psychologist is interested in studying children's _____, which is the term we use for the sense of hearing.
   a. wavelength
   b. amplitude
   c. pitch
   d. audition

8. Frequency theory of pitch perception suggests it is the number of _____ that allows us to perceive differences in pitch.
   a. sound waves greater
      than 1,000 Hz
   b. the timbre
   c. neural impulses
      firing
   d. the amplitude

9. People with the rare condition of *anosmia* are unable to perceive odors. They have lost their sense of smell, which is considered a:
   a. perceptual set.
   b. vestibular sense.
   c. chemical sense.
   d. hue.

10. The wiring of the olfactory system is unique, because other sensory systems relay data through the _____ before information is passed along to higher brain centers, but this is not the case for olfactory information.
    a. thalamus
    b. corpus callosum
    c. reticular formation
    d. basilar membrane

11. _____ specialize in recognizing specific characteristics of your visual experience, such as angles, lines, and movements.
    a. Feature detectors
    b. Rods
    c. Cones
    d. Photoreceptors

12. We are aware of where the parts of our bodies are in space because of specialized nerve endings called _____, which are primarily located in the joints and muscles.
    a. proprioceptors
    b. Meissner's corpuscles
    c. Pacinian corpuscles
    d. nociceptors

13. Hector is staring at the small print on the back of a credit card. Which of the following would be a binocular cue to indicate how close the credit card is to his face?

14. One of the gestalt organizational principles suggests that objects close to each other are perceived as a group. This is known as:
    a. continuity.
    b. closure.
    c. similarity.
    d. proximity.

15. When two objects are similar in actual size and one of these objects is farther away than the other, the object at a distance appears to be smaller than the closer object. This is a monocular cue called:
    a. linear perspective.
    b. interposition.
    c. relative size.
    d. texture gradient.

16. Use the evolutionary perspective of psychology to explain the importance of any two aspects of human taste.

17. How is extrasensory perception different from the perception of subliminal stimuli?

18. The transformation of a sound wave into the experience of something heard follows a complicated path. To better understand the process, draw a diagram starting with a sound in the environment and ending with the sound heard by an individual.

19. Why does placing ice on a sore shoulder stop the pain?

20. Describe the difference between absolute threshold and difference threshold.

✓ CHECK YOUR ANSWERS IN APPENDIX C.

YOUR SCIENTIFIC WORLD

Apply psychology to the real world!
Go to LaunchPad for access.

Gianni Dagli Orti/Corbis.

San Diego History Center.

UniversalImagesGroup/Getty Images.

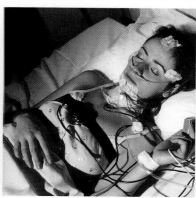

Garo/Phanie/Superstock.

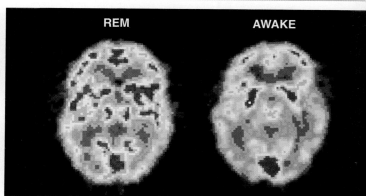

REM   AWAKE

Hank Morgan/Science Source.

4 consciousness

luckyraccoon/Shutterstock.

An Introduction to Consciousness

EXPLORING OUTER AND INNER SPACE Dr. Divya Chander was in first grade when she decided to become an astronaut. Her dream nearly came true at the age of 32, when she made it to the final round of astronaut selection for NASA. Although she did not end up traveling to outer space (not yet, at least), her exploration continued. Rather than studying far-flung corners of the solar system, Dr. Chander has been investigating a dark and mysterious place right here on Earth—the human brain.

Every day that Dr. Chander walks into the hospital, she assumes a tremendous responsibility: keeping people alive and comfortable as they are sliced, prodded, and stitched back together by surgeons. Dr. Chander is an anesthesiologist, a medical doctor whose primary responsibility is to oversee a patient's vital functions and manage pain before, during, and after surgery. Using powerful drugs that manipulate the nervous system, she makes sure a patient's heart rate, blood pressure, and other critical processes remain in a safe range. Her anesthetic drugs also block pain, paralyze muscles, and prevent memory formation (temporarily, of course). Without the work of anesthesiologists like Dr. Chander, many of today's common medical procedures would be too painful or emotionally traumatic for patients to tolerate.

The Explorer
Dr. Divya Chander at the age of 3 or 4 (left). A couple of years after this photo was taken, young Divya decided she would become a neuroscientist and an astronaut. She went on to earn both an MD and a PhD in neuroscience and now practices anesthesiology at Stanford University. As for the astronaut dream, it nearly became reality when she made it to the final round of NASA's astronaut selection. Dr. Chander still aspires to become a space explorer, but for now her exploration centers on what you might call "inner space"—uncovering the mysteries of consciousness. Left: Dr. Divya Chander. Right: Macmillan Learning, photo by Norbert von der Groeben.

Ancient Opium
Wall art from the Tomb of Horemheb in Egypt's Valley of the Kings depicts a person holding two round vessels representing poppy flowers. The ancient Egyptians used the poppy opiate morphine for pain relief, but its therapeutic role was controversial (El Ansary, Steigerwald, & Esser, 2003). Gianni Dagli Orti/Corbis.

It's Written All Over the EEG
Dr. Chander and a colleague review an electroencephalogram (EEG), the technology she uses to monitor her patients' level of consciousness. By observing the changes in wave frequency, she can tell if the patient is in a deep unconscious state, approaching wakefulness, or somewhere in between. Macmillan Higher Education photo by Norbert von der Groeben.

consciousness The state of being aware of oneself, one's thoughts, and/or the environment; includes various levels of conscious awareness.

Anesthesiology is as old as recorded history. In ancient times, people may have sought pain relief by dipping their wounds in cold rivers and streams. They concocted mixtures of crushed roots, barks, herbs, fruits, and flowers to ease pain and induce sleep in surgical patients (Keys, 1945). Many of the plant chemicals discovered by these early peoples are still given to patients today, although in slightly different forms. Opium was used by the ancient Egyptians (Schroeder, 2013), and its chemical relatives are employed by modern-day physicians and hospitals all over the world (for example, *morphine* for pain relief and *codeine* for cough suppression).

But it took many centuries for anesthesia to become a regular part of surgery. Before the mid-1800s, surgery was so painful that patients writhed and screamed on operating tables, sometimes held down by four or five people (Bynum, 2007). During the Mexican-American War, a band would play when Mexican soldiers had their limbs amputated so the men's cries would not be heard by others (Aldrete, Marron, & Wright, 1984). The only anesthetic available may have been whiskey, wine, or a firm blow to the head that literally knocked the patient out.

Fortunately, the science of anesthesia has come a long way. It is now possible to have a tooth extracted or a mole removed without a twinge of discomfort. A patient undergoing open heart surgery can lie peacefully as surgeons pry open his chest and poke around with their instruments, then leave the hospital with no memory of the actual operation.

"I am very, very privileged that, as an anesthesiologist, I have access to these drugs that I use on a regular basis in order to make [patients'] lives better, to make surgery possible for them," Dr. Chander explains. These same drugs also enable Dr. Chander to observe the brain as it falls into the deeper-than-sleep state of general anesthesia, losing awareness of the outside world, and then emerges from the darkness, awake and alert. In other words, she can study human brains as they pass through various levels of *consciousness.* ●

What Is Consciousness?

LO 1 Define consciousness.

Consciousness is a concept that can be difficult to pinpoint. Psychologist G. William Farthing offers a good starting point: **Consciousness** is "the subjective state of being currently aware of something either within oneself or outside of oneself" (1992, p. 6). Thus, consciousness might be conceived as a state of being aware of oneself, one's thoughts, and/or the environment. According to this definition of subjective awareness, one can be asleep and still be aware (Farthing, 1992). Indeed, says Dr. Chander, "there are neuroscientists who believe that dreaming should be considered a conscious state." Take this example: You are dreaming about a siren blaring and you wake up to discover it is your alarm clock; you were clearly asleep but aware at the same time, as the sound registered in your brain. This ability to register a sound while asleep helps us be vigilant about dangers day and night. For our primitive

Note: Quotations attributed to Dr. Divya Chander and Matt Utesch are personal communications.

ancestors, this might have meant hearing a predator rustling in the bushes, and for modern people, hearing a fire alarm or smoke detector. Researchers have conducted numerous studies to determine the types of sounds most likely to arouse a sleeping person, as well as individual differences (for example, age, gender, sleep deprivation, hearing ability, and sleep stage) that affect whether a person will register and/or wake up to a sound (Thomas & Bruck, 2010). This type of work is done by human factors engineers, who explore the interaction of consciousness and the design of machines.

"Sometimes people think that when you lose consciousness, or you go to sleep, that your brain is less active," explains Dr. Chander. "In some dimensions it is less active," she notes, "[but] a better characterization might be that it's less functionally connected to itself." In other words, there is less communication occurring between different parts of the brain. As a person lies on the operating table, in a "less conscious" state, the brain also seems to be doing fewer calculations, processing less information. "When I say 'less conscious,' I do literally mean that because I do think it's an entire spectrum," Dr. Chander explains. "There isn't just 'unconscious' and 'conscious.' There are varied depths of consciousness."

NIGHTMARE ON THE OPERATING TABLE   For a patient undergoing major surgery, the goal is to decrease the level of consciousness to a point where pain is no longer felt and awareness of the outside world dissipates. But the anesthesiologist must be careful; giving too much anesthetic can suppress vital functions and kill a person. (Musical legend Michael Jackson died from an overdose of the commonly used anesthetic propofol.) To reduce consciousness and keep patients safe, the anesthesiologist must give just the right combination, and proper dosage, of anesthetic drugs.

On very rare occasions (about 1 in 10,000, according to some research), the anesthetic cocktail does not work as intended—patients become aware during general anesthesia (Mashour & Avidan, 2015). For some, this could simply mean hearing the voices of surgeons and nurses as they work; other people actually wake up, or become completely aware, and perhaps even feel pain during the procedure (Cook et al., 2014). Just imagine lying on the operating table, unable to move or speak (you've been paralyzed by the anesthetic drugs). Meanwhile, the surgical team is sawing through your femur bone or cutting into your eye. For some patients, this horrifying experience leads to posttraumatic stress syndrome (Cook et al., 2014).

None of Dr. Chander's patients have reported this type of "accidental awareness" during surgery, and they probably never will. That's because Dr. Chander is constantly monitoring their brain activity with an electroencephalogram (EEG), which picks up electrical signals from the brain's surface (the cortex) and displays this information on a screen. Looking at the EEG monitor, Dr. Chander can determine a patient's depth of anesthesia, or the degree to which the drugs have induced a "hypnotic state," or changed his level of consciousness. The changes in wave frequency on the EEG monitor tell her when a patient is becoming "light" (getting close to waking up), "deep" (in a profound slumber, deeper than sleep), and even when he is receiving a particular drug.

Dr. Chander is unusual in this respect; most anesthesiologists are not trained to read an EEG with this level of precision (Dr. Chander is both an anesthesiologist and a neuroscientist). Instead they rely on other, less direct, indicators of consciousness, such as blood pressure and heart rate. This approach actually works very well because the amount of anesthetic needed to suppress blood pressure, heart rate, and movement is greater than that required to suppress consciousness (Aranake, Mashour, & Avidan, 2013). Dr. Chander's ability to read raw EEG data, and her deep knowledge of neuroscience, put her in an ideal position to track levels of consciousness in her patients—and discover the secrets of consciousness in general. ●

CONNECTIONS

In **Chapter 1,** we introduced the evolutionary perspective. The adaptive trait to remain aware even while asleep has evolved through natural selection, allowing our ancestors to defend against predators and other dangerous situations.

CONNECTIONS

Anesthetic drugs can lower blood pressure and heart rate by suppressing the sympathetic nervous system. In **Chapter 2,** we discussed how the sympathetic nervous system orchestrates the "fight-or-flight" response, prepping the body to respond to stressful situations. Surgery would certainly qualify as a stressful situation.

CONNECTIONS

In **Chapter 1,** we discussed the contributions of these early psychologists. Wundt founded the first psychology laboratory, edited the first psychology journal, and used experimentation to measure psychological processes. Titchener was particularly interested in examining consciousness and the "atoms" of the mind.

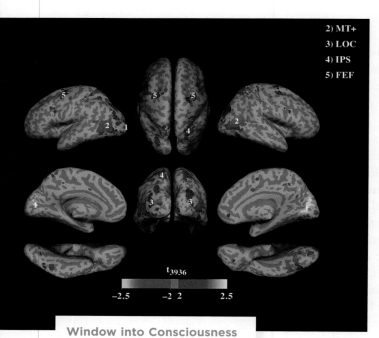

2) MT+
3) LOC
4) IPS
5) FEF

t_{3936}

−2.5   −2 2   2.5

Window into Consciousness
Using fMRI, researchers showed it was possible to monitor participants' conscious perceptions of ambiguous images in real time. The red areas indicate areas of high blood flow, while blue areas signal lower blood flow (Reichert et al., 2014). © 2014 Reichert C., Fendrich R., Bernarding J., Tempelmann C., Hinrichs H. and Rieger J.W. (2014) Online tracking of the contents of conscious perception using realtime fMRI. *Front. Neurosci. 8,* 116. doi: 10.3389/fnins.2014.00116.

CONNECTIONS

In **Chapter 1,** we presented the concept of objective reports, which are free of opinions, beliefs, expectations, and values. Here, we note that descriptions of consciousness are subjective (unique or personal), and do not lend themselves to objective reporting.

Studying Consciousness

The field of psychology began with the study of consciousness. Wilhelm Wundt and his student Edward Titchener founded psychology as a science based on exploring consciousness and its contents. Another early psychologist, William James, regarded consciousness as a "stream" that provides a sense of day-to-day continuity (James, 1890/1983). Think about how this "stream" of thoughts is constantly rushing through your head. An e-mail from an old friend appears in your inbox, jogging your memory of the birthday party she threw last month, and that reminds you that tomorrow is your mother's birthday (better not forget that one). You notice your shoe is untied, think about school starting tomorrow, and remember the utility bill sitting on the counter, all within a matter of seconds. Thoughts interweave and overtake each other like currents of flowing water; sometimes they are connected by topic, emotion, events, but other times they don't seem to be connected by anything other than your stream of consciousness.

Although psychology started with the introspective study of consciousness, American psychologists John Watson, B. F. Skinner, and other behaviorists insisted that the science of psychology should restrict itself to the study of observable behaviors. This attitude persisted until the 1950s and 1960s, when psychology underwent a revolution of sorts. Researchers began to direct their focus back on the unseen mechanisms of the mind. **Cognitive psychology**, the scientific study of conscious and unconscious mental processes such as thinking, problem solving, and language, emerged as a major subfield. Today, understanding consciousness is an important goal of psychology, and many believe science can be used to investigate its mysteries.

In her neuroscience research, Dr. Chander has used a cutting-edge technology called optogenetics to search for groups of neurons that may act as "on" or "off" switches for different states of consciousness (asleep versus awake, for example). With optogenetics, researchers can activate or deactivate neurons or groups of neurons over milliseconds (the timescale in which neurons fire), and see how it affects animals' behavior (Deisseroth, 2015). Technologies like optogenetics and functional magnetic resonance imaging (fMRI) have added to our growing knowledge base (Reichert et al., 2014; Song & Knöpfel, 2016), yet barriers to studying consciousness remain. One is that consciousness is subjective, pertaining only to the individual who experiences it. Thus, some have argued it is impossible to *objectively* study another's conscious experience (Blackmore, 2005; Farthing, 1992). To make matters more complicated, one's consciousness changes from moment to moment. Right now you are concentrating on these words, but in a few seconds you might be thinking of something else or slip into light sleep. In spite of these challenges, researchers around the world are inching closer to understanding consciousness by studying it from many perspectives. Welcome to the world of consciousness and its many shades of gray.

The Nature of Consciousness

There are many elements of conscious experience, including desire, thought, language, sensation, perception, and knowledge of self. Memory is also involved, as conscious experiences usually involve the retrieval of memories. Essentially, any cognitive process is potentially a part of your conscious experience. Let's look at what this means, for example, when you go shopping on the Internet. Your ability to navigate from page to page hinges on your recognition of visual images (*Is that the PayPal home page or my e-mail log-in?*), language aptitude (for reading), and motor skills (for typing and clicking). While browsing products, you access various memories (which link you just clicked, the shoes you saw last week, and so on)—all of this is part of your consciousness, your stream of thought.

LO 2 Explain how automatic processing relates to consciousness.

AUTOMATIC PROCESSING Stop reading and listen. Do you hear background sounds you didn't notice before—a soft breeze rustling through the curtains, a clock ticking? You may not have picked up on these sounds, because you were not paying attention to them, but your brain was monitoring all this activity. In describing consciousness, psychologists often distinguish between cognitive processes that occur *automatically* (without effort, awareness, or control) and cognitive activity that requires us to focus our attention on specific sensory input (with effort and awareness, we choose what to attend to and where to direct our focus). Our sensory systems absorb an enormous amount of information, and the brain must sift through these data and determine what is important and needs immediate attention, what can be ignored, and what can be processed and stored for later use. This **automatic processing** allows information to be collected and saved (at least temporarily) with little or no conscious effort (McCarthy & Skowronski, 2011; Schmidt-Daffy, 2011). Without automatic processing, we would be overwhelmed with data.

Automatic processing can also refer to the involuntary cognitive activity guiding some behaviors. We are seemingly able to carry out routine tasks without focusing our attention. Behaviors seem to occur without intentional awareness, and without getting in the way of our other activities (Hassin, Bargh, & Zimerman, 2009). Do you remember the last time you walked a familiar route, checking your phone and daydreaming the entire time? Somehow you arrived at your destination without noticing much about your surroundings or the traffic. You were conscious enough to complete complex tasks, but not enough to realize that you were doing so. This type of multitasking is commonplace, although the great majority of people have difficulty trying to accomplish more than one demanding task (Medeiros-Ward, Watson, & Strayer, 2015). See **TABLE 4.1** on the next page for solutions to some multitasking problems.

> ### In Class: Collaborate and Report
>
> In your group, discuss and record examples of **A)** when it is to your advantage to use automatic processing and **B)** when automatic processing could be risky or problematic. **C)** Decide if you think the benefits outweigh the risks.

Although unconscious processes direct various behaviors, we can also make conscious decisions about where to focus our attention. While walking to class, you might focus intently on a conversation you just had with your friend or an exam you will take in an hour. In these cases, we deliberately channel or direct our attention.

LO 3 Describe how we narrow our focus through selective attention.

SELECTIVE ATTENTION Although we have access to a vast amount of information in our internal and external environments, we can only focus our attention on a small portion at one time. This narrow focus on specific stimuli is known as **selective attention**. Talking to someone in a crowded room, you are able to block out the chatter and noise around you and immerse yourself in the conversation. This efficient use of selective attention is known as the *cocktail-party effect,* and it is evident in the way the brain responds to speech that is attended to and speech that is ignored (Golumbic et al., 2013; Koch, Lawo, Fels, & Vorländer, 2011). Studies suggest selective attention

CONNECTIONS

In **Chapter 3,** we introduced the concept of sensory adaptation, which is the tendency to become less sensitive to and less aware of constant stimuli over time. This better prepares us to detect changes in the environment, which can signal important activities that require attention. Here, we see how this can occur with automatic processing.

Acting Without Thinking
Do you recall dropping your keys in your bag this morning? Many routine activities, such as putting away keys and locking the door, occur without our awareness. We might not remember these events because we never gave them our attention in the first place. Ariel Skelley/Blend Images/Getty Images.

cognitive psychology The scientific study of mental processes such as thinking, problem solving, and language.

automatic processing Collection and sometimes storage of information without conscious effort or awareness.

selective attention The ability to focus awareness on a small segment of information that is available through our sensory systems.

TABLE 4.1 BE SMART ABOUT MULTITASKING

Problem	Solution
You think you can drive safely while using your phone, because you can text and talk without even looking at the screen.	If you're like the overwhelming majority of drivers (97.5%, according to one study), you cannot drive safely while using a cell phone (Watson & Strayer, 2010). Those of us who feel most confident in our multitasking abilities are often the worst at doing so (Sanbonmatsu, Strayer, Medeiros-Ward, & Watson, 2013; Strayer, 2015). The only safe way to use a phone when behind the wheel is to pull over and off the road.
Sometimes you can't resist checking Instagram and Facebook during study sessions.	Intersperse your study sessions with "media breaks." For example, allow yourself 5 minutes of screen time for every 1 hour of studying. This is better than constantly switching your focus between studying and media, because every little adjustment requires time (Carrier, Rosena, Cheeverb, & Lima, 2015).
You know you shouldn't text during class, but you must respond to a time-sensitive message before the lecture is over.	If you must text during class, and you know your instructor will permit this, choose a strategic time to do so. Rather than replying instantly, wait until your instructor has finished expressing a thought or explaining a concept (Carrier et al., 2015).
You know it's rude, but you can't help glancing at your phone while talking to your partner.	Put away your phone or turn down the volume during face-to-face conversations, especially with the people you love. Snubbing someone with your phone ("phubbing") can cause conflict in romantic relationships, which may lead to lower levels of "life satisfaction" (Roberts & David, 2016).

Multitasking with technology cannot always be avoided. But with strategies like those listed above, you can avoid some of the negative effects of juggling media with other tasks.

can be influenced by emotions. Anger, for example, increases our ability to selectively attend to something or someone (Finucane, 2011). So, too, does repeated exposure to important stimuli (Brascamp, Blake, & Kristjánsson, 2011). We also get better at ignoring distractions as we age (Couperus, 2011).

This doesn't mean other information goes undetected (remember, the brain is constantly gathering data through automatic processing). Our tendency is to adapt to continuous input, and ignore the unimportant sensory stimuli that bombard us at every moment. We are designed to pay attention to abrupt, unexpected **changes in the environment**, and to stimuli that are unfamiliar or especially strong (Bahrick & Newell, 2008; Daffner et al., 2007; Parmentier & Andrés, 2010). Imagine you are studying in a busy courtyard. You are aware the environment is bustling with activity, but you fail to pay attention to every person—until something changes (someone yells, for example). Then your attention might be directed to that specific event.

INATTENTIONAL BLINDNESS Selective attention is great if you need to study for a psychology test as people around you are playing video games, but it can also be dangerous. Suppose a friend sends you a hilarious text message while you are walking toward a busy intersection. Thinking about the text can momentarily steal your attention away from signs of danger, like a car turning right on red without stopping. While distracted by the text message, you might step into the intersection—without seeing the car turning in your path. This "looking without seeing" is referred to as inattentional blindness, and it can have serious consequences (Mack, 2003).

Ulric Neisser illustrated just how blind we can be to objects directly in our line of vision. In one of his studies, participants were instructed to watch a video of men passing a basketball from one person to another (Neisser, 1979; Neisser & Becklen, 1975). As the participants diligently followed the basketball with their eyes, counting each pass, a partially transparent woman holding an umbrella was superimposed walking

CONNECTIONS

In **Chapter 2,** we described the reticular formation, an intricate web of neurons responsible for levels of arousal. It also plays a role in selectively attending to important information by sifting through sensory data, picking out what's relevant, and ignoring the rest. Here, we see how the brain pays attention to unexpected changes in the environment.

What Umbrella?
In an elegant demonstration of inattentional blindness, researchers asked a group of participants to watch a video of men passing around a basketball. As the participants kept careful tabs on the players' passes, a semi-transparent image of a woman with an umbrella appeared among them. Only 21% of the participants (1 out of 5) even noticed; the others had been focusing their attention elsewhere (Most et al., 2001).

across the basketball court. Only 21% of the participants even noticed the woman (Most et al., 2001; Simons, 2010); the others had been too fixated on counting the basketball passes to see her (Mack, 2003). It turns out even experts can fall prey to this phenomenon. In one study, researchers embedded an image of a gorilla on a CAT scan of a lung. Twenty out of 24 expert radiologists failed to detect the gorilla (Drew, Vo, & Wolfe, 2013).

LEVELS OF CONSCIOUSNESS People often equate consciousness with being awake and alert, and unconsciousness with being passed out or comatose. But the distinction is not so clear, because there are different *levels of conscious awareness,* including wakefulness, sleepiness, dreaming, as well as drug-induced, hypnotic, and meditative states. One way to define these levels of consciousness is to determine how much control you have over your awareness. A high level of awareness might occur when you focus intensely on a task (using a sharp knife); a lower level might occur as you daydream, although you are able to snap out of it as needed. Sometimes we can identify an agent that causes a change in the level or state of consciousness. Psychologists typically delineate between *waking consciousness* and *altered states of consciousness* that may result from drugs, alcohol, or hypnosis—all topics covered in this chapter.

Wherever your attention is focused at this moment, that is your conscious experience —but there are times when attention essentially shuts down. What's going on when we lie in bed motionless, lost in a peaceful slumber? Sleep, fascinating sleep, is the subject of our next section.

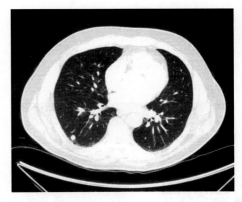

Is That a Gorilla in My Lung?
Look on the upper right side of this lung scan. Do you see a gorilla? Researchers showed this image to a group of radiologists, medical professionals who specialize in reading computerized axial tomography (CAT) scans like this. A whopping 83% did not notice the gorilla, even though it was 48 times bigger than the lung nodules they identify on a regular basis (Drew, Vo, & Wolfe, 2013). A beautiful illustration of inattentional blindness. Trafton Drew.

 show what you know

1. _____ is the state of being aware of oneself, one's thoughts, and/or the environment.

2. While studying for an exam, your sensory systems absorb an inordinate amount of information from your surroundings, most of which escapes your awareness. Because of _____, you generally do not get overwhelmed with incoming sensory data.

    a. consciousness
    b. automatic processing
    c. depressants
    d. inattentional blindness

3. Inattentional blindness is the tendency to "look without seeing." Given what you know about selective attention, how would you advise someone to avoid inattentional blindness?

√ CHECK YOUR ANSWERS IN APPENDIX C.

Sleep Troubles

Matt Utesch was active and full of energy as a child, but come sophomore year in high school, he periodically fell asleep throughout the day. Matt was beginning to experience the symptoms of a serious sleep disorder. Courtesy Matthew Utesch.

Matt, in His Own Words

http://qrs.ly/mx5a5ag

Croc Sleep

A crocodile dozes while swimming, one eye cracked open and the other closed. Researchers suspect that saltwater crocs are able to sleep with just one brain hemisphere at a time. The eye linked to the awake hemisphere remains open, allowing the animal to maintain awareness of its surroundings (Kelly et al., 2015). Westend61/Getty Images.

Sleep

 **ASLEEP AT THE WHEEL** When Matt Utesch reminisces about childhood, he remembers having a lot of energy. "I was the kid that would wake up at 6:00 A.M. and watch cartoons," Matt recalls. As a teenager, Matt channeled his energy through sports—playing basketball, running cross-country, and competing in one of the nation's top-ranking private soccer leagues. But everything changed during Matt's sophomore year of high school. That was the year the sleepiness hit.

At first it seemed like nothing serious. Matt just dozed off in class from time to time. But his mininaps gradually became more frequent. Eventually, the sleepiness would take hold of him in every class except physical education. "Matt, you just fell asleep," his friends would say. "No I didn't," he would shoot back, unaware he had nodded off. Most of Matt's teachers assumed he was just another teenager exhausted from late-night partying. Nobody, not even Matt's doctor, suspected he had a serious medical condition—until the accident happened.

It was the summer before his junior year, and Matt was driving his truck home from work at his father's appliance repair shop. One moment he was rolling along the street at a safe distance from other cars, and the next he was ramming into a brown Saturn that had slowed to make a left turn. What had transpired in the interim? Matt had fallen asleep. He slammed on the brake pedal, but it was too late; the two vehicles collided. Unharmed, Matt leaped out of his truck and ran to check on the other driver—a woman who, as he remembers, "was totally out of it." Her backrest had broken, and her back had nearly broken along with it. A few weeks after the accident, Matt went to the woman's home to bring her flowers. She invited him inside, and they sat down and began to chat. Then, right in the midst of their conversation, Matt fell asleep. ●

An Introduction to Sleep

Most animals sleep or engage in some rest activity that resembles sleep, and the amount they need varies across species (Siegel, 2008). Crocodiles snooze keeping one eye cracked open most of the time; horses can sleep standing up (although they also lay down to sleep); and some birds appear to doze mid-flight (Kelly, Peters, Tisdale, & Lesku, 2015; U.S. Fish & Wildlife Service, 2006). There are animals that require plenty of sleep—bats and opossums sleep 18 to 20 hours a day—and those that need barely any—elephants and giraffes get by on 3 or 4 hours (Siegel, 2005). Sleep needs vary greatly among people, but the National Sleep Foundation recommends adults get between 7 and 9 hours per night (Hirshkowitz et al., 2015). Do the math and that translates to about a third of the day, and therefore a third of your *life*. Clearly, sleep serves some important function, but what is it? And how does it relate to consciousness? How can sleep go so wrong, as happened for Matt? Before tackling these questions, let's get a handle on the basics.

LO 4 Identify how circadian rhythm relates to sleep.

CIRCADIAN RHYTHM Have you ever noticed that you often get sleepy in the middle of the afternoon? Even if you had a good sleep the night before, you inevitably begin feeling tired around 2:00 or 3:00 P.M.; it's like clockwork. That's because it is clockwork. Many things your body does, including sleep, are regulated by a biological clock. Body temperature rises during the day, reaching its maximum in the early evening. Hormones are secreted in a cyclical fashion. Growth hormone is released at night, and the stress hormone cortisol soars in the morning, reaching levels 10 to 20 times higher than at night (Wright, 2002). These are just a few of the body functions that follow predictable daily patterns, affecting our behaviors, alertness, and activity levels. Such patterns in our physiological functioning roughly follow the 24-hour cycle of daylight and darkness; they follow a **circadian rhythm** (ser-KAY-dee-an).

In the circadian rhythm for sleep and wakefulness, there are two times when the desire for sleep hits hardest. The first is between 2:00 and 6:00 A.M., the same window of time when most car accidents caused by sleepiness occur (Horne, 2006). The second, less intense desire for sleep strikes midafternoon, between 2:00 and 4:00 P.M. (Lohr, 2015, September/October), when many college students seem to have trouble keeping their eyes open in class. This is a time when many, but not all, people nap. One study found that members of "preindustrial societies," who were hunter-gatherers/horticulturalists living in Tanzania, Bolivia, and Namibia, slept between 6 and 7 hours daily, with minimal napping. Temperature seemed to regulate their sleep duration and timing (Yetish et al., 2015).

Not all biological rhythms are circadian. Some occur over longer time intervals (monthly menstruation), and others cycle much faster (90-minute sleep cycles, to be discussed shortly). Many animals migrate or hibernate during certain seasons and mate according to a yearly pattern. Even when deprived of cues like changing levels of sunlight, some animals continue to follow these cycles. Birds caged indoors, for example, exhibit mood and behavioral changes at the times of year when they would normally be migrating. Biological clocks are everywhere in nature, acting as day planners for organisms as basic as bacteria and slime mold (Wright, 2002; Summa & Turek, 2015, February).

SUPRACHIASMATIC NUCLEUS Where in the human body do these inner clocks and calendars dwell? Miniclocks are found in cells all over your body, but a master clock is nestled deep within the hypothalamus, a brain structure whose activities revolve around maintaining homeostasis, or balance, in the body's systems. This master of clocks, known as the *suprachiasmatic nucleus (SCN),* actually consists of two clusters, each no bigger than an ant, totaling around 20,000 neurons (Bedrosian, Fonken, & Nelson, 2016; Forger & Peskin, 2003; Wright, 2002). The SCN plays a role in our circadian rhythm by communicating with other areas of the hypothalamus, which regulates daily patterns of hunger and temperature, and the reticular formation, which regulates alertness and sleepiness (**INFOGRAPHIC 4.1** on the next page).

Although tucked away in the recesses of the brain, the SCN knows the difference between day and night by receiving signals from a special type of light-sensing cells in the eye, called *retinal ganglion cells.* One way the SCN keeps you on schedule is by indirectly communicating with the pineal gland, a part of the endocrine system, to regulate the release of *melatonin,* a hormone that promotes sleep (Bedrosian et al., 2016). In dark conditions, the clock commands the pineal gland to produce melatonin, making it easier to sleep. When light hits the eye, melatonin secretion slows down. So if you want to sleep, turn down the lights, and let the melatonin get to work.

Digital technology is great for helping us monitor the time, and therefore keeping our internal clocks on schedule. But we must be careful about when and where we use them.

DIDN'T SEE THAT COMING
Are Screens Ruining Your Rhythm?

It's been a long day, and you're ready to snuggle under your soft, warm covers. On the way to your bedroom, you pass by your phone. *Let me check my e-mail one last time,* you think to yourself as you crawl into bed. One e-mail turns into two, two into three, and before you know it, you're logging into Facebook to see if you missed any good posts since you brushed your teeth. Your desire to sleep has now been replaced by excitement over new videos, photos, and status updates.

PROTECT YOUR CLOCK.

CONNECTIONS

In **Chapter 2,** we explained the functions of the hypothalamus. For example, it maintains blood pressure, temperature, and electrolyte balance. It also is involved in regulating sleep-wake cycles, sexual arousal, and appetite.

CONNECTIONS

In **Chapter 3,** we described how light enters the eye and is directed to the retina. The rods and cones in the retina are photoreceptors, which absorb light energy and turn it into electrical and chemical signals. Here, we see how light-sensing cells relay information to the SCN.

CONNECTIONS

In **Chapter 2,** we presented the endocrine system, a communication system that uses glands to convey messages within the body. The messages are delivered by hormones, which are chemicals released in the bloodstream. The pineal gland, a part of the endocrine system, secretes melatonin, a hormone that is involved in sleep-wake cycles.

circadian rhythm The daily patterns roughly following the 24-hour cycle of daylight and darkness; a 24-hour cycle of physiological and behavioral functioning.

The Suprachiasmatic Nucleus

The suprachiasmatic nucleus (SCN) of the hypothalamus is the body's internal master clock, playing a role in regulating our circadian rhythms. These rhythms roughly follow the 24-hour cycle of daylight and darkness. But one doesn't have to consciously perceive light for the SCN to function properly; there is a dedicated, *nonvisual* pathway that carries light information from the eyes to the SCN.

Pineal gland
produces melatonin

Hypothalamus
regulates patterns of hunger and temperature

Reticular formation
regulates alertness and sleepiness

The SCN is located deep in the brain, far away from visual processing areas. So how does it get information about light? Our eyes contain a separate nonvisual pathway made of retinal ganglion cells. This pathway goes directly to the SCN.

SCN

Suprachiasmatic nucleus (SCN)

The SCN is actually two tiny bundles of neurons within the hypothalamus. The SCN sends messages about light to the rest of the hypothalamus and the reticular formation, and regulates the pineal gland's production of melatonin, a sleep-inducing hormone.

Pathway for visual information

Optic chiasm

Supra is Latin for "above."
Suprachiasmatic means "above the chiasm." The SCN's long name helps you find it in the brain!

Visual processing area

Nonvisual pathway for signals about light

For the 20% of the U.S. workforce doing shift work, normal sleep schedules are disrupted. This leads to health problems and increased accidents (Harrington, 2001). Using what we know about how the SCN works, researchers are helping industries ease these effects. Bright lights, such as those installed in this power station control room, contain a high proportion of the blue light found in morning sun, fooling the SCN into thinking it is daytime. That makes it easier for workers to synchronize sleep patterns with work activities.

If this experience sounds familiar, you are not alone. Many Americans (as many as 90% of adults) use smartphones, tablets, and computers within 1 hour of bedtime, often to the detriment of their sleep (Bedrosian et al., 2016). Researchers have found that the blue light wavelengths emitted by LEDs (light-emitting diodes) may suppress the sleep-promoting hormone melatonin (Galbraith, 2015, April 7; Wood, Rea, Plitnick, & Figueiro, 2013). This finding is particularly relevant for adolescents, who tend to stay up later and need to wake early for school. For these young people, screen time before bed may lead to less sleep, sleepiness during the day, and reduced cognitive performance (van der Lely et al., 2015). Those over the age of 45 may be less vulnerable to such effects because, as we age, the eye filters out some of the blue light coming from the environment. This is partly a result of the pupil constricting and the lens becoming more yellow (Turner & Mainster, 2008). Regardless of your age, staring at LED screens close to bedtime can disrupt circadian rhythms (Wood et al., 2013). The brighter the light and the closer the device to the eye, the greater the impact (Galbraith, 2015, April 7).

How can we take this knowledge gleaned from research and use it to improve our sleep quality? The National Sleep Foundation (2016) suggests removing electronics from the bedroom a minimum of 1 hour before sleep. If you must check your e-mail close to bedtime, be quick and turn down the backlight, which gives off blue wavelengths. You may even consider using a "warm white" lightbulb (they emit a lower percentage of blue wavelengths) to illuminate your bedroom (Galbraith, 2015, April 7). 👁!

Want to Sleep Tight? Cut Out the Blue Light
The blue light emitted by LED screens of smartphones, computers, and other electronics may suppress the sleep hormone melatonin, and thereby disrupt sleep–wake cycles. Sam Diephuis/ Getty Images.

LARKS AND OWLS Everyone has her own unique clock, which helps explain why some of us are "morning people" or so-called larks, and others are "night owls." If you are a lark, you roll out of bed feeling energized and alert, get more accomplished early in the day, yet grow weary as the day drags on (Ferrante et al., 2015). Owls, on the other hand, get up late and hit the sack late. If you slam the "snooze" button on your alarm clock five times every morning, shower with your eyes closed, and act like a grouch at breakfast, you're probably an owl. But being an owl often means your energy level builds later in the day (Ferrante et al., 2015), making it easy to stay up late posting to Instagram or reading your textbook. These types of circadian rhythms impact peak performance in athletes (Facer-Childs & Brandstaetter, 2015) as well as college students.

 **In Class: Collaborate and Report**

College students are often portrayed as owls, but is this just a stereotype? In your group, discuss **A)** whether something in the college environment influences sleep–wake cycles, or is there a biological explanation. **B)** If you were to use the experimental method to explore this question, what would your independent and dependent variables be? **C)** What variables would you have to control for to make sure your groups are similar to each other?

JET LAG AND SHIFT WORK Whether you are a lark or an owl, your biological clock is likely to become confused when you travel across time zones. Your clock does not automatically reset to match the new time. The physical and mental consequences of this delayed adjustment, known as "jet lag," may include difficulty concentrating, headaches, and gastrointestinal distress. Fortunately, the biological clock can readjust by about 1 or 2 hours each day, eventually falling into step with the new environmental schedule (Cunha & Stöppler, 2016, June 6). Jet lag is frustrating, but at least it's only temporary, and there are things that can help lessen its effects. Researchers recommend strategies such as getting as much sleep as possible before traveling, avoiding caffeine and alcohol during your trip, and shifting your sleep schedule ahead of time so that it's more aligned with the time zone of your destination (Weingarten & Collop, 2013).

Night Shift

A young man works the night shift at the Jia Ling motorcycle factory in Chongqing, China. Factory workers are among the many professionals who clock in and out at all hours of the day. Working alternating or night shifts can disrupt circadian rhythms, leading to fatigue, irritability, and diminished mental sharpness. Physical activity and good sleep habits will help counteract the negative effects (Costa, 2003).
China Photos/Getty Images.

A related phenomenon, *social jet lag,* affects 70% of the U.S. population and occurs when we use our alarm clocks to get up to go to work or school, and then sleep later on the days we have off (Baron & Reid, 2014). Our day-to-day responsibilities can make it difficult to support our natural sleeping routines, so we are not getting as much sleep as we need (Bedrosian et al., 2016).

Now imagine plodding through life with a case of jet lag you just can't shake. This is the tough reality for some of the world's shift workers—firefighters, nurses, miners, power plant operators, and other professionals who work while the rest of the world snuggles under the covers. Shift workers represent about 20% of the workforce in the United States and other developed countries, or 1 in 5 people who are employed (Di Lorenzo et al., 2003; Wright, Bogan, & Wyatt, 2013). Some work rotating shifts, which means they are constantly going to bed and waking up at different times; others consistently work the overnight shift, so their sleep–wake cycles are permanently out-of-step with the light and dark cycles of the earth. Constantly fighting the clock takes a heavy toll on the mind and body. An irregular sleep schedule may lead to symptoms of *insomnia,* or difficulty falling asleep and sleeping soundly. Picture yourself coming off the night shift and arriving home at 7:00 A.M.: The sun is shining brightly, the birds are chirping, and the rest of the family is chatting over their cornflakes. This is not an ideal environment for sleep. Insomnia resulting from shift work can lead to mood disorders, diabetes, and other chronic diseases (Baron & Reid, 2014; Bedrosian et al., 2016; Wright et al., 2013). Shift workers also face an elevated risk of becoming overweight, and of developing stomach ulcers and heart disease (Baron & Reid, 2014; Monk & Buysse, 2013). In addition, an estimated 5% to 10% of shift workers have been diagnosed with *circadian rhythm sleep–wake disorders,* characterized by excessive sleepiness at work and insomnia at home (American Psychiatric Association, 2013).

Because of the varied schedules shift workers endure, it is difficult to minimize circadian disturbances. Remember that light is the master clock's most important external cue. Maximizing light exposure during work time and steering clear of it close to bedtime can help (Bedrosian et al., 2016). Some night shifters don sunglasses on their way home, to block the morning sun, and head straight to bed in a quiet, dark room (Epstein & Mardon, 2007). Taking 20- to 30-minute power naps in the middle of a night shift can also help shift workers stay awake and alert, as can getting regular exercise (Bedrosian et al., 2016; Harvard Medical School, 2007).

The Stages of Sleep

LO 5   **Summarize the stages of sleep.**

Have you ever watched someone sleeping? The person looks blissfully tranquil: body still, face relaxed, chest rising and falling like a lazy ocean wave. Don't be fooled. Underneath the body's quiet front is a very active brain, as revealed by an electroencephalogram (EEG), monitoring activity on the surface of the brain. If you could look at an EEG trace of your brain right at this moment, you would probably see a series of tiny, short spikes in rapid-fire succession. These high-frequency brain waves are called **beta waves,** and they appear when you are solving a math problem, reading a book, or any time you are alert (**INFOGRAPHIC 4.2**). Researchers call this Stage W, indicating a "waking state," and this stage can range from being fully alert to slightly drowsy (Berry et al., 2016). Now let's say you climb into bed, close your eyes, and relax. As you become more and more drowsy, the EEG would likely begin showing **alpha waves**, which are lower in frequency than beta waves (Cantero, Atienza, Salas, & Gómez, 1999; Silber et al., 2007). At some point, you drift into a different level of

beta waves Brain waves that indicate an alert, awake state.

alpha waves Brain waves that indicate a relaxed, drowsy state.

Sleep

Looking in on a sleep study, you'll see that the brain is actually very active during sleep, cycling through non-REM stages and ending in REM sleep approximately five times during the night. Transitions between stages are clearly visible as shifts in EEG patterns.

Graphs illustrating the human sleep cycle typically present an 8-hour time span, as shown below. But this doesn't tell the whole story of sleep. The amount of time spent sleeping and the content of our sleep changes across the life span. Currently, only two thirds of U.S. adults get the recommended minimum of 7 hours per night (Liu et al., 2016).

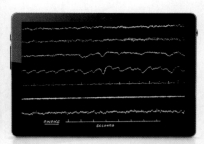

This sleep study participant wears electrodes that will measure her brain waves and body movements during sleep.

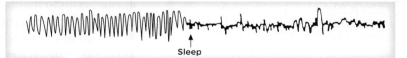

Sleep

Looking at brain waves allows us to trace a person's stage of sleep. Here we can see a clear shift from waking to sleeping patterns.
(FROM DEMENT & VAUGHAN, 1999.)

Human Sleep Stages

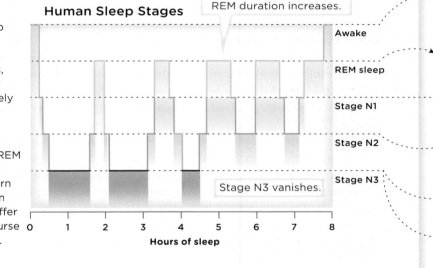

A typical night's sleep has 4 or 5 multistage sleep cycles, each lasting approximately 90 minutes. Each cycle includes at least 1 non-REM and 1 REM stage. Pattern and duration of stages differ over the course of the night.

REM duration increases.
Stage N3 vanishes.

Awake / REM sleep / Stage N1 / Stage N2 / Stage N3

Hours of sleep

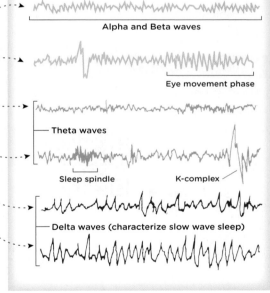

Alpha and Beta waves / Eye movement phase / Theta waves / Sleep spindle / K-complex / Delta waves (characterize slow wave sleep)

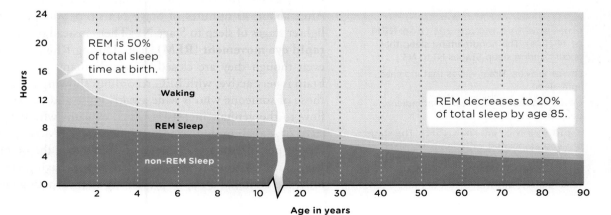

As we age, we need fewer hours of sleep, and the proportion of time spent in REM diminishes.

REM is 50% of total sleep time at birth.
REM decreases to 20% of total sleep by age 85.

Waking / REM Sleep / non-REM Sleep

Age in years

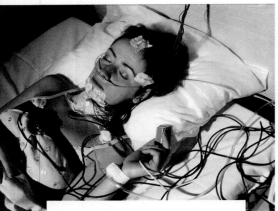

Sleep Waves
A sleep study participant undergoes an EEG. Electrodes attached to her head pick up electrical activity from her brain, which is transformed into a series of spikes on a computer screen. Through careful study of EEG data, researchers have come to understand the various stages of sleep. Garo/Phanie/Superstock.

You Asked, Matt Answers

http://qrs.ly/di5a5ak

In hindsight, did you notice any changes that may have foreshadowed the onset of narcolepsy?

scan this →

non-rapid eye movement (non-REM or NREM) The nondreaming sleep that occurs during sleep Stages N1 to N3.

theta waves Brain waves that indicate light sleep.

delta waves Brain waves that indicate a deep sleep.

rapid eye movement (REM) The stage of sleep associated with dreaming; sleep characterized by bursts of eye movements, with brain activity similar to that of a waking state, but with a lack of muscle tone.

consciousness known as sleep. Over the years, researchers have developed a variety of methods to study sleep and diagnose sleep disorders. These technologies have helped researchers characterize the different stages of sleep, and create standard procedures for studying sleep (Berry et al., 2016).

NON-REM SLEEP A normal sleeper begins the night in **non-rapid eye movement (non-REM** or **NREM)**, or nondreaming, sleep, which has three stages (Berry et al., 2016; Infographic 4.2). The first and lightest is Stage N1 (NREM 1 sleep), also known as "light sleep." During Stage N1, muscles go limp and body temperature starts to fall. The eyeballs may move gently beneath the lids. If you looked at an EEG of a person in Stage N1, you would likely see **theta waves**, which are lower in frequency than both alpha and beta waves. This is the type of sleep many people deny having. Example: Your friend begins to snooze while watching TV, so you poke her in the ribs and say, "Wake up!" but she swears she wasn't asleep. It is also during this initial phase of sleep that *hallucinations,* or imaginary sensations, can occur. Do you ever see blotches of color or bizarre floating images as you drift off to sleep? Or perhaps you have felt a sensation of falling or swinging and then jerked your arms or legs in response? False perceptions that occur during the limbo between wakefulness and sleep are called *hypnagogic* (hip-nuh-GOJ-ik) *hallucinations,* and they are no cause for concern—in most cases. More on this when we return to Matt's story.

After a few minutes in Stage N1, you move on to the next phase of non-REM sleep, called Stage N2 (NREM 2 sleep), which is slightly deeper than Stage N1, so you are harder to awaken. Theta waves continue showing up on the EEG, along with little bursts of electrical activity called *sleep spindles* and large waves called *K-complexes* appearing every 2 minutes or so. Researchers suspect sleep spindles are associated with memory consolidation and intelligence (Fogel & Smith, 2011; Laventure et al., 2016). The exact function of K-complexes is up for debate: Some suggest they are the brain's way of being ready to awaken when the need arises, while others believe they are the mechanism for remaining asleep in spite of disturbing stimuli (Colrain, 2005). They are also thought to be involved in the consolidation of some types of memories (Caporro et al., 2012).

After passing through Stages N1 and N2, the sleeper descends into Stage N3 (NREM 3 sleep), when it can be most difficult to awaken. Stage N3 is considered slow-wave sleep, because it is characterized by tall, low-frequency **delta waves**. Stage N3 contains a higher proportion of delta waves than the prior stages (at least 20%; Berry & Wagner, 2015). Waking a person from slow-wave sleep is not easy. Most of us feel groggy, disoriented, and downright irritated when jarred from a slow-wave slumber. This is also the peak time for the secretion of growth hormone, which helps children to grow taller and stronger, and to build tissue (Awikunprasert & Sittiprapapom, 2012).

REM SLEEP You don't stay in deep sleep for the remainder of the night, however. After about 40 minutes of Stage N3 sleep, you work your way back through the lighter stages of sleep to Stage N2. Then, instead of waking up, you enter Stage R, or **rapid eye movement (REM)** sleep. During REM sleep, the eyes often dart around, even though they are closed (hence the name "rapid eye movement" sleep). The brain is very active, with EEG recordings showing faster and shorter waves similar to those of someone who is wide awake. Pulse and breathing rate fluctuate, and blood flow to the genitals increases, which explains why people frequently wake up in a state of sexual arousal. Another name for REM sleep is *paradoxical sleep,* because the sleeper appears to be quiet and resting, but the brain is full of electrical activity. People roused from REM sleep often report having vivid, illogical dreams. Thankfully, the brain has a way of preventing us from acting out our dreams. During REM sleep, certain neurons in the brainstem control the voluntary muscles, keeping most of the body still.

What would happen if the neurons responsible for disabling the muscles during REM sleep were destroyed or damaged? Researchers led by Michel Jouvet in France and Adrian Morrison in the United States found the answer to that question in the 1960s and 1970s. Both teams showed that severing these neurons in the brains of cats caused them to act out their kitty dreams. Not only did the sleeping felines stand up; they arched their backs in fury, groomed and licked themselves, and hunted imaginary mice (Jouvet, 1979; Sastre & Jouvet, 1979).

Kitty Dreams
This cat may be dreaming of chasing mice and birds, but its body is essentially paralyzed during REM sleep. Disable the neurons responsible for this paralysis and you will see some very interesting behavior—the cat will act out its dream. iStock/Getty Images.

SLEEP ARCHITECTURE Congratulations. You have just completed one sleep cycle, working your way through Stages N1, N2, and N3 of non-REM sleep and ending with a dream-packed episode of REM. Each of these cycles lasts about 90 minutes, and the average adult sleeper loops through five of them per night. The composition of these 90-minute sleep cycles changes during the night. During the first two cycles, a considerable amount of time is devoted to the deep sleep Stage N3. Halfway through the night, however, Stage N3 vanishes. Meanwhile, the REM periods become progressively longer, with the first REM episode lasting only 5 to 10 minutes, and the final one lasting nearly a half-hour (Siegel, 2005). Therefore, we pack in most of our non-REM sleep early in the night and most of the dreaming toward the end; and the sleep stage we spend the most time in—nearly half the night—is Stage N2 (Epstein & Mardon, 2007).

The makeup of our sleep cycles, or *sleep architecture,* changes throughout life. Infants spend almost half of their sleep in REM periods (Skeldon, Derks, & Dijk, 2016). Older people spend far less time in REM sleep and the deeply refreshing stages of non-REM sleep (N3). Instead, they experience longer periods of light sleep (Stages N1 and N2), which can be interrupted easily by noises and movements, and a decrease in the deeper sleep stages that include the slow brain waves (Cirelli, 2012; Ohayon, Carskadon, Guilleminault, & Vitiello, 2004; Scullin & Bliwise, 2015). Could this be the reason many older people complain of sleeping poorly, waking up often, and feeling drowsy during the day? Not all elderly people have trouble sleeping, of course. Like most everything in life, sleep patterns vary considerably from one individual to the next.

On a typical weeknight, the average American sleeps 6 hours and 40 minutes, but there is significant deviation from this "average" (National Sleep Foundation, 2009). A large number of people—about 28% of the population—get fewer than 6 hours, and another 9% snooze longer than 8 hours (Schoenborn, Adams, & Peregoy, 2013).

Wake Up!
Some of us feel refreshed after sleeping 6 or 7 hours. Others can barely grasp a glass of orange juice without a solid 8. Sleep habits appear to be a blend of biological and environmental forces—both nature and nurture. Ariel Skelley/Corbis.

PROBLEM IDENTIFIED: NARCOLEPSY Shortly after the car accident, Matt was diagnosed with **narcolepsy,** a neurological disorder characterized by excessive daytime sleepiness and other sleep-related disturbances. The most striking symptoms of narcolepsy include the "irrepressible need to sleep, lapsing into sleep, or napping occurring within the same day" (American Psychiatric Association, 2013, p. 372). With narcolepsy, sleepiness can strike anytime, anywhere—during a job interview, while riding a bicycle, or in the midst of a passionate kiss. One time Matt fell asleep while making a sandwich. When he awoke, he was still holding a slice of meat in his hand. Some people with narcolepsy report a waking alert level and then falling asleep, while others report an overwhelming feeling of sleepiness all the time. "Sleep attacks" can occur several times a day. Most are measured in seconds or minutes, but episodes of an hour or

narcolepsy A neurological disorder characterized by excessive daytime sleepiness, which includes lapses into sleep and napping.

longer have been reported (National Institute of Neurological Disorders and Stroke, 2013, September). By the time Matt was a junior in high school, his uncontrollable naps were striking upward of 20 to 30 times a day. ●

Sleep Disturbances

LO 6 Recognize various sleep disorders and their symptoms.

CATAPLEXY And that wasn't all. Matt developed another debilitating symptom of narcolepsy: *cataplexy*, an abrupt loss of strength or muscle tone that occurs when a person is awake. During a severe cataplectic attack, some muscles go limp, and the body may collapse slowly to the floor like a rag doll. One moment Matt would be standing in the hallway laughing with friends; the next he was splayed on the floor unable to move a muscle. "It was like a tree being cut down [and] tipping over," he recalls. Cataplexy attacks come on suddenly, usually during periods of emotional excitement (American Psychiatric Association, 2013). The effects usually wear off after several seconds, but severe attacks can immobilize a person for minutes.

Cataplexy may completely disable the body, but it produces no loss in consciousness. Even during the worst attack, Matt remained completely aware of himself and his surroundings. He could hear people talking about him; sometimes they snickered in amusement. "Kids can be cruel," Matt says. By junior year, Matt was having 60 to 100 attacks a day.

SLEEP PARALYSIS AND HYPNAGOGIC HALLUCINATIONS Matt also developed two other common narcolepsy symptoms: sleep paralysis and hypnagogic hallucinations. *Sleep paralysis* is a temporary paralysis that strikes just before falling asleep or upon waking (American Psychiatric Association, 2013). Recall that the body becomes paralyzed during REM sleep, but sometimes this paralysis sets in prematurely or fails to turn off on time. Picture yourself lying in bed, awake and fully aware yet unable to roll over, climb out of bed, or even wiggle a toe. You want to scream for help, but your lips won't budge. Sleep paralysis is a common symptom of narcolepsy, but it can also strike ordinary sleepers. Researchers have found that a wide range of people have experienced sleep paralysis at least once in their lives: from around 8% of the general population to 28% of college students (Jalal & Ramachandran, 2014; Jalal, Taylor, & Hinton, 2014; Sharpless & Barber, 2011). Episodes usually last a few seconds, but some go on for several minutes—a terrifying experience for most people.

Sleep paralysis may seem scary, but now imagine seeing bloodthirsty vampires standing at the foot of your bed just as you are about to fall asleep. Earlier we discussed the *hypnagogic hallucinations* people can experience during Stage N1 sleep (seeing strange images, for example). But not all hypnagogic hallucinations involve harmless blobs. They can also be realistic visions of axe murderers or space aliens trying to abduct you (McNally & Clancy, 2005). Matt had a recurring hallucination of a man with a butcher knife racing through his doorway, jumping onto his bed, and stabbing him in the chest. Upon awakening, Matt would often quiz his mother with questions like, "When is my birthday?" or "What is your license plate number?" He wanted to verify she was real, not just another character in his dream. Like sleep paralysis, vivid hypnagogic hallucinations can occur in people without narcolepsy, too. Shift work, insomnia, and sleeping face-up are all factors that appear to heighten one's risk (Cheyne, 2002; McNally & Clancy, 2005).

BATTLING NARCOLEPSY Throughout junior year, Matt took various medications to control his narcolepsy, but his symptoms persisted. Narcolepsy was beginning to interfere with virtually every aspect of his life. At the beginning of high school, Matt had

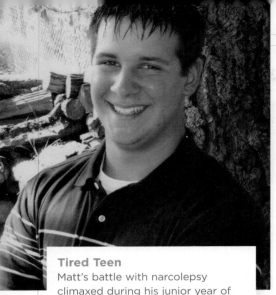

Tired Teen
Matt's battle with narcolepsy climaxed during his junior year of high school. In addition to falling asleep 20 to 30 times a day, he was experiencing frequent bouts of cataplexy, an abrupt loss of muscle tone that occurs while one is awake. Cataplexy struck Matt anytime, anywhere—up to 100 times a day. Courtesy Matthew Utesch.

Did She Have Narcolepsy?
Harriet Tubman is famous for helping hundreds of people escape slavery through the Underground Railroad. But few people know that Tubman suffered from symptoms of narcolepsy. Her sleep problems began after an incident that occurred when she was still a slave: An overseer struck her in the head as punishment for protesting the beating of a fellow slave (Michals, 2015; Poole, 2016, April 20). UniversalImagesGroup/Getty Images.

a 4.0 grade point average; now he was working twice as hard and earning lower grades. Playing sports had become a major health hazard because his cataplexy struck wherever and whenever, without notice. If he collapsed while sprinting down the soccer field or diving for a basketball, he might twist an ankle, break an arm, or worse. It was during this time that Matt realized who his true friends were. "The people that stuck with me [then] are still my close friends now," he says. Matt's loyal buddies learned to recognize the warning signs of his cataplexy (for example, when he suddenly stands still and closes his eyes) and did everything possible to keep him safe, grabbing hold of his body and slowly lowering him to the ground. His buddies had his back—literally.

Approximately 1 in 2,500 people suffers from narcolepsy (Ohayon, 2011). It is believed to result from a failure of the brain to properly regulate sleep patterns. Normally, the boundaries separating sleep and wakefulness are relatively clear—you are awake, in REM sleep, or in non-REM sleep. With narcolepsy, the lines separating these different realms of consciousness fade, allowing sleep to spill into periods of wakefulness. The loss of muscle tone during cataplexy, sleep paralysis, and dreamlike hypnagogic hallucinations may be explained by occurrences of REM sleep in the midst of wakefulness (Attarian, Schenck, & Mahowald, 2000). In other words, REM sleep occurs in the wrong place, at the wrong time (see a summary of this and other sleep disturbances in **TABLE 4.2** on the following page).

REM SLEEP BEHAVIOR DISORDER Problems with REM regulation can also lead to other sleep disturbances, including **REM sleep behavior disorder**. The defining characteristics of this disorder include "repeated episodes of arousal often associated with vocalizations and/or complex motor behaviors arising from REM sleep" (American Psychiatric Association, 2013, p. 408). People with REM sleep behavior disorder are much like the cats in Morrison's and Jouvet's experiments; something has gone awry with the brainstem mechanism responsible for paralyzing their bodies during REM sleep, so they are able to move around and act out their dreams (Schenck & Mahowald, 2002). This is not a good thing, since the dreams of people with REM sleep behavior disorder tend to be unusually violent and action-packed, involving fights with wild animals and other attackers (Fantini, Corona, Clerici, & Ferini-Strambi, 2005). According to some research, up to 65% of REM sleep behavior disorder sufferers have injured either themselves or their bedmates at one point or another. Scrapes, cuts, and bruises are common, and traumatic brain injuries have also been reported (American Psychiatric Association, 2013; Aurora et al., 2010). REM sleep behavior disorder primarily affects older men (age 50 and up) and frequently foreshadows the development of serious neurodegenerative disorders—conditions such as Parkinson's disease and dementia that are associated with the gradual decline and death of neurons (Boeve et al., 2007; Fantini et al., 2005; Postuma et al., 2009; Schenck & Mahowald, 2002). Women and younger people are diagnosed with this disorder as well (American Psychiatric Association, 2013).

BREATHING-RELATED SLEEP DISORDERS There are several breathing-related sleep disorders, but the most common is **obstructive sleep apnea hypopnea** (hi-POP-nee-uh), characterized by a complete absence of air flow (apnea) or reduced air flow (hypopnea). During normal sleep, the airway remains open, allowing air to flow in and out of the lungs. With obstructive sleep apnea hypopnea, the upper throat muscles go limp, allowing the upper airway to close shut (American Psychiatric Association, 2013). Breathing stops for 10 seconds or more, causing blood oxygen levels to drop (Chung & Elsaid, 2009; Teodorescu et al., 2015). The brain responds by commanding the body to *wake up and breathe!* The sleeper awakes and gasps for air, sometimes with a noisy nasal sound, and then drifts back to sleep. This process can repeat itself several hundred times per night, preventing a person from experiencing the deep

You Asked, Matt Answers

http://qrs.ly/xs5a5ao

What kind of physician did you visit in order to be diagnosed with narcolepsy?

scan this ➡

Does Rosie Snore?
Actor and TV personality Rosie O'Donnell is among the millions of Americans who suffer from obstructive sleep apnea hypopnea (Schocker, 2012, September 25). Research suggests this sleep disorder affects between 3% and 7% of the adult population (Punjabi, 2008). Steve Mack/FilmMagic/Getty Images.

REM sleep behavior disorder
A sleep disturbance in which the mechanism responsible for paralyzing the body during REM sleep is not functioning, resulting in the acting out of dreams.

obstructive sleep apnea hypopnea
A serious disturbance of non-REM sleep characterized by complete absence of air flow (apnea) or reduced air flow (hypopnea).

TABLE 4.2 SLEEP DISTURBANCES

Sleep Disturbance	Definition	Defining Characteristics
Narcolepsy	Neurological disorder characterized by excessive daytime sleepiness, which includes lapses into sleep and napping.	Irrepressible need to sleep; daytime napping; cataplexy; sleep paralysis; hypnagogic hallucinations.
REM Sleep Behavior Disorder	The mechanism responsible for paralysis during REM not functioning, resulting in the acting out of dreams.	Dreamers vocalize and act out dreams; violent and active dreams are common; upon awakening, the dream is remembered; risk of injury to self and sleeping partners.
Obstructive Sleep Apnea Hypopnea	Serious disturbance characterized by a complete absence of air flow (apnea) or reduced air flow (hypopnea).	Upper throat muscles go limp; airway closes; breathing stops for 10 seconds or longer; sleeper awakens, gasping for air.
Insomnia	Inability to fall asleep or stay asleep.	Poor sleep quantity or quality; tendency to wake up too early; cannot fall back asleep; not feeling refreshed after a night's sleep.
Sleepwalking	Disturbance of non-REM sleep characterized by complex motor behavior during sleep.	Expressionless face; open eyes; may sit up in bed, walk around, or speak gibberish; upon awakening, has limited recall.
Sleep Terrors	Disturbance of non-REM sleep generally occurring in children.	Screaming, inconsolable child; usually, no memory of the episode the next day.

Problems can arise during both REM and non-REM sleep. This table outlines some of the most common sleep disturbances and their defining characteristics.

stages of sleep so crucial for feeling reenergized in the morning. Most people have no memory of the repeated awakenings and wonder why they feel so exhausted during the day; they are completely unaware that they suffer from this serious sleep disturbance. Obstructive sleep apnea hypopnea is more common among men than women and is more prevalent in the obese, and in women after menopause. This condition is linked to increased risk of death in the elderly, traffic accidents, and reduced quality of life, as well as elevated blood pressure, which increases the risk of cardiovascular disease (American Psychiatric Association, 2013). These risks are not limited to adults; researchers have noted a correlation between obstructive sleep apnea and sudden infant death syndrome (SIDS), failure-to-thrive, and other developmental issues (Katz, Mitchell, & D'Ambrosio, 2012).

INSOMNIA The most prevalent sleep disturbance is **insomnia**, which is characterized by an inability to fall asleep or stay asleep. Those experiencing this condition may complain of waking up in the middle of the night or arising too early, and not being able to fall back asleep. People with insomnia often report that the quantity or quality of their sleep is not good. Sleepiness during the day and difficulties with cognitive tasks are also reported (American Psychiatric Association, 2013). About a third of adults experience some symptoms of insomnia, and 6% to 10% meet diagnostic criteria for *insomnia disorder* (American Psychiatric Association, 2013; Mai & Buysse, 2008; Roth, 2007). Insomnia is, to a certain degree, inherited (Van Someren et al., 2015), but its symptoms can be triggered by many factors, including the stress of a new job, college studies, depression, anxiety, jet lag, aging, drug use, and chronic pain.

OTHER SLEEP DISTURBANCES A common sleep disturbance that can occur during non-REM sleep (typically Stage N3) is *sleepwalking*. A quarter of all children will experience at least one sleepwalking incident, and it seems to run in families (Licis, Desruisseau, Yamada, Duntley, & Gurnett, 2011; Petit et al., 2015). Here are some

Synonyms

sleepwalking somnambulism (som-NAM-byuh-liz-um)

sleep terrors night terrors

insomnia Sleep disturbance characterized by an inability to fall asleep or stay asleep, impacting both the quality and quantity of sleep.

sleep terrors A disturbance of non-REM sleep, generally occurring in children; characterized by screaming, staring fearfully, and usually no memory of the episode the following morning.

nightmares Frightening dreams that occur during REM sleep.

ways to spot a sleepwalker: Her face is expressionless; her eyes are open; and she may sit up in bed, walk around in confusion, or speak gibberish. (The garbled speech of sleepwalking is different from sleep *talking,* which can occur in either REM or non-REM sleep, but is not considered a sleep disturbance.) Sleepwalkers may have "limited recall" of the event upon awakening (American Psychiatric Association, 2013). They are capable of accomplishing a variety of tasks such as opening doors, going to the bathroom, and getting dressed, all of which they are likely to forget by morning. Most sleepwalking episodes are not related to dreaming, and contrary to urban myth, awakening a sleepwalker will not cause sudden death or injury. What's dangerous is leaving the front door unlocked and the car keys in the ignition, as sleepwalkers have been known to wander into the streets and even attempt driving (American Psychiatric Association, 2013).

Sleep terrors are non-REM sleep disturbances primarily affecting children. A child experiencing a night terror may sit up in bed, stare fearfully at nothing, and scream. Parents may find the child crying hysterically, breathing rapidly, and sweating. No matter what the parents say or do, the child remains inconsolable. Fortunately, sleep terrors only last a few minutes, and most children outgrow them. Children generally do not remember the episode the next day (American Psychiatric Association, 2013).

Nightmares are frightening dreams that occur in REM sleep. Nightmare disorder affects approximately 4% of the population (Aurora et al., 2010). And unlike night terrors, nightmares can often be recalled in vivid detail. Because nightmares usually occur during REM sleep, they are generally not acted out (American Psychiatric Association, 2013). Recent research suggests that people who frequently experience nightmares may be "more susceptible to daily stressors" and are associated with a variety of other problems like depression and insomnia (Hochard, Heym, & Townsend, 2016, p. 47; Nadorff, Nadorff, & Germain, 2015). In some cases, nightmares may not have an apparent cause; in other cases, they may be related to issues such as posttraumatic stress disorder (PTSD; see Chapter 12), substance abuse, and anxiety. Approximately 80% of people with PTSD report having nightmares (Aurora et al., 2010).

Who Needs Sleep?

Matt's worst struggle with narcolepsy stretched through the last two years of high school. During this time, he was averaging 20 to 30 naps a day. You might think that someone who falls asleep so often would at least feel well rested while awake. This was not the case. Matt had trouble sleeping at night, and it was taking a heavy toll on his ability to think clearly. He remembers nodding off at the wheel a few times but continuing to drive, reassuring himself that everything was fine. He forgot about homework assignments and couldn't recall simple things people told him. Matt was experiencing two of the most common symptoms of sleep deprivation: impaired judgment and lapses in memory (Goel, Rao, Durmer, & Dinges, 2009, September).

Let's face it. No one can function optimally without a good night's sleep. But the expression "good night's sleep" can mean something quite different from one person to the next. Newborns sleep anywhere from 10.5 to 18 hours per day, toddlers 11 to 14 hours, school-aged children 9 to 11 hours, and teens 8 to 10 hours (National Sleep Foundation, 2015a, 2015c). The average adult needs between 7 and 8 hours to feel restored, though some (including Madonna and Jay Leno) claim they get by on just 4 (Breus, 2009, May 6). Adults who average less than 4 or more than 11 hours of sleep are very rare (Horne, 2006).

SLEEP DEPRIVATION What happens to animals when they don't sleep at all? Laboratory studies show that sleep deprivation kills rats faster than starvation (Rechtschaffen & Bergmann, 1995; Siegel, 2005). Curtailing sleep in humans leads to rapid

"Disturbia" or Insomnia?
Rihanna appears to get plenty of beauty sleep, but her social media activity suggests otherwise. The singer/songwriter has been known to Tweet about her sleep troubles: "Waited all yr + Finally I have time off, time 4 rest n quiet. Suddenly all the silence is being drowned by my thoughts! No sleep" (Klein, 2014, March 6; Rihanna, 2012, January 4). Kevin Mazur/Getty Images for FENTY PUMA.

"Wake up, Tom. You're having the American dream again."

Peter Steiner/The New Yorker Collection/www.cartoonbank.com.

Sleep Culture
A rickshaw driver in New Delhi, India, snoozes in the bright sun. Afternoon siestas are common in countries such as India and Spain, but atypical in the United States (Randall, 2012, September 22). Cultural norms regarding sleep vary significantly around the world. Christine Welman/Alamy.

Record-Breaking Randy
A half-century ago, 17-year-old Randy Gardner set the record for the longest documented period of self-imposed sleep deprivation. With the help and encouragement of two friends, and no caffeine or stimulants of any sort, the young man went 11 consecutive days without snoozing (Gulevich et al., 1966). San Diego History Center.

REM rebound An increased amount of time spent in REM after sleep deprivation.

deterioration of mental and physical well-being. Stay up all night for 48 hours and you can expect your memory, attention, reaction time, and decision making to suffer noticeably (Goel et al., 2009, September; Van Someren et al., 2015). Sleepy people find it especially challenging to accomplish tasks that are monotonous and boring; those deprived of sleep have trouble focusing on a single activity, like keeping their eyes on the road while driving (Lim & Dinges, 2010). Using driving simulators and tests to measure alertness, hand-eye coordination, and other factors, researchers report that getting behind the wheel while sleepy is similar to driving drunk. Staying awake for just 17 to 19 consecutive hours (which many of us with demanding jobs, children, and social lives do regularly) produces the same effect as having a blood alcohol content (BAC) of 0.05%, the legal limit in many countries—driving under these circumstances is dangerous (Watson et al., 2015; Williamson & Feyer, 2000). Sleep loss also makes you more prone to *microsleeps,* or uncontrollable mininaps lasting several seconds—enough time to miss a traffic light turning red. Staying awake for several days at a time (11 days is the current world record, based on experimental data; Gillin, 2002, March 25) produces a host of disabling effects, including fragmented speech, cognitive deficits, mood swings, and hallucinations (Gulevich, Dement, & Johnson, 1966).

A more chronic form of sleep deprivation results from insufficient sleep night-upon-night for weeks, months, or years. People in this category are less likely than their well-rested peers to exercise, eat healthy foods, have sex, and attend family events (National Sleep Foundation, 2009). They also face a greater risk for heart disease, diabetes, cancer, and weight gain (Luyster, Strollo, Zee, & Walsh, 2012), and have decreased immune system responses and slower reaction times (Besedovsky, Lange, & Born, 2012; Orzeł-Gryglewska, 2010). Many researchers suspect the obesity epidemic currently plaguing industrialized countries like the United States is partially linked to chronic sleep deprivation. Skimping on sleep appears to disrupt appetite-regulating hormones, which may lead to excessive hunger and overeating (Van Someren et al., 2015; Willyard, 2008).

REM DEPRIVATION So far we have only covered sleep loss in general. What happens if REM sleep is compromised? Preliminary research suggests depriving people of REM sleep can cause emotional overreactions to threatening situations (Rosales-Lagarde et al., 2012). REM deprivation can also lead to **REM rebound**, an increased amount of time spent in REM sleep when one finally gets an opportunity to sleep in peace. Researchers report that sleep disturbances following surgery, for example, often result in REM sleep rebound (Chouchou, Khoury, Chauny, Denis, & Lavigne, 2014).

WHY DO WE SLEEP? The purpose of sleep has yet to be conclusively identified (Assefa, Diaz-Abad, Wickwire, & Scharf, 2015). Drawing from sleep deprivation studies and other types of experiments, researchers have constructed various theories to explain *why* we spend so much time sleeping (**TABLE 4.3**). Here are three of the major ones:

- The *restorative theory* says we sleep because it allows for growth and repair of the body and brain. Growth hormone is secreted during non-REM sleep and protein production ramps up in the brain during REM. Some have suggested that sleep is a time for rest and replenishment of neurotransmitters, especially those important for attention and memory (Borbély, Daan, Wirz-Justice, & Deboer, 2016; Hobson, 1989).

- An *evolutionary theory* says sleep serves an adaptive function; it evolved because it helped us survive. For much of human history, nighttime was very dark—and very unsafe. Humans have poor night vision compared to animals hunting for prey, so it was adaptive for us to avoid moving around our environments in the dark of night. The development of our circadian rhythms driving us to sleep at night has served an important evolutionary purpose (Barton & Capellini, 2016).

TABLE 4.3 THEORIES OF SLEEP

Theory	Description	Explanation
Restorative	Sleep allows for growth and repair of the body and brain.	Growth hormone secreted during non-REM sleep; protein production increases during REM; replenishment of neurotransmitters.
Evolutionary	Sleep serves adaptive function; evolved as it helped survival.	Dark environments were unsafe; humans have poor night vision compared to animals hunting at night.
Consolidation	Sleep aids in the consolidation of memories and learning.	Assists in creation of memories, learning difficult concepts; similar patterns of brain activity when learning and sleeping afterward.

We spend approximately a third of our lives sleeping, yet the precise purpose of sleep is still to be established. Above are three of the dominant theories.

- Another popular theory suggests that sleep helps with the *consolidation* of memories and learning (Tononi & Cirelli, 2014). Researchers disagree about which stage of sleep might facilitate such a process, but one thing seems clear: Without sleep, our ability to lay down complex memories, and thus learn difficult concepts, is hampered (Farthing, 1992). Studies show that areas of the brain excited during learning tasks are reawakened during non-REM sleep. When researchers monitored the neuronal activity of rats exploring a new environment, they noticed certain neurons firing. These same neurons became active again when the rats fell into non-REM sleep, suggesting that the neurons were involved in remembering the experience (Diekelmann & Born, 2010). Similarly, in humans, positron emission tomography (PET) scans have shown common patterns of brain activity when research participants were awake and learning and later while asleep (Maquet, 2000).

Whatever the purpose of sleep, there is no denying its importance. After a couple of sleepless nights, we are grumpy, clumsy, and unable to think straight. Although we may appreciate the value of sleep, we don't always practice the best sleep habits—or know what they are. Read on to discover some behaviors and assumptions you should avoid.

THINK IT THROUGH
9 Sleep Myths

Everyone seems to have their own bits of "expert knowledge" about sleep. Read on to learn about claims (in **bold**) that are false.

NO IPADS ALLOWED IN THE BED!

- **Drinking alcohol before bed helps you sleep better:** Alcohol helps you fall asleep, but it undermines sleep quality and may cause you to awaken in the night (Ebrahim, Shapiro, Williams, & Fenwick, 2013). So, too, can one or two cups of coffee. Although moderate caffeine consumption heightens alertness (Epstein & Mardon, 2007; Volkow et al., 2015), be careful not to drink too much or too close to bedtime; either action may lead to further sleep disruption (Drake, Roehrs, Shambroom, & Roth, 2013).

- **Yawning means you are exhausted:** It likely means you are hot. Yawning appears to be related to temperature, and functions to help keep the brain cool (Massen, Dusch, Eldakar, & Gallup, 2014).

- **Exercising right before bed sets you up for a good night's sleep:** Generally speaking, exercise promotes slow-wave sleep, the type that makes you feel bright-eyed and bushy-tailed in the morning (Driver & Taylor, 2000; Youngstedt & Kline, 2006; Uchida et al., 2012). However, working out too close to bedtime (2 to 3 hours beforehand) may prevent good sleep (National Institutes of Health [NIH], 2012).

- **Everyone needs 8 hours of sleep each night:** Experts recommend that we get more than 7 hours of sleep each night (Watson et al., 2015), but sleep needs can range greatly from person to person. Some people do fine with 6 hours; others genuinely need 9 or 10 (Schoenborn et al., 2013).

- **Watching TV or using your computer just before bed helps get you into the sleep zone:** Screen time is not advised as a transition to sleep time. The stimulation of TV and computers can inhibit sleep (National Sleep Foundation, 2015b).

- **You can catch up on days or weeks of sleep loss with one night of "super-sleep":** Settling any sleep debt is not easy. You may feel refreshed upon waking from 10 hours of "recovery" sleep, but the effects of sleep debt will likely creep up later on (Cohen et al., 2010).

- **Pressing snooze is a good way to catch a few more minutes of rest:** Because we need more than a few minutes of sleep to feel rested, hitting snooze is a good indication that you are not getting enough sleep (Oexman, 2013, May 5).

- **Insomnia is no big deal. Everyone has trouble sleeping from time to time:** Insomnia disorder is a mentally and physically debilitating condition that can result in mood changes, memory problems, difficulty with concentration and coordination, physical injuries, and other life-altering impairments (Kessler et al., 2012; Pavlovich-Danis & Patterson, 2006).

- **Sleep aids are totally safe:** When taken according to prescription, sleep aids are relatively safe and effective, although they do not guarantee a normal night of sleep. That being said, research has linked some of these medications to an increased risk of death (Kripke, Langer, & Kline, 2012), as well as an increased risk of sleep eating, sleep sex, and "driving while not fully awake" (U.S. Food and Drug Administration, n.d., para. 5).

Before moving on to the next section, look at **TABLE 4.4** for some ideas on how to get better sleep.

TABLE 4.4 HOW TO GET A GOOD NIGHT'S SLEEP

To Get Good Sleep	Reasoning
Get on a schedule.	The body operates according to daily cycles, or circadian rhythms. Putting your body and brain on a regular schedule—going to bed and waking up at roughly the same time every day—is critical.
Set the stage for sleep.	Turn down the lights, turn off your phone, and slip into soft pajamas. Do everything possible to create a quiet, dark, and comfortable sleeping environment.
Watch your eating, drinking, and smoking.	Beware of foods that create heartburn, and avoid excessive use of alcohol, caffeine, and nicotine (known enemies of sleep) especially late in the day.
Move it or lose it.	Exercise is associated with better sleep, but not right before bed. Exercising 2 to 3 hours before bed can actually prevent good sleep.

If you frequently wake up feeling groggy and unrestored, there are several simple measures you can take to improve the quality of your sleep.
Information from: NIH, 2012.

 ○ ☑ ○ ○ **show what you know**

1. The suprachiasmatic nucleus obtains its information about day and night from:
   a. circadian rhythms.
   b. beta waves.
   c. K-complexes.
   d. retinal ganglion cells.

2. In which of the following stages of sleep do adults spend the most time at night?
   a. Stage N1
   b. Stage N2
   c. Stage N3
   d. Stage W

3. Narcolepsy is a neurological disorder characterized by excessive daytime sleepiness and other sleep-related disturbances such as _____, which refers to an abrupt loss of muscle tone that occurs when a person is awake.

4. Make a drawing of the 90-minute sleep cycle. Label each stage with its associated brain wave(s).

√ CHECK YOUR ANSWERS IN APPENDIX C.

Dreams

Sleep is an exciting time for the brain. As we lie in the darkness, eyes closed and bodies limp, our neurons keep firing. REM is a particularly active sleep stage, characterized by brain waves that are fast and irregular. During REM, anything is possible. We can soar through the clouds, kiss superheroes, and ride roller coasters with frogs. Time to explore the weird world of dreaming.

SLEEP, SLEEP, GO AWAY Just 2 months before graduating from high school, Matt began taking a new medication that vastly improved the quality of his nighttime sleep. He also began strategic power napping, setting aside time in his schedule to go somewhere peaceful and fall asleep for 15 to 30 minutes. "Power naps are probably the greatest thing a person with narcolepsy can do," Matt insists. The naps helped eliminate the daytime sleepiness, effectively preempting all those unplanned naps that had fragmented his days. Matt also worked diligently to create structure in his life, setting a predictable rhythm of going to bed, taking medication, going to bed again, waking up in the morning, attending class, taking a nap, and so on.

Now a college graduate and working professional, Matt manages his narcolepsy quite successfully. All of his major symptoms—the spontaneous naps, cataplexy, sleep paralysis, and hypnagogic hallucinations—have faded. "Now if I fall asleep, it's because I choose to," Matt says. "Most people don't even know I have narcolepsy."

Not everyone with narcolepsy is so fortunate. The disorder is often mistaken for another ailment, such as depression or insomnia. Most people with narcolepsy don't even know they have it, and by the time an expert offers them a diagnosis (sometimes years after the symptoms began), they have already suffered major social and professional consequences (Stanford School of Medicine, 2015 n.d.). Although several medications are available to help control symptoms, there is no known cure for narcolepsy.

Now when Matt goes to sleep at night, he no longer imagines people coming to murder him. In dreams, he soars through the skies like Superman, barreling into outer space to visit the planets. "All my dreams are now pleasant," says Matt, "[and] it's a lot nicer being able to fly than being stabbed by a butcher knife." If you wonder what Matt is doing these days, he works at a credit union (he is one of the top producers in his company) and is pursuing his master's of business administration (MBA). Onward and upward, like Superman. ●

In Your Dreams

LO 7 Summarize the theories of why we dream.

What are dreams, and why do we have them? People have contemplated the significance of dreams for millennia, and scholars have developed many intriguing theories to explain them.

You Asked, Matt Answers

http://qrs.ly/hh5a5ar

What sorts of medications help to control narcolepsy?

scan this →

Under Control
After a few very challenging years, Matt developed effective strategies for managing his narcolepsy. In addition to using a medication that helps him sleep more soundly at night, Matt takes strategic power naps and sticks to a regular bedtime and wake-up schedule. Courtesy Matthew Utesch.

PSYCHOANALYSIS AND DREAMS The first comprehensive theory of dreaming was developed by the father of psychoanalysis, Sigmund Freud. In 1900 Freud laid out his theory in the now-classic *The Interpretation of Dreams,* proposing that dreams were a form of "wish fulfillment," or a playing out of unconscious desires. As Freud saw it, many of the desires expressed in dreams are forbidden and would produce great anxiety in a dreamer if she were aware of them. In dreams, these desires are disguised so they can be experienced without danger of discovery. Freud believed dreams have two levels of content: *manifest* and *latent.* **Manifest content**, the apparent meaning of a dream, is the actual story line of the dream itself—what you remember when you wake up. **Latent content** is the hidden meaning of a dream, and represents unconscious conflicts and desires. During therapy sessions, psychoanalysts look deeper than the actual story line of a dream, using its latent content to uncover what's occurring unconsciously. Critics of Freud's approach to dream analysis would note there are an infinite number of ways to interpret any dream, all of which are impossible to prove wrong.

ACTIVATION-SYNTHESIS MODEL In contrast to Freud's theory the **activation–synthesis model** suggests that dreams have no meaning whatsoever (Hobson & McCarley, 1977). During REM sleep, the motor areas of the brain are inhibited (remember, the body is paralyzed), but sensory areas of the brain hum with a great deal of neural activity. According to the activation–synthesis model, we create meaning in response to this activity, even though this sensory excitement is only random chatter among neurons (Hobson & Pace-Schott, 2002). Our creative minds make up stories to match this activity, and these stories are our dreams. During REM sleep, the brain is also trying to make sense of neural activity in the vestibular system. If the vestibular system is active while we are lying still, then the brain may interpret this as floating or flying—both common experiences reported by dreamers. As advances in research have enabled further study on dreaming, researchers have built upon the activation–synthesis model of dreaming. We not only create meaning in response to the neural activity, but our recent waking experiences influence our dreams as well (Hobson, 2009; Hobson & Friston, 2012).

NEUROCOGNITIVE THEORY OF DREAMS The neurocognitive theory of dreams proposes that a network of neurons exists in the brain, including some areas in the limbic system and the forebrain, that is necessary for dreaming to occur (Domhoff, 2001). People with damage to these brain areas either do not have dreams, or their dreams are not normal. Research suggests that dreaming and daydreaming activate similar brain regions (Domhoff & Fox, 2015), suggesting that this network of neurons is common to both mind-wandering and dreaming.

Additional support for this theory comes from studies of children; it turns out that the dreams of children differ from those of adults. Before about 13 to 15 years of age, children report dreams that are less vivid and seem to have less of a story line. Apparently, an underlying neural network must develop or mature before a child can dream like an adult.

The neurocognitive theory of dreams does not suggest that dreams necessarily serve a purpose. Instead, they seem to be the result of how sleep and consciousness have evolved in humans and are a by-product of how memories are consolidated (Domhoff, 2001; Murkar et al., 2014). As noted earlier, memory consolidation seems to be facilitated by sleep, with some theorists emphasizing the important role of REM (Murkar, Smith, Dale, & Miller, 2014).

In Class: Collaborate and Report

Team up and discuss the three models of dreaming. Use at least two of the eight perspectives introduced in Chapter 1 (see Table 1.4) to explain dreams.

CONNECTIONS

In **Chapter 3,** we noted that the vestibular system is responsible for balance. Accordingly, if its associated area in the nervous system is active while we are asleep, the sensations we normally feel when we are awake may be interpreted in a congruent manner.

manifest content The apparent meaning of a dream; the remembered story line of a dream.

latent content The hidden meaning of a dream, often concealed by the manifest content of the dream.

activation-synthesis model Theory proposing that humans respond to random neural activity while in REM sleep as if it has meaning.

Dream a Little Dream

Most dreams feature ordinary, everyday scenarios like driving a car or sitting in class. The content of dreams is repetitive and frequently in line with our activities, emotions, and what we think about when we are awake. In particular, intense emotional "waking-life experiences" are incorporated more often in the content of dreams (Malinowski & Horton, 2014). The content of dreams is relatively consistent across cultures. For example, dreams about teachers, school, flying, being chased, sexual experiences, and eating delicious foods were the most frequent themes for both Chinese and German participants across dream studies (Mathes, Schredl, & Göritz, 2014; Yu, 2015). Dreams are more likely to include sad events than happy ones and, contrary to popular assumption, less than 12% of dream time is devoted to sexual activity (Yu & Fu, 2011). If you're one of those people who believe they don't dream, you are most likely wrong. Most individuals who insist they don't dream simply fail to remember their dreams. If awakened during a dream, one is more likely to recall it at that moment than if asked to remember it at lunchtime. Typically, the ability to remember dreams is dependent on the length of time since the dream.

Most dreaming takes place during REM sleep and is jam-packed with rich sensory details and narrative. Dreams also occur during non-REM sleep, but they lack the vivid imagery and storylike quality of REM dreams. The average person starts dreaming about 90 minutes into sleep, then goes on to have about four to six dreams during the night. Add up the time and you get a total of about 1 to 2 hours of dreaming per night. An interesting feature of dreams is that they happen in real time. In one early study investigating this phenomenon, researchers roused a small number of sleepers after they had been in a 5-minute REM cycle and again after a 15-minute REM cycle, asking them how long they had been dreaming (5 or 15 minutes). Eighty percent of the participants gave the right answer (Dement & Kleitman, 1957).

Have you ever realized that you are in the middle of a dream? A *lucid dream* is one that you are aware of having, and research suggests that about half of us have had one (Gackenbach & LaBerge, 1988). There are two parts to a lucid dream: the dream itself and the awareness that you are dreaming. Some suggest lucid dreaming is actually a way to direct the content of dreams (Gavie & Revonsuo, 2010), but this is a potentially contentious claim because dreams cannot be experienced by an outsider, making them challenging to "verify objectively" (LaBerge, 2014). Fantastical, funny, or frightening, dreams represent a distinct state of consciousness, and consciousness is a fluid, ever-changing entity. Now it's time to explore how consciousness transforms when chemicals are introduced into our bodies, or when we undergo hypnosis. On to the "altered states". . . .

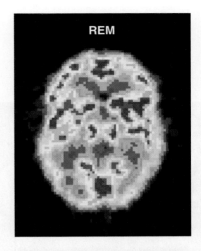

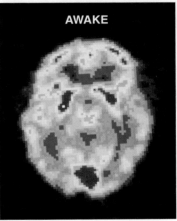

Dreaming Brain
PET scans reveal the high levels of brain activity during REM sleep (top) and wakefulness (bottom). During REM, the brain is abuzz with excitement. (This is especially true of the sensory areas.) According to the activation–synthesis model, dreams may result when the brain tries to make sense of all this neural activity. Hank Morgan/Science Source.

---

  show what you know

1. Freud believed dreams have two levels. The _____ refers to the apparent meaning of the dream, whereas the _____ refers to its hidden meaning.

2. According to the _____, dreams have no meaning whatsoever. Instead, the brain is responding to random neural activity as if it has meaning.

   a. psychoanalytic perspective
   b. neurocognitive theory
   c. activation–synthesis model
   d. evolutionary perspective

3. What occurs in the brain when you dream?

4. Your 6-year-old cousin does not have dreams with a true story line; her dreams seem to be fleeting images. This supports the neurocognitive theory of dreams, as does the fact that:

   a. until children are around 13 to 15 years old, their reported dreams are less vivid.
   b. dream content is not the same across cultures.
   c. children younger than 13 can report very complicated story lines from their dreams.
   d. dream content is the same for people, regardless of age.

✓ CHECK YOUR ANSWERS IN APPENDIX C.

Altered States of Consciousness

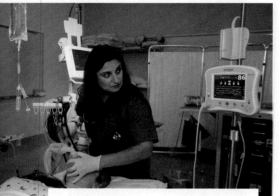

Going Under
Dr. Chander uses various drugs to lull her surgical patients into a deeper-than-sleep state. She may administer a gas, such as nitrous oxide, or a volatile liquid, such as isoflurane, through a mask (as demonstrated here). In other instances, she delivers drugs through injection. Macmillan Learning, photo by Norbert von der Groeben.

UNDER THE KNIFE You awake in the morning with a dull pain around your belly button. By the time you get to your 10:00 A.M. class, the pain is sharper and has migrated to your lower right abdomen, so you head to the local emergency room. Doctors diagnose you with appendicitis, an inflammation of the appendix often caused by infection (and potentially fatal, if allowed to progress too far). You need an emergency operation to remove your appendix. You've never had surgery, and the prospect of "going under" is making you very nervous: *I hate needles—do I have to have an IV? What if I wake up in excruciating pain? What if I never wake up?*

Dr. Chander, introduced at the start of the chapter, is your anesthesiologist. She is there to keep you safe and comfortable throughout the process; she also may be able to ease your anxiety by connecting with you on a human level. "The most important thing, in addition to assessing what their surgical and anesthetic risk is, is to form that quick bond, and rapport with that patient," Dr. Chander explains. "If you're an anesthesiologist that can really connect to humans . . . you can really make a difference in someone's life," she adds. "I think you can impact their entire healing process by taking away a lot of their fear in the beginning."

After taking notes on your medical history and examining your heart, lungs, and airways, Dr. Chander explains the procedure you are about to undergo. When you're ready, she starts an IV, delivering a drug such as Versed (midazolam) to ease your anxiety and interfere with your ability to form new memories for the next 20 minutes or so. Why the need for this temporary memory block? The moments before surgery are terrifying; many patients tremble and cry in anticipation. But everyone is different; a small number of Dr. Chander's patients refuse the Versed because they want to remember their presurgery experience.

The Versed kicks in; you start to feel relaxed and sleepy; and before you know it, you're in the operating room, hooked up to all sorts of tubes and monitors. Dr. Chander lulls you into unconsciousness with a drug called propofol, and blunts your perception of pain with a powerful narcotic such as fentanyl. She also paralyzes your muscles with drugs such as rocuronium or vecuronium, whose effects are readily reversible. These drugs are modern derivatives of *curare,* an arrowhead poison used by South American natives. Curare works by blocking the activity of the neurotransmitter acetylcholine, which stimulates muscle contractions. But curare does not cross into the brain, and therefore it does not have the power to transport you to another level of consciousness (Czarnowski, Bailey, & Bal, 2007).

A few minutes ago, you were awake, sensing, perceiving, thinking, and talking. Now you see nothing, hear nothing, feel nothing. It's like you are gone. The anesthetics Dr. Chander used to produce these effects are called *psychoactive drugs.* ●

CONNECTIONS

In **Chapter 2,** we described neurotransmitters and their role in the nervous system. Acetylcholine is a neurotransmitter that relays messages from motor neurons to muscles, enabling movement. Here, we see how drugs can block the normal activity of acetylcholine, causing the paralysis useful during surgery.

Psychoactive Drugs

LO 8 Define psychoactive drugs.

Psychoactive drugs cause changes in psychological activities such as sensation, perception, attention, judgment, memory, self-control, emotion, thinking, and behavior—all of which are associated with our conscious experiences. You don't have to visit a hospital to have a psychoactive drug experience. Mind-altering drugs are everywhere—in the coffee shop around the corner, at the liquor store down the street, and probably in your own kitchen. About 90% of people in the United States regularly use *caffeine,* a psychoactive drug found in coffee, soda, tea, and some medicines (Alpert, 2012; Gurpegui, Aguilar, Martínez-Ortega, Diaz, & de Leon, 2004). Trailing close behind caffeine are *alcohol* (found in beer, wine, and liquor) and *nicotine* (in cigarettes and other tobacco products), two substances that present serious health risks. Another huge category of psychoactive drugs is prescription medications—drugs for pain relief, depression, insomnia, and just about any ailment you can imagine. Don't forget the illicit, or illegal, drugs like LSD and Ecstasy. In one study, 9.4% of Americans aged 12 and older reported that they had used illegal drugs over the past month (Substance Abuse and Mental Health Services Administration [SAMHSA], 2014).

Psychoactive drugs alter consciousness in an untold number of ways. They can rev you up, slow you down, let down your inhibitions, and convince you that the universe is on the verge of collapse. We will discuss the three major categories of psychoactive drugs—depressants, stimulants, and hallucinogens—but keep in mind that some drugs fall into more than one group.

Depressants

LO 9 **Identify several depressants and stimulants and know their effects.**

In the operating room, Dr. Chander relies heavily on a group of psychoactive drugs that suppress certain kinds of activity in the central nervous system, or slow things down. They are known as sedative-hypnotics or, more broadly, **depressants**. In the example above, you learned how she used Versed to ease anxiety. Versed is a benzodiazepine, which acts as a *tranquilizer*—a type of depressant with a calming, sleep-inducing effect. Other examples of tranquilizers are Valium (diazepam) and Xanax (alprazolam), used to treat anxiety disorders. A more recent addition to the tranquilizer family is Rohypnol (flunitrazepam), also known as the "date rape drug" or "roofies," which is legally manufactured and approved as a treatment for insomnia in other countries, but banned in the United States (Drug Enforcement Administration [DEA], 2012). Sex predators have been known to slip roofies into their victims' drinks (a potentially deadly combination), especially darker-colored cocktails where the blue pills dissolve unseen. Rohypnol can cause confusion, amnesia, lowered inhibitions, and sometimes loss of consciousness, preventing victims from defending themselves or remembering the details of a sexual assault.

BARBITURATES Once a patient is in the operating room and ready for surgery, Dr. Chander puts him "to sleep," a process called *induction*. In the past, anesthesiologists sometimes induced patients with another type of depressant termed a **barbiturate** (bar-BICH-er-it), which is a sedative (calming or sleep-inducing) drug that decreases neural activity. In low doses, barbiturates cause many of the same effects as alcohol (discussed below)—relaxation, lowering of spirits, or alternatively, aggression (Julien, Advokat, & Comaty, 2014)—which may explain why they have become so popular among recreational users. But these substances are addictive and extremely dangerous when taken in excess or mixed with other drugs. If barbiturates are taken with alcohol, for example, the muscles of the diaphragm may relax to the point of suffocation (**INFOGRAPHIC 4.3** on the next page).

OPIOIDS Putting a patient to sleep is not enough to prepare him for a major surgery; he also needs drugs that combat pain. Even when a patient is out cold on the operating table, his brain can receive pain impulses, and pain during surgery can lead to greater pain during recovery. "When the surgeon's cutting, it causes trauma to the body whether or not you're consciously perceiving it," explains Dr. Chander. "If you don't block pain receptors up front, you could have significant pain afterwards, sometimes lasting well beyond the period of healing from the surgery. We call this conversion from acute to chronic pain." For this purpose, Dr. Chander may use an **opioid**, a drug

Vulnerable Youth
Young smokers are more inclined than their nonsmoking peers to use illegal drugs, display aggression, and develop mental health problems. They also have a harder time quitting than those who start smoking in adulthood (American Cancer Society, 2013, November 15). National Geographic/Getty Images.

Synonyms

depressants downers

barbiturates yellow jackets, pink ladies, goof balls, reds, rainbows

psychoactive drugs Substances that can cause changes in psychological activities such as sensation, perception, attention, judgment, memory, self-control, emotion, thinking, and behavior; substances that cause changes in conscious experiences.

depressants A class of psychoactive drugs that *depress* or slow down activity in the central nervous system.

barbiturates Depressant drugs that decrease neural activity and reduce anxiety; a type of sedative.

opioids A class of psychoactive drugs that minimize perceptions of pain.

The Dangers of Drugs in Combination

Taking multiple drugs simultaneously can lead to unintended and potentially fatal consequences because of how they work in the brain. Drugs can modify neurotransmission by increasing or decreasing the chemical activity. When two drugs work on the same system, their effects can be additive, greatly increasing the risk of overdose. For example, alcohol and barbiturates both bind to GABA receptors. GABA's inhibitory action has a sedating effect, which is a good thing when you need to relax. But too much GABA will relax physiological processes to the point where unconscious, life-sustaining activities shut down, causing you to stop breathing and die.

Hundreds of deaths are caused annually in the U.S. when drugs like alcohol and barbiturates are taken in combination (Kochanek et al., 2012). In 2009 alone, 519,650 emergency room visits were attributed to use of alcohol in combination with other drugs (SAMHSA, 2010).

NORMAL GABA ACTIVITY

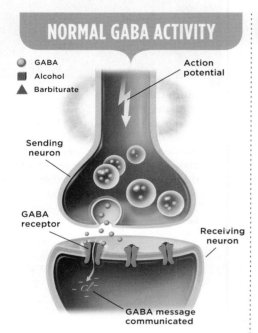

- ● GABA
- ■ Alcohol
- ▲ Barbiturate

Action potential

Sending neuron

GABA receptor

Receiving neuron

GABA message communicated

GABA activation, which calms nervous system activity, is essential for proper functioning of the central nervous system. Without GABA, nerve cells fire too frequently.

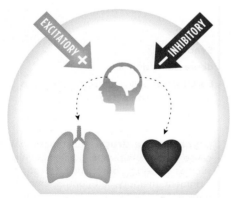

When systems are functioning normally, GABA's inhibitory signals perfectly balance excitatory signals in the central nervous system (CNS). This results in regular breathing and heart rate.

ALCOHOL

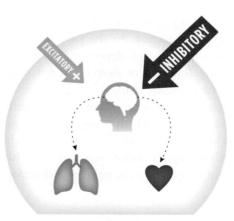

Alcohol activates the same receptors, increasing GABA's activity.

When alcohol increases GABA's inhibitory signals, excitatory and inhibitory signals in the CNS are out of balance. Along with increased relaxation, heart and breathing rates decrease. Increasing levels of alcohol could eventually lead to stupor and coma.

ALCOHOL + BARBITURATE

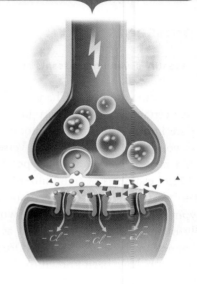

Barbiturates bind to and activate GABA receptors too, creating even more GABA-related inhibition.

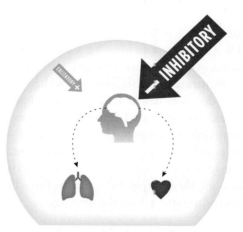

Together, alcohol and barbiturates further unbalance excitatory and inhibitory signals, suppressing heart rate and the impulse to breathe.

that minimizes the brain's perception of pain. "Opioid" is an umbrella term for a large group of similarly acting drugs, some found in nature and others concocted in laboratories (synthesized replacements such as methadone). Opioids block pain, induce drowsiness and euphoria, and slow down breathing (Julien et al., 2014). There are two types of naturally occurring opioids: the endorphins produced by your body, and the **opiates** found in the opium poppy. Morphine, which is derived from the opium poppy, is used to alleviate pain in medical settings; it also serves as the raw material for making the street drug heroin, which enters the brain more quickly and has 3 times its strength (Julien et al., 2014).

PRESCRIPTION DRUG ABUSE It was once believed that few people in the United States actually use heroin (less than 1%; SAMHSA, 2014), but studies now suggest the numbers are on the rise (Cicero, Ellis, Surratt, & Kurtz, 2014). It seems that another class of opioids is serving as a gateway to heroin—synthetic painkillers such as Vicodin (hydrocodone) and OxyContin (oxycodone; Cicero et al., 2014; Fischer & Rehm, 2007; SAMHSA, 2010). Unlike heroin, these medications are legally manufactured by drug companies and legitimately prescribed by physicians. Intentionally using a medication without a doctor's approval or in a way not prescribed by a doctor (for example, taking too much of a medication) can lead to *prescription drug abuse,* and this behavior is shockingly common among teenagers, who are more vulnerable to becoming hooked or addicted (Santye, 2013, July 14; Zhang et al., 2009). Where are teens getting prescription meds? The majority obtain these drugs from friends and family members (National Institute on Drug Abuse, 2014a). Opioid abuse is an epidemic among high school students, and many don't understand how easy it is to become hooked on these drugs. Sadly, drug overdose deaths have surpassed the number of deaths resulting from car accidents in the United States (Moisse, 2011, September 20). Opioids were implicated in 28,647 deaths in 2014 alone (Rudd, Aleshire, Zibbell, & Gladden, January 2016).

Alcohol

We end our coverage of depressants with alcohol, which, like other drugs in its class, has played a central role in the history of anesthesia. The ancient Greek doctor Dioscorides gave his surgical patients a special concoction of wine and mandrake plant (Keys, 1945), and 19th-century Europeans used an alcohol-opium mixture called *laudanum* for anesthetic purposes (Barash, Cullen, Stoelting, & Cahalan, 2009). These days, you won't find anesthesiologists knocking out patients with alcohol, but you will encounter plenty of people intoxicating themselves.

BINGE DRINKING Alcohol is the most commonly used depressant in the United States. Around 15% of adults and 25% of teenagers report that they *binge drink* (consuming four or more drinks for women and five or more for men, on one occasion or within a short time span) at least once a month (Naimi et al., 2003; Wen et al., 2012). Many people think binge drinking is fun, but they might change their minds if they reviewed the research. Studies have linked binge drinking to poor grades, aggressive behavior, sexual promiscuity, and accidental death. Each year, almost 2,000 college students in the United States die in alcohol-related accidents (Hingson, Zha, & Weitzman, 2009; National Institute on Alcohol Abuse and Alcoholism, n.d.). Think getting wasted is sexy? Consider this: Too much alcohol impairs sexual performance, particularly for men, who may have trouble obtaining and sustaining an erection.

You don't have to binge drink in order to have an alcohol problem. Some people cannot get through the day without a midday drink; others need alcohol to unwind or fall asleep. The point is there are many forms of alcohol misuse. About 8.5% of the adult population in the United States (nearly 1 in 10 people) struggle with alcohol dependence

Opium Poppy
Naturally occurring opioids, or opiates, are found in the opium poppy, the same plant that produces those little black seeds on your breakfast bagel. Doctors have been using the poppy opiate morphine to alleviate pain since the 1800s (Julien et al., 2014). AtWaG/Getty Images.

Shooting Up
Heroin is one of the most pleasure-inducing—and dangerous—drugs in the world. About 23% of heroin users get hooked, and the consequences of chronic use are serious: boils on the skin, HIV and hepatitis (from contaminated needles), liver disease, spontaneous abortion, to name but a few (National Institute on Drug Abuse, 2013b). PhotoAlto/Alamy.

opiates A class of psychoactive drugs that cause a sense of euphoria; a drug that imitates the endorphins naturally produced in the brain.

FIGURE 4.1
Blood Alcohol Concentration (BAC)

The effects of one drink—a 12-oz bottle of beer, 4-oz glass of wine, or 1-oz shot of hard liquor—vary depending on weight, ethnicity, gender, and other factors. Across most of the United States, a BAC of .08 is the legal limit for driving. But even at lower levels, our coordination and focus may be impaired. Data from Centers for Disease Control and Prevention, 2011, February 11. Photos: (left & center) Danny Smythe/Shutterstock; (right) Thinkstock.

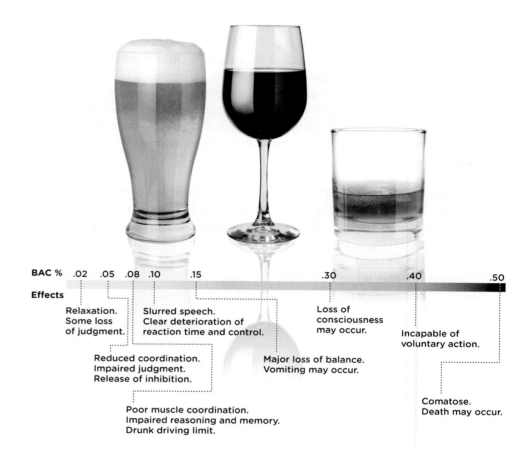

| BAC % | .02 | .05 | .08 | .10 | .15 | .30 | .40 | .50 |

Effects

Relaxation. Some loss of judgment.

Slurred speech. Clear deterioration of reaction time and control.

Loss of consciousness may occur.

Incapable of voluntary action.

Reduced coordination. Impaired judgment. Release of inhibition.

Major loss of balance. Vomiting may occur.

Comatose. Death may occur.

Poor muscle coordination. Impaired reasoning and memory. Drunk driving limit.

Binge Drinking
Binge drinking has been associated with reduced mental and physical health. This effect appears to intensify with increasing levels of alcohol ingestion (Wen et al., 2012). Pascal Deloche/GODONG/Corbis.

or some other type of drinking problem (American Psychiatric Association, 2013; Grant et al., 2004). Drinking can destroy families, careers, and human lives.

ALCOHOL AND THE BODY Let's stop for a minute and examine how alcohol influences consciousness (**FIGURE 4.1**). People sometimes say they feel "high" when they drink. How can such a statement be true when alcohol is a *depressant,* a drug that slows down activity in the central nervous system? Alcohol boosts the activity of GABA, a neurotransmitter that dampens activity in certain neural networks, including those that regulate social inhibition—a type of self-restraint that keeps you from doing things you will regret the next morning. This release of social inhibition can lead to feelings of euphoria. Drinking affects other conscious processes, such as reaction time, balance, attention span, memory, speech, and involuntary life-sustaining activities like breathing (Howland et al., 2010; McKinney & Coyle, 2006). Drink enough, and these vital functions will shut down entirely, leading to coma and even death (Infographic 4.3).

The female body is less efficient at breaking down (metabolizing) alcohol. Even when we control for body size and muscle-to-fat ratio, we see that women achieve higher blood alcohol levels (and thus a significantly stronger "buzz") than men who have consumed equal amounts. Why? Because men have more of an alcohol-metabolizing enzyme in their stomachs, which means they start to break down alcohol almost immediately after ingestion. In a woman, most of the alcohol clears the stomach and enters the bloodstream and brain before the liver finally breaks it down (Toufexis, 2001, June 24).

THE CONSEQUENCES OF DRINKING Light alcohol consumption by adults—one to two drinks a day—may boost cardiovascular health, although some of the observed benefits may be specific to red wine (American Heart Association, 2015).

However, if you look at the overall impact of alcohol consumption among people worldwide, the risks outweigh the benefits (Rehm, Shield, Roerecke, & Gmel, 2016). Excessive drinking is associated with a host of health problems. Overuse of alcohol can lead to malnourishment, cirrhosis of the liver, and *Wernicke–Korsakoff syndrome,* whose symptoms include confusion and memory problems. Excessive drinking has also been linked to heart disease, various types of cancer, tens of thousands of yearly traffic deaths, and *fetal-alcohol syndrome* in children whose mothers drank during pregnancy. Deaths due to overuse of alcohol number about 88,000 annually, shortening people's lives, on average, by 30 years (Centers for Disease Control and Prevention [CDC], 2016b). These types of deaths have been reported as the fourth most common type of preventable death in the United States (Stahre, Roeber, Kanny, Brewer, & Zhang, 2014). If you suspect that you or someone you care about is overusing alcohol, take a look at the warning signs of problematic drinking presented in **FIGURE 4.2.**

- Having your friends or relatives express concern.
- Becoming annoyed when people criticize your drinking behavior.
- Feeling guilty about your drinking behavior.
- Thinking you should drink less but being unable to do so.
- Needing a morning drink as an "eye-opener" or to relieve a hangover.
- Not fulfilling responsibilities at work, home, or school because of your drinking.
- Engaging in dangerous behavior (like driving under the influence).
- Having legal or social problems due to your drinking.

FIGURE 4.2
Warning Signs of Problematic Drinking
The presence of one or more of these warning signs could indicate a developing problem with alcohol. *Sources:* APA, 2012, March; NIH, National Institute on Alcohol Abuse and Alcoholism, 2013.

Stimulants

Not all drugs used in anesthesia are depressants. Did you know that some doctors use cocaine as a local anesthetic for nose and throat surgeries (MedicineNet, 2015, June 1)? Cocaine is a **stimulant**—a drug that increases neural activity in the central nervous system, producing heightened alertness, energy, elevated mood, and other effects (Julien et al., 2014). When applied topically, cocaine blocks sensation in the peripheral nerves and thereby numbs the area.

COCAINE The first to tap into cocaine's pain-zapping potential were the ancient Peruvians, who chewed the leaves of the coca plant (which contain about 1% cocaine) and then applied their saliva to surgical incisions (Schroeder, 2013). The coca plant, they believed, was a divine gift; chewing the leaves quenched their hunger, reduced their sadness, and restored their energy. Thousands of years later, in 1860, a German chemist named Albert Niemann extracted an active part of the coca leaf and dubbed it "cocaine" (Julien et al., 2014; Keys, 1945). Within a few decades, doctors were using cocaine for anesthesia, Sigmund Freud was giving it to patients (and himself), and Coca-Cola was putting it in soda (Keys, 1945; Musto, 1991).

While cocaine is illegal in the United States and most other countries, it is among the most widely used illicit drugs. Depending on the form in which it is prepared (powder, rocks, and so on), it can be snorted, injected, or smoked. The sense of energy, euphoria, and other alterations of consciousness that cocaine induces after entering the bloodstream and infiltrating the brain last anywhere from 5 to 30 minutes (National Institute on Drug Abuse, 2013a). Cocaine produces a rush of pleasure and excitement by amplifying the effects of dopamine and norepinephrine. But the coke high comes at a steep price. Any time you take cocaine, you put yourself at risk for suffering a stroke or heart attack, even if you are young and healthy. Cocaine has been implicated in

Cocaine in Cola
The original recipe for Coca-Cola included cocaine, but the company removed the drug from its cola in 1900, one year before the city of Atlanta banned its nonprescription use (Musto, 1991). Corbis.

stimulants A class of drugs that increase neural activity in the central nervous system.

This Is Your Face on Meth
This woman appears to have aged 15 or 20 years, but the time elapsed between these two photos is just 2 1/2 years. Methamphetamine ravages the body, the brain, and one's overall appearance. Some meth users have lingering symptoms: Imagine experiencing horrific tactile hallucinations that cause you to believe bugs have invaded your skin and are crawling underneath it, and that in response you tear your skin to the bone in order to kill them. Multnomah County Sheriff/Splash/Newscom.

Uncertain About "Heisenberg"
How accurately did the AMC series *Breaking Bad* portray the methamphetamine underworld? The show got some things wrong; for example, there is no such thing as pure blue meth (Wickman, 2013, September 26). But as far as representing the horrors of drug trafficking, Breaking Bad comes uncomfortably close to the truth (Keefe, 2012, July 13). AMC-TV/THE KOBAL COLLECTION at Art Resource, NY.

more emergency room visits than any other illegal drug (Drug Abuse Warning Network, 2011). It is also extremely addictive. Many users find they can never quite duplicate the high they experienced the first time, so they take increasingly higher doses, developing a physical need for the drug, increasing their risk of effects such as anxiety, insomnia, and schizophrenia-like psychosis (Julien et al., 2014).

Cocaine use grew rampant in the 1980s. That was the decade *crack*—an ultra-potent (and ultra-cheap) crystalline form of cocaine—began to ravage America's inner cities. Although cocaine is still a major problem, another stimulant—methamphetamine—has come to rival it in popularity.

AMPHETAMINES *Methamphetamine* belongs to a family of stimulants called the **amphetamines** (am-FET-uh-meens). In the 1930s and 1940s, doctors used amphetamines to treat medical conditions as diverse as excessive hiccups and hypotension (unusually low blood pressure; Julien et al., 2014). During World War II, soldiers and factory workers used methamphetamine to increase energy and boost performance (Lineberry & Bostwick, 2006). Nonprescription use of methamphetamine is illegal, but people have learned how to brew this drug in their own laboratories, using ingredients from ordinary household products such as drain cleaner, battery acid, and over-the-counter cough medicines. "Cooking meth" is a dangerous enterprise. The flammable ingredients, combined with the reckless mentality of "tweaking" cookers, make for toxic fumes and thousands of accidental explosions every year (Lineberry & Bostwick, 2006; Melnikova et al., 2011). Despite the enormous risk, many people continue to cook meth at home, endangering and sometimes killing their own children.

Ridiculously cheap, easy to make, and capable of producing a euphoric high lasting many hours, methamphetamine stimulates the release of the brain's pleasure-producing neurotransmitter dopamine, causing a surge in energy and alertness similar to a cocaine high. It also tends to increase sex drive and suppress one's appetite for food. But unlike cocaine, which the body eliminates quickly, meth lingers in the body (National Institute on Drug Abuse, 2013d). Brain-imaging studies show that chronic meth use causes serious brain damage in the frontal lobes and other areas, still visible even among those who have been clean for 11 months. This may explain why so many meth users suffer from lasting memory and movement problems (Krasnova & Cadet, 2009; Volkow et al., 2001). Other severe consequences of meth use include extreme weight loss; tooth decay ("meth mouth"); and psychosis with hallucinations that can come and go for months, if not years, after quitting (National Institute on Drug Abuse, 2013d).

CAFFEINE Most people have not experimented with illegal stimulants like cocaine and meth, but many are regular users of caffeine. We usually associate caffeine with beverages like coffee, but this pick-me-up drug also lurks in places you wouldn't expect, such as in over-the-counter cough medicines, chocolate, and energy bars. Caffeine works by blocking the action of adenosine, a neurotransmitter that normally muffles the activity of excitatory neurons in the brain (Julien et al., 2014). By interfering with adenosine's calming effect, caffeine makes you feel physically and mentally wired. A cup of coffee might help you stay up later, exercise longer and harder, and get through more pages in your textbooks.

Moderate caffeine use (up to four cups of coffee per day) has been associated with increased alertness, enhanced recall ability, elevated mood, and greater endurance during physical exercise (Ruxton, 2008). Some studies have also linked moderate long-term consumption with lower rates of depression

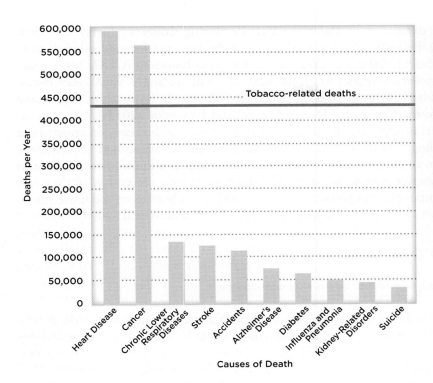

FIGURE 4.3
Leading Causes of Death in the United States
The leading killers in this country—heart disease, cancer, and chronic lower respiratory diseases—are largely driven by smoking. Tobacco exposure is behind nearly half a million deaths every year. Data from Kochanek et al., 2011. Photo: David J. Green—Lifestyle/Alamy.

and suicide, and reduced cognitive decline with aging (Lara, 2010; Rosso, Mossey & Lippa, 2008). But just because researchers find a link between caffeine and positive health outcomes, we should not necessarily conclude that caffeine is responsible for it. We need to remember that correlation does not prove causation. What's more, too much caffeine can make your heart race, your hands tremble, and your mood turn irritable. It takes several hours for your body to metabolize caffeine, so a late afternoon mocha latte may still be present in your system as you lie in bed at midnight counting sheep—with no luck.

TOBACCO What do you think is the number one cause of premature death worldwide—AIDS, illegal drugs, road accidents, murder . . . suicide? None of the above (**FIGURE 4.3**). Tobacco causes more deaths than any of these other factors combined (BBC News, 2010, November 20; World Health Organization [WHO], 2008). Cigarette smoking claims over 480,000 "premature deaths" every year in the United States (CDC, 2015f). Smoking can lead to lung cancer, emphysema, heart disease, and stroke (American Lung Association, 2014). The average smoker loses approximately 10 to 15 years of her life.

Despite these harrowing statistics, about 17% of adults in the United States continue to light up (CDC, 2015, November 13). They say it makes them feel relaxed yet more alert, less hungry, and more tolerant of pain. And those who try to kick the habit find it exceedingly difficult. Cigarettes and other tobacco products contain a highly addictive stimulant called *nicotine,* which sparks the release of epinephrine and norepinephrine. Nicotine use appears to be associated with activity in the same brain area activated by cocaine, another drug that is extremely difficult to give up (Pich et al., 1997; Zhang, Dong, Doyon, & Dani, 2012). The few who succeed face a steep uphill battle. Around 90% of quitters relapse within 6 months (Nonnemaker et al., 2011), suggesting that relapse is a normal experience when quitting, not a sign of failure.

Smoking is not just a problem for the smoker. It is a problem for spouses, children, friends, and anyone who is exposed to the *secondhand smoke.* Secondhand smoke is

CONNECTIONS

In **Chapter 1,** we discussed the problem with possible third variables and correlations. Here, we need to be cautious about making too strong a statement about coffee causing positive health outcomes, because third variables could be involved in increased caffeine consumption and better health.

CONNECTIONS

In **Chapter 2,** we discussed how caffeine acts as an antagonist, blocking the receptors for the neurotransmitter adenosine. We also noted some benefits and negative consequences of its use.

Synonyms

methamphetamines meth, crystal meth, crank

amphetamines speed, uppers, bennies

secondhand smoke passive smoke

amphetamines Stimulant drugs; methamphetamine falls in this class of drugs.

particularly dangerous for children, whose developing tissues are highly vulnerable (Chapter 8). By smoking, parents increase their children's risk for sudden infant death syndrome (SIDS), respiratory infections, asthma, and bronchitis (CDC, 2014a). Secondhand smoke contributes to 21,400 lung cancer deaths and 379,000 heart disease deaths worldwide (Öberg, Jaakkola, Woodward, Peruga, & Prüss-Ustün, 2011), and according to the Centers for Disease Control and Prevention (2014a), "There is no risk-free level of exposure" (para. 3). Researchers have also become concerned about the health implications of thirdhand smoke (especially in infants and children), the combination of cigarette toxins (including lead, which is a known neurotoxin) that lingers in rooms, elevators, and other small spaces long after a smoker has left the scene. Thirdhand smoke is what you smell when you walk into a hotel room and think, *Hmm, someone's been smoking in here* (Ferrante et al., 2013; Winickoff et al., 2009).

Hallucinogens

LO 10 Discuss how hallucinogens alter consciousness.

We have learned how various depressants and stimulants are used in anesthesia. Believe it or not, there is also a place for **hallucinogens** (huh-LOO-suh-nuh-gens)—drugs that produce hallucinations (sights, sounds, odors, or other sensations of things that are not actually present), altered moods, and distorted perception and thought. Phencyclidine (PCP or *angel dust*) and ketamine (*Special K*) are sometimes referred to as *psychedelic anesthetics* because they were developed to block pain in surgical patients during the 1950s and 1960s (Julien et al., 2014). PCP is highly addictive and extremely dangerous. Because users cannot feel normal pain signals, they run the risk of unintentionally harming or killing themselves. Long-term use can lead to depression and memory impairment. Doctors stopped giving PCP to patients long ago; its effect was just too erratic.

Ketamine, on the other hand, continues to be used in hospitals across the country. Unlike many of the depressants used in anesthesia, which can reduce respiratory drive to the point of death (hence the need for the breathing tube and ventilator), ketamine causes less interference with breathing and respiratory reflexes. "Ketamine is an amazing drug for preventing pain," Dr. Chander says. "It's great to use in trauma. You can give it in the muscle, especially if somebody can't start an IV . . . and help them go to sleep that way," she adds. "But used in medicinal ways, or even for recreational purposes, it can have long-lasting effects, much like LSD, a structurally analogous drug, which can cause later flashbacks. Ketamine can in fact induce lasting plastic changes in the brain. Some of these changes can be positive. Interestingly, researchers are finding that ketamine may contribute antidepressant effects through different brain networks than the ones that provide analgesia (pain relief). The drug is being investigated further for this."

LSD Sheets
Lysergic acid diethylamide, or LSD, is usually taken by mouth, administered through candy, sugar cubes, or blotter sheets like the one pictured here. A popular drug during the "hippie" era of the 1960s and 1970s, LSD has now fallen out of favor. Science Source.

LSD The most well-known hallucinogen is probably **lysergic acid diethylamide (LSD;** lih-SER-jic; die-eth-ul-AM-ide)—the odorless, tasteless, and colorless substance that produces extreme changes in sensation and perception. People using LSD may report seeing "far out" colors and visions of spirals and other geometric forms. Some experience a crossover of sensations, such as "tasting sound" or "hearing colors." Emotions run wild and bleed into one another; the person "tripping" can quickly flip between depression and joy, excitement and terror (Julien et al., 2014). Trapped on this sensory and emotional roller coaster, some people panic and injure themselves. Others believe that LSD opens their minds, offers new insights, and expands their consciousness. The outcome of a "trip" depends a great deal on the environment and people who are there. LSD is not often overused, and its reported use has remained at an all-time low (Johnston, O'Malley, Bachman, & Schulenberg, 2012). Long-term use may be associated with depression and other psychological problems, including flashbacks that can occur weeks, months, or years after taking the drug (Centre for Addiction and Mental Health, 2010).

MDMA In addition to the traditional hallucinogens, there are quite a few "club drugs," or synthetic "designer drugs," used at parties, raves, and dance venues. The most popular among them is **methylenedioxymethamphetamine** (MDMA; meth-ul-een-die-ox-ee-meth-am-FET-uh-meen), commonly known as *Ecstasy* or *Molly*. Ecstasy is chemically similar to the stimulant methamphetamine and the hallucinogen *mescaline*, and thus produces a combination of stimulant and hallucinogenic effects (Barnes et al., 2009; National Institute on Drug Abuse, 2013c).

An Ecstasy trip might bring on feelings of euphoria, love, openness, heightened energy, and floating sensations. Ecstasy has also been found to have "unusual sociability-enhancing effects," meaning it seems to increase behaviors that benefit others. Some researchers are exploring the potential therapeutic use of MDMA for people dealing with trauma, for example (Kamilar-Britt & Bedi, 2015). But Ecstasy can also cause a host of troubling changes in the body, including decreased appetite, lockjaw, blurred vision, dizziness, heightened anxiety, rapid heart rate, and dehydration. Dancing in hot, crowded conditions while on Ecstasy can lead to severe heat stroke, seizures, even cardiac arrest and death (Gordon, 2001, July 5; Noller, 2009; Parrott, 2004, 2015). Despite its dangers, Ecstasy continues to be a popular illicit drug (Roberts, Jones, & Montgomery, 2016; SAMHSA, 2012).

Ecstasy triggers a sudden general unloading of serotonin in the brain, after which serotonin activity is temporarily depleted until its levels are restored (Klugman & Gruzelier, 2003; Roberts et al., 2016). Studies of animals have shown that even short-term exposure to MDMA can result in long-term, perhaps even permanent, damage to the brain's serotonin pathways, and there is evidence that a similar type of damage affecting reuptake from the synapse and storage of serotonin occurs in humans as well (Campbell & Rosner, 2008; Reneman et al., 2001). The growing consensus is that even light to moderate Ecstasy use can handicap the brain's memory system, and heavy use may impair higher-level cortical functions, such as planning for the future and shifting attention (Klugman & Gruzelier, 2003; Parrott, 2015; Roberts et al., 2016). Studies also suggest that Ecstasy users are more likely to experience symptoms of depression (Guillot, 2007; Parrott, 2015).

MARIJUANA The most widely used illegal (in most of the United States) drug, and one of the most popular in all the Western world, is *marijuana* (Compton, Grant, Colliver, Glantz, & Stinson, 2004; Degenhardt & Hall, 2012; SAMHSA, 2014). Forty-four percent of high school seniors in the United States have tried this drug (National Institute on Drug Abuse, 2014b). "It's no big deal," a user might say, "you can't get addicted." But these kinds of assumptions are misleading. Studies suggest that marijuana use can lead to dependence, memory impairment, and deficits in attention and learning (Harvey, Sellman, Porter, & Frampton, 2007; Kleber & DuPont, 2012). Impairments in learning and memory may persist for days in adults (weeks for adolescents), and long-term use may lead to addiction (National Institute on Drug Abuse, 2015a; Schweinsburg, Brown, & Tapert, 2008). Some identify marijuana as a cause of several chronic psychological disorders (Reece, 2009). Long-term use has been associated with reduced motivation (Reece, 2009), as well as respiratory problems, impaired lung functioning, and suppression of the immune system (Iversen, 2003; Pletcher

CONNECTIONS

In **Chapter 2,** we reported that serotonin is critical for the regulation of mood, appetite, aggression, and automatic behaviors like sleep. Here, we see how the use of Ecstasy can alter levels of this neurotransmitter.

Synonyms

hallucinogens psychedelic drugs

methylenedioxymethamphetamine E, X

mescaline peyote

marijuana Mary Jane, M.J., grass, reefer, weed, pot, ganja, hemp

hallucinogens A group of psychoactive drugs that can produce hallucinations (auditory, visual, or kinesthetic), distorted sensory experiences, alterations of mood, and distorted thinking.

lysergic acid diethylamide (LSD) A synthetically produced, odorless, tasteless, and colorless hallucinogen that is very potent; produces extreme changes in sensations and perceptions.

methylenedioxymethamphetamine (MDMA) A synthetic drug chemically similar to the stimulant methamphetamine and the hallucinogen mescaline; produces a combination of stimulant and hallucinogenic effects.

Cannabis

Marijuana is the most commonly used illicit drug in the world, consumed by 2.6% to 5% of the adult population. It is also the primary reason people seek drug treatment in many regions of the world, including North America (United Nations, 2012). Its use in the treatment of a variety of illnesses, including arthritis and multiple sclerosis, is still controversial (Feinstein, Freeman, & Lo, 2015; Kalant, 2015). iStock/Getty Images.

et al., 2012). In addition, the smoke from marijuana contains 50% to 70% more cancer-causing hydrocarbons than tobacco (Kothadia et al., 2012). Smoking marijuana also causes a temporary dip in sperm production and a greater proportion of abnormal sperm (Brown & Dobs, 2002).

Marijuana comes from the hemp plant, *Cannabis sativa,* which has long been used as—surprise—an anesthetic (Keys, 1945). These days, doctors prescribe marijuana to stimulate patients' appetites and suppress nausea, but its medicinal use is not without debate. Studies suggest that marijuana does effectively reduce the nausea and vomiting linked to chemotherapy (Grotenhermen & Müller-Vahl, 2012; Iversen, 2003), but there is conflicting evidence about its long-term effects on the brain (Schreiner & Dunn, 2012).

Marijuana's active ingredient is **tetrahydrocannabinol** (**THC**; te-truh-high-druh-kuh-NAB-uh-nawl), which toys with consciousness in a variety of ways, making it hard to classify the drug into a single category (for example, stimulant, depressant, or hallucinogen). In addition to altering pain perception, THC can induce mild euphoria, and create intense sensory experiences and distortions of time. At higher doses, THC may cause hallucinations and delusions (Murray, Morrison, Henquet, & Di Forti, 2007). It's important to recognize that not all products called "marijuana" contain THC. A relatively new group of psychoactive drugs collectively known as "synthetic marijuana" target the same receptors as THC, but they do not come from the hemp plant, or any plant for that matter (National Institute on Drug Abuse, 2015b).

from the pages of
SCIENTIFIC AMERICAN

Fake Weed, Real Crisis

Synthetic cannabinoids are cheap, widespread, hard to track and highly toxic.

When powerful street drugs collectively known as synthetic pot are smoked, the resulting high mimics the effects of marijuana. Yet these man-made cannabinoids are not marijuana at all. The drugs, more commonly called spice, fake weed or K2, are made up of any number of dried, shredded plants sprayed with chemicals that live in a murky legality zone. They are highly dangerous—and their use is on the rise.

Synthetic pot, which first hit the market in the early 2000s, has especially caught the attention of public health officials in the past couple of years, stemming from a surge in hospitalizations and violent episodes. Although the drugs act on the same brain pathway as weed's active ingredient, they can trigger harsher reactions, including heart attacks, strokes, kidney damage and delusions. Between June and early August usage of these drugs led to roughly 2,300 emergency room visits in New York State alone. Nationwide more than 6,000 incidents involving spice have been reported to U.S. poison-control centers this year—about double the number of calls in 2013.

Ever changing recipes make it possible for spice sellers to elude the authorities. Each time an ingredient is banned, producers swap in another compound. The drugs are then sold on the Internet or at gas stations and convenience stores at prices lower than genuine marijuana. The changing formulations also pose a challenge for researchers trying to match the chemicals with their side effects or to develop tests to identify them in a user's system. "The drugs are present in blood for only a short period, so it's very difficult to detect them," says Marilyn Huestis, chief of the Chemistry and Drug Metabolism Section at the National Institute on Drug Abuse. Huestis is now working to identify synthetic cannabinoid by-products via a method that captures all ions present in a single test sample. It can take a month to evaluate one compound, but to keep up with the influx of pot knockoffs, she says, "I think this [method] is our only hope." **Dina Fine Maron. Reproduced with permission. Copyright © 2015 Scientific American, a division of Nature America, Inc. All rights reserved.**

Dangerous Habit

A man lies on the sidewalk in New York City, apparently unconscious after using synthetic marijuana. Use of this drug, also called "Spice" or "K2," may lead to a variety of undesirable outcomes, including paranoia, violent behavior, seizures, dangerous increases in blood pressure, and sometimes death (National Institute on Drug Abuse, 2015b). Spencer Platt/Getty Images.

Overuse and Addiction

We often joke about being "addicted" to our coffee or soda, but do we understand what this really means? In spite of frequent references to *addiction* in everyday conversations, the term has been omitted from the American Psychiatric Association's diagnostic manual due to its "uncertain definition and potentially negative connotation" (American Psychiatric Association, 2013, p. 485). Historically, the term addiction has been used (both by laypeople and professionals) to refer to the urges people experience to use a drug or engage in an activity to such an extent that it interferes with their functioning or is dangerous. This could mean a gambling habit that depletes your bank account, a sexual appetite that destroys your marriage, or perhaps even a social media fixation that prevents you from holding down a job. Social media addiction . . . really?

SOCIAL MEDIA AND PSYCHOLOGY
Can't Get Enough

 Is it difficult for you to sit through a movie without checking your Twitter "Mentions"? Are you constantly looking at your Facebook News Feed in between work e-mails? Do you sleep with your iPhone? If you answered "yes" to any of the above, you are not alone. People around the world, from Indonesia to the United Kingdom, are getting hooked on social media—so

> **THE URGE TO USE MEDIA WAS HARDER TO RESIST THAN SEX, SPENDING MONEY, ALCOHOL. . . .**

hooked in some cases that they are receiving treatment for social media *addiction* (Maulia, 2013, February 15; NBC Universal, 2013, February 12).

Facebook and Twitter may be habit forming, but you would think these sites would be easier to resist than, say, coffee or cigarettes. Such is not the case, according to one study. With the help of smartphones, researchers kept tabs on the daily desires of 205 young adults and found the urge to use media was harder to resist than sex, spending money, alcohol, coffee, or cigarettes (Hofmann, Vohs, & Baumeister, 2012). These findings are thought provoking, and this line of research is something to follow, but don't allow one study to minimize the serious and long-standing issue of drug addiction. The American Psychiatric Association (2013) does not consider *behavioral* addictions to be mental disorders. Further, the National Institute on Drug Abuse (2014c) defines addiction to drugs, in particular, as "a chronic, relapsing brain disease that is characterized by compulsive drug seeking and use, despite harmful consequences" (para. 1). You read it right: Addiction changes your brain. ●

👥 In Class: Collaborate and Report

With your group, design a study using the correlational method to examine the potential impact of social media use. **A)** List measurable variables of social media use (for example, amount of time spent on social media; time lapsed between checking social media). **B)** List measurable variables you think might be associated with social media use (for example, GPA; time spent studying; number of friends). **C)** Record several examples of two variables (one from each list) and the predicted direction of their correlation (for example, hours on social media and GPA expected to have a negative correlation). **D)** Why can't we prove that the variables listed in **A** cause changes to the variables listed in **B**?

LO 11 Explain how physiological and psychological dependence differ.

PHYSIOLOGICAL AND PSYCHOLOGICAL DEPENDENCE Substance use can be fueled by both *physiological* and *psychological* dependence. **Physiological dependence** means the body no longer functions normally without the drug (see **FIGURE 4.4** on the next page). Want to know if you are physiologically dependent on your morning cup of Joe? Try removing it from your routine for a few days and see if you get a headache or feel fatigued. If your answers are yes and yes, odds are that you have experienced *withdrawal*,

tetrahydrocannabinol (THC)
The active ingredient of marijuana.

physiological dependence With constant use of some psychoactive drugs, the body no longer functions normally without the drug.

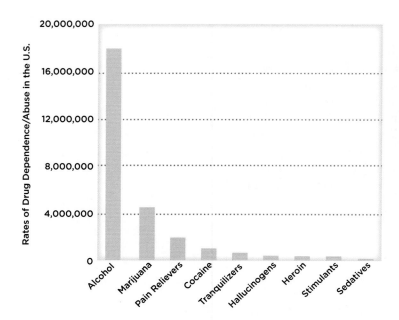

FIGURE 4.4
Rates of Drug Dependence in the United States
This graph depicts the rates of drug dependence/ abuse in the United States. As you can see, alcohol tops the list, followed by marijuana, and then pain relievers such as Vicodin and Oxycontin. The sedatives category includes barbiturates, which are powerful nervous system depressants. Data from National Institute on Drug Abuse, 2012, July. Photo: Alec Macdonald/Alamy.

a sign of physiological dependence. **Withdrawal** is the constellation of symptoms that surface when a drug is removed or withheld from the body, and it's not always as mild as a headache and fatigue. If a person who is physiologically dependent on alcohol suddenly stops drinking, she may suffer from **delirium tremens (DTs)**, withdrawal symptoms that include sweating, restlessness, hallucinations, severe tremors, seizures, and even death. Withdrawal symptoms disappear when you take the drug again, and this of course makes you more likely to continue using it. (The removal of the unpleasant symptoms acts as negative reinforcement for taking the drug, a process you can learn about in Chapter 5.) In this way, withdrawal powers the addiction cycle.

Another sign of physiological dependence is **tolerance**. Persistent use of alcohol and other drugs alters the chemistry of the brain and body. Over time, your system adapts to the drug and therefore needs more and more to re-create its original effect. If it once took you 2 beers to unwind, but now it takes you 4, then tolerance has probably set in. Tolerance increases the risk for accidental overdose, because more of the drug is needed to obtain the desired effect.

Psychological dependence is indicated by a host of problematic symptoms distinct from tolerance and withdrawal. Individuals with psychological dependence believe, for example, they need the drug because it will increase their emotional or mental well-being. The "pleasant" effects of a drug can act as positive reinforcement for taking the drug (Chapter 5). Let's say a smoker has a cigarette, fulfilling her physical need for nicotine. If the phone rings, she might answer it and light up a cigarette, because she has become accustomed to smoking and talking on the phone at the same time. Psychological dependence is an urge or craving, not a physical need. The cues associated with using the telephone facilitate the smoker's urge to light up (Bold, Yoon, Chapman, & McCarthy, 2013).

Psychologists and psychiatrists use specific criteria for drawing the line between use and overuse of drugs. Overuse is maladaptive and causes significant impairment or distress to the user and/or his family: problems at work or school, neglect of children or household duties, physically dangerous behaviors, and so forth. In addition, the behavior has to be sustained for a certain period of time (that is, over a 12-month period). The American Psychiatric Association (2013) has established these criteria to help professionals distinguish between drug use and substance use disorder.

WE'RE ALL DIFFERENT We have discussed the general effects of psychoactive drugs, but keep in mind that people respond to drugs in distinct, and sometimes unpredictable,

withdrawal With constant use of some psychoactive drugs, a condition in which the body becomes dependent and then reacts when the drug is withheld; a sign of physiological dependence.

delirium tremens (DTs) Withdrawal symptoms that can occur when a person who is physiologically dependent on alcohol suddenly stops drinking; can include sweating, restlessness, hallucinations, severe tremors, and seizures.

tolerance With constant use of some psychoactive drugs, a condition in which the body requires more and more of the drug to create the original effect; a sign of physiological dependence.

psychological dependence With constant use of some psychoactive drugs, a strong desire or need to continue using the substance occurs without the evidence of tolerance or withdrawal symptoms.

ways. Dr. Chander sees evidence of this in her daily practice. For example, patients require varying doses of Versed in order to become calm and drowsy before going into the operating room. Similarly, patients have distinct ways of waking up from anesthesia; their EEGs look different, and these differences seem to be linked to their pain experience during recovery (Chander, Garcia, MacColl, Illing, & Sleigh, 2014).

Some of the variability in drug response relates to gender, age, body weight, and other easy-to-identify characteristics. But our reactions to drugs also seem to be inherited; in other words, they are determined by our genes. Wouldn't it be wonderful if doctors had a way of predicting drug responses *before* patients went under anesthesia? Imagine taking a drop of blood, putting it on a chip, analyzing it, and producing a genetic profile that indicates how a person will react to different drugs. This concept of "personalized medicine" is the future, and Dr. Chander is bringing us closer to it with her Anesthesia and Pharmacogenomics Initiative at Stanford University.

Depressants, stimulants, hallucinogens, marijuana—every drug we have discussed, and every drug imaginable—must gain entrance to the body in order to access the brain. Some are inhaled, others snorted or injected directly into the veins—all altering the state of consciousness of the user (**TABLE 4.5**). But is it possible to enter an altered state of consciousness without using a substance? It is time to explore hypnosis.

TABLE 4.5 PSYCHOACTIVE DRUGS

Drug	Classification	Effects	Potential Harm
Alcohol	Depressant	Disinhibition, feeling "high"	Coma, death
Barbiturates	Depressant	Decreased neural activity, relaxation, possible aggression	Loss of consciousness, coma, death
Caffeine	Stimulant	Alertness, enhanced recall, elevated mood, endurance	Heart racing, trembling, insomnia
Cocaine	Stimulant	Energy, euphoria, rush of pleasure	Heart attack, stroke, anxiety, psychosis
Heroin	Depressant	Pleasure-inducing, reduces pain, rush of euphoria and relaxation	Boils on the skin, hepatitis, liver disease, spontaneous abortion
LSD	Hallucinogen	Extreme changes in sensation and perception, emotional roller coaster	Depression, long-term flashbacks, other psychological problems
Marijuana	Hallucinogen	Stimulates appetite, suppresses nausea, relaxation, mild euphoria, distortion of time, intense sensory experiences	Respiratory problems, immune system suppression, cancer, memory impairment, deficits in attention and learning
MDMA	Stimulant; hallucinogen	Euphoria, heightened energy, and anxiety	Blurred vision, dizziness, rapid heart rate, dehydration, heat stroke, seizures, cardiac arrest, and death
Methamphetamine	Stimulant	Energy, alertness, increases sex drive, suppresses appetite	Lasting memory and movement problems, severe weight loss, tooth decay, psychosis, sudden death
Opioids	Depressant	Blocks pain, induces drowsiness, euphoria, slows down breathing	Respiratory problems during sleep, falls, constipation, sexual problems, overdose
Tobacco	Stimulant	Relaxed, alert, more tolerant of pain	Cancer, emphysema, heart disease, stroke, reduction in life span

Most drugs can be classified under one of the major categories listed above, but there are substances, such as MDMA, that fall into more than one class. Psychoactive drugs carry serious risks.

Hypnosis

LO 12 Describe hypnosis and explain how it works.

The term *hypnosis* was taken from the Greek root word for "sleep," but hypnosis is by no means the equivalent of sleep. Most would agree **hypnosis** is an altered state of consciousness in which changes in perceptions and behaviors result from suggestions made by a hypnotist. "Changes in perceptions and behaviors" can mean a lot of things, of course, and there is some debate about what hypnosis is. Before going any further, let's be clear about what hypnosis *is not*.

CONTROVERSIES
False Claims About Hypnosis

➡️⬅️ Popular conceptions of hypnosis often clash with scientists' understanding of the phenomenon. Let's take a look at some examples.

NO ONE CAN FORCE YOU TO BECOME HYPNOTIZED

- **People can be hypnotized without consent:** You cannot force someone to be hypnotized; they must be willing.
- **Hypnotized people will act against their own will:** Stage hypnotists seem to make people walk like chickens or miscount their fingers, but these are things they would likely be willing to do when not hypnotized.
- **Hypnotized people can exhibit "superhuman" strength:** Hypnotized or not, people have the same capabilities (Druckman & Bjork, 1994). Stage hypnotists often choose feats that their hypnotized performers could achieve under normal circumstances.
- **Hypnosis helps people retrieve lost memories:** Studies find that hypnosis may actually promote the formation of false memories and one's confidence in those memories (Kihlstrom, 1985, 2014).
- **Hypnotized people experience age regression. In other words, they act childlike:** Hypnotized people may indeed act immaturely, but the underlying cognitive activity is that of an adult (Nash, 2001).
- **Hypnosis induces long-term amnesia:** Hypnosis cannot make you forget your first day of kindergarten or your wedding. Short-term amnesia is possible if the hypnotist specifically suggests that something will be forgotten after the hypnosis wears off. ➡️⬅️

Now that some misconceptions about hypnosis have been cleared up, let's focus on what we know. Researchers propose the following characteristics are evident in a hypnotized person: (1) ability to focus intently, ignoring all extraneous stimuli; (2) heightened imagination; (3) an unresisting and receptive attitude; (4) decreased pain awareness; and (5) high responsivity to suggestions (Hoeft et al. 2012; Kosslyn, Thompson, Costantini-Ferrando, Alpert, & Spiegel, 2000; Silva & Kirsch, 1992).

Does this process have any application to real life? With some limited success, hypnosis has been used therapeutically to treat phobias and commercially to help people change lifestyle habits (Green, 1999; Kraft, 2012). Some have found hypnotherapy beneficial in helping people confront their fear of going to the dentist (Butler, 2015). Hypnosis has also been used on children to alleviate chronic pain insomnia, and anxiety related to routine medical procedures (Adinolfi & Gava, 2013). And, others have demonstrated the benefits of hypnosis in conjunction with traditional therapies for the treatment of chronic issues such as tension headaches (Shahkhase, Gharaei, Fathi, Yaghoobi, & Bayazi, 2014). Some research suggests that hypnosis can ease the pain associated with childbirth and surgery, reducing the need for painkillers (Cyna,

Mesmerizing
A 19th-century doctor attempts to heal a patient using the hypnotic techniques created by Franz Mesmer in the 1770s. Mesmer believed that every person was surrounded by a magnetic field, or "animal magnetism," that could be summoned for therapeutic purposes (Wobst, 2007). The word "mesmerize" derives from Mesmer's name. Jean-Loup Charmet/ Science Source.

hypnosis An altered state of consciousness allowing for changes in perceptions and behaviors, which result from suggestions made by a hypnotist.

McAuliffe, & Andrew, 2004; Wobst, 2007), although more recent research finds that hypnosis did not reduce the use of painkillers during labor and childbirth (Cyna et al., 2013; Wemer, Uldbjerg, Zachariae, Rosen, & Nohr, 2013).

A SESSION WITH A HYPNOTIST Imagine you are using hypnosis for one of these purposes—to address constant headaches, for example. How would a session with a hypnotist proceed? Probably something like this: The hypnotist talks to you in a calm, quiet voice, running through a list of suggestions on how to relax. She might suggest that you sit back in your chair and choose a place to focus your eyes. Then she quietly suggests that your eyelids are starting to droop, and you feel like you need to yawn. You grow tired and more relaxed. Your breathing slows. Your arms feel so heavy that you can barely lift them off the chair. Alternatively, the hypnotist might suggest that you are walking down steps, and ask you to focus attention on her voice. Hypnotists who are very good at this procedure can perform an induction in less than a minute, especially if they know the individual being hypnotized.

People in hypnotic states sometimes report having sensory experiences that deviate from reality; they may, for example, see or hear things that are not there. In a classic experiment, participants were hypnotized to believe they wouldn't experience pain when asked to place one hand in a container filled with ice-cold water. With their other hand, they were asked to press a button if they experienced pain. Amazingly, the participants gave spoken reports of feeling no pain. However, they actually did press the button, indicating pain during their hypnotic session (Hilgard, Morgan, & Macdonald, 1975). This suggests a "divided consciousness," that is, part of our consciousness is always aware, even when hypnotized and instructed to feel no pain. People under hypnotic states can also experience temporary blindness and deafness.

With the help of PET scans, some researchers have found evidence that hypnosis induces changes in the brain that might explain this diminished pain perception (Faymonville et al., 2000; Rainville, Duncan, Price, Carrier, & Bushnell, 1997, August 15). The perception of pain is complex, and "virtually all of the brain areas involved in the processing of pain have been shown to be impacted by hypnosis" (Jensen et al., 2015, p. 41). Hypnosis, meditation, and other relaxation techniques can indeed reduce anxiety and pain. But if you plan to go under the knife with hypnosis as your sole form of pain management, don't be surprised if you feel the piercing sensation of the scalpel.

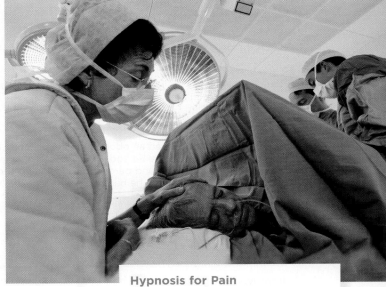

Hypnosis for Pain
A doctor in Belgium performs hypnosis on a patient undergoing a painful procedure. For those who are susceptible to hypnosis, this approach may diminish the need for anesthesia.
Universal Images Group/Getty Images.

THEORIES OF HYPNOSIS There are many theories to explain hypnosis. One hypothesis, referred to briefly above, is that hypnotized people experience a "split" in awareness or consciousness (Hilgard, 1977, 1994). According to this perspective, there is an ever-present "hidden observer" that oversees the events of our daily lives. You are listening to a boring lecture, picking up a little content here and there, but also thinking about that juicy gossip you heard before class. Your mind is working on different levels, and the hidden observer is keeping track of everything. In a hypnotic state, the hidden observer is still aware of what is transpiring in the environment, while another stream of mental activity focuses on the hypnotic suggestions.

Some researchers have suggested that hypnosis is not a distinct state of consciousness, but more of a role-play (Crabtree, 2012; Lynn, Rhue, & Weekes, 1990). Have you ever watched a little boy pretend he was a firefighter? He becomes so enthralled in his play that he really believes he is a firefighter. His tricycle is now his fire engine; his baseball cap his firefighter's hat. He *is* the firefighter. Something similar happens when we are hypnotized. We have an expectation of how a hypnotized person should act or behave; therefore, our hypnotized response is nothing more than fulfilling the role we think we should assume. And this is particularly true when good rapport exists between the hypnotist and the person being hypnotized.

FADE TO BLACK It is almost time to conclude our discussion of consciousness, so let's run through some of the big picture concepts you should take away from this chapter. Consciousness refers to a state of awareness—awareness of self and things outside of self—that has many gradations and dimensions. During sleep, awareness decreases, but it does not fade entirely (remember that alarm clock that becomes part of your dream about a wailing siren). Sleep has many stages, but the two main forms are non-REM and REM. Dreams may serve a purpose, but they may also be nothing more than your brain's interpretation of neurons signaling in the night. You learned from Dr. Chander that anesthetic drugs can profoundly alter consciousness. The same is true of drugs used outside of medical supervision; legal or not, many drugs can lead to dependence, health problems, and death. And although somewhat controversial and misunderstood, hypnosis appears to induce an altered state of consciousness and may have useful applications.

◯ ✓◯◯ show what you know

1. Match the drug in the left column with an outcome on the right:

_____1. depressant   **a.** blocks pain

_____2. opioid   **b.** slows down activity in the CNS

_____3. alcohol   **c.** increases neural activity in the CNS

_____4. cocaine   **d.** cirrhosis of the liver

2. An acquaintance described an odorless, tasteless, and colorless substance he took many years ago. He discussed a variety of changes to his sensations and perceptions, including seeing colors and spirals. It is likely he had taken which of the following hallucinogens?

a. alcohol   **c.** LSD

b. nicotine   **d.** cocaine

3. Dr. Chander uses a range of _____ to inhibit memories of surgery and change levels of consciousness.

4. People often describe dangerous or risky behaviors as being addictive. You might hear a character in a movie say that he is addicted to driving fast, for example. Given what you have learned about physiological and psychological dependence, how would you determine if behaviors are problematic?

✓ CHECK YOUR ANSWERS IN APPENDIX C.

Improve your grade! Use 🔷 **LearningCurve** adaptive quizzing to create your personalized study plan, which will direct you to the resources that will help you most in 🔷 **LaunchPad**

4 summary of concepts

LO 1 Define consciousness. (p. 144)

Consciousness is the state of being aware of oneself, one's thoughts, and/or the environment. There are various levels of conscious awareness, including wakefulness, sleepiness, drug-induced states, dreaming, hypnotic states, and meditative states.

LO 2 Explain how automatic processing relates to consciousness. (p. 147)

Because our sensory systems absorb large amounts of information, being consciously aware of all of it is not possible. Without our awareness, the brain determines what is

important, what requires immediate attention, and what can be processed and stored for later use if necessary.

LO 3 Describe how we narrow our focus through selective attention. (p. 147)

We can only direct our attention toward a small portion of the information that is available to us. This narrow focus on specific stimuli is referred to as selective attention. In particular, we are designed to pay attention to changes in environmental stimuli, to unfamiliar stimuli, and to especially strong stimuli.

LO 4 Identify how circadian rhythm relates to sleep. (p. 150)

Predictable daily patterns influence our behaviors, alertness, and activity levels in a cyclical fashion. These circadian rhythms in our physiological functioning roughly follow the 24-hour cycle of daylight and darkness. In the circadian rhythm for sleep and wakefulness, there are two times when the desire for sleep hits hardest. The first occurs in the early hours of the morning, between about 2:00 to 6:00 A.M., and the second, less intense desire for sleep strikes midafternoon, around 2:00 or 3:00 P.M.

LO 5 Summarize the stages of sleep. (p. 154)

Sleep begins in non-rapid eye movement (non-REM), or nondreaming sleep, which has three stages. The lightest is Stage N1; this is the time during which imaginary sensations can occur. Stage N1 lasts only a few minutes before Stage N2 begins. At this point, it is more difficult to rouse the sleeper before she drifts even further into Stage N3, also known as slow-wave sleep. The sleeper then works her way back up to Stage N2. And instead of waking up, she enters the R Stage, known as rapid eye movement (REM) sleep. During this stage, closed eyes dart around, and brain activity changes. People awakened from REM sleep often report having vivid dreams. Each cycle, from Stage N1 through REM, lasts about 90 minutes, and the average adult loops through five complete cycles per night. The composition of these cycles changes as the night progresses.

LO 6 Recognize various sleep disorders and their symptoms. (p. 158)

Narcolepsy is a neurological disorder characterized by excessive daytime sleepiness and other sleep-related disturbances. REM sleep behavior disorder occurs when the mechanism responsible for paralyzing the body during REM sleep does not function properly. As a result, the individual is able to move around and act out dreams. Obstructive sleep apnea hypopnea is a serious disturbance of non-REM sleep characterized by periodic blockage of breathing. The upper throat muscles go limp, allowing the airway to close. The sleeper awakens and gasps for air, then drifts back to sleep. Insomnia is the inability to fall asleep or stay asleep. People with insomnia report poor quantity or quality of sleep, and some may complain about waking up too early and being unable to fall back to sleep.

LO 7 Summarize the theories of why we dream. (p. 165)

Freud believed dreams have two levels of content. Manifest content, the apparent meaning of the dream, is the actual story line of the dream itself. Latent content contains the hidden meaning of the dream, consisting of unconscious conflicts and desires. The activation–synthesis model suggests that dreams have no meaning whatsoever: We respond to random neural activity of the sleeping brain as if it has meaning. Neurocognitive theory suggests there is a network of neurons in the brain necessary for dreaming to occur. According to this theory, dreams are the result of how sleep and consciousness have evolved in humans.

LO 8 Define psychoactive drugs. (p. 168)

Psychoactive drugs can cause changes in psychological activities such as sensation, perception, attention, judgment, memory, self-control, emotion, thinking, and behavior. These drugs alter consciousness in an untold number of ways. They can, for example, depress activity in the central nervous system, produce hallucinations, or cause a sense of euphoria.

LO 9 Identify several depressants and stimulants and know their effects. (p. 169)

Depressants decrease activity in the central nervous system. These include barbiturates, opioids, and alcohol. Stimulants increase activity in the central nervous system, producing effects such as heightened alertness, energy, and mood. These include cocaine, amphetamines, methamphetamine, caffeine, and nicotine.

LO 10 Discuss how hallucinogens alter consciousness. (p. 176)

Hallucinogens produce hallucinations, altered moods, and distorted perception and thought. The most well-known is lysergic acid diethylamide (LSD). This odorless, tasteless, and colorless substance often produces extreme changes in sensation and perception. Others are the "club drugs," or synthetic "designer drugs," used at parties, raves, and dance venues. Of these, the most popular is methylenedioxymethamphetamine (MDMA), which is chemically similar to the stimulant methamphetamine, producing a combination of stimulant and hallucinogenic effects. The most widely used illegal (in most of the United States) drug is marijuana. At high doses, its tetrahydrocannabinol (THC) can induce mild euphoria and create intense sensory experiences.

LO 11 Explain how physiological and psychological dependence differ. (p. 179)

With constant use of some psychoactive drugs, a condition can develop in which the body becomes dependent on the drug. Signs of this physiological dependence include tolerance and withdrawal. Psychological dependence occurs without the evidence of tolerance or withdrawal symptoms, but is indicated by many other problematic symptoms. People with psychological dependence believe they need the drug because it increases their emotional or mental well-being. Physiological dependence is physical and has serious health consequences.

LO 12 Describe hypnosis and explain how it works. (p. 182)

Hypnosis is an altered state of consciousness that can create changes in perceptions and behaviors, usually resulting from suggestions made by a hypnotist. Hypnosis has been used during childbirth and surgery to reduce pain. One theory suggests that hypnotized people experience a "split" in awareness or consciousness. Others suggest hypnosis is not a distinct state of consciousness, but more of a role-play.

key terms

activation–synthesis model, p. 166
alpha waves, p. 154
amphetamines, p. 174
automatic processing, p. 147
barbiturates, p. 169
beta waves, p. 154
circadian rhythm, p. 151
cognitive psychology, p. 146
consciousness, p. 144
delirium tremens (DTs), p. 180

delta waves, p. 156
depressants, p. 169
hallucinogens, p. 176
hypnosis, p. 182
insomnia, p. 160
latent content, p. 166
lysergic acid diethylamide (LSD), p. 176
manifest content, p. 166
methylenedioxymethamphetamine (MDMA), p. 177
narcolepsy, p. 157
nightmares, p. 161

non-rapid eye movement (non-REM), p. 156
obstructive sleep apnea hypopnea, p. 159
opiates, p. 171
opioids, p. 169
physiological dependence, p. 179
psychoactive drugs, p. 168
psychological dependence, p. 180
rapid eye movement (REM), p. 156

REM rebound, p. 162
REM sleep behavior disorder, p. 159
selective attention, p. 147
sleep terrors, p. 161
stimulants, p. 173
tetrahydrocannabinol (THC), p. 178
theta waves, p. 156
tolerance, p. 180
withdrawal, p. 180

test prep *are you ready?*

1. William James proposed that _____ is like a "stream" that provides a sense of day-to-day continuity.
   a. dreams
   b. automatic processing
   c. selective attention
   d. consciousness

2. A great deal of information is available in our internal and external environments, but we can only focus on a small portion of it. This narrow focus on specific stimuli is known as:
   a. stream of consciousness.
   b. selective attention.
   c. waking consciousness.
   d. creation of memories.

3. Turrell was able to focus on talking with his friend while they were at a loud fraternity fundraiser. His ability to ignore everything else and focus on their conversation is known as:
   a. the cocktail-party effect.
   b. inattentional blindness.
   c. automatic processing.
   d. the circadian rhythm.

4. Sleep-wake cycles, body temperature, and growth hormone secretion follow predictable patterns over a 24-hour period. These patterns are driven by our:
   a. blood pressure.
   b. need for sleep.
   c. levels of consciousness.
   d. circadian rhythm

5. The suprachiasmatic nucleus (SCN) can be thought of as a master clock for our daily rhythm. The SCN sends messages to the _____, which regulates patterns of hunger and temperature, and the _____, which regulates alertness and sleepiness.
   a. reticular formation; retinal ganglion cells
   b. retinal ganglion cells; hypothalamus
   c. hypothalamus; reticular formation
   d. thalamus; hypothalamus

6. Mary Ann is a shift worker and is having problems with her sleep-wake cycle. This often results in _____, which refers to difficulty falling asleep and sleeping soundly.
   a. insomnia
   b. cataplexy
   c. narcolepsy
   d. hypnagogic hallucinations

7. If we hook you up to an electroencephalogram (EEG) as you become drowsy, the EEG would begin to show _____ waves.
   a. fast
   b. alpha
   c. beta
   d. theta

8. The fourth stage of sleep is known as _____, when brain activity looks similar to that of someone who is wide awake.
   a. sleep paralysis
   b. cataplexy
   c. non-REM sleep
   d. REM sleep

9. Depriving people of REM sleep can result in:
   a. REM rebound.
   b. insomnia.
   c. more beta waves while they sleep.
   d. increased energy levels

10. According to Sigmund Freud's theory, dreams are a form of:
    a. REM rebound.
    b. wish fulfillment.
    c. microsleep.
    d. sleep terror.

11. People with damage to specific areas of the limbic system and forebrain do not have dreams or experience abnormal dreams. Which of the following explains this finding?
    a. the theory of evolution
    b. the activation–synthesis model
    c. the psychoanalytic theory
    d. the neurocognitive theory

12. _____ such as caffeine, alcohol, and hallucinogens can cause changes in psychological activities, for example, sensation, perception, attention, and judgment.
    a. Tranquilizers
    b. Depressants
    c. Psychoactive drugs
    d. Stimulants

13. Methamphetamine stimulates the release of the brain's pleasure-producing neurotransmitter _____, causing a surge in energy and alertness.
    a. dopamine
    b. serotonin
    c. acetylcholine
    d. adenosine

14. Which is the number one cause of premature death worldwide?
    a. AIDS
    b. tobacco
    c. road accidents
    d. illegal drugs

15. Drug use can be fueled by dependence. _____ dependence means the body no longer functions normally without the drug, and one sign of this type of dependence is _____, as indicated by the symptoms that occur when the drug is withheld.
    a. Psychological; tolerance
    b. Physiological; substance abuse
    c. Physiological; withdrawal
    d. Psychological; withdrawal

16. Give an example showing that you are still conscious when asleep.

17. Describe automatic processing, and give two reasons why it is important.

18. Interns and residents in hospitals sometimes work 48-hour shifts. Why would you not want a doctor keeping such a schedule to care for you at the end of her shift?

19. Name and describe four different sleep disturbances. Differentiate them by describing their characteristics.

20. Give four examples of drugs that people use legally on a daily basis.

✓ CHECK YOUR ANSWERS IN APPENDIX C.

YOUR SCIENTIFIC WORLD

Apply psychology to the real world! Go to LaunchPad for access.

Kiko Jimenez/Shutterstock.

AP Photo/TT News Agency, Anders Wiklund.

Mathew Imaging/FilmMagic for Academy of Television Arts and Sciences/Getty Images.

Hulton Archive/Getty Images.

Mark Weber/The Commercial Appeal via ZUMA Wire.

Design Pics/Ron Nickel/Getty Images.

AP Photo/Wilfredo Lee.

5 learning

SteffiMueller/
Shutterstock.

An Introduction to Learning

BEFORE HE WAS THE DOG WHISPERER   December 23, 1990: Cesar Millan had made up his mind; it was time to leave Mexico and start a new life in America. He was 21 years old, spoke no English, and had exactly $100 in his pocket. Since the age of 13, Cesar had dreamed of becoming the greatest dog trainer in the world. Now he was ready to pursue that goal, even if it meant saying goodbye to everything he knew and cherished—his family, his homeland, and his culture (Millan & Peltier, 2006).

From his home in Mazatlan, Cesar traveled to the dangerous border city of Tijuana, where he spent two weeks sleeping in the back of a nightclub. After three unsuccessful attempts crossing the border on his own, Cesar met a human smuggler, or "coyote," who said he would get him into the United States for a fee of—you guessed it—$100. Trudging over muddy terrain, darting across a busy freeway, and hiding in a frigid trench of water, Cesar stuck with the coyote. At last they reached a tunnel leading to a gas station, where the coyote paid a taxi driver to take Cesar into San Diego (Partisan Pictures, 2012; Millan & Peltier, 2006). "He drove me to San Diego and dropped me off there—dripping wet, filthy, thirsty, hungry, my boots covered with mud," Cesar recalls in his book *Cesar's Way.* "I was the happiest man in the world. I was in the U.S." (Millan & Peltier, 2006, p. 39).

For more than a month, Cesar slept under a freeway and lived on hotdogs from 7-Eleven (Partisan Pictures, 2012). Technically, he was "homeless," but he didn't feel like a drifter. "I never felt lost," Cesar

No Dream Is Too Big
Young Cesar Millan works with a dog on a treadmill. Early on Cesar knew he wanted to devote his life to dogs. He remembers himself as a 13-year-old asking his mother, "Mom, you think I can be the best dog trainer in the world?" She responded, "You can do whatever you want" (NPR, 2014, March 30). Eight years later, at the age of 21, Cesar arrived in the United States with no money, no acquaintances, and virtually no knowledge of English. But he had a dream, and that was more powerful than anything.
Courtesy of Cesar's Way Inc.

Dog's Best Friend
Cesar walks a pack of large and powerful dogs. They follow Cesar because he emanates the confidence and "calm, assertive energy" of a pack leader; if a dog owner fails to provide this type of leadership, a dog will attempt to become pack leader, and this can lead to anxiety, aggression, and other problems (Millan, 2013, p. 76). Gregg Cobarr/WireImage/Getty Images.

Top Dog
The world's most famous dog expert doesn't train dogs—he trains people. "I'm training humans to understand how dogs react, how dogs behave, what is their communication, and what makes them happy," Cesar explains. It's all about bringing balance to dogs' lives and promoting more fulfilling relationships between dogs and their owners. Mathew Imaging/FilmMagic for Academy of Television Arts and Sciences/Getty Images.

recalls, "I always knew what I wanted." One day, while exploring the city, Cesar came upon a pet-grooming parlor. Using the few words of English he had learned, he asked for a job application. The kind women who ran the parlor not only hired him; they gave him a place to sleep in the shop. "I call these women my American guardian angels," Cesar writes. "They trusted me and acted as if they'd known me all their lives" (Millan & Peltier, 2006, p. 41).

A couple of years later, Cesar moved to Los Angeles, where he worked as a kennel boy, a limousine washer, and eventually a self-employed dog trainer. His dog-training business was based in Inglewood, a city just south of Los Angeles with a strong gang presence and many dogs trained to protect and fight (Fine, 2013, February 7; Lopez, 2012, March 18; Millan & Peltier, 2006). Capable of pacifying even the fiercest of dogs, Cesar could be seen strolling through the city with a pack of Rottweilers and pit bulls—off leash (Millan, n.d.)! Word spread about the "Mexican guy who has a magical way with dogs" (Millan & Peltier, 2006, p. 50), and Cesar accumulated more and more clients, including rapper Redman and actor Jada Pinkett Smith. The *Los Angeles Times* got wind of Cesar's work and profiled him in 2002, sparking the interest of several television producers (Levine, 2002, September 25).

Fast-forward 15 years. Cesar Millan is perhaps the most famous dog expert on the planet. His résumé includes nine seasons of the Emmy-nominated reality television series *Dog Whisperer with Cesar Millan* (broadcast in more than 100 countries), along with other TV series such as *Cesar Millan's Leader of the Pack* and *Cesar 911*. A best-selling author, Cesar travels the world, from Idaho to Singapore, giving seminars in auditoriums packed with thousands of eager listeners. Fans flood his website with comments, some of them desperate ("HEY Ceser! I really need HELP! I have a 10 month old pit mix. . . ."), others adoring ("Dear Cesar, keep doing what you're doing. . . . You've got a believer in me and millions of others"; Millan, n.d.).

How do you explain Cesar's rise from poverty to superstardom? This man is clearly hardworking, motivated, and blessed with an innate gift for understanding dogs. But Cesar's life, and the lives of countless dogs and dog owners he has helped, have also been shaped by *learning*. ●

What Is Learning?

LO 1 Define learning.

Psychologists define **learning** as a relatively enduring change in behavior or thinking that results from our experiences. Studies suggest that learning

Note: Unless otherwise specified, quotations attributed to Cesar Millan are personal communications.

can begin before we are even born—fetuses can hear voices from inside the womb, and it appears they learn basic speech sounds and are able to distinguish among vowels used in their native language (Moon, Lagercrantz, & Kuhl, 2013; Partanen et al., 2013). Learning occurs every day, and may continue until our dying breath. Even though learning leads to changes in the brain, including alterations to individual neurons and their networks, these modifications of behavior and thinking are not always permanent.

The ability to learn is not unique to humans. Dogs can learn to dance salsa and drive cars (Goldman, 2012, December 13); orangutans can pick up whistling (Wich et al., 2009); and fruit flies can be trained to avoid smells associated with electrical shocks (Dissel, Melnattur, & Shaw, 2015). One of the most basic forms of learning occurs during the process of **habituation** (huh-bich-oo-EY-shun), which is evident when an organism does not respond as strongly or as often to an event following multiple exposures to it. This type of learning is apparent in a wide range of living beings, from humans to sea slugs. An animal might initially *respond* to a **stimulus,** which is an event that generally leads to a response, but with repeated exposures, the stimulus is increasingly ignored and habituation occurs. Essentially, an organism learns about a stimulus but begins to ignore it as the stimulus is repeated.

Researchers have used a variety of animals to study learning. The history of psychology is full of stories about scientists who began studying animal *biology*, but then switched their focus to animal *behavior* as unexpected events unfolded in the laboratory. These scientists were often excited to see the connections between biology and experience that became evident as they explored the principles of learning.

Animals are often excellent models for studying and understanding human behavior, including learning. Conducting animal research sidesteps many of the ethical dilemmas that arise with human research. It's generally considered okay to keep rats, cats, and birds in cages to ensure control over experimental variables (as long as they are otherwise treated humanely), but locking up people in laboratories would obviously be unacceptable.

This chapter focuses on three major types of learning: classical conditioning, operant conditioning, and observational learning. As you make your way through the pages discussing each, you will begin to realize that learning is very much about creating associations. Through *classical conditioning,* we associate two different stimuli: for example, the sound of a buzzer and the arrival of food. In *operant conditioning,* we make connections between our behaviors and their consequences: for example, through rewards and punishments. With *observational learning,* we learn by watching and imitating other people, establishing a closer link between our behavior and the behavior of others.

Learning can occur in predictable or unexpected ways. It allows us to grow and change, and it is a key to achieving goals. Let's see how learning has shaped the life and work of Cesar Millan.

PATRIOT WITH A PROBLEM Every year around July 4th, animal shelters around the country report a surge in the number of runaway dogs and other pets (Humane Society, 2015, June 26). The banging and popping of fireworks are so terrifying to some dogs, they flee their homes to escape the sounds. A dog that fears fireworks or thunder is nothing out of the ordinary. But what if the animal went into panic mode every time he heard the beep of a microwave, cell phone, or elevator? This was the sad reality for Gavin, a sweet and gentle yellow Labrador retriever who worked as a bomb-sniffing dog for the Bureau of Alcohol, Tobacco, Firearms and Explosives (ATF).

Cesar, in His Own Words

http://qrs.ly/ae5a5au

Photo: Vincent Sandoval/ WireImage/Getty Images.

CONNECTIONS

In **Chapter 2,** we described circumstances in which learning alters the brain and vice versa. For example, dopamine plays an important role in learning through reinforcement. Neurogenesis (the generation of new neurons) is also thought to be associated with learning.

CONNECTIONS

In **Chapter 3,** we discussed sensory adaptation, which is the tendency to become less aware of constant stimuli. Becoming habituated to sensory input keeps us alert to *changes* in the environment.

CONNECTIONS

In **Chapter 1,** we discussed Institutional Review Boards, which must approve all research with human participants *and* animal subjects to ensure safe and humane procedures.

learning A relatively enduring change in behavior or thinking that results from experiences.

habituation A basic form of learning evident when an organism does not respond as strongly or as often to an event following multiple exposures to it.

stimulus An event or occurrence that generally leads to a response.

Serving His Country
Special Agent L. A. Bykowsky works with Gavin in an explosives-detecting exercise. During his five years with the Bureau of Alcohol, Tobacco, Firearms and Explosives (ATF), Gavin helped ensure the safety of people attending Super Bowls and NASCAR races; then he went on a mission in Iraq, where his problems with noises seemed to begin (Millan & Peltier, 2010). AP Photo/Wilfredo Lee.

When Cesar first met Gavin, the yellow Lab had already retired from the ATF, but the poor dog couldn't relax and enjoy his golden years because he was so traumatized by events from the past. While on a tour in the Iraq War, Gavin had witnessed several loud explosions. Whenever an explosion occurred, "he quivered and shook," but then was able to carry on with his duties, according to his handler, Special Agent L. A. Bykowsky (Millan & Peltier, 2010, p. 58). Gavin may have been able to hold it together in Iraq, but the experience had a profound impact on his mental health. "He came back with a post-traumatic stress [disorder]," explains Cesar. Shortly after returning to his home in Pompano Beach, Florida, Gavin lived through two consecutive hurricanes (Millan & Peltier, 2010), which "just took him to the roof," according to Cesar. After that, anything that made a beeping noise would trigger Gavin's fear response: the sound of a voicemail ringtone might cause whole-body muscle contractions and uncontrollable shaking.

Clearly, Gavin was suffering from severe anxiety, but how did he come to associate harmless, everyday sounds with danger? To answer this question, we need to travel back in time and visit the lab of an aspiring Russian scientist: Ivan Pavlov. ●

 **show what you know**

1. Learning is a relatively enduring change in _____ that results from our _____.

2. Learning is often described as the creation of _____, for example, between two stimuli or between a behavior and its consequences.

   a. habituation   **c.** associations
   b. ethical dilemmas   **d.** unexpected events

✓ CHECK YOUR ANSWERS IN APPENDIX C.

Classical Conditioning

LO 2   **Explain what Pavlov's studies teach us about classical conditioning.**

The son of a village priest, Ivan Pavlov had planned to devote his life to the church. He changed his mind at a young age, however, due to a combination of the changing political times in Russia and the readings that challenged his worldview (Todes, 2014). His primary interest was physiology, a branch of biology that investigates the physical and chemical mechanisms underlying life's processes. Although he won a Nobel Prize in 1904 for his research on the physiology of digestion, Pavlov's most enduring legacy was his trailblazing research on learning (Fancher & Rutherford, 2012). This research "would raise him far above the status of a mere Nobel Prize winner to a cultural symbol of twentieth-century science" (Todes, 2014, p. 265).

Pavlov spent the 1890s studying the digestive system of dogs at Russia's Imperial Institute of Experimental Medicine, during which he had around 100 people working for him in the laboratory (Todes, 2014; Watson, 1968). Many of his early experiments involved measuring how much dogs salivate in response to food. Initially, the dogs salivated as expected, but as the experiment progressed, they began salivating to other stimuli as well. After repeated trials with an assistant giving food and then measuring the dog's saliva output, Pavlov realized that instead of salivating the moment food was

---

CONNECTIONS

A dog naturally begins to salivate when exposed to the smell of food, even before tasting it. This is an involuntary response of the autonomic nervous system, which we explored in **Chapter 2**. Dogs do not normally salivate at the sound of footsteps, however. This response is a *learned* behavior, as the dog salivates without tasting or smelling food.

neutral stimulus (NS) A stimulus that does not cause a relevant automatic or reflexive response.

served, the dog began to salivate at the mere sight or sound of the lab assistant arriving to feed it. The assistant's footsteps, for example, might act like a trigger (*stimulus*) for the dog to start salivating (*response*). Pavlov realized that the dogs' "psyche," or personality, and their "thoughts about food" were interfering with the collection of objective data on their digestion (Todes, 2014, p. 158). In other words, the dogs' psychological activities were affecting their physiology, making it difficult for the researchers to study digestion as an isolated phenomenon. Pavlov had discovered that associations develop through the process of learning, which we now refer to as *conditioning*. The dog was associating the sound of footsteps or the sight of the bowl with the arrival of food; it had been *conditioned* to link certain sights and sounds with eating. Intrigued by his discovery, Pavlov began to shift the focus of his research and investigate the dogs' salivation (which he termed "psychic secretions") in these types of scenarios (Fancher & Rutherford, 2012; Todes, 2014).

Pavlov's Basic Research Plan

Pavlov followed up on his observations about psychic secretions with numerous studies starting in the early 1900s, examining the link between stimulus (for example, the sound of human footsteps) and response (how much the dog salivates). The type of behavior Pavlov was studying (salivating) is not voluntary, but involuntary or reflexive (Pavlov, 1906). The connection between food and salivating is innate and universal (occurs in all members of the species), whereas the link between the sound of footsteps and salivating is learned. Learning has occurred whenever a new, nonuniversal link between stimulus (footsteps) and response (salivation) is established.

Many of Pavlov's studies had the same basic format (**INFOGRAPHIC 5.1** on the next page). Prior to the experiment, the dog had a tube surgically inserted into its cheek so researchers could determine exactly how much saliva the dog was producing. Once the dog had recovered from the surgery, it was placed alone in a soundproof room and outfitted with equipment to keep it from moving around. Because Pavlov was interested in exploring the link between a stimulus and the dog's response, he had to pick a stimulus that was more controlled than the sound of someone walking into a room. Pavlov used a variety of stimuli, such as sounds produced by metronomes and buzzers, and flashing lights, which under normal circumstances have nothing to do with food or salivation. In other words, they are *neutral* stimuli in relation to feeding and responses to food.

On numerous occasions during an experimental trial, Pavlov and his assistants presented a dog with a chosen stimulus—the sound of a buzzer, for instance—and then moments later gave the dog a piece of meat. Each time the buzzer was sounded, the assistant would wait a couple of seconds and then offer the dog meat. All the while, its drops of saliva were being measured. After repeated pairings, the dog began to link the buzzer with the meat; it would salivate in response to the sound alone, with *no* meat present, evidence that learning had occurred. The dog had *learned* to associate the tone with food. Remember, we call this type of learning *conditioning*.

Time for Some Terms

LO 3 Identify the differences between the US, UR, CS, and CR.

Now that you know Pavlov's basic research procedure, it is important to learn the specific terminology psychologists use to describe what is happening (Infographic 5.1). Before the experiment began, the tone was a **neutral stimulus (NS)**—something in the environment that *does not* normally cause a relevant *automatic* or reflexive response. In this case, that automatic, unlearned response is salivation; dogs do not normally

What Is a Metronome?
Pavlov conditioned his dogs to salivate in response to auditory stimuli, such as buzzers and ticking metronomes. A metronome is a device that musicians often use to maintain tempo. This "old-fashioned" metronome has a wind-up knob and a pendulum that ticks at various speed settings. Modern metronomes are digital and often come with additional features such as adjustable volume. Perhaps Pavlov could have used these new features to test different aspects of classical conditioning. Galina Ermolaeva/ Dreamstime.com.

CONNECTIONS

In **Chapter 1,** we discussed the importance of control in the experimental method. Here, if the sound of footsteps is the stimulus, then Pavlov would need to *control* the number of steps taken and the type of shoes worn to ensure the stimulus was identical across trials. Otherwise, he would be introducing extraneous variables, or characteristics that interfere with the research outcome, making it difficult to determine what caused the dog to salivate.

CONNECTIONS

In **Chapter 1,** we discussed operational definitions, which are the precise ways in which characteristics of interest are defined and measured. Although earlier we described the research in everyday language, here we provide operational definitions for the procedures of the study.

Learning Through Classical Conditioning

During his experiments with dogs, Ivan Pavlov noticed them salivating before food was even presented. Somehow the dogs had learned to associate the lab assistant's approaching footsteps with eating. This observation led to Pavlov's discovery of classical conditioning, in which we learn to associate a neutral stimulus with an unconditioned stimulus that produces an automatic, natural response. The crucial stage of this process involves repeated pairings of the two stimuli.

PAVLOV'S EXPERIMENT

Before conditioning

Dog salivates automatically when food is presented.

Unconditioned stimulus → Unconditioned response (salivates)

Buzzer means nothing to dog, so there is no response.

Neutral stimulus (buzzer sound) — No response

During conditioning

In the process of conditioning, buzzer is repeatedly sounded right before dog receives food. Over time, dog learns that buzzer signals arrival of food.

Neutral stimulus (buzzer sound) + Unconditioned stimulus = Unconditioned response (salivates)

repeated over time

After conditioning

Dog has now learned to associate buzzer with food and will begin salivating when buzzer sounds.

Conditioned stimulus (buzzer sound) — Conditioned response (salivates)

HAVE YOU BEEN CONDITIONED?

Before conditioning

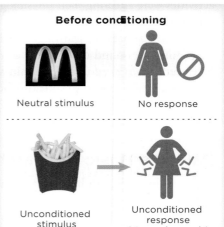

Neutral stimulus — No response

Unconditioned stimulus — Unconditioned response (stomach growls)

During conditioning

Neutral stimulus + Unconditioned stimulus

Unconditioned response (stomach growls) — repeated over time

After conditioning

Conditioned stimulus — Conditioned response (stomach growls)

Classical conditioning is an involuntary form of learning that happens every day. Does your stomach rumble when you see the McDonald's "golden arches"? Just like Pavlov's dogs, we learn through repeated pairings to associate neutral stimuli (the golden arches) with food (French fries). Once this association is formed, the sight of the golden arches can be enough to get our stomachs rumbling.

respond to the tone of a buzzer by salivating. But through experience, they learned to link this neutral stimulus (the tone) with another stimulus (food) that normally prompts salivation. This type of learning is called **classical conditioning**, and it is evident when an originally neutral stimulus triggers an involuntary response, such as salivation, eye blinks, and other types of *reflex* reactions.

US, UR, CS, AND CR At the start of a trial, before a dog was conditioned or had learned anything about the neutral stimulus, it salivated when it smelled or received food, in this case meat. The meat is considered an **unconditioned stimulus (US)** because it triggers an automatic response without any learning needed. The dog's salivation when exposed to food is an **unconditioned response (UR)** because it doesn't require any learning; the dog just does it involuntarily. Salivation (the UR) is an automatic reaction elicited by the smell or taste of meat (the US). After conditioning has occurred, the dog responds to the buzzer tone almost as if it were food. The tone, previously a *neutral stimulus,* has now become a **conditioned stimulus (CS)** because it triggers the dog's salivation. When the salivation occurs in response to the tone, it is a learned behavior; we call it a **conditioned response (CR).**

THE ACQUISITION PHASE The pairings of the neutral stimulus (the tone) with the unconditioned stimulus (the meat) occur during the **acquisition** or initial learning phase. Some points to remember:

- The meat is always an unconditioned stimulus (the dog never has to learn how to respond to it).

- The dog's salivating is initially an unconditioned response to the meat, but eventually becomes a conditioned response as well; it occurs when the tone is sounded (without the sight or smell of meat).

- The unconditioned stimulus is always different from the conditioned stimulus; the unconditioned stimulus automatically triggers the response, while the conditioned stimulus elicits a response that has been *learned* by the organism.

Pavlov's work paved the way for a new generation of psychologists who considered behavior to be a topic of objective, scientific study. Like many scientists who would follow, he focused on the objective recording of measurable behaviors, in this case counting the exact number of saliva drops produced by the dogs. His work transformed our understanding of learning and our approach to psychological research.

Nuts and Bolts of Classical Conditioning

We have learned about Pavlov's dogs and their demonstration of classical conditioning, defining terms along the way. Now it's time to take our learning (about learning) to the next level and examine some of the principles guiding the process.

LO 4 Recognize and give examples of stimulus generalization and stimulus discrimination.

STIMULUS GENERALIZATION What would happen if a dog in one of Pavlov's experiments heard a slightly higher-frequency buzzer tone? Would the dog still salivate? Pavlov (1927/1960) asked this same question and found that a stimulus similar to the conditioned stimulus (CS) caused the dogs to salivate as well. This is an

CONNECTIONS

In **Chapter 1,** we discussed extraneous variables, characteristics of the environment or participants that interfere with the research outcome. Here, the sight and smell of meat are potential extraneous variables that could affect the conditioning procedure. These were carefully controlled to avoid interference with measurements of the dependent variables.

CONNECTIONS

In **Chapter 1,** we described the scientific method and its dependence on *objective* observation. This approach requires us to observe and record free from personal opinion or expectations. We are all prone to biases, but the scientific method helps minimize their effects. Pavlov was among the first to insist that behavior must be studied objectively.

Synonyms

classical conditioning Pavlovian conditioning, respondent conditioning

classical conditioning Learning process in which two stimuli become associated with each other; when an originally neutral stimulus is conditioned to elicit an involuntary response.

unconditioned stimulus (US) A stimulus that automatically triggers an involuntary response without any learning needed.

unconditioned response (UR) A reflexive, involuntary response to an unconditioned stimulus.

conditioned stimulus (CS) A previously neutral stimulus that an organism learns to associate with an unconditioned stimulus.

conditioned response (CR) A learned response to a conditioned stimulus.

acquisition The initial learning phase in both classical and operant conditioning.

Layland Masuda/Shutterstock.

CONNECTIONS

In **Chapter 3,** we introduced the concept of a difference threshold, the minimum difference between two stimuli noticed 50% of the time. Here, we see that difference thresholds can play a role in stimulus discrimination. The difference between the conditioned stimulus and the comparison stimuli must be greater than the difference threshold.

stimulus generalization The tendency for stimuli similar to the conditioned stimulus to elicit the conditioned response.

stimulus discrimination The ability to differentiate between a conditioned stimulus and other stimuli sufficiently different from it.

extinction In classical conditioning, the process by which the conditioned response decreases after repeated exposure to the conditioned stimulus in the absence of the unconditioned stimulus; in operant conditioning, the disappearance of a learned behavior through the removal of its reinforcer.

example of **stimulus generalization.** Once an association is forged between a CS and a conditioned response (CR), the learner often responds to similar stimuli as if they were the original CS. When Pavlov's dogs learned to salivate in response to a metronome ticking at 90 beats per minute, they also salivated when the metronome ticked a little more quickly (100 beats per minute) or slowly (80 beats per minute; Hothersall, 2004). Their response was *generalized* to metronome speeds ranging from 80 to 100 beats per minute. Perhaps you have been classically conditioned to salivate at the sight of a tall glass of lemonade. Stimulus generalization predicts you would now salivate when seeing a shorter glass of lemonade, or even a mug, if you knew it contained your favorite drink.

STIMULUS DISCRIMINATION Next let's see what would happen if you presented Pavlov's dogs with two stimuli that differed significantly. Suppose the dogs have learned to associate the meat with a high-pitched sound; they salivate whenever they hear it. Expose these same dogs to lower-pitched sounds, and they may not salivate. If so, they are demonstrating **stimulus discrimination,** the ability to distinguish between a particular conditioned stimulus (CS) and other stimuli sufficiently different from it. With enough training, Pavlov's dogs could distinguish between a metronome beating 96 times per minute and one beating 104 times per minute (Todes, 2014). Similarly, someone who's been stung by a bee might only have an involuntary fear response to the sight of bees (and not flies) because he has learned to discriminate among various flying insects. He has only been conditioned to fear bees.

EXTINCTION Once the dogs in a classical conditioning experiment associate the tone of a buzzer with meat, can they ever listen to the sound without salivating? The answer is yes—if they are repeatedly exposed to the buzzer *without* the meat. Present the conditioned stimulus (CS) without the unconditioned stimulus (US), over and over, and the association may fade. The conditioned response (CR) decreases and eventually disappears in a process called **extinction.** In general, if dogs are repeatedly exposed to a CS (for example, a metronome or buzzer) without any tasty treats to follow, they produce progressively less saliva in response to the stimulus and, eventually, none at all (Watson, 1968).

SPONTANEOUS RECOVERY But take note: Even with extinction, the connection is not necessarily gone forever. After conditioning a dog to associate the tone of a buzzer with meat, Pavlov (1927/1960) stopped presenting the meat, and the association was extinguished (the dog didn't salivate in response to the tone). Two hours following this extinction, Pavlov presented the tone again and the dog salivated. This reappearance of the conditioned response (CR) following its extinction is called **spontaneous recovery.** With the presentation of a conditioned stimulus (CS) after a period of rest, the conditioned response (CR) reappears. The dog had not "forgotten" the association when the pairing was extinguished. Rather, the CR was suppressed or inhibited when the dog was not being exposed to the unconditioned stimulus (US). When the buzzer (the CS) sounded in the absence of food (the US), the association reemerged; the link between the tone and the food had remained, simply simmering beneath the surface. Let's return to that tall refreshing glass of lemonade—a summer drink you may not consume for 9 months out of the year. It is possible that your CR (salivating) will be suppressed by extinction from September to the end of May, but when June rolls around, spontaneous recovery may occur, and once again you are salivating at the sight of that lemonade glass (the CS).

HIGHER ORDER CONDITIONING Is it possible to add another layer to the conditioning process? Absolutely. Suppose the tone of the buzzer has become a conditioned stimulus (CS) for the dog. Now the researcher adds a new neutral stimulus, such as

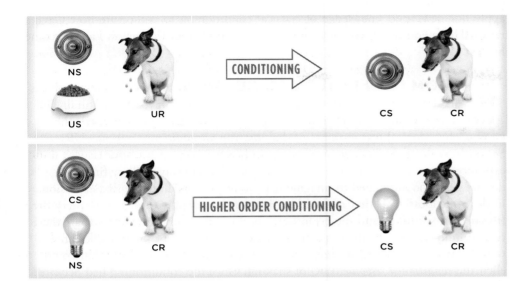

a light flashing, every time the dog hears the buzzer. After pairing the buzzer and the light (without the meat anywhere in sight or smell), the light becomes associated with the sound and the dog will begin to salivate in response to seeing the light alone. This is called **higher order conditioning** (FIGURE 5.1). With repeated pairings of the CS (buzzer tone) and a new neutral stimulus (the light), the second neutral stimulus becomes a CS as well. When all is said and done, both stimuli (the buzzer and the light) have gone from being neutral stimuli to conditioned stimuli, and either of them can elicit the conditioned response (CR; salivation). Note that in higher order conditioning, the second neutral stimulus is paired with a CS instead of being paired with the original unconditioned stimulus (Pavlov, 1927/1960). In our example, the light is associated with the buzzer sound, not with the food directly.

How might higher order conditioning figure into everyday life? Suppose your nightly routine includes making dinner during television commercial breaks. The sight and smell of food make your mouth water, and since cooking exposes you to these delicious stimuli, it causes salivation as well. But that's not all. Over time, you have come to associate cooking with commercial breaks, so the commercials (originally neutral stimuli) also have the power to trigger salivation. Cooking (CS) prompts you to salivate (CR), and because dinner preparation always happens during commercial breaks, the commercials make you salivate (CR) as well, even if there is no food present. Here, we have an example of higher order conditioning, whereby additional stimuli elicit the CR.

Classical conditioning is not limited to salivation. It affects you in ways you may not even realize. Just think of what happens to your heart rate when you walk into a room where you have had a bad experience, or when you come face to face with a person (perhaps a boss) who has caused you great anxiety. When Cesar Millan is about to go on stage and give a seminar, his heart races; his throat gets dry; and his stomach feels uneasy. Could these be classically conditioned responses? Perhaps Cesar has learned to associate certain backstage sights, sounds, and smells with the anxiety of not knowing how people will react to him. "Every time you perform in a new environment, you don't know how the audience is going to take it," Cesar says. "The energy of people in Florida is completely different than the energy of people in New York . . . . Same topic, same show, but the audience is going to respond different[ly]."

We launched the discussion of classical conditioning with the story of Gavin, the ATF dog who became fearful of everyday sounds after serving in the Iraq War. Let's

spontaneous recovery The reappearance of a conditioned response following its extinction.

higher order conditioning With repeated pairings of a conditioned stimulus and a second neutral stimulus, that second neutral stimulus becomes a conditioned stimulus as well.

Calm in the Water
According to Cesar, being in the
water brings out the instinctual
side of dogs, connecting them
with nature and making them feel
calm. To help Gavin the ATF dog
overcome his fear of everyday
noises (the CS), Cesar paired the
disturbing sounds with activities
that were relaxing and pleasurable
for Gavin. MPH/Emery Sumner JV.

conditioned taste aversion A form of
classical conditioning that occurs when an
organism learns to associate the taste of a
particular food or drink with illness.

adaptive value The degree to which a
trait or behavior helps an organism survive.

apply our newfound knowledge of classical conditioning to conjecture how Gavin's
unusual behaviors developed, and discover how Cesar helped this yellow Lab overcome
his fear.

 FROM IVAN PAVLOV TO CESAR MILLAN An explosion is
an alarming event, and Gavin's response (shaking) only seems natural. The
sound of the explosion is an *unconditioned stimulus* (US) that elicits the
physiological fear response of shaking (the *unconditioned response;* UR).
Somewhere along the line, we suspect Gavin heard another sound paired with the
explosion—perhaps the rhythmic, popping sound of faraway artillery fire. (It
doesn't seem too farfetched to imagine you would hear artillery fire and explosions
in the same location.) After repeated pairings of the popping of distant artillery fire
(the neutral stimulus) and the explosion sound (US), Gavin came to associate these
two stimuli; we call this the acquisition phase. The sound of distant artillery fire
went from being a *neutral stimulus* (NS) to a *conditioned stimulus* (CS) that could
elicit the *conditioned response* (CR) of shaking. Once the conditioning had occurred,
the sound of artillery fire would evoke the same physiological response (shaking) as
an explosion.

So what does all this have to do with Gavin's fear of beeping microwaves, cell
phones, and elevators? Again, we can only speculate because we weren't there to
observe Gavin in Iraq. But suppose he was conditioned to fear the sound of distant
artillery fire. Then it's possible that this fear became generalized to other rhythmic,
mechanical sounds, such as beeping cell phones and elevators. Through *stimulus
generalization,* these non-dangerous sounds began to evoke a *conditioned response*
(CR) as well.

However, Gavin did not shake in response to every sound he heard. The voice of
Cesar and the panting sounds of nearby dogs did not seem to faze him (Millan &
Peltier, 2010). Thus, Gavin demonstrated a certain degree of *stimulus discrimination.*
His conditioned response (CR) seemed to be reserved for rhythmic sounds.

When Cesar first met Gavin, he immediately sensed that this exquisitely trained
animal had lost touch with the instinctual dog within. ATF Agent Gavin could sniff
out the odors of 19,000 bomb chemicals, yet he seemed to have forgotten how to
enjoy life as a dog—one that follows the scents of animals (rather than bombs) and
interacts with members of a pack. To help Gavin regain his canine identity, Cesar
brought the yellow Lab to his Dog Psychology Center in Santa Clarita, California.
Gavin was well received by the dogs in Cesar's pack, and being in this natural social
environment helped him move into a more relaxed state. "As I've seen hundreds of
times, a pack of dogs can do more rehab in a few hours than I can do alone in a few
days," Cesar writes in his book *Cesar's Rules* (Millan & Peltier, 2010, p. 59). Spending
time with Cesar and his pack helped Gavin become more relaxed in general, but
he still exhibited the same fear response when he heard beeping elevators and other
sounds. How might you eliminate this classically conditioned response?

If Gavin were to go many months without hearing any noise that triggered his
fear reaction (not very realistic, given the variety of sounds that provoked it), the
association might fade away through *extinction.* But quite often, this type of avoidance
behavior does not extinguish a classically conditioned response, as the possibility
of *spontaneous recovery* always exists. (Recovery in this sense means recovering the
conditioned response of fear, not the more familiar sense of "getting better.")

The second option would be to pair a new response with the unconditioned
stimulus (US) or the conditioned stimulus (CS). Cesar took this approach, and it
worked wonders. To help Gavin overcome his fear of everyday loud noises (the CS),
Cesar combined those sounds with something relaxing or pleasurable. For example,

he would create a loud noise just as he presented Gavin with his favorite food (carrots). To reduce Gavin's fear of truly frightening sounds like thunder, fireworks, and explosions (the US), Cesar placed him in a virtual reality environment. As Gavin walked on a treadmill (an enjoyable activity for him), Cesar exposed him to the sounds he feared most (not all at once, but in small steps). Eventually, Gavin's fear response diminished and he could visit a firing range without shutting down and shaking (Millan & Peltier, 2010). In Chapter 14, we present similar techniques used by therapists to help clients struggling with anxiety and fear. ●

We've learned how classical conditioning can cause a variety of reflexive responses, including salivation (Pavlov's dogs), increased heart rate (Cesar), and shaking (Gavin). Would you believe that this form of learning can also make you feel nauseous?

Yuck: Conditioned Taste Aversion

LO 5 Summarize how classical conditioning is dependent on the biology of the organism.

Have you ever experienced food poisoning? After falling ill from something you ate, whether it was sushi, uncooked chicken, or tainted peanut butter, you probably steered clear of that particular food for a while. This is an example of **conditioned taste aversion,** a powerful form of classical conditioning that occurs when an organism learns to associate a particular food or drink with illness. Often, it only takes a single pairing between a food and a bad feeling—that is, one-trial learning—for an organism to change its behavior. Imagine a grizzly bear that avoids poisonous berries after vomiting from eating them. In this case, the unconditioned stimulus (US) is the poison in the berries; the unconditioned response (UR) is the vomiting. After acquisition, the conditioned stimulus (CS) would be the sight of the berries, and the conditioned response (CR) would be a nauseous feeling. In all likelihood, the bear would avoid the berries in the future.

Avoiding foods that induce sickness has **adaptive value,** meaning it helps organisms survive, upping the odds they will reproduce and pass their genes along to the next generation. According to the evolutionary perspective, humans and other animals have a powerful drive to ensure that they and their offspring reach reproductive age, so it's critical to steer clear of tastes that have been associated with illness.

How might conditioned taste aversion play out in your life? Suppose you eat a hot dog a few hours before coming down with a stomach virus that's coincidentally spreading throughout your college. The hot dog isn't responsible for your illness—and you may be aware of this—but thereafter, the slightest taste of one, or the thought of eating one, can make you feel sick even after you have recovered. Physical experiences like this can sometimes be so strong that they override our knowledge of the facts.

RATS WITH BELLYACHES American psychologist John Garcia (1917–2012) and his colleagues demonstrated conditioned taste aversion in their well-known studies with laboratory rats (Garcia, Ervin, & Koelling, 1966). They designed a series of experiments to explore how rats would respond to eating and drinking foods that would become associated with sickness. In one study, Garcia and his colleagues provided the animals with flavored water followed by injections of a drug that upset their stomachs. The animals rejected that flavored drink thereafter.

The rats in Garcia's studies seemed naturally inclined to link their "internal malaise" (sick feeling) to tastes and smells and less likely to associate their nausea with things they heard or saw (Garcia et al., 1966). This is clearly adaptive, because nausea often

CONNECTIONS

In **Chapter 1,** we introduced the evolutionary perspective, which suggests that adaptive behaviors and traits are shaped by natural selection. Here, this perspective helps clarify why some types of learning are so powerful. In the case of conditioned taste aversion, species gain an evolutionary advantage through quick and efficient learning about poisonous foods.

try this ↓

Identify the neutral stimulus (NS), the unconditioned stimulus (US), the unconditioned response (UR), the conditioned stimulus (CS), and the conditioned response (CR) in the hot dog scenario.

√ CHECK YOUR ANSWERS IN APPENDIX C.

results from ingesting food that is poisonous or spoiled. In order to survive, an animal must be able to recognize and shun the tastes of dangerous substances. Garcia's research highlights the importance of **biological preparedness,** the predisposition or inclination of animals (and people) to form certain kinds of associations through classical conditioning. Conditioned taste aversion is a powerful form of learning. Would you believe it can be used to save endangered species?

THINK IT THROUGH
Rescuing Animals with Classical Conditioning

Using your newfound knowledge of conditioned taste aversion, imagine how you might solve the following problem: An animal is in trouble in Australia. The northern quoll, a meat-eating marsupial that might be described as a cute version of an opossum, is critically endangered

EATING A POISONOUS TOAD CAN TAKE A QUOLL!

because a non-native "cane toad" is invading its territory. Cane toads may look delicious (at least to the quolls, who eat them right up), but they pack a lethal dose of poison—often enough to kill a quoll in just one eating. Wherever the toads have settled, quoll populations have diminished or disappeared (Lewis, 2014; O'Donnell, Webb, & Shine, 2010). The quolls are now in danger of becoming extinct. How could you use conditioned taste aversion to save them?

Remember that conditioned taste aversion occurs when an organism rejects a food or drink after consuming it and becoming very sick. To condition the quolls to stop eating the toxic toads, you must teach them to associate the little amphibians with nausea. You could do this by feeding them non-poisonous cane toads containing a drug that causes nausea. A group of researchers from the University of Sydney used this approach with the quolls, and the strategy turned out to be quite successful. Quolls that experienced conditioned taste aversion were less likely than their unconditioned comrades to eat the poisonous toads and die (O'Donnell et al., 2010).

Similar approaches are being tried across the world. In Africa, ranchers often kill lions for preying upon cattle (Platt, 2015, June 24). But researchers have shown that the big cats can learn to avoid beef through conditioned taste aversion (Platt, 2011, December 27). Another example comes from California, where researchers are trying to save an endangered bird called a marbled murrelet by feeding its predator murrelet look-alike eggs that make them vomit (Oskin, 2013, May 17). As you see, lessons learned by psychologists working in a lab can have far-reaching applications.

CONNECTIONS

In **Chapter 1,** we introduced two types of research. Basic research is focused on gathering knowledge for the sake of knowledge. Applied research focuses on changing behaviors and outcomes, often leading to real-world applications. Here, we see how classical conditioning principles are *applied* to help save wildlife.

Learning to the Rescue
Australia's northern quoll (left) is threatened by the introduction of an invasive species known as the cane toad (right). The quolls eat the toads, which carry a lethal dose of poison, but they can learn to avoid this toxic prey through conditioned taste aversion (O'Donnell et al., 2010). Left: David Hosking/Corbis. Right: Chris Mattison/FLPA/Science Source.

Little Albert and Conditioned Emotional Response

LO 6 Describe the Little Albert study and explain how fear can be learned.

So far, we have focused chiefly on the classical conditioning of physical responses—salivation, nausea, and shaking. Now let's take a closer look at how classical conditioning can influence emotions. A **conditioned emotional response** occurs when a neutral stimulus is paired with an emotional reaction.

The classic case study of "Little Albert," conducted by John B. Watson and Rosalie Rayner (1878–1958, 1898–1935), provides a famous illustration of a conditioned emotional response (Watson & Rayner, 1920). Little Albert was around 9 months old when first tested by Watson and Rayner (Griggs, 2015d; Powell, Digdon, Harris, & Smithson, 2014). Initially, he had no fear of rats; in fact, he was rather intrigued by the little white critters and sometimes reached out to touch them. But all this changed when Albert was about 11 months old; that's when the researchers began banging a hammer against a steel bar (an unconditioned stimulus [US] for a fear response in younger children) whenever he reached for the rat (Harris, 1979). After seven pairings of the loud noise and the appearance of the rat, Albert began to fear rats and generalized this fear to other furry objects, including a sealskin coat and a rabbit (Harris, 1979). The sight of the rat went from being a neutral stimulus (NS) to a conditioned stimulus (CS), and Albert's fear of the rat became a conditioned response (CR).

Nobody knows exactly what happened to Little Albert after he participated in Watson and Rayner's research. Some psychologists believe Little Albert's true identity is still unknown (Powell, 2010; Reese, 2010). Others have proposed Little Albert was Douglas Merritte, who had a neurological condition called hydrocephalus and died at age 6 (Beck & Irons, 2011; Beck, Levinson, & Irons, 2009; Fridlund, Beck, Goldie, & Irons, 2012). Still others suggest Little Albert was a healthy baby named William Albert Barger (later known as William Albert Martin), who lived until 2007 and reportedly had an "aversion to dogs" (Bartlett, 2014; Digdon, Powell, & Harris, 2014; Powell et al., 2014). Did Barger's distaste for dogs and other animals stem from his supposed participation in Watson and Rayner's experiment, his dislike of messiness, or was it the result of seeing a childhood pet killed in an accident (Powell et al., 2014)? Researchers cannot be sure, and we may never know the true identity of Little Albert or the long-term effects of his conditioning through this unethical study. Although Watson and Rayner (1920) discussed how they might have reduced Little Albert's fear of rats (for example, giving him candy while presenting the rat), they were never able to provide him with such treatment (Griggs, 2014a).

The Little Albert study would never happen today; at least, we hope it wouldn't. Contemporary psychologists conduct research according to stringent ethical guidelines, and instilling terror in a baby would not be considered acceptable (nor would it be allowed at research institutions).

Poor Albert
"Little Albert" was a baby who developed a fear of rats through his participation in an ethically questionable experiment conducted by John B. Watson and Rosalie Rayner (Watson & Rayner, 1920). Watson and Rayner repeatedly showed the child a rat while terrifying him with a loud banging sound. Albert quickly learned to associate the sight of the rat with the scary noise, and his resulting fear of rats is known as a conditioned emotional response. The Drs. Nicholas and Dorothy Cummings Center for the History of Psychology, The University of Akron.

 In Class: Collaborate and Report

Discuss the Little Albert case study in your group, answering the following questions: **A)** How would you change the conditions to make the study ethical? **B)** What contributions to psychology does this case study offer? **C)** Imagine a parent repeatedly shouting "NO!" at his toddler when she reaches to touch a rat. Identify the NS, US, UR, CS, and CR in this scenario. (*Hint:* A loud sound scared Little Albert.) **D)** How could you stop the behavior without frightening the child?

biological preparedness The tendency for animals to be predisposed or inclined to form certain kinds of associations through classical conditioning.

conditioned emotional response An emotional reaction acquired through classical conditioning; process by which an emotional reaction becomes associated with a previously neutral stimulus.

Classical Conditioning: Do You Buy It?

Classical conditioning has applications in marketing and sales (TABLE 5.1). Have you ever noticed that baseball, basketball, and other sports events are often promoted by celebrity athletes? In one study, researchers had some participants view images of sports events paired with famous athletes, while others viewed the same events without celebrity endorsement. As you might expect, participants exposed to celebrity endorsement developed more favorable attitudes toward the events (Chen, Lin, & Hsiao, 2012). Through classical conditioning, the sports events had become associated with the famous people.

Celebrities also come in handy for selling products. Cover Girl makeup looks very appealing on the face of Sofia Vergara, and who can resist Nike gear worn by soccer star Cristiano Ronaldo? Advertisements can instill emotions and attitudes toward product brands, and these classically conditioned responses may linger as long as 3 weeks (Grossman & Till, 1998). In one study, some participants were shown pictures of pleasant scenes (such as a tropical location or a panda in a natural setting) paired with a fictitious mouthwash brand. Participants who were exposed to the mouthwash (originally a neutral stimulus) and the favorable pictures (the unconditioned stimulus)

TABLE 5.1   REAL-LIFE EXAMPLES OF CLASSICAL CONDITIONING

Type	NS and US	Expected Response
Advertising	Repeated pairing of products such as cars (NS) with celebrities (US)	Automatic response to celebrity may include sexual desire and arousal, or increased heart rate (UR); pairing leads to a similar response (CR) to the product (CS).
Fears	Pairing of a dog lunging (US) at you, and the street where the dog lives (NS)	Automatic response to the dog lunging at you is fear (UR); pairing leads to similar response of fear (CR) to the street (CS) where the dog lives.
Fetishes	Repeated pairings of originally nonsexual objects like shoes (NS) and sexual activity (US)	Automatic response to sexual activity is sexual arousal (UR); pairing leads to sexual arousal (CR) in response to the objects (CS).
Romance	Repeated pairings of a cologne (NS) with your romantic partner (US)	Automatic response to your feelings for your partner is sexual arousal (UR); pairing leads to sexual arousal (CR) in response to the cologne (CS).
Pet behavior	Repeated pairings of an electric can opener sound (NS) and the serving of food (US)	Automatic response to food is the dog/cat's salivation (UR); pairing leads to salivation (CR) in response to the sound of the can opener (CS).
Startle reaction	Repeated pairings of the toilet flushing sound (NS) with the sudden rise in water temperature in the shower (US)	Automatic response to the sensation of scalding water is jumping back (UR); pairing causes the person showering to jump back (CR) in response to the sound of the toilet flushing (CS).

The implications of classical conditioning extend far beyond salivating dogs. Here are just a few examples illustrating its widespread relevance.

were more likely to retain a positive enduring attitude (now the conditioned response) toward the mouthwash (which became a conditioned stimulus) than participants who were exposed to the same set of pictures paired in random order. In other words, the researchers were able to create "favorable attitudes" toward the fictitious mouthwash brand by pairing pictures of the mouthwash with scenery that evoked positive emotions (Grossman & Till, 1998). The study did not address whether this favorable attitude leads to a purchase, however.

What if classically conditioned attitudes did lead to changes in purchasing behavior? The implications could be far-reaching. Imagine, for example, that consumers made decisions based on medical advice offered by celebrities, as opposed to health professionals (Hoffman & Tan, 2013).

Do you think you are susceptible to this kind of conditioning? We would venture to say that we all are. Complete the following Try This to see if classical conditioning affects your attitudes and feelings toward everyday products.

try this ↓

Marketers use classical conditioning to instill positive emotions and attitudes toward product brands. List examples of recent advertisements you have seen on television or the Internet that use this approach to get people to buy products. Which of your recent purchases may have been influenced by such ads?

Remember that classical conditioning is a type of learning associated with automatic (or involuntary) behaviors. You don't "learn" to go out and buy a particular brand of mouthwash through classical conditioning. Classical conditioning can influence our attitudes toward products, but it can't teach us voluntary behaviors. Well then, how do we learn these types of deliberate behaviors? Read on.

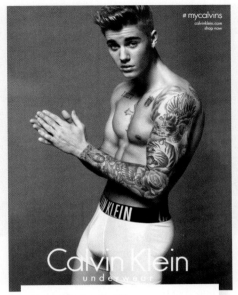

Does Sexy Sell?
Justin Bieber models underwear for Calvin Klein's spring 2015 ad campaign. Research suggests that advertisements may instill attitudes toward brands through classical conditioning (Grossman & Till, 1998), but how do these attitudes affect sales? Now that is a question worth researching. The Advertising Archives.

○◉○○ **show what you know**

1. _____ is the learning process in which two stimuli become associated.

2. Because of _____, animals and people are predisposed to form associations that increase their chances of survival.

3. Hamburgers were once your favorite food, but ever since you ate a burger tainted with salmonella (which causes food poisoning), you cannot smell or taste one without feeling

nauseous. Which of the following is the unconditioned stimulus?
   a. salmonella   c. hamburgers
   b. nausea   d. the hamburger vendor

4. Watson and Rayner used classical conditioning to instill fear in Little Albert. Create a diagram of the NS, US, UR, CS, and CR in their experiment. In what way does Little Albert show stimulus generalization?

√ CHECK YOUR ANSWERS IN APPENDIX C.

Operant Conditioning

WE'VE GOT DOG PROBLEMS Cesar spent much of his early life on his grandfather's cattle ranch in Ixpalino, a small town in Sinaloa, Mexico. He loved being around the ranch animals, especially the dogs. They lived in a pack of about 5 to 7 members, slept outside, hunted wild animals, and ate scraps of human food. Cesar's family depended on the dogs to herd cattle and guard the property, but also gave them plenty of "free time" to splash around in the creek and play with each other. The ranch dogs organized their activities as a pack, as wolves do in nature, and their needs for daily exercise were satisfied (Fine, 2013, February 7; Millan & Peltier, 2006).

Only in America
Where else do dogs wear diamond-studded tiaras and have their own birthday parties? People in the United States have a tendency to humanize dogs, but this approach does not benefit the dog (Millan, 2013). "Every single species has its own psychology," Cesar explains. "But when it comes to a dog, we say 'no, don't be a dog, be a human.' *Why*? Why would a dog want to be a human? We're the most unstable species on the planet!" Kiko Jimenez/Shutterstock.

When Cesar arrived in the United States, he encountered quite a different type of dog. Many pooches in America were *humanized,* or treated like people. They dined on gourmet biscuits, slept on memory foam mattresses, and got their hair blown dry at doggie salons. It was not unusual for owners to attribute human emotions to their dogs' behavior ("Sparkie is whining right now because he feels sad"), and respond to them as they might a child ("Sparkie needs affection"). Cesar began to realize that many American owners didn't understand their dogs or know how to communicate with them. Because the owners didn't know what their dogs needed, the dogs were unsatisfied with their lives. Consequently, they suffered from an untold number of "issues," including anxiety, aggression, and hyperactivity (Millan & Peltier, 2006). In order to "fix" the dogs' misbehaviors, Cesar would have to teach their human owners a few things. As Cesar often says, "I rehabilitate dogs, and I train people" (Millan, 2013, March 26, para. 3).

So how exactly does Cesar train humans? We can't possibly cover the myriad approaches Cesar employs, but we can explore how he uses *operant conditioning* to change behavior. ●

The Shaping of Behavior

Operant conditioning is a type of learning whereby people or animals come to associate their voluntary actions with consequences. Whether pleasant or unpleasant, the effects of a behavior influence future actions. Think about the many consequences of Cesar's hard work. Helping people understand and connect with their dogs is one positive consequence: "When I show them how the brain of a dog works, when I show them what makes a dog happy, when I show them how dogs communicate, and how we can communicate with [dogs]," Cesar explains, "then [I] see people understanding and making sense of what's happening." This is a rewarding experience for Cesar, one that makes him more likely to continue his work in the future. Now suppose all dog owners ignored his advice and continued with their bad habits. How do you think this consequence would influence Cesar's future behaviors—would he be more or less likely to continue his work rehabilitating dogs and training people?

LO 7 Describe Thorndike's law of effect.

THORNDIKE AND HIS CATS One of the first scientists to objectively study how consequences affect behavior was American psychologist Edward Thorndike (1874–1949). Thorndike's early research focused on chicks and other animals, which he sometimes kept in his apartment. But after an incubator almost caught fire, his landlady insisted he get rid of the chicks (Hothersall, 2004). Thorndike was assisted by William James, whose "habitual kindness and devotion to underdogs" led him to house the chickens in his basement for a time (Thorndike, 1936, p. 264).

Thorndike's research with the chicks was only a starting point, as his most famous studies involved cats. One of his experimental setups involved putting a cat in a latched cage called a "puzzle box" and planting enticing pieces of fish outside the door. When first placed in the box, the cat would scratch and paw around randomly, but after a while, just by chance, it would pop the latch, causing the door to release. The cat would then escape the cage to devour the fish (**FIGURE 5.2**). The next time the cat was put in the box, it would repeat this random activity, scratching and pawing with no particular direction. And again, just by chance, the cat would pop the latch that released the door and freed it to eat the fish. Each time the cat was returned to the

operant conditioning Learning that occurs when voluntary actions become associated with their consequences.

law of effect Thorndike's principle stating that behaviors are more likely to be repeated when followed by pleasurable outcomes, and less likely to be repeated when followed by unpleasant outcomes.

reinforcers Consequences, such as events or objects, that increase the likelihood of a behavior reoccurring.

reinforcement Process by which an organism learns to associate a voluntary behavior with its consequences.

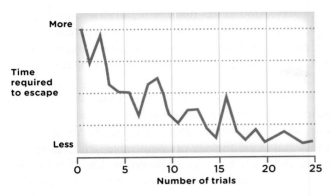

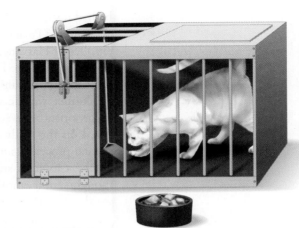

FIGURE 5.2
Puzzle Box
Early psychologist Edward Thorndike conducted his well-known cat experiments using "puzzle boxes" like the one shown here. At the start of the experiment, Thorndike's cats pawed around haphazardly until they managed to unlatch the door and then eat the fish treats placed outside. As the trials wore on, the felines learned to free themselves more quickly. After several trials, the amount of time needed to escape the box dropped significantly (see the graph above). Thorndike attributed this phenomenon to the *law of effect,* which states that behaviors are more likely to reoccur if they are followed by pleasurable outcomes. Information from Thorndike, 1898.

box, the number of random activities decreased until eventually it was able to break free almost immediately (Thorndike, 1898).

We should highlight a few important issues relating to this early research. First, these cats discovered the solution to the puzzle box accidentally, while exhibiting their naturally occurring behaviors (scratching and exploring). So, they initially obtained the fish treat by accident. The other important point is that the measure of learning was not a grade or score of some sort, but the amount of time it took the cats to break free.

The cats' behavior, Thorndike reasoned, could be explained by the **law of effect,** which says that a behavior (opening the latch) is more likely to happen again when followed by a pleasurable outcome (delicious fish). Behaviors that lead to pleasurable results will be repeated, while behaviors that don't lead to pleasurable results (or are followed by something unpleasant) will not be repeated. The law of effect is not limited to cats. When was the last time your behavior changed as a result of a pleasurable outcome?

Most contemporary psychologists would call the fish in Thorndike's experiments **reinforcers,** because these treats increased the likelihood that the preceding behavior (escaping the cage) would occur again. Reinforcers are consequences that follow behaviors, and they are a key component of operant conditioning. Our daily lives abound with examples of reinforcers. Praise, hugs, good grades, enjoyable food, and attention can all be reinforcers that increase the probability that the behaviors they follow will be repeated. Through the process of **reinforcement,** target behaviors become more frequent. A dog praised for sitting is more likely to obey the "sit" command in the future. An Instagram user who is reinforced with a lot of "likes" is more apt to post photos and videos in the future.

SKINNER AND BEHAVIORISM Some of the earliest and most influential research on operant conditioning came from the lab of B. F. Skinner. Like Pavlov, Skinner had not planned to study learning. Upon graduating from college, Skinner decided to become a writer and a poet, but after a year of trying his hand at writing, he decided

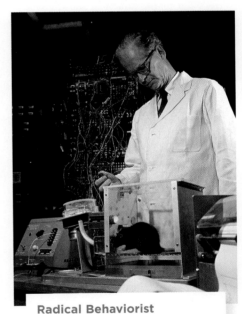

Radical Behaviorist
American psychologist Burrhus Frederic Skinner, or simply B. F. Skinner, is one of the most influential psychologists of all time. Skinner believed that every thought, emotion, and behavior (basically anything psychological) is shaped by factors in the environment. Using animal chambers known as "Skinner boxes," he conducted carefully controlled experiments on animal behavior. Nina Leen/Time & Life Pictures/Getty Images.

he had nothing to say (Skinner, 1976). Around this time, he began to read the work of Watson and Pavlov, which inspired him to pursue a graduate degree in psychology. He enrolled at Harvard, took some psychology classes that he found "dull," and eventually joined a lab in the Department of Biology, where he could study the subject he found most intriguing: animal behavior.

Skinner was devoted to *behaviorism,* the scientific study of observable behavior. Behaviorists believed that psychology could only be considered a "true science" if it was based on the study of behaviors that could be seen and documented. And although mental processes such as memory and emotion were not observable (and thus should not be a topic of study), Skinner and other behaviorists proposed that *all* behaviors, thoughts, and emotions are shaped by factors in the external environment. In other words, they are learned.

LO 8 Explain shaping and the method of successive approximations.

SHAPING AND SUCCESSIVE APPROXIMATIONS Building on Thorndike's law of effect and Watson's approach to research, Skinner demonstrated, among other things, that rats can learn to push levers and pigeons can learn to bowl (Peterson, 2004). Animals cannot immediately perform such complex tasks, but they can learn through **successive approximations,** the use of reinforcers to change behaviors through small steps toward a desired behavior (see **INFOGRAPHIC 5.2**). In the photo on page 205, you can see that Skinner placed animals in chambers, or *Skinner boxes,* which were outfitted with food dispensers the animals could activate (by pecking a target or pushing on a lever, for instance) and recording equipment to monitor these behaviors. Such boxes allowed Skinner to conduct carefully controlled experiments, measuring activity precisely and advancing the scientific and systematic study of behavior.

Some of Skinner's most incredible results occurred through **shaping,** a process in which a person observes the behaviors of another organism (an animal, for example) and provides reinforcers if the organism performs at a required level (Peterson, 2000). Through shaping by successive approximations, Skinner taught a rat to "play basketball" (dropping a marble through a hole) and pigeons to "bowl" (nudging a ball down a miniature alley).

Let's unpack this concept using the bowling pigeons example. Skinner's first task was to break the bowling lessons into activities the birds could accomplish. Next, he introduced reinforcers (usually food) as consequences for behaviors that came closer and closer to achieving the desired goal—bowling a strike! Choosing the right increments for the behaviors was crucial. If his expectations started too high, the pigeons would never receive any reinforcers. If his expectations were too low, the pigeons would get reinforcers for everything they did. Either way, they would be unable to make the critical connection between desired behavior and reward. Every time the animals did something that brought them a step closer to completing the desired behavior, they would get a reinforcer. The first reward might be given for simply looking at the ball; the second, for bending down and touching it; and the third, for nudging the ball with their beaks. By the end of the experiment, the pigeons were repeatedly driving balls down miniature alleys, knocking down pins with a swipe of the beak (Peterson, 2004).

Shaping by successive approximations can also be used with humans, who are sometimes unwilling or unable to change problematic behaviors overnight. For example, psychologists have employed this approach to change truancy behavior in adolescents (Enea & Dafinoiu, 2009). The truant teens were provided reinforcers for consistent attendance, but with small steps requiring increasingly more days in school.

It is amazing that the principles of animal training can also be harnessed to keep teenagers in school. Is there anything operant conditioning *can't* accomplish?

Synonyms

Skinner boxes operant chambers

successive approximations A method that uses reinforcers to condition a series of small steps that gradually approach the target behavior.

shaping Process by which a person observes the behaviors of another organism, providing reinforcers if the organism performs at a required level.

Learning Through Operant Conditioning

Operant conditioning is a type of learning in which we associate our voluntary actions with their consequences. For example, a pigeon naturally pecks things. But if every time the pigeon pecks a ball, he is given a *reinforcer,* the pigeon will soon learn to peck the ball more frequently.

B. F. Skinner showed that operant conditioning could do more than elicit simple, isolated actions. Through the process of *shaping,* Skinner provided his pigeons with reinforcers when they performed at a desired level, teaching them behaviors that involved a series of actions, like bowling and tennis. Today, shaping is used routinely by parents, teachers, coaches, and employers to train all kinds of complex behaviors.

SKINNER'S EXPERIMENT: TRAIN A PIGEON TO PLAY TENNIS

Pigeon is rewarded with seeds for pecking the ball.

peck **REINFORCEMENT**

reinforcement with seeds

Ball-pecking behavior increases.

peck **REINFORCEMENT** peck **REINFORCEMENT** peck **REINFORCEMENT**

Now only the next step toward "tennis" is rewarded.

peck peck pushing the ball **REINFORCEMENT**

reinforcement with seeds

Ball-pushing behavior increases.

pushing the ball **REINFORCEMENT** pushing the ball **REINFORCEMENT** pushing the ball **REINFORCEMENT**

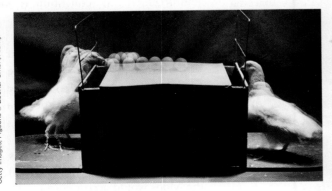

After behavior has been shaped through reinforcement, the pigeon has learned to play "tennis."

HAVE YOU BEEN TRAINED?

Not every child is born loving the healthy foods his parent offers. But shaping can help a child learn to eat his vegetables. Over a period of time, reinforcement is given for behaviors that are closer and closer to this goal. Can you think of anything that would be a reward for eating vegetables? Praise or the excitement of a contest may work in this way.

1 Child refuses to eat vegetables.

2 YES! Reinforced for touching fork

3 GOOD JOB! Now, reinforced for touching vegetables

4 After behavior has been shaped through reinforcement, the child has learned to eat his vegetables.

THINK IT THROUGH
Chickens Can't Play Baseball

BASEBALL? NO. PIANO? YES.

Rats can be conditioned to press levers; pigeons can be trained to bowl; and—believe it or not—chickens can learn to dance and play the piano (Breland & Breland, 1951). Keller and Marian Breland (1915–1965, 1920–2001), a pair of Skinner's students, managed to train 6,000 animals not only to boogie but also to vacuum, dine at a table, and play sports and musical instruments (Breland & Breland, 1961). But as hard as they tried, the Brelands could not coax a chicken to play baseball.

Here's a rundown of what happened: The Brelands placed a chicken in a cage adjacent to a scaled down "baseball field," where it had access to a loop attached to a baseball bat. If the chicken managed to swing the bat hard enough to send the ball into the outfield, a food reward was delivered at the other end of the cage. Off the bird would go, running toward its meal dispenser like a baseball player sprinting to first base—or so the routine was supposed to go. But as soon as the Brelands took away the cage, the chicken behaved nothing like a baseball player; instead, it madly chased and pecked at the ball (Breland & Breland, 1961).

How did the Brelands explain the chickens' behavior? They believed that the birds were demonstrating **instinctive drift,** the tendency for instinct to undermine conditioned behaviors. A chicken's pecking, for example, is an instinctive food-getting behavior. Although it's useful for opening seeds and killing insects (Breland & Breland, 1961), pecking won't help the bird get to first base. Animal behavior can be shaped by forces in the environment (nurture), but instinct (nature) may interfere with the process.

The above examples involve researchers deliberately shaping behaviors with reinforcers in a laboratory setting. Many behaviorists believe behaviors are being shaped all of the time, both in and out of the laboratory. Sometimes the outcome is favorable, but not always.

THE SHAPING OF BAD BEHAVIOR Have you ever wondered why some dogs are annoyingly hyper? We're talking about the ones who greet you on two hind legs, jumping, pawing, and nearly pushing you over as they pant and slobber in your face. Most dogs that act this way are not getting enough exercise, a problem that stems from their owners' failure to recognize their need for physical activity. Some breeds, like golden retrievers and Siberian huskies, may require more than an hour of walking or running each day (Millan, 2013). But other factors, including misdirected reinforcement, can contribute to the problem as well.

Consider the case of Takis Stathoulis and his three fluffy white bichons frises, who appeared in the first season of *Cesar 911.* The three little fluffballs, collectively known as "The Moos," were extremely loud and high-strung. Every time Takis walked into the restaurant he owns (Frisco's in Long Beach, California), the Moos would accost customers

Musical Bunny
Keller and Marian Breland observe one of their animal performers at the IQ Zoo in Hot Springs, Arkansas, circa 1960. Using the operant conditioning concepts they learned from B. F. Skinner, the Brelands trained ducks to play guitars, raccoons to shoot basketballs, and chickens to tell fortunes. But their animal "students" did not always cooperate; sometimes their instincts interfered with the conditioning process (Bihm, Gillaspy, Lammers, & Huffman, 2010). The Central Arkansas Library System/Courtesy of Bob Bailey.

Trouble with the Moos
Cesar works with the three bichons frises owned by Takis Stathoulis and his wife Joanne. The dogs, affectionately referred to as "the Moos," were notorious for their obnoxious barking and hyperactivity. Takis unwittingly reinforced their bad behaviors with his approving body language and verbal feedback (Furtado, 2014). By acting like everything was normal, Takis was essentially telling the dogs, "This behavior is good. Please continue."

and bark in their faces. Takis did nothing to stop them; actually, he reinforced their behaviors by smiling, patting them, and emanating the same type of boisterous energy (Furtado, 2014). "Dog lovers, they have a tendency to reinforce excited behavior," explains Cesar, "and that's where it gets tricky." Here, we see how reinforcement can perpetuate undesirable behaviors. ●

Types of Reinforcement

Like most people who have achieved a high level of success and fame, Cesar has accumulated a fair number of critics. Some claim he is too physical with the animals, forcing them into submission with foot taps to the area above the hind leg and vibrating collars (Grossman, 2012, June 9; Hanna, 2012, October 27). Cesar has defended himself by saying he reserves these techniques for "red zone" dogs—those that pose a threat to other animals and/or people and therefore may be at risk for being euthanized. "My mission has always been to save dogs—especially troubled and abandoned dogs," he said in an interview with the *Daily Mail*. "I've dedicated my life to this" (Barber, 2012, October 27, para. 4).

We are not interested in taking sides here, but it is surprising how little attention Cesar receives for using other, non-forceful approaches. Watch Cesar closely, and you'll see that he employs quite a bit of *positive reinforcement*.

LO 9 **Identify the differences between positive and negative reinforcement.**

POSITIVE REINFORCEMENT Earlier, we explained that a reinforcer is a consequence that increases the likelihood of a behavior being repeated. *Any* stimulus, good or bad, is considered a reinforcer if it eventually increases the behavior that had immediately preceded it. What we haven't addressed is that a reinforcer can be something added or something taken away. In the process of **positive reinforcement,** reinforcers are presented (added) following the target behavior, and they are generally pleasant (see Infographic 5.2). By presenting positive reinforcers following a target behavior, we are increasing the chances that the target behavior will occur again. If the behavior doesn't increase after the stimulus is presented, that particular stimulus should not be considered a reinforcer. The fish treats that Thorndike's cats received immediately after escaping the puzzle box and the morsels of bird feed that Skinner's pigeons got for bowling are examples of positive reinforcement. In both cases, the reinforcers were *added* following the desired behavior and were pleasurable.

What reinforcers does Cesar employ in dog rehabilitation? Sometimes it's not as obvious as a biscuit or bone. Before giving reinforcement, Cesar explains, you have to help your dog feel calm and happy, and that requires exercise and mental stimulation. Once the dog reaches that tranquil state, you can reinforce it with affection. However, petting and praising may not even be necessary, according to Cesar; you can also reinforce the dog's behavior with your own "calm and confident" demeanor. Do you recall the example of Takis and his rambunctious trio of bichons frises? When Cesar showed Takis how to become a calm and confident leader, the little white dogs finally chilled out and stopped barking (Furtado, 2014). Perhaps Takis' new relaxed disposition reinforced the dogs' own calm behavior. It's important to remember that the definition of "positive reinforcer" depends entirely on the organism receiving it (Skinner, 1953). If the dog finds his owner's calm and confident demeanor reinforcing, then the owner's demeanor is a reinforcer.

For some dogs, playtime is a powerful positive reinforcer. Remember Gavin, the ATF agent with the classically conditioned response to certain noises? After Gavin completed his sessions in the virtual reality environment, Cesar would reinforce the Lab's good work with "a vigorous play period," which often meant a dip in the pool (Millan & Peltier, 2010, p. 63).

Rewards! Rewards!
Restaurants, stores, and other businesses use mobile apps to reward patrons for their loyalty. Customers rack up rewards by making purchases or, in some cases, by simply walking into a store. These rewards can serve as positive reinforcement for buying behavior—assuming the customer finds them reinforcing. Remember, a consequence qualifies as a reinforcer only if the organism finds it reinforcing—now that's a tongue twister! mimagephotography/Shutterstock.

instinctive drift The tendency for animals to revert to instinctual behaviors after a behavior pattern has been learned.

positive reinforcement The process by which reinforcers are added or presented following a target behavior, increasing the likelihood of it occurring again.

Dogs offer positive reinforcement to humans as well; you just have to be perceptive enough to notice. Consider this example from Cesar: "Your dog wants to go outside and pee. He sits by the door. You open the door. The dog walks out, but as he passes by you, he looks up at you for a moment and makes eye contact. He just rewarded you" (Millan & Peltier, 2010, p. 121). Why is eye contact reinforcing? When you gaze into your dog's eyes, both you and the dog release the hormone *oxytocin,* which plays an important role in social bonding. Oxytocin increases "social reward" and enhances attachment between infants and their mothers, and between sexual partners. Eye contact is just one of the ways dogs and humans have established mutually reinforcing relationships during the course of evolution (MacLean & Hare, 2015; Nagasawa et al., 2015).

We should point out that not all positive reinforcers are pleasant; when we refer to *positive* reinforcement, we mean that something has been *added*. For example, if a child is starved for attention, then any kind of attention (including a reprimand) might act as a positive reinforcer. Every time the child misbehaves, she gets reprimanded, and reprimanding is a form of attention, which the child craves. The scolding reinforces the misbehavior.

NEGATIVE REINFORCEMENT We have established that behaviors can be increased or strengthened by the addition of a stimulus. But it is also possible to increase a behavior by taking something away. Behaviors increase in response to **negative reinforcement,** through the process of *taking away* (or subtracting) something unpleasant. Skinner used negative reinforcement to shape the behavior of his rats. The rats were placed in Skinner boxes with floors that delivered a continuous mild electric shock—except when they pushed on a lever. The animals would begin the experiment scampering around the floors to escape the electric current, but every once in a while, they would accidentally hit the lever and turn off the current. Eventually, they learned to associate pushing the lever with the removal of the unpleasant stimulus (the mild electric shock). After several trials, the rats would push the lever immediately, reducing their shock time.

Think about some examples of negative reinforcement in your own life. If you try to drive your car without your seat belt, does your car make an annoying beeping sound? If so, the automakers have employed negative reinforcement to *increase* your use of seat belts. The beeping provides an annoyance (an unpleasant stimulus) that prompts most people to put on their seat belts (the desired behavior increases) to make the beeping stop, and thus remove the unpleasant stimulus. The next time you get in the car, you will more quickly put on your seat belt, because you have learned that buckling up immediately makes the annoying sound go away. Another example is putting the lid on a garbage can to cover its awful smell. Here, the desired behavior is to put the lid on the can, and the unpleasant stimulus that goes away is the bad smell. Finally, think about a dog that constantly begs for treats. The begging (an unpleasant stimulus) stops the moment the dog is given a treat, a pattern that increases *your* treat-giving behavior. Meanwhile, the dog's begging behavior is being strengthened through positive reinforcement; the dog has learned that the more it begs, the more treats it receives.

Notice that with negative reinforcement, the desired behaviors increase in order to remove an unwanted condition. Let's say a dog is barking on and off all day—an undesired behavior for most owners. According to Cesar, constant barking is the dog's way of communicating, "My needs are not being met" (Millan, 2013, p. 127). If the dog is a high-energy Australian shepherd whose biggest unfulfilled need is exercise, then the owner would be wise to lace up her Nikes and take her dog for a spin around the park. In doing so, she performs a desired behavior herself (walking or jogging for exercise). The removal of the annoying stimulus (dog barking) increases a desirable behavior in

Synonyms

negative reinforcement omission training

secondary reinforcers conditioned reinforcers

negative reinforcement The removal of an unpleasant stimulus following a target behavior, which increases the likelihood of it occurring again.

primary reinforcer A reinforcer that satisfies a biological need, such as food, water, physical contact; innate reinforcer.

secondary reinforcer Reinforcers that do not satisfy biological needs but often gain power through their association with primary reinforcers.

the owner (exercising). Thus, the owner's exercise is negatively reinforced by the dog's excessive barking. Keep in mind that the goal of negative reinforcement (and positive reinforcement) is to *increase* a desired behavior.

 In Class: Collaborate and Report

Imagine you have an elderly relative or friend who is hard-of-hearing, but won't admit it. Team up with classmates and **A)** design a positive reinforcement system to encourage her to use hearing aids, and **B)** explain how you could use negative reinforcement to increase this behavior.

LO 10 Distinguish between primary and secondary reinforcers.

PRIMARY AND SECONDARY REINFORCERS There are two major categories of reinforcers: primary and secondary. The food Skinner used to reward his pigeons and rats is considered a **primary reinforcer,** because it satisfies a biological need. Food, water, and physical contact are considered primary reinforcers (for both animals and people) because they meet essential requirements. **Secondary reinforcers** do not satisfy biological needs, but often derive their power from their connection with primary reinforcers. Although money is not a primary reinforcer, we know from experience that it gives us access to primary reinforcers, such as food, a safe place to live, and perhaps even the ability to attract desirable mates. Thus, money is a secondary reinforcer. Good grades might also be considered secondary reinforcers, because doing well in school leads to job opportunities, which provide money to pay for food and other basic needs.

Secondary reinforcers are evident in everyday social interactions. Think about how your behaviors change in response to praise from a boss, a pat on the back from a co-worker, or even a nod of approval from a friend on Twitter or Instagram.

SOCIAL MEDIA AND PSYCHOLOGY
Contagious Behaviors

In some respects, the behavioral effects of social media are obvious. Why do you keep glancing at Facebook, and what compels you to check your phone 10 times an hour? All those little tweets and updates you receive are reinforcing. It feels good to be re-tweeted, and it's nice to see people "like" your wall posts and photos.

With its never-ending supply of mini-rewards, social media often absorbs time that would otherwise be devoted to offline relationships and work—a clear drawback. But

WHY DO YOU CHECK YOUR PHONE 10 TIMES AN HOUR? | the reinforcing power of social media can also be harnessed to promote positive behaviors. A study by MIT researcher Damon Centola found that people are more likely to explore healthy behaviors when alerted that others in their social media networks are doing the same. This is especially true for those in "clustered" networks, where people share many of the same contacts. As Centola observed: "People usually require contact with multiple sources of 'infection' before being convinced to adopt a behavior" (Centola, 2010, p. 1194). Each of these sources of infection, it seems, provides social reinforcement for the positive behavior. Others have concluded that using social media "campaigns" to promote healthy behavior is a great way to generate initial participation, but encouragement from "friends" seems to keep people engaged (Zhang, Brackbill, Yang, & Centola, 2015). Thus, if you want to develop a healthier lifestyle, it can't hurt to surround yourself with online friends who exercise, eat well, and don't smoke.

Now that we have a basic understanding of reinforcement, let's explore the various ways it can be delivered.

Reinforced Through Social Media
Healthy living apps such as MyFitnessPal and PumpUp enable users to share their exercise accomplishments and get feedback from friends and family members. Can the reinforcing power of social media be harnessed to promote exercise and other healthy behaviors? Such potential exists, but further research is needed (Centola, 2010; Maher et al., 2014). Courtesy Jack Stone.

The Power of Partial Reinforcement

HIGHLY TRAINED, BUT UNSTABLE Shortly after arriving in Los Angeles, Cesar began working for a very popular dog-training establishment. He encountered dogs with impeccable training, capable of executing any number of commands, such as "sit" and "stay." Yet some of these highly trained animals were psychologically unstable. "Many of the dogs were fearful and insecure, and the process of training made them worse," Cesar recalls. "They might have left the facility being able to respond to commands, but they still had the behavior problem they'd come in with" (Millan & Peltier, 2010, p. 22). What these animals needed, Cesar eventually concluded, was a better relationship with their owners: a human–dog bond based on trust, understanding, and good communication (Millan & Peltier, 2010). ●

LO 11 Describe continuous reinforcement and partial reinforcement.

CONTINUOUS REINFORCEMENT Once that positive relationship is established between dog and owner, obedience training is likely to proceed more smoothly. (Here, we could draw an analogy with parenting; enforcing rules is much easier when the caregiver–child relationship is based on mutual love and respect; Kochanska, Kim, & Boldt, 2015.) When it comes to teaching new behaviors to dogs, children, and other organisms, most psychologists would agree that positive reinforcement is extremely effective. Let's say you are teaching your puppy to "sit." You begin the process by giving her a treat every time she obeys the "sit" command. Rewarding the pup in this manner is called **continuous reinforcement,** because the reinforcer is presented *every* time the desired behavior occurs. Continuous reinforcement can be used in a variety of settings: a child getting praise every time he does the dishes; a salesperson receiving a bonus every time she makes a sale. You get the commonality: reinforcement every time the behavior occurs.

PARTIAL REINFORCEMENT Continuous reinforcement comes in handy for a variety of purposes and is ideal for establishing new behaviors during the acquisition phase. But delivering reinforcers intermittently, or every once in a while, works better for maintaining behaviors. We call this approach **partial reinforcement.** Returning to the examples of continuous reinforcement, we can also imagine applying partial reinforcement: The child gets praise almost every time he does the dishes; a salesperson gets a bonus for every third sale she makes. The reinforcer is not given every time the behavior is observed, only on some occasions.

How might partial reinforcement apply to dog training? Continuous reinforcement can work wonders when a dog is first learning commands, but switching to partial reinforcement may be more practical in the long run (who wants to walk around with hundreds of doggie treats in his pocket?). The amazing thing about partial reinforcement is that it happens to all of us, in an infinite number of settings, and we might never know how many times we have been partially reinforced for any particular behavior. Common to all of these partial reinforcement situations is that the target behavior is exhibited, but the reinforcer is not supplied each time it occurs.

PARTIAL REINFORCEMENT EFFECT Skinner used partial reinforcement to train his pigeons to peck at a target. Once the behavior had been learned, they would continue to peck at the target up to 10,000 times with no further reinforcers

"Sit!"
Rewarding a dog with a treat every time she follows the "sit" command is a form of continuous reinforcement. This is a great approach for establishing a desired behavior, but partial reinforcement may work better for sustaining behaviors.
Yuri_Arcurs/Getty Images.

Synonyms

partial reinforcement intermittent reinforcement

continuous reinforcement A schedule of reinforcement in which every target behavior is reinforced.

partial reinforcement A schedule of reinforcement in which target behaviors are reinforced intermittently, not continuously.

given (Skinner, 1953). According to Skinner, "Nothing of this sort is ever obtained after continuous reinforcement" (p. 99). The same seems to be true with humans. In one study from the mid-1950s, researchers observed college students playing slot machines. Some of the slot machines provided continuous reinforcement, delivering pretend coins every time students pulled their levers. Other slot machines provided partial reinforcement, dispensing coins only some of the time. After the students played eight rounds, all of the machines stopped giving coins. Without any coins to reinforce them, the students stopped pulling the levers—but not at the same time. Those who had received coins with every lever pull gave up more quickly than did those rewarded intermittently. In other words, lever-pulling behavior took longer to extinguish when established through partial reinforcement (Lewis & Duncan, 1956). Psychologists call this phenomenon the **partial reinforcement effect:** Behaviors take longer to disappear (through the process of *extinction*) when they have been acquired or maintained through partial, rather than continuous, reinforcement. Some people, in particular those who gamble frequently, seem to be especially responsive to partial reinforcement, though it's not clear whether this tendency is a precursor to gambling or the result of it (Horsley, Osborne, Norman, & Wells, 2012).

Remember, partial reinforcement works very well for maintaining behaviors, but not necessarily for establishing behaviors. Imagine how long it would take Skinner's pigeons to accomplish the first step in learning how to bowl if they were rewarded for looking at the ball only every fifth time. The birds learn fastest when reinforced every time, but their behavior will persist longer if they are given partial reinforcement thereafter.

Timing Is Everything: Partial Reinforcement Schedules

LO 12   Name the schedules of reinforcement and give examples of each.

Skinner identified various ways to administer partial reinforcement, or *partial reinforcement schedules.* As often occurs in scientific research, he stumbled on the idea by chance. Late one Friday afternoon, Skinner realized he was running low on the food pellets he used as reinforcers for his laboratory animals. If he continued rewarding the animals on a continuous basis, the pellets would run out before the end of the weekend. With this in mind, he decided only to reinforce some of the desired behaviors (Skinner, 1956, 1976). The new strategy worked like a charm. The animals kept performing the desired behaviors, even though they weren't given reinforcers every time.

Clearly, partial reinforcement is effective, but how exactly should it be delivered? Four different reinforcement schedules can be used: fixed-ratio, variable-ratio, fixed-interval, and variable-interval (**INFOGRAPHIC 5.3** on the next page).

FIXED-RATIO SCHEDULE   In some situations, the best approach to reinforcement is a **fixed-ratio schedule.** With this arrangement, the subject must exhibit a predetermined number of desired responses or behaviors before a reinforcer is given. A pigeon in a Skinner box, for example, must peck a spot five times in order to score a delicious pellet. Generally, the fixed-ratio schedule produces a high response rate, but with a characteristic dip immediately following the reinforcement. Pigeons rest briefly before pecking away at the target again. Some instructors use the fixed-ratio

Hope Springs Eternal
Why are slot machines so enticing? The fact that they deliver rewards occasionally and unpredictably makes them irresistible to many gamblers. Slot machines take advantage of the partial reinforcement effect, which states that behaviors are more persistent when reinforced intermittently, rather than continuously. The Image Bank/Getty Images.

partial reinforcement effect The tendency for behaviors acquired through intermittent reinforcement to be more resistant to extinction than those acquired through continuous reinforcement.

fixed-ratio schedule A schedule in which the subject must exhibit a predetermined number of desired behaviors before a reinforcer is given.

Partial Reinforcement: Schedules of Reinforcement

Continuous reinforcement is ideal for establishing new behaviors. But once learned, a behavior is best maintained through partial reinforcement. Partial reinforcement can be delivered according to four schedules: fixed-ratio, variable-ratio, fixed-interval and variable-interval.

TIMING IS EVERYTHING

Fixed-Ratio

peck peck peck peck peck
reinforcement with food pellet on 5th peck
REINFORCEMENT

peck peck peck peck peck
reinforcement with food pellet on 5th peck
REINFORCEMENT

peck peck peck peck peck
reinforcement with food pellet on 5th peck
REINFORCEMENT

Fixed-Ratio
Subject must exhibit a predetermined number of desired responses before a reinforcer is given.

Variable-Ratio

peck peck peck
reinforcement with food pellet on 3rd peck
REINFORCEMENT

peck peck peck peck peck peck peck peck
reinforcement with food pellet on 8th peck
REINFORCEMENT

peck peck peck peck
reinforcement with food pellet on 4th peck
REINFORCEMENT

Variable-Ratio
Reinforcement is unpredictable, that is, the number of desired responses that must occur before a reinforcer is given changes across trials and is based on an average number of responses to be reinforced.

Fixed-Interval

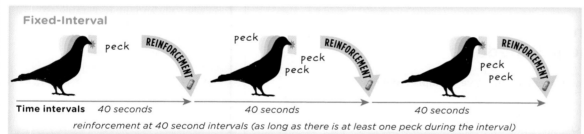

peck
REINFORCEMENT

peck peck peck
REINFORCEMENT

peck peck peck
REINFORCEMENT

Time intervals   40 seconds   40 seconds   40 seconds
reinforcement at 40 second intervals (as long as there is at least one peck during the interval)

Fixed-Interval
The reinforcer comes after a preestablished interval of time; the target response is only reinforced after the given time period is over.

Variable-Interval

peck peck
REINFORCEMENT

peck
REINFORCEMENT

peck peck
REINFORCEMENT

Time intervals   41 seconds   43 seconds   40 seconds
reinforcement at variable intervals (as long as there is at least one peck during the interval)

Variable-Interval
Reinforcement follows the first target response after the time interval has elapsed. The length of the time interval changes from trial to trial.

---

test yourself

Which schedule of reinforcement matches each of the following examples? Choose from **fixed-ratio**, **variable-ratio**, **fixed-interval**, and **variable-interval**.

1. Checking the clock more frequently as the time for your favorite television show approaches is an example of _____ .

2. You listen intently to your favorite radio show because they will randomly select times throughout the day for listeners to call in to win free tickets to a concert. This is an example of _____ .

3. Finding it difficult to walk away from the slot machine because you think the next pull will be a winner is an example of _____ .

4. You consistently submit your chapter summaries to your instructor because you can earn 5 points for every 4 summaries submitted. This is an example of _____ .

Answers 1. fixed-interval, 2. variable-interval, 3. variable-ratio, 4. fixed-ratio

schedule to reinforce attendance. For example, treats are provided when all students show up on time for three classes in a row.

VARIABLE-RATIO SCHEDULE Other times, it is best to use reinforcement that is unpredictable. In a **variable-ratio schedule,** the number of desired responses or behaviors that must occur before a reinforcer is given changes across trials. (This number is based on an average number of responses to be reinforced.) If the goal is to train a pigeon to peck a spot on a target, a variable-ratio schedule can be used as follows: Trial 1, the pigeon gets a pellet after pecking the spot twice; Trial 2, the pigeon gets a pellet after pecking the spot once; Trial 3, the pigeon gets a pellet after pecking the spot three times; and so on. Here's another example: To encourage on-time attendance, an instructor provides treats after several classes in a row, but students don't know if it will be on the third class, the second class, or the fifth class. This variable-ratio schedule tends to produce a high response rate (pecking in our example) and behaviors that are difficult to extinguish because of the unpredictability of the reinforcement schedule.

FIXED-INTERVAL SCHEDULE In some cases, it might be important to focus on the interval of time between reinforcers, as opposed to the number of desired responses. In a **fixed-interval schedule,** the reinforcer comes after a preestablished interval of time; a reinforcer is given for the first target behavior *after* that period has elapsed. If a pigeon is on a fixed-interval schedule of 30 seconds, it can peck at the target as often as possible once the interval starts, but it will only get a reinforcer following its first response after the 30 seconds have ended. With this schedule, the target behavior tends to increase as each time interval comes to an end. The pigeon pecks the spot more often when the time nears 30 seconds. Do you want to increase your focus while studying? Reinforce yourself with a treat after each hour you have worked without digital distractions.

VARIABLE-INTERVAL SCHEDULE In a **variable-interval schedule,** the length of time between reinforcers is unpredictable. In this schedule, the reinforcer comes after an interval of time goes by, but the length of the interval changes from trial to trial (within a predetermined range based on an average interval length). Training a pigeon to peck a spot on a target using a variable-interval schedule might include the following: Trial 1, the pigeon gets a pellet after 41 seconds; Trial 2, the pigeon gets a pellet after 43 seconds; Trial 3, the pigeon gets a pellet after 40 seconds; and so on. As with the fixed-interval schedule, the pigeon is rewarded for the first response it makes after the interval of time has passed (but in this case, the interval length varies from trial to trial). The variable-interval schedule tends to encourage steady patterns of behavior. The pigeon tries its luck pecking a target once every 40 seconds or so. Do you want to increase your study group's focus? Reinforce them with a treat following 45 minutes of steady work; then maybe after 30 minutes of studying, give them another treat (keep them guessing!).

 In Class: Collaborate and Report

Imagine you are teaching math to third-grade students. In your groups, **A)** explain how you would use each of the four reinforcement schedules to increase the amount of time students study for math quizzes; **B)** describe how each schedule might affect student behavior; and **C)** predict the problems that could arise with each schedule.

Reinforcement schedules may come in handy when you're studying with friends. Read on to discover a great strategy for quizzing each other on the material.

variable-ratio schedule A schedule in which the number of desired behaviors that must occur before a reinforcer is given changes across trials and is based on an average number of behaviors to be reinforced.

fixed-interval schedule A schedule in which the reinforcer comes after a preestablished interval of time; the behavior is only reinforced after the given interval is over.

variable-interval schedule A schedule in which the reinforcer comes after an interval of time, but the length of the interval changes from trial to trial.

from the pages of
SCIENTIFIC AMERICAN

Wait for It: Delayed Feedback Enhances Learning—But Only If You're Curious

When answers to questions come at unpredictable intervals, memory improves.

It may seem that getting instant results would enhance learning, but various studies indicate a benefit to feedback that is delayed. Test takers are more likely to retain the correct answer if they receive it several seconds after providing their answers rather than immediately.

To understand why delayed answers improve learning, researchers at Iowa State University asked college students to give their best guess to trivia questions such as "Who coined the word 'nerd'?" and "What color is a grasshopper's blood?" and to rate how curious they were about each answer. For half of the items, participants learned the correct answer immediately after responding to the question. For the remaining items, the answers either followed a four-second delay or an unpredictable interval of two, four or eight seconds. The students were then tested on the questions after engaging in unrelated distracting tasks.

The results, which were published in the November 2014 issue of *Memory & Cognition,* confirm the benefit of delayed feedback and show that it hinges on curiosity: in follow-up tests, participants answered more accurately when feedback arrived later but only for items that piqued their interest. The researchers suggest that delayed feedback encourages learners to anticipate the answer, which may increase their level of attention to it when they receive it. The effect was strongest when feedback was presented at unpredictable intervals, which is in line with previous studies showing that attention is enhanced when an upcoming event's timing is uncertain. So if you are studying with a buddy, ask that person to give you the answers after an unpredictable delay of a few seconds. If you are working alone, resist the urge to Google or look up an answer immediately and take a guess first.

By the way, Dr. Seuss coined the word "nerd," and a grasshopper's blood is white. If you were wondering about these answers, that delay may have just sealed them in your memory forever.

So far, we have learned about *increasing* behaviors through reinforcement, but sometimes we need to *decrease* behaviors. Let's turn our attention to techniques used for this purpose.

The Trouble with Punishment

In contrast to reinforcement, which makes a behavior more likely to recur, the goal of **punishment** is to decrease or stop a behavior (**INFOGRAPHIC 5.4**). Punishment accomplishes this by instilling an association between a behavior and some unwanted consequence (for example, between stealing and going to jail, or between misbehaving and loss of screen time). Punishment isn't always effective, however; people are sometimes willing to accept unpleasant consequences to get something they really want.

POSITIVE AND NEGATIVE PUNISHMENT There are two major categories of punishment: *positive* and *negative.* With **positive punishment,** something aversive or disagreeable is applied following a target behavior. For example, getting scolded by your instructor when your cell phone rings is a positive punishment, the goal of which is to decrease disruptions during class. For some dogs, the owner's disapproval, as expressed through facial expressions and body language, may serve as a positive punishment, according to Cesar. So, too, may the jerk of a leash; as a dog runs toward the street, the owner gives it a good yank, and this creates an unpleasant sensation for the dog. The disapproving "Tsch" sound Cesar uses with dogs might also be considered a form of positive punishment. When delivered in the right way, the "Tsch" causes the dog to feel tension, and therefore stop the undesirable behavior it initiated. Here, the *addition*

punishment The application of a consequence that decreases the likelihood of a behavior recurring.

positive punishment The addition of something unpleasant following an unwanted behavior, with the intention of decreasing that behavior.

Learning: Reinforcement and Punishment

Behavior: *Driving Fast*

Do you want to increase this behavior?

YES!
It's NASCAR! You have to drive faster than anyone else to win.
We will apply a reinforcer to **increase** the behavior.

NO!
We're not at the racetrack! Speeding is dangerous and against the law.
We will apply a punishment to **decrease** the behavior.

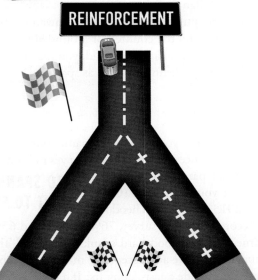

REINFORCEMENT

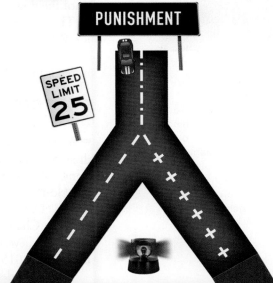

PUNISHMENT

SPEED LIMIT 25

Negative Reinforcement

You don't like working in the family auto-body shop. Your family says you can work fewer hours if you win the next race. **Taking away** unwanted work increases the speeding behavior.

Positive Reinforcement

You win a trophy and a cash prize for going fast at the race. **Adding** desirable rewards increases your speeding behavior.

Negative Punishment

The police officer confiscates your license. **Taking away** something desirable decreases your speeding behavior.

DRIVER LICENSE
2340596837485960043
SUSPENDED
JEAN DOE
23 1st Street
New York, NY

Positive Punishment

The police officer gives you a citation. **Adding** something undesirable decreases your speeding behavior.

Credits: Red and green sports cars, Jenka/Fotolia LLC; Police officer writing a ticket, © Lisa F. Young - Fotolia.com; Flags, © FreeSoulProduction - Fotolia.com; Green Traffic Light, Thinkstock; Red Traffic Light, Thinkstock; Wrench, Thinkstock; Green highway sign isolated, Thinkstock; Speed limit road sign with post and different numbers, © Thomaspajot/Dreamstime.com; Red flashing light on a white background, © Fotovika/Dreamstime.com; Trophy, Stockbyte/Thinkstock; Falling money, istockphoto/Thinkstock; Vector design set of racing flags, freesoulproduction/Shutterstock

---

✓ **test yourself**

Which process matches each of the following examples?
Choose from **positive reinforcement**, **negative reinforcement**, **positive punishment**, and **negative punishment**.

1. Carlos' parents grounded him the last time he stayed out past his curfew, so tonight he came home right on time.

2. Jinhee spent an entire week helping an elderly neighbor clean out her basement after a flood. The local newspaper caught wind of the story and ran it as an inspiring front-page headline. Jinhee enjoyed the attention and decided to organize a neighborhood work group.

3. The trash stinks, so Sheri takes it out.

4. Gabriel's assistant had a bad habit of showing up late for work, so Gabriel docked his pay.

5. During food drives, the basketball team offers to wash your car for free if you donate six items or more to the local homeless shelter.

6. Claire received a stern lecture for texting in class. She doesn't want to hear that again, so now she turns off her phone when she enters the classroom.

Answers 1. negative punishment, 2. positive reinforcement, 3. negative reinforcement, 4. negative punishment, 5. positive reinforcement, 6. positive punishment

Time-Out
Sending a child to a corner for a "time-out" is an example of negative punishment because it involves removing something (the privilege to play) in order to decrease a behavior. Spanking is a positive punishment because it involves the addition of something (a slap on the bottom) to discourage a behavior. Design Pics/Ron Nickel/Getty Images.

CONNECTIONS

In **Chapter 2,** we noted the primary roles of the frontal lobes: to organize information processed in other areas of the brain, orchestrate higher-level cognitive functions, and direct behaviors associated with personality. Here, we note that harsh physical punishment may interfere with normal development of the frontal lobes.

negative punishment The removal of something desirable following an unwanted behavior, with the intention of decreasing that behavior.

of something aversive (the tension-causing "Tsch" sound) is used with the intention of decreasing a behavior (jumping up, running away, acting aggressively)

The goal of **negative punishment** is also to reduce a behavior, but in this case, it is done by *taking away* something pleasant or valuable. A person who drives while inebriated runs the risk of negative punishment, as his driver's license may be taken away. If you show up late for class, you may suffer the negative punishment of missing that day's lecture altogether, as many instructors lock the door at the beginning of class. The goal is to decrease behaviors that lead to being tardy to class. What kind of negative punishment might be used to rein in the misbehavior of dogs? Ignoring a dog (withholding the positive stimulus of affection) is a very effective approach (*I will not pay attention to you until you stop jumping on me*). Other examples of negative punishment include restricting access to desired objects and activities (for example toys and games) until the dog gives up the bad behavior (Milllan & Peltier, 2010).

Think about the last time you tried using punishment to reduce unwanted behavior. Perhaps you scolded your cat for jumping on the counter, or grounded your child for missing curfew. If you are a parent or caregiver of a young child, you may have tried to reign in misbehavior with various types of punishment, such as spanking.

CONTROVERSIES
Spotlight on Spanking

➡️ ⬅️ Were you spanked as a child? Would you or do you spank your own children? Statistically speaking, there is a good chance your answer will be yes to both questions. Studies suggest that most American parents use corporal (physical) punishment to discipline their young children (Child Trends Databank, 2015; Gershoff, 2013; Zolotor, Theodore, Runyan, Chang, & Laskey, 2011). According to one survey, 76% of men and 65% of women believe that "a child sometimes needs a 'good hard spanking'" (Child Trends Databank, 2015, p. 2). But is spanking an effective and acceptable means of discipline?

| TO SPANK OR NOT TO SPANK . . .

There is little doubt that spanking can provide a fast-acting fix: If a child is beating up his brother, a swift slap on his bottom will probably make him stop pronto. But think about the larger lesson the boy learns in the process. His parents are trying to teach him not to be aggressive toward his brother, but in doing so, they demonstrate an aggressive behavior (hitting). Children are experts at mimicking adults' behaviors (see the next section on observational learning), and several studies suggest that spanking is linked to future aggression and other antisocial behaviors (Gershoff, 2013; MacKenzie, Nicklas, Waldfogel, & Brooks-Gunn, 2013; Taylor, Manganello, Lee & Rice, 2010).

Apart from sending children the message that the use of physical force is okay, corporal punishment may promote serious long-term mental health problems. Harsh physical punishment, which includes spanking, grabbing, and pushing, has been linked to an elevated risk for developing mood, anxiety, and personality disorders (Afifi, Mota, Dasiewicz, MacMillan, & Sareen, 2012). It may also interfere with cognitive development, retarding growth in various parts of the frontal lobes, a region of the brain that processes complex thoughts, and impact areas associated with emotions and social behaviors (Lim, Radua, & Rubia, 2014; Tomoda et al., 2009). One study even found that spanked children score lower on intelligence tests than their nonspanked peers (Straus & Paschall, 2009).

But some scholars are skeptical of such findings, as they contend that spanking studies have methodological problems (for example, the selection of participants is not totally random). What's more, critics say, these studies are primarily *correlational*, and therefore reveal associations—not necessarily cause-and-effect relationships—between physical punishment and negative outcomes (Larzelere, Cox, & Swindle, 2015). Can you think of any other factors that might explain some of the problems spanked children seem to develop? Perhaps these kids are aggressive and antisocial to begin with (that would explain why they were spanked in the first place), or maybe their parents are more likely to be abusive, and the abuse (not the spanking) is to blame (Baumrind, Larzelere, & Cowan, 2002).

Spanking, or "striking a child with an open hand on the buttocks or extremities with the intention of modifying behavior without causing physical injury" (American Academy of Pediatrics, 1998, pp. 725–726), may be an effective way to modify young children's behavior, according to certain experts (Baumrind et al., 2002; Larzelere & Baumrind, 2010). But it must be delivered by a parent whose approach is "warm, responsive, rational, and temperate" (Baumrind, 1996, p. 857). However, researchers have found that "maternal warmth does not moderate the influence of spanking on child aggression"; in other words, children who are spanked by mothers showing high levels of warmth are still more likely to be aggressive (Lee, Altschul, & Gershoff, 2013, p. 2026).

Scholars on both sides make valid points, but the debate is somewhat lopsided, as an increasing number of studies suggest that spanking generally fails to achieve the desired behavior modification, and may harm children (Durrant & Ensom, 2012; Ferguson, 2013; Smith, 2012, April). ➤◄

LO 13 **Explain how punishment differs from negative reinforcement.**

PUNISHMENT VERSUS NEGATIVE REINFORCEMENT Punishment and negative reinforcement are two concepts that students often find difficult to distinguish (**TABLE 5.2**; also see Infographic 5.4 on page 217). Remember that punishment (positive or negative) is designed to *decrease* the behavior that it follows, whereas reinforcement (positive or negative) aims to *increase* the behavior.

If all the positives and negatives are confusing you, just think in terms of math: Positive always means adding something, and negative means taking it away. Punishment can be positive, which means the addition of something viewed as unpleasant ("Because you made a mess of your room, you have to clean the toilets!"), or negative, which involves the removal of something viewed as pleasant or valuable ("Because you made a mess of your room, no ice cream for you!"). For dogs, a positive punishment might take the form

---

TABLE 5.2 REINFORCEMENT VERSUS PUNISHMENT

Term	Defined	Goal	Example
Positive reinforcement	Addition of a pleasant stimulus following a target behavior	Increase desired behavior	Students who complete an online course 15 days before the end of semester receive 10 points of extra credit.
Negative reinforcement	Removal of an unpleasant stimulus following a target behavior	Increase desired behavior	Students who have perfect attendance for the semester do not have to take the final exam.
Positive punishment	Addition of something unpleasant following an unwanted behavior	Decrease undesired behavior	Students who are late to class more than two times have to write an extra paper.
Negative punishment	Removal of something pleasant following an unwanted behavior	Decrease undesired behavior	Students late to class on exam day are not allowed to use their notes when taking the exam.

The positive and negative forms of reinforcement and punishment are easy to confuse. Above are some concrete definitions, goals, and examples to help you sort them out.

of a disapproving "Tsch" or leash pull. Negative punishment would involve withholding something pleasurable (affection or toys) to decrease an unwanted behavior.

Operant Conditioning Every Day

With all our talk about chickens, pigeons, and dogs, you may be wondering how operant conditioning applies to you. Just think about the last time you earned a good grade on a test after studying really hard. How did this grade affect your preparation for the next test? If it made you study more, then it served as a positive reinforcer. A little dose of positive reinforcement goes a long way when it comes to increasing productivity. Let's examine a couple of everyday dilemmas and brainstorm ways we could use positive reinforcers to achieve better outcomes.

Problem 1: Your housemate frequently goes to sleep without washing his dinner dishes. Almost every morning, you walk into the kitchen and find a tower of dirty pans and plates in the sink. No matter how much you nag and complain, he simply will not change his ways. *Solution:* Nagging and complaining are getting you nowhere. Try positive reinforcers instead. Wait until a day your housemate takes care of his dishes and then pour on the praise. You might be pleasantly surprised the next morning.

Problem 2: Your child is annoying you with her incessant whining. She whines for milk, so you give it to her. She whines for someone to play with, so you play with her. Why does your child continue to whine when you respond to all her needs? *Solution:* Here, we have a case in which positive reinforcers are driving the problem. When you react to your child's gripes and moans, you are reinforcing them. Turn off your ears to the whining. You might even want to say something like, "I can't hear you when you're whining. If you ask me in a normal voice, I'll be more than happy to help." Then reinforce her more mature behavior by responding attentively. This way, you are reinforcing the behavior you want to see repeated, not the one that's irritating you so much!

Common Features of Operant and Classical Conditioning

Both operant and classical conditioning are forms of learning, and they share many common principles (**TABLE 5.3**). As with classical conditioning, behaviors learned through operant conditioning go through an *acquisition* phase. It takes a certain number of practice sessions for a dog to learn a new command, such as "stay" or "down." Similarly, the cats in Thorndike's experiments learned how to escape their puzzle boxes after a series of trials. In both cases, the acquisition stage occurs gradually. Behaviors learned through operant conditioning are also subject to *extinction*— that is, they may fade in the absence of reinforcers. A rat in a Skinner box eventually gives up pushing on a lever if there is no longer a reinforcer awaiting. But that same lever-pushing behavior can make a sudden comeback through *spontaneous recovery*. After a rest period, the rat returns to his box and reverts to his old lever-pushing ways.

With operant conditioning, stimulus generalization is seen when a previously learned response to one stimulus occurs in the presence of a similar stimulus. A rat is conditioned to push a particular type of lever, but it may push a variety of other lever types similar in shape, size, and color. In certain situations, stimulus generalization through operant conditioning can be a problem. Suppose a person has a disappointing experience with a taco truck. The tacos she bought from one particular vendor are bland and soggy, so now she has forsworn all food trucks. As a result, she may miss out on some tasty tacos and other mouthwatering meals. This type of overgeneralization

---

try this ↓

Choose a bad habit that you would like to change. Design a program to achieve this goal using positive reinforcement and negative punishment. *Hint:* Remember, continuous reinforcement is most effective for establishing behaviors, but a variable schedule (that is, giving treats intermittently) is a good bet if you want to make the behavior stick. You are also more likely to succeed if you take things "one step at a time," that is, use successive approximations.

TABLE 5.3 CONDITIONING BASICS

Concept	Classical Conditioning	Operant Conditioning
The association	Links different stimuli, often through repeated pairings	Links behaviors with consequences, often through repeated pairings
Response	Involuntary behavior	Voluntary behavior
Acquisition	The initial learning phase	The initial learning phase
Extinction	The disappearance of a conditioned response after repeated exposure to the conditioned stimulus in the absence of the unconditioned stimulus	The disappearance of a learned behavior through the removal of its reinforcer
Spontaneous recovery	The reappearance of the conditioned response following its extinction	The reappearance of a behavior following its extinction; often occurs in a setting similar to that where learning occurred

These fundamental learning concepts apply to both classical and operant conditioning.

may occur when a person has trouble ignoring irrelevant information in the memory system (Lenaert, van de Ven, Kaas, & Vlaeyen, 2016).

Stimulus discrimination is also at work in operant conditioning, as organisms can learn to discriminate between behaviors that do and do not result in reinforcement. With the use of reinforcers, turtles can learn to discriminate among black, white, and gray paddles. In one study, researchers rewarded a turtle with morsels of meat when it chose a black paddle over a white one; subsequently, the turtle chose the black paddle over other-colored paddles (Leighty et al., 2013). In this example, the turtles learned stimulus discrimination with the help of *positive reinforcement,* one of the most effective ways to change behavior.

Classical and Operant Conditioning: What's the Difference?

Students sometimes have trouble differentiating classical and operant conditioning (**FIGURE 5.3**). After all, both forms of conditioning—classical and operant—involve forming associations. In classical conditioning, the learner links different *stimuli;* in operant conditioning, the learner connects her behavior to its *consequences* (reinforcement and punishment). Another key similarity is that the principles of acquisition, stimulus discrimination, stimulus generalization, extinction, and spontaneous recovery apply to both types of conditioning.

But there are also key differences between classical and operant conditioning. In classical conditioning, the learned behaviors are involuntary, or reflexive. Gavin the ATF agent could not directly control his shaking any more than Pavlov's dogs could decide when to salivate. Operant conditioning, on the other hand, concerns voluntary behavior. Cesar had power over his decision to work with problem dogs, just as Skinner's pigeons had control over swatting bowling balls with their beaks. In short, classical conditioning is an involuntary form of learning, whereas operant conditioning requires active effort.

FIGURE 5.3

Differences Between Classical and Operant Conditioning

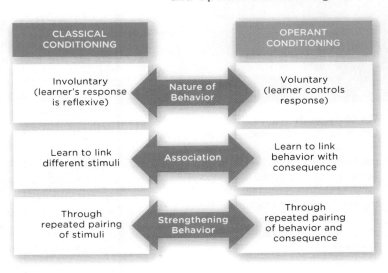

Another important distinction is the way in which behaviors are strengthened. In classical conditioning, behaviors become more established with repeated pairings of stimuli. The more often the sight of the "golden arches" is paired with the taste of french fries, the tighter the association between these stimuli (recall the stomach rumbling example from Infographic 5.1). Behaviors established through operant conditioning are also strengthened by repeated pairings, but in this case, the connection is between a behavior and its consequences. Reinforcers strengthen the behavior; punishment weakens it. The more benefits (reinforcers) Cesar accrues by working with people and dogs, the greater the likelihood he will continue cultivating his career.

Often, classical conditioning and operant conditioning occur simultaneously. A baby learns that he gets fed when he cries; getting formula or breast milk reinforces the crying behavior (operant conditioning). At the same time, the baby learns to associate formula or breast milk with the appearance of the bottle or breast; the moment he sees either, he begins salivating in anticipation of being fed (classical conditioning).

Classical and operant conditioning are not the only ways we learn. There is another major category of learning we have yet to cover. Use this hint to guess what it might be: How did you learn to peel a banana, trim your fingernails, and throw a Frisbee? Somebody must have shown you.

 **show what you know**

1. According to Thorndike and the _____, behaviors are more likely to be repeated when they are followed by pleasurable outcomes.

2. A third-grade teacher gives her students prizes for passing math tests. Not only do the students improve their math scores, they also begin studying harder for spelling tests as a result of this reinforcement schedule. Their increased studying of spelling is an example of:
   a. classical conditioning.
   b. an unconditioned response.
   c. an unconditioned stimulus.
   d. stimulus generalization.

3. A child disrupts class and the teacher writes her name on the board. For the rest of the week, the child does not act up. The teacher used _____ to decrease the child's disruptive behaviors.
   a. positive punishment
   b. negative punishment
   c. positive reinforcement
   d. negative reinforcement

4. Think about a behavior you would like to change (either yours or someone else's). Devise a schedule of reinforcement using positive and negative reinforcement to change that behavior. Also contemplate how you might use successive approximations. What primary and secondary reinforcers would you use?

5. How do continuous and partial reinforcement differ?

✓ CHECK YOUR ANSWERS IN APPENDIX C.

On the Ranch
Left to right: Cesar's mother, grandmother, sister, cousin, grandfather, and Cesar on the family farm in Ixpalino. Many of the behaviors Cesar learned in childhood came from observing role models on the family farm. His mother, for example, always worked hard and never complained about not having enough food or money.
Courtesy Cesar's Way Inc.

Observational Learning and Cognition

CESAR'S ROLE MODELS Growing up in Mexico, Cesar loved watching reruns of the dog shows *Lassie* and *The Adventures of Rin Tin Tin* from the 1950s and 60s. The dogs in these shows performed incredible physical and intellectual feats—behaviors young Cesar imagined were typical of all American dogs. The dogs of Hollywood continued to inspire Cesar when he first came to the United States. "I really believed that everybody in America had a dog just like Lassie and Rin Tin Tin," he recalls. "I really believed that I was going to learn from Americans." And so Cesar began searching for a mentor, someone who could school him in the art of American dog training. "You have to look for a master. You have to look for a sensei; you have to look for somebody with wisdom," Cesar says. "And so that's what kept me going."

But Cesar would eventually discover that his most important teachers were back in Mexico, and he had already learned from them. His grandfather Teodoro had taught him what it means to be pack leader, and how to interact effectively with dogs. A veteran of the Mexican revolution, Teodoro was a proud and grateful man, a "spiritual warrior," according to Cesar. He didn't talk much, but he demonstrated behaviors that Cesar could observe and imitate. "Never work against Mother Nature," Teodoro would say, or "you have to be calm." Then, after stating these tenets, Teodoro would execute them, and the dogs would trot after him and perform desired behaviors. "When you're on the farm, you hear very [few] words and [see] a lot of action," Cesar explains. "It was very hands on."

The ranch dogs also served as role models for young Cesar. "From the time I was very little, I found joy in dogs simply by observing them" (Millan & Peltier, 2006, p. 25). Cesar spent hours studying how the dogs interacted, and adopted some of these behaviors himself. If you watch Cesar meet a dog for the first time, you'll see he demonstrates "no talk, no touch, no eye contact" (Millan & Peltier, 2006, p. 46). This is exactly how dogs greet one another with respect.

Cesar's grandfather and the ranch dogs served as **models,** demonstrating behaviors that could be observed and imitated. We call this process **observational learning,** as it results from watching the behavior of others. According to Bandura (1986), this type of learning is more likely to occur when the learner: (1) is paying attention to the model; (2) remembers what she observed (Bahrick, Gogate, & Ruiz, 2002); (3) is capable of performing the behavior she has observed; and (4) is motivated to demonstrate the behavior. ●

Learning from the Pack
Cesar works with members of his pack at the Dog Psychology Center in Santa Clarita, California. His dogs are excellent role models for troubled dogs that come to the Center for rehabilitation. As he explains, "Dogs are great at copying behavior—that's one of the many ways in which they learn from one another when they are pups" (Millan & Peltier, 2010, p. 15). Courtesy Cesar's Way Inc.

The Power of Observational Learning

Think about how observational learning impacts your own life. Unlocking doors, using utensils, and singing are all skills you probably picked up by watching and mimicking others. Do you ever use slang? Phrases like "gnarley" (cool) from the 1980s, "Wassup" (What is going on?) from the 1990s, and "peeps" (my people, or friends) from the 2000s caught on because people copy what they observe others saying and writing. What are some of today's trending phrases that people won't recognize 20 years from now?

LO 14   **Summarize what Bandura's classic Bobo doll study teaches us about learning.**

PLEASE PLAY NICELY WITH YOUR DOLL Just as observational learning can lead to positive outcomes like effective leadership (Cesar adopting the ways of his grandfather), it can also breed undesirable behaviors. The classic Bobo doll experiment by American psychologist Albert Bandura (1925–) and his colleagues reveals just how fast children can adopt aggressive ways they see modeled by adults, as well as exhibit their own novel aggressive responses (Bandura, Ross, & Ross, 1961). In one of Bandura's studies, 76 preschool children were placed in a room one at a time with an adult and allowed to play with stickers and prints for making pictures. During their playtime, some of the children were paired with adults who acted aggressively toward a 5-foot-tall inflatable Bobo doll—punching it in the nose, hitting its head with a mallet, kicking it around the room, and yelling phrases such as "Sock him in the nose" and "Pow!" The other children in the study were paired with adults who played with toys peacefully (Bandura et al., 1961).

At the end of the experiment, all the children were allowed to play with a Bobo doll themselves. Those who had observed adults attacking and shouting were much more likely to do the same. Boys were more likely than girls to mimic physical aggression,

You Asked, Cesar Answers

http://qrs.ly/tj5a5cz

Who has had the greatest influence on your life?

scan this →

Synonyms
observational learning social learning

model The individual or character whose behavior is being imitated.
observational learning Learning that occurs as a result of watching the behavior of others.

Bobo Doll

Preschool children in Albert Bandura's famous Bobo doll experiment performed shocking displays of aggression after seeing violent behaviors modeled by adults. The children were more likely to copy models who were rewarded for their aggressive behavior and less likely to mimic those who were punished (Bandura, 1986). Dr. Albert Bandura.

try this ↓

Identify the independent variable and dependent variable in the experiment by Bandura and colleagues. What might you change if you were to replicate this experiment?

✓ CHECK YOUR ANSWERS IN APPENDIX C.

especially if they had observed it modeled by men. And boys and girls were about equally likely to imitate verbal aggression (Bandura et al., 1961).

VIOLENCE IN THE MEDIA Psychologists have followed up on Bandura's research with studies investigating how children are influenced by violence they see on television, the Internet, and in movies and video games. One study conducted in New Zealand followed over 1,000 children from as early as birth until they were around 26 years old. The researchers found that the more television the children watched, the more likely they were to exhibit antisocial behaviors as young adults. Interestingly, this association was between antisocial behaviors and excessive television viewing, regardless of the content (Robertson, McAnally, & Hancox, 2013). Another study of over 5,000 fifth graders found strong associations between physical aggression and exposure to violent music, video games, and TV. The researchers concluded that media violence was just as strongly linked to physical aggression as other well-known factors, such as neighborhood and domestic violence (Coker et al., 2015, January/February).

Critics caution, however, that an *association* between media portrayals and violent behaviors doesn't mean a cause-and-effect relationship exists. (Establishing an association is not the same as pinning down a cause.) There are other factors related to parenting that could influence *both* television viewing and aggression (Gentile, Reimer, Nathanson, Walsh, & Eisenmann, 2014; Huesmann, Moise-Titus, Podolski, & Eron, 2003). If a parent is emotionally neglectful and places a child in front of the television all day, the child may eventually imitate some of the aggression she sees on TV. At the same time, the child may resent the parent for ignoring her, and this resentment could lead to aggression. But how do you know which of these factors—television exposure or parenting approach—is more important in the development of aggressive tendencies? This is an active area of psychological research, but experts agree that exposure to media violence is one of the factors that may lead to aggression in children (American Psychological Association, 2013c; Beresin, 2015; Coyne, 2016). The American Academy of Pediatrics sums it up nicely: "Extensive research evidence indicates that media violence can contribute to aggressive behavior, desensitization to violence, nightmares, and fear of being harmed" (American Academy of Pediatrics, 2009, p. 1495).

How can parents and caregivers deal with this problem? One approach is to limit the amount of time children spend with electronic media. The American Academy of Pediatrics recommends minimal screen time for children under the age of 2, a

prosocial behaviors Actions that are kind, generous, and beneficial to others.

maximum 1 hour per day for preschoolers, and parental supervision for all age groups (American Academy of Pediatrics, 2016a & b). Unfortunately, children and their parents have not followed these guidelines. The average American child spends 7 hours per day watching TV, and using tablets, cell phones, and other electronic media (American Academy of Pediatrics, n.d.). Instead of focusing on total screen time, some researchers suggest we direct our attention toward media content, and try to reduce exposure to violence and increase exposure to prosocial behaviors (Christakis et al., 2013; McCarthy, 2013). We should also consider the positive impact of sending children outdoors to play—it improves their sleep, health, and social well-being (Alexander, Frohlich, & Xu Fusco, 2014; Xu, Wen, Hardy, & Rissel, 2016).

PROSOCIAL BEHAVIOR AND OBSERVATIONAL LEARNING **Prosocial behaviors** are actions that are kind, generous, and beneficial to others, and children can easily pick them up by observing models. TV shows like *Sesame Street* can encourage prosocial behaviors (Cole, Labin, & del Rocio Galarza, 2008). In one study, researchers had parents change the television shows their preschoolers were viewing, substituting "aggression-laden programming" with "high quality prosocial and educational programming" (Christakis et al., 2013, p. 431). When assessed 6 and 12 months after the intervention, the children who had switched to prosocial/educational programming showed more behavioral improvement than those in the control group. This effect was pronounced for boys from low-income households (Christakis et al., 2013). Perhaps the prosocial messages of shows like *Dora the Explorer* and *Super Why* had made a difference.

Adults can also pick up prosocial messages from media. In a multipart study, researchers exposed adults to prosocial song lyrics (as opposed to neutral lyrics). They found that listening to prosocial lyrics increased the frequency of prosocial thoughts, promoted empathy (the ability to feel what another person is experiencing), and encouraged helping behavior. The researchers only looked at the short-term effects, but "repeated exposure" to prosocial lyrics may have a lasting impact (Greitemeyer, 2009). Another study explored the impact of different types of music that customers heard while on hold with a call center. Contrary to what you might expect, customers were less aggressive with employees when they heard "popular music with neutral lyrics" as opposed to music with prosocial lyrics (Niven, 2015). The impact of prosocial lyrics is still being researched, so stay tuned for future studies. In the meantime, try to observe your own behavior after listening to different types of song lyrics. Do certain types of songs seem to make you more irritable, while others inspire you to be kind?

In Class: Collaborate and Report

A camp director wants to teach campers to come quickly when the dinner bell rings. Team up and discuss **A)** how she could use operant conditioning and observational learning to accomplish this, **B)** why classical conditioning may not be an appropriate technique here, and **C)** what kind of classically conditioned behavior they might learn, without even realizing it.

Earlier, we pointed out that Cesar focuses on rehabilitating dogs and training people. When did his unique philosophy take form? When Cesar began working at a dog-training facility in Los Angeles, he awed the other workers with his ability to placate out-of-control dogs. His approach was simple: If he noticed a dog was afraid or on edge, he would quietly open the door, avoid eye contact, turn his back, and allow the dog to come to him. "Unconsciously, I was beginning to apply the dog psychology I had learned from my years observing dogs on my grandfather's farm," Cesar writes. "I was interacting with the dogs the way they interacted with one another" (Millan & Peltier, 2006, p. 47). Here, we have an example of *latent learning*.

Sunny Days
The prosocial behaviors demonstrated by *Sesame Street* friends such as Elmo and Big Bird (and sometimes even Oscar the Grouch!) appear to have a meaningful impact on child viewers. Children have a knack for imitating positive behaviors like sharing and caring (Cole et al., 2008). Hulton Archive/ Getty Images.

Whistling Ape
Bonnie the orangutan seems to have learned whistling by copying workers at the Smithsonian National Zoological Park in Washington, D.C. Her musical skill is the result of observational learning (Stone, 2009; Wich et al., 2009). Jennifer Zoon/Courtesy of Smithsonian's National Zoological Park.

Latent Learning

LO 15 Describe latent learning and explain how cognition is involved in learning.

Latent learning is a type of learning that occurs without awareness and regardless of reinforcement, and that is not evident until there is a need to use it. You experience latent learning all the time. For example, any time you explore a new park, neighborhood, or shopping mall, you are unconsciously gathering data from your senses—sights, sounds, smells, touch, and perhaps even taste if you stop for a bite to eat.

RATS THAT KNOW WHERE TO GO American psychologist Edward Tolman (1886–1959) and his colleague C. H. Honzik demonstrated latent learning in rats in their classic 1930 maze experiment (**FIGURE 5.4**). The researchers took three groups of rats and let them run free in mazes for several days. One group received food for reaching the goal boxes in their mazes; a second group received no reinforcement; and a third group received nothing until the 11th day of the experiment, when they, too, received food after finding the goal box. As you might expect, rats getting the treats from the onset solved the mazes more quickly as the days wore on. Meanwhile, their unrewarded compatriots wandered through the twists and turns. But on Day 11 when the researchers started to give treats to the third group of rats, their behavior changed markedly. After just one round of treats, the rats were scurrying through the mazes and scooping up the food as if they had been rewarded throughout the experiment (Tolman & Honzik, 1930). They had apparently been learning, even when there was no reinforcement for doing so—or in simpler terms, learning just for the sake of learning.

A MAP THAT CANNOT BE SEEN Like Tolman's rats, we remember locations, objects, and details of our surroundings without realizing it, and bring this information together in a mental layout (Lynch, 1960). This latent learning is evident in our ability to form **cognitive maps,** or mental representations of the physical surroundings. Although we form cognitive maps through latent learning, there are individual differences in how we learn about our surroundings (Weisberg & Newcombe, 2016).

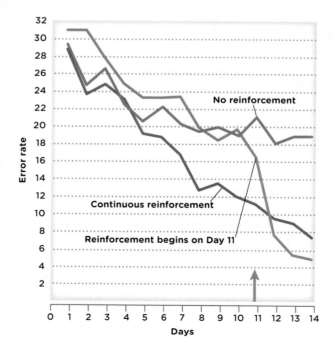

FIGURE 5.4

Latent Learning

In a classic experiment, groups of rats learned how to navigate a maze at remarkably different rates. Rats in a group receiving reinforcement from Day 1 (the green line on the graph) initially had the lowest rate of errors and were able to work their way through the maze more quickly than the other groups. But when a group began to receive reinforcement for the first time on Day 11, their error rate dropped immediately. This shows that the rats were learning the basic structure of the maze even when they weren't being reinforced. Information from Tolman, 1948.

Research suggests that visually impaired people forge cognitive maps without the use of visual information. Instead, they use "compensatory sensorial channels" (hearing and sense of touch, for example) to gather information about their environments (Lahav & Mioduser, 2008).

These findings highlight the importance of cognitive processes underlying behavior and suggest that learning can occur in the absence of reinforcement. Because of the focus on cognition, this research approach conflicts with the views of Skinner and some other 20th-century psychologists who adhered to a strict form of behaviorism.

Many other studies have challenged Skinner's views. German psychologist Wolfgang Köhler's (1925) research on chimpanzees suggests that animals are capable of thinking through a problem before taking action. Köhler (1887–1967) designed an experiment in which chimps were presented with out-of-reach bananas, and showed that the animals were able to plan a variety of banana-fetching strategies, including stacking crates to climb on. Here, the chimps displayed *insight,* a sudden coming together of awareness of a situation, leading to the solution of a problem (Chapter 7).

Today, most psychologists agree that both observable, measurable behaviors and internal cognitive processes such as insight are necessary and complementary elements of learning. Environmental factors have a powerful influence on behavior, as Pavlov, Skinner, and others discovered, but every action can be traced to activity in the brain. Understanding how cognitive processes translate to behaviors remains one of the great challenges facing psychologists.

NATURE AND NURTURE
Natural Born Learners

Cesar is known around the world as an exceptional teacher and dog expert. In order to achieve that status, he had to master the art of learning. As early as he can remember, Cesar studied the dogs on his grandfather's farm in Ixpalino (Millan & Peltier, 2006). He learned by observing their behaviors, and those of human role models as well. Arriving in the United States as a young man, he was eager to soak up knowledge and cultivate new skills, and his ability to learn seems to be ever-present. It's almost as if Cesar has an innate propensity for learning. Is it possible that some of us are natural born learners?

HOW MUCH OF OUR LEARNING ABILITY IS INHERITED?

Research suggests that one very important component of learning in school is conscientiousness, which refers to organizational tendencies and attention to detail (Dumfart & Neubauer, 2016). And as we will discuss in Chapter 11, this type of personality trait is shaped in part by nature (genes). In reality, much of what students are able to achieve is related to a variety of factors that are inherited to some degree, including intelligence, personality characteristics, and beliefs about one's ability to be effective and reach goals (Krapohl et al., 2014). But these facets of our nature should not be considered barriers to our growth; our nature refers to "what is; it does not predict what could be" (Krapohl et al., 2014, p. 15276). While it seems Cesar has a natural ability to learn from those around him, environmental factors also played an important role in his success.

Discovering the Brain's "GPS"
John O'Keefe (left), May-Britt Moser, and Edvard Moser won the 2014 Nobel Prize in Physiology or Medicine for discovering the "place cells" and "grid cells" in the brain that allow us to form cognitive maps of our surroundings (Vogel, 2014, October 6). Thanks to the brain's "GPS system," we can find our way around the world. AP Photo/TT News Agency, Anders Wiklund.

For the Love of Dogs
Cesar walks with other proponents of pet adoption at the Great Dog Adventure in San Diego. In addition to his hands-on work with dogs and owners, Cesar leads a non-profit called the Cesar Millan PACK Project, which promotes dog welfare through a variety of programs, one of which pairs shelter dogs with foster children. Using positive reinforcement, the children teach the dogs behaviors needed for successful placement in new homes (Cesar Millan PACK Project, n.d.). AP Photo/Sandy Huffaker for Warner Bros.

latent learning Learning that occurs without awareness and regardless of reinforcement, and is not evident until needed.
cognitive map A mental representation of physical space.

26 Years Later
Cesar enjoys the company of his right-hand dog Junior. It has now been over two decades since this celebrated dog expert illegally crossed the border into the United States. And although he became a U.S. citizen in 2009, Cesar really views himself as a citizen of the world. "I belong to a worldwide community of people who love dogs," he writes. "This is my pack" (Millan, 2013, p. 12). Vincent Sandoval/ WireImage/Getty Images.

Imagine you could sit down and talk with Cesar Millan. What advice might he offer about lifelong learning and career goals?

THINK POSITIVE

You Are a Valuable Member of the Pack

 Each of us plays a unique and important role in society, or the "human pack," as Cesar might describe it. "I see that we're all part of a pack," Cesar explains. "You have to find your place in the pack. And once you find your place in the pack, you serve a big purpose." Some of us are leaders, others are not, but every pack member has equal value. "You can't feel less than the guy in the top because the guy in the top won't do what he's doing without you."

> **FIND YOUR PASSION AND NEVER STOP LEARNING.**

What would Cesar say to those of us still struggling to find our place in the pack, or purpose in life? It may sound like a platitude, but find your passion, figure out what makes you happy, and pursue a path that allows you to nurture it. "Once you find your passion, you don't think you're working," Cesar says. Indeed, research suggests that people who are satisfied at work often feel more satisfied in their personal lives (Allen & McCarthy, 2016). If you ever find yourself lost, focus your energy on learning. "I think the listening is more powerful than anything else," Cesar explains. "When you're lost, when you're sad, you have to ask questions." In other words, learning should be a continuous, lifelong activity. 👍

◯◉◯◯ show what you know

1. You want to learn how to play basketball, so you watch videos of Seth Curry executing plays. If your game improves as a result, this would be considered an example of:
   a. observational learning.
   b. association.
   c. prosocial behavior.
   d. your cognitive map.

2. Bandura's Bobo doll study shows us that observational learning results in a wide variety of learned behaviors. Describe several types of behaviors you have learned by observing others.

3. Although Skinner believed that reinforcement is the cause of learning, there is robust evidence that reinforcement is not always necessary. This comes from experiments studying:
   a. positive reinforcement.
   b. negative reinforcement.
   c. latent learning.
   d. stimulus generalization.

✓ CHECK YOUR ANSWERS IN APPENDIX C.

Improve your grade! Use 🅜 **LearningCurve** macmillan learning adaptive quizzing to create your personalized study plan, which will direct you to the resources that will help you most in 🅜 **LaunchPad** macmillan learning

5

summary of concepts

LO 1 Define learning. (p. 190)

Learning is a relatively enduring change in behavior or thinking that results from experiences. Organisms as simple as fruit flies and as complex as humans have the ability to learn. Learning is about creating associations. Sometimes we associate two different stimuli (classical conditioning). Other times we make connections between our behaviors and their consequences (operant conditioning). We can also learn by watching and imitating others (observational learning), creating a link between our behavior and the behavior of others.

LO 2 Explain what Pavlov's studies teach us about classical conditioning. (p. 192)

The dogs in Pavlov's studies learned to link various stimuli with the anticipation of food, which caused them to salivate when the stimuli were introduced. He discovered that associations develop through the process of learning, which we now refer to as conditioning. With classical conditioning, two stimuli become associated; once this association has been established, an originally neutral stimulus elicits an involuntary response.

LO 3 Identify the differences between the US, UR, CS, and CR. (p. 193)

In classical conditioning, a neutral stimulus (NS) is something in the environment that does not normally cause a relevant automatic or reflexive response. This neutral stimulus is repeatedly paired with an unconditioned stimulus (US) that triggers an unconditioned response (UR). The neutral stimulus thus becomes a conditioned stimulus (CS) that the organism has learned to associate with the US. This CS elicits a conditioned response (CR). The initial pairing of a neutral stimulus with a US is called acquisition. In Pavlov's experiment with dogs, the US was the meat; the UR was the dog's salivation. After repeated pairings with the meat, the buzzer (originally, a NS) becomes a CS, and when the salivation occurs in response to the buzzer, it is a learned behavior (a CR).

LO 4 Recognize and give examples of stimulus generalization and stimulus discrimination. (p. 195)

Once an association is forged between a CS and a CR, the learner often responds to similar stimuli as if they are the original CS. This is called stimulus generalization. For example, someone who has been bitten by a small dog and reacts with fear to all dogs, big and small, demonstrates stimulus generalization. Stimulus discrimination is the ability to differentiate between a CS and other stimuli sufficiently different from it. Someone who was bitten by a small dog may be afraid of small dogs, but not large dogs, thus demonstrating stimulus discrimination.

LO 5 Summarize how classical conditioning is dependent on the biology of the organism. (p. 199)

Animals and people show biological preparedness, meaning they are predisposed to learn associations that have adaptive value. For example, a conditioned taste aversion is a form of classical conditioning that occurs when an organism learns to associate the taste of a particular food or drink with illness. Avoiding foods that induce sickness increases the odds the organism will survive and reproduce, passing its genes along to the next generation.

LO 6 Describe the Little Albert study and explain how fear can be learned. (p. 201)

The case study of Little Albert illustrates the conditioned emotional response, an emotional reaction (fear in Little Albert's case) acquired via classical conditioning. When Little Albert heard a loud bang (US), he exhibited a fear response (UR). Through conditioning, the sight of a rat became paired with the loud noise and went from being a neutral stimulus to a CS. Little Albert's fear of the rat became a CR.

LO 7 Describe Thorndike's law of effect. (p. 204)

Thorndike's law of effect was important to the study of operant conditioning, a type of learning in which people or animals come to associate their voluntary actions with consequences. The law of effect states that if a behavior is followed by a pleasurable outcome, that behavior is more likely to reoccur. Thorndike's cats learned that if they escaped the puzzle box, they would get to eat fish; this increased the speed with which they opened the puzzle box.

LO 8 Explain shaping and the method of successive approximations. (p. 206)

Building on Thorndike's law of effect and Watson's behaviorism, Skinner used shaping through successive approximations to mold the behavior of animals. With shaping, a person observes the behaviors of animals, providing reinforcers when they perform at a required level. Successive approximations refers to the series of small steps leading to a desired behavior. Animal behavior can be shaped using successive approximations, but instinct can interfere with the process. This instinctive drift is the tendency for animals to revert to instinctual behaviors after a behavior pattern has been learned.

LO 9 Identify the differences between positive and negative reinforcement. (p. 209)

Positive reinforcement is a process by which reinforcers are presented following a target behavior. The addition of these reinforcers, which generally are pleasant stimuli, increases the likelihood of the behavior recurring. The fish treats that Thorndike gave his cats are examples of positive reinforcers (they increased the likelihood of the cats opening the latch). Behaviors can also increase in response to negative reinforcement, or the removal of something unpleasant. Putting on a seat belt to stop an annoying beep is an example of negative reinforcement (it increases the likelihood of wearing a seat belt). Both positive and negative reinforcement increase desired behaviors.

LO 10 Distinguish between primary and secondary reinforcers. (p. 211)

There are two major categories of reinforcers. Primary reinforcers satisfy biological needs. Food, water, and physical contact are considered primary reinforcers. Secondary reinforcers do not satisfy biological needs, but often derive their power from their connection with primary reinforcers. Money is an example of a secondary reinforcer; we know from experience that it gives us access to primary reinforcers, such as food, a safe place to live, and perhaps even the ability to attract desirable mates.

LO 11 Describe continuous reinforcement and partial reinforcement. (p. 212)

Reinforcers can be delivered on a constant basis (continuous reinforcement) or intermittently (partial reinforcement). Continuous reinforcement is generally more effective for establishing a behavior, whereas learning through partial reinforcement is more resistant to extinction (the partial reinforcement effect) and useful for maintaining behavior.

LO 12 Name the schedules of reinforcement and give examples of each. (p. 213)

In a fixed-ratio schedule, reinforcement follows a predetermined number of desired responses or behaviors. In a variable-ratio schedule, the number of desired responses or behaviors that must occur before a reinforcer is given changes across trials and is based on an average number of responses to be reinforced. In a fixed-interval schedule, the reinforcer comes after a preestablished interval of time; the response or behavior is only reinforced after the given interval passes. In a variable-interval schedule, the reinforcement comes after an interval of time passes, but the length of the interval changes from trial to trial. The lengths of these intervals are within a predetermined range based on an average interval length.

LO 13 Explain how punishment differs from negative reinforcement. (p. 219)

In contrast to reinforcement, which makes a behavior more likely to recur, the goal of punishment is to decrease a behavior. Negative reinforcement strengthens a behavior that it follows by removing something aversive or disagreeable. Punishment decreases a behavior by instilling an association between a behavior and some unwanted consequence (for example, between stealing and going to jail, or between misbehaving and loss of screen time).

LO 14 Summarize what Bandura's classic Bobo doll study teaches us about learning. (p. 223)

Observational learning can occur when we watch a model demonstrate a behavior. Albert Bandura's classic Bobo doll experiment showed that children readily imitate aggression when they see it modeled by adults. Studies suggest that children and adults may be inclined to mimic aggressive behaviors seen in TV shows, movies, video games, and on the Internet. Observation of prosocial behaviors, on the other hand, can encourage kindness, generosity, and other forms of behavior that benefit others.

LO 15 Describe latent learning and explain how cognition is involved in learning. (p. 226)

Learning can occur without reinforcement. Edward Tolman showed that rats could learn to navigate mazes even when given no rewards. Their learning only became apparent when it was needed (latent learning). The rats were learning without reinforcement, just for the sake of learning. This cognitive approach reminds us that measurable behaviors and cognitive processes are necessary and complementary elements in the study of learning.

key terms

acquisition, p. 195
adaptive value, p. 199
biological preparedness, p. 200
classical conditioning, p. 195
cognitive map, p. 226
conditioned emotional response, p. 201
conditioned response (CR), p. 195
conditioned stimulus (CS), p. 195
conditioned taste aversion, p. 199

continuous reinforcement, p. 212
extinction, p. 196
fixed-interval schedule, p. 215
fixed-ratio schedule, p. 213
habituation, p. 191
higher order conditioning, p. 197
instinctive drift, p. 208
latent learning, p. 226
law of effect, p. 205
learning, p. 190
model, p. 223

negative punishment, p. 218
negative reinforcement, p. 210
neutral stimulus (NS), p. 193
observational learning, p. 223
operant conditioning, p. 204
partial reinforcement, p. 212
partial reinforcement effect, p. 213
positive punishment, p. 216
positive reinforcement, p. 209
primary reinforcer, p. 211
prosocial behaviors, p. 225
punishment, p. 216
reinforcement, p. 205

reinforcers, p. 205
secondary reinforcer, p. 211
shaping, p. 206
spontaneous recovery, p. 196
stimulus, p. 191
stimulus discrimination, p. 196
stimulus generalization, p. 196
successive approximations, p. 206
unconditioned response (UR), p. 195
unconditioned stimulus (US), p. 195
variable-interval schedule, p. 215
variable-ratio schedule, p. 215

test prep *are you ready?*

1. One basic form of learning occurs during the process of _____, which is evident when an organism does not respond as strongly or as often to an event following multiple exposures to it.
   - a. insight
   - b. habituation
   - c. classical conditioning
   - d. operant conditioning

2. Even turtles can learn through operant conditioning, as evidenced by their:
   - a. innate urge to get food.
   - b. reaction to an unconditioned stimulus.
   - c. ability to learn through positive reinforcement.
   - d. reactions to predators

3. The behaviors learned with classical conditioning are _____, whereas those learned with operant conditioning are _____.
   - a. involuntary; voluntary
   - b. voluntary; involuntary
   - c. voluntary; innate
   - d. involuntary; innate

4. Every time you open the pantry where dog food is stored, your dog starts to salivate. His reaction is a(n):
   - a. unconditioned response.
   - b. conditioned response.
   - c. stimulus discrimination.
   - d. reaction based on observational learning.

5. Your first love wore a musky-scented perfume, and your heart raced every time he or she appeared. Even now when you smell that scent, your heart speeds up, suggesting the scent is a(n):
   - a. unconditioned stimulus.
   - b. conditioned stimulus.
   - c. conditioned response.
   - d. unconditioned response.

6. Avoiding foods that induce sickness has _____. This taste aversion helps organisms survive.
   - a. adaptive value
   - b. stimulus generalization
   - c. stimulus discrimination
   - d. higher order conditioning

7. Little Albert was a baby who originally had no fear of rats. In an experiment conducted by Watson and Rayner, he was classically conditioned to fear white rats through the pairing of a loud noise with exposure to a rat. His resulting fear is an example of a(n):
   - a. unconditioned stimulus.
   - b. operant conditioning.
   - c. conditioned emotional response.
   - d. biological preparedness.

8. _____ indicates that if a behavior is followed by a pleasurable outcome, it likely will be repeated.
   - a. Latent learning
   - b. Classical conditioning
   - c. Biological preparedness
   - d. The law of effect

9. Which of the following is an example of negative reinforcement?
   - a. working hard to get an A on a paper
   - b. a child getting more computer time when he finishes his homework
   - c. a dog whining in the morning, leading an owner to wake up and take it outside
   - d. getting a speeding ticket and then not exceeding the speed limit afterward

10. All your friends tell you that you look fabulous in your new jeans, so you start wearing them all the time. This is an example of:
    - a. positive reinforcement.
    - b. negative reinforcement.
    - b. positive punishment.
    - d. negative punishment.

11. A child is reprimanded for misbehaving, but then she seems to misbehave even more! This indicates that reprimanding her was:
    - a. negative punishment.
    - b. positive reinforcement.
    - c. positive punishment.
    - d. an unconditioned response.

12. In Bandura's Bobo doll study, children who saw an adult attacking and shouting at the doll_____.
    - a. were more likely to display aggressive behavior
    - b. were less likely to display aggressive behavior
    - c. did not play with the Bobo doll at all
    - d. began to cry when they saw the adult acting aggressively

13. According to research, there is a strong association between physical aggression and exposure to violent music, video games, and TV. However, this association between media portrayals and violent behaviors does not mean a _____ exists. There could be other factors like parenting involved.
    - a. cause-and-effect relationship
    - b. prosocial relationship
    - c. neutral stimulus
    - d. conditioned emotional response

14. Rats allowed to explore a maze, without getting reinforcers until the 11th day of the experiment, subsequently behaved in the maze as if they had been given reinforcers throughout the entire experiment. Their behavior is evidence of:
    - a. latent learning.
    - b. observational learning.
    - c. classical conditioning.
    - d. operant conditioning.

15. Wolfgang Köhler's research on chimpanzees suggests that animals are capable of thinking through a problem before taking action, and having a sudden coming together of awareness of a situation, leading to a solution. This is called:
    - a. observational learning.
    - b. insight.
    - c. modeling.
    - d. higher order conditioning.

16. What is the difference between stimulus generalization and stimulus discrimination?

17. Give an example showing how you have used shaping and partial reinforcement to change your behavior. Which schedule of reinforcement do you think you were using?

18. What is the difference between primary reinforcers and secondary reinforcers? Give an example of each and explain how they might be used to change a behavior.

19. How are punishment and negative reinforcement different? Give examples of negative reinforcement, positive punishment, and negative punishment and explain how they aim to change behavior.

20. Describe conditioned taste aversion and provide an example. Label each of the components using the terminology of classical conditioning.

✓ CHECK YOUR ANSWERS IN APPENDIX C.

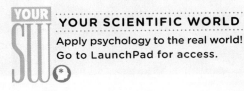

YOUR SCIENTIFIC WORLD
Apply psychology to the real world!
Go to LaunchPad for access.

John Gibbins/ZUMApress/ffi.

Courtesy of Carolyn Buckley, www.carolbuckley.com.

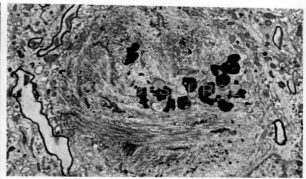

Thomas Deerinck, NCMIR/Science Source.

CHAPTER OUTLINE AND LEARNING OBJECTIVES

An Introduction to Memory

LO 1 Define memory.

LO 2 Describe the processes of encoding, storage, and retrieval.

Flow With It: Stages of Memory

LO 3 Explain the stages of memory described by the information-processing model.

LO 4 Describe sensory memory.

LO 5 Summarize short-term memory.

LO 6 Give examples of how we can use chunking to improve our memory span.

LO 7 Describe working memory and its relationship to short-term memory.

LO 8 Describe long-term memory.

Retrieval and Forgetting

LO 9 Illustrate how encoding specificity relates to retrieval cues.

LO 10 Identify and explain some of the reasons why we forget.

The Reliability of Memory

LO 11 Explain how the malleability of memory influences the recall of events.

LO 12 Define and explain the significance of rich false memory.

The Biology of Memory

LO 13 Compare and contrast anterograde and retrograde amnesia.

LO 14 Identify the brain structures involved in memory.

LO 15 Describe long-term potentiation and its relationship to memory.

Jiri Rezac/Polaris/Newscom.

Ros Drinkwater/Alamy.

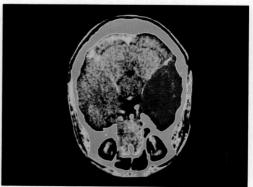

Airelle-Joubert/Science Source.

6 memory

An Introduction to Memory

MEMORY BREAKDOWN: THE CASE OF CLIVE WEARING

Monday, March 25, 1985: Deborah Wearing awoke in a sweat-soaked bed. Her husband, Clive, had been up all night perspiring, vomiting, and with a high fever. He said that he had a "constant, terrible" headache, like a "band" of pain tightening around his head (Wearing, 2005, p. 27). The symptoms worsened over the next few days, but the two doctors caring for Clive reassured Deborah that it was just a bad case of the flu. By Wednesday, Clive had spent three nights awake with the pain. Confused and disoriented, he turned to Deborah and said, "Er, er, darling. . . . I can't . . . think of your name" (p. 31).

The doctor arrived a couple of hours later, reassured Deborah that her husband's confusion was merely the result of sleep deprivation, and prescribed sleeping pills. Deborah came home later that day, expecting to find her husband in bed. But no Clive. She shouted out his name. No answer, just a heap of pajamas. After the police had conducted an extensive search, Clive was found when a taxi driver dropped him off at a local police station; he had gotten into the cab and couldn't remember his address (Wearing, 2005). Clive returned to his flat (which he did not recognize as home), rested, and took in fluids. His fever dropped, and it appeared that he was improving. But when he awoke Friday morning, his confusion was so severe he could not identify the toilet among the various pieces of furniture in his bathroom. As Deborah placed urgent calls to the doctor, Clive began to drift away. He lost consciousness and was rushed to the hospital in an ambulance (Wearing, 2005; Wilson & Wearing, 1995).

Prior to this illness, Clive Wearing had enjoyed a fabulous career in music. As the director of the London Lassus Ensemble, he spent his days leading singers and instrumentalists through the emotionally complex music of his favorite composer, Orlande de Lassus. A renowned expert on Renaissance music, Clive produced music for the prestigious British Broadcasting Corporation (BBC), including that which aired on the wedding day of Prince Charles and Lady Diana Spencer (Sacks, 2007, September 24; Wilson, Baddeley,

The Conductor
In 1985 conductor Clive Wearing (pictured here with his wife, Deborah) developed a brain infection—viral encephalitis—that nearly took his life. Clive recovered physically, but his memory was never the same. Ros Drinkwater/Alamy.

C Squared Studios/Getty Images.

Clive and Deborah, in Their Own Words

http://qrs.ly/8m5a5d1

& Kapur, 1995; Wilson, Kopelman, & Kapur, 2008). But Clive's work—and his whole life—tumbled into chaos when a virus that normally causes blisters on the mouth invaded his brain.

Millions of people carry herpes simplex virus type 1 (HSV-1). Usually, it causes unsightly cold sores on the mouth and face. (There is also HSV-2, more commonly associated with genital herpes.) But for a small minority of the adult population—as few as 1 in 500,000 annually—the virus invades the central nervous system and causes a life-threatening infection called *encephalitis.* Left untreated, herpes encephalitis causes death in over 70% of its victims. Most who survive have lasting neurological deficits (Sabah, Mulcahy, & Zeman, 2012; Sili, Kaya, Mert, & HSV Encephalitis Study Group, 2014).

Although Deborah saw to it that Clive received early medical attention, having two doctors visit the house day and night for nearly a week, these physicians mistook his condition for the flu with meningitis-like symptoms (Wilson & Wearing, 1995). Misdiagnosis is common with herpes encephalitis (even to this day), as its symptoms resemble those of other conditions, including the flu, meningitis, a stroke, and epilepsy (Sabah et al., 2012). When Clive and Deborah arrived at the hospital on the sixth day of his illness, they waited another 11 hours just to get a proper diagnosis (Wearing, 2005; Wilson & Wearing, 1995).

Clive survived, but the damage to his brain was extensive and profound; the virus had destroyed a substantial amount of neural tissue. And though Clive could still sing and play the keyboard (and spent much of the day doing so), he was unable to continue working as a conductor and music producer (D. Wearing, personal communication, June 13, 2013; Wilson & Wearing, 1995). In fact, he could barely get through day-to-day life. In the early stages of recovery, simple activities like eating baffled him. He ate the menu and attempted to spread cottage cheese on his bread, apparently mistaking it for butter. He confused basic concepts such as "scarf" and "umbrella," and shaved his eyebrows and nose (Wearing, 2005; Wilson & Wearing, 1995).

The Diary
Looking at a page from Clive's diary, you can see the fragmented nature of his thought process. He writes an entry, forgets it within seconds, and then returns to the page to start over, often writing the same thing. Encephalitis destroyed areas of Clive's brain that are crucial for learning and memory, so he can no longer recall what is happening from moment to moment. Jiri Rezac/Polaris/Newscom.

In the months following his illness, Clive was overcome with the feeling of just awakening. His senses were functioning properly, but every sight, sound, odor, taste, and feeling registered for just a moment, and then vanished. As Deborah described it, Clive saw the world anew with every blink of his eye (Wearing, 2005). The world must have seemed like a whirlwind of sensations, always changing. Desperate to make sense of it all, Clive would pose the same questions time and again: "How long have I been ill?" he would ask Deborah and the hospital staff members looking after him. "How long's it been?" (Wearing, 2005, p. 181). For much of the first decade following his illness, Clive repeated the same few phrases almost continuously in his conversations with people. "I haven't heard anything, seen anything, touched anything, smelled anything," he would say. "It's just like being dead" (p. 160).

The depth of Clive's impairment is revealed in his diary, where he wrote essentially the same entries all day long. On August 25, 1985, he wrote, "I woke at 8:50 A.M. and baught [sic] a copy of *The Observer*," which is then crossed out and followed by "I woke at 9:00 A.M. I had already bought a copy of *The Observer*." The next line reads, "This (officially) confirms that I awoke at 9:05 A.M. this morning" (Wearing, 2005, p. 182). Having forgotten all previous entries, Clive reported throughout the day that he had just become conscious. His recollection of writing in his journal—along with every experience in his life—came and went in a flash. The herpes virus had ravaged his memory system. ●

The story of Clive Wearing launches our journey through *memory*. This chapter will take us to the opposite ends of a continuum: from memory loss to exceptional feats of remembering. We will explore the world of memory sport, learning tricks from some of the greatest memory athletes in the world. These strategies could help you remember material for exams and everyday life: terms, concepts, passwords, pin numbers, people's names, and where you left your keys. You, too, can develop superior memorization skills; you just have to practice using memory aids. But beware: No matter how well you exercise your memory "muscle," it does not always perform perfectly. Like anything human, memory is prone to error.

Three Processes: Encoding, Storage, and Retrieval

LO 1 Define memory.

Memory refers to the brain processes involved in the encoding (collection), storage, and retrieval of information. Much of this process has gone haywire for Clive. You may be wondering why we chose to start this chapter with the story of a person whose memory system failed. When it comes to understanding complex cognitive processes like those of memory, sometimes it helps to examine what happens when elements of the system are not working.

What is your earliest memory and how was it created? Do you know if it is accurate? And how can you recall it after so many years? Psychologists have been asking questions like these since the 1800s. Exactly how the brain absorbs information from the outside world and files it for later use is still not completely clear, but scientists have proposed many theories and models to explain how the brain processes, or works on, data on their way to becoming memories. As you learn about various theories and models, keep in mind that none of them are perfect. Rather than labeling one as *right* and another as *wrong*, most psychologists embrace a combination of approaches, taking into consideration their various strengths and weaknesses.

One often-used model likens the brain's memory system to a computer. Think about how a computer operates: It receives data from external sources, like your fingers typing on the keyboard, and converts that data into a code it can manipulate. Once this is accomplished, the information can be saved on the hard drive so you can open up the documents, MP3s, and other data files you need. The brain's memory system accomplishes similar tasks, but it is very different from a computer. **Communication among neurons** in the brain is more complicated than signals running between electrical components in a circuit. And unlike a computer, which maintains your files exactly how you last saved them, memories are subject to modifications over time, and this

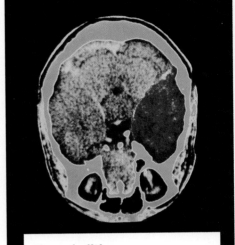

Encephalitis
The red area in this computerized axial tomography (CAT) scan reveals inflammation in the temporal lobe. The cause of this swelling is herpes simplex virus, the same virus responsible for Clive's illness. Many people carry this virus (it causes cold sores), but herpes encephalitis is extremely rare, affecting as few as 1 in 500,000 people annually (Sabah et al., 2012). Even with early treatment, this brain infection frequently leaves its victims with cognitive damage (Kennedy & Chaudhuri, 2002). Airelle-Joubert/Science Source.

CONNECTIONS

In **Chapter 2,** we described the electrical and chemical processes involved in communication between neurons. We also reported that the human brain contains billions of cells interlinked by trillions of connections.

memory Brain processes involved in the encoding, storage, and retrieval of information.

means they may be somewhat different each time you access them. Finally, the brain has seemingly unlimited storage capabilities, and the ability to process many types of information simultaneously, both consciously and unconsciously. We don't completely understand how a functioning memory system works, but there is basic agreement on its general processes, particularly *encoding, storage,* and *retrieval.*

LO 2   **Describe the processes of encoding, storage, and retrieval.**

ENCODING   During the course of a day, we are bombarded with information coming from all of our senses and internal data from thoughts and emotions. Some of this information we will remember, but the majority of it will not be retained for long. What is the difference between what is kept and what is not? Most psychologists agree that it all starts with **encoding,** the process through which information enters our memory system. Think about what happens when you pay attention to an event unfolding before you; stimuli associated with that event (sights, sounds, smells) are taken in by your senses and then converted to neural activity that travels to the brain. The information is processed and takes one of two paths: Either it enters our memory system (it is encoded to be stored for a longer period of time) or it slips away. For Clive Wearing, much of this information slips away.

STORAGE   For information that is successfully encoded, the next step is **storage.** Storage is exactly what it sounds like: preserving information for possible recollection in the future. Before Clive Wearing fell ill, his memory was excellent. His brain was able to encode and store a variety of events and learned abilities. Following his bout with encephalitis, however, his ability for long-term storage of new memories was destroyed—he could no longer retain new information for more than seconds at a time.

RETRIEVAL   After information is stored, how do we access it? Perhaps you still have a memory of your first-grade teacher's face, but can you remember his or her name? This process of coming up with stored information (Ms. Nautiyal! Mr. Kopitz!) is called **retrieval.** Sometimes information is encoded and stored in memory but cannot be accessed, or retrieved. Have you ever felt that a person's name or a certain vocabulary word was just sitting "on the tip of your tongue"? Chances are you were struggling from a retrieval failure, which we will discuss later in this chapter.

Before taking a closer look at the processes of memory, let's give your memory system a little workout. Ready for a challenge?

 MEMORY: IT'S A SPORT   Give yourself 5 minutes to study the row of ones and zeros below. When 5 minutes are up, look away from your textbook and try to write down the exact sequence on a blank piece of paper.

000101101011010011010101011100110001010100011100100100100100

How did you do? Most people have a hard time remembering all 60 digits in 5 minutes, but there are individuals who can memorize *hundreds* in this short time. The current world record, held by Johannes Mallow of Germany, is 1,080. Here are a few other accomplishments of the world's leading "memory athletes" (World Memory Sports Council, 2016a & b):

CONNECTIONS

In **Chapters 2** and **3,** we described how sensory information is taken in by sensory receptors and transduced; that is, transformed into neural activity. Here, we explore what happens *after* transduction, when information is processed in the memory system.

Memory Jocks

Competitors at the 2013 World Memory Championships study stacks of playing cards. Many wear earmuffs and other devices to block out background noises that might interfere with their concentration. Matthew Lloyd/The Times/Newscom.

- Alex Mullen of the United States memorized 3,029 decimal digits in 1 hour (for example, "2 7 6 4 3 0 9 7 2 8 8 4 3. . .").

- Simon Reinhard of Germany memorized an entire deck of playing cards in 20.44 seconds (for example, "7 of spades, jack of hearts, 3 of diamonds. . .").

- Purevjav Erdenesaikhan of Mongolia memorized 112 random words in 5 minutes (for example, "dog, now, is, notebook, stinging. . ."). ●

MEMORY COMPETITORS AND THE REST OF US Who are these memory athletes, and how do they manage to pack so much information into their brains in so little time? Most are ordinary people—college students, accountants, writers, scientists, and others—who have become interested in memory training and memory competitions, such as the World Memory Championships. Ordinary people they may be, but extraordinary brains they must have . . . right?

Not necessarily. According to eight-time World Memory Champion Dominic O'Brien, most anyone can acquire an exceptional memory. When O'Brien first began to train his memory at age 30, he could remember no more than 6 or 7 playing cards in a row. Eventually, he was able to memorize 2,808 cards (54 decks) after looking at each card only once. "I transformed my memory power very quickly as a result of applying simple techniques and practicing regularly," Dominic says. "If I can become a memory champion then anybody can" (D. O'Brien, personal communication, December 4, 2015). Just like a gymnast or wrestler, a memory athlete prepares, trains, and practices. A powerful memory takes work!

THE BRAINS OF MEMORY EXPERTS Researchers comparing a small sample of memory competitors to "normal" people found nothing extraordinary about their intelligence or brain structure. What they did find was heightened activity in specific brain areas, particularly in regions used for "spatial memory" (Maguire, Valentine, Wilding, & Kapur, 2003). This activity seems to be associated with the use of a strategy in which items to be remembered are placed along points of an imagined "journey" (Mallow, Bernarding, Luchtmann, Bethmann, & Brechmann, 2015). As it turns out, memory athletes rely heavily on this type of imagined journey, which is rich with visual images (Mallow et al., 2015; Martin, 2013). We will learn about this memory aid later in the chapter, when we discuss memory improvement, but first let's get a grasp of how memories are processed.

Levels of Processing

One way to conceptualize memory is from a processing standpoint. To what degree does information entering the memory system get worked on? According to the *levels of processing* framework, there is a "hierarchy of processing stages" corresponding to different depths of information processing (Craik & Lockhart, 1972). Thus, processing can occur along a continuum from shallow to deep (**FIGURE 6.1** on page 238). Shallow-level processing is primarily concerned with physical features (structural), such as the brightness or shape of an object, or the number of letters in a word, and generally results in short-lived memories. Deeper-level processing relies on characteristics related to patterns, like rhymes (phonemic) and meaning (semantic), and generally results in longer-lasting and easier-to-retrieve memories. So when you give little attention to data entering your sensory system, shallow processing occurs, resulting in more transient memories. If you really contemplate incoming information and relate it to memories you already have, deeper processing occurs, and the new memories are more likely to persist (Craik & Tulving, 1975; Francis & Gutiérrez, 2012; Newell & Andrews, 2004).

2,808 Cards
Memory master Dominic O'Brien took 54 decks of shuffled cards and memorized their correct order after flipping through them just once. By practicing memory techniques, Dominic went from being a person with an average memory to an eight-time World Memory Champion. musk/Alamy.

encoding The process through which information enters our memory system.

storage The process of preserving information for possible recollection in the future.

retrieval The process of accessing information encoded and stored in memory.

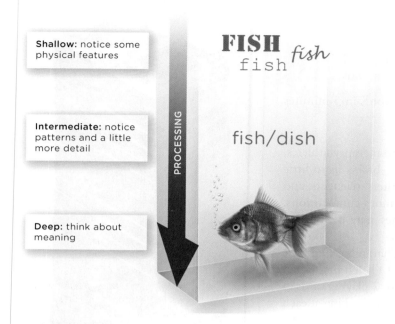

Shallow: notice some physical features

Intermediate: notice patterns and a little more detail

Deep: think about meaning

PROCESSING

FISH fish *fish*

fish/dish

FIGURE 6.1

The Levels of Processing Framework of Memory

Information can be processed along a continuum from shallow to deep, affecting the probability of recall. Shallow processing, in which only certain details like the physical appearance of a word might be noticed, results in brief memories that may not be recalled later. We are better able to recall information we process at a deep level, thinking about meaning and tying it to memories we already have. Goldfish: Gunnar Pippel/Shutterstock.

Synonyms

information-processing model modal model of memory

sensory memory sensory register

sensory memory A stage of memory that captures near-exact copies of vast amounts of sensory stimuli for a very brief period of time.

short-term memory A stage of memory that temporarily maintains and processes a limited amount of information.

long-term memory A stage of memory with essentially unlimited capacity that stores enduring information about facts and experiences.

Suppose you are trying to remember the names of the three processes involved in memory: encoding, storage, and retrieval. You could try to memorize the words based on a shallow, structural characteristic (storage has seven letters, encoding has eight letters, and retrieval has nine letters), or you could think about the words on a deeper level, connecting them to concepts already stored in your memory system. Memory champion Dominic O'Brien came up with this one: *Encoding* makes him think of codes and secret agents, so he imagines a James Bond character going into a huge warehouse (*storage* facility) and seeing a golden retriever (*retrieval*) run out the door (D. O'Brien, personal communication, December 4, 2015). The more deeply you think about incoming information, considering its meaning or personal relevance, the greater success you will have learning and remembering it.

Fergus Craik and Endel Tulving explored levels of processing in their classic 1975 study. After presenting college students with various words, the researchers asked them yes or no questions, prompting them to think about and encode the words at three different levels: shallow, intermediate, and deep. The shallow questions required the students to study the appearance of the word: "Is the word in capital letters?" The intermediate-level questions related to the sound of the word: "Does the word rhyme with 'weight'?" And finally, the deep questions challenged students to consider the word's meaning: "Is the word a type of fish?" When the researchers surprised the students with a test to see which words they remembered without any cues or clues, the students were best able to recall words whose meaning they had thought about (Craik & Tulving, 1975). The take-home message: Deep thinking helps create stronger memories (Dunlosky, Rawson, Marsh, Nathan, & Willingham, 2013; Foos & Goolkasian, 2008).

try this ↓

Ask several people to remember the name "Clive Wearing." (1) Tell some of them to picture it written out in uppercase letters (CLIVE WEARING). (2) Tell others to imagine what it sounds like (*Clive Wearing rhymes with dive daring*). (3) Ask a third group to contemplate its underlying significance (*Clive Wearing is the musician who suffers from an extreme case of memory loss*). Later, test each person's memory for the name and see if a *deeper* level of processing leads to better encoding and a stronger memory.

Most people have the greatest success with (3) deep processing, but it depends somewhat on how they are prompted to retrieve information. For example, if someone asks you to remember any words that rhyme with "dive daring," the name "Clive Wearing" will probably pop into your head regardless of whether you used deep processing.

The levels of processing model helps us understand why testing, which often requires you to connect new and old information, can improve memory and help you succeed in school. Research strongly supports the idea that "testing improves learning," as long as the stakes are low (Dunlosky et al., 2013). The Show What You Know and Test Prep resources in this textbook are designed with this in mind. Repeated testing, or the *testing effect,* results in a variety of benefits: better information retention; identification of areas needing more study; and increased self-motivated studying (Roediger, Putnam, & Smith, 2011). Speaking of testing, why not take a moment and show what you know?

 show what you know

1. _____ refers to the information that your brain collects, stores, and may use at a later time.

2. _____ is the process whereby information enters the memory system.
   a. Retrieval
   b. Encoding
   c. Communication
   d. Spatial memory

3. How might you illustrate shallow processing versus deep processing as it relates to studying?

✓ CHECK YOUR ANSWERS IN APPENDIX C.

Flow With It: Stages of Memory

Psychologists use **several models** to explain how the memory system is organized. Among the most influential is the _information-processing model_ first developed by Richard Atkinson and Richard Shiffrin. This model conceptualizes memory as a _flow of information_ through a series of stages: _sensory memory, short-term memory,_ and _long-term memory_ (**FIGURE 6.2**) (Anderson, 1971; Atkinson & Shiffrin, 1968, January 31; Wood & Pennington, 1973).

> **CONNECTIONS**
>
> In **Chapter 3,** we described the importance of using theories and models to organize and conceptualize observations. In this chapter, we present several of these to explain the human memory system.

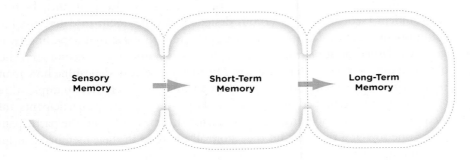

Sensory Memory → Short-Term Memory → Long-Term Memory

FIGURE 6.2
The Information-Processing Model of Memory

The Information-Processing Model

LO 3 Explain the stages of memory described by the information-processing model.

According to the information-processing model, each stage of memory has a certain type of storage with distinct capabilities: **Sensory memory** can hold vast amounts of sensory stimuli for a sliver of time, **short-term memory** can temporarily maintain and process limited information for longer periods (about 30 seconds, if there are no distractions), and **long-term memory** has essentially unlimited capacity and can hold onto information indefinitely. In the sections that follow, we will flesh out these concepts of sensory, short-term, and long-term memory, which are incorporated in most memory models.

The information-processing model is a valuable tool for learning about and researching memory, but like any scientific model, it has flaws. Some critics contend that _sensory memory_ is really a primary component of **perception**. Others doubt that a clear boundary exists between _short-term_ and _long-term_ memory (Baddeley, 1995). Still others argue that this "pipeline" model is a simplistic representation because information does not necessarily flow through the memory system in a straight-line path (Cowan, 1988). Despite its weaknesses, the information-processing model remains an essential tool for explaining how memory works. As you read about Clive Wearing in the pages to come, you will see how both his short- and long-term memory are severely impaired.

> **CONNECTIONS**
>
> In **Chapter 3,** we defined sensation as the process by which receptors receive and detect stimuli. Perception is the process through which sensory information is organized, interpreted, and transformed into something meaningful. Some critics of the information-processing model suggest that sensory memory is an important component of perception, not a stage of memory.

Sensory Memory: The Here and Now

LO 4   Describe sensory memory.

Think of all the information streaming through your sensory channels at this very moment. Your eyes may be focused on this sentence, but you are also collecting data through your peripheral vision. You may be hearing noises (voices in the distance), smelling odors (the scent of lotion or deodorant you applied earlier today), tasting foods (if you are snacking), and even feeling things (shoes gently squeezing your feet). Many of these sensory stimuli never catch your attention, but some are being registered in your *sensory memory,* the first stage of the information-processing model. The bulk of information entering sensory memory comes and goes like images flitting by in a movie. A few things catch your attention—the beautiful eyes of Zoe Saldana, the sound of her voice, and perhaps the color of her shirt—but not much more before the frame switches and you're looking at another image. Information floods our sensory memory through multiple channels—what we see enters through one channel, what we taste through another, and so on.

ICONIC MEMORY: "MORE IS SEEN THAN CAN BE REMEMBERED" Interested in understanding how the brain processes data entering the visual channel, Harvard graduate student George Sperling (1960) designed an experiment to determine how much information can be detected in a brief exposure to visual stimuli. Sperling set up a screen that flashed multiple rows of letters for one-twentieth of a second, and then asked participants to report what they saw. His first goal was to determine how many letters the participants could remember when an *array* of letters (for example, three rows of four letters) was flashed briefly; he found that, on average, the participants only reported four letters. But Sperling wasn't sure what this meant: Could the participants only store one row at a time, or did they store all the rows in their memory, but just not long enough to recite them before they were forgotten?

Sperling suspected that "more is seen than can be remembered" (1960, p. 1), so he devised a clever method called *partial report* to provide evidence. As with the original experiment, he briefly flashed an array of letters (for example, three rows of four letters), with all rows visible. But instead of having the participants report what they remembered from all the rows, he asked them to report what they remembered from just one row at a time (**FIGURE 6.3**).

Here's how the study went: The array of letters was flashed, and once it disappeared, a tone was sounded. When participants heard a high-pitched tone, they were to report the letters in the top row; with a medium-pitched tone, the letters in the middle row; and with a low-pitched tone, the letters in the bottom row. The participants were only

FIGURE 6.3
How Fast It Fades
How do we know how long iconic memory lasts? George Sperling developed a creative way to measure how quickly iconic memories fade from awareness. Participants were shown an array of letters and were asked to recall one row. Participants performed well when recalling that one row, but couldn't recall other letters: Their sensory memory had faded (Sperling, 1960). This technique is still used today to study fleeting sensory memories.

Letters flash on screen, then disappear.

A tone sounds. Participants report only the row associated with that tone.

Participants can report row associated with tone, but no other row. All letters initially registered in their sensory memory, but the iconic memory dissolves before more letters can be reported.

asked to give a partial report, that is, to report on just one of the rows, but they did not know which row ahead of time. In this version of the study, the participants doubled their performance, recalling approximately 76% of the letters regardless of which row they were asked to recall (Sperling, 1960). Sperling's research suggests that the *visual impressions* in our sensory memory, also known as **iconic memory**, are photograph-like in their accuracy but dissolve in less than a second. Given the short duration of iconic memory, can you predict what would happen to the participants' performance if there were a delay before they reported what they saw?

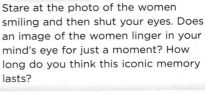

try this ⬇

Stare at the photo of the women smiling and then shut your eyes. Does an image of the women linger in your mind's eye for just a moment? How long do you think this iconic memory lasts?

EIDETIC IMAGERY Perhaps you have heard friends talk about someone who claims to have a "photographic memory" that can record and store images with the accuracy of a camera: "My cousin Dexter can look at a textbook page, remember exactly what it says in a few seconds, and then recall the information days later, seeing the pages exactly as they were." That may be what Dexter claims, but is there scientific evidence to back up such an assertion? Not at this time (Gordon, 2012, December 19; MacLeod, Jonker, & James, 2013).

Bartosz Hadyniak/Getty Images

According to some reports, though, researchers have documented a phenomenon that comes fairly close to photographic memory. It's called *eidetic imagery* (ahy-DET-ik), and the rare "handful" who have this ability can "see" an image or object sometimes long after it has been removed from sight, describing its parts with amazing specificity. For example, architect Stephen Wiltshire is an *autistic savant,* who reportedly can create detailed and accurate drawings of entire "cityscapes after a single helicopter ride" (Martin, 2013, p. R732). This ability seems to occur primarily in children, with some suggesting that this type of memory is lost as a child's brain grows and develops (Ko, 2015; Searleman, 2007, March 12).

ECHOIC MEMORY Exact copies of the sounds we hear linger longer than visual impressions; **echoic memory** (eh-KOH-ik) can last from about 1 to 10 seconds (Lu, Williamson, & Kaufman, 1992; Peterson, Meagher, & Ellsbury, 1970), and it can capture very subtle changes in sound. Research has shown that the introduction of a **single tone** played for 300 milliseconds initiates changes in brain activity (Inui et al., 2010). Even if you are not aware of it, your auditory system is picking up slight changes in stimuli and storing them in echoic memory for a brief moment. In this way, you don't have to pay attention to every incoming sound. Perhaps you have had the following experience: During class, your instructor notices a classmate daydreaming and tries to bring her back to reality: "Olivia, could you please restate the question for us?" Her mind was indeed wandering, but amazingly she can recall the instructor's last sentence, responding, "You asked us if brain scans should be allowed as evidence in courtrooms." For this, Olivia can thank her echoic memory.

Although brief, sensory memory is critical to the creation of memories. Without it, how would information enter the memory system in the first place? The bulk of research has focused on iconic and echoic memories, which register sights and sounds, but memories can also be rich in smells, tastes, and touch. Data received from all of the senses are held momentarily in sensory memory. Yet at any given moment, you can only concentrate on a tiny percentage of the data flooding your sensory memory, and most of this information disappears quickly. Items that capture your attention can move into the next stage of information-processing: short-term memory.

CONNECTIONS

In **Chapter 3,** we described sensory adaptation, the process by which we become less aware of constant stimuli. This allows us to focus on changes in our environment, an ability invaluable to survival. Humans are exquisitely sensitive to the slightest changes in auditory stimuli, and our echoic memory allows us to store and follow changes in sounds.

iconic memory Visual impressions that are photograph-like in their accuracy but dissolve in less than a second; a form of sensory memory.

echoic memory Exact copies of the sounds we hear; a form of sensory memory.

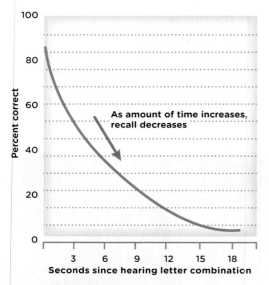

FIGURE 6.4

Duration of Short-Term Memory
Distraction can reduce the amount of time information remains in short-term memory. When performing a distracting cognitive task, most people were unable to recall a letter combination beyond 18 seconds. Information from Peterson and Peterson (1959), Figure 3, p. 195.

CONNECTIONS

Here, we see how memory is related to attention. In **Chapter 4,** we discussed the limited capacity of human attention. At any given point in time, there are only so many items you can attend to and thus move into your memory system.

Synonyms

maintenance rehearsal rote rehearsal

maintenance rehearsal Technique of repeating information to be remembered, increasing the length of time it can be held in short-term memory.

chunking Grouping numbers, letters, or other items into meaningful subsets as a strategy for increasing the quantity of information that can be maintained in short-term memory.

working memory The active processing of information in short-term memory; the maintenance and manipulation of information in the memory system.

Short-Term Memory: It Doesn't Last Long

LO 5   Summarize short-term memory.

When information enters your sensory memory, it does not linger. So where does it go next? If not lost in the overwhelming array of sensory stimuli, the data proceed to *short-term memory,* the second stage in the information-processing model proposed by Atkinson and Shiffrin (1968). The amount of time information is maintained and processed in short-term memory depends on how much you are distracted by other cognitive activities, but the duration can be about 30 seconds (Atkinson & Shiffrin, 1968). You can stretch short-term memory further with **maintenance rehearsal**, a technique of repeating what you want to remember over and over in your mind. Using maintenance rehearsal, you can theoretically hold onto information as long as you desire. This strategy comes in handy when you need to remember a series of numbers or letters (for example, phone numbers or zip codes). Imagine the following: While strolling down the street, you witness a hit-and-run accident. A truck runs a red light, smashes into a car, and then speeds away. As the truck zooms off, you manage to catch a glimpse of the license plate number, but how will you remember it long enough before reaching the 911 operator? If you're like most people, you will say the plate number to yourself over and over, either aloud or in your mind, using maintenance rehearsal.

But maintenance rehearsal does not work so well if you are distracted. In a classic study examining the duration of short-term memory, most participants were unable to recall three-letter combinations beyond 18 seconds while performing another task (Peterson & Peterson, 1959; **FIGURE 6.4**). The task (counting backward by 3s) interfered with their natural inclination to mentally repeat the letter combinations; in other words, they were limited in their ability to use maintenance rehearsal. What this study reveals is that short-term memory has a limited capacity. Please remember this if you are tempted to text during class or watch TV while studying; if your goal is to remember what you *should be* concentrating on, you need to give it your full attention.

LO 6   Give examples of how we can use chunking to improve our memory span.

With maintenance rehearsal, you try to remember numbers and letters, for example, by repeating them over and over in your mind. But how many items can we realistically hold in our short-term memory at one time? Using a task called the Digit Span Test (**FIGURE 6.5**), cognitive psychologist George Miller (1956) determined that most people can retain only five to nine digits: He called this the "magical number seven, plus or minus two." Indeed, researchers following up on this discovery have found that most people can only attend to about five to nine *items* at one time (Cowan, Chen, & Rouder, 2004; Cowan, Nugent, & Elliott, 2000). But what exactly constitutes an item? Must it be a single-digit number? Not necessarily; we can expand short-term memory by packing more information into the items to be remembered.

Consider this example: Your friend has just gotten a new phone number, which she rattles off as the elevator door closes between you. How are you going to remember her number long enough to create a new entry in your cell phone? You could try memorizing all 10 digits in a row (8935550172), but a better strategy is to break the number into more manageable pieces (893-555-0172). Here, you are using **chunking**, Miller's (1956) name for grouping numbers, letters, or other types of information into meaningful "chunks," or units of information (Cowan, 2015). Can you think of situations in which you might chunk information to help you remember it more easily?

Short-term memory can only hold so much, but we can expand its storage capacity by chunking. The fact that short-term memory is actively processing information and is flexible in this regard suggests that it may be more than just a stage in which information is briefly stored. Indeed, many psychologists believe that short-term memory is hard at work.

Working Memory: Where the Action Is

LO 7 Describe working memory and its relationship to short-term memory.

Updated versions of the information-processing model include a concept known as **working memory** (Baddeley, 2012; Baddeley & Hitch, 1974), which refers to what is *going on* in short-term memory. Working memory is the active processing through which we maintain and manipulate information in the memory system. Let's use an analogy of a "bakery" and what goes on inside it. Short-term memory is the bakery, that is, the place that hosts your current thoughts and whatever your brain is working on at this very moment. Working memory is what's going on inside the bakery—making bread, cakes, and pastries. Some psychologists use the terms short-term and working memory interchangeably. For our purposes, we will identify "short-term memory" as a stage in the original information-processing model as well as the "location" where information is temporarily held, and "working memory" as the activities and processing occurring within.

According to the model of working memory originally proposed by psychologists Alan Baddeley and Graham Hitch (1974; Baddeley, 2012), the purpose of working memory is to actively maintain information, and thus enable complex cognitive tasks. To accomplish this, working memory has four components: the phonological loop, visuospatial sketchpad, central executive, and episodic buffer (Baddeley, 2002; **FIGURE 6.6**).

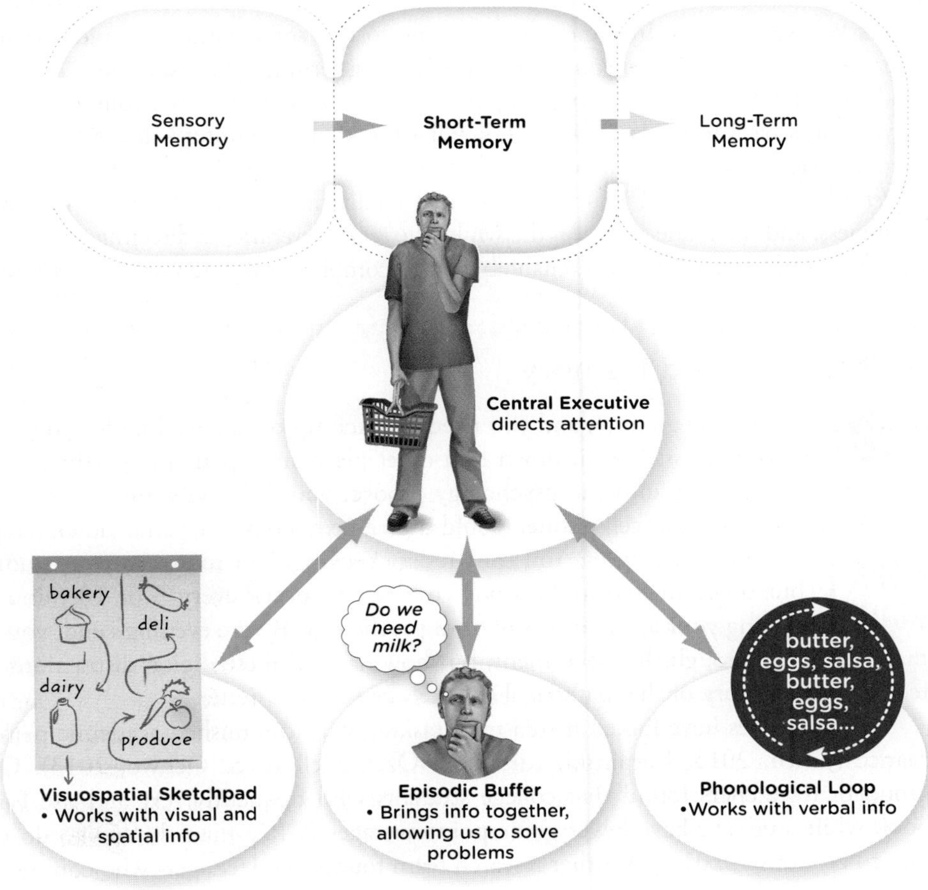

2390
45791
340982
0128957
93781256
501298347

FIGURE 6.5
Digit Span Test
The Digit Span Test is a simple way to assess memory. Participants are asked to listen to a string of numbers and then repeat them. The string of numbers grows longer as the test progresses. Ask a friend to give you this test and see how many numbers you can remember. For a real challenge, you can even try to recite the list backward!

FIGURE 6.6
Working Memory
Working memory represents the active processing occurring in short-term memory. Overseeing the big picture is the central executive, which directs attention and integrates processing among three subsystems: the phonological loop, visuospatial sketchpad, and episodic buffer. To see how this model works, imagine you have stopped by the supermarket to pick up groceries. You rehearse the shopping list with your phonological loop, produce a mental layout of the store with your visuospatial sketchpad, and use the episodic buffer to access long-term memories and determine whether you need any additional items. Tying together all these activities is the central executive.
Information from Baddeley (2002).

PHONOLOGICAL LOOP The *phonological loop* is responsible for working with verbal information for brief periods of time; when exposed to verbal stimuli, we "hear" an immediate corollary in our mind. This component of working memory is what we use, for example, when we are reading, trying to solve problems, or learning new vocabulary.

VISUOSPATIAL SKETCHPAD The *visuospatial sketchpad* is where visual and spatial data are briefly stored and manipulated, including information about your surroundings and where things are in relation to each other and you. This working memory component allows you to close your eyes and reach for the coffee mug you just set down. We can also use information from long-term memory in our visuospatial sketchpad (Baddeley, 1999, 2006).

CENTRAL EXECUTIVE The *central executive* has responsibilities similar to those of the chief executive in any organization—it directs attention, makes plans, and coordinates activities (Baddeley, 2002). Part of its role is to determine what information is important, and to help organize and manipulate consciousness. Why is it that we cannot actually text, eat, and safely drive all at once? Like a juggler, the central executive can only catch and toss one ball at a time. We may think we are doing all three tasks at once, but we are really just swapping the alternatives in and out at a fast pace.

EPISODIC BUFFER The *episodic buffer* is the part of working memory where information from the phonological loop, visuospatial sketchpad, and long-term memory can be brought together temporarily, under the direction of the central executive (Baddeley, 2000). The episodic buffer forms the bridge between memory and conscious awareness. It enables us to assign meaning to past events, solve problems, and make plans for the future.

LET'S WORK IT OUT Imagine you are trying to buy some running sneakers online. You need your password, so you retrieve it from long-term memory and then "hear" the ten letters and numbers played in your *phonological loop*. Now you need your credit card, so you think back to the last place you saw it—the kitchen counter—and bring forth a mental image of how your kitchen is laid out in your *visuospatial sketchpad*. The *episodic buffer* allows memories of your password and credit card location to come into your awareness, and then fade away. All the while, the *central executive* is directing your attention from one place to the next, enabling you to complete every step of the purchase.

SOCIAL MEDIA AND PSYCHOLOGY
Multitasking and Memory

It's Sunday evening, and you need to catch up on the reading for your psychology class. You sit down in a quiet place and open your textbook. But just as you are getting into the psychology groove, you feel a vibration inside your pocket—your cell phone. Could it be a text, a new Snapchat video, a reply to your latest tweet? You can't resist checking. You return to your studies, but social media notifications continue to occur every 5 or 10 minutes, pulling your attention away from psychology. By the evening's end, you do manage to get through the assignment, but how have all these digital distractions affected your memory of the material? Definitely not for the better.

HOW TO LOWER YOUR GPA USING FACEBOOK

Various studies have linked media multitasking with diminished academic performance (Junco, 2015; Karpinski, Kirschner, Ozer, Mellott, & Ochwo, 2013). One group of researchers found that college students who frequently text and use Facebook while studying have lower grade point averages (GPA) than those who do not (Junco & Cotten, 2012). Another research team found that teenagers who commonly

Synonyms

explicit memory declarative memory

explicit memory A type of memory you are aware of having and can consciously express in words or declare, including memories of facts and experiences.

multitask with media perform worse on math and English achievement tests than those who multitask less (Cain, Leonard, Gabrieli, & Finn, 2016). Many of these studies are correlational, making it difficult to untangle cause-and-effect relationships. Does media multitasking make it harder to remember material and thus lead to inferior academic performance, or do lower-achieving students simply have a more difficult time resisting the lure of Twitter, Snapchat, and Instagram? Perhaps students with lower GPAs spend more time on social media (Michikyan, Subrahmanyam, & Dennis, 2015).

Controlled experiments do suggest that digital distractions have the potential to impair memory and learning. In one study, researchers had university students sit through lectures and then quizzed them on their memory of the material. Students who had used instant messaging (IM) or Facebook during the lecture performed worse than those who had taken notes with a pencil and paper (Wood et al., 2011). Their diminished performance may have to do with the burden that social media imposes on working memory. Reading a funny post or responding to a message requires a shift in attention—hard work for the brain, which has to engage and disengage different networks (Courage, Bakhtiar, Fitzpatrick, Kenny, & Brandeau, 2015; de Fockert, 2013; Junco, 2015). What does this mean for you? If you're multitasking with media, you are likely missing important information from lectures and readings. One of the most remarkable findings from a recent study might come as a surprise to you: Even when students use their laptops only for note-taking, they perform more poorly on conceptual questions than students who take notes by longhand (Mueller & Oppenheimer, 2014).

👥 In Class: Collaborate and Report

Find a partner and complete the following memory task: **A)** Choose an activity that requires your attention (for example, texting each other the names of your favorite TV show characters; taking turns naming books you have read). **B)** As you perform this task, try to memorize the 40 key terms listed at the end of the chapter. **C)** After 5 minutes, close your textbook and write the key terms (in order) on a blank sheet of paper. **D)** Discuss how multitasking affected your maintenance rehearsal of the key terms.

As you know, short-term memory is limited in its capacity and duration, and working memory has its limitations as well. So how do we maintain so much information over the years? What aspect of memory makes it possible to memorize thousands of vocabulary words, scores of names and facts, and lyrics to your favorite songs? Enter long-term memory.

Long-Term Memory: Save It for Later

Items that enter short-term memory have two possible fates: Either they fade away or they move into *long-term memory* (**FIGURE 6.7** on page 246). Think of how much information is stored in your long-term memory: funny jokes, important conversations, images of faces, song lyrics, multiplication tables, and so many words—around 10,000 to 11,000 word families (such as "smile," "smiled," "smiling") for English-speaking college students (Treffers-Daller & Milton, 2013). Could it be that long-term memory has an endless holding capacity? It may be impossible to answer this question, but for all practical purposes our long-term memory has no limits. Some memories stored there, such as street names from your childhood, may even last a lifetime (Reber, 2010, May/June; Schmidt, Peeck, Paas, & van Breukelen, 2000).

LO 8 Describe long-term memory.

Long-term memory can be described in a variety of ways, but psychologists often distinguish between two categories: explicit and implicit. **Explicit memory** is the type

CONNECTIONS

In **Chapter 1,** we discussed negative correlations, or the inverse link between two variables. Here we see that as time spent using Facebook goes up, GPA goes down. But correlation does not prove causation; perhaps people with lower GPAs have less interest in studying, and thus more time to socialize. Or, maybe there is a third factor, such as the ability to manage time effectively, influencing both variables.

Don't Do It
Media multitasking doesn't just threaten your academic performance; it can endanger your life, too. Picture this crumpled car next time you consider using your smartphone behind the wheel. Texting while driving increases the likelihood of crashing by four times (National Safety Council, 2015), and studies show that using a cell phone impairs driving to the same degree as drunkenness (Strayer & Watson, 2012, March). AP Photo/Jeff Roberson.

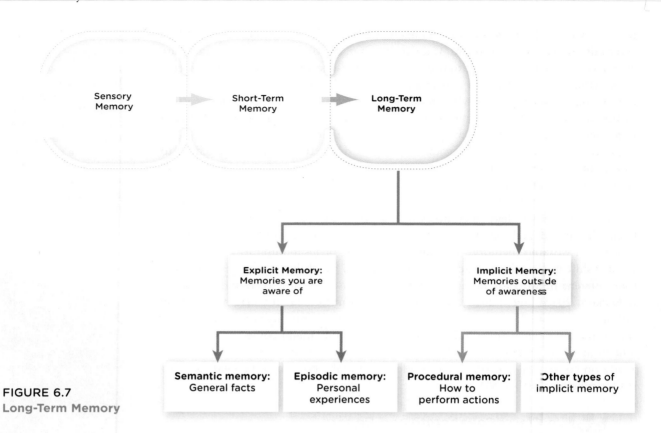

FIGURE 6.7
Long-Term Memory

Turbulent Memories of Helicopters?
Perhaps you have heard about the "memory problems" of former NBC news anchor Brian Williams. During the Iraq War in 2003, Williams rode in a military helicopter not far from the site where another helicopter came under attack. Williams' chopper was never hit, yet he claimed it was in a 2013 interview with David Letterman, and made similar statements at other times (Steel, 2015, June 19). Could it be that Williams experienced a distorted flashbulb memory—his recollection of learning about an actual event was conflated with his own memory of riding in a military helicopter? Patrick Andrade/Newscom/Polaris Images/United States.

of memory you are aware of having and can consciously express in words or declare: *Roses are red, guacamole is made with avocados; I wore faded jeans yesterday.* **Implicit memory** is a memory of something you know or know how to do, which may be automatic, unconscious, and difficult to bring to awareness and express.

EXPLICIT MEMORY Endel Tulving (1972) proposes there are two forms of explicit memory: semantic and episodic. **Semantic memory** pertains to general facts about the world (*the Earth is located in the Milky Way; the United States holds presidential elections every four years; the brain has two hemispheres*). But there is also a type of memory you can call your own. Your first experience riding a bike, the time you got lost in the supermarket, the sandwich you ate yesterday—all of these personal memories are part of your **episodic memory** (ep-uh-SOD-ik). You can think of episodic memory as the record of memorable experiences, or "episodes," in your life, including when and where they occurred (Tulving, 1985). One could say that semantic memories are verifiable, but episodic memories are not.

FLASHBULB MEMORIES Often, our most vivid episodic memories are associated with intense emotion. Think about an emotionally charged experience from your past: learning about a terrorist attack, getting news that someone you love has been in an accident, or hearing that your favorite sports team has won a historic championship. If recollecting these moments feels like watching a 4-D movie, you might be experiencing what psychologists call a **flashbulb memory**, a detailed account of circumstances surrounding an emotionally significant or shocking, sometimes historic, event (Brown & Kulik, 1977). With flashbulb memories, you often recall the precise moment you learned of an event—where you were, who or what source relayed the news, how it made you feel, what you did next, and other random details about the experience (Brown & Kulik, 1977). Perhaps you have a flashbulb memory of hearing about the horrific shootings at Sandy Hook Elementary School in Newtown, Connecticut, in 2012, or learning that

Donald Trump won the 2016 presidential election or the Chicago Cubs won the World Series; you recall whom you were with, what you were drinking and eating, what music was playing. Note that a flashbulb memory is a specific type of episodic memory of the experiences associated with *learning about* an event rather than "first-hand memories" of *experiencing* the event (Hirst & Phelps, 2016).

Because flashbulb memories seem so strong, vivid, and rich in detail, we often place great confidence in them, but research suggests that we should be cautious about doing this. Flashbulb memories sometimes include inaccuracies or lack specific details (Neisser, 1991; Hirst et al., 2015).

IMPLICIT MEMORY Unlike explicit memory, which can easily flow into conscious thought, implicit memory is difficult to bring into awareness and express. It is a memory for something you know or know how to do, but which might be automatic or unconscious. Many of the physical activities we take for granted, such as playing an instrument, driving a car, and dribbling a basketball, use a special type of implicit memory called **procedural memory,** that is, the memory of how to carry out an activity without conscious control or attention. After his illness, Clive Wearing could still pick up a piece of music and play it on the piano. He had no recollection of learning to sight-read or play, yet he could execute these skills like the professional he had always been (Vennard, 2011, November 21). Therefore, Clive's procedural memory was still working.

Memories acquired through classical conditioning are also implicit. Let's say you enjoy eating food at McDonald's and the very sight of the golden arches makes you salivate like one of Pavlov's dogs. Somewhere along the line, you formed an association, a memory linking the appearance of that restaurant to juicy hamburgers and creamy shakes, but the association does not require your conscious awareness (Cowan, 1988). It is implicit.

Improve Your Memory

How does the process of moving data into the memory system create long-term memories? Some activities work well for keeping information in short-term memory (maintenance rehearsal, for example). Others involve moving information from short-term memory to long-term memory. Let's take a look at some of these processes, kicking off our discussion with a little test.

> **try this ↓**
>
> Take 15 seconds and try to memorize these seven words in the order they appear:
>
> **puppy stop sing sadness soccer kick panic**
>
> Now close your eyes, and see how many you recall. How did you do?

You just completed a miniversion of "Random Words," an event in the World Memory Championships. One memory champion memorized 300 words in 15 minutes. What is the secret? Many memory athletes use **mnemonic** (nih-MON-ik) devices—techniques for improving memory. You have probably used several mnemonic devices in your own life. For example, have you ever relied on the *first-letter technique* to remember the order of operations in math (Please Excuse My Dear Aunt Sally)? Or perhaps you have used an *acronym,* such as ROY G BIV, to remember the colors of the rainbow (**FIGURE 6.8** on page 248)? Chunking, which we discussed earlier, is also a mnemonic technique. As you can see in **INFOGRAPHIC 6.1** (page 251), mnemonic devices and other memory strategies can enhance the retention of material as you study.

METHOD OF LOCI One of the mnemonics memory athletes rely on most is the *method of loci* (LOH-sahy, meaning "places"). Here's how it works: When presented with a series

Effortless
Following his bout with encephalitis in 1985, Clive could still read music and play the piano, demonstrating that his procedural memory was not destroyed. Researchers documented a similar phenomenon in a professional cello player who battled herpes encephalitis in 2005 (Vennard, 2011, November 21). Jiri Rezac/Polaris/Newscom.

CONNECTIONS

In **Chapter 5,** we introduced the concept of classical conditioning, which occurs when an originally neutral stimulus is conditioned to elicit or induce an involuntary response, such as salivation, eye blinks, and other types of reflex reactions. Here, we can see how closely linked learning and memory are.

Synonyms
implicit memory nondeclarative memory

implicit memory A memory of something you know or know how to do, which may be automatic, unconscious, and difficult to bring to awareness and express.

semantic memory The memory of information theoretically available to anyone, which pertains to general facts about the world; a type of explicit memory.

episodic memory The record of memorable experiences or "episodes" including when and where an experience occurred; a type of explicit memory.

flashbulb memory A detailed account of circumstances surrounding an emotionally significant or shocking, sometimes historic, event.

procedural memory The unconscious memory of how to carry out a variety of skills and activities; a type of implicit memory.

mnemonic Technique to improve memory.

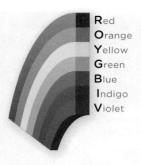

FIGURE 6.8
Mnemonics
Mnemonics enable us to translate information into a form that is easier to remember. For example, the common acronym ROY G BIV helps us remember the order of the seven colors in the rainbow. And when music students have trouble remembering the notes on the lines of the treble clef (EGBDF), they often rely on the first-letter technique, creating a sentence out of words beginning with these letters: *Every Good Boy Deserves Fudge.*

try this ↓

Try to remember the various divisions of the nervous system. Sketch a diagram like the one here (this is from Figure 2.2 in Chapter 2) showing the relationships among the concepts, starting with the most general and ending with the most specific.

of words to remember, the competitors take the words on a mental journey through a place they know well. For example, memory expert Dorothea Seitz goes on a mental journey through her bedroom and bathroom. Walking through her room, she puts the items-to-be-remembered at predetermined spots along the way. Let's say she is trying to remember the seven words from the Try This exercise on the previous page. Dorothea visualizes herself entering her bedroom. The first thing she comes upon is the bed, so she might imagine a cute *puppy* playing with the pillow. Then she encounters a bedside table, which suddenly becomes a bus *stop* with a bus parked in front. She walks over to the sofa, climbs up onto it, and begins to *sing*. The next object on her path is a box, but not an ordinary box, because it's weeping tears of *sadness*. Next in her path is a mirror that she shatters to pieces with a *soccer* ball. When she gets to the sink, she *kicks* it with her foot. Finally, she imagines aliens climbing out of the toilet, causing her to *panic*. If she needs to remember the items, she retraces the journey, stopping at each point to observe the image she left there (D. Seitz, personal communication, December 13, 2009).

You can use the method of loci, too. Just pick a familiar route—through your favorite restaurant, college campus, even your body parts—and mentally place things you need to remember at points along the way. For remembering short lists, memory champion Dominic O'Brien suggests tagging items to pre-established points along the body (O'Brien, 2013). Suppose you need to pick up five items at the grocery: *milk, eggs, olive oil, bananas,* and *cherries.* Choose some body parts and then visually connect them to the items you need. For example, your hair is slicked back in *olive oil;* your nose is a big long *banana;* you can't see because someone threw *eggs* in your eyes; *cherries* dangle from your ears like earrings; and you have a *milk* mustache. The method of loci works very well for memorizing lists, especially if you practice often.

HIERARCHICAL STRUCTURES Another way to boost your memory is to arrange the material you are trying to memorize into a hierarchy, or a system of meaningful categories and subcategories. In one classic study, researchers found that if participants were given a list of words that followed a hierarchical structure, they were better able to recall the words than a similar group of participants who were asked to memorize the same words that had not been organized in any meaningful way. In fact, the participants who had learned the words using the hierarchy were able to recall three times as many words as the other group (Bower, Clark, Lesgold, & Winzenz, 1969).

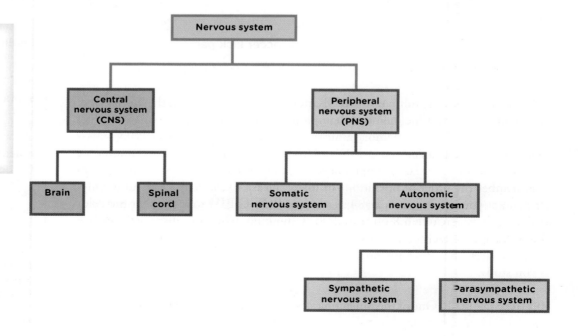

AUTOMATIC AND EFFORTFUL PROCESSING As you recall from earlier in the chapter, the levels of processing framework suggests that stronger memories result when you think about information on a deep level. Memory experts come to the championships ready to use **effortful processing**. As the name implies, effortful processing is not only intentional but also requires "cognitive effort," which broadly refers to the "degree of engagement with demanding tasks" (Westbrook & Braver, 2015, p. 396). In other words, how much you are willing to buckle down and put your mind to a task. Some types of effortful processing, such as maintenance rehearsal, are useful for extending the amount of time you can hold onto information in short-term memory. Others employ patterns and meaning to encode information for longer storage. As mentioned earlier, one expert links hundreds of elaborate images (like the puppy playing on the pillow, or aliens rising out of the toilet) on a mental journey—not an easy task to perform in 15 minutes. Her effortful processing occurs at a deep level and, as the levels of processing framework suggests, results in more successful learning and retention of information.

Your decisions to use (or not use) effortful processing may impact your academic achievement, performance on standardized tests, and ability to solve everyday problems. But despite your best intentions, you may not always choose the effortful path, particularly if the "cost" is too high and the effort feels "aversive" (Westbrook & Braver, 2015). For example, your psychology writing assignment is so cognitively taxing that you decide it's not worth the effort; you'd rather spend your time creating a new photo album on Facebook. Even deciding whether to use effortful processing takes effort, putting a strain on working memory, which has limited resources (Boureau, Sokol-Hessner, & Daw, 2015). What can a student do to make effortful processing less daunting and concentrating easier? Here are a few things that may help: Work in a quiet room, keep cell phones and TVs out of sight, sit at the front of the classroom, and keep your eye on a clock so you can use your time wisely (Duckworth, Gendler, & Gross, 2016).

We should note that some encoding occurs through automatic processing—that is, with little or no conscious effort or awareness (Evans & Stanovich, 2013; Hasher & Zacks, 1979). For example, if you walked into the conference room at the World Memory Championships, you might process all sorts of information without even trying—like the fact that most of the people milling around the room are men, and that some teams wear matching outfits. You would not make an effort to pick up on these details, but you remember them nevertheless. Your memory system absorbs the data automatically.

ELABORATIVE REHEARSAL AND VISUALIZATION Effortful processing is evident in **elaborative rehearsal**, the method of connecting incoming information to knowledge in long-term memory. Here, we can see that the *level of processing* occurs at a deep level, which suggests the encoding of information will be more successful. The memory champions' mental walks involve this type of deeper processing (elaborative rehearsal) because they take new information and put it in the familiar framework of places they know. By picturing the journey and the objects-to-be-remembered in their minds' eye, they take advantage of *visualization,* another effective encoding strategy. People tend to remember verbal information better when it's accompanied by vivid imagery. Some research suggests, for example, that children recall news stories better when they see them presented on television, as opposed to reading about them in a printed article (Walma van der Molen & van der Voort, 2000).

DISTRIBUTED PRACTICE What other learning strategies might improve encoding and help you move information into long-term memory? You've probably heard this before, but you should avoid cramming when trying to learn new material.

CONNECTIONS

In **Chapter 4,** we described automatic processing, the collection and retention of information with little or no conscious effort. Automatic processing can also refer to the automatic cognitive activity that guides some behaviors, enabling us to act without focusing attention on what we are doing. Without our awareness, the brain determines what needs attention and what can be processed for later use.

effortful processing The encoding and storage of information with conscious effort, or awareness.

elaborative rehearsal The method of connecting incoming information to knowledge in long-term memory; a deep level of encoding.

TABLE 6.1 SLEEP AND MEMORY

	Sleep	Impact on Memory
Get Adequate Sleep	Get sleep before you learn something new.	Readies brain for "initial formation of memories" (Contie, Defibaugh, Steinberg, & Wein, 2013, April).
	Get sleep after you learn something new.	Sleeping increases potential for retention of newly acquired information. Saves and strengthens information in the brain, which means you will be more likely to remember what you learned (Contie et al., 2013, April).
Impact of Sleep Deprivation	Sleep deprivation associated with increased risk for heart disease, stroke, and type 2 diabetes (LeWine, 2014, May 2).	These diseases can decrease blood flow, preventing cells from receiving oxygen and glucose, which can affect proper brain function (LeWine, 2014, May 2).
	Staying up all night can interfere with learning.	May reduce ability to learn new information by 40% (Contie et al., 2013, April).
Impact of Sleep on Emotions	Sleep can increase durability of memories for fear-laden events.	Sleep "strengthens fear memories." Conditioned fear memories are consolidated while we sleep, helping us to distinguish between what is threatening and what is not (Goldstein & Walker, 2014).
	Sleep can reduce the strength of emotional reactions to events.	REM sleep helps to reduce or dampen emotional reactions to events, while still consolidating memories (Goldstein & Walker, 2014).

Get 7–8 hours of sleep every night; too much (over 9 or 10 hours) and too little (less than 5 hours) impact cognitive activity. In general, sleep helps sustain memory in "later life" (LeWine, 2014, May 2; Devore et al., 2014).

Psychologists don't call it cramming, though; instead, we refer to it as **massed practice**, meaning that learning sessions occur generally within the same day, "back-to-back or in relatively close succession" (Dunlosky et al., 2013, p. 36). The other approach to learning uses **distributed practice** by spreading study sessions over the course of many days. Research starting as early as the 1800s resoundingly shows that distributed practice is much more effective for learning material than cramming sessions at the last minute (Dunlosky et al., 2013; Ebbinghaus, 1885/1913; Rohrer & Taylor, 2006). When researchers asked students to learn a new mathematical skill, they found that participants who practiced the new skill in two sessions (separated by a week) did better on a practice test (4 weeks later) than those who spent the same amount of time practicing in one session (Pashler, Rohrer, Cepeda, & Carpenter, 2007). Similarly, students who reviewed material from a natural science class 8 days after the original lectures did better on final exams than students who reviewed the material 1 day after the lectures (Kapler, Weston, & Wiseheart, 2015).

 In Class: Collaborate and Report

In your groups, **A)** discuss your daily routines. **B)** Create a weekly calendar showing when you study and how much time you devote to each study session. **C)** Determine whether you are using distributed practice.

CONNECTIONS

In **Chapter 4,** we discussed how sleep and dreams relate to memory. For example, researchers suspect that sleep spindles are associated with memory consolidation, and some theorists emphasize the importance of REM sleep in this process.

Synonyms

distributed practice spacing effect

massed practice Studying for long periods of time without breaks.

distributed practice Spreading out study sessions over time with breaks in between.

SLEEP AND MEMORY We have touched on many strategies for boosting memory, from chunking to visualization to distributed practice. If we could leave you with one final piece of advice, it would be the following: SLEEP. Exactly how sleep promotes memory is still not completely understood, but there is no question that good sleep makes for better processing of memories (TABLE 6.1; Diekelmann & Born, 2010; Marshall & Born, 2007; Rasch & Born, 2013). The relationship between sleep and memory formation also is evident in non-mammals, such as birds, and perhaps even invertebrates, such as bees (Vorster & Born, 2015). Even periods of "wakeful resting"

Study Smarter: Methods of Improving Your Memory

You may never need to memorize the order of 2,808 playing cards as memory champion Dominic O'Brien did. But you do need to be able to understand and recall hundreds of details when your teacher hands you an exam. Luckily, research shows that certain strategies and memory techniques will help you retain information when you study.

start studying

Recall details

Mnemonics translate information into a more easily remembered form.

ROYGBIV

Acronyms and first-letter technique
It's easier to remember a short phrase than a string of information.

Chunking
It's easier to remember a few chunks than a long string.

8935550172
893-555-0172

Method of loci
It's easier to remember information when you deliberately link it to locations along a familiar route.

Organize information

Hierarchical structures organize information into a meaningful system. The process of organizing aids encoding and, once encoded, the information is easier to recall.

furniture

fruit

flowers

Make connections

Elaborative rehearsal is deep processing that boosts transfer to long-term memory by connecting new information to older memories.

Give yourself time

Distributed practice creates better memory than study crammed into a single session.

NOVEMBER **13**   NOVEMBER **15**
NOVEMBER **18**   NOVEMBER **21**
↶ study ↷
NOVEMBER **23**   ← test

Get some rest

Sleep, or even wakeful resting after study, allows newly learned material to be encoded better.

zzz

A test

Credits: Single lotus flower, fanedison/Shutterstock; Pine chest of drawers, Paul Maguire/Shutterstock; Pansy, AndreyKlepikov/Shutterstock; Green sofa, Shutterstock; Alexander Mozymov/Marigold, Shutterstock; City map with labels, Laralova/Shutterstock; Vintage wooden rocking chair, eurobanks/Shutterstock; Red grape, HeinzTeh/Shutterstock; Peach, Nattika/Shutterstock; November calendar icon, DVARG/Shutterstock; Banana, Tatiana Popova/Shutterstock; Portrait of teenage girl with hand on chin, BLOOMimage/Getty Images; High education (student with chemical models and chemical formula on the blackboard), zorani/Getty Images.

can be of benefit. In one study, participants who experienced a 15-minute period of wakeful resting (sitting in a dark quiet room) displayed better retention of newly learned material than those who played a game for 15 minutes. Wakeful resting seems to allow newly learned material to be encoded better, and thus retained in memory longer (Dewar, Alber, Butler, Cowan, & Della Sala, 2012). What might this mean for you? Make sure you allow yourself some quiet time following the learning of new material. Of course, it takes more than good rest to succeed in college; you need to be able to analyze, apply, and synthesize material, not just remember it.

"Wow, that's a lot to remember," you may be saying. Hopefully, you can retain it with the help of some of the mnemonic devices we have presented. You might also take a wakeful resting break in preparation for the next section, which focuses on the topic of memory retrieval.

In Class: Collaborate and Report

In your group, describe three strategies you could use to memorize the list of key terms at the end of this chapter. (*Hint:* Refer to the section "Improve Your Memory.")

 show what you know

1. According to the information-processing model, our short-term memory can hold onto information for up to about _____ if we are not distracted by something else.
   a. 10 seconds
   b. 30 seconds
   c. 45 seconds
   d. 60 seconds

2. As you enter the airport, you try to remember the location of the baggage claim area. You remember the last time you picked up your friend at this airport, and using your visuospatial sketchpad, realize the area is to your left. This ability demonstrates the use of your:
   a. sensory memory.
   b. working memory.
   c. phonological loop.
   d. flashbulb memory.

3. If you are trying to memorize a long password, you could use _____, by grouping the numbers and symbols into meaningful units of information.

4. Develop a mnemonic device to help you memorize the following terms from this section: sensory memory, long-term memory, explicit memory, semantic memory, episodic memory, flashbulb memory, implicit memory, and procedural memory.

✓ CHECK YOUR ANSWERS IN APPENDIX C.

Friends Forever
Elephants Jenny and Shirley remembered each other after being separated for 23 years. Reunited at the Elephant Sanctuary in Hohenwald, Tennessee, they examined one another's trunks and hollered with joy (Ritchie, 2009, January 12). Courtesy of Carolyn Buckley, www.carolbuckley.com.

Retrieval and Forgetting

Have you ever heard the saying "An elephant never forgets"? Granted, this might be somewhat of an overstatement, but as far as animals go, elephants do have remarkable memories. Consider the story of two elephants that briefly worked together in the circus and then were separated for 23 years. When they re-encountered one another at an elephant sanctuary in Tennessee, the two animals started to inspect each other's trunk scars and "bellowed" in excitement: The long-lost friends had recognized one another (Ritchie, 2009, January 12)! An elephant's memory—and yours, too—is only as good as its ability to retrieve stored memories. Let's return to the World Memory Championships and examine the critical process of retrieval.

What Can You Retrieve?

Every event in the World Memory Championships begins with encoding data into the memory system and storing that information for later use. Contestants are presented with information—numbers, words, historic dates, and the like—and provided a certain amount of time to file it away in long-term memory. But no matter how much information they absorb, the contestants' efforts are meaningless if they can't *retrieve* it in the recall phase of the event.

RETRIEVAL CUES AND PRIMING One of the most grueling events in the World Memory Championships is "One Hour Numbers," a race to see who can memorize the greatest number of random digits in an hour. Contestants are given four sheets of paper, each containing 1,000 random digits, and 1 hour to cram as many digits as possible into their long-term memories. During the recall phase that follows, they get 2 hours to scrawl the correctly ordered numbers on blank sheets of paper. This is a backbreaker because there are no reminders, or *retrieval cues,* to help contestants locate the information in their long-term memory. **Retrieval cues** are stimuli that help you retrieve stored information that is difficult to access (Tulving & Osler, 1968). For example, let's say you were trying to remember the name of the researcher who created the working memory model introduced earlier in the chapter. If we gave you the first letter of his last name, *B,* would that help you retrieve the information? If your mind jumped to "Baddeley" (the correct answer), then *B* served as your retrieval cue. You probably create your own retrieval cues to memorize important information. When you take notes, for example, you don't copy everything you are reading; you write down enough information (the cue) to help you later retrieve what you are trying to learn. Or you might name a photo file in your computer "JoseBday4" so you can remember that the photo was taken on José's 4th birthday. Remember, "a good external cue can sustain memory retrieval in the face of considerable forgetting" (Tullis & Benjamin, 2015, p. 922).

Even Clive Wearing, who could not remember what was happening from one moment to the next, showed evidence of using retrieval cues. For instance, Clive spent 7 years of his life at St. Mary's Hospital in Paddington, London, yet had no conscious memory of living there. And, according to his wife, Deborah, Clive was "completely devoid" of knowledge of his own location; the hospital name was not at all connected with his sense of location (D. Wearing, personal communication, June 25, 2013). But if Deborah prompted him with the words "St. Mary's," he would chime back, "Paddington," oblivious to its connection (Wearing, 2005, p. 188). In this instance, the *retrieval cue* in Clive's environment (the sound of the word "St. Mary's") was **priming** his memory of the hospital name. Priming, a type of implicit memory, awakens memories with the help of retrieval cues.

At this point, you may be wondering how priming can occur in a person with severe amnesia. Clive's conscious, *explicit* memory is diminished, but his unconscious, *implicit* memory still functions, evidenced by his response to priming. Just because he could not articulate, or "declare," the name of the hospital does not mean that the previously known word combination had vanished from his memory system.

RECALL AND RECOGNITION Now let's return to the "One Hour Numbers" event of the World Memory Championships. This type of challenge relies on pure **recall**, the process of retrieving information held in long-term memory without the help of explicit retrieval cues. Recall is what you depend on when you answer fill-in-the-blank or short-answer essay questions on exams. Say you are given the following prompt: "Using a computer metaphor, what are the three processes involved in memory?" In this situation, you must come up with the answer from scratch: "The three processes are *encoding, storage,* and *retrieval.*"

Now let's say you are faced with a multiple-choice question: "One proven way to help you retain information is: (a) distributed practice, (b) massed practice, or (c) eidetic imagery." Answering this question relies on **recognition**, the process of matching incoming data to information stored in long-term memory. Recognition is generally a lot easier than recall because the information is right before your eyes; you

The Ultimate Test
"One Hour Numbers" is one of the most demanding events in the World Memory Championships. Contestants are given 1 hour to memorize as many random digits as possible, and then 2 hours to write them in order on paper. The current world record, held by Alex Mullen of the United States, is 3,029 digits (World Memory Sports Council, 2016b). The World Memory Championships.

retrieval cues Stimuli that help in the retrieval of stored information that is difficult to access.

priming The stimulation of memories as a result of retrieval cues in the environment.

recall The process of retrieving information held in long-term memory without the help of explicit retrieval cues.

recognition The process of matching incoming data to information stored in long-term memory.

just have to identify it (*Hey, I've seen that before*). Recall, on the other hand, requires you to come up with information on your own. Most of us find it easier to recognize the correct answer from a list of possible answers in a multiple-choice question than to recall the same correct answer for a fill-in-the-blank question.

SERIAL POSITION EFFECT Recall and recognition come into play outside of school as well. Just think about the last time someone asked you to pick up some items at the store. In order to find the requested goods, you had to recognize them (*There's the ketchup*), but even before that you had to recall them—a much harder task if they are not written down. The ability to recall items from a list depends on where they fall in the list, a phenomenon psychologists call the **serial position effect** (FIGURE 6.9). When given a list of words to memorize, research participants are better able to remember items at the beginning of the list, which is known as the **primacy effect**, as well as items at the end, which is called the **recency effect** (Deese & Kaufman, 1957; Kelley, Neath, & Surprenant, 2015; Murdock, 1962).

Imagine you are on your way to the store to buy supplies for a dinner party, but your cell phone battery is about to die. Your phone rings; it's your housemate asking you to pick up the following items: napkins, paper towels, dish soap, butter, laundry soap, paper plates, sparkling water, ice cream, plastic spoons, bread, pickles, and flowers. Without any way to write down this list, you are at the mercy of the serial position effect. In all likelihood (and if you don't use mnemonics), you will return home with napkins, paper towels, and a bottle of dish soap (due to the primacy effect), as well as bread, pickles, and flowers (due to the recency effect); the items in the middle will more likely be forgotten. Similarly, items are more "popular" when listed at the beginning or end of a menu, as opposed to the middle, presumably due to the serial position effect; they pop into your head more easily when you are ordering your meal (Bar-Hillel, 2015).

MEMORY AND CULTURE Research also suggests that culture plays a role in the types of recollections people have. Chinese people, for example, are more likely than Americans to remember social and historical occurrences and focus their memories on other people. Americans, on the other hand, tend to recall events as they relate to their individual actions and emotions (Wang & Conway, 2004). This may have something to do with the fact that China has a *collectivist* culture, whereas the United States is more *individualistic*. People in collectivist societies tend to prioritize the needs of family and community over those of the individual. Individualistic cultures are more "me" oriented, or focused on autonomy and independence. It thus makes sense that people from the collectivist culture of China would have more community-oriented memories than their American counterparts.

The Encoding Specificity Principle

When it comes to retrieving memories, context matters. Where were you when you encoded the information, and what was occurring around you? Researchers have found that environmental factors play a key role in determining how easily memories are retrieved.

LO 9 Illustrate how encoding specificity relates to retrieval cues.

CONTEXT IS EVERYTHING In a classic study by Godden and Baddeley (1975), participants learned lists of words under two conditions: while underwater (using scuba gear) and on dry land. They were then tested for recall in both conditions: If they learned the list underwater, they were tested underwater and on dry ground; if they learned the list on dry ground, they were tested on dry ground and underwater. The participants were better able to retrieve words when the learning and recall

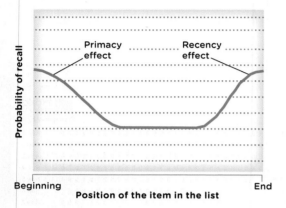

FIGURE 6.9
The Serial Position Effect
Items at the beginning and end of a list are more likely to be recalled.

serial position effect The ability to recall items in a list depends on where they are in the series.

primacy effect The tendency to remember items at the beginning of a list.

recency effect The tendency to remember items at the end of a list.

encoding specificity principle Memories are more easily recalled when the context and cues at the time of encoding are similar to those at the time of retrieval.

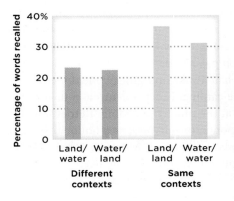

FIGURE 6.10

Does Context Influence Memory Retrieval?

Researchers asked participants to learn a list of words in two contexts, underwater and on dry land. The participants had an easier time recalling words when learning and recall happened in the same setting: learning underwater and recalling underwater, or learning on dry land and recalling on dry land. Information from Godden and Baddeley (1975). Photo: Sergey Dubrov/Shutterstock.

occurred in the same location (**FIGURE 6.10**). If they learned the words underwater, they had an easier time recalling them underwater. Words learned on land were easier to recall on land. Here, we have an example of *context-dependent memory;* memories are easier to access when the encoding and retrieval occur in similar contexts.

Context-dependent memory is part of a broader phenomenon conveyed by the **encoding specificity principle,** which states that memories are more easily recalled when the context and cues at the time of encoding are similar to those at the time of retrieval (Smith, Glenberg, & Bjork, 1978; Tulving & Thomson, 1973). There is even evidence that summoning a memory for an event reactivates the same brain areas that became excited during the event itself (Danker & Anderson, 2010). This suggests that the activity in your brain at the time of encoding is similar to that at retrieval, and researchers using **fMRIs** have found support for this (Gottfried, Smith, Rugg, & Dolan, 2004).

CONNECTIONS

In **Chapter 2,** we presented a variety of technologies used to explore the brain. fMRI captures changes in brain activity by revealing patterns of blood flow in a particular area. This is a good indicator of how much oxygen is being used as a result of activity there.

In Class: Collaborate and Report

Team up and discuss **A)** how the encoding specificity principle might help you remember people's names; and **B)** how you might use the encoding specificity principle to improve your retention of course information.

IT ALL COMES FLOODING BACK In your own life, you may have noticed that old memories tend to emerge from the woodwork when you return to the places where they were created. Dining at a restaurant you once frequented with an ex-boyfriend or girlfriend probably sparks memories of romantic moments (or perhaps a bitter argument) you had there. Going to a high school reunion might bring back memories of football games, dances, and classrooms not recalled in years. How does returning to the birthplace of a memory help bring it to mind? Places where memories are created often abound with retrieval cues—sights, sounds, tastes, smells, and feelings present at the time of encoding. These retrieval cues help awaken stored memories.

Suppose you go to a friend's house to watch the movie *50 First Dates* starring Adam Sandler and Drew Barrymore. While encoding a memory of the movie, you are exposed to all sorts of stimuli in the environment, such as the hum of an air conditioner, the taste of the chips and salsa you are munching on, the tabby cat purring next to you on the sofa. All these stimuli have nothing to do with *50 First Dates,* but they are strongly linked to your experience of watching the film. So the next time you are at your friend's house and you see that tabby cat purring on the sofa, thoughts of "Ten Second Tom" might come back to you.

MOODS, INTERNAL STATES, AND MEMORY The encoding specificity principle does not merely apply to the context of the surroundings. Remembering things is also easier when physiological and psychological conditions, including moods and emotions,

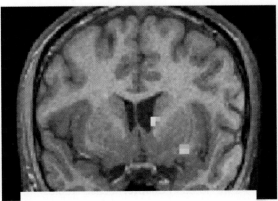

Context Matters

Using fMRI scans, researchers observed the brain activity of people trying to remember images they had first viewed in the presence of a specific scent (Gottfried, Smith, Rugg, & Dolan, 2004). When recalling images they had linked to smells, odor-processing areas of the brain became noticeably excited, even in the absence of any odors. The scan shows the activity in the brain (see yellow on scan) of a person recalling an odor-linked image (Gottfried et al., 2004). Republished with permission of Gottfried, J. A., Smith, A. P. R., Rugg, M. D., & Dolan, R. J. (2004). Remembrance of odors past: Human olfactory cortex in cross-modal recognition memory. *Neuron, 42,* 687–895; permission conveyed through Copyright Clearance Center, Inc.

are similar at the time of encoding and retrieval. Sometimes memories can be best retrieved under such circumstances; we call this *state-dependent memory.* One morning upon awakening, you spot a red cardinal on your window ledge. You forget about the cardinal for the rest of the day—even when you pass the very same window. But come tomorrow morning when you are once again half-awake and groggy, memories of the red bird return. Here, your ability to recall the cardinal is dependent on your internal or physiological state being the same as it was at the time of encoding. Retrieval is also easier when the content of a memory corresponds to our present emotional state, a phenomenon known as *mood congruence* (Bower, Gilligan, & Menteiro, 1981; Drace, Ric, & Desrichard, 2010). If you are in a happy mood, you are more likely to recollect a happy-go-lucky character from a book, but if you are in a sour mood, you are more inclined to remember the character whose bad mood matches yours.

How Easily We Remember: Memory Savings

Retrieval is clearly at work in recall and recognition, the two processes we compared above. But there is another, less obvious form of retrieval that occurs in the process of **relearning.** Perhaps you've noticed that you learn material much more quickly a second time around. Math equations, vocabulary, and grammar rules seem to make more sense if you've been exposed to them before. Some information seems to stick better when we learn it twice (Storm, Bjork, & Bjork, 2008).

HERMANN EBBINGHAUS The first person to quantify the effect of relearning was Hermann Ebbinghaus (1850–1909), a German psychologist and pioneering researcher of human memory. Ebbinghaus was the sole participant in his experiments, so his research actually shed light on *his* memory, although the trends he uncovered in himself seem to apply to human memory in general (Murre & Dros, 2014).

Thorough scientist that he was, Ebbinghaus spent hour upon hour, day after day memorizing lists of "nonsense syllables"—meaningless combinations of vowels and consonants such as DAZ and MIB. Once Ebbinghaus had successfully remembered a list, meaning he could recite it smoothly and confidently, he would put it aside. Later, he would memorize it all over again and calculate how much time he had saved in Round 2, a measure called the "savings score" (Ebbinghaus, 1885/1913). In a study that supports Ebbinghaus' theory of savings in relearning, participants who were asked to memorize number–word pairs (for example, 17-snake, 23-crown) showed significant savings in the amount of time needed to relearn the number–word pairs 6 weeks later (Marmurek & Grant, 1990).

Since no one spends all day memorizing nonsense syllables, you may wonder how Ebbinghaus' research and the "savings score" apply to real life. At some point in school, you probably had to memorize a famous speech like Dr. Martin Luther King's "I Have a Dream." Let's say it took you 100 practice sessions to recite the speech flawlessly. Then, a month later, you tried memorizing it again and it only took 50 attempts. Because you cut your learning time in half (from 100 practice sessions to 50), your savings score would be 50%.

A FOREIGN LANGUAGE? Learning is a lot like blazing a trail through freshly fallen snow. Your first attempt plowing through the powder is hard work and slow going, but the second time (relearning) is easier and faster because the snow is packed and the tracks already laid down. This also seems to be true for relearning a forgotten childhood language. One small study focused on native English speakers who as children had been exposed to either Hindi or Zulu to varying degrees. Although none of the adults in the study had any *explicit* memories of the languages, those who were under 40 were still able to distinguish sounds from their childhood languages better than members of a control group with no exposure to these languages (Bowers, Mattys & Gage, 2009).

ADAMSANDLER   **DREW**BARRYMORE

Imagine having to win over
the girl of your dreams...
every friggin' day.

50FIRSTDATES

Retrieval Cues
While watching your favorite Adam Sandler movie, you pick up on all sorts of background stimuli from the environment. These sights, sounds, smells, tastes, and feelings have become entwined with your memory of the movie, so they can serve as retrieval cues for scenes in the film. Next time you smell buttery popcorn, don't be surprised if the lyrics to "Forgetful Lucy" pop into your head. THE KOBAL COLLECTION/ COLUMBIA at Art Resource, NY.

CONNECTIONS
As we noted in **Chapter 1,** case studies generally have only one participant. Here, we see that Ebbinghaus, the researcher, was the sole participant. It is important to consider this when interpreting the findings, especially as we try to generalize to the population.

relearning Material learned previously is acquired more quickly in subsequent exposures.

The implication is that people who have some knowledge of a language (even if they don't realize it) benefit from this memory, by showing a "memory savings" if they try to learn the language again. They are a step ahead of other adults learning that language for the first time.

How Easily We Forget: Memory Slips

LO 10　Identify and explain some of the reasons why we forget.

Once the memory athletes have memorized numbers, images, and other bits of information for the World Memory Championships, how long does such data remain in their minds—an hour, a day, a week? One memory champion, Dorothea Seitz, reports that images and words can last for several days, but meaningless strings of numbers, like the hundreds of digits memorized for the "One Hour Numbers" event, tend to fade within a day (D. Seitz, personal communication, December 13, 2009).

This would probably come as no surprise to Hermann Ebbinghaus, who, in addition to demonstrating the effects of relearning, was the first to illustrate just how rapidly memories vanish. Through his experiments with nonsense syllables, Ebbinghaus (1885/1913) found that the bulk of forgetting occurs immediately after learning. If you look at his *curve of forgetting* (**FIGURE 6.11**), you will see his memory of word lists plunging downward the hour following learning, then leveling off thereafter. Think about how the curve of forgetting applies to you. Some of what you hear in a psychology lecture may disappear from memory as soon as you walk out the door, but what you remember a week later will probably not differ much from what you recall in a month.

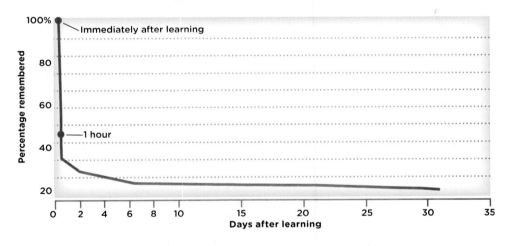

FIGURE 6.11

Ebbinghaus' Curve of Forgetting
Ebbinghaus discovered that most forgetting occurs within 1 hour of learning and then levels off.

ENCODING FAILURE What exactly causes us to forget? That may depend on the stage of memory processing—encoding, storage, or retrieval—at which a given instance of memory failure occurs. Sometimes details and events we think we have forgotten were actually never encoded in the first place. Take this example: After a long and stressful day, you stop at the supermarket to pick up some blackberries and dark chocolate. While fumbling through your bag in search of your wallet, you take out your gloves and place them on the cashier's counter, but because your attention is focused on finding your wallet, you don't even notice where you've placed the gloves. Then you pay and walk out the door, only to wake up the next morning wondering where you left your gloves! This is an example of *encoding failure* because the data never entered your memory system. You never registered putting your gloves on the counter in the first place, so how can you expect to remember where you left them? For a demonstration of encoding failure, take a look at the four images appearing in the Try This. You've looked at the Apple logo countless times, so it should be easy to tell if you're looking at one that's phony, right?

try this ⬇

Are any of these the correct Apple logo?

Research from Adam B. Blake and Alan D. Castel, 2015.

Who Are They?
Sometimes a name we are trying to remember feels so close, yet we cannot quite pull it out of storage. This feeling of near-retrieval is known as the tip-of-the-tongue phenomenon, and it happens frequently when we try to recall the names of celebrities. Top: Corbis. Middle: AP Images. Bottom: WireImage/Getty Images.

If you're like most people, you identified one of the wrong logos as correct (real Apple logo not shown), perhaps because there is no "functional reason" for you to *encode* the logo's visual elements. Or maybe you have been exposed to the logo so many times that you no longer attend to its details (Blake, Nazarian, & Castel, 2015).

STORAGE FAILURE AND MEMORY DECAY Memory lapses can also result from *storage* failure. Take a moment and try to remember your high school locker combination. At one point, you knew these numbers by heart, but they have slipped your mind because you no longer use them. Many memories decay over time, but there is plenty of evidence that we can store a vast fund of information, sometimes for very long periods. Such memories might include the name of the street where you grew up (Schmidt et al., 2000), grades in college (Bahrick, Hall, & Da Costa, 2008), and factual knowledge from college courses (Conway, Cohen, & Stanhope, 1991). However, these types of memories are subject to a variety of inaccuracies and distortions, and tapping into them is not always easy.

TIP-OF-THE-TONGUE PHENOMENON Sometimes we know that we have knowledge of something but just can't pull it out of storage, or retrieve it. The name of that college classmate or that new blockbuster movie, it's just sitting on the tip of your tongue but it won't slide off! This simple *retrieval* failure is called the *tip-of-the-tongue phenomenon.* Most of us have this feeling about once a week, but luckily we are able to retrieve the elusive phrase approximately 50% of the time (James & Burke, 2000; Schwartz, 2012). Often, we can correctly guess the first letter of the word or how many syllables it has (Hanley & Chapman, 2008). Studies suggest that the tip-of-the-tongue phenomenon becomes more common with age (Brown & Nix, 1996).

HIGHLY SUPERIOR AUTOBIOGRAPHICAL MEMORY What would happen if you had the opposite problem—that is, instead of forgetting all the time, you remembered everything? Imagine how overwhelming it would be to remember all the experiences you have had, all the people you have met, all the meals that you have eaten over the years, and so on. The ability to forget seems to have great adaptive value, because forgetting allows you to attend to what's going on in the here and now. In simple terms, forgetting is adaptive because it clears the way for new memories (Wimber, Alink, Charest, Kriegeskorte, & Anderson, 2015). Some people, however, have an inherent ability to "retain and retrieve vast amounts of public and autobiographical events," without trying (LePort et al., 2012, p. 13). This type of memory ability is very rare, and is known as *highly superior autobiographical memory* (HSAM; LePort et al., 2012; McGaugh & LePort, 2014). People with HSAM can easily recall details about personal and news events from almost every day starting in middle childhood (Patihis, 2016). In contrast, memory champions generally use mnemonics to improve their memory, and children with eidetic imagery mostly are remembering images or objects. Interestingly, individuals with this type of superior memory can remember what they had for lunch a decade ago, but when asked to remember a word list, they make a similar amount of errors as members of a control group (Patihis et al., 2013). Like the rest of us, people with HSAM can suffer from "memory distortions."

PROACTIVE INTERFERENCE You now know that forgetting can stem from problems in encoding and storage. And the tip-of-the-tongue phenomenon tells us that it can also result from glitches in *retrieval.* Studies also show that retrieval is influenced, or in some cases blocked, by information we learn before and after a memory is made, which we refer to as *interference* (Waugh & Norman, 1965). If you have studied more than one foreign language, you have probably experienced interference. Suppose you take Spanish in middle school, and then begin studying Italian in college. As you try to learn Italian, you may find Spanish words creeping into your mind and confusing you;

FIGURE 6.12
Proactive and
Retroactive Interference

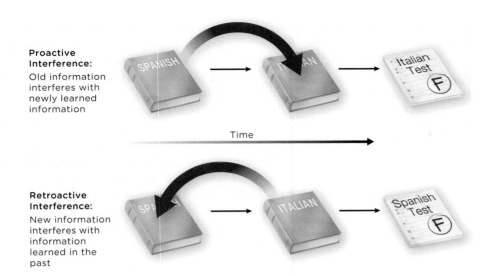

Proactive Interference: Old information interferes with newly learned information

Time

Retroactive Interference: New information interferes with information learned in the past

this is an example of **proactive interference**, the tendency for information learned in the past to interfere with the retrieval of new material. People who learn to play a second musical instrument experience the same problem; the fingering of the old instrument interferes with the retrieval of new fingering.

RETROACTIVE INTERFERENCE Now let's say you are going on a trip to Mexico and need to use the Spanish you learned back in middle school. As you approach a vendor in an outdoor market in Costa Maya, you may become frustrated when the only words that come to mind are *ciao bello* and *buongiorno* (Italian for "hello handsome" and "good day"), when you really are searching for phrases with the same meaning in Español. Here, recently learned information interferes with the retrieval of things learned in the past. We call this **retroactive interference**. This type of interference can also impact the musician; when she switches back to her original instrument, the fingering techniques she uses to play the new instrument interfere with her old techniques. Thus, proactive interference results from knowledge acquired in the past and retroactive interference is caused by information learned recently (**FIGURE 6.12**).

Although our memories fail us all the time, we manage to get by with a little help from our friends, who remind us to set our alarm clocks, study for tests, and say "happy birthday" to so and so. We have cell phones to store phone numbers and e-mail accounts to maintain addresses. The news media remind us what day it is. And then of course, there is Google.

DIDN'T SEE THAT COMING
Google Brain

Google. What would life be like without it? Every day, we use Google to find the answers to questions we are too embarrassed to ask out loud. It enables us to stay abreast of the latest news, provides us with immediate access to the voices and faces of friends, and helps us schedule our lives. Google is, without doubt, one of the modern brain's greatest helpers. But here's the question: Is all of Google's hard work making us lazy?

IS GOOGLE MAKING US LAZY?

Maybe "resourceful" is a better word. People essentially use computers as storage places for information they would otherwise have to remember (Sparrow & Chatman, 2013b; Sparrow, Liu, & Wegner, 2011). When researchers asked participants to read and type 40 statements referring to trivia-like information (for example, "An ostrich's eye is bigger than its brain"), those who were told they would need the information later *and* that it would be available on the computer were less likely to try memorizing it than

proactive interference The tendency for information learned in the past to interfere with the retrieval of new material.

retroactive interference The tendency for recently learned information to interfere with the retrieval of things learned in the past.

those denied computer access. Even those who were *not* asked to remember the information showed better recall if they had no expectations of searching for it on the computer (Sparrow et al., 2011). We have exceptional memory systems. But if information is not applicable to us, there is no need to remember it, especially when we can search for it online (Sparrow & Chatman, 2013b). Being able to continually access information may allow us to retrieve more of it over time, perhaps overestimating how much we remember, and thus influencing how much we actually study (Sparrow & Chatman, 2013a).

Thanks to Siri, Echo, and smartphones, it seems our culture has adapted to being constantly "plugged in" and having information at our fingertips. Remember the last time you lost Internet or cell phone service? "The experience of losing our Internet connection becomes more and more like losing a friend" (Sparrow et al., 2011, p. 4).👁❗

 **show what you know**

1. The _____ suggests that retrieving memories is easier in the context in which they were made.
   a. encoding specificity principle
   b. retroactive interference
   c. proactive interence
   d. curve of forgetting

2. Your friend remarks that her scores are better when she studies and takes the quiz in Starbucks than if she studies in Starbucks but takes the quiz at home. Lauren is exhibiting:
   a. context-dependent memory.
   b. proactive interference.
   c. retroactive interference.
   d. mood-congruent memory.

3. Ebbinghaus reported that his memory of word lists plunged the first hour after he learned them; he displayed this in his:
   a. encoding-specificity principle.
   b. curve of forgetting.
   c. recency effect.
   d. serial position effect.

4. What are some approaches you can use to make retrieving memories easier?

✓ CHECK YOUR ANSWERS IN APPENDIX C.

The Reliability of Memory

CONNECTIONS

In **Chapter 1,** we introduced the concepts of expectations and bias, noting that these can produce inaccuracies in thinking and research. Here, we describe the ways in which our memories can fail. As accurate as our thoughts and memories may seem, we must be aware that they are vulnerable to error.

Why do we need computers to help us keep track of the loads of information flooding our brains throughout the day? The answer is simple. We can't remember everything. We forget, and we forget often. Sometimes it's obvious an error has occurred (*I can't remember where I left my cell phone*), but other times it's less apparent. Have you noticed that when you recall a shared event, your version is not always consistent with those of other people? As you will soon discover, memories are not reliable records of reality. They are *malleable* (that is, capable of being changed or reshaped by various influences) and constantly updated and revised, like a wiki. Let's see how this occurs.

Misinformation: Can Memories Be Trusted?

LO 11 Explain how the malleability of memory influences the recall of events.

Elizabeth Loftus, a renowned psychologist and law professor, has been studying memory and its reliability for the last four decades. During the course of her career, she has been an expert witness in over 200 trials. The main focus of her work is the very problem we just touched upon: If two people have different memories of an event, whom do we believe?

MEMORY RECONSTRUCTED Loftus suggests that we should not expect our accounts of the past to be identical to those of other people or to even match our own previous renditions of events. According to Loftus, episodic memories are not exact duplicates of past events (recent or distant). Instead, she and others propose a *reconstructionist* model of memory "in which memories are understood as creative blendings of fact and fiction" (Loftus & Ketcham, 1994, p. 5). Over the course of time, memories can fade, and

misinformation effect The tendency for new and misleading information obtained after an incident to distort one's memory of it.

because they are permeable, they become more vulnerable to the invasion of new information. In other words, your memory of some event might include revisions to what really happened, based on knowledge, opinions, and information you have acquired since the event occurred.

Suppose you watch a debate between two presidential candidates on live television. A few days later, you see that same debate parodied on *Saturday Night Live.* Then a few weeks later, you try to remember the details of the actual debate—the topics discussed, the phrases used by the candidates, the clothes they wore. In your effort to recall the real event, you may very well incorporate some elements of the *Saturday Night Live* skit (for example, words or expressions used by the candidates). The memories we make are not precise depictions of reality, but representations of the world as we perceive it. With the passage of time, we lose bits and pieces of a memory, and unknowingly we replace them with new information. So if you need an accurate account of an event, you better get it right way. Eyewitnesses to crimes are often asked to rate their confidence in identifying a suspect. Researchers have found that "eyewitness confidence" is linked to the accuracy of the eyewitness account, but only when the confidence level is assessed at the time of the event. Simply stated, if the eyewitness has a high level of confidence in identifying a suspect *at the time of the crime,* her identification is more accurate (Wixted, Mickes, Clark, Gronlund, & Roediger, 2015).

THE MISINFORMATION EFFECT If you witnessed a car accident, how accurately would you remember it? Elizabeth Loftus and John Palmer (1974) tested the reliability of people's memories for such an event in a classic experiment. After showing participants a short film clip of a multiple-car accident, Loftus and Palmer quizzed them about what they had seen. They asked some participants, "About how fast were the cars going when they smashed into each other?" Replacing the word "smashed" with "hit," they asked others, "About how fast were the cars going when they hit each other?" Can you guess which version resulted in the highest estimates of speed? If you guessed "smashed," you are correct.

One week later, the researchers asked the participants to recall the details of the accident, including whether they had seen any broken glass in the film. Although no broken glass appears in the film, the researchers nevertheless predicted there would be some "yes" answers from participants who had initially been asked about the speed of the cars that "smashed" into each other. Their predictions were correct. Participants who had heard the word "smashed" apparently incorporated a faster speed in their memories, and were more likely to report having seen broken glass. Participants who had not heard the word "smashed" seemed to have a more accurate memory of the filmed car collision. The researchers concluded that memories can change in response to new information, and specifically that the participants' recollections were altered by the wording of a questionnaire (Loftus & Palmer, 1974). This research suggests that eyewitness accounts of accidents, crimes, and other important events might be altered by factors that come into play *after* the event occurs. Because memories are malleable, the wording of questions can change the way events are recalled, and care must be taken when questioning people about the past, whether it's in a therapist's office, a social service agency, or a police station.

Researchers have since conducted numerous studies on the **misinformation effect**, or the tendency for new and misleading information to distort one's memory of an incident. Studies with a variety of participants have resulted in their "remembering" a stop sign that was really a yield sign, a screwdriver that was really a hammer, and a barn that did not actually exist (Loftus, 2005).

Prosecutors often tell people who have witnessed crimes not to speak to each other, and with good reason. Suppose two people witnessed an elderly woman being robbed.

Fact or Fiction?
Hollywood doesn't always get the facts right, but moviegoers are not so good at ignoring false information conveyed by historical films. In fact, we often incorporate movie fallacies into our memories of historical events (Butler, Zaromb, Lyle, & Roediger, 2009; Zacks, 2015, February 13). For example, the 2014 movie *Selma* portrays a rocky relationship between President Lyndon B. Johnson and Martin Luther King Jr., but in reality the two men cooperated quite well (Kaiser, 2015, January 9). Nevertheless, many people would unknowingly conflate this movie portrayal with true historical knowledge they gathered through reading and school. © Paramount Pictures/Courtesy Everett Collection.

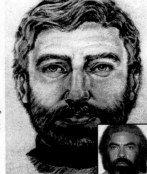

Memory Sketches
Comparing the two police sketches (left) and the more accurate drawing by sketch artist Jeanne Boylan (right), you see how renderings of the same individual can be dramatically different, even though all three were based on eyewitness information. Police sketches are based on the memories of eyewitnesses, each of whom has a unique—and potentially erroneous— memory of the suspect. COMPOSITE BY NATE CAPLIN/KRT/Newscom.

One eyewitness remembers seeing a bearded man wearing a blue jacket swiping the woman's purse. The other noticed the blue jacket but *not* the beard. If, however, the two eyewitnesses exchange stories of what they saw, the second eyewitness may unknowingly incorporate the beard into his "memory." Information learned after the event (that is, the "fact" that the thief had a beard) can get mixed up with memories of that event (Loftus, 2005; Loftus, Miller, & Burns, 1978). If we can instill this type of "false" information into a "true" memory, do you suppose it is possible to give people memories for events that never happened? Indeed, it is.

False Memories

LO 12 Define and explain the significance of rich false memory.

Elizabeth Loftus knows firsthand what it is like to have a memory implanted. Tragically, her mother drowned when she was 14 years old. For 30 years, she believed that someone else had found her mother's body in a swimming pool. But then her uncle, in the middle of his 90th birthday party, told her that she, Elizabeth, had found her mother's body. Loftus initially denied any memory of this horrifying experience, but as the days passed, she began to "recall" the event, including images of the pool, her mother's body, and numerous police cars arriving at the scene. These images continued to build for several days, until she received a phone call from her brother informing her that her uncle had been wrong, and that all her other relatives agreed Elizabeth was not the one who found her mother. According to Loftus, "All it took was a suggestion, casually planted" (Loftus & Ketcham, 1994, p. 40), and she was able to create a memory of an event she never witnessed. Following this experience, Loftus began to study **rich false memories**, that is, "wholly false memories" characterized by "the subjective feeling that one is experiencing a genuine recollection, replete with sensory details, and even expressed with confidence and emotion, even though the event never happened" (Loftus & Bernstein, 2005, p. 101).

Would you believe that about 25% of participants in rich false memory studies are able to "remember" an event that never happened? Using the "lost in the mall" technique, Loftus and Pickrell (1995) showed just how these imaginary memories take form. The researchers recruited a pair of family members (for example, parent–child or sibling–sibling) and then told them they would be participating in a study on memory. With the help of one of the members of the pair (the "relative"), the researchers recorded three true events from the pair's shared past and created a plausible story of a trip to a shopping mall that never happened. Then they asked the true "participant" to recall as many details as possible about each of the four events (remember, only three of the events were real), which were presented in a book provided by the researchers. If the participant could not remember any details from an event, he was instructed to write, "I do not remember this." In the "lost in the mall" story, the participant was told that he had been separated from the family in a shopping mall around the age of 5. According to the story, the participant began to cry, but was eventually helped by an elderly woman and was reunited with his family. Mind you, the "lost in the mall" episode was pure fiction, but it was made to seem real through the help of the participant's relative (who was working with the researchers). Following a series of interviews, the researchers concluded that 29% of the participants were able to "recall" either part or all of the fabricated "lost in the mall" experience (Loftus & Pickrell, 1995). These findings may seem shocking (they certainly caused a great uproar in the field), but keep in mind that a large majority of the participants did not "remember" the fabricated event (Hyman, Husband, & Billings, 1995; Loftus & Pickrell, 1995).

False Memories
Would you believe that looking at photo-shopped pictures can lead to the creation of false memories? In one study, researchers discovered that participants could "remember" hot air balloon rides they never took after looking at doctored photos of themselves as children on balloon rides. The researchers speculate that a photo "helps subjects to imagine details about the event that they later confuse with reality" (Garry & Gerrie, 2005, p. 321). Mike Sonnenberg/Getty Images.

CONTROVERSIES

The Debate over Repressed Childhood Memories

➡️⬅️ Given what you learned from the "lost in the mall" study, do you think it's possible that false memories can be planted by psychotherapy? Imagine a clini-

REAL OR IMAGINED? | cal psychologist or psychiatrist who firmly believes that her client was sexually abused as a child. The client has no memory of abuse, but the therapist is convinced that the abuse occurred and that the traumatic memory for it has been *repressed,* or unconsciously pushed below the threshold of awareness (see Chapter 11). Using methods such as hypnosis and dream analysis, the therapist helps the client resurrect a "memory" of the abuse (that presumably never occurred). Angry and hurt, the client then confronts the "abuser," who happens to be a close relative, and forever damages the relationship. Believe it or not, this scenario is very plausible. Consider these true stories picked from a long list:

- With the help of a psychiatrist, Nadean Cool came to believe that she was a victim of sexual abuse, a former member of a satanic cult, and a baby killer. She later claimed these to be false memories brought about in therapy (Loftus, 1997).

- Under the influence of prescription drugs and persuasive therapists, Lynn Price Gondolf became convinced that her parents molested her during childhood. Three years after accusing her parents of such abuse, she concluded the accusation was a mistake (Loftus & Ketcham, 1994).

- Laura Pasley "walked into her Texas therapist's office with one problem, bulimia, and walked out with another, incest" (Loftus, 1994, p. 44).

In the history of psychology, few topics have stirred up as much controversy as repressed memories, and the debate is still ongoing today (Brewin & Andrews, 2014; Patihis, Ho, Tingen, Lilienfeld, & Loftus, 2014; Patihis, Lilienfeld, Ho, & Loftus, 2014). Some psychologists believe that painful memories can indeed be repressed and recovered years or decades later, with a distinct gap between scientists who are skeptical of this and practitioners who are less so (Knapp & VandeCreek, 2000; Patihis, Ho, et al., 2014). The majority, however, would agree that the studies supporting the existence of repressed memories have many shortcomings (Piper, Lillevik, & Kritzer, 2008). Although childhood sexual abuse is shockingly common, with approximately 18% of girls and 8% of boys being affected worldwide (Stoltenborgh, Bakermans-Kranenburg, Alink, & IJzendoorn, 2015), there is *not* good evidence that these traumas are repressed. Even if they were, many believe retrieved memories of them would likely be inaccurate (Patihis, Ho, et al., 2014; Roediger & Bergman, 1998). Many trauma survivors face quite a different challenge—letting go of painful memories that continue to haunt them. (See the discussion of posttraumatic stress disorder in Chapter 12.)

The American Psychological Association (APA) and other authoritative mental health organizations have investigated the repressed memory issue at length. In 1998 the APA issued a statement offering its main conclusions, summarized below:

- Sexual abuse of children is very common and often unrecognized, and the repressed memory debate should not detract attention from this important issue.

- Most victims of sexual abuse have at least some memory of the abuse.

- Memories of past abuses can be forgotten and remembered at a later time.

CONNECTIONS

In **Chapter 4,** we described an altered state of consciousness called hypnosis that allows for changes in perceptions and behavior, resulting from suggestions made by the hypnotist. Here, we discuss the use of hypnosis in a therapeutic setting; the hypnotist is a therapist trying to help a client "remember" an abuse that the therapist believes has been repressed.

rich false memories Recollections of an event that never occurred, which are expressed with emotions and confidence and include details.

- People sometimes do create false memories of experiences they never had.

- We still do not completely understand how accurate and flawed memories of childhood abuse are formed (APA, 1998a).

Keep these points in mind next time you hear the term "repressed memory" tossed around in television talk shows, Internet posts, or casual conversations. You are now prepared with scientific knowledge to evaluate claims about repressed memories, so ask critical questions and maintain a healthy degree of skepticism. If you or someone you know is dealing with issues related to abuse, seek help from a licensed psychotherapist (APA, n.d.-c). ➜ ←

The main message of this section is that memory is malleable, or changeable. What are the implications for eyewitness accounts, especially those provided by children? If we are aware of how questions are structured and understand rewards and punishments from the perspective of a child, then the interview will produce fewer inaccuracies (Sparling, Wilder, Kondash, Boyle, & Compton, 2011). Researchers have found that having children close their eyes increases the accuracy of the testimony (Vredeveldt, Baddeley, & Hitch, 2014), but relying solely on their accounts has contributed to many cases of mistaken identity. In addition, the presence of someone in a uniform appears to put added pressure on child eyewitnesses, resulting in more guessing and inaccurate recall (Lowenstein, Blank, & Sauer, 2010).

The interrogation of people at any age can lead to serious, lifelong consequences. Following a series of interviews using suggestive memory-retrieval methods, 70% of the young adults participating in one study generated rich false memories of criminal behavior they had *not* committed during adolescence. They recalled incidents involving theft and assault, including interactions with the police that never happened! The implication is that some false confessions might be influenced by interrogation techniques that result in the false recall of crimes that were not committed. A person can believe he committed a crime that never happened, falsely confess to it, and then be wrongly convicted (Porter & Baker, 2015; Shaw & Porter, 2015).

Before you read on, take a minute and allow the words of Elizabeth Loftus to sink in: "Think of your mind as a bowl filled with clear water. Now imagine each memory as a teaspoon of milk stirred into the water. Every adult mind holds thousands of these murky memories. . . . Who among us would dare to disentangle the water from the milk?" (Loftus & Ketcham, 1994, pp. 3–4). What is the basis for all this murkiness? Time to explore the biological roots of memory.

Innocent
February 2016: Vanessa Gathers leaves a Brooklyn courthouse after her 1998 manslaughter conviction was overturned. Gathers served 10 years in prison after a detective manipulated her into giving a false confession (Nir, 2016, February 23). AP Photo/Seth Wenig.

○ ✓ ○ ○ **show what you know**

1. Your uncle claims he attended a school play in which you played the "Cowardly Lion." He has described the costume you wore, the lines you mixed up, and even the flowers he gave you. At first you can't remember the play, but eventually you seem to. Your mother insists you were never in that school play, and your uncle wasn't in the country that year, so he couldn't have attended the performance at all. Instead, you have experienced a:
   a. curve of forgetting.
   b. state-dependent memory.
   c. savings score.
   d. rich false memory.

2. The _____ refers to the tendency for new and misleading information to distort memories.

3. Loftus and Palmer (1974) conducted an experiment in which the wording of a question (using "smash" versus "hit") significantly influenced participants' recall of the event. What does this suggest about the malleability, or changeability, of memory?

✓ CHECK YOUR ANSWERS IN APPENDIX C.

The Biology of Memory

What did you do today? Did you have breakfast, brush your teeth, put your clothes on, drive your car, read an assignment, text a friend? Whatever you did, we are sure of one thing: It required a whole lot of memory. You could not send a text message without knowing how to spell, read, and use a cell phone—all things you had to learn and remember. Likewise, you could not drive without remembering how to unlock your car, start the engine, use the pedals. Memory is involved in virtually everything you do.

If memory is behind all your daily activities, important processes must be occurring in the brain to make this happen: both on the macro (large) and micro (small) scale. But as we learned from Clive's example, these processes are fragile and can be profoundly disrupted. Exploring the causes of memory failure can help us understand the biological basis of memory.

Amnesia

THE AFTERMATH In the months and years following Clive's illness, researchers administered many tests to assess his cognitive functioning. They found his IQ to be within an average range but his ability to remember past events deeply impaired. When prompted to name as many musical composers as possible in 1 minute, Clive—a man who had devoted his career to the study of music—could only produce four: Mozart, Beethoven, Bach, and Haydn. He denied that dragonflies have wings and claimed he had never heard of John F. Kennedy (Wilson et al., 1995).

Clive was even more disabled when it came to developing new memories. Initially, he could not hold onto incoming information for more than a blink of an eye. If his wife Deborah left the room, even for a short trip to the restroom, he would welcome her back as if she had been away for years—embracing, celebrating, sometimes weeping. "How long have I been ill?" he would ask, forgetting the answer and repeating himself within seconds (Wearing, 2005, p. 181). ●

Love Triumphs
Clive forgot many things, but not the love he has for his wife. Every time Deborah came to visit, he recognized her but could not recall their last meeting, even if it had happened just minutes before. Hugging, kissing, and sometimes twirling Deborah in the air, he would ask how much time had passed (Wearing, 2005). Jiri Rezac/ Polaris/Newscom.

LO 13 Compare and contrast anterograde and retrograde amnesia.

Amnesia, or memory loss, can result from either a physical or psychological condition. There are different types and degrees of amnesia, ranging from extreme (losing decades of autobiographical memories) to mild (temporarily forgetting people's names after a concussion).

ANTEROGRADE AMNESIA According to researchers, Clive suffers from "a more severe anterograde amnesia than any other patient previously reported" (Wilson et al., 1995, p. 680). **Anterograde amnesia** (ANT-er-oh-grade) is the inability to "lay down" or create new long-term memories (**FIGURE 6.13** on page 266), and it is generally caused by damage or injury to the brain, resulting from surgery, alcohol, head trauma, or illness. Someone with anterograde amnesia cannot form memories of events and experiences that occur following the brain damage, regardless of its cause. People affected by anterograde amnesia may be incapable of holding down a job, as their inability to lay down new memories affects their capacity to remember daily tasks. For Clive, his short-term memory still functioned to a certain extent, but he could only absorb and process information for several seconds before it was lost. From his perspective, every experience was fresh, and every person (with the exception of some he knew well from the past) a total stranger.

anterograde amnesia A type of memory loss; an inability to create new memories following damage or injury to the brain.

FIGURE 6.13
Retrograde and Anterograde Amnesia
Retro means "before," so retrograde amnesia is the inability to retrieve memories for events that occurred *before* an amnesia-causing injury. *Antero* means "after," so anterograde amnesia is the inability to form memories for events that occur *after* an injury. Photo: Getty Images Sport/ Getty Images.

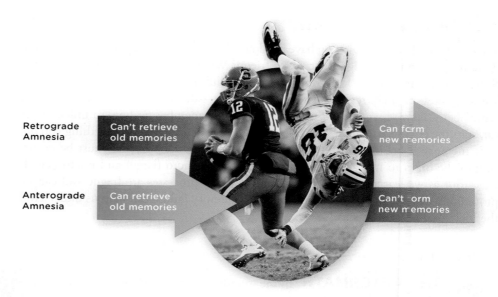

Retrograde Amnesia — Can't retrieve old memories → Can form new memories

Anterograde Amnesia — Can retrieve old memories → Can't form new memories

RETROGRADE AMNESIA A second type of memory loss is **retrograde amnesia**, an inability to access memories created before a brain injury or surgery (Brandt & Benedict, 1993; Figure 6.13). With retrograde amnesia, a person has difficulty retrieving old memories, though how "old" depends on the extent of trauma to the brain. People with retrograde amnesia generally remember who they are and the most important events of their earlier lives (Manns, Hopkins, & Squire, 2003; Squire & Wixted, 2011). Remember that *retrograde* refers to the inability to access old memories (think of "retro," meaning in the past, to help you distinguish between the terms), and *anterograde* refers to the inability to create new memories.

Clive suffered from retrograde amnesia in addition to his anterograde amnesia. While he appeared to retain a vague outline of his past (hazy information about his childhood, the fact that he had been a choral scholar at Clare College, Cambridge, and so on), he could not retrieve the names of his children unless prompted. And although Clive's children were all adults when he developed encephalitis, he came out of the illness thinking they were young children. The retrograde amnesia has improved, but only minimally. In 2005, for example, Clive asked his 40-something son what subjects he was studying in grammar school (equivalent to American high school). Nowadays when inquiring about his children, Clive simply asks, "What are they doing?" (D. Wearing, personal communication, June 18 and 25, July 11, 2013).

In spite of the severe retrograde and anterograde amnesia, some of Clive's memory functions continued to operate quite well. At one point, Deborah arranged for Clive to be reunited with the singers from the London Lassus Ensemble, a group he had conducted for more than a decade before his illness. At first, Clive paused and looked at the musicians with uncertainty, but then he raised his hands and began conducting, leading them through the music with precision and grace. Remembering the piece (which he had edited himself), Clive mouthed its words in Latin and employed the same tempo and conducting style he had used in the past (D. Wearing, personal communication, July 11, 2013). After the performance, the musicians left and Clive sat in the empty chapel wondering what had gone on there earlier (Wearing, 2005). When shown a video of himself leading the chorus, he remarked, "I wasn't conscious then" (Wilson et al., 2008). Clive's explicit memory of the event vanished in seconds, but his implicit memory—knowing how to conduct—was intact.

How is it possible that some of Clive's long-term memories were blotted out, while others, such as how to conduct music, remained fairly clear? The evidence

Synonyms

connectionism parallel distributed processing (PDP)

retrograde amnesia A type of memory loss; an inability to access memories formed prior to damage or injury to the brain, or difficulty retrieving them.

memory trace The location where memories are etched in the brain via physiological changes.

suggests that different types of long-term memories have distinct processing routes in the brain. Thus, damage to one area of the brain may impair some types of memory but not others. Let's take a closer look at where memories seem to be stored in the brain.

Where Memories Live in the Brain: A Macro Perspective

LO 14 Identify the brain structures involved in memory.

A few years after the onset of Clive's illness, doctors evaluated his brain using an MRI scan. A troubling picture emerged; the virus had destroyed many parts of his brain, notably the hippocampus, which plays a vital role in the creation of new memories (Wilson et al., 2008).

Only in the last 50 years have scientists come to appreciate the role of the hippo-campus in memory (**INFOGRAPHIC 6.2** on page 268). Back in the 1920s, psychologist Karl Lashley set out to find a **memory trace:** the physical spot where memories are etched in the brain, also called an *engram*. Lashley selected a group of rats that had learned the layout of specific mazes, and then made large cuts at different places in their cortices to see how this affected their memory of the mazes. No matter where Lashley sliced, the rats still managed to maneuver their way through the mazes (Costandi, 2009, February 10; Lashley, 1950). These findings led Lashley and other scientists to believe that memory is spread throughout the brain rather than local-ized in a particular region (Costandi, 2009, February 10; Kandel & Pittenger, 1999). *Connectionism* is a model that suggests our memories are distributed throughout the brain in a network of interlinked neurons.

CONNECTIONS

In **Chapter 2,** we described the hippocampus as a pair of curved structures buried deep within the temporal lobes. The hippocampus is primarily responsible for processing and making new memories, but is not where memories are permanently stored. It is also one of the brain areas where neurogenesis occurs, that is, where new neurons are generated.

THE CASE OF H.M. Henry Molaison (better known as "H.M.") forced scientists to completely reevaluate their understanding of the brain's memory system. From the onset of his amnesia in 1953 until his death in 2008, H.M. served as a research participant for some 100 scientists (Corkin, 2002), making him the most exten-sively studied amnesic patient.

H.M.'s brain troubles began at the age of 10, a year or so after being knocked unconscious in a bicycle accident. He began to experience seizures, which worsened with age and eventually be-came so debilitating that he could no longer hold a steady job. Antiseizure medications were unsuccessful in controlling his sei-zures, so at the age of 27, H.M. opted for an experimental surgery to remove parts of his brain: the temporal lobes (just beneath the temples), including the hippocampus (Scoville & Milner, 1957).

H.M.'s surgery succeeded in reining in his epilepsy but left his memory in shambles. Upon waking from the operation, he could no longer find his way to the bathroom or recognize the hospital workers car-ing for him. He played with the same jigsaw puzzles and read the same magazines day after day as if he were seeing them for the first time (Scoville & Milner, 1957). Like Clive, H.M. suffered from profound *anterograde amnesia,* the inability to encode new long-term memories, and a milder form of *retrograde amnesia,* trouble retrieving existing memories from storage. Although H.M. had difficulty recalling what occurred during the few years leading up to his surgery (Scoville & Milner, 1957), he did remember events from the more distant past, for example, the 1929 stock market crash and the events of World War II (Carey, 2008, December 4).

Project H.M.

Dr. Jacopo Annese, director of the Brain Observatory at the University of San Diego, stands in front of a massive digital image rendered from a slice of brain tissue preserved on a slide. Dr. Annese and his team carved the brain of amnesiac Henry Molaison, or "H.M.," into 2,401 slices to create a digital model (Annese et al., 2014). John Gibbins/ ZUMApress/Newscom.

Tracking Memory in the Brain

Whether with lab rats or case studies, psychologists have spent decades tracking the location of memory in the brain. What they've found so far should be no surprise: Memory is a complex system involving multiple structures and regions of the brain. Memory is formed, processed, and stored throughout the brain, and different types of memory have different paths. So to find memory in the brain, it helps to know your way around the brain's structures. Remembering the amygdala's role in processing basic emotion, for instance, can help you understand its role in processing the emotional content of memories.

Forming New Memories

In an attempt to control the disabling seizures of a man named Henry Molaison (H.M.) doctors surgically removed portions of his brain, including the hippocampus. The surgery affected H.M.'s memory. He had profound anterograde amnesia: He could tap into old memories, but he could no longer make new explicit memories. However, he could still create implicit memories. Using information gathered about H.M.'s brain, scientists have been able to directly connect the hippocampus to the creation of new explicit memories.

After his death, H.M.'s brain was cut into over 2,000 slices that were preserved and digitized for research.

John Gibbins/ZUMApress/Newscom.

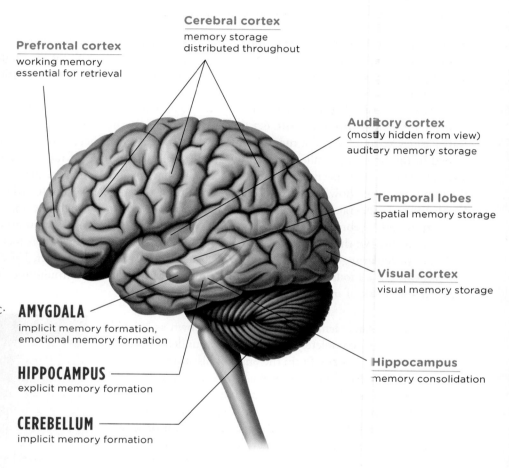

Prefrontal cortex
working memory
essential for retrieval

Cerebral cortex
memory storage
distributed throughout

Auditory cortex
(mostly hidden from view)
auditory memory storage

Temporal lobes
spatial memory storage

Visual cortex
visual memory storage

AMYGDALA
implicit memory formation,
emotional memory formation

HIPPOCAMPUS
explicit memory formation

CEREBELLUM
implicit memory formation

Hippocampus
memory consolidation

Journal of Comparative Neurology, K. S. Lashley,
L. E. Wiley, Copyright © 1933 The Wistar Institute
of Anatomy and Biology.

Lashley kept a careful record of the sizes and locations of lesions made in each rat as part of his experiments.

Storing Memories

Through his experiments slicing the cortices of rats that had learned to navigate mazes, Karl Lashley concluded that complex memories are not localized to a particular region in the cortex, but are instead widely distributed. Later research has established the interrelated roles of specific structures in the process of encoding, storing and retrieving memories.

In a process called *memory consolidation,* which occurs in the hippocampus, memories are moved to other parts of the cerebral cortex for long-term storage. Research on this topic is ongoing. For instance, scientists have been able to link explicit memory storage to areas of the brain where the original sensation was processed (see Harris, Petersen, & Diamond, 2001).

H.M. maintained a working implicit memory, which he demonstrated in an experiment involving the complex task of tracing a pattern reflected in a mirror. With repeated practice sessions (none of which he remembered), H.M. improved his performance on the drawing task, learning it as well as someone without amnesia (Gabrieli, Corkin, Mickel, & Growdon, 1993). Clive can also acquire new implicit memories, but his ability is very limited. According to Deborah, it took years for Clive to learn how to get to his bedroom in the small community residence where he moved after leaving the hospital (Wearing, 2005).

THE ROLE OF THE HIPPOCAMPUS Imagine you are a scientist trying to figure out exactly what role the hippocampus plays in memory. Consider the facts you know about H.M.: (1) He has virtually no hippocampus; (2) he has lost the ability to make new *explicit* memories, yet can create *implicit* memories; and (3) he can still tap into memories of the distant past. So what do you think the hippocampus does? Evidence suggests that the hippocampus is essential for creating new explicit memories but *not* implicit memories. Researchers have also shown that explicit memories are processed and stored in other parts of the brain, including the temporal lobes and areas of the frontal cortex (García-Lázaro, Ramirez-Carmona, Lara-Romero, & Roldan-Valadez, 2012).

As in H.M.'s case, Clive's ability to form explicit memories is profoundly compromised, largely a result of the destruction of his hippocampus. Yet Clive also struggles with the creation of implicit memories—not surprising given the extensive damage to other regions of his brain, such as the amygdala and temporal lobes (Wilson et al., 2008). Studies have zeroed in on other brain areas, such as the cerebellum and amygdala, as processing hubs for implicit memory (Thompson & Kim, 1996; Thompson & Steinmetz, 2009). The amygdala plays a central role in the processing of emotional memories (García-Lázaro et al., 2012). See Infographic 6.2 for more information about memory processing in the brain.

So although the hippocampus plays a central role in laying down new memories, it does not appear to serve as their ultimate destination. This process of memory formation, which moves a memory from the hippocampus to other areas of the brain, is called *memory consolidation* (Squire & Bayley, 2007). The consolidation that begins in the hippocampus allows for the long-term storage of memories. According to Kandel and Pittenger (1999): "The final locus of storage of memory is widely assumed to be the cerebral cortex, though this is a difficult assertion to prove" (p. 2041). As for retrieval, the hippocampus appears to be in charge of accessing young memories, but then passes on that responsibility to other brain regions as memories grow older (Smith & Squire, 2009).

This idea that the hippocampus is essential for creating explicit memories (as opposed to implicit memories) is supported by what we know about *infantile amnesia,* that is, the inability to remember events from our earliest years. Most adults cannot remember events before the age of 3, though it is not clear why. Some researchers suggest that it is because the hippocampus and frontal cortex, both important for the creation of long-term explicit memories, are not fully developed in children (Bauer, 2006; Willoughby, Desrocher, Levine, & Rovet, 2012). Simply stated, young children do not construct complete episodic memories of their experiences (Bauer & Larkina, 2014). We are less likely to forget memories starting around age 7 due to the type of memories we begin generating (more elaborate and personally relevant). The efficiency of how the memories are formed (more effective neural processes) also make these memories "more impervious to the ravages of forgetting" (Bauer, 2015, p. 225).

For most people, the average age of first memory is from an event that happened around the age of 3 or 4. What's your first memory?

What's Your First Memory?

You might expect that your earliest recollection would be dramatic—yet for most of us, it is fairly mundane. Only about a quarter of people report a first memory that involves a trauma, according to a 2005 study. *Scientific American Mind*'s online survey of readers' first memories uncovered the same pattern [*see chart below*].

Young children are more likely to recall an event if they are prompted to talk about it and probed for details. Perhaps that is why the age at which a memory first sticks varies across cultures. Among the Maori of New Zealand, for example, most children's memories start a year earlier than they do in North America—a function of a culture in which memories are honored and much discussed, according to researcher Carole Peterson of Memorial University in Newfoundland. —*V.S.* **Victoria Stern. Reproduced with permission. Copyright © 2014 Scientific American, a division of Nature America, Inc. All rights reserved.**

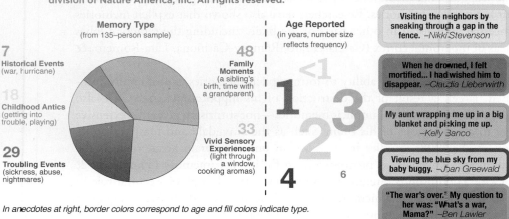

Memory Type
(from 135–person sample)

7
Historical Events
(war, hurricane)

18
Childhood Antics
(getting into trouble, playing)

29
Troubling Events
(sickness, abuse, nightmares)

48
Family Moments
(a sibling's birth, time with a grandparent)

33
Vivid Sensory Experiences
(light through a window, cooking aromas)

Age Reported
(in years, number size reflects frequency)

<1 1 2 3 4 6

In anecdotes at right, border colors correspond to age and fill colors indicate type.

I remember the long dirt road leading to the house, and thinking that the other way might lead to heaven. –*Ben Alon*

Running toward the edge of a steep cliff. My father ran and caught me. –*Amalia Liontaki*

My mother came home from the hospital with my brother... a small, white bundle. –*A. Adams*

Visiting the neighbors by sneaking through a gap in the fence. –*Nikki Stevenson*

When he drowned, I felt mortified... I had wished him to disappear. –*Claudia Lieberwirth*

My aunt wrapping me up in a big blanket and picking me up. –*Kelly Banco*

Viewing the blue sky from my baby buggy. –*Joan Greewald*

"The war's over." My question to her was: "What's a war, Mama?" –*Ben Lawler*

. . . .

The macrolevel perspective presented in this section allows us to see the "big picture" of memory, but what's going on microscopically? Next we will focus on the important changes occurring in and between neurons.

Where Memories Live in the Brain: A Micro Perspective

LO 15 Describe long-term potentiation and its relationship to memory.

How does your brain change when you learn a new driving route to school? If we could peer into your skull, we might see a change in your hippocampus. Now imagine what might happen in the brain of a taxicab driver in London, who must memorize the 25,000 streets in the city, including their businesses and landmarks. As one study found, London taxicab drivers with greater time spent on the job had structural changes in some regions of the hippocampus, particularly to an area that processes "spatial knowledge" (Maguire, Woollett, & Spiers, 2006; Rosen, 2014, November 10). Zooming in for a closer look, we might actually see changes at the level of the neuron. If you are looking for a memory imprint, the best place to look is the synapse.

LONG-TERM POTENTIATION As it turns out, the more neurons communicate with each other, the better the connections between them. **Long-term potentiation** occurs when sending neurons release neurotransmitters more effectively, and receiving neurons become more sensitive, boosting synaptic strength for days or even weeks (Lynch, 2002;

CONNECTIONS

In **Chapter 2,** we introduced the synapse: the tiny gap between two neurons. Neurons communicate with each other via chemicals called neurotransmitters, which are released into the synapse. Here, we see how the activities at the neural level are related to the formation and maintenance of memories.

long-term potentiation The increased efficiency of neural communication over time, resulting in learning and the formation of memories.

Malenka & Nicoll, 1999; Whitlock, Heynen, Shuler, & Bear, 2006). In other words, long-term potentiation refers to the increased efficiency of neural communication over time, resulting in learning and the formation of memories. Researchers suggest long-term potentiation may be the biological basis for many kinds of learning. As you

Smart Slug
Studying the neurons of sea slugs, researchers have observed the synaptic changes that underlie memory. Long-term potentiation enables a sea slug to retract its gills in anticipation of being squirted with water.
NaturePL/Superstock.

learn a new skill, for example, the neurons involved in performing that skill increase their communication with each other. It might start with a somewhat random firing of neurons, but eventually the neurons responsible for the new skill develop pathways through which they communicate more efficiently. Having trouble visualizing the process? Imagine this scenario: Your college has opened a new campus with an array of brand-new buildings, but it has yet to construct the sidewalks connecting them. In order to go from one class to the next, students have to wade through tall grass and weeds. All the trampling eventually gives way to a system of paths linking the buildings, including a multitude of efficient paths that develop among them. Long-term potentiation of neural connections occurs in a similar fashion: Over time, the communication among neurons improves and strengthens, allowing for the skill to develop and become more natural (Whitlock et al., 2006). These paths represent how a skill, whether tying your shoes or driving a stick shift, is learned and thus becomes a memory.

APLYSIA Amazingly, we have learned much about long-term potentiation from the sea slug *Aplysia,* which has only about 20,000 neurons (Kandel, 2009)—a little easier to work with than the billions of neurons in a human brain. The fact that the sea slug's synapses are relatively easy to examine individually also allows for the intensive study of habituation and other processes involved in classical conditioning. Studies using sea slugs as their subjects indicate that long-term potentiation, or increases in synaptic "strength," is associated with learning and memory. **What can a sea slug learn**? They can be classically conditioned to retract their gills in response to being squirted with water, resulting in structural changes to both presynaptic and postsynaptic cells, including changes to connections between neurons (Kandel, 2009)—evidence of long-term potentiation. So never, ever complain that you cannot learn: If a sea slug can do it, so can you!

CONNECTIONS

In **Chapter 5,** we discussed classical conditioning and how a neutral stimulus can be paired with an unconditioned stimulus, ultimately leading to a conditioned stimulus resulting in a conditioned response. In the case of the sea slug, the squirt of water is the conditioned stimulus and its involuntary response of retracting its gills is the conditioned response.

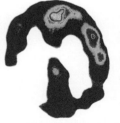

ALZHEIMER'S DISEASE On a less positive note, disruptions in long-term potentiation appear to be at work in *Alzheimer's disease,* a progressive, devastating brain illness that causes cognitive decline, including memory, language, and thinking problems. Alzheimer's affects upwards of 5 million Americans (National Institute on Aging, n.d.). The disease was first discovered by Alois Alzheimer, a German neuropathologist, in the early 1900s. He had a patient with severe memory problems whose autopsy revealed that neurons in her brain had become tangled like the wires of your earbud headphones. These *neurofibrillary tangles,* as they came to be called, were eventually shown to result from twisted protein fibers accumulating inside brain cells. In addition to the tangles, the other distinctive sign of Alzheimer's is the presence of *amyloid plaques,* protein clumps that build up between neurons, blocking their lines of communication (Vingtdeux, Davies, Dickson, & Marambaud, 2011).

NATURE AND NURTURE
Why Alzheimer's?

By the year 2050, Alzheimer's disease is expected to affect approximately 106 million people in the United States, with an associated annual cost of $1.2 trillion (Alzheimer's Association, 2013b; Demartini, Schilling, da Costa, & Carlini, 2014). Clearly, it is imperative that we uncover the causes of Alzheimer's disease and take steps to prevent it.

IF YOUR FATHER OR SISTER HAS ALZHEIMER'S, ARE YOU AT HIGHER RISK?

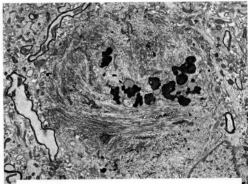

Inside Alzheimer's
The PET scan (top left) depicts the brain of a normal person, while the scan to the right shows that of a person with Alzheimer's. Studies using PET suggest a slowing of brain activity in certain regions of the Alzheimer's brain (Alzheimer's Association, 2013a). The neurofibrillary tangles (bottom image, with tangles in pink) result from twisted protein fibers accumulating inside brain cells. Top: Jessica Wilson/Science Source. Bottom: Thomas Deerinck, NCMIR/Science Source.

While we still don't have a solid understanding of what causes Alzheimer's, we know some forms of the disease are inherited. People who have a first-degree relative (a parent, sibling, or child) with Alzheimer's have a higher risk for developing the disease. Researchers have zeroed in on a certain gene, APOEε4, which seems to predispose people to Alzheimer's (Liu, Kanekiyo, Xu, & Bu, 2013). But we also know that factors such as diet and exercise can influence the development and progression of the disease (Alzheimer's Association, 2013b). Being obese and sedentary can heighten one's risk; in fact, studies suggest that the standard American diet (one that is high in sugar, fats, and processed food, and low in fruits, vegetables, and whole grains) can cause "nutrient deficiency and inflammation that could impact cognition directly" (Graham et al., 2016, p. 2). Even the air we breathe may play a role, as long-term exposure to air pollution has been linked to cognitive decline in older adults (Ailshire & Clarke, 2014; Gatto et al., 2014; Weuve et al., 2012).

Alzheimer's disease clearly results from a combination of nature and nurture. While we can't change our genetic code, we can take preventative measures to reduce our risk of cognitive decline in general. Healthy eating; staying physically, mentally, and socially active; and doing our part to reduce pollution are good places to start. ◐ ♠

No cure for Alzheimer's disease exists, and current treatments focus only on reducing the severity of symptoms rather than correcting the brain damage responsible. But there is also reason to be hopeful. Promising new drugs are coming down the pipeline, and some preliminary evidence suggests that simple lifestyle changes, like becoming more physically active and pursuing intellectually and socially stimulating activities, may actually decrease the speed and severity of cognitive decline (Hertzog, Kramer, Wilson, & Lindenberger, 2009, July/August; Walsh, 2011; Wilson & Bennett, 2003). Additional good news comes from research suggesting that we should not think of cognitive decline as inevitable in aging. We have more control of aging than previously thought, especially when we focus on the lifelong possibilities of learning and independence (Hertzog et al., 2009). Furthermore, it's not only the strengthening of synapses that makes for enduring memories, but also the activation of new ones (Yu, Ponomarev, & Davis, 2004), and this process could offset cognitive decline (**TABLE 6.2**).

TABLE 6.2   FACTS ABOUT MEMORY LOSS

Category	Facts
Family	There is no definitive way to know whether you or a family member will suffer from a neurocognitive disorder; most cases result from a complex combination of genetic, environmental, and lifestyle factors.
Exercise	Studies of both animals and people have linked physical exercise to a variety of positive changes in the brain, including enhanced blood flow, increased thickness of the cortex, and less age-related deterioration of the hippocampus (Polidori, Nelles, & Pientka, 2010). Some research suggests that people who begin exercising in their thirties (and stick with it) experience less cognitive decline than their sedentary peers by the time they reach their forties and fifties (Hertzog, Kramer, Wilson, & Lindenberger, 2009, July/August), although consistent exercise at any age has lasting cognitive benefits (Cotman & Berchtold, 2002; Kramer, Erickson, & Colcombe, 2006).
Intellectual stimulation	Intellectually engaging activities such as reading books and newspapers, writing, drawing, and solving crossword puzzles have been associated with a lower risk of memory loss (Hertzog et al., 2009, July/August; Wang, Karp, Winblad, & Fratiglioni, 2002).
Social activity	Being socially active and hooked into social networks may reduce the risk of developing dementia (Fratiglioni, Paillard-Borg, & Winblad, 2004).

Memory loss needn't be an inevitable part of aging. Above are some facts you should know.

CHRONIC TRAUMATIC ENCEPHALOPATHY Similar in some ways to Alzheimer's disease, *chronic traumatic encephalopathy* (CTE) is distinct in its progression and impact on memory (McKee et al., 2013). CTE is a neurodegenerative disease that leads to atypical deposits of the tau protein throughout various regions in the brain as a result of repeated mild traumatic brain injury. This disease affects football players, soccer players, wrestlers, rugby players, boxers, hockey players, lacrosse players, combat war veterans, and many other people who have suffered impact to the head (Maroon et al., 2015; McKee et al., 2016). Symptoms include significant memory issues, impulsivity, aggression, insomnia, and depression. CTE is progressive, and symptoms may not appear for months to years following the impact, and can only be diagnosed after death (Kirk, Gilmore, & Wiser, 2013; McKee et al., 2013). Who's at risk and what are some of the more obvious symptoms of CTE? Discover the answers in **INFOGRAPHIC 6.3** on page 274.

As we continue to learn more about CTE, parents must make difficult decisions about the type of sports they encourage their children to participate in. Approximately 4 million concussions are reported every year as a result of playing sports, but it is estimated that 50% of all concussions may not be reported (Harmon et al., 2013). Further, the subconcussive hits (those not hard enough to cause a concussion) may also put athletes at risk for the development of this disease (Harmon et al., 2013).

Like many topics psychologists study, the biological mechanisms that give rise to memory remain somewhat mysterious. We know we have memories, we know they are formed in the brain, and we know the brain is a physical entity; yet we still don't know exactly how we go from an array of firing neurons to a vivid recollection of your 21st birthday bash, your high school prom, or the image of Bruno Mars banging on his drums at the Super Bowl halftime show. Studies attempting to test the various theories of memory formation are inconclusive, often generating more questions than answers. But one thing seems certain: Memory researchers face plenty of important work ahead.

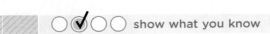 **show what you know**

1. _____ refers to the inability to lay down new long-term memories, generally resulting from damage to the brain.
   a. Anterograde amnesia   **c.** Infantile amnesia
   b. Retrograde amnesia   **d.** Long-term potentiation

2. The _____ is a pair of curved structures in the brain that play a central role in memory.
   a. engram   **c.** hippocampus
   b. temporal lobe   **d.** aplysia

3. _____ is the process of memory formation, which moves a memory from the hippocampus to other areas of the brain.
   a. Long-term potentiation   **c.** Priming
   b. Memory consolidation   **d.** The memory trace

4. Infantile amnesia makes it difficult for people to remember events that occurred before the age of 3. What is your earliest memory and how old were you when that event occurred?

✓ CHECK YOUR ANSWERS IN APPENDIX C.

FINAL THOUGHTS At this point, you may be wondering what became of Clive Wearing. After living in the hospital for 7 years, Clive moved to a country residence specially designed for people suffering from brain injuries. As he left the hospital, some of the staff members offered him a farewell and said they would miss him. Addressing them with a polite bow, Clive exclaimed, "You're the first people I've seen!" When Deborah would visit Clive in his new home, she found him happy and relaxed, spending much of his time on walks through gardens and the local village (Wearing, 2005, p. 293). In 2002 Clive and Deborah renewed their marriage vows. Clive participated fully in the service, reciting scripture he had memorized during his career as a professional singer decades before (D. Wearing, personal communication, June 10, 2013). After the ceremony, he had no recollection of what had taken place but nevertheless was very happy, laughing and devouring sponge cake (Wearing, 2005). ●

Onward
Nearly two decades after falling ill, Clive renewed his wedding vows with Deborah. Now in his seventies, Clive lives in a country residence for people suffering from brain injuries (Vennard, 2011, November 21). Jiri Rezac/Polaris/Newscom.

Chronic Traumatic Encephalopathy

Chronic Traumatic Encephalopathy (CTE) is a progressive neurodegenerative disease caused by a single or repeated blow to the head. CTE affects athletes of many types, combat war veterans, and many others who experience head trauma (Maroon et al., 2015; McKee et al., 2016). The symptoms, which may not appear for months or years after the injury, include changes to memory, emotions, thinking, and personality. CTE is somewhat similar to other neurodegenerative diseases like Alzheimer's and Parkinson's in that it can impair memory, movement, and the ability to plan and carry out everyday tasks (McKEE, et al., 2013).

In 2012, after 20 seasons as an NFL player, **Junior Seau** committed suicide at age 43. In the years leading to his death, Seau's family noticed a change in his thinking, personality, and enthusiasm for the game. Impulsive gambling, alcoholism and violence became the new conversation around the man once known as a beloved philanthropist (FAINARU-WADA, 2013 FEBRUARY 15). Upon his death, his brain showed the hallmarks of CTE (NINDS, 2013 JANUARY 10).

Retired soccer star **Brandi Chastain** has announced she will donate her brain to research. Chastain believes this will be a bigger legacy than her goal-winning shot in the 1999 World Cup. Like many soccer players, Chastain advocates the banning of headers in youth soccer. (BRANCH, 2016 MARCH).

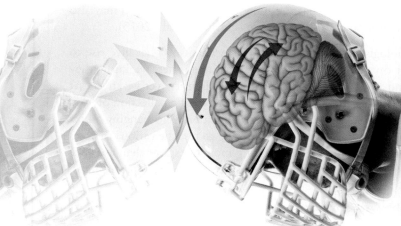

THE PROGRESSION OF CTE

Stage 1
Tau protein accumulates locally in the cortex.

Symptoms: headaches, and difficulty maintaining focus.

Stage 2
The damage spreads to surrounding areas.

Symptoms: short-term memory impairment, mood swings, depression, explosive temper, and continued headaches and trouble focusing.

Stage 3
Damage continues to spread, reaching areas such as the hippocampus, amygdala, and brainstem.

Symptoms: memory loss, difficulty planning and carrying out tasks, "visuospatial abnormalities," and ongoing difficulties with mood and attention.

Stage 4
Widespread damage across many regions of the brain, including the medial temporal lobe, hypothalamus, and thalamus.

Symptoms: worsening of existing symptoms, along with language difficulties and paranoia. Severe memory loss.

How does CTE differ from other neurodegenerative diseases such as Alzheimer's? Symptoms associated with CTE typically present around age 40, while those of Alzheimer's generally appear around 60. Changes in thinking, cognition, and personality are common symptoms of CTE, while Alzheimer's is typically associated with memory problems (FREQUENTLY ASKED QUESTIONS, n.d). However, emerging research suggests that behavioral changes and "neuropsychiatric symptoms" (depression or anxiety, for example) may signal the beginning of the disease process in Alzheimer's patients (DONOVAN et al., 2014; ISMAIL, 2016).

6

summary of concepts

LO 1 Define memory. (p. 235)

Memory refers to the information collected and stored in the brain that is generally available for later use. Exactly how the brain absorbs information from the outside world and files it for later use is still not completely understood. However, scientists have proposed many theories and constructed various models to help explain how the brain processes, or works on, data on their way to becoming memories.

LO 2 Describe the processes of encoding, storage, and retrieval. (p. 236)

Encoding is the process through which new information enters our memory system. Information is taken in by our senses and converted into neural activity that travels to the brain, and if successfully encoded, it is stored. Storage preserves the information for possible recollection in the future. Retrieval is the process of accessing information stored in memory.

LO 3 Explain the stages of memory described by the information-processing model. (p. 239)

According to the information-processing model, the brain has three types of memory storage associated with the stages of memory: sensory memory, short-term memory, and long-term memory.

LO 4 Describe sensory memory. (p. 240)

Data picked up by the senses enter sensory memory, where sensations are registered. Here, almost exact copies of our sensations are processed for a very brief moment. Information from the outside world floods our sensory memory through multiple channels. Although this stage of memory is fleeting, it is critical to the creation of memories.

LO 5 Summarize short-term memory. (p. 242)

Short-term memory is the second stage of the original information-processing model. This is where information is temporarily maintained and processed before moving on to long-term memory or leaving the memory system. Short-term memory has a limited capacity; how long and how much it can hold depends on how much you are distracted by other cognitive activities. Through maintenance rehearsal, we can prolong short-term memory.

LO 6 Give examples of how we can use chunking to improve our memory span. (p. 242)

Grouping numbers, letters, or other items into meaningful subsets, or "chunks," is an effective strategy for juggling and increasing the amount of information in short-term memory. In addition, chunking can help nudge the same information into long-term memory.

LO 7 Describe working memory and its relationship to short-term memory (p. 243).

The active processing component of short-term memory, working memory, has four important parts. The phonological loop is responsible for working with verbal information for brief periods of time. The visuospatial sketchpad is where visual and spatial data are briefly stored and manipulated. The central executive directs attention, makes plans, coordinates activities, and determines what information should be ignored. The episodic buffer is where information from the phonological loop, visuospatial sketchpad, and long-term memory can all be brought together temporarily, as directed by the central executive.

LO 8 Describe long-term memory. (p. 245)

Long-term memory is a stage of memory with essentially unlimited capacity. Long-term memories may be explicit or implicit. Explicit memory is the type of memory you are aware of having and can consciously express, and can be further divided into semantic and episodic memory. Semantic memory pertains to general facts about the world, while episodic memory is your record of the memorable experiences in your life. Implicit memory is for something you know or you know how to do, but that might be automatic or unconscious, and therefore difficult to articulate.

LO 9 Illustrate how encoding specificity relates to retrieval cues. (p. 254)

Retrieval cues are stimuli that help you retrieve stored information that is difficult to access. The encoding specificity principle states that memories are more easily recalled when the context and cues at the time of encoding are similar to those at the time of retrieval. Thus, the context (external or internal) at the time of encoding and retrieval provides retrieval cues. Priming, recall, and recognition also play a role in the retrieval of stored information.

LO 10 Identify and explain some of the reasons why we forget. (p. 257)

Memory failure may occur during any of the three stages of memory processing: encoding, storage, and retrieval. One example of memory failure is the tip-of-the-tongue phenomenon, which occurs when we cannot retrieve a stored memory.

LO 11 Explain how the malleability of memory influences the recall of events. (p. 260)

Eyewitness accounts are not always reliable because people's memories are far from perfect. Memories can change over time, which means we lose bits and pieces of a memory, and unknowingly replace them with new information; this can influence the recall of the event.

LO 12 Define and explain the significance of rich false memory. (p. 262)

Rich false memories are experienced as true recollections of an event, including details, emotions, and confidence that the event occurred, although it never did. Some researchers have managed to implant false memories in the minds of participants.

LO 13 Compare and contrast anterograde and retrograde amnesia. (p. 265)

There are varying degrees of amnesia, or memory loss, due to medical or psychological conditions. Anterograde amnesia is the inability to "lay down" or create new long-term memories, and is generally caused by damage to the brain resulting from surgery, alcohol, head trauma, or illness. Retrograde amnesia is an inability to access memories created before a brain injury or surgery.

LO 14 Identify the brain structures involved in memory. (p. 267)

Researchers have identified many brain structures involved in the processing and storage of memory. The hippocampus is essential for creating new explicit memories, as are the temporal lobes and frontal cortex. Other areas, such as the cerebellum and amygdala, are integral in the processing of implicit memories.

LO 15 Describe long-term potentiation and its relationship to memory. (p. 270)

Long-term potentiation refers to the increased efficiency of neural communication over time, resulting in learning and the formation of memories. The communication among neurons improves and strengthens, allowing for new skills to develop and become more natural. These new pathways explain how a skill, for example, is learned and thus becomes an implicit memory.

key terms

anterograde amnesia, p. 265
chunking, p. 242
distributed practice, p. 250
echoic memory, p. 241
effortful processing, p. 249
elaborative rehearsal, p. 249
encoding, p. 236
encoding specificity principle, p. 255
episodic memory, p. 246
explicit memory, p. 245

flashbulb memory, p. 246
iconic memory, p. 241
implicit memory, p. 246
long-term memory, p. 239
long-term potentiation, p. 270
maintenance rehearsal, p. 242
massed practice, p. 250
memory, p. 235
memory trace, p. 267

misinformation effect, p. 261
mnemonic, p. 247
primacy effect, p. 254
priming, p. 253
proactive interference, p. 259
procedural memory, p. 247
recall, p. 253
recency effect, p. 254
recognition, p. 253
relearning, p. 256

retrieval, p. 236
retrieval cues, p. 253
retroactive interference, p. 259
retrograde amnesia, p. 266
rich false memories, p. 262
semantic memory, p. 246
sensory memory, p. 239
serial position effect, p. 254
short-term memory, p. 239
storage, p. 236
working memory, p. 243

test prep *are you ready?*

1. You try to remember the name of a movie you watched last year, but struggle to recall it. When you do finally remember the film was *The Martian,* which memory process were you using?
   a. short-term memory
   b. sensory memory
   c. encoding
   d. retrieval

2. According to the levels of processing framework, there is a _____ that corresponds to the depth at which information is processed, as well as reflecting how durable and retrievable a memory may be.
   a. hierarchy of processing
   b. computer metaphor
   c. method of loci
   d. phonological loop

3. Using the partial report method, Sperling (1960) showed that participants could recall 76% of the letters briefly flashed on a screen. The findings from this study indicate the capabilities of:

    a. eidetic imagery.
    b. depth of processing.
    c. iconic memory.
    d. the phonological loop.

4. Miller (1956) reviewed findings from the Digit Span Test and found that short-term memory capacity is limited to between 5 and 9 numbers, that is, the "magical number seven, plus or minus two." However, through the use of _____, we can improve the span of our short-term memory.

    a. echoic memory
    b. iconic memory
    c. multitasking
    d. chunking

5. Baddeley and colleagues proposed that the purpose of _____ is to actively maintain information while the mind is performing complex tasks. The phonological loop, visuospatial sketchpad, central executive, and episodic buffer all play a role in this process.

    a. eidetic imagery
    b. working memory
    c. short-term memory
    d. semantic memory

6. In a classic study, Godden and Baddeley (1975) asked participants to learn lists of words under two conditions: while underwater and on dry land. Participants were better able to recall the information in the same context in which it was encoded. This finding supports:

    a. the encoding specificity principle.
    b. Baddeley's working memory model.
    c. the serial position effect.
    d. the information-processing model of memory.

7. Your friend tells you she prefers multiple-choice tests because she is able to identify an answer when she sees it listed as one of the choices for a question. She is describing her _____, which is the process of matching incoming data to information stored in long-term memory.

    a. relearning
    b. recall
    c. recognition
    d. retrieval

8. _____ causes problems with the retrieval of memories because of information you learned in the past and _____ causes problems with retrieval due to recently learned information.

    a. The recency effect; the primacy effect
    b. The primacy effect; the recency effect
    c. Proactive interference; retroactive interference
    d. Retroactive interference; proactive interference

9. According to _____, memories can fade over time, becoming more vulnerable to new information. Thus, your memory of an event might include revisions of what really happened.

    a. the information-processing model of memory
    b. the levels of processing framework
    c. Baddeley's model of working memory
    d. a reconstructionist model of memory

10. In studies by Loftus and colleagues, around 25% of participants are able to "remember" an event that never happened. This type of _____ shows us how the malleability of memory can influence recall.

    a. hyperthymestic syndrome
    b. rich false memory
    c. proactive interference
    d. serial position effect

11. In one study, Loftus and Palmer (1974) found that when they told participants two cars had "smashed" into each other, these same participants were more likely to report they had seen broken glass in a previously viewed film than participants who were told the cars had "hit" each other. This tendency for new and possibly deceptive information to distort one's memory of a past incident is known as:

    a. the misinformation effect.
    b. retroactive interference.
    c. proactive interference.
    d. the serial position effect.

12. Traumatic experiences that are thought to be pushed out of consciousness are often referred to as _____ memories.

    a. long-term
    b. short-term
    c. repressed
    d. sensory

13. Retrograde amnesia is generally caused by some sort of trauma to the brain. People with retrograde amnesia generally cannot:

    a. form memories of events that occur following the trauma.
    b. access memories of events created before the trauma.
    c. form semantic memories following the trauma.
    d. use procedural memories.

14. _____ refers to the increased efficiency of neural communication over time, resulting in learning and the formation of memories.

    a. Memory consolidation
    b. Long-term potentiation
    c. Memory trace
    d. Priming

15. The _____ is essential for creating new explicit memories, but not implicit memories.

    a. parietal lobe
    b. amygdala
    c. cerebellum
    d. hippocampus

16. A friend says, "My grandmother has terrible short-term memory. She can't remember anything from a couple of hours ago." This statement represents a very common mistake people make when discussing memory. How would you explain this confusion about short-term memory versus long-term memory?

17. How are iconic memory and echoic memory different from each other?

18. How does working memory differ from short-term memory?

19. Create a mnemonic to help you remember the process of encoding, storage, and retrieval.

20. Imagine you are a teacher creating a list of classroom rules in case of an emergency. If you were expecting your students to remember these rules after only reading through them once, where in the list would you position the most important rules? Why?

✓ CHECK YOUR ANSWERS IN APPENDIX C.

YOUR SCIENTIFIC WORLD

Apply psychology to the real world! Go to LaunchPad for access.

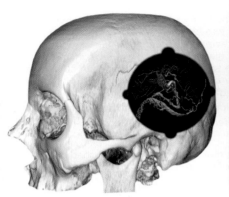

Medical Body Scans/Science Source.

Mark Olencki~Wofford College.

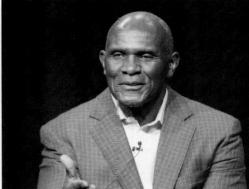

Frederick M. Brown/Getty Images.

CHAPTER OUTLINE AND LEARNING OBJECTIVES

An Introduction to Cognition

LO 1   Give the definition of cognition and explain how it is related to thinking.

LO 2   Demonstrate an understanding of concepts and how they are organized.

LO 3   Differentiate between formal concepts and natural concepts.

LO 4   Describe the biological processes associated with cognition.

Problem Solving

LO 5   Explain how trial and error and algorithms can be used to solve problems.

LO 6   Identify different types of heuristics used to solve problems.

Decision Making

LO 7   Describe the process of decision making and explain how heuristics can lead us astray.

Head Trauma and Cognition

LO 8   Identify the causes and symptoms of chronic traumatic encephalopathy (CTE).

Language

LO 9   Define language and give examples of its basic elements.

LO 10   Explain the linguistic relativity hypothesis and how language influences thought.

Intelligence

LO 11   Examine and distinguish among various theories of intelligence.

LO 12   Describe how intelligence is measured and identify the important characteristics of assessment.

LO 13   Define creativity and its associated characteristics.

Pete Marovich/Getty Images.

Jonathan Daniel/Getty Images.

© My Stroke of Insight, Inc._Photo by Kip May.

7 cognition, language, and intelligence

londoneye/
Getty Images.

An Introduction to Cognition

BLEEDING BRAIN   December 10, 1996, was the day a blood vessel in Dr. Jill Bolte Taylor's brain began to bleed. At approximately 7:00 A.M., Dr. Taylor awoke to a pain behind her left eye, a stabbing sensation she found similar to the "brain freeze" felt after a hasty gulp of ice cream. It seemed strange for a healthy 37-year-old woman to experience such a terrible headache, but Dr. Taylor was not the type to lounge in bed all day. Pushing through the pain, she got up and climbed onto her exercise machine.

But as soon as she began moving her limbs back and forth, a weird out-of-body sensation took hold. "I felt as though I was observing myself in motion, as in the playback of a memory," Dr. Taylor writes in her book *My Stroke of Insight.* "My fingers, as they grasped on to the handrail, looked like primitive claws" (Taylor, 2006, p. 37).

The pain, meanwhile, kept hammering away at the left side of her head. She stepped off the workout machine and headed toward the bathroom, but her steps seemed plodding, and maintaining balance demanded intense concentration. Finally reaching the shower, Dr. Taylor propped herself against the wall and turned on the faucet, but the sound of the water splashing against the tub was not the soothing *whoosh* she had expected to hear. It was more like an earsplitting roar. Dr. Taylor's brain was no longer processing sound in a normal way. For the first time that morning, she began to wonder if her brain was in serious trouble (Taylor, 2006).

"What is going on?" she thought. "What is happening in my brain?" (Taylor, 2006, p. 41). If anyone was poised to answer these questions, it was Dr. Taylor herself. A devoted neuroanatomist, she spent her days studying neurons at a laboratory affiliated with Harvard Medical School. She now imagined herself rummaging through her mental library for any memories that might help diagnose her condition. This method of **recall** was something

Dr. Taylor, in Her Own Words

http://qrs.ly/1v5a5d3

Photo: AJ Mast/The New York Times/ Redux.

CONNECTIONS

In **Chapter 6,** we presented the process of retrieval in memory. Dr. Taylor was having difficulty retrieving her memories. We assume that the information she was trying to access had been successfully encoded and stored prior to the stroke.

The Brain Scientist
An accomplished neuroanatomist, Dr. Jill Bolte Taylor had devoted her career to studying the brains of others. But one winter morning in 1996, she was given the frightening opportunity to observe her own brain in the midst of a meltdown. AJ Mast/The New York Times/Redux.

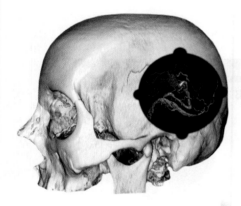

Tangled
The tangled intersection of arteries (red) and veins (blue) is an arteriovenous malformation (AVM), the anatomical abnormality that led to Dr. Taylor's stroke. An AVM is essentially a clump of blood vessels that results when there are no capillaries linking arteries to veins. Sometimes the vessels of an AVM burst under pressure, allowing blood to pool in the brain; this is called a *hemorrhagic stroke* (American Stroke Association, 2012; National Institute of Neurological Disorders and Stroke, n.d.-a). Medical Body Scans/Science Source.

she habitually used, but all the files seemed to be locked. The knowledge was there, but she could not tap into it (Taylor, 2006).

Dr. Taylor sensed that something was terribly wrong, but she could not help feeling mesmerized by the "tranquil euphoria" of her new state of consciousness. She no longer felt separate from the outside world. Like a fluid running fast and free, her body drifted in and out of surrounding space. Memories of the past floated into the distance, everyday worries evaporated, and the little voices in her mind that normally narrated her train of thought fell silent (Taylor, 2006).

Wading in a dreamlike fog, Dr. Taylor managed to shower and put on clothes. Then, just as she began visualizing the journey to work, her right arm fell limp like a dead fish. It was paralyzed. At that moment she knew: "Oh my gosh, I'm having a stroke! I'm having a stroke!" (Taylor, 2006, p. 44). Her next thought was: "Wow this is so cool! . . . How many scientists have the opportunity to study their own brain function and mental deterioration from the inside out?" (p. 44).

Dr. Taylor was indeed having a rare form of stroke caused by a defective linkage between blood vessels in the brain. This faulty connection in the central nervous system, known as an arteriovenous malformation (AVM), is present in a substantial number of people—about 300,000 in the United States alone (around 0.1% of the population). Most individuals born with AVMs are symptomless and unaware of their condition, but about 12% (36,000 people) experience effects ranging from annoying headaches to life-threatening brain bleeds like the kind Dr. Taylor was experiencing (National Institute of Neurological Disorders and Stroke, n.d.-a).

Having a backstage pass to her own stroke was a once-in-a-lifetime learning opportunity for a neuroanatomist, but it was also a serious condition requiring an immediate response. Aware of this urgency, Dr. Taylor walked into her home office and took a seat by the phone, racking her brain for ideas of how to get help. The usual strategies like calling 911 or knocking on a neighbor's door simply did not cross her mind. As she gazed at the phone keypad, a string of digits materialized in her brain. It was the phone number of her mother in Indiana. Calling her mom was certainly an option, but what would she say? Dr. Taylor didn't want to worry her mother, so she sat and waited, hoping that another set of digits would appear (Taylor, 2006).

Finally, another number flickered by in two separate chunks—it was her work number. She scrawled the digits as fast as she could, but looking at what she had written, she only saw cryptic lines and curves. Fortunately, those lines and curves matched the figures she saw on the phone keypad. Dr. Taylor picked up the receiver and dialed her coworker and friend Dr. Stephen Vincent (Taylor, 2006). Steve answered the phone immediately, but his words were incomprehensible to Dr. Taylor. "Oh my gosh, he sounds like a golden retriever!" she thought. Mustering all her mental might, she opened her mouth and said, "This is Jill, I need help!" Well, that's what she hoped she had said. Her own voice sounded like a golden retriever as well (Taylor, 2006, p. 56; 2008, February). Luckily, Steve recognized that the murmurs and cries belonged to his friend Jill, and before long he was driving her to the hospital (Taylor, 2006).

As blood hemorrhaged into Dr. Taylor's brain, she became increasingly unable to process sensory information, tap into memories, and use language. As she later reflected: "In the course of four hours, I watched my brain completely deteriorate in its ability to process all information" (Taylor, 2008, February). The bleeding was beginning to limit her capacity for cognition. ●

Cognition. You've probably heard the word tossed around in conversation, and perhaps you know that it has something to do with thinking. But what exactly do we mean by cognition, and where does it figure in the vast landscape of psychology?

Cognition and Thinking

The study of cognition is deeply rooted in the history of psychology. Early psychologists were intensely focused on understanding the mysterious workings of the mind, often using introspection (examination of one's own conscious activities) in their studies. With the rise of behaviorism in the 1930s, the emphasis shifted away from internal processes and on to behavior. Researchers shunned the study of thoughts, emotions, and anything they could not observe or measure objectively. In the 1950s, psychologists once again began to probe the private affairs of the mind. Psychology experienced a *cognitive revolution,* and research on cognition and thinking has flourished ever since.

LO 1	Give the definition of cognition and explain how it is related to thinking.

Cognition is the mental activity associated with obtaining, converting, and using knowledge. But how is this different from *thinking?* Thinking is a specific type of cognition that requires us to "go beyond" information or to manipulate information to reach a goal. **Thinking** involves transforming information to make a decision, reach a solution, or form a belief (Matlin & Farmer, 2016). Cognition is a broad term that describes mental activity, and thinking is a subset of cognition. Dr. Taylor was clearly experiencing significant impairments in both cognition and thinking on the morning of her stroke.

HOSPITAL HUBBUB Upon arriving at Mount Auburn Hospital, Dr. Taylor had a computerized axial tomography (CAT) brain scan. The cross-sectional slices provided by the scan merged into a troubling picture: a giant hemorrhage in the left side of her brain. According to Dr. Taylor, "My left hemisphere was swimming in a pool of blood and my entire brain was swollen in response to the trauma" (Taylor, 2006, p. 68).

Dr. Taylor was rushed by ambulance to Massachusetts General Hospital, which has a neurological intensive care unit. The hospital scene, with its blinding lights and loud noises, was far too hectic for Dr. Taylor's fragile sensory systems, which had become ultra-sensitive to stimulation. Light assaulted her eyes and scorched her brain "like fire" (Taylor, 2006, p. 67). Hospital workers grilled her with questions that seemed nothing more than a bewildering racket. "Sound streaming in through my ears blasted my brain senseless so that when people spoke, I could not distinguish their voices from the underlying clatter of the environment," she remembers (p. 75). Some of the

CONNECTIONS

In **Chapter 1,** we described how Wundt used introspection to examine psychological responses to stimuli. Titchener used introspection to determine the structure of the mind. These early psychologists paved the way for cognitive psychology, the study of mental processes, and cognitive neuroscience, which explores their physiological basis.

CONNECTIONS

In **Chapter 1,** we discussed critical thinking, an important component of the scientific method. This type of thinking involves the process of weighing and synthesizing evidence—thinking clearly, rationally, and with an open mind. Here, we explore thinking more broadly.

CONNECTIONS

In **Chapter 2,** we described CAT scans. This technology uses X-rays to create cross-sectional "slices" of the brain that come together to form a three-dimensional image. CAT scans can detect tumors and brain damage and display the brain's structural features.

cognition The mental activity associated with obtaining, converting, and using knowledge.

thinking Mental activity associated with coming to a decision, reaching a solution, or forming a belief.

Bleeding Brain

The red zone on the right of the CAT scan shows a hemorrhage on the left side of the brain. (Note that the patient's left is your right.) In Dr. Taylor's case, the bleeding interfered with activity in Broca's and Wernicke's areas, impairing her ability to produce and understand language. Her frontal lobe function also deteriorated the morning of the stroke, as illustrated by the difficulty she had in devising a coherent strategy to get medical help. Scott Camazine/Science Source.

You Asked, Dr. Taylor Answers

http://qrs.ly/165a5dl

How did you communicate thoughts and ideas to others when you weren't able to effectively express yourself?

scan this →

Synonyms

formal concepts artificial concepts

concepts Mental representations of categories of objects, situations, and ideas that belong together based on their central features or characteristics.

formal concepts The mental representations of categories that are created through rigid and logical rules or features.

natural concepts The mental representations of categories resulting from experiences in daily life.

hospital personnel, who didn't understand Dr. Taylor's condition and were insensitive to her vulnerability, tried to communicate by speaking louder and louder, as if she were hearing impaired, but this only upset and confused her more. What she needed was for those addressing her to speak slowly, pronounce clearly, and show a bit of compassion (Taylor, 2006). Fortunately, the neurologist overseeing her case was one of the few people who saw what Dr. Taylor needed. Dr. Anne Young looked into Dr. Taylor's eyes, spoke quietly, and touched her body with respect. "Although I could not completely understand her words, I completely understood her intention," Dr. Taylor recalls. "This woman understood that I was not stupid but that I was wounded" (p. 86). ●

Concepts

On Day 2 in the hospital, Steve told Dr. Taylor that her mother, who went by the name of "G.G.," would be coming to visit. Dr. Taylor found the news perplexing (Taylor, 2006). What on Earth was a *mother,* and who or what was a *G.G.?* "Initially, I didn't understand the significance of G.G.—as I had lost the concept of what a mother was," she writes (p. 88). The following day, G.G. appeared at the doorway, walked over to her daughter's bed, and climbed in alongside her. As Dr. Taylor recalls, "She immediately wrapped me up in her arms and I melted into the familiarity of her snuggle" (p. 90).

LO 2 **Demonstrate an understanding of concepts and how they are organized.**

Although the touch of G.G. felt familiar, the *concept* of her had slipped away, at least temporarily. Concepts are a central ingredient of cognitive activity, and are used in important processes such as memory, reasoning, and language (McCaffrey & Machery, 2012; Slaney & Racine, 2011). We can define **concepts** as mental representations of categories of objects, situations, and ideas that belong together based on their central features or characteristics. The concept of *superhero,* for example, includes a variety of recognizable characteristics, such as: has supernatural powers, battles villains, and protects innocent people. Abstract concepts (such as *love, belonging,* and *honesty*) are far harder to pinpoint than concrete concepts (like *animals, furniture,* and *telephones*). Personal experiences and culture shape the construction of abstract concepts, and we don't always agree on their most important characteristics.

Without concepts, it would be quite difficult to understand the tidal wave of data flooding our brains every day. For example, we all know what a *cat* is. But if the concept *cat* did not exist, we would have to describe all the characteristics that we expect of a cat whenever one comes up in conversation: "Yesterday I saw the cutest animal—you know, those furry, four-legged creatures with pointy ears and long tails, the ones that say *meow?*" Thanks to our *cat* concept, however, we can simply use the word "cat" as shorthand for all of them ("Yesterday I saw the cutest cat"). And even if you encounter a cat breed you have never seen before (for example, a hairless Sphynx cat), you still know it's a cat. Concepts allow us to organize and synthesize information, and to draw conclusions about specific objects, situations, and ideas that we have never encountered before (Yee & Thompson-Schill, 2016). Imagine how exhausting thinking and talking would be if we did not have concepts to fall back on.

HIERARCHIES OF CONCEPTS One way to understand concepts is to consider how they can be organized in *hierarchies,* or rankings. Generally, psychologists use a three-level concept hierarchy to categorize information.

At the top of the hierarchy are *superordinate* concepts. This is the broadest category, encompassing all the objects belonging to a concept. The superordinate concept of furniture is depicted at the top of the hierarchy in **INFOGRAPHIC 7.1** on the next page. This is a very broad group, including everything from couches to nightstands.

Narrowing our focus to include only couches, we are considering the *midlevel* or basic level of our hierarchy. This is still a fairly general grouping, but not as broad as a superordinate concept such as furniture.

Subordinate-level concepts are even narrower, in this case referring to specific types or instances of couches, such as a loveseat, a La-Z-Boy, or my own couch with crumbs between the cushions.

The midlevel category is what we use most often to identify objects in everyday experience. Most children learn the midlevel concepts first, followed by the superordinate and subordinate concepts (Mandler, 2008; Rosch, Mervis, Gray, Johnson, & Boyes-Braem, 1976). Although a child might grasp the meaning of *couch*, she may not understand *furniture* (the superordinate level) or *chaise lounge* (the subordinate level).

In Class: Collaborate and Report

As a team, **A)** pick a superordinate concept. **B)** Record midlevel concepts and subordinate-level concepts that would fall in this hierarchy. **C)** Discuss how you might use this type of hierarchy to help you study.

Reconstructing concept hierarchies was a formidable task for Dr. Taylor, because so many of their layers had been washed away by the hemorrhage. But with hard work, relentless optimism, and the help of G.G., she slowly reconstructed concepts as diverse as *alphabet letters* and *tuna salad*. Using children's books like *The Puppy Who Wanted a Boy*, G.G. helped her daughter retrain her brain to read, and by putting together puzzles, Dr. Taylor was able to re-create concepts such as *right side up* and *edge* (Taylor, 2006). A trip to the laundromat became a lesson in first-grade math concepts—and in the challenges of learning concepts all over again. Putting a few coins in her daughter's hand, G.G. posed the following question: "What's one plus one?" Perplexed, Dr. Taylor came back with a more basic question: "What's a one?" (p. 108).

LO 3 Differentiate between formal concepts and natural concepts.

FORMAL CONCEPTS Now let's take a look at the way concepts develop. **Formal concepts** are based on rigid and logical rules (or "features" of a concept). When a child learns that 5 is an odd number because, like all other odd numbers, it cannot be divided evenly by 2 without a remainder, she is developing a simple formal concept. An object, idea, or situation must explicitly adhere to strict criteria in order to meet the definition of a particular formal concept. Science uses formal concepts to develop laws, theorems, and rules. An example of a formal concept you may have learned in school is an *isosceles triangle,* which refers to a three-sided polygon with at least two equal-length sides. If you were taking a geometry test and needed to identify an isosceles triangle among various shapes, you could pick out the members of this formal concept using these criteria.

NATURAL CONCEPTS In contrast to formal concepts, **natural concepts** are defined by general characteristics and are acquired during the course of our daily lives (Rosch, 1973; Yee & Thompson-Schill, 2016). We've already discussed several natural concepts, including *superhero, furniture,* and *love,* which are all mental representations of categories formed through each person's unique experience. Your concept of *superhero,* for example, is likely based on stories you've heard, books you've read, and movies you've seen; there are no universal or fixed rules for what constitutes a superhero, as they are

Cool Cats
Perhaps you've never come face to face with a Red Self Longhair (top), a Devon Rex (middle), or a hairless Sphynx (bottom). However, you immediately know they are cats because you have developed a "cat" concept, which specifies the defining features of these animals. Red Self Longhair: Dave King/Getty Images. Devon Rex and Sphynx: Jagodka/Shutterstock.

CONNECTIONS

In **Chapter 1,** we introduced operational definitions, which specify the precise manner in which a variable is defined and measured. Creating operational definitions for formal concepts is relatively straightforward, because they are already defined by rigid and logical rules. Natural concepts are more challenging, as experts do not always agree on how to define or measure them.

Concepts and Prototypes

Concepts are used to organize information in a manner that helps us understand things even when we are encountering them for the first time. *Formal concepts,* like "circle," allow us to categorize objects and ideas in a very precise way— something either meets the criteria to be included in that category, or it doesn't. *Natural concepts* develop as a result of our everyday encounters, and vary according to our culture and individual experiences. We tend to use *prototypes,* ideal representations with features we associate most with a category, to identify natural concepts.

formal
CONCEPT

Defined by rigid, precise rules

A circle is a two-dimensional shape in which all points are the same distance from its center.

natural
CONCEPT

Defined by general characteristics established through everyday encounters

A couch is a large piece of furniture used for sitting.

Concepts can be organized into **HIERARCHIES**

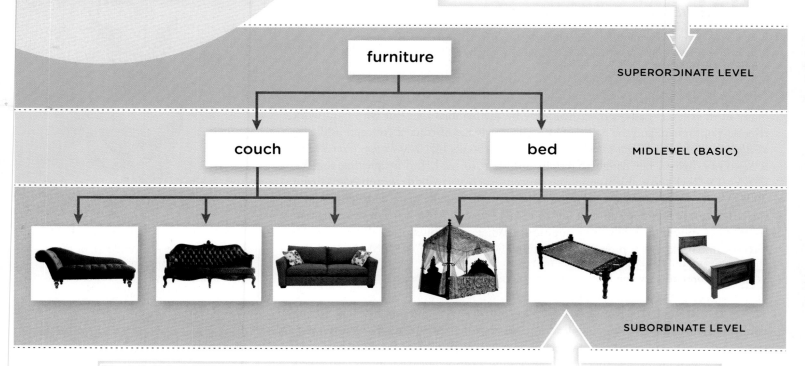

furniture — SUPERORDINATE LEVEL

couch — bed — MIDLEVEL (BASIC)

SUBORDINATE LEVEL

Did you think of this? Maybe not. But if you're from India, the traditional charpai may be your prototype—the first image that comes to mind when someone says "bed." What comes to mind when you think of the concept "fruit"? Researchers studying the development of categories organized a group of items from the most prototypical to the least prototypical (Rosch & Mervis, 1975). How long would it take you to think of an olive?

most prototypical   least prototypical

orange   apple   banana   strawberry   pineapple   lemon   date   coconut   tomato   olive

"constantly changing and are inextricably linked to their contexts" (Yee & Thompson-Schill, 2016, p. 1015). Identifying objects that fall into such categories is more difficult because their boundaries are imprecise and harder to define; natural concepts don't have the same types of rigid rules for identification that formal concepts do (Hampton, 1998).

Consider the natural concept of *mother*. Your concept of *mother* may be quite different from that of your classmate. What criteria do you use to determine if someone is a mother? Is it necessary for a person to get pregnant and have a baby? If so, the large group of women who adopt children are not included. What about someone who gives birth but then immediately puts the baby up for adoption—is she a mother?

PROTOTYPES In our daily use of natural concepts, we rely on **prototypes**, which are the ideal or most representative examples of natural concepts (Mervis & Rosch, 1981). In other words, a prototype is the image or definition that quickly comes to mind when considering the concept. Prototypes help us categorize or identify specific members of a concept. If you were asked to identify the ideal example of a mother, you might very well begin describing the characteristics of your *own* mother, because she is probably the mother with whom you are most familiar. If we asked you to name an example of a fruit, you would most likely say apple or orange—and *not* rambutan, unless you happen to be from Indonesia, where this sweet fruit with a spiky covering is eaten on a regular basis. Infographic 7.1 presents a list of fruit organized from the most frequently suggested prototype—orange—to the least frequently suggested prototype—olive (Rosch & Mervis, 1975).

Items are easier to identify when they closely resemble prototypes. If shown an image of a papaya, many people in the United States would take longer to identify it as belonging to the fruit category than if they were shown an image of a peach (which is more similar to the common prototypes of apples and oranges). We suspect it would take them even longer to identify a durian or rambutan. Let's consider the concept of hero (scaling back from superheroes), which has been the subject of much research over the years. The natural concept of hero can be defined by its "most prototypical features," including bravery, moral integrity, conviction, self-sacrifice, honesty, altruism, and determination (Kinsella, Ritchie, & Igou, 2015). But such qualities do not constitute "rigid boundaries" for identifying a hero.

We now know how the brain organizes information into meaningful categories, or concepts. But how is that information represented inside our heads, even for concepts related to people, places, and things that aren't present? With the help of *mental imagery*, another key ingredient of cognition, we see them in our mind's eye and imagine how they look, sound, smell, taste, and feel.

Mental Imagery

Dr. Taylor's stroke devastated certain aspects of her cognitive activity, such as language and memory. But some functions, like her ability to think visually, continued humming along quite smoothly (Taylor, 2006). If asked a question, she would search for answers in her arsenal of mental images. As Dr. Taylor describes it, "Language with linear processing was out. But thinking in pictures was in" (p. 78).

When people try to describe cognitive activity, they often provide descriptions of images from the "mind's eye," or *mental images*. Try to imagine, for instance, where your cell phone is right now. Did a picture of your beloved mobile device suddenly materialize in your head? If so, you have just created a mental image. Whether contemplating the whereabouts of cell phones or daydreaming about celebrities walking the red carpet, our brains are constantly whipping up vivid pictures. These mental images are not two-dimensional scenes frozen in time. Our brains have an amazing knack for manipulating them in three dimensions.

Unfamiliar Fruits
If we asked you to classify a durian (top) or a rambutan (bottom), you might pause before saying the word "fruit"! This is because durians and rambutans do not closely resemble our typical fruit prototypes, apples and oranges. If we showed you a peach, however, your response might be faster because peaches are more similar to apples and oranges.
Top: Mrs_ya/Shutterstock. Bottom: tarapong srichaiyos/Shutterstock.

prototype The ideal or most representative example of a natural concept; helps us categorize or identify specific members of a concept.

FIGURE 7.1
Manipulating Mental Images
Can you tell which object pair is congruent? In order to figure this out, you must hold images of these figures in your mind and mentally manipulate them. (The answer appears at the bottom of this page.) Information from Shepard and Metzler (1971).

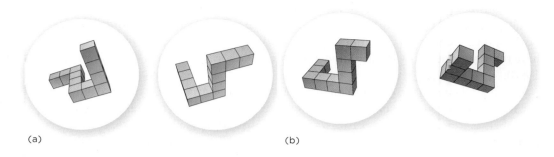

(a)   (b)

Let's consider what we do when we examine a new object for the first time. We typically hold the object in our hands (if it's not too heavy) and rotate it to get a better sense of what we are looking at. If the object is too large to hold, we often walk around it to see how it looks from various angles. Researchers are particularly interested in finding out if we *mentally* behave this way as well, and they have spent a great deal of time studying mental imagery and the rotation of objects.

IMAGINING OBJECTS AND MAPS In one of the earliest studies on this topic, Roger Shepard and Jacqueline Metzler (1971) had eight participants look at 1,600 pairs of object drawings like those displayed in **FIGURE 7.1** and then asked them to mentally rotate one of the objects in the pair to determine if they were identical. In calculating the reaction times, the researchers discovered that the amount of time it took participants to rotate the object depended on the degree of difference between the orientations of the two objects. The greater the rotation, the longer it took participants to decide if the objects were identical.

The ability to mentally rotate objects is extremely useful in everyday life. Remember the last time you tried to fit a large piece of furniture through a doorway, squeeze rolling luggage into the overhead bin of an airplane, or cram just one more container of leftovers into an overflowing refrigerator. In each case, you probably relied on some type of mental rotation to plan how to get each of these objects into or through a small space. Educators are also using this type of mental rotation to help students learn about organic chemistry, geometry, and geology. Being able to interact with concrete and virtual models "enable[s] students to internalize a mental model of these transformations," which helps them to use more accurate mental rotation when the models are not physically present (Stull & Hegarty, 2016, p. 521).

In another fascinating study on mental imagery, participants were instructed to study a map of a small fictional island (**FIGURE 7.2**). The researchers then asked them to close their eyes and imagine the map, first picturing one object (the hut) and then scanning across their mental image of the map until they "arrived" at a second object (the rock). The researchers found that it took longer for participants to "find" objects on the mental map when the objects were farther apart. As with the scanning of real objects, the amount of time it takes to scan a mental image is relative to the distances between the objects in the image (Kosslyn, Ball, & Reiser, 1978). In addition, Kosslyn (1978) suggests that the size of the image is connected to how much detail people can see in their mind's eye. Fewer details can be detected on smaller images.

FIGURE 7.2
Scanning Mental Images
Researchers asked participants to imagine this fictional map and "find" objects there. As with a real object, it took longer to find objects that were farther apart. Information from Kosslyn, Ball, and Reiser (1978).

Answer to Figure 7.1: a

AUDITORY IMAGERY Stop for a moment and imagine the smell of chocolate chip cookies baking in the oven, the tang of lemon on your tongue, or the sound of a cat meowing. It is important to remember that not all imagery is visual; other sensory experiences can be used to construct imagery in our minds. A review of research on auditory imagery indicates that auditory images are similar to true auditory stimuli (such as music and language) in their properties (for example, pitch and loudness), and that auditory images involve the brain regions used in auditory perception, such as Broca's area (Hubbard, 2010). Interestingly, auditory imagery is associated with a person's musical background and ability. When asked to think about two known song lyrics, study participants with musical training were better than other participants at identifying which of the songs would be sung in a higher pitch (Janata & Paroo, 2006).

We use mental images all the time—so often it's hard to conceive of thinking without them. Imagine reading this chapter without being able to visualize Dr. Taylor staggering around her house the morning of her stroke. How would your brain interpret the description of Steve's voice sounding like a golden retriever if you could not "hear" the sound in your mind? Mental images, like concepts, lie at the heart of cognition.

Every cognitive activity we have discussed thus far, from establishing prototypes of fruit to mentally rotating leftovers in the refrigerator, is made possible by the electric and chemical bustle of billions of neurons. Let's dive into that bustle and get acquainted with the biology of cognition.

Biology of Cognition

LO 4   **Describe the biological processes associated with cognition.**

Dr. Taylor's story provides a stark illustration of the following principle: If the brain's biological integrity is compromised, cognition is likely to suffer. The bleeding in her brain began in a small region on the left side of her cerebral cortex but soon spread across large areas of her brain (Taylor, 2006). Among those affected was her left frontal lobe, a part of the brain critical for a broad array of higher cognitive functions such as processing emotions, controlling impulses, and making plans. Remember that Dr. Taylor experienced enormous difficulty devising a simple plan to save her own life (for example, she was unable to think of calling 911).

The stroke also ravaged brain regions critical for another major element of cognition: language processing. "As the blood interrupted the flow of information transmission between my two language centers (Broca's anteriorly and Wernicke's posteriorly) . . . I could neither create/express language nor understand it," Dr. Taylor recalls in her book (Taylor, 2006, p. 62). Broca's and Wernicke's areas work with other parts of the brain to generate and understand language.

COGNITION AND NEURONS The biology of cognition can also be observed on a micro scale. Normally, changes at the level of neurons make it possible to store and retrieve information—like how to call 911 in a dire emergency. Apparently, the stroke had interfered with neurons involved in the retrieval of memories. It is also at the neuronal level where we see the amazing plasticity of the brain at work. Following a stroke, healing and regeneration begin with changes to neurons. These changes include greater excitability of the neurons, rewiring to take advantage of both hemispheres, increases in dendritic connections, and increased efficiency of communication at the synapses (Dobkin, 2005).

MEASURING COGNITION IN THE BRAIN Reading Dr. Taylor's CAT scans, the doctors were able to see the cause of all these cognitive malfunctions—an enormous hemorrhage on the left side of her brain: "It didn't take someone with a Ph.D. in neuroanatomy to figure out that the huge white hole in the middle of the brain scan didn't belong there!" (Taylor, 2006, p. 68).

CAT scans are extremely useful for detecting abnormalities like strokes and tumors, while other technologies help us study cognitive activity in the brain. Many interesting studies on cognition have investigated the biological basis of mental imagery. As it turns out, the brain often displays similar patterns of activity, whether we are imagining something or seeing it in real life (Lisman, 2015).

CONNECTIONS

In **Chapter 1,** we emphatically noted that a correlation does not prove a cause-and-effect link between variables. Here, we need to determine if musical training made participants better at identifying the pitch, or whether some other third variable was involved. Perhaps the musicians had better auditory abilities to begin with and decided to study music because of that.

CONNECTIONS

In **Chapter 2,** we described the association areas, which integrate information from all over the brain. Dr. Taylor's stroke impacted her ability to use language, presumably by disrupting the normal activities of two association areas: Broca's area, pivotal for speech production, and Wernicke's area, for language comprehension.

CONNECTIONS

In **Chapter 6,** we described how learning and memory are evident at the neural level. Through the process of long-term potentiation, communication between sending and receiving neurons is enhanced. This increased synaptic strength facilitates learning and memory formation, and is apparent in the aftermath of a stroke.

In one study, researchers implanted electrodes in the brains of participants with severe epilepsy. This allowed the researchers to monitor individual neurons as participants looked at houses, animals, famous people, and other images. They found that some neurons responded to certain objects but not to others. A neuron would fire when the participant was looking at a picture of a baseball but not at an image of a face, for example. The researchers could identify the image the person was viewing simply by observing his brain activity. They also observed that *the same* neurons that became excited when the person looked at an actual object were active when the person was merely imagining that object (Kreiman, Koch, & Fried, 2000).

Using technologies such as positron emission tomography (PET) and functional magnetic resonance imaging (fMRI), researchers have found that the visual cortex can be activated by mental imagery as well as by external stimuli (Ganis, Thompson, & Kosslyn, 2004; Lisman, 2015). Information (from either an external stimulus or a mental image) is processed by the visual cortex, which works with other areas of the brain to identify images based on knowledge stored in memory. Researchers have noted that similar areas of the frontal and parietal regions of the brain are activated when study participants look at, for example, an image of a tree *and* when they imagine a tree. Once again, it appears that perception and imagery use many of the same neural mechanisms (Ganis et al., 2004; Lisman, 2015).

CONNECTIONS

In **Chapter 2,** we reported that the visual cortex is the part of the brain where visual information is received, interpreted, and processed. Here, we see that the information processed by the visual cortex does not always arise from visual stimuli.

 show what you know

1. _____ is the mental activity associated with obtaining, converting, and using knowledge.

2. If you were to define the _____ of *superhero,* you might suggest that characters in this category have supernatural powers, battle villains, and protect people.
   a. cognition
   b. concept
   c. hierarchy
   d. mental imagery

3. Your instructor explains that the pitch of a sound is defined by the frequency of the sound wave. She is describing a _____, which is created through rigid rules or features.
   a. prototype
   b. natural concept
   c. formal concept
   d. cognition

4. Give two examples of how biology is associated with cognition.

✓ CHECK YOUR ANSWERS IN APPENDIX C.

Problem Solving

THE BIG DILEMMA On Day 3 at the hospital, a team of doctors arrived at Dr. Taylor's bedside to discuss the possibility of performing surgery. One of the doctors, an expert in AVMs (the blood vessel abnormality responsible for her stroke), informed Dr. Taylor that there was a blood clot as big as a "golf ball" on the left side of her brain. Both the clot and the remainder of the AVM needed to be extracted; otherwise, she risked suffering another stroke (Taylor, 2006).

Dr. Taylor did not understand much of what she heard from the doctors because her language-processing neurons were, as she puts it, "swimming in a pool of blood" (Taylor, 2006, p. 91). But she did catch the part about slicing open her skull, a prospect that she found quite unappealing. "Any self-respecting neuroanatomist would *never* allow anyone to cut their head open!" she writes (p. 91). Dr. Taylor had good reason to worry, for brain surgery involves considerable risks. When surgeons go into the brain to fix one problem, there is always the possibility that they will unintentionally create a new one. No one could be certain of the operation's outcome. ●

Dr. Taylor had a very big problem on her hands and a very important decision to make. This section of the chapter is devoted to problem solving and decision making, two distinct yet tightly interwoven topics. Read carefully: The knowledge we are about to share may be very useful to you. Understanding problems and how they are solved can make life's difficulties a lot more manageable.

What's the Problem?

Have you ever considered the multitude of problems you encounter and solve every day? Problems crop up when something gets in the way of a goal, like a computer crashing when you are racing to finish a project or a tricky scheduling situation at work. Problems range from the mundane (*the printer is jammed*) to the potentially overwhelming (*I have a life-threatening brain bleed*). In psychology, **problem solving** refers to the variety of approaches we can use to achieve a goal.

COMPONENTS OF PROBLEM SOLVING Problem solving has intrigued psychologists for generations. Newell, Shaw, and Simon (1958) developed an information-processing model, suggesting that problem solving proceeds from an initial state (the situation at the start of a problem) to a goal state (the situation when the problem is solved; Matlin & Farmer, 2016). Think about how this model applies to Dr. Taylor. Her *initial state* included two very big problems: a massive blood clot and a troublesome clump of blood vessels in the left hemisphere of her brain. The *goal state* was maximizing her health, both physically and cognitively.

Another crucial component of problem solving is recognizing obstacles that block the path to a solution (Matlin & Farmer, 2016). Think about a problem you want to solve and try to identify the initial state, the goal state, and the obstacles in your way. If your initial state is unfinished homework and your goal state is the completion of your homework in a timely manner, the obstacles might include the competing duties of household chores or something more internal, like sleepiness or lack of motivation.

STEPS TO SOLVING PROBLEMS The first step in problem solving is understanding the problem (see **INFOGRAPHIC 7.2** on page 291). If you can't identify or label a problem, then solving it is going to be difficult. Once you grasp the problem, you must choose one of many available approaches or strategies to tackle it. Which strategy you settle on—and the speed, accuracy, and success of your solution—will depend on many factors, including your reservoir of knowledge, your organization of knowledge, and the amount of time you spend assessing the problem (Ericsson, 2003; Goldstein, 2011).

Problems are a constant part of life, but they are much easier to manage if we understand the strategies available to solve them. The aim of the upcoming discussion is to provide you with several approaches for solving problems, while also examining the various factors that come into play during the process.

Approaches to Problem Solving

LO 5 Explain how trial and error and algorithms can be used to solve problems.

TRIAL AND ERROR One common approach to problem solving is **trial and error**, the process of finding a solution through a series of attempts. Mistakes will likely be made along the way, but attempts that don't work are simply eliminated. Let's say you have a HUGE set of keys and you have to unlock a door you don't use very often. With the trial-and-error approach, you would insert keys, one by one, hoping the correct key is on the ring.

Trial and error is only useful in certain circumstances. It should not be used if the stakes are extremely high, particularly in situations where a wrong selection could be harmful or life-threatening. Imagine, for example, if Dr. Taylor's physicians had used trial and error to figure out what procedure she needed. *Let's try this surgery first: If it*

No Problem!
When Shawn Mendes first posted a 6-second video of himself on Vine, he had no intention of becoming a world famous pop artist. Soon it occurred to him that Vine might be his ticket to superstardom. Mendes recognized his primary challenge—getting recognized by a record label. And he solved that problem by posting videos of himself on Vine, and accumulating millions of followers, including his future manager. Mendes ended up signing with Island Records and soaring to the top of the pop charts with his single "Stitches" (Howard & Inverso, 2016; Sisario, 2015, April 24). Johnny Louis/Getty Images.

problem solving The variety of approaches that can be used to achieve a goal.

trial and error An approach to problem solving that involves finding a solution through a series of attempts and eliminating those that do not work.

64,000 Combos
Forgot your lock combination? Trying to figure it out by trial and error is not an effective strategy, as there are 64,000 possible solutions. Better buy a new lock. Pixel Embargo/Shutterstock.

doesn't work, we'll try a different one next week, and then another the following week. When an individual's health and well-being are on the line, trial and error is clearly not the way to go.

Nor is this approach recommended for problems with too many possible solutions. If your keychain has 50 keys, you probably would not want to spend your time randomly selecting keys until one fits (potentially trying the same key more than once). Trial and error is somewhat of a gamble because there is no guarantee it will lead to a solution. By the way, computer hackers may use this approach to get your password and gain uninvited access to your digital world. More about this to come.

ALGORITHMS If you're looking for a problem-solving approach that is more of a sure thing, an *algorithm* is probably your best bet. **Algorithms** (AL-guh-rith-umz) use formulas or sets of rules that provide solutions to problems. Unlike trial and error, algorithms ensure a solution, as long as you choose the right one and follow all its steps. Examples of algorithms are all around us: following the instructions on prepackaged boxes of food, installing software through a series of drags and clicks, and locating a book in the library. Sometimes the steps are not written out; you just have to remember them. Suppose you are trying to figure out a 20% tip for a server at a restaurant. Here's an easy algorithm to calculate your tip—take the total amount of your bill, move the decimal to the left one space, and multiply by 2. This will result in 20% of your bill. Such an algorithm provides a guaranteed "correct" solution to the problem.

As reliable as algorithms may be, they are not always practical. You can only use an algorithm if you know its formula, and there may be occasions when the steps of an algorithm require too much time. Let's return to our example of computer hacking. After losing patience with trial and error, the hacker designs an algorithm that generates a series of possible passwords made up of letters, numbers, and symbols. Because algorithms guarantee solutions, the hacker eventually will generate your password. But the question is: Will it happen in this century? If you have chosen your password wisely, the algorithm may not work within a time frame that the hacker is willing—or able—to wait. For example, simply changing your eight-letter password by one character (lowercase to uppercase) and adding an asterisk can increase a hacker's processing time from 2.4 days to 2.1 centuries (Mahmood, 2010, March 31). And rest assured, most password-protected accounts block access after a set number of failed attempts. Ha ha, hacker!

LO 6 Identify different types of heuristics used to solve problems.

HEURISTICS If using an algorithm is not an option, which is often the case with everyday problems, we can turn to **heuristics** (hyoo-RISS-tiks). A heuristic is a problem-solving approach that employs a "rule of thumb" or broad application of a strategy. Although heuristics are not always reliable in their results, they do help us identify and evaluate possible solutions to our problems. Let's say you are cooking rice, but the instructions are unavailable. One good rule of thumb is to use 2 cups of water for every cup of rice. Another heuristic is to put the rice in the pot and add water until it is one thumb-knuckle above the rice. But unlike algorithms, which use formulas and sets of rules, there is no guarantee a heuristic will yield a correct solution. The advantage of heuristics is that they allow you to shrink the pool of possible solutions to a size that is manageable. Sometimes you must choose from among a handful of heuristics to solve a problem. Let's say you are trying to figure out how much money you should set aside for emergencies; one financial consultant suggests you save enough money to pay your bills for 3 months, and another suggests you stash away 6 to 8 months of your total income. Which heuristic is right for you?

algorithm An approach to problem solving using a formula or set of rules that, if followed, ensures a solution.

heuristics Problem-solving approaches that incorporate a rule of thumb or broad application of a strategy.

Problem Solving

Problem solving involves figuring out how to achieve a goal. Once you understand a problem, you can identify an approach to solving it. A successful approach will help you manage obstacles that come from the problem itself, such as a rigid deadline for an essay you're struggling to write. But sometimes the way we think about a problem can itself be a barrier, preventing us from identifying available approaches.

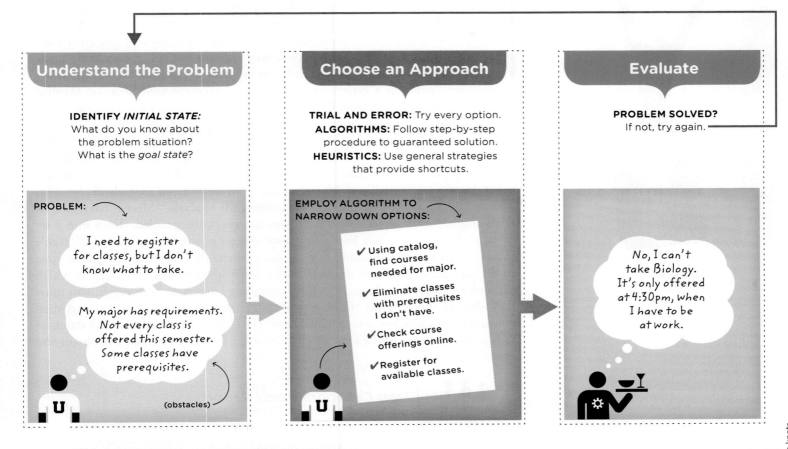

Understand the Problem

IDENTIFY *INITIAL STATE:* What do you know about the problem situation? What is the *goal state*?

PROBLEM:

> I need to register for classes, but I don't know what to take.

> My major has requirements. Not every class is offered this semester. Some classes have prerequisites.

(obstacles)

Choose an Approach

TRIAL AND ERROR: Try every option.
ALGORITHMS: Follow step-by-step procedure to guaranteed solution.
HEURISTICS: Use general strategies that provide shortcuts.

EMPLOY ALGORITHM TO NARROW DOWN OPTIONS:

✔ Using catalog, find courses needed for major.

✔ Eliminate classes with prerequisites I don't have.

✔ Check course offerings online.

✔ Register for available classes.

Evaluate

PROBLEM SOLVED? If not, try again.

> No, I can't take Biology. It's only offered at 4:30pm, when I have to be at work.

Barriers to Problem Solving

Being stuck in a certain way of thinking about a problem can limit what we see as available approaches. For example, our student registering for classes may assume that "classes" must be in-person meetings with an instructor on campus. This assumption prevents the student from investigating more flexible online classes, hybrid classes, or classes that could be transferred from another college.

Sticking with our usual solution strategies is called a *mental set*. To see if you can overcome your mental set, try solving this problem:

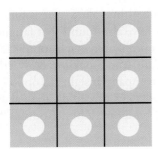

Without lifting your pencil, can you connect all nine dots using only 4 straight lines and without crossing any dot more than once? *(Solution on page 294.)*

Functional fixedness is another barrier in which we can only imagine using familiar objects in their usual way. Say you need to tie two ropes together, but you can't reach them both at the same time. Will functional fixedness keep you from solving this problem? *(Solution on page 294.)*

Heuristics provide shortcuts, allowing you to ignore the many approaches you know will not work and move on to solutions more likely to be successful. But you might need to use trial and error to choose the best solution from that smaller pool of possibilities. A hacker might use a heuristic that combines a commonly used password (123456, password, football) and then add something from the domain itself. For example, if the hacker is trying to break into a Sony PlayStation account, her heuristic might be to try a variety of commonly used passwords and add "PS" at the end (123456PS, passwordPS, footballPS). She would then use trial and error until she breaks into the account. Most problems in life do not come with ready-made algorithms for reaching a correct solution, so we tend to fall back on heuristics.

Heuristics come in a variety of forms. One commonly used heuristic involves *creating subgoals* or *subproblems.* In the days following her stroke, Dr. Taylor had a great deal of trouble moving her body. One of her main challenges was sitting up, but she was able to solve this problem "by breaking the effort of sitting up into the smaller steps of rocking and then rolling upward" (Taylor, 2006, p. 93). When writing your last term paper, did you break it into shorter, more achievable parts? If so, you were using this type of heuristic, which instructors often recommend to students.

Another frequently used heuristic is **means–ends analysis.** "Means" refers to how to reach your goal, or "end." To start, you can break the problem down into a set of subproblems. Once you have formulated this set of smaller problems, you tackle them one by one, determining how to decrease the distance from the initial state to the goal state (Matlin & Farmer, 2016). Often the challenge is to decide which subproblem to address first. If you are struggling with your term paper, you must first identify the problem (finding appropriate support for your thesis) and then divide the problem into two subproblems: (1) identifying an appropriate database to search for articles in the field; and (2) finding a library where you can obtain and read the articles.

I Want a Banana

In a classic study, Gestalt psychologist Wolfgang Köhler provided chimpanzees with some out-of-reach bananas and materials that could potentially be used to fetch them. Resourceful chimps they were, building towers of crates and poking at the fruit with sticks. Rather than using trial and error to solve the problem, they seemed to rely on intelligence and insight (Köhler, 1925).

 **In Class: Collaborate and Report**

You have an appointment on Saturday afternoon, and traffic is really bad! With your group, use the following approaches to solve this problem: **A)** trial and error, **B)** an algorithm, and **C)** heuristics. **D)** Decide which of these approaches would work the best in this situation.

INSIGHT Another manner of reaching a solution is through **insight**, an understanding that occurs in a sudden stroke of clarity (that oh-so-satisfying "aha!" or "eureka!" moment). It can stem from experience solving previous problems, or it can be totally new. Insight often comes as a pleasant surprise because we are not aware of the mental "work" we did to achieve it.

Insight happens so suddenly that we sometimes say to ourselves *Why did it take me so long to figure that out? The answer seems so obvious now.* Theories suggest that, without our conscious awareness, our minds are busy reorganizing the way the problem is represented, and this allows us suddenly and inexplicably to see things in a new light. Sometimes stepping away from a problem for a short time allows the solution to instantly appear (Sio & Ormerod, 2009). Researchers have also found that fatigue, moderate alcohol consumption, and letting go of complex problem-solving approaches may sometimes increase "insight problem solving" (DeCaro, Van Stockum, & Wieth, 2016). A unique pattern of neural activity appears to accompany insight (as opposed to a more analytical problem-solving approach); immediately preceding the "aha!" moment, we see increased activation in the frontal and temporal lobes (Kounios & Beeman, 2009).

means–ends analysis Heuristic used to determine how to decrease the distance between a goal and the current status (the means), leading to the solution of a problem (the end).

insight An understanding or solution that occurs in a sudden stroke of clarity (the feeling of "aha!").

functional fixedness A barrier to problem solving that occurs when familiar objects can only be imagined to function in their normal or usual way.

As you probably know from personal experience, great ideas do not always material-ize when we need them. How might we increase the chances of having keen insights? When struggling with a problem, sometimes the best thing to do is let loose and laugh.

Laughter Leads to Insight

Happy moods facilitate aha! moments.

from the pages of
SCIENTIFIC AMERICAN

Stumped by a crossword puzzle? Try taking a break to watch a funny TV show. Recent research shows that people in a lighthearted mood more often have eureka moments of sudden inspiration.

Karuna Subramaniam, then at Northwestern University, and her colleagues found that boosting the mood of volunteers increased their likelihood of having an aha! moment that helped solve a word association puzzle. Those who watched a Robin Williams comedy special did measurably better at the task using insight than those who watched a quantum electronics talk or a scary movie. The games, in which players must find a word that connects three seemingly unrelated words, have been used for decades to demonstrate creative problem solving. In the brain, sudden insight is accompanied by increased activity in the brain's anterior cingulate cortex (ACC) prior to solving each problem. The region is involved in regulating attention; in problem solving, it seems to work in conjunction with other brain areas either to stay focused on a particular strategy or to switch to a new one. Subramaniam found with functional MRI that people in a positive mood had more ACC activity going in to the task, which probably helped prepare the brain to find novel solutions. Participants who watched anxiety-producing movies such as *The Shining,* however, showed less activity in the ACC and less creativity in solving the puzzles. **Elizabeth King Humphrey, Reproduced with permission. Copyright © 2011 Scientific American, a division of Nature America, Inc. All rights reserved.**

Barriers to Problem Solving

With the capacity for insight, we can be masterful problem solvers, but there are many barriers to problem solving (Infographic 7.2). One such barrier is **functional fixedness**, which occurs when we can only imagine using familiar objects in their usual way. This *fixation* can hinder problem solving, because it stops us from being able to find other, creative uses for objects. Suppose the hem of your pants gets caught on something and the thread starts unraveling. A roll of tape and a stapler are on your desk, and both could be used to "fix" your wardrobe malfunction. But because of functional fixedness, you only view these items in their "usual" capacities. Children have less trouble with functional fixedness than adults because they have not become accustomed to using familiar objects in a fixed way (German & Defeyter, 2000). Yet, the more they observe others using objects, the less likely they are to be innovative. Sometimes observation and pedagogy can get in the way, leading to "restricted exploration and learning" (Carr, Kendal, & Flynn, 2015, p. 331).

Mental sets represent another barrier to problem solving. When faced with a problem, we tend to fall back on solution strategies we have always used—even if they don't work so well. For example, after successfully completing high school, freshmen often start their first semester believing they can succeed in college courses using strategies that worked in the past. For many students though, the requirements and expectations in college cannot be met using the same strategies. In high school, students might have gotten homework done during class, but this is not a winning strategy in college. With mental sets, an approach that has worked in the past will often come immediately to mind and be reused, preventing us from seeing other solutions.

CONNECTIONS

In **Chapter 3,** we described the phenomenon of perceptual set, which is the tendency to perceive stimuli in a specific manner based on past experiences and expectations. With functional fixedness, we can only imagine using objects in their usual way.

Think Outside the Box
Who knew that a paint roller could be used for holding toilet paper and that car tires doubled as planters? Sometimes it's hard to imagine using objects for unconventional purposes. Our resistance toward using familiar objects in new ways is known as functional fixedness, and it can get in the way of problem solving. Left: Andreas Schlegel/AGE Fotostock. Right: Andrea Jones/AGE Fotostock.

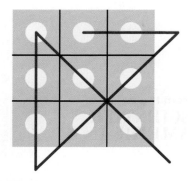

FIGURE 7.3

Solution to the Dot Problem in Infographic 7.2

Did your mental set cause you to assume the square implied boundaries? If so, it may not have occurred to you that one could draw lines extending outside the square.

FIGURE 7.4

Solution to the Two-Rope Problem in Infographic 7.2

Using a shovel to create a pendulum will allow you to swing the second rope. When it swings near you, you can grab it and hold both ropes at the same time. Ropes: Seregam/Shutterstock. Bushes: 3dmentor/Shutterstock.

Emotional barriers can also get in the way of problem solving. If you are trying to figure out how to fix the dripping faucet and someone is peering over your shoulder saying, "Hurry up! What's taking you so long?," you may feel rushed, anxious, and annoyed. These negative emotions affect your ability to think clearly and creatively. Positive emotions, on the other hand, may set the stage for innovative thinking. Good feelings are thought to promote a "flexible" way of thinking, one that enables quick attention shifting and the ability to develop new strategies in response to a changing environment (Isen, 2008). Keep this in mind when you are trying to help someone solve a problem.

 In Class: Collaborate and Report

In your team, identify a familiar object and **A)** list its conventional uses; then **B)** brainstorm as many creative uses as possible. **C)** Discuss the ways that functional fixedness has interfered with your ability to solve problems in the past.

ACROSS THE WORLD
Problem Solving in Different Cultures

Another factor influencing problem solving is culture. People from "relatively unpredictable cultural environments" tend to use short-term planning, while members of "stable cultures" take a longer-term approach (Güss & Robinson, 2014, p. 3). Those from stable cultures have the luxury of long-term planning because they don't have to worry about the political, social, or economic environment drastically changing (Güss & Robinson, 2014). Another important factor is cultural orientation. Research suggests that people from highly individualistic, or self-focused societies, such as the United States, tend to be action-oriented in their problem solving, making a lot of decisions in a short amount of time. In contrast, those from more collectivist, or community-focused countries, such as Brazil, tend to be more careful in their approach, making fewer decisions when faced with a problem (Güss, 2011; Ohbuchi, Fukushima, & Tedeschi, 1999). Why do you think this is so? People from collectivist (as opposed to individualistic) cultures are more inclined to consider how their decisions impact relationships (Güss & Robinson, 2014). This awareness of the social factors of the problem results in a careful approach when making decisions (Güss, 2004).

Think about the last time you faced a difficult problem. In what ways do you think your cultural background might have influenced your approach to solving it?

CRANKING OUT DECISIONS ACROSS CULTURES

 show what you know

1. Imagine it is the first day of classes, but you forgot to write down the number of the room where your psychology class is meeting. You decide you will try to find your classroom by sticking your head in a random number of rooms until you see the assigned psychology textbook on someone's desk. This approach to finding your classroom uses:

   a. means–ends analysis.　　**c.** trial and error.
   b. an algorithm.　　**d.** heuristics.

2. One assignment in your psychology class is to design an experiment. Describe how you would use means–ends analysis to choose a topic for your experiment and write a review of the literature.

3. One common barrier to problem solving is_____, which occurs when we can only imagine using familiar objects in their usual way.

   a. functional fixedness　　**c.** an algorithm
   b. cultural orientation　　**d.** a goal state

✓ CHECK YOUR ANSWERS IN APPENDIX C.

Decision Making

UNDER THE KNIFE With the help of her mother's gentle coaxing, Dr. Taylor made the decision to go through with surgery. On the afternoon of December 27, 1996, she awoke in the recovery room with the left side of her head shaved clean and a 9-inch wound in the shape of a horseshoe (Taylor, 2006). Dr. Taylor had survived the operation, and she didn't feel drained and confused, as you might expect: "Upon awakening, I realized that I felt different now. There was brightness in my spirit again and I felt happy" (p. 112).

"Say something!" demanded G.G. as she approached her daughter's bedside (Taylor, 2006, p. 113). G.G. needed to know that her daughter could still use language. Surgeons had just spent hours poking around her left hemisphere, home to the language-processing regions of Broca's and Wernicke's areas. The surgeons might have inadvertently damaged one of these key regions, compromising her ability to understand or produce words. Dr. Taylor opened her mouth and responded, and she and G.G. both became teary-eyed. The operation appeared to have gone well; Dr. Taylor, it seemed, had made the right decision (Taylor, 2006). ●

Decisions, Decisions

LO 7 Describe the process of decision making and explain how heuristics can lead us astray.

You may be wondering how decision making differs from problem solving. As you now know, problem solving refers to the variety of approaches we can use to achieve a goal. **Decision making** is the cognitive process of choosing from those alternative approaches. Thus, problem solving and decision making can occur at the same time.

PREDICTING THE FUTURE Decision making often involves predicting the future: What is the likelihood that Event A will occur under these circumstances? How about Event B? In cases like these, we can make an educated guess, but some situations lend themselves to more accurate guesses than others. If the Weather Channel predicts there is a 99% chance of thunderstorms today, it's fairly safe to assume it's going to rain. Better bring your umbrella.

But there are many times when predicting the future is like rolling dice—you have almost no way of knowing the outcome. Suppose you are searching for a used car on craigslist. How do you choose a "gently used" car from among the hundreds listed in your locality? With no prior knowledge of the cars or their owners (apart from whatever information they decide to post on craigslist), all you can do is hope the car you choose is not a lemon. But who knows if your gamble is going to work? Choices that hinge on unknowns can be very risky, and we sometimes make the wrong decision.

SINGLE FEATURE There are many ways to go about making decisions. One way is to focus on a single aspect, or feature, of the situation. Let's say you are trying to decide where to stop for gas. If your only criterion is cost, you will seek out the gas station with the cheapest gasoline, paying no attention to what kind of donuts it sells inside or how clean its bathroom may be. The *single feature* on which you are basing your decision (where to stop for gas) is the price of the fuel (not tasty donuts or a clean bathroom).

ADDITIVE MODEL The single-feature approach may not be effective for making complex decisions, in which there are *many* features to consider. With a more complex decision, such as which car to purchase, you might create a list of the primary features

Brightness in Her Spirit
Dr. Taylor poses with her mother, G.G., who played an instrumental role in the recovery process. When Dr. Taylor emerged from surgery, G.G. was anxious to know whether her daughter's language-processing abilities were still intact. When Dr. Taylor opened her mouth and spoke, it seemed clear that everything was going to be okay.
© My Stroke of Insight, Inc. Photo by Kip May.

You Asked, Dr. Taylor Answers

http://qrs.ly/dg5a5do

Did you fully recover language and cognition after the surgery?

scan this →

decision making The cognitive process of choosing from alternatives that might be used to reach a goal.

you consider important (gas mileage, safety ratings, sound system, and so on). Using this list, you could rate each of the possible choices (for example, Ford Focus versus Toyota Prius) according to their features, and then tally these ratings to see which car comes out on top. This method of calculating the highest rating is often referred to as an *additive model* of decision making.

The Trouble with Heuristics and the Confirmation Bias

At the start of the section, we mentioned that decision making often involves making predictions, and different scenarios afford different levels of certainty about the future. Heuristics, which involve a rule of thumb or a broad application of a strategy, can help predict the probability of an event occurring. Unfortunately, heuristics can also lead us astray in our assessment of situations and prediction of outcomes. Daniel Kahneman and Amos Tversky (1973) were among the first to systematically research the ways in which heuristics can be ineffective. They found that people are prone to ignore important information while using heuristics (Kahneman & Tversky, 1996). This is particularly true for the *availability heuristic* and the *representativeness heuristic*.

Outbreak of Panic
In the fall of 2014, Ebola arrived in the United States. Although the virus was ravaging parts of West Africa, experts said a U.S. epidemic was unlikely (BBC News, 2014, October 16). Still, many Americans perceived Ebola as an imminent threat. This may have something to do with the availability heuristic: We tend to overestimate the odds of something occurring if we can easily recall similar events ("events" being alarming media reports, in this case). JOHN SPINK/MCT/Newscom.

THE AVAILABILITY HEURISTIC Using the **availability heuristic**, we predict the probability of something happening in the future based on how easily we can recall a similar type of event from the past. The availability heuristic is essentially a decision-making strategy that relies on memory. If we can easily recall a certain event, then we tend to base our decisions on the assumption that it can happen again. Many factors make an event more available, including its recency, frequency, familiarity, and vividness. Let's look at each of these categories.

Imagine it is October 2014 and you have recently seen hundreds of news reports about the dreadful Ebola virus arriving in the United States. Every time you turn on the news, you see images of health-care workers in Hazmat suits and interviews with infectious disease experts. If you are like many Americans (33% according to one poll), you worry that you or someone in your family will become infected (Pew Research Center, 2014, October 6), even though the likelihood of this occurring is "very low"—1 in 13.3 million, according to one estimate (Centers for Disease Control and Prevention [CDC], 2016g; Doucleff, 2014, October 23). Because of all the media reports, Ebola is fresh in your mind, and this makes you overestimate the likelihood of it touching your own life. Events that happened *recently* tend to be more easily recalled, causing us to overestimate the chances of their re-occurrence.

Now imagine that you were asked to decide the following: Do more students at your college use Macs or PCs? Before deciding how to answer, you would probably think about the number of students you have seen using these types of computers and make an estimation based on that tally. In this case, the *frequency* of occurrence influences your decision. You rely on your recall of seeing students using computers in the halls, classrooms, and library. If you are in the graphic design department, for example, chances are you'll see more Macs than PCs. (Historically, more people in art departments use Macs.) Based strictly on your observations from a single department, your sample would not be representative of the entire college, and the availability heuristic would lead you to the wrong answer. The availability heuristic can be accurate, but only when based on appropriate information.

The *familiarity* of an event might also lead to inaccurate estimates. If you and your friends are all avid PC users, you may tend to overestimate the extent to which others

CONNECTIONS

In **Chapter 6,** we described the recency effect, which is the tendency to remember items more accurately when they appear at the end of a list or series. Here, we discuss the tendency to remember similar events better if they have occurred recently.

CONNECTIONS

In **Chapter 1,** we discussed the importance of using a representative sample when making generalizations about a population. Here we must be careful that our observations are representative, and not chosen because of their recency, frequency, familiarity, and vividness.

are using PCs. The more familiar you are with a situation, the more likely you are to predict a similar occurrence in the future.

Finally, the *vividness* of an event can influence our recall. Try to conjure up an image of someone winning the "big one" at a casino. There are lights, sounds, and a lot of hub-bub. The prizewinner jumps joyfully in the air, hollering and crying at the top of her lungs, with onlookers clapping and shouting in approval. This type of dramatic display never occurs when some poor guy loses his last $100; the details of a losing bet would consequently be far more difficult to recall. Because the winning image is more vivid, we are more likely to recall it and thus overestimate the likelihood of a win occurring in our own lives. Memorable imagery leads us to believe that these types of wins happen all the time, when in fact they are very rare. If an event has made a striking impression on you, even a rare occurrence such as an airplane crash, you will be more likely to overestimate the probability of it happening again (Tversky & Kahneman, 1982).

THINK IT THROUGH
Fearing the Friendly Skies

Are people generally more afraid of flying in an airplane or riding in a car? Airplanes seem frightening to many people, yet the statistics suggest we should be more concerned about driving. The odds of getting into a fatal traffic accident are 1 in 113, compared to about 1 in 9,737 for a plane crash (National Safety Council, 2016).

Now consider the weeks and months following the terrorist attacks of September 11, 2001. How did people feel about flying after seeing what happened to the hijacked planes on the news? Countless people stayed away from airports and airplanes. So many would-be air travelers took to the roads after 9/11 that there was a temporary surge in traffic fatalities. In the 3 months following September 11, more people died in car accidents (apparently trying to avoid air travel) than did in the four hijacked airplanes (Gigerenzer, 2004). In this unfortunate case, people increased their risk of death by trying to reduce it.

Risk perception is complex. A number of factors contribute to an overblown fear of flying. The fact that airplane crashes and terrorist attacks are beyond one's control and represent the potential for enormous disaster tends to increase many people's perceptions of risk (Slovic & Weber, 2002, April). And, as we've learned from our earlier discussion of the availability heuristic, people tend to deem events more probable when similar scenarios are easy to recall.

THE REPRESENTATIVENESS HEURISTIC Often we have to make decisions based on our judgment of a situation or person. The **representativeness heuristic** evaluates the degree to which their primary characteristics are similar to our prototypes (ideal or most representative examples). With the representativeness heuristic, we make quick, effortless judgments about how closely a person or situation fits our preconceived prototype (Lerner, Li, Valdesolo, & Kassam, 2015; Shah & Oppenheimer, 2008). In contrast, the availability heuristic requires us to access information from long-term memory and use it to make predictions about events.

Let's examine how the representativeness heuristic works in practice. Peter is a middle-aged man. He is conservative, a lovely speaker, thoughtful, and well read. He lives alone in an apartment in the city. Is Peter a truck driver or a poet? Forced to choose between these two occupations and using the representativeness heuristic, the majority of people would likely guess that Peter is a poet because his description better matches their prototype of a poet than their prototype of a truck driver. But this approach fails to consider the *base rate* (the prevalence of features or events in the population) of these

SIT BACK, RELAX, AND ENJOY THE FLIGHT.

Safer Than a Car
The odds of dying in a plane crash are extremely low—lower than perishing in a fall, a drowning incident, or a car accident (National Safety Council, 2016). Still, many people are petrified of flying. This is partly a result of the availability heuristic; we tend to overestimate the likelihood of events that easily spring to mind. ssuaphotos/Shutterstock.

availability heuristic A decision-making strategy that predicts the likelihood of something happening based on how easily a similar type of event from the past can be recalled.

representativeness heuristic A decision-making strategy that evaluates the degree to which the primary characteristics of a person or situation are similar to our prototype of that type of person or situation.

occupations. There are far more truck drivers than poets, suggesting the better guess would be that Peter is a truck driver. The representativeness heuristic can be useful, but the accuracy of our information must also be taken into account; our conclusions should be drawn from base rates, not stereotypes (more on this in Chapter 15). The other limitation of the representativeness heuristic is that prototypes are based on exposure to limited samples, which may not provide a good representation of the population.

THE CONFIRMATION BIAS We can also miss important information through the **confirmation bias,** when we unintentionally look for evidence that upholds our beliefs. People tend to overlook or discount evidence that runs counter to their original views or convictions. For example, you decide to go on a date with someone you are *really* interested in, even though you don't know him very well. You Google stalk him and look on his Facebook page, and immediately connect with one of his "likes." With this information in hand, you stop your search, convinced you now have evidence to support your decision to go out with him. We tend to focus on information that supports favorable outcomes (Krizan & Windschitl, 2007; Scherer, Windschitl, O'Rourke, & Smith, 2012), but what other sources of information could you use to avoid the confirmation bias in this case?

Although we don't deliberately set out looking for information to support what we already think, it does happen, and because of this, we often miss or ignore important information. Most of us read about these types of heuristic errors and think *that wouldn't happen to me!* But rest assured, it does.

You've Been Framed!

We have spent a great deal of time discussing factors that impede the decision maker. But in many situations, the characteristics of the problem itself, or the presentation of the problem, are to blame.

WHAT'S IN A FRAME? The **framing effect** demonstrates how the presentation or context of a problem can influence the outcome of a decision. Consider the following study, which demonstrates how the framing effect influences our decision making in ways beyond our awareness. Researchers instructed participants to imagine that they had purchased a $10 ticket to attend a show, but lost their ticket on the way to the theater. Each participant was then asked whether he or she would be willing to pay $10 for another ticket. Only 46% of participants indicated that they would spend another $10 for a new ticket. Participants were next instructed to imagine another situation: In it, they planned to buy a $10 ticket to attend a show, but once they got in the ticket line, they suddenly realized that they had lost one of their $10 bills. Faced with this second scenario, 88% of the participants were willing to fork over the $10. In each case, the participants were faced with the proposition of spending an additional and

confirmation bias The tendency to look for evidence that upholds our beliefs and to overlook evidence that runs counter to them.

framing effect Occurs when the wording of questions or the context of a problem influences the outcome of a decision.

unexpected $10, but they tended to make different decisions in response to the different circumstances. The background information framing these hypothetical scenarios influenced the decisions made, even though the outcomes would have been identical —a net loss of $10 (Kahneman & Tversky, 1984; Tversky & Kahneman, 1981).

WHAT'S IN A QUESTION? The specific wording of questions should also be considered. One study found that people are more likely to prefer ground beef if it is described as "80% lean," as opposed to "20% fat." Although 80% lean and 20% fat describe exactly the same product, these phrases evoke very different responses (Johnson, 1987). Another study demonstrated how the wording of a question can influence people's descriptions of themselves. Researchers prompted college students to describe themselves using one of two questions: "Please take five minutes and write what you *think* about yourself," or "Please take five minutes and write what you *feel* about yourself." The group assigned to the "feel" condition evaluated themselves in a more negative way than the group assigned to the "think" condition. This may be because those in the "feel" condition were focusing on emotions, and the English language has more words to describe negative emotions than positive emotions (Holtgraves, 2015). As this study demonstrates, researchers must carefully choose their words when designing questionnaires, as "subtle variations in the wording of questions" can greatly influence how participants think about the questions and their answers (p. 9).

The story of Jill Bolte Taylor has helped us understand some basic cognitive processes—concepts, imagery, problem solving, and decision making. We learned how quickly cognitive functions can deteriorate when the brain faces an emergency. But not all lapses in cognition stem from catastrophic events like strokes. Brain injuries can also occur in small increments, accumulating over time and triggering gradual changes in cognition and behavior.

Imagine you spent 21 years playing a game that required slamming your body against muscular, 200- to 300-pound men. How would the rapid changes in speed and direction, and the constant banging of your skull, affect the delicate brain inside? Football Hall of Famer Harry Carson is here to tell you.

CONNECTIONS

In **Chapter 1,** we presented the survey method, descriptive research that relies on questionnaires and interviews. A survey is a series of questions that can be administered in a variety of settings. People are not always forthright in their responses to questions. Here, we see that the wording of questions can lead to biases as well.

✓ **show what you know**

1. _____ refers to the cognitive process of choosing from a variety of alternatives you might use to reach your goal.

2. We often predict the probability of an event happening in the future based on how easily we can recall a similar type of event from the past. This is known as the:
   a. framing effect.
   b. confirmation bias.
   c. representativeness heuristic.
   d. availability heuristic.

3. A good friend is terrified of flying. How would you use your knowledge of heuristics to make him feel less afraid?

✓ CHECK YOUR ANSWERS IN APPENDIX C.

Head Trauma and Cognition

ostill/Shutterstock.

"I SAW STARS" Harry Carson was 14 years old when he first stepped onto the football field. It was August in Florence, South Carolina; the air was warm, moist, and steeped in the scent of freshly cut grass. Wearing 20 pounds of football equipment was uncomfortable, but Harry felt proud having it on, especially the imposing shoulder pads and helmet (Carson, 2011).

During that first practice at Wilson High School, the coaches assigned the players to a man-on-man blocking drill. Young Harry was pitted against "Bubble Gum," a bigger, more experienced player. "As he came off the ball to block me, I

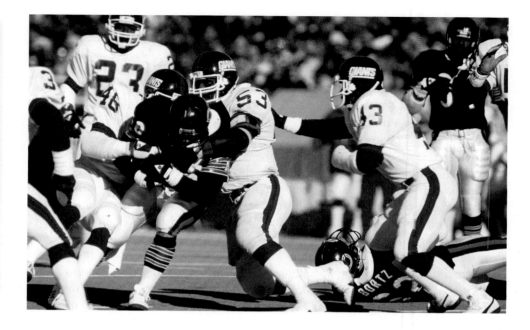

Hard-Hitting Legend

Harry Carson's football career spanned 21 years. How many blows to the head do you think he sustained during that time? Using data from a study of collegiate players, which found the number of head impacts per season to be as high as 1,444 (Crisco et al., 2010), we estimate that Harry took as many as 30,000 hits to the head. The overwhelming majority of those hits were not forceful enough to cause concussions, but that does not mean they didn't cause damage. Subconcussive blows may put athletes at risk for chronic traumatic encephalopathy (CTE; Harmon et al., 2013). Jonathan Daniel/Getty Images.

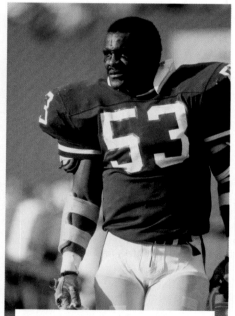

The Captain Pays a Price

During his career with the New York Giants, Harry began to experience periodic lapses in speech and language comprehension. Were these difficulties associated with the repeated head trauma he sustained on the field? This is quite possible, as head trauma has been linked with subsequent speech and language disturbances (McKee et al., 2009; Vas, Chapman, & Cook, 2015). PCN Photography/Alamy Stock Photo.

could do little to defend myself," Harry recalls in his memoir *Captain for Life*. "He must have blocked me three or four times, and with each block I felt like a rag doll being chewed up by a pit bull" (Carson, 2011, p. 12).

Colliding with Bubble Gum was not only painful; it jarred Harry's brain, causing immediate changes in perception. "I was conscious," Harry recalls, '[but] I saw little stars twinkling before my eyes." Like most players of his time, Harry didn't realize that "seeing stars" or momentarily "blacking out" was a sign of concussion, a brain injury that is not fatal but can have life-changing consequences.

Harry ended up quitting the team that day, and although he felt ashamed and defeated, he didn't give up on football. The following year, he returned to that practice field and dominated in the same drill, aweing the coaches with his power and agility. Harry continued to play through high school, and went on to become a star lineman and team captain at South Carolina State. Then he achieved what many American boys only dream about—he was drafted into the National Football League (NFL). During his 13-year career with the New York Giants, Harry established himself as one of the greatest middle linebackers in the history of professional football. Eventually, he was inducted into the Pro Football Hall of Fame, joining other greats like Walter Payton and Joe Montana. But becoming a football legend came at a price.

About halfway through his professional career, Harry starting having unexplained mood swings and suicidal thoughts. Driving across the Tappan Zee Bridge north of New York City, he pictured himself turning the wheel and plummeting into the river below. In addition to the emotional ups and downs, Harry began having periodic migraines and difficulty using language. While giving media interviews, he sometimes had trouble processing and responding to reporters' questions. There he stood in the locker room, the team captain surrounded by cameras and microphones, searching for vocabulary words that normally rolled off his tongue with ease. Maybe no one else noticed the problem, because Harry did a good job filling in the gaps with standard expressions like "um" and "you know." But he knew something was wrong.

It was not until his retirement from pro football that Harry began to connect his symptoms with the repeated brain trauma he had sustained on the field. In

1990, two years after he left the NFL, a neuropsychologist diagnosed him with *post-concussion syndrome,* a collection of physical and psychological symptoms that linger long after a concussion occurs (Institute of Medicine [IOM] & National Research Council [NRC], 2014). After his diagnosis, Harry began going to the library to research sports-related brain injuries. "I came to realize that all of this stuff that I was experiencing was a result of the dings, the bell-ringers, the concussions that I sustained as a player." As Harry learned more about his condition, he began sharing his story at conferences and in media interviews. "There were people who probably thought I was crazy for even talking about it," he says. "Football players are very proud individuals, and they do not go around talking about being brain damaged." ●

Chronic Traumatic Encephalopathy (CTE)

LO 8   **Identify the causes and symptoms of chronic traumatic encephalopathy (CTE).**

In 2005, a decade after Harry began raising awareness about sports-related brain injuries, a groundbreaking scientific report came out in the journal *Neurosurgery.* The study, led by pathologist Bennet Omalu at the University of Pittsburgh, detailed the extensive brain damage of deceased NFL player Mike Webster (Omalu et al., 2005). It was the first time a retired pro football player had been diagnosed with **chronic traumatic encephalopathy (CTE)**, a neurodegenerative disease caused by repeated head trauma. One of the telltale signs of CTE is abnormal accumulation of *tau,* a protein also implicated in Alzheimer's disease (McKee et al., 2013; Turner et al., 2013). The symptoms of CTE may include headaches, depression, anger, aggression, and a host of cognitive problems (McKee, Cantu et al., 2009; McKee, Stein et al., 2013). Advanced cases of CTE have been associated with "severe memory loss with dementia" (McKee et al., 2013, p. 59).

Following the initial reports by Omalu and colleagues, a team led by Dr. Ann McKee at Boston University discovered CTE in the brains of football players, hockey players, boxers, combat veterans, and others who had sustained repetitive head trauma; of the 85 brains they examined, 68 of them (or 80%) showed evidence of CTE (McKee et al., 2013). Many prominent football players have had confirmed cases of CTE, among them Junior Seau and Dave Duerson, who both died of self-inflicted gunshot wounds. In his suicide note, Duerson wrote, "Please, see that my brain is given to the N.F.L.'s brain bank" (New York Times, 2016, February 13, para. 5).

The discovery of CTE in professional football players came as no surprise to Harry Carson. In fact, he is relatively confident he suffers from CTE as well: "I don't really worry about it, because I think that, with the information that has already been presented, we all probably have it." The damage Harry sustained cannot be undone, but he doesn't seem bitter or hardened. Instead, he focuses on managing his life in a positive way—eating healthy foods, exercising, and educating others about sports-related brain injuries. "Periodically, I have not-so-good days," Harry explains, "and when those days show up, I'm ready." During those tough times, Harry tries to minimize interviews and speaking engagements. "That's sort of a quiet time that I enter," he says, "and I just sort of roll with it until I'm sort of rolling out of that phase."

We have no way of knowing whether Harry suffers from CTE (at this point, the disease can only be diagnosed after death), but one thing seems clear: He is managing his post-concussion syndrome with grace and dignity. Watch him in an interview and you would never suspect he has any cognitive deficiency. Why is Harry doing so

CONNECTIONS

In **Chapter 6,** Infographic 6.3 describes the stages and symptoms of CTE and its impact on memory. Here we explore the history that led to the discovery of this neurodegenerative disease and its impact on cognition.

Discoverer of CTE
Pathologist Bennet Omalu was the first to identify chronic traumatic encephalopathy (CTE) in the brain of a former football player. His research sparked the ongoing conversation about the neurological risks of football and other contact sports. Omalu, now a professor at the University of California, Davis, says he cannot bear to watch football games: "When I watch and see them meeting head onto head, helmet onto helmet, what flashes through my mind is what's going on in their brains," Omalu said in an interview with the *Los Angeles Times.* "It's like torture to me" (Morrison, 2016, February 3, para. 3).
Pete Marovich/Getty Images.

well, while other NFL retirees are facing early-onset dementia? Could it be that certain people are more susceptible to CTE than others?

NATURE AND NURTURE
Are Some People at Greater Risk for CTE?

Does hitting your head mean you are going to be diagnosed with chronic traumatic encephalopathy (CTE)? Should parents allow their children to play sports that put them at risk for head trauma? These are the questions researchers and parents face every day.

. . . IT'S NOT JUST ABOUT CONTACT SPORTS.

There is little doubt that environmental factors, namely head trauma, contribute to the development of this disease (Montenigro, Bernick, & Cantu, 2015; McKee et al., 2013). Injury to the brain is the one factor associated with all diagnosed cases of CTE. Brain trauma can result from falls, car crashes, physical violence, and contact sports (Bieniek et al., 2015). However, just because you play a contact sport does not mean CTE is in your future (Hay, Johnson, Smith, & Stewart, 2016). People exhibit different responses to head trauma.

Could it be that some people are genetically predisposed to developing CTE? The studies to date are small and inconclusive, but research suggests certain genes play a role (Bieniek et al., 2015; McKee et al., 2013). CTE can only be diagnosed after death, making it difficult to determine the relative contributions of nature and nurture; it is possible, however, that the same blow to the head could trigger the development of CTE in one person but not another. The gene–environment interaction is different from person to person.

 **show what you know**

1. The symptoms of _____ may include headaches, depression, anger, aggression, memory impairment, and many types of cognitive problems.

2. In your own words, explain the cause(s) of CTE.

√ CHECK YOUR ANSWERS IN APPENDIX C.

Language

SEE THE WORDS When Harry gets a headache, it often starts on the left side (Kirk & Carson, 2013, September 4). Perhaps it's no coincidence that his pain originates in the brain hemisphere where language processing occurs. As you may recall, Harry periodically struggled with media interviews, taking extra time to digest journalists' questions and articulate his responses. These language roadblocks continued popping up when Harry left the NFL and began a career as a sports commentator. "Once football was over, I went into broadcasting," he says, "and that was something that I failed at horribly because I would lose my train of thought live on the air." Even today, Harry has days when it's hard to access the words needed to express his thoughts. But he has developed a cognitive strategy for dealing with it: "Sometimes when I am trying to make the points that I want to make . . . I have to visualize each word that I want to use in my brain before I allow it to leave my lips," he says. "When I do that, I probably speak more deliberately." ●

The Power of Language

Until something goes wrong, it's easy to take language for granted. Words are so much a part of our daily routines that it's difficult to imagine life without them. What if we couldn't have e-mail exchanges, job interviews, and work meetings? Without words, there would be no books, legal codes, news reports, instruction manuals, social media, and song lyrics. We wouldn't be able to say, "I love you" or "Why are you looking at me like that?" Language gives us the power to explicitly convey complex thoughts and feelings to others, and that is a remarkable feat.

LO 9   Define language and give examples of its basic elements.

Language can be defined as a system for using symbols to think and communicate. These symbols are words, gestures, or sounds put together according to specific rules. Within a language, speakers generally agree on the meaning of these symbols, and use them to think, solve problems, make decisions, and daydream. Language is the ultimate medium for creativity. We can use words, gestures, and sounds to create an infinite number of statements.

The average English-speaking college student is familiar with around 10,000 to 11,000 word families (groups of related words such as "smile," "smiled," "smiling"; Treffers-Daller & Milton, 2013). What's more, humans are always finding new meanings for old words or inventing new ones. Over the years, football players and coaches have fine-tuned their communication with highly specialized words and phrases. In a "horse collar tackle," for example, a player is seized by the neck and taken down from behind (fortunately, this dangerous strategy was prohibited beginning in 2005). There are also names for different kicks, plays, and players. Perhaps you have heard of a "squib kick," a "pooch punt," or a "flea flicker" (Kostora, 2012, May 16)?

The Basic Elements of Language

Language can be written, spoken, and signed. Speaking comes naturally to us because we are born with brains evolved for that purpose (Shaywitz, 1996). Children learn to speak, in large part, by hearing others talk. (In Chapter 8, we will describe the consistent pathways through which language develops for children.)

Children may not need speaking and listening lessons, but they do require instruction in learning to read. Think back to your first reading lesson. Your teacher probably introduced you to written language by teaching you to break words into their basic sound units (for example, the combination of *kuh, aah,* and *tuh* to form the word "cat"; Shaywitz, 1996). Your teacher was introducing you to *phonemes.*

PHONEMES **Phonemes** (FOH-neemz) are units of sound that serve as the basic building blocks of all *spoken* languages (**INFOGRAPHIC 7.3** on page 306). The symbols we call words are made up of phonemes (when referring to how they sound). Examples of English phonemes include the sounds made by the letter *t* in the word "tail" and the letter *s* in the word "sail." Some letters can represent more than one phoneme. For example, the letter *i* can represent two clearly different phonemes, as in the words "bit" and "bite." Keep in mind that we don't use phonemes to compose written words; the basic units that make up written words are called *graphemes.*

Infants between 6 and 8 months can recognize all phonemes from all languages, but this ability begins to diminish at about 10 months. At this point, infants show the first signs of being "culture-bound listeners" (Kuhl, 2015, p. 67). Their ability to distinguish between phonemes that are not in the language(s) they regularly hear spoken declines (de Boysson-Bardies, Halle, Sagart, & Durand, 1989; Werker & Tees, 1984). This is what makes it so difficult for older children and adults to learn to speak a foreign language without an accent.

If you have children (or plan to have them), it would be a great idea to teach them more than one language very early in life. Not only will their pronunciation sound natural; they may enjoy some cognitive perks, too.

language A system for using symbols to think and communicate.

phonemes The basic building blocks of spoken language.

DIDN'T SEE THAT COMING
The Perks of Being Bilingual

DOES BEING BILINGUAL CLUTTER YOUR BRAIN?

Psychologists once thought that the brain was best suited for learning a single language, and that exposing children to more than one language frustrated their intellectual development (Klass, 2011, October 10). Researchers are now uncovering evidence that learning two languages does not lead to word mix-ups and other cognitive troubles; it may actually improve a child's communication skills (Fan, Liberman, Keysar, & Kinzler, 2015). What's more, juggling two languages could potentially lead to improved performance on various cognitive tasks (Westly, 2011, July/August).

Bilingualism has been associated with enhanced creativity, abstract thought, and working memory. Among the most striking qualities associated with bilingualism are strong executive control and more efficient *executive functioning* (Bialystok, 2011; Engel de Abreu, Cruz-Santos, Tourinho, Martin, & Bialystok, 2012; Westly, 2011, July/August). As the name implies, executive control is concerned with managing the brain's precious resources, deciding what's important and where to focus attention. Executive functioning refers to abilities related to planning ahead and solving problems.

A study of 7-month-old babies found that those growing up in bilingual homes already had an executive control advantage over their peers from monolingual environments. They could, for example, adjust their responses in order to get a reward (the appearance of a puppet) in ways that the monolingual babies could not (Kovács & Mehler, 2009). Research further demonstrates that bilingual children carry this executive control advantage into early adulthood and beyond (Bialystok, 2011; Bialystok, Poarch, Luo, & Craik, 2014).

Why is this so? The bilingual brain is constantly exercising its executive control system. A person who speaks two languages cannot just turn on one language and turn off the other; the knowledge of both is always present and awake. The speaker is eternally torn between the competing languages. Resolving this ongoing conflict seems to keep the executive control system very busy and always practicing (Bialystok, 2011).

Bilingual Bonus
A sign conveys a message in English and Spanish, suggesting that both languages are spoken in the place shown. Speaking two languages may boost the brain's ability to manage many different activities (Bialystok, 2011). glenda/ Shutterstock.

MORPHEMES **Morphemes** (MOR-feemz) represent the next level of language. They consist of one or more phonemes. It is the morpheme that brings meaning to a language. For example, the word "unimaginable" has three morphemes: *un, imagine,* and *able.* Each morpheme has a meaning and communicates something. Remove just one, and the word takes on a whole new significance. Clipping off *un,* for example, produces the word "imaginable," which means the exact opposite of the word you started with.

SYNTAX The **syntax** of a language is the collection of rules dictating where words and phrases should be placed. Syntax guides both word choice and word order, providing consistency in sentence organization (Brandone, Salkind, Golinkoff, & Hirsh-Pasek, 2006). We say, "I love you," not "Love you I," because English syntax demands that the words appear in this order. Different languages have different syntaxes. In German, helping verbs often come toward the end of sentences, a variation in syntax that is striking to English speakers learning to speak German.

GRAMMAR AND SEMANTICS **Grammar** refers to the rules associated with both word and sentence structure (Evans & Green, 2006). It tells us how words are made from sounds, how sentences are formed with words, where to place punctuation, and which word tenses to use. It combines syntax (the rules governing word choice and word order) and semantics. **Semantics** represents the rules used to bring meaning to

morphemes The fundamental units that bring meaning to language.

syntax The collection of rules concerning where to place words or phrases.

grammar The rules associated with word and sentence structure.

semantics The rules used to bring meaning to words and sentences.

pragmatics The social rules that help to organize language.

words and sentences. Here are two sentences with different syntax, but the same semantics: *Jane kicked the ball. The ball was kicked by Jane.* Now, here are two sentences with the same word order, but slightly different grammar: "Some people enjoy cooking, their families, and their dogs." "Some people enjoy cooking their families and their dogs" (Oxford Royale Academy, 2014, October 15, para. 3).

Semantics also refers to the context in which words appear. Let's consider the word "snap":

- Can you *snap* your fingers?
- He got the job done in a *snap.*
- The football player crouched down to *snap* the ball.
- Oh *snap!*
- Don't *snap* at me!
- It's cold outside; *snap* up your jacket.
- She stepped on the branch and it went *snap.*

In each instance, we determine the meaning of the word "snap" based on the context in which it is used in the sentence.

PRAGMATICS Language is used in social interactions, which are governed by certain norms and expectations. **Pragmatics** are the social rules that help organize language. We have to learn how to take turns in a conversation, what gestures to use and when, and how to address people according to social standing (speaking with someone who occupies a higher status, an equal status, and so on) (Steiner, 2012, September 4; Yule, 1996). When addressing the Queen of Denmark, you would say, "Good day, Your Majesty," but when addressing your friend, you might say, "Hey, there."

How do we "know" these rules for language? Learning theorists propose that children learn language just like they learn other behaviors, through processes such as reinforcement and modeling (Bandura, 1977; Skinner, 1957). In contrast, linguist Noam Chomsky (1928–) suggests that humans are born with innate language abilities. Children needn't be taught the basics of language, according to Chomsky (2000); language develops like other organs in the body. Chomsky's position is based on the observation that children possess a much deeper knowledge of language than that which could have been acquired through experience. Their knowledge of language is not simply the result of hearing and imitating; it is hardwired within the brain. A built-in *language acquisition device* (LAD) accounts for the universality of language development. In fact, researchers have observed this innate capacity for language across cultures and in nonhearing children (Chomsky, 2000; Petitto & Marentette, 1991).

THINK IT THROUGH
Language Without Sound

If Chomsky is right, then children would learn all languages, including signed languages, in basically the same way. Evidence suggests this is exactly what happens.

DEAF BABIES BABBLE WITH THEIR HANDS.

No one sat down with you and "taught" you language. You just picked it up because people around you were using it. The same is true for all native speakers (those who have spoken a certain language since infancy), whether they converse in Russian, Mandarin, or American Sign Language (ASL). ASL is a language with symbols, syntax, and a grammatical structure that parallels spoken language (Petitto, 1994). When people use sign language, some of the same regions of the brain are activated as when spoken language is used (Emmorey, 2015; Horwitz et al., 2003; Levänen, Uutela, Salenius, & Hari, 2001).

The Building Blocks of Language

Language is made up of a collection of units and rules. These build upon each other to help us think and communicate. At the base are phonemes, which combine to make up morphemes, the smallest unit of language that carries meaning. At the top is displacement, which is the human ability to refer to things that are abstract or hypothetical.

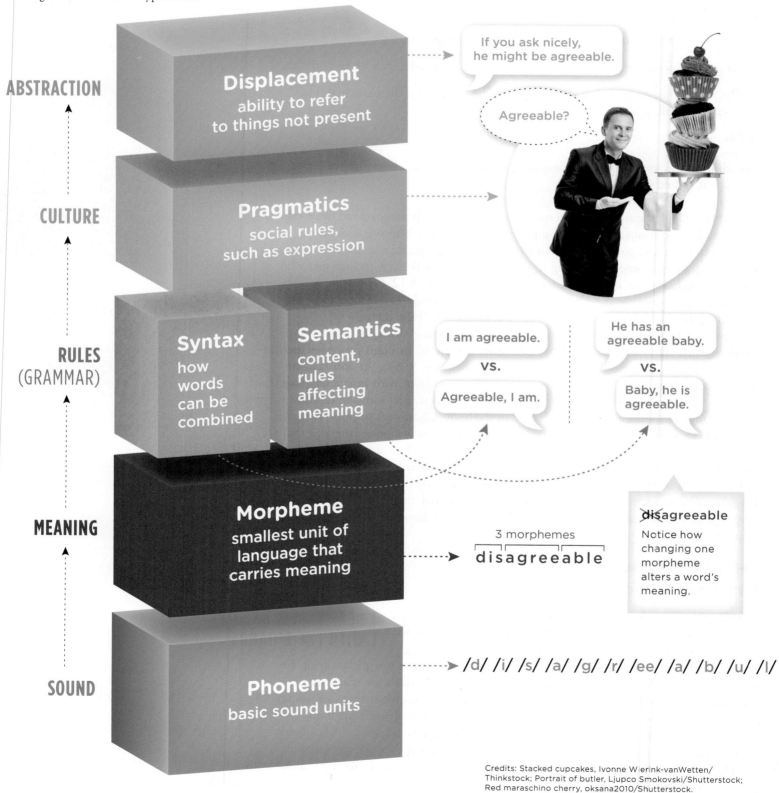

ABSTRACTION

Displacement
ability to refer to things not present

If you ask nicely, he might be agreeable.

Agreeable?

CULTURE

Pragmatics
social rules, such as expression

RULES (GRAMMAR)

Syntax
how words can be combined

Semantics
content, rules affecting meaning

I am agreeable.
vs.
Agreeable, I am.

He has an agreeable baby.
vs.
Baby, he is agreeable.

MEANING

Morpheme
smallest unit of language that carries meaning

3 morphemes
disagreeable

~~dis~~agreeable
Notice how changing one morpheme alters a word's meaning.

SOUND

Phoneme
basic sound units

/d/ /i/ /s/ /a/ /g/ /r/ /ee/ /a/ /b/ /u/ /l/

Credits: Stacked cupcakes, Ivonne Wierink-vanWetten/ Thinkstock; Portrait of butler, Ljupco Smokovski/Shutterstock; Red maraschino cherry, oksana2010/Shutterstock.

Spoken and signed languages also share the same important time frame for acquisition. Between birth and 5 years old, the brain is highly plastic and ready to incorporate any language, but after that period, fluency is difficult to develop (Humphries et al., 2012).

Even the stages of language acquisition appear to proceed along the same path (Emmorey, 2015). Research suggests, for example, that babies who are deaf pass through a babbling stage around the same time as hearing babies. If you are unfamiliar with babbling, we are referring to the *ba-ba-ba* or *dah-dah-dah* sounds babies like to make while cruising on all fours. Babbling is accompanied by activation of the left hemisphere of the brain, a clue that it represents a step in language acquisition, not simply a new motor skill (Holowka & Petitto, 2002). Babies who are deaf and exposed to ASL engage in "manual babbling," using their hands to repeat the fundamental units of sign language (Petitto & Marentette, 1991).

With the increased use of handheld devices, adults are focusing more attention on "events outside their immediate social context" (Przybylski & Weinstein, 2012). This could result in caregivers spending less time talking with babies. How might this impact the development of language in babies, both those who are deaf and those with normal hearing? 🧠

DISPLACEMENT   Many scientists argue that language, more than any other human ability, truly sets us apart from other species. Animals have evolved complex systems of communication, but some features of human language appear to be unique. One of these unique features is *displacement*—the ability to talk and think about things that are not present at the moment. "I wonder if it's going to rain today," you might say to a friend. This statement demonstrates displacement, because it refers to an abstract concept and a hypothetical event. Displacement allows us to communicate about the future and the past, and fantasize about things that may or may not exist.

Thinking What We Say or Saying What We Think?

LO 10   Explain the linguistic relativity hypothesis and how language influences thought.

For many years, psychologists have tried to understand the relationship between language and thought. According to the *linguistic relativity hypothesis* developed by Benjamin Lee Whorf (1956), languages have different effects on thinking and perception. For example, the Inuit and other Alaska Natives have many terms that refer to "snow" (in contrast to the single word used in English). This may cause them to perceive and think about snow differently than English speakers. Whorf's hypothesis is not universally accepted, however. Critics suggest that he exaggerated the number of words the Inuit and other Alaska Natives have for "snow" and underestimated the number of words in English (Pullum, 1991).

Although language might not *determine* thinking and perception, it certainly has an influence (Kersten et al., 2010). Consider the role of gender in language. The English language tends to use "he" and "his" when gender is unspecified. Research indicates that the use of masculine pronouns often results in people ignoring females and focusing on males when forming mental images (Gastil, 1990; Hegarty & Buechel, 2006). "He" and "his" in these situations theoretically refer to either males or females, but the majority of English-speaking Americans think of males. Perhaps you can predict the potential downside of this tendency. Narrowing the focus to male images inevitably promotes gender bias and stereotyping. Consider a study of Dutch and German schoolchildren who were either exposed to occupational titles in their plural forms or pairs of the titles in their female and male forms. (The equivalent in English might be

Babble
Deaf babies who are exposed to sign language develop their own version of babbling. Instead of rattling off spoken syllables (*da-da-da* or *ma-ma-ma*) as hearing infants typically do, they babble with their hands, repeating the basic units of sign language (Petitto & Marentette, 1991). Boaz Rottem/Alamy.

Synonyms
linguistic relativity hypothesis linguistic determinism theory, Sapir–Whorf hypothesis

firefighters versus *fireman* and *firewoman*.) Children who were exposed to the title pairs in their male and female forms were more confident about their ability to be successful in traditionally male jobs (Vervecken & Hannover, 2015).

In Class: Collaborate and Report

Consider how language influences thinking. In your group, **A)** discuss the implications of using terms like spokes*man*, *man*kind, and *man*made. **B)** What other potential biases can you identify in English words and phrases? **C)** How can we counter their influences?

The capacity for language is one of the defining characteristics of humanity. But it is not certain whether this capacity is unique to human beings. Animals communicate with a variety of instinctual (unlearned) behaviors (for example, chirping, whistling, tail slapping, and dancing). Is it possible they use language as well? Read on and draw your own conclusions.

CONTROVERSIES
Do Animals Use Language, Too?

➡️⬅️ Rico was a border collie in Germany who knew 200 vocabulary words, including the name of a bunny toy, "Kaninchen," and a little Santa Claus named "Weihnachtsmann" (Newsweek, 2004, June 20). When Rico's owners instructed him to fetch a certain toy, he would run into the next room and race back with that exact toy in his mouth. So impressive was the dog's verbal comprehension that a team of researchers decided to make him the focus of a case study. They concluded that Rico was capable of "fast-mapping," the ability to deduce the meaning of a word by hearing someone use it just once (Kaminski, Call, & Fischer, 2004). Rico's accomplishments were eventually eclipsed by those of another border collie, Chaser, who learned 1,022 words (Pilley & Reid, 2011). In addition to her impressive vocabulary, Chaser demonstrated a rudimentary understanding of grammar, distinguishing between commands such as "to ball take Frisbee" and "to Frisbee take ball" (Bower, 2013, May 21, para. 2).

HOT DOG!

Rico and Chaser are not alone in possessing exceptional communication skills. The green-rumped parrotlet of Venezuela learns its early contact calls, or socially meaningful songs, from its parents. In other words, it learns to communicate through social interaction as opposed to instinct (Berg, Delgado, Cortopassi, Beissinger, & Bradbury, 2012). Kanzi the bonobo can create simple sentences with the help of pictograms, or images that represent words (Lessmoellmann, 2006, October 4). And Sarah the chimpanzee reportedly learned to read 130 word symbols and connect them into meaningful combinations, such as "Mary give raisin Sarah" (Premack & Premack, 1972, p. 6).

Sharp Canine
If you were impressed with Rico's 200-word vocabulary, you will be astonished by the skills of Chaser, pictured here with her owner John Pilley. With the help of Pilley and others, this border collie learned to recognize the names of 1,022 objects (Pilley & Reid, 2011). Mark Olencki–Wofford College.

There is no question that animals are capable of sophisticated communication. But does that communication qualify as *language?* Keep in mind that animals need extensive training to learn and use vocabulary (you don't think Rico learned 200 words on his own, do you?), while human children pick up language through exposure. To our knowledge, only people have the ability to convey a vast number of ideas through complex grammatical constructs, and apply those constructs to critical thinking. The ability to create a limitless number of original sentences distinguishes human communication from that of dogs and other animals. Even if animals do possess rudimentary language abilities, humans appear to be the only species capable of grasping and using intricate sentence structures (Lessmoellmann, 2006, October 4; Pinker, 2003). ➡️⬅️

1. _____ are the basic building blocks of spoken language.

2. According to the linguistic relativity hypothesis, language differences lead to differences in:
   a. phonemes.
   b. thinking and perception.
   c. the language acquisition device.
   d. displacement.

3. The Dutch word *gezelligheid* does not really have a one-word counterpart in English. It refers to a primary component of Dutch culture: a cozy type of setting that can be quaint, fun, and intimate. Most languages have these types of untranslatable words. How might this be an advantage for people who know more than one language?

✓CHECK YOUR ANSWERS IN APPENDIX C.

Intelligence

INTELLIGENT ATHLETES What adjectives come to mind when you picture a football superstar? Is he big, strong, and fast . . . how about intelligent? Great ball players are often admired for their physical prowess, but playing good football also requires mental mastery of the sport. Once you get to the level of the NFL, the game is "80% mental and 20% physical," according to Harry. "The reason why a lot of players don't make it on the professional level is they're not able to make that transition to how mentally tough it is to play," he says. "The speed is faster, the talent is greater. . . . You have to know what you're doing, and you can't really stop to think about it, because if you stop to think about it, it's too late."

In high school and college, Harry was a defensive lineman, one of the guys who tries to disrupt the opposing team's offense before they can execute their play. When drafted by the Giants, Harry was challenged to learn a new position: middle linebacker. "It was a position that basically, I had to become the leader, the quarterback of the defense," he explains. When Harry arrived in New York, he spent many hours taking cognitive tests and meeting with the team psychologist. It was the psychologist's job to determine whether Harry was cognitively fit to play the demanding position of middle linebacker. As history shows, Harry was more than qualified. A fast-thinking problem solver, he proved he could multitask and make sound judgments on the fly. For any given play, he was able to remember what every defensive player was supposed to be doing, and he learned from past experiences, rarely making the same mistake twice. Harry demonstrated a high level of *intelligence.* ●

What Is Intelligence?

LO 11 **Examine and distinguish among various theories of intelligence.**

Generally speaking, **intelligence** is one's innate ability to solve problems, adapt to the environment, and learn from experiences. Intelligence relates to a broad array of psychological processes, including memory, learning, perception, and language, and how it is defined may sometimes depend on the variable being measured.

In the United States, intelligence is often associated with "book smarts." We think of "intelligent" people as those who score high on tests measuring academic abilities. But intelligence is more complicated than that—so complicated, in fact, that psychologists have yet to agree on precisely what it encompasses. It is not even clear whether intelligence is a single unified entity, or a collection of capabilities.

We do know that intelligence is, to a certain degree, a cultural construct. So although people in the United States tend to equate intelligence with school smarts, this is not the case everywhere in the world. Children living in a village in Kenya on the African continent, for example, grow up using herbal medicine to treat

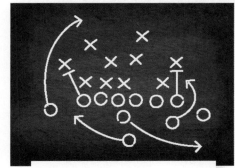

Play It Smart
A play diagram illustrates the positions and movements of football players on the field. A defense playbook may contain as many as 300 plays, and members of the defense are expected to learn all of them, according to Harry. "You are ultimately responsible for everything in that book, and if you don't know it, and if you're not able to compete, then you become a liability." Memorizing plays and mentally adjusting when things don't go as planned require a certain level of intelligence. Alex Belomlinsky/ Getty Images.

intelligence Innate ability to solve problems, adapt to the environment, and learn from experiences.

Are Intelligent People Happier?

Research suggests that intelligence is positively correlated with life satisfaction; people living in countries with high average IQ scores tend to be happier. But the strength of this relationship varies from culture to culture. Intelligence seems to be more important for the happiness of people in individualistic societies, as opposed to those in collectivist (community-oriented) societies. Perhaps this is because collectivist societies prioritize social harmony over individual achievements, such as job promotions and big paychecks, that demand a certain level of intelligence (Stolarski, Jasielska, & Zajenkowski, 2015). Jeremy Woodhouse/Getty Images.

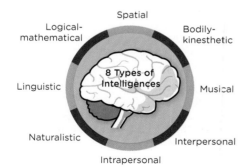

FIGURE 7.5

Gardner's Revised Theory of Multiple Intelligences

parasitic diseases in themselves and others. Identifying illness and developing treatment strategies are a regular part of life. These children would score much higher on tests of intelligence relating to practical knowledge than on tests assessing vocabulary (Sternberg, 2004). Even within a single culture, the meaning of intelligence changes across time. "Intelligence" for modern Kenyans may differ from that of their 14th-century ancestors.

As we explore the theories of intelligence below, please keep in mind that intelligence does not always go hand in hand with *intelligent behavior.* People can score high on intelligence measures but exhibit poor judgment. Perhaps you know a straight-A student who is somewhat lacking in common sense?

THE *G*-FACTOR   What makes it possible for someone to be highly intelligent? Very early in the history of intelligence measurement, Charles Spearman (1863–1945), an English psychologist known for his work in statistics, speculated that humans have a **general intelligence** (or ***g*-factor**), by which he meant a singular underlying aptitude or intellectual ability. This *g*-factor, Spearman asserted, drives capabilities in many areas, including verbal, spatial, and reasoning competencies. The *g*-factor is the common link.

MULTIPLE INTELLIGENCES   American psychologist Howard Gardner (1943–) suggests that intelligence can be divided into *multiple intelligences* (Gardner, 1999, 2011; **FIGURE 7.5**). He originally proposed seven types of intelligences or "frames of mind": linguistic (verbal), logical-mathematical, spatial, bodily-kinesthetic, musical, intrapersonal, and interpersonal. Take a look at **TABLE 7.1** and consider how different occupations might be well suited for individuals who excel in Gardner's original seven intelligences. Later in his career, Gardner added an eighth intelligence: naturalistic, which primarily refers to the "capacity to categorize objects according to salient similarities and differences among them" (Visser, Ashton, & Vernon, 2006, p. 491). He has proposed that there also may be an existential intelligence (the tendency to question one's existence), but the evidence of it, at least for now, is only suggestive (Gardner, 2011; Visser, Ashton, & Vernon, 2006).

According to Gardner (2011), partial evidence for multiple intelligences comes from studying people with brain damage. Some mental capabilities are lost, whereas others remain intact, suggesting that they are really distinct categories. Further evidence for multiple intelligences (as opposed to just a *g*-factor) comes from observing people with *savant syndrome.* Individuals with savant syndrome have some area of extreme singular ability (calendar calculations, art, mental arithmetic, and so on; Treffert, 2015). The late Kim Peek, for example, was able to simultaneously read two pages of a book—one with each eye—and memorize nearly all the information it contained. Like the movie character he inspired ("Raymond Babbitt" in the movie *Rain Man*), Peek had extraordinary intellectual abilities (Brogaard & Marlow, 2012, December 11; Treffert, 2015).

Some psychologists question whether these abilities qualify as intelligence, as opposed to skills. Critics contend that there is little empirical support for the existence of multiple intelligences (Geake, 2008; Waterhouse, 2006).

THE TRIARCHIC THEORY OF INTELLIGENCE   Robert Sternberg (1949–) proposed three kinds of intelligence. Sternberg's (1988) **triarchic theory of intelligence** (trahy-AHR-kik) suggests that humans have varying degrees of analytical, creative, and practical competencies (**FIGURE 7.6**). *Analytic intelligence* refers to our capacity to solve problems. *Creative intelligence* represents the knowledge and skills we use to handle new situations. *Practical intelligence* includes our ability to adjust to different environments.

TABLE 7.1   GARDNER'S ORIGINAL MULTIPLE INTELLIGENCES

Logical-mathematical	Scientist Mathematician	Sensitivity to, and capacity to discern logical or numerical patterns; ability to handle long chains of reasoning.
Linguistic	Poet Journalist	Sensitivity to the sounds, rhythms, and meanings of words; sensitivity to the different functions of language.
Musical	Composer Violinist	Abilities to produce and appreciate rhythm, pitch, and timbre; appreciation of the forms of musical expressiveness.
Spatial	Navigator Sculptor	Capacities to perceive the visual-spatial world accurately and to perform transformations on one's initial perceptions.
Bodily-kinesthetic	Dancer Athlete	Abilities to control one's body movements and to handle objects skillfully.
Interpersonal	Therapist Salesman	Capacities to discern and respond appropriately to the moods, temperaments, motivations, and desires of other people.
Intrapersonal	Person with detailed, accurate self-knowledge	Access to one's own feelings and the ability to discriminate among them and draw on them to guide behavior; knowledge of one's own strengths, weaknesses, desires, and intelligences.

This table presents Gardner's original seven intelligences. Each intelligence has associated strengths and capabilities. Reprinted with permission from Gardner and Hatch (1989).

Let's take a moment and see how the triarchic theory of intelligence relates to Harry's experience on the football field. The Giants were playing on the big stage of Monday night football against the San Francisco 49ers. Harry was going one-on-one with the 49ers running back near the sideline, trying to stop him from taking the ball down the field. But rather than forcing his opponent out of bounds, Harry attempted to tackle him. The running back gave him a fake and ended up scoring a touchdown. It was embarrassing for Harry to make that mistake, especially with so many people watching the game on TV.

One year later, the Giants were playing the 49ers in the playoffs, and Harry made an interception (caught a pass intended for the other team). He looked up and saw that same running back who had faked him out the year before. "Automatically, my brain went back to that play that he beat me on the previous year," Harry says. Using the same strategy the running back had used on him, Harry avoided the tackle and scored a touchdown. "I was able to sort of give back to him what he gave to me."

In this situation, Harry was demonstrating *analytic intelligence;* he faced a problem (the other player was trying to stop him), but he swiftly produced a solution, drawing on knowledge he had acquired through past experience. This play also showcases Harry's *practical intelligence;* finding himself in a novel situation (essentially switching roles with the running back), he adjusted his behavior to accomplish his goal.

Needless to say, there are different ways to conceptualize intelligence (**TABLE 7.2**, on the following page), none of which appear to be categorically "right" or "wrong." Given these varied approaches, you might expect there are also many tools to measure intelligence. Let's explore several ways psychologists assess intellectual ability.

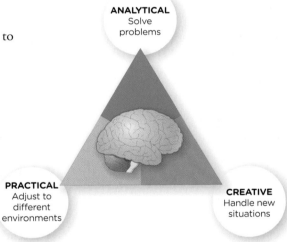

FIGURE 7.6
Sternberg's Triarchic Theory of Intelligence

general intelligence (*g*-factor) A singular underlying aptitude or intellectual competence that drives abilities in many areas, including verbal, spatial, and reasoning.

triarchic theory of intelligence Sternberg's theory suggesting that humans have varying degrees of analytical, creative, and practical abilities.

TABLE 7.2 THEORIES OF INTELLIGENCE

Theory	Advantages	Further Questions
Spearman's general intelligence (*g*-factor): There is a general intelligence driving abilities in many areas.	A connection exists among different abilities, such as verbal, spatial, and reasoning competencies.	Given the complexity of the mind, can intelligence really be explained by a single general factor?
Gardner's multiple intelligences: There are eight types of intelligences, each associated with certain strengths and capabilities.	Different "frames of mind" that allow humans to succeed.	What differentiates intelligence from skills?
Sternberg's triarchic theory: Humans have varying degrees of analytical, creative, and practical competencies.	Analytic intelligence allows us to solve problems, creative intelligence represents knowledge and skills used to handle new situations, and practical intelligence includes the ability to adjust to different environments, all of which can be assessed.	Are each of these areas separate, or do they share something in common (like a *g*-factor)?

Above is a summary of the main theories of intelligence, each with its own set of strengths and other considerations.

Measuring Brainpower

LO 12 Describe how intelligence is measured and identify the important characteristics of assessment.

Tests of intelligence generally aim to measure **aptitude**, or a person's potential for future learning. On the other hand, measures of **achievement** are designed to assess acquired knowledge (what a person has previously learned). It is possible to perform poorly on achievement tests but very well on aptitude tests. The writer John Irving received a low score on the verbal portion of the SAT, and the renowned physician Delos Cosgrove performed poorly on the Medical College Admission Test. These individuals, both of whom have dyslexia, did not allow a single test to deter them (Shaywitz, 2003). The line between aptitude and achievement tests is somewhat hazy; most tests are not purely one or the other.

A BRIEF HISTORY OF INTELLIGENCE TESTING Intelligence testing is more than a century old. In 1904 psychologist Alfred Binet (1857–1911) joined a commission of the French government that sought to create a way to identify students who might have trouble learning in regular classroom settings. A new French law had recently required school attendance by all children. The Ministry of Public Instruction recognized that this transition would be difficult because some French children had never attended school. For the law to be implemented successfully, it was necessary to identify children who had the potential to succeed. A measure was needed to predict the performance of these schoolchildren (Fancher & Rutherford, 2012; Watson, 1968).

Binet worked with one of his students, Théodore Simon (1872–1961), to construct an assessment of intelligence. They studied Binet's daughters and Parisian schoolchildren, coming up with the 30 items in the original assessment. These items were designed to be of increasing difficulty, starting with a simple test to see if a child could follow a lit match that the tester moved in front of her. The items became more difficult as testing progressed—explaining how paper and cardboard are different, and making rhymes with words, for instance (Fancher & Rutherford, 2012).

Binet and Simon assumed that children generally follow the same path of intellectual development. Their primary goal was to compare a child's mental ability with

aptitude An individual's potential for learning.

achievement Acquired knowledge, or what has been learned.

mental age (MA) A score representing the mental abilities of an individual in relation to others of a similar chronological age.

intelligence quotient (IQ) A score from an intelligence assessment; originally based on mental age divided by chronological age, multiplied by 100.

the mental abilities of other children of the same age. They would determine the **mental age (MA)** of a child by comparing his performance to that of other children in the same age category. For example, a 10-year-old boy with average intellectual abilities would score similarly to other 10-year-old children and thus would have a *mental age* of 10. An intelligent 10-year-old boy would score better than other 10-year-old children and thus have a higher mental age (for example, a mental age of 12) compared to his chronological age. Similarly, a child who was intellectually delayed would have a mental age lower than his chronological age. Although Binet and Simon's measure of intelligence was groundbreaking at the time, it had many shortcomings that were eventually addressed by others.

One of the problems with relying on mental age as an index is that it cannot be used to compare intelligence levels across age groups. For example, you can't use mental age to compare the intelligence levels of an 8-year-old girl and a 12-year-old girl. In 1912 German psychologist William Stern (1871–1938) solved this problem by devising the **intelligence quotient (IQ)**. To calculate IQ, a child's mental age is divided by her chronological age and multiplied by 100. A 10-year-old girl with a mental age of 8 would have an IQ score of (8 ÷ 10) × 100 = 80. If her mental age and chronological age were the same, her IQ would be 100. The IQ score can be used to compare the level of intelligence of this 10-year-old girl with children of other ages.

This method does not apply to adults, however. It wouldn't make sense to give a 60-year-old man who scores the same as a 30-year-old man an IQ score of 50 (that is, 30 ÷ 60 × 100 = 50). Modern intelligence tests still assign a numerical score (which we continue to refer to as "IQ"), although they no longer use the actual quotient score.

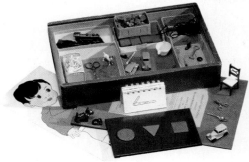

What's Your IQ?
French psychologist Alfred Binet collaborated with one of his students, Théodore Simon, to create a systematic assessment of intelligence. The materials pictured here come from Lewis Terman and Maude Merrill's 1937 version of Binet and Simon's test. Using these materials, the test administrator prompts the test taker with statements such as "Point to the doll's foot," or "What advantages does an airplane have over a car?" (Sattler, 1990). Top: Albert Harlingue/Roger-Viollet/The Image Works. Bottom: Science & Society Picture Library/Getty Images.

THE STANFORD–BINET TEST American psychologist Lewis Terman (1877–1956) revised Stern's work so that Binet's test could be used in the United States, where it came to be known as the Stanford–Binet. Terman (1916) changed some items, added items, developed standards based on American children, and extended the test to include teens and adults. *The Stanford–Binet Intelligence Scales,* as it is now known in its fifth edition (Roid, 2003), includes the assessment of verbal and nonverbal abilities (for instance, defining words, tracing paths in a maze). The Stanford–Binet yields an overall score for general intelligence as well as scores relating to more specific abilities, such as knowledge, reasoning, visual processing, and working memory (Becker, 2003).

THE WECHSLER TESTS In the late 1930s, American psychologist David Wechsler (1896–1981) began creating intelligence tests for adults (Anastasi & Urbina, 1997). Although many had been using the Stanford–Binet with adults, it was not an ideal measure, given that adults might react negatively to the questions geared to the daily experiences of school-age children. The Wechsler Adult Intelligence Scale (WAIS) was published in 1955 and has since been revised numerous times (1981, 1997), with the most recent revision in 2008 (WAIS–IV). In addition to creating assessments for adults, Wechsler also developed scales for older children (Wechsler Intelligence Scale for Children, WISC–V) and younger children (Wechsler Preschool and Primary Scale of Intelligence, WPPSI–IV).

The Wechsler assessments of intelligence consist of a variety of subtests designed to measure different aspects of intellectual ability. The 10 subtests on the WAIS–IV target four domains of intellectual performance: verbal abilities, perceptual reasoning,

working memory, and processing speed. Results from the WAIS–IV include an overall intelligence quotient (IQ) score, as well as scores on the four domains. Psychologists look for consistency among the domain scores and subtest scores, as opposed to focusing only on the overall IQ score. Substantial inconsistency may suggest an issue that should be further explored, such as a reading or language disability. In the United States, Wechsler tests are now used more frequently than the Stanford–Binet.

Let's Test the Intelligence Tests

As you read about the history of intelligence assessment, did you wonder how effective those early tests were? We hope so, because this would indicate you are thinking critically. Psychologists make great efforts to ensure the accurate assessment of intelligence, paying close attention to three important characteristics: validity, reliability, and standardization (**INFOGRAPHIC 7.4** on page 316).

VALIDITY **Validity** is the degree to which an assessment measures what it intends to measure. If you are looking for a valid intelligence test, then it must measure intelligence, and not something else. We can assess the validity of a measure by comparing its results to those of other assessments that have been found to measure the factor of interest. In addition, we determine the validity of an assessment by seeing if it can predict what it is designed to measure, or its *predictive validity.* Thus, to determine if an intelligence test is valid, we would check to see if the scores it produces are consistent with those of other intelligence tests. A valid intelligence test should also be able to predict future performance on tasks related to intellectual ability.

RELIABILITY Another important characteristic of assessment is **reliability,** the ability of a test to provide consistent, reproducible results. If given repeatedly, a reliable test will continue producing similar scores. If we administer an intelligence test to an individual, we would expect (if it is reliable) that the person's scores will remain consistent across time, as someone's intelligence is not expected to vary much over time. We can also determine the reliability of an assessment by splitting the test in half and then determining whether the findings of the first and second halves of the test agree with each other (this is called *split-half reliability*).

It is important to note that it is possible to have a reliable test that is not valid. For this reason, we always have to determine *both* reliability and validity. Imagine a psychologist using a reliable test that claims to measure intelligence (provides similar scores when people are retested), but the test is not valid and is actually measuring reading level instead. The test reliably measures reading level (achievement), but is not a measure of intelligence (aptitude).

STANDARDIZATION In addition to being valid and reliable, a good intelligence test provides standardization. Perhaps you have taken a test that measured your achievement in a particular area (for example, an ACT or SAT), or an aptitude test to measure your innate abilities (for example, an IQ test). Upon receiving your scores, you may have wondered how you performed in comparison to other people in your class, college, or state. Most aptitude and achievement tests allow you to make these judgments through the use of **standardization.** Standardization occurs when test developers administer a test to a large sample of people and then publish the average scores, or *norms,* for specified groups. The sample must be representative of the population of interest; that is, it must include a variety of individuals who are similar to the population using the test. This allows you to compare your own score with people of the same age, gender, socioeconomic status, or region. Test norms permit evaluation of the relative performance (often provided as percentiles) of an individual compared to others with similar characteristics.

It is also critical that assessments are given and scored using standard procedures. This ensures that no one is given an unfair advantage or disadvantage. Intelligence tests are subject to tight control. The public does not have access to the questions or answers, and all testing must be administered by a professional. What about those IQ tests found on the Internet? They simply are not valid due to lack of standardization.

THE NORMAL CURVE Have you ever wondered how many people in the population are really smart? Or perhaps how many people have average intelligence? With aptitude tests like the Wechsler assessments and the Stanford–Binet, we can predict what percentage of the population will have scores between two intervals by using a **normal curve,** which depicts the frequency of values along a continuum (Infographic 7.4 on the next page). The normal curve is symmetrical and shaped like a bell. The highest point on the graph reflects the average score.

The normal curve shown in Infographic 7.4 portrays the distribution of scores for the Wechsler tests. As you can see, the *mean* or average score is 100. As you follow the horizontal axis, notice that the higher and lower scores occur less and less frequently in the population. A score of 145 or 70 is far less common than a score of 100, for example.

The normal curve applies to a variety of traits, including IQ, height, weight, and personality characteristics, and we can use it to make predictions about these traits. Consult Appendix A for more information on the normal curve and a variety of other topics associated with statistics.

BUT ARE THEY FAIR? One important responsibility of test developers is to ensure that they do not promote any test-based biases. A major concern with cognitive tests, like those that measure intelligence, is that scores consistently differ across certain groups of people. For example, researchers have reported that Black Americans, in general, score lower on cognitive tests than do White Americans (Cottrell, Newman, & Roisman, 2015). Differences in the averages of these two groups have been found to be around 10 to 15 IQ points (Ceci & Williams, 2009; Dickens & Flynn, 2006). Group differences are also apparent for East Asians, who score around 6 points higher than average White Americans, and for Hispanics, who score around 10 points lower than average White Americans (Rushton & Jensen, 2010). Although researchers disagree about what causes these gaps in IQ scores, they are in general agreement that there is *no* evidence to support a "genetic hypothesis" across races (Nisbett et al., 2012). Researchers generally attribute these group differences to environmental factors, not to race-wide genetics.

The evidence for environmental influence contributing to this gap in IQ scores is strong and points to a variety of factors (Cottrell et al., 2015). Differences in environments can account for disparities in IQ and other cognitive test scores. Factors like maternal disadvantages (income, mother's education, and verbal ability) can lead to parenting factors (such as maternal sensitivity, acceptance, and safe environment), which ultimately "could account for the association between race and cognitive test scores" (Cottrell et al., 2015, p. 1723).

Socioeconomic status (SES) is an important variable to consider. The disproportionate percentage of minorities in the lower strata may, in fact, mask the critical issue of environmental factors and their relationship with IQ. For example, children raised in homes with lower SES tend to watch more TV, have less access to books and technology, and are not read to as often. In addition, individuals with lower SES frequently live in disadvantaged neighborhoods and have limited access to quality schools (Hanscombe et al., 2012).

Another likely environmental explanation for the IQ gap is stress. Research suggests that Black families, "on average, tend to live in more stressful environments than do" White families (Nisbett et al., 2012, p. 152). Chronic stress can have a negative impact on the function of the brain, particularly those areas responsible for attention

CONNECTIONS

In **Chapter 1,** we discussed the importance of operational definitions, which specify the precise manner in which variables are defined and measured. Here we note that standard procedures are important when administering assessments as well. Data must be collected in a controlled fashion to ensure errors don't arise from unknown environmental factors.

Synonyms
normal curve normal distribution

validity The degree to which an assessment measures what it intends to measure.

reliability The ability of an assessment to provide consistent, reproducible results.

standardization Occurs when test developers administer a test to a large sample and then publish the average scores for specified groups.

normal curve Depicts the frequency of values of a variable along a continuum; bell-shaped symmetrical distribution, with the highest point reflecting the average score.

How Smart Are Intelligence Tests?

Tests that claim to measure intelligence are everywhere—online, in your favorite magazine, at job interviews, and in many elementary and secondary schools. But can all of these tests be trusted? The results of an intelligence test aren't meaningful unless the test is *valid*, *reliable*, and *fair*. But what do those concepts mean, and how can we be sure whether a test is valid, reliable, or fair—let alone all three? Let's take a look.

validity DOES THE TEST MEASURE WHAT IT INTENDS TO MEASURE?

Is a bathroom scale valid for measuring height?

How about a ruler missing its first inch?

A shortened ruler would not be a valid measure because it would provide different results than other rulers.

A valid intelligence test will provide results that:

✔ agree with the results of other valid intelligence tests

✔ predict performance in an area related to intelligence, such as academic achievement

reliability WILL YOUR SCORE BE CONSISTENT EVERY TIME YOU TAKE THE TEST?

A shortened ruler isn't valid, but it is *reliable* because it will give the same result every time it's used.

A reliable intelligence test will provide results that:

✔ are reproducible (produce a similar score if taken a second time)

✔ show the first and second halves of the test are consistent with each other

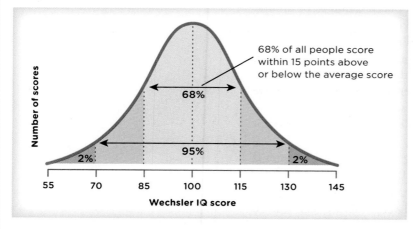

68% of all people score within 15 points above or below the average score

68%

2%   95%   2%

55   70   85   100   115   130   145

Wechsler IQ score

Number of scores

Because most intelligence tests are *standardized*, you can determine how well you have performed in comparison to others. Test scores tend to form a bell-shaped curve—called the normal curve—around the average score. Most people (68%) score within 15 points above or below the average. If the test is reliable, each person's score should stay around the same place on the curve across multiple testings.

fairness IS THE TEST VALID FOR THE GROUP?

An animal weighing 2 stone is likely to be a:
(a) sparrow   (c) mature lion
(b) small dog   (d) blue whale

Unless you live in the United Kingdom, where the imperial system of weights is used, you probably wouldn't know that a stone is approximately 14 pounds, and therefore the correct answer is B. Does this mean that you are less intelligent, or that the test is biased against people without a specific background? A test that is culture-fair is designed to minimize the bias of cultural background.

3 inches   2.286 Chinese Imperial cùn   .1667 cubits

and memory (short-term, long-term, and working memory), which are vulnerable to sustained high levels of stress (McEwen, 2000).

CULTURE-FAIR INTELLIGENCE TESTS It has not yet been determined whether group differences in IQ scores also reflect biases of the tests themselves. Can an assessment tool be valid for some groups but not others? For example, are these IQ tests solely aptitude tests, or do they incorporate some level of achievement (learned content)? If that is the case, then people with limited exposure to certain types of test content may be at a disadvantage. Early versions of the IQ tests exhibited some bias against individuals from rural areas, people of lower socioeconomic status, and African Americans. Bias may result from language, dialect, or the culture of those who have created the tests (Sattler, 1990; Sternberg, 2004).

To address these problems, psychologists have tried to create **culture-fair intelligence tests,** designed to measure intelligence without putting people at a disadvantage because of their cultural backgrounds. One way to avoid bias is to use questions that would be familiar to people from a variety of backgrounds. Another method is to use nonverbal questions. (The Raven's Progressive Matrices uses this approach; see **FIGURE 7.7.**) Since intelligence is defined within a culture and tests are created within a culture, some have suggested that we can only create culture-relevant tests, not culture-fair or culture-free assessments (Sternberg, 2004).

CONNECTIONS

In **Chapter 6,** we discussed the biology of memory, exploring areas of the brain responsible for memory formation and storage (hippocampus, cerebellum, and amygdala) as well as changes at the level of the neuron (long-term potentiation). Here, we note that stressful environments can impact the functioning of the memory system.

FIGURE 7.7
Nonverbal Intelligence
The Raven's Progressive Matrices test (left) and the Matrix Reasoning subtest of the WISC–IV (right) are used to assess components of nonverbal intelligence. For both sample questions pictured here, the test taker is required to choose the item that completes the matrix pattern. The correct answer for the Raven's is choice 2; the correct answer for the Matrix Reasoning is choice 4. These types of tests are generally considered culturally fair, meaning they do not favor certain cultural groups over others.

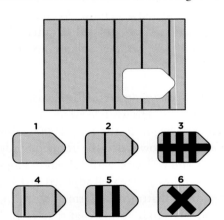

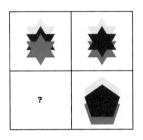

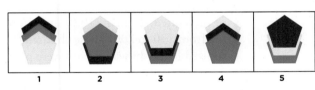

Sample items similar to those found in the Wechsler Intelligence Scale for Children, Fourth Edition (WISC-IV). Copyright © 2003 NCS Pearson, Inc. Reproduced with permission. All rights reserved. Sample items similar to those found in the Raven's® Progressive Matrices. Copyright © 1998 NCS Pearson, Inc. Reproduced with permission. All rights reserved. "Wechsler Intelligence Scale for Children", "WAIS", and "Raven's" are trademarks, in the US and/or other countries, of Pearson Education, Inc. or its affiliates(s).

Ultimately, IQ tests are good at predicting academic success. They are highly correlated with SATs, ACTs, and Graduate Record Examinations (GRE), for example, and the correlations are stronger for the higher and lower ranges of IQ scores. Strong correlations help us make predictions about future behavior. Some researchers have found, however, that self-discipline may be a better predictor of success than IQ tests (Duckworth & Seligman, 2005).

The study of intelligence is far from straightforward. Assessing a concept with no universally accepted definition is not an easy task, but these tests do serve useful purposes. The key is to be mindful of their limitations, while appreciating their ability to measure an array of cognitive abilities.

The Diversity of Human Intelligence

Once called mental retardation, *intellectual disability* consists of a delay in thinking, intelligence, and social and practical skills that is evident before age 18. Psychologists can assess intellectual functioning with IQ scores; for example, disability is identified as an

culture-fair intelligence tests
Assessments designed to minimize cultural bias.

Gifted Artist
Chinese conductor Hu Yizhou rehearses for an upcoming concert in Korea. Yizhou, who has Down syndrome, is part of the China Disabled Peoples Performing Art Troupe. REUTERS/ You Sung-Ho KKH/SH.

gifted Highly intelligent; defined as having an IQ score of 130 or above.

emotional intelligence The capacity to perceive, understand, regulate, and use emotions to adapt to social situations.

heritability The degree to which hereditary factors (genes) are responsible for a particular characteristic observed within a population; the proportion of variation in a characteristic attributed to genetic factors.

IQ score below approximately 70 on the Wechsler tests. It can also be assessed in terms of one's ability to adapt; for example, being able to live independently, and understanding number concepts, money, and hygiene. Both low IQ scores and adaptive functioning deficits are evident in intellectual disability (American Psychiatric Association, 2013). Although intellectual disability is the preferred term, prior to October 5, 2010, references to "mental retardation" existed in many laws and policies relating to intellectual disability (Schalock et al., 2010). On that special day in 2010, President Barack Obama signed Rosa's Law declaring that all earlier references to this phrase be removed from federal, health, education, and labor laws (Ford, Acosta, & Sutcliffe, 2013).

There are many causes of intellectual disability, but we cannot always pinpoint them. According to the American Association on Intellectual and Developmental Disabilities (AAIDD), nearly half of intellectual disability cases have unidentifiable causes (Schalock et al., 2010). Known causes include Down syndrome (an extra chromosome in what would normally be the 21st pair), fetal alcohol syndrome (exposure to alcohol while in utero), and fragile X syndrome (a defect in a gene on the X chromosome leading to reductions in protein needed for development of the brain). There are also known environmental factors, such as lead and mercury poisoning, lack of oxygen at birth, various diseases, and exposure to alcohol and other drugs during fetal development.

At the other end of the intelligence spectrum are the intellectually **gifted,** those who have IQ scores of 130 or above. Above 140, one is considered a "genius." As you might imagine, very few people—about 2% of the population—are classified as gifted. An even smaller proportion falls in the genius range: only 1% of the population (Simonton, 2012, November/December).

TERMAN'S STUDY OF THE GIFTED Lewis Terman was interested in discovering if gifted children could function successfully in adulthood. His work led to the longest-running longitudinal study on genius and giftedness, begun in the early 1900s. This study, formerly called the Genetic Studies of Genius, is now called the Terman Study of the Gifted. Terman (1925) monitored 857 boys and 671 girls with IQ scores ranging from 130 to 200. These children (known as "Termites") were well adjusted socially, showed leadership skills, and were physically healthy and attractive (Terman & Oden, 1947). Following the participants into adulthood, the study found that they earned more academic degrees and achieved more financial success than their nongifted peers (Fancher & Rutherford, 2012; Holahan & Sears, 1995). Compelling as these findings may be, they do not necessarily indicate that high IQ scores guarantee success in all areas of life.

LIFE SMARTS The ability to function in everyday life also is influenced by *emotional intelligence* (Goleman, 1995). **Emotional intelligence** is the capacity to perceive, understand, regulate, and use emotions to adapt to social situations. People with emotional intelligence use information about their emotions to direct their behavior in an efficient and creative way (Salovey, Mayer, & Caruso, 2002). They are self-aware and can properly judge how to behave in social situations. A high level of emotional intelligence is indicated by self-control—the ability to manage anger, impulsiveness, and anxiety. Other attributes include empathy, awareness of emotions, and persistent self-motivation. Research suggests that emotional intelligence is related to performance on the job and at school (Joseph, Jin, Newman, & O'Boyle, 2015; MacCann, Fogarty, Zeidner, & Roberts, 2011).

As you may have observed in your own life, people display varying degrees of emotional intelligence. Where does this diversity in emotional intelligence—or any characteristic of intelligence—arise? Like many topics in psychology, it comes down to nature and nurture.

Origins of Intelligence

Now let's examine how nature and nurture impact intelligence in general. Twin studies (research involving identical and fraternal twins) are an excellent way to evaluate the relative weights of nature and nurture for virtually any psychological trait. The Minnesota Study of Twins Reared Apart (MISTRA) indicates there are strong correlations between the IQ scores of identical twins—stronger than the correlations between the IQ scores of fraternal twins or other siblings. In other words, the closer the genetic relationship (identical twins have identical genes at conception), the more similar their IQ scores are (Johnson & Bouchard, 2011; McGue, Bouchard, Iacono, & Lykken, 1993; Shakeshaft et al., 2015). This suggests that genes play a major role in determining intellectual abilities. According to the Minnesota twin studies, identical twins' IQ scores have correlations as high as .86 (remembering that ±1.00 is a perfect correlation) (**FIGURE 7.8**).

Heritability refers to the degree to which heredity is responsible for a particular characteristic or trait in the population. As psychologists study the individual differences associated with a variety of traits, they try to determine the heritability of each one. Many traits have a high degree of heritability (for example, eye color, height, and other physical characteristics), but others are determined by the environments in which we are raised (for example, manners; Dickens & Flynn, 2001). Results from twin and adoption studies suggest that heritability for "general cognitive abilities" is about 50% (Plomin & DeFries, 1998; Plomin, DeFries, Knopik, & Niederhiser, 2013). In other words, about half of the variation in intellectual or cognitive ability can be attributed to genetic make-up, and the other half to environment. However, with twin studies, it is impossible to completely isolate the impact of the shared environment, which would require genetic analyses of people who do not belong to the same family (von Stumm & Plomin, 2015). Evidence from direct genetic analyses indicates that between 40% and 51% of the variation in intelligence between individuals is due to "many genes of small effects" (Davies et al., 2011, p. 996).

We should close this discussion with a few important conclusions: (1) It is important to emphasize that heritability applies to groups of people, not individuals. We cannot say, for example, that an individual's intelligence level is 40% due to genes and 60% the result of environment. We can only make general predictions about groups and how they are influenced by genetic factors (Dickens & Flynn, 2001). (2) We must also remember that although there are gaps in cognitive test results across groups of people, these are not considered to be due to genetics, as socioeconomic factors seem to play a critical role in such differences (Cottrell et al., 2015). (3) Cognitive abilities do

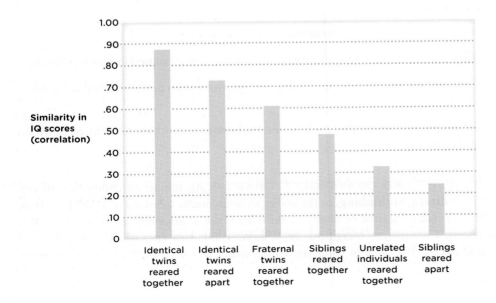

FIGURE 7.8

The Impact of Nature and Nurture on Intelligence

The most genetically similar people, identical twins, have the strongest correlation between their scores on IQ tests. This suggests that genes play a major role in determining intelligence. But if identical twins are raised in different environments, the correlation is slightly lower, showing some environmental effect. McGue et al., 1993.

run in families, with approximately 40–50% of these differences due to genes (Davies et al., 2011).

We have now explored the various approaches to assessing and conceptualizing intelligence. Let's shift our focus to a quality that is associated with intelligence but far more difficult to measure: *creativity*.

Creativity

Harry never approached football in a conventional way. When he was learning the ropes in his new middle linebacker position with the Giants, the coach provided specific instructions to accomplish his objectives. Harry would execute the task, but not always the way the coach had prescribed. "Everything he tried to get me to do, I did it [backwards], but I got the same or better results," Harry explains. Eventually, the coach gave up and allowed Harry the freedom to think outside the box. He threw up his hands and said, "As long as you get the job done, I can't fault you!"

LO 13   **Define creativity and its associated characteristics.**

Harry was using creativity to solve problems on the football field, just as you might use creativity to resolve a tricky situation in school or spice up a bland recipe in your kitchen. In a problem-solving scenario, **creativity** is the ability to construct valuable results in innovative ways. Creativity and intelligence are not equivalent, but they are correlated, and a basic level of intelligence is necessary for creativity to flow (Jaarsveld et al., 2015). For example, you need to have a certain level of intelligence to generate original ideas, as opposed to just more ideas (Benedek, Franz, Heene, & Neubauer, 2012; Nusbaum & Silvia, 2011).

CHARACTERISTICS OF CREATIVITY Because creativity doesn't present itself in a singular or uniform manner, it is difficult to measure. Most psychologists agree that there are several basic characteristics associated with creativity (Baer, 1993; Sternberg, 2006a, 2006b):

- *Originality:* the ability to come up with unique solutions when trying to solve a problem

- *Fluency:* the ability to create many potential solutions

- *Flexibility:* the ability to use a variety of problem-solving tactics to arrive at solutions

- *Knowledge:* a sufficient base of ideas and information

- *Thinking:* the ability to see things in new ways, make connections, see patterns

- *Personality:* characteristics of a risk taker, someone who perseveres and tolerates ambiguity

- *Intrinsic motivation:* influenced by internal rewards, motivated by the pleasure and challenge of work

DIVERGENT AND CONVERGENT THINKING An important component of creativity is **divergent thinking,** or the ability to devise many solutions to a problem (Baer, 1993). A classic measure of divergent thinking is the *unusual uses test* (Guilford, 1967; Guilford, Christensen, Merrifield, & Wilson, 1960; **FIGURE 7.9**). A typical prompt would ask the test taker to come up with as many uses for a brick as she can imagine.

In this test, you will be asked to consider some common objects. Each object has a common use, which will be stated. You are to list as many as six other uses for which the object or parts of the object could serve.

Example:

Given: A NEWSPAPER (used for reading). You might think of the following other uses for a newspaper.

a. Start a fire

b. Wrap garbage

c. Swat flies

d. Stuffing to pack boxes

e. Line drawers or shelves

f. Make a kidnap note

Notice that all of the uses listed are different from each other and different from the primary use of a newspaper. Each acceptable use must be different from others and from the common use.

FIGURE 7.9

Instructions for Guilford's Alternate Uses Task

The sample question above is from Guilford's Alternate Uses Task, a revised version of the *unusual uses test,* which is designed to gauge creativity. Reproduced by special permission of the Publisher, MIND GARDEN, Inc., www.mindgarden.com from the Alternate Uses by J.P. Guilford, Paul R. Christensen, Philip R Merrifield, & Robert C. Wilson. Copyright 1960 by Sheridan Supply Co. Further reproduction is prohibited without the Publisher's written consent.

(What ideas do you have? Paperweight? Shot put? Stepstool?) Remember that we often have difficulty thinking about how to use familiar objects in atypical ways because of functional fixedness.

In contrast to divergent thinking, **convergent thinking** focuses on finding a single best solution by converging on the correct answer. Here, we fall back on previous experience and knowledge. This conventional approach to problem solving leads to one solution, but, as we have noted, many problems have multiple solutions.

Creativity comes with many benefits. People with this ability tend to have a broader range of knowledge and interests. They are open to new experiences and often are less inhibited in their thoughts and behaviors (Feist, 2004; Simonton, 2000). The good news is that we can become more creative by practicing divergent thinking, taking risks, and looking for unusual connections between ideas (Baer, 1993).

 In Class: Collaborate and Report

In your groups, **A)** create a game that reinforces your learning of the key concepts and terms used in the chapter (*Hint:* charades, Pictionary, hang-man). **B)** How did you incorporate convergent and divergent thinking?

DR. TAYLOR'S NEWFOUND INTELLIGENCE It took Dr. Taylor 8 years to recuperate from what she now calls her "stroke of insight," and it was not smooth sailing. Regaining her physical and cognitive strength required steadfast determination and painstaking effort. "Recovery was a decision I had to make a million times a day," she writes (Taylor, 2006, p. 115). She also had many people cheering her on—family and friends who had faith in her brain's plasticity, or ability to repair and rewire (Taylor, 2006).

If stroke victims fail to regain all faculties by 6 months, they never will. At least that is what Dr. Taylor remembers hearing her doctors say. But she proved all the naysayers wrong. Within 2 years, Dr. Taylor was living back in her home state of Indiana and teaching college courses in anatomy/physiology and neuroscience. Four years after the operation, she had retrained her body to walk gracefully and her brain to multitask. By Year 5, she could solve math problems, and by Year 7, she had accepted another teaching position, this time at Indiana University (Taylor, 2006).

Today, Dr. Taylor is working on various projects aimed at increasing awareness and understanding of the brain, and supporting those recovering from neurological damage (drjilltaylor.com, 2015). Dr. Taylor finds she has become more open to new experiences and ways of thinking (a prerequisite for creativity), and that she has emerged from her ordeal more empathetic and emotionally aware. ●

A CAPTAIN OFF THE FIELD In 2006 Harry Carson was inducted into the Pro Football Hall of Fame, but he was not in the mood for celebrating. As he recalled in an interview with *PBS Frontline*, "I wasn't happy about being a Hall of Famer knowing that so many of my brethren were struggling. They were suffering" (Kirk & Carson, 2013, September 4; 4:19). Harry used his enshrinement speech to advocate on behalf of the players who had made the NFL into the multibillion-dollar enterprise it is today: "I would hope that the leaders of the NFL, the future commissioner, and the player[s] association do a much better job of looking out for those individuals. . . . If we made the league what it is, you have to take better care of your own" (Pro Football Hall of Fame, n.d.).

New Beginnings
Dr. Taylor currently serves as the national spokesperson for the Harvard Brain Tissue Resource Center, where scientists conduct research on brain tissue from cadavers. It took 8 years for Dr. Taylor to recover from her stroke. © My Stroke of Insight, Inc. Photo by Kip May.

You Asked, Dr. Taylor Answers

http://qrs.ly/q15a5d4

Did you undergo any psychological treatment during your recuperation?

scan this →

creativity In problem solving, the ability to construct valuable results in innovative ways; the ability to generate original ideas.

divergent thinking The ability to devise many solutions to a problem; a component of creativity.

convergent thinking A conventional approach to problem solving that focuses on finding a single best solution to a problem by using previous experience and knowledge.

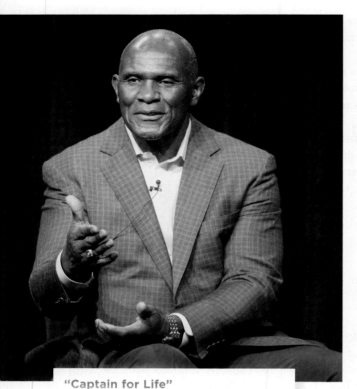

"Captain for Life"
Harry participates in the League of Denial: The NFL's Concussion Crisis panel discussion at the 2013 Summer Television Critics Association tour. Since his retirement in 1988, Harry has become a powerful voice in the conversation about sports-related head injuries. He continues to lead and advocate for generations of football players who are facing the repercussions of brain injury. The title of his memoir, *Captain for Life,* could not be more fitting. Frederick M. Brown/Getty Images.

It would take another decade for the NFL to finally admit that head injuries sustained in football are associated with chronic traumatic encephalopathy (CTE; Fainaru, 2016, March 15). Although this represents a positive shift in the discussion about football-related brain injuries, Harry's work is far from done. One of his main goals is to help other NFL retirees see that they are not alone in their struggles with mood swings, cognitive impairment, and other symptoms of traumatic brain injury—and that these challenges can become manageable. Another of his major objectives is to educate parents about the neurological consequences of contact sports. "There are a lot of misconceptions out there about this issue," Harry explains. "One is that it is an NFL problem." Traumatic brain injuries can occur in football players at all levels: in college, in high school, even at the Pop Warner level (ages 5 to 16). And it's not limited to football. Brain injuries may happen in a variety of sports, including soccer, lacrosse, hockey, boxing, wrestling, and horseback riding. "There needs to be a warning to parents to understand that in signing [their] kids up to play ice hockey or football or some other sport where their child might sustain neurological damage . . . that [this] young person might not be the same after they've been concussed." As for his own grandson, football is not in his future. "I cannot in good conscience allow my grandson to play knowing what I know," Harry said in an interview with *PBS Frontline* "This young, smart black kid, I want him to be intelligent, I want him to be brilliant, I want him to be able to use his brain, not his brawn. . . . I want him to be the best that he can be" (Kirk & Carson, 2013, 20:33-21:35).

When it comes to his own well-being, Harry will be in good shape if his brain is anything like his right shoulder. Decades ago, during a practice with the Giants, Harry severed a nerve serving his posterior deltoid muscle. After the destruction of that nerve, the muscle withered and became useless. But over a period of time, the surrounding muscles got stronger, compensating for the loss. Harry hopes his brain displays a similar degree of plasticity: "I would like to think that any kind of deficiency that I might have neurologically . . . that other parts of the brain might take over." ●

◯◯✔◯◯ show what you know

1. Sternberg believed that intelligence is made up of three types of competencies, including:
   a. linguistic, spatial, musical.
   b. intrapersonal, interpersonal, existential.
   c. analytic, creative, practical.
   d. achievement, triarchic, prototype.

2. Some tests of intelligence measure _____, or a person's potential for learning, and other tests measure _____, or acquired knowledge.

3. Define IQ. How is it derived?

4. An artist friend of yours easily comes up with unique solutions when trying to solve problems. This _____ is one of the defining characteristics of creativity.

✔ CHECK YOUR ANSWERS IN APPENDIX C.

Improve your grade! Use 📖 **LearningCurve** macmillan learning adaptive quizzing to create your personalized study plan, which will direct you to the resources that will help you most in 📖 **LaunchPad** macmillan learning

summary of concepts

LO 1 Give the definition of cognition and explain how it is related to thinking. (p. 281)

Cognition is the mental activity associated with obtaining, converting, and using knowledge. Thinking is a specific type of cognition, which involves coming to a decision, reaching a solution, forming a belief, or developing an attitude. Cognition is a broad term that describes mental activity, and thinking is a subset of cognition.

LO 2 Demonstrate an understanding of concepts and how they are organized. (p. 282)

Concepts are mental representations of categories of objects, situations, and ideas that belong together based on their central features or characteristics. Psychologists often use a three-level hierarchy to categorize objects. At the top of the hierarchy are superordinate concepts, the broadest category encompassing all the objects belonging to it. Below is the more specific midlevel of the hierarchy, the category used most often to identify objects. At the bottom of the hierarchy is the subordinate level, the most specific category.

LO 3 Differentiate between formal concepts and natural concepts. (p. 283)

Formal concepts are created through rigid and logical rules or features of a concept. Natural concepts, on the other hand, are acquired through everyday experience. Natural concepts don't have the same types of rigid rules for identification that formal concepts do, and this makes them harder to outline. We organize our worlds with the help of prototypes, which are the ideal or most representative examples of particular natural concepts.

LO 4 Describe the biological processes associated with cognition. (p. 287)

The biology of cognition is evident in the brain, both on a micro and macro level. Changes at the level of the neuron, whether through rewiring, heightened excitability, or increased efficiency of synaptic transmission, make it possible to store, retrieve, and manipulate information. The plasticity of the brain enables dramatic recoveries from trauma.

LO 5 Explain how trial and error and algorithms can be used to solve problems. (p. 289)

Problem solving refers to the variety of approaches used to achieve goals. One approach to problem solving is trial and error, which involves finding a solution through a series of attempts. Algorithms provide a virtually guaranteed solution to a problem by using formulas or sets of rules. Unlike trial and error, algorithms ensure that you will reach a solution if you follow all the steps correctly.

LO 6 Identify different types of heuristics used to solve problems. (p. 290)

Heuristics are problem-solving approaches that incorporate a rule of thumb or broad application of a strategy. One commonly used heuristic involves creating subgoals or subproblems. Another commonly used heuristic is means–ends analysis, which involves figuring out how to decrease the distance between a goal and the current status. Using means–ends analysis, you can break a problem into subproblems and solve them independently.

LO 7 Describe the process of decision making and explain how heuristics can lead us astray. (p. 295)

Decision making generally refers to the cognitive process of choosing among various ways to reach a goal. Sometimes a decision is based on a single feature. With more complex decisions, we tend to consider a variety of features. Using the availability heuristic, we predict the probability of something happening in the future based on how easily we can recall a similar type of event from the past. If we can easily recall a similar type of event, then we judge that event as being more likely to occur. With the representativeness heuristic, we evaluate the degree to which the primary characteristics of an event, person, or situation are similar to our prototype.

LO 8 Identify the causes and symptoms of chronic traumatic encephalopathy (CTE). (p. 301)

Chronic traumatic encephalopathy (CTE) is a neurodegenerative disease caused by repeated head trauma. The telltale sign of CTE is abnormal accumulation of the protein tau in the brain. This disease has been identified in deceased boxers, football players, and others who have sustained traumatic head injuries. Symptoms include headaches, depression, anger, and a host of cognitive problems.

LO 9 Define language and give examples of its basic elements. (p. 303)

Language is a system for using symbols to think and communicate. These symbols are words, gestures, or sounds, and there are specific rules for putting them together. Phonemes are the basic building blocks of spoken language. Morphemes consist of one or more phonemes and represent the fundamental units of meaning. The syntax of a language refers to the collection of rules guiding word choice and word order. Grammar refers to the rules associated with word and sentence structures and how these are formed from their components. Semantics refers to rules that are used to bring meaning to words and sentences. Pragmatics refers to the social rules for using language.

LO 10 Explain the linguistic relativity hypothesis and how language influences thought. (p. 307)

The linguistic relativity hypothesis proposes that language differences lead to disparities in thinking and perception. Most psychologists agree that although language might not determine thinking and perception, it certainly can influence it.

LO 11 Examine and distinguish among various theories of intelligence. (p. 309)

Charles Spearman speculated that intelligence consists of a general intelligence (or g-factor), which refers to a singular underlying aptitude or intellectual ability. Howard Gardner suggested we have multiple intelligences, proposing eight different types of intelligences or "frames of mind": linguistic (verbal), logical-mathematical, spatial,

bodily-kinesthetic, musical, intrapersonal, interpersonal, and naturalist. Robert Sternberg proposed three kinds of intelligences. His triarchic theory of intelligence suggests that humans have varying degrees of analytical, creative, and practical abilities.

LO 12 Describe how intelligence is measured and identify the important characteristics of assessment. (p. 312)

Some tests of intelligence aim to measure aptitude, or a person's potential for learning. Measures of achievement are designed to assess acquired knowledge (what a person has learned). Psychologists must ensure the accurate assessment of intelligence by determining validity, that is, the degree to which the test measures what it intends to measure. Another important characteristic is reliability, the ability of a test to provide consistent, reproducible results. A reliable test, given repeatedly, will result in similar scores.

LO 13 Define creativity and its associated characteristics. (p. 320)

Creativity is the ability to construct valuable results in innovative ways. Most psychologists agree on the basic characteristics of creativity, including originality, fluency, and flexibility. Because creativity is not evident in a singular or uniform manner, it is difficult to measure.

key terms

achievement, p. 312
algorithm, p. 290
aptitude, p. 312
availability heuristic, p. 296
cognition, p. 281
concepts, p. 282
confirmation bias, p. 298
convergent thinking, p. 321
creativity, p. 320
culture-fair intelligence test, p. 317
decision making, p. 295

divergent thinking, p. 320
emotional intelligence, p. 318
formal concepts, p. 283
framing effect, p. 298
functional fixedness, p. 293
general intelligence (*g*-factor), p. 310
gifted, p. 318
grammar, p. 304
heritability, p. 319
heuristics, p. 290
insight, p. 292

intelligence, p. 309
intelligence quotient (IQ), p. 313
language, p. 303
means–ends analysis, p. 292
mental age (MA), p. 313
morphemes, p. 304
natural concepts, p. 283
normal curve, p. 315
phonemes, p. 303
pragmatics, p. 305
problem solving, p. 289

prototypes, p. 285
reliability, p. 314
representativeness heuristic, p. 297
semantics, p. 304
standardization, p. 314
syntax, p. 304
thinking, p. 281
trial and error, p. 289
triarchic theory of intelligence, p. 310
validity, p. 314

test prep *are you ready?*

1. _____ is a mental activity associated with obtaining, converting, and using knowledge, and _____ refers to coming to a decision, reaching a solution, or forming a belief.
   a. Thinking; formal concept
   b. Cognition; superordinate concept
   c. Thinking; cognition
   d. Cognition; thinking

2. _____ are the mental representations of categories of objects, situations, and ideas that belong together based on their central features or characteristics.
   a. Concepts
   b. Prototypes
   c. Algorithms
   d. Heuristics

3. The boundaries of _____ are imprecise and hard to define, because they do not have rigid rules for identification. For example, not everyone agrees with what qualities make a *mother.*
   - a. algorithms
   - b. heuristics
   - c. natural concepts
   - d. formal concepts

4. Following a stroke, the neurons in the brain exhibit greater excitability, rewiring occurs, and there is increased efficiency of synaptic connections, all indicating _____ of the brain.
   - a. algorithms
   - b. the plasticity
   - c. means–ends analysis
   - d. the functional fixedness

5. You are at dinner with a friend and you are struggling to determine the tip you should leave. Your friend suggests you do what she does to calculate a 20% tip: Move the decimal to the left one space and multiply by 2. This is an example of using _____ to solve the problem.
   - a. prototypes
   - b. a heuristic
   - c. trial and error
   - d. an algorithm

6. The _____ suggests that language can affect thinking and perception.
   - a. confirmation bias
   - b. *g*-factor
   - c. triarchic theory
   - d. linguistic relativity hypothesis

7. Factors such as the frequency and vividness of an event make us more likely to predict such an event will occur in the future. This is known as using the:
   - a. representativeness heuristic.
   - b. availability heuristic.
   - c. additive model.
   - d. confirmation bias.

8. Sometimes we do not gather important information when making decisions because we are only looking for evidence that upholds our beliefs. This is known as the:
   - a. availability heuristic.
   - b. framing effect.
   - c. single-feature approach to decision making.
   - d. confirmation bias.

9. The wording of a question can influence the outcome of a decision. People are more likely to prefer ground beef if it is described as 80% lean as opposed to 20% fat. This is an example of:
   - a. insight.
   - b. the confirmation bias.
   - c. the framing effect.
   - d. the vividness of an event.

10. Infants can recognize and distinguish among all _____ from all languages until about 10 months of age. This is why it is so much more difficult for older children and adults to learn to speak a foreign language without an accent.
    - a. morphemes
    - b. phonemes
    - c. words
    - d. semantics

11. One of the telltale signs of chronic traumatic encephalopathy (CTE) is abnormal accumulation of _____, a protein also implicated in Alzheimer's disease.
    - a. brain bleeds
    - b. tau
    - c. arteriovenous malformations
    - d. phoneme

12. The word "unexcitable" can be broken into three parts (*un, excite, able*). Remove one of these and the meaning of the word changes. These three parts represent _____, the fundamental units that bring meaning to a language.
    - a. grammar
    - b. phonemes
    - c. morphemes
    - d. semantics

13. _____ is one's innate ability to solve problems, adapt to the environment, and learn from experience.
    - a. Heritability
    - b. Giftedness
    - c. Insight
    - d. Intelligence

14. To determine the _____ of an intelligence test, you could give the assessment to a sample of participants and then compare the results with another assessment of intelligence to make sure the test is measuring what it intends to measure.
    - a. reliability
    - b. validity
    - c. standardization
    - d. norms

15. Although there is a consistent gap between how Black Americans and White Americans score on IQ tests, research suggests there is *no* evidence to support a(n) _____ across races.
    - a. split-half reliability
    - b. normal curve
    - c. genetic hypothesis
    - d. emotional intelligence

16. How are formal and natural concepts different? Give examples of each.

17. Compare the theories of intelligence presented in this chapter.

18. Many people on the Jersey Shore had to leave their homes when Hurricane Irene hit in 2001. On returning home, they found that no significant damage had occurred. When told to evacuate for Superstorm Sandy in 2012, many of these same residents did not leave. What heuristic do you think they used?

19. Why are reliability and validity important in test construction? What is at risk if you have developed an unreliable IQ test? Can you think of any negative consequence of using an IQ test that is not valid?

20. Using divergent thinking, how many uses can you think of for a hammer?

✓ CHECK YOUR ANSWERS IN APPENDIX C.

YOUR SCIENTIFIC WORLD

Apply psychology to the real world!
Go to LaunchPad for access.

Mel Yates/Getty Images.

Mario Tama/Getty Images.

Robert van der Hilst/Corbis.

CHAPTER OUTLINE AND LEARNING OBJECTIVES

The Study of Human Development

LO 1 Define human development.

LO 2 Outline the three longstanding discussions in developmental psychology.

LO 3 Identify the types of research psychologists use to study developmental processes.

Genetics, Conception, and Prenatal Development

LO 4 Examine the role genes play in our development and identify the biological factors that determine sex.

LO 5 Discuss how genotype and phenotype relate to development.

LO 6 Describe the progression of prenatal development.

Infancy and Child Development

LO 7 Summarize the physical changes that occur in infancy.

LO 8 Distinguish among the theories explaining language acquisition.

LO 9 Outline the universal sequence of language development.

LO 10 Discuss the key elements of Piaget's and Vygotsky's theories of cognitive development.

LO 11 Explain Erikson's theory of psychosocial development up until puberty.

Adolescence

LO 12 Give examples of significant physical changes that occur during adolescence.

LO 13 Summarize Piaget's description of cognitive changes that take place during adolescence.

LO 14 Detail how Erikson explained changes in identity during adolescence.

LO 15 Examine Kohlberg's levels of moral development.

Adulthood

LO 16 Name several of the most important physical changes that occur across adulthood.

LO 17 Identify the most significant cognitive changes that occur across adulthood.

LO 18 Explain some of the socioemotional changes that occur across adulthood.

LO 19 Describe Kübler-Ross' theory regarding reactions to imminent death.

Nina Leen/Getty Images.

AP Photo/Kyodo News.

Christian Kober/Corbis.

8 human development

Yuriy Ruddy/Shutterstock.

The Study of Human Development

COLLEGE DOWN THE DRAIN? Joan Brown was 18 years old when she became pregnant for the first time. Beginning with the birth of her first child, she devoted her life to motherhood, putting her personal ambitions on hold. She worked as a waitress, took a job at Kmart, and spent several years at home with her three kids. When her middle child Ericka began preschool, Joan went along with her. She never intended to accompany her daughter to preschool 6 hours a day for the entire year, but if it eased Ericka's anxiety, Joan was willing to do it.

By the time Ericka was 16, the insecurity of her preschool days had vanished. Ericka was now a strong and independent young woman with the ability to accomplish most anything she wanted. "She was very smart, and I saw potential in her," Joan says. "And I knew that she was going to be better than I was, and that's what I always wanted."

But Joan's expectations were shattered one summer day at the doctor's office. Ericka had not been feeling well, though she couldn't quite articulate what was wrong, so Joan took her in for a checkup. When the doctor emerged from the examination room and said, "Ericka wants me to tell you something," Joan knew immediately: "What, she's pregnant?"

The car ride home was very quiet. Other than asking Ericka if she was hungry, Joan didn't say much of anything, and she remained withdrawn for a couple days. "I was furious because, you know, you have that talk so many times," Joan recalls. "I figured no college; [it's] gone down the drain."

Joan had reason to be concerned, as the statistics were not in Ericka's favor. According to one study, less than 2% of women having babies at the age of 17 or younger earn a college degree by the time they are 30 (Hoffman, 2006). Half of all teenage moms don't even graduate from high school by 22. By comparison, 90% of women who don't have babies in their teenage years earn high school diplomas (Centers for Disease Control and Prevention [CDC], 2016a).

Girl with Potential
Ericka Harley was 16 years old and starting her junior year of high school when she found out she was pregnant. Her mother, Joan, was disappointed to discover that her daughter, an honor-roll student, would soon be a mom; she had hoped Ericka might attend college and enjoy a successful career. Would Ericka ever make it to college? Courtesy Ericka Harley.

Ericka had reached a crossroads, both in her relationship with her mom and in her life. How would she face the challenge of teen pregnancy? What kinds of physical, mental, and social changes would she experience in the months and years ahead? In other words, how would this major life event affect Ericka's *development?* ●

Developmental Psychology

LO 1 Define human development.

When psychologists use the word "development," they are referring to the changes that occur in our bodies, minds, and social functioning from conception to death. The goal of **developmental psychology** is to examine these changes. Research in developmental psychology helps us understand the struggles and triumphs of everyday people, such as Ericka and Joan, as they journey through the different stages of life. Psychologists often focus their studies on "typical" or "average" individuals, as it helps them uncover common themes and variations across the life span.

Various topics discussed in this chapter, including personality, learning, and emotion, are covered elsewhere in the book. Here, we focus on how humans change over the course of a lifetime, homing in on three major categories of developmental change: physical, cognitive, and socioemotional.

THREE CATEGORIES OF DEVELOPMENT *Physical development* begins the moment a sperm unites with an egg, and it continues until we take our final breath. The physical growth beginning with conception and ending when the body stops growing and developing is referred to as **maturation**. For the most part, maturation follows a progression that is universal in nature and biologically driven, as these changes are common across all cultures and ethnicities, and generally follow a predictable pattern. After maturation, physical changes continue, but not necessarily in a positive or growth direction. Some people, for example, experience vision loss as they age, and this requires changes to their everyday activities and goals (Schilling et al., 2016). Changes in memory, problem-solving abilities, decision making, language, and intelligence all fall under the umbrella of *cognitive development*. Like physical development, cognitive development tends to follow a universal course early in life, but there is enormous variation in the way cognitive abilities change, particularly as people get older (Skirbekk, Loichinger, & Weber, 2012; Small, Dixon, & McArdle, 2011; von Stumm & Deary, 2012). *Socioemotional development* refers to social behaviors, emotions, and the changes people experience with respect to their relationships, feelings, and overall disposition.

Ericka, in Her Own Words

http://qrs.ly/6v5a5dq

CONNECTIONS

In **Chapter 5,** we described how various types of learning result in changes to behavior. Here, we are describing maturation, which also results in behavioral changes. Although some activities like sitting up alone appear to be learned, they are the result of maturation, as these changes are biologically driven.

We Can Sit!
Most babies begin sitting up on their own around 6 months (CDC, 2016f). Sitting upright is one of the milestones of physical development. Maturation tends to follow a predictable pattern, regardless of ethnicity or culture.
Mel Yates/Getty Images.

Note: Quotations attributed to Ericka Harley and Joan Brown are personal communications.

BIOPSYCHOSOCIAL PERSPECTIVE In this chapter, we draw on the biopsychosocial perspective, which recognizes the contributions of biological, psychological, and social forces shaping human development. We consider the intricate interplay of heredity, chemical activity, and hormones (biological factors); learning and personality traits (psychological factors); and family, culture, and media (social factors).

Three Debates

LO 2 Outline the three longstanding discussions in developmental psychology.

Science is, at its core, a work in progress, full of unresolved questions and areas of disagreement. In developmental psychology, longstanding debates and discussions tend to cluster around three major themes: stages and continuity, nature and nurture, and stability and change. Each of these themes relates to a basic question: (1) Does development occur in separate or discrete stages, or is it a steady, continuous process? (2) What are the relative roles of heredity and environment in development? (3) How stable is one's personality over a lifetime and across situations?

STAGES OR CONTINUITY Some aspects of development occur in discrete stages; others in a steady, continuous process. Abrupt changes are often related to environmental circumstances. High school graduation, for example, marks the time when many young people feel free to move out of the family home. This response is not universal, however. Ericka continued to live with her mom until she was 25—not unusual among today's young adults. As of 2014, 36.4% of women and 42.8% of men between the ages of 18 and 34 live with parents and other family members (Fry, 2015, November 11). Physical changes may also occur in stages, such as learning to walk and talk, or developing the physical characteristics of a sexually mature adult.

One line of evidence supporting developmental stages with definitive beginnings and endings comes to us indirectly through the animal kingdom. Konrad Lorenz (1937) documented the *imprinting* phenomenon, showing, for example, that when baby geese hatch, they become attached to the first "moving and sound-emitting object" they see, whether it's their mother or a nearby human (p. 269). Lorenz made sure he was the first moving creature several goslings saw, and he found that they followed him as soon as they could stand up and walk, becoming permanently attached to him because he was that first "object." But there appeared to be a limited time frame within which this imprinting occurred. Experiences during a **critical period** for this type of automatic response result in permanent and "irreversible changes" in brain function (Knudsen, 2004). Unlike baby geese, humans do not exhibit dramatic behavioral changes resulting from experiences that occur during critical periods. However, some researchers hypothesize that there are critical periods for the normal development of vision, attachment, and language (Hensch, 2004; Myers, 1987/2014).

Although some developmental changes occur stepwise, others happen gradually, without clear beginnings and endpoints (McAdams & Olson, 2010). Observing a toddler making her transition into early childhood, you probably won't be able to pinpoint her shift from the "terrible twos" to the more emotionally self-controlled young child.

NATURE AND NURTURE Psychologists also debate the degree to which heredity (nature) and environment (nurture) influence behavior and development, but few

He Must Be My Mother
A brood of baby geese follows scientist Konrad Lorenz. The goslings treated Lorenz like a mother because he was the first "moving and sound-emitting" object with whom they had contact (Lorenz, 1937, p. 269). As Lorenz discovered, there appears to be a critical period during which imprinting occurs.
Nina Leen/Getty Images.

developmental psychology A field of psychology that examines physical, cognitive, and socioemotional changes across the life span.

maturation Physical growth beginning with conception and ending when the body stops growing.

critical period Specific time frame in which an organism is sensitive to environmental factors, and certain behaviors and abilities are readily shaped or altered by events or experiences.

CONNECTIONS

Nature and nurture are discussed starting in **Chapter 1,** where we noted the debates of ancient philosophers. In **Chapter 7,** we introduced the concept of heritability, or the degree to which heredity (nature) is responsible for a particular characteristic. Here, we examine how nature and nurture influence human development.

CONNECTIONS

In **Chapter 6,** we described recall as the process of retrieving information held in long-term memory without the help of explicit retrieval cues. Here, we will see how these memory processes change as a function of development.

CONNECTIONS

In **Chapter 1,** we described confounding variables as unaccounted factors that change in sync with the independent variable, making it very hard to discern which one is causing changes in the dependent variable. Here, we consider how a cohort can act as a confounding variable.

cross-sectional method A research design that examines people of different ages at a single point in time.

cohort effect The differences across groups that result from common experiences within the groups.

longitudinal method A research design that examines one sample of people over a period of time to determine age-related changes.

would dispute the important contributions of both (Moore, 2013; Mysterud, 2003). Researchers can study a trait like impulsivity, which is the tendency to act before thinking, to determine the extent to which it results from hereditary factors and from the environment. In this particular case, nature and nurture appear to both play a substantial role (Anokhin, Grant, Mulligan, & Heath, 2015; Bezdjian, Baker, & Tuvblad, 2011). Later in this chapter, we will examine the balance of nature and nurture in relation to brain and language development, a longstanding, sometimes controversial debate in psychology and beyond.

STABILITY AND CHANGE How much does a person change from childhood to old age? Some researchers suggest that personality traits identified early in life can be used to predict behaviors across the life span (Allemand, Steiger, & Hill, 2013; McAdams & Olson, 2010). Others report that personality characteristics change as a result of relationships and other experiences. The way we adapt to aging may also influence personality development (Kandler, Kornadt, Hagemeyer, & Neyer, 2015; Specht, Egloff, & Schmukle, 2011). Psychologists often discuss how experiences in infancy can set the stage for stable cognitive characteristics, particularly when it comes to early enrichment and its long-term impact on intellectual abilities.

Three Methods

LO 3   **Identify the types of research psychologists use to study developmental processes.**

Developmental psychologists use a variety of methods to study differences across ages and time (**INFOGRAPHIC 8.1**).

THE CROSS-SECTIONAL METHOD The **cross-sectional method** enables researchers to examine people of different ages at a given point in time. In one study, for example, researchers used the cross-sectional method to investigate developmental changes in the efficiency of memory recall (Castel et al., 2011). They divided their 320 participants into groups according to age (children, adolescents, younger adults, middle-aged adults, young-old adults, and old-old adults) and compared the scores of the different groups to see if changes occur across the life span. One advantage of the cross-sectional method is that it can provide a great deal of information quickly; by studying differences across age groups, we don't have to wait for people to get older.

But a major problem with the cross-sectional method is that it doesn't tell us whether differences across age groups result from actual developmental changes or from common experiences within groups, a phenomenon known as the **cohort effect.** Members of each age group, or cohort, have lived through similar historical and cultural eras, and these common experiences may be responsible for some differences across groups. For example, the "old-old adults" in the memory recall study described above were not raised on cell phones, iPads, Google, or Facebook, so they probably have different perspectives than those in the younger adult group. The authors of the study were quick to point out this pitfall: "The present design was cross-sectional, whereas (in some ways) a longitudinal design would allow for stronger conclusions regarding . . . *changes* with age" (Castel et al., 2011, p. 1562).

THE LONGITUDINAL METHOD Researchers can avoid the cohort effect by using the **longitudinal method,** which follows one group of individuals over a period of time. Curious to find out what "lifestyle activities" are associated with age-related cognitive decline, one team of researchers studied 952 individuals over a 12-year period (Small, Dixon, McArdle, & Grimm, 2012). Every three to four years, they administered tests

Research Methods in Developmental Psychology

Developmental psychologists use several research methods to study changes that occur with age. Imagine you want to know whether using social media helps protect against feelings of loneliness over time. How would you design a study to measure that? Let's compare methods.

Longitudinal

Measure a **single group** at **different points in time**

Example: Researchers follow a sample of participants, interviewing them every decade for a total of three measurements. As they age, participants report lower levels of loneliness than expected. But because the study is longitudinal, we can't eliminate the possibility that this particular group of participants is less lonely because of some historically specific effect.

GROUP 1 · 20 YEARS OLD · 30 YEARS OLD · 40 YEARS OLD

2005 · 2015 · 2025

BENEFITS
+ Can track age-related changes.

PROBLEMS
− Measured changes could be specific to the particular group of participants.
− Takes a long time, leading some participants to drop out before study is complete.

Cross-sectional

Measure groups of people of **different ages** (for example, 20-, 40-, and 60-year-olds) at a **single point in time**

Example: Researchers interview participants in three different age groups: 20-, 40-, and 60-year-olds. The oldest group reports higher levels of loneliness. But because the study is cross-sectional, we can't be sure if this finding reflects a cohort effect, in which differences may be due to age or to common experiences within the group, as opposed to developmental changes in physical, cognitive, or socioemotional functioning.

GROUP 3 · 60 YEARS OLD

GROUP 2 · 40 YEARS OLD

GROUP 1 · 20 YEARS OLD

2005 · 2015 · 2025

BENEFITS
+ Allows comparison between age groups.
+ Can be completed relatively quickly.

PROBLEMS
− Susceptible to cohort effect.

Cross-sequential

Measure groups of people of **different ages,** following them across **different points in time**

Example: Researchers interview participants from three age groups every decade for a total of three measurements. This results in data showing how social media use and loneliness change within each group as they age.

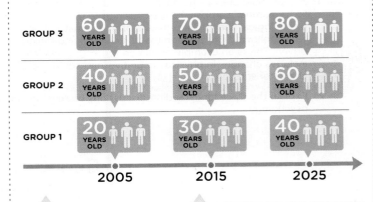

GROUP 3 · 60 YEARS OLD · 70 YEARS OLD · 80 YEARS OLD

GROUP 2 · 40 YEARS OLD · 50 YEARS OLD · 60 YEARS OLD

GROUP 1 · 20 YEARS OLD · 30 YEARS OLD · 40 YEARS OLD

2005 · 2015 · 2025

BENEFITS
+ Shows changes within individuals and between groups.
+ Better addresses cohort effect.

PROBLEMS
− Requires substantial resources and many participants.
− Takes a long time, leading some participants to drop out before study is complete.

to all participants, assessing, for example, cognitive abilities and health status. The more engaged and socially active the participants were, the better their long-term cognitive performance. Using the longitudinal method, we can compare the same individuals over time, identifying similarities and differences in the way they age. But these studies are difficult to conduct because they require a great deal of money, time, and participant investment. Common challenges include attrition (people dropping out of the study) and practice effects (people performing better on measures as they get more "practice").

THE CROSS-SEQUENTIAL METHOD The **cross-sequential method**, also used by developmental psychologists, is a mixture of the longitudinal and cross-sectional methods. You might call it the best of both worlds. Participants are divided into age groups and followed over time, so researchers can examine developmental changes within individuals and across different age groups. One team of researchers used this approach to identify the age at which cognitive decline becomes evident (Singh-Manoux et al., 2012). They recruited 10,308 participants, assigning each to a 5-year age group (45–49, 50–54, 55–59, 60–64, and 65–70), and then followed them for 10 years. Using this approach, they could observe changes in individuals as they aged *and* identify differences across age groups.

Human development is very complex. Some processes are universal; others are specific to an individual, and it is this combination that makes the field so fascinating. As you learn about the development of Ericka and her family, you may be struck by the degree of similarity (or differences) in your own family.

In Class: Collaborate and Report

The entire population of Flint, Michigan, was exposed to lead-contaminated drinking water for about 1 year in 2014–2015. You want to study how exposure to lead impacted the intellectual development of children in the area. Team up and **A)** formulate a hypothesis for your study. **B)** Discuss the three research designs described above (cross-sectional, longitudinal, and cross-sequential). **C)** Decide which of the designs would be best for testing your hypothesis and explain why.

  show what you know

1. A 3-year-old decides he doesn't need diapers, and much to his parents' surprise, he starts using the toilet. This physiological change likely results from his maturation, which follows a progression that is universal and biologically driven. This is an example of human _____, which includes changes in physical, cognitive, and socioemotional characteristics.

2. Explain the three longstanding discussions of developmental psychology.

3. A researcher is interested in studying developmental changes in memory recall. She asks 300 participants to take a memory test and then compares the results across five different age groups. This researcher is using which of the following methods?
   a. cross-sequential
   b. longitudinal
   c. cross-sectional
   d. biopsychosocial

✓ CHECK YOUR ANSWERS IN APPENDIX C.

Genetics, Conception, and Prenatal Development

LIFE GOES ON Ericka suspected she was pregnant weeks before visiting the doctor's office with her mom. "I felt like something was different, but even before the missed period," she recalls. "I just ate everything, and I was like, 'I'm still hungry!'" Around this same time, Ericka was beginning to have doubts about her relationship with the baby's father. The whole situation was unsettling, and Ericka just wanted to push the subject out

cross-sequential method A research design that examines groups of people of different ages, following them across time.

of her mind. "It was almost like, *if I just don't think about being pregnant, it'll go away*," she explains. "But it didn't quite work that way."

On the drive to the doctor's office, Ericka sat in terror as she anticipated her mother's response. "I didn't know what she was going to think or how she was going to react," says Ericka, who had heard stories of pregnant teens getting kicked out of their homes. Joan was initially angry and disappointed, but a talk with her own mother (Ericka's grandmother) changed her outlook: "I remember having a conversation with my mom," Joan recalls, "and she said, '[Ericka is] not the first, and she won't be the last,' and something just clicked." What was it about Grandma's comment that completely shifted Joan's frame of mind? Maybe she realized that some aspects of her children's lives were beyond her control. No matter how hard she tried to steer Ericka on the straight path toward college, Ericka would ultimately set her own course.

From that point on, Joan continued to do what she had always done as a mother—give Ericka unconditional emotional support. She also made it clear that Ericka would be taking full responsibility for herself and her child. Ericka was welcome to live at home, but there would be no complimentary babysitting or financial assistance.

As the pregnancy progressed, Ericka began to experience some of the common side effects of pregnancy, like changes in eating habits and aversions to certain smells and tastes. Her go-to meal became salad and french fries. Toothpaste made her nauseous. She suffered from dizziness and headaches, which triggered a frightening fall down the stairs, and prevented her from attending school. But Ericka, always a bright and motivated student, kept up with her classmates by doing schoolwork from home.

Meanwhile, she began imagining the little person developing inside of her. "I wondered about everything," Ericka says. "How she would sound? . . . Would she smile like me? Would she act like me? Would she love me back?" Ericka aspired to be a good parent, to provide a happy life for her child. "I hoped and wished for a girl," she says. "I found out at about 5 months that I was having a girl. My heart melted and I was even more in love." ●

The qualities Ericka imagined in her baby—the smile, the voice, the sex, and even to some degree the behaviors—would be influenced by the *genes* found in every cell of the developing baby's body. Now let's venture inside the cell and find out where those genes dwell.

Chromosomes and Genes

LO 4   **Examine the role genes play in our development and identify the biological factors that determine sex.**

With the exception of red blood cells, every cell in the human body has a nucleus at its center. Within this nucleus is material containing the blueprint or plan for the building of a complete person. This material is coiled tightly into 46 **chromosomes,** the thread-like structures we inherit from our biological parents (23 from our father and 23 from our mother). A chromosome contains one molecule of **deoxyribonucleic acid (DNA).** Looking at the DNA molecule in **FIGURE 8.1**, on the next page, you can see a specific section along its length has been identified. This section corresponds to a **gene,** and genes provide the instructions for making proteins. The proteins encoded by genes determine the texture of your hair, the color of your eyes, and some aspects of your personality. Genes influence nearly every dimension of the complex living system known as YOU.

Your chromosomes, and all the genes they contain, come from your biological parents. In the moment of conception, your father's sperm united with your mother's egg to

chromosomes Inherited threadlike structures composed of deoxyribonucleic acid (DNA).

deoxyribonucleic acid (DNA) A molecule that provides instructions for the development of an organism.

gene Specified segment of a DNA molecule.

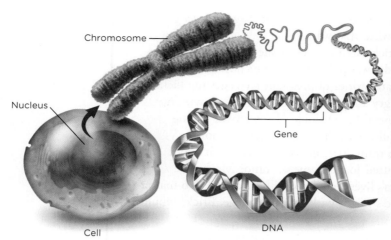
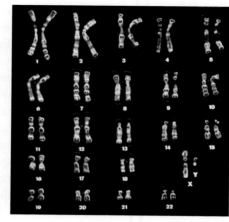

FIGURE 8.1

Chromosomes, DNA, and Genes

Every cell in your body, except red blood cells and sex cells (sperm or egg), contains a full set of 23 chromosome pairs like those shown in the photo on the right. These 23 chromosome pairs contain the full blueprint for you as a complete, unique person. The primary component of each chromosome is a single, tightly wound molecule of DNA. Within that DNA are around 21,000 genes (Pennisi, 2012, September 5), each determining specific traits such as hair texture. Note the sex chromosomes (X and Y) on the lower right, indicating that the sex is male. Photo: CNRI/Science Source.

form a **zygote** [ZAHY-goht], a single cell that eventually gave rise to the trillions of cells that now make up your body (Sherwood, 2016). Typically, both sperm and egg contain 23 chromosomes, so the resulting zygote has 23 *pairs* of chromosomes, or a total of 46. The 23rd pair of chromosomes, also referred to as the *sex chromosomes,* includes specific instructions for the zygote to develop into a male or female, determining genetic sex (the *XX* for a female, and *XY* for a male; Chapter 10).

LO 5 Discuss how genotype and phenotype relate to development.

GENOTYPE AND PHENOTYPE As stated, the cells in your body have 23 chromosome pairs (46 chromosomes total). These chromosomes contain all of your genes, which are collectively known as your **genotype**. Genotypes do not change in response to the environment, but they do interact with the environment. Because so much variability exists in the surrounding world, the outcome of this interaction is not predetermined. The color and appearance of your skin, for example, result from an interplay between your genotype and a variety of environmental factors including sun and wind exposure, age, nutrition, and smoking—all of which can impact how your genes are expressed (Kolb, Whishaw, & Teskey, 2016; Rees, 2003). The product of this interaction is the **phenotype**—a person's observable characteristics. Your phenotype is apparent in your unique physical, psychological, and behavioral characteristics (Plomin, DeFries, Knopik, & Neiderhiser, 2016; Scarr & McCartney, 1983).

You might be wondering what all this talk of genotype and phenotype has to do with psychology. Our genetic make-up influences our behavior, and psychologists are interested in learning how this process occurs. Consider schizophrenia, a disabling psychological disorder (Chapter 13) with symptoms ranging from hallucinations to disorganized thinking. A large body of evidence now suggests that a person's genotype may predispose him to developing schizophrenia, with heritability rates between 60% and 80% (Cardno & Owen, 2014; Edwards et al., 2016; Matheson, Shepherd, & Carr, 2014). But the expression or manifestation of the disorder results from a combination of genotype and experience, including diet, stress, toxins, and childhood adversity (Hameed & Lewis, 2016; Zhang & Meaney, 2010). Identical twins, who have the same genotype, may display different phenotypes, including distinct expressions of schizophrenia if they both have developed this disorder. This is because schizophrenia, or any psychological phenomenon, results from complex relationships between genes and environment (Kremen, Panizzon, & Cannon, 2016). Understanding these relationships is the main thrust of **epigenetics**, a field that examines the processes involved in the development of phenotypes.

CONNECTIONS

In **Chapter 7,** we described heritability as the degree to which heredity is responsible for a particular characteristic. Here, we see that around 60–80% of the population-wide variation in schizophrenia can be attributed to genetic make-up and 20–40% to the environment.

DOMINANT AND RECESSIVE GENES Genes are behind just about every human trait you can imagine—from height, to shoe size, to behavior. But remember, you possess two copies of each chromosome (one from mom, one from dad), and therefore two of each gene. Sometimes the genes in a pair are identical (both of them encode dimples, for instance). In other cases, the two genes differ, providing dissimilar instructions about the outcome (one encodes dimples, while the other encodes no dimples). Often one gene variant has more power than the other. This **dominant gene** governs the expression of the inherited characteristic, overpowering the recessive, or subordinate, gene in the pair. A **recessive gene** cannot overcome the influence of a dominant gene. For example, "dimples" are dominant, and "no dimples" are recessive. If one gene encodes for dimples and the other no dimples, then dimples will be expressed. If both genes encode for no dimples, no dimples will be expressed. This all sounds relatively straightforward, but it's not. Psychological traits—and the genetics behind them—are exceedingly complex. Characteristics such as intelligence and aggressive tendencies are influenced by multiple genes (also known as *polygenic inheritance*), most of which have yet to be identified.

Now that we have a basic handle on genetics, let's shift our attention toward the developmental changes that occur within the womb.

Seas of DNA
The colored lights are an artistic representation of the human genome, the complete set of DNA found in most cells in the body. Researchers with the Human Genome Project have decoded the entire human genome, which contains about 21,000 DNA segments known as genes (Pennisi, 2012, September 5). Genes are the blueprints for proteins that endow you with a unique set of traits, including eye color, hair texture, and—to a certain extent—psychological characteristics.
Mario Tama/Getty Images.

Have a Peak?
Some traits are determined by the presence of a single, dominant gene. The "widow's peak," or V-shaped hairline, is thought to be one of them (Chiras, 2015). The man on the left must have at least one dominant widow's peak gene, while the person on the right has two recessive straight hairline genes. Left: Johner Images/Getty Images. Right: Dougal Waters/Getty Images.

From Zygote to Embryo to Fetus

LO 6 Describe the progression of prenatal development.

As you may recall, Ericka experienced occasional headaches and dizziness during her pregnancy. But she was able to function quite well, never falling behind in her schoolwork. It's actually quite remarkable how Ericka (and many women, for that matter) can breeze through pregnancy with such ease, because the changes occurring in the body are phenomenal. In less than a year, Ericka's body built a living, breathing human being with 10 little fingers and toes, fully functional organ systems, and a brain equipped with 86 to 100 billion neurons (Herculano-Houzel, 2012; Toga, Thompson, & Sowell, 2006). How does an infant emerge from a single cell roughly the size of the dot at the bottom of this question mark? It's time to explore *prenatal development,* the 39–40 weeks between conception and birth for a full-term baby (Spong, 2013).

THE ZYGOTE In the beginning, before you became you, an egg (also known as an *ovum*) from your biological mother and a sperm cell from your biological father came together at the moment of *conception.* Together, the egg and sperm formed a single cell called a zygote, which is barely visible to the naked eye. Under normal circumstances,

zygote A single cell formed by the union of a sperm cell and egg.

genotype An individual's complete collection of genes.

phenotype The observable expression or characteristics of one's genetic inheritance.

epigenetics A field of study that examines the processes involved in the development of phenotypes.

dominant gene One of a pair of genes that has power over the expression of an inherited characteristic.

recessive gene One of a pair of genes that is overpowered by a dominant gene.

a zygote immediately begins to divide into two cells, then each of those cells divides, and so on.

Conception sometimes results in twins or multiples. Identical or **monozygotic twins** develop from one egg inseminated at conception. This egg is fertilized by one sperm and then it splits, forming separate zygotes with identical sets of 46 chromosomes. Eventually these zygotes develop into identical twin infants who have the same sex and almost identical features. Fraternal or **dizygotic twins,** on the other hand, occur when two eggs are inseminated by two different sperm, leading to the development of two distinct zygotes. This can occur naturally, but assisted reproductive technology may increase the odds of a woman releasing more than one egg (Manninen, 2011). Over the past four decades, the number of twin births in developed countries has "nearly doubled," in large part due to medically assisted reproduction (Pison, Monden, & Smits, 2015). Twins and multiples resulting from the distinct sperm–egg combinations are like other biological siblings; they share around 50% of their genes.

GERMINAL AND EMBRYONIC PERIODS From conception to the end of the 2nd week is the *germinal period,* during which the rapidly dividing zygote implants in the uterine wall. Between the 3rd and 8th weeks of development, the growing mass of cells is called an **embryo.** The embryo develops in the *amniotic sac,* which is the "bag" of fluids that provides protection. An organ called the *placenta* provides the embryo with oxygen and nourishment, disposes of waste, and prevents mixing between the mother's and baby's blood. The embryo receives its nourishment, hydration, and oxygen through the *umbilical cord,* which is attached to the placenta. During the germinal period, all the cells are identical. In the *embryonic period,* the cells differentiate and the major organs and systems begin to form (**FIGURE 8.2**).

FIGURE 8.2
Prenatal Development and Periods of Critical Growth
During prenatal development, individual structures form and are fine-tuned at different times. As each structure is being established, it is particularly vulnerable to interference. Once their critical periods are complete, the structures are fully established. Photos: (left) Omikron/Science Source; (center) Anatomical Travelogue/Science Source; (right) Neil Bromhall/Science Source.

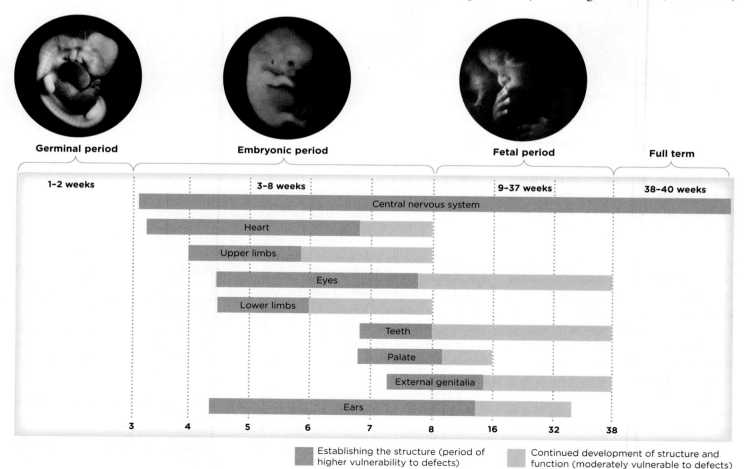

Germinal period	Embryonic period	Fetal period	Full term
1–2 weeks	3–8 weeks	9–37 weeks	38–40 weeks

Central nervous system
Heart
Upper limbs
Eyes
Lower limbs
Teeth
Palate
External genitalia
Ears

3   4   5   6   7   8   16   32   38

■ Establishing the structure (period of higher vulnerability to defects)   ■ Continued development of structure and function (moderately vulnerable to defects)

TABLE 8.1　THE DANGERS OF TERATOGENS

Category	Teratogen	Potential Effects
Drugs	Acne medication (isotretinoin)	Heart defects, neurological, musculoskeletal, and liver issues
	Alcohol	Fetal alcohol syndrome: intellectual disability, poor growth, heart problems, growth delay
	Caffeine	High exposure associated with miscarriage
	Cocaine	Birth defects, miscarriage, placental abruption
	Marijuana	Low birth weight, small skull, tremors
	Nicotine	Malformations, low birth weight, cleft lip or palate, heart defects
Environmental factors	Lead	High exposure linked with miscarriage and stillbirth, intellectual disability
	Mercury	Cerebral palsy, intellectual disability, blindness
	Radiation exposure	Small skull, blindness, spina bifida, cleft palate
Infections	Rubella	Heart disease, small skull, liver issues
	Syphilis	Inflamed joints, rash, swollen liver and spleen
	Toxoplasmosis	Small skull, intellectual disability, malformations of the eye
Maternal disease	Diabetes (insulin-dependent)	Abnormal tissue formation, death, birth defects
	Epilepsy (antiepileptic drugs and seizures)	Miscarriages, spina bifida, heart defects, small skull, cleft lip, cleft palate, developmental delays

From conception until birth, the developing human is nestled deep inside a woman's body, but it remains vulnerable to threats from the outside. Listed here are some common teratogens and their effects. Information from Brent (2004), Huizink (2014), and Jamkhande, Chintawar, & Chandak (2014).

This differentiation allows for the heart to begin to beat, the arms and legs to grow, and the spinal cord and intestinal system to develop. But less than half of all zygotes actually implant in the uterine wall (Gold, 2005). Of reported pregnancies, around 21% end in a miscarriage (Buss et al., 2006), many of which result from genetic abnormalities of the embryo (Velagaleti & Moore, 2011).

TERATOGENS The embryo may be safely nestled in the amniotic sac, but it is not protected from all environmental dangers. **Teratogens** [tuh-RAT-uh-jenz] are agents that can damage a zygote, embryo, or fetus (**TABLE 8.1**). Radiation, viruses, bacteria, chemicals, and drugs are all considered teratogens. The damage depends on the agent, as well as the timing and duration of exposure, and can result in miscarriage, decreased birth weight, heart defects, long-term behavioral problems, and other adverse outcomes (Jamkhande, Chintawar, & Chandak, 2014). One well-known teratogen is alcohol, which can lead to *fetal alcohol spectrum disorders (FASD)*. In particular, **fetal alcohol syndrome (FAS)** is the result of moderate to heavy alcohol use during pregnancy, which can cause delays in normal development, a small head, lower intelligence, and distinct facial characteristics (for example, wide-spaced eyes, flattened nose). Researchers continue to debate what constitutes an acceptable amount of alcohol use during pregnancy, but they do agree that even a small amount poses risks, warning that "no

monozygotic twins Identical twins who develop from one egg inseminated at conception, which then splits into two separate cells.

dizygotic twins Fraternal twins who develop from two eggs inseminated by two sperm, and are as genetically similar as any sibling pair.

embryo The unborn human from the beginning of the 3rd week of pregnancy, lasting through the 8th week of prenatal development.

teratogens Environmental agents that can damage the growing zygote, embryo, or fetus.

fetal alcohol syndrome (FAS) Delays in development that result from moderate to heavy alcohol use during pregnancy.

Dad and Daughter

A father enjoys time with his 25-year-old adopted daughter. The young woman has fetal alcohol syndrome, a condition that results from exposure to alcohol during fetal development. The symptoms of fetal alcohol syndrome—which can be avoided by abstaining from alcohol during pregnancy—include delays in physical growth, learning disabilities, and problems with anxiety, attention, and impulse regulation (Mayo Clinic, 2014, June 2). STUART WONG/Newscom/Tribune News Service/COLORADO SPRINGS/CO/USA.

CONNECTIONS

In **Chapter 4,** we noted that the daily patterns in some of our physiological functioning roughly follow the 24-hour cycle of daylight and darkness, driven by our circadian rhythm. Here, we can see that even before birth, sleep–wake cycles are becoming evident.

amount of alcohol is safe during pregnancy" (O'Brien, 2007; Vall, Salat-Batlle, & Garcia-Algar, 2015, p. 928). The National Institute on Alcohol Abuse and Alcoholism (NIAAA, 2015) is very clear in its advice to pregnant women and women trying to get pregnant: Quit drinking alcohol.

THE FETAL PERIOD Between 2 months and birth, the growing human is called a **fetus** (Figure 8.2). During the *fetal period,* the developing person grows from the size of a pumpkin seed to a small watermelon, the average birth weight being approximately 7 pounds (by North American standards). It is also during this time that the developing person begins to demonstrate clear sleep–wake cycles (Suwanrath & Suntharasaj, 2010). Most systems and structures are fully developed, and the baby is ready for the outside world.

If you step back and contemplate the baby-making phenomenon, it's really quite amazing. But many more exciting developments are in store. Are you ready for some shrieking, babbling, and a little game of peekaboo? Let's move on to infancy and childhood.

◯◉◯◯ **show what you know**

1. _____ are threadlike structures humans inherit from their biological mothers and fathers.
   a. Teratogens
   b. Zygotes
   c. Genes
   d. Chromosomes

2. _____ represents a complete collection of genes, and _____ represents the observed expression of inherited characteristics.

3. A coworker tells you that she is in her 6th week of pregnancy. She is excited because she has learned that during this _____, her baby is developing a spinal cord, its heart is beginning to beat, and its intestinal system is forming.
   a. embryonic period
   b. phenotype
   a. germinal period
   d. genotype

√ CHECK YOUR ANSWERS IN APPENDIX C.

Infancy and Child Development

BABY'S COMING! April, 18, 2006: Ericka's baby was already three days late. Doctors were concerned the baby was growing too big, so they planned to induce labor at 5 P.M. ("Induction" means using medications to activate contractions of the uterus, and thereby start the labor.) But just a few hours before the scheduled induction, Ericka was roused from a nap by strange sensations in her abdomen. She remembers calling Joan at work and saying, "I think there's something going on, because I have this weird feeling in my belly and I don't like it very much." The baby was on her way.

Twenty hours and many painful contractions later, Ericka was in the final stages of labor. As she strained to push the baby out, doctors asked if she wanted to feel the baby's head. "I don't want to feel her head. I just want it to be over!" Ericka remembers saying. Within minutes, she was looking into the eyes of her baby girl.

fetus The unborn human from 2 months following conception to birth.

"She was just perfect," Ericka recalls. "I couldn't believe how tiny her fingers were, and I counted them, and I touched all of them."

Ericka cried as she watched Joan take the baby in her arms. Then the baby's father held her, and he looked like he might cry, too. It was an emotional, almost surreal moment. After nine months of anticipation, a new little person had finally arrived. They named her Aa'Niyah. ●

Newborn Growth and Development

LO 7 **Summarize the physical changes that occur in infancy.**

At 7 pounds, 13 ounces, Aa'Niyah (affectionately called "Niyah") was within the average weight range for babies born in North America. She was also hungry, and drinking twice the amount of milk as other babies her age, according to Ericka. Unfortunately, breast-feeding was extremely painful because Niyah was born with two teeth ("natal teeth" are rare, affecting 1 in 2,000 to 3,000 babies; National Library of Medicine [NLM], 2016, February 22). But Ericka held out as long as she could, and nursed baby Niyah for the first two weeks—a worthy sacrifice, since breast milk is thought to have important effects on growth and cognitive development (Chaimay, 2011; de Lauzon-Guillain et al., 2012; Horwood & Fergusson, 1998).

Newborns exhibit several *reflexes,* or automatic responses to stimuli, some of which facilitate feeding. Certain reflexes are necessary for survival, while others serve no obvious purpose (**TABLE 8.2**). A few fade away in the first weeks and months of life, but many will resurface as voluntary movements as the infant grows and develops motor

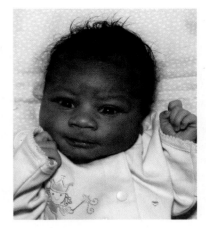

Introducing . . . Aa'Niyah!
After 40 weeks and 4 days of anticipation, Aa'Niyah finally arrived. Niyah was full-term, but many babies are born before the typical 39–41 weeks of gestation. In the past (and in many developing nations today), some of these premature babies would not survive outside the womb. Thanks to advances in medicine, the *age of viability* has dropped to approximately 23 weeks in the United States (Seri & Evans, 2008). Courtesy Ericka Harley.

TABLE 8.2 NEWBORN REFLEXES

Reflex	The Response	See It	Reflex	The Response	See It
Rooting	When cheek is touched, newborn turns head toward stimulus.		Babinski (toes curl)	When sole of newborn foot is stroked, big toe bends toward ankle and other toes fan out.	
Sucking	Mouth area touched by object, then newborn sucks on object.		Stepping	Newborn will take steps when feet are put on hard surface.	
Grasping	Newborn actively grasps when object is placed in palm of hand.		Moro (startle)	Abrupt extension of head, arms, and legs after a sudden noise or movement.	

Newborns exhibit various reflexes, or automatic responses to stimuli. Listed here are some of the reflexes first evident at birth. Information from Zafeiriou (2004). Photos: (Left column, top to bottom) Christine Hanscomb/Science Source; BSIP SA/Alamy Stock Photo; Michelle Gibson/Getty Images. (Right column, top to bottom) Ray Ellis/Science Source; Picture Partners/Alamy; ASTIER/age fotostock.

control (Thelen & Fisher, 1982). Let's take a look at the two reflexes important for feeding—rooting and sucking.

ROOTING AND SUCKING REFLEXES What does a newborn do when you stroke her cheek? She opens her mouth and turns her head in the direction of your finger, apparently in search of a nipple. This *rooting reflex* typically disappears at 4 months, never to be seen again. The *sucking reflex,* evident when you touch her lips, also appears to be a feeding reflex. Sucking and swallowing abilities don't fully mature until the gestational age of 33 to 36 weeks, so babies who are born before that time may struggle with feeding (Lee et al., 2011). But many mothers pump their breast milk, making it possible for their premature babies to get its nutritional benefits through a feeding tube.

A newborn spends most of his time eating, sleeping, and crying. Sounds like a simple routine, but waking every 2 to 3 hours to feed a wailing baby can be very exhausting. Nevertheless, this stage soon gives way to a period of change that is far more interactive, and includes waving, clapping, walking, and dangerous furniture climbing. **INFOGRAPHIC 8.2** details some of the sensory and motor milestones of infancy. Keep in mind that the listed ages are averages; significant variation does exist across infants. The general sequence and timing, however, are fairly universal.

THE NEWBORN SENSES From the moment Niyah was born, she was intensely interested in people. She made a lot of eye contact, listened closely to voices, and responded with her own little noises. Babies come into the world equipped with keen sensory capabilities that seem to be designed for facilitating relationships. As Niyah's example illustrates, infants are visually drawn to people; in fact, they prefer to look at human faces over geometric shapes (Salva, Farroni, Regolin, Vallortigara, & Johnson, 2011; Simion & Di Giorgio, 2015). Within hours of birth, infants can discriminate their mother's voice from those of other women, and they show a preference for her voice (DeCasper & Fifer, 1980; Moon, Zernzach, & Kuhl, 2015). They may even come to recognize their mother's voice while in the womb (Kisilevsky et al., 2003; Moon et al., 2015). This occurs despite the fact that sounds initially heard by newborns are distorted. Although hearing is developed and functioning before birth, it takes some time for amniotic fluid to dry up so the baby can hear clearly (Hall, Smith, & Popelka, 2004).

Smell and taste are also well developed in newborn infants. These tiny babies can distinguish the smell of their own mothers' breast milk from that of other women within days of birth (Nishitani et al., 2009). Babies prefer sweet tastes, react strongly to sour tastes, and notice certain changes to their mothers' diets because those tastes are present in breast milk. If a mother has eaten something very sweet, for instance, the infant tends to breastfeed longer.

The sense of touch, and thus the ability to feel pain, are evident before birth (Marx & Nagy, 2015). It was once believed that newborns were incapable of experiencing pain, but research now suggests otherwise. Newborns respond to pain with reactions similar to those of older infants, children, and adults (Gradin & Eriksson, 2011; Urso, 2007).

Sight is the weakest sense in newborns, who have difficulty seeing things that are not in their immediate vicinity. The optimal distance for a newborn to see an object is approximately 8–14 inches away from his face (Cavallini et al., 2002), which happens

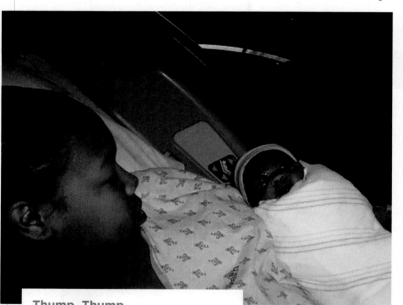

Thump, Thump
Ericka holds Niyah a few minutes after she was born. Niyah came into the world eager to interact with people. Like other full-term newborns, her sense of hearing was well developed. She especially liked listening to human voices and the rhythmic beat of her mother's heart. Lying on Ericka's chest, where she could hear her mom's heartbeat, Niyah would fall asleep almost immediately. Courtesy Ericka Harley.

Infant Brain and Sensorimotor Development

As newborns grow, they progress at an astounding rate in seen and unseen ways. When witnessing babies' new skills, whether it be reaching for a rattle or pulling themselves into a standing position, it's easy to marvel at how far they have come. But what you can't see is the real action. These sensorimotor advancements are only possible because of the incredible brain development happening in the background.

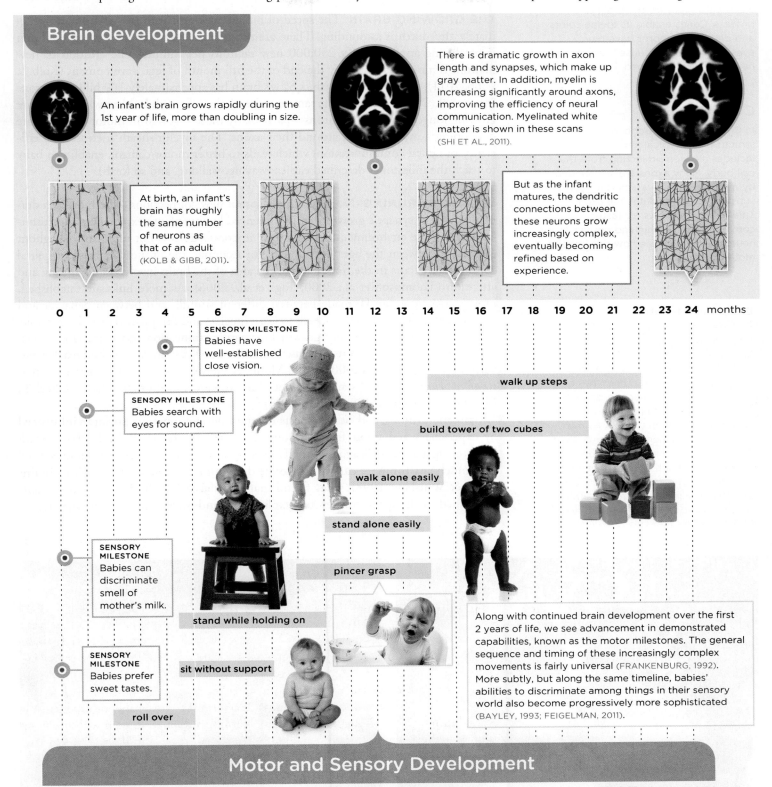

Brain development

An infant's brain grows rapidly during the 1st year of life, more than doubling in size.

At birth, an infant's brain has roughly the same number of neurons as that of an adult (KOLB & GIBB, 2011).

There is dramatic growth in axon length and synapses, which make up gray matter. In addition, myelin is increasing significantly around axons, improving the efficiency of neural communication. Myelinated white matter is shown in these scans (SHI ET AL., 2011).

But as the infant matures, the dendritic connections between these neurons grow increasingly complex, eventually becoming refined based on experience.

0 1 2 3 4 5 6 7 8 9 10 11 12 13 14 15 16 17 18 19 20 21 22 23 24 months

SENSORY MILESTONE Babies have well-established close vision.

SENSORY MILESTONE Babies search with eyes for sound.

SENSORY MILESTONE Babies can discriminate smell of mother's milk.

SENSORY MILESTONE Babies prefer sweet tastes.

walk up steps

build tower of two cubes

walk alone easily

stand alone easily

pincer grasp

stand while holding on

sit without support

roll over

Along with continued brain development over the first 2 years of life, we see advancement in demonstrated capabilities, known as the motor milestones. The general sequence and timing of these increasingly complex movements is fairly universal (FRANKENBURG, 1992). More subtly, but along the same timeline, babies' abilities to discriminate among things in their sensory world also become progressively more sophisticated (BAYLEY, 1993; FEIGELMAN, 2011).

Motor and Sensory Development

Credits: Brain Scans, Shi, F., Yap, P.-T., Wu, G., Jia, H., Gilmore, J. H., Lin, W., & Shen, D. (2011). Infant brain atlases from neonates to 1- and 2-year-olds. PLoS One, 6. doi:10.1371/journal.pone.0018746. Real People: Boy with boots and orange hat, Jani Bryson/Thinkstock; Small child, Jaroslaw Wojcik/Getty Images; Baby boy (12-15 months) close-up, portrait, Photodisc/Getty Images; Baby boy eating, © sanapadh/Alamy; Baby learning to stand assisted by a stool, Aseph/Shutterstock; Little boy playing with colorful cubes, Sergiy Bykhunenko/Shutterstock.

CONNECTIONS

In **Chapter 3,** we reported that cones are specialized neurons called photoreceptors, which absorb light energy and turn it into chemical and electrical signals for the brain to process. Cones enable us to see colors and details. Newborns have blurry eyesight, in part, because their cones have not fully developed.

CONNECTIONS

In **Chapter 2,** we described the structure of a typical neuron, which includes an axon projecting from the cell body. Many axons are surrounded by a myelin sheath, which is a fatty substance that insulates the axon. This insulation allows for faster communication within and between neurons. Here, we see how this impacts motor development.

Environment Matters

A kindergarten teacher leads students through dance movements (left) in what appears to be an enriched environment. Opportunities for physical exercise, social interaction, and other types of stimulating activity characterize enriched environments, which promote positive changes in the brain (Khan & Hillman, 2014; van Praag, Kempermann, & Gage, 2000). Fewer signs of enrichment appear in the photo on the right, which shows another teacher with her class of preschoolers in a sparse room without books or even furniture. Left: GOH CHAI HIN/ Getty Images. Right: Robert van der Hilst/Corbis.

to be the approximate distance between the face of a nursing baby and his mother. Eye contact is thought to strengthen the relationship between mother and baby. A newborn's vision can be blurry for several months, one reason being that the light-sensitive cones in the back of the eye are still developing (Banks & Salapatek, 1978).

THE GROWING BRAIN The speed of brain development in the womb and immediately after birth is astounding. There are times in fetal development when the brain is producing approximately 250,000 new neurons per minute! The creation of new neurons is mostly complete by the end of the 5th month of fetal development (Kolb & Gibb, 2011). At the time of birth, a baby's brain has approximately 100 billion neurons (Toga et al., 2006)—roughly the same number as that of an adult. Meanwhile, axons are growing longer, and more neurons—particularly those involved in motor control—are developing a myelin sheath around their axons. The myelin sheath increases the efficiency of neural communication, which leads to better motor control, enabling a baby to reach the milestones described earlier (waving, walking, and so forth).

SYNAPTIC PRUNING Neurons rapidly sprout new connections to each other, a dramatic phase of synaptic growth that is influenced by the infant's experiences and stimulation from the environment. The increase in connections is not uniform throughout the brain. Between the ages of 3 and 6, for example, the greatest increase in neural connections occurs in the frontal lobes, the area of the brain involved in planning and attention (Thompson et al., 2000; Toga et al., 2006). As more links are established, more associations can be made between different stimuli, and between behavior and consequences. A young person needs to learn quickly, and this process makes it possible.

However, the extraordinary growth in synaptic connections does not last forever, as the number of connections decreases by 40% to 50% by the time a child reaches puberty (Thompson et al., 2000; Webb, Monk, & Nelson, 2001). In a process known as *synaptic pruning,* unused synaptic connections are downsized or eliminated (Chechik, Meilijson, & Ruppin, 1998; Spear, 2013).

Synaptic pruning and other aspects of brain development are strongly influenced by experiences and input from the outside world. In the 1960s and 1970s, Mark Rosenzweig and his colleagues at the University of California, Berkeley, demonstrated how much environment can influence the development of nonhuman animal brains (Kolb & Whishaw, 1998). They found that rats placed in stimulating environments (furnished with opportunities for exploration and social interaction) experience

greater increases in brain weight and synaptic connections than those put in non-stimulating environments (Barredo & Deeg, 2009, February 24; Kolb & Whishaw, 1998; Rosenzweig, 1984). Environmental stimulation (or lack thereof) also appears to influence the brain development of infants and children. Researchers have found startling problems with brain development for infants who were exposed to "severe deprivation" early in life (Kennedy et al., 2016). For example, babies raised in orphanages that provide minimal care and human interaction not only experience "deficits" in cognitive, social, and physical development, they also face "life-long risks of chronic disorders of mental and physical health" (Kumsta et al., 2016, p. 5).

The Language Explosion

The brain development that occurs during childhood and the cognitive changes associated with it are remarkable. Consider the fact that babies come into the world incapable of using language, yet by the age of 6, most have amassed a vocabulary of about 13,000 words—that represents about one new word every 2 hours awake (Pinker, 1994). Let's take a look at some of the theories that attempt to explain the language explosion.

LO 8   Distinguish among the theories explaining language acquisition.

BEHAVIORISM AND LANGUAGE   Behaviorists propose that all behavior—including the use of language—is learned through associations, reinforcers, and observation. Infants and children learn language in the same way they learn everything else, through positive attention to correct behavior (for example, praising correct speech), unpleasant attention to incorrect behavior (for example, criticizing incorrect speech), and the observation of others.

LANGUAGE ACQUISITION DEVICE   But the behaviorist theory cannot explain all the complexities of language acquisition. If a young child tries to imitate a particular sentence structure, such as "I am going to the kitchen," he might instead say something grammatically incorrect, "I go kitchen." Children are not directly taught the structure of grammar, because its rules are too difficult for their developing brains to understand. Linguist Noam Chomsky (1959) suggested humans have a language acquisition device (LAD) that provides an innate mechanism for learning language. With the LAD, children compare the language they hear in their environment to a framework already hardwired in their brains. The fact that children all over the world seem to learn language in a fixed sequence, and during approximately the same time period, is evidence that this innate language capacity exists.

INFANT-DIRECTED SPEECH   More recent theories of language acquisition focus on parents' and other caregivers' use of _infant-directed speech (IDS)_. High-pitched and repetitious, infant-directed speech is observed throughout the world (Singh, Nestor, Parikh, & Yull, 2009). Can't you just hear Ericka saying to baby Niyah, "Who's my baby girl?" Researchers report that infants as young as 5 months old pay more attention to people who use infant-directed speech, which allows them to choose "appropriate social partners," or adults who are more likely to provide them with chances to learn and interact (Schachner & Hannon, 2011). Infants who don't show this preference for infant-directed speech later develop "seriously disrupted" language skills. When they pay attention to people talking in their environment, infant-directed and otherwise, they are better able to "uncover" elements of language and engage in social interactions (Golinkoff, Can, Soderstrom, & Hirsh-Pasek, 2015).

LANGUAGE IN THE ENVIRONMENT   Infants may not be the best conversation partners, but they benefit from a lot of chatter. It turns out that the amount of language

CONNECTIONS

In **Chapter 7,** we introduced the basic elements of language, such as phonemes, morphemes, and semantics, and explored how language relates to thought. In this chapter, we discuss how language develops.

CONNECTIONS

Chapter 5 presented the principles of learning. Here, we see how operant conditioning, through reinforcement and punishment, and observational learning, through modeling, can be used to understand how language is acquired.

Synonyms

infant-directed speech motherese

spoken in the home correlates with socioeconomic status. Children from high-income families are more likely to have parents who engage them in conversation. Just look at findings from early studies of parents of toddlers: 35 words a minute spoken by high-income parents; 20 words a minute spoken by middle-income parents; 10 words a minute spoken by low-income parents (Hoff, 2003). The consequences of such interactions are apparent, with toddlers from high-income households having an average vocabulary of 766 words, and those from low-income homes only 357 (Hart & Risley, 1995). How might this disparity in exposure, also referred to as the *30-million-word gap,* impact these same children when they start school (Hirsh-Pasek et al., 2015)? Research suggests that children from lower socioeconomic households begin school already lagging behind in reading, math, and academic achievement in general, all of which could potentially be linked to decreased verbal interactions (Hoff, 2013; Lee & Burkan, 2002).

We have noted the benefits of infant-directed speech, and the importance of exposing young children to a large number of words (particularly in the first 18 months), but the quality of speech input is also critical to language development (Golinkoff et al., 2015; Hirsh-Pasek et al., 2015). Research suggests that children in their third year benefit from exposure to diverse and sophisticated vocabulary words, while those in their fourth year gain from listening to discussions of the past or future (Rowe, 2012).

LO 9 Outline the universal sequence of language development.

THE SEQUENCE OF ACQUISITION Coo. Babble. Talk. No matter what language infants speak, or who raises them, you can almost be certain they will follow the universal sequence of language development (Chomsky, 2000). At the age of 2 to 3 months, infants typically start to produce vowel-like sounds known as *cooing.* These "oooo" and "ahhh" sounds are often repeated in a joyful manner. Every time Ericka put Niyah down to sleep, she would coo like a songbird in her bassinet. "She was one of those babies who didn't want to go to sleep because they felt like they would miss something," Ericka says. Even when it wasn't sleep time, Niyah made her presence known. "She was always, kind of like, letting you know she was in the room, making little sounds," Ericka recalls. "You couldn't forget that she was in the room."

When infants reach the age of 4 to 6 months, they begin to combine consonants and vowels in the *babbling* stage. These sounds are meaningless, but babbling can resemble real language ("ma, ma, ma, ma, ma" *Did you say . . . mama?*). Nonhearing infants also go through this babbling stage, but they move their hands instead of babbling aloud (Petitto & Marentette, 1991). For both infants with normal hearing and infants who are deaf, the babbling stage becomes an important foundation for speech production; when infants babble, they are on their way to their first words.

When do real words begin? At around 12 months, infants typically begin to utter their magical first words. Often these are nouns used to convey an entire message, or *holophrase.* Perhaps you have heard an infant say something emphatically, such as "JUICE!" or "UP!" What she might be trying to say is "I am thirsty, could I please have some juice?" or "I want you to pick me up."

At about 18 months, infants start to use two-word phrases in their **telegraphic speech.** These brief statements might include only the most important words of a sentence, such as nouns, verbs, and adjectives, but no prepositions or articles. "Baby crying" might be a telegraphic sentence meaning the baby at the next table is crying loudly. As children mature, they start to use more complete sentences. Their grammar becomes more complex and they pack more words into statements. A "vocabulary explosion" tends to occur around 2 to 3 years of age (McMurray, 2007; **FIGURE 8.3**). It was around this time that Niyah began asking a lot of questions: "What did you do today? Where are we going? Is this the way to Grandma's house? Why are we buying that?" As Ericka tried to keep pace with Niyah's inquiries, she wondered how this little person came up

Benefits of Sign
A baby and a caregiver communicate with sign language. Introducing sign to children as young as 6 months may help them communicate before they use verbal speech (Doherty-Sneddon, 2008). Early use of sign may also provide a verbal advantage down the road when they enter elementary school (Barnes, 2010). Christina Kennedy/Alamy Stock Photo.

telegraphic speech Two-word phrases typically used by infants around the age of 18 months.

with such questions. *Why are you asking me that? How do you know to ask me that?* By 5 to 6, most children are fluent in their native language, although their vocabulary does not match that of an adult.

There are two important components of normal language acquisition: (1) physical development, particularly in the language-processing areas of the brain (Chapter 2); and (2) exposure to language. If a child does not observe people using language during the first several years of life, normal language skills will not develop. Evidence for this phenomenon comes from case studies of people who were deprived of language in childhood (Goldin-Meadow, 1978). One of the most well-documented—and deeply troubling—cases of childhood deprivation centers on a young girl known as Genie.

NATURE AND NURTURE
Genie the "Feral Child"

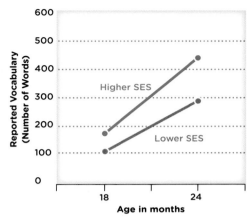

In 1970 a social worker in Arcadia, California, discovered a most horrifying case of child neglect and abuse. "Genie," as researchers came to call her, was 13 at the time her situation came to the attention of the authorities, though she barely looked 7. Feeble and emaciated, the child could not even stand up straight. Genie was not capable of chewing food or using a toilet. She could not articulate a single word (Curtiss, Fromkin, Krashen, Rigler, & Rigler, 1974; PBS, 1997, March 4).

AT AGE 13, GENIE COULD NOT EVEN SPEAK.

Between the ages of 20 months and 13 years, Genie had been locked away in a dark room, strapped to a potty chair or confined in a cagelike crib. Her father beat her when she made any type of noise. There, Genie stayed for 12 years, alone in silence, deprived of physical activity, sensory stimulation, and affection (Curtiss et al., 1974).

When discovered and brought to a hospital at age 13, Genie would not utter a sound (Curtiss et al., 1974). She did seem to understand simple words, but that was about it for her language comprehension. Researchers tried to build Genie's vocabulary, teaching her basic principles of syntax, and she made considerable gains, eventually speaking meaningful sentences. But some aspects of language, such as the ability to use the passive tense ("The carrot was given to the rabbit") or words such as "what" and "which" continued to mystify her (Goldin-Meadow, 1978). Why couldn't Genie master certain linguistic skills? Was it because she missed important experiences during the normal period for language development?

This is a real possibility. Similar outcomes have been observed in other "feral" children. Consider the example of 6-year-old Danielle Crockett of Florida, discovered by authorities in 2005. Living among cockroaches and excrement in her mother's home, Danielle was starving and unable to speak (DeGregory, 2008, July 31). After being removed from the home and adopted by a loving family, she learned a variety of skills, such as brushing her teeth and using a computer. However, Danielle's speech is extremely limited; she can only articulate short phrases such as "I love you" (Owen, 2016, June 22; Times Staff Writer, 2014, June 18).

There are other variables to consider in the Genie case, like the possibility that she may have suffered from an underlying intellectual disability, or that she never developed the throat muscles required for normal speech (Curtiss et al., 1974; James, 2008, May 7). Could it be that nature played a role in her difficulty with language? It's almost impossible to say, given the extreme environmental circumstances of Genie's case. We should note nevertheless that Genie's story does end with a glimmer of hope. Genie is reported to be "happy," living in a group home for adults with intellectual disabilities (James, 2008, May 7).

Some psychologists suggest there is a *critical period* for language acquisition. Until a certain age, children are highly receptive to learning language, but after that period ends,

FIGURE 8.3
The Vocabulary Explosion
During the second year of life, a child's vocabulary increases dramatically. In one study, parents identified the words understood and spoken by their children (from a list of 680 items). As shown above, the vocabulary gap between children of higher and lower socioeconomic status (SES) widened between 18 and 24 months. Information from Fernald, Marchman, and Weisleder (2014).

"Modern-Day Genie"?
Danielle Crockett (now Danielle Lierow) with her adoptive parents and brother. There are many parallels between the cases of Danielle and Genie the "feral child." Both were found living alone in small rooms, deprived of stimulation and affection, and severely malnourished. At the time of their discovery, they were unable to eat solid foods, use the bathroom, stand upright without assistance, and communicate with language (Curtiss et al., 1974; DeGregory, 2008, July 31). Tampa Bay Times/Melissa Lyttle/The Image Works.

it is difficult for them to acquire a first language that is age-appropriate and "normal" (Friedmann & Rusou, 2015; Kuhl, Conboy, Padden, Nelson, & Pruitt, 2005). Critical periods are times during development, in which "certain capacities are readily shaped or altered by experience" (Knudsen, 2004, p. 1412). These critical periods are accompanied by "irreversible changes in brain function" (p. 1412). Others suggest that language acquisition is not subject to a hard-and-fast critical period, but rather to *sensitive periods* that all children experience (Knudsen, 2004). For an example of a sensitive period, we can look to young barn owls, which use auditory information to create a mental map of their environment during a certain stage of development. This period is not characterized by irreversible brain changes, so it would qualify as a sensitive period rather than a critical period (Knudsen, 2004).

Piaget and Cognitive Development

LO 10 Discuss the key elements of Piaget's and Vygotsky's theories of cognitive development.

Language is just one domain of cognitive development. How do other processes like memory and problem solving evolve through childhood? As noted earlier, psychologists do not always agree on whether development is continuous or occurs in steps. Swiss biologist and developmental psychologist Jean Piaget (pee-uh-ZHAY; 1896–1980) was among the first to suggest that infants have cognitive abilities, a notion that was not widely embraced at the time. Children do not think like adults, suggested Piaget, and their cognitive development takes place in stages.

One important component of cognition, according to Piaget (1936/1952), is the **schema** [SKEE-muh], a collection of ideas or notions that serves as a building block of understanding. Young children create these schemas by learning about functional relationships. The schema "toy," for example, might include any object that can be played with (such as dolls, trucks, and balls). As children mature, so do their schemas, which begin to organize and structure their thinking around more abstract categories, such as "love" (romantic love, love for one's country, and so on). As they grow, children expand their schemas in response to interactions with the environment and other life experiences.

Piaget (1936/1952) believed humans are biologically driven to advance intellectually, partly as a result of an innate need to maintain *cognitive equilibrium,* or a feeling of cognitive balance. Suppose a toddler's schema of house pets only includes small dogs like his own, which he recognizes as having fur, four legs, and a tail. When he sees a very large kitten at a neighbor's house for the first time, he looks to his mother and says "Puppy," because he notices it, too, has fur, four legs, and a tail. This is an example of **assimilation;** the child attempts to understand new information (the sight of an unfamiliar small animal) using his already existing knowledge base, or schema (the characteristics of small animals familiar to him). Hearing the mistake, his mother responds, "That's a kitty, and kitties say 'meow.' 'Woof' is what puppies say." This shakes up his notion of what a house pet is, causing an uncomfortable sense of *disequilibrium* that motivates him to restore cognitive balance. The new information about this four-legged creature is so disconcerting that it cannot be assimilated, so he must instead use **accommodation**, the restructuring of old notions to make a place for new information. With accommodation, we remodel old schemas or create new ones. The child had never seen a kitten before, causing him some confusion. To eliminate this, he created a new schema (*Small furry animals with four legs and a tail that say "meow" are cats*). Both assimilation and accommodation allow us to make great strides in cognitive growth. We assimilate information to fit new experiences into our old ways of thinking, and we accommodate our old way of thinking to understand new information.

Piaget (1936/1952) also proposed that cognitive development occurs in four periods or stages, and these stages have distinct beginnings and endings (**INFOGRAPHIC 8.3**).

At Play with Piaget
Developmental psychologist Jean Piaget (center) works with students in a New York City classroom. Piaget's research focused on school-age children, including his own three, who became participants in some of his studies. Children think differently from adults, Piaget proposed, and they experience cognitive development in distinct stages. Bill Anderson/Science Source.

schema A collection of ideas that represents a basic unit of understanding.

assimilation Using existing information and ideas to understand new knowledge and experiences.

accommodation A restructuring of old ideas to make a place for new information.

Piaget's Theory of Cognitive Development

Jean Piaget proposed that children's cognitive development occurs in stages characterized by particular cognitive abilities. These stages have distinct beginnings and endings.

Formal Operational
Child is now able to think logically and systematically and is capable of hypothetical thinking.

Concrete Operational
Child understands operations and thinks more logically in reference to concrete objects and circumstances.

Preoperational
Child uses symbolic thinking to explore and understand the world. Children at this stage are known for magical thinking and egocentrism.

Sensorimotor
Child uses sensory capabilities and motor activities to learn about the world; develops object permanence.

Piaget's four stages of cognitive development

Sensorimotor
birth–2 yrs

Preoperational
2–7 yrs

Concrete Operational
7–11 yrs

Formal Operational
11 yrs and up

Credits: Child playing peekaboo, © Peter Polak/Fotolia.com; Child playing vet with Teddy bear, © Gina Sanders/Fotolia.com; Object permanence test, Doug Goodman/Science Source; Blocks, pavel siamionau/Thinkstock; Teenage girl writing on chalkboard, Creatas/Thinkstock; Boy pouring oil into cake batter, AnnWorthy/istockphoto/Thinkstock; Open hand, zveiger alexandre/istockphoto/Thinkstock; Piaget Conservation-Girl with milk glasses, Bianca Moscatelli/Worth Publishers. Eye featured in the hand: © Flashon Studio/Dreamstime.com.

How do we assess a child's stage of cognitive development?

Piaget developed techniques to test characteristic capabilities associated with each stage.

Object permanence test: Does the child realize objects continue to exist when they are hidden? Infants who have developed object permanence will search for an object.

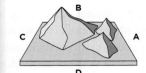

Three Mountains task tests egocentrism. Can the child imagine a perspective different than her own? "What would you see if you were standing at Point B?"

Conservation of Volume test assesses understanding of operations. Does a child understand that the amount of liquid remains constant when it is poured into a container with a different shape?

Third Eye task tests formal operational thought. "If you had a third eye, where would you put it?" Children at this stage come up with logical, innovative answers.

Does That Taste Good?
Babies are notorious for putting just about everything, including toys, shoes, and sand, in their mouths. Mouthing is one of the main ways babies experience their worlds, and it is an important aspect of cognitive development. It also provides exposure to viruses and other environmental pathogens, which helps prepare the developing immune system to fight infections (Fessler & Abrams, 2004). Kaori Ando/agefotostock.

Hello, Doctor
During the preoperational stage (ages 2–7), many children relish imaginative play. In addition to pretending to be a "baker" in her kitchen, Niyah played the role of the family "doctor," nursing the wounds of grandmothers, aunts, uncles, and, of course, her mom. "She would always fix my boo boos, even if I didn't have any," Ericka says. "She was very nurturing." Courtesy Ericka Harley.

SENSORIMOTOR STAGE According to Piaget, from birth to about 2 years old is the **sensorimotor stage.** Infants use their sensory abilities and motor activities (such as reaching, crawling, and handling things) to learn about the surrounding world, exploring objects with their mouths, fingers, and toes. It's a nerve-racking process for parents ("Please do *not* put that shoe in your mouth!"), but an important part of cognitive development.

One significant milestone of the sensorimotor stage is **object permanence,** or an infant's realization that objects and people still exist when they are out of sight or touch. While playing with babies, Piaget observed how they react when a toy is placed under a blanket. Those who had reached the object permanence milestone realized the toy still existed even though it could not be seen. The toy was out of sight but not out of mind, so the baby would actively look for it (Piaget, 1936/1952). A baby who had not reached this stage would continue playing as if nothing were missing.

PREOPERATIONAL STAGE The next stage in Piaget's cognitive development theory is the **preoperational stage,** which applies to children from 2 to 7 years old. During this time, children start using language to explore and understand their worlds (rather than relying primarily on sensory and motor activities). They ask questions and use symbolic thinking in their make believe play. The concoction of dirt and sticks in the bowl becomes symbolic of food for the baby doll. This is a time for pretending and engaging in fantasy play. Children in the preoperational stage tend to be somewhat limited by their **egocentrism;** they primarily imagine the world from their own perspective (see the Three Mountains task in Infographic 8.3). This type of egocentrism refers to their *cognitive ability* to understand another person's point of view, which is not the same as a child being selfish or spoiled.

According to Piaget (1936/1952), children in this stage have not yet mastered *operations* (hence, the name *preoperational* stage), which are the logical reasoning processes that older children and adults use to understand the world. For example, these children have a difficult time understanding the *reversibility* of some actions or events. They may have trouble comprehending that vanilla ice cream can be refrozen after it melts, but not turned back into sugar, milk, and vanilla. This difficulty with operations is also apparent in errors involving **conservation,** which refers to the unchanging properties of volume, mass, or amount in relation to appearance (**FIGURE 8.4**). For example, if you take two masses of clay of the same shape and size, and then roll only one of them out into a hotdog shape, a child in this stage may think that the longer-shaped clay is now made up of more clay than the undisturbed clump of clay. Or, the child may see that the newly formed clump of clay is skinnier and therefore assume it is smaller. Why is this so? Children at this age generally focus on only one characteristic of an object. They do not understand how the object stays fundamentally the same, even if it is manipulated or takes on a different appearance.

CONCRETE OPERATIONAL STAGE Around age 7, children enter what Piaget called the **concrete operational stage.** They begin to think more logically, but mainly in reference to concrete objects and circumstances: things that can be seen or touched, or are well defined by strict rules. Children in this stage tend to be less egocentric and can understand the concept of conservation. However, they still have trouble with abstract ideas and hypothetical thinking. For example, a 7-year-old may respond with a blank stare when asked a question such as "What would you do if you could travel to the future?" or "If you had to choose between losing your eyebrows or your eyelashes, which one would you give up?" If you ask Niyah, who is now 10 years old, what she imagines herself doing in 20 years, she will say, "I want to be a baker, a school bus driver, and a teacher." At this stage in her cognitive development, Niyah may not realize how difficult it would be to perform all three jobs simultaneously.

Type of Conservation Task	Original Presentation	Alteration	Question	Preoperational Child's Answer
Volume	Two equal beakers of liquid	Pour one into a taller, narrower beaker.	Does one beaker have more liquid?	The taller beaker has more liquid.
Mass	Two equal lumps of clay	Roll one lump into a long, hotdog shape.	Does one lump weigh more?	The original lump weighs more.

FIGURE 8.4

Conservation Tasks

Children in the preoperational stage don't realize that properties like volume and mass stay constant when items are only rearranged or reshaped. Tasks like those outlined here are used to test children's understanding of conservation.

FORMAL OPERATIONAL STAGE According to Piaget, children enter the **formal operational stage** at age 11; they begin to think more logically and systematically. They can solve problems such as those in the Third Eye task in Infographic 8.3. This activity asks a child where she would put a third eye, and why (*I'd put it in the back of my head so that I could see what is going on behind my back*). These types of capabilities do not necessarily develop overnight, and logical abilities are likely to advance in relation to interests and to skills developed in a work setting. Piaget suggested that not everyone reaches this stage of formal operations. But to succeed in most colleges, this type of logical thinking is essential; students need to think critically and use abstract ideas to solve problems.

THE CRITICS Critics of Piaget suggest that although cognitive development might occur in stages with distinct characteristics, the transitions from one stage to the next are likely to be gradual, and do not necessarily represent a complete leap from one type of thinking to the next. Some believe Piaget's theory underestimates children's cognitive abilities. For example, some researchers have found that object permanence occurs sooner than suggested by Piaget, depending on factors such as the length of time an object is out of sight (Baillargeon, Spelke, & Wasserman, 1985; Bremner, Slater, & Johnson, 2015). Others question Piaget's assertion that the formal operational stage is reached by 11 to 12 years of age, and that no further delineations can be made between the cognitive abilities of adolescents and adults of various ages. One solution is to account for cognitive changes occurring in adulthood by considering stages beyond Piaget's original formulation.

Vygotsky and Cognitive Development

One other major criticism of Piaget's work is that it does not take into consideration the social interactions that influence the developing child. Russian psychologist Lev Vygotsky (vie-GOT-skee) was particularly interested in how social and cultural factors affect a child's cognitive development (Vygotsky, 1934/1962).

As Vygotsky saw it, children are like apprentices in relation to others who are more capable and experienced (Zaretskii, 2009). Those children who receive help from older children and adults progress more quickly in their cognitive abilities. For example, when parents help their children solve puzzles by providing support for them to succeed on their own, the children show advancement in goal-directed behavior and the ability to plan ahead (Bernier, Carlson, & Whipple, 2010; Hammond, Müller, Carpendale, Bibok, & Liebermann-Finestone, 2012).

One way we can support children's cognitive development is through **scaffolding:** pushing them to go just beyond what they are competent and comfortable doing, but

sensorimotor stage Piaget's stage of cognitive development during which infants use their sensory capabilities and motor skills to learn about the surrounding world.

object permanence A milestone of the sensorimotor stage of cognitive development; an infant's realization that objects and people still exist even when out of sight or touch.

preoperational stage Piaget's stage of cognitive development during which children can start to use language to explore and understand their worlds.

egocentrism When a person is only able to imagine the world from his or her own perspective.

conservation Refers to the unchanging properties of volume, mass, or amount in relation to appearance.

concrete operational stage Piaget's stage of cognitive development during which children begin to think more logically, but mainly in reference to concrete objects and circumstances.

formal operational stage Piaget's stage of cognitive development during which children begin to think more logically and systematically.

scaffolding Pushing children to go just beyond what they are competent and comfortable doing, while providing help in a decreasing manner.

Culture and Cognition
A man and a boy work together threshing rice in the fields of Madagascar. What this child learns and how his cognitive development unfolds are shaped by the circumstances of his environment. Children reared in agricultural societies may acquire different cognitive skill sets than those raised in urban, industrialized settings. Yvan Travert/Corbis.

You Asked, Ericka Answers

http://qrs.ly/db5a5dv

How did being a single mother influence your daughter's development?

scan this →

zone of proximal development
The range of cognitive tasks that can be accomplished alone and those that require the guidance and help of others.

temperament Characteristic differences in behavioral patterns and emotional reactions that are evident from birth.

also providing help in a decreasing manner. A parent or caregiver provides support when necessary, but allows a child to solve problems independently: "Successful scaffolding is like a wave, rising to offer help when needed and receding as the child regains control of the task" (Hammond et al., 2012, p. 275).

In order to scaffold effectively, the caregiver must be familiar with the "the discrepancy between a child's actual mental age and the level he reaches in solving problems with assistance" (Vygotsky, 1934/1962, p. 103). According to Vygotsky, we should consider not only what children know, but also where they are in their current development and what remains to be learned. In other words, the child's **zone of proximal development** includes cognitive tasks that can be accomplished alone and those that require the guidance and help of others. To facilitate a child's cognitive development, we should create an environment that provides activities they can accomplish alone, and challenges they can overcome with help. For example, a fifth grader learning the principles of the scientific method can design a very basic experiment, but only with the help of an older child or adult can he accomplish a more complex research design.

Vygotsky also emphasized that learning always occurs within the context of a child's culture. Children across the world have different sets of expected learning outcomes, from raising sheep to weaving blankets to completing a geometry proof. We need to keep these cross-cultural differences in mind when exploring cognitive development in children.

Until now, we have mostly discussed physical and cognitive development, but recall we are also interested in *socioemotional* development.

Temperament and Attachment

 "THE BEST BABY EVER" After Niyah was born, Ericka finished high school and began working full-time. "She went to school, she worked, she took care of Niyah, and she took her to the baby sitter," says Joan. "She lived in my house, but she took full responsibility for everything." Niyah spent only 2–3 days a month with her father, so Ericka was essentially a single parent. But it was manageable (and even fun!) because Niyah was such a good-natured and happy baby. She was, according to Ericka, "the best baby ever."

Ericka was lucky, because not all babies are so easygoing. It's not uncommon for newborns to wake up crying every 2 hours during the night. Niyah began sleeping solid 8-hour stretches when she was just 3 months old. Some babies want to be held a large part of the day, and will cry hysterically if they are put down. Others experience *separation anxiety,* which typically peaks at approximately 13 months (Hertenstein & McCullough, 2005). Many babies cry for no obvious reason, or can only fall asleep when nursing or riding in a car. "I don't ever remember there being a situation where she would just not stop crying," Ericka says. Apparently, Niyah was born with a calm and happy *temperament.* ●

HIGH-REACTIVE AND LOW-REACTIVE **Temperament,** which refers to one's distinct patterns of emotional reactions and behaviors, is apparent across all developmental stages. We begin to see evidence of temperament in the first days of life. Some babies can be categorized as having an exuberant temperament, showing an overall positive attitude and sociability (Degnan et al., 2011). "High-reactive" infants exhibit a great deal of distress when exposed to unfamiliar stimuli, such as new sights, sounds, and smells. "Low-reactive" infants do not respond to new stimuli with great distress (Kagan, 2003). Classification as high- and low-reactive is based on measures of behavior, emotional response, and physiological factors, such as heart rate and blood pressure (Kagan, 1985, 2003).

These different characteristics seem to be innate, as they are apparent from birth and consistent in the infants' daily lives (Plomin, DeFries, Knopik, & Neiderhiser, 2013). There is also evidence that some of these characteristics remain fairly stable throughout life (Kagan & Snidman, 1991). However, the environment can influence temperament (Briley & Tucker-Drob, 2014; Caspi, Roberts, & Shiner, 2005). Factors such as maternal education, neighborhood, and paternal occupation through adolescence can predict characteristics of adult temperament, such as persistence, shyness, and impulsiveness (Congdon et al., 2012).

EASY, DIFFICULT, OR SLOW TO WARM UP We can characterize babies according to their reactivity, or we can focus on how easy they are to care for. Researchers have found that the majority of infants can be classified as having one of three fundamental temperaments (Thomas & Chess, 1986). Around 40% are considered "easy" babies; they are easy to care for because they follow regular eating and sleeping schedules. These happy babies can be soothed when upset and don't appear to become rattled by transitions or changes in their environments. Ericka would put Niyah in this category. "She didn't cry a lot," Ericka explains, but if she did get upset, there would always be a clear reason. "It had to be [a] 'I'm hungry, I'm wet' type of thing."

"Difficult" babies (around 10%) are more challenging because they don't seem to have a set schedule for eating and sleeping. And they don't deal well with transitions or changes in the environment. Difficult babies are often irritable and unhappy, and compared to easy babies, they are far less responsive to the soothing attempts of caregivers. They also tend to be very active, kicking their legs on the changing table and wiggling like mad when you try to put on their clothes. Joan's recollections suggest that Ericka could possibly be placed in this category. "Ericka cried about everything when she was a baby," Joan says. "I never knew why she cried so much."

"Slow to warm up" babies (around 15%) are not as irritable (or active) as difficult babies, but they are not fond of change. Give them enough time, however, and they will adapt.

These categories of baby temperaments are useful, but we should remember that 35% of babies are considered hard to classify because they share the characteristics of more than one type.

Easy, difficult, or slow to warm up, all babies are sensitive to input from parents and other caregivers. But what exactly makes a good parent? The adjectives or phrases that come to our minds are "patience," "sensitivity," "acceptance," "strength," and "unconditional love." It also helps to be soft, warm, and snuggly—especially if you happen to be a monkey.

THE HARLOWS AND THEIR MONKEYS Research suggests that physical touch is a very important part of infant development. Among the first to explore this topic in an experimental situation were Harry Harlow, Margaret Harlow, and their colleagues at the University of Wisconsin (Harlow, Harlow, & Suomi, 1971). The researchers were initially interested in learning how physical contact affects the development of loving relationships between infants and mothers. But they realized this would be **difficult to study** with human infants; instead, they turned to newborn macaque monkeys (Harlow, 1958).

Easy, Baby
Most babies can be classified according to one of three fundamental temperaments: About 40% are "easy," meaning they are generally content and follow predictable schedules; approximately 10% are "difficult," or hard to please and irregular in their schedules; and another 15% are "slow to warm up," meaning they struggle with change but eventually adjust. The remaining 35% do not fall into any one category. YinYang/Getty Images.

CONNECTIONS

In **Chapter 1,** we discussed the importance of ensuring the ethical treatment of research participants (human and animal). Psychologists must do no harm and safeguard the welfare of participants. The Harlows obviously could not take human newborns from their parents to study the importance of physical contact. Many question the ethics of using newborn monkeys in this manner.

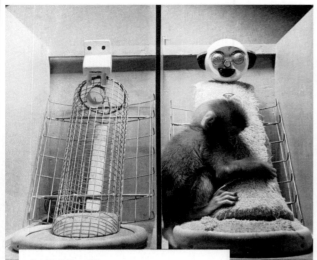

Soft Like Mommy
A baby monkey in a laboratory experiment clings to a furry mother surrogate. Research by Harry and Margaret Harlow and colleagues at the University of Wisconsin showed that physical comfort is important for the socioemotional development of these animals. When given the choice between a wire mesh "mother" that provided milk and a cloth-covered "mother" without milk, most of the monkeys opted to snuggle with the cuddly cloth-covered one (Harlow, 1958). SCIENCE SOURCE/Getty Images.

Here's how the experiment worked: Infant monkeys were put in cages alone, each with two artificial "surrogate" mothers. One surrogate was outfitted with a soft cloth and heated with a bulb. The other surrogate mother was designed to be lacking in "contact comfort," as she was made of wire mesh and not covered in cloth. Both of these surrogates could be set up to feed the infants. In one study, half the infant monkeys received their milk from the cloth surrogates and the other half got their milk from the wire surrogates. The great majority of the infant monkeys spent most of their time clinging to or in contact with the cloth mother, even if she was not the mother providing the milk. The baby monkeys spent 15 to 18 hours a day physically close to the cloth mother, and only 1 to 2 hours touching the wire mother.

Harlow and colleagues also created situations in which they purposefully scared the infants with a moving toy bear, and found that the great majority of the infant monkeys (around 80%) ran to the cloth mother, regardless of whether she was a source of milk. In times of fear and uncertainty, these infant monkeys found more comfort in the soft, cloth mothers. Through their experiments, Harlow and his colleagues showed how important physical contact is for these living creatures (Harlow, 1958; Harlow & Zimmerman, 1959).

ATTACHMENT Physical contact plays an important role in **attachment,** or the degree to which an infant feels an emotional connection with primary caregivers. Using a research procedure called the *Strange Situation,* American-Canadian psychologist Mary Ainsworth (1913–1999) studied the attachment styles of infants between 12 and 18 months (Ainsworth, 1979, 1985; Ainsworth & Bell, 1970; Ainsworth, Blehar, Waters, & Wall, 1978). In one study using the Strange Situation, (1) a mother and child are in a room alone. (2) A stranger enters, and (3) the mother then exits the room, leaving the child in the unfamiliar environment with the stranger, who tries to interact with the child. (4) The mother returns to the room but leaves again, and then returns once more. At this point, (5) the stranger departs. During this observation, the researchers note the amount of anxiety displayed by the child before and after the stranger arrives, the child's willingness to explore the unfamiliar environment, and the child's reaction to the mother's return. The following response patterns were observed:

- **Secure attachment:** The majority of the children were upset when their mothers left the room, but were easily soothed upon her return, quickly returning to play. These children seemed confident that their needs would be met and felt safe exploring their environment, using the caregiver as a "secure base."

- **Avoidant attachment:** Some of the children displayed no distress when their mothers left, and they did not show any signs of wanting to interact with their mothers when they returned, seemingly happy to play in the room without looking at their mothers or the stranger. They didn't seem to mind when their mothers left, or fuss when they returned.

- **Ambivalent:** Children in this group were quite upset and very focused on their mothers, showing signs of wanting to be held, but unable to be soothed by their mothers. These children were angry (often pushing away their mothers) and not interested in returning to play.

Ideally, parents and caregivers provide a *secure base* for infants, and are ready to help regulate emotions (soothe or calm) or meet other needs. This makes infants feel comfortable exploring their environments. Ainsworth and colleagues (1978) suggested that development, both physical and psychological, is greatly influenced by the quality of

attachment The degree to which an infant feels an emotional connection with primary caregivers.

an infant's attachment to caregivers. But much of the early research in this area focused on infants' attachment to their mothers. Subsequent research suggests that we should examine infants' attachment to multiple individuals (mother, father, caregivers at day care, and close relatives), as well as cross-cultural differences in attachment (Field, 1996; Rothbaum, Weisz, Pott, Miyake, & Morelli, 2000).

Critics of the Strange Situation method suggest it creates an artificial environment and does not provide good measures of how infant–mother pairs act in their natural settings. Some suggest that the temperament of infants predisposes them to react the way they do in this setting. Infants prone to anxiety and uncertainty are more likely to respond negatively to such a scenario (Kagan, 1985). More generally, attachment theories are criticized for not considering cross-cultural differences in relationships (Rothbaum et al., 2000).

Attachments are formed early in childhood, but they have implications for a lifetime: "Experiences in early close relationships create internal working models that then influence cognition, affect [emotions], and behavior in relationships that involve later attachment figures" (Simpson & Rholes, 2010, p. 174). Some people who experienced ambivalent attachment as infants have been described as exhibiting an "insatiability for closeness" in their adult relationships. Those who had secure attachments are more likely to expect that they are lovable and that others are capable of love. They are aware that nobody is perfect, and this attitude allows for intimacy in relationships (Cassidy, 2001). Infant attachment may even have long-term health consequences. One 32-year longitudinal study found that adults who had been insecurely attached as infants were more likely to report inflammation-based illnesses (for example, asthma, cardiovascular disease, and diabetes) than those with secure attachments (Puig, Englund, Simpson, & Collins, 2013).

 **In Class: Collaborate and Report**

What makes a good parent? In your group, **A)** list the characteristics of an effective caregiver, and **B)** support this list using the lessons you learned from Vygotsky, Ainsworth, and the Harlow experiments.

Feeling Secure
A childcare worker plays with toddlers at Moore Community Center's Early Head Start program in Biloxi, Mississippi. Children are more willing to explore their environments when they have caregivers who consistently meet their needs and provide a secure base. Jim West/PhotoEdit.

Erikson's Psychosocial Stages

LO 11 Explain Erikson's theory of psychosocial development up until puberty.

You may recall that Piaget proposed that cognitive development proceeds in stages. German-born American psychologist Erik Erikson (1902–1994) believed that socio-emotional development progresses stepwise as well. According to Erikson, human development is marked by eight psychosocial stages, spanning infancy to old age (**TABLE 8.3**, on the next page; Erikson & Erikson, 1997). Each of these stages is marked by a developmental task or an emotional crisis that must be handled successfully to allow for healthy psychological growth. The crises, according to Erikson, stem from conflicts between the needs of the individual and the expectations of society (Erikson, 1993). Successful resolution of a stage enables an individual to approach the following stage with more tools. Unsuccessful resolution leads to more difficulties during the next stage. Let's take a look at the stages associated with infancy and childhood.

- **Trust versus mistrust (birth to 1 year):** In order for an infant to learn to trust, her caregivers must attend to her needs. If caregivers are not responsive, she will develop in the direction of mistrust, always expecting the worst of people and her environment.

- **Autonomy versus shame and doubt (1 to 3 years):** If his caregivers provide freedom to explore, a child will learn how to be autonomous and independent. If exploration is restricted and the child is punished, he will likely learn to feel shame and doubt.

- **Initiative versus guilt (3 to 6 years):** During this time, children have more experiences that prompt them to extend themselves socially. Often they become more responsible and capable of creating and executing plans. If a child does not have responsibilities or cannot handle them, she will develop feelings of guilt and anxiety.

- **Industry versus inferiority (6 years to puberty):** Children in this age range are generally engaged in a variety of learning tasks. When successful, they feel a sense of accomplishment and self-esteem increases. If success is not achieved, the child feels a sense of inferiority or incompetence, theoretically leading to unstable work habits or unemployment later on.

TABLE 8.3 ERIKSON'S EIGHT STAGES

Stage	Age	Positive Resolution	Negative Resolution
Trust versus mistrust	Birth to 1 year	Trusts others, has faith in others.	Mistrusts others, expects the worst of people.
Autonomy versus shame and doubt	1 to 3 years	Learns to be autonomous and independent.	Learns to feel shame and doubt when freedom to explore is restricted.
Initiative versus guilt	3 to 6 years	Becomes more responsible, shows the ability to follow through.	Develops guilt and anxiety when unable to handle responsibilities.
Industry versus inferiority	6 years to puberty	Feels a sense of accomplishment and increased self-esteem.	Feels inferiority or incompetence, which can later lead to unstable work habits.
Ego identity versus role confusion	Puberty to twenties	Tries out roles and emerges with a strong sense of values, beliefs, and goals.	Lacks a solid identity, experiences withdrawal, isolation, or continued role confusion.
Intimacy versus isolation	Young adulthood (twenties to forties)	Creates meaningful, deep relationships.	Lives in isolation.
Generativity versus stagnation	Middle adulthood (forties to mid-sixties)	Makes a positive impact on the next generation through parenting, community involvement, or work that is valuable and significant.	Experiences boredom, conceit, and selfishness.
Integrity versus despair	Late adulthood (mid-sixties and older)	Feels a sense of accomplishment and satisfaction.	Feels regret and dissatisfaction.

These are the eight stages of psychosocial development proposed by Erik Erikson. Each stage is marked by a developmental task or an emotional crisis that must be handled successfully to allow for healthy psychological growth. Information from Erikson and Erikson (1997).

This introduction to development during childhood provides an opportunity to understand the physical, cognitive, and socioemotional changes from birth to late childhood. But enough about children. The time has come to explore the exciting period of adolescence.

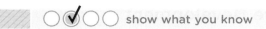 ◯ ✓ ◯ ◯ **show what you know**

1. The _____ reflex occurs when you stroke a baby's cheek; she opens her mouth and turns her head toward your hand. The _____ reflex occurs when you touch the baby's lips; this reflex helps with feeding.

2. Your instructor describes how he is teaching his infant to learn new words by showing her flashcards with images. Every time the infant uses the right word to identify the image, he gives her a big smile. When she uses an incorrect word, he frowns. Your instructor is using which of the following to guide his approach?
   a. theories of behaviorism
   b. Chomsky's language acquisition device
   c. infant-directed speech
   d. telegraphic speech

3. Piaget suggested that when we try to understand new information and experiences by incorporating them into our existing knowledge and ideas, we are using:
   a. the rooting reflex.
   b. schemas.
   c. accommodation.
   d. assimilation.

4. Vygotsky recommended supporting children's cognitive development by _____, pushing them a little harder than normal while gradually reducing the amount of help you give them.

5. Erikson proposed that socioemotional development comprises eight psychosocial stages, and these stages include:
   a. scaffolding.
   b. physical maturation.
   c. developmental tasks or emotional crises.
   d. conservation.

6. What can new parents expect regarding the sequence of their child's language development, and how might they help encourage it?

✓ CHECK YOUR ANSWERS IN APPENDIX C.

Adolescence

WALKING ON PINS AND NEEDLES Recall that Ericka got pregnant with Niyah when she was 16 years old. Was it a conscious choice, or was the pregnancy unplanned? "It was very much a surprise," says Ericka, who had been using birth control, just not consistently. Like many teenagers, Ericka was probably living in the moment, and not too worried about the long-term consequences of her decisions.

Ericka was also rebellious in her teen years. Although she kept up with her schoolwork and made honor roll each semester, skipping school was one of her favorite escapes (Ericka estimates she skipped about 100 days during ninth and tenth grade). Joan had no idea her daughter was home watching TV during school hours, because all the evidence was destroyed. When the school's automated system called to report the absence, Ericka (home alone) would pick up the phone before it went to voicemail. Then she would erase the school phone number from the caller ID.

Adolescence also brought out the emotional side of Ericka. Unable to predict what might trigger one of Ericka's angry outbursts, Joan often felt like she was "walking on pins and needles" in her own house. "I don't want to talk about it," Ericka would say defensively, or "I want to go to Grandma's." ●

Behaviors like these are stereotypical of teenagers, or *adolescents*. **Adolescence** refers to the transition period between late childhood and early adulthood, and it can be challenging for both parents and kids.

In the United States, adult responsibilities often are distant concepts for adolescents. But this is not universal. For example, in underdeveloped countries, children take on adult responsibilities as soon as they are able. In some parts of the world, girls younger than 18 are already married and dealing with grown-up responsibilities. In Bolivia, girls can legally marry at 14 years old (Nour, 2009). However, in America, adolescence generally allows for a much slower transition to adult duties. Although adolescents might develop adult bodies, including the ability to become parents, the more extensive schooling and training they must complete in order to perform at an adult level keep them dependent on parents and caregivers for a longer time.

You Asked, Ericka Answers

http://qrs.ly/xq5a5e0

Do you wish you would have had a "typical" adolescence?

scan this →

adolescence The transition period between late childhood and early adulthood.

Physical and Cognitive Development in Adolescence

LO 12 Give examples of significant physical changes that occur during adolescence.

PHYSICAL DEVELOPMENT Adolescence is a time of dramatic physical growth, comparable to that which occurs during fetal development. The "growth spurt" includes rapid changes in height, weight, and bone growth, and usually begins between ages 9 and 10 for girls and ages 12 and 16 for boys. Sex hormones, which influence this growth and development, are at high levels.

Puberty is the period during which the body changes and becomes sexually mature and able to reproduce. During puberty, the **primary sex characteristics** (reproductive organs) mature; these include the ovaries, uterus, vagina, penis, scrotum, and testes. At the same time, the **secondary sex characteristics** (physical features not associated with reproduction) become more distinct; these include pubic, underarm, and body hair. Breast changes also occur in boys and girls (with the areola increasing in size), and fat increases in girls' breasts. Adolescents experience changes to their skin and overall body hair. Girls' pelvises begin to broaden, while boys experience a deepening of their voices and broadening of their shoulders.

It is during this time that girls experience **menarche** (meh-NAR-key), the point at which menstruation begins. Menarche can occur as early as age 9 or after age 14, but typical onset is around 12 or 13. Boys experience **spermarche** (sper-MAR-key), their first ejaculation, during this time period as well (Ladouceur, 2012). But when it occurs is more difficult to specify, as boys may be reluctant to talk about the event (Mendle, Harden, Brooks-Gunn, & Graber, 2010).

Not everyone goes through puberty at the same time. Researchers have linked the timing of puberty to diet, exercise, and exposure to chemicals such as pesticides (Seltenrich, 2015, October; Windham et al., 2015). Genetics also may play a role, as the timing of puberty for both mom and dad may be a "strong influence" on that of their children (Wohlfahrt-Veje et al., 2016, p. 7). Some evidence suggests that adolescents who mature earlier face a greater risk of engaging in unsafe behaviors, such as drug and alcohol use (Shelton & van den Bree, 2010). Compared to their peers, girls who mature early seem to experience more negative outcomes than those who mature later, including increased anxiety, particularly social anxiety; they also appear to face a higher risk of emotional problems and delinquent behaviors (Blumenthal et al., 2011; Harden & Mendle, 2012). Early maturing girls are more likely to smoke, drink alcohol, have lower self-confidence, and later take on jobs that are "less prestigious." There are certain factors that can reduce such risks, though, including parents who show warmth and support (Shelton & van den Bree, 2010).

Boys who mature early generally do not show evidence of increased anxiety (Blumenthal et al., 2011). But, when researchers examine the "tempo," or speed, with which boys reach full sexual maturity, they find that rapid development can be associated with a range of problems, including aggressive behavior, cheating, and temper tantrums (Marceau, Ram, Houts, Grimm, & Susman, 2011). One interesting theory about the rate of male maturation suggests that it is linked to the context of the time period and its environment: "Humans evolved the capacity to accelerate pubertal maturation in response to contextual factors" (Kogan et al., 2015, p. 616). For example, early sexual maturation may be an adaptation to "harsh, unpredictable community environments" (p. 609).

Adolescence is a time when sexual interest peaks, yet teenagers don't always make the best choices when it comes to sexual activity. Over half of new _sexually transmitted infections_ affect young people ages 15–24; keep in mind that this group represents only 25% of the sexually active population (CDC, 2015e; see Chapter 10). Sexually transmitted infections are especially risky for adolescents because such infections often go untreated and can lead to a host of problems, including long-term sterility.

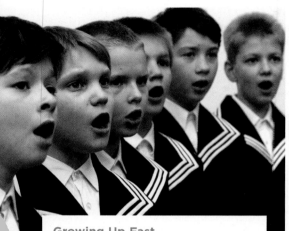

Growing Up Fast
Members of the St. Thomas Boys Choir in Leipzig, Germany, practice a chant in rehearsal. Choir directors are struggling with the fact that young boys' voices are deepening earlier as the years go by. In the mid-1700s, voice changes reportedly occurred in singers aged 17 or 18; these days, the average age is closer to 10 (Mendle & Ferrero, 2012). No one is certain why boys are hitting puberty sooner, but some researchers point to a correlation with an increasing body mass index (Sørensen, Aksglaede, Petersen, & Juul, 2010). Wolfgang Kluge/picture-alliance/dpa/AP Images.

Synonyms

sexually transmitted infections sexually transmitted diseases

puberty The period of development during which the body changes and becomes sexually mature and capable of reproduction.

primary sex characteristics Organs associated with reproduction, including the ovaries, uterus, vagina, penis, scrotum, and testes.

secondary sex characteristics Body characteristics, such as pubic hair, underarm hair, and enlarged breasts, that develop in puberty but are not associated with reproduction.

menarche The point at which menstruation begins.

spermarche A boy's first ejaculation.

identity A sense of self based on values, beliefs, and goals.

LO 13 Summarize Piaget's description of cognitive changes that take place during adolescence.

COGNITIVE DEVELOPMENT Alongside the remarkable physical changes of adolescence are equally remarkable cognitive developments. As noted earlier, children in this age range are better able to distinguish between abstract and hypothetical situations. This ability is an indication that a teenager has entered Piaget's formal operational stage, which begins in adolescence and continues into adulthood. During this period, the adolescent begins to use deductive reasoning to draw conclusions and critical thinking to approach arguments. She can reason abstractly, classify ideas, and use symbols. The adolescent can think beyond the current moment, pondering the future and considering many possibilities. She may begin to contemplate what will happen beyond high school, including career choices and education.

A specific type of egocentrism emerges in adolescence. Before this age, children can only imagine the world from their own perspective, but during adolescence they begin to become aware of others' perspectives. Egocentrism is still apparent, however, as they believe others share their preoccupations. For example, a teenager who focuses on his appearance will think that others are focusing on his appearance as well (Elkind, 1967). Adolescents also tend to believe that most of their peers think the same way they do.

This intense focus on the self may lead to a feeling of immortality, which can result in risk-taking behaviors (Elkind, 1967). Because they have not had many life experiences, adolescents may fail to consider the long-term consequences of their behaviors. They may neglect to consider the repercussions of unprotected sex or drug use, for instance. Their focus on the present (for example, having fun in the moment) outweighs their ability to assess the potential harm in the future (pregnancy or addiction). So to help adolescents stop engaging in risky behaviors such as smoking, we might focus on short-term consequences, like bad breath when kissing a partner, in addition to the long-term dangers such as lung cancer (Robbins & Bryan, 2004).

THE ADOLESCENT BRAIN Risk taking in adolescence is thought to result from characteristics of the adolescent brain. The limbic system, which is responsible for processing emotions and perceiving rewards and punishments, undergoes significant development during adolescence. Another important change is the increased myelination of axons in the prefrontal cortex, which improves the connections within the brain involved in planning, weighing consequences, and multitasking (Steinberg, 2012). But the relatively quicker development of the limbic system in comparison to the prefrontal cortex can lead to risk-taking behavior. Because the prefrontal cortex has not yet fully developed, the adolescent may not foresee the possible consequences of reward-seeking activities. Activity in the limbic system overrides that in the prefrontal cortex, sometimes resulting in poor decisions. Changes to the structure of the brain continue through adolescence, resulting in a fully adult brain between the ages of 22 and 25, and a decline in risk-taking behaviors (Giedd et al., 2009; Steinberg, 2010, 2012). But the studies on brain structure provide results for groups, which may not apply to every person. We cannot use such findings to draw definitive conclusions about individual teenagers (Bonnie & Scott, 2013).

Socioemotional Development in Adolescence

Adolescence is also a time of great socioemotional development. During this period, children become more independent from their parents. Conflicts may result as an adolescent searches for his **identity,** or sense of who he is based on his values, beliefs, and goals. Until this point in development, the child's identity was based primarily on the parents' or caregivers' values and beliefs. Adolescents explore who they are by

Too Young
A teen inmate sits in her room at a maximum-security juvenile facility in Illinois. As a result of the 2005 *Roper v. Simmons* decision (Borra, 2005), defendants being tried for crimes committed before age 18 are no longer candidates for the death penalty. The U.S. Supreme Court arrived at this decision after carefully weighing evidence submitted by the American Psychological Association (APA) and others, which suggests that the juvenile mind is still developing and vulnerable to impulsivity and poor decision making (APA, 2013d).
Chicago Tribune/Getty Images.

trying out different ideas in a variety of categories, including politics and religion. Once these areas have been explored, they begin to commit to a particular set of beliefs and attitudes, making decisions to engage in activities related to their evolving identity. However, their commitment may shift back and forth, sometimes on a day-to-day basis (Klimstra et al., 2010).

LO 14 Detail how Erikson explained changes in identity during adolescence.

ERIKSON AND ADOLESCENCE Erikson's theory of development addresses this important issue of identity formation (Erikson & Erikson, 1997). The time from puberty to the twenties is the stage of *ego identity versus role confusion,* which is marked by the creation of an adult identity. The adolescent strives to define himself. If the tasks and crises of Erikson's first four psychosocial stages have not been successfully resolved, the adolescent may enter this stage with distrust toward others, and feelings of shame, guilt, and inadequacy (see Table 8.3 on p. 354). In order to gain acceptance, he may try to be all things to all people.

It is during this period that one wrestles with some important life questions: *What career do I want to pursue? What kind of relationship should I have with my parents? What religion (if any) is compatible with my views, beliefs, and goals?* This stage often involves "trying out" different roles. A person who resolves this stage successfully emerges with a stronger sense of her values, beliefs, and goals. One who fails to resolve *role confusion* will not have a solid sense of identity and may experience withdrawal, isolation, or continued role confusion. However, just because we reach adulthood doesn't mean our identity stops evolving. As we will soon see, there is still plenty of growth throughout life.

PARENTS AND ADOLESCENTS What role does a parent play during this dynamic period? Generally speaking, parent–adolescent relationships are positive (Paikoff & Brooks-Gunn, 1991), but conflict does increase during early adolescence (Van Doorn, Branje, & Meeus, 2011), and it frequently relates to issues of control and parental authority. Often these parent–teen struggles revolve around everyday issues such as curfews, chores, schoolwork, and personal hygiene. Parents are routinely faced with decisions that impact the health, safety, and well-being of their children: *Should I allow my child to* play a contact sport? *How much screen time should I allow per day? Is a midnight curfew too late?* Dilemmas like these can potentially create conflict between parents and teens. The turmoil serves an important purpose, however; it gives teenagers practice dealing with conflict and negotiation in the context of the family (Moed et al., 2015). Fortunately, conflict tends to decline as both parties become more comfortable with the adolescent's growing sense of autonomy and self-reliance (Lichtwarck-Aschoff, Kunnen, & van Geert, 2009; Montemayor, 1983).

FRIENDS Friends become increasingly influential during adolescence. Some parents express concern about the negative influence of peers; however, it is typical for adolescents to form relationships with others of the same age and with whom they might share beliefs and interests. These friendships tend to support the types of behaviors and beliefs parents encouraged during childhood (McPherson, Smith-Lovin, & Cook, 2001). Adolescents tend to behave more impulsively in front of their peers than do adults. It appears that perceived social pressure may inhibit their ability to "put the brakes on" impulsivity in decision making (Albert, Chein, & Steinberg, 2013). But peers can also have a positive influence, supporting prosocial behaviors—getting good grades or helping others, for example (Roseth, Johnson, & Johnson, 2008; Wentzel, McNamara Barry, & Caldwell, 2004). With the use of smartphones and tablets, these negative and positive influences are often transmitted through digital space.

It's My Life!
Relationships between teens and parents are generally positive, but most involve some degree of conflict. Many disputes center on everyday issues, like clothing and chores, but the seemingly endless bickering does have a deeper meaning. The adolescent is breaking away from his parents, establishing himself as an autonomous person. SW Productions/Getty Images.

CONNECTIONS

In **Chapters 6** and **7,** we discussed chronic traumatic encephalopathy (CTE), a neurodegenerative disease caused by head trauma. Researchers have found people who play contact sports are at a higher risk for CTE. Parents must weigh the risks and benefits of allowing children to participate in contact sports, including the potential risk for CTE.

SOCIAL MEDIA AND PSYCHOLOGY
The Social Networking Teen Machine

 Social media provides an easy way for young people to create and cultivate relationships, but the quality of some of these associations is questionable. Many recent events have confirmed the fears experts expressed early on regarding its potential use in negative behaviors such as bullying. According to one survey, approximately 8% of Internet-using teenagers say they have been bullied online in the past year; 88% have observed others being "mean or cruel" on a social media site (Lenhart et al., 2011). Being a target of online bullying makes children and teens more vulnerable to depression and suicidal thoughts (van Geel, Vedder, & Tanilon, 2014; Best, Manktelow, & Taylor, 2014). The bullies themselves may also suffer, as studies have linked "cyberbullying involvement as victim and/or perpetrator" to a variety of negative outcomes, including substance use, diminished self-esteem, and feelings of loneliness (Kowalski, Giumetti, Schroeder, & Lattanner, 2014, p. 1114).

NETWORK BULLIES AND FRIENDS

But it's not all bad news. The majority of teens who use social media indicate that their interactions through these networks have made them feel better about themselves and more deeply connected to others (Best et al., 2014; Lenhart et al., 2011). Online communities provide teens with a space to explore their identities and interact with people from diverse backgrounds. They serve as platforms for the exchange of ideas and art (sharing music, videos, and blogs), and places for students to study and collaborate on school projects (O'Keeffe, Clarke-Pearson, & Council on Communications and Media, 2011).

Social media is here to stay, and will continue to impact the socioemotional development of adolescents. The challenge for parents is to find ways to monitor and direct this online activity while giving the child sufficient space to "experience some level of risk, and form coping strategies for protecting themselves from harm" (Wisniewski, Jia, Xu, Rossen, & Carrroll, 2015, p. 12). What steps do you think parents should take to ensure that their teenage offspring are using social media in a positive way?

Kohlberg's Stages of Moral Development

LO 15   Examine Kohlberg's levels of moral development.

Moral development is another important aspect of socioemotional growth. Lawrence Kohlberg (1927–1987), influenced by the work of Piaget, proposed three levels of moral development that occur in sequence over the life span. These levels focus on specific changes in beliefs about right and wrong (**TABLE 8.4**, on page 360).

Kohlberg used a variety of fictional stories about moral dilemmas to determine the stage of moral reasoning of participants in his studies. The *Heinz dilemma* is a story about a man named Heinz who was trying to save his critically ill wife. Heinz did not have enough money to buy a drug that could save her, so after trying unsuccessfully to borrow money, he finally decided to steal the drug. The two questions asked of individuals in Kohlberg's studies were these: "Should the husband have done that? Was it right or wrong?" (Kohlberg, 1981, p. 12). Kohlberg was not really interested in whether his participants thought Heinz should steal the drug or not; instead, the goal was to determine the moral reasoning behind their answers.

Although Kohlberg described moral development as sequential and universal in its progression, he noted that environmental influences and interactions with others (particularly those at a higher level of moral reasoning) support its continued development. Additionally, not everyone progresses through all three levels; an individual may get stuck at an early stage and remain at that level of morality throughout life. Let's look at these three levels.

TABLE 8.4 KOHLBERG'S STAGES OF MORAL DEVELOPMENT

Level	Moral Understanding	What Should Heinz Do?
Preconventional moral reasoning	Right and wrong are determined by the consequences.	Heinz should not steal the drug because he may go to jail if caught.
Conventional moral reasoning	Right and wrong are informed by the expectations of society and important others, not simply personal consequences.	Because society says a husband must take care of his wife, Heinz should steal the drugs so that others won't think poorly of him. or Heinz should not steal because stealing is against the law.
Postconventional moral reasoning	Right and wrong are determined by the individual's beliefs about morality, which may be inconsistent with society's rules and regulations.	Heinz should steal the drug because the laws of society fail to consider his unique situation. or Heinz should thoughtfully consider all possible options, but ultimately decide that human life overrides societal laws.

Kohlberg believed that people pass through different stages of moral development, described above. Information from Kohlberg and Hersh (1977).

Kohlberg at Work
American psychologist Lawrence Kohlberg proposed that moral reasoning progresses through three major levels: preconventional, conventional, and postconventional. The rate at which we move through these developmental levels partly depends on environmental factors, such as interactions with parents and siblings. Critics contend that Kohlberg's research focused too heavily on men in Western cultures (Endicott, Bock, & Narvaez, 2003; Gilligan, 1982).
The LIFE Images Collection/Getty Images.

• **Preconventional moral reasoning** usually applies to young children, and it focuses on the consequences of behaviors, both good and bad. For children, "goodness" and "badness" are determined by whether a behavior is punished. Consequences drive the belief about what is right and wrong. Children behave in accordance with a "marketplace" mentality, looking out for their own needs most of the time. The world is seen as an exchange of goods and services, so giving to others does not occur out of loyalty or fairness, but for the hope of reciprocity—"You scratch my back and I'll scratch yours" (Kohlberg & Hersh, 1977, p. 55).

• **Conventional moral reasoning** emerges around puberty, and determining right and wrong is informed by expectations from society and important adults, not simply personal consequences. The emphasis is on conforming to society's rules and regulations. Duty and obedience to authorities define what is right (Kohlberg & Hersh, 1977).

• **Postconventional moral reasoning** suggests right and wrong are determined by the individual's beliefs about morality, which may be inconsistent with society's rules and regulations. Laws should be followed when they are upheld by society as a whole; but, if a law does not exhibit "social utility," it should be changed to meet the needs of society. In other words, a law-and-order approach isn't always morally right. Moral behavior is determined by universal principles of justice, equality, and respect for human life. An understanding of the "right" thing to do is guided not only by what is universally regarded as right, but also by one's conscience and personal ethical perspective.

preconventional moral reasoning
Kohlberg's stage of moral development in which a person, usually a child, focuses on the consequences of behaviors, good or bad, and is concerned with avoiding punishment.

 In Class: Collaborate and Report

In your group, **A)** choose three people in the news whose behaviors exemplify one of Kohlberg's stages of moral development. **B)** Justify your selections with specific examples of those behaviors. **C)** Team up with another group and compare and contrast your results.

CRITICISMS Kohlberg's theory of moral development has not been without criticism. American psychologist Carol Gilligan (1936–) leveled a number of serious critiques, suggesting that the theory did not represent women's moral reasoning (1982). She noted that Kohlberg's initial studies included only male participants, introducing bias into his research findings. Gilligan suggested that Kohlberg had discounted the importance of caring and responsibility and that his choice of an all-male sample was partially to blame. Another issue with Kohlberg's theory is that it focuses on the moral reasoning of individuals, and thus is primarily applicable to Western cultures; in more collectivist cultures, the focus is on the group (Endicott, Bock, & Narvaez, 2003). One last concern about Kohlberg's theory is that we can define and measure moral reasoning, but predicting moral behavior is not always easy. Research that examines moral reasoning and moral behavior indicates that the ability to predict moral behavior is weak at best (Blasi, 1980; Krebs & Denton, 2005).

Emerging Adulthood

Childhood and adolescence pave the way for the stage of life known as *adulthood.* In the United States, the legal age of adulthood is 18 for some activities (voting, military enlistment) and 21 for others (drinking, financial responsibilities). These ages are not consistent across cultures and countries (the legal drinking age in some nations is as young as 16). Many cultures and religions mark the transition into adulthood by ceremonies and rituals (for example, Jewish *bar/bat mitzvahs,* Australian walkabouts, Christian confirmations, Latin American *quinceañeras*), starting as early as age 12.

CONNECTIONS

In **Chapter 1,** we discussed the importance of collecting data from a representative sample, whose members' characteristics closely reflect the population of interest. Kohlberg's early research included only male participants, but he and others generalized his findings to females. Generalizing from an all-male sample to females in the population may not be justifiable.

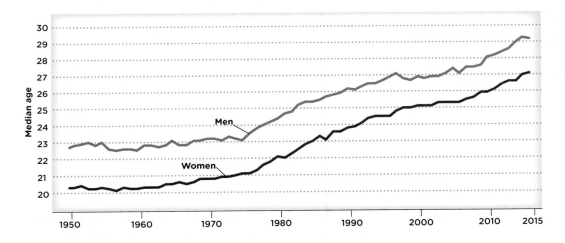

FIGURE 8.5
Age of First Marriage
Many developmental psychologists consider marriage a marker of adulthood because it can represent the first time a person leaves the family home to set out on his or her own. Since the 1950s and 1960s, the median age at which men and women marry for the first time has increased, a trend that appears likely to continue. Information from the U.S. Census Bureau (2015).

Complicating the demarcation between adolescence and adulthood is the fact that young people in today's Western societies are marrying much later (Arnett, 2000; Elliott, Krivickas, Brault, & Kreider, 2012), and remaining dependent on their families for longer periods of time (**FIGURE 8.5**). Psychologists now propose a phase known as **emerging adulthood,** which is the time of life between 18 and 25 years of age. Emerging adulthood is neither adolescence nor early adulthood, and it is a period of exploration and opportunity. The emerging adult has neither the permanent responsibilities of adulthood nor the dependency of adolescence. By this time, most adolescent egocentrism has disappeared, which is apparent in intimate relationships and empathy (Elkind, 1967). During this stage, one can seek out loving relationships, education, and new views of the world before settling into the relative permanency of family and career (Arnett, 2000).

conventional moral reasoning Kohlberg's stage of moral development that determines right and wrong from the expectations of society and important others.

postconventional moral reasoning Kohlberg's stage of moral development in which right and wrong are determined by the individual's beliefs about morality, which sometimes do not coincide with society's rules and regulations.

emerging adulthood A phase of life between 18 and 25 years that includes exploration and opportunity.

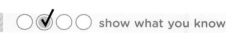 show what you know

1. The physical features not associated with reproduction, but that become more distinct during adolescence, are known as:
   a. primary sex characteristics.
   b. secondary sex characteristics.
   c. menarche.
   d. puberty.

2. Your cousin is almost 14, and she has begun to use deductive reasoning to draw conclusions and critical thinking to support her arguments. Her cognitive development is occurring in Piaget's:
   a. formal operational stage.
   b. concrete operational stage.
   c. ego identity versus role confusion stage.
   d. instrumental–relativist orientation.

3. _____ moral reasoning usually is seen in young children, and it focuses on the consequences of behaviors, both good and bad.

4. "Helicopter" parents pave the way for their children, troubleshooting problems for them, and attempting to make certain they are successful in every endeavor. How might this type of parenting impact an adolescent in terms of Erikson's stage of ego identity versus role confusion?

✓ CHECK YOUR ANSWERS IN APPENDIX C.

Support System
(Left to right, and front) Joan, Ericka, Ericka's mentor Aisha, and Niyah. In addition to Ericka's grandmother, these are the people who helped keep Ericka motivated and inspired throughout college. Ericka considered withdrawing from college at one point, but then she discovered Generation Hope, a non-profit organization devoted to supporting teen parents as they work toward college degrees. In addition to graduating cum laude, Ericka served as president of the Student Government Association and belonged to two honor societies.
Courtesy Ericka Harley.

menopause The time when a woman no longer ovulates, her menstrual cycle stops, and she is no longer capable of reproduction.

Adulthood

"SHE PROVED ME WRONG" Ten years ago, when Joan learned of Ericka's pregnancy, she assumed college was no longer an option. But today, Joan is proud to say, "She proved me wrong."

When Niyah was 3 years old, Ericka enrolled at Trinity Washington University in Washington, D.C. Juggling a full-time job and college was not easy, but Ericka "planned out every minute, every hour" to maximize her time with Niyah. In the morning, they would get up early to talk about their day. Then Ericka would drop off Niyah at school, go to work, and pick her up in the late afternoon. After a few more hours of mother–daughter time, Ericka would go to her night classes. In 2011, Ericka earned her associate's degree, and in 2014 graduated cum laude with her bachelor's degree in business administration.

Ericka proved that she could do it all, and do it all well—motherhood, college, and career. Her accomplishments speak to her own hard work and resolve, and also to the dedicated support of three strong women: her mother Joan, her grandmother Katherine, and a PhD student named Aisha. Ericka met Aisha through her participation in Generation Hope, a non-profit organization devoted to helping teen parents get through college. Like every Generation Hope scholar, Ericka was paired with a mentor (Aisha) who provided financial assistance from her own personal funds and emotional support during college. "She's really helped me to focus on me and what I want," Ericka explains. "My issue has always been being worried about being accepted by other people." With Aisha's guidance, Ericka learned to embrace the person she is, and go after what she wants in life.

Now in her late twenties, Ericka is married and expecting a second baby. She is immersed in young adulthood, a stage of life when many people are forging their identities and laying the groundwork for lifelong relationships. While others her age are still exploring the "Who am I?" type of questions that emerged in adolescence, Ericka already seems to know the answers. "I am pretty confident, and I believe what I believe," Ericka says. "I'm not afraid to express those opinions or tell you why I believe it." Parenthood has a way of making you grow up fast. ●

Whatever you want from life, you are most likely to pursue and attain it during the developmental stage known as adulthood. Developmental psychologists have identified various stages of this long period, each corresponding to an approximate age group: *early adulthood* spans the twenties and thirties, *middle adulthood* the forties to mid-sixties, and *late adulthood* everything beyond.

Physical Development

LO 16 Name several of the most important physical changes that occur across adulthood.

The most obvious signs of aging tend to be physical in nature. Often you can estimate a person's age just by looking at his hands or facial lines. Let's get a sense of some of the basic body changes that occur through adulthood. Remember, physical development is important because it impacts behavior and mental processes.

EARLY ADULTHOOD During early adulthood, the sensory systems are sharp, and we are at the height of our muscular and cardiovascular ability. Other systems have already begun their downhill journey, however. One example is hearing, which often starts to decline as a result of noise-induced damage beginning in early adolescence (Niskar et al., 2001; World Health Organization [WHO], 2015). The body is fairly resilient at this stage, but lifestyle choices can have profound health consequences. Heavy drinking, poor eating habits, obesity, lack of exercise, and smoking can make a person look, feel, and function like someone much older. All these factors have been associated with high risk for cardiovascular disease and premature death in middle adulthood (Hulsegge et al., 2016; Liu et al., 2012). These factors may determine if you spend your later adulthood volunteering at a local nursing home, or living in one.

As we head toward our late thirties, fertility-related changes occur for both men and women. Women experience a 6% reduction in fertility in their late twenties, 14% in their early thirties, and 31% in their late thirties (Menken, Trussell, & Larsen, 1986; Nelson, Telfer, & Anderson, 2013). Men also experience a fertility dip, but it appears to be gradual and results from fewer and poorer-quality sperm (Sloter et al., 2006). It is not until age 50 that male fertility declines substantially (Kidd, Eskenazi, & Wyrobek, 2001).

MIDDLE ADULTHOOD In middle adulthood, the skin wrinkles and sags due to loss of collagen and elastin, and skin spots may appear (Bulpitt, Markowe, & Shipley, 2001). Hair starts to turn gray and may fall out. Hearing loss continues and may be exacerbated by exposure to loud noises (Kujawa & Liberman, 2006). Eyesight may decline. The bones weaken, and osteoporosis can occur (Kaczmarek, 2015). Oh, and did we mention you might shrink? But do not despair. There are measures you can take to slow the aging process. For example, genes influence height and bone mass, but research suggests we can limit the shrinking process through continued exercise. In one study, researchers followed over 2,000 people for three decades. Everyone in the study got shorter (the average height loss being 4 centimeters, or about 1.6 inches), but those who had engaged in "moderate vigorous aerobic" exercise lost significantly less height (Sagiv, Vogelaere, Soudry, & Ehrsam, 2000). To maintain your stature and overall physique, you would be wise to participate in lifelong moderate endurance activities such as jogging, walking, and swimming.

For women, middle adulthood is a time of major physical change. Estrogen production decreases, the uterus shrinks, and menstruation no longer follows a regular pattern. This marks the transition toward **menopause**, the time when ovulation and

CONNECTIONS

In **Chapter 3,** we described the causes of hearing impairment. Sensorineural deafness results from damage to the hair cells or auditory nerve. Conduction hearing impairment occurs when the eardrum or middle-ear bones are compromised. Exposure to loud sounds may play a role in hearing impairment that begins in adolescence.

He's 100!
Don Pellmann, 100 years old, hurls the shot put at the 2015 San Diego Senior Games. Exercise is one of the best ways to fight the aging process. Working out on a regular basis improves cardiovascular health, bone and muscle strength, and mood. A study of more than 400,000 people in Taiwan found that those who exercised just 15 minutes a day lived an average of 3 years longer than their sedentary peers (Wen et al., 2011). SANDY HUFFAKER/The New York Times.

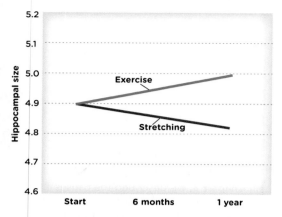

FIGURE 8.6

Exercise to Build Bigger . . . Brains?
Researchers interested in the effects of exercise on the aging brain randomly assigned participants to two groups: One group engaged in a program of gentle stretching exercises, and the other began doing more aerobic activity. During the course of the yearlong study, the researchers found typical levels of age-related shrinkage in the hippocampi of the stretching group. However, in the group that exercised more vigorously, not only was age-related deterioration prevented, hippocampal volume actually increased, with corresponding improvements in memory. Information from Erickson et al. (2011).

CONNECTIONS

In **Chapter 2,** we reported that studies with nonhuman animals and humans have shown that some areas of the brain are constantly generating new neurons, in a process known as neurogenesis. As we age, this production of new neurons seems to be supported by physical exercise.

crystallized intelligence Knowledge gained through learning and experience.

fluid intelligence The ability to think in the abstract and create associations among concepts.

menstruation cease, and reproduction is no longer possible. Menopausal women can experience hot flashes, sweating, vaginal dryness, and breast tenderness (Kaczmarek, 2015; Newton et al., 2006). These symptoms may sound unpleasant, but many women report a sense of relief following the cessation of their menstrual periods, as well as increased interest in sexual activity (Etaugh, 2008).

Men experience their own constellation of midlife physical changes, sometimes referred to as male menopause or *andropause* (Kaczmarek, 2015). Some suggest calling it *androgen decline,* as there is a reduction in testosterone production, not an end to it (Morales, Heaton, & Carson, 2000). Men in middle adulthood may complain of depression, fatigue, and cognitive difficulties, which might be associated with lower testosterone. But research suggests this link between hormones and behavior is evident in only a tiny proportion of aging men (Pines, 2011).

LATE ADULTHOOD Late adulthood, which begins around 65, is also characterized by the decline of many physical and psychological functions. Eye problems, such as cataracts and impaired night vision, are common. Hearing continues on a downhill course, and reaction time increases (Fozard, 1990). The brain processes information more slowly, and brain regions responsible for memory deteriorate (Eckert, Keren, Roberts, Calhoun, & Harris, 2010).

Some physical decline is inevitable with age, but it is possible to grow old gracefully. One of the best ways to fight aging is to get your body moving. Aerobic exercise improves bone density and muscle strength, and lowers the risk for cardiovascular disease and obesity. It's good for your brain, too. "A single bout of moderate [aerobic] exercise" seems to provide a short-term boost in working memory for adults of various ages (Hogan, Mata, & Carstensen, 2013, para. 1). Maintaining a certain level of day-to-day aerobic activity also appears to make a difference, as older people who are physically active tend to perform better on working memory tasks (Guiney & Machado, 2013). We cannot offer a surefire biological explanation for these findings, but it is interesting to note that exercise might foster the development of neural networks, helping with the production of **new hippocampus nerve cells**, which are important in memory (Deslandes et al., 2009; Erickson et al., 2011; **FIGURE 8.6**). Would you believe that working out may even reduce the risk of Alzheimer's disease and other disorders of the nervous system (Radak et al., 2010)? When you take good care of your body, you're also taking good care of your mind.

Cognitive Development

What goes on in the brain as we pass through the various stages of adulthood, and how do these changes affect our ability to function? Let's explore cognitive development in adulthood.

LO 17 Identify the most significant cognitive changes that occur across adulthood.

EARLY ADULTHOOD Measures of aptitude, such as intelligence tests, indicate that cognitive ability remains stable from early to middle adulthood (Larsen, Hartmann, & Nyborg, 2008), though processing speed begins to decline (Schaie, 1993). Young adults are theoretically in Piaget's formal operational stage, which means they can think logically and systematically, but some researchers estimate that only 50% of adults ever exhibit formal operational thinking (Arlin, 1975).

MIDDLE AND LATE ADULTHOOD Much of the discussion of middle adulthood has focused on decline: declining skin elasticity, testosterone, cardiovascular health, and so on. Yet cognitive function does not necessarily decrease during middle adulthood. Longitudinal studies indicate that decreases in cognitive abilities cannot be reliably measured before 60 (Gerstorf, Ram, Hoppmann, Willis, & Schaie, 2011; Schaie, 1993, 2008). There are some exceptions, however. Midlife is a time when information processing and memory can decline, particularly the ability to remember past events (Ren, Wu, Chan, & Yan, 2013).

After the age of 70, cognitive decline is more apparent. The Seattle Longitudinal Study has shown that the cognitive performance of today's 70-year-old participants is similar to the performance of 65-year-olds tested 30 years ago (Gerstorf et al., 2011; Schaie, 1993, 2008). So from a cognitive abilities perspective, turning 65 does not mean it is time to retire. Processing speed may slow with old age, but older adults are still capable of amazing accomplishments. Frank Lloyd Wright finished designing New York's Guggenheim Museum when he was 89 years old and Nelson Mandela became president of South Africa when he was 76.

Some types of cognitive skills diminish in old age and others become more refined. Older people may not remember all of their academic knowledge, but their practical abilities seem to grow. Life experiences allow people to develop a more balanced understanding of the world around them, one that only comes with age (Sternberg & Grigorenko, 2005).

If you look at intelligence scores from the 1950s, 1970s, and 1990s, you will see the average intelligence score increasing over the generations. These differences are so impressive that many people taking IQ tests in the 1930s would be considered cognitively delayed by today's standards (Flynn, 2009). We call this global phenomenon the *Flynn effect* (Flynn, 2012). Does this mean that people today are smarter than they were in decades past? Researcher James Flynn (2012) suggests that this is not the case. Intelligence scores are most likely increasing because we confront a larger spectrum of "cognitive problems" than those who came before us. In other words, people today encounter more issues that require abstract thinking.

When studying cognitive changes across the life span, psychologists frequently describe two types of intelligence: **crystallized intelligence**, the knowledge we gain through learning and experience, and **fluid intelligence**, the ability to think in the abstract and create associations among concepts. As we age, the speed with which we acquire new material and create associations decreases (von Stumm & Deary, 2012). In one study, researchers examined performance on fluid and crystallized intelligence tasks in adults between the ages of 20 and 78. Crystallized abilities increased with age, whereas fluid abilities increased from 20 to 30 years of age and remained stable until age 50 (Cornelius & Caspi, 1987). Working memory, the active processing component of short-term memory that maintains and manipulates information, becomes less efficient with age (Nagel et al., 2008; Reuter-Lorenz, 2013).

Earlier we mentioned that physical exercise provides a cognitive boost. The same appears to be true of mental exercises, such as those required for playing a musical instrument (Hanna-Pladdy & MacKay, 2011). That said, there does appear to be a lot of hype surrounding the "use it or lose it" mantra of aging. The declaration that exercising the brain will stop cognitive decline might be a slight overstatement (Salthouse, 2006). Although there are clear benefits to doing crossword puzzles and reading the newspaper, the evidence is not conclusive that this activity has the same effect it would have on a child, for example. When older adults exercise their brains in a particular domain (for example, playing a musical instrument or using Wii *Big Brain Academy* software), the results do not necessarily transfer to other general abilities, such as cognitive and perceptual information processing (Ackerman, Kanfer, & Calderwood, 2010). However, tasks that specifically focus on training working memory may improve fluid intelligence,

Golden Years
Late adulthood can be a time of great intellectual, humanitarian, and physical achievement. Ingeborg Syllm-Rapoport (top) was 102 when she earned her doctorate degree; Nelson Mandela (middle) was 76 when he became the first Black president of South Africa; and Katsusuke Yanagisawa was 71 when he climbed Mount Everest.
Top: Bodo Marks/picture-alliance/dpa/AP Images.
Center: Per-Anders Pettersson/Getty Images.
Bottom: AP Photo/Kyodo News.

CONNECTIONS

Here, we are reminded of an issue presented in **Chapter 1:** We must be careful not to equate correlation with causation. In this case, if you experience a decline in cognitive ability, you are less likely to work. Thus, it is the cognitive decline that would lead to the lack of work.

even into older age (Nisbett et al., 2012). But research suggests that people who continue to work, both physically and mentally, and remain in good physical shape are less likely to experience significant cognitive decline (Rohwedder & Willis, 2010). Thus, if your goal is to maintain a sharp mind as you age, don't just increase your Sudoku playing or reading time. You need to maintain a balanced approach incorporating a broad range of activities and interests, including those that provide social stimulation.

**from the pages of
SCIENTIFIC
AMERICAN**

Join a Club, Stay Sharp

Group social activity beats one-on-one encounters for preventing cognitive decline.

Social activity is well known to influence mental health, particularly as people age—but the details behind this phenomenon are unclear. Different types of social interactions may be more or less important, depending on the circumstances. One-on-one relationships, such as those between spouses, may yield specific emotional benefits. When it comes to slowing cognitive decline, however, group interactions have more power, according to a recent study published in *Social Science & Medicine*.

The study analyzed data from more than 3,400 adults aged 50 and older. Subjects who reported high engagement with social groups such as book clubs and community organizations performed better on tests measuring cognitive skills such as working memory. Individual relationships such as friendships, meanwhile, appeared to have no effect on cognitive ability. The mental boost from group activity was also more pronounced with age: group-connected subjects closer to age 50 had the cognitive capacities of someone about five years younger, whereas those near 80 years old were rejuvenated by about 10 years, putting them mentally closer to a 70-year-old.

Group relationships require effort to maintain, and they reinforce self-identity, both of which may sharpen thinking skills, says Catherine Haslam, a clinical psychology professor at the University of Queensland in Australia and lead author of the study. Conversely, the ease of interactions with spouses or family members may make them less stimulating. "The difference in terms of keeping mentally active is those group relationships," Haslam says. Erica Westly.

Socioemotional Development

Socioemotional development does not always occur in a neat, stepwise fashion. This next section describes a host of social and emotional transformations that typically occur during adulthood.

LO 18 Explain some of the socioemotional changes that occur across adulthood.

ERIKSON AND ADULTHOOD Earlier we described Erikson's approach to explaining socioemotional development from infancy through adolescence, noting that unsuccessful resolution of prior stages has implications for the stages that follow (see Table 8.3 on page 354). During young adulthood (twenties to forties), people are challenged by *intimacy versus isolation*. Young adults tend to focus on creating meaningful, deep relationships, and failing at this endeavor may lead to a life of isolation. Erikson also believed that we are unable to form these relationships if identity has not been clearly established in the identity versus role confusion of adolescence. The focus shifts away from fun-filled first experiences with sex and love to deeper connections. For many people, the twenties represent a transition between the "here and now" type of relationships of adolescence to the serious, long-term partnerships of adulthood (Arnett, 2000).

Moving into middle adulthood (forties to mid-sixties), we face the crisis of *generativity versus stagnation*. Positive resolution of this stage includes feeling like you have made a real impact on the next generation, through parenting, community involvement, or work that is valuable and significant. Those who do not have a positive resolution of this stage face stagnation, characterized by boredom, conceit, and selfishness.

In late adulthood (mid-sixties and older), we look back on life and evaluate how we have done; we call this the crisis of *integrity versus despair*. If previous stages have resulted in positive resolutions, we feel a sense of accomplishment and satisfaction. A negative resolution of this stage indicates that we have regrets and dissatisfaction.

Before we further explore socioemotional development in adulthood, we must note that Erikson's theory, though very important in the field of developmental psychology, has provided more framework than substantive research findings. His theory was based on case studies, with limited supporting research. In addition, the developmental tasks of Erikson's stages might not be limited to the particular time frame proposed. For example, creating an adult identity is not limited to adolescence, as this stage may resurface at any point in adulthood (Schwartz, 2001).

One drastic change in identity that many people consider the most challenging, yet rewarding, is parenthood. We touched on parenting in earlier sections, but let's revisit this topic with a discussion on childrearing styles.

PARENTING STYLES Do you ever find yourself watching parent–child interactions at the grocery store? You likely have noticed a vast spectrum of child-rearing approaches. American psychologist Diana Baumrind (1927–) has been studying parenting for over four decades, and her work has led to the identification of four parenting behavioral styles (1966, 1971). These styles seem to be stable across situations, and are distinguished by levels of warmth, responsiveness, and control (Maccoby & Martin, 1983).

Parents who insist on rigid boundaries, show little warmth, and expect high control exhibit **authoritarian parenting**. They want things done in a certain way, no questions asked. "Because I said so" is a common justification used by such parents. Authoritarian parents are extremely strict and demonstrate poor communication skills with their children. Their kids, in turn, tend to have lower self-assurance and autonomy, and experience more problems in social settings (Baumrind, 1991). Researchers have found that there are exceptions to this rule, however. In situations where "societal conformance or . . . safety of the child" is vital, "authoritarian parenting is actually more adaptive" (Herzog, Hill-Chapman, Hardy, Wrighten, & El-Khabbaz, 2015, p. 121).

Authoritative parenting may sound similar to authoritarian parenting, but it is very different. Parents who practice authoritative parenting set high expectations, demonstrate a warm attitude, and are responsive to their children's needs. Being supported and respected, children of authoritative parents are quite responsive to their parents' expectations. They also tend to be self-assured, independent, responsible, and friendly (Baumrind, 1991). In one study, researchers found that the more education the parents had, the more likely they were to be authoritative in their parenting (Anton, Jones, & Youngstrom, 2015).

With **permissive parenting,** the parent demands little of the child and imposes few limitations. These parents are very warm but often make next to no effort to control their children. Ultimately, their children tend to lack self-control, act impulsively, and show no respect for boundaries.

Uninvolved parenting describes parents who seem indifferent to their children. Emotionally detached, these parents exhibit minimal warmth and devote little time to their children, although they do provide for their children's basic needs. Children raised by uninvolved parents tend to exhibit behavioral problems, poor academic performance, and immaturity (Baumrind, 1991).

authoritarian parenting A rigid parenting style characterized by strict rules and poor communication skills.

authoritative parenting A parenting style characterized by high expectations, strong support, and respect for children.

permissive parenting A parenting style characterized by low demands of children and few limitations.

uninvolved parenting A parenting style characterized by a parent's indifference to a child, including a lack of emotional involvement.

Keep in mind that the great majority of research on these parenting styles has been conducted in the United States, which should make us wonder how applicable these categories are in other countries and cultures (Grusec, Goodnow, & Kuczynski, 2000). Additional factors to consider include the home environment, the child's personality and development, and the unique parent–child relationship. Children with irritable and easygoing dispositions will not exhibit the same reactions to the restrictions imposed by authoritarian parents, for example (Grusec & Goodnow, 1994).

CONNECTIONS

In **Chapter 3,** we discussed subliminal stimuli, which are well beneath absolute thresholds. Nevertheless, the brain does register subliminal messages and these can influence moods and attitudes. Here, we see how they can lead to changes in physical functioning.

GROWING OLD WITH GRACE When many people think of growing older, they imagine a disabled frail old woman or man sitting in a bathrobe and staring out the window. This stereotype is not accurate. As of 2014, fewer than 1% of Americans lived in a nursing home (CDC, 2014b). Most older adults in the United States enjoy active, healthy, independent lives. They are involved in their communities, faiths, and social lives, and contrary to popular belief—a large number have active sex lives (Lindau et al., 2007). Moreover, negative stereotypes are known to be "detrimental" to the physical functioning of elderly people. But researchers have found that subliminal exposure to positive age stereotypes can improve physical functioning (Levy, Pilver, Chung, & Slade, 2014).

Researchers have discovered that happiness generally increases with age (Jeste et al., 2013). Positive emotions become more frequent than negative ones, and emotional stability increases, meaning that we experience fewer extreme emotional swings (Carstensen et al., 2011). Stress and anger begin to diminish in early adulthood, and worry becomes less apparent after age 50 (Stone, Schwartz, Broderick, & Deaton, 2010).

Older people might feel happy because they no longer care about proving themselves in the world, they are pleased with the outcome of their lives, or they have developed a strong sense of emotional equilibrium (Jeste et al., 2013). Research suggests that older adults who are healthy, independent, and engaged in social activities also report being happy, and there is some evidence that this increased happiness may result in a longer life (Oerlemans, Bakker, & Veenhoven, 2011). Americans are now living longer than ever, with the average life expectancy of women being 81.1 years and men 76.3 years (Hoyert & Xu, 2012).

In Class: Collaborate and Report

Most of us know older people for whom we have a great deal of respect and hope to be like when we reach their age. In your group, **A)** describe some of the current accomplishments of these older individuals. **B)** Discuss the factors that you think have led to their successful aging. **C)** How would you define successful aging? **D)** What would you say to someone who holds stereotypical ideas of what it means to be old?

THE LIFE OF KAT WRIGHT "My grandmother passed away on September 5, 2011," Ericka says. "I really remember it like it was yesterday."

It was Labor Day weekend and the family was hoping to have a cookout at Grandma's house, just as they did every year. But Grandma wasn't feeling well and asked for a small family dinner instead. When Ericka and her relatives arrived, Grandma wanted to stay in bed—unusual for the woman who was the focal point of every family get-together. Eventually, she got up, but her breathing was not normal. The family called 911, and medical workers arrived on the scene but soon left, not finding evidence of any major problem. Ericka wasn't too worried because Grandma had experienced health issues in the past, problems from which she had always recovered.

Night soon fell and it was time to go home. "Okay Grandma, I'll see you tomorrow," Ericka said. "I love you." Grandmother told Ericka she loved her, too, and said "goodbye" (odd, because she usually said "see you later"). Later that night,

Courtesy Ericka Harley.

Ericka awoke to the sound of her mom getting ready to go visit Grandma, now in the hospital. Assuming her grandmother would pull through as always, Ericka went back to bed, although her mind was spinning. She headed for the hospital around 2:00 A.M., but by the time she arrived, Grandma was already gone. "I couldn't like breathe, I couldn't say anything," Ericka recalls. "I knew that one day she would pass away, but I wasn't ready for it."

The death of Katherine Wright had a profound impact on Joan, Ericka, and the whole family. One of the hardest parts of grieving was the sudden loss of everyday contact—Joan stopped receiving Grandma's morning phone calls, and suddenly Ericka was no longer visiting Grandma 6 days a week. Ericka's pregnancy had brought together four generations of women—Katherine, Joan, Ericka, and Niyah—and they were as close as ever. But now their leader was gone.

"I remember the first couple months I was really angry at God," Ericka explains. "I felt like, if God loves us, why would he take her away? . . . . He knew I wanted her to see me graduate and, I was just questioning everything." ●

Death and Dying

LO 19   Describe Kübler-Ross' theory regarding reactions to imminent death.

Ericka eventually came to the realization that having her grandmother for the first 22 years of life had been a great gift, but the anger she felt is relatively typical for a person in mourning. Those who are dying may also experience anger. As psychiatrist Elisabeth Kübler-Ross (2009) observed in the early 1960s, people often have similar reactions when confronted with the news they are dying: stages of denial, anger, bargaining, depression, and acceptance. These stages, Kübler-Ross suggested, are coping mechanisms for dealing with what is to come.

- **Denial:** In the denial stage, a person may react to the news with shock and disbelief, perhaps even suggesting the doctors are wrong. Unable to accept the diagnosis, he may seek other medical advice.

- **Anger:** A dying person may feel anger toward others who are healthy, or toward the doctor who does not have the cure. *Why me?* she may wonder, projecting her anger and irritability in a seemingly random fashion.

- **Bargaining:** This stage may involve negotiating with God, doctors, or other powerful figures for a way out. Usually, this involves some sort of time frame: *Let me live to see my firstborn get married,* or *Just give me one more month to get my finances in order.*

- **Depression:** There comes a point when a dying person can no longer ignore the inevitable. Depression may be due to the symptoms of the patient's actual illness, but it can also result from the overwhelming sense of loss—the loss of the future.

- **Acceptance:** Eventually, a dying person accepts the finality of his predicament; death is inevitable, and it is coming soon. This stage can deeply impact family and close friends, who, in some respects, may need more support than the person who is dying. According to one oncologist, the timing of acceptance is quite variable. For some people, it occurs in the final moments before death; for others, soon after they learn there is no chance of recovery from their illness (Lyckholm, 2004).

Kübler-Ross was instrumental in bringing attention to the importance of attending to the dying person (Charlton & Verghese, 2010; Kastenbaum & Costa, 1977). The stages she proposed provide a valuable framework for understanding death, but keep in mind that every person responds to death in a unique way. For some people, the stages are overlapping; others don't experience the stages at all (Schneidman, 1973). We should also note that there is little research supporting the validity of stages of death, and that the theory arose in a Western cultural context. Evidence suggests that people from other backgrounds may view death and dying from very different perspectives.

ACROSS THE WORLD
Death in Different Cultures

What does death mean to you? Some of us believe death marks the beginning of a peaceful afterlife. Others see it as a crossing over from one life to another. Still others believe death is like turning off the lights; once you're gone, it's all over.

DEALING WITH DEATH IN DIFFERENT WAYS

Views of death are very much related to religion and culture. A common belief among Indian Hindus, for example, is that one should spend a lifetime preparing for a "good death" (*su-mrtyu*). Often this means dying in old age, after conflicts have been put to rest, family matters settled, and farewells said. To prepare a loved one for a good death, relatives place the person on the floor at home (or on the banks of the Ganges River, if possible) and give her water from the hallowed Ganges. If these and other rituals are not carried out, the dead person's soul may become trapped and the family suffers the consequences: nightmares, infertility, and other forms of misfortune (Firth, 2005). In Korea and Taiwan, where practices of Confucianism are strongly held, family members show great respect, taking care of parents at the end of their lives: "In Korea and Taiwan, dying and death is perceived not as a personal issue, but rather a family issue" (Cheng et al., 2015, p. 4). Imagine a psychologist trying to assist grieving relatives without any knowledge of these beliefs and traditions, or the culture-specific ways people show sympathy and compassion for others (Koopmann-Holm & Tsai, 2014).

In Japan and other parts of East Asia, families often make medical decisions for the dying person, although attitudes regarding patient autonomy have changed significantly over the past decade (Matsumura et al., 2002; Morita et al., 2015). Family members may avoid using words like "cancer" to shield the dying person from the bad news, believing this knowledge may cause her to lose hope and deteriorate further (Koenig & Gates-Williams, 1995; Searight & Gafford, 2005). Yet, healthy East Asians are more likely than European Americans to engage in and enjoy life when reminded of the imminence of death (Ma-Kellams & Blascovich, 2012).

Interesting as these findings may be, remember they are only cultural trends. Like any developmental step, the experience of death is shaped by countless social, psychological, and biological factors.

Celebrating the Dead
A mariachi band plays at a cemetery in Mexico's Michoacan state on Dia de los Muertos, "Day of the Dead." During this holiday, people in Mexico and other parts of Latin America celebrate the lives of the deceased. Music is played, feasts are prepared, and graves are adorned with flowers to welcome back the spirits of relatives who have passed. In this cultural context, death is not something to be feared or dreaded, but rather a part of life that is embraced (National Geographic, 2015). Christian Kober/Corbis.

THINK POSITIVE
Resilient in the Face of Hardship

Ericka may never get completely accustomed to the idea that her grandmother is gone. Sometimes while cooking, Ericka thinks to herself, *I just need to call Grandma and ask her how she would make this dish.* But then reality sets in, and she calls Joan to ask what Grandma would do. This is how the whole family deals with the loss—by leaning on each other during times they would normally rely on Grandma. When one person in the family is faced with a dilemma, the other members look at each other and say, "What would Kat Wright do?" This type of social support is important for people who are recovering from the sudden loss of a loved one (Barlé, Wortman, & Latack, 2016).

GETTING THROUGH IT TOGETHER

Sometimes we try to avoid thinking about a person who has died; this may reduce distress temporarily, but a better long-term approach is to confront our feelings of loss (Barlé et al., 2016). Joan and Ericka couldn't stop thinking about Kat Wright if they tried, because Niyah has inherited so many of her qualities. Just like Grandma, Niyah sits down at the table with a newspaper, reading articles (especially those on politics) and searching the weekly ads for sales; she loves trivia, crossword puzzles, and making lists; and she's curious about everything. But perhaps most important, Niyah possesses Grandma's special brand of kindness. If a classmate forgets her lunch at home, Niyah will share everything in her lunch bag. When she sees homeless people, she wants to use her own money to buy them food. "She's very compassionate and grateful for what she does have," says Ericka.

Now, when Ericka reflects on her pregnancy with Niyah, she is nothing but grateful: "Even though it was really unexpected, I think it might have been one of the best things that ever happened."

Ericka is in good company, as many young women demonstrate resiliency when faced with the stigma of teen pregnancy. How do these teenage moms achieve successful outcomes? Those who are resilient tend to resist stereotypes about teenage mothers and maintain a positive attitude; they are driven to reach educational goals and willing to put the needs of their children above their own. "Strong social support systems" and quality health care are also important (Solivan, Wallace, Kaplan, & Harville, 2015, p. 352). If we focus on resiliency, we start to see "what is 'right' instead of what is 'wrong'" (p. 354). 👍

Kat Wright Lives On
Ericka's grandmother (left) suddenly passed away at the age of 72, leaving behind a huge family that loved and depended on her. Six years later, Kat Wright is still very much alive in the thoughts and memories of Joan, Ericka, and the rest of the family. She lives on through Niyah, who inherited many of her best qualities, including a seemingly endless capacity for love. As Joan puts it, "We love. We love hard." Left: Courtesy Ericka Harley. Right: Emily Weiss Photography.

○◉○○ **show what you know**

1. Physical changes during middle adulthood include declines in hearing, eyesight, and height. Which of the following does research suggest can help limit the shrinking process?
   a. physical exercise
   b. elastin
   c. andropause
   d. collagen

2. As we age, our _____ intelligence, or ability to think abstractly, decreases, but our knowledge gained through experience, our _____ intelligence, increases.

3. When faced with death, a person can go through five stages. The final stage is _____, and sometimes family members need more support during this stage than the dying person.
   a. denial
   b. anger
   c. bargaining
   d. acceptance

4. An aging relative in his mid-seventies is looking back on his life and evaluating what he has accomplished. He feels satisfied with his work, family, and friends. Erikson would say that he has succeeded in solving the crisis of _____ versus _____.

✓ CHECK YOUR ANSWERS IN APPENDIX C.

Improve your grade! Use 🅜 **LearningCurve** macmillan learning adaptive quizzing to create your personalized study plan, which will direct you to the resources that will help you most in 🅜 **LaunchPad** macmillan learning

summary of concepts

LO 1 Define human development. (p. 328)

Development refers to the changes that occur in physical, cognitive, and socioemotional functioning over the course of the life span. These changes begin at conception and end at death. The goal of developmental psychology is to examine such changes.

LO 2 Outline the three longstanding discussions in developmental psychology. (p. 329)

Developmental psychologists' longstanding debates and discussions have centered on three major themes: stages and continuity; nature and nurture; and stability and change. Each

of these themes relates to a basic question: (1) Does development occur in separate or discrete stages, or is it a steady, continuous process? (2) What are the relative roles of heredity and environment in human development? (3) How stable is one's personality over a lifetime and across situations?

LO 3 Identify the types of research psychologists use to study developmental processes. (p. 330)

Developmental psychologists use several methods to explore changes across the life span. The cross-sectional method examines people of different ages at one point in time, and the longitudinal method follows one sample of individuals over a period of time. In the cross-sequential method, participants are divided into age groups as well as followed over time, so researchers can examine developmental changes within individuals and across different age groups.

LO 4 Examine the role genes play in our development and identify the biological factors that determine sex. (p. 333)

All the cells in the human body (except for red blood cells) include a nucleus at their center. Inside this nucleus are our chromosomes, which contain genes made of deoxyribonucleic acid (DNA). Genes provide the blueprint for our physiological development and structure, the inherited framework for how we will develop. At conception, when the sperm and egg merge, they form a single cell called a zygote. The 23rd pair of chromosomes, also referred to as the sex chromosomes, provides specific instructions for the individual to develop into a female or male. The egg from the mother contributes an X chromosome to the 23rd pair, and the sperm from the father contributes either an X chromosome or a Y chromosome. When both members of the 23rd pair are X chromosomes (XX), the zygote generally develops into a female. When the 23rd pair contains an X chromosome and a Y chromosome (XY), the zygote generally develops into a male.

LO 5 Discuss how genotype and phenotype relate to development. (p. 334)

Genotype refers to the 23 chromosome pairs that are unique to each individual and do not change in response to the environment. The genotype interacts with the environment, which results in a phenotype. This phenotype consists of a person's unique physical, psychological, and behavioral characteristics resulting from his or her particular combination of genotype and experiences.

LO 6 Describe the progression of prenatal development. (p. 335)

At the moment of conception, an egg from the mother and sperm cell from father come together to form a zygote. Under normal circumstances, the zygote immediately begins to divide into two cells, then each of those cells divides, and so on. During the germinal period, the zygote grows through cell division and eventually becomes implanted in the uterine wall. Between the 3rd and 8th weeks of development, the mass of cells is called an embryo. From 2 months following conception to birth, the growing human is identified as a fetus. The amniotic sac serves as a protective barrier; however,

harmful environmental agents called teratogens can damage the growing embryo or fetus. Radiation, viruses, bacteria, chemicals, alcohol, and drugs are all considered teratogens.

LO 7 Summarize the physical changes that occur in infancy. (p. 339)

As newborns grow, they experience astounding changes both seen and unseen. We see advancement in demonstrated capabilities, known as the motor milestones, and an increasingly sophisticated ability to discriminate among sensory stimuli. These sensorimotor advancements are made possible by the incredible brain development that is occurring. Neurons rapidly sprout new connections, and this dramatic synaptic growth is influenced by experiences and stimulation from the environment.

LO 8 Distinguish among the theories explaining language acquisition. (p. 343)

The behaviorist's view of language development proposes that infants and children learn language in the same way they learn everything else—through positive attention from others for correct behavior, unpleasant attention for incorrect behavior, and their own observations. Chomsky suggested that humans have a language acquisition device (LAD), an innate mechanism that provides a framework for children to learn language. Infant-directed speech (IDS) also plays a role in language acquisition. Infants pay more attention to adults who use IDS. These same adults are more likely to provide them with chances to learn and interact, thus allowing more exposure to language.

LO 9 Outline the universal sequence of language development. (p. 344)

At age 2–3 months, infants typically start to produce vowel-like sounds known as cooing. At 4–6 months, in the babbling stage, infants combine consonants with vowels. This progresses to their first words around 12 months, followed by two-word telegraphic speech at approximately 18 months. As children mature, they start to use more complete sentences. A "vocabulary explosion" tends to occur around 2 to 3 years of age. Most children are fluent in their native language by age 5 or 6.

LO 10 Discuss the key elements of Piaget's and Vygotsky's theories of cognitive development. (p. 346)

Piaget proposed that one important component of cognition is the schema, the collection of ideas or notions that serve as a building block of understanding. Humans are driven to advance intellectually, partly as a result of an innate need to maintain cognitive equilibrium. With assimilation, we understand new information using an already existing schema. With accommodation, we restructure old notions to make a place for new information. Piaget proposed that cognitive development occurs in four stages: sensorimotor, preoperational, concrete operational, and formal operational. Vygotsky was interested in how social and cultural factors affect cognitive development. He proposed that one way to help children's cognitive development is through scaffolding—pushing them to go just beyond what they are competent and comfortable doing, but also providing help, when needed, in a decreasing manner.

LO 11 Explain Erikson's theory of psychosocial development up until puberty. (p. 353)

According to Erikson, human development is marked by eight psychosocial stages, spanning infancy through old age. Each stage is marked by a developmental task or an emotional crisis that must be handled successfully to allow for healthy psychological growth: trust versus mistrust, autonomy versus shame and doubt, initiative versus guilt, and industry versus inferiority are the stages up to puberty.

LO 12 Give examples of significant physical changes that occur during adolescence. (p. 356)

Adolescence is characterized by many physical changes: a growth spurt in height, weight, and bones; sex hormones, which influence this growth and development, are also at high levels. In addition, primary sex characteristics (features associated with reproductive organs) and secondary sex characteristics (features not associated with reproductive organs) mature in both boys and girls.

LO 13 Summarize Piaget's description of cognitive changes that take place during adolescence. (p. 357)

During the formal operational stage of cognitive development, adolescents begin to use deductive reasoning and logic to draw conclusions. A specific type of egocentrism also emerges in adolescence. Adolescents may believe that most of their peers think the same way they do. Because they have not had a lot of life experiences, they may fail to consider long-term consequences associated with their behaviors.

LO 14 Detail how Erikson explained changes in identity during adolescence. (p. 358)

The stage of ego identity versus role confusion occurs during adolescence and is marked by the creation of an adult identity. During this stage, the adolescent seeks to define himself through his values, beliefs, and goals. Erikson believed that the period of role confusion is important for the

adolescent to navigate, as it provides a chance to "try out" different roles. Successful resolution of this stage results in stronger fundamental values, beliefs, and goals with a firmer sense of identity.

LO 15 Examine Kohlberg's levels of moral development. (p. 359)

Kohlberg proposed three levels of moral reasoning that occur in sequence. Preconventional moral reasoning usually applies to young children and focuses on the personal consequences of behaviors, both good and bad. At puberty, conventional moral reasoning is used, with the determination of right and wrong based on the expectations of society and important others. In postconventional moral reasoning, right and wrong are determined by the individual's beliefs about morality, which may not coincide with society's rules and regulations.

LO 16 Name several of the most important physical changes that occur across adulthood. (p. 363)

Adulthood brings about many physical changes. We are physically at our peak in early adulthood, but that typically declines as we reach late adulthood. Gradual physical changes occur, including hearing and vision loss, wrinkles, graying hair, reduced stamina, and for women menopause. Lifestyle choices can have significant influences on health. Heavy drinking, drug use, poor eating habits, and sleep deprivation can make one look, feel, and function like someone much older.

LO 17 Identify the most significant cognitive changes that occur across adulthood. (p. 364)

Cognitive ability remains stable from early to middle adulthood, but midlife is a time when information processing and memory can decline, particularly the ability to remember past events. Processing speed may slow with old age. Crystallized intelligence refers to the knowledge we gain through experience, and fluid intelligence refers to the ability to think in the abstract and create associations among concepts. As we age, the speed with which we learn new material and create associations decreases, but crystallized intelligence increases.

LO 18 Explain some of the socioemotional changes that occur across adulthood. (p. 366)

According to Erikson, during young adulthood, people face the crisis of intimacy versus isolation, and failure to create meaningful, deep relationships may lead to a life of isolation. In middle adulthood, we face the crisis of generativity versus stagnation. Positive resolution of this stage includes feeling like one has made a valuable impact on the next generation. In late adulthood, in the crisis of integrity versus despair, we look back on life and evaluate how we have done.

LO 19 Describe Kübler-Ross' theory regarding reactions to imminent death. (p. 369)

Kübler-Ross documented similar reactions among people faced with the news of their imminent death: denial (reacting with shock and disbelief), anger (toward others who are healthy, or about the lack of a cure), bargaining (negotiating for more time), depression (due to illness or the overwhelming sense of loss), and acceptance (accepting death is inevitable). Yet people vary greatly in how they deal with and experience dying. Many of these reactions or coping mechanisms may occur simultaneously or in stages, or the dying individual might not experience any of these stages.

key terms

accommodation, p. 346
adolescence, p. 355
assimilation, p. 346
attachment, p. 352
authoritarian parenting, p. 367
authoritative parenting, p. 367
chromosomes, p. 333
cohort effect, p. 330
concrete operational stage, p. 348
conservation, p. 348
conventional moral reasoning, p. 360
critical period, p. 329
cross-sectional method, p. 330

cross-sequential method, p. 332
crystallized intelligence, p. 365
deoxyribonucleic acid (DNA), p. 333
developmental psychology, p. 328
dizygotic twins, p. 336
dominant gene, p. 335
egocentrism, p. 348
embryo, p. 336
emerging adulthood, p. 361
epigenetics, p. 334
fetal alcohol syndrome (FAS), p. 337
fetus, p. 338
fluid intelligence, p. 365

formal operational stage, p. 349
gene, p. 333
genotype, p. 334
identity, p. 357
longitudinal method, p. 330
maturation, p. 328
menarche, p. 356
menopause, p. 363
monozygotic twins, p. 336
object permanence, p. 348
permissive parenting, p. 367
phenotype, p. 334
postconventional moral reasoning, p. 360
preconventional moral reasoning, p. 360

preoperational stage, p. 348
primary sex characteristics, p. 356
puberty, p. 356
recessive gene, p. 335
scaffolding, p. 349
schema, p. 346
secondary sex characteristics, p. 356
sensorimotor stage, p. 348
spermarche, p. 356
telegraphic speech, p. 344
temperament, p. 350
teratogens, p. 337
uninvolved parenting, p. 367
zone of proximal development, p. 350
zygote, p. 334

test prep *are you ready?*

1. A researcher is interested in studying changes across the life span with regard to memory, problem solving, and language. She chooses a large sample of college seniors and decides to follow them for the next 30 years. This is an example of:
   a. socioemotional development.
   b. longitudinal research.
   c. cross-sectional research.
   c. epigenetics.

2. Ricardo's grandfather suffers from Alzheimer's disease. Ricardo wonders if he will experience a similar future because of his biological connection to his grandfather. What Ricardo is contemplating is similar to which of the following debates in developmental psychology?
   a. stability and change
   b. stages or continuity
   c. critical or sensitive period
   d. nature and nurture

3. DNA molecules include sections corresponding to _____, which encode proteins that determine the texture of hair, color of eyes, and some aspects of personality.
   a. phenotypes
   b. epigenetics
   c. zygotes
   d. genes

4. Your psychology instructor often discusses the factors in the environment that can influence how genes are expressed. This topic is a part of the field studying:
   a. epigenetics.
   b. maturation.
   c. the cohort effect.
   d. prenatal development.

5. Human development is influenced by the interaction of many factors. Brain development, for example, is influenced by biological maturation and experiences in the

environment. This is evident in _____, which occurs when unused synaptic connections are eliminated.

a. myelin
c. synaptic pruning
b. socioemotional development
d. the rooting reflex

6. _____ are agents that can damage a growing embryo or fetus.

a. Phenotypes
c. Zygotes
b. Genotypes
d. Teratogens

7. Children all over the world seem to learn language in a fixed sequence. This provides evidence in support of Noam Chomsky's theory that humans have a _____ that provides an innate mechanism for learning language.

a. sensorimotor stage
b. language acquisition device
c. zone of proximal development
d. rooting reflex

8. Erikson proposed that human development is characterized by eight psychosocial stages, each marked by a developmental task or emotional crisis. In the first stage, the infant must resolve the _____ conflict. Caregivers who are not responsive might lead the infant to always expect the worst in people.

a. autonomy versus shame and doubt
b. industry versus inferiority
c. trust versus mistrust
d. ego identity versus role confusion

9. According to Vygotsky, _____ is an approach that helps children learn, providing support when necessary but allowing them to problem solve as much as possible on their own.

a. assimilation
c. phenotype
b. scaffolding
d. schema

10. _____ further develop during adolescence. These changes are associated with reproductive organs, such as the maturation of ovaries, uterus, penis, and testes.

a. Gender schemas
b. Temperaments
c. Primary sex characteristics
d. Secondary sex characteristics

11. Adolescents begin thinking more logically and systematically, and start to use deductive reasoning to draw conclusions. They have entered what Piaget would refer to as the:

a. formal operational stage.
b. postconventional moral reasoning stage.
c. industry versus inferiority stage.
d. concrete operational stage.

12. One of the important tasks of adolescence is to search for identity, that is, to find a sense of self based on values, beliefs, and goals. This task falls under which of the following categories of development?

a. physical
c. maturation
b. socioemotional
d. cognitive

13. During middle adulthood, one major physical change for women is _____, which is often preceded by a decrease in estrogen production and a reduction in the size of the uterus.

a. andropause
c. shrinking in height
b. menarche
d. menopause

14. Which of the following represents the correct order of the universal sequence of language development?

a. root; babble; coo
c. coo; babble; first words
b. babble; coo; first words
d. coo; root; babble

15. A woman learns that her death is imminent. According to Kübler-Ross, her initial reaction to this news will likely be shock and disbelief, which are common in the _____ stage.

a. denial
c. late adulthood
b. conventional moral reasoning
d. preoperational

16. During adolescence, a specific type of egocentrism emerges that is different from that experienced by younger children. Describe both of these types of egocentrism and explain how they differ from what might be described as a spoiled or entitled child.

17. Draw a diagram that outlines how Erikson's stages of psychosocial development, Piaget's stages of cognitive development, and Kohlberg's stages of moral development fit together on a developmental timeline.

18. Describe and give examples of crystallized intelligence and fluid intelligence. Discuss how these types of intelligence change across the life span.

19. Describe the types of crises that adults face using Erikson's stages of socioemotional development.

20. We have described how cognitive abilities tend to decline with age. What kinds of cognitive activities might actually improve with age?

✓ CHECK YOUR ANSWERS IN APPENDIX C.

YOUR SCIENTIFIC WORLD
Apply psychology to the real world!
Go to LaunchPad for access.

Courtesy of Mohamed Dirie.

Universal/The Kobal Collection at Art Resource.

Jump Run Productions/Getty Images.

CHAPTER OUTLINE AND LEARNING OBJECTIVES

Motivation

LO 1 Define motivation.

LO 2 Explain how extrinsic and intrinsic motivation impact behavior.

Theories of Motivation

LO 3 Summarize instinct theory.

LO 4 Describe drive-reduction theory and explain how it relates to motivation.

LO 5 Explain how arousal theory relates to motivation.

LO 6 Outline Maslow's hierarchy of needs.

LO 7 Explain how self-determination theory relates to motivation.

Back to Basics: Hunger

LO 8 Discuss how the stomach and the hypothalamus make us feel hunger.

Emotion

LO 9 Define emotions and explain how they are different from moods.

Theories of Emotion

LO 10 List the major theories of emotion and describe how they differ.

LO 11 Discuss evidence to support the idea that emotions are universal.

LO 12 Indicate how display rules influence the expression of emotion.

Types of Emotion

LO 13 Describe the role the amygdala plays in the experience of fear.

LO 14 Summarize evidence pointing to the biological basis of happiness.

Rodrigo Friscione/Getty Images.

Johan Spanner/Polaris.

M Lohmann/agefotostock.

9 motivation and emotion

Jose Luis Pelaez Inc./
Getty Images.

Motivation

FIRST DAY OF SCHOOL When Mohamed Dirie started first grade, he did not know his ABCs or 123s. He had no idea what the words "teacher," "cubby," or "recess" meant. In fact, he spoke virtually no English. As for his classmates, they were beginning first grade with basic reading and writing skills from preschool and kindergarten. Mohamed's early education had taken place in an Islamic school, where he spent most of his time learning to read and recite Arabic verses of the Qur'an (kuh-RAHN). But Arabic wasn't going to be much help to a 6-year-old trying to get through first grade in St. Paul, Minnesota.

Months earlier, Mohamed and his mother, father, and older sister had arrived in St. Paul from the East African nation of Kenya, some 8,000 miles across the globe. Kenya was not their native country, just a stopping point between their homeland, Somalia, and a new life in America.

Perhaps you have heard about Somalia. Many of the news stories coming out of this nation in past decades have told of bloody clashes between rival factions, kidnappings by pirates, suicide bombings, and

War-Torn Somalia
Mohamed's family comes from the East African nation of Somalia (shaded red on the map). They fled their homeland in 1991 during a violent government overthrow that led to more than 20,000 civilian deaths (Gassmann, 1991, December 21). The photo shows a group of Somali rebels in the capital city of Mogadishu about a month after the regime was toppled. Map: Globe Turner, LLC/Getty Images. Photo: AP Images.

Note: Quotations attributed to Mohamed Dirie are personal communications.

The Scholar
Four-year-old Mohamed (left) dressed in special attire to celebrate his completion of a *surah,* or chapter in the Qur'an. When this photograph was taken, the Dirie family had left Somalia and was living in a temporary home in Kenya. Some 14 years later, Mohamed graduated from high school in St. Paul, Minnesota (right). Courtesy of Mohamed Dirie.

Mohamed, in His Own Words

http://qrs.ly/zu5a5ee

Photo: Macmillan Learning.

CONNECTIONS

In **Chapter 7,** we described intellectually gifted people as those with very high IQ scores. We also presented the concept of emotional intelligence. Here, we see that in addition to intelligence, motivation plays a role in success.

starving children. Somalia's serious troubles began in 1991 when rebel forces overthrew the government of President Siad Barre. With gunshots ringing through the streets of their home city of Mogadishu, Mohamed's family, like thousands of others, fled the country, narrowly escaping death.

The first day of school in St. Paul, little Mohamed strapped on his backpack and walked with his mother to the bus stop. When the yellow bus pulled up to the curb, Mohamed's mother followed him inside and insisted on accompanying him to school. But Mohamed was ready to make the journey alone. "No, Mom, I got this," he remembers saying in his native Somali.

When Mohamed arrived at his new school, he found his way to the first-grade classroom and discovered a swarm of children chattering and making friends. Mohamed wanted to mingle, too, so he endeared himself to the other kids the best way he could—by smiling. Flashing a grin was Mohamed's way of communicating, *Hey, I am a good person and you should get to know me.* His strategy worked. "I really felt like other people approached me better," he says. Mohamed's warm and welcoming demeanor may have been one reason his teacher took a special interest in him, providing the individual attention he needed to catch up to his peers. And Mohamed caught up quickly.

By the end of third grade, he had graduated from an English as a Second Language (ESL) program and could converse fluently with classmates. He sailed through the rest of elementary school with As and Bs in all subjects. Middle school presented new challenges, as Mohamed attended one of the poorest schools in the district and occasionally got picked on, but he continued to excel academically, taking the most challenging classes offered. In high school, he took primarily international baccalaureate (IB) or pre-IB classes, which prepped him for his undergraduate work at the University of Minnesota. Now with his bachelor's degree in scientific and technical communication, Mohamed is contemplating his next step. Will it be law school? A master's degree? Maybe a PhD?

If you think about where Mohamed began and where he is today, it's hard not to be awed. He entered the United States' school system 2 years behind his peers, unable to speak a word of English, an outsider in a culture radically different from his own. Without any tutoring from his parents (who couldn't read the class assignments, let alone help him with schoolwork), he managed to propel himself to the upper levels of the nation's educational system in just 12 years.

How do you explain Mohamed's success? This young man is definitely intelligent. You can tell he is bright after 5 minutes of conversation. But intelligence is not the only ingredient in the recipe for outstanding achievement. Other factors are important as well, including something psychologists consider essential for success in school: *motivation* (Conley, 2012; Hodis, Meyer, McClure, Weir, & Walkey, 2011; Linnenbrink & Pintrich, 2002). ●

What Is Motivation?

There are people who get kicks from bungee jumping out of helicopters, and those who feel completely invigorated by a rousing match of chess. Human behaviors can be logical: We eat when hungry, sleep when tired, and go to work to pay the rent. Our behaviors can also be senseless and destructive: A beautiful fashion model starves herself, or an aspiring politician throws away an entire career for a fleeting sexual adventure. Why do people spend their hard-earned money on lottery tickets when the chances of winning may be 1 in 175 million (Wasserstein, 2013, May 16)? And what in the world drives teenagers to wrap houses in toilet paper on Halloween night?

One way to explain human behavior is through learning. We know that people (not to mention dogs, chickens, and slugs) can *learn* to behave in certain ways through classical conditioning, operant conditioning, and observational learning (Chapter 5). But learning isn't everything. Another way to explain behavior is to consider what might be motivating it. In the first half of this chapter, you will learn about different forms of motivation and the theories explaining them. Keep in mind that human behavior is complex and should be studied in the context of culture, biology, and environmental factors. Every behavior is likely to have a multitude of causes (Maslow, 1943).

LO 1 Define motivation.

Psychologists propose that **motivation** is a stimulus or force that can direct the way we behave, think, and feel. A motivated behavior tends to be guided (that is, it has a direction), energized, and persistent. Mohamed's academic behavior exhibits all three features: *guided* because he sets specific goals like getting into graduate school, *energized* because he goes after those goals with zeal, and *persistent* because he sticks with his goals even when challenges arise.

INCENTIVE Let's take a look at how operant conditioning, particularly the use of *reinforcers,* can help us understand the relationship between learning and motivation. When a behavior is reinforced (with positive or negative reinforcers), an association is established between the behavior and its consequence. If we consider motivated behavior, this association becomes the **incentive**, or reason, to repeat the behavior. Imagine you have been avoiding a particular term paper assignment. You decide you will treat yourself to an hour of watching Netflix for every three pages you write. Adding a reinforcer (Netflix) increases your writing behavior; thus, we call it a *positive reinforcer.* The association between the behavior (writing) and the consequence (watching your favorite show) is the incentive. Before you know it, you begin to expect this break from work, which motivates you to write.

LO 2 Explain how extrinsic and intrinsic motivation impact behavior.

EXTRINSIC MOTIVATION When a learned behavior is motivated by the incentive of external reinforcers in the environment, we would say there is an **extrinsic motivation** to continue that behavior (Deci, Koestner, & Ryan, 1999; TABLE 9.1 on the next page). In other words, the motivation comes from consequences that are found in the environment or situation. Bagels and coffee might provide extrinsic motivation for people to attend a boring meeting. Sales commissions provide

You Asked, Mohamed Answers

http://qrs.ly/wb5a5en

What motivated you to go to college and better your education?

scan this ➔

Adrenaline Junkies
Why are some people drawn to thrill-seeking activities like skydiving? In this chapter, we will discuss "sensation seeking," which appears to be an inherited trait associated with certain patterns of dopamine activity in the brain (Norbury & Husain, 2015). Jump Run Productions/Getty Images.

CONNECTIONS

In **Chapter 5,** we introduced positive and negative reinforcers, which are stimuli that increase future occurrences of target behaviors. In both cases, the behavior becomes associated with the reinforcer. Here, we see how these associations become incentives.

motivation A stimulus that can direct behavior, thinking, and feeling.

incentive An association established between a behavior and its consequences, which then motivates that behavior.

extrinsic motivation The drive or urge to continue a behavior because of external reinforcers.

TABLE 9.1 EXAMPLES OF INTRINSIC, EXTRINSIC, AND NEUTRAL PHRASES USED IN A MOTIVATION STUDY

Intrinsic Motivation Phrases	Extrinsic Motivation Phrases	Neutral Phrases
Writing an enjoyable paper	Writing an extra-credit paper	Writing an assigned paper
Working on the computer out of curiosity	Working on the computer for bonus points	Working on the computer to meet a deadline
Participating in a fun project	Participating in a money-making project	Participating in a required project
Pursuing my personal interests in class	Pursuing an attractive reward in class	Pursuing a routine task in class
Working with freedom	Working for incentives	Working with pressure
Having options and choices	Having prizes and awards	Having pressures and obligations
Working because it's fun	Working because I want money	Working because I have to
Feeling interested	Anticipating a prize	Feeling frustrated

Listed above are descriptions of activities that typically arouse intrinsic motivation, extrinsic motivation, or no motivation. Reproduced with permission of Elsevier Science/The Lancet/Japan Neurosciences Society from Lee, Reeve, Xue, and Xiong (2012).

extrinsic motivation for salespeople to sell more goods. For most of us, money serves as a powerful form of extrinsic motivation.

INTRINSIC MOTIVATION But learned behaviors can also be motivated by personal satisfaction, interest in a subject matter, and other variables that exist within a person. When the urge to continue a behavior comes from within, we call it **intrinsic motivation** (Deci et al., 1999). Reading a textbook because it is inherently interesting exemplifies intrinsic motivation. The reinforcers originate inside of you (learning feels good and brings you satisfaction), and not from the external environment.

What compels you to offer your seat to an older adult on a bus: Is it because you've been praised for helping others before (extrinsic motivation), or because it simply feels good to help someone (intrinsic motivation)? Perhaps your response is a combination of both.

EXTRINSIC VERSUS INTRINSIC Many behaviors are inspired by a blend of extrinsic and intrinsic motivation, but there do appear to be potential disadvantages to extrinsic motivation, especially when performance (for example, on a presentation) is a factor (Cerasoli, Nicklin, & Ford, 2014; Deci et al., 1999). Researchers have found that using rewards, such as money and marshmallows, to reinforce already interesting activities (like doing puzzles, playing word games, and so on) can lead to a decrease in what was initially intrinsically motivating. Perhaps the use of external reinforcers causes people to feel less responsible for initiating their own behaviors.

In general, behavior resulting from intrinsic motivation is likely to include "high-quality learning," but only when the activities are novel, challenging, or have aesthetically pleasing characteristics. Extrinsic motivation may be less effective, resulting in resentment or disinterest (Ryan & Deci, 2000). "Tangible rewards—both material rewards, such as pizza parties for reading books, and symbolic rewards, such as good student awards—are widely advocated by many educators and are used in many classrooms, yet the evidence suggests that these rewards tend to undermine intrinsic

intrinsic motivation The drive or urge to continue a behavior because of internal reinforcers.

motivation" (Deci, Koestner, & Ryan, 2001, p. 15). More recent research suggests that the relationship may not be that simple; extrinsic motivators such as merit-based salary increases do not always undermine intrinsic motivation (Gerhart & Fang, 2015).

For Mohamed, the most powerful source of extrinsic motivation was the approval of his mother. He recalls how proud she was after returning from a parent–teacher conference in which his first-grade teacher said, "Your child is as bright as the sun." Mohamed doesn't remember his mom rewarding him with material things like toys and candy; apparently, making her proud was gratifying enough. But there were also forces driving Mohamed from within (intrinsic motivation). He enjoyed the process of learning. It was rewarding to master a second language and nail down his multiplication tables. Outside of class, Mohamed read books for fun. He still enjoys reading science fiction, so much that he hopes to write his own novel one day. Says Mohamed, "I want to be the first Somali to write a science fiction [book] in Somali."

 In Class: Collaborate and Report

Imagine you are a psychology instructor and your goal is to motivate your students to perform better on exams. Using Table 9.1 as your guide, team up and discuss **A)** extrinsic motivation strategies you could implement, and **B)** ways to encourage intrinsic motivation. **C)** Which do you think would be more effective in the long term?

We now have developed a basic understanding of what motivation is: a stimulus or force that can direct the way we behave, think, and feel. We also have established that motivation may stem from factors outside of ourselves (extrinsic) or from within (intrinsic). But what underlies motivation? Let's take a look at the major theories.

  show what you know

1. _____ is a stimulus or force that directs the way we behave, think, and feel.

2. Behavior that is motivated by internal reinforcers is considered to be the result of:
   a. extrinsic motivation.
   b. intrinsic motivation.
   c. persistence.
   d. external consequences.

3. Imagine you are a teacher trying to motivate your students. Explain why you would want them to be influenced by intrinsic motivation as opposed to extrinsic motivation.

✓ CHECK YOUR ANSWERS IN APPENDIX C.

Theories of Motivation

GOODBYE, SOMALIA Somalia was not a safe place in 1991. The groups that orchestrated the revolution began warring among themselves, and the country plunged into bloody chaos. Over 20,000 innocent people were killed in the crossfire (Gassmann, 1991, December 21). A famine and food crisis ensued, which, in addition to the ongoing fighting, led to 240,000 to 280,000 deaths within the next 2 years (Gundel, 2003). It is easy to understand why Mohamed's parents, or anyone, would want to remove their family from Somalia during this period. Faced with a life-or-death situation, they were motivated by what you might call a "survival" instinct. ●

Hungry and Waiting
Somali refugees wait in line for food aid in Mogadishu during a severe drought in July, 2011. Food shortages have been a recurrent problem in Somalia. epa european pressphoto agency b.v./Alamy.

Turtles on a Mission
Baby loggerhead sea turtles instinctually crawl toward the ocean after hatching. When the females reach adulthood, they return to the same beach to lay their own eggs, finding their way "home" with the help of the earth's magnetic field (Brothers & Lohmann, 2015). Elena Tyapkina/Alamy.

CONNECTIONS

In **Chapter 1,** we presented the evolutionary perspective, which suggests humans have evolved adaptive traits through natural selection. Behaviors that improve the chances of survival and reproduction are most likely to be passed along to offspring, whereas less adaptive behaviors decrease in frequency.

You Asked, Mohamed Answers

http://qrs.ly/fs5a5ej

How have your childhood experiences impacted you as an adult?

scan this ➔

Instinct Theory

LO 3 **Summarize instinct theory.**

Instinct. You hear that word used all the time in everyday conversation: "Trust your instincts," people say in times of uncertainty. "That fighter has a killer instinct," a sports commentator remarks during a boxing match. But what exactly are instincts, and do humans really have them?

First observed by scientists studying animals, **instincts** are complex behaviors that are fixed, unlearned, and consistent within a species. Instincts motivate honeybees' communication through a "waggle dance," and prompt sea turtles to swim to the ocean after they have hatched (Malkemus, 2015). No one teaches the bees to dance or the turtles to swim to the ocean; through evolution, these behaviors appear to be etched into their genetic make-up.

Instincts form the basis of one of the earliest theories of motivation. Inspired in part by Charles Darwin's theory of evolution, early scholars proposed that a variety of instincts motivate human behavior (Krueger & Reckless, 1931; McDougall, 1912). William James (1890/1983) suggested we could explain some human behavior through instincts such as attachment and cleanliness. At the height of instinct theory's popularity, several thousand human "instincts" had been named, among them curiosity, flight, and aggressiveness (Bernard, 1926; Kuo, 1921). Yet there was little evidence they were true instincts—that is, complex behaviors that are fixed, unlearned, and consistent within a species. Only a handful of human activities, among them rooting behavior in newborn infants, might be considered instincts (Chapter 8). But even these behaviors are more akin to reflexes than complex activities like honeybee waggle dancing.

Although instinct theory faded into the background, some of its themes are apparent in the evolutionary perspective. A substantial body of research suggests that evolutionary forces influence human behavior. For example, emotional responses, such as fear of snakes, heights, and spiders, may have evolved to protect us from danger (Plomin, DeFries, Knopik, & Neiderhiser, 2013). But these fears are not instincts, because they are not universal. Not everyone is afraid of snakes and spiders; some of us have learned to fear (or not fear) them through experience. When trying to pin down the motivation for behavior, it is difficult to determine the relative contributions of learning (nurture) and innate factors (nature) such as instinct (Malkemus, 2015).

FOUR YEARS IN KENYA   After fleeing the bullet-riddled city of Mogadishu, Mohamed and his family made their way across the border into the neighboring country of Kenya, where they lived for about 4 years.

Mohamed considers himself one of the "more fortunate ones." Many Somalis had no choice but to settle in squalid, overcrowded refugee camps, while Mohamed's family had the means to rent a small apartment in the capital city of Nairobi.

Being an outsider in Kenya was not easy, however. Back in Somalia, Mohamed's father had earned a solid living constructing buildings, and his mother had been a successful entrepreneur selling homemade food from their house. In Kenya, neither parent could find employment. They had no choice but to live off "remittances," or money sent from family members outside of Africa, and relying on other people was not their style. "You're waiting on other people to feed you," Mohamed says, "and [my father] didn't like that."

Daily life presented its fair share of challenges, too. Mohamed's diet was painfully monotonous, with most meals centering on *ugali,* a dense gruel made of corn or millet flour—similar to oatmeal, but harder in consistency. At times, the apartment building where they lived lost electricity for weeks, or water stopped flowing from faucets. During water shortages, the whole family would carry empty buckets and tubs to a nearby army base and ask for water. Despite these difficulties, Mohamed never went hungry or thirsty. His basic *physiological needs* were usually met. ●

Drive-Reduction Theory

Humans and nonhuman animals have basic physiological **needs** or requirements that must be maintained at some baseline or constant state to ensure continued existence. **Homeostasis** refers to the way in which our bodies maintain these constant states through internal controls. In order to survive, there is a continuous monitoring of oxygen, fluids, nutrients, and other physiological variables. If these fall below desired or necessary levels, an urge to restore equilibrium surfaces. And this urge motivates us to act.

LO 4 Describe drive-reduction theory and explain how it relates to motivation.

The **drive-reduction theory** proposes that this biological balancing act (homeostasis) is the basis for motivation (Hull, 1952). According to this theory, behaviors are driven by the need to maintain homeostasis—that is, to fulfill basic biological needs for nutrients, fluids, oxygen, and so on (see **INFOGRAPHIC 9.1** on the next page). If a need is not fulfilled, this creates a **drive**, or state of tension, that pushes us or motivates behaviors to meet the need. The urges to eat, drink, sleep, or have sex are associated with physiological needs. Once a need is satisfied, the drive is reduced, but not forever. The need inevitably returns, and you feel driven to meet it once again. A good example is hunger. You wake up with an empty stomach, fill it with breakfast foods, but then find yourself hungry at noon; so you eat lunch, but the hunger returns in the evening, and the cycle continues.

Let's look at another concrete example of drive reduction. Imagine you visit a mountainous area 6,500 feet above sea level, which puts a strain on breathing. While jogging, you find yourself gasping for air because your oxygen levels have dropped. Motivated by the need to maintain homeostasis, you stop what you are doing until your oxygen levels return to normal. Having an unfulfilled *need* (not enough oxygen) creates a *drive* (state of tension) that pushes you to modify your behavior in order to restore homeostasis (you stop and breathe deeply, allowing your blood oxygen levels to return to a normal level). The drive-reduction theory helps us understand how physiological needs can be motivators, but it is less useful for explaining why we buy new clothes, go to college, or drive cars too fast.

Arousal Theory

Mohamed arrived in America when he was 6 years old. Stepping off the plane in the Twin Cities (Minneapolis/St. Paul) was quite a shock for a young boy who had lived most of his childhood in the crowded, pavement-covered city of Nairobi. "It was really strange to me," Mohamed says. "At that time, I hadn't really seen a place that had space." How odd it was to see patches of green grass in front of every house. "Everything looked like it sparkled."

New places, people, and experiences can be frightening. They can also be delightfully exhilarating. Humans are fascinated by novelty, and you see evidence of this innate curiosity in the earliest stages of life. Babies grab, taste, smell, and climb on just about everything they can get their hands on, including dangerous electrical devices

instincts Complex behaviors that are fixed, unlearned, and consistent within a species.

needs Physiological or psychological requirements that must be maintained at some baseline or constant state.

homeostasis The tendency for bodies to maintain constant states through internal controls.

drive-reduction theory Suggests that homeostasis motivates us to meet biological needs.

drive A state of tension that pushes us or motivates behaviors to meet a need.

Theories of Motivation

Motivational forces drive our behaviors, thoughts, and feelings. Psychologists have proposed different theories addressing the needs that create these drives within us. Let's look at the three most prominent theories of motivation. Some theories, like drive-reduction theory, best explain motivation related to physiological needs. Other theories focus on psychological needs, such as the need for an optimum level of stimulation, as described in arousal theory. In his hierarchy of needs, Abraham Maslow combined various drives and proposed that we are motivated to meet some needs before others.

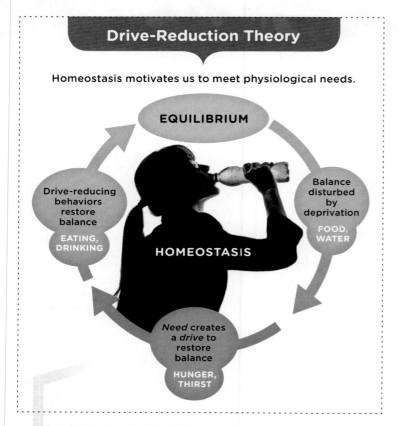

Drive-Reduction Theory

Homeostasis motivates us to meet physiological needs.

EQUILIBRIUM

Drive-reducing behaviors restore balance
EATING, DRINKING

HOMEOSTASIS

Balance disturbed by deprivation
FOOD, WATER

Need creates a *drive* to restore balance
HUNGER, THIRST

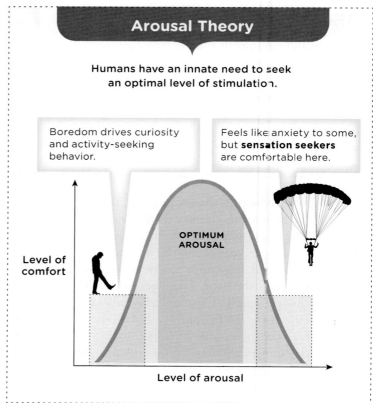

Arousal Theory

Humans have an innate need to seek an optimal level of stimulation.

Boredom drives curiosity and activity-seeking behavior.

Feels like anxiety to some, but **sensation seekers** are comfortable here.

OPTIMUM AROUSAL

Level of comfort

Level of arousal

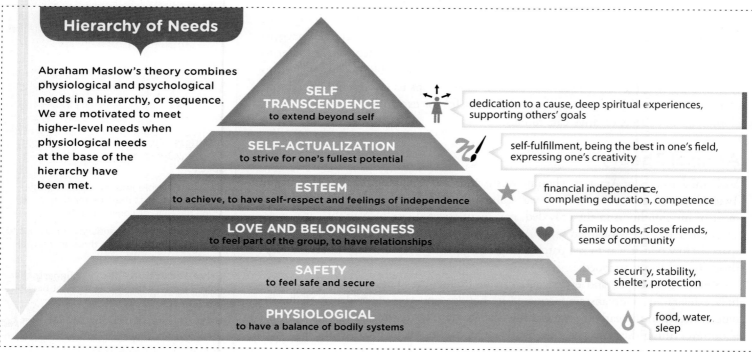

Hierarchy of Needs

Abraham Maslow's theory combines physiological and psychological needs in a hierarchy, or sequence. We are motivated to meet higher-level needs when physiological needs at the base of the hierarchy have been met.

SELF TRANSCENDENCE
to extend beyond self
— dedication to a cause, deep spiritual experiences, supporting others' goals

SELF-ACTUALIZATION
to strive for one's fullest potential
— self-fulfillment, being the best in one's field, expressing one's creativity

ESTEEM
to achieve, to have self-respect and feelings of independence
— financial independence, completing education, competence

LOVE AND BELONGINGNESS
to feel part of the group, to have relationships
— family bonds, close friends, sense of community

SAFETY
to feel safe and secure
— security, stability, shelter, protection

PHYSIOLOGICAL
to have a balance of bodily systems
— food, water, sleep

and household chemicals. Ignoring the most forceful parental warnings (*Do NOT touch that hot pan!*), many toddlers still reach out and touch extremely hot cookware or recklessly leap between pieces of furniture. But mind you, children are not the only ones seeking new experiences. Adults will pay hundreds of dollars to parachute out of airplanes or float over jagged mountains in hot-air balloons. They also spend hours tooling around websites like Wikipedia and YouTube—just to learn about new things. Why engage in activities that have little, if anything, to do with satisfying basic biological needs? Humans are driven by other types of urges, including the apparent need for stimulation.

Our primate cousins are also inquisitive, which suggests that they, too, have an innate need for enrichment and sensory stimulation. Researchers have found that monkeys will attempt to open latches without extrinsic motivation; apparently, their curiosity motivates their behavior (Butler, 1960; Harlow, Harlow, & Meyer, 1950).

LO 5 Explain how arousal theory relates to motivation.

According to **arousal theory**, humans (and perhaps other primates) seek an optimal level of arousal, as not all motivation stems from physical needs. Arousal, or engagement in the world, can be a product of anxiety, surprise, excitement, interest, fear, and many other emotions. Have you ever had an unexplained urge to make simple changes to your daily routines, like taking a new route to work, preparing your morning eggs differently, or adding new clothes to your wardrobe? These behaviors may stem from your need to increase arousal. Optimal arousal is a personal or subjective matter that is not the same for everyone (Infographic 9.1). Evidence suggests that some people are *sensation seekers;* that is, they appear to seek activities that increase arousal (Zuckerman, 1979, 1994, 2015). The heritability of this trait appears to be quite high, ranging from 58% to 67% (Zuckerman, 2015). Popularly known as "adrenaline junkies," these individuals relish activities like cliff diving, racing motorcycles, and watching horror movies. High sensation seeking is not necessarily a bad thing, as it may be associated with a higher tolerance for stressful events (Roberti, 2004). Some research findings indicate that sensation seeking can decrease during later adolescence, suggesting that as sensation seekers mature, they might be taking more responsible risks (Lauriola, Panno, Levin, & Lejuez, 2014).

Needs and More Needs: Maslow's Hierarchy

LO 6 Outline Maslow's hierarchy of needs.

Have you ever been in a car accident, lived through a hurricane, or witnessed a violent crime? At the time, you probably did *not* think about what show you were going to watch on HBO that night. When physical safety is threatened, everything else tends to take a backseat. This is one of the themes underlying the **hierarchy of needs** theory of motivation proposed by Abraham Maslow, a leading figure in the humanistic movement. Maslow organized human needs into a hierarchy of biological and psychological needs, often depicted as a pyramid (Infographic 9.1). The needs in the hierarchy are considered universal and are ordered according to the strength of their associated drives, with the most critical needs at the bottom. Food and water, for example, are situated at the base of the hierarchy, and generally take precedence over higher-level needs.

PHYSIOLOGICAL NEEDS *Physiological needs,* as stated earlier, include the requirements for food, water, sleep, and an overall balance of bodily systems. If a life-sustaining need such as fluid intake goes unsatisfied, other needs are placed on hold and the person is motivated to find ways to satisfy it. Maslow suggested that the basic physiological needs of most North Americans are "relatively well gratified" (Maslow, 1943), but this is not always the case. The 2014–2015 water crisis in Flint, Michigan, is a prime example. During this time, Flint residents were supplied with lead-contaminated

Dangerous Fun
Babies and toddlers are notorious for climbing on furniture, mouthing nonfood items, and reaching for hazardous objects (this is why many parents "baby proof" their homes). Like adults looking for exciting places to travel and new electronic gadgets to own, these babies may be searching for novel forms of stimulation. BSIP/Phototake.

CONNECTIONS

In **Chapter 7,** we presented heritability, the degree to which heredity is responsible for a particular characteristic in a population. The heritability for sensation seeking indicates that 58–67% of the population-wide variation can be attributed to genes, and 33–42% to environmental influences.

CONNECTIONS

In **Chapter 1,** we discussed Maslow and his involvement in humanistic psychology. The humanists suggest that people are inclined to grow and change for the better, and this perspective is apparent in the hierarchy of needs. Humans are motivated by the universal tendency to move up the hierarchy and meet needs toward the top.

arousal theory Suggests that humans are motivated to seek an optimal level of arousal, or alertness and engagement in the world.

hierarchy of needs A continuum of needs that are universal and ordered in terms of the strength of their associated drives.

water—the result of government negligence and ineptitude (Bosman, 2016, March 23). Another example is the widespread need for adequate nutrition. In 2015 the U.S. Department of Agriculture reported that 14% of American households were "food insecure at least some time during the year . . . . meaning they lacked access to enough food for an active, healthy life for all household members" (Coleman-Jensen, Rabbitt, Gregory, & Singh, 2015, p. i).

SAFETY NEEDS If physiological needs are satisfied, human behavior is motivated by the next level in the hierarchy: *safety needs.* But how you define safety depends on the circumstances of your life. If you were living in Mogadishu during the 1991 revolution (and many times subsequent to that period), staying safe might have involved dodging bullets and artillery fire. For those currently living in Somalia, safety includes having access to safe drinking water and disease-preventing vaccines. Most people living in America do not have to worry about access to clean water or routine vaccinations. Here, safety is more likely equated with the need for predictability and order: having a steady job, a home in a safe neighborhood, health insurance, and living in a country with a stable economy. What does safety mean for you?

LOVE AND BELONGINGNESS NEEDS If safety needs are being met, then people will be motivated by *love and belongingness needs.* Maslow suggested this includes the need to avoid loneliness, to feel like part of a group, and to maintain affectionate relationships. Except for a rare run-in with neighborhood bullies, Mohamed enjoyed a fairly secure existence in Minnesota. His need for safety was met, so he was motivated at this next level of the hierarchy. In addition to cultivating deep family bonds, Mohamed befriended two boys he met in middle school, one who had emigrated from Bangladesh and the other a first-generation Mexican American. The three pals all ended up going to the University of Minnesota, and they remain very close to this day.

We all want to belong, and failing to meet this need has significant consequences. People who feel disconnected or excluded may demonstrate less prosocial behavior (Twenge, Baumeister, DeWall, Ciarocco, & Bartels, 2007) and act more aggressively and less cooperatively, which only tends to intensify their struggle for social acceptance (DeWall, Baumeister, & Vohs, 2008; Stenseng, Belsky, Skalicka, & Wichstrøm, 2014). However, this effect is reduced when ostracized (excluded) people think about the future and consider the long-term implications of their actions (Balliet & Ferris, 2013).

ESTEEM NEEDS If the first three levels of needs are being met, then the individual might be motivated by *esteem needs,* including the need to be respected by others, to achieve, and to have self-respect, self-confidence, and feelings of independence. Cultivating and fulfilling these needs foster a sense of confidence and self-worth, both qualities that Mohamed seems to possess. It was early in life that Mohamed began doing things for himself. His parents may have been there to encourage him, but they could not hold his hand when it came to tasks demanding proficiency in English—like filling out employment applications. But Mohamed did just fine on his own, landing his first job at a nonprofit student loan company just after ninth grade, and performing so well that the company employed him throughout college. Mohamed, it appears, began meeting esteem needs very early on.

SELF-ACTUALIZATION Even with the above-mentioned needs actively being met, Maslow suggested that the need for **self-actualization** would provide motivation "to become more and more what one is, to become everything that one is capable of becoming" (Maslow, 1943, p. 382). Self-actualization is the need to reach one's fullest potential. Some will meet this need by being the best possible parent, while others will strive to be the best artist or musician. Self-actualization is at the

Love, Affection, and Belongingness
Relationships with friends help fulfill what Maslow called love and belongingness needs. Leonardo Patrizi/ Getty Images.

heart of the humanistic movement: It represents the human tendency toward growth and self-discovery (Chapter 11). For Mohamed, self-actualization means being an exceptional scholar, employee, and father.

SELF-TRANSCENDENCE Toward the end of his life, Maslow proposed an additional need: that for *self-transcendence*. This need motivates us to go beyond our own needs and feel outward connections through "peak experiences" of ecstasy and awe. Fulfilling this need might mean devoting oneself to a humanitarian cause, pursuing a lofty ideal, or achieving spiritual enlightenment. If you walk into Mohamed's home, you will see a poster on the wall that says, "Live a simple life so others can simply live." What this means, explains Mohamed, is that you should do the best you can in life, but also strive to allow others to do the same. "It's balancing your life so that you're always doing the most positive good," he says. As president of the University of Minnesota's Somali Student Association, Mohamed put this slogan to work, organizing activities to support Somali students, and arranging cultural awareness events at the university and in the greater Twin Cities communities.

EXCEPTIONS TO THE RULE Maslow's hierarchy provides suggestions for the order of needs, but this sequence is not set in stone. In some cases, people abandon physiological needs in order to meet a self-actualization need—going on a hunger strike or giving up material possessions, for example. The practice of fasting, which occurs in Islam, Christianity, Hinduism, and Judaism, illustrates how basic physiological needs (food and water) can temporarily be placed on hold for a greater purpose (religion).

Safety is another basic need often relegated in the pursuit of something more transcendent. Just think of all the soldiers who have given their lives fighting for causes like freedom and social justice. Parents living in a war zone and battling hunger may neglect their own basic needs to ensure their children's well-being, thus fulfilling higher needs such as love and esteem.

LO 7 | Explain how self-determination theory relates to motivation.

SELF-DETERMINATION THEORY Building on the ideas of both Maslow and Erik Erikson, Edward Deci and Richard Ryan (2008) proposed the **self-determination theory (SDT)**, which suggests that humans are born with three universal, fundamental needs that are always driving us in the direction of optimal functioning: competence, relatedness, and autonomy (Stone, Deci, & Ryan, 2009). Competence represents the need to reach our goals through successful mastery of day-to-day responsibilities. Imagine a college student preparing for a psychology exam and passing with flying colors. She takes on the challenge while gaining the skills needed to accomplish her goal. Relatedness is the need to create meaningful and lasting relationships. We are all intrinsically motivated to establish bonds that allow us to share our deepest thoughts and hurts. Autonomy means managing one's behavior to reach personal goals. Deciding on a major as you move one step closer to a career is an example of autonomy. When autonomy is threatened (for example, when parents are strict and controlling of their adolescent children), frustration may increase (Van Petegem, Soenens, Vansteenkiste, & Beyers, 2015). Self-determination theory does not focus on overcoming one's shortcomings, but on moving in a positive direction.

NEED FOR ACHIEVEMENT In the early 1930s, Henry Murray proposed that humans are motivated by 20 fundamental needs. One of these has been the subject of a great deal of research: the **need for achievement (n-Ach)**, or a drive to reach attainable and challenging goals, especially in the face of competition. Other researchers suggested that people tend to seek out situations that provide

Breaking Fast
Iraqi families gather for Iftar, the evening meal eaten after the daytime fast. During the holy month of Ramadan, Muslims foreswear food, water, tobacco, and chewing gum from dawn to dusk. "As defined in the Qur'an, fasting is a strict practice of deep personal worship in which Muslims seek the highest level of awareness of the Divine" (Ilias, Tayeh, & Pachoundakis, 2016, p. 147). Here, basic needs (food and water) are put on hold for something more transcendent. Johan Spanner/Polaris.

CONNECTIONS

In **Chapter 8,** we introduced Erikson's theory of psychosocial development, which suggests that stages of development are marked by a task or emotional crisis. These crises often touch on issues of competence, relatedness, and autonomy.

self-actualization The need to be one's best and strive for one's fullest potential.

self-determination theory (SDT) Suggests that humans are born with the needs for competence, relatedness, and autonomy, which are always driving us in the direction of growth and optimal functioning.

need for achievement (n-Ach) A drive to reach attainable and challenging goals, especially in the face of competition.

opportunities for satisfying this need (McClelland, Atkinson, Clark, & Lowell, 1976). A child who aspires to become a professional basketball player might start training at a very young age, read books about the sport, and apply for basketball camp scholarships. A high school student dead set on going to college may schedule meetings with the college counselor, take practice SATs, and read books about how to write an exceptional application essay.

NEED FOR POWER Some people are motivated by a **need for power (n-Pow)**, or a drive to control and influence others (McClelland et al., 1976). People with this need may project their importance through outward appearances. They may drive around in luxury cars, wear flashy designer clothing, and buy expensive houses.

👥 In Class: Collaborate and Report

In your groups, **A)** discuss the major theories of motivation. **B)** Choose a behavior you would like to increase through motivation. **C)** Apply each of the different theories to the selected behavior and discuss their advantages and disadvantages.

Whatever your needs may be, there is a good chance you try to fulfill some of them with the help of digital technology. Ninety percent of adults between the ages of 18 and 29 use Facebook and other social media sites (Pew Research Center, 2015, October 8). What needs are these young people trying to satisfy?

SOCIAL MEDIA AND PSYCHOLOGY
Network Needs

Social media users are driven by the desire for love and belongingness—the third level from the bottom on Maslow's hierarchy. Facebook, in particular, seems to appeal to people who struggle to get those needs met offline. As one group of researchers put it, "Lonely individuals who are shy and have low social support may turn to Facebook to compensate for their lack of social skills and/or social networks in [face-to-face] settings" (Song et al., 2014, p. 450). This begs the question: Does using Facebook help people feel less lonely?

FACEBOOK: A CURE FOR LONELINESS?

Social media can either intensify or reduce feelings of loneliness, and this partly depends which activities you choose to engage in. Using social media to strengthen offline relationships appears to be beneficial (DiSalvo, 2010). So, too, is *active Facebook use,* or engaging others with messages, comments, and other communication tools. On the other hand, *passive Facebook use,* or consuming content created by others, is more apt to make you sad. This activity, which includes viewing other people's photos and status updates, may lead to feelings of envy, and thereby decrease "affective well-being" (Verduyn et al., 2015). In other words, it diminishes positive emotions. Perhaps you have experienced this firsthand: While browsing through the Facebook and Instagram posts of friends, you get the impression that their lives are more exciting and interesting than your own. If ever you find yourself in this scenario, remember that people often use these platforms to portray themselves in the most flattering ways. Perhaps more importantly, recognize that passively viewing other people's content is unlikely to satisfy your need for love and belongingness. Find a way to connect with friends more directly, online and offline. Comment on a new post, send a message, or make plans to spend time together in person. 💬

In the next section, we return our focus to the base of Maslow's pyramid, where basic drives such as hunger and thirst are represented. Sadly, many people in the world do not get those needs fulfilled.

Does It Make You Sad?
Social media may be a great way to keep up with friends and family, but how does it affect your well-being? In one study, researchers asked Facebook users to abstain from using the site for one week. Meanwhile, the control group continued using Facebook as usual. At the end of the experiment, those who had taken a break from Facebook reported "a significantly higher level of life satisfaction" (The Happiness Research Institute, 2015, p. 6). Martin Dimitrov/Getty Images.

need for power (n-Pow) A drive to control and influence others.

 **show what you know**

1. Your instructor suggests that gender differences in dating behavior are ultimately motivated by evolutionary forces. She is using which of the following to support her explanation?
   a. operant conditioning
   b. arousal theory
   c. instinct theory
   d. homeostasis

2. The _____ theory of motivation suggests that the need to maintain homeostasis motivates us to meet our biological needs.
   a. arousal
   b. instinct
   c. incentive
   d. drive-reduction

3. According to Maslow, the biological and psychological needs that motivate us to behave are arranged in a _____.

4. Self-determination theory proposes that we are motivated by three universal, fundamental needs: competence, relatedness, and autonomy. Describe one example for each of these needs.

5. How does drive-reduction motivation differ from arousal motivation?

✓ CHECK YOUR ANSWERS IN APPENDIX C.

Back to Basics: Hunger

STARVING IN SOMALIA Like many Somali Americans, Mohamed regularly sends money back home to relatives in need. Without assistance from family members living in more prosperous countries like the United States, many Somalis would not be able to afford food, medicine, and other necessities. As Mohamed says, "You can't just leave your family back home to starve."

In the spring of 2011, the Horn of Africa was hit by a drought that plunged Somalia into one of the greatest humanitarian crises of our time—a famine responsible for the starvation deaths of 250 children every day, or 1 child every 6 minutes (British Broadcasting Corporation [BBC], 2011, July 22). Refugees poured out of Somalia by the thousands. Desperate for food, they walked for weeks to reach refugee camps in neighboring countries. Aid workers said they encountered wounded children, dehydrated and emaciated, arriving at the camps with no shoes (BBC, 2011, June 28). According to a 2011 report, nearly half of Somalia's population was in need of "lifesaving assistance" (United Nations Office for the Coordination of Humanitarian Affairs, 2011, September 5). The situation has since improved, but food shortages continue (BBC, 2016, September 20). ●

Food Aid
A Somali woman hauls a bag of food aid through the massive Dadaab refugee settlement in Kenya. When famine struck the Horn of Africa in 2011, tens of thousands of Somalis fled their homeland and resettled in overcrowded refugee camps like Dadaab (Gettleman, 2011, July 15). Oli Scarff/Getty Images.

In the coming pages, we will explore hunger, one of the most powerful motivators of human behavior. You will learn what happens in the brain and body when a person is in dire need of food, or eating in excess. Let's start our exploration, beginning with the stomach.

Hungry Brain, Hungry Body

It's midnight; you are struggling to get through the final pages of your psychology chapter. Suddenly, your stomach lets out a desperate gurgling cry. "Feed me!" *Time to heat up that frozen burrito,* you say to yourself as you head into the kitchen. But wait! Are you really hungry?

LO 8 Discuss how the stomach and the hypothalamus make us feel hunger.

THE STOMACH AND HUNGER In a classic study, Walter Cannon and A. L. Washburn (1912) sought to answer this question (well, not this *exact* question, but they did want to learn what causes stomach contractions). Here's a brief synopsis of the experiment: To help monitor and record his stomach contractions, Washburn swallowed a balloon that the researchers could inflate. The researchers also kept track of Washburn's hunger levels, having him push a button anytime he felt "hunger pangs." What did the experiment reveal? Anytime he felt those hunger pangs, his stomach

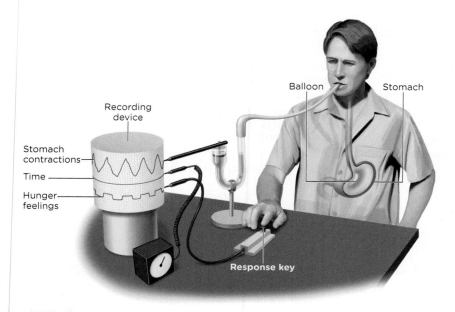

FIGURE 9.1

Cannon and Washburn's Classic Hunger Study

Washburn swallowed a special balloon attached to a device designed to monitor stomach contractions. While the balloon was in place, he pressed a key every time he felt hungry. Comparing the record of key presses against the balloon measurements, Washburn was able to show that stomach contractions accompany feelings of hunger.

CONNECTIONS

In **Chapter 2,** we described hormones as chemical messengers released in the bloodstream. Hormones do not act as quickly as neurotransmitters, but their messages are more widely spread throughout the body. Here, we see how hormones are involved in communicating information about hunger and feeding behaviors.

CONNECTIONS

In **Chapter 1,** we discussed naturalistic observation, which studies participants in their natural environments. One important feature of this descriptive research is that the experimenters do not disturb participants or their environment. Here, we assume the researchers measured and recorded the meals without interfering with participants' behaviors.

indeed contracted. Do stomach contractions always mean that we are hungry? The answer is yes . . . and no (**FIGURE 9.1**).

BLOOD SUGAR AND HUNGER Cannon and Washburn's experiment demonstrates that the stomach plays an important role in hunger, but it's just one small piece of the puzzle. One reason we know this is that most cancer patients who have had their stomachs surgically removed do not differ from people with their stomachs intact in regard to feelings of satiety (that is, feeling full) or the amount of food eaten during a meal (Bergh, Sjöstedt, Hellers, Zandian, & Södersten, 2003; Karanicolas et al., 2013). We also must consider the chemicals in the blood, such as glucose, or blood sugar. When glucose levels dip, the stomach and liver send signals to the brain that something must be done about this reduced energy situation. The brain, in turn, initiates a sense of hunger.

THE HYPOTHALAMUS AND HUNGER One part of the brain that helps regulate hungry feelings is the hypothalamus, which can be divided into functionally distinct areas. When the *lateral hypothalamus* is activated, appetite increases. Such occurs even in well-fed animals if this region is stimulated electrically. Destroy this area of the brain, and animals lose interest in food, even to the point of starvation. The lateral hypothalamus is also involved in motivating behavior, ultimately helping to preserve the balance between energy supply and demand (Leinninger, 2011; Stamatakis et al., 2016).

If the *ventromedial hypothalamus* becomes activated, appetite declines, causing an animal to stop eating. Disable this region of the brain, and the animal will overeat to the point of obesity. The ventromedial hypothalamus receives information about levels of blood glucose and other feeding-related stimuli, as it, too, works to maintain the body's energy balance (Drougard, Fournel, Valet, & Knauf, 2015; King, 2006).

The hypothalamus has a variety of sensors that react to information about appetite and food intake. Once this input is processed, appropriate responses are communicated via hormones in the bloodstream (**INFOGRAPHIC 9.2**). One such hormone is *leptin,* a protein emitted by fat cells that plays a role in suppressing hunger. Another is *insulin,* a pancreatic hormone involved in controlling levels of glucose in the bloodstream. With input from these and other hormones, the brain can monitor energy levels and respond accordingly. This complex system enables us to know when we are hungry, full, or somewhere in between.

Let's Have a Meal: Cultural and Social Context

Biology is not the only factor influencing eating habits. We must also consider the culture and social context in which we eat. In the United States, most of our social activities, holidays, and work events revolve around food. We may not even be hungry, but when presented with a spread of food, we find ourselves eating. All too often we eat too fast, rushing to our next event, class, or meeting, not taking the time to experience the sensation of taste. We tend to match our food intake to those around us, although we may not be aware of their influence (Herman, Roth, & Polivy, 2003; Vartanian, Spanos, Herman, & Polivy, 2015). Gender plays a role in eating habits as well. Using naturalistic observation, researchers found that women choose lower-calorie meals or eat less when trying to impress others (Young, Mizzau, Mai, Sirisegaram, & Wilson, 2009; Vartanian, 2015).

Mechanisms in Hunger Regulation

We are all aware—sometimes uncomfortably so—when our stomachs are grumbling. But most hunger signals are communicated in an imperceptible cycle throughout our bodies. Feelings of hunger and satisfaction are the result of many independent signals. Different organs are involved in monitoring blood chemistry, prompting the communication of hunger or satiety signals to the brain. These messages are received by the hypothalamus, which regulates basic physiological needs. Separate areas of the hypothalamus then send signals to other parts of the brain, motivating us to increase or decrease eating.

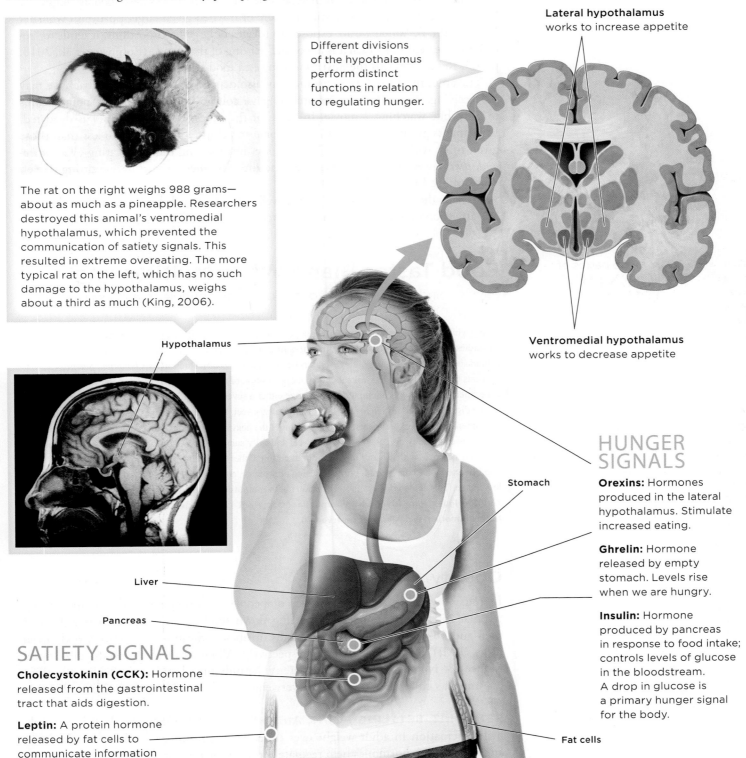

The rat on the right weighs 988 grams—about as much as a pineapple. Researchers destroyed this animal's ventromedial hypothalamus, which prevented the communication of satiety signals. This resulted in extreme overeating. The more typical rat on the left, which has no such damage to the hypothalamus, weighs about a third as much (King, 2006).

Different divisions of the hypothalamus perform distinct functions in relation to regulating hunger.

Lateral hypothalamus works to increase appetite

Ventromedial hypothalamus works to decrease appetite

Hypothalamus

Liver

Pancreas

Stomach

Fat cells

SATIETY SIGNALS

Cholecystokinin (CCK): Hormone released from the gastrointestinal tract that aids digestion.

Leptin: A protein hormone released by fat cells to communicate information about the body's fat stores.

HUNGER SIGNALS

Orexins: Hormones produced in the lateral hypothalamus. Stimulate increased eating.

Ghrelin: Hormone released by empty stomach. Levels rise when we are hungry.

Insulin: Hormone produced by pancreas in response to food intake; controls levels of glucose in the bloodstream. A drop in glucose is a primary hunger signal for the body.

Credits: Young woman eating red apple, © Piotr Marcinski/Agefotostock; Rats, The rise, fall, and resurrection of the ventromedial hypothalamus in the regulation of feeding behavior and body weight, Bruce M. King, *Physiology & Behavior*, Volume 87, Issue 2, 28 February 2006, pages 221–244; MRI, midsagittal section, showing a normal brain, highlighting the hypothalamus (orange), © ISM/Phototake.

PORTION DISTORTION A variety of factors drive our decisions to eat, including social influence, hunger, and satiety (Vartanian, Herman, & Polivy, 2016). But more subtle variables, such as portion size, also come into play. In one study, participants at a movie theater were given free popcorn; some received medium-sized buckets and others large buckets. Some of the buckets contained popcorn that was fresh, and others were filled with popcorn that was 14 days old. Participants given large buckets consistently ate 33% more than those who received medium-size buckets, regardless of whether the popcorn was fresh or stale. The stale popcorn was described as "soggy" or "terrible," yet the participants still ate more of it when given larger portions (Wansink & Kim, 2005). When we are exposed to images of large food portions, it tends to "recalibrate perceptions of what is a 'normal' serving of that food" (Robinson et al., 2016, p. 32). Remember this the next time you see a food commercial on TV.

The amount of food we consume may also depend on the visual feedback we may be receiving. To study this, researchers gave college students tubes of potato chips to eat while watching a movie. In some of the tubes, every 7th chip was dyed red. Participants given tubes with the occasional red chips consumed 50% less than those given tubes with no red chips. Thus we see, interrupting mindless eating (*Wait a second, that's a red chip*) can decrease the amount of food consumed in one sitting (Geier, Wansink, & Rozin, 2012).

Perhaps the best strategy for eating well is to savor each bite, rather than dividing our attention between meals and other activities.

from the pages of
SCIENTIFIC AMERICAN

Food Tastes Bland While Multitasking

Paying mindful attention to one's food leads people to eat less but savor it more.

Eating while distracted is well known to cause overindulgence, as confirmed by a recent review of 24 studies published in April 2013 in the *American Journal of Clinical Nutrition*. The exact mechanism behind such mindless bingeing, however, has been unclear. A recent study in *Psychological Science* suggests that mentally taxing tasks dampen our perception of taste, causing us to eat more. In four experiments, participants attempted to memorize either a seven-digit number (a heavy load on the brain) or one digit (a light cognitive load) while tasting salty, sweet, and sour substances and rating each food's taste intensity. In all experiments, participants under the heavy cognitive load rated each type of taste as less intense, and they also ate more of the sweet and salty substances. The researchers believe cognitive load may compete with sensory input for our attention. Other studies have found that simply paying mindful attention to one's food—fully focusing on its taste, aroma and texture, for example—leads to less intake. This study adds yet another reason not to multitask at mealtime: your food will taste better.

Obesity

In today's world, a growing number of people are struggling with obesity, fueling popular interest in strategies for cutting down food intake. Approximately 37% of men and 38% of women are overweight or obese—meaning they have a body mass index (BMI) that exceeds 25 or 30, respectively (Albuquerque, Stice, Rodríguez-López, Manco, & Nóbrega, 2015). Adults aren't the only ones battling the bulge; one-third of America's children and teens are overweight (American Heart Association, 2014b).

SET POINT, SETTLING POINT, AND HEREDITY Surprisingly, there is relatively little fluctuation in adult weight over time. The communication between the brain and the appetite hormones help regulate the body's **set point**, or stable weight that we tend to maintain despite variability in day-to-day exercise and intake of food. This "antiquated but still popular" theory states that if you don't consume enough calories and your weight falls below this set point, metabolism decreases, causing you to gain weight and return to your set point (deShazo, Hall, & Skipworth, 2015, p. 457). Exceed the set point, and metabolism increases, once again moving you back toward your stable weight (deShazo et al., 2015; Keesey & Hirvonen, 1997). The set point acts like a thermostat, helping to maintain a consistent weight in part through changes in metabolism.

Some critics of the set point model suggest that it fails to appreciate the importance of social and environmental influences (Stroebe, van Koningsbruggen, Papies, & Aarts, 2013). These theorists suggest we should consider a *settling point,* which is less rigid and might explain how the "set" point can actually change based on the relative amounts of food consumed and energy used. A settling point may also help us understand how body weight can shift to a newly maintained weight, and why so many people are overweight as a result of environmental factors, such as bigger meal portions, calorie-dense foods, increased dining at restaurants, and eating while engaged in another activity like watching television. This brings us to an important point: Eating can become a learned behavior. If you always have dinner while

Before and After

NBC *Today* co-anchor Al Roker before (left) and after his 2002 gastric bypass surgery. The procedure, which reduces the volume of the stomach and changes the way food is absorbed by the digestive system, helps people lose weight and may lead to improvements in cardiovascular health (Adams et al., 2012; Medline Plus, 2015, March 31). But Roker cautions that surgery is not a magic bullet for people struggling with obesity. "You can defeat the bypass, just as you can defeat any diet you're on," he said in an interview with *Today.* "You have to be constantly vigilant" (Celizic, 2010, June 7). In other words, exercise and healthy eating are essential even after you have had the procedure. Left: RJ Capak/WireImage/Getty Images. Right: Jason LaVeris/FilmMagic/Getty Images.

watching TV, or habitually snack before going to sleep, these activities become associated with "hunger." Conditioning is an important part of emotional eating, or eating because you feel depressed or upset (Bongers, van den Akker, Havermans, & Jansen, 2015).

Whatever your settling point may be, it is partly a result of your genetic make-up. Studies suggest that the heritability of BMI is around 65% (Speakman et al., 2011). Researchers using a longitudinal study (following participants for 25 years) reported even higher heritability (84%), and at least one study of monozygotic twins found heritability for fat mass to be as high as 90% (Albuquerque et al., 2015). More research is needed, but it seems we may be genetically predisposed to stay within a certain weight range.

OVEREATING, SLEEP, AND SCREEN TIME As you well know, deciding what and when to eat does not always come down to being hungry or full. We must consider how motivation plays a role in our eating patterns. Some people eat not because they are hungry, but because they are bored, sad, or anxious. Others eat simply because the clock indicates that it is mealtime. Higher brain regions involved in eating decisions can override the hypothalamus, driving you to devour that cheesy burrito even when you don't need the calories.

This type of overeating is one factor contributing to the growing public health problem of *obesity.* Obesity is both a physiological and psychological issue. There is some evidence that genes play a role, and we also know some illnesses (such as Cushing's disease) can lead to weight gain (Geer et al., 2016; Plomin et al., 2013). But one often overlooked lifestyle factor related to obesity is sleep. Preliminary research suggests that

set point The stable weight that is maintained despite variability in exercise and food intake.

TABLE 9.2 WEIGHT LOSS: MAKING IT FIT

Strategies	Description
Set realistic goals.	Set goals and expectations that are specific, realistic, and flexible.
Get regular exercise.	Exercising 30 minutes a day 5 times a week can help with weight loss. Add a variety of physical activities to your daily routines.
Eat regularly and track intake.	Eat on a set schedule to minimize mindless eating. Eat only when hungry, and write down what and how much you consume by keeping a food diary.
Control portions.	Watch your portions. This is the amount you decide to eat. Read labels to determine the recommended serving size.
Drink water.	Eliminate sweetened beverages like soda.
Join a weight-loss support group.	Social support helps promote healthier coping strategies and accountability.

Losing weight is not an easy task, but it doesn't have to be painful. Making basic lifestyle changes in your daily routines can have significant benefits. Information from Kruger, Blanck, and Gillespie (2006).

inadequate sleep is linked to weight problems (a negative correlation exists between sleep and weight gain). In contrast, individuals who sleep between 6 and 8 hours are more likely to lose weight. Additionally, a positive correlation exists between screen time (that is, using a tablet, smartphone, computer, or television) and weight gain: The more screen time, the more weight gain. It seems that screen time interferes with making healthy eating choices and getting regular exercise (Buchanan et al., 2016; Elder et al., 2012; Elder, Ammar, & Pile, 2015).

To lose weight, one must eat less and move more (**TABLE 9.2**); in other words, use more calories than you are taking in. Our ancestors didn't have to worry about this. They *had* to choose foods rich in calories to give them energy to sustain themselves. Although this was a very efficient means of survival for them, it doesn't work out so well for us. When experiencing a "famine" (a decrease in the caloric intake our bodies are accustomed to), our metabolism naturally slows down; we require fewer calories and have a harder time losing weight.

In response to the obesity problem in the United States, policies have been implemented to raise awareness and discourage overeating. One such intervention is requiring information about calories to be clearly labeled, which can serve as a visual cue or reminder. Providing this information can impact healthy food choices. However, accessibility to comparably priced healthy alternatives must be increased (in vending machines, for example)—but this, too, may require changes in policy (Stroebe et al., 2013).

 show what you know

1. Washburn swallowed a special balloon to record his stomach contractions. He also pressed a button to record his feelings of hunger. The findings indicated that whenever he felt hunger, his:
   a. stomach was contracting. c. blood sugar went up.
   b. stomach was still. d. ventromedial hypothalamus was active.

2. Describe how the hypothalamus triggers hunger and influences eating behaviors.

3. Let's revisit the case of your hypothetical midnight burrito craving presented on page 389. Considering the physical, cultural, and social factors that cause hunger, would you say you were truly hungry? Why?

✓ CHECK YOUR ANSWERS IN APPENDIX C.

Emotion

Rubberball/
Superstock.

SHARK ATTACK For those longing for a quiet beach escape, Ocracoke Island on the North Carolina coast is hard to beat. Wrapped in 16 miles of pristine beach, Ocracoke is a perfect place for building sandcastles, collecting seashells, and riding waves. Circumstances are ideal for young children, except for the occasional rip current. Oh, and there's one more thing: Beware of sharks.

One summer night, 6-year-old Lucy Mangum was splashing around on her boogie board at her family's favorite Ocracoke beach. She was close to shore in water no deeper than 2 feet. Suddenly, Lucy let out a spine-chilling scream. Her mother Jordan, just feet away, spotted the fin of a shark cutting through the water. Running to swoop up her daughter, Jordan did not realize what had occurred—until she saw the blood streaming from her daughter's right leg, which was "completely open" from heel to calf (Allegood, 2011, July 27). The shark had attacked Lucy.

Jordan did the right thing. She applied pressure to the gushing wound and called for help. Lucy's father Craig, who happens to be an emergency room doctor, rushed over and looked at the wound. Right away, he knew it was severe and needed immediate medical attention (Stump, 2011, July 26). In the moments following the attack, Lucy was remarkably calm. "Am I going to die?" she asked her mom. "Absolutely not," Jordan replied. "Am I going to walk?" Lucy asked. "Am I going to have a wheelchair?" It was too early to know (CBS News, 2011, July 26, para. 16). ●

Lucy the Brave
Lucy Mangum was just 6 years old when she was attacked by a shark in the shallow waters of Ocracoke Island in North Carolina. Mangum family archives.

What Is Emotion?

Unprovoked shark attacks are extremely uncommon, occurring less than 100 times per year worldwide. And most attacks are not fatal. To put things in perspective, you are 75 times more likely to be killed by a bolt of lightning and 33 times more likely to be killed by a dog (Florida Museum of Natural History, 2014). Despite their rarity, shark attacks seem to be particularly fear provoking. Maybe the thought of becoming the prey of a wild creature reminds us that we are still, at some level, animals: vulnerable players in the game of natural selection.

Fear is an emotion you experience throughout your life. When you were a baby, you might have been afraid of the vacuum cleaner or the hair dryer. As you matured, your fears may have shifted to the dog next door or the monster in the closet. These days, you might be scared of growing older, being diagnosed with a serious disease, or losing someone you love.

LO 9 Define emotions and explain how they are different from moods.

What exactly is fear? That's an easy question: Fear is an emotion. Now here's the hard question: What is an *emotion?* An **emotion** is a psychological state that includes a subjective or inner experience. In other words, emotion is intensely personal; we cannot actually feel each other's emotions firsthand. Emotion also has a physiological component; it is not only "in our heads." For example, anger can make you feel hot, anxiety might cause sweaty palms, and sadness may sap your physical energy. Finally, emotion entails a behavioral expression often seen in our faces. We scream and run when frightened, gag in disgust, and shed tears of sadness. Think about the last time you felt joyous. What was your inner experience of that joy, how did your body react, and what would someone have noticed about your behavior?

emotion A psychological state that includes a subjective or inner experience, a physiological component, and a behavioral expression.

Thus, emotion is a subjective psychological state that includes both physiological and behavioral components. But are these three elements—psychology, physiology, and behavior—equally important, and in what order do they occur? Experts agree on some fronts, but these "big questions" are still being explored (Davidson, Scherer, & Goldsmith, 2002; Ekman, 2016). Given the complexity of emotion, it should come as no surprise that its definition is debated and that academics and scientists from many fields and perspectives study it (Coan, 2010; Ekman, 2016).

MOODS VERSUS EMOTIONS Most psychologists agree that emotions are different from moods. Emotions are quite strong, but they don't generally last as long as moods, and they are more likely to have an identifiable cause. An emotion is initiated by a stimulus, and it is more likely than a mood to motivate someone to action. Moods are longer-term emotional states that are less intense than emotions and do not appear to have distinct beginnings or ends (Kemeny & Shestyuk, 2008; Matlin & Farmer, 2016; Oatley, Keltner, & Jenkins, 2006). An example might help clarify: Imagine your mood is happy, but a car cuts you off on the highway, creating a negative emotional response like anger. Fortunately, this flash of anger is likely to vanish as quickly as it appeared, and your happy mood persists.

Now let's see how the three distinguishing characteristics of emotion (as opposed to moods) might apply to Lucy's situation. When Lucy's mother saw the wound from the shark bite, she remembers feeling "afraid" (CBS News, 2011, July 26). Her emotion (1) had a clear cause (the shark attacking her daughter), (2) likely produced a physiological reaction (heart racing, for example), and (3) motivated her to action (applying pressure to the wound and calling for help).

LANGUAGE AND EMOTION If you were Lucy's mom, what words would you have used to describe your fear—"frightened," "terrified," "horrified," "scared," "petrified," "spooked," "aghast"? Having a variety of labels at your disposal certainly helps when it comes to communicating your emotions. "I feel *angry* at you" conveys a slightly different meaning than "I feel *resentful* of you," or "I feel *annoyed* by you." Words not only facilitate communication; they also influence our perceptions of emotions, and "perhaps even emotional experiences" (Lindquist, Satpute, & Gendron, 2015, p. 1). Imagine that diamonds were called "doodleboogers"—do you think they would inspire the same emotions as "diamonds"?

The English language includes about 200 words to describe emotions. But does that mean we are capable of feeling only 200 emotions? Probably not. Words and emotions are not one and the same, but they are closely linked. In fact, their relationship has captivated the interest of linguists from fields as different as anthropology, psychology, and evolutionary biology (Majid, 2012).

Rather than focusing on words or labels, scholars typically characterize emotions along different dimensions. American psychologist Carroll Izard (2007) suggests that we can describe emotions according to valence and arousal (**FIGURE 9.2**). The *valence* of an emotion refers to how pleasant or unpleasant it is. Happiness, joy, and satisfaction are on the pleasant end of the valence dimension; anger and disgust lie on the unpleasant end. The *arousal level* of an emotion describes how active, excited, and involved a person is while experiencing the emotion, as opposed to how calm, uninvolved, or passive she may be. With valence and arousal level, we can compare and contrast emotions. The emotion of ecstasy, for example, has a high arousal level and a positive valence. Feeling relaxed has a low arousal level and a positive valence.

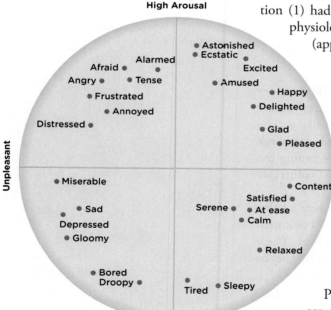

FIGURE 9.2
Dimensions of Emotion
Emotions can be compared and contrasted according to their valence (how pleasant or unpleasant they are) and their arousal level. Copyright © 2005 by the American Psychological Association. Adapted with permission from Lyubomirsky, S., Sheldon, S.M., & Schkade, D. (2005). Pursuing happiness: The architecture of sustainable change. *Rev Gen Psychol*, 9, 111–131.

When Lucy looked down and saw the shark, she likely experienced an intense fear—high arousal, but negative valence. Fortunately, for Lucy and her family, fear eventually gave way to more positive emotions. Let's find out what happened.

○ ✓ ○ ○ **show what you know**

1. _____ is a psychological state that includes a subjective or inner experience, physiological component, and behavioral expression.
   a. Valence
   b. Instinct
   c. Mood
   d. Emotion

2. Emotions can be described along two dimensions: valence and _____.

3. On the way to a wedding, you get mud on your clothing. Describe how your emotion and mood would differ.

✓ CHECK YOUR ANSWERS IN APPENDIX C.

Theories of Emotion

FIGHT BACK Within 35 minutes of the attack, Lucy was lifted off Ocracoke Island by helicopter and on her way to a trauma center in Greenville, North Carolina. The damage to her leg was extensive, with large tears to the muscle and tendons. She would need two surgeries, extensive physical therapy, and a wheelchair for some time after leaving the hospital (WRAL.com, 2011, July 26).

How did Lucy hold up during this period of extreme stress? According to lead surgeon Dr. Richard Zeri, the 6-year-old was "remarkably calm" (Allegood, 2011, July 27). She even forgave the shark: "I don't care that the shark bit me," she told reporters, "I forgive him" (Stump, 2011, July 26, para. 4). But Lucy also seemed to harbor some negative feelings, at least initially. "I hate sharks," she told her parents (Stump, 2011, July 26, para. 2). "I should have kicked him in the nose," she reportedly said (Allegood, 2011, July 27, para. 3). Fighting back is not an unusual response; some victims have prevented sharks from attacking by grabbing their tails, punching them in the gills, and gouging their eyes (Cabanatuan & Sebastian, 2005, October 19; Caldicott, Mahajani, & Kuhn, 2001). ●

Emotion and Physiology

Such acts of self-defense are mediated by the sympathetic nervous system's **fight-or-flight** response (Chapter 12). When faced with a crisis situation like a shark attack, stress hormones are released into the blood; breathing rate increases; the heart pumps faster and harder; blood pressure rises; the liver releases extra glucose into the bloodstream; and blood surges into the large muscles. All these physical changes prepare the body for confronting or fleeing the threat; hence the expression "fight or flight." But fear is not the only emotion that involves dramatic physical changes. Tears pour from the eyes during intense sadness and joy. Anger is associated with sweating, elevated heart rate, and heightened blood flow to the hands, apparently in anticipation of a physical confrontation (Ekman, 2003). If you find yourself angry and want to bring your heart rate and blood flow back down to normal, take a moment and focus on your breathing. Researchers have shown that just a single meditation session can help reduce the physiological responses to anger (Fennell, Benau, & Atchley, 2016).

CONNECTIONS

In **Chapter 2,** we explained how the sympathetic nervous system prepares the body to respond to an emergency, whereas the parasympathetic nervous system brings the body back to a noncrisis mode through the "rest-and-digest" process. Here, we see how the autonomic nervous system is involved in physiological experiences of emotion.

LO 10   List the major theories of emotion and describe how they differ.

Most psychologists agree that emotions and physiology are deeply intertwined, but they have not always agreed on the precise order of events. What happens first: the

Ha Ha Ha!
Does laughing make you happy? According to the James-Lange theory of emotion, yes. It suggests that a behavioral response such as laughing paves the way for an emotion (happiness). Some clinicians actually incorporate "laugh therapy" into their treatment, and encouraging results have been seen in cancer patients and elderly people (Demir, 2015; Ko & Youn, 2011). Blend Images/ Shutterstock.

James–Lange theory of emotion
Suggests that a stimulus initiates the experience of a physiological and/or behavioral reaction, and this reaction leads to the feeling of an emotion.

Cannon–Bard theory of emotion
Suggests that environmental stimuli are the starting point for emotions, and physiological or behavioral responses occur at the same time emotions are felt.

body changes associated with emotion or the emotions themselves? That's a no-brainer, you may be thinking. Emotions occur first, and then the body responds. American psychologist William James would have disagreed.

JAMES–LANGE THEORY In the late 1800s, William James and Danish physiologist Carl Lange (1834–1900) independently derived similar explanations for emotion (James, 1890/1983; Lange & James, 1922). What is now known as the **James–Lange theory of emotion** suggests that a stimulus initiates a physiological reaction (for example, the heart pounding, muscles contracting, a change in breathing) and/or a behavioral reaction (such as crying or striking out) *before* we feel an emotion (**INFOGRAPHIC 9.3**). Emotions *do not* cause physiological or behavioral reactions to occur, as common sense might suggest. Instead, "we feel sorry because we cry, angry because we strike, afraid because we tremble" (James, 1890/1983, p. 1066). In other words, changes in the body and behavior pave the way for emotions. Our bodies automatically react to stimuli, and awareness of this physiological response leads to the subjective experience of an emotion.

How might the James–Lange theory apply to our shark attack victim Lucy? It all begins with a stimulus—in this case, the appearance of the shark and the pain of the bite. Next occur the physiological reactions (increased heart rate, faster breathing, and so on) and the behavioral responses (screaming, trying to swim away). Finally, the emotion registers. Lucy feels fear. Imagine that Lucy, for some reason, had no physiological reaction to the shark—no rapid heartbeat, and so forth. Would she still experience the same degree of terror? According to the James–Lange theory, no. Lucy might see the shark and decide to flee, but she wouldn't *feel* afraid.

The implication of the James–Lange theory is that each emotion has its own distinct physiological fingerprint. If this were the case, it would be possible to identify an emotion based on a person's physiological/behavioral responses. Sadness and anger, for example, would have distinct physiological and behavioral characteristics. PET scans have confirmed that different emotions such as happiness, anger, and fear do indeed have distinct activation patterns in the brain, lending evidence in support of the James–Lange theory (Berthoz, Blair, Le Clec'h, & Martinot, 2002; Carlsson et al., 2004; Damasio et al., 2000; Salimpoor, Benovoy, Larcher, Dagher, & Zatorre, 2011). As proponents of the James–Lange theory explain, "Feelings are the consequences, not the causes, of emotional behavior and bodily response" (Laird & Lacasse, 2014, p. 32).

However, critics of the James–Lange theory of emotion suggest it cannot fully explain emotional phenomena because (1) people who are incapable of feeling physiological reactions of internal organs (as a result of surgery or spinal cord injuries, for example) can still experience emotions; (2) the speed of an emotion is much faster than physiological changes occurring in internal organs; and (3) when physiological functioning of internal organs is altered (through a hormone injection, for instance), emotions do not necessarily change (Bard, 1934; Cannon, 1927; Hilgard, 1987). In one experiment, researchers used surgery to stop animals from becoming physiologically aroused, yet the animals continued to exhibit behaviors associated with emotions, such as growling and posturing (Cannon, 1927).

CANNON–BARD THEORY American physiologist Walter Cannon (1871–1945) and his student Philip Bard (1898–1977) were among those who believed the James–Lange theory could not explain all emotions (Bard, 1934; Cannon, 1927). The **Cannon–Bard theory of emotion** suggests that we do not feel emotion as a result of physiological and behavioral reactions; instead, the emotions and the body

Theories of Emotion

Imagine you are swimming and you think you see a shark. Fear pierces your gut, sending your heart racing as you swim frantically to shore. Or is it actually your churning stomach and racing heart that cause you to feel so terrified? And what part, if any, do your thoughts play in this process?

Psychologists have long debated the order in which events lead to emotion. Let's compare four major theories, each proposing a different sequence of events.

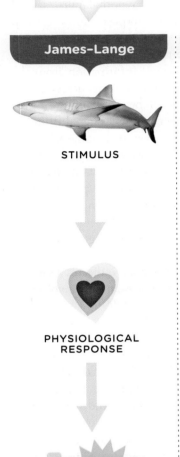

Body changes lead to emotions.

James-Lange

STIMULUS

↓

PHYSIOLOGICAL RESPONSE

↓

FEAR

EMOTION

Body changes and emotions happen together.

Cannon-Bard

STIMULUS

PHYSIOLOGICAL RESPONSE   EMOTION
                                FEAR

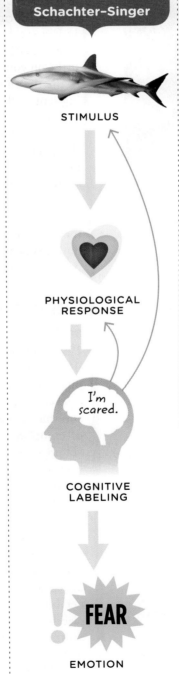

Our thoughts about our body changes lead to emotions.

Schachter-Singer

STIMULUS

↓

PHYSIOLOGICAL RESPONSE

↓

I'm scared.
COGNITIVE LABELING

↓

FEAR

EMOTION

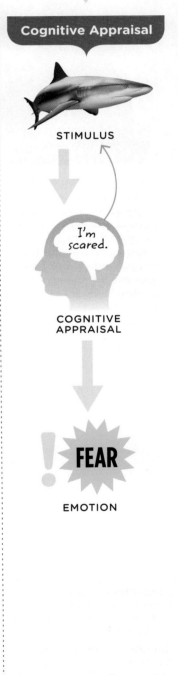

Our thoughts about our situation lead to emotions.

Cognitive Appraisal

STIMULUS

↓

I'm scared.

COGNITIVE APPRAISAL

↓

FEAR

EMOTION

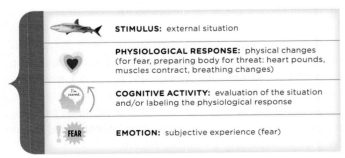

STIMULUS: external situation

PHYSIOLOGICAL RESPONSE: physical changes (for fear, preparing body for threat: heart pounds, muscles contract, breathing changes)

COGNITIVE ACTIVITY: evaluation of the situation and/or labeling the physiological response

EMOTION: subjective experience (fear)

Credits: Sharks, Rich Carey/Shutterstock.

How Would You Feel?
A diver comes face-to-face with a crocodile while swimming off the coast of Quintana Roo, Mexico. If you were this unlucky diver, what would you experience first—the emotion of fear, a physiological response (increased heart rate), or a behavioral reaction (flinching)? The Cannon–Bard theory of emotion suggests that all these events would occur simultaneously. Rodrigo Friscione/Getty Images.

Schachter–Singer theory of emotion Suggests that the experience of emotion is the result of physiological arousal and a cognitive label for this physiological state.

cognitive appraisal approach Suggests that the appraisal or interpretation of interactions with surroundings causes an emotional reaction.

responses occur *simultaneously* (Infographic 9.3). The starting point of this response is a stimulus in the environment.

Let's use the Cannon–Bard theory to see how the appearance of a snake might lead to an emotional reaction. Imagine you are about to crawl into bed for the night. You pull back the sheets, and there, in YOUR BED, is a snake! According to the Cannon–Bard theory, the image of the snake will stimulate sensory neurons to relay signals in the direction of your cortex. But rather than rushing to the cortex, these signals pass through the thalamus, splitting in two directions—one toward the cortex and the other toward the hypothalamus.

When the neural information reaches the cortex and hypothalamus, several things could happen. First, the "thalamic–hypothalamic complex will be thrown into a *state of readiness*" (Krech & Crutchfield, 1958, p. 343), in a sense, waiting for the determination of whether the message will continue to the skeletal muscles and internal organs, instructing them to react. The neural information from the thalamus will arrive in the cortex at the same time, enabling you to "perceive" the snake on your bed. If it is just a rubber snake, this news will be sent from the cortex to the thalamic–hypothalamic complex, preventing the emergency signal from being sent to the skeletal muscles and internal organs. However, if the object in your bed is a real snake, then the emergency message will be forwarded to your skeletal muscles and internal organs, prompting a physiological and/or behavioral response (heart racing, jumping backward). It is at this point, along with the perception of the snake, that an emotion is experienced. The emotion and physiological reaction occur simultaneously.

Critics of the Cannon–Bard theory suggest that the thalamus might not be capable of carrying out this complex processing on its own and that other brain areas may contribute (Beebe-Center, 1951; Hunt, 1939). Research indicates that the limbic system, hypothalamus, and prefrontal cortex are also substantially involved in processing emotions (Kolb & Whishaw, 2015; Northoff et al., 2009).

Cognition and Emotion

SCHACHTER–SINGER THEORY American psychologists Stanley Schachter (1922–1997) and Jerome E. Singer (1934–2010) also took issue with the James–Lange theory, primarily because different emotions do not have distinct and recognizable physiological responses (Schachter & Singer, 1962). They suggested there is a *general* pattern of physiological arousal caused by the sympathetic nervous system, and this pattern is common to a variety of emotions. The **Schachter–Singer theory of emotion** proposes that the experience of emotion is the result of two factors: (1) physiological arousal, *followed by* (2) a cognitive label for this physiological state (the arousal). According to this theory, if someone experiences physiological arousal, but doesn't know why it has occurred, she will label the arousal and explain her feelings based on her "knowledge" of the environment and previous experiences (that is, in recognition of the context of the situation). Depending on the "cognitive aspects of the situation," the physiological arousal might be labeled as joy, fear, anxiety, fury, or jealousy (Infographic 9.3).

To test their theory, Schachter and Singer injected participants (male college students) with either epinephrine to mimic physiological reactions of the sympathetic nervous system (such as increased blood pressure, respiration, and heart rate) or a placebo. The researchers also divided the participants into the following groups: those who were informed correctly about possible side effects (for example, tremors, palpitations, flushing, or accelerated breathing), those who were misinformed about side effects, and others who were told nothing about side effects.

The participants were left in a room with a "stooge," a confederate secretly working for the researchers, who was either euphoric or angry. When the confederate behaved euphorically, the participants who had been given no explanation for their physiological arousal were more likely to report feeling happy or appeared happier. When the confederate behaved angrily, participants given no explanation for their arousal were more likely to appear or report feeling angry. Through observation and self-report, it was clear the participants who did not receive an explanation for their physiological arousal could be manipulated to feel either euphoria or anger, depending on the confederate they were paired with. The participants who were accurately informed about side effects did not show signs or report feelings of euphoria or anger. Instead, they accurately attributed their physiological arousal to the side effects clearly explained to them at the beginning of the study (Schachter & Singer, 1962).

Some have criticized the Schachter–Singer theory, suggesting it overstates the link between physiological arousal and the experience of emotion (Reisenzein, 1983). Studies have shown that people can experience an emotion without labeling it, especially if neural activity sidesteps the cortex, heading straight to the limbic system (Dimberg, Thunberg, & Elmehed, 2000; Lazarus, 1991a). We will discuss this process in the upcoming section on fear.

COGNITIVE APPRAISAL AND EMOTION Rejecting the notion that emotions result from cognitive labels of physiological arousal, American psychologist Richard Lazarus (1984, 1991a) suggested that emotion is the result of the way people appraise or interpret interactions they have in their surroundings. It doesn't matter if someone can label an emotion or not; he will experience the emotion nonetheless. We've all felt emotions such as happiness, anxiety, and shame, and we don't need an agreed upon label or word to experience them. Babies, for example, can feel emotions long before they are able to label them with words.

Lazarus also suggested that emotions are adaptive, because they help us cope with the surrounding world. In a continuous feedback loop, as an individual's appraisal or interpretation of his environment changes, so do his emotions (Folkman & Lazarus, 1985; Lazarus, 1991b). Emotion is a very personal reaction to the environment. This notion became the foundation of the **cognitive appraisal approach** to emotion (Infographic 9.3), which suggests that the appraisal causes an emotional reaction. In contrast, the Schachter–Singer theory asserts the arousal comes first and then has to be labeled, leading to the experience of an emotion.

Responding to the cognitive-appraisal approach, social psychologist Robert Zajonc (ZI-yunce; 1984) suggested that thinking does not always have to be involved when we experience an emotion. As Zajonc (1980) saw it, emotions can precede thoughts and may even cause them. He also suggested we can experience emotions without interpreting what is occurring in the environment. Emotion can influence cognition, and cognition can influence emotion.

One of the main areas of disagreement among the theories just described concerns the role of cognition. Forgas (2008) proposed that the association between emotion and cognitive activity is complex and bidirectional: "Cognitive processes determine emotional reactions, and, in turn, affective states influence how people remember, perceive, and interpret social situations and execute interpersonal behaviors" (p. 99).

Emotions are complex and closely related to cognition, physiology, and perception (Farb, Chapman, & Anderson, 2013). We know, for example, that certain physiological changes are likely to occur when a person is frightened, anxious, or attempting to conceal deceit. In fact, some important technologies are built on this very premise. Perhaps you've heard of the polygraph?

Do Polygraphs Work?
A new recruit undergoes a polygraph, or "lie detector," test at the FBI Academy. The polygraph operates on the premise that emotions are accompanied by measurable physiological changes. When some people lie, they experience changes in breathing rate, blood pressure, and other variables controlled by the autonomic nervous system (Nelson, 2014). By monitoring these variables, the polygraph can theoretically detect when a person feels stressed from lying (APA, 2004). However, critics are skeptical of the findings often used to endorse this technology (Nelson & Handler, 2013; Rosky, 2013). Anna Clopet/Getty Images.

CONNECTIONS

In **Chapter 2,** we described how fMRI technology reveals patterns of blood flow in areas of the brain, which is a good indicator of how much oxygen is being used as a result of activity there. Here, we see how researchers are trying to use this technology to detect lying.

CONTROVERSIES
Problems with Polygraphs

➡️ ⬅️ Since its introduction in the early 1900s, the polygraph, or "lie detector," test, has been used by government agencies for a variety of purposes, including job screening, crime investigation, and spy identification (Department of Justice, 2006; Nelson, 2014). The FBI (along with many police departments) will not even hire applicants for certain positions unless they undergo a thorough background check, which includes a polygraph (Federal Bureau of Investigation n.d.). Despite the widespread use of this technology, many scientists have serious doubts about its validity, and emphasize the importance of considering the complex interactions of the brain and the body ("True Lies," 2004, April 15; Palmatier & Rovner, 2015).

JUST HOW ACCURATE ARE POLYGRAPH TESTS?

What is this so-called lie detector and how does it work? The polygraph is a machine that attempts to determine if someone is lying by measuring physiological arousal presumed to be associated with deceit. When people lie, they often experience changes in breathing rate, blood pressure, and other variables controlled by the autonomic nervous system (Nelson, 2014). By monitoring such variables, the polygraph can theoretically detect when a person is being honest or deceitful.

But here's the problem: Biological signs of anxiety do not always go hand-in-hand with deception. There are many other reasons one might experience physiological changes while taking a polygraph test, among them "fear, anxiety, anger, and many medical or mental conditions" (Rosky, 2013, p. 2). Some estimates of polygraph accuracy are as high as 90%, but critics contend that studies often cited to justify the use of the polygraph are riddled with methodological problems and have not been subjected to proper peer review (Nelson & Handler, 2013; Rosky, 2013). Searching for a better alternative, some have turned to fMRI lie detection, but the accuracy and validity of this technology have also been questioned (Farah, Hutchinson, Phelps, & Wagner, 2014). According to one group of researchers, the ability of fMRI to detect lying is "better than chance but far from perfect" (Monteleone et al., 2009, p. 537). Currently, neither polygraph nor fMRI evidence is considered admissible in court, but that doesn't mean lie detectors will never serve a role in our judicial system (Stroud, 2015, February 2). The technology is evolving fast, so stay tuned for future developments. ➡️ ⬅️

👥 In Class: Collaborate and Report

Team up and discuss the use of polygraphs. **A)** Should polygraphs be used as a measure of lie detection? Why or Why not? **B)** Discuss other ways people try to detect when someone is lying. Are they more or less effective than polygraphs? **C)** Given what you have just read about polygraphs, why do you think they continue to be used in various settings?

Thus, it appears that current lie detection technologies are not much better than old-fashioned observation. If we rely on body language, facial expressions, and other social cues, our lie-detection accuracy is no more than 60% (Gamer, 2009). We may not be skilled at spotting dishonesty, but we are pros at identifying basic emotions like happiness, anger, and fear.

It's Written All Over Your Face

We now know that emotions are complex and closely related to cognition, physiology, and perception. But how do these internal activities affect a person's appearance? Think about the clues you rely on when trying to "read" another person's emotions. Where do you look for signs of anger, sadness, or surprise? It's written all over his face, of course.

FACE VALUE Lucy was lucky. With a 90% tear to the muscle and tendon and a severed artery, she could have easily lost her leg. But the surgeries went well. Just a week after the horrific incident, she was flashing a bashful grin on national television. Seated between mom and dad, Lucy played with her mother's fingers, squirmed, and then nestled her head under her father's arm. She looked as bright-eyed and vibrant as any child her age (MSNBC.com, 2011, July 26).

"The prognosis is great," Lucy's father, Craig, told *Today*'s Ann Curry. "It's going to take some time and some physical therapy, but she's going to be, you know, back and running and playing like she should" (MSNBC.com, 2011, July 26). The look on Craig's face was calm, happy. Jordan also appeared relieved. Their little girl was going to be okay.

Suppose you knew nothing about Lucy's shark attack, and someone showed you an image of Lucy's parents during that television interview. Would you be able to detect the relief in their facial expressions? How about someone from Nepal, Trinidad, or Bolivia: Would a cultural outsider also be able to "read" the emotions written across Craig and Jordan's faces? ●

Road to Recovery
Despite the large cast on her leg, Lucy looks happy and healthy. Her shark-bite injuries were severe, but she received prompt, high-quality medical care. Mangum family archives.

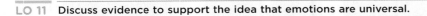

LO 11 Discuss evidence to support the idea that emotions are universal.

Writing in *The Expression of the Emotions in Man and Animals* (1872/2002), Charles Darwin suggested that interpreting facial expressions is not something we learn but rather is an innate ability that evolved because it promotes survival. Sharing the same facial expressions allows for communication. Being able to identify the emotions of others—like fear in a friend who has just spotted a snake slithering your way—would seem to come in handy. If facial expressions are truly unlearned and universal, then people from all different cultures ought to interpret them in the same way. A "happy face" should look much the same wherever you go, from the United States to the Pacific island of New Guinea.

EKMAN'S FACES Some five decades ago, American psychologist Paul Ekman (1934–) traveled to a remote mountain region of New Guinea to study an isolated group of indigenous peoples. Ekman and his colleagues were very careful in selecting their participants, choosing only those who were unfamiliar with *Western facial behaviors*—people who were unlikely to know the signature facial expressions we equate with basic emotions like disgust and sadness. The participants didn't speak English, nor had they watched Western movies, worked for anyone with a Caucasian background, or lived among Westerners. The study went something like this: The researchers told the participants stories conveying various emotions such as fear, happiness, and anger. In the story conveying fear, for example, a man is sitting alone in his house with no knife, axe, bow, or any weapon to defend himself. Suddenly, a wild pig appears in his doorway, and he becomes frightened that the pig will bite him. Next, the researchers asked the participants to match the emotion described in the story to a picture of a person's face (choosing from 6–12 sets of photographs). The results indicated that the same facial expressions represent the same basic emotions across cultures—and this finding has been replicated approximately 200 times (Ekman & Friesen, 1971; Ekman & Keltner, 2014, April 10). And so it seems, a "happy face" really does look the same to people in the United States and New Guinea.

Further evidence for the universal nature of these facial expressions is apparent in children born blind; although they have never seen a human face demonstrating

Universal Expressions

A smile in Kenya (top left) means the same thing as a smile in Lithuania (top middle) or India (top right). Facial expressions for other basic emotions such as sadness (middle row) and anger (bottom row) are also strikingly similar across cultures (Ekman & Friesen, 1971). Top row, left to right: M Lohmann/agefotostock; Wojtek Buss/agefotostock; Design Pics Inc/Alamy Stock Photo. Middle row, left to right: Rieko Honma/Getty Images; Giantstep Inc/Getty Images; Ravi Shekhar/Dinodia Photo/AGE Fotostock. Bottom row, left to right: khoa vu/Getty Images; Kerry Lorimer/Getty Images; Ezra Bailey/Getty Images.

an emotion, their smiles and frowns are similar to those of sighted children (Galati, Scherer, & Ricci-Bitti, 1997; Matsumoto & Willingham, 2009).

In Class: Collaborate and Report

In your groups, have everyone take out a piece of paper and sketch faces (or emoticons) demonstrating happiness, sadness, disgust, anger, surprise, and fear. Compare your faces with others in your group. Describe the similarities. Are there many differences?

LO 12 Indicate how display rules influence the expression of emotion.

ACROSS THE WORLD
Can You Feel the Culture?

Although the expression of some basic emotions appears to be universal, culture acts like a filter, determining the appropriate contexts in which to exhibit them. According to Mohamed (the Somali American we introduced earlier in the chapter), people from Somalia tend to be much less expressive than those born in the United States. "I have | **WHEN TO REVEAL, WHEN TO CONCEAL** cousins who have just come to America, and even [now] when they have been here for about five years, they still like to keep to themselves about personal feelings," says Mohamed. This is especially true when it comes to interacting with people outside the immediate family.

These differences Mohamed observes are probably reflections of display rules. A culture's **display rules** provide the framework or guidelines for when, how, and where an emotion is expressed. Think about some of the display rules in American culture. Negative emotions such as anger are often hidden in social situations. Suppose you are

display rules Framework or guidelines for when, how, and where an emotion is expressed.

facial feedback hypothesis The facial expression of an emotion can affect the experience of that emotion.

furious at a friend for embarrassing you at a party. You probably won't reveal your anger when you encounter her in class, surrounded by other students. Other times, display rules compel you to express an emotion you are *not* feeling. Your friend gives you a birthday gift that really isn't your style. Do you say, "Thank you, but this isn't really me. I think I'll exchange it for a store credit," or "Thank you so much" and smile graciously?

In North America, where individualism prevails, people tend to be fairly expressive. Showing emotion, particularly positive emotions, is socially acceptable. This is less the case in the collectivist societies of East Asia, where concealing emotions is more the norm. Display rules are taught early in life, as parents show approval or disapproval of children's emotional expressions. For example, Korean and Asian American parents appear more inclined than European American parents to favor "modesty and suppression of children's emotions and to use shaming and love withdrawal to control children" (Louie, Oh, & Lau, 2013, p. 429). Why do collectivist cultures tend to discourage emotional displays? Showing emotions, particularly anger, can threaten the social harmony that is highly valued by collectivist cultures (Louie et al., 2013).

However, we cannot solely attribute variations in display rules to collectivism and individualism because there are key distinctions within these two categories. For example, the United States and Germany (both considered individualistic) appear to have different display rules for contempt and disgust, with Americans being more inclined to reveal these emotions (Koopmann-Holm & Matsumoto, 2011). To fully understand the origins of display rules, we must explore how expressions of *specific* emotions (not simply emotions in general) are influenced by a variety of cultural values (Hareli, Kafetsios, & Hess, 2015; Koopmann-Holm & Matsumoto, 2011). 🌐

FACIAL FEEDBACK HYPOTHESIS While we are on the topic of emotional displays, let's take a brief detour back to the very beginning of the chapter when Mohamed arrived in his first-grade classroom speaking no English. Without a common language to communicate, Mohamed turned to a more universal form of communication: smiling. It is probably safe to assume that most of Mohamed's classmates took this to mean he was enjoying himself, as smiling is viewed as a sign of happiness in virtually every corner of the world. It also seems plausible that Mohamed's smiling had a positive effect on his classmates, making them more likely to approach and befriend him. But how do you think the act of smiling affected Mohamed?

Believe it or not, the simple act of smiling can make a person *feel* happier. Although facial expressions are caused by the emotions themselves, they sometimes affect the experience of those emotions. This is known as the **facial feedback hypothesis** (Buck, 1980), and if it is correct, we should be able to manipulate our emotions through our facial activities. Try this for yourself.

> *try this* ➜ Take a pen and put it between your teeth, with your mouth open for about half a minute. Now, consider how you are feeling. Next, hold the pen with your lips, making sure not to let it touch your teeth, for half a minute. Again, consider how you are feeling.

If you are like the participants in a study conducted by Strack, Martin, and Stepper (1988), holding the pen in your teeth should result in your seeing the objects and events in your environment as funnier than if you hold the pen with your lips. Why would that be? Take a look at the photo to the right and note how the person holding the pen in his teeth seems to be smiling—the feedback of those smiling muscles leads to a happier mood.

We are now nearing the end of this chapter—and what an emotional one it has been! Before wrapping things up, let's examine various kinds of emotions humans can experience, narrowing our gaze onto fear and happiness.

Facial Feedback
Holding a pencil between your teeth (top) will probably put you in a better mood than holding it with your lips closed (bottom). This is because the physical act of smiling, which occurs when you place the pencil in your teeth, promotes feelings of happiness. So next time you're feeling low, don't be afraid to flex those smile muscles! Robert M. Errera.

◯ ✓ ◯ ◯ show what you know

1. The _____ theory of emotion suggests that changes in the body and behavior lead to the experience of emotion.

2. _____ of a culture provide a framework for when, how, and where an emotion is expressed.
   a. Beliefs
   b. Display rules
   c. Feedback loops
   d. Appraisals

3. The _____ suggests the expression of an emotion can affect the experience of an emotion.
   a. James–Lange theory
   b. Cannon-Bard theory
   c. Schachter–Singer theory
   d. facial feedback hypothesis

4. Name two ways in which the Cannon–Bard and Schachter–Singer theories of emotion are different.

5. What evidence exists that emotions are universal?

✓ CHECK YOUR ANSWERS IN APPENDIX C.

Types of Emotions

Imagine the whirlwind of emotions you would feel if you witnessed a loved one being attacked by a shark. Fear is probably the most obvious, but there may be others, including *anger* toward the shark, *disgust* at the sight of blood, *anxiety* about the outcome, *gratitude* toward those who came to the rescue, and *guilt* ("it should have been me").

Are such feelings common to all people? Some researchers have proposed that there is a set of "biologically given" emotions, which includes anger, fear, disgust, sadness, and happiness (Coan, 2010). However, some who study facial expressions contend there may be only four patterns of universally recognized emotions—happiness, sadness, surprise/fear, and disgust/anger (Jack, Sun, Delis, Garrod, & Schyns, 2016). These types of feelings are considered *basic emotions* because people all over the world experience and express them in similar ways; they appear to be innate and have an underlying neural basis (Izard, 1992). The fact that children born deaf and blind have the same types of emotional expressions (happiness, anger, and so on) suggests these emotions are universal (Hess & Thibault, 2009).

It is also noteworthy that unpleasant emotions (fear, anger, disgust, and sadness) have survived throughout our evolutionary history, and are more prevalent than positive emotions such as happiness, surprise, and interest (Ekman, 1992; Forgas, 2008; Izard, 2007). This suggests that negative emotions have "adaptive value"; in other words, they may be useful in dangerous situations, like those that demand a fight-or-flight response (Adolphs, 2013; Forgas, 2008; Friedman, Stephens, & Thayer, 2014).

Jaws the Terrible
The 1975 movie *Jaws* was America's first "summer blockbuster." *Jaws* told the tale of a great white shark that stalked beachgoers in a summer vacation spot. So frightening were the film's story and imagery that many Americans stopped going to the beach that summer (BBC, 2001, November 16). Universal/The Kobal Collection at Art Resource.

The Biology of Fear

LO 13   Describe the role the amygdala plays in the experience of fear.

Have you ever wondered what takes place in your brain when you feel afraid? Researchers certainly have. With the help of brain-scanning technologies, they have zeroed in on an almond-shaped structure in the limbic system (Cheng, Knight, Smith, & Helmstetter, 2006; Pape & Pare, 2010). This structure, known as the amygdala, is central to our experience of fear (Méndez-Bértolo et al., 2016; Davis & Whalen, 2001; Hariri, Tessitore, Mattay, Fera, & Weinberger, 2002). If a person views threatening images, or even looks at an image of a frightened face, the amygdala is activated (Chiao et al., 2008; Laeng et al., 2010; Méndez-Bértolo et al., 2016).

PATHWAYS TO FEAR What exactly does the amygdala do? When confronted with a fear-provoking situation, the amygdala enables an ultrafast and unconscious response. Sensory information (sights, sounds) entering the thalamus can either go to the cortex for processing, or head straight for the amygdala without stopping at the cortex (LeDoux, 1996, 2000, 2012). The direct path that goes from the thalamus to the amygdala conveys raw information about the threat, enabling your brain and body to respond to danger without your awareness. Like a panic button, the amygdala issues an alert, summoning other parts of the brain that play a role in the experience of fear (for example, the hypothalamus and medulla), which then alert the sympathetic nervous system. A pathway also goes to the pituitary gland, resulting in the secretion of stress hormones (LeDoux, 2012).

Let's see how this immediate fear response might play out using the snake-in-the-bed example from earlier in the chapter. Visual information about the snake goes directly to the thalamus, and from there to the amygdala, which triggers an alarm reaction. Your heart rate increases and breathing becomes rapid, preparing you to flee the slithery reptile. Meanwhile, information that was sent to the sensory processing centers of the visual cortex results in a visual representation of the snake. Let's suppose the "snake" is merely a rubber toy planted by a mischievous child. In this case, your cortex sends a message to the amygdala: "False alarm. The snake in the bed is a rubber toy." The key thing to note is that it takes longer for neural information to go from the thalamus to the cortex than from the thalamus to the amygdala. This explains why one generally needs a moment to calm down: The physiological reaction starts before the false alarm message from the cortex reaches the amygdala (**INFOGRAPHIC 9.4** on the next page).

EVOLUTION AND FEAR American neuroscientist Joseph LeDoux suggests an evolutionary advantage to having direct and indirect routes for processing information about potential threats (2012). The direct route (thalamus to amygdala, causing an emotional reaction) enables us to react quickly to threats for which we are biologically prepared (snakes, spiders, aggressive faces). The other pathway allows us to evaluate more complex threats (such as nuclear weapons, job layoffs) with our cortex, overriding the fast-response pathway when necessary.

The amygdala also plays an important role in the creation of "emotional memories," which are fairly robust and detailed (Johnson, LeDoux, & Doyère, 2009; LeDoux, 2002). This is useful because we are more likely to survive if we remember threats in our environments. For some people, however, emotional memories cause troublesome fear and anxiety (Chapter 12).

AUTONOMIC NERVOUS SYSTEM AND FEAR Earlier in the chapter, we discussed the fight-or-flight response. In a stressful situation, the sympathetic nervous system, which is a part of the autonomic nervous system, automatically and quickly activates a variety of physiological responses. Blood pressure increases, goose bumps appear, hair stands on end, pupils dilate, digestion stops, blood sugar increases, and so on. A similar response can also occur with some other emotions such as love and joy (Adolphs, 2013; Levenson, 1992; Shiota, Neufeld, Yeung, Moser, & Perea, 2011). But separating the physiological profiles of emotions can get tricky, as they often overlap. For example, fear, anger, and sadness are all accompanied by an increased heart rate (Ekman, 2003; Rhudy & Meagher, 2000). Anger is associated with heightened skin temperature and a greater increase in heart rate than fear. Meanwhile, fear promotes increased blood flow to the legs and decreased skin temperature in the hands (Ekman, Levenson, & Friesen, 1983).

Research suggests that the biological response patterns accompanying basic emotions are innate and universal (they appear to be preprogrammed and shared by all). These patterns are the same irrespective of gender or age, although responses in older adults tend to be less extreme (Levenson, Carstensen, Friesen, & Ekman, 1991).

What happens to these automatic responses when the amygdala is not working? Animal studies suggest that damage to the amygdala impairs the fear response (Bliss-Moreau, Bauman, & Amaral, 2011; Phillips & LeDoux, 1992). Similarly, people

The Anatomy of Fear

You instantly recoil when you spot a snake—then sigh with relief just a moment later when it registers that the snake is a rubber toy. Have you ever wondered why you react with fear when a "threat" turns out to be nothing? Why does it take longer for you to process a threat than react to it? Sensory information (sight, sound) entering the brain travels to the thalamus and is then routed to the cortex for processing. Sensory information can also go directly to the amygdala. In the case of a threat, the amygdala alerts other areas of the brain and the endocrine system instantly without waiting for a conscious command. This enables a response to fear before you are even fully aware of what you are reacting to.

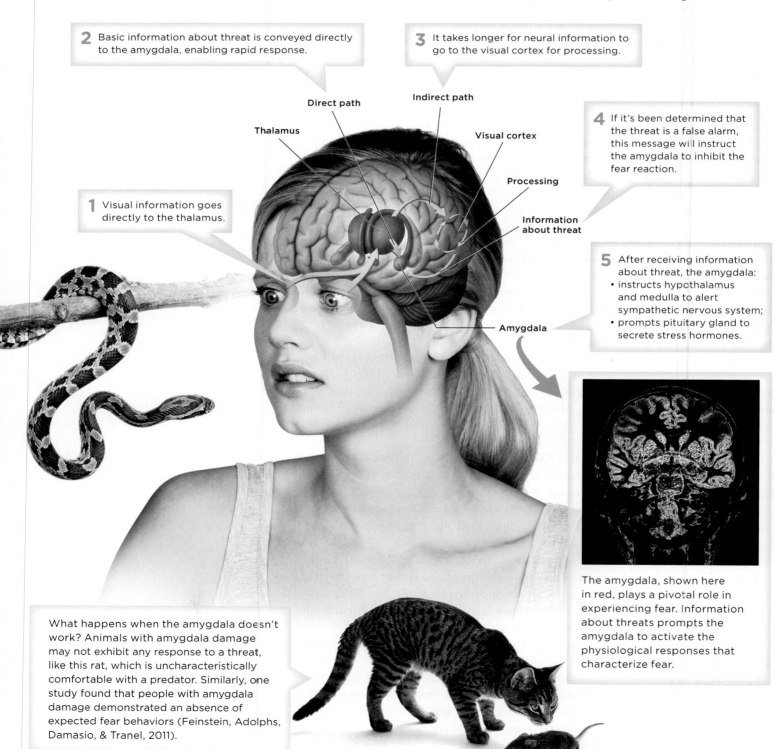

2 Basic information about threat is conveyed directly to the amygdala, enabling rapid response.

3 It takes longer for neural information to go to the visual cortex for processing.

Direct path

Indirect path

Thalamus

Visual cortex

4 If it's been determined that the threat is a false alarm, this message will instruct the amygdala to inhibit the fear reaction.

Processing

1 Visual information goes directly to the thalamus.

Information about threat

5 After receiving information about threat, the amygdala:
• instructs hypothalamus and medulla to alert sympathetic nervous system;
• prompts pituitary gland to secrete stress hormones.

Amygdala

What happens when the amygdala doesn't work? Animals with amygdala damage may not exhibit any response to a threat, like this rat, which is uncharacteristically comfortable with a predator. Similarly, one study found that people with amygdala damage demonstrated an absence of expected fear behaviors (Feinstein, Adolphs, Damasio, & Tranel, 2011).

The amygdala, shown here in red, plays a pivotal role in experiencing fear. Information about threats prompts the amygdala to activate the physiological responses that characterize fear.

Credits: T1 weighted MRI image of the brain demonstrates normal cerebral anatomy, Living Art Enterprises/Science Source; Alarmed woman, Brand New Images/Getty Images; Snake, Eric Isselee/Shutterstock; Mouse, S-F/Shutterstock; Cat, Kitchin & Hurst/Agefotostock.

with a damaged amygdala exhibit weaker-than-normal responses to stimuli that inspire fear or disgust (Buchanan, Tranel, & Adolphs, 2004). They also have difficulty perceiving emotion and comprehending nonverbal behavior associated with emotion (Adolphs, 2008).

Happiness

In the very first chapter of this book, we introduced the field of positive psychology, "the study of positive emotions, positive character traits, and enabling institutions" (Seligman & Steen, 2005, p. 410). Rather than focusing on mental illness and abnormal behavior, positive psychology emphasizes human strengths and virtues. The goal is well-being and fulfillment, and that means "satisfaction" with the past, "hope and optimism" for the future, and "flow and happiness" at the current time (Seligman & Csikszentmihalyi, 2000). Let's take a moment to explore that flow and happiness of the present.

THINK POSITIVE
Going with the Flow

👍 People often make the mistake of viewing happiness as a goal they will attain at some point in the future, when all of life's pieces fall into place: "Once I start making a lot of money and buy a house, I will be happy," or, "If I just lose 10 pounds, I will finally be content." What they don't realize is that happiness may be within grasp, right here and right now. Sometimes it's just a matter of getting into the "flow."

IS IT THE SECRET TO ACHIEVING HAPPINESS?

Have you ever felt completely absorbed in a challenging task, guided by a focus so intense that everything else, including the past and future, faded from your awareness? Some people call it being "in the zone"; Hungarian-born psychologist Mihaly Csikszentmihalyi (me-HIGH CHEEK-sent-me-hi-ee; 1934–) refers to it as "flow" and considers it a prerequisite for happiness (Csikszentmihalyi, 1999). To get into the flow, you must be engaged in a task that is intrinsically rewarding and challenging (but not so challenging that it makes you feel anxious); aware of what you need to accomplish from one minute to the next; and receiving feedback during the process (Csikszentmihalyi, 1975, 1999).

Activities that lend themselves to flow include "fun activities" such as chess, rock climbing, dancing, and composing music, but it can also be achieved during more ordinary tasks associated with work and school (Csikszentmihalyi, 1990; Culbertson, Fullagar, Simmons, & Zhu, 2015). In the classroom, you are most likely to experience flow while performing tasks that afford you some control and require active participation, such as group work and individual assignments (Shernoff, Csikszentmihalyi, Shneider, & Shernoff, 2003). So next time the opportunity arises, try to get into the flow by giving the activity your undivided attention and being fully present in the moment. You may become more interested in the material and enjoy the process. What's more, your positive experience may rub off on those around you, as flow appears to be somewhat contagious (Culbertson et al., 2015). 👍

Flow is one of the secrets to achieving happiness, and it can be experienced by anyone. However, some of us seem more inclined toward happiness than others. Why is this so?

The Brighter Side
Psychologist Martin Seligman is a leading proponent of positive psychology, which emphasizes the goodness and strength of the human spirit. Getting the most out of life, according to Seligman, means not only pursuing happiness, but also cultivating relationships, achieving goals, and being deeply engaged in meaningful activities (Szalavitz, 2011, May 13). Courtesy Positive Psychology Center, University of Pennsylvania/ Martin Seligman.

LO 14 Summarize evidence pointing to the biological basis of happiness.

THE BIOLOGY OF HAPPINESS To what degree do we inherit happiness? Happiness has heritability estimates between 35% and 50%, and as high as 80% in longitudinal

CONNECTIONS

In **Chapter 8,** we described some of the temperaments exhibited by infants. About 40% can be classified as easy babies, meaning they are relatively happy and easy to soothe, follow regular schedules and quickly adjust to changes in the environment. This early evidence of temperament lends support to the biological basis of happiness discussed here.

CONNECTIONS

In **Chapter 5,** we presented the concept of habituation, a basic form of learning in which repeated exposure to an event generally results in a reduced response. Here, we see the same effect can occur with events that result in happiness. With repeated exposure, we will habituate to an event that initially elicited happiness.

studies (Nes, Czajkowski, & Tambs, 2010). In other words, a sizable proportion of the population-wide variation in happiness, life satisfaction, and well-being can be explained by genetic make-up, as opposed to environmental factors.

Research suggests that the biological basis of happiness may include a "set point" similar to the set point for body weight (Bartels et al., 2010; Lyubomirsky, Sheldon, & Schkade, 2005). Happiness tends to fluctuate around a fixed level, which is influenced by genes and related to temperament. We may experience periodic ups and downs, but ultimately we move back toward that fixed level of happiness.

Some researchers suggest that the set point theory fails to account for the variety of events that impact well-being over a lifetime. One such event is marriage. Research suggests that people who marry are generally happier than those who remain single throughout life. This disparity appears to result from differences in experience rather than variations in happiness set points (Anusic, Yap, & Lucas, 2014).

INCREASING HAPPINESS That being said, the happiness brought about by positive life events does not seem to last forever (Diener, Lucas, & Scollon, 2006; Mancini, Bonanno, & Clark, 2011). We tend to become habituated to events that make us feel happy rather quickly. If you win the lottery, get a new job, or buy a beautiful house, you will likely experience an increased level of happiness for a while, but then go back to your baseline, or "set point," of happiness (Lyubomirsky et al., 2005). Things that feel new and improved or life-changing quickly become mundane, suggesting that happiness will not be found in new possessions or shopping sprees. The implication is that we need to be careful when pursuing happiness as a goal in life, as we don't want to emphasize obtaining a specific outcome (like moving to a house near the ocean) or acquiring a desired object (Lyubomirsky et al., 2005). Our focus should not be on becoming happier, but rather on being content with what we have (Lyubomirsky, Dickerhoof, Boehm, & Sheldon, 2011).

With this in mind, there are many steps you can take to maximize enjoyment of your life right now. Engaging in physical exercise, showing kindness, and getting involved in activities that benefit others are all linked to increased positive emotions (Lyubomirsky et al., 2011; Lyubomirsky & Layous, 2013; Walsh, 2011). The same can be said for recording positive thoughts and feelings of gratefulness in a journal. One group of researchers asked participants to write down in a diary those aspects of their lives for which they were grateful each day. The researchers measured well-being and found that the participants in the diary group were better off than those not counting their blessings. The participants who recorded their blessings were also more likely to report they had helped or offered emotional support to another person (Emmons & McCullough, 2003). An additional way to increase happiness is to identify and actively pursue goals that will have an important effect on your life (Brunstein, 1993). Write down what you are trying to accomplish and take action to make it happen. Researchers have found that "simple intentional changes in one's thoughts and behaviors can precipitate meaningful increases in happiness" (Lyumbomirsky & Layous, 2013, p. 60). Knowing what you are actively working toward and committing to attainable goals are associated with increased feelings of well-being and happiness. There may be a genetic component to happiness, but nature isn't everything. Life is what you make of it, and happiness is yours to discover.

We can better understand happiness with the *broaden-and-build model* of positive emotions, first introduced by American psychologist Barbara Fredrickson (1998, 2000, 2004, 2013). This model suggests that positive emotions *broaden,* or expand, our focus and awareness, enabling us to see the big picture. "Joy sparks the urge to play, interest sparks the urge to explore, contentment sparks the urge to savour and integrate, and love sparks a recurring cycle of each of these urges within safe, close relationships" (Fredrickson, 2004, p. 1367). As our focus and awareness broaden, we are able to identify possibilities and resources that would otherwise go unrecognized. For example, children's physical play may strengthen their gross motor, cognitive, and social skills, which might come in handy in future situations that don't involve play.

In Class: Collaborate and Report

Can money buy happiness? Team up and **A)** discuss how money can be used to influence happiness. **B)** Imagine your group has been given $200 to spend in a way that impacts the happiness of everyone in your group. How will you spend that money? **C)** How would you spend $2000? **D)** How did the different amounts influence your spending? **E)** Compare your answers with those of other groups in the class.

Gender and Emotions

Urban myth, common sense, stereotypes, and our daily experiences in North America all lead us to believe that men and women experience and express their emotions differently, but is this true? Are women really more "emotional" than men? Do men hide their emotions? In a study that set out to examine some of these beliefs, participants were shown pictures of faces expressing emotions such as anger, happiness, and sadness (Barrett & Bliss-Moreau, 2009). Each of the faces was paired with a label stating some situational cause for its emotion (for example, a face showing anger was paired with the phrase "insulted by a stranger"). Then the participants were shown the same images without any label, and asked to state whether the individual depicted was "emotional" or "having a bad day." Female expressions were more likely to be described as emotional, whereas the male faces were more likely to be labeled as having a bad day. Apparently, the participants assumed that the female emotions stemmed from some internal characteristic (being an "overly emotional female"). Meanwhile, the men's emotions were presumed to be responses to situations or environments.

The gender differences suggested by the participants' beliefs are not necessarily accurate, however. Most psychologists studying this topic suggest that men and women are more similar than different when it comes to experiencing and expressing emotion (Else-Quest, Higgins, Allison, & Morton, 2012). As noted earlier, there are universal facial expressions, and these are similar across gender. But the notion that women are more emotional is a gross overgeneralization at best.

Who Is Emotional?
Both of these individuals appear angry, but why are they feeling this way? Research suggests that people are more likely to attribute a woman's unpleasant expression to her "emotional" disposition and a man's angry face to "having a bad day" (Barrett & Bliss-Moreau, 2009). These assumptions rest on the stereotype that women are more emotional than men. Nicole Betz, Lab Coordinator/Research Technician Interdisciplinary Affective Science Lab, Northeastern University, photo courtesy of Dr. Lisa Feldman Barret.

Happy As Ever
Mohamed got married in 2011 and graduated from the University of Minnesota in 2013. He now has three children (two girls and a boy) and is working toward his master's degree in Management of Technology at the University of St. Thomas. He also works full-time as an information technology analyst at the Minneapolis Public Housing Authority. Courtesy of Mohamed Dirie.

You Asked, Mohamed Answers

http://qrs.ly/1y5a5ef

Did you do extracurricular activities in high school, and did they help make you feel connected?

scan this ➜

That being said, research has uncovered some interesting gender disparities related to emotion. In Western cultures, girls are expected to show more positive emotions (happiness) and boys more negative ones (anger). This may be related to society's gender role expectations and stereotypes (Chaplin, 2015). Some evidence suggests that women tend to feel more guilt, shame, and embarrassment than men (Else-Quest et al., 2012). They also seem to be more adept at identifying the emotion behind a particular face (Hall & Matsumoto, 2004). We don't know if this results from biological or cultural differences (perhaps women start practicing earlier, and this ability becomes more automatic for them). Women who paid closer attention to eyes, in one study, were able to discern emotional expressions more quickly and correctly than men, suggesting that the eyes are especially important for conveying emotions (Hall, Hutton, & Morgan, 2010). With that thought in mind, take a minute and look into the eyes of Mohamed (in the photograph above). Do you see a look of happiness and tranquility? We certainly do.

 **show what you know**

1. Researchers have found that when people view images that are threatening, or when they see images of faces of people who are afraid, the _____ becomes active.

2. "Happiness has heritability estimates as high as 80%." How would you explain this statement to a fellow student?

3. When confronted by a potential threat, such as a crocodile, your heart starts pounding, your breathing speeds up, and your pupils dilate. These changes are activated by:
   a. the cognitive appraisal approach.
   b. the cortex.
   c. the sympathetic nervous system.
   d. gender differences.

✓ CHECK YOUR ANSWERS IN APPENDIX C.

Improve your grade! Use **LearningCurve** macmillan learning adaptive quizzing to create your personalized study plan, which will direct you to the resources that will help you most in **LaunchPad** macmillan learning

summary of concepts

LO 1 Define motivation. (p. 379)

Motivation is a stimulus that can direct the way we behave, think, and feel. A motivated behavior tends to be guided (that is, it has a direction), energized, and persistent. When a behavior is reinforced, an association is established between the behavior and its consequence. With motivated behavior, this association becomes the incentive, or reason, to repeat the behavior.

LO 2 Explain how extrinsic and intrinsic motivation impact behavior. (p. 379)

When a learned behavior is motivated by the incentive of external reinforcers in the environment, there is an extrinsic motivation to continue that behavior. Intrinsic motivation occurs when a learned behavior is motivated by the prospect of internal reinforcers. Performing a behavior because it is inherently interesting or satisfying exemplifies intrinsic motivation; the reinforcers originate from within.

LO 3 Summarize instinct theory. (p. 382)

Instinct theory proposes that through evolution some behaviors are etched into our genetic make-up, and are consistent from one member of the species to the next. Instincts, then, are complex behaviors that are fixed, unlearned, and consistent within a species. Although they apply to other nonhuman animals, there are limited data suggesting that humans display instincts.

LO 4 Describe drive-reduction theory and explain how it relates to motivation. (p. 383)

The drive-reduction theory of motivation suggests that human behaviors are driven by the need to maintain homeostasis—that is, to fulfill basic biological needs for nutrients, fluids, oxygen, and so on. If a need is not fulfilled, this creates a drive, or state of tension, that pushes us or motivates behaviors to meet it. Once a need is satisfied, the drive is reduced, but not forever. The need inevitably returns, and you feel driven to meet it once again.

LO 5 Explain how arousal theory relates to motivation. (p. 385)

According to arousal theory, humans seek an optimal level of arousal, which is a level of alertness and engagement in the world. What constitutes an optimal level of arousal is variable, and depends on individual differences. Some people seem to be sensation seekers; that is, they seek activities that increase arousal.

LO 6 Outline Maslow's hierarchy of needs. (p. 385)

The needs in Maslow's hierarchy, often depicted as a pyramid, are considered to be universal and are ordered in terms of the strength of their associated drive, with the most critical needs, those that are physiological, at the bottom. Moving up the pyramid are increasingly higher-level needs: safety needs; love and belongingness needs; esteem needs; self-actualization; and self-transcendence. Maslow suggested that basic needs must be met before higher-level needs motivate behavior. In some cases, people abandon their lower-level needs for a greater purpose (religion or adherence to an ideology, for example).

LO 7 Explain how self-determination theory relates to motivation. (p. 387)

This theory suggests that humans are motivated in the direction of growth and optimal functioning. According to the self-determination theory, we are born with three universal, fundamental needs: competence (reaching goals through mastery of day-to-day responsibilities), relatedness (creating meaningful and lasting relationships), and autonomy (managing behavior to reach personal goals). The focus is not on overcoming one's shortcomings, but on moving in a positive direction.

LO 8 Discuss how the stomach and the hypothalamus make us feel hunger. (p. 389)

In a classic experiment, researchers confirmed that activities in the stomach and brain accompany hunger. When glucose levels dip, the stomach and liver send signals to the brain that something must be done about this reduced energy source. The brain, in turn, initiates a sense of hunger. Signals from the digestive system are sent to the hypothalamus, which then transmits signals to higher regions of the brain. When the lateral hypothalamus is activated, appetite increases. If the ventromedial hypothalamus becomes activated, appetite declines, causing an animal to stop eating.

LO 9 Define emotions and explain how they are different from moods. (p. 395)

An emotion is a psychological state that includes a subjective or inner experience. It also has a physiological component and a behavioral expression. Emotions are quite strong, but they don't generally last as long as moods. In addition, emotions are more likely to have identifiable causes (they are reactions to stimuli), and they are more likely to motivate a person to action. Moods are longer-term emotional states that are less intense than emotions and do not appear to have distinct beginnings or ends.

LO 10 List the major theories of emotion and describe how they differ. (p. 397)

The James–Lange theory of emotion suggests there is a stimulus that initiates the experience of a physiological reaction and/or a behavioral reaction, and it is this reaction that leads to an emotion. The Cannon–Bard theory of emotion suggests that we do not feel emotion as a result of physiological and behavioral reactions; instead, all these experiences occur simultaneously. The Schachter–Singer theory of emotion suggests there is a general pattern of physiological arousal caused by the sympathetic nervous system, and this pattern is common to a variety of emotions. The experience of emotion is the result of two factors: (1) physiological arousal and (2) a cognitive label for this physiological state (the arousal). The cognitive appraisal theory suggests that the appraisal or interpretation of interactions with surroundings causes an emotional reaction.

LO 11 Discuss evidence to support the idea that emotions are universal. (p. 403)

Darwin suggested that interpreting facial expressions is not something we learn, but rather an innate ability that evolved because it promotes survival. Sharing the same facial expressions allows for communication. Research conducted among an isolated group of indigenous peoples in New Guinea indicated that the same facial expressions represent the same basic emotions across cultures. In addition, the fact that children born deaf and blind have the same types of expressions of emotion (for example, happiness and anger) suggests the universal nature of such displays.

LO 12 Indicate how display rules influence the expression of emotion. (p. 404)

Although the expression of basic emotions appears, in many cases, to be universal, culture acts like a filter to determine the specific context in which to exhibit them. That is, the display rules of a culture provide the framework or guidelines for when, how, and where an emotion is expressed.

LO 13 Describe the role the amygdala plays in the experience of fear. (p. 406)

The amygdala is an almond-shaped structure found in the limbic system and appears to be central to our experience of fear. When people view threatening images, or even look at an image of a frightened face, the amygdala is activated. When confronted with a fear-provoking situation, the amygdala enables an ultrafast and unconscious response. The amygdala also plays an important role in the creation of emotional memories. This is useful because we are more likely to survive if we remember threats in our environments.

LO 14 Summarize evidence pointing to the biological basis of happiness. (p. 409)

Happiness has heritability estimates between 35% and 50%, and as high as 80% in longitudinal studies. There may be a set point for happiness, or level around which our happiness tends to fluctuate. As we strive for personal happiness, we should keep in mind that our set point is strong, and directed by our genes and temperament.

key terms

arousal theory, p. 385
Cannon–Bard theory of emotion, p. 398
cognitive appraisal approach, p. 401
display rules, p. 404
drive, p. 383
drive-reduction theory, p. 383

emotion, p. 395
extrinsic motivation, p. 379
facial feedback hypothesis, p. 405
hierarchy of needs, p. 385
homeostasis, p. 383
incentive, p. 379

instincts, p. 382
intrinsic motivation, p. 380
James–Lange theory of emotion, p. 398
motivation, p. 379
needs, p. 383
need for achievement (n-Ach), p. 387

need for power (n-Pow), p. 388
Schachter–Singer theory of emotion, p. 400
self-actualization, p. 386
self-determination theory (SDT), p. 387
set point, p. 392

test prep *are you ready?*

1. If a mother wants her son to practice his math facts, she could allow him to play his favorite game on her tablet when he is done studying. Playing the game eventually will represent _____ for him to study his math facts.
   a. negative reinforcement
   b. intrinsic motivation
   c. satiety
   d. an incentive

2. The entire week before final exams, the resident advisor (RA) in your dorm provides delicious cookies for students who come to group study sessions in the common room. The RA seems to be using _____ to encourage students to study together.
   a. extrinsic motivation
   b. intrinsic motivation
   c. negative reinforcment
   d. instincts

3. _____ are complex behaviors that are fixed, unlearned, and consistent within a species.
   a. Drives
   c. Instincts
   b. Motivators
   d. Needs

4. Biological needs and homeostasis motivate us to meet our needs. If a need is not fulfilled, this creates a state of tension that pushes us to meet it. This describes the _____ theory of motivation.
   a. self-actualization
   c. cognitive-appraisal
   b. drive-reduction
   d. Schachter–Singer

5. Humans have different optimal levels of need for arousal. These individual differences indicate that some people are _____; they appear to seek out activities that increase arousal.
   a. sensation seekers
   c. driven by extrinsic motivation
   b. externally motivated
   d. sympathetic

6. When the _____ is stimulated electrically, it sends a hormone signal to decrease appetite. If this region of the brain is destroyed, an animal will drastically overeat.
   a. limbic system
   c. lateral hypothalamus
   b. amygdala
   d. ventromedial hypothalamus

7. Self-determination theory suggests that humans are born with three universal, fundamental needs that are always driving us in the direction of optimal functioning. These three needs are:
   a. homeostasis, drive-reduction, optimal arousal.
   b. competence, relatedness, autonomy.
   c. incentive, arousal, reflex.
   d. need for power, need for achievement, need for self-actualization.

8. According to Mihaly Csikszentmihalyi, one prerequisite for happiness is the experience of _____, which occurs when you feel completely absorbed and engaged in a challenging task that is intrinsically rewarding.
   a. homeostasis
   c. flow
   b. adaptive value
   d. tend and befriend

9. Emotion is a psychological state that includes a subjective experience, a physiological component, and a(n):
   a. mood.
   c. behavioral expression.
   b. drive.
   d. incentive.

10. To study the universal nature of emotions, Paul Ekman traveled to New Guinea to explore indigenous peoples' detection of facial expressions. Although unfamiliar with Western facial behaviors, the participants in his study:
    a. could not identify the facial expressions in the photos he showed them.
    b. could identify the facial expressions common across the world.
    c. could understand English.
    d. had no display rules.

11. The Schachter–Singer theory suggests that the experience of emotion is the result of:
    a. physiological arousal.
    b. cognitive labeling.
    c. physiological arousal and cognitive labeling.
    d. an appraisal of the environment.

12. The _____ suggests that emotion is a very personal reaction to and interpretation of the environment, and that emotion does not result from a cognitive label of physiological arousal.
    a. James–Lange theory
    b. cognitive-appraisal approach
    c. Schachter–Singer theory
    d. Cannon–Bard theory

13. The polygraph is used to determine if someone is lying by measuring:
    a. physiological arousal.
    c. activity in the amygdala.
    b. cognitive appraisal.
    d. activity in the thalamus.

14. In a fear-provoking situation, initial processing can be unconscious. Information from the thalamus can take two paths: It may go to the _____ for processing, or directly to the _____, which sets the stage by preparing the body for response to a threat.
    a. cortex; amygdala
    b. parasympathetic nervous system; cortex
    c. hypothalamus; parasympathetic nervous system
    d. parasympathetic nervous system; sympathetic nervous system

15. Evidence from research on emotions suggests that when looking at faces, women seem to:
    a. spend less time paying attention to eyes than men.
    b. be less likely to feel embarrassment than men.
    c. be less able to identify what emotion is being felt than men.
    d. be better able to identify what emotion is being felt than men.

16. What type of evidence is there for the biological basis of happiness?

17. Describe a situation you experienced in which someone's motivation did not follow the order outlined in Maslow's hierarchy of needs.

18. What role do the stomach and hypothalamus play in hunger? How do cultural and social factors influence our eating habits?

19. Describe some of the display rules you adhere to on a daily basis. Do you follow different display rules at school and at home?

20. We discussed the concept of set point for both body weight and happiness. Describe what these mean and explain how you might use this knowledge to help someone struggling with weight and/or happiness.

✓ CHECK YOUR ANSWERS IN APPENDIX C.

YOUR SCIENTIFIC WORLD
Apply psychology to the real world!
Go to LaunchPad for access.

Steve Russell/Getty Images.

BSIP SA/Alamy.

Biosphoto/Superstock.

CHAPTER OUTLINE AND LEARNING OBJECTIVES

Sex and Sexuality

LO 1 Define sex and distinguish it from gender.

LO 2 Identify the biological factors that determine sex.

LO 3 Explain some of the causes of intersexual development.

Gender

LO 4 Define gender and explain how culture plays a role in its development.

LO 5 Distinguish between transgender and transsexual.

The Birds and the Bees

LO 6 Describe the human sexual response as identified by Masters and Johnson.

LO 7 Define sexual orientation and summarize how it develops.

The Trouble with Sex

LO 8 Identify the symptoms of sexual dysfunctions.

Sex, Its Consequences, and Culture

LO 9 Classify sexually transmitted infections and identify their causes.

LO 10 Describe human immunodeficiency virus (HIV) and its role in acquired immune deficiency syndrome (AIDS).

LO 11 Define sexual scripts and describe some of the ways people deviate from sex-related cultural norms.

Wallace Kirkland/Getty Images.

Mark Buehler.

Leren Lu/Getty Images.

10 sexuality and gender

Sex and Sexuality

GUESS THE PROFESSION Stephen Patten usually walks into Portland's veteran's hospital around 6:00 A.M. Then he checks his e-mail, puts on his scrubs, and heads to the operating room to prepare for the day's surgeries. What do you think Stephen does for a living?

Stephanie Buehler spends much of her workday discussing erections, orgasms, and relationship woes. People of all different ages, ethnicities, and cultural backgrounds come to her for help with their most intimate problems. What is Stephanie's profession?

Stephen Patten is a nurse. But if you guessed he is a doctor, you're not alone. Many of Stephen's patients jump to the same conclusion when they see a man in his mid-fifties approach their bedside. Stephen is indeed unusual in his field: More than 93% of nurses in the United States are women, according to a 2013 survey (Budden, Zhong, Moulton, & Cimiotti, 2013). But there is another reason patients do a double take when this 200-pound lumberjack type walks through the door and says, "Hi, I'm Stephen. I'll be your nurse today." It has to do with our notions of masculine and feminine. In other words, it relates directly to *gender,* a concept we will explore in the upcoming pages.

Dr. Stephanie Buehler is a certified sex therapist, a psychotherapist who specializes in helping individuals and couples resolve sexual issues. You may think your secret sexual fantasies are unusual, but Dr. Buehler would probably not be surprised if you shared them with her. It takes a lot to shock a woman who spends 8 hours a day discussing sexual concerns with all types of people. Her clients range in age from 18 to 80 and come from all walks of life. She sees firefighters, physicians, homemakers, and college students like you; she sees heterosexual, homosexual, and bisexual clients. Her work has afforded her a privileged view of human *sexuality*—a slice of which we are going to share with you. ●

Note: Quotations attributed to Stephen Patten and Dr. Stephanie Buehler are personal communications.

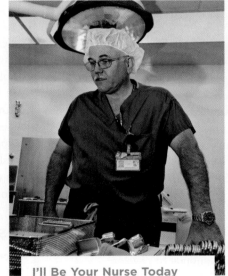

I'll Be Your Nurse Today
A nurse for over three decades, Stephen Patten has worked in a variety of different settings. He has treated gunshot and stab wounds in trauma centers, and he has held important leadership positions, serving as director of a hospital tissue bank and president of the National Association of Clinical Nurse Specialists (2012–2013). Stephen Patten/D. Michael Moody Medical Photographer, Medical Media Production Service.

CONNECTIONS

In **Chapter 8,** we noted that the 23rd pair of chromosomes is referred to as the sex chromosomes. In this chapter, we will discuss how this genetic composition influences human sexuality.

CONNECTIONS

In **Chapter 1,** we described variables as measurable characteristics that can vary or change over time. Some variables, like sex and gender, vary across groups, and we study their impact on the members of those groups. Here, we will explore sex and gender as they relate to a variety of topics in psychology.

Sexual Healing
Dr. Stephanie Buehler is a certified sex therapist. She helps couples and individuals resolve sexual problems, including low desire, erectile dysfunction, pain during intercourse, and confusion about sexual orientation. Sex therapy is a rapidly advancing field, as researchers continue to develop and test new approaches to treatment. Mark Buehler.

Dr. Buehler, in Her Own Words

http://qrs.ly/jk5a5eq

Photo: Mark Buehler.

Let's Talk About Sex

LO 1 Define sex and distinguish it from gender.

Sexuality is an important dimension of human nature; it refers to everything that makes us sexual beings, including our sexual activities, attitudes, and behaviors. When people talk about **sex,** they often are referring to a sexual act such as intercourse. But "biological sex" refers to the classification of people based on their **sex chromosomes** and their internal and external reproductive organs. According to the American Psychological Association (APA, 2012b), this "biological status" includes the categories of male, female, and intersex. **Gender,** on the other hand, refers to the categories or dimensions of masculinity and femininity based on social, cultural, and psychological characteristics. The American Psychological Association (APA, 2010, 2012, 2014) recommends using the term "sex" when referring to biological status and "gender" for the cultural roles and expectations that distinguish males and females. According to the American Psychiatric Association (which also goes by the acronym APA), "gender" also indicates the public and often legally recognized role a person has as a man or woman, boy or girl (APA, 2013).

What are the topics of sex and gender doing in a psychology textbook, and are they sufficiently important to merit their own chapter? Sex and gender are critical **variables** in the scientific study of behavior and mental processes, influencing us in our schooling, careers, parenting, memories, emotions, and sexual activities. And you know intuitively that relationships and emotions related to sexuality are a part of what makes us human.

Sexuality is one of the most intimate—and fascinating—dimensions of human behavior. It is also one of the most difficult to study. A very personal topic for most people, sex is not openly discussed in many homes, schools, doctors' offices, or even bedrooms in North America (Byers, 2011). This is ironic, as North American culture supplies a steady stream of sexual imagery, words, and media. Many parents feel embarrassed discussing sex with their children. Medical and mental health professionals find it difficult to communicate with patients about sexual issues (Bauer, Haesler, & Fetherstonhaugh, 2015). Some of us cannot even talk honestly about sex with our sexual partners. But none of this has stopped psychologists from trying to explore human sexuality.

Research and Sex

When did researchers begin exploring sexuality in a systematic way? As early as the 1900s, some began studying the sexual behavior of rats, and by 1921, several research programs were using funding from the Committee for Research on Problems of Sex to study humans (Hegarty, 2012; Pettit, 2012). Perhaps the most famous early studies were those by Alfred Kinsey and colleagues. Beginning in the 1940s, this group endeavored to study human sexuality in an objective, scientific manner (Kinsey, Pomeroy, & Martin, 1948; Kinsey, Pomeroy, Martin, & Gebhard, 1953). With the survey method, the researchers collected data on the sexual behaviors of 5,300 White male and 5,940 White female Americans. Their findings were fascinating: Both men and women masturbated, and participants had experiences with premarital sex, adultery, and sexual activity with someone of the same sex. Perhaps most surprising was the fact that so many people were willing to talk about their personal sexual behavior in post–World War II America.

Researchers now use a variety of approaches to study human sexuality, including surveys, interviews, case studies, and the experimental method. There are also many technologies to observe and measure the physiological responses of participants

(Chivers, Seto, Lalumière, Laan, & Grimbos, 2010). For example, an electro-encephalogram (EEG), magnetic resonance imaging (MRI), and functional magnetic resonance imaging (fMRI) can be used to study sexual arousal during intercourse and other sexual activities (Alho, Salminen, Sams, Hietanen, & Nummenmaa, 2015; Castillo, 2014).

But as you can imagine, studying sexual behavior has its difficulties. People are often uncomfortable discussing sex, especially their own sex lives, so getting them to talk freely can be tricky. The extremely intimate nature of sexuality can also make research that includes the *observation* of sexual behavior especially challenging. As a result, our knowledge of sexual behavior is often limited to self-reporting. Yet there are problems with relying on self-reported data, including the tendency for some people to be dishonest or portray themselves in the best possible light. There are ways to sidestep these issues, however. For example, Rieger and Savin-Williams (2012) had participants view short video clips of images that were neutral (landscapes) or sexually explicit (male or female models masturbating). Given that our pupils dilate when we are sexually aroused, the researchers were able to use this variable as an index of sexual arousal. They measured the degree to which participants' pupils dilated when they looked at neutral versus sexually explicit images, gauging the participants' sexual arousal without being too intrusive.

Not everyone is shy about personal sexual behavior, of course, and that is good news for researchers. Participants in human sexuality studies engage in a variety of sexual activities, including sexual intercourse and masturbation, with approval from Institutional Review Boards (IRBs) to ensure ethical treatment.

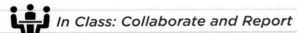 **In Class: Collaborate and Report**

In your group, discuss **A)** why you think it is difficult to talk about sex and **B)** the types of difficulties researchers could encounter studying it. **C)** Consider which of the research designs described in Chapter 1 could be used to study human sexuality.

Now it's time to delve into the heart of the chapter. Get ready to explore the many facets of sexuality and gender.

Sex: It's in Your Biology

A person's sex (male or female) depends on both genes and hormones. *Sex determination* refers to the designation of genetic sex, which guides the activity of hormones that direct the development of reproductive organs and structures (Ngun, Ghahramani, Sánchez, Bocklandt, & Vilain, 2011). Let's take a closer look at how all this works.

LO 2   Identify the biological factors that determine sex.

Your genetic sex was determined by your father's sperm. In the moment of conception, dad's sperm united with mom's egg to form a zygote. A zygote contains genetic material from both parents in the form of 46 chromosomes—23 from mom, 23 from dad. These chromosomes provide the blueprint for biological development, including that of the physiological structures associated with sex. The 23rd pair of chromosomes (sex chromosomes) includes specific instructions for the zygote to develop into a female or a male. It's as simple as X and Y.

SEX CHROMOSOMES The egg from the mother contributes an X chromosome, and the sperm from the father contributes either an X chromosome or a Y chromosome. If the sperm carries an X chromosome to the 23rd pair, the genetic sex is *XX,* and the zygote generally develops into a female. If the sperm

CONNECTIONS

In **Chapter 1,** we discussed the importance of using representative samples. Here, we refer to participants who have chosen to take part in human sexuality research. We must interpret findings cautiously as their behaviors may not reflect those of the general population.

CONNECTIONS

In **Chapter 8,** we learned that the mother's ovum and the father's sperm come together and form a single cell. Under normal circumstances, this zygote divides as it moves through the fallopian tube toward the uterus. The resulting mass of cells eventually implants in the uterine wall.

sexuality A dimension of human nature encompassing everything that makes us sexual beings; sexual activities, attitudes, and behaviors.

sex The classification of someone as male or female based on biological characteristics; a sexual act such as intercourse.

gender The dimension of masculinity and femininity based on social, cultural, and psychological characteristics.

23 Pairs
A typical person has 23 pairs of chromosomes (46 total) in almost every cell. The 23rd pair, also referred to as the sex chromosomes, contains genes that determine the sex of the developing person. If the 23rd pair is XY, then the zygote will develop into a male; if XX, it will become a female. Can you tell what genetic sex is represented here? (See the bottom of the column on page 425 for the correct answer.) BSIP SA/Alamy.

CONNECTIONS

In **Chapter 8,** we noted that primary sex characteristics, including the ovaries, uterus, vagina, penis, scrotum, and testes, are related to reproduction. Secondary sex characteristics, such as deepening of the voice in males and breast development in females, are physical features not associated with reproduction.

CONNECTIONS

In **Chapter 9,** we described one robust gender difference relating to social cognition: Women are better and faster than men at identifying emotional expressions. However, it is not clear if these differences result from biological or cultural influences.

carries a Y chromosome, the genetic sex is *XY,* and the zygote typically develops into a male. About 50% of sperm carry the X chromosome, and 50% carry the Y chromosome. This is the reason the population is approximately half male and half female.

GENES AND HORMONES From the moment a zygote is formed, genetic sex is constant. In other words, the composition of the 23rd pair of chromosomes remains female (XX) or male (XY). We should note, however, that the structure and function of the reproductive organs do not always match the original *genetic* sex (XX or XY). The development of reproductive anatomy is influenced by a variety of factors, including interactions among genes and the activity of hormones produced by the sex glands (also known as *gonads*) of the fetus (Arnold, Chen, & Itoh, 2012; Blecher & Erickson, 2007; Dennis, 2004). For the sake of the discussion here, we'll assume that the genetic sex matches the developing physical characteristics.

In a genetic male, the presence of the Y chromosome causes the gonads to become testes. If the Y chromosome is not present, as in the case of a genetic female, then the gonads develop into ovaries (Hines, 2011a; Koopman, Sinclair, & Lovell-Badge, 2016). Both the testes and ovaries secrete hormones that influence the development of reproductive organs: **androgens** in the case of the testes and **estrogen** in the case of the ovaries. These sex hormones are also secreted by the adrenal glands in both males and females. **Testosterone** is an androgen that influences whether the fetus develops male or female genitals.

DISTINGUISHING BETWEEN MALES AND FEMALES The genetic sex of the fetus is determined at conception, and although it is possible to ascertain sex as early as 7 weeks after conception through blood tests, the most reliable blood tests are done after 20 weeks (Devaney, Palomaki, Scott, & Bianchi, 2011). Fetal genital anatomy can be determined by ultrasound by the end of the first trimester with about 70% accuracy (Kong, Tong, Lam, Chan, & To, 2016). But it is usually not until adolescence that the sex organs kick into reproductive action. Puberty begins, and the cycle of life is poised to continue.

Puberty is a period when notable changes occur in physical development, ultimately leading to sexual maturity and the ability to reproduce. During this time, the *primary and secondary sex characteristics* further develop (**FIGURE 10.1**). In addition, one of the most significant changes for males is *spermarche,* or first ejaculation (often occurring during sleep). The equivalent for females is *menarche,* or first menstruation (Ladouceur, 2012; Mendle, Harden, Brooks-Gunn, & Graber, 2010).

Vive la Différence

Apart from the obvious physical differences between the sexes, what else distinguishes males and females? Adult male brains, on average, are approximately 10% larger than adult female brains (Feis, Brodersen, von Cramon, Luders, & Tittgemeyer, 2013). There are also structural disparities in the brain; for example, the cerebral hemispheres are not completely symmetric, and males and females differ somewhat in these asymmetries (Tian, Wang, Yan, & He, 2011). MRI analyses point to sex differences in the brain networks involved in social cognition and visual-spatial abilities (Feis et al., 2013). Some distinctions between male and female brains are believed to be influenced by hormones secreted prenatally, suggesting they have a biological basis (Berenbaum & Beltz, 2016; Hines, Constantinescu, & Spencer, 2015; Sanders, Sjodin, & de Chastelaine, 2002).

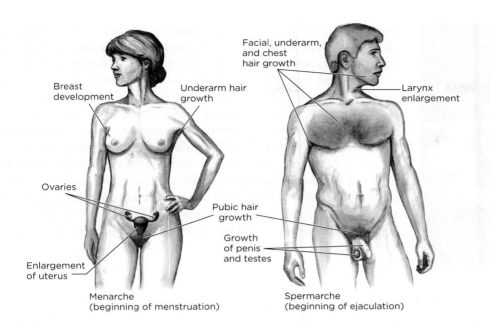

FIGURE 10.1
Physical Changes at Puberty
During puberty, the body changes and becomes sexually mature and able to reproduce. The primary sex characteristics (reproductive organs), including the ovaries, uterus, vagina, penis, scrotum, and testes, mature. Meanwhile, secondary sex characteristics, such as breasts and pubic hair, become more distinct.

COGNITION Despite these contrasts in brain size and structure, males and females do *not* differ significantly in terms of general intelligence (Burgaleta et al., 2012; Halpern et al., 2007; Koch, 2016, January 1). "Apparently, males and females can achieve similar levels of overall intellectual performance by using differently structured brains in different ways" (Deary, Penke, & Johnson, 2010, p. 209). Researchers do find different patterns of neurological activity in males and females, but remember that brains can change in response to experience, a phenomenon called neuroplasticity. These differences may be due to changes in synaptic connections and neural networks that result from the different experiences of being male or female (Hyde, 2007; Shors, 2016).

Although gender has little impact on general intelligence, males and females may differ slightly in certain areas of cognitive performance. Studies suggest that males are better than females at mentally rotating objects (Hines et al., 2015; Maeda & Yoon, 2013, 2016). This difference seems to emerge in infancy, although both men and women can improve their mental rotation skills and general spatial abilities with training (Cherney, 2008; Lauer, Udelson, Jeon, & Lourenco, 2015; Uttal et al., 2013). Another area of difference is verbal competence (Hines et al., 2015). In childhood, girls tend to perform better on tests of verbal ability, but the discrepancies are so small that they don't provide useful information for making educational decisions (Hyde & Linn, 1988; Wallentin, 2009). Boys, on the other hand, seem to perform better than girls on complex arithmetic problems—but only under certain environmental circumstances. One study found evidence of this gender gap among first graders in the United States and Russia, but not in Taiwan. Could this have something to do with the educational systems in these countries? Taiwanese boys and girls are taught to solve problems with similar strategies, whereas children in the United States and Russia may be given more leeway in choosing their approach. This suggests that input from the outside world (teacher instruction, in this case) interacts with culture to shape certain types of math skills (Shen, Vasilyeva, & Laski, 2016). And research suggests that environmental factors such as mother's education, the learning environment of the home, and effectiveness of the elementary school are "far stronger predictors" of math performance than gender (Lindberg, Hyde, Petersen, & Linn, 2010).

Any differences in cognitive development that exist between boys and girls are "minimal," and account for only a small proportion of the variability in children's

CONNECTIONS

In **Chapter 7,** we explored mental imagery, which is involved in the cognitive task of mental rotation. Here, we see that this visual-spatial ability seems to be different for men and women, although it is not clear how much is due to biology or to environmental influences.

CONNECTIONS

In **Chapter 2,** we learned there are many similarities between male and female brains, but some disparities do exist. Differences in brain structure and function, while biological, can be shaped by experience.

androgens The male hormones secreted by the testes in males and by the adrenal glands in both males and females.

estrogen The female hormone secreted primarily by the ovaries and by the adrenal glands in both males and females.

testosterone An androgen produced by the testes.

Closing the Gender Gap
The male–female gender gap in math performance is not apparent among first graders in Taiwan. Some researchers suspect that certain educational environments can level the playing field for boys and girls: "Even if boys and girls differ in certain aspects of mathematical skills or cognitive processes, instruction can minimize or eliminate the subsequent differences in performance" (Shen, Vasilyeva, & Laski, 2016, p. 63). Leren Lu/Getty Images.

CONNECTIONS

In **Chapters 7** and **8,** we presented the concept of heritability (in relation to intelligence and schizophrenia, for example). Here, we note that around half of the variability in aggressive behavior in the population can be attributed to genes and the other half to environment.

scores on cognitive tasks (Ardila, Rosselli, Matute, & Inozemtseva, 2011). Some of these minor disparities carry over into adulthood, with women outperforming men in verbal tasks and men excelling in spatial and mathematical abilities. Such differences have declined over the past several decades, however. This may be a result of socio-cultural factors, such as greater availability of advanced math courses and more support for both men and women to pursue careers that interest them (Deary et al., 2010; Wai, Cacchio, Putallaz, & Makel, 2010). While these changes are valuable, true equality can only be achieved when we adjust our mindsets. Women perceive their math performance fairly accurately, while men tend to overestimate their performance. Could this difference in attitude help explain why more men pursue careers oriented toward math and science (Bench, Lench, Liew, Miner, & Flores, 2015)?

AGGRESSION We've discussed disparities in brain anatomy and cognitive abilities, but how do males and females differ in terms of behavior? Men tend to demonstrate more physical aggression (such as hitting) (Ainsworth & Maner, 2012; see Chapter 15), but that doesn't mean women aren't aggressive. Some researchers report that women exhibit more *relational aggression,* or aggressive behaviors that are indirect and aimed at relationships, such as spreading rumors or excluding certain group members, although men clearly exhibit this type of aggression as well (Archer, 2004; Archer & Coyne, 2005; Crick & Grotpeter, 1995; Kuppens, Laurent, Heyvaert, & Onghena, 2013; Vaillancourt, 2013). These differences typically appear early in life (Card, Stucky, Sawalani, & Little, 2008; Hanish, Sallquist, DiDonato, Fabes, & Martin, 2012).

What causes these gender disparities? One hormonal candidate is testosterone, which has been associated with aggression (Montoya, Terburg, Bos, & van Honk, 2012) and, as discussed earlier, exists at higher levels in males. Studies of identical twins suggest that approximately 50% of aggressive behavior in the population can be explained by genetic factors, although specific genes associated with aggression have not yet been identified (DiLalla, 2002; Tackett, Waldman, & Lahey, 2009; Vassos, Collier, & Fazel, 2014). This implies that a significant proportion of gender differences in aggressive behavior results from an interaction between environmental factors and genetics (Brendgen et al., 2005; Rowe, Maughan, Worthman, Costello, & Angold, 2004; Vassos et al., 2014). Media portrayals of violence include both physical and relational aggression, and we know that observational learning is a potent environmental factor. Interestingly, the media rating system used in the United States focuses on physical aggression, but not relational aggression, even though both types of aggression appear in media content created for children. Parents and caregivers should consider this when making decisions about media use for children and teens (Coyne, 2016). We should all be concerned about the impact of "surveillance reality" television programs, which are chock full of verbal and relational aggression. In one study, participants who watched this type of show were more aggressive than participants who viewed other types of programs (Gibson, Thompson, Hou, & Bushman, 2016).

Does aggression vary across cultures? Research suggests that boys tend to be more aggressive when raised in nonindustrial societies; patriarchal societies, where women have less power and are considered inferior to men; and polygamous societies, where men can have more than one wife. Why are men in these societies more aggressive? Evolutionary psychology would suggest that competition for resources (including suitable mates) increases the likelihood of aggression, with revenge as a possible motivating force (Wilkowski, Hartung, Crowe, & Chai, 2012; Wood & Eagly, 2002).

One thing to keep in mind is that, overall, the variation within a gender is much greater than the variation between genders: "Males and females are similar on most, but not all, psychological variables" (Hyde, 2007, p. 260). This *gender similarities hypothesis* proposed by Hyde (2005) states that males and females exhibit large differences in only a few areas, including some motor behaviors (throwing distance), some characteristics of sexuality (frequency of masturbation), and to a moderate degree, aggression.

We should acknowledge that all the gender differences described above were detected by *measurements* of characteristics, rather than the characteristics themselves. You cannot directly measure verbal ability, for example, but you can design a test to measure it. Measuring tools are invaluable, but they are not immune to flaws and biases. That being said, studies on gender disparities often produce similar results. One analysis of over 20,000 studies involving more than 12 million participants found gender differences to be consistent across culture, age groups, and generations (Zell, Krizan, & Teeter, 2015).

Comparing men and women may be interesting, but note that many people cannot be boxed into the "male" or "female" categories prescribed by society. These gender non-conforming individuals help us understand the limitations of the "gender binary system," that is, the classification of people as male or female without recognition of alternate gender identities.

Diversity of Sex Development

LO 3   Explain some of the causes of intersexual development.

In some cases, irregularities in genes or hormone activity can lead to differences of sex development (DSD), or the emergence of "physical sex characteristics" that are not typical (APA, 2015a; Topp, 2013; **INFOGRAPHIC 10.1**, on the next page). Such disparities result from inherited "conditions in which development of chromosomal, gonadal, or anatomic sex is atypical" (Lee, Houk, Ahmed, & Hughes, 2006, p. e488). According to the American Psychiatric Association (2013, p. 451), **intersexual** refers to having "conflicting or ambiguous biological indicators" of male or female in sexual structures and organs. For example, intersexual development would be apparent in a genetic female (XX) or male (XY) who has sexual structures and organs that are ambiguous or inconsistent with genetic sex. Intersex traits are commonly referred to as "disorders of sexual development," but this terminology has "pathologising implications"; in other words, it may suggest intersex traits are medical problems that need to be fixed (Schweitzer, Brunner, Handford, & Richter-Appelt, 2014).

Around 1% of infants are found to have intersex traits at birth. These individuals might once have been called "hermaphrodites," but this term is outdated, derogatory, and misleading because it refers to the impossible condition of being both fully male and fully female (Vilain, 2008). Differences of sex development may be traced to irregularities in the sex chromosomes, as the creation of the 23rd pair does not always follow the expected pattern of XX or XY (Juul, Main, & Skakkebaek, 2011; Wodrich & Tarbox, 2008). In the case of *Klinefelter's syndrome,* a male is born with at least one extra X chromosome in the 23rd pair (for example, XXY). A boy with Klinefelter's syndrome typically develops normally until puberty, but then has a

intersexual Having ambiguous or inconsistent biological indicators of male or female in the sexual structures and organs.

Different Layers of Sexual Determination

When thinking about the biological factors that determine sex, most people envision the primary sex characteristics that indicate our assignment at birth. But one's sex is made up of many layers with different influences. Though they often all combine in a predictable way, there can be exceptions at any point. Looking at variations at each layer demonstrates the complex reality of sex that goes far beyond what is declared on our birth certificates.

Primarily influenced by **genes**

CHROMOSOMES

One chromosome from each parent combines to determine genetic sex: XX (female) or XY (male).

exceptions:
Boys with *Klinefelter's syndrome* (XXY) develop normally until puberty, but can have underdeveloped male characteristics or additional female secondary sex characteristics because of the extra X chromosome. Also: *Turner's syndrome* (female born with an absent or incomplete X chromosome).

exception:
Those with *5-alpha reductase deficiency* appear female at birth. At puberty, hormonal surges cause external masculinization sufficient to make them indistinguishable from other men.

SECONDARY SEX CHARACTERISTICS

Prompted by hormonal changes, these characteristics appear at puberty and are only indirectly involved with reproduction.

GONADS

Presence of Y chromosome causes gonads to become testes. If Y chromosome is not present, gonads develop into ovaries.

PRIMARY SEX CHARACTERISTICS

Testes secrete androgens that influence the development of male genitals. The absence of this signal leads to the development of female genitals.

exception:
Intersexual development is apparent when individuals are born with sexual structures and organs that are ambiguous or inconsistent with genetic sex.

exception:
Though genetically male and possessing testes, those with *androgen-insensitivity syndrome* do not respond to androgens and develop more femalelike sex organs and other characteristics.

Primarily influenced by **hormones**

greater chance of developing female sex characteristics such as breasts. He will be infertile and may have underdeveloped sexual organs and secondary sex characteristics (Mandoki, Sumner, Hoffman, & Riconda, 1991; Manning, Kilduff, & Trivers, 2013). In *Turner's syndrome,* a female is born with only one X chromosome (as opposed to two X chromosomes), anatomically normal genitals, ovaries that are not fully developed, and infertility. Girls with this syndrome who go undiagnosed or untreated are at increased risk for estrogen deficiency, hypothyroidism, cardiovascular issues, and short stature (Hjerrild, Mortensen, & Gravholt, 2008). Despite the possibility of developmental delays in cognitive, social, and emotional functioning, women with Turner's syndrome who receive treatment can lead independent, stable, and productive lives (McCauley & Sybert, 2006).

Beautiful Bodies

Intersex advocate Sean Saifa Wall (the feature subject of Chapter 11) is changing the way people view intersex traits: "Accepting myself as intersex and advocating for intersex people and children, I really put forward that our bodies are our mosaic. There is no such thing as a 'normal body,'" Saifa says. "We get so many messages in society that tell us that we're too fat, too skinny, not pretty enough, that we need straight hair, that we need fair skin, that we need smooth skin. . . . We're constantly bombarded with these images of what perfection looks like, and it's all warped." Courtesy Sean Saifa Wall.

Differences in sensitivity to hormones may also lead to intersex traits. If a male fetus is partly or completely insensitive to androgens, for example, he may develop more female-like sex organs (known as *androgen insensitivity syndrome;* Gottlieb, Beitel, & Trifiro, 2014). Additionally, an *androgenized female* develops more male-like sex organs as a result of being exposed to excess androgens (Dessens, Slijper, & Drop, 2005).

 **show what you know**

1. _____ refers to our sexual activities, attitudes, and behaviors.
   a. Sex
   b. Sex determination
   c. Sexuality
   d. Gender

2. A physician attempts to explain to a young couple some of the biological factors that determine sex. She states that when the 23rd chromosome pair contains an X and a Y, the zygote generally develops:
   a. into a female.
   b. into a male.
   c. ovaries.
   d. the anatomy of both sexes.

3. How are chromosomes involved in differences of sex development?

✓ CHECK YOUR ANSWERS IN APPENDIX C.

Gender

With the prior biology lesson under our belt, let's consider its implications for psychology. What does it mean to be a "man" or "woman" in today's world? Many think of men as being assertive, logical, and in charge, whereas women are perceived as more caring, sensitive, and emotional. But such characterizations are simplistic and frequently inaccurate. Just ask Stephen Patten.

A MASCULINE TOUCH Have you ever been hospitalized? If so, you probably remember your nurses—perhaps better than your doctors. The role of the nurse is extremely important. Nurses are the people who make sure you are clean, comfortable, and properly medicated at all hours of the day. When you press the call button at 2:00 A.M., it is the nurse who appears at your bedside. As you undergo a frightening or painful procedure, it is typically the nurse who holds your hand. Few professions demand such a high level of sensitivity and compassion.

Above and to the right of the 22nd chromosome pair is the 23rd pair (sex chromosomes). Since one is X and the other is Y, we can conclude the gender is male.

The field of nursing is dominated by women, who are sometimes perceived as being more caring and nurturing than men. But according to Stephen Patten, the ability to care and nurture has little to do with gender. The son of a minister, Stephen was raised to believe that men have the capacity for deep compassion—and he has put this lesson to work in his 32-year career.

Nothing is more rewarding than the nurse–patient relationship, according to Stephen. Nursing, he says, is "the most intimate of any of the health-care professions." Doctors diagnose and treat diseases (an important job indeed), but the nurse is the patient's advocate and lifeline. Lying on an operating table unable to move and unconscious, you are in no position to help yourself, but the nurse is there to make sure you are hydrated, to cover you with a warming blanket, and to ensure that hospital staff use proper sterilization techniques so you do not acquire a dangerous infection, among other things.

Some patients are pleasantly surprised to discover a man will be caring and advocating for them in their most vulnerable state. But others have trouble accepting the idea that Stephen could serve in such a capacity. "What are you, some sort of lesbian trapped in a man's body?" one patient demanded to know. Another flat-out refused to have a male nurse participate in her care. Why do you think these patients reacted to Stephen this way? We suspect it has something to do with their preconceived notions about *gender roles*. ●

Gender: Beyond Biology

LO 4 Define gender and explain how culture plays a role in its development.

Earlier, we described gender as the categories or dimensions of masculinity and femininity. Men are often expected to be masculine in their "attitudes, feelings, and behaviors," while women are expected to be more feminine (APA, 2015a). But concepts of masculine and feminine vary according to culture, social context, and the individual. We learn how to behave in gender-conforming ways through the **gender roles** designated by our culture. This understanding of expected male and female behavior is generally demonstrated by around age 2 or 3. So, too, is the ability to differentiate between boys and girls, and men and women (Zosuls, Miller, Ruble, Martin, & Fabes, 2011). Gender roles are demonstrated through the actions, general beliefs, and characteristics associated with masculinity and femininity. Within a culture, gender roles guide how we are expected to look and behave; they even influence our social responsibilities (APA, 2015a). For example, women in the United States traditionally take on more childcare responsibilities. Our laws protect the rights of mothers, allowing them to take time off following the birth or adoption of a baby. In Scandinavian countries such as Sweden and Denmark, however, both mothers and fathers are encouraged and given financial support to leave the workplace to care for their babies, sometimes "stretching well beyond the first year of the child's life" (Rostgaard, 2014, p. 14).

LEARNING AND GENDER ROLES Children learn gender roles through a process called *gender typing*, "the development of traits, interests, skills, attitudes, and behaviors that correspond to stereotypical masculine and feminine social roles" (Mehta & Strough, 2010, p. 251). These roles can be acquired through observational learning, as explained by social-cognitive theory (Bussey & Bandura, 1999; Else-Quest, Higgins, Allison, & Morton, 2012; Tenenbaum & Leaper, 2002). We learn from our observations of others in our environment, particularly by watching those of the same gender. Children also learn and model the behaviors represented in electronic media and books (Kingsbury & Coplan, 2012). Many kids go through a phase of *appearance rigidity*

CONNECTIONS

In **Chapter 5,** we described how learning can occur by observing and imitating a model. Here, we see how this type of learning can shape the formation of gender roles.

gender roles The collection of actions, beliefs, and characteristics that a culture associates with masculinity and femininity.

during early childhood (around 3–4 years old), when they closely adhere to gender-stereotyped dress. For girls, this has been referred to as the "pink, frilly dress" phase, when nothing else will do regardless of weather, occasion, or repetition of the outfit. For boys, appearance rigidity may involve superhero costumes and strict avoidance of anything considered "girly." Young children are "active self-socializing agents, picking up clues on what gender looks like and doggedly following their deductions" (Halim et al., 2014, p. 1100).

Operant conditioning is also involved in the development of gender roles. Children often receive reinforcement for behaviors considered gender-appropriate and punishment for those viewed as inappropriate. Parents, caregivers, relatives, and peers reinforce gender-appropriate behavior by smiling, laughing, or encouraging. But when children exhibit gender-inappropriate behavior (a boy playing with a doll, for example), the people in their lives might frown, get worried, or even put a stop to it. Through this combination of encouragement and discouragement, a child learns to conform to society's expectations.

A person's **gender identity** is the feeling or sense of being either male or female, and compatibility, contentment, and conformity with one's gender (APA, 2015a; Egan & Perry, 2001; Tobin et al., 2010). Gender identity is often reinforced by learning and parental stereotyping of appropriate girl/boy behaviors, but not always. Children raised in environments where gender roles are not strictly specified seem to develop more fluid ideas about gender-appropriate behavior (Hupp, Smith, Coleman, & Brunell, 2010). For example, kids who grow up in single-parent homes will likely see their parents taking on the traditional gender roles of both men and women, and will be more comfortable stepping outside the boundaries prescribed by such roles.

Gender-Free
Toronto parents Kathy Witterick and David Stocker decided to raise their third child gender-free. When baby Storm was born, Witterick and Stocker informed family and friends that the sex of the child would remain a secret for some time; they wanted Storm to make his or her own decision about gender identity (Poisson, 2013, November 5). Pictured here is Storm with big brother Jazz. Steve Russell/Getty Images.

 **In Class: Collaborate and Report**

With your group, **A)** describe how gender roles have changed during your lifetime. **B)** Identify the benefits or drawbacks of these changes. **C)** Ask yourself if anything makes you uncomfortable about these shifts (for example, do you approve of the growing number of women engaged in military combat?), and consider the reasons for your discomfort.

COGNITION AND GENDER SCHEMAS In addition to learning by observation and reinforcement, children seem to develop gender roles by actively processing information (Bem, 1981). In other words, children think about the behaviors they observe, including the differences between males and females. They watch their parents' behavior, often following suit (Tenenbaum & Leaper, 2002). Using the information they have gathered, they develop a variety of gender-specific rules they believe should be followed (for example, girls help around the house, boys play with model cars; Yee & Brown, 1994). These rules provide the framework for **gender schemas,** which are the psychological or mental guidelines that dictate how to be masculine or feminine. Gender schemas also impact how we process information or remember events (Barberá, 2003). For example, Martin and Halverson (1983) found that children were more likely to remember events incorrectly if those events violated gender stereotypes. If they saw a little girl playing with a truck and a little boy playing with a doll, they were likely to recall the girl having the doll and the boy having the truck when tested several days later. In a more recent study, children were asked to recall information from storybooks they had just heard on audiotape. Immediately afterward, their recall of the stories was "often imprecise," most likely because their notions of gender-appropriate behavior (gender schemas) colored their memories. For example, one of the stories told of a little girl who was trying to help an adult male overcome his fear of walking on a high wire. Yet many children inaccurately remembered the little girl being afraid,

CONNECTIONS

In **Chapter 5,** we discussed operant conditioning, which is learning that results from consequences. Here, the positive reinforcer is encouragement, which leads to an increase in a desired behavior. The punishment is discouragement, which reduces the unwanted behavior.

CONNECTIONS

In **Chapter 8,** we stated that schemas are a component of cognition. Schemas are collections of ideas or notions representing a basic unit of understanding. Here, we see a specific type of schema that influences conceptions of gender and memories.

gender identity The feeling or sense of being either male or female, and compatibility, contentment, and conformity with one's gender.

gender schemas The psychological or mental guidelines that dictate how to be masculine and feminine.

Monkey Play

A male vervet monkey rolls a toy car on the ground (left), and a female examines a doll (right). When provided with a variety of toys, male vervet monkeys spend more time playing with cars and balls, whereas females are drawn to dolls and pots (Alexander & Hines, 2002). Similar behaviors have been observed in rhesus monkeys (Hassett, Siebert, & Wallen, 2008). These studies suggest a biological basis for the gender-specific toy preferences often observed in human children. Left: MCT/Getty Images. Right: MCT/MCT via Getty Images.

or thought that the man was protecting her (Frawley, 2008). Apparently, their gender schemas incorporated the assumption that men are brave, and this interfered with their ability to recall the story correctly.

BIOLOGY AND GENDER Clearly, culture and learning influence the development of gender-specific behaviors and interests, but could biology play a role, too? Research on nonhuman primates suggests this is the case (Hines, 2011a). A growing body of literature points to a link between testosterone exposure *in utero* and specific play behaviors (Swan et al., 2010). For example, male and female infants as young as 3 to 8 months demonstrate gender-specific toy preferences that cannot be explained by mere socialization or learning (Hines, 2011b). Research using eye-tracking technology reveals that baby girls spend more time looking at dolls, while boys tend to focus on toy trucks (Alexander, Wilcox, & Woods, 2009). When given a choice, babies prefer stimuli that include faces, so both infant boys and girls show *greater* preference for a doll in comparison to a truck, but infant boys tend to show "relatively greater visual attention" to a truck than do infant girls (Lauer et al., 2015). Although these early differences seem to be unlearned, infants as young as 6 months can learn to discriminate between male and female faces and voices. Perhaps their toy interests have a learned component as well (Martin, Ruble, & Szkrybalo, 2002). But the bottom line is, not all gender-specific behaviors can be attributed to culture and upbringing—a principle well illustrated by the heartbreaking story of Bruce Reimer.

NATURE AND NURTURE
The Case of Bruce Reimer

Bruce Reimer and his twin brother were born in 1965. During a circumcision operation at 8 months, Bruce's penis was almost entirely burnt away by electrical equipment used in the procedure. When he was about 2 years old, his parents took the advice of Johns Hopkins psychologist John Money and decided to raise Bruce as a girl (BBC, 2005, September). The thinking at the time was that what made a person a male or female was not necessarily the original structure of the genitals, but rather how he or she was raised (Diamond, 2004).

> HIS PARENTS . . . DECIDED TO RAISE BRUCE AS A GIRL.

Just before Bruce's second birthday, doctors removed his testicles and used the tissues to create the beginnings of female genitalia. His parents began calling him Brenda, dressing him like a girl and encouraging him to engage in stereotypically "girl" activities such as baking and playing with dolls (BBC, 2005, September). But Brenda did not adjust so well to her new gender assignment. An outcast at school, she was called cruel names like "caveman" and "gorilla." She brawled with both boys and girls alike, and eventually got kicked out of school (CBC News, 2004, May 10; Diamond & Sigmundson, 1997).

When Brenda hit puberty, the problem became even worse. Despite ongoing psychiatric therapy and estrogen replacement, she could not deny what was in her *nature*—she refused to consider herself female (Diamond & Sigmundson, 1997). Brenda became suicidal, prompting her parents to tell her the truth about the past (BBC, 2005, September).

You Asked, Dr Buehler Answers

http://qrs.ly/1l5a5ez

What made you choose this field of study?

scan this →

At age 14, Brenda decided to "reassign himself" to be a male. He then changed his name to David, began taking male hormones, and underwent a series of penis construction surgeries (Colapinto, 2000; Diamond & Sigmundson, 1997). At 25, David married and adopted his wife's children, and for some time it appeared he was doing quite well (Diamond & Sigmundson, 1997). But sadly, at the age of 38, he took his own life.

We are in no position to explain the tragic death of David Reimer, but we cannot help but wonder what role his traumatic gender reassignment might have played. Keep in mind that this is just an isolated *case*. As discussed in Chapter 1, we should be extremely cautious about making generalizations from case studies, which may or may not be representative of the larger population. ◊🏠

GENDER-ROLE STEREOTYPES The case of Bruce Reimer touches on another important topic: gender-role stereotypes. Growing up, David (who was called "Brenda" at the time) did not enjoy wearing dresses and playing "girl" games. He didn't adhere to the *gender-role stereotypes* assigned to little girls. Gender-role stereotypes, which begin to take hold around age 3, are strong ideas about the nature of males and females—how they should dress, what kinds of games they should like, and so on. Decisions about children's toys, in particular, follow strict gender-role stereotypes (boys play with trucks, girls play with dolls), and any crossing over risks ridicule from peers, sometimes even adults. Gender-role stereotypes are apparent in toy commercials, toy packaging, and pictures in coloring books (Auster & Mansbach, 2012; Fitzpatrick & McPherson, 2010; Kahlenberg & Hein, 2010; Owen & Padron, 2016). They also manifest themselves in academic settings. For example, many girls have negative attitudes about math, which seem to be associated with parents' and teachers' expectations about gender differences in math competencies (Gunderson, Ramirez, Levine, & Beilock, 2012).

Children, especially boys, are judged more harshly for veering from gender-role stereotypes. You are much more likely to see a girl playing with a "boy" toy than a boy playing with a "girl" toy (Weisgram, Fulcher, & Dinella, 2014). Society, in turn, is more tolerant of girls who cross gender stereotypes. In many cultures, the actions of a tomboy (a girl who behaves in ways society considers masculine) are more acceptable than those of a "sissy" (a derogatory term for a boy who acts in a stereotypically feminine way; Martin & Ruble, 2010; Thorne, 1993). Despite such judgments, some children do not conform to societal pressure (Tobin et al., 2010).

ANDROGYNY Those who cross gender-role boundaries and engage in behaviors associated with both genders are said to exhibit **androgyny**. An androgynous person might be nurturing (generally considered a feminine quality) and assertive (generally considered a masculine quality), thus demonstrating characteristics associated with both genders (Johnson et al., 2006; Wood & Eagly, 2015). But concepts of masculine and feminine—and therefore what constitutes androgyny—are not consistent across cultures. In North America, notions about gender are revealed in clothing colors; parents frequently dress boy babies in blue and girl babies in pink. In the African nation of Swaziland, children are dressed androgynously (at least in the eyes of North Americans), wearing any color of the rainbow (Bradley, 2011).

Androgynous Actor
Academy Award–winning Tilda Swinton embraces androgyny through her hairstyle, clothing, and make-up choices. Some would say she is beautiful and handsome at the same time.
Riccardo Ghilardi/Getty Images.

Transgender and Transsexual

LO 5 Distinguish between transgender and transsexual.

The development of gender identity and the acceptance of gender roles go relatively smoothly for most people. But sometimes societal expectations of being male or female differ from what an individual is feeling inwardly, leading to discontent. At

androgyny The tendency to cross gender-role boundaries, exhibiting behaviors associated with both genders.

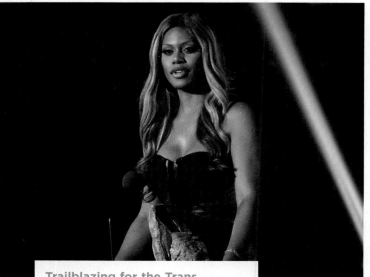

Trailblazing for the Trans Community

Actress Laverne Cox is the first transgender person to appear on the cover of *TIME Magazine* and receive a nomination for a primetime Emmy. The *Orange Is the New Black* star has helped bring transgender people into the mainstream media, but she points out that there is much progress to be made: "In terms of the day-to-day lives of trans people, we still experience violence at a disproportionate rate, as well as homelessness, unemployment, the denial of health care, and being criminalised and incarcerated" (Mulkerrins, 2016, June 10, para. 3). Larry Busacca/Getty Images.

birth, most infants are identified as "boy" or "girl"; this is referred to as a person's *natal gender,* or gender assignment. When natal gender does not feel right, an individual may have *transgender* experiences. According to the American Psychological Association, **transgender** refers to people "whose *gender identity, gender expression,* or behavior does not conform to that typically associated with the sex to which they were assigned at birth" (APA, 2014a, p. 1). Remember that gender identity is the feeling or sense of being either male or female. For a person who is transgender a mismatch occurs between that sense of identity and the gender assignment at birth. This disparity can be temporary or persistent (American Psychiatric Association, 2013). Approximately 700,000 individuals in the United States (around 0.2% of the population) consider themselves to be transgender (Gates, 2011).

The American Psychological Association (2015b) acknowledges that there are occasions when it is "medically and therapeutically" appropriate for some people to "transition from one gender to another," and this may involve medical treatments and changes to names, pronouns, hair, and clothing (p. 422). According to the American Psychiatric Association (2013), a person is considered **transsexual** if he or she seeks or undergoes "a social transition from male to female or female to male, which in many, but not all, cases also involves a somatic transition by cross-sex hormone treatment and genital surgery (*sex reassignment surgery*)" (p. 451, italics in original). Using "medical intervention" to make this type of transition is also termed *gender affirmation* (APA, 2014a).

We have discussed the meaning of transgender and transsexual, both of which fall into the larger classification of *trans.* Generally speaking, *trans* refers to "all people whose gender identity, gender expression, or both, fall outside social norms" (Hendricks & Testa, 2012, p. 461). Since there is inconsistency in the labeling of trans people, we should be sensitive in our use of terminology and, when possible, ask people who are trans how they would like to be identified (Hendricks & Testa, 2012). Note that *trans* is included in the acronym LGBTQ, an even larger category encompassing lesbian, gay, bisexual, transgender, and questioning/queer (Grisham, 2016, July 22).

What do trans experiences feel like? Every person is different, but many people who are transsexual say they have always felt they were born into the wrong-sex body. For example, a person feels male but his body is female, or vice versa. When the discrepancy between natal gender and gender identity leads to significant experiences and/or expression of distress, an individual might meet the criteria for a *gender dysphoria* diagnosis (American Psychiatric Association, 2013). Although gender dysphoria does not affect all transgender people, many still face a lack of "affordable resources, such as counseling, hormone therapy, medical procedures, and the social support necessary to freely express their gender identity and minimize discrimination" (APA, 2014a, p. 3).

As you may realize, gender is a complex and intangible social construct. Now it's time to tackle something a little more concrete. Are you ready for sex?

show what you know

1. A sixth grader states that men are more assertive, logical, and in charge than women. She has learned about this _____ from a variety of sources in her immediate setting and culture.
   a. gender identity
   b. observational learning
   c. gender role
   d. androgyny

2. The psychological or mental rules that dictate how to be masculine and feminine are known as _____.

3. Describe the difference between transgender and transsexual.

✓ CHECK YOUR ANSWERS IN APPENDIX C.

The Birds and the Bees

THE MAKING OF A SEXPERT Dr. Stephanie Buehler grew up in California's San Fernando Valley during the 1970s, when the sexual revolution was in full gear. During this time in American history, many people questioned conventional notions about sex and explored different avenues of sexual expression. "There was a lot of sexual activity at that time," explains Dr. Buehler, who had many gay, bisexual, and transgender friends. "I was really exposed to a lot of different aspects of sexuality." At home, she knew it was okay to ask her parents questions about sex and birth control. So, it was no big deal when Stephanie's family allowed her to watch the avant-garde and sexually explicit movie *Last Tango in Paris* (which received an X rating at the time of its release, and currently has an NC-17 rating).

With this upbringing, Dr. Buehler was fairly relaxed talking about sex, and therefore her pursuit of a career as a sex therapist would seem like a plausible path. But graduate school was a long shot for a girl growing up in the 1970s, when women were just beginning to establish themselves as a major presence in the workforce. After graduating from college, the first person in her immediate family to do so, she became a teacher at an inner-city elementary school, and then decided to pursue a master's degree and eventually a doctorate in psychology. Her PsyD concentration was family therapy, but another interest was brewing beneath the surface. During couples' role-playing sessions in class, Dr. Buehler always was the sole student asking questions about sex: "What about your sex life? What's going on in the bedroom?" She recalls her classmates looking at her and asking, "Why are you bringing that up? What does that have to do with anything?" The answer, she can now state with confidence, is a whole lot.

After working as a licensed psychotherapist for several years, Dr. Buehler began her sex therapy training. She found it so rewarding that she launched her own sex therapy institute, The Buehler Institute in Newport Beach, California. "I just find I'm never, ever bored with my work," says Dr. Buehler. Sexuality is quite personal . . . and that means everyone is quite different. ●

Everything You Always Wanted to Know About Sex

When you think of sex, what comes to mind? Genitals? Intercourse? To grasp the complexity of sexual experiences, we must understand the basic physiology of the sexual response. Enter William Masters (1915–2001) and Virginia Johnson (1925–2013) and their pioneering laboratory research, which included the study of approximately 10,000 distinct sexual responses of 312 male and 382 female participants (Masters & Johnson, 1966).

LO 6 **Describe the human sexual response as identified by Masters and Johnson.**

HUMAN SEXUAL RESPONSE CYCLE Masters and Johnson made some of the most important contributions to the study of the human sexual response. Their research commenced in 1954, not exactly a time when sex was thought to be an acceptable subject for dinner conversation. Nevertheless, almost 700 people volunteered to participate in their study, which lasted a little more than a decade (Masters & Johnson, 1966). In particular, Masters and Johnson were interested in determining the physiological responses that occurred during sexual activity, such as masturbation and intercourse. They used a variety of instruments to measure blood flow, body temperature, muscular changes, and heart rate. What they discovered is that most people experience a similar

Therapist at Work
Dr. Buehler found sex therapy so rewarding that she established her own sex therapy practice, The Buehler Institute, in Newport Beach, California. In addition to meeting with clients, Dr. Buehler trains and oversees other psychotherapists, and is the author of the book, *What Every Mental Health Professional Needs to Know about Sex.* Mark Buehler.

You Asked, Dr. Buehler Answers

http://qrs.ly/jz5a5er

Which gender visits your office more frequently?

scan this ➔

transgender Refers to people whose gender identity and expression do not match the gender assigned to them at birth.
transsexual An individual who seeks or undergoes a social transition to the other gender, and who may make changes to his or her body through surgery and medical treatment.

FIGURE 10.2

Masters and Johnson's Human Sexual Response Cycle
In the male sexual response (left), excitement is typically followed by a brief plateau, orgasm, and then a refractory period during which another orgasm is not possible. In the female sexual response (right), there is no refractory period. Orgasm is typically followed by resolution (A) or, if sexual stimulation continues, additional orgasms (B).

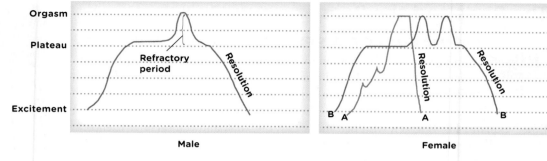

Male Female

Sexy Science
In the mid-1950s, William Masters teamed with Virginia Johnson to study the bodily changes that occur during masturbation and sex. Their research was groundbreaking, and it upended many long-held misconceptions about sex. For example, Masters and Johnson found that the length of a man's penis does not determine his ability to give pleasure (Fox, 2013, July 25). Art Phillips/Corbis.

CONNECTIONS

In **Chapter 9,** we noted that Maslow emphasized our deep-seated need to feel loved, to experience affection, and to belong to a group. These needs motivate us to seek out relationships, which can include sexual activities.

physiological sexual response, which can result from oral stimulation, manual stimulation, vaginal intercourse, or masturbation. Men and women tend to follow a similar pattern or cycle: *excitement, plateau, orgasm,* and *resolution* (**FIGURE 10.2**). It is important to note, though, that these phases vary for each individual in terms of duration.

Sexual arousal begins during the *excitement phase.* This is when physical changes start to become evident. Muscles tense, the heartbeat quickens, breathing accelerates, the nipples become firm, and blood pressure rises a bit. In men, the penis becomes erect, the scrotum constricts, and the testes pull up toward the body. In women, the vagina lubricates and the clitoris swells (Levin, 2008).

Next is the *plateau phase.* There are no clear physiological signs to mark the beginning of this phase, but it is the natural progression from the excitement phase. During the plateau phase, the muscles continue to tense, breathing and heart rate increase, and the genitals begin to change color as blood fills this area. This phase is usually quite short-lived, lasting only a few seconds to minutes.

The shortest phase of the sexual response cycle is the *orgasm phase.* As the peak of sexual response is reached, an **orgasm** occurs, which is a powerful combination of extremely gratifying sensations and a series of rhythmic muscular contractions. When men and women are asked to describe their orgasmic experiences, it is very difficult to differentiate between them. Their brain activity, observed via PET scans, is also very similar (Georgiadis, Reinders, Paans, Renken, & Kortekaas, 2009; Mah & Binik, 2001).

The final phase of the sexual response cycle, according to Masters and Johnson, is the *resolution phase.* This is when bodies return to a relaxed state. Without further sexual arousal, the body will immediately begin the resolution phase. The blood flows out of the genitals, and blood pressure, heart rate, and breathing slow to normal. Men lose their erection, the testes move down, and the skin of the scrotum loosens. Men will also experience a **refractory period**, an interval during which they cannot attain another orgasm. This can last from minutes to hours, and typically the older the man is, the longer the refractory period lasts. For women, the resolution phase is characterized by a decrease in clitoral swelling and a return to the normal labia color. Women do not experience a refractory period, and if sexual stimulation continues, some are capable of having multiple orgasms.

Armed with this knowledge about the physiology of sex, let's move on to its underlying psychology. How are sexual activities shaped by learning, relationships, and the need to be loved and belong?

Sexual Orientation

LO 7   Define sexual orientation and summarize how it develops.

Sexual orientation refers to "the sex of those to whom one is sexually and romantically attracted" (APA, 2015a, p. 22). This "enduring pattern" of sexual, romantic, and emotional attraction generally involves someone of the same sex, opposite sex, or both sexes (APA, 2008). When attracted to members of the opposite sex, sexual orientation is **heterosexual.** When attracted to members of the same sex, sexual orientation is **homosexual.** When attracted to members of the same sex *and* members of the opposite sex, sexual orientation is **bisexual.** Sexual orientation, however, does not necessarily fit into these neat categories. Some describe it as a continuum that includes many dimensions of our sexuality, including attraction, desire, emotions, and all the behaviors that result. Others suggest it is more akin to a mosaic; as Dr. Buehler's mentor once explained, "There is a universe of orientations and identities, and each person gets to put him or herself in the constellation." Human beings can be "attracted to men, women, both, neither, genderqueer, androgynous or have other gender identities" (APA, 2015a, p. 22). The use of rigid categories to describe a continuous variable is misleading: If sexual orientation is "more like height than eye color—why should we try to force it into a small number of categories?" (Epstein, McKinney, Fox, & Garcia, 2012, p. 1377).

Those who do not feel sexually attracted to others are referred to as *asexual.* Lack of interest in sex does not necessarily prevent a person from maintaining relationships with spouses, partners, or friends, but little is known about the impact of asexuality because research on the topic is scarce. We can't be sure how many people would consider themselves asexual, but by some estimates, they constitute as low as 0.6% and as high as 5.5% of the population (Crooks & Baur, 2017).

There is also a universe of labels for different sexual orientations. In America, the most common terminology refers to a homosexual woman as a "lesbian," and a homosexual man as "gay" (APA, 2012b). Some people refer to themselves as "queer," thereby avoiding the "gender binaries of male and female or … the perceived restrictions imposed by lesbian, gay, and bisexual orientations" (APA, 2015a, p. 22). In other words, such individuals choose not to be boxed into a certain category.

WHAT'S IN A NUMBER? What percentage of the population is heterosexual? How about homosexual and bisexual? These questions may seem straightforward, but they are not easy to answer. This is partly because there are no clear-cut criteria for identifying individuals as homosexual, heterosexual, or bisexual. In other words, a vast continuum representing sexual orientation exists. At one end are people who are "exclusively heterosexual" and at the other end are those considered "exclusively homosexual." Between these two poles is considerable variation (Kinsey, Pomeroy, & Martin, 1948; **FIGURE 10.3**). Some people might be exploring their sexuality, but not necessarily exhibiting a particular orientation, and this adds to the variability of rates. Estimates are available, but definitions of sexual orientation vary across cultures, and findings can be inconsistent as a result of differing survey designs: data collection in different years, the use of different age groups, different wording of questions, and so forth (Mosher, Chandra, & Jones, 2005, September 15).

In one study of 18–44 year olds, 1.3% of women and 1.9% of men reported they were "homosexual, gay, or lesbian." And, 5.5% of women and 2.0% of men said they were bisexual (Copen, Chandra, & Febo-Vazquez, 2016). Some research suggests that up to 7% of the population is "exclusively attracted" to same-sex partners (Epstein, 2016). Other estimates put the homosexual population as low as 1% (referring only to same-sex behavior) and as high as 24% (defined as any sexual attraction to the same sex). This high end refers specifically to young women, who show greater fluidity in their sexual attractions and orientations (Ainsworth & Baumeister, 2012; Epstein, 2016; Savin-Williams, 2009).

FIGURE 10.3
The Sexual Orientation Continuum
We can think of sexual orientation as a continuum rather than a set of discrete categories. This graph shows the range of orientations that might characterize a population (Epstein, 2016). Information from Epstein (2016).

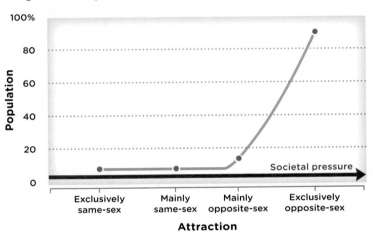

orgasm A powerful combination of extremely gratifying sensations and a series of rhythmic muscular contractions.

refractory period An interval of time during which a man cannot attain another orgasm.

sexual orientation A person's enduring sexual attraction to individuals of the same sex, opposite sex, or both sexes; a continuum that includes dimensions of sexuality, attraction, desire, and emotions.

heterosexual Attraction to members of the opposite sex.

homosexual Attraction to members of the same sex.

bisexual Attraction to members of both the same and opposite sex.

As you digest these statistics, remember that sex is, first and foremost, a human experience. We may have different preferences, but our bodies react to sexual activity in similar ways. As Masters and Johnson (1979) demonstrated, we all experience a similar sexual response cycle, regardless of orientation. Even our brains display similar patterns of activity, apparent from fMRI and PET studies, when we feel sexual desire (Diamond & Dickenson, 2012). What makes us different is what we find sexually arousing (Cerny & Janssen, 2011).

How Sexual Orientation Develops

We are not sure how sexual orientation develops, but many professionals in the field agree that it is not a matter of choice. Consistent with this perspective, most people feel they do not have control over whom they find attractive. Research suggests sexual orientation results from an interaction of many biological and environmental factors—nature *and* nurture (APA, 2008; Epstein, 2016).

GENETICS AND SEXUAL ORIENTATION To determine the influence of genes in sexual orientation, we turn to twin studies, which are commonly used to examine the degree to which nature and nurture contribute to psychological traits. Since monozygotic twins share 100% of their genetic make-up at conception, we expect them to share more genetically influenced characteristics than dizygotic twins, who only share about 50% of their genes. In a large study of Swedish twins, researchers explored the impact of genes and environment on "same-sex sexual behavior" (among 2,320 monozygotic twin pairs, 1,506 dizygotic twin pairs). In their sample, the monozygotic twins were moderately more likely than the dizygotic twins to have the same sexual orientation. They also found that same-sex sexual behavior for monozygotic twins had heritability estimates around 34–39% for men, and 18–19% for women (Långström, Rahman, Carlström, & Lichtenstein, 2010). Others report heritability estimates ranging from 25% to 50% for men, and "substantially lower" percentages for women (Epstein, 2016). Overall, people are more likely to be homosexual if they have close relatives who are homosexual, suggesting there is a genetic component for sexual orientation (close relatives share many common genes; Epstein, 2016). These findings highlight two important factors: Men and women differ in terms of the heritability of same-sex sexual behavior, and both genes and environment (nature and nurture) contribute to sexual orientation.

Researchers have searched for specific genes that might influence sexual orientation. Some have suggested that genes associated with male homosexuality might be transmitted by the mother. In one key study, around 64% of male siblings who were both homosexual had a set of several hundred genes in common, and these genes were located on the X chromosome (Hamer, Hu, Magnuson, Hu, & Pattatucci, 1993). But critics suggest this research was flawed, and no replications of this "gay gene" have been published since the original study (O'Riordan, 2012).

THE BIOLOGY OF SEXUAL ORIENTATION Can sexual orientation be detected in the brain? Research in this area is inconclusive. LeVay (1991) discovered that a "small group of neurons" in the hypothalamus of homosexual men was almost twice as big as that found in heterosexual men. However, he did not suggest this size difference was indicative of homosexuality; it may have resulted from factors unrelated to sexual orientation. Others have used MRI technology to demonstrate that the corpus callosum is thicker in homosexual men (Witelson et al., 2008).

If there really are brain differences associated with sexual orientations, they may emerge before birth. As noted earlier, the fetal gonads secrete hormones (estrogen and androgens) that influence the development of reproductive anatomy. These same hormones may help determine sexual orientation. For example, the presence of androgens (hormones secreted primarily by the male gonads) may steer the development of a sexual orientation toward women. This would lead to heterosexual orientation in men, but homosexual orientation in women (Mustanski, Chivers, & Bailey, 2002). Because it would be unethical to manipulate hormone levels in pregnant women, researchers rely on cases in which hormones are elevated because of a genetic abnormality or medication taken by a mother. For example, high levels of androgens early in a pregnancy may cause girls to be more "male-typed," and promote the development of a homosexual orientation (Berenbaum, Blakemore, & Beltz, 2011; Jordan-Young, 2012).

Interestingly, having older brothers in the family seems to be associated with homosexuality in men, particularly in right-handed men (Blanchard, 2008; **FIGURE 10.4**). Why would this be? Evolutionary theory would suggest that the more males there are in a family, the more potential for "unproductive competition" among the male siblings. If sons born later in the birth order were less aggressive, the result would be fewer problems among siblings, especially related to competition for mates and resources to support offspring. A homosexual younger brother would be less of a threat to an older brother than would a heterosexual younger brother.

How does right-handedness play a role? Some of the same genes associated with handedness are also linked to immune responses. If the fetus carries these genes, the mother may produce an anti-male antibody that impacts the development of brain structures hypothesized to play a role in sexual orientation, such as the hypothalamus. The mother's immune response increases with each additional son (Bogaert & Skorska, 2011), which would explain why younger sons are more likely to be homosexual. Although research has supported the birth order effect, the handedness link has been more difficult to replicate (Bogaert, 2007).

Despite numerous attempts to identify genetic markers for homosexuality, researchers have had very little success (Dar-Nimrod & Heine, 2011). Some suggest that the search for genes underlying homosexuality is misguided. Why do we spend so much time and money seeking biological explanations for a "valid alternative lifestyle" (Jacobs, 2012, p. 393)?

WHERE'S THE NURTURE? We have spent a great deal of time discussing the potential role of nature in sexual orientation. How does nurture fit into the picture? Earlier, we noted that sexual orientation might be understood as a continuum. At one end of the continuum are people who are strictly heterosexual; and at the other end are those who are undeniably homosexual. Many people fall somewhere in the middle of these two extremes. These middle-ground individuals have some flexibility in their orientation, particularly when they are young, and environmental factors (nurture) help determine where they fall on the continuum. Because we live in a *homomisic society*— one that strongly favors heterosexuality—most people in the middle will be pushed toward a heterosexual orientation. Those at either end of the continuum are less likely to be flexible in their orientation, in part due to the strong genetic component of sexual orientation (Epstein, 2016).

While we're on the subject of environment, we should note that children raised in same-sex parent households do not appear to be at a disadvantage compared to those from opposite-sex parent households. In fact, one study found that teens raised by lesbian mothers tended to score higher on measures of self-esteem and had fewer behavioral problems than those reared in comparable heterosexual households (Bos, van Gelderen, & Gartrell, 2015; Perrin, Cohen, & Caren, 2013).

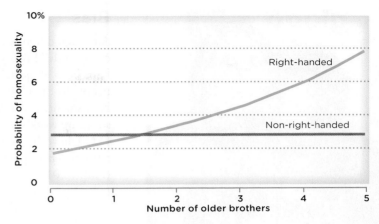

FIGURE 10.4
How Many Older Brothers?
The probability of a man's being homosexual may be associated with the number of older brothers he has, particularly if he is right-handed; however, the research is inconclusive.
Reproduced/adapted with permission of Psychology Press/Taylor & Francis Ltd (informaworld.com) from Blanchard (2008).

Love and Marriage

Comedian Wanda Sykes (left) and her wife, Alex Sykes, were married in 2008, when same-sex marriage was banned throughout most of the country (Jordan, 2009, May 13). In 2015 the Supreme Court legalized same-sex marriage across the nation, a legal shift that seems to parallel the changing attitudes of Americans. Between 2004 and 2015, support for same-sex marriage grew from 30% to 59% (Hook, 2015, March 9). Jason LaVeris/FilmMagic/Getty Images.

---

try this ↓

Ask yourself the following questions: (1) When did you choose your sexual orientation? (2) How can you be sure you made the right choice for yourself? (3) Imagine you have a different sexual orientation, and repeat Steps 1 and 2, noting any difference in the way you feel.

✓ CHECK YOUR ANSWERS IN APPENDIX C.

Bias

Although differences in sexual orientation are universal and have been evident throughout recorded history, individuals identified as members of the nonheterosexual minority have been subjected to stereotyping, prejudice, and discrimination. Nonheterosexual people in the United States, for example, have been, and continue to be, subjected to harassment, violence, and unfair practices related to housing and employment. Many states are working to amend these practices. "In total, 32 states (including Washington, D.C.) have implemented at least one kind of workplace nondiscrimination law or administrative policy that protects gay and transgender workers from discrimination" (Hunt, 2012, p. 2). Those in other states are left to fend for themselves, however, as federal protection is lacking (Kite & Bryant-Lees, 2016).

Counter to some stereotypes, a homosexual or bisexual orientation does not serve as a barrier to maintaining long-lasting relationships. Most same-sex couples experience the same ups and downs as heterosexual couples.

ACROSS THE WORLD
Homosexuality and Culture

When it comes to homosexuality in some parts of the world—particularly in developing nations—acceptance is lacking. One survey found that homosexuality is more widely accepted in North America, Europe, and Latin America than in Africa, Russia, and various regions of Asia. Age may be a factor in people's attitudes. For people under the age of 30 in Japan, almost 83% believe homosexuality should be accepted. In contrast, only 39% of Japanese men and women over 50 years had similar feelings about homosexuality. The numbers are similar all over the world; younger people are more accepting (Pew Research Center, 2013, June 4).

> **... PEOPLE ACROSS THE GLOBE ARE ROUTINELY VICTIMIZED FOR THEIR SEXUALITY. ...**

Still, people across the globe are routinely victimized for their sexuality. In Nigeria, men are physically beaten for homosexuality; in Iran, men are murdered for homosexuality; and in places like Russia and Uganda, the nations' "anti-homosexual laws" have resulted in citizens fleeing to other, more accepting, cultures to preserve their lives. "There is an urgent need for strategic reflection on how best to promote greater acceptance of sexual rights in a world in which too often sexuality has become a touchstone for fear, prejudice and hatred" (Altman & Beyrer, 2014, p. 19244).

What would happen if we lived in a world where sexual orientation was a completely neutral characteristic? Do you think the percent of people reporting homosexual versus heterosexual orientations would change?

Evolutionary Psychology and Sex

What is the purpose of sex? Evolutionary psychology would suggest that humans have sex to make babies and ensure the survival of the species (Buss, 1995). But if this were the only reason, then why would so many people choose same-sex partners? Some researchers believe it has something to do with "kin altruism," which suggests that homosexual men and women support reproduction in the family by helping relatives care for their children. Homosexual individuals may not "spend their time reproducing," but they can nurture the reproductive efforts of their "kin" (Erickson-Schroth, 2010).

Male orgasm has a clear evolutionary purpose, but female orgasm has been a mystery . . . perhaps until now. According to a recently proposed model, the female orgasm began as a reflex to induce ovulation (Pavličev & Wagner, 2016). Our mammalian ancestors would only ovulate in response to hormonal changes triggered by the physical stimulation of intercourse. "The female orgasm-like trait may have been adaptive . . . for inducing ovulation," the authors of the model explain (p. 1). At some point, our ancestors began ovulating spontaneously (without the need for physical stimulation), but the female orgasm remained.

There are other reasons to believe that human sex involves more than making babies. If sex were purely for reproduction, we would expect to see sexual activity occurring only during the fertile period of the female cycle. Obviously, this is not the case. Couples have sex throughout a woman's monthly cycle and long after she goes through menopause. Through sex, people feel pleasure, express affection, and form social bonds. In this respect, we are different from other members of the animal kingdom, who generally mate to procreate. There is at least one notable exception, however. If you could venture deep into the forests of the Democratic Republic of Congo, you might be surprised at what you would see happening between our close primate cousins, the bonobos.

DIDN'T SEE THAT COMING
Great Ape Sex

Bonobos are tree- and land-dwelling great apes that look like small and lanky versions of chimpanzees. And like chimps, these animals are closely related to humans, sharing 98.7% of our genetic material (Prüfer et al., 2012). Bonobos and people also happen to share some sexual behaviors.

BONOBOS HAVE BOTH ORAL AND VAGINAL SEX.

Bonobos have both oral sex and vaginal sex. They enjoy a variety of positions, including the so-called missionary style commonly favored by people. They French kiss and fondle each other. Males mate with females, but pairs of females also rub their genitals together, a phenomenon known as *genito–genital rubbing,* or *G–G rubbing.* Males engage in similar activities called *scrotal rubbing* and *penis fencing* (De Waal, 2009).

In bonobo society, sex happens at the times you might least suspect. Imagine two female bonobos simultaneously discovering a delicious piece of sugarcane. Both of them want it, so you might expect a little aggression to ensue. But what do the bonobos do instead? They rub their genitals together, of course! Now picture two males competing for the same female. They could fight over her, but why fight when you can make love? The vying males set aside their dispute and engage in a friendly scrotal rub (De Waal, 2009).

Sex Conquers All?
Two bonobos enjoy a slobbery kiss. In bonobo society, sexual activity appears to reduce social tension and promote unity—a strategy that seems to work very well, because bonobos rarely fight. Females are the dominant sex, and the bonds between them hold communities together (Santa Maria, 2012, February 14). Biosphoto/Superstock.

As these examples illustrate, bonobo sex has a lot to do with maintaining social harmony. Sex is used to defuse the tension that might arise over competition for food and mates (De Waal, 2009). It helps younger females bond with the dominant females in a new community—an important function given the supremacy of females in this species (Clay & Zuberbühler, 2012). Female relationships, it seems, are the glue holding together bonobo society.

What kinds of similarities do you detect between the sex lives of bonobos and humans?

The Sex We Have

Thus far we have discussed sex in broad terms, but let's get into some specifics. What constitutes "normal," or typical, sexual behavior? Alfred Kinsey (1894–1956) and his colleagues, whose work was mentioned earlier, went to great lengths to answer this question and others.

In **Chapter 1,** we emphasized that representative samples enable us to generalize findings to populations. Here, we see that inferences about sexual behaviors for groups other than White, well-educated Protestants could be problematic, as few members of these groups participated in the Kinsey study.

GATHERING SEX DATA The Kinsey study was groundbreaking in terms of its data content and methodology, which included accuracy checks and assurances of confidentiality. The Kinsey data continue to serve as a valuable reference for researchers studying how sexual behaviors have evolved over time. However, Kinsey's work was not without limitations. For example, Kinsey and colleagues (1948, 1953) utilized a biased sampling technique that resulted in a sample that was not representative of the population. It was a completely White sample, with an overrepresentation of well-educated Protestants (Potter, 2006; Wallin, 1949). Another criticism of the Kinsey study is that it failed to determine the context in which orgasms occurred. Was a partner involved? Was the orgasm achieved through masturbation (Potter, 2006)?

Subsequent research has been better designed, including samples more representative of the population. Robert Michael and colleagues (1994) conducted the now-classic National Health and Social Life Survey (NHSLS), which examined the sexual activities of a representative sample of some 3,000 Americans between the ages of 18 and 59. A more recent study included a sample of approximately 5,800 men and women between the ages of 14 and 94 years (Herbenick et al., 2010).

What patterns of sexual activity do we see today? Most people in the United States start out relatively young, with about 77% of adults reporting they engaged in intercourse by age 20, and 95% by age 44. The overwhelming majority are not waiting for marriage (Finer, 2007; see **FIGURE 10.5**). That being said, married people do have more sex than those who are unmarried (Laumann et al., 1994). Good for them, because sex has many benefits beyond pure pleasure. According to a large study of Swedish adults, the frequency of penile–vaginal intercourse is associated with sexual satisfaction, as well as satisfaction with relationships, mental health, and life in general (Brody & Costa, 2009). Frequency of penile–vaginal sex has also been correlated with greater life expectancy, lower blood pressure, slimmer waistline, and lower risk of prostate and breast cancer (Brody, 2010). Other sexual activities, such as masturbation, may be inversely related to measures of life satisfaction (Regnerus &

Radical Research

Alfred Kinsey interviews a subject in his office at the Institute for Sex Research, now The Kinsey Institute. Kinsey began investigating human sexuality in the 1930s, when talking about sex was taboo. He started gathering data with surveys, but then switched to personal interviews, which he believed to be more effective. These interviews often went on for hours and included hundreds of questions (PBS, 2005, January 27). Wallace Kirkland/ Getty Images.

FIGURE 10.5

Premarital Sex in the United States
Looking across adolescence and into adulthood, the number of people having sex increases steadily with age. Of those currently having sex, 97% engaged in sex before marriage. Information from Finer (2007), Figure 1.

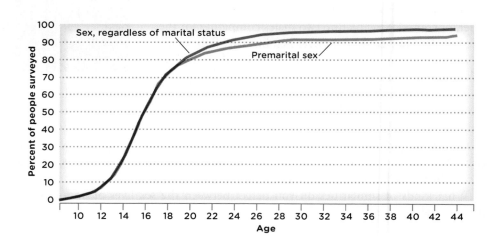

Gordon, 2013; see **TABLE 10.1** for reported gender differences in frequency of sexual activity).

SEXUAL ACTIVITY IN RELATIONSHIPS In the United States, the average age at first marriage is around 27 for women and 29 for men (Fry, 2015, November 11). The odds of a first marriage lasting at least 10 years is 68% for women and 70% for men, and the probability of a first marriage lasting 20 years is only 52% for women and 56% for men (Copen, Daniels, Vespa, & Mosher, 2012). Most Americans are monogamous (one partner at a time), and 65–85% of married men and approximately 80% of married women report that they have always been faithful to their spouses (Laumann, Gagnon, Michael, & Michaels, 1994). Of course, not everyone agrees that marriage goes hand–in–hand with monogamy. In one study, 4–5% of the participants reported they are in "open" relationships, that is, consensually nonmonogamous relationships (Conley, Ziegler, Moors, Matsick, & Valentine, 2013).

TABLE 10.1	**WHAT'S GOING ON?**	
Sexual Activity	Average Frequency in Prior Month for Men	Average Frequency in Prior Month for Women
Penile–vaginal intercourse	5.2	4.8
Oral sex	2.3	1.9
Anal sex	0.10	0.08
Masturbation	4.5	1.5

How often do people engage in different types of sexual activity? Here are the monthly self-reported averages for adult men and women (the average age being 41). Keep in mind that significant variation exists around these averages. Information from Brody and Costa (2009), Table 1, p. 1950.

Keeping Up with the Joneses—in Bed

Couples who have sex at least once a week are happiest, perhaps because that rate is thought to be the norm.

from the pages of
SCIENTIFIC AMERICAN

How much sex is enough? You might question the premise of that query, but new research reports that there's a limit to the benefits of carnal pleasures. Beyond a certain frequency, more sex does not mean more happiness. One possible reason: as long as we are doing it as often as our neighbors are, we're content.

For a recent paper in *Social Psychological and Personality Science,* Amy Muise, Ulrich Schimmack and Emily Impett, all at the University of Toronto Mississauga, analyzed three survey samples comprising more than 30,000 Americans. They found that among couples, sex frequency positively correlated with satisfaction in life, confirming earlier reports. (They found no such link for singles.) The difference in happiness between those who had sex less than once a month and those who had sex once a week was at least as great as that between those earning less than $15,000 a year and those earning more than $100,000. Direction of causality is unclear; their analysis suggested that sex frequency increases relationship satisfaction, which increases happiness, but they also found evidence for the reverse pathway, in which general life satisfaction increases relationship satisfaction, which in turn increases sex frequency.

Unlike in previous studies, a subtler pattern also appeared: at frequencies greater than once a week, the happiness graph flattened out. The reason "is an open question that we are exploring," Muise says. Her team thinks one possibility is that people are satisfied when they are doing it as much as they think they should be, a standard set by their peers. Indeed, the average for couples is once a week.

In support of this idea, Tim Wadsworth, a sociologist at the University of Colorado Boulder, reported in 2014 in *Social Indicators Research* that happiness is positively correlated with sex frequency but negatively correlated with the sex frequency of others in the same demographic group, a rate people probably surmise from conversation and media. "How much sex is appropriate, like so many other questions, depends on what we think is 'normal,'" Wadsworth says. One sees the same trend with income: a 2010 paper in *Psychological Science* reported that income rank among peers predicted happiness better than did absolute income. So if you are worried you and your sweetheart are failing to keep up with the Joneses, there is an easy solution: just tell yourself you're having *better* sex than all those once-a-weekers. **Matthew Hutson. Reproduced with permission. Copyright © 2016 Scientific American, a division of Nature America, Inc. All rights reserved.**

TABLE 10.2 HOOKUP BEHAVIOR

Behavior	% Undergraduates
Kissing	98
Sexual touching above waist	58
Sexual touching below the waist	53
Performed oral sex	36
Received oral sex	35
Sexual intercourse	34

What exactly do college students mean when they say they "hooked up" with someone? As you can see from the data presented here, hooking up can signify anything from a brief kiss to sexual intercourse. Information from Garcia et al. (2012).

SEXUAL ACTIVITY AND GENDER DIFFERENCES As stereotypes suggest, men think about sex more often than women. In the United States, 54% of men report thinking about sex "every day or several times a day"; 67% of women report thinking about sex only "a few times a week or a few times a month" (Laumann et al., 1994). One other notable gender difference is that men consistently report a higher frequency of masturbation (Peplau, 2003), a finding that has been replicated with a British sample (Gerressu, Mercer, Graham, Wellings, & Johnson, 2008). Decades ago in the United States, men tended to be more tolerant than women about casual sex before marriage, as well as more permissive in their attitudes about extramarital sex (Laumann et al., 1994). But these differences in attitude are not apparent in heterosexual teenagers and young adults, as young men and women more commonly engage in hookups, or "brief uncommitted sexual encounters among individuals who are not romantic partners or dating each other" (Garcia, Reiber, Massey, & Merriwether, 2012, p. 161). For these young people, attitudes about casual sex are apparent in their "hookup" behavior (**TABLE 10.2**). Researchers have shown that physical strength and attractiveness are positively linked to casual sex in men, but not in women (Lukaszewski, Larson, Gildersleeve, Roney, & Haselton, 2014). From an evolutionary perspective, this would serve men well, as the more sex they have, the greater the opportunity for reproduction; women, on the other hand, would not benefit in the same way.

SEXUAL ACTIVITY AND AGE What sexual encounters do people commonly have? Herbenick and colleagues (2010) used a cross-sectional survey study to provide a snapshot of the types and rates of sexual behaviors across a wide range of ages in the United States. They found that masturbation is more common than partnered sexual activities among adolescents and people over the age of 70. They also discovered that more than half of the participants aged 18 to 49 had engaged in oral sex over the past year, with a lower proportion of the younger and older age groups engaging in this activity. Penetrative sex (vaginal and anal) was most common among adults ages 20 to 49. In another study of around 3,000 adults (57 to 85 years old), researchers reported that aging did not seem to adversely affect interest in sexual activity; many of the respondents in their sixties, seventies, and eighties were still sexually active. These findings challenge the popular assumption that elderly people are "asexual." Sexual problems are common in older people, but many have vibrant and satisfying sex lives (Taylor & Gosney, 2011).

ACROSS THE WORLD

What They Are Doing in Bed . . . or Elsewhere

WHICH COUNTRY'S POPULATION HAS THE MOST SEX?

How often do people in New Zealand have sex? How many lovers has the average Israeli had? And are Chileans happy with the amount of lovemaking they do? These are just a few of the questions answered by the Global Sex Survey (2005), which, we dare to say, is one of the sexiest scientific studies out there (and which was sponsored by Durex, a condom manufacturer). We cannot report all the survey results, but here is a roundup of those we found most interesting:

- People in Greece have the most sex—an average of 138 times per year, or 2 to 3 times per week.

- People in Japan have the least amount of sex—an average of 45 times per year, or a little less than once per week.

- The average age for losing one's virginity is lowest among Icelanders (between 15 and 16) and highest for those from India (between 19 and 20).

- Across nations, the average number of sexual partners is 9. If gender is taken into account, that number is a little higher for men (11) and lower for women (7).

- Of respondents, 50% reported having sex in cars, 39% in bathrooms, and 2% in airplanes.

- Across the world, many people use sexual aids such as pornography (41%), massage oils and creams (31%), lubricants (30%), and vibrators (22%).

- Approximately 13% of adults say they have had a sexually transmitted infection.

- Nearly half the people around the world are happy with their sex lives.

As you reflect on these results, remember that surveys have limitations. People are not always honest when it comes to answering questions about personal issues (like sex), and the wording of questions can influence people's responses. Even if responses are accurate, we can only speculate about the beliefs and attitudes underlying them. 🌐→

Contemporary Trends in Sexual Behavior

As noted earlier, we can define sex as an activity (for example, she had *sex*), but how we define what constitutes sex is not always consistent (Hill, Sanders, & Reinisch, 2016; Schwarz, Hassebrauck, & Dörfler, 2010). If you ask one teenager whether she has had "sex," she might say no, even if she has had oral sex, whereas another teen might say yes, thinking that oral sex does count as sex. Such variability may explain why teenagers are more likely to participate in oral sex than intercourse, and to have more oral sex partners because they are not defining it as sex (Hans, Gillen, & Akande, 2010; Prinstein, Meade, & Cohen, 2003). It is important for researchers, medical professionals, and those in-volved in health promotion to use "clear behaviorally-specific terminology" when com-municating about sex (Hill et al., 2016, p. 36).

If oral sex doesn't qualify as "sex," as some teenagers believe, then it doesn't pose a health risk . . . right? Wrong. Many diseases can be transmitted through oral sex—among them HIV, herpes, syphilis, genital warts, and hepatitis (Saini, Saini, & Sharma, 2010). Needless to say, it is crucial for teen-targeted sex education programs to spread the word about the risks associated with oral sex (Brewster & Tillman, 2008).

THINK IT THROUGH
Sext You Later

🧠 What kinds of environmental factors encourage casual attitudes about sex among teens? Most adolescents have cell phones these days, and around 73% have access to smartphones (Lenhart, 2015, April 9). A large num-ber of those young people are using their phones to exchange text messages with sexually explicit words or images. In other words, today's teenagers are doing a lot of *sexting*. One study found that 20% of high school students have used their cell phones to share sexual pictures of themselves, and twice as many have received such images from others (Strassberg, McKinnon, Sustaíta, & Rullo, 2013). Teens who sext are more likely to have sex and take sexual risks, such as having unprotected sex (Rice et al., 2012). Sex-ting has also led to "criminal and civil legal charges" against minors (Lorang, McNiel, & Binder, 2016).

ARE TEENS WHO SEXT MORE LIKELY TO HAVE SEX?

Sexting carries another set of risks for those who are married or in committed relationships. As many people see it, sexting outside a relationship is a genuine form of cheating. And because text messages can be saved and forwarded, it becomes an easy and effective way to damage the reputations of people, sometimes famous ones. Perhaps you have read about the sexting scandals associated with golfer Tiger Woods, ex-footballer Brett Favre, and former U.S. Congressman Anthony Weiner?

Happy Between the Sheets
Nearly half (44%) of adults participating in the Global Sex Survey said they were happy with their sex lives. Men were more likely than women to say they wanted to have sex more often (Global Sex Survey, 2005). East/Shutterstock.

CONNECTIONS

In **Chapter 1,** we discussed limitations of using self-report surveys. People often resist revealing attitudes or behaviors related to sensitive topics, such as sexual activity. The risk is gathering data that do not accurately represent participants' attitudes and beliefs, particularly with face-to-face interviews.

I'll Show You Mine if You Show Me Yours
Media reports often shine the spotlight on adolescent sexting, but adults are the ones who sext the most. Some research suggests that women may be more likely to send sext messages, while men are more apt to be on the receiving end (Klettke, Hallford, & Mellor, 2014). What could be the cause of this gender disparity? spyarm/Shutterstock.

Now that's a lot of bad news about sexting. But can it also occur in the absence of negative behaviors and outcomes? When sexting occurs between two consenting, or shall we say "consexting," adults, it may be completely harmless (provided no infidelity is involved). According to one survey of young adults, sexting was not linked to unsafe sex or psychological problems such as depression and low self-esteem (Gordon-Messer, Bauermeister, Grodzinski, & Zimmerman, 2013). For some, sexting is just a new variation on flirting; for others, it may fulfill a deeper need, like helping them feel more secure in their romantic attachments (Weisskirch & Delevi, 2011).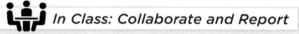

SEX EDUCATION One way to learn about this intriguing phenomenon of sexting —or any sexual topic, for that matter—is through sex education in the classroom. School is the primary place where American children get information about sex (Byers, 2011), yet sex education is somewhat controversial. Some parents are afraid that it essentially condones sexual activity among young people. Until 2010, Title V federal funding was limited to states that taught abstinence only (Chin et al., 2012). Yet, research suggests that programs promoting abstinence are associated with more teenage pregnancies: States with a greater emphasis on abstinence (as reflected in state laws and policies) have higher teenage pregnancy and birthrates (Stanger-Hall & Hall, 2011).

Teenagers who receive a thorough education on sexual activity, including information on how to prevent pregnancy, are less likely to become pregnant (or get someone pregnant). Research shows that formal sex education increases safe-sex practices, reducing the likelihood of disease transmission (Kohler, Manhart, & Lafferty, 2008; Stanger-Hall & Hall, 2011). Sex education clearly impacts the behaviors of teenagers and young adults. In some European nations, "openness" and "comfort" about sex lead to an understanding that sexuality is "a lifelong process." Sex education programs in these countries aim "to create self-determined and responsible attitudes and behavior with regard to sexuality, contraception, relationships and life strategies and planning" (Advocates for Youth, 2009; Stanger-Hall & Hall, 2011, p. 9).

👥 In Class: Collaborate and Report

In your groups, discuss **A)** what kind of formal sex education you received, **B)** the pros and cons of such a program, and **C)** what you would do to improve it. **D)** Using the ideas you just discussed, design a campaign to promote sex education for teens.

 show what you know

1. Masters and Johnson studied the physiological changes that accompany sexual activity. They determined that men and women experience a similar sexual response cycle, including the following ordered phases:
   a. excitement, plateau, orgasm, and resolution.
   b. plateau, excitement, orgasm, relaxation.
   c. excitement, plateau, orgasm.
   d. excitement, orgasm, resolution.

2. Some have suggested that "kin altruism" may explain how homosexual men and women contribute to the overall reproduction of the family, by helping to care for children of relatives. This explanation draws on the _____ perspective.

3. Explain how twin studies have been used to explore the development of sexual orientation.

✓ CHECK YOUR ANSWERS IN APPENDIX C.

The Trouble with Sex

 NOT TONIGHT, BABE *Ever since we had kids, my husband never seems to want sex. What can we do to rekindle his interest?*

My boyfriend used to get really turned on by me, but now he seems to be more interested in Internet porn. What happened?

Low desire is the number one sexual problem facing Dr. Buehler's clients. What's behind the decline in libido? "It's generally different for men and women," Dr. Buehler says. Every case is unique, but a common explanation for low desire might be called *The Woman Wearing Too Many Hats.* "What I frequently find is that women have a need to be perfect in everything they do, and women also have a lot of demands put on them (or they put them on themselves)," Dr. Buehler explains. "They don't leave any energy left over for pleasure." So when their partners want sex, it just becomes another demand.

Is it possible a woman might be avoiding sex by packing her schedule with activities? Perhaps she does not derive much pleasure from sex (she may have trouble achieving orgasm), or maybe there is a problem in the relationship that makes her want to push away her partner. Dr. Buehler is always on the lookout for relationship problems that have infiltrated the bedroom.

Low libido is much less common in men, and when present, often results from low testosterone levels. If the problem isn't biological, then there may be a relationship issue, Dr. Buehler explains. "You know, just not participating in sex as a way of communicating that 'I'm not interested in being with you right now. I don't like things that are going on in our relationship.'"

One of the most challenging scenarios, according to Dr. Buehler, is when the man has lower desire than the woman. This often leads to feelings of rejection on the woman's part: *He's not into me anymore. He's mad at me. He's having an affair!* "Everybody thinks it's normal for men to have more desire, but you know, there are individual variations for both sexes," Dr. Buehler explains. (The assumption that all men are sex machines is a prime example of a *gender-role stereotype,* a concept presented earlier in the chapter.) Some men want sex twice a day, whereas others are perfectly satisfied with once a week. "If everybody is happy and fulfilled," Dr. Buehler notes, "it's normal." ●

"I really think you should see a specialist about your lack of libido, Sharon."

Sexual Dysfunctions

LO 8 Identify the symptoms of sexual dysfunctions.

When there is a "significant disturbance" in the ability to respond sexually or to gain pleasure from sex, we call this **sexual dysfunction** (APA, 2013). In the National Health and Social Life Survey, researchers found 43% of women and 31% of men suffered from some sort of sexual dysfunction (Laumann, Paik, & Rosen, 1999).

Everyday stressors or situational issues may cause temporary sexual difficulties, which can be resolved once the stress or the situation has passed. Then there are the longer-term sexual difficulties, which can stem from a variety of issues, including beliefs about sex, ignorance about sexual practices, and even performance expectations. Health conditions can also give rise to sexual difficulties. The *biopsychosocial* perspective is invaluable for helping to untangle the roots of sexual problems.

Sexual dysfunctions may result from problems with desire, arousal, orgasm, and pain, but these are not mutually exclusive categories (**TABLE 10.3**, on the next page). Let's examine each one more carefully.

DESIRE Situational issues such as illness, fatigue, or frustration with one's partner can lead to temporary problems with desire. In some cases, however, lack of desire is persistent and distressing. Although low desire can affect both men and women, women tend to report desire problems more frequently (Brotto, 2010; Heiman, 2002).

AROUSAL Problems with arousal occur when the psychological desire to engage in sexual behavior is present, but the body does not cooperate. Men may have trouble

You Asked, Dr. Buehler Answers

http://qrs.ly/db5a5eu

How do you make sexual topics more approachable as a discussion?

scan this →

sexual dysfunction A significant disturbance in the ability to respond sexually or to gain pleasure from sex.

TABLE 10.3 SEXUAL DYSFUNCTIONS

Dysfunction	Description
Delayed ejaculation	Frequent delayed ejaculation or failure to ejaculate
Erectile disorder	Issues in getting or maintaining an erection, or a decrease in penile rigidity
Female orgasmic disorder	Consistent inability to reach orgasm, reduced orgasmic intensity, or not reaching orgasm quickly enough during sexual activity
Female sexual interest/arousal disorder	Reduced interest in sex, lack of initiation of sexual activity, lack of sexual excitement during sexual activity, or lack of genital sensations during sexual activity
Genito-pelvic pain/penetration disorder	Refers to four types of co-occurring symptoms specific to women: difficulty having intercourse, genito-pelvic pain, fear of pain or vaginal penetration, and tension of pelvic floor muscles
Male hypoactive sexual desire disorder	Reduced interest in and desire for sex; lacking or absent sexual/erotic thoughts or fantasies
Premature (early) ejaculation	Related to the timing of, or the inability to control, ejaculation when it occurs, specifically in relation to vaginal sex

Sexual dysfunction can stem from problems with desire, arousal, orgasm, and pain. Above are some of the most common sexual dysfunctions. Information from APA (2013) and Goshtasebi, Gandevani, and Foroushani (2011).

getting or maintaining an erection, or they may experience a decrease in rigidity, which is called *erectile disorder* (APA, 2013). As many as 20% of all men report they have occasionally experienced problems with erections (Hock, 2016). Women can also struggle with arousal. *Female sexual interest/arousal disorder* is apparent in reduced interest in sex, lack of initiation of sexual activities, reduced excitement, or decreased genital sensations during sexual activity (APA, 2013).

ORGASM Disorders related to orgasm are yet another category of dysfunction. *Female orgasmic disorder* is diagnosed when a woman is consistently unable to reach orgasm, has reduced orgasmic intensity, or does not reach orgasm quickly enough during sexual activity (APA, 2013). Men who experience frequent delay or inability to ejaculate might have a condition known as *delayed ejaculation* (APA, 2013; Segraves, 2010). With this disorder, the ability to achieve orgasm and ejaculate is inhibited or delayed during partnered sexual activity. Men who have trouble controlling when they ejaculate (particularly during vaginal sexual activity) may suffer from *premature (early) ejaculation* (APA, 2013).

PAIN The final category of sexual dysfunction is painful intercourse. Women typically report more problems with intercourse-related pain than men. *Genito-pelvic pain/penetration disorder* refers to four types of co-occurring symptoms specific to women: difficulty having intercourse, pain in the genitals or pelvis, fear of pain or vaginal penetration, and tension of the pelvic floor muscles (APA, 2013). Up to 15% of women in North America report frequent pain during intercourse, and issues related to pain are associated with reduced desire and arousal.

Chris Wildt/CartoonStock.com.

"This stuff isn't selling. Maybe we should switch to Viagra."

Sexual dysfunction is surprisingly common and often related to psychological and social variables such as anxiety and relationship troubles. The good news is that many of these conditions can be resolved with interventions that target their biological, psychological, and social roots. Unfortunately, we cannot say the same for some of the diseases transmitted through sex. As you will learn in the next section, some sexually transmitted infections have no cures.

 **show what you know**

1. Difficulties related to sexual activity can be divided into four categories:
   a. being heterosexual, homosexual, bisexual, and nonsexual.
   b. excitement, plateau, orgasm, and relaxation.
   c. desire, arousal, orgasm, and pain.
   d. desire, arousal, orgasm, and the sexual response cycle.

2. A man in his late fifties is concerned because he has occasional troubles with delayed ejaculation and his wife is not interested in sex. They have three small children and both work full time. Many of their friends are "empty nesters" whose grown children have moved out, and they seem to be celebrating their second honeymoons. Use the biopsychosocial perspective to help understand what might be contributing to this couple's sexual problems.

√ CHECK YOUR ANSWERS IN APPENDIX C.

Sex, Its Consequences, and Culture

Sexually Transmitted Infections

LO 9 Classify sexually transmitted infections and identify their causes.

Although sex is pleasurable and exciting for most, it is not without risks. Many people carry **sexually transmitted infections (STIs)**—diseases or illnesses passed on through sexual activity (Workowski & Bolan, 2015). The more sexual partners you have, the greater your risk of acquiring an STI. But you can lower your risk by communicating with your partner. People who know that their partners have had (or are having) sex with others face a lower risk of acquiring an STI than those who do not know. Why is this so? If you are aware of your partner's activities, you may be more likely to take preventative measures, such as using condoms. Of course, there is always the possibility that your sexual partner (or you) has a disease but doesn't know it. Some people with STIs are asymptomatic, meaning they have no symptoms. There are many causes of STIs, but we will focus on two of the most common types: *bacterial* and *viral* (see **TABLE 10.4** on the next page for data on their prevalence).

BACTERIAL INFECTIONS *Syphilis* is a bacterial infection. Initial signs of syphilis might include sores on the genitals, breasts, anus, lips, or in the mouth. If the infection proceeds untreated over the course of years, it can lead to heart failure, blindness, liver damage, severe mental disturbance, or death. Another bacterial infection is *gonorrhea*, one of the most pervasive STIs in the United States. The initial symptoms of gonorrhea are more obvious for men than women. For a man, the first sign might be painful urination and cloudy discharge with a bad odor. Early symptoms in women, such as unusual discharge from the vagina, might go unnoticed or be mistaken for a less serious problem. Without treatment, men can become sterile and develop problems with the prostate and testes. Untreated gonorrhea can also lead to sterility in women. Like other bacterial infections, *gonorrhea* is treated with antibiotics, but resistance to these medications is becoming a problem (Centers for Disease Control [CDC], 2015b; 2016h).

Another common bacterial infection is *chlamydia*. Teenage girls and young women are the most susceptible to this infection due to the immature development of the

sexually transmitted infections (STIs) Diseases or illnesses transmitted through sexual activity.

TABLE 10.4 SEXUALLY TRANSMITTED INFECTIONS (STIs)

STI	Symptoms	Estimated Annual Prevalence of New Infections in the U.S.
Chlamydia	Women often have no symptoms; men can experience discharge from penis, burning when urinating, and pain/swelling of the testicles.	2.86 million
Gonorrhea	No symptoms may be present in men or women. Men can experience burning when urinating; white, yellow, or green discharge. Women can experience pain/burning when urinating, or vaginal discharge.	820,000
Herpes	Blisters on the genitals, rectum, or mouth; painful sores after blisters break; fever, body aches, and swollen glands can occur.	776,000
Human papillomavirus (HPV)	Genital warts; certain cancers; warts growing in the throat.	14 million
Syphilis	Firm, round sores that first appear where the infection enters the body and can then spread to other parts of the body.	63,450

Sexually transmitted infections (STIs) are extremely common. HPV, for example, is so widespread that nearly all sexually active people are infected at one time or another. Information from CDC (2013; 2015a, b; 2016a, b, c).

cervix. Chlamydia can affect the urethral tube and cervix, but it may spread to the uterus and fallopian tubes, leading to *pelvic inflammatory disease,* which can result in lower back pain, menstrual difficulties, and headaches. Around 80–90% of women with chlamydia are asymptomatic, and 80% of women with gonorrhea are asymptomatic (CDC, 2015d).

VIRAL INFECTIONS One of the most common viral STIs is *genital herpes,* caused by *herpes simplex virus two (HSV-2).* HSV-2 results in sores and lesions. Herpes can also infect other parts of the body, such as the mouth (CDC, 2015a).

Even more common than herpes is the *human papillomavirus (HPV),* which can cause genital warts. Over 100 types of HPV have been identified, and research shows that untreated HPV can lead to the development of cervical, vaginal, urethral, penile, and anal cancers. One of the most worrisome aspects of HPV is that many carriers have no symptoms, so they can spread the infection without even knowing they have it. Although bacterial infections often clear up with antibiotics, viral infections like herpes and HPV have no cure, only treatments to reduce symptoms (CDC, 2016e).

LO 10 **Describe human immunodeficiency virus (HIV) and its role in acquired immune deficiency syndrome (AIDS).**

HIV AND AIDS Perhaps the most feared STI is **human immunodeficiency virus (HIV).** This virus is spread through the transfer of bodily fluids (such as blood, semen, vaginal fluid, or breast milk) and eventually causes the breakdown of the immune system. HIV often will not show up on blood tests for up to 6 months after infection, which means that even if you have had a negative test result for HIV, you cannot assume you are "safe"—hence, the importance of having protected sex. HIV eventually progresses to **acquired immune deficiency syndrome (AIDS),** which generally results in a severely compromised immune system. A weakened immune system makes the body much more susceptible to opportunistic infections caused by bacteria, viruses, or fungi, and this vulnerability increases as the disease progresses.

human immunodeficiency virus (HIV) A virus transferred via bodily fluids (blood, semen, vaginal fluid, or breast milk) that causes the breakdown of the immune system, eventually resulting in AIDS.

acquired immune deficiency syndrome (AIDS) This condition, caused by HIV, generally results in a severely compromised immune system, which makes the body vulnerable to other infections.

The World Health Organization (WHO) reported in 2016 that approximately 78 million people were infected with HIV and some 35 million had died of HIV complications since it was first identified in 1981. In addition, the WHO (2016b) reported that approximately 1.1 million people died AIDS-related deaths in 2015. In the United States, approximately 1.2 million people have HIV, and it's likely that around 13% of these people are unaware they have the infection (CDC, 2015c). Worldwide, HIV is a leading cause of death, and in sub-Saharan Africa it is *the* leading killer (Kendall, 2012). **INFOGRAPHIC 10.2**, on the next page, provides a closer examination of regional statistics.

Apparently, knowing the dangers of HIV does not motivate most people to change their risky habits. Unprotected sex and intravenous drug use (through a needle) are the most common forms of transmission. There is no cure for HIV/AIDS, but anti-HIV drugs have been developed to help reduce viral levels in the blood. These medications are very expensive, with a cost of approximately $20,000 per year per person, and funding shortfalls result in over 2,000 people in the United States not being able to get the treatments they need (Maxmen, 2012). The problem is global. In 2015 approximately 20 million HIV sufferers around the world were not receiving treatment (WHO, 2016b).

Many people are uncomfortable discussing HIV and other STIs, and often those who suffer from these conditions are stigmatized. But everyone—with the exception of those who practice abstinence—is vulnerable. When it comes to STIs, or any aspect of human sexuality, be careful about passing judgment.

AIDS in Africa
This young woman in Johannesburg, South Africa, was orphaned when HIV/AIDS claimed the lives of her parents. She is now the guardian of her younger sisters and her own baby. In South Africa, HIV/AIDS affects about one in five adults between the ages of 15 and 49 (UNAIDS, 2015).
Pep Bonet/NOOR/Redux.

"Normal" Is Relative

LO 11   Define sexual scripts and describe some of the ways people deviate from sex-related cultural norms.

It is only natural for us to wonder if what we are doing between the sheets (or elsewhere) is normal or healthy. Is it normal to masturbate? Is it normal to fantasize about sex with strangers? The answers to these types of questions depend somewhat on cultural context. Most of us unknowingly learn *sexual scripts,* or cultural rules that tell us what types of activities are "appropriate" and don't interfere with healthy sexual intimacy. In some cultures, the sexual script suggests that women should have minimal, if any, sexual experience before marriage, but men are expected to explore their sexuality, or "sow their wild oats."

FETISHES AND PARAPHILIA   There are some behaviors that most people would consider unusual, regardless of culture. **Paraphilia** is the term used to describe these uncommon sexual acts (**TABLE 10.5**, on page 449). An example would be *fetishism,* a sexual fixation with an object or nongenital body part (APA, 2013). Fetishes center on just about any object you can imagine, from stuffed animals, to bald heads, to red toenails.

How do sex therapists deal with these sexual obsessions? According to Dr. Buehler, therapists and clients in past decades would spend years trying to understand and eliminate fetishes. "These days the thinking is, if it doesn't hurt anybody, who cares," she says. "You like shoes? Okay. You like latex? Great. Whatever it is, it's fine, as long as whatever activity you're involved [in] is consensual" (and does not involve children). The issue is usually a couple's issue, Dr. Buehler adds. Can the partner accept the fetish, and if so, is there a way to integrate it into the couple's sex life? If not, perhaps the partner can tolerate the other person masturbating with the fetish object.

As already mentioned, many people are not comfortable discussing their *own* sexual activities, which often leaves them wondering if what they do is appropriate. Sexual

paraphilia Uncommon sexual acts.

STIs Around the World

Should you be concerned about sexually transmitted infections (STIs)? Every year in the U.S., new STI cases number 20 million. Half of these new infections occur among people aged 15 to 24 (CDC, 2013). The graph at right shows estimated numbers of people living with selected STIs in the Americas. The bacterial STIs shown here in teal are curable, but can have serious health consequences if left untreated. Viral STIs, shown in red, have no cures. The map below provides estimated numbers for HIV worldwide.

SOURCES: CDC (2013); LOOKER, GARNETT, AND SCHMID (2008); UNAIDS (2012b); WHO (2008c).

STIs in the Americas

(INCLUDES NORTH, SOUTH, AND CENTRAL AMERICA)

SYPHILIS	2,800,000
HIV	2,800,000
GONORRHEA	11,000,000
CHLAMYDIA	26,500,000
HPV (U.S. ONLY)	79,000,000
HERPES	83,500,000

BACTERIAL   **VIRAL**

HIV Around the World

EASTERN EUROPE AND CENTRAL ASIA
1,400,000

WESTERN AND CENTRAL EUROPE
900,000

EAST ASIA
830,000

NORTH, SOUTH, AND CENTRAL AMERICA
2,800,000

MIDDLE EAST AND NORTH AFRICA
300,000

SOUTH AND SOUTHEAST ASIA
4,000,000

SUB-SAHARAN AFRICA
23,500,000

 STIs can have serious implications, especially for young women.

 Some people with STIs are asymptomatic. Many infections are never diagnosed.

 Serious health consequences can be avoided if curable STIs are treated in time. The CDC recommends screening for chlamydia and other STIs depending on risk factors.

HIV will not show up on blood tests for up to 6 months after infection. Protected sex is important even if a recent test showed a negative result.

 STIs are preventable. You can lower your risk by communicating with your partner.

TABLE 10.5 PARAPHILIAS

Type	Description	Prevalence
Exhibitionism	Sexual arousal as a result of exposing oneself to an unwilling bystander	Males: 2–4% Females: number unknown; believed to be lower than males
Fetishism	Sexual arousal with an object or nongenital body part	Unknown
Frotteurism	Sexual arousal as a result of touching or rubbing against an unwilling person	Males: as high as 30% Females: unreported
Klismaphilia	Sexual arousal associated with receiving enemas	Unknown
Pedophilia	Sexual arousal associated with sexual fantasies or urges involving prepubescent children	Males: 3–5% Females: uncertain; reportedly much lower than males
Sexual masochism	Sexual arousal as a result of experiencing pain or suffering	Unknown
Sexual sadism	Sexual arousal as a result of inflicting pain or suffering	Varies anywhere from 2% to 30%
Telephone scatologia	Sexual arousal as a result of making obscene phone calls to an unwilling person	Unknown
Voyeurism	Sexual arousal as a result of watching unsuspecting individuals undress or engage in sexual activity	Males: 12% Females: 4%

Shown above are the prevalence rates for *paraphilias*, or unusual sexual interests. Prevalence rates are rough estimates in the general population, but given the intimate nature of sexuality and people's reluctance to self-disclose, these numbers should be interpreted with caution. Information from APA (2013), Crooks and Baur (2017), McAnulty, Dillon, and Adams (2002).

behavior is as varied as any other type of human behavior. As with any definition of appropriate versus inappropriate, deviant versus normal, we must always consider the sociocultural context and whether the behavior is harmful to oneself or others.

What we want to emphasize is that there is a range of sexual behavior, and the overwhelming majority of it is perfectly healthy. But some fetishes and other sexual behaviors are rare and/or problematic. Here, the sexual activity might involve nonhuman objects, and sometimes results in the suffering or humiliation of those involved. Often, the behavior is repeated and compulsive (Kafka, 2009).

Pedophilia is a paraphilia in which a person at least 16 years old has sexual fantasies or urges about children (usually younger than 14). In some cases, the person never acts on the urges or fantasies. Others, however, victimize children and develop techniques to gain access to them. Pedophilia is more common in men and appears to last throughout life (APA, 2013).

CULTURE AND SEX Culture plays a role in determining what sexual behaviors are deemed acceptable, and there is considerable variation in this regard. Whereas some cultures abhor nudity and view sex only as a means of reproduction, others believe that children should be educated about sex early in life. It was reported for many years that Inis Beag (a pseudonym for an island off the coast of Ireland) was a "sex-negative" society, known for abstinence, monogamy, and infrequent sexual encounters. In contrast, the "sex-positive" culture of Mangaia in the South Pacific was known for frequent sexual encounters and reports of multiple orgasms each night (Levine & Troiden, 1988).

What about Americans? Do you think we tend to promote sexual modesty? Or is the sexually explicit content of *Game of Thrones* more representative of our attitudes?

It's Medieval Sexy
Americans can't seem to get enough of *Game of Thrones,* the HBO series known for its steamy sex scenes and raw violence. Do you think erotic content encourages people to explore new sexual experiences, or does the act of watching quench the need for novelty? Ian G Dagnall/Alamy.

Americans generally value sexual modesty, but we are also exposed to a broad spectrum of sexual expression via the media (although variation abounds based on subcultural and regional differences within the United States). In one study from 1998, researchers examined attitudes regarding nonmarital sex in 24 different countries. They reported that the United States belonged to a cluster of countries referred to as "sexual conservatives," with the great majority of people disapproving of any form of nonmarital sex—both premarital and extramarital (Widmer, Treas, & Newcomb, 1998). Do you think this attitude still prevails?

People engage in sexual activity for procreation, recreation, and everything in between. Sexual desires and preferences vary from person to person and across time, but are also based on culture. What motivates individuals to engage in sexual activity? Women seem more likely to be looking for love and commitment, intimacy, or to solidify a relationship. Men report being motivated by the physical appearance of their partner, pleasure, and the desire to reduce stress. While such gender disparities do exist, research reveals they are quite small (Hatfield, Luckhurst, & Rapson, 2010).

Choosing a Mate: Are You My Natural Selection?

Many people are very particular when it comes to choosing long-term sexual partners. What selection criteria do we use when filtering all the candidates? In Chapter 15, we discuss the various factors important for interpersonal attraction, including proximity, similarity, and physical attractiveness. These variables are shaped by culture, but they may also be dependent on biology. According to one controversial theory, mate choices are guided by the forces of evolution.

If we look at things from a purely evolutionary standpoint (ignoring all social, emotional, and cultural factors), men and women both have the same goals: to ensure that their genes outlast them. However, they have different roles in reproduction. Women generally invest more in childbearing and rearing (pregnancy, breastfeeding, and so on) and they are limited in the number of offspring they can produce. Men are capable of fathering hundreds, if not thousands, of children, and they are not hampered by the biological constraints of pregnancy and breastfeeding. Under these circumstances, a woman's best strategy is to find a mate who will ensure that her children have all the resources they need to survive and reproduce. A man, on the other hand, should be on the lookout for a woman who can bear many children—someone who shows signs of fertility, like youth and beauty (Geary, Vigil, & Byrd-Craven, 2004).

Do people really choose partners according to these criteria? One study of over 10,000 participants from 37 cultures concluded that women around the world do indeed favor mates who appear to be good providers, whereas men place greater value on good looks and youth (Buss, 1989). Subsequent studies have produced similar results (Buss, Shackelford, Kirkpatrick, & Larsen, 2001; Schwarz & Hassebrauck, 2012; Shackelford, Schmitt, & Buss, 2005).

"Marry me, Virginia. My genes are excellent and, as yet, unpatented."

Keep in mind that these are just general trends; sometimes the reverse is true. We all know there are many women in search of "hot men," and men in pursuit of "sugar mamas." Over the past several decades, in fact, a woman's financial security has become an increasingly important criterion for male suitors (Buss et al., 2001). In today's ever-changing social and cultural environment, evolution is just one potential variable influencing our mate choices.

BACK TO THE FUTURE You may be wondering what the future holds for Stephen Patten and Dr. Stephanie Buehler. Stephen is retiring and relocating to the Florida Keys, where he plans to teach part time at a local community college.

Dr. Buehler's book, *What Every Mental Health Professional Needs to Know about Sex,* is now in its second edition. She also has a new title, *Counseling Couples Before, During, and After Pregnancy: Intimacy and Sexuality.* In addition to her writing projects and international speaking engagements, Dr. Buehler is Director of The Buehler Institute, which offers sex and relationship therapy as well as continuing education for psychotherapists. ●

○ ✓ ○ ○ **show what you know**

1. _____ and _____ are both bacterial infections spread through unprotected sexual activity.

   a. Syphilis; gonorrhea
   b. Pelvic inflammatory disease; herpes
   c. Human papillomavirus; herpes
   d. Syphilis; acquired immune deficiency syndrome

2. Most people learn _____, which are the rules our culture has taught us about what is "appropriate" for sexual activity.

3. Describe how HIV is transmitted and how it progresses to AIDS.

✓ CHECK YOUR ANSWERS IN APPENDIX C.

Improve your grade! Use ⬛ **LearningCurve** macmillan learning adaptive quizzing to create your personalized study plan, which will direct you to the resources that will help you most in ⬛ **LaunchPad** macmillan learning

summary of concepts

10

LO 1 Define sex and distinguish it from gender. (p. 418)

Sexuality is an important dimension of human nature; it refers to everything that makes us sexual beings, including our sexual activities, attitudes, and behaviors. Sex can refer to a sexual act such as intercourse or masturbation. Sex also refers to the classification of someone as male or female based on genetic composition and structure and/or function of reproductive organs. Gender refers to the dimensions of masculinity and femininity based on social, cultural, and psychological characteristics. The term "sex" is used when referring to biological status and "gender" for the cultural roles and expectations that distinguish males and females.

LO 2 Identify the biological factors that determine sex. (p. 419)

The 23rd pair of chromosomes, also referred to as the sex chromosomes, provides specific instructions for the zygote to develop into a female or male (the biological sex of the individual). The egg from the mother carries an X chromosome, and the sperm from the father carries either an X chromosome or a Y chromosome. When both members of the 23rd pair are X chromosomes (XX), the zygote will generally develop into a female. When the 23rd pair contains an X chromosome and a Y chromosome (XY), the zygote generally develops into a male.

LO 3 Explain some of the causes of intersexual development. (p. 423)

Intersexuality can result from genetic irregularities, hormone activity early in development, and/or environmental factors. In some cases, there are too many sex chromosomes, or one missing. In other cases, the sex chromosomes are normal, but the developing fetus does not respond to hormones in a typical way.

LO 4 Define gender and explain how culture plays a role in its development. (p. 426)

Gender refers to the dimension of masculinity and femininity based on social, cultural, and psychological characteristics. It is often used in reference to the cultural roles that distinguish males and females. We generally learn by observing other people's behavior and by internalizing cultural beliefs about what is appropriate for men and women.

LO 5 Distinguish between transgender and transsexual. (p. 429)
Sometimes societal expectations of being male or female differ from what an individual is feeling inwardly, leading to feelings of discontent. Transgender refers to the mismatch between a person's gender assignment at birth and his or her gender identity. Some transgender people try to resolve this discontent through medical interventions. A transsexual person seeks or undergoes a social transition to an alternative gender by making changes to his or her body through sex reassignment surgery and/or medical treatment.

LO 6 Describe the human sexual response as identified by Masters and Johnson. (p. 431)
The human sexual response is the physiological pattern that occurs during sexual activity. Men and women tend to experience a similar pattern or cycle of excitement, plateau, orgasm, and resolution, but the duration of these phases varies from person to person.

LO 7 Define sexual orientation and summarize how it develops. (p. 432)
Sexual orientation refers to the sex of those to whom you are attracted. This enduring pattern of sexual, romantic, and emotional attraction generally involves someone of the same sex, opposite sex, or both sexes—meaning you are heterosexual, homosexual, or bisexual. Sexual orientation is a continuum that includes many dimensions of our sexuality, attraction, desire, emotions, and the resulting behaviors. Research has focused on the causes of sexual orientation, but there is no strong evidence pointing to any one factor or factors. Sexual orientation is the result of a complex interaction between nature and nurture.

LO 8 Identify the symptoms of sexual dysfunctions. (p. 443)
Difficulties related to sexual activity can be divided into four sometimes overlapping categories: desire, arousal, orgasm, and pain. Problems associated with desire must be persistent to be considered a dysfunction. When an individual has the desire to engage in sexual behavior, but his or her body does not cooperate, an arousal problem exists. Difficulties with orgasm may include reduced orgasmic intensity and the inability to reach orgasm. Problems associated with pain are more frequently reported by women, and may also be associated with reduced desire and arousal.

LO 9 Classify sexually transmitted infections and identify their causes. (p. 445)
Sexually transmitted infections (STIs) are infections caused by viruses and bacteria and are contracted through sexual activity. Having multiple sexual partners increases the risk of getting an STI; however, awareness that a partner has had (or is having) sex with other partners lowers the risk somewhat. Once aware of a partner's activities, one is more inclined to take preventive measures, such as using condoms. Syphilis, gonorrhea, and chlamydia are bacterial infections. Genital herpes, human papillomavirus, and human immunodeficiency virus (HIV) are viral infections.

LO 10 Describe human immunodeficiency virus (HIV) and its role in acquired immune deficiency syndrome (AIDS). (p. 446)
Human immunodeficiency virus (HIV) is spread through the transfer of bodily fluids (blood, semen, vaginal fluid, or breast milk) and eventually causes the breakdown of the immune system. HIV often does not show up on blood tests for up to 6 months after infection occurs; it eventually progresses to acquired immune deficiency syndrome (AIDS), which generally results in a severely compromised immune system. A weakened immune system makes the body much more susceptible to opportunistic infections caused by bacteria, viruses, or fungi, and this vulnerability increases as the disease progresses.

LO 11 Define sexual scripts and describe some of the ways people deviate from sex-related cultural norms. (p. 447)
Sexual scripts are cultural rules about what is and is not appropriate sexual activity. There is a range or continuum of sexual behavior, and the overwhelming majority of it is perfectly normal. Yet some sexual behaviors are rare and/or problematic. For example, paraphilia refers to uncommon sexual behaviors that are repeated and compulsive. Paraphilia sometimes involves nonhuman objects and may cause suffering or humiliation for those involved.

key terms

acquired immune deficiency syndrome (AIDS), p. 446
androgens, p. 420
androgyny, p. 429
bisexual, p. 433
estrogen, p. 420
gender, p. 418

gender identity, p. 427
gender roles, p. 426
gender schemas, p. 427
heterosexual, p. 433
homosexual, p. 433
human immunodeficiency virus (HIV), p. 446

intersexual, p. 423
orgasm, p. 432
paraphilia, p. 447
refractory period, p. 432
sex, p. 418
sexual dysfunction, p. 443

sexual orientation, p. 432
sexuality, p. 418
sexually transmitted infections (STIs), p. 445
testosterone, p. 420
transgender, p. 430
transsexual, p. 430

test prep *are you ready?*

1. _____ refers to a sexual act or the classification of male or female. _____ refers to masculinity and femininity based on social, cultural, and psychological characteristics.
   a. Gender; Sex
   b. Sex; Gender
   c. Sex; Sexuality
   d. Gender; Sexuality

2. The _____ provide(s) specific instructions on whether a zygote will develop into a male or female, that is, the genetic sex of the individual.
   a. 23rd pair of chromosomes
   b. gonads
   c. primary sex characteristics
   d. secondary sex characteristics

3. The sensitivity of a fetus to _____ produced during its early development can play a role in the development of intersexuality.
   a. the X chromosome
   b. the Y chromosome
   c. secondary sex characteristics
   d. hormones

4. A psychologist refers to biological characteristics when discussing a client's _____, but when talking about sexual attitudes and behaviors, a psychologist is referring to _____.
   a. sex; sexuality
   b. primary sex characteristics; secondary sex characteristics
   c. secondary sex characteristics; primary sex characteristics
   d. heterosexuality; homosexuality

5. The general beliefs, in American culture, that men are assertive and logical, and women are caring and emotional represent:
   a. gender identity.
   b. gender schemas.
   c. androgyny.
   d. gender roles.

6. The acquisition of gender roles can occur through _____, as explained by social-cognitive theory. That is, we are shaped by models in our environment.
   a. genes
   b. chromosomes
   c. observational learning
   d. paraphilias

7. According to Masters and Johnson, sexual arousal begins in the _____ phase, when physical changes begin to take place.
   a. excitement
   b. plateau
   c. resolution
   d. orgasm

8. A family friend confides that he has always had the feeling he was born in the body of a female and that he has started cross-sex hormone treatment. Your friend would be considered _____ by the American Psychiatric Association.
   a. homosexual
   b. heterosexual
   c. transsexual
   d. bisexual

9. Having older brothers in a family seems to be associated with homosexuality in men. One explanation for this is the maternal immune hypothesis, which suggests that:
   a. older mothers become immune to homosexuality while pregnant.
   b. mothers develop an anti-male antibody while pregnant.
   c. mothers with brothers of their own develop an anti-male antibody while pregnant.
   d. children with no siblings will not be homosexual.

10. Research regarding the sexual response cycle indicates:
    a. it should not be treated with psychotherapy.
    b. the orgasm phase is the longest phase.
    c. it is experienced more frequently by men.
    d. men and women experience a similar pattern or cycle.

11. Some men experience problems getting or maintaining an erection, which is referred to as:
    a. hypoactive sexual desire.
    b. erectile disorder.
    c. male orgasmic disorder.
    d. premature ejaculation.

12. _____ is spread through the transfer of bodily fluids, such as blood, semen, and breast milk, and it eventually progresses to _____.
    a. Human immunodeficiency virus; acquired immune deficiency syndrome
    b. Acquired immune deficiency syndrome; human immunodeficiency virus
    c. Human papillomavirus; chlamydia
    d. Chlamydia; human papillomavirus

13. People who know their partners have had (or are having) sexual activity with others will:
    a. definitely see symptoms of an STI in themselves or their partners.
    b. have an equal risk of acquiring an STI than those who don't know of this activity.
    c. have a lower risk of acquiring an STI than those who don't know of this activity.
    d. have a higher risk of acquiring an STI than those who don't know of this activity.

14. A friend of yours shies away from some of the more daring sexual escapades her husband suggests. For example, yesterday he asked her to engage in a "threesome." She unknowingly has learned _____ from her culture, telling her that such sexual behavior is not appropriate.
    a. sexual scripts
    b. paraphilia
    c. fetishes
    d. gender dysphoria

15. _____ refers to uncommon sexual acts that might involve nonhuman objects, and sometimes results in the suffering or humiliation of those involved.
    a. Sex determination
    b. Spermarche
    c. A sexual script
    d. Paraphilia

16. We have noted how difficult it can be to get people to participate in a study, but also to be open and honest in research examining sexual activity. If you were planning to conduct this type of research, how would you go about convincing potential participants that their involvement will be worthwhile and that they should be honest in their responses?

17. Explain how gender roles are acquired through culture and learning.

18. How would an evolutionary psychologist explain extramarital sex?

19. Describe the four areas in which sexual dysfunction can occur.

20. Describe three paraphilias.

✓ CHECK YOUR ANSWERS IN APPENDIX C.

YOUR SCIENTIFIC WORLD
Apply psychology to the real world!
Go to LaunchPad for access.

© Mary Evans/Sigmund Freud Copyrights/The ImageWorks.

LWA/Getty Images.

James Whitlow Delano/Redux.

CHAPTER OUTLINE AND LEARNING OBJECTIVES

An Introduction to Personality

LO 1 Define personality.

LO 2 Distinguish how the perspectives of psychology explain personality development.

Psychoanalytic Theories

LO 3 Illustrate Freud's models for describing the mind.

LO 4 Summarize Freud's use of psychosexual stages to explain personality.

Humanistic Theories

LO 5 Explain how the neo-Freudians' theories of personality differ from Freud's.

LO 6 Summarize Maslow's hierarchy of needs, and describe self-actualizers.

Learning and Social-Cognitive Theories

LO 7 Discuss Rogers' view of self-concept, ideal self, and unconditional positive regard.

LO 8 Use the behavioral perspective to explain personality development.

LO 9 Summarize Rotter's view of personality.

LO 10 Discuss how Bandura uses the social-cognitive perspective to explain personality.

Trait Theories and Their Biological Basis

LO 11 Distinguish trait theories from other personality theories.

LO 12 Identify the biological roots of the five-factor model of personality.

Personality Assessment

LO 13 Explain why reliability and validity are important in personality assessment.

LO 14 Define projective personality tests and evaluate their strengths and limitations.

LO 15 Describe objective personality tests and evaluate their strengths and limitations.

Courtesy of Sean Saifa Wall.

Jamie Squire/Allsport/Getty Images.

Susan Chiang/Getty Images.

11 personality

MSF/Shutterstock.

An Introduction to Personality

WHO IS SAIFA? Sometimes a simple question can change your life. For Sean Saifa Wall, the critical question came in 2007. He was 28 years old and appeared to have his life in order. A graduate of Williams College (one of the highest-ranked liberal arts institutions in the nation), Saifa had built an impressive résumé, acquired a desirable job, and amassed a large number of social contacts. But he was tormented on the inside. Unable to make sense of his thoughts, Saifa felt he was losing control, and he worried that something terrible would happen if he didn't seek help: "I was just like, either someone's going to kill me, or I'm going to kill myself."

In a move that may have saved his life, Saifa picked up the phone and made an appointment to talk with a psychotherapist. A few days later, he was sitting on the therapist's couch beginning to unravel his complicated life story. Apparently, the therapist was perceptive, because during that first appointment, he posed a question that set Saifa's healing process in motion and changed the course of his life: "When did you realize love was not possible?" Saifa broke down and began weeping. "I don't know," he said in between tears. The weeping continued for many sessions.

Eyes of Discontent
Sean Saifa Wall was 26 years old when this picture was taken. Looking at this photo today, Saifa sees a young man who is "performing masculinity" to compensate for feelings of insecurity.
Courtesy Sean Saifa Wall.

For years leading to that moment, Saifa had wrestled with feelings of loneliness, isolation, and self-hatred. He tried to fill the void with new relationships and sex, but the emptiness persisted. "I thought that if I just had more sex, that I would eventually be full," Saifa explains. "But I think the scary more terrifying part, was that there wasn't enough sex to be had, and the more sex I had from all sources (casual sex, relationship sex, pornography), the more miserable and lonely I felt." Saifa's focus on sex was a symptom of something much bigger. "For me, sexual addiction is not about sex," Saifa explains. "Sexual addiction is me dealing with something that is so, so visceral, and so deep. It's such a well of hurt and shame that some places I can't access."

This hurt and shame had prevented Saifa from loving himself, but he went to great lengths to attain approval from others. "I was trying to impress the women I dated," he explains. "I wanted all these material things that I thought would bring me happiness . . . that

455

Saifa, in His Own Words

http://qrs.ly/rx5a5f0

would bring me more self-esteem, but the more I got these things, the more I realized I wasn't really happy, 'cause I wasn't myself." Like a chameleon, Saifa adjusted his roles and behaviors to please other people. As he explains, "I could be whatever you wanted me to be, because that would garner your acceptance."

Who was the person beneath the chameleon, and how did he fall into that crater of self-hatred? Perhaps most importantly, did he ever climb out? Let's start with the first question: Who is Sean Saifa Wall? ●

What Is Personality?

LO 1 Define personality.

If you ask Saifa to describe himself, he will use words like "vivacious," "loud," "charismatic," "direct," and "empathetic." He might also mention that he has a strong sense of fairness, and always leans in the direction of justice. These attributes have been apparent for much of Saifa's life, and therefore would be considered facets of his *personality*. Generally speaking, **personality** refers to the unique, core set of characteristics that influence the way one thinks, acts, and feels—characteristics many psychologists would agree are relatively consistent and enduring throughout the life span and in a variety of settings.

We should point out that personality is not the equivalent of *character*. When people discuss character, they often are referring to qualities of morality or culture-specific ideas about what makes a person "good" or "bad." A person who is untrustworthy or makes "poor" choices might be described as having a weak character, while someone who stands up for what she believes might be said to have a strong character. You may hear that the guy with the blue mohawk or the woman with the multiple body piercings is a "real character." Psychologists try not to make such judgments; our goal is to describe behaviors and personality characteristics objectively. Unlike character, which is essentially a label based on superficial observations, personality is defined by an influential core set of characteristics that often become apparent early in life.

TEMPERAMENT Certain aspects of adult personality appear to derive from temperament, the distinct patterns of emotional reactions and behaviors observed early in life (Soto & Tackett, 2015). Some infants are easy to calm, others cranky, sociable, or highly reactive. Because various temperaments are evident in infants, they appear to have a genetic basis (Plomin, DeFries, Knopik, & Neiderhiser, 2013). Although behavioral patterns of temperament remain somewhat stable across the life span, they can be molded by the environment (Briley & Tucker-Drob, 2014; Caspi, Roberts, & Shiner, 2005; Kagan & Snidman, 1991; Soto, 2016). There is not complete agreement about where child temperament ends and adult personality begins, but we can think of temperament as an important, stable aspect of the broader notion of personality (Goldsmith et al., 1987; Soto & Tackett, 2015).

CONNECTIONS

In **Chapter 8,** we described various infant temperaments. Humans are born with certain temperaments, and many of the attending characteristics seem to persist throughout life. Here, we introduce child temperament in the context of the development of personality.

LO 2 Distinguish how the perspectives of psychology explain personality development.

PERSPECTIVES ON PERSONALITY Psychologists explain the development of personality in a variety of ways, often in accordance with certain theoretical perspectives (**TABLE 11.1**). None of the perspectives can completely account for the development and expression of personality, but they do help describe, explain, and predict behavior.

personality The unique, core set of characteristics that influence the way one thinks, acts, and feels, and that are relatively consistent and enduring throughout the life span.

Note: Unless otherwise specified, quotations attributed to Sean Saifa Wall are personal communications.

TABLE 11.1 THEORETICAL PERSPECTIVES ON PERSONALITY

Personality Theory	Main Points	Criticisms
Psychoanalytic	Personality develops early in life; we are greatly influenced by processes of which we are unaware (e.g., internal conflicts, aggression, sexual urges).	Ignores importance of current experiences; overemphasis on the unconscious and the role of sexuality in personality; theory based on a biased, nonrepresentative sample; concepts difficult to operationally define and empirically test.
Behavioral	Personality is shaped by interactions with the environment, specifically through learning (classical conditioning, operant conditioning, and observational learning).	Narrow focus on behavioral processes; ignores influence of unconscious processes and emotional factors.
Humanistic	We are innately good and control our destinies; we have a force moving us toward growth.	Concepts difficult to operationally define and empirically test; ignores the negative aspects of human nature.
Social-cognitive	Focuses on social influences and mental processes that affect personality; emphasis on the combination of environment, cognitive activity, and individual behavior.	Narrow focus on social-cognitive factors; ignores influence of unconscious processes and emotional factors.
Biological	Emphasizes the physiological and genetic influences on personality development; incorporates gene–environment explanations for the emergence of certain characteristics.	Inconsistent findings regarding the stability of the personality dimensions; varying estimates of environmental influences.
Trait	Looks at current traits of the individual to describe personality and predict behaviors.	Underestimates the environmental influences on personality; neglects to explain foundations of personality.

Psychology uses a variety of theoretical perspectives to explain the development of personality. Listed here are the major theories and some of their key limitations.

Most have strong ties to their founders, all of whom were influenced by their life experiences and the historical period in which they lived. Sigmund Freud's emphasis on sexuality, for example, was partly a reaction to the proper Victorian cultural climate into which he was born.

In the next section, we will examine these theories of personality in greater depth, but first let's take a quick detour somewhere fun. How would you describe your sense of humor?

NATURE AND NURTURE
The Funny Thing About Personality

Some of us rely on humor to connect with other people, cracking jokes and acting silly for their enjoyment. Others use it as a way to cope with challenges. (We must admit, it does feel good to let loose and laugh when we're feeling overwhelmed.) Both of these styles of humor are viewed as positive, as they strengthen social bonds and promote personal well-being. There are also negative forms of humor, like ridiculing another person to make yourself look good, or poking fun at yourself in a way that seems to erode self-esteem (Hunter, Fox, & Jones, 2016; Martin, Puhlik-Doris, Larsen, Gray, & Weir, 2003; McCosker & Moran, 2012).

WHERE DID YOU GET THAT SENSE OF HUMOR?

Where do these styles of humor originate? According to one large study conducted in Australia, identical twins (who have nearly identical genes) are more likely to share humor styles than fraternal (nonidentical) twins. What this tells

Silly Genes
Identical twins, who have nearly all the same genes, are more likely to have similar humor styles than fraternal twins, who share only about half their genes (Baughman et al., 2012). This suggests that sense of humor is to some degree inherited. Susan Chiang/Getty Images.

you is that genes matter. In fact, the study suggests that 30–47% of population-wide variation in humor styles can be attributed to genetics (Baughman et al., 2012), and some research shows an even higher proportion (Vernon, Martin, Schermer, Cherkas, & Spector, 2008).

But how do you explain the other 53–70% of the variation? Chalk it up to nurture. Some research suggests that close friendships play an important role in the development of humor. A study of 11- to 13-year-olds found that the humor styles of best friends tend to become more alike over time. However, this finding only applied to humor that enhances relationships, not negative humor styles that can hurt feelings and damage friendships (Hunter, Fox, & Jones, 2016). Further evidence for this learned aspect of humor comes from research on gender. Many people believe that men are funnier than women, but this appears to be more of a stereotype than a true phenomenon. In one study, researchers showed participants cartoon captions written by men and women. Participants unknowingly rated men's and women's captions to be equally funny, but they were more likely to credit the funniest captions to male authors (Hooper, Sharpe, & Roberts, 2016). Humor is very much like other aspects of personality—grounded in biology, but chiseled and refined by a lifetime of experiences. ⏀🏠

 In Class: Collaborate and Report

In your group, **A)** pick a well-known fairy tale figure and describe some of his or her personality characteristics. **B)** Now consider the six theoretical perspectives presented in Table 11.1, and pick at least three of them to explain how such characteristics might develop in your fairy tale figure. **C)** Decide which perspective you think is the best fit and briefly explain how the fairy tale might change.

Over 7 billion human beings inhabit this planet, and no two of them have the same personality. Each individual's personality reflects a distinct interplay of inborn characteristics and life experiences. Consider this nature-and-nurture dynamic as you explore the theories of personality in the pages to come. To what degree does each perspective recognize the contributions of nature and nurture, and how do these forces interact? We'll get this discussion rolling with the help of Saifa.

 show what you know

1. _____ is the unique, core set of characteristics that influence the way one thinks, acts, and feels.

2. Use three theoretical perspectives presented in this section to explain how personality develops.

✓ CHECK YOUR ANSWERS IN APPENDIX C.

Psychoanalytic Theories

CONNECTIONS

In **Chapter 10,** we discussed differences of sex development. People with intersex traits may have internal and external reproductive organs that are not clearly male or female.

psychoanalysis Freud's views regarding personality as well as his system of psychotherapy and tools for the exploration of the unconscious.

BEFORE SAIFA, THERE WAS SUSANNE Saifa was born on December 28, 1978, at Columbia–Presbyterian Hospital in New York City. Unlike most babies, who are readily identified as "boy" or "girl," Saifa had ambiguous genitalia (not clearly male, not clearly female). Doctors assigned him female and instructed his mother to raise him as a girl, indicating that he would "function as such" (Wall, 2015, p. 118). During this era, many psychologists and medical professionals believed that human behaviors were primarily shaped by environmental input, or nurture (Schultz & Schultz, 2016; Segal, 2012). But as you will learn from Saifa's story, nature can sometimes overpower nurture.

Saifa was, and still is, genetically male (XY). He has an intersex trait called androgen insensitivity syndrome (AIS), characterized by reduced sensitivity to male hormones, or androgens. People with AIS are genetically male, but their bodies do not follow the typical "male" or "female" path of sexual development. Some are designated "male" at birth, others "female." These gender assignments appear to work out for some people (about 75%, according to one study), but a substantial minority feel unsatisfied (Schweizer, Brunner, Handford, & Richter-Appelt, 2014).

Saifa was raised as a little girl named "Susanne," but fulfilling society's gender expectations did not come naturally. He didn't like feminine clothes or crossing his legs like a lady, and he certainly was not attracted to boys. "I knew from, like the age of five, that I liked girls," Saifa recalls. "When I could walk and talk, started thinking for myself, I was like, *I like girls!*" His parents accepted this nonconformist approach to girlhood, but within limits. One of Saifa's first memories is from the age of 4 or 5; he was getting ready to visit his grandmother and wanted to wear overalls. "As a kid, I loved to wear corduroys, jeans, pants," Saifa says. "You name it, I'm in it." But his mom insisted he wear a sundress with spaghetti straps and put his hair in pigtails. Saifa protested and cried, but ended up complying—and feeling miserably out of his element: "I remember being on the train going downtown and just feeling so vulnerable."

Childhood presented other challenges for Saifa. He grew up in the Bronx during the 1980s, when crack cocaine was devastating urban communities and crime was rampant (New York City's murder rate hit an all-time high in 1990, with 2,245 killings in one year; City of New York, 2012). Saifa witnessed trauma and suffering not only in his neighborhood, but also within his family: "If we're talking about the most formative experiences I had, if we're talking about between the ages of 0 and 6," Saifa explains, "[It] was seeing my dad drunk, witnessing the domestic violence that took place in the home." ●

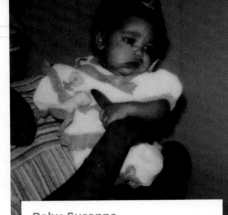

Baby Susanne
What is the first question most people ask when they hear someone had a baby? They want to know if it's a boy or a girl, but the answer is not always straightforward. About 1 in 1,500 newborns have ambiguous genitalia, meaning they are not clearly identifiable as male or female (American Psychological Association, 2006). Saifa was one of these babies. Although he has XY (male) sex chromosomes, he was assigned female and raised as "Susanne." Courtesy Sean Saifa Wall.

How did these early childhood experiences impact Saifa in the long term, and what role did they play in the development of his personality? If we could pose this question to Sigmund Freud, he would probably say they were critical. Freud believed that childhood is the prime time for personality development, the early years and basic drives being particularly important because they shape our thoughts, emotions, and behaviors in ways beyond our awareness. **Psychoanalysis** refers to Freud's theories about personality as well as his system of psychotherapy and tools for the exploration of the unconscious. (See Chapter 14 for more on Freud's theory and techniques for treatment.) In the next section, we will present an overview of Freud's psychoanalysis as it relates to personality and some of the later personality theories it influenced.

Growing Up Susanne
(Left) Five-year-old Susanne (now Saifa) with friends. "When I was growing up, I felt more connected to boyhood," Saifa explains. "Innately, I felt more masculine, more male [but] externally, what I was presenting to the world based on my body, based on my physical characteristics, was female." As you read the next section, ask yourself what Freud might have thought of this conflict between Susanne's physical characteristics and her innate sense of gender. Courtesy Sean Saifa Wall.

Freud and the Mind

Sigmund Freud spent the majority of his life in Vienna, Austria. A smart, ambitious young man, Freud attended medical school and became a physician and researcher with a primary interest in physiology and later neurology. Freud loved doing research, but he soon came to realize that the anti-Semitic culture in which he lived would drastically interfere with his ability to work as a researcher (Freud was Jewish). So, instead of pursuing the career he loved, he opened a medical practice in 1881, specializing in clinical neurology. Working with patients, he noted that many had unexplained or unusual symptoms that seemed related to emotional problems. He also observed (along with colleagues) that the basis of the problems appeared to be sexual in nature, although his patients weren't necessarily aware of this (Freud, 1900/1953). Thus began Freud's lifelong journey to untangle the mysteries of the unconscious mind.

CONNECTIONS

In **Chapter 6,** we presented a component of working memory called the episodic buffer, which allows information from long-term memory to reach conscious awareness. Although Freud did not refer to this buffer, the preconscious level includes activities somewhat similar to those of the episodic buffer.

Little Freud
Looking at this photo of Sigmund Freud and his father, Jacob, we can't help but wonder how this father–son relationship influenced the development of the younger Freud's personality. Freud believed that events and conflicts from childhood—particularly those involving parents and other caregivers—have a powerful impact on adult personality. Imagno/Getty Images.

LO 3 Illustrate Freud's models for describing the mind.

CONSCIOUS, PRECONSCIOUS, AND UNCONSCIOUS Freud (1900/1953) proposed that the mind has three levels of consciousness—conscious, preconscious, and unconscious—and that mental processes occurring on these levels guide behaviors and personality.

Everything you are aware of at this moment exists at the *conscious* level, including thoughts, emotions, sensations, and perceptions. At the preconscious level are the mental activities outside your current awareness, which can be brought easily to your attention. (You are studying Freud's theory at this moment, but your mind begins to wander and you start thinking about what you did yesterday.) The **unconscious** level is home to activities outside of your awareness, such as feelings, wishes, thoughts, and urges, which are very difficult to access without concerted effort and/or therapy. To gain access to the unconscious level, Freud (1900/1953) used a variety of techniques, such as dream interpretation (Chapter 4), hypnosis (Chapter 4), and free association (Chapter 14). Freud did suggest, however, that some content of the unconscious can enter the conscious level through manipulated and distorted processes beyond a person's control or awareness (more on this shortly).

This *topographical model* was Freud's earliest attempt to explain the bustling activity occurring within the head (Westen, Gabbard, & Ortigo, 2008). It describes the *levels* of the mind; hence the reference to topography. Freud was influenced by Gustav Fechner's idea that the great majority of the mind is "hidden below the surface where it is influenced by unobservable forces" (Schultz & Schultz, 2016, p. 290). Many who describe Freud's model compare it to an iceberg. According to this analogy, what we see on the surface is just the "tip of the iceberg" (the conscious level), small in comparison to the vast and influential unconscious mind (Schultz & Schultz, 2017; **FIGURE 11.1**).

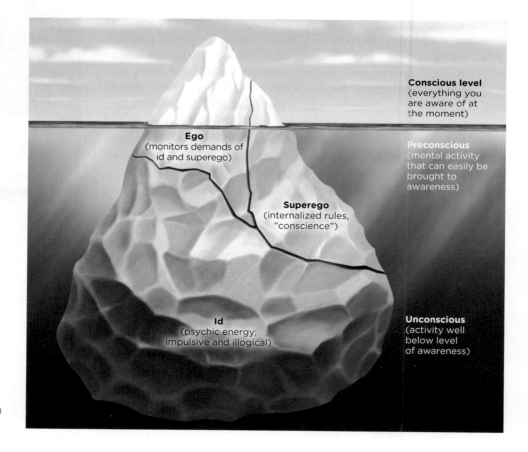

FIGURE 11.1
Psychoanalytic Description of the Mind

Id, Ego, and Superego:
The Structural Model of the Mind

In addition to the topographical model, Freud proposed a *structural model,* which describes the "functions or purposes" of the mind's components (Westen et al., 2008, p. 65). As Freud saw it, the human mind is composed of three structures: the *id,* the *ego,* and the *superego.* These components lie at the core of the unconscious conflicts influencing our thoughts, emotions, and behaviors—that is, our personality (Westen et al., 2008).

THE ID   The **id** is the most primitive structure of the mind. It is present from birth, and its activities occur at the unconscious level. The infant-like part of our mind and personality (being impulsive, illogical, pleasure seeking) results from the workings of the id. Our biological drives and instincts, which motivate us, derive from the id. Freud proposed that the id represents the component of the mind that forms the primary pool of *psychic energy* (Freud, 1923/1961, 1933/1964). Included in that pool is sexual energy, which motivates much of our behavior. The primary goal of the id is to ensure that the individual's needs are being met, helping to maintain homeostasis. The id is not rational, and unfulfilled needs or urges compel it to insist on immediate action. It is ruled by the **pleasure principle**, which guides behavior toward instant gratification—and away from contemplating consequences. The id seeks pleasure and avoids pain.

THE EGO   As an infant grows and starts to realize that the desires of the id cannot prevail in all situations, her **ego**, which is not present from birth, begins to develop from the id (Freud, 1933/1964, 1940/1949). The ego manipulates situations, plans for the future, solves problems, and makes decisions to satisfy the needs of the id. The goal is to make sure that the id is not given free rein over behavior, as this would cause problems. Adults know they can't always get what they want when they want it, but the id does not know or care. Imagine what a busy supermarket would be like if we were all ruled by our ids, ignoring societal expectations to stand in line, speak politely, and pay for food; the store would be full of adults having toddler-like tantrums. To negotiate between the id and the environment, and thereby control the id's psychic energy, the ego uses the **reality principle**. This requires knowledge of the rules of the "real" world and allows most of us to delay gratification as needed (Freud, 1923/1960). The reality principle works through an awareness of potential consequences; the ego can predict what will happen if we act on an urge. We are aware of the ego's activities, although some happen at the preconscious level, and even fewer at the unconscious level (Figure 11.1).

THE SUPEREGO   The **superego** is the structure of the mind that develops last, guiding behavior to follow the rules of society, parents, or other authority figures (Freud, 1923/1960). The superego begins to form as the toddler starts moving about on his own, coming up against rules and expectations (*No, you cannot hit your sister! You need to put your toys away*). Around age 5 or 6, the child begins to incorporate the morals and values of his parents or caregivers, including their expectations and ideas about right and wrong, colloquially known as the *conscience.* Once the superego is rooted, it serves as a critical internal guide to the values of society (not just those of the parents) so that the child can make "good" choices without constant reminders from a parent, caregiver, or religious leader. The rules and expectations now come from an internal voice citing right and wrong. Sometimes, the superego can be harsh and judgmental, and it may set unrealistic standards. For example, married men and women may feel

CONNECTIONS

In **Chapter 9,** we discussed the concept of drive reduction, which suggests that if a need is not fulfilled, a state of tension results that motivates behavior. Once the need is met, the drive is reduced. Meeting the demands of the id is similar to this drive reduction model; in this case, the id is in charge of making sure needs are met and homeostasis is maintained.

S. Harris/CartoonStock.com.

unconscious According to Freud, the level of consciousness outside of awareness, which is difficult to access without effort or therapy.

id According to Freud, the most primitive structure of the mind, the activities of which occur at the unconscious level and are guided by the pleasure principle.

pleasure principle Collection of rules that guide the id, resulting in behavior to achieve instant gratification without thought to consequences.

ego According to Freud, the structure of the mind that uses the reality principle to manipulate situations, plan for the future, solve problems, and make decisions.

reality principle Collection of rules that guide the ego as it negotiates between the id and the environment.

superego According to Freud, the structure of the mind that guides behavior to follow the rules of society, parents, or other authority figures.

some guilt when they fix their eyes on attractive people who are not their spouses. When this happens, their judgmental superego might say, *What's wrong with you? Are you a cheater?* The superego is an internalized version of what you have been *taught* is right and wrong, not necessarily an independent moral authority. Some of the activities of the superego are conscious, but the great majority occur at the preconscious and unconscious levels.

CAUGHT IN THE MIDDLE The ego monitors the demands of both the id and the superego, trying to satisfy both. The ego must handle rules and expectations as it maneuvers between the wishes of the id and the requirements of the environment. Think of the energy of the id, pushing to get all desires met instantly. The ego must ensure needs are met in a manner acceptable to the superego, reducing tension as much as possible. But not all urges and desires can be met (sometimes not instantly, sometimes never), so when the ego cannot satisfy the id, it must do something with the unsatisfied urge or unmet need. One solution is to remove it from the conscious part of the mind.

Defense Mechanisms

As you have figured out by now, the job of the ego is not easy. It must balance the infantile demands of the id with the perfectionist authority of the superego, and deal with the resulting conflict. This is feasible, but it takes some fancy footwork on the part of the ego. Freud proposed that **ego defense mechanisms** distort our perceptions and memories of the real world, without our awareness, to reduce the anxiety created by the conflicts among the id, ego, and superego.

Imagine you are about to leave for class and you get a text from a good friend, inviting you to a movie. You are torn, because you know an exam is coming up and you should not skip today's class. Your id is demanding a movie, some popcorn, and freedom from work. Your superego demands that you go to class so that you will be fully prepared for the exam. Clearly, your ego can't satisfy both of these demands. The ego must also deal with the external world and its requirements (for example, getting points for attendance). Freud (1923/1960) proposed that this sort of struggle is an everyday, recurring experience that is not always won by the ego. Sometimes, the id will win, and the person will act in an infantile, perhaps even destructive manner (you give in to the pressures of your friend and your id, and happily decide to skip class). Occasionally, the superego will prevail, and the person will feel a great deal of remorse or guilt for not living up to some moral ideal (you skip class, but you feel so guilty you can't enjoy the movie). Sometimes, the anxiety associated with the conflict between the id and the superego, which generally is unconscious, will surface to the conscious level. The ego will then have to deal with this anxiety and make it more bearable (perhaps by suggesting that a day off will help you study, because you haven't had any free time all semester). The ego must come up with a way to decrease the tension, but if it can't find a compromise, the anxiety may become overwhelming, and the ego will turn to defense mechanisms to reduce it.

Freud proposed a variety of defense mechanisms, which were expanded upon by his daughter, psychoanalyst Anna Freud (1895–1982). Some of these are shown in **INFOGRAPHIC 11.1**. There are two important points to remember about defense mechanisms. First, we are often unaware of using them, even if they are brought to our attention. Second, using defense mechanisms is not necessarily a bad thing (Vaillant, 2000). In some cases, distortions are helpful; if anxiety seeps to the surface, defense mechanisms can bring it down to a more manageable level. However, when conflicts between the id and the superego become overwhelming and the anxiety is too much for the ego, we tend to overuse defense mechanisms. This is when behaviors may turn inappropriate or unhealthy (Cramer, 2000, 2008; Tallandini & Caudek, 2010).

ego defense mechanisms Distortions of perceptions and memories of the real world, without one's awareness, to reduce the anxiety created by the conflict among the id, ego, and superego.

Ego Defense Mechanisms

The impulsive demands of the id sometimes conflict with the moralistic demands of the superego, resulting in anxiety. When that anxiety becomes excessive, the ego works to relieve this uncomfortable feeling through the use of defense mechanisms (Freud, 1923/1960). Defense mechanisms give us a way to "defend" against tension and anxiety, but they are only sometimes adaptive, or helpful. Defense mechanisms can be categorized ranging from less adaptive to more adaptive (Vaillant, 1992). More adaptive defense mechanisms help us deal with our anxiety in more productive and mature ways.

EGO relieves anxiety by employing a defense mechanism.

I really should get this mole checked. If it's cancerous, it would be better to get it treated right away.

Doctors freak me out! There's no way I'm going to see one.

EGO

anxiety

ID

SUPEREGO

Credit: Sad Young Woman, Tom Fullum/Getty Images.

✱ We may get better at dealing with stress and anxiety as we age. In a study comparing the use of defense mechanisms in different age groups, older participants were found to use fewer maladaptive defense mechanisms (Segal, Coolidge, & Mizuno, 2007).

MORE ADAPTIVE

SUBLIMATION
Redirecting unacceptable impulses into acceptable outlets.

Example: Instead of worrying about cancer risk, spend time researching clinics and selecting a highly trained dermatologist who specializes in mole analysis.

IDENTIFICATION
Unconsciously modeling our feelings or actions on the behaviors of someone we admire.

Example: Feeling worried about sun exposure, begin sporting the floppy hat and sunglasses frequently worn by a famous model.

DISPLACEMENT
Shifting negative feelings and impulses to an acceptable target.

Example: When scheduling appointment with dermatologist, complain to receptionist about the long wait and inconvenient hours.

REPRESSION
Anxiety-producing information is pushed into the unconscious.

Example: Continually forget to make an appointment.

RATIONALIZATION
Creating an acceptable excuse for an uncomfortable situation.

Example: "I've always had that mole. There's nothing to worry about."

PROJECTION
Attributing your own anxiety-provoking thoughts and impulses to someone else.

Example: "My girlfriend spends too much time sunbathing. I'll tell her she should get screened for skin cancer!"

DENIAL
Refusing to recognize a distressing reality.

Example: Ignore the mole. "I'm way too young. It can't be cancer."

LESS ADAPTIVE

CONNECTIONS

In **Chapter 6,** we presented the controversy surrounding repressed memories of childhood abuse. Many psychologists question the validity of research supporting the existence of repressed memories. Freud's case studies describing childhood sexual abuse have been questioned as well.

Oops

A "Freudian slip" occurs when an unintended word accidentally slips off the tongue, shedding light on unconscious thoughts. Here, the woman reassures the balding man he still has plenty of hair, but her Freudian slip reveals she thinks otherwise. Naf/CartoonStock.com.

repression The way the ego moves uncomfortable thoughts, memories, or feelings from the conscious level to the unconscious.

psychosexual stages According to Freud, the stages of development, from birth to adulthood, each of which has an erogenous zone as well as a conflict that must be dealt with.

fixation Being stuck in a particular psychosexual stage of development as a result of unsuccessfully dealing with the conflict characteristic of that stage.

REPRESSION One of the more commonly known defense mechanisms is **repression**, which refers to the way the ego moves uncomfortable thoughts, memories, or feelings from the conscious level to the unconscious. With anxiety-provoking memories, the reality of an event can become distorted to such an extreme that you don't even remember it. Saifa, for example, witnessed many violent incidents as a child, but he may have unconsciously or automatically repressed the memories surrounding some of these traumas. The repressed memories do not cease to exist, however, and they may pop up in unexpected forms. "Even though I may have one part of my life that is totally repressed . . . . It's going to leak out, and it might leak out in these weird ways," Saifa says. "It may be manifested in controlling or being abusive toward other people, or being abusive toward myself."

Repressed thoughts are like ping-pong balls held below the surface of the water. As long as you hold them down, they stay submerged; but if you let go, they pop up to the surface. The balls didn't cease to exist—they were simply just below the surface, out of sight and awareness.

 *In Class: Collaborate and Report*

It's Saturday morning and you have an important paper due this week. You could spend the day at the library gathering research and writing the paper, but there is tail-gaiting to do, a football game to attend, and a post-game party to go to with your friends. Team up and explain how at least four ego defense mechanisms might be used to justify your decision to avoid the library.

Freud's Stages of Development

LO 4 Summarize Freud's use of psychosexual stages to explain personality.

Freud's structural and topographical models of the mind provide frameworks for studying personality, but he didn't stop there. Freud (1905/1953) also conceived a *developmental* model to explain how personality is formed through experiences in childhood, with a special emphasis on sexuality. The development of sexuality and personality follows a fairly standard path through what Freud termed the **psychosexual stages**, which all children experience as they mature into adulthood (**TABLE 11.2**). The sexual energy of the id is a force behind this development, and because children are sexual beings starting from birth, this indicates a strong biological component to personality development. Associated with each of the psychosexual stages is a specific *erogenous zone,* or area of the body that when stimulated provides more sexual pleasure than other areas.

If the idea of a preschooler getting sexual pleasure from a body part makes you uncomfortable, then you can relate to the child's feeling of conflict between pleasurable

TABLE 11.2　FREUD'S PSYCHOSEXUAL STAGES

Stage	Age	Erogenous Zone	Focus	Type of Conflict	Results of Fixation
Oral	Birth–1$\frac{1}{2}$ years	Mouth	Sucking, chewing, and gumming	Weaning	Smoking, drinking, nail biting, excessive talking
Anal	1$\frac{1}{2}$–3 years	Anus	Eliminating bodily waste and controlling bodily functions responsible for this process	Toilet training	Being rule-bound, stingy, chaotic, destructive
Phallic	3–6 years	Genitals	Sexual feelings and awareness of self	Autoeroticism	Promiscuity, flirtation, vanity, or overdependence, and a focus on masturbation
Latency Period	6 years–puberty	Period during which children develop mentally, socially, and physically			
Genital	Puberty and beyond	Genitals	Reawakening of sexuality, with focus on relationships	Sexuality and aggression	Inability to thrive in adult activities such as work and love

According to Freud, psychological and sexual development proceeds through distinct stages. Each stage is characterized by a certain pleasure area, or "erogenous zone," and a conflict that must be resolved. If resolution is not achieved, the person may develop a problematic "fixation."

sexual feelings and the restrictions and potential disapproval of caregivers. Along with each psychosexual stage comes a conflict that must be successfully resolved in order for an individual to become a well-adjusted adult. If these conflicts are not suitably addressed, one may suffer from a **fixation** and get stuck in that particular stage, unable to progress smoothly through the remaining stages. Freud believed that fixation at a psychosexual stage during the first 5 to 6 years of life can dramatically influence an adult's personality. Let's look at each stage, its erogenous zone, conflicts, and some consequences of fixation.

THE ORAL STAGE The *oral stage* is the first psychosexual stage, beginning at birth and lasting until the infant is 1 to 1.5 years old. As its name suggests, the erogenous zone for this stage is the mouth. During this period, the infant gets his greatest pleasure from sucking, chewing, and gumming. According to Freud, the conflict during this stage generally centers on weaning. Infants must stop nursing or using a bottle or pacifier, and the timing of this weaning is often decided by the caregiver. Here is a possible conflict: The infant wants to continue using the bottle because it is a pleasurable activity, but his parent believes he is old enough to switch to a cup. How the caregiver handles this conflict (weaning too early or too late) can have long-term consequences for personality development. Freud suggested that certain behavior patterns and personality traits are associated with an oral fixation, and these might include smoking, nail biting, excessive talking, and increased alcohol consumption.

THE ANAL STAGE Following the oral stage, a child enters the *anal stage,* which lasts approximately until the age of 3. During this stage, the erogenous zone is the anus, and pleasure is derived from eliminating bodily waste as well as learning to control the body parts responsible for this process. The conflict during this stage centers on toilet training: The parents want their child to use a toilet, but the child is not necessarily

Oral Fixation
The average baby (birth to 18 months) spends 108 minutes per day sucking on a pacifier and another 33 minutes mouthing other objects (Juberg, Alfano, Coughlin, & Thompson, 2001). Freud identified this phase of life with the oral stage of psychosexual development. Natalia Campbell of NC Photography/Getty Images.

ready. Once again, how caregivers deal with this learning task may have long-term implications for personality. Freud suggested that toilet training can set the stage for power struggles between child and adult; the child ultimately will gain control over her bodily functions, and then she can use this control to manipulate caregivers (not always "going" at the appropriate time and place). If a parent is too harsh about toilet training (growing angry when there are accidents, forcing a child to sit on the toilet until she goes) or too lenient (making excuses for accidents, not really encouraging the child to learn control), the child might grow up with an *anal-retentive* personality (rule-bound, stingy) or an *anal-expulsive* personality (chaotic, destructive).

PHALLIC STAGE Ages 3 to 6 years mark the *phallic stage* (*phallus* means "penis" in Latin). During this period, the erogenous zone is the genitals, and many children begin to discover that self-stimulation is pleasurable. Freud (1923/1960) assigned special importance to the conflict that occurs in the phallic stage.

During this time, little boys develop a desire to replace their fathers. These feelings are normal, according to Freud, but they lead to boys becoming jealous of their fathers, who are now considered rivals for their mothers' affection. This pattern, referred to as the **Oedipus complex** (ED-uh-puss), is named for a character in a complicated Greek myth. Oedipus was abandoned by his parents when he was a newborn, so he did not know their identities. As an adult, he unknowingly married his mother and killed his father. Freud named the Oedipus complex after this Greek tragedy, as it mirrors how boys behave and feel during the phallic stage. Freud believed that when a little boy becomes aware of his attraction to his mother, he realizes his father is a formidable rival and experiences jealousy and anger toward him. He also begins to fear his father, who is so powerful, and worry that his father might punish him. Specifically, he fears that his father will castrate him (Freud, 1917/1966). In order to reduce the tension, the boy must identify with and behave like his father, a process known as *identification*. This defense mechanism resolves the Oedipus complex by allowing the boy to take on or internalize the behaviors, mannerisms, morals, and standards of his father. Freud proposed that the fear of castration causes a great deal of anxiety, but with successful resolution of the Oedipus complex, this anxiety is reduced. The boy realizes that sexual affection should only be between his father and mother, and the incest taboo develops.

Freud (1923/1960) believed that little girls experience a different type of conflict during this period. Little girls feel an attraction to their fathers, and become jealous and angry toward their mothers. Around the same time, they realize that they do not have a penis. This leads to feelings of loss and jealousy, known as *penis envy*. The girl responds with anger, blaming her mother for her missing penis. Realizing she can't have her father, she begins to act like her mother through the process of *identification*. She takes on her mother's behaviors, mannerisms, morals, and standards. Some of Freud's followers labeled this conflict the Electra complex (Kilmartin & Dervin, 1997; Schultz & Schultz, 2017). Freud's theory of female development is now regarded as a product of its historical and social context, as opposed to objective observation.

If children do not resolve the sexual conflicts that arise during the phallic stage, they develop a fixation, which can lead to promiscuity, flirtation, vanity, overdependence, bravado, and an increased focus on masturbation.

LATENCY PERIOD Freud proposed that from 6 years old to puberty, children remain in a *latency period* (not a "stage" according to Freud's definition, as there is no erogenous zone, conflict, or fixation). During this time, psychosexual development slows. Where does the child's sexual energy go during this period? According

Just Like Dad
Young boys often look up to their fathers and strive to be like them. Freud believed this is the way boys resolve the Oedipus complex. Unable to displace his powerful father, the son stops trying to compete and begins to identify with him. LWA/Getty Images.

Oedipus complex According to Freud, the attraction a child feels toward the opposite-sex parent, along with the resentment or envy directed toward the same-sex parent.

to Freud, it is repressed: Although children develop mentally, socially, and physically, their sexual development is on hold. This idea seems to be supported by the fact that most prepubertal children tend to gravitate toward same-sex friends and playmates.

GENITAL STAGE Following the calm of the latency period, a child's psychosexual development picks up speed again. The *genital stage* begins at puberty and is the final stage of psychosexual development. During this time, there is a reawakening of sexuality. The erogenous zone is centered on the genitals, but now in association with relationships, as opposed to masturbation. Adolescents become interested in partners, whereas earlier their focus was family members. This is a time when one resolves the Oedipus or Electra complex and often becomes attracted to partners who resemble the opposite-sex parent, according to Freud (1905/1953). Because of the ever-present *id* and its requirement for satisfaction, there still are unconscious conflicts to be addressed, including the continual battle against hidden sexual and aggressive urges. The resolution of these conflicts impacts the types of relationships we seek and cultivate. If earlier conflicts are resolved, then it is possible to thrive in adult activities such as work and love.

Taking Stock: An Appraisal of Psychoanalytic Theory

Freud's psychoanalytic theory has been the subject of much criticism (Bornstein, 2005; Strenger, 2015). Some of Freud's own followers (a few of whom we will discuss shortly) recognized several key weaknesses. For example, psychoanalysis does not take into account the possibility that people can change; we are not predestined to develop certain personality types simply because we had specific childhood experiences. Thus, psychoanalysis ignores the importance of development beyond childhood. Critics also contend that Freud placed too much weight on the unconscious forces guiding behavior, instead proposing that we can be conscious of our motivations and change our behaviors. Many have objected to Freud's emphasis on sexuality and its role in personality development.

Another concern is that Freud's theory to a large degree is male-centered and based on a biased, nonrepresentative sample—a handful of middle- and upper-class Viennese women and Freud himself. His theory of development, for example, frames female sexuality as a deficiency: Women lack a penis rather than have a vagina. According to psychoanalytic theory, women are considered inferior in their "character development" and should accept their "passive position in a world that is male-dominated" (Tummala-Narra, 2016, p. 18). Many have raised concerns about Freud's one-sided male perspective, though not necessarily dismissing the potential utility of psychoanalysis for women (Young-Bruehl, 2009).

Given the amount of attention Freud's concepts have received, one might expect a great deal of research supporting or refuting aspects of his theory. But where would a researcher start? For example, how would you go about designing an experiment to test whether early weaning causes later problems in relationships? How about persuading an ethics committee to approve a study with an independent variable that manipulates toilet training? With these types of difficulties, it is no surprise there is limited published research on Freudian concepts themselves, although numerous researchers have conducted studies on their effectiveness when incorporated into psychotherapy (Fonagy, 2015; Shedler, 2010).

Many students have trouble understanding why we should study Freud, whose ideas they consider sexist, perverse, and outdated. Freud is an important historical figure in

Who Is Anna O.?
"Anna O." is the alias for Bertha Pappenheim (1859–1936), whose case study appears in the 1895 book *Studies on Hysteria* by Josef Breuer and Sigmund Freud. Although Anna O. inspired Freud's psychoanalytic theory, the facts of her case remain foggy. What type of disorder did she have, and did psychoanalytic methods really help her? Scholars have been discussing Anna O. for decades, but the answers to such questions are still up in the air (Hurst, 1982; Spitz, 2016). © Mary Evans/Sigmund Freud Copyrights/The ImageWorks.

CONNECTIONS

In **Chapter 1,** we introduced the case study, a form of descriptive research. A major weakness of the case study is its failure to provide a representative sample, or sample whose characteristics reflect the population. Freud's case studies focused on a particular subgroup; thus, his findings might not be generalizable.

psychology, and we can't ignore his legacy just because we may disagree with him. You wouldn't find many history teachers ignoring world leaders whose policies they dislike, would you? The same principle applies to Freud; his impact was huge and cannot be overlooked.

A DARK PERIOD Young childhood was no picnic for Saifa. In addition to witnessing violence and suffering, he faced an ongoing conflict between his innate sense of gender and society's expectations for him as a "girl." But the early years were also a time of great freedom. "When I was a young child, when I was like 5, 6, 7, I was the adult that I am now," Saifa says. "I was very uninhibited; I was very loud; I was very free; I was weird; I was quirky. I was just in my edges" (being bold, brave, and the complete person he was).

Life took a dramatic turn on October 30, 1989, when police showed up at Saifa's building and took away his father. Saifa, 10 years old, observed the whole event. "I saw my father arrested, and that image was kind of seared into my mind," Saifa says. "That's the last time I saw him alive, [he] was being taken away in handcuffs."

While Saifa's mother dealt with the aftermath of the arrest, Saifa went to live with his sister in North Carolina. She was 23 years old, busy with work, and not available to give Saifa the love and nurture he needed. In addition to being separated from his parents, Saifa was relentlessly teased and bullied at his new school. "I think living in North Carolina just really killed my fire as a child," Saifa says. "I was still that quirky, weird, loud kid, but then I was teased, I was bullied, my self-esteem was really low."

A year or two after moving to North Carolina, Saifa began to experience puberty. His voice deepened; he began growing facial hair; and his muscles became more defined—all changes associated with *male* puberty. But Saifa was still a "girl" at this point; as you may recall, he had been assigned female at birth and raised as "Susanne." The masculinization of his body was fueled by testosterone from his undescended testes. (People with AIS are born with internal testes, in contrast to typical males whose testes descend into the scrotum during fetal development.) "I didn't know how to think about it as a young person, given that I was assigned female, but yet I was experiencing this male puberty," Saifa says. "But it felt normal; it felt good."

The male puberty Saifa enjoyed came to an abrupt halt at age 13, when he moved back to New York City and doctors removed his testes. The purpose of the operation was to eliminate the pain he had been feeling in his groin, possibly the result of hernias in his testes. The other reason, so doctors informed Saifa's mother, was that the internal gonads would likely become cancerous. Following the surgery, Saifa's doctor put him on female hormones, which feminized his face and body. "[The doctors] wanted to create this feminine body that was going against what my body was naturally doing… I was developing with both male and female characteristics, and that's what makes my particular intersex trait so beautiful," Saifa says. "The right to my body was taken away from me. No one asked me what I wanted to do with my body." ●

According to Freud, personality is largely shaped by early childhood experiences and sexual impulses. Yet, some of the most transformative experiences in Saifa's life—the arrest of his father, the bullying at school, and the surgery to remove his testes—occurred later in life and had little to do with sexual urges. Some personality theorists might argue

What's Beneath That Smile?
Saifa, 18, poses for his high school graduation photo (top) and a portrait with his sister. After doctors removed his internal testes, Saifa fell into a deep depression. "I didn't comb my hair, I didn't brush my teeth, I didn't shower," Saifa explains. "It was so bad, I wouldn't even go outside." This depression landed him in therapy, which helped him get back into the world. However, the therapist was not honest with Saifa about the circumstances of his birth. She suggested he was a female born with an underdeveloped uterus and ovaries, and pushed him to adopt a female gender identity. Courtesy of Sean Saifa Wall.

that these types of events are important factors in the development of personality. We now turn to the neo-Freudians, who agree with Freud on many points, but depart from his intense emphasis on early childhood experiences, aggression, and sexuality.

The Neo-Freudians

LO 5   Explain how the neo-Freudians' theories of personality differ from Freud's.

Not surprisingly, Freud's psychoanalytic theory was quite controversial, but he did have a following of students who adapted some of the main aspects of his theory. Erik Erikson, for example, considered himself a "loyal Freudian," yet he took Freud's ideas in a new direction (Schultz & Schultz, 2017). **Erikson** suggested psychosocial development occurs throughout life, with eight stages each marked by a conflict between the individual's needs and society's expectations. Some who disagreed with Freud on key points broke away to develop their own theories; they are often referred to as neo-Freudians (neo = "new").

ALFRED ADLER One of the first followers to forge his own path was a fellow Austrian physician, Alfred Adler (1870–1937), whose own theory conflicted with the Freudian notion that personality is, to a large degree, shaped by unconscious motivators. As Adler saw it, humans are not just pleasure seekers, but conscious and intentional in their behaviors. We are motivated by the need to feel superior—to grow, overcome challenges, and strive for perfection. This drive originates during childhood, when we realize that we are dependent on and inferior to adults. Whether imagined or real, our sense of inferiority pushes us to compensate, so we cultivate our special gifts and skills. This attempt to balance perceived weaknesses with strengths is not a sign of abnormality, but a natural response.

Adler's theory of *individual psychology* focuses on each person's unique struggle with feelings of inferiority. Unfortunately, not everyone is successful in overcoming feelings of helplessness and dependence, but instead may develop what is known as an *inferiority complex* (Adler, 1927/1994). Someone with an inferiority complex feels incompetent, vulnerable, and powerless, and cannot achieve his full potential.

Perhaps you can imagine how feelings of inferiority might arise in sibling relationships. The firstborn child receives all his parents' attention for the first years of life. Then along comes a baby brother or sister, and suddenly mom and dad must divide their attention. How might this affect the older child's sense of worth? Younger siblings have their own reasons for feeling inferior. They are, after all, the newcomers, smaller and less developed than their older siblings. And unlike the firstborn, who enjoyed being an only child for some time, younger siblings never had that special alone time with mom and dad. They always had to share their parents' love.

Adler was one of the first to theorize about the psychological repercussions of birth order. He believed that firstborn children experience different environmental pressures than youngest and middle children, and these pressures can set the stage for the development of certain personality traits (Ansbacher & Ansbacher, 1956).

CONNECTIONS

In **Chapter 8,** we discussed Erikson's views of growth and development. Building on the views of Freud, Erikson believed every developmental stage is marked by a task or emotional crisis that must be handled successfully to allow for healthy psychological growth.

An Individual Psychology
Alfred Adler studied with Freud but ultimately broke from his teacher and created his own theory. According to Adler, personality is strongly influenced by the drive to conquer feelings of inferiority. Failure to succeed at this endeavor paves the way for an inferiority complex. Imagno/Getty Images.

CONTROVERSIES

How Birth Order May—or May Not— Affect Your Personality

➡️⬅️ Firstborns are conscientious and high achieving. They play by the rules, excel in school, and become leaders in the workforce. The youngest children, favored and

DO MIDDLE CHILDREN GET LOST IN THE SHUFFLE?

Caught in the Middle?
In the popular television show *Modern Family,* the middle child Alex (left) is portrayed as hard driven, conscientious, and high achieving— but these characteristics are more commonly associated with firstborn children. Do you think stereotypes about birth order are valid? ABC/Photofest.

CONNECTIONS

In **Chapter 1,** we discussed confounding variables, which are a type of extraneous variable that changes in sync with an independent variable (IV), making it difficult to discern which variable—the IV or the confounding variable—is causing changes in the dependent variable. Here, family size is a potential confounding variable.

collective unconscious According to Jung, the universal experiences of humankind passed from generation to generation, including memories.

archetypes Primal images, patterns of thoughts, and storylines stored in the collective unconscious, with themes that may be found in art, literature, music, dreams, and religions.

coddled by their parents, grow up to be gregarious and rebellious. Middle children tend to get lost in the shuffle, but they learn to be self-sufficient.

Have you heard these stereotypes about birth order and personality? How well do they match your personal experience, and do you think they are valid?

If you search the scientific literature, you will indeed find research supporting such claims. According to one analysis of 200 studies, firstborns (as well as only children) are often accomplished and successful; middle children are sociable but tend to lack a sense of belonging; and last-born children are agreeable and rebellious (Eckstein et al., 2010). Others have found that later-born children, particularly those who are middle siblings, often go out of their way to help others (Salmon, Cuthbertson, & Figueredo, 2016). These findings are intriguing and often seem consistent with our everyday observations. However, birth order studies have historically been riddled with confounding variables, such as the number of siblings in a family, and designing studies to circumvent these variables has proven difficult. In 2015 researchers carried out a study that controlled for many of these factors, subduing the longstanding debate. Reviewing studies that include over 20,000 participants, these researchers could not find any connection between birth order and specific personality characteristics (Bakalar, 2015, October 28; Damian & Roberts, 2015; Rohrer, Egloff, & Schmukle, 2015). ➜ ⬅

CARL GUSTAV JUNG Another influential neo-Freudian was Swiss psychiatrist Carl Gustav Jung (yoong; 1875–1961). Jung's focus was on growth and self-understanding. Although he agreed with Freud about the importance of the unconscious, in his *analytic psychology* he placed less emphasis on biological urges (sex and aggression), proposing more positive and spiritual aspects of human nature. Critical of Freud's overemphasis on the sex drive, Jung claimed that Freud viewed the brain as "an appendage to the genital glands" (Westen et al., 2008, p. 66). Jung (1969) proposed we are driven by psychological energy (not sexual energy) that promotes growth, insight, and balance. He also believed personality development is not limited to childhood; adults continue to evolve throughout life.

Jung also differed from Freud in his view of the unconscious. Jung believed personality is made up of the ego (at the conscious level), a *personal unconscious,* and a *collective unconscious.* The personal unconscious is akin to Freud's notion of the preconscious and the unconscious mind; items from the personal unconscious range from easily retrievable memories to anxiety-provoking repressed memories. The **collective unconscious**, according to Jung, holds the universal experiences of humankind passed from generation to generation, memories that are not easily retrieved without some degree of effort or interpretation. We inherit a variety of primal images, patterns of thought, and storylines. The themes of these **archetypes** (AHR-ki-types) may be found in art, literature, music, dreams, and religions across time, geography, and culture. Some of the consistent archetypes include the nurturing mother, powerful father, innocent child, and brave hero. Archetypes provide a blueprint for us as we respond to situations, objects, and people in our environments (Jung, 1969). The *anima* refers to the part of our personality that is feminine, and the *animus* to that which is masculine. Jung believed both of these parts exist in everyone's personality, and we must acknowledge and appreciate them. Failure to accept the anima and animus can result in an imbalance, which prevents us from being whole.

KAREN HORNEY Karen Horney (HOR-nahy; 1885–1952) was a German psychoanalyst who immigrated to the United States in the early 1930s. As a neo-Freudian,

she emphasized the role of relationships between children and their caregivers, not erogenous zones and psychosexual stages. She agreed with Freud, however, that our early years play an important role in shaping adult personality, and that conflict arises between individual desires and the needs of society (Schultz & Schultz, 2017; Tummala-Narra, 2016). Horney believed that personality development is driven by the social environment, particularly that of the family. Inadequate parenting can create feelings of helplessness and isolation, which she referred to as *basic anxiety* (Horney, 1945). In order to deal with this anxiety, Horney suggested that people use three strategies: moving toward people (looking for affection and acceptance), moving away from people (looking for isolation and self-sufficiency), or moving against people (looking to control others). Horney believed that a balance of these three strategies is important for psychological stability and a core component of healthy personality development. She was also a strong critic of Freud's sexist approach to the female psyche, pointing out that women are not jealous of the penis itself, but rather what it represents in terms of power and status in society. Horney (1926/1967) also proposed that boys and men can envy women's ability to bear and breastfeed children.

Freud's Legacy

Freud's psychoanalytic theory was groundbreaking and controversial, and it led to a variety of extensions and permutations through neo-Freudians such as Adler, Jung, Horney, and Erikson. Freud's theories are considered among the most important in the field of personality development. He called attention to the existence of infant sexuality at a time when sex was a forbidden topic of conversation. He recognized the importance of infancy and early childhood in the unfolding of personality, and appreciated the universal stages of human development. It was a blow to our collective self-esteem to realize that so much of our thinking occurs without conscious awareness, but this notion has been widely accepted, even among psychologists who reject the Freudian perspective. Some suggest Freud's work has "become so pervasive in Western thinking that he is to be ranked with Darwin and Marx for introducing new—and often disturbing—modes of thought in Western culture" (Hilgard, 1987, p. 99).

⭕✅⭕⭕ **show what you know**

1. According to Freud, all children go through _____ stages as they mature into adulthood. If conflicts are not resolved, a child may suffer from a _____.

2. Freud's _____ includes three levels: conscious, preconscious, and unconscious.
   a. structural model of the mind
   b. developmental model
   c. individual psychology
   d. topographical model of the mind

3. Jung believed personality is made up of the ego, a personal unconscious, and the:
   a. id.
   c. superego.
   b. collective unconscious.
   d. preconscious.

4. How did the theories of the neo-Freudians differ from Freud's psychoanalytic theory in regard to personality development?

✓ CHECK YOUR ANSWERS IN APPENDIX C.

Humanistic Theories

ON A POSITIVE PATH After Saifa's testes were removed and he began taking female hormones, doctors expected (or hoped) he would blossom into a lovely young woman. The pediatrician told Saifa's mom that AIS was common among fashion models, and assured her that her daughter would be pretty. But as Saifa recalls, "I did not succumb to the pressure to be more feminine, but actually gravitated toward masculinity" (Wall, 2015, p. 118). At age 14, Saifa came out as a gay woman. He excelled in school and became a leader at Williams College, spearheading campus demonstrations against police brutality and anti-gay hate crimes ("About Sean Saifa Wall," 2016). A few years after graduating, Saifa decided to make the biological and social transition to manhood; he changed his name to Sean Saifa Wall, began taking testosterone, and underwent a double-mastectomy.

Saifa assumed control of his body and his life like never before, yet he could not shake the feelings of loneliness and self-hatred. To do this, he would need to confront a lifetime of trauma, which included the loss of his father—first to prison and then to AIDS—and life-changing medical interventions before he was old enough to give informed consent. Saifa courageously faced these traumas by going to psychotherapy, and enrolling in a 12-step recovery program for sex addiction. He also got involved in an Oakland-based organization called Generative Somatics, which he says "offers an alternative healing modality to create personal and political transformation in the individual and community."

For the last 10 years, Saifa has been on a journey to heal himself and help others. Through his research, writing, and public speaking, he has established himself as an expert on intersex traits. In 2012 Saifa became the board president of Advocates for Informed Choice (now interACT), an organization devoted to protecting the legal rights of intersex children. More recently, his focus has shifted to his collage art, writing, and advisory work for the Astraea Intersex Fund for Human Rights. "I've definitely been on this journey . . . looking outward about how I can change the world around me, but also this inward journey of how I can change the world within me," Saifa explains. "Because I think that the work we do inside of us informs the work that we do outside of us."

Saifa is now 37 and seems to have reached a point of self-acceptance and love. "I still have more work to do and more growing to do, as we all do," Saifa says, "but I can see that I have returned to that child of like 7 who is just in the world . . . totally free." ●

Every Body Is Beautiful
Saifa advocates for the legal rights of children with intersex traits. "Accepting myself as intersex and advocating for intersex people and children, I really put forward that our bodies are our mosaic," Saifa says. "There is no such thing as a 'normal body' . . . . This variation is what makes us, as a species, beautiful."
Courtesy of Sean Saifa Wall.

The Brighter Side: Maslow and Rogers

If you asked a humanistic theorist to explain Saifa's evolution, she would likely say that his drive to grow and improve is, and has always been, the main force shaping his personality. According to the humanistic perspective, not only are we innately good; we are also in control of our destinies, and these positive aspects of human nature drive the development of personality. This perspective began gaining momentum in the 1960s and 1970s in response to the negative, mechanistic view of human nature apparent in other theories. According to leading humanists Abraham Maslow and Carl Rogers, our natural tendency is to grow in a positive direction.

LO 6 Summarize Maslow's hierarchy of needs, and describe self-actualizers.

MASLOW AND PERSONALITY Abraham Maslow is considered by some to be the "single person most responsible for creating humanistic psychology" (Moss, 2015, p. 13). As a humanist, he believed that psychology should also study human creativity, growth, and healthy functioning, not just mental illness and maladaptive personality traits. Probably best known for his theory of motivation, Maslow (1943) proposed that human behaviors are motivated by biological and psychological needs. When a need is not being met, a state of tension motivates us to meet it, and this causes the tension to diminish. Maslow's hierarchy of needs explains the organization of human needs, which are universal and ordered in terms of their strength (from basic physiological needs to self-actualization and self-transcendence). How does this relate to personality? As you learned earlier, personality is the unique core set of characteristics that influence the way we think, act, and feel. Although we tend to respond to needs in a universal order, Maslow suggested that we all have the ability to reorder them. Maslow was particularly interested in *self-actualizers,* or people who are continually seeking to reach their fullest potential, one of the guiding principles of the humanistic perspective. If you're looking for an example of a self-actualizer, you needn't look beyond this chapter.

THINK POSITIVE

Saifa the Self-Actualizer

According to Maslow, mentally healthy people are able to satisfy their self-focused needs and direct their attention toward helping others and making the world a better place (D'Souza & Gurin, 2016). Saifa began to

HEALTHY PEOPLE HELP THEMSELVES BY HELPING OTHERS

move in this direction early in life, volunteering at the Gay Men's Health Crisis, an organization devoted to preventing HIV/AIDS and supporting families impacted by the epidemic. (This work was motivated by personal experience; Saifa lost his own father to AIDS.) He continued on this path as a young adult, working with women in prison, conducting HIV research at the University of California at San Francisco (UCSF), and helping lesbian, gay, bisexual, and transgender (LGBT) high school students advocate for their legal rights based on gender identity and sexual orientation. His current work as an intersex advocate is inspired by not only his own story but also the struggles of others: "When I started connecting and really hearing the stories of other people, I think that's what motivated me to action," asserts Saifa, who has devoted his life to making the world a fair and just place, a pursuit that Maslow associated with self-actualization (Duff, Rubenstein, & Prilleltensky, 2016). Says Saifa, "Activism for me is motivated by love and truth and the desire for justice."

Have a look at some of the attributes of self-actualizers presented in **TABLE 11.3** on the following page. Do you recognize any of them in yourself?

Transcendent Art
This artwork by Saifa shows the profile of an African American child surrounded by a border of razors, and filled with words from a newspaper article describing the 1901 race riots that occurred in Pierce City, Missouri. It represents the many young black men who end up behind bars or lose their lives to violence before reaching adulthood. Saifa's artwork may reveal *self-transcendence,* an additional need proposed by Maslow toward the end of his life. Self-transcendence means going beyond oneself and connecting with the world through "peak experiences" that may be mystical, aesthetic, or emotional in nature (Koltko-Rivera, 2006). And they stay hungry for dark meat, 2013, Sean Saifa Wall. Mixed media, 9.5 × 8.25 inches, Atlanta, GA.

TABLE 11.3 ARE YOU A SELF-ACTUALIZER?

Tendencies	Characteristics	Example
Realistic perceptions of reality	Nonjudgmental, objective, and acutely aware of others	An individual who is empathetic and unbiased
Acceptance of self, others, and nature	Has patience with weaknesses of self, others, and society	Someone who is forgiving and accepting of others
Spontaneity and creativeness	Original, flexible, and willing to learn from mistakes	Someone who is self-sufficient and lives in unconventional ways
Independent and private	Not reliant on others, enjoys time alone	A person with a strong sense of self who doesn't conform to peer pressure
Freshness of appreciation	Views each experience as if it was the first time (e.g., a sunrise), is grateful for what he has	An individual who lives life thankful for each day
Peak experiences	Has moments of ecstasy and transcendence	A highly spiritual individual who experiences intense happiness in day-to-day activities
Social interest and fellowship	Empathic and sympathetic toward others	A person who is devoted to helping others
Profound interpersonal relations	Maintains deep and lasting friendships	Someone with intense, lifelong friendships
A democratic character structure	Tolerant and accepting of others	A person who is open-minded and humble
Autonomous and resistant to enculturation	Independent and free from cultural pressures	An individual who is self-sufficient in thought and behavior and resists social pressure

According to Maslow, a "self-actualizer" is someone who continually strives to achieve his maximum potential. Listed above are the common traits and examples of self-actualizers. Perhaps some of these qualities characterize you. Information from Schultz & Schultz (2013).

LO 7 Discuss Rogers' view of self-concept, ideal self, and unconditional positive regard.

ROGERS AND PERSONALITY Carl Rogers was another humanist who had great faith in the essential goodness of people and their ability to make sound choices (Rogers, 1979). This humanistic perspective colored both his theory of personality as well as the work he did as a therapist. According to Rogers, we all have an innate urge to move toward situations and people that will help us grow and to avoid those with the potential to inhibit growth. Starting in infancy, we have an inborn tendency not only to survive but also to enhance ourselves, and this continues throughout life (Murphy & Joseph, 2016). He believed we should trust our ability to find happiness and mental balance, that is, to be *fully functioning*, and strive to really experience life, not just be passive participants. At the same time, we must also be sensitive to the needs of others.

Rogers highlighted the importance of **self-concept**, which refers to a person's knowledge of her own strengths, abilities, behavior patterns, and temperament. Problems arise when a person's self-concept is *incongruent* with, or does not correspond to, her experiences in the world (Rogers, 1959). If a woman believes she is kind and sociable but fails to get along with most people in her life, this incongruence will produce tension and confusion. Rogers also proposed that people often develop an **ideal self**, which is the *self-concept* a person fervently strives to achieve. Problems arise when the ideal self is unattainable or incongruent with one's self-concept, a topic we will discuss further in Chapter 14 (Rogers, 1959).

self-concept The knowledge an individual has about his strengths, abilities, behavior patterns, and temperament.

ideal self The self-concept a person strives for and fervently wishes to achieve.

unconditional positive regard According to Rogers, the total acceptance or valuing of a person, regardless of behavior.

Like Freud, Rogers believed caregivers play a vital role in the development of personality and self-concept. Ideally, caregivers should show **unconditional positive regard**, or total acceptance of a child regardless of her behavior. According to Rogers, people need to feel totally accepted and valued for who they are, not what they do. Caregivers who place too much emphasis on rules, morals, and values, ignoring a child's innate goodness, can cause the child to experience *conditions of worth*. Stated differently, the child feels as if she is worthy of being loved only when she acts in accordance with how her parents' want her to behave. When our behaviors are judged to be bad or wrong, we feel unworthy, so we may try to please others by hiding or repressing these "unacceptable" behaviors and emotions. Seeking approval from others, we deny our true selves, and anxiety is ever-present in our lives. As caregivers, it is important to show children that we value them all the time, not just when they obey us and act the way we want them to. Of course, children behave in ways we dislike, but parents should love their children unconditionally, because it is the behavior that is unacceptable, not the child.

Unconditional Love?
Marge Simpson of *The Simpsons* loves and accepts her children no matter how they behave. Does this cartoon mother demonstrate unconditional positive regard? © 20th Century Fox Film Corp. All rights reserved./Courtesy Everett Collection.

 *In Class: Collaborate and Report*

Before meeting with your group, **A)** briefly outline the definitions of self-concept, ideal self, conditions of worth, and unconditional positive regard. **B)** Team up and write a short users' manual for new parents. Provide instructions for how to raise a "fully functioning" child using these principles and any other appropriate concepts from humanistic psychology. **C)** Are there situations in which you think unconditional positive regard is not appropriate?

Taking Stock: An Appraisal of the Humanistic Theories

The humanistic approach may not be as well known as psychoanalysis, but its influence is far reaching. From psychotherapy to research on human strengths and optimal functioning, we can see the "resurgence" of the humanists' work in the field (DeRobertis, 2016). The humanistic perspective has led to a more positive and balanced view of human nature, influencing approaches to parenting, education, and research. Its legacy is alive and well in the emerging field of positive psychology.

Now let's step back and review the potential weaknesses of the humanistic approach. For humanistic and psychoanalytic theories alike, creating operational definitions can be challenging. How can you use the experimental method to test a subjective approach whose concepts are open to interpretation (Schultz & Schultz, 2017)? Imagine submitting a research proposal that included two randomly assigned groups of children: one group whose parents were instructed to show them *unconditional positive regard* and the other group whose parents were told to instill *conditions of worth*. The proposal would never amount to a real study, not only because it raises ethical issues, but also because it would be impossible to control the experimental conditions. Another problem with unconditional positive regard in particular is that constantly praising, attempting to boost self-esteem, and withholding criticism can be counterproductive. Some even believe the use of unconditional positive regard is a "narcissist's dream" (Paris, 2014). And while it is important to recognize that humans have great potential to grow and move forward, we should not discount the developmental impact of early experiences. Finally, some have argued that humanism almost ignores the negative aspects of human nature evident in war, greed, abuse, and aggression (Burger, 2015). This may be true, but some humanistic psychologists are actually "inspired by the challenges" presented by the darker side of humanity (Stern, 2016, xi).

CONNECTIONS

In **Chapter 1,** we described positive psychology as a relatively new approach. The humanists' optimism struck the right chord with many psychologists, who wondered why the field was not focusing on human strengths and virtues.

In the next section, we will explore how personality is influenced by forces in the outside world. How do you think your interactions with the environment have shaped your personality?

 show what you know

1. _____ was a humanist who was interested in exploring people who are self-actualizers. _____, also a humanist, explored the difficulties people face when their self-concept is incongruent with life experiences.

2. The total acceptance of a child regardless of her behavior is known as:
   a. conditions of worth.
   b. repression.
   c. the real self.
   d. unconditional positive regard.

3. How do the psychoanalytic and humanistic perspectives differ in regard to personality development?

✓ CHECK YOUR ANSWERS IN APPENDIX C.

You Asked, Saifa Answers

http://qrs.ly/w15a5f3

Does your social media accurately reflect who you are?

scan this ➜

Learning and Social-Cognitive Theories

 NANA LIVES ON A decade has passed since Saifa's therapist asked him the crucial question: "When did you realize love was not possible?" Even today, those words strike Saifa in a deep and vulnerable place. But he no longer falls apart—perhaps because he knows that love *is* possible. There is no doubt he pours love into the world, advocating for the rights of intersex children and others who don't fit neatly into society's male and female gender categories. For those in his close circle, Saifa demonstrates love by cooking and hosting—making sure they are comfortable and happy. He learned these nurturing behaviors from his grandmother, who passed away in 2003.

"One of my role models was my Nana," Saifa says. "She didn't really talk much, she was kind of shy . . . . but she was an amazing cook." Preparing meals and cleaning were the ways she expressed her love. "To speak to her history, she was a domestic worker for most of her life, so that's what she knew," Saifa explains. "She showed her love by doing rather than saying." ●

The Role of Learning, Thought, and Environment

LO 8 Use the behavioral perspective to explain personality development.

The behaviors Saifa learned from his Nana are expressions of his personality, yet none of the personality theories we have explored emphasize the importance of learning through role models, or through classical and operant conditioning. These processes are a primary focus of the behavioral perspective.

When we consider the definition of personality—the core set of characteristics that influence the way one thinks, acts, and feels—there is only one aspect that behaviorists would be willing to study: the way a person acts. Behaviorists like B. F. Skinner are not interested in studying the thoughts and emotions typically equated with expressions of personality; instead, they measure observable behaviors. Personality is a collection of behaviors, all of which have been shaped through a lifetime of learning: Each person "develops under a different or unique set of stimulus conditions and consequently his resulting personality becomes uniquely his own" (Lundin, 1963, p. 265). In some cases, operant conditioning shapes personality characteristics that influence the way we act, for example through the use of reinforcement. When Saifa's friends praise the meals he makes, this surely acts as a positive reinforcer for his cooking and the way he nurtures others. Saifa's nurturing behavior also provides an example of a personality

expectancy A person's predictions about the consequences or outcomes of behavior.

social-cognitive perspective Suggests that personality results from patterns of thinking (cognitive) as well as relationships and other environmental factors (social).

self-efficacy Beliefs one has regarding how effective he or she will be in reaching a goal.

characteristic that has been shaped by the environment through observational learning. In this case, Saifa's Nana modeled behaviors that he followed. These behaviors are learned; they follow a predictable pattern and thus constitute part of Saifa's personality. Of course, not everyone agrees with this behaviorist view of personality development.

LO 9   Summarize Rotter's view of personality.

ROTTER AND PERSONALITY American psychologist Julian Rotter (1916–2014) was one of the early social learning theorists who suggested that not all aspects of behavior and personality can be directly observed (Rotter, 1990). He proposed several important cognitive aspects of personality, including *locus of control* and *expectancy*. According to Rotter, a key component of personality is locus of control, a pattern of generalized beliefs about where control or responsibility for outcomes resides. If a person has an *internal* locus of control, she believes that the causes of her life events generally reside within her, and that she has some control over them. For example, such a person would say that her career success depends on how hard she works, not on luck (Rotter, 1966). Someone with an *external* locus of control generally believes that causes for outcomes reside outside of him; he assigns great importance to luck, fate, and other features of the environment, over which he has little control. As this person sees it, getting a job occurs when all the circumstances are right and luck is on his side (Rotter, 1966). A person's locus of control refers to beliefs about the self, not about others.

Rotter also explored how personality is influenced by thoughts about the future. **Expectancy** refers to the predictions we make about the outcomes and consequences of our behaviors (**INFOGRAPHIC 11.2** on the following page). A woman who is considering whether she should confront the manager of a restaurant over a bad meal will decide her next move based on her expectancy: Does she expect to be thrown out the door, or does she believe complaining will lead to a free meal? In these situations, there is an interaction among expectancies, behaviors, and environmental factors.

LO 10   Discuss how Bandura uses the social-cognitive perspective to explain personality.

BANDURA AND PERSONALITY Another early critic of the behaviorist approach was Albert Bandura. Bandura rejected the notion that psychologists should only focus on observable behavior, and recognized the importance of cognition, reinforcers, and environmental factors (Bandura, 2006). This **social-cognitive perspective** suggests that personality results from patterns of thinking (cognitive) as well as relationships and other factors in the environment (social). Prior experiences have shaped, and will continue to shape, your personality. Our cognitive abilities and knowledge are partly the result of interactions with others (Bandura, 1977b, 2006). We don't spend much time in isolation; in fact, almost everything we do involves some sort of collaboration. We are social creatures who mostly work together and live in family units.

Bandura also pointed to the importance of **self-efficacy,** which refers to beliefs about our ability and effectiveness in reaching goals (Bandura, 1977a, 2001). People who exhibit high self-efficacy often achieve greater success at work because they are more likely to be flexible and open to new ideas (Bandura, 2006). A person who demonstrates low self-efficacy generally believes he will not succeed in a particular situation, regardless of his abilities or experience. Beliefs about self-efficacy are influenced by experience and may change across situations. Generally speaking, people who believe they can change and progress are more likely to persevere in difficult situations.

Beliefs play a key role in our ability to make decisions, problem-solve, and deal with life's challenges. The environment also responds to our behaviors. In essence,

It's a Social-Cognitive Thing
Psychologist Albert Bandura asserts that personality is molded by a continual interaction between cognition and social interactions, including observations of other people's behaviors. His approach is known as the social-cognitive perspective. Jon Brenneis/Getty Images.

The Social-Cognitive Perspective on Personality

Social-cognitive theorists rejected behaviorists' exclusive focus on observable behavior. Acknowledging that personality may be shaped through learning, social-cognitive theorists such as Albert Bandura also emphasized the roles of cognition and environmental influences on behavior. Bandura's theory of reciprocal determinism shows how cognition, behaviors, and the environment all interact to determine our personality.

"Good job!"

Child is praised for reading quietly.

Child receives attention for effort in school.

Child is rewarded for school achievement.

Behaviorists believe personality is the compilation of behaviors shaped through a lifetime of learning. A child who receives reinforcement for studying and effort in school will repeat this behavior, eventually exhibiting the personality characteristic "studious."

cognition

Thinking about behaviors and what they have led to in the past creates expectancies, predictions about what future outcomes will result from a behavior. When we recognize that past efforts to study usually resulted in good grades, we will expect that studying will lead to good grades in the future. Bandura calls this learned expectation of success *self-efficacy*.

I succeed because I am a studious person.

I will apply to college because I can succeed there.

I get good grades when I study, so I will continue to do this.

I am in college, so I know I can handle a busy schedule like other college students.

EXPECTANCIES INFLUENCE BEHAVIOR.

ENVIRONMENT INFLUENCES EXPECTANCIES.

EXPECTANCIES INFLUENCE THE ENVIRONMENT YOU SEEK OUT.

When I study, I get good grades.

PRIOR EXPERIENCES CREATE EXPECTANCIES.

environment

I'm a college student now, so I need to spend more time studying.

behavior

Reinforced behaviors become more consistent over time. When an instructor praises our participation in class, that reinforcement will lead us to participate again. We also learn by observing others' behaviors. If our classmates form a study group that helps them better understand the material, we may learn to adopt that technique.

ENVIRONMENT INFLUENCES BEHAVIOR.

BEHAVIOR INFLUENCES ENVIRONMENT.

The environment can include the college you choose, the major you select, the classes you enroll in, and also the culture where you are a student. For example, in Chinese classrooms, struggle is assumed to be part of the learning process. However, in Western classrooms, struggle is often seen as a sign of lower ability (Li, 2005; Schleppenbach, Flevares, Sims, & Perry, 2007). The culture you live in—your environment—can influence how you think about your own skills and behaviors, and how hard you work at something that is difficult for you.

I study hard and am a successful student, so I've chosen to go to college.

we have internal forces (beliefs, expectations) directing our behavior, external forces (reinforcers, punishments) responding to those behaviors, and the behaviors themselves influencing our beliefs and the environment. Beliefs, behavior, and environment form a complex system that determines our behavior patterns and personality (Infographic 11.2). Bandura (1978, 1986) refers to this multidirectional interaction as **reciprocal determinism.**

Let's use an example to see how reciprocal determinism works. A student harbors a certain belief about herself (*I am going to graduate with honors*). This belief influences her behavior (she studies hard and reaches out to instructors), which affects her environment (instructors take note of her enthusiasm and offer support). Thus, you can see, personality is the result of an ongoing interaction among cognition, behaviors, and the environment. Bandura's reciprocal determinism resembles Rotter's view. Both suggest that personality is shaped by an ongoing interplay of cognitive expectancies, behaviors, and environment.

Taking Stock: An Appraisal of Learning and Social-Cognitive Theories

Like any theory of personality, behaviorism has limitations. Critics contend that behaviorism essentially ignores anything that is not directly observable and thus portrays humans too simplistically, as passive and unaware of what is going on in their internal and external environments. The learning and social-cognitive theorists were among the first to realize that we are not just products of our environments, but dynamic agents capable of altering the environment itself. Their focus on research and testable hypotheses provides a clear advantage over the psychoanalytic and humanistic theories. Some critics argue that these approaches minimize the importance of unconscious processes and emotional influences (Schultz & Schultz, 2017; Westen, 1990), but overall, the inclusion of cognition and social factors offers valuable new ways to study and understand personality.

So far, our main focus has been understanding the origins of personality. In the next section, we direct our attention away from theories explaining personality and onto those describing it.

You Asked, Saifa Answers

http://qrs.ly/yv5a5f6

Has someone shown you unconditional love?

scan this ➡

Learning from Role Models
Orange Is the New Black actress Uzo Aduba may have developed some personality traits by observing and imitating her mother, a role model who appreciated the value of hard work (Lewis, 2016, August 11). As Aduba recalls in an interview with the *New York Daily News,* "When I first moved to New York, she dropped me off at the train and she turned off the car, and she said, 'Uzo. Just work hard. I don't care what you do, as long as you work hard. I never heard of 'nothing' come from hard work'" (Daily News Staff, 2015, May 4). Kevork Djansezian/ Getty Images.

  show what you know

1. According to _____, personality is the compilation of behaviors that have been shaped via reinforcement and other forms of conditioning.

2. Julian Rotter proposed that personality is influenced by _____, one's beliefs about where responsibility or control exists.
   a. reinforcement expectancy
   b. locus of control
   c. expectancy
   d. reinforcement value

3. Reciprocal determinism represents a complex multidirectional interaction among beliefs, behavior, and environment. Draw a diagram illustrating how reciprocal determinism explains one of your behavior patterns.

✓ CHECK YOUR ANSWERS IN APPENDIX C.

Trait Theories and Their Biological Basis

Earlier in the chapter, we used some words to describe Saifa's personality—"vivacious," "loud," "charismatic," "direct," and "empathetic." All these might be considered examples of **traits,** the relatively stable properties that describe elements of personality. The **trait theories** presented here are different from the theories discussed earlier; they focus less on explaining why and how personality develops and more on describing personality and predicting behaviors.

reciprocal determinism According to Bandura, multidirectional interactions among cognition, behaviors, and the environment.

traits The relatively stable properties that describe elements of personality.

trait theories Theories that focus on personality dimensions and their influence on behavior; can be used to predict behaviors.

Who's Who in Trait Theory?

LO 11 **Distinguish trait theories from other personality theories.**

ALLPORT AND PERSONALITY One of the first trait theorists was American psychologist Gordon Allport (1897–1967), who compiled a comprehensive list of traits to describe personality. This list was developed to operationalize the terminology used in personality research; when researchers study a topic, they should agree on definitions. If two psychologists are studying a trait called "vivacious," they will have an easier time comparing results if they use the same definition. Allport and his colleague carefully reviewed *Webster's New International Dictionary* (1925) and identified 17,953 words (out of approximately 400,000 entries in the dictionary) that they proposed were "descriptive of personality or personal behavior" (Allport & Odbert, 1936, p. 24). The list contained terms that were considered to be personal traits (such as "acrobatical" and "zealous"), temporary states (such as "woozy" and "thrilled"), social evaluations (such as "swine" and "outlandish"), and words that were metaphorical and doubtful (such as "mortal" and "middle-aged"). Most relevant to personality were the personal traits, of which they identified 4,504—a little over 1% of all the entries in the dictionary. Surely, this long list could be condensed, reduced, or classified to make it more manageable. Enter Raymond Cattell.

CATTELL AND PERSONALITY Raymond Cattell (1905–1998) was a British psychologist who moved to the United States in the early 1940s. Cattell proposed grouping the long list of personality traits into two major categories: surface traits and source traits (Cattell, 1950). **Surface traits** are the easily observable personality characteristics we commonly use to describe people: *Josie is quiet. Amir is friendly.* **Source traits** are the foundational qualities that give rise to surface traits. For example, "extraversion" is a source trait, and the surface traits it produces may include "warm," "gregarious," and "assertive." There are thousands of surface traits but only a few source traits. Cattell (1950) proposed that source traits are the product of both heredity and environment (nature and nurture), and surface traits are the "combined action of several source traits" (p. 34).

Cattell also condensed the list of surface traits into a much smaller set of 171. Realizing that some of these surface traits would be correlated, he used a statistical procedure known as *factor analysis* to group them into a smaller set of dimensions according to common underlying properties. With factor analysis, Cattell was able to produce a list of 16 personality factors.

These 16 factors, or personality dimensions, can be considered primary source traits. Looking at **FIGURE 11.2**, you can see that the ends of the dimensions represent polar extremes. On one end of the first dimension is the reserved and unsocial person; at the other end is the "social butterfly." Based on these factors, Cattell developed the Sixteen Personality Factor Questionnaire (16PF), which is described in greater detail in the upcoming section on objective personality tests.

EYSENCK AND PERSONALITY Psychologist Hans Eysenck (AHY-sengk; 1916–1997) was born in Germany, but in 1934 moved to England. Eysenck continued to develop our understanding of source traits, proposing that we could describe personalities using three dimensions: introversion–extraversion (E), neuroticism (N), and psychoticism (P) (**FIGURE 11.3**).

People high on the *extraversion* end of the introversion–extraversion (E) dimension tend to display a marked degree of sociability and are outgoing and active with others in their environment. Those on the *introversion* end of the dimension tend to be quiet and careful and enjoy time alone. Having high *neuroticism* (N) typically goes hand in hand with being restless, moody, and excitable, while low neuroticism means being calm,

CONNECTIONS

In **Chapter 1,** we described a correlation as a relationship between two variables. Here, we explain factor analysis, which examines the relationships among an entire set of variables.

1.	Reserved	⟷	Outgoing
2.	Concrete thinker	⟷	Abstract thinker
3.	Affected by feelings	⟷	Emotionally stable
4.	Submissive	⟷	Dominant
5.	Serious	⟷	Happy-go-lucky
6.	Expedient	⟷	Conscientious
7.	Timid	⟷	Bold
8.	Tough-minded	⟷	Sensitive
9.	Trusting	⟷	Suspicious
10.	Practical	⟷	Imaginative
11.	Forthright	⟷	Shrewd
12.	Self-assured	⟷	Insecure
13.	Conservative	⟷	Experimenting
14.	Group-dependent	⟷	Self-sufficient
15.	Undisciplined	⟷	Controlled
16.	Relaxed	⟷	Tense

FIGURE 11.2

Cattell's 16 Personality Factors
Raymond Cattell produced personality profiles by measuring where people fell along each of these 16 dimensions, or personality factors. Information from Cattell (1973b) and Cattell, Eber, and Tatsuoka (1970).

reliable, and emotionally stable. A person who is high on the *psychoticism* dimension is likely to be cold, impersonal, and antisocial, whereas someone at the opposite end of this dimension is warm, caring, and empathetic. (The psychoticism dimension is not related to psychosis, which is described in Chapter 13.)

In addition to identifying these dimensions, Eysenck worked diligently to unearth their biological basis. For example, he proposed a direct relationship between the behaviors associated with the introversion–extraversion dimension and the reticular formation (Eysenck, 1967). According to Eysenck (1967, 1990), introverted people display higher reactivity in their reticular formation. With their higher arousal levels, introverts are more likely to react to stimuli, and thus develop patterns of coping with arousal. An introvert may be more careful or restrained, for example. An extravert has lower levels of arousal, and thus is less reactive to stimuli. Extraverts seek stimulation because their arousal levels are low, so they tend to be more impulsive and outgoing.

FIGURE 11.3
Eysenck's Dimensions of Personality
Psychologist Hans Eysenck described personality using three dimensions. This figure displays only Eysenck's original dimensions; years later, he proposed an additional dimension called psychoticism. People who score high on the psychoticism trait tend to be impersonal and antisocial. Information from Eysenck and Eysenck (1968). Reproduced from Schultz and Schultz (2013) with permission.

CONNECTIONS

In **Chapter 1,** we described the reticular formation, a network of neurons responsible for levels of arousal. It also plays a role in selectively attending to important information by sifting through sensory data. Eysenck suggested that the reticular formation is also associated with the introversion-extraversion dimension of personality.

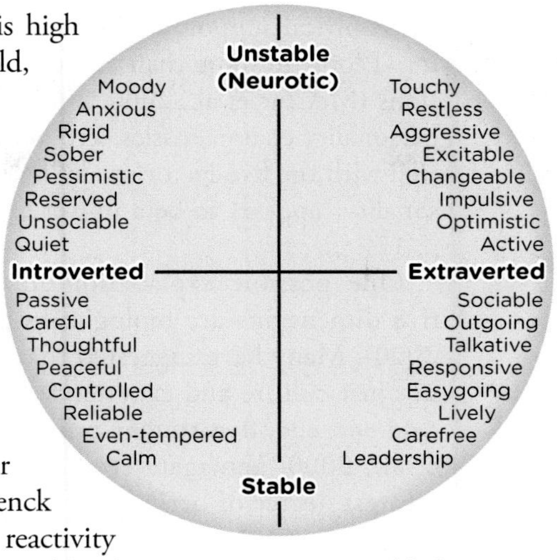

The theories of Allport, Cattell, and Eysenck paved the way for the trait theories commonly used today. Let's take a look at one of the most popular models.

LO 12 **Identify the biological roots of the five-factor model of personality.**

THE BIG FIVE The **five-factor model of personality**, also known as the Big Five, is a current trait approach for explaining personality (McCrae, 2011; McCrae & Costa, 1987; McCrae et al., 2013). This model, developed using factor analysis, indicates there are five factors, or dimensions, to describe personality. Although there is not 100% agreement on the names of these factors, in general, trait theorists propose they are (1) openness to experience, (2) conscientiousness, (3) extraversion, (4) agreeableness, and (5) neuroticism (McCrae et al., 2013; McCrae, Scally, Terracciano, Abecasis, & Costa, 2010). Openness is the degree to which someone is willing to try new experiences. Conscientiousness refers to someone's attention to detail and organizational tendencies. The extraversion and neuroticism dimensions are similar to Eysenck's dimensions noted earlier: Extraversion refers to degree of sociability and outgoingness; neuroticism, to emotional stability (the degree to which a person is calm, secure, and even tempered). Agreeableness indicates how trusting and easygoing a person is. To remember these factors, students sometimes use the mnemonic OCEAN: Openness, Conscientiousness, Extraversion, Agreeableness, and Neuroticism (FIGURE 11.4).

Openness	Conforming Uncreative Practical	⟷	Unconforming Creative Imaginative
Conscientiousness	Unreliable Lazy Spontaneous	⟷	Reliable Ambitious Punctual
Extraversion	Loner Quiet Reserved	⟷	Sociable Talkative Affectionate
Agreeableness	Rude Uncooperative Critical	⟷	Good-natured Trusting Helpful
Neuroticism	Calm Even-tempered Secure	⟷	Emotional Temperamental Worried

FIGURE 11.4
The Five-Factor Model of Personality
The mnemonic OCEAN will help you remember these factors. Information from McCrae and Costa (1990).

surface traits Easily observable characteristics that derive from source traits.

source traits Basic underlying or foundational characteristics of personality.

five-factor model of personality A trait approach to explaining personality, including dimensions of openness to experience, conscientiousness, extraversion, agreeableness, and neuroticism; also known as "the Big Five."

CONNECTIONS

Chapters 1 and 7 describe twin studies, which indicate that genes play an important role in intelligence. Identical twins share 100% of their genes at conception, fraternal twins about 50%, and adopted siblings are genetically very different. Comparing personality traits among these siblings can show the relative importance of genes and the environment.

TABLE 11.4	HERITABILITY AND THE BIG FIVE
Big Five Personality Dimensions	**Heritability**
Openness	.61
Conscientiousness	.44
Extraversion	.53
Neuroticism	.41
Agreeableness	.41

Heritability is the degree to which heredity is responsible for a particular characteristic in the population. Studies suggest a substantial proportion of variation in the Big Five traits can be attributed to genes; the remainder is explained by environmental influences (Bouchard, 2004; Power & Pluess, 2015). Information from Jang, Livesley, and Vernon (1996).

Empirical support for this model has been established using cross-cultural testing. People in more than 50 cultures have been shown to exhibit these five dimensions (McCrae et al., 2000, 2005, 2010). Even the everyday terms used to describe personality characteristics across continents (North America, Europe, and Asia) fit well with the five-factor model (McCrae et al., 2010). The five-factor model of personality "appears to be a universal aspect of human nature" (McCrae et al., 2013, p. 17).

One possible explanation for such cross-cultural similarities is that these five dimensions are biologically based (Allik & McCrae, 2004; McCrae et al., 2000). Many have suggested that these personality traits are influenced by genes, not just culture and experience (Karwowski & Lebuda, 2016). Three decades of **twin and adoption studies** point to a genetic basis for the five factors (McCrae et al., 2000; Yamagata et al., 2006), with openness to experience showing the greatest degree of heritability (McCrae et al., 2000; **TABLE 11.4**). Some researchers suggest that dog personalities can be described using similar dimensions, such as extraversion and neuroticism (Ley, Bennett, & Coleman, 2008). And this kind of research is not limited to canines; animals as diverse as squid and orangutans seem to display personality characteristics that are surprisingly similar to those observed in humans (Sinn & Moltschaniwskyj, 2005; Weiss, King, & Perkins, 2006). For example, some squid respond to stimuli "boldly or aggressively," while others act more shyly (Sinn & Moltschaniwiskyj, 2005, p. 105).

The biological basis of these five factors is further supported by their general stability over time, for periods as long as 40 years (Kandler et al., 2010; McCrae et al., 2000, 2013; Terracciano, Costa, & McCrae, 2006). This implies that the dramatic environmental changes most of us experience in life do not have as great an impact as our inherited characteristics. Such does not mean personalities are completely static, however; people can experience changes in these five factors over the life span (Specht, Egloff, & Schmukle, 2011). For example, as people age, they tend to score higher on agreeableness and lower on neuroticism, openness, extraversion, and conscientiousness. They also seem to become happier and more easygoing with age, displaying more positive attitudes (Marsh, Nagengast, & Morin, 2013).

Impact on Personality

Despite the general stability of inherited personality characteristics, environmental factors such as chronic head trauma can sometimes alter personality. BMX racer Dave Mirra suffered multiple head injuries during his 41 years of life, beginning with a car accident at age 19 and continuing throughout his biking career. This repetitive head trauma may be associated with personality changes his wife observed in the year leading to his suicide: "I started to notice changes in his mood. And then it quickly started to get worse," his wife told ESPN. "He wasn't able to be present in any situation or conversation, so it was hard to be in a relationship with him to any degree" (Roenigk, 2016, May 24, para. 13). After his death, Mirra was diagnosed with chronic traumatic encephalopathy (CTE; Mather, 2016, May 24). Jamie Squire/Allsport/Getty Images.

Personality traits impact your life in ways you may find surprising. Would you believe that creativity—a facet of the personality trait openness—has been linked to longer life span in some men? Apparently, creative thinking helps lower stress (good for overall health) and stimulates the brain by activating a variety of circuits (Rodriguez, 2012; Turiano, Spiro, & Mroczek, 2012). Another personality trait, conscientiousness, has been associated with certain measures of success, including income level and life satisfaction (Duckworth, Weir, Tsukayama, & Kwok, 2012). Even the personality traits of other people, such as romantic partners, may influence you. One study suggests that marrying a conscientious person could benefit your career; conscientious husbands and wives support their spouses' professional lives by taking care of household chores, and by modeling conscientious behaviors, for example (Solomon & Jackson, 2014). How might such information be useful in everyday life? You have a great deal of control over your actions. This means you have the ability to cultivate behaviors associated with the personality traits you find desirable. You can also seek out those desirable traits in others.

👥 In Class: Collaborate and Report

In your group, **A)** discuss the most important features of the traits discussed in this section, including the ends of each continuum (for example, differences between high and low neuroticism). **B)** Choose three of the traits and write up a brief scenario about a fictitious college student. **C)** Team up with another group and see if you can determine the traits used in each other's case studies.

Men and women appear to differ with respect to the five factors, although there is not total agreement on how. A review of studies from 55 nations reported that, across cultures, women score higher than men on conscientiousness, extraversion, agreeableness, and neuroticism (Schmitt, Realo, Voracek, & Allik, 2008). Men, on the other hand, seem to demonstrate greater openness to experience. These disparities are not extreme, however; the variation within the groups of males and females is greater than the differences between males and females. Critics suggest that using such rough measures of personality may conceal some of the true differences between men and women; in order to shed light on such disparities, they suggest investigating models that incorporate 10 to 20 traits rather than just 5 (Del Giudice, Booth, & Irwing, 2012).

Maybe you would have predicted women score higher on measures of agreeableness and neuroticism; perhaps you would have guessed the opposite. Research suggests that

Mountains or Beach?
When given a choice between the mountains and the beach, introverts tend to show a preference for the mountains, while extroverts gravitate toward the beach. Mountains are perceived as quiet places to unwind, and beaches are associated with social activity (Oishi, Talhelm, & Lee, 2015). Left: Roman Khomlyak/Shutterstock. Right: Vibrant Image Studio/Shutterstock.

— CONNECTIONS

In **Chapter 10,** we presented the gender similarities hypothesis, which states that, overall, the variation within a gender is greater than the variation between genders. Here, we see how this applies to the five factors of personality.

some gender stereotypes do indeed contain a kernel of truth (Costa, Terracciano, & McCrae, 2001; Terracciano et al., 2005). Let's find out if this principle holds true for cultural stereotypes as well.

ACROSS THE WORLD
Culture of Personality

PLEASE LEAVE YOUR STEREOTYPES AT THE BORDER!

Have you heard the old joke about European stereotypes? It goes like this: In heaven, the chefs are French, the mechanics German, the lovers Italian, the police officers British, and the bankers Swiss. In hell, the cooks are British, the police officers German, the mechanics French, the lovers Swiss, and the bankers Italian (Mulvey, 2006, May 15). This joke plays upon what psychologists might call "national stereotypes," or preconceived notions about the personalities of people belonging to certain cultures. The joke assumes, for example, that Italian people have some underlying quality that makes them excel in romance but not money management. Are such national stereotypes accurate?

To get to the bottom of this question, a group of researchers used personality tests to assess the Big Five traits of nearly 4,000 people from 49 cultures. When they compared the results of the personality tests to national stereotypes, they found no evidence that the stereotypes mirrored reality (Terracciano et al., 2005). Subsequent research supports this conclusion (McCrae et al., 2013).

Are any personality stereotypes accurate across cultures? Research suggests that, throughout much of the world, adolescents are perceived as rebellious and sensation-seeking, while older people are viewed as sedentary and comfortable with routine. There may be some element of truth in these age-related stereotypes (Chan et al., 2012). But beware: Accurate or inaccurate, stereotypes can have lasting adverse effects and should be avoided.

Taking Stock: An Appraisal of the Trait Theories

As you can see from the examples above, trait theories have facilitated important psychological research. One important finding that could have useful applications is the evident continuum with "normal personality traits" at one end and symptoms of some mental illnesses at the other (DeYoung, Carey, Krueger, & Ross, 2016). This has the potential for clarifying the causes of some disorders, and maybe even reducing stigma—we all share these traits to some extent.

But like any scientific approach, the trait theories have their flaws. One major criticism is that they fail to explain the origins of personality. What aspects of personality are innate, and which are environmental? How do unconscious processes, motivations, and development influence personality? If you're looking to answer these types of questions, trait theories might not be your best bet. Critics have also argued that the samples used in many of the cross-cultural studies on the five-factor model may not be representative of their respective populations (for example, most of the participants were college students). Researchers examining the universality of the five dimensions in non-industrialized cultures, such as the Bolivian Tsimane culture, found little support for the five-factor model (Gurven, von Rueden, Massenkoff, Kaplan, & Lero Vie, 2013).

Trait theories also tend to underestimate environmental influences on personality. As psychologist Walter Mischel (1930–) pointed out, environmental circumstances can affect the way traits manifest themselves (Mischel & Shoda, 1995). A person who is high on the openness factor may be nonconforming in college, wearing unique clothing and pursuing unusual hobbies, but put her in the military and her noncon-formity will probably assume a new form.

We are about to wrap up our discussion of the trait theories and move on to the intriguing topic of personality testing. Before we do so, let's take a closer look at an example mentioned earlier. What do researchers have to say about the link between openness and life span?

Open Mind, Longer Life

The trait of openness improves health through creativity.

from the pages of
SCIENTIFIC AMERICAN

Researchers have long been studying the connection between health and the five major personality traits: agreeableness, extraversion, neuroticism, openness and conscientiousness. A large body of research links neuroticism with poorer health and conscientiousness with superior health. Now openness, which measures cognitive flexibility and the willingness to entertain novel ideas, has emerged as a lifelong protective factor. The linchpin seems to be the creativity associated with the personality trait—creative thinking reduces stress and keeps the brain healthy.

A study published in the June issue of the *Journal of Aging and Health* found that higher openness predicted longer life, and other studies this year have linked that trait with lower metabolic risk, higher self-rated health and more appropriate stress response.

The June study sought to determine whether specific aspects of openness better predicted survival rates than overall openness, using data on more than 1,000 older men collected between 1990 and 2008. The researchers found that only creativity—not intelligence or overall openness—decreased mortality risk. One possible reason creativity is protective of health is because it draws on a variety of neural networks within the brain, says study author Nicholas Turiano, now at the University of Rochester Medical Center. "Individuals high in creativity maintain the integrity of their neural networks even into old age," Turiano says—a notion supported by a January study from Yale University that correlated openness with the robustness of study subjects' white matter, which supports connections between neurons in different parts of the brain.

Because the brain is the command center for all bodily functions, exercising it helps all systems to continue running smoothly. "Keeping the brain healthy may be one of the most important aspects of aging successfully —a fact shown by creative persons living longer in our study," Turiano says.

He also cites creative people's ability to handle stress—they tend not to get as easily flustered when faced with an emotional or physical hurdle. Stress is known to harm overall health, including cardiovascular, immune and cognitive systems. "Creative people may see stressors more as challenges that they can work to overcome rather than as stressful obstacles they can't overcome," Turiano says. Although studies thus far have looked at those who are naturally open-minded, the results suggest that practicing creative-thinking techniques could improve anyone's health by lowering stress and exercising the brain. **Tori Rodriguez.**

Better with Age
Japanese calligrapher Kawamata-sensei paints a giant character that will go on display at an upcoming event. Creativity is associated with the personality trait of openness, which has been linked to longevity. James Whitlow Delano/Redux.

 show what you know

1. The relatively stable properties of personality are:
   a. traits.
   b. expectancies.
   c. reinforcement values.
   d. ego defense mechanisms.

2. The traits we easily observe and quickly describe based on someone's behavior or characteristics are called

   _____.

3. Name the Big Five traits and give one piece of evidence for their biological basis.

 CHECK YOUR ANSWERS IN APPENDIX C.

You Asked, Saifa Answers

http://qrs.ly/4t5a5fb

Is there something in your personality that you have tried to change?

scan this →

CONNECTIONS

In **Chapter 1,** we noted that people are prone to the hindsight bias, the feeling that "I knew it all along." Researchers, in particular, can introduce observer bias into the recording of observations. When choosing a personality assessment, it is important to be alert to the biases that can interfere with objective data collection.

CONNECTIONS

In **Chapter 7,** we discussed ways to determine the reliability of intelligence tests. In addition to test–retest reliability, we can split a test in half to see if the findings of the two halves agree. This type of reliability can be determined with personality assessment as well.

CONNECTIONS

An important factor to consider in the interview procedure is the malleability of memory, which we discussed in **Chapter 6.** The interviewer should avoid posing questions that might lead to the misinformation effect, the tendency for new or misleading information to distort memories.

Personality Assessment

Personality tests can be broadly classified as objective or subjective in nature. Findings from subjective assessments are based, in part, on personal intuition, clinical judgment, opinions, or interpretations. With objective assessments, findings are based on a standardized procedure in which the scoring is free of opinions, personal beliefs, expectations, and values. Critics of subjective assessments suggest that there is not enough consistency across findings, as a result of nonstandard scoring procedures (see interrater reliability, discussed below). And as noted in earlier chapters, humans are prone to a variety of biases and cognitive errors that can interfere with their ability to accurately assess people and situations. Critics of objective assessments contend that the standardization of these tests does not allow for flexibility and fails to appreciate the diversity of individual experiences. Despite these alleged flaws, many psychologists use a mixture of objective and subjective assessment techniques with their clients.

Not everyone agrees about the effectiveness of personality assessment, in terms of both reliability and validity. Even so, it is used in many contexts and in ways that have profound implications. Psychologists use personality tests to get to know their clients and diagnose mental disorders. Companies use them to make decisions about new hires and promotions (*Does this person have what it takes to be a manager?*). Personality tests are part of the battery of assessments used to evaluate the functioning of parents embroiled in custody disputes: *Is Mom depressed? Can she care for this child?* (Lilienfeld, Wood, & Garb, 2005).

Reliability and Validity

LO 13 Explain why reliability and validity are important in personality assessment.

Before we discuss the various types of personality tests, let's get a handle on the qualities that render these tests effective—reliability and validity. Reliability can refer to two aspects of an assessment. *Test–retest reliability* is how consistent results are when the same person takes the test more than once. Suppose you take the same personality test today and tomorrow. From one day to the next, your personality is unlikely to change, so your results shouldn't either. With a reliable test, the scores should be very similar at different points in time. *Interrater reliability* refers to the consistency across people scoring an assessment. With high interrater reliability, the results are the same regardless of who scores the test.

The other important quality of a personality assessment is validity. A valid test is one that can be shown to measure what it intends to measure. Let's say a psychologist develops an assessment for extraversion. In order for her test to be considered valid, it must yield results that are similar to already established and valid assessments of extraversion. If her test can predict future scores on tasks related to extraversion, this would indicate it has *predictive validity.*

In the next section, we will explore the major types of personality tests that psychologists employ: interviews, projective personality tests, and objective personality tests. Many of these are aligned with specific perspectives (psychoanalytic or behavioral, for example), but most psychologists use an integrative approach, drawing on multiple perspectives in their assessment of clients.

What Brings You Here Today?

One way to gather information about personality is through a face-to-face interview. In an unstructured, or open-ended, interview, there is no predetermined path. A psychologist might begin with a question like "What brings you here today?" and then gently direct the conversation in a way that helps her understand her client's strengths and weaknesses, hopes and plans. Semistructured and structured interviews, on the other hand, employ specific paths of questioning that hinge on the respondent's answers. This format provides a more systematic means of comparing behaviors across individuals.

One great advantage of the interview is that it allows a psychologist to see a client in a relatively natural, realistic setting. Talking with a client face to face, a psychologist can observe facial expressions and body language, which may offer clues to what's going on inside. There are drawbacks, however. Interview subjects may lie to the interviewer (in some cases without even realizing it), spin the facts to misrepresent themselves, or share memories that are distorted or incomplete. Another source of error is the interviewer. She may, for example, lead the interview in a particular direction or interpret responses in a way that reinforces her own beliefs about personality. Clients can also be influenced by the interviewers' nonverbal language. The desire to answer "correctly" is strong in an interview format. Just as in surveys, the way a question is asked can have a profound influence on the answer. For example, do you think people would provide identical responses to these two questions? "Are you happy in your marriage?" or "Are you unhappy in your marriage?"

What Do *You* See? Projective Personality Tests

LO 14 Define projective personality tests and evaluate their strengths and limitations.

It's a hot summer's day and you're lying on the beach, gazing at the clouds. "What do you see?" you ask your friend. "I see the profile of a Doberman pinscher," she replies. "That's funny," you say. "I see a child doing jumping jacks."

How can two people look at the same image and come away with such different impressions? Some would argue that it has a lot to do with personality. The idea that personality influences perception is the premise of **projective personality tests**, which psychologists use to explore characteristics that might not be accessible through interview or observation, as they attempt to access aspects of the unconscious (**INFOGRAPHIC 11.3** on the following page). With this type of assessment, the test taker is shown a stimulus without a specified meaning and then prompted to *project* meaning onto it. Projective personality tests assume that people harbor anxiety and unresolved conflicts, often beneath conscious awareness. Because these tests attempt to uncover such issues indirectly, they are less threatening than other methods, and therefore provoke less resistance. The goal of the test administrator is to take the manifest content (what the person reports seeing) and try to understand its underlying meaning.

THE RORSCHACH INKBLOTS The best-known projective personality test is the Rorschach. The original version of the test was developed by Swiss psychiatrist Hermann Rorschach (1884–1922). Today's psychologists typically use Rorschach inkblots with a comprehensive coding system introduced in the 1970s (Exner, 1980, 1986).

Here is a rough description of how the test is administered: Imagine someone hands you a series of cards covered in odd-looking blotches of ink—five cards with black-and-white blotches, and another five with color. Presenting the cards one by one, he asks you to report what you see. The images you describe and the details on which you focus will be important factors in the assessment of your personality, which involves a systematic comparison with answers given by other test takers who have known personality characteristics and diagnoses. Do you see bears playing patty cake? Seeing animals in motion might be interpreted as a sign of rashness. Are you homing in on the black areas? This could suggest a feeling of melancholy or sadness (Lilienfeld et al., 2005).

THE THEMATIC APPERCEPTION TEST (TAT) In the mid-1930s, Henry Murray and his colleagues developed the Thematic Apperception Test (TAT), a projective

Tell Me About Yourself
Psychologists assess personality using a variety of tools, including personal interviews. These face-to-face sessions range from open-ended and exploratory to highly structured. Wavebreakmedia Ltd/Getty Images.

projective personality tests Assessments that present stimuli without a specified meaning to test takers, whose responses can then be interpreted to uncover underlying personality characteristics.

Examining the Unconscious: Projective Personality Tests

The psychoanalytic perspective holds that some aspects of personality exist beneath conscious awareness. Projective personality tests seek to uncover these characteristics. Ideas and anxieties in the unconscious will appear in descriptions of ambiguous stimuli, revealing previously hidden conflicts that the test administrator can evaluate.

◄ Test administration ►

The best-known projective tests, the Thematic Apperception Test (TAT) and the Rorschach Inkblot Test, are both conducted in the same way (Lilienfeld, Wood, & Garb, 2005): The test administrator presents a series of picture cards, one at a time, then records the participant's responses. The administrator also notes behaviors such as gestures, tone of voice, and facial expressions.

The standard administration of the TAT presents a selection of 5 to 12 cards. The participant is asked to tell a story for each scene, including what the characters are feeling and how the story might end.

The Rorschach has 10 cards with symmetrical inkblots, 5 in color and 5 in black-and-white. The participant is prompted to give multiple responses for each image, identifying details.

Test Interpretation

To help decrease the influence of administrator bias in interpretation of projective tests, comprehensive systems have been developed to standardize scoring and interpretation of some tests. For the Rorschach Inkblot Test, responses are coded on dimensions such as location (whole inkblot or one detail), themes (unique or consistent), and thought processes (Erdberg, 1990). The use of a comprehensive system allows administrators to compare typical and atypical responses.

PARTICIPANT RESPONSES

"Looks like two people."

"The people are fighting over something."

"Or they're carrying something heavy together."

"Maybe it's one person looking in a mirror."

"I also see a butterfly."

These sample responses are representative for this inkblot. Most participants interpret this Rorschach inkblot as two figures (Burstein & Loucks, 1989).

EXAMINER RESPONSES

Participant mentions the typical response of two figures.

Suggestion that the people are fighting could indicate issues with aggression or an aggressive personality.

Focus on individuals working together could represent a need for social connection.

However, seeing one person alone could indicate social anxiety.

Now participant switches to a specific part of the image, which could also show that he is uncomfortable thinking about others, perhaps related to introversion.

assessment that consists of 20 cards containing black-and-white illustrations of ambiguous scenes. When shown a card, the test taker is asked to tell a story about it. The story might incorporate a description of the people in the scene, and should include what led up to the scene, the emotions and thoughts of the characters, and a conclusion. The assumption is that the test taker will project underlying conflicts onto the ambiguous stimuli of the picture; the job of the test administrator is to unearth them.

Taking Stock: An Appraisal of Projective Personality Tests

One criticism of projective personality tests is that they can take a lot of time. However, because the test taker may be willing to speak openly, honestly, and freely due to the unstructured nature of the assessment, the benefits seem to outweigh the costs. Another major concern, mentioned earlier, is the subjectivity of interpreting results, which can lead to reliability problems. Test administrators may score differently, and test takers may not get the same results when they take the test on different occasions. Even the comprehensive scoring system for the Rorschach inkblots has not resolved concerns about projective tests, because the issue of validity remains. Many critics suggest projective tests are not valid because they do not measure what they claim to be measuring (Schultz & Schultz, 2017). Nonetheless, clinicians continue using projective tests because they often provide a way to begin forming a picture of a client. Due to the concerns noted above, these tests should be used cautiously in other situations, such as with employment decisions.

What tools do you use to get a feel for a person? Do you ever try to size up someone's personality by looking at his Facebook page? In many cases, personality characteristics projected through social media bear close resemblance to real-world identities.

SOCIAL MEDIA AND PSYCHOLOGY
It's Written All Over Your Facebook

Facebook profiles reveal a great deal about the personalities of their owners. In one study, researchers assessed the offline personalities of American Facebook users and German StudiVZ users (StudiVZ is a popular European network), and then compared those results with the impressions of people checking out their profiles. Their readings of the profiles turned out to be quite accurate, particularly when it came to the traits of extraversion and openness (Back et al., 2010).

DO NARCISSISTS FLOCK TO INSTAGRAM?

This tendency for Facebook to reveal one's true personality may not be a good thing if you happen to be narcissistic. Narcissism is a personality trait often equated with vanity, self-absorption, and feelings of superiority and entitlement. Strangers can easily pick out real-life narcissists by viewing their Facebook profiles (Buffardi & Campbell, 2008). People who post narcissistic status updates are likely to be perceived as "less likeable, less successful, and less worthy of friendship" (Kauten, Lui, Stary, & Barry, 2015). In addition to Facebook, many narcissists flock to Instagram, a photo-sharing platform where they can easily edit photos to promote themselves (Sheldon & Bryant, 2016).

"But... your Facebook profile says you're a vegetarian!"

Dominique Deckmyn/CartoonStock.com.

Objective Personality Tests

LO 15 Describe objective personality tests and evaluate their strengths and limitations.

Earlier, we mentioned that clinicians use a variety of tools to assess the personalities of their clients. (They are also used in many other areas, such as industrial and organizational psychology; see Appendix B: Careers in Psychology). Among those tools

Personality Assessments in the Workplace

In addition to running criminal background checks and credit scores, some employers use objective personality assessments to screen job applicants (Weber, 2015, April 15). For example, police departments use assessments such as the MMPI-2-RF to help evaluate future performance as a police officer (Detrick & Chibnall, 2014).
CSP_mybaitshop/AGE Fotostock.

FIGURE 11.5

Example Profiles Generated by the 16PF

On Cattell's 16PF, writers appear to be more reserved, sensitive, and imaginative than airline pilots. Pilots, on the other hand, tend to fall on the tough-minded end of the continuum. Are you surprised that they also appear to be more relaxed?
Information from Cattell (1973b).

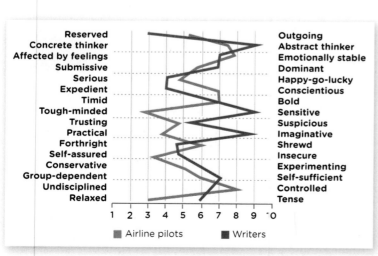

are *objective personality tests,* assessments made up of a standard set of questions with answer choices (true/false, multiple choice, circle the number). These tests are called *objective* because the results are assessed in a standardized way, predominantly free of personal bias. In contrast to the projective inventories, which often seem to be overly subjective, objective personality tests have clear scoring instructions that are identical for anyone taking the test. Often, scores are calculated by a computer. In addition to being convenient, objective tests have a solid base of evidence supporting their reliability and validity (Anastasi & Urbina, 1997). Some of these tests may focus on a particular personality characteristic or trait (such as locus of control); others might assess a group of characteristics (such as the Big Five traits). For example, the Big Five Inventory (BFI) is a short assessment that is self-administered and designed to be completed quickly, reducing testing fatigue and boredom in the test taker (John, Naumann, & Soto, 2008).

THE MMPI The most commonly used objective personality test is the Minnesota Multiphasic Personality Inventory (MMPI–2-RF; Ben-Porath, 2012, Butcher & Rouse, 1996). This self-report questionnaire includes 338 statements to which the individual responds "true," "false," or "cannot say." Some of the items you might see on the MMPI–2-RF include statements such as "I often wake up rested and ready to go" or "I want to work as a teacher." Since the original purpose of the MMPI was to identify disorders and abnormal behavior, it included 10 clinical scales (such as cynicism and antisocial behavior). It also has validity scales (such as the Lie scale and the Defensiveness scale) to assess the degree to which the results are useful. These validity measures help ensure that the person taking the assessment is not trying to appear either more disturbed or more healthy than she actually is. It is important to control for manipulation by the test taker because the MMPI is used in a variety of nonclinical settings—to inform decisions about custody or other legal matters, for example. Like other personality assessments, the MMPI has its share of criticisms. Since it was designed to help make diagnoses, many feel its application outside of therapeutic settings is inappropriate. The scales are based on groups of people exhibiting abnormalities, and therefore they may not translate to nonclinical populations.

16PF Another objective assessment of personality is the Sixteen Personality Factor Questionnaire (16PF), originally created by Raymond Cattell and based on his trait theory. With the 16PF, the test taker must select one of three choices in response to 185 questions. Ultimately, a profile is constructed, which indicates where the person falls along the continuum of each of the 16 dimensions. Take a look at **FIGURE 11.5** and you can see how pilots and writers compare on the 16 factors. For example, airline pilots tend to fall on the tough-minded end of the continuum, whereas writers tend to be located on the sensitive, tender-minded end (Cattell, 1973a).

MYERS–BRIGGS One very popular objective assessment of personality is the Myers–Briggs Type Indicator (MBTI) (Briggs & Myers, 1998). Katherine Briggs and her daughter Isabel Briggs-Myers created this assessment in the 1940s. It designates a personality "type" as it relates to the following four dimensions: extraversion (E) versus introversion (I); sensing (S) versus intuiting (N); thinking (T) versus feeling (F); and judgment (J) versus perception (P). For example, someone characterized as ISTP would be introverted, rely on the senses (rather than intuition) to understand the environment, favor logic over emotion, and focus on using perception as opposed to judgment.

Problems arise when assessments incorporate somewhat vague descriptions of personality traits. Some would even liken it to the Barnum effect, which was named after P. T. Barnum (1810–1891), the American showman and founder of the Barnum and Bailey Circus. He was famous for his ability to convince people he could read minds. Essentially, he did this by making generally complimentary and vague statements that could be true about anyone (*You are creative and work well with others and you sometimes procrastinate, but ultimately you get the job done*). Similarly, with the MBTI, the personality type descriptions are "generally flattering and sufficiently vague so that most people will accept the statements as true of themselves" (Pittenger, 1993, November, p. 6). Although the MBTI is quite popular, the research supporting it is weak, especially as it relates to job performance, career choices, and related matters (Pittenger, 2005). Because the test results don't always correlate with job success, the validity of the assessment is questionable. In addition, the test–retest reliability is not always strong. A person can take the test twice and end up with different results (Hunsley, Lee, & Wood, 2003; Pittenger, 2005).

Taking Stock: An Appraisal of Objective Personality Tests

We have noted specific criticisms of the MMPI-2-RF and Myers–Briggs tests, but there are other serious drawbacks of objective assessments. Although many of these tests include some sort of mechanism for checking the validity of the test taker's answers, people may lie (and get away with it), particularly when the assessment results might impact some important aspect of their lives, such as work or a child custody case. In addition, social desirability can influence the results; individuals may unintentionally answer questions in a way that makes them "look better" to others. Despite many criticisms, these tests are the best tools we have to evaluate personality.

FEARLESS AND HONEST You may be wondering why we chose to feature the story of an intersex man in this chapter on personality. Wouldn't Sean Saifa Wall's story be a better fit for the sexuality and gender chapter? We don't believe that gender nonconforming people should be confined to discussions of sex and gender. We chose to include Saifa here because we were captivated by him, and his rare ability to reflect on his personality development in a fearless and honest way. ●

 show what you know

1. _____ personality tests present ambiguous stimuli to the test taker, so the administrator can interpret and uncover underlying personality characteristics based on that participant's responses.
   a. Objective
   b. Projective
   c. 16PF
   d. Myers–Briggs

2. A psychologist gives a client several personality tests to help her choose a career path. What might the consequences be if the tests are not valid? How would the client know if the tests were not reliable?

3. Critics of objective personality tests report that the _____ of these tests does not allow for flexibility and fails to consider the diversity of individual experiences.
   a. standardization
   b. extraversion
   c. neuroticism
   d. factor analysis

✓ CHECK YOUR ANSWERS IN APPENDIX C.

summary of concepts

LO 1 Define personality. (p. 456)

Personality refers to the unique, core set of characteristics that influence the way one thinks, acts, and feels—characteristics many psychologists would agree are consistent and enduring throughout the life span.

LO 2 Distinguish how the perspectives of psychology explain personality development. (p. 456)

The psychoanalytic perspective suggests that personality development is heavily influenced by processes of which we are unaware, how those processes manifest early in life, and the way caregivers respond. The behavioral perspective describes and explains how the environment shapes personality, and specifically, how reinforcers influence behaviors. The humanistic perspective suggests that we should take advantage of our capabilities as we strive for personal growth, and that the choices we make in life influence our personalities. The social-cognitive perspective focuses on relationships, environmental influences, cognitive activity, and individual behavior as they come together to form personality. The biological perspective suggests physiological and genetic factors affect personality development. Trait theories look at current characteristics of the individual to describe personality and predict behaviors.

LO 3 Illustrate Freud's models for describing the mind. (p. 460)

Psychoanalysis refers to Freud's views regarding personality as well as his system of psychotherapy and tools for the exploration of the unconscious. According to his topographical model, our personalities and behaviors result from mental processes that occur at three levels: the conscious, preconscious, and unconscious. The structural model of the mind describes the functions of the mind's components. The id is the most primitive component of the mind, and its activities occur at the unconscious level. The ego develops as the infant grows, finding ways to manipulate situations, plan for

the future, solve problems, and make decisions to satisfy the needs of the id. The superego develops last and guides our behavior to follow the rules of society, parents, or other authority figures.

LO 4 Summarize Freud's use of psychosexual stages to explain personality. (p. 464)

The developmental model helps explain personality and sexuality in terms of a standard developmental path through what Freud called the psychosexual stages. He believed all children must go through these stages as they mature into adulthood. Associated with each stage is an erogenous zone as well as a conflict that must be dealt with. If the conflict is not successfully resolved, the child may suffer from a fixation and get "stuck" in that particular stage, not able to progress smoothly through the remaining stages. The stages include the oral stage, anal stage, phallic stage, latency period, and genital stage.

LO 5 Explain how the neo-Freudians' theories of personality differ from Freud's. (p. 469)

Some of Freud's followers branched out on their own due to disagreements about certain issues, such as his focus on sex and aggression, his idea that personality is determined by the end of childhood, and his somewhat negative view of human nature. Adler proposed that humans are conscious and intentional in their behaviors. Jung suggested that we are driven by a psychological energy (as opposed to sexual energy), which encourages positive growth, self-understanding, and balance. Horney emphasized the role of relationships between children and their caregivers, not erogenous zones and psychosexual stages.

LO 6 Summarize Maslow's hierarchy of needs, and describe self-actualizers. (p. 473)

Maslow proposed a hierarchy of needs, which represents a continuum of drives that are universal and ordered in terms of their strength. He suggested that we typically, but not always, respond to these needs in a predictable order. Self-actualizers are those who continually seek to reach their fullest potential.

LO 7 Discuss Rogers' view of self-concept, ideal self, and unconditional positive regard. (p. 474)

Rogers proposed that the development of personality is highly influenced by the role of caregivers in a child's life. He suggested humans have an innate urge to move toward and be attracted to situations and people that will help us grow, and to avoid those that have the potential to stop our growth. Self-concept is knowledge of one's strengths, abilities, behavior patterns, and temperament. Rogers believed that individuals develop an ideal self, which refers to the self-concept we strive for and fervently wish to achieve. Ideally, caregivers should show unconditional positive regard, which is the total acceptance of a child regardless of behavior. People need to feel completely accepted and valued for who they are, not what they do.

LO 8 Use the behavioral perspective to explain personality development. (p. 476)

According to learning theory, personality is a compilation of behaviors, all of which have been shaped through a lifetime of reinforcement and conditioning. Some behaviorists use learning principles to explain personality, including those of classical conditioning, operant conditioning, and observational learning.

LO 9 Summarize Rotter's view of personality. (p. 477)

Rotter suggested that not all aspects of behavior and personality can be directly observed. He believed a key component of personality is locus of control, which is a pattern of beliefs regarding where responsibility or control for an outcome exists. Rotter explored how these beliefs can influence behavior. Expectancy refers to the predictions we make about the consequences or outcomes of our behavior.

LO 10 Discuss how Bandura uses the social-cognitive perspective to explain personality. (p. 477)

Bandura rejected the notion that psychologists should only focus on observable behavior; he realized behavior is determined by cognition as well as reinforcers and other environmental influences. He used this social-cognitive perspective to explain personality. Personality results from patterns of thinking (cognitive) in addition to our relationships and other environmental factors (social). Bandura refers to this multidirectional interaction among beliefs, behaviors, and the environment as reciprocal determinism.

LO 11 Distinguish trait theories from other personality theories. (p. 480)

Traits are the relatively stable properties that describe elements of personality. The trait theories are different from other personality theories in that they focus less on explaining why and how personality develops, and more on describing personality and predicting behaviors. Allport created a comprehensive list of traits to help operationalize the terminology used in personality research. Cattell grouped the traits into two categories: surface traits and source traits. He used factor analysis to uncover the relationships among surface traits, resulting in 16 personality factors, and developed the Sixteen Personality Factor Questionnaire (16PF) to measure them. Eysenck proposed that we could describe personalities using three dimensions: introversion–extraversion, neuroticism, and psychoticism. He also worked to understand the biological basis of these dimensions.

LO 12 Identify the biological roots of the five-factor model of personality. (p. 481)

The five-factor model of personality, also known as the Big Five, is another trait approach to explaining personality and includes the following factors: openness to experience, conscientiousness, extraversion, agreeableness, and neuroticism. Twin and adoption studies conducted across the world point to a genetic basis for the five factors. These characteristics are stable over time, suggesting that the environmental changes we experience over the life span have less of an impact on personality than inherited characteristics.

LO 13 Explain why reliability and validity are important in personality assessment. (p. 486)

Reliability generally refers to two aspects of a personality assessment: test–retest reliability and interrater reliability. Test–retest reliability is consistency of results when the same person takes a test more than once. Interrater reliability refers to the consistency across people scoring an assessment. Validity refers to the degree to which an assessment measures what it is intended to measure. A valid test must yield results similar to established assessments. Both reliability and validity are important in the assessment of personality because they help render the assessments effective.

LO 14 Define projective personality tests and evaluate their strengths and limitations. (p. 487)

Personality influences perceptions. With projective personality tests, a test taker is shown a stimulus that has no specified meaning and then is prompted to respond, thus projecting meaning onto it. Testers interpret and uncover underlying personality characteristics from these responses—characteristics that might not be accessible through interview or observation. One strength of this type of assessment is its unstructured nature, which makes it less threatening to test takers, therefore provoking less resistance. Limitations include the amount of time needed to administer the assessment as well as the subjective nature of its interpretation, which can lead to problems with reliability. Some of the best-known projective tests are the Rorschach Inkblot Test and the Thematic Apperception Test (TAT).

LO 15 Describe objective personality tests and evaluate their strengths and limitations. (p. 489)

Objective personality tests are made up of a standard set of questions with answer choices (true/false, multiple choice, circle the number). One strength of this type of personality test is that it is scored in a standardized way, free of any personal intuition or bias. Limitations include the potential for dishonesty on the part of test takers as well as their tendency to unintentionally answer questions in a way that causes them to be viewed in a more favorable light (social desirability). Two commonly used objective personality tests are the Minnesota Multiphasic Personality Inventory (MMPI–2) and the Sixteen Personality Factor Questionnaire (16PF).

key terms

archetypes, p. 470
collective unconscious, p. 470
ego, p. 461
ego defense mechanisms, p. 462
expectancy, p. 477
five-factor model of personality, p. 481

fixation, p. 465
id, p. 461
ideal self, p. 474
Oedipus complex, p. 466
personality, p. 456
pleasure principle, p. 461
projective personality tests, p. 487
psychoanalysis, p. 459

psychosexual stages, p. 464
reality principle, p. 461
reciprocal determinism, p. 479
repression, p. 464
self-concept, p. 474
self-efficacy, p. 477
social-cognitive perspective, p. 477

source traits, p. 480
superego, p. 461
surface traits, p. 480
traits, p. 479
trait theories, p. 479
unconditional positive regard, p. 475
unconscious, p. 460

test prep *are you ready?*

1. The _____ perspective of personality suggests that personality is shaped by interactions with the environment, specifically through learning.
   - a. trait
   - b. humanistic
   - c. biological
   - d. behavioral

2. A professor doing research on personality development insists personality develops early in life and that we are greatly influenced by conflicts and urges of which we are unaware. This professor appears to be proposing which of the following perspectives?
   - a. humanistic
   - b. behavioral
   - c. psychoanalytic
   - d. social-cognitive

3. Freud's topographical model suggests our personalities and behaviors result from:
   - a. components of the mind, including the id, ego, and superego.
   - b. the reality principle.
   - c. the pleasure principle.
   - d. mental processes that occur at three levels of consciousness.

4. Which of the following form the basis for Freud's structural model of the mind?
   - a. superego, preconscious, unconscious
   - b. id, preconscious, ego
   - c. id, ego, superego
   - d. temperament, unconscious, character

5. According to Freud, all children progress through _____ as they mature into adulthood, although sometimes their progress is not smooth and they may suffer from a _____.
   - a. psychosexual stages; fixation
   - b. three levels of consciousness; superego
   - c. defense mechanisms; locus of control
   - d. erogenous zones; reciprocal determinism

6. _____ refer(s) to the drive to achieve one's full potential.
   - a. Repression
   - b. Conditions of worth
   - c. Self-actualization
   - d. Reciprocal determinism

7. Rogers believed that problems can develop when a person's self-concept is _____ with his experiences in the world.

   a. incongruent
   b. in harmony
   c. self-actualized
   d. conditioned

8. A person high in _____ strongly believes she will succeed in a particular situation even if she has experienced failure in similar circumstances.

   a. reciprocal determinism
   b. reinforcers
   c. self-efficacy
   d. source traits

9. _____ refers to the unique, core set of characteristics that influence how we think, act, and feel.

   a. Personality
   b. Ego defense mechanism
   c. Reciprocal determinism
   d. Expectancy

10. Cattell proposed there are 16 personality dimensions that can be considered primary _____, and these are the product of both nature and nurture.

    a. source traits
    b. conditions of worth
    c. Big Five traits
    d. defense mechanisms

11. According to Eysenck, we can describe personalities based on:

    a. three dimensions of traits.
    b. self-actualization.
    c. locus of control.
    d. reinforcement value.

12. Evidence for the biological basis of the five-factor model of personality includes:

    a. the instability of personality characteristics over time.
    b. the stability of personality characteristics over time.
    c. the fact that there are no gender differences in personality characteristics.
    d. the absence of heritability of personality characteristics.

13. _____ can be determined when someone takes the same personality assessment more than once and the results do not change.

    a. Heritability
    b. Effectiveness
    c. Reliability
    d. Validity

14. The idea that personality traits influence perception is part of the logic underlying _____, which attempt to explore characteristics that might not be accessible through interview or observation.

    a. projective personality tests
    b. semistructured interviews
    c. structured interviews
    d. fMRI studies

15. The neo-Freudians agree with Freud on many issues, but tend to disagree with which of the following?

    a. his belief in the positive aspect of human nature
    b. his belief in the importance of personality growth throughout life
    c. his intense emphasis on sex and aggression
    d. his notion that caregivers cannot shape personality

16. Think about a friend you know who is outgoing. How would a behaviorist explain the development of your friend's personality characteristics.

17. What is the difference between the humanistic perspective and the social-cognitive perspective of personality development?

18. Describe the Oedipus complex and the Electra complex. How are they different?

19. Consider how you are doing in your college courses. Name three causes for your successes that represent an internal locus of control. Name three causes for your successes that represent an external locus of control.

20. Describe the differences between objective and subjective approaches to the assessment of personality.

✓ CHECK YOUR ANSWERS IN APPENDIX C.

YOUR SCIENTIFIC WORLD

Apply psychology to the real world! Go to LaunchPad for access.

Courtesy of Veronica Garfield Newhoff.

Andy Katz/Pacific Press/Sipa USA/Newscom.

Juan Manuel Silva/AGE Fotostock.

CHAPTER OUTLINE AND LEARNING OBJECTIVES

An Introduction to Stress

LO 1 Define stress and stressors.

LO 2 Describe the relationship between major life events and illness.

LO 3 Summarize how poverty, adjusting to a new culture, and daily hassles affect health.

Responding to Stressors

LO 4 Identify the brain and body changes that characterize the fight-or-flight response.

LO 5 Outline the general adaptation syndrome (GAS).

LO 6 Explain the function of the hypothalamic–pituitary–adrenal (HPA) system.

Stress and Your Health

LO 7 Explain how stressors relate to health problems.

LO 8 List some consequences of prolonged exposure to the stress hormone cortisol.

Can You Deal?

LO 9 Illustrate how appraisal influences coping.

LO 10 Describe Type A and Type B personalities and explain how they relate to stress.

LO 11 Discuss several tools for reducing stress and maintaining health.

LO 12 Describe mindfulness meditation and its benefits.

John Moore/Getty Images.

Richard Graulich/ZUMA Press/Newscom.

Code 4 Photography (Kyler Hewes).

12 stress and health

An Introduction to Stress

A DAY NOT TO REMEMBER Thursday, October 9, 2014: Christy Sheppard can only recall bits and pieces of that rainy day in Colorado Springs. She remembers leaving her house just before 9:00 A.M., and glancing in the rearview mirror to see if the garage door was closed. Yet, she has no memory of driving to a local school building, getting out of her car, and finding her way to the room where she took the Physical Abilities Test (PAT), a fitness exam administered by the Colorado Springs Police Department. Christy doesn't recall interacting with her fellow officers, or anything about the test itself—not one push-up, sit-up, agility exercise, or shuttle run.

Throughout the morning, Christy asked the test administrators the same questions over and over: "How many sit-ups did I do? Did I pass?" The other officers, some of them close friends, found Christy's behavior strange and annoying, but didn't make much of it. After the test, Christy and her friends arranged to meet at the Black-eyed

Feeling the Pressure
A 25-year veteran of the Colorado Springs Police Department, Christy Sheppard has taken—and passed—many police fitness exams. Yet, the stakes seemed higher on that testing day in the fall of 2014. "I was worried, being a minority, a female, and a brand new lieutenant," Christy explains. "In my mind I was thinking, *I don't want to be the guy that fails.*" Courtesy of Veronica Garfield Newhoff.

Fit for Duty?
Applicants for the New Jersey state police take a physical qualification exam. Police officers around the nation must periodically take fitness tests to demonstrate they are physically capable of carrying out their duties. The test required by the Colorado Springs Police Department includes push-ups, sit-ups, an agility test, and a shuttle run known as the Beep Test. "You have to pass the PT [physical training] test," Christy explains. "If you don't pass it, then you have to retake it every 30 days, and after 6 months, they can proceed with termination." AP Photo/Mel Evans.

Christy, in Her Own Words

http://qrs.ly/wr5a5ff

Pea, a restaurant they had been frequenting for 25 years. She has no recollection of driving there, though she clearly remembers sitting in the parking lot and wondering, *What am I doing here?* That's when she called her husband Ron. "What's today's date?" she asked. Ron told her it was October 9. "Yeah, but what's the day of the week?"

At first, Ron thought Christy was just being funny, as they always joked around with each other. But when Christy began repeating herself ("What's today's date? What's the day of the week?"), Ron knew something was wrong. "Where are you?" he asked.

"I'm at the Black-eyed Pea," said Christy, beginning to cry. "Why am I at the Black-eyed Pea?"

"I'm coming right there," Ron reassured her. "Don't go anywhere." Thinking Christy was having a stroke, Ron called for an ambulance. Meanwhile, Christy's friends (the ones she had arranged to meet for lunch) coaxed her out of the car and into the restaurant. The ambulance crew arrived soon after and began assessing her physical and cognitive health. Apart from having abnormally high blood pressure, Christy was physically okay, and she could answer general questions like "How many quarters are in two dollars?" and "Who is the president?" Yet, her knowledge of recent events was clearly impaired. In the emergency room, Christy told doctors she was a police sergeant and that her oldest daughter lived at home. She had no recollection of being promoted to lieutenant or dropping off her daughter at college a few months earlier. As Christy explains, "I had completely lost 6 months."

It didn't take long for the neurologist overseeing Christy's case to make a diagnosis: *transient global amnesia,* a mysterious type of memory loss that begins suddenly and lasts no more than 24 hours. People suffering from this rare condition cannot lay down new memories and may have trouble retrieving long-term memories (Romero et al., 2013). Fortunately, transient global amnesia is not a sign of a serious medical condition, and most people fully recover (Mayo Clinic, 2014, July 18). Researchers have yet to nail down the cause of transient global amnesia, but some evidence suggests that stress could be a trigger (Griebe et al., 2015). ●

There is no question that Christy was experiencing stress at that point in her life. But what exactly is stress, and how does it arise?

Stress and Stressors

LO 1 Define stress and stressors.

We all have an intuitive sense of how stress feels, and many of us are more familiar with it than we would like. Some people report they experience the *feeling* of stress, almost as if stress were an emotion. Others describe stress as if it were a force that needs to be resisted. An engineer might refer to stress as the application of a force on a target, such as the wing of an airplane, to determine how much load it can handle before breaking (Lazarus, 1993). Do you ever feel you might "break" because the load you bear causes such great strain (**INFOGRAPHIC 12.1**)?

Stress is defined as the response to perceived threats or challenges resulting from stimuli or events that cause strain, analogous to the airplane wing bending because of an

CONNECTIONS

In **Chapter 9**, we defined emotion as a psychological state that includes a subjective or inner experience. Emotion also has a physiological component and a behavioral expression. Here, we discuss stress responses, which are psychological, physiological, and emotional in nature.

stress The response to perceived threats or challenges resulting from stimuli or events that cause strain.

Note: Quotations attributed to Christy Sheppard and Kehlen Kirby are personal communications.

Stressed Out

Periodically, the American Psychological Association (APA) commissions a survey investigating perceived stress among adults in the United States. In addition to measuring attitudes about stress, the survey identifies leading sources of stress and common behaviors used to manage stressors. The resulting picture shows that stress is a significant issue for many people in the United States and that we are not always managing it well (APA, 2016c). Even when we acknowledge the importance of stress management and resolve to make positive lifestyle changes, many adults report barriers such as a lack of time or willpower that prevent them from achieving their goals. The good news? Our ability to manage stress appears to improve with age. (ALL INFORMATION PRESENTED BELOW, EXCEPT THE PERCEIVED STRESS SCALE, IS FROM APA, 2013e)

Credits: Strawberry-flavored donut with a bite taken out, Lucie Lang/Shutterstock; Torn, crumpled dollar, Dimedrol68/Shutterstock.

4 OUT OF 5
Number of people reporting their **stress level has increased** or stayed the same in the past year.

TOP SOURCES OF STRESS

money **69%**

work **65%**

the economy **61%**

family responsibilities **57%**

relationships **56%**

family health problems **52%**

Number experiencing **responses to stress**, including **anger, fatigue** and **feeling overwhelmed.**

NEARLY 7 IN 10

People with high stress also report poor health behaviors.

Only **30%** of adults with high stress report eating healthy and getting enough sleep.

IN PREVIOUS 5 YEARS

60%

60% of people have tried to reduce their stress

53%

53% are still trying

STRESS OVER THE LIFE SPAN

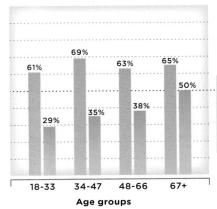

Age groups	18-33	34-47	48-66	67+

61% 69% 63% 65%
29% 35% 38% 50%

50% Oldest people report highest rate of meeting stress management goals.

■ Managing stress is very important
■ Doing a very good job managing stress

People across all age groups agree that managing stress is very important. However, the ability to manage stress varies with age. Younger adults are more likely to rely on unhealthy behaviors like drinking alcohol and smoking for stress management. Older adults report more success in achieving healthy lifestyle goals such as eating healthy and getting enough sleep. They also report higher rates of religious participation.

DO **YOU** FEEL STRESSED?

Psychologist Sheldon Cohen and colleagues (1983) developed the Perceived Stress Scale to measure the degree to which we appraise situations as stressful. By comparing your score against others tested in your age group, you are able to assess the amount of perceived stress in your life. Simply knowing you find your life uncontrollable or overloaded can be a trigger to seek help implementing positive lifestyle change.

For each question, indicate how often you felt or thought a certain way. The best approach is to answer each question fairly quickly, choosing the alternative that seems like a reasonable estimate.

0=never   3=fairly often
1=almost never   4=very often
2=sometimes

1. In the last month, how often have you been upset because of something that happened unexpectedly?

2. In the last month, how often have you felt that you were unable to control the important things in your life?

3. In the last month, how often have you felt nervous and "stressed"?

4. In the last month, how often have you felt confident about your ability to handle your personal problems?

5. In the last month, how often have you felt that things were going your way?

6. In the last month, how often have you found that you could not cope with all the things that you had to do?

7. In the last month, how often have you been able to control irritations in your life?

8. In the last month, how often have you felt that you were on top of things?

9. In the last month, how often have you been angered because of things that were outside of your control?

10. In the last month, how often have you felt difficulties were piling up so high that you could not overcome them?

CONNECTIONS

In **Chapter 2,** we discussed hormones, which are the chemical messengers of the endocrine system released into the bloodstream. Hans Selye was an endocrinologist who studied hormones and physiological reactions to stressors. His work describes human behavior from the biological perspective of psychology.

applied load. For humans, these stimuli, or **stressors**, can cause psychological, physiological, and emotional reactions. As you read this chapter, be careful not to confuse *how we react to stressors* with the *stressors* themselves; stress is the response and stressors are the cause (Harrington, 2013). Hans Selye (ZEL-yeh; 1907–1982), an endocrinologist who studied the impact of hormones and stress, proposed that "stress is the nonspecific response of the body to any demand. A stressor is an agent that produces stress at any time" (1976, p. 53).

We should note that not all experts agree on definitions for stress and stressors. Some contend that commonly used definitions are far too broad, which complicates the collection and interpretation of data (Kagan, 2016). For example, how can you create an operational definition for a "stressor" if researchers use it to describe phenomena as diverse as "a rat restrained in a tube for several hours, a mouse exposed to bright light, and an adolescent bullied by a peer, as well as an adult asked to prepare a speech to be given to strangers" (p. 443)?

Stressors take countless forms. Many of the stressors acting on Christy originate from her job as a police officer. A few months before the fitness test, Christy started working the midnight shift, which begins around 8:00 P.M. and ends at about 6:00 A.M. During those 10-hour nights, Christy and one other lieutenant are the highest-ranking officers on duty; they oversee all police activity in Colorado Springs, a city of almost a half million people. "On the midnight shift, the lieutenant is responsible for making decisions or deciding if those higher up should be woken, consulted, and informed," Christy explains. "No matter what happens, I have to make the decisions." Here is an everyday type of decision Christy makes on her nightshift: A patrol officer pulls over an older woman for a traffic violation. He runs a background check and finds out that the state of Florida has a 20-year-old warrant for her arrest. The officer calls Christy and says, "I feel like maybe this is a mistake that this warrant is in the system. . . . I don't feel right arresting someone's grandma." Christy also experiences sympathy for this elderly woman, but she must follow protocol. "The law says, if you contact someone with a warrant, you will arrest," Christy explains. "I can't let them let her go even if it is a really nice grandma," she adds. "But, at the same time, I'm human and. . . . [I] feel bad for people." After calling the Florida police to verify the warrant's legitimacy, Christy tells the officer to make the arrest. The decision is made, but it continues to act as a stressor. When Christy goes home and lies down to sleep, her mind spins as she replays all those decisions she made that night on the job.

More than anything, Christy worries about the safety of the officers she supervises. "Every day I come in, my biggest worry is that one of these officers is going to get hurt or killed," she says. The risk of this happening increases when multiple incidents occur simultaneously and police resources are spread thin across the city. One summer night in 2012, for example, three separate homicides involving multiple victims and a shooting involving an officer took place—all within hours of each other. When this type of scenario occurs, the nightshift lieutenant works with Communications Center supervisors to decide where, when, and how many officers to deploy across the city. If there is a shortage of personnel, officers may enter dangerous situations without proper backup, and as Christy puts it, "The potential for something to go south is great."

What are the stressors in your life? Some exist outside of you, like homework assignments, job demands, and dead phone batteries. Others are more internal, like the *thought* that your partner deceived you or the *realization* that you're not ready for your exam this afternoon. Generally, we experience stress in response to stressors, although there is at least one exception to this rule: People with anxiety disorders can feel intense anxiety in the absence of any apparent stressors (Chapter 13). Which brings us to another point: Stress is very much related to how one perceives the surrounding world.

In many cases, stress results from a *perceived* threat, because what constitutes a threat differs from one person to the next. You might find the idea of undercover police work very threatening; the thought of posing as a drug user and purchasing methamphetamine from a heavily armed dealer seems frightening. Or perhaps you're more like Christy, and you relish this type of challenge. "The undercover work is just fun. It's acting. It's going in some place, acting like someone you're not," Christy says. "Plus you get to wear dirty clothes to work."

Remember that stress can have psychological, physiological, and emotional effects. Christy's transient global amnesia may have been a psychological consequence of stress. During that episode, emergency medical workers determined she had abnormally high blood pressure; this may have been a physiological component of stress. Christy was also uncharacteristically emotional, shedding tears as she sat in the car talking on the phone with her husband—an emotional aspect of stress. Fortunately for Christy, the condition was only temporary.

PICKING UP THE PIECES Christy ended up being admitted to the hospital overnight and undergoing a series of tests to rule out a stroke or another serious medical condition. Her memory recovered within 24 hours, though it took days for her thought process to return to its normal speed and efficiency. "I just had to sit on my couch, and I couldn't do anything," Christy recalls. "I stayed in my pajamas for a good week." The cause of transient global amnesia remains unknown, but Christy believes her case was triggered by the stressors brought on by police work, and the constant sleep deprivation associated with the midnight shift (she was averaging no more than 4 or 5 hours per night).

"We laugh about it now, and talk about the day my marbles rolled down the street," Christy says, "but when I seriously think about it, it was very, very scary." As traumatic as this experience was, Christy bounced back and resumed her job as a police officer. Do you think everyone would have recovered so easily? As you will learn in this chapter, people experience and cope with stressors in diverse ways. ●

EUSTRESS AND DISTRESS Thus far, we have focused on negative stressors and their consequences, but some stressors are positive. For Christy, getting married and having three babies were enjoyable stressors. So, too, was dropping off her oldest daughter at college. "You know what else is a positive stressor?" Christy says. "Preparing for a vacation." Every year, Christy and her husband take their three children to a warm and peaceful place, often on a cruise ship or beautiful beach. "I think vacations are important, and I think doing it with your family is important," says Christy, who encourages her colleagues to do the same with their families. Getting married, having kids, and planning for vacations are "good" stressors that can lead to positive results. This stress response to agreeable or positive events is called **eustress** (YOO-stress) and can also lead to psychological, physiological, and emotional reactions. Think about the last time you faced a challenge and hoped it would lead to personal growth or improved performance. Maybe your challenge was a final exam. You studied so hard that you were actually looking forward to proving yourself at the end of the semester. Here, the exam prep is the positive stressor; deep learning might be a psychological consequence; and happy anticipation an emotional response. Of course, most people view stress in a negative context. Undesirable or disagreeable occurrences lead to a stress response known as **distress**. This type of negative stress may occur if you put off studying for your final exam, cram the night before, and show up to the exam sleep-deprived and underprepared.

stressors Stimuli that cause psychological, physiological, and emotional reactions.

eustress The stress response to agreeable or positive stressors.

distress The stress response to unpleasant or undesirable stressors.

In one study, researchers found that work groups experiencing eustress demonstrated more dedication and engagement (Kozusznik, Rodríguez, & Peiró, 2015). Those feeling distress not only showed less engagement; they experienced more fatigue throughout the workday (Kozusznik et al., 2015; Parker & Ragsdale, 2015).

Now that we have a basic understanding of stress, let's explore the various types of stressors and how they impact the mind and body. We'll start big, focusing our attention on major life events.

Major Life Events

LO 2   Describe the relationship between major life events and illness.

Holmes and Rahe (1967) were among the first to propose that life-changing events can be stressors. In other words, any event that requires a life adjustment, such as the birth of a child, the death of a spouse, or a change in financial status, can cause a stress reaction. They also suggested that these life-changing events have a cumulative effect; the more events you experience in a row or within a brief period of time, the greater the potential for increased stress and negative health outcomes. Recall the analogy of applying a force to an airplane wing. The degree to which the wing bends (or breaks) indicates the strain it is under (Lazarus, 1993). Studies have uncovered associations between certain life events (the force causing strain) and illnesses (the response), such as heart attack, leukemia, diabetes, influenza, and psychiatric disorders (Hatch & Dohrenwend, 2007; Rabkin & Struening, 1976; Ridout, Carpenter, & Tyrka, 2016).

SOCIAL READJUSTMENT RATING SCALE Illnesses can be clearly identified and defined, but how do psychologists measure life events? Holmes and Rahe (1967) developed the Social Readjustment Rating Scale (SRRS) to do just that. With the SRRS, participants are asked to read through a list of events and experiences, and determine which happened during the previous year and how many times they occurred. A score is then calculated based on severity ratings of events and the frequency of their occurrence. An event like the death of a spouse has a greater severity rating than something like a traffic violation. Participants are also asked to report any illnesses or accidents they experienced during the same period. Researchers then use this information to look at the correlation between life events and health problems, exploring whether there is a positive link between the two variables (Kobasa, 1979). But remember, a correlation between life events and illness (or any correlation for that matter) is not proof of causality. The possibility always exists that a third variable, such as poverty, may be causing both illnesses and life-changing events. Someone who is impoverished might not have a job or access to good health care, nutrition, and so forth. In this case, poverty is leading to stressful life events *and* poor health outcomes.

First used in the late 1960s, the SRRS has been updated over the years. (For example, the original scale included a "mortgage over $10,000" as an event.) The rating scale has also been adapted to better match the life events of specific populations; an example is the College Undergraduate Stress Scale (CUSS; Renner & Mackin, 1998; **FIGURE 12.1**). Even with this degree of specificity, the scale may not be suitable for every person. In addition to dealing with term papers, midterms, and other college-related life events, many of today's college students face a host of other potential stressors, such as raising children and caring for elderly family members.

Another possible problem with self-report scales such as the SRRS and the CUSS is that people tend to forget events over time, or the opposite—they tend to focus more on past events than recent ones (Pachana, Brilleman, & Dobson, 2011). What's

---

CONNECTIONS

In **Chapter 1,** we explained that a positive correlation indicates that as one variable increases, so does the other variable. Here, we see a positive correlation between life events and health problems: The more life events people have experienced, the more health problems they are likely to have.

---

posttraumatic stress disorder (PTSD) A psychological disorder characterized by exposure to or being threatened by an event involving death, serious injury, or sexual violence; can include disturbing memories, nightmares, flashbacks, and other distressing symptoms.

more, not all negative life-changing events lead to bad outcomes. Some have even suggested that moderate exposure to stress makes us stronger, a view described as *stress inoculation*. Someone with a "low to moderate" degree of stress may end up with "better mental health and well-being" and a greater ability to cope with pain than those who either have faced no hardships or have had to handle an overwhelming level of adversity (Seery, 2011).

Looking across cultures, we see that most people rate the weight of life-changing events very similarly (Leontopoulou, Jimerson, & Anderson, 2011; Scully, Tosi, & Banning, 2000). For example, people from France, Belgium, Switzerland, and Malaysia are similar to Americans in their views about the readjustment required for life events (Harmon, Masuda, & Homes, 1970; Woon, Masuda, Wagner, & Holmes, 1971).

 **In Class: Collaborate and Report**

Imagine you were tasked with redesigning the College Undergraduate Stress Scale (CUSS) to bring it up to date. With your group, **A)** discuss how to decide what items to include in your rating scale. **B)** Suggest additional events for inclusion in a new inventory. **C)** Team up with other groups in your class to see if you have any new events in common.

Posttraumatic Stress Disorder

One type of event not included in the SRRS, but which is familiar to police officers and other first responders, is a major disaster. These cataclysmic events include natural catastrophes such as hurricanes, earthquakes, and tornadoes, as well as multicar accidents, war, and terrorist attacks. The emotional and physical responses to such occurrences can last for many years, manifesting themselves in nightmares, flashbacks, depression, grief, anxiety, and other symptoms related to *posttraumatic stress disorder*.

In order to be diagnosed with **posttraumatic stress disorder (PTSD)**, a person must be exposed to or threatened by an event involving death, serious injury, or some form of sexual violence. Someone could develop PTSD after witnessing a violent assault or accident, or upon learning about the traumatic experiences of family members, close friends, perhaps even strangers. In some cases, the exposure to trauma is ongoing. Police officers, firefighters, and other first responders may witness disturbing scenarios on a weekly basis. Rates of PTSD among firefighters, for example, may be as high as 37% (Henderson, Van Hasselt, LeDuc, & Couwels, 2016). Another group disproportionately affected is the prison population; in one study, 48% of the inmate sample received a PTSD diagnosis (Briere, Agee, & Dietrich, 2016). For U.S. veterans 21–59 years old, current rates of PTSD are around 8% (Hoge & Warner, 2014). In contrast, around 3.5% to 4% of the general population is estimated to have received a PTSD diagnosis during the previous 12 months (American Psychiatric Association, 2013; Briere et al., 2016).

However, not everyone exposed to trauma will develop PTSD. Over the course of a lifetime, most people will experience an event that qualifies as a "psychological trauma," yet the majority will not meet the diagnostic criteria for PTSD (Bonanno, Westphal, & Mancini, 2011). To be diagnosed with this disorder, a person must experience at least one of the following symptoms: (1) distressing, disturbing, and spontaneously recurring memories of an event; (2) dreams with content or emotions associated with the event; (3) "dissociative reactions" that include feeling as if the event is happening again (flashbacks); (4) extreme psychological distress when reminded of the event; or (5) obvious physical reactions to cues related to the event (American Psychiatric Association, 2013).

FIGURE 12.1

Sample Items from the College Undergraduate Stress Scale

Event	Rating
Being raped	100
Death of a close friend	97
Contracting a sexually transmitted infection (other than AIDS)	94
Finals week	90
Flunking a class	89
Financial difficulties	84
Writing a major term paper	83
Talking in front of class	72
Difficulties with a roommate	66
Maintaining a steady dating relationship	55
Commuting to campus or work, or both	54
Getting straight As	51
Falling asleep in class	40

Reprinted by permission of SAGE Publications/APA/ LAWRENCE/ERLBAUM ASSOCIATES, INC. from Renner and Mackin (1998).

Invisible Wounds of War
An Iraqi refugee carries his blind wife and infant onto the shores of Lesvos, Greece, in June 2016. Ongoing fighting in Iraq has forced 4.2 million citizens to leave their homes and resettle elsewhere. The prevalence of PTSD among Iraqi refugees living in Western countries may be as high as 37.2% (Slewa-Younan, Uribe Guajardo, Heriseanu, & Hasan, 2015). STRATIS TSOULELIS/EPA/Newscom.

CONNECTIONS

In **Chapter 7,** we discussed the relationship between poverty and cognitive abilities. In **Chapter 8,** we presented evidence suggesting that isolation and lack of stimulation can hamper the development of young brains. Here, we highlight the link between poverty-related stressors and neurocognitive development.

acculturation The process of cultural adjustment and adaptation, including changes to one's language, values, cultural behaviors, and sometimes national identity.

acculturative stress Stress that occurs when people move to new countries or cultures and must adjust to a new way of life.

Many people with PTSD try to avoid environmental cues (people, places, or objects) linked to the trauma. If someone were involved in a serious car accident on U.S. Highway 101, then simply driving along that freeway may trigger unwanted memories. Other symptoms include difficulty remembering the details of the event, unrealistic self-expectations, ongoing self-blame, and loss of interest in activities that once were enjoyable. Someone with PTSD might be irritable or aggressive, lashing out at loved ones for no apparent reason. She may have trouble sleeping and concentrating. Also associated with PTSD are *dissociative symptoms,* which may include distorted perceptions of the world, and the feeling of observing oneself from the outside (American Psychiatric Association, 2013; Müllerová, Hansen, Contractor, Elhai, & Armour, 2016; Powers, Cross, Fani, & Bradley, 2015).

As we mentioned earlier, PTSD is a concern for police officers (Berger et al., 2011), many of whom bear witness to bloody crime scenes, traumatized victims, and gun violence. But it is not just these types of traumas that impact police officers; just as important are the more chronic stressors, like being overworked, lacking social support from superiors, colleagues, and the larger community, and not spending enough time with family (Collins & Gibbs, 2003; Habersaat, Geiger, Abdellaoui, & Wolf, 2015; Maguen et al., 2009).

It's Nonstop: Chronic Stressors

You don't have to be a police officer to appreciate the burden of everyday stress. For some of us, stressors come from balancing school and work, or taking care of young children. Many face the constant stressor of battling a chronic illness such as diabetes, asthma, or cancer (Sansom-Daly, Peate, Wakefield, Bryant, & Cohn, 2012), or caring for an adult child with a severe mental disorder (Barker, Greenberg, Seltzer, & Almeida, 2012). And for a growing number of people in the United States and around the world, poverty is an overwhelming stressor.

LO 3 Summarize how poverty, adjusting to a new culture, and daily hassles affect health.

POVERTY The number of Americans living at or below the poverty line is significant. The poverty threshold in the United States is defined as an individual income of less than $12,071 or less than $24,230 for a family of four. As of 2014, 21.1% of children under 18 years in the United States were living below the poverty level (DeNavas-Walt & Proctor, 2015). People struggling to make ends meet experience numerous stressors, including poor health care and nutrition, noisy living situations, overcrowding, violence, and underfunded schools (Blair & Raver, 2012; Mistry & Wadsworth, 2011; Schickedanz, Dreyer, & Halfon, 2015). The cycle of poverty is difficult to break, so these stressors often persist across generations. The longer people live in poverty, the more exposure they have to stressors, and the greater the likelihood they will become ill (Miller, Chen, & Parker, 2011).

For children in particular, the impact of socioeconomic status (SES) can have lifelong repercussions because environmental stressors affect the developing brain. Factors linked to poverty have been associated with differences in the development of cognitive and socioemotional abilities, which can impact performance in school and at work (Blair & Raver, 2015; Javanbakht et al., 2015). Results from scanning technology indicate that children from lower-SES families have reduced volume in the frontal and parietal cortex compared with higher-SES children. These reductions are linked to behavior problems, aggression, significantly smaller vocabularies, language processing problems, and poorer results on a variety of cognitive tests. What's causing these differences? One possible variable is related to caregiver interactions—low-SES children are exposed to far fewer words than high-SES children. The other important variable is stress; low-SES children are exposed to a greater number of stressors, which can cause changes to normal brain development (Kolb & Gibb, 2015).

In Class: Collaborate and Report

In your groups, **A)** discuss why poverty is hard to escape (*Hint:* List the stressors associated with an income of less than $24,230 for a family of four). **B)** Consider how poverty affects the health and intelligence of children (use the information presented in this chapter). **C)** Use at least three of the eight perspectives introduced in Chapter 1 (see Table 1.4) to explain the causes of poverty. **D)** Create a list of reasonable responses to those who suggest that people living in poverty should just "fix" their lives.

ACCULTURATIVE STRESS Another increasingly common source of stress is migration. As of 2015, there were 244 million migrants dispersed across the world (United Nations Population Fund, n.d., para. 1). Moving to a new country frequently involves a process of cultural adjustment and adaptation. This **acculturation** can result in changes to language, values, cultural behaviors, and sometimes even national identity (Schwartz et al., 2014). Acculturation is often accompanied by **acculturative stress** (uh-KUHL-chur-a-tiv), or stress associated with adjusting to a new way of life. How would it feel to leave behind your extended family and close friends, and move to a foreign land where the language, customs, holidays, and belief systems are new and different? Perhaps you have had this experience; over 41 million people living in the United States were born in another country (Pew Research Center, 2015, September 28). Even those who have lived on American soil their whole life can experience acculturative stress. For example, Asian American men whose parents, or even grandparents, were born in the United States are still influenced in some ways by acculturation—these men may feel pressure to develop the highly muscular male body-type often portrayed by American media (Cheng, McDermott, Wong, & La, 2016).

People respond to acculturative stress in a variety of ways (Berry, 1997). Some try to assimilate, letting go of old ways and adopting those of the new culture. But assimilation can cause problems if family members or friends from the old culture reject the new one, or have trouble assimilating themselves. Other people cling to their roots and remain *separated* from the new culture. Such an approach can become very problematic if the new culture does not support this type of separation and requires assimilation. A combination of these two approaches is *integration,* or holding onto some elements of the old culture, but also adopting aspects of the new one.

The degree of acculturative stress varies greatly from one individual to the next. Some people thrive on new soil (a prime example being Mohamed Dirie from Chapter 9), while others struggle with the stress of starting over. What determines the intensity of acculturative stress, and why do some people seem to have an easier time with it than others?

ACROSS THE WORLD
The Stress of Starting Anew

Imagine trying to get a job, pay your bills, or simply make friends in a world where most everyone speaks a foreign language. Familiarity with language appears to play a key role in determining acculturative stress levels. A study of Haitian immigrants in the United States determined lower levels of acculturative stress among those who spoke English (Belizaire & Fuertes, 2011). "The ability to speak English is crucial to the adjustment and well-being of immigrants in the United States," the authors wrote, "and some researchers see this ability as the best indicator of acculturation" (p. 93).

CONNECTIONS

In **Chapter 8,** we discussed Piaget's concept of assimilation, which refers to a cognitive approach to dealing with new information. This suggests that a person attempts to understand new information using her existing knowledge base. Here, assimilation means letting go of old ways and adopting the customs of a new culture.

Celebration of Culture
Young people celebrate the Hindu Holi fest in the Richmond Hill neighborhood of Queens, New York. The style of their clothing suggests they have embraced aspects of American culture, but their participation in the festival indicates they have not abandoned their roots. Queens is ranked among the top five most diverse counties in the United States (Narula, 2014, April 29).
Andy Katz/Pacific Press/Sipa USA/Newscom.

Another important determinant is the degree of difference between old and new cultures. Chinese graduate students appear to experience less acculturative stress studying in Hong Kong as opposed to Australia. Presumably, this is because the cultures of China and Hong Kong are more similar (Pan & Wong, 2011). Finally, we cannot forget the unpleasant reality of discrimination, which causes great stress for the world's immigrant populations. Common targets of discrimination in the United States are people of Arab and/or South Asian descent. Discrimination against these groups, which appears to have grown after the terrorist attacks of 9/11, may increase acculturative stress, erode psychological well-being, and possibly promote the development of depression (Goforth Oka, Leong, & Denis, 2014; Kaduvettoor-Davidson & Inman, 2013; Tummala-Narra, Alegria, & Chen, 2012).

Fortunately, there are ways to combat acculturative stress. One of the best defenses is **social support,** or assistance from others. (Here, we mean positive social support, not the type of support provided by gangs and other groups that engage in antisocial behaviors.) A small study of refugees in Austria indicated that those who could count on social support from a sponsor experienced less anxiety and depression and had an easier time adapting (Renner, Laireiter, & Maier, 2012). 🌐➤

Now that we have described some dramatic stressors like immigration and natural disasters, let's shift our discussion to a more mundane source of stress. Have you ever wondered how life's little annoyances impact your mind and body?

TORNADO IN MY KITCHEN "Today, I woke up, I went downstairs, and I walk into my kitchen, and it looks like somebody had a party in there," says Christy. "[They] ate up all this food, and not one person bothered to do any dishes. . . . My kitchen looks like a tornado went off in it." On top of the mess left by her family, Christy cannot get her coffeemaker to function, and the dog is hungry because no one else in the family bothered to feed it.

Functioning on 5 hours of unsatisfying sleep (she went to sleep at 7 A.M. and woke up at noon), Christy heads to the police station, where she finds a heap of paperwork sitting on her desk. An officer calls to report that she twisted her ankle at the gym, and will not be able to report for duty this evening. Now there is a hole in the schedule, and Christy needs to fix it ASAP; otherwise, there won't be an adequate number of police officers working in the city tonight. Are you feeling stressed yet? Christy certainly is. All these *daily hassles* compound, and she becomes exasperated. ●

What a Hassle, What a Joy

Daily hassles are the minor problems or irritants we deal with on a regular basis, such as traffic, financial worries, misplaced keys, messy roommates—a list that does not seem to end. These hassles, although seemingly minor, are repetitive and ever-present. It's a good thing that the weight of our daily hassles is counterbalanced by the uplifts in our lives.

Uplifts are positive experiences that have the potential to make us happy. For Christy, it might be a text from her daughter joking about the family dog: "Shasta has gas again!" Think about the last time you smiled; it was likely in response to an uplift, such as a funny comment on your latest Instagram post, a surprise phone call

---

IMMIGRATION IS STRESSFUL, ESPECIALLY IF YOU DON'T SPEAK THE NEW LANGUAGE.

"Monday I woke up at noon and I've been cussing ever since."
Getting 4 to 5 hours of sleep makes Christy feel irritable, moody, and physically exhausted. "Irritable doesn't even cover it," Christy says. "I bet my family wants me to move out!" The constant sleep deprivation also makes it difficult to deal with the daily hassles of home life and police work. Courtesy of Veronica Garfield Newhoff.

social support The assistance we acquire from others.

daily hassles Minor and regularly occurring problems that can act as stressors.

uplifts Experiences that are positive and have the potential to make one happy.

from an old friend, or waking up to the sunshine flooding through your window. We all experience hassles and uplifts, but how do they interact to affect our health and well-being? Researchers have been asking this question for decades.

DeLongis and colleagues (1988) developed a scale of daily hassles and uplifts, and used it to explore the relationship between stress and illness (**FIGURE 12.2**). They asked participants to read through a list of 53 items that could be either hassles or uplifts, such as meeting deadlines, maintaining a car, interacting with fellow workers, and dealing with the weather. Participants then rated these items on a 4-point scale indicating "how much of a hassle" and "how much of an uplift" each was on that particular day (0 = none or not applicable, to 3 = a great deal). They also asked participants to report any illness, injuries, or symptoms they experienced that same day. What did they find? Over a 6-month period, there was a significant link between hassles and health problems. The more daily stressors the participants reported, the more likely they were to suffer from sore throats, headaches, influenza, back problems, and other health issues. As subsequent research suggests, dealing with daily hassles may increase the risk of catching contagious diseases and could prolong the course of illness (Glaser & Kiecolt-Glaser, 2005). A link may even exist between daily stressors and cardiovascular risk factors, such as high blood pressure (Uchino, Berg, Smith, Pearce, & Skinner, 2006). Thus it appears that the strain of managing daily hassles can take a toll on our health and well-being (DeLongis, Coyne, Dakof, Folkman, & Lazarus, 1982; DeLongis, Folkman, & Lazarus, 1988). This may be especially true for first responders who deal with long hours and shift work (Larsson, Berglund, & Ohlsson, 2016).

How do hassles and uplifts affect psychological and social health? One group of researchers studied two Israeli populations (Jewish and Arab), exploring the similarities and differences within subgroups living in the same country. While disparities existed, the researchers noted some important similarities. In both groups, for example, daily uplifts had a positive impact on "family satisfaction," while daily hassles had a negative effect on "life satisfaction," though the meaning of "uplift" differed between the two groups (Lavee & Ben-Ari, 2008).

How might you increase the uplifts in your life? Research suggests that people who demonstrate kindness and generosity, and act in ways that benefit others are more likely to experience happiness and other "positive emotions." Thus, by paying it forward, you create uplifts for others and perhaps even yourself: "As people do nice things for others, they may feel greater joy, contentment, and love, which in turn promote greater overall well-being and improve social relationships and [more]" (Nelson, Layous, Cole, & Lyubomirsky, 2016, p. 7).

Hassles					Uplifts			
0	1	2	3	Your child(ren)	0	1	2	3
0	1	2	3	Your friend(s)	0	1	2	3
0	1	2	3	Your work load	0	1	2	3
0	1	2	3	Enough money for emergencies	0	1	2	3
0	1	2	3	Financial care for someone who doesn't live with you	0	1	2	3
0	1	2	3	Your drinking	0	1	2	3
0	1	2	3	Your physical appearance	0	1	2	3
0	1	2	3	Political or social issues	0	1	2	3
0	1	2	3	Amount of free time	0	1	2	3
0	1	2	3	Being organized	0	1	2	3

FIGURE 12.2

The Hassles and Uplifts Scale
Research participants were instructed to circle a number rating the degree to which each item was a hassle (left column) and an uplift (right column). Numbers range from 0 ("none or not applicable") to 3 ("a great deal"). The scale includes 53 items, a sample of which are shown here. © 1988 by the American Psychological Association. Data from DeLongis, Folkman, and Lazarus (1988).

CONNECTIONS

In **Chapter 9,** we discussed different ways that we can increase our well-being. Keeping a journal and recording feelings of gratefulness are associated with increased happiness. Here, we see that uplifts are linked to family satisfaction. Being mindful of the good things in our lives has many benefits.

In Class: Collaborate and Report

In your group, **A)** come up with 10 daily hassles and 10 uplifts that do not already appear in the scale above and to the right. **B)** Discuss how we can create more uplifts and reduce hassles in our lives.

Conflicts

We have discussed a variety of stressors, from major life events to daily hassles. Conflicts can also serve as stressors. When people think of conflict, they may imagine arguments and fistfights, but conflict can also refer to the discomfort one feels when

Tricky Situation
Police officers deal with a variety of conflicts in their daily work. Imagine you are an officer trying to decide whether to arrest a parent suspected of child abuse. If you make the arrest, the child may be removed from the home and placed in foster care—not an ideal scenario, but at least the threat of abuse is removed. This is an approach-avoidance conflict, meaning the outcome has both positive and negative elements. LifetimeStock/Shutterstock.

making tough choices. In an **approach–approach conflict**, two or more favorable alternatives are pitted against each other. Here, you must choose between two options you find attractive. Imagine this situation: You have to pick only one course this semester, and to fit it into your schedule, you must choose between two classes you would really like to take. An **approach–avoidance conflict** occurs when you face a choice or situation that has both favorable and unfavorable characteristics. For example, you are required to take a biology lab class, and although you like biology, you do not enjoy working with other students in a lab setting. A third type of conflict is the **avoidance–avoidance conflict**, which occurs when you are faced with two or more alternatives that are unattractive. In order to fulfill a requirement, you must choose between two courses that you really dread taking.

Let's see how these types of conflict might arise in police work:

- *approach–approach conflict:* Suppose you are a 30-year veteran of the police department. You can either retire now and begin receiving a pension, or continue working in a profession you find rewarding. Both options are positive.

- *approach–avoidance conflict:* Now imagine you are a police officer contemplating whether to arrest a mother and father suspected of child abuse. If you make the arrest, all of the children in the home will be placed in foster care, an unfamiliar, often frightening environment for children. Something good will come out of the change (the children are no longer at risk of suspected abuse), but the downside is that they will be thrust into an unfamiliar environment.

- *avoidance–avoidance conflict:* You are new to the police force. It is your second day on the job, and you are given a choice between the following two tasks: ride in the squad car with a partner you dislike or stay in the station all day and answer calls (a very boring activity). Both decisions lead to negative outcomes.

Now that we have examined different types of stressors, let's explore how the brain and body respond to them.

 show what you know

1. _____ is a response to perceived threats or challenges resulting from stimuli that cause strain.

2. The Social Readjustment Rating Scale was created to measure the severity and frequency of life events. This scale is most often used to examine the relationship between stressors and which of the following?
   a. aging
   b. levels of eustress
   c. perceived threats
   d. illness

3. _____ can occur when a person must adjust to life in a new country, often due to unfamiliar language, religious beliefs, and holidays.
   a. Eustress
   b. Acculturative stress
   c. Uplifts
   d. Posttraumatic stress disorder

4. Reflect on the last few days. Can you think of three uplifts and three hassles you experienced during this period?

✓ CHECK YOUR ANSWERS IN APPENDIX C.

approach–approach conflict A type of conflict in which one must choose between two or more options that are attractive.

approach–avoidance conflict A type of conflict that occurs when one is faced with a choice or situation that has favorable and unfavorable characteristics.

avoidance–avoidance conflict A type of conflict in which one is faced with two or more options that are unattractive.

Responding to Stressors

TROUBLE UNDERCOVER In her 25 years as a police officer, Christy has faced stressors that are completely unfamiliar to the average person. Imagine knocking on someone's door at 3:00 A.M. and delivering a death notice. ("Mrs. X, I regret to inform you that your son died in an accident tonight.") Or, picture yourself entering a home and discovering a toddler covered in bruises and other injuries indicative of child abuse. These types of experiences are emotionally disturbing and stressful. However, they don't bring on the intense, fear-for-your-life type of stress Christy experienced at other points in her career, like the time her cover was nearly blown in an operation to bust crack-cocaine dealers.

Posing as a buyer, Christy walked into a house where a suspected dealer was selling. One of the men hanging out in the house gave her a funny look, and she instantly realized that he recognized her as a police officer. Fortunately, the man did not give her away (who knows what the dealer would have done had her identity been revealed), and Christy escaped the situation unscathed. But we can only imagine what she must have felt at that moment.

Faced with the prospect of being gunned down by a drug dealer, Christy most likely experienced the sensations associated with the **fight-or-flight** response, such as increased pulse, breathing rate, and mental alertness. A coordinated effort of the sympathetic nervous system and the endocrine system, the fight-or-flight reaction primes the body to respond to danger, either by confronting the threat head on (in Christy's case, defending herself against a physical attack) or escaping (bolting out of the crack house). Let's take a closer look at this survival mechanism. ●

Too Stressful? Depends Who You Are
An undercover police officer posing as a prostitute (right) is photographed alongside the "john" who attempted to buy her services in Van Nuys, California. Some people, like Christy, appear to be cut out for undercover police work; they enjoy the excitement, bounce back from traumatic experiences, and adapt when things don't go as planned. Others find the stress overwhelming. David Bro/ZUMA Press/Newscom.

Fight or Flight

LO 4 Identify the brain and body changes that characterize the fight-or-flight response.

When faced with a threatening situation, portions of the brain, including the hypothalamus, activate the sympathetic nervous system, which leads to the secretion of catecholamines such as epinephrine and norepinephrine. These hormones cause heart rate, blood pressure, respiration, and blood flow to the muscles to increase. Meanwhile, digestion slows and the pupils dilate.

Once the emergency has ended, the **parasympathetic system** reverses these processes by reducing heart rate, blood pressure, and so on. If a person is exposed to a threatening situation for long periods of time, the fight-or-flight system remains active. This, in turn, can have detrimental effects on health (Shonkoff et al., 2012), an issue we will explore later.

LO 5 Outline the general adaptation syndrome (GAS).

GENERAL ADAPTATION SYNDROME Hans Selye, introduced earlier in the chapter, identified police work "as likely the most stressful occupation in the world" (according to Violanti, 1992, p. 718). As noted, Selye (1976) proposed that stress is a "nonspecific response" to a stressor, which is "an agent that produces stress." Selye (1936) was also one of the first to suggest the human body responds to prolonged stressors in a predictable way (Selye, 1976). This specific pattern of physiological reactions is called the **general adaptation syndrome (GAS)**.

CONNECTIONS

We introduced the fight-or-flight response in **Chapter 2**. The sympathetic nervous system is a division of the autonomic nervous system, which regulates the body's involuntary activity (such as digestion and the beating of the heart). In this chapter, we learn how this automatic activity may relate to illness.

CONNECTIONS

In **Chapter 2,** we introduced the parasympathetic nervous system, which is responsible for the "rest-and-digest" process following activation of the fight-or-flight response. The parasympathetic nervous system works with the sympathetic nervous system to prepare us for crises and then to calm us when danger has passed.

general adaptation syndrome (GAS)
A specific pattern of physiological reactions to stressors that includes the alarm stage, resistance stage, and exhaustion stage.

Selye's Stages
Endocrinologist Hans Selye proposed that the body passes through a predictable sequence of changes in response to stressors. Selye's general adaptation syndrome includes three phases: the alarm stage, the resistance stage, and the exhaustion stage. Corbis.

According to this theory, the body passes through three stages (**INFOGRAPHIC 12.2**). The first is the *alarm stage,* or the body's initial response to a threatening situation, similar to the fight-or-flight response. Arousal increases, and the body prepares to deal with the threat. Following the alarm stage is the *resistance stage.* During this period, the body maintains a high level of arousal (though not as high as that of the *alarm stage*), but with a decreased response to new stressors. Under such intense physiological demands, the body simply cannot address any new threatening situations that might arise. According to Selye, this is when some people start to show signs of *diseases of adaptation,* such as hypertension and arthritis (Selye, 1953; Selye & Fortier, 1950). If the threat remains and the person can no longer adapt, Selye suggested that the body then moves into the *exhaustion stage.* At this point, the body's resources become depleted, resulting in vulnerability to illnesses, physical exhaustion, and even death.

LO 6 Explain the function of the hypothalamic–pituitary–adrenal (HPA) system.

HYPOTHALAMIC–PITUITARY–ADRENAL SYSTEM Overseeing the sympathetic nervous system's response to stress is the *hypothalamic–pituitary–adrenal (HPA) system* (Infographic 12.2). This HPA system helps to maintain balance in the body by directing not only the sympathetic nervous system, but also the neuroendocrine and immune systems (Ben-Zvi, Vernon, & Broderick, 2009; Spencer, Emmerzaal, Kozicz, & Andrews, 2015). (The immune system defends the body from bacteria, viruses, and other types of invaders by deploying cells and chemicals to confront these threats.) When a stressful situation arises, the hypothalamus alerts the pituitary gland, prompting it to send signals to the adrenal cortex, which secretes corticosteroids such as cortisol. These hormones summon the immune system to fend off a threat and reduce the amount of energy used for nonessential activities (that is, those not associated with the threat), such as digestion and bladder control. The HPA system responds to a stressor in the same way it would to a pathogen—by mobilizing a defense response. You might say it's working overtime. How do you think this affects a person's health?

 **show what you know**

1. According to the _____, the human body responds in a predictable way to stressors, following a specific pattern of physiological reactions.

2. As a police officer, Christy has found herself in life-threatening situations. When faced with danger, Christy's body initially exhibits a fight-or-flight reaction, which is equivalent to the _____ of the general adaptation syndrome.
   a. alarm stage
   b. exhaustion stage
   c. diseases of adaptation
   d. acculturative stress

3. _____ helps maintain balance in the body by overseeing the sympathetic nervous system as well as the neuroendocrine and immune systems.
   a. The general adaptation syndrome
   b. The exhaustion stage
   c. The hypothalamic-pituitary-adrenal system
   d. Eustress

4. Explain the processes that occur in the human body when it is faced with a life-threatening situation.

✓ CHECK YOUR ANSWERS IN APPENDIX C.

Synonyms

hypothalamic–pituitary–adrenal (HPA) system hypothalamic–pituitary–adrenal axis (HPA axis)

health psychology behavioral medicine

health psychology The study of the biological, psychological, and social factors that contribute to health and illness.

Stress and Your Health

For decades, psychologists have been trying to understand how stress impacts human health. Early in the 1960s, the field of **health psychology** began to gather momentum, exploring the biological, psychological, and social factors that contribute to health and illness. Health psychology seeks to explain how food choices, social interactions, and living environments affect our predisposition to illness. Research in this field informs public policy and health education, leading to changes in health-related guidelines and the promotion of positive eating and exercise habits. Health psychologists also study the impact of personality factors,

Physiological Responses to Stress

When faced with an emergency, our bodies go through a series of physiological responses that assist us in coping with a stressor. Activation of the *fight-or-flight* response and *hypothalamic-pituitary-adrenal (HPA)* systems gives us the energy and resources we need to cope with a temporary stressor. Studying these physiological responses, Hans Selye (1956) found that the sequence follows the same path no matter the stressor. Selye called this sequence the general adaptation syndrome (GAS). He found that when the stressor remains, our bodies can no longer adapt.

GENERAL ADAPTATION SYNDROME (GAS)

In the alarm stage, the short-term responses are activated, giving us the energy to combat a threat. In the resistance stage, resources remain mobilized, and we continue to cope with the stressor. But eventually we enter the exhaustion stage, becoming weak and susceptible to illness, and less able to cope with the stressor (Selye, 1956).

STRESSOR

Resistance to stress — high / low

normal level of resistance to stress

Alarm stage
(stress response activated)

Resistance stage
(coping with stressor)

Exhaustion stage
(reserves diminished)

SHORT-TERM RESPONSES TO STRESS

Amygdala processes information about stressor. If threat is perceived, hypothalamus triggers short-term stress response.

STRESSOR

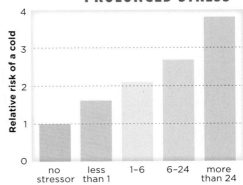

Hypothalamus

Pituitary gland

Adrenal glands

kidneys

FIGHT-OR-FLIGHT SYSTEM

ACTIVATES

Sympathetic Nervous System

SENDS SIGNAL TO

Adrenal Medulla
(core of adrenal glands)

RELEASES

Catecholamines
epinephrine, norepinephrine

CAUSES

Efficient management of bodily resources so they are available for emergency action:
- increased heart rate
- increased respiration
- increased blood flow to muscles
- digestion slows
- pupils dilate

HYPOTHALAMIC-PITUITARY-ADRENAL (HPA) SYSTEM

ALERTS

Pituitary gland

SENDS SIGNAL TO

Adrenal Cortex
(outside layer of adrenal glands)

RELEASES

Corticosteroids
including cortisol

CAUSES

Efficient management of bodily resources; immune system activation

✱ The HPA system manages resources like the fight-or-flight system does, but it takes longer to mobilize these processes, and the effects are more sustained.

PROLONGED STRESS

Relative risk of a cold — 0, 1, 2, 3, 4

Duration of stressor (in months): no stressor / less than 1 / 1–6 / 6–24 / more than 24

Prolonged stress can cause the immune system to break down. As you can see, the risk of becoming sick is directly related to the duration of a stressor. This effect is seen even when the stressor is not traumatic. Data in this study were collected from people reporting on interpersonal conflicts and problems concerning work (Cohen et al., 1998).

Credit: Firefighter, Colin Anderson/AGE Fotostock; Firefighter crouching, Alan Bailey/Shutterstock; Firefighter fighting fire, Chuckmoser/Thinkstock/Getty Images.

TABLE 12.1 LIVING LONGER

Characteristics	Benefits	Application
Innate movement	You don't have to join a gym or compete in triathlons; every physical activity counts.	Walk to work or to the store, bike to school. Find ways to incorporate natural movement into your daily life.
Find meaning	Purpose outside of your job makes it easier to wake up each morning; knowing your purpose can extend life expectancy.	Find your motivation for life. What energizes you?
Slow down	Stress affects everyone, but slowing down reduces inflammation that can lead to many age-related illnesses.	Meditate, pray, or nap.
"80% rule"	Helps prevent weight gain and overeating.	Stop eating when you feel 80% full.
Eat more plants	Inexpensive source of complex carbs, fiber, and protein.	Eat lean; make beans and vegetables the bulk of your diet. Limit your intake of meat.
Social support	Healthy friends encourage healthy behaviors.	Surround yourself with people who encourage healthy living and happiness.
Family first	Time spent with grandparents, parents, and a committed life partner can extend life expectancy.	Create strong family ties, and keep loved ones in close proximity.

Can you live a long, healthy, low-stress life? It is possible, according to Dan Buettner, especially if you adopt the characteristics listed above, which are commonly observed in "blue zone" regions of the world. Information from Buettner, 2015.

coping style, cognitive appraisal, poverty, culture, social support, and religion—all topics addressed in this chapter (**INFOGRAPHIC 12.3** on page 514).

ACROSS THE WORLD
The "Blue Zones"

Can the place you reside contribute to your level of stress and overall health? A group of researchers working with the National Geographic Society set out to identify regions of the world with the highest number of people living over 100 years.

"BLUE ZONES" OFFER CLUES ON HOW TO LIVE A LONG AND HEALTHY LIFE.

(These locations came to be called "blue zones" because someone used a blue pen to circle one of them on a map; Buettner, 2015).

To qualify as a blue zone, an area had to be inhabited by people reaching old age without health issues such as diabetes, cancer, obesity, and heart trouble. Five areas in the world made the cut: Ikaria, Greece; Okinawa, Japan; Ogliastra Region, Sardinia; Loma Linda, California; Nicoya Peninsula, Costa Rica. What unique features of these areas allow for such longevity (Buettner, 2015; see **TABLE 12.1**)?

Are these characteristics for a long, healthy life limited to blue zones? Apparently not. If you stay physically active, limit stress, eat locally grown foods, and surround yourself with strong social support, you, too, might live to be a centenarian (Govindaraju, Atzmon, & Barzilai, 2015; Poulain, Herm, & Pes, 2013).

Is Stress Making You Sick?

LO 7 **Explain how stressors relate to health problems.**

Before we further explore the connection between stress and illness, we must understand how the body deals with illness. Let's take a side trip into introductory biology

Synonyms

B lymphocytes B cells

T lymphocytes T cells

lymphocyte Type of white blood cell produced in the bone marrow whose job is to battle enemies such as viruses and bacteria.

and learn about the body's main defense against disease—the immune system (**FIGURE 12.3**). The immune system is made up of the spleen, lymph nodes, and bone marrow. When disease-causing invaders threaten the body, the immune system deploys a special army of white blood cells called **lymphocytes**. Lymphocytes are produced in bone marrow, and their job is to battle enemies such as viruses and bacteria. When the body is expending its resources to deal with an ongoing stressor, the immune system is less powerful, and the work of lymphocytes is compromised.

Like a platoon of soldiers, the immune system has a defense team to fight off invaders. Should the intruder(s) get past the skin, the *macrophages* ("big eaters") are ready to attack. These cells hunt and consume invaders as well as worn-out cells in the body. Cells that have been affected by invaders, such as viruses and cancer, are the targets of *natural killer cells* (*NK cells*), which inject compromised cells with a deadly chemical. In addition, NK cells release a protein that prevents the infection from spreading to other cells. In some cases, the body must call on its "special ops" teams. These are the _B lymphocytes_ and _T lymphocytes_. The B lymphocytes mature in the bone marrow and produce antibodies that chemically inhibit bacteria. The T lymphocytes mature in the thymus and play an integral role in fighting cancer, viruses, and other disease-causing agents that the B lymphocytes have not been successful in warding off (Matloubain et al., 2004; Straub, 2014).

With that immunology lesson under our belt, let's examine some of the diseases thought to be associated with stressors.

GASTRIC ULCERS AND STRESSORS Gastric ulcers have long been thought to be associated with stress, but the nature of this link has not always been clear. For many years, it was believed that stress alone caused gastric ulcers, but researchers then started to suspect other culprits. They found evidence that the bacterium *H. pylori* plays an important role. This does not mean that *H. pylori* is always to blame, however. Some people who carry the bacteria never get ulcers, while others develop ulcers in its absence. It seems that many factors influence the development of ulcers—among them, tobacco use, family history, and excess gastric acid (Fink, 2011).

CANCER AND STRESSORS Cancer has also been associated with stress, both in terms of risk and development. Specifically, stress has been linked to the suppression of T lymphocytes and NK cells, which help monitor immune system reactions to the invasion of developing tumors. When a person is exposed to stressors, the body is less able to mount an effective immune response, which increases the risk of cancer (Reiche, Nunes, & Morimoto, 2004).

In the United States and other Western countries, breast cancer is the greatest cancer risk for women. Researchers have identified a number of stressors related to cancer (specifically breast and ovarian). Cancer often causes financial stress due to the high costs of treatment, the limited amount of sick leave one might have, and the physical pain associated with the illness (Andreotti, Root, Ahles, McEwen, & Compas, 2015).

Stress has been correlated with other types of cancer, though not always in the expected direction. One group of researchers examined the relationship between chronic

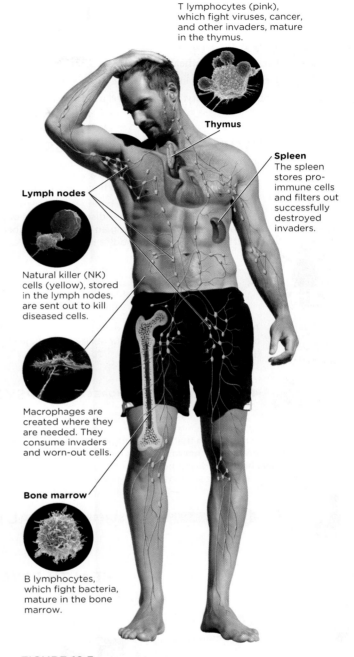

T lymphocytes (pink), which fight viruses, cancer, and other invaders, mature in the thymus.

Thymus

Spleen
The spleen stores pro-immune cells and filters out successfully destroyed invaders.

Lymph nodes

Natural killer (NK) cells (yellow), stored in the lymph nodes, are sent out to kill diseased cells.

Macrophages are created where they are needed. They consume invaders and worn-out cells.

Bone marrow

B lymphocytes, which fight bacteria, mature in the bone marrow.

FIGURE 12.3
The Immune System
Our immunity derives from a complex system involving structures and organs throughout the body that support the work of specialized cell types to keep us healthy. Man: B2M Productions/Getty Images. T lymphocytes & B lymphocytes: Steve Gschmeissner/ Science Source. Natural killer cell & macrophage: Eye of Science/Science Source.

Health Psychology

Health psychology is the study of the biological, psychological, and social factors that contribute to health and illness. Using the biopsychosocial perspective, health psychologists examine how a variety of factors, including diet, physical activity, and social relationships, impact our predisposition to illness. One of the primary goals is to increase positive health behaviors and decrease negative ones. Research in this field can benefit the health and well-being of individuals and the community at large through changes to public policy and health education.

Understanding Stress: The Biopsychosocial Perspective

Stress has been linked to a variety of negative health outcomes. The biopsychosocial perspective helps us understand how the interaction between these factors contribute to our vulnerability.

Viruses, bacteria, and other disease-causing organisms invade the body, triggering an immune response and putting a strain on the body's resources.

Exercise is one of the best ways to buffer against stress and its negative effects (MILANI & LAVIE, 2009).

MORE STRESS **BIOLOGY** LESS STRESS

A perceived lack of control, even in mundane aspects of life, profoundly impacts our ability to manage stress (PAGNINI, BERCOVITZ, & LANGER, 2016; RODIN, 1986).

Research has shown that mindfulness meditation helps ease anxiety and depression (GOYAL ET AL., 2014).

 OH NO!

MORE STRESS **PSYCHOLOGY** LESS STRESS

OM

Research has shown that feeling judged on one's race, gender, income level and other factors has a negative impact on physical health and well-being (CLARK, DesMEULES, LUO, DUNCAN, & WIELGOSZ, 2009; WILLIAMS & MOHAMMED, 2009).

As a species, human beings are social and benefit from interaction with other humans and even animals (ALLEN, 2003; JOHN-HENDERSON, STELLAR, MENDOZA-DENTON, & FRANCIS, 2015).

MORE STRESS **SOCIAL INTERACTION** LESS STRESS

HEALTH PSYCHOLOGY APPLIED

BIOLOGY
What's in a Color?

PANTONE 448C

With public health in mind, Australia and the United Kingdom have begun requiring cigarette packs to be wrapped in "Opaque Couché" (Pantone 448C), deemed the ugliest color across the globe (BLAKEMORE, 2016, JUNE 9, PARA. 2). The packaging also features shocking images of smoking-related health consequences. Smoking rates in Australia fell after the new packaging was implemented and tobacco taxes were raised (AUSTRALIAN DEPARTMENT OF HEALTH, 2016, MAY 27; BLAKEMORE, 2016, JUNE 9).

PSYCHOLOGY
The Power of Thinking "Beyond the Now"

College students who were able to think about and plan for their futures showed an increase in positive health behaviors, such as exercise and conscientious eating habits (VISSER & HIRSH, 2014).

SOCIAL INTERACTION
Animal Therapy in Crisis Management

Recognizing how animals can help people manage stress, professionals now use therapy dogs to facilitate coping (ALLEN, 2003; ASSOCIATED PRESS, 2014, MAY 8; CUNNINGHAM & EDELMAN, 2012, DECEMBER 17; FIEGL, 2012, DECEMBER 12).

daily stressors and the development of colorectal cancer using a prospective study in which nearly 12,000 Danes (who had never been diagnosed with colorectal cancer) were followed for 18 years (Nielsen et al., 2008). The researchers noted some surprising findings, particularly with respect to females. Women who reported higher levels of "stress intensity" and "daily stress" were less likely to develop colon cancer during the course of the study. In contrast, men with "high stress intensity" experienced higher levels of rectal cancer, although this association was not considered to be strong because only a small number actually developed this kind of cancer. The authors suggested that a variety of physiological, mental, and behavioral factors (for example, sex hormones, burnout, and increased alcohol intake) were involved in the relationship between high stress and lower rates of colon cancer in the women.

Why can't researchers definitively characterize the link between cancer and stressors? Part of the problem is that studies frequently focus on stressors of different durations. Short- and long-term stressors have distinct effects on the immune system, and thus its ability to combat cancer (Dhabhar, 2014; Segerstrom & Miller, 2004). For short-lived stressors such as midterm exams, public speaking, and other activities lasting between 5 and 100 minutes, the body responds by increasing the number of NK cells and deploying other immune cells where needed. In other words, short-term stressors tend to augment immune functioning. The situation is quite different with long-term stressors such as military deployment or caring for someone with dementia, which are associated with decreases in NK cells. In order to appreciate the complex relationship between stress, immune function, and cancer, we must also consider biopsychosocial influences. Factors such as age, medical history, social support, and mental health can mediate the link between stressors and cancer (Reiche et al., 2004; Segerstrom & Miller, 2004).

CARDIOVASCULAR DISEASE AND STRESSORS The same is true for the relationship between stressors and cardiovascular disease. Dimsdale (2008) noted that over 40,000 citations popped up in a medical database when the search terms "stress" and "heart disease" were used. What constitutes a stressor in this context? Earthquakes, unhappy marriages, and caregiving burdens are just a few stressors associated with a variety of outcomes or vulnerabilities, ranging from abnormalities in heart function to sudden death. Earlier, we discussed socioeconomic status and stress; it turns out that both of those variables are factors in cardiovascular disease. Joseph and colleagues reported fivefold higher odds of experiencing "cardiometabolic events" (within 5 years) for people who became unemployed as a result of Hurricane Katrina, a devastating natural disaster that occurred in 2005 (Joseph, Matthews, & Myers, 2014). The faster people get support to decrease "socioeconomic disruptions" related to a disaster, the better their health outcomes.

Other stressors have also been linked to heart disease. "Social-evaluative threats," or concerns about being judged by others (about physical appearance or behaviors in a social context, for example), are associated with increases in blood pressure and consequently an elevated risk of heart disease (Smith, Birmingham, & Uchino, 2012). One model suggests that increased job stress can put people at greater risk for developing coronary heart disease, particularly those who perceive a significant degree of job "strain" resulting from high demands, lack of control, and other factors (Ferris, Kline, & Bourdage, 2012).

The exact nature of the relationship between stressors, high blood pressure, and cardiovascular disease is not totally understood (Straub, 2014). However, we do know that an increase of fatty deposits, inflammation, and scar tissue within artery walls, that is, *atherosclerosis,* is a dangerous risk factor for stroke and heart disease (Go et al., 2013). With this type of damage, blood flow in an artery may become blocked

CONNECTIONS

In **Chapter 6,** we discussed the malleability of memory. Problems may arise when study participants are asked to remember events and illnesses from the past. Here, we describe a prospective study, which does not require participants to retrieve information from the distant past, thus reducing opportunities for error.

Battling Stress
A group of Marines practice patrolling techniques as part of their combat training. Long-term stressors such as military deployment are associated with declines in activity of NK cells, which help the body fight infections (Dhabhar, 2014). Scott Olson/Getty Images.

or reduced. Researchers are not sure exactly how atherosclerosis starts, but one theory suggests that it begins with damage to the inner layer of the artery wall, which may be caused by elevated cholesterol and triglycerides, high blood pressure, and cigarette smoke (American Heart Association, 2014a). It is important to note that stressors cannot be shown to *cause* changes in cardiovascular health (Dimsdale, 2008). Although there is a clear correlation between biopsychosocial stressors and cardiovascular disease, we cannot say with certainty that these stressors are responsible (Ferris et al., 2012).

Stress and Substances

A great way to promote cardiovascular health and reduce stress is exercise. Both Christy and her husband, Ron, who also works in law enforcement, combat stress with regular workouts. They also unwind by sharing food and drink with friends. "A good way to deal with stress is laughter, or working out, getting together with your friends, enjoying a good meal," says Christy, but she is careful to point out the importance of moderation. Christy and her husband do not drink excessively, but they have seen how the overindulgence of alcohol can ruin careers.

In Chapter 4, on consciousness, we described how people use alcohol and other drugs for recreational purposes, and how anesthesiologists rely on drugs to alleviate pain, block memories, and toy with various aspects of consciousness. But a discussion of drugs is also in order here, because many people mistakenly view substances as stress relievers. Psychologists explain this type of behavior with *the self-medication hypothesis,* which suggests that people turn to drugs and alcohol to reduce anxiety (Swendsen et al., 2000).

As you can see, stress often exerts its harmful effects indirectly (Cohen, Miller, & Rabin, 2001). When faced with stressors, we may sleep poorly, eat erratically, and perhaps abuse substances. These behavioral tendencies can lead to significant health problems (Benham, 2010; Ng & Jeffery, 2003).

SMOKING AND STRESS Smokers report that they smoke more cigarettes in response to stressors, as they believe it improves their mood. The association between lighting up and feeling good is one reason smokers have such a hard time quitting (Lerman & Audrain-McGovern, 2010). One study found that when participants were forced to abstain from smoking for some time (a half day, for example), their mood improved when they finally puffed on a cigarette. However, forgoing cigarettes was the only stressful condition of the study in which smoking heightened mood; the effect was not observed when participants were made to prepare for a public-speaking task, for example (Perkins, Karelitz, Conklin, Sayette, & Giedgowd, 2010). Yet, such findings are inconsistent with the self-reports of smokers, who claim that they smoke to feel better in a variety of stressful situations. And, due to the extreme health problems that smoking creates, smoking itself may eventually become the stressor.

How do we get people to kick a habit that is perceived as so pleasurable? One effective way is to meet them where they are, rather than taking a one-size-fits-all approach (Mahoney, 2010; Prochaska, Velicer, Prochaska, Delucchi, & Hall, 2006). In other words, we should recognize that not all smokers need the same type of help. Some need assistance with smoking only; others engage in additional risky behaviors, like eating high-fat diets or getting too much sun. Yet, even if we tailor interventions to address the needs of the individual, the road to recovery may be bumpy. Remember that nicotine is extremely addictive. Repeated use can lead to tolerance; the more you use a drug, the more you need to achieve the same effect.

ALCOHOL AND STRESS Much the same could be said for alcohol, another drug frequently used to "take the edge off," or counteract, the unpleasant feelings

It's Not Medicine
Some people turn to alcohol and other drugs for stress relief, but the self-medication approach is not effective. A better strategy might be jogging in the park, laughing with a friend, or doing some deep breathing exercises.
Image Source/Alamy.

CONNECTIONS

In **Chapter 4,** we discussed the concept of tolerance. When we use drugs, such as nicotine, they alter the chemistry of the brain and body. Over time, the body adapts to the drug and therefore needs more and more of it to create the original effect.

associated with stress. Perhaps you know someone who "needs" a drink to relax after a rough day. Teenagers, in particular, appear to rely on alcohol to cope with daily hassles (Bailey & Covell, 2011). Adolescents frequently face disagreements with family members, teachers, and peers. They may worry about how they look and whether they are succeeding in school. We need to help adolescents find new and more "healthy" ways to handle these hassles. This means providing more support in schools, and perhaps educating teachers and counselors about the tendency to self-medicate with drugs and alcohol. Researchers have found that people who start using alcohol early in life and have a "greater number of stressful life events demonstrated the highest consumption of alcohol in early adulthood" (Stanger, Abaied, & Wagner, 2016, p. 483).

Later, we will discuss some positive coping strategies for teens and adults alike, but first let's see how some people seem to thrive under stress. Get ready to meet Kehlen Kirby, our next first responder.

Tetra Images/
Superstock.

ADRENALINE JUNKIES Kehlen Kirby sees more pain and suffering in one month than most people do in a lifetime. Working as an emergency medical services (EMS) provider in Pueblo, Colorado, this young man has witnessed the highest highs and lowest lows of human experience. He has rescued people from flaming car wrecks, treated teenage gang members for stab and gunshot wounds, and watched chain-smokers who are dying from emphysema beg for cigarettes en route to the hospital. In between the sadness and suffering, there are also stories of hope and inspiration, as when Kehlen and his colleagues delivered a baby on the shoulder of U.S. Route 50, and the mother went from a state of screaming hysteria to smiling, laughing bliss.

The reward of alleviating human suffering is "incredible," according to Kehlen. Imagine walking into the home of a diabetic who is lying on the floor, unconscious and surrounded by trembling family members. You insert an IV line into the patient's vein and deliver D50, a dextrose solution that increases blood sugar. In a few moments, the person is awake as if nothing happened. The family is ecstatic; you have saved their loved one from potential brain damage or death. "People that like to do selfless acts, I think, are made for this job," Kehlen says. And for those who enjoy a good challenge, both physical and mental, an EMS career will not disappoint. Try working for 24 hours in a row, making life-and-death decisions, hoisting heavy bodies onto stretchers, and crouching over patients until your joints burn.

But there appears to be something else drawing people into the EMS profession. You might call it the "adrenaline junkie" factor. Ever since Kehlen was a small boy, he enjoyed a certain amount of risk taking. He was the kid who fearlessly scaled the monkey bars and leaped off the jungle gym, and many of his colleagues claim they were the same way. "All of us probably thought we were 10 feet tall and made of steel," Kehlen says, careful to note that "daring" is not the same as "reckless." One must be calculating when it comes to determining what risks are worth taking.

The adrenaline junkie quality is also apparent in some police officers, according to Christy. An officer patrolling a city beat probably experiences the so-called adrenaline rush at least a few times per week. "When a hot call comes in, anyone worth their salt wants to go," Christy explains ("hot call" meaning anything full of excitement and drama, like a robbery in progress).

Is there really some common adrenaline junkie tendency among police officers, EMS providers, and other first responders? That remains an open question.

Life Saver
Kehlen Kirby has one of the most stressful jobs imaginable—providing emergency medical services to people injured in car accidents, fires, and other traumatic incidents. The constant exposure to pain and suffering helps Kehlen maintain perspective on the hassles of daily life; he doesn't sweat the small stuff. Leslie Nazario/Portraits by Leslie.

CONNECTIONS

In **Chapter 9,** we introduced arousal theory, which suggests behaviors can arise out of the need for stimulation or arousal. Here, we point out that some people seek stressors in order to maintain a satisfying level of arousal.

Arousal theory tells us that humans seek an optimal level of arousal, and what is *optimal* differs from person to person. We also know that first responders are frequently exposed to highly stressful events (Anderson, Litzenberger, & Plecas, 2002; Gayton & Lovell, 2012). Could it be that people like Kehlen and Christy are drawn to these careers because they satisfy a need for arousal? Perhaps, but even adrenaline junkies have their limits. When stress is constant, the body and mind begin to suffer. ●

Too Much Cortisol

LO 8	**List some consequences of prolonged exposure to the stress hormone cortisol.**

Earlier, we discussed the stress hormone cortisol, which plays an important role in mobilizing the body to react to threats and other stressful situations. Cortisol is useful if you are responding to immediate danger, like a raging fire or ruthless assailant. However, you don't want cortisol levels to remain high for long. Both body and brain are impacted when the cortisol system flips into overdrive.

CORTISOL AND KIDS The negative effects of stress are apparent very early in life. Infants born to mothers subjected to natural disasters, trauma, and other extreme stressors are more likely to be born prematurely, have low birth weights, exhibit behavioral difficulties, and perhaps even show problems with cognitive development (Davis & Sandman, 2010; Tollenaar, Beijers, Jansen, Riksen-Walraven, & De Weerth, 2011). Prenatal stressors have also been associated with fussing and crying, but this link might be indirect (Field & Diego, 2008); such temperamental difficulties could be due to preterm birth (Baibazarova et al., 2013).

Now consider the types of stressors some preschool children confront every day. Research shows that conflicts at home can increase cortisol levels in children (Slatcher & Robles, 2012). Verbal exchanges such as the child exclaiming, "No! I don't want to!" and parents saying, "You are going to shut your mouth and be quiet!" are exactly the types of conflicts associated with increased cortisol levels. Cortisol activity may help explain why exposure to conflict during childhood seems to pave the way for health problems (Slatcher & Robles, 2012).

There is little doubt that cortisol plays a role in early development. But how does this stress hormone affect teens?

THINK IT THROUGH
Waking Up Is Hard to Do

Think back to your days in high school. Like many of today's teens, you probably balanced multiple responsibilities—schoolwork, extracurricular activities, and perhaps a part-time job. After doing homework late into the night, you drifted off to sleep, only to have your slumber rudely cut short by an annoying alarm clock. You scrambled to get to school before the first bell rang (usually well before 8:00 A.M.), and slogged through your morning classes feeling tired and exhausted because you simply did not get enough sleep.

LATER SCHOOL START TIMES ARE LINKED TO IMPROVED ACADEMIC AND HEALTH OUTCOMES FOR TEENS.

Many U.S. high school students deal with this type of scenario on a regular basis, and their sleep deprivation may have serious consequences. Evidence suggests that inadequate sleep and other sleep issues lead to heightened levels of cortisol, which could play a role in "academic, behavioral and health problems" (Mrug, Tyson, Turan, & Granger, 2016, p. 95). For example, teens who get less than 8 hours of sleep are more likely to experience symptoms of depression, use caffeine, and have an elevated risk for substance use (Wahlstrom et al., 2014).

One way to help teenagers get more sleep is to push back school start times. According to a study by researchers at the University of Minnesota, more than 60% of high school students would be able to get 8 hours of sleep if classes started after 8:30 A.M. Such an intervention could reduce absenteeism and tardiness and potentially improve grades and performance on standardized tests. It may even help young people stay safe; the researchers also found there was a 70% decrease in the number of car accidents among drivers ages 16 to 18 when school start times changed from 7:35 A.M. to 8:55 A.M. (Wahlstrom et al., 2014). Evaluating this evidence, the American Academy of Pediatrics "urges middle and high schools to aim for start times that allow students to receive 8.5–9.5 hours of sleep at night" (American Academy of Pediatrics, 2014, August 25, para. 10).

With all of this research pointing to the benefits of a later start time, why haven't more school districts implemented this change? Many are resistant to changing start times because it may complicate school bus transportation, parents' work schedules, child care, and school sports (Wahlstrom et al., 2014). Do you think the benefits of later start times outweigh the costs? 🧠

Now that we have explored how excess cortisol impacts children and teens, let's see how it might affect the functioning of adults. We'll use a law enforcement scenario as our example.

CORTISOL ON THE JOB How might heightened cortisol levels impact the behaviors of police officers making on-the-spot safety decisions? In one study, researchers had police officers participate in a realistic simulation of being targeted by shooters. Not only did the officers' cortisol levels rise, but the functioning of their working memory decreased (Taverniers, Smeets, Van Ruysseveldt, Syroit, & von Grumbkow, 2011). Can you imagine the implications of being in a dangerous situation with impaired working memory? Think of the last time you were really afraid, and how difficult it was to think clearly. Your working memory was probably compromised.

Other research suggests that heightened cortisol levels may decrease errors in decision making. When police officers had to make threat-related decisions in a video simulation, they were better able to discern whether an individual was armed when their cortisol levels were high. But this accuracy increased when the officer faced a simulation involving a Black suspect, and decreased when the suspect was White. This finding was the same for the White officers and minority officers participating in the study. The researchers concluded that higher cortisol levels, which were caused by the stressful situation, resulted in "heightened vigilance for danger" (Akinola & Mendes, 2012, p. 172). Apparently, the *perceived* threat of Black men was greater, which is consistent with what social psychologists have learned about the conscious and unconscious reactions many people have to racial minorities (Chapter 15). A more recent meta-analysis of studies concluded that participants engaged in shooting tasks were "quicker to shoot armed Black targets, slower to not shoot unarmed Black targets, and were more likely to have a liberal shooting threshold for Black targets" (Mekawi & Bresin, 2015, p. 128).

PSYCHONEUROIMMUNOLOGY We have now discussed some of the effects of short- and long-term stressors. You know that a spurt of cortisol steps up immunity and prepares the body to confront a threat. You also know that if cortisol levels remain high for prolonged periods (as occurs with chronic stressors), the immune system may not function at an optimal level. We discussed how this affects one's risk for developing gastric ulcers, cancer, and heart disease, but the list of negative health effects is much

Performance Anxiety
Heightened cortisol levels can help or hinder a person studying for a math test. For people with "higher working memory" and low math anxiety, cortisol seems to boost performance, but it has the opposite effect when math anxiety is high (Mattarella-Micke, Mateo, Kozak, Foster, & Beilock, 2011). Alejandro Rivera/Getty Images.

CONNECTIONS

In **Chapter 6,** we presented the concept of working memory, which refers to how we actively maintain and manipulate information in short-term memory. Here, we see how these activities can be impacted by stressful situations.

You Asked, Christy Answers

http://qrs.ly/745a5fk

How do you unwind from the daily stresses of work?

scan this ➜

longer. According to a meta-analysis of over 300 studies, chronic stressors were found to be associated with problematic immune system responses, which may increase the risk for various illnesses involving inflammation, including asthma, allergies, multiple sclerosis, and rheumatoid arthritis (Segerstrom & Miller, 2004). The exact nature of these relationships has yet to be determined, but researchers are working hard to uncover them, especially for people who are aging and have vulnerable immune systems (Cohen et al., 2001). It is an exciting time for those who specialize in the field of **psychoneuroimmunology** (SI-koh-NUR-oh-IM-mu-NOL-oh-gee), which examines the relationships among psychological factors (such as coping, emotions, and beliefs), the nervous system, and the functioning of the immune system (Slavich, 2016).

The field of health psychology, which draws on the biopsychosocial model and psychoneuroimmunology, has shed light on the complex relationship between stress and health (Havelka, Lučanin, & Lučanin, 2009). Now that we understand how profoundly stressors can impact physical well-being, let's explore how different people tolerate and respond to stress.

 show what you know

1. When everyday stressors get to be too much, some people seek relief in alcohol. The _____ suggests that people turn to drugs and alcohol to ease anxiety.

2. Infants born to mothers subjected to extreme stressors may be born prematurely, have low birth weight, and exhibit

behavioral difficulties. These outcomes result from increased levels of the stress hormone _____.
   a. *H. pylori*   c. cortisol
   b. lymphocytes   d. NK cells

3. Why are people under stress more likely to get sick?

√ CHECK YOUR ANSWERS IN APPENDIX C.

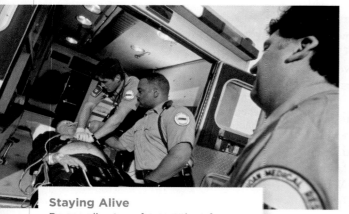

Staying Alive
Paramedics transfer a patient from ambulance to emergency room. The patient is clearly experiencing a health crisis, but the paramedics face their own set of health risks. Working odd hours, not getting enough exercise, eating poorly, and dealing with the ongoing stressors of paramedic work make staying healthy a challenge.
Juan Manuel Silva/AGE Fotostock.

psychoneuroimmunology The field that studies the relationships among psychological factors, the nervous system, and immune system functioning.

burnout Emotional, mental, and physical fatigue that results in reduced motivation, enthusiasm, and performance.

Can You Deal?

First responders encounter a variety of disturbing scenarios, from accidents involving children to the injury or death of close colleagues. Sometimes stressors pile up so high they become difficult to tolerate. When we can no longer deal with stress in a constructive way, we experience what psychologists call *burnout*.

AMBULANCE BURNOUT Kehlen has been in the EMS field for nearly a decade, and most of that time he has spent working for a private ambulance company. He estimates that the average ambulance worker lasts about 8 years before quitting to pursue another line of work. What makes this career so hard to endure? The pay is modest, the 24-hour shifts grueling, and the constant exposure to trauma profoundly disturbing. The pressure to perform is enormous, but there is seldom a "thank-you" or recognition for a job well done. Perhaps no other profession involves so much responsibility—combined with so little appreciation. "The ambulance crews, they're kind of like the silent heroes," Kehlen explains. "You work so hard and you don't get any thanks at the end of the day."

It might not surprise you that the EMS profession has one of the highest rates of *burnout* (Gayton & Lovell, 2012). **Burnout** refers to emotional, mental, and physical fatigue that results from repeated exposure to challenges, leading to reduced motivation, enthusiasm, and performance. People who work in the helping professions, such as nurses, mental health professionals, and child protection workers, are clearly at risk for burnout (Jenaro, Flores, & Arias, 2007; Linnerooth, Mrdjenovich, & Moore, 2011; Rupert, Stevanovic, & Hunley, 2009). Some of the factors contributing to burnout include the substantial demands of the job, long work shifts, insufficient support from coworkers and supervisors, and lack of ongoing education. At times burnout is a sign of something worse to come, like substance abuse or thoughts of suicide (Bragard, Dupuis, & Fleet, 2015). ●

I Can Deal: Coping with Stress

Police officers are also susceptible to burnout. The nature of the work they do, the size of the department they work in, and the amount of trust they must place in their coworkers all play a role (McCarty, Schuck, Skogan, & Rosenbaum, 2011, January 7). To survive and thrive in this career, you must excel under pressure. Police departments need officers who are emotionally stable and capable of making split-second decisions with potentially serious ethical implications. If a tired, stressed-out officer makes one bad decision, the reputation of the entire police department could be tarnished. No wonder over 90% of city police departments in the United States require job applicants to take psychological tests, such as the Minnesota Multiphasic Personality Inventory (MMPI–2–RF; Ben-Porath, 2012; Butcher & Rouse, 1996; Cochrane, Tett, & Vandecreek, 2003). Psychological testing is just one hurdle facing the aspiring police officer; some departments also insist on full-length meetings with a psychologist. Most city agencies require criminal background checks, polygraph (lie detector) tests, and physical fitness assessments. Then there are the 1,000-or-so hours of training at the police academy (Cochrane et al., 2003). But even after overcoming all the hurdles of the hiring process, some police officers end up struggling with stress management. In this respect, police work is like any other field; there will always be people who have trouble coping with the stress of their job. As Christy explains, "Officers are just a segment of society. Some people deal with stuff really well, and others, they can't get past it, they can't put it out of their mind."

Drained
A nurse holds a patient's IV bag in the emergency room. Nursing is one of the professions associated with a high rate of burnout—the emotional, mental, and physical exhaustion that develops when a person faces constant challenges. Lisa Krantz/San Antonio Express-News/Zuma Press.

LO 9   Illustrate how appraisal influences coping.

APPRAISAL AND COPING Needless to say, people respond to stress in their own unique ways. Psychologist Richard Lazarus (1922–2002) suggested that stress is the result of a person's appraisal of a stressor, not necessarily the stressor itself (Folkman & Lazarus, 1985; Lazarus & Folkman, 1984). This viewpoint stands in contrast to Selye's suggestion (noted earlier) that we all react to stressors in a similar manner. **Coping** refers to the cognitive, behavioral, and emotional abilities used to manage something that is perceived as difficult or challenging. In order to cope, we must determine if an event is harmful, threatening, or challenging (**INFOGRAPHIC 12.4** on the next page). A person making a **primary appraisal** of a situation determines how the event will affect him. He must decide if it is irrelevant, positive, challenging, or harmful. Next, the individual makes a **secondary appraisal**, or decides how to respond, considering what resources are available. If he believes he can cope with virtually any challenge that comes his way, the impact of stress remains low. If he thinks his coping abilities are poor, then the impact of stress will be high. These differences in appraisals help explain why two people can react to the same event in dramatically different ways.

There are two basic types of coping. **Problem-focused coping** means taking a direct approach, confronting a problem head-on. Suppose you are having trouble in a relationship; an example of problem-focused coping might be reading self-help books or finding a counselor. **Emotion-focused coping** involves addressing the emotions that surround a problem, rather than trying to solve it or change the situation. With a troubled relationship, you might think about your feelings, look to friends for support, or exercise to take your mind off it, instead of addressing the problem directly. Sometimes it's better to use emotion-focused coping—when an emotional reaction might be too stressful or interferes with daily functioning, or when a problem cannot be solved (for example, the death of a loved one). In the long run, however, problem-focused coping is usually more productive.

CONNECTIONS

In **Chapter 9,** we described the cognitive appraisal theory of emotion, which suggests that emotion results from the way people appraise or interpret interactions they have. We appraise events based on their significance, and this subjective appraisal influences our response to stressors.

coping The cognitive, behavioral, and emotional abilities used to manage something that is perceived as difficult or challenging.

primary appraisal One's initial assessment of a situation to determine its personal impact and whether it is irrelevant, positive, challenging, or harmful.

secondary appraisal An assessment to determine how to respond to a challenging or threatening situation.

problem-focused coping A coping strategy in which a person deals directly with a problem by attempting to solve and address it head-on.

emotion-focused coping A coping strategy in which a person addresses the emotions that surround a problem, as opposed to trying to solve it.

The Process of Coping

Coping refers to the cognitive, emotional, and behavioral methods we employ to manage stressful events. But we don't always rely on the same strategies to manage stressors in our lives. Coping is an individual *process* through which we appraise a stressor to determine how it will affect us and how we can respond.

I have a final exam!

stressful encounter

MAY **12** Math Final

How will this affect me?

BEFORE TEST

PRIMARY APPRAISAL

DURING TEST

PRIMARY APPRAISAL

***Now** how will this affect me?*

Most stressful events are not static. Therefore, we may appraise them at different stages with different results. For example, you will appraise the challenge of a test differently before you take it, while you are taking it, and after you have taken it but are waiting to receive a grade.

There will be independent responses from each instance of primary appraisal.

I missed a lot of classes and don't understand the material.

STRESS!

I don't know how to manage this.

PERSON "X"

CHALLENGING

PERSON "Y"

POSITIVE

I'm doing well in class. I will still get a good grade for the class even if I don't do that well on the final.

not too stressed

I can cope with this.

People respond differently to stressors depending on how they appraise them. A student who is struggling in a class because she hasn't worked hard may find a test even more challenging than a student who has been working hard all semester.

SECONDARY APPRAISAL

What can I do?

SECONDARY APPRAISAL

What can I do?

Once we know how an event will affect us, we use secondary appraisal to determine our response, taking into consideration what resources are available.

✳ problem focused

Seek help from friends

emotion focused

Seek emotional support

✳ problem focused

Planning

emotion focused

Emphasize the positive

I'll get notes from a classmate.

I'll feel better after venting.

First I'll take the online self-quiz, then I'll look up incorrect answers in my textbook.

I feel so much better when I study.

In response to a stressor, most people use several coping strategies, including both problem-focused and emotion-focused coping. Problem-focused coping involves doing something to deal with the source of stress. People who do not feel they can solve the problem tend to rely more on emotion-focused coping to manage their feelings about the situation.

emotion focused

Mental disengagement

✳ problem focused

Suppress competing activities

I don't care about this class anyway.

I won't go out this weekend so I can focus on studying.

✳ **Problem-focused coping is usually the most productive. Here are some other problem-focused strategies:**

➡ Restraint (wait to act until all relevant data has come to light)

➡ Break the problem into manageable chunks

➡ Research the situation

➡ Pursue alternatives

In Class: Collaborate and Report

Team up and **A)** explain the meaning of primary and secondary appraisal, as well as problem- and emotion-focused coping. **B)** Follow the steps outlined in Infographic 12.4 using a different stressful encounter (for example, an upcoming marriage, a new job, or a newborn baby).

We all have distinct ways of dealing with stress, and these coping styles appear to be related to our personalities. In fact, personality appears to have a profound effect on our predispositions to stress-related illness.

LO 10 Describe Type A and Type B personalities and explain how they relate to stress.

TYPE A AND TYPE B PERSONALITIES For decades, researchers have known that people with certain personality types are prone to developing cardiovascular disease. Cardiologists Meyer Friedman (1910–2001) and Ray Rosenman (1920–2013) were among the first to suspect a link between personality type and the cardiovascular problems they observed in their patients (Friedman & Rosenman, 1974). In particular, they noted that many of the people they treated were intensely focused on time and always in a hurry. This characteristic pattern of behaviors eventually was referred to as **Type A personality**. Someone with a Type A personality is competitive, aggressive, impatient, and often hostile (Diamond, 1982; Smith & Ruiz, 2002). Through numerous studies, Friedman and Rosenman discovered that people with Type A personality were twice as likely to develop cardiovascular disease as those with **Type B personality**. People with Type B personality are often more relaxed, patient, and non-aggressive (Rosenman et al., 1975). There appear to be various reasons people with Type A personality suffer disproportionately from cardiovascular disease: They are more likely to have high blood pressure, an elevated heart rate, and increased stress hormone levels. Type A individuals are also prone to more interpersonal problems (for example, arguments, fights, or hostile interactions), which increase the time their bodies are prepared for fight or flight.

Although many years of research confirmed the relationship between Type A behavior and coronary heart problems, some researchers began to report findings inconsistent with this assessment (Smith & MacKenzie, 2006). Failure to reproduce the results led some to question the validity of this relationship, with one major factor being lack of consistency in research methodology. For example, some studies used samples with high-risk participants, whereas others included healthy people. As researchers continued to probe the relationship between personality type and coronary heart disease, they found that the component of *hostility* in Type A personality was the strongest predictor of coronary heart disease.

TYPE D PERSONALITY Another personality type associated with poor cardiovascular outcomes is the *Type D personality*, where the "D" refers to distress (Denollet & Conraads, 2011). A Type D individual frequently experiences emotions like worry, tension, bad moods, and social inhibition (avoids confronting others, poor social skills). There is a clear link between Type D characteristics and a "poor prognosis" in patients with coronary heart disease (Denollet & Conraads, 2011). In other words, people who have heart problems and exhibit these Type D qualities are more likely to struggle with their illness. It could be that people with Type D personality tend

Laid-Back Bolt
The fastest man alive, Usain Bolt (right), may have what psychologists call a Type B personality—he appears to be relaxed and easygoing, even during a race! Here, the Jamaican sprinter exchanges smiles with his competitor, Canadian Andre De Grasse, during the 200-meter semifinal at the 2016 Olympics in Rio de Janeiro (Ng, 2016, August 18). AP Photo/Matt Dunham.

Type A personality A person who exhibits a competitive, aggressive, impatient, and often hostile pattern of behaviors.

Type B personality A person who exhibits a relaxed, patient, and nonaggressive pattern of behaviors.

Documenting War

Lynsey Addario (second from left) poses with fellow photojournalists on March 11, 2011, in Ras Lanuf, Libya. Four days later, Addario was kidnapped along with three colleagues from *The New York Times*. It was the second time Addario had been abducted while covering conflicts abroad. She survived the kidnapping and continues her work as a photojournalist (King & Laurent, 2016, February 6). Addario seems to display a high level of resilience, or the ability to bounce back from stressful experiences. John Moore/Getty Images.

to avoid dealing with their problems directly and don't take advantage of social support. Such an approach might lead to poor choices about coping with stressors over time (Martin et al., 2011).

THE THREE Cs OF HARDINESS Clearly, not everyone has the same tolerance for stress (Ganzel, Morris, & Wethington, 2010; Straub, 2014). Some people seem capable of handling intensely stressful situations, such as war and poverty. These individuals appear to have a personality characteristic referred to as **hardiness**, meaning that even when functioning under a great deal of stress, they are very resilient and tend to remain positive. Kehlen, who considers himself "a very optimistic person," may fit into this category, and findings from one study of Scottish ambulance personnel suggest that EMS workers with this characteristic are less likely to experience burnout (Alexander & Klein, 2001).

Others have studied how some executives seem to withstand the effects of extremely stressful jobs (Kobasa, 1979). Their hardiness appears to be associated with three characteristics: feeling a strong *commitment* to work and personal matters; believing they are in *control* of the events in their lives and not victims of circumstances; and not feeling threatened by *challenges,* but rather seeing them as opportunities for growth. Sometimes the best way to deal with stressors is to embrace them with excitement.

from the pages of
SCIENTIFIC AMERICAN

Performance Anxiety

Call it excitement and psych yourself up.

Pounding heart, rapid breath, racing thoughts—is it anxiety or excitement? New studies at Harvard University found that by interpreting these sensations as excitement instead of anxiety, people performed better in three types of stressful situations: singing in front of strangers, speaking in public and solving difficult math problems.

In the experiments, some participants were told to either try to calm down or try to get excited before the task; others were given no such instructions. People who viewed their anxious arousal as excitement not only reported feeling more excited, they also performed better on all tasks than the other participants: their singing was about 30 percent more accurate, their scores on several dimensions of public speaking were approximately 20 percent higher, and their performance on a timed math test was about 15 percent better, according to the paper, which ran in the *Journal of Experimental Psychology* last June. Another Harvard study, published in *Emotion* in August 2014, also found performance-boosting effects for people with social anxiety who thought of their stress as being helpful during a public performance.

Most people try to calm down when facing high-stakes situations, but that approach backfires by increasing rumination about what could go wrong. Instead choose to focus on the potential high points of the scenario—for instance, look forward to making colleagues laugh during a presentation or knowing how to solve some problems on a test. "Getting excited about how things can go well will give you confidence and energy and increase the likelihood that the positive outcomes you imagine will actually happen," says Alison Wood Brooks, an assistant professor of business administration at Harvard Business School and author of the June paper. **Tori Rodriguez. Reproduced with permission. Copyright © 2015 Scientific American, a division of Nature America, Inc. All rights reserved.**

I Am in Control

The ability to manage stress is very much dependent on one's perceived level of personal control. Psychologists have consistently found that people who believe they have control over their lives and circumstances are less likely to experience the negative impact of stressors than those who do not feel the same control. For example, Langer and Rodin (1976) conducted a series of studies using nursing home residents as participants. Residents in a "responsibility-induced" group were allowed to make a variety of choices about their daily activities and their environments. Members of the "comparison" group were not given these kinds of choices; instead, the nursing home staff made all of these decisions for them (the residents were told the staff was responsible for their happiness and care). After following the residents for 18 months, the researchers found that members of the responsibility-induced group were more lively, active in their social lives, and healthier than the residents in the comparison group. And twice as many of the residents in the comparison group died during this period (Rodin & Langer, 1977).

Researchers have examined how having a sense of personal control relates to a variety of health issues across all ages. Feelings of control are linked to how patients fare with some diseases. Cancer patients who exhibit a "helpless attitude" regarding their disease seem more likely to experience a recurrence of the cancer than those with perceptions of greater control. Why would this be? Women who have had breast cancer and believe they maintain control over their lifestyle, through diet and exercise, are more likely to make proactive changes related to their health (Costanzo, Lutgendorf, & Roeder, 2011). Ultimately, these changes may reduce the risk factors associated with cancer (Simon, 2015, January 16). The same type of relationship is apparent in cardiovascular disease; the less control people feel they have, the greater their risk (Shapiro, Schwartz, & Astin, 1996).

Feelings of control may also have a more direct effect on the body; for example, a sense of powerlessness is associated with increases in catecholamines and corticosteroids, both key players in a physiological response to stressors. Some have suggested a causal relationship between feelings of perceived control and immune system function; the greater the sense of control, the better the functioning of the immune system (Shapiro et al., 1996). But these are correlations, and the direction of causality should not be assumed. Could it be that better immune functioning, and thus better health, might increase one's sense of control?

We must also consider cross-cultural differences. Individual control is emphasized and valued in individualist cultures like our own, but not necessarily in collectivistic cultures, where people look to "powerful others" and "chance factors" to explain events and guide decision making (Cheng, Cheung, Chio, & Chan, 2013).

LOCUS OF CONTROL Differences in perceived sense of control stem from beliefs about where control resides (Rotter, 1966). Someone with an *internal locus of control* generally feels she is in control of life and its circumstances; she probably believes it is important to take charge and make changes when problems occur. A person with an *external locus of control* generally feels as if chance, luck, or fate is responsible for her circumstances; there is no point in trying to change things or make them better. Imagine that a doctor tells a patient he needs to change his lifestyle and start exercising. If the patient has an internal locus of control, he will likely take charge and start walking to work or hitting the gym; he expects his actions will impact his health. If the patient has an external locus of control, he is more apt to think his actions won't make a difference and may not attempt lifestyle changes. In the 1970 British Cohort Study, researchers examined over 11,000 children at age 10, and then assessed their health at age 30.

CONNECTIONS

In **Chapter 11,** we discussed locus of control, a key component of personality. People with an internal locus of control believe causes of events in their lives reside within them. Those with an external locus of control think causes reside on the outside. Here, higher personal control is associated with better health outcomes.

We Can Do This!

People gather in support of breast cancer research at the Komen South Florida Race for the Cure. Receiving a cancer diagnosis and undergoing cancer treatments are significant stressors, but a patient's capacity to cope can affect her physical and psychological health (Andreotti et al., 2015). Cancer survivors who believe they have control over their health may be inclined to make healthy lifestyle choices such as choosing to exercise and eat well (Costanzo, Lutgendorf, & Roeder, 2011). Ultimately, these choices may reduce the risk factors associated with cancer (Simon, 2015, January 16). Richard Graulich/ZUMA Press/Newscom.

hardiness A personality characteristic indicating an ability to remain resilient and optimistic despite enduring intensely stressful situations.

Camaraderie
Firefighters climb the notoriously difficult "Incline," a seemingly endless set of stairs up Pikes Peak in Manitou Springs, Colorado. Every year on the morning of September 11, the firefighters walk up the 1-mile path to commemorate those who died in the 9/11 terrorist attacks. The tight-knit community at the firehouse provides Kehlen with friendship, emotional support, and a great deal of stress reduction Nicole Pritts.

Participants with an internal locus of control, measured at 10 years of age, were less likely as adults to be overweight or obese, and had lower levels of psychological problems. They were also less likely to smoke and more likely to exercise regularly than people with a more external locus of control (Gale, Batty, & Deary, 2008).

FROM AMBULANCE TO FIREHOUSE

Kehlen's original career goal was to become a firefighter, but jobs are extremely hard to come by in this field. Fresh out of high school, Kehlen joined an ambulance crew with the goal of moving on to the firehouse. Seven years later, he reached his destination. Kehlen is now a firefighter paramedic with the Pueblo Fire Department. His job description still includes performing CPR, inserting breathing tubes, and delivering lifesaving medical care. But now he can also be seen handling fire hoses and rushing into 800-degree buildings with 80 pounds of gear.

Compared to an ambulance, the firehouse environment is far more conducive to managing stress. For starters, there is enormous social support. Fellow firefighters are a lot like family members. They eat together, go to sleep together, and wake to the same flashing lights and tones announcing the latest emergency. "The fire department is such a brotherhood," Kehlen says. Spending a third of his life at the firehouse with colleagues, Kehlen has come to know and trust them on a deep level. They discuss disturbing events they witness and help each other recover emotionally. "If you don't talk about it," says Kehlen, "it's just going to wear on you." Another major benefit of working at the firehouse is having the freedom to exercise, which Kehlen considers a major stress reliever. The firefighters are actually required to work out 1 hour per day during their shifts.

Ambulance work is quite another story. Kehlen and his coworkers were friends, but they didn't share the tight bonds that Kehlen now has with fellow firefighters. And eating healthy and exercising were almost impossible. Ambulance workers don't have the luxury of making a healthy meal in a kitchen. They often have no choice but to drive to the nearest fast-food restaurant and wipe the crumbs off their faces as they race to the next emergency. One of the worst aspects of the job was the lack of exercise. Says Kehlen, "That killed me when I was in the ambulance." ●

Tools for Healthy Living: Everyday Stress Relievers

LO 11 Discuss several tools for reducing stress and maintaining health.

Dealing with stressors can be challenging, but you don't have to grin and bear it. There are many ways to manage and reduce stress. Let's take a look at several powerful stress-fighting weapons: good nutrition, physical exercise, and relaxation techniques.

NUTRITION Think about the last time you felt stressed. What kinds of food did you crave? Probably not kale salad, whole grains, and walnuts. If you're like most people, you longed for something more along the lines of potato chips and chocolate chip cookies. Unfortunately, stress can lead to poor health choices.

Perhaps you've heard of the "Freshman 15"? The popular assumption that students often put on pounds during their first year of college appears to be more than an urban myth. Weight gain does seem to be a common factor for approximately two thirds of freshmen students, and it has been associated with stress, poor nutrition, inadequate exercise, and alcohol consumption (Vadeboncoeur, Townsend, & Foster, 2015). As the semester progresses, students report choosing unhealthier foods—especially around finals (Wansink, Cao, Saini, Shimizu, & Just, 2013).

Weight gain among college freshmen is almost 5 times higher than that of the general population (Vadeboncoeur et al., 2015). Just under 2 billion people over the age of 18 are considered overweight, a number that has "more than doubled since 1980" (World Health Organization, 2016a, para. 1).

Stress is inevitable, but eating unhealthy food is unlikely to make it disappear. A well-balanced diet is important for long-term health. Reducing sugar and carbs, increasing lean proteins, and eating more vegetables may allow us to live longer (Jankovic et al., 2014). But, good nutrition is just the beginning. If you really want to battle stress, get your heart pumping.

EXERCISE You are feeling the pressure. Exam time is here, and you haven't cracked open a book because you've been so busy at work. The holidays are approaching, you have not purchased a single present, and the pile of unpaid bills on your desk is starting to build. With so much to do, you feel paralyzed. In these types of situations, the best solution may be to drop to the floor to do some push-ups, or run out the door and take a jog. When you come back, you feel a new sense of calm. *I can handle this,* you'll think to yourself. *One thing at a time.*

How does exercise work its magic? Physiologically, we know exercise increases blood flow, activates the autonomic nervous system, and helps initiate the release of several hormones. These physiological reactions help the body defend itself against potential illnesses, especially those that are stress related. Exercise also spurs the release of the body's natural painkilling and pleasure-inducing neurotransmitters, the endorphins (Daenen, Varkey, Kellmann, & Nijs, 2015; Salmon, 2001).

When it comes to choosing an exercise regimen, the tough part is finding an activity that is intense enough to reduce the impact of stress, but sufficiently enjoyable to keep you coming back for more. Research suggests that only 30 minutes of daily exercise is needed to decrease the risk of heart disease, stroke, hypertension, certain types of cancer, and diabetes (Warburton, Charlesworth, Ivey, Nettlefold, & Bredin, 2010) and improve mood (Bryan, Hutchison, Seals, & Allen, 2007; Hansen, Stevens, & Coast, 2001). Exercise needn't be a chore. Your daily 30 minutes could mean dancing to *Just Dance 2017* on the Wii, going for a bike ride, raking leaves on a beautiful fall day, or shoveling snow in a winter wonderland. Exercising outdoors improves not only your physical health, but your mental health as well (Pasanen, Tyrväinen, & Korpela, 2014).

RELAX Exercise is all about getting the body moving, but relaxing the muscles can also relieve stress. "Just relax." We have heard it said a thousand times, but do we really know how to begin? Physician and physiologist Edmund Jacobson (1938) introduced a technique known as *progressive muscle relaxation,* which has since been expanded upon. With this technique, you begin by tensing a muscle group (for example, your toes) for about 10 seconds, and then releasing as you focus on the tension leaving. Next you progress to another muscle group, such as the calves, and then the thighs, buttocks, stomach, shoulders, arms, neck, and so on. After several weeks of practice, you will begin to recognize where you hold tension in your muscles—at least this is the goal. Once you become aware of that tension, you can focus on relaxing those specific muscles without going through the entire process. Progressive muscle relaxation has been shown to defuse anxiety in highly stressed college students. In one study, researchers found that just 20 minutes of progressive muscle relaxation had "significant short-term effects," including decreases in anxiety, blood pressure, and heart rate (Dolbier & Rush, 2012). Participants also reported a feeling of increased control and energy.

Wash the Stress Away?
Next time you wash dishes, focus on the experience of this activity. Feel the weight of the bowls and plates in your hands, notice the water running over your skin, and take in the clean scent of soap. Be aware of your breathing and stay fully present in the moment—not thinking about something else you'd rather be doing. Turning the everyday chore of dishwashing into a mindful activity may help decrease feelings of nervousness and make you feel inspired (Hanley, Warner, Dehili, Canto, & Garland, 2015). Jonathan Knowles/Getty Images.

You Asked, Christy Answers

http://qrs.ly/jg5a5fo

What advice would you give to people who deal with high amounts of stress on a daily basis?

scan this →

Inducing this *relaxation response* may also serve as an effective way to reduce pain (Benson, 2000; Dusek et al., 2008).

try this ➜ Using a clock or watch to time yourself, breathe in slowly for 5 seconds. Then exhale slowly for 5 seconds. Do this for 1 minute. With each breath, you begin to slow down and relax. The key is to breathe deeply. Draw your breath deep into the diaphragm and avoid shallow, rapid chest breathing.

BIOFEEDBACK A proven method for reducing physiological responses to stressors is **biofeedback**. This technique builds on learning principles to teach control of seemingly involuntary physiological activity (such as heart rate, blood pressure, and skin temperature). The biofeedback equipment monitors internal responses and provides visual or auditory signals to help a person identify those that are maladaptive (for example, tense shoulder muscles). The person begins by focusing on a signal (a light or tone, for example) that indicates when a desired response occurs. By learning to control this biofeedback indicator, the person learns to maintain the desired response (relaxed shoulders in this example). The goal is to be able to tap into this technique outside of the clinic or lab, and translate what has been learned into real-life practice.

The use of biofeedback can decrease the frequency of headaches and chronic pain (Flor & Birbaumer, 1993; Sun-Edelstein & Mauskop, 2011). It appears to be useful for all age groups, including children, adolescents, and the elderly (Morone & Greco, 2007; Palermo, Eccleston, Lewandowski, Williams, & Morley, 2010).

SOCIAL SUPPORT Up until now, we have discussed ways to manage the body's physiological response to stressors. There are also situational methods to deal with stressors, like maintaining a social support network. Researchers have found that proactively participating in positive enduring relationships with family, friends, and religious groups can generate a health benefit similar to exercise and not smoking (House, Landis, & Umberson, 1988). People who maintain positive, supportive relationships have better overall health (Walsh, 2011).

You might expect that receiving support is the key to lowering stress, but research suggests that *giving* support also really matters. In a study of older married adults, researchers reported reduced mortality rates for participants who indicated that they helped or supported others, including friends, spouses, relatives, and neighbors. There were no reductions in mortality, however, associated with receiving support from others (Brown, Nesse, Vinokur, & Smith, 2003).

Helping others because it gives you pleasure, and expecting nothing in return, is known as *altruism,* and it appears to be an effective stress reducer and happiness booster (Schwartz, Keyl, Marcum, & Bode, 2009; Schwartz, Meisenhelder, Yunsheng, & Reed, 2003). When we care for others, we generally don't have time to focus on our own problems; we also come to recognize that others may be dealing with more troubling circumstances than we are.

FAITH, RELIGION, AND PRAYER Psychologists are also discovering the health benefits of faith, religion, and prayer. Research suggests elderly people who actively participate in religious services or pray experience improved health and noticeably lower rates of depression than those who don't participate in such activities (Lawler-Row &

What Goes Around
Volunteers in Chongqing, China, celebrate Father's Day with elderly men in a nursing home. Altruism, or helping others because it feels good, is an excellent stress reliever. TopPhoto via AP Images.

biofeedback A technique that involves providing visual or auditory information about biological processes, allowing a person to control physiological activity (for example, heart rate, blood pressure, and skin temperature).

mindfulness meditation Being fully present in the moment; focusing attention on the here-and-now without passing judgment.

Elliott, 2009; Powell, Shahabi, & Thoresen, 2003). In fact, religious affiliation is associated with increased reports of happiness and physical health (Green & Elliott, 2010).

These proactive, stress-reducing behaviors reflect a certain type of attitude. You might call it a positive psychology attitude.

LO 12 Describe mindfulness meditation and its benefits.

THINK POSITIVE

Right Here, Right Now

In the very first chapter of this book, we introduced a field of study known as *positive psychology,* "the study of positive emotions, positive character traits, and enabling institutions" (Seligman & Steen, 2005, p. 410). Rather than focusing on mental illness and abnormal behavior, positive psychology emphasizes human strengths and virtues. The goal is well-being and fulfillment, and that means "satisfaction" with the past, "hope and optimism" for the future, and "flow and happiness" at the current time (Seligman & Csikszentmihalyi, 2000, p. 5).

As we wrap up this chapter on stress and health, we encourage you to focus on that third category: flow and happiness in the present moment. No matter what stressors come your way, try to stay grounded in the here and now. The past is the past, the future is uncertain, but this moment is yours. Finding a way to enjoy the present is one of the best ways to reduce stress. Easier said than done, you may be thinking.

If "being in the moment" does not come naturally, you might try **mindfulness meditation**—the practice of focusing attention on current experiences without passing judgment (Tang, Hölzel, & Posner, 2015). You don't have to be a Buddhist monk or yoga master to stay in the moment and focus your attention. Practicing meditation may be as easy as following these steps, provided by Diana Winston of the UCLA Mindful Awareness Research Center (Fully Present: The Book, 2010, August 3):

- Sit on a chair or a pillow. Keep your back straight but relaxed, close your eyes, and place your hands on your knees or thighs.

- Feel the weight of your body and focus on whatever sensations you are experiencing right now.

- Breathe naturally, and focus on the sensation of inhaling and exhaling; this might mean the rise and fall of your abdomen or chest, or the air entering and exiting your nostrils.

- Continue to focus on breathing, and if a thought enters your mind, try to observe it as if you were a nonjudgmental outsider. Then calmly direct your attention back to the sensation of breathing.

- Continue this practice for 5 minutes.

If you're feeling relaxed after this activity, we wouldn't be surprised. Research suggests that "brief mindfulness training can help college students manage their stress in response to the ubiquitous academic and cognitive challenges of college life" (Shearer, Hunt, Chowdhury, & Nicol, 2016, p. 232). This practice may even promote psychological

FOCUS ON YOUR BREATHING. . . .

Inhale, Exhale
How does mindfulness meditation impact the brain? Brain imaging research suggests that engaging in this practice for 2 months may cause structural changes in the amygdala (a structure involved in the stress response) and the pre-frontal cortex (an area important for higher cognitive functions; Ireland, 2014, June 12). Further research is needed, but "there is emerging evidence that mindfulness meditation might cause neuroplastic changes in the structure and function of brain regions involved in regulation of attention, emotion and self-awareness" (Tang, Hölzel, & Posner, 2015, p. 10). Philip Lee Harvey/Getty Images.

Happy at Work
Christy Sheppard (top) and
Kehlen Kirby have devoted their
careers to keeping the public safe.
The work of a first responder can
be extremely stressful, but the
reward of helping people makes
it worthwhile. Top: Macmillan Learning/
Photo by Mark Alamo. Bottom: Code 4
Photography (Kyler Hewes).

health by reducing depression, stress, and anxiety (Dimidjian et al., 2016; Goldin et al., 2016; Harrington & Dunne, 2015).

If you look online, you will find countless stories of people who have discovered peace and happiness with the help of mindfulness meditation. Consider these reflections from Karen Gifford, who turned to meditation when she was overwhelmed by stressors associated with raising small children, having a spouse who traveled frequently, and dealing with her own high-pressure legal practice. "For one thing, meditation changed my home life," Gifford writes. "I enjoyed the time I had with my kids and spouse more fully, without being so pulled into work problems, or worse, stressing out over how little time we had together" (Gifford, 2013, March 22, para. 9). Meditation also helped Gifford take pleasure in an extremely stressful job. Rather than viewing her work as a burden, she began to relish the challenges it presented (Gifford, 2013, March 22). 👍

**TO PROTECT, SERVE, AND NOT
GET TOO STRESSED** If you're wondering how Christy
Sheppard and Kehlen Kirby are doing these days, both are thriving
in their careers. After spending nearly a year and a half on the night shift,
Christy was assigned to the technical investigations unit. She now oversees
20 officers performing a variety of tasks, from monitoring illegal Internet activity to investigating financial crimes such as identity theft and embezzlement. Any case that involves extracting evidence from phones, computers, and other digital devices is within her purview. The new job is demanding and, at times, stressful, but it's much better than working nights. "I am much happier on days," Christy says. "I'm a nicer person!"

Kehlen is currently working at the busiest fire station in Pueblo County. The department responds to over 20,000 calls per year, and that number appears to be growing. "There is some speculation it may be due to the recent legalization of marijuana," says Kehlen, who is now working as an "engineer." One of the most important people in the fire department, the engineer drives the fire truck in addition to carrying out regular firefighting and paramedic responsibilities. As the demand on firefighters increases, the department is "pushing mental health very hard," according to Kehlen. "This is a major nationwide push, but it just emphasizes the amount of stress that EMS personnel have." ●

 show what you know

1. Having to choose between two options that are equally attractive to you is called a(n) _____ conflict.

2. _____ is apparent when a person deals directly with a problem by attempting to solve it.
   a. Emotion-focused coping
   b. Positive psychology
   c. Support seeking
   d. Problem-focused coping

3. Individuals who are more relaxed, patient, and nonaggressive are considered to have a:
   a. Type A personality.
   b. Type B personality.
   c. Type C personality.
   d. Type D personality.

4. Describe three "tools" for healthy living that you could use to improve your health.

√ CHECK YOUR ANSWERS IN APPENDIX C.

Improve your grade! Use 🔁 **LearningCurve** adaptive quizzing to create your personalized study plan, which will direct you to the resources that will help you most in 🔁 **LaunchPad**

summary of concepts

LO 1 Define stress and stressors. (p. 498)

Stress is the response to perceived threats or challenges resulting from stimuli or events that cause strain, analogous to an airplane wing bending in response to an applied load. For humans, these stimuli, or stressors, can cause physiological, psychological, and emotional reactions. We must be careful not to confuse how we react to stressors and the stressors themselves; stress is the response, stressors are the cause. Stress primarily occurs in reaction to a perceived threat.

LO 2 Describe the relationship between major life events and illness. (p. 502)

Holmes and Rahe developed the Social Readjustment Rating Scale (SRRS) to measure the impact of life events. The score is based on the severity of events and their frequency of occurrence. Researchers use this to examine relationships between life events and health problems. Although correlations do exist, they are not necessarily indicative of cause and effect.

LO 3 Summarize how poverty, adjusting to a new culture, and daily hassles affect health. (p. 504)

People living in poverty, moving to a new culture, and dealing with everyday hassles are faced with a number of stressors that increase the likelihood of illness. Unlike major life changes and catastrophes, daily hassles occur on a more constant basis. Moving to a new country is a major life change that can result in acculturative stress; however, integrating the old and new cultures and developing social support helps combat the effects. With all the stressors in our lives, we should be grateful for the positive experiences, or uplifts, that can serve to balance them.

LO 4 Identify the brain and body changes that characterize the fight-or-flight response. (p. 509)

When faced with a threatening situation, portions of the brain, including the hypothalamus, activate the sympathetic nervous system, which then leads to the secretion of catecholamines such as epinephrine and norepinephrine. These hormones cause heart rate, blood pressure, respiration, and blood flow to the muscles to increase. At the same time, the digestive system slows down and the pupils dilate. These physiological responses prepare us for an emergency by efficiently managing the body's resources.

LO 5 Outline the general adaptation syndrome (GAS). (p. 509)

The human body responds in a predictable way to stressors. The general adaptation syndrome suggests that the body passes through three stages. The first is the alarm stage, or initial response to a threatening situation. This stage includes an increase in arousal, during which the body prepares to deal with a threat. Next is the resistance stage, during which the body maintains a high level of arousal (although not as high as that of the alarm stage) as it deals with a threatening situation; at this point, there is a decreased response to new stressors. During the resistance stage, some people start to show signs of diseases of adaptation. Finally, the exhaustion stage occurs; the body's resources become depleted, resulting in vulnerability to illnesses, physical exhaustion, and even death.

LO 6 Explain the function of the hypothalamic–pituitary–adrenal (HPA) system. (p. 510)

Overseeing the sympathetic nervous system's activity is the HPA system. When a stressful situation arises, the hypothalamus initiates a cascade of responses by alerting the pituitary gland, which then sends signals to the adrenal cortex. In turn, the cortex orders the secretion of corticosteroids (for example, cortisol). These hormones summon the immune system to fight off a threat and reduce the amount of energy used on nonessential activities. When faced with a stressor, the body responds in the same way it would to a pathogen—by mobilizing a defense response.

LO 7 Explain how stressors relate to health problems. (p. 512)

When the body is continually mobilizing its resources for fight or flight, the immune system becomes taxed, and the work of the lymphocytes is compromised. During times of stress, people tend to sleep poorly and eat erratically, and may increase their drug and alcohol use, along with other poor behavioral choices. These tendencies can lead to health problems. In particular, stressors have been linked to ulcers, cancer, and cardiovascular disease.

LO 8 List some consequences of prolonged exposure to the stress hormone cortisol. (p. 518)

Cortisol steps up immunity and prepares the body to confront a threat. But when cortisol levels remain high for prolonged periods (which is the case with chronic stressors and threatening situations), the functioning of the immune system may decrease. Elevated cortisol has been associated with premature birth and low birth weight in infants. For workers who have to make on-the-spot safety decisions, high cortisol levels can decrease working memory. The field of psychoneuroimmunology explores the complex interplay of psychological, neurological, and immunological factors involved in stress.

LO 9 Illustrate how appraisal influences coping. (p. 521)

Coping refers to the cognitive, behavioral, and emotional abilities used to manage something that is perceived as difficult or challenging. We must decide whether an event is irrelevant, positive, challenging, or harmful (primary appraisal) and how we will respond (secondary appraisal). If we determine that we have the ability to cope, then the impact of stress will remain low. We can choose to deal directly with a problem (problem-focused coping), or to address the emotions surrounding the problem (emotion-focused coping).

LO 10 Describe Type A and Type B personalities and explain how they relate to stress. (p. 523)

Personality appears to have a profound effect on coping style and predispositions to stress-related illnesses. People with Type A personalities are competitive, aggressive, impatient, often hostile, and twice as likely to develop cardiovascular disease as people with Type B personalities, who are more relaxed, patient, and nonaggressive. The presence of Type D personality may be a better predictor of how patients fare when they already have heart disease,

and it is characterized by emotions such as worry, tension, bad moods, and social inhibition. People who exhibit a personality characteristic referred to as hardiness seem to be more resilient, optimistic, and better able to handle a great deal of stress.

LO 11 Discuss several tools for reducing stress and maintaining health. (p. 526)

Stress management incorporates tools to lower the impact of possible stressors. Exercise, meditation, progressive muscle relaxation, biofeedback, and social support all have positive physical and psychological effects. Caring for and giving to others are also effective ways to reduce the impact of stress.

LO 12 Describe mindfulness meditation and its benefits. (p. 529)

Mindfulness meditation means being fully present in the moment, or focusing attention on the here-and-now without passing judgment. This practice has been found to have a powerful calming effect, and can serve to promote psychological health through the reduction of depression, stress, and anxiety.

key terms

acculturation, p. 505
acculturative stress, p. 505
approach–approach conflict, p. 508
approach–avoidance conflict, p. 508
avoidance–avoidance conflict, p. 508
biofeedback, p. 528

burnout, p. 520
coping, p. 521
daily hassles, p. 506
distress, p. 501
emotion-focused coping, p. 521
eustress, p. 501
general adaptation syndrome (GAS), p. 509

hardiness, p. 524
health psychology, p. 510
lymphocyte, p. 513
mindfulness meditation, p. 529
posttraumatic stress disorder (PTSD), p. 503
primary appraisal, p. 521
problem-focused coping, p. 521

psychoneuroimmunology, p. 520
secondary appraisal, p. 521
social support, p. 506
stress, p. 498
stressors, p. 500
Type A personality, p. 523
Type B personality, p. 523
uplifts, p. 506

test prep *are you ready?*

1. Stress is the response to perceived threats resulting from stimuli that can cause physiological, psychological, and emotional reactions. In this context, these stimuli are known as:
   a. conflicts.
   b. eustress.
   c. assimilation.
   d. stressors.

2. Last year, when Christy dropped off her oldest daughter at college, she felt happy, proud, and somewhat worried. This kind of "good" stressor leads to a stress response known as:
   a. eustress.
   b. distress.
   c. perceived threats.
   d. optimal arousal.

3. A researcher using the Social Readjustment Rating Scale predicts that the more _____ people have, the greater the potential for increased stress and negative health outcomes.
   a. assimilation
   b. stress inoculation
   c. social support
   d. life-changing events

4. When faced with a threat, portions of the brain, including the hypothalamus, activate the _____, which leads to the secretion of epinephrine and norepinephrine.
   a. parasympathetic nervous system
   b. sympathetic nervous system
   c. general adaptation syndrome
   d. lymphocytes

5. Once an emergency has ended, the _____ reverses the processes set in motion through the fight-or-flight reaction. Heart rate and blood pressure start to decrease and respiration returns to normal.
   a. parasympathetic nervous system
   b. sympathetic nervous system
   c. general adaptation syndrome
   d. resistance stage

6. According to the general adaptation syndrome, if a threat remains constant, the body's resources become depleted during the _____, resulting in a vulnerability to illnesses, physical exhaustion, and even death.
   a. alarm stage
   b. resistance stage
   c. exhaustion stage
   d. diseases of adaptation stage

7. The hypothalamic–pituitary–adrenal system plays an important role in stress reactions. This system helps to maintain balance in the body by overseeing the neuroendocrine and _____ while monitoring the immune system.
   a. diseases of adaptation
   b. gastric ulcers
   c. assimilation
   d. sympathetic nervous system

8. Stressors can lead to health problems, because as the body mobilizes its resources for fight or flight, _____ is less powerful, and the work of its lymphocytes is reduced.
   a. the immune system   c. atherosclerosis
   b. *H. pylori*   d. cortisol

9. Physical exercise is a powerful way to reduce the impact of stress, by increasing blood flow, activating the autonomic nervous system, and initiating the release of _____, the body's natural painkilling neurotransmitters.
   a. macrophages   c. B lymphocytes
   b. endorphins   d. natural killer cells

10. The students in your study group are extremely worried about tomorrow's final exam. One student has been seeing a counselor all semester because of her anxiety. When she walks into class tomorrow, she will use what she has learned about _____ to help reduce tension in her body.
    a. the hypothalamic–pituitary–adrenal system
    b. macrophages
    c. stress inoculation
    d. progressive muscle relaxation

11. Your friend is worried he will lose his job, so he goes home and drinks too much alcohol. His reaction may be explained by the self-medication hypothesis, and his behavior is an example of how:
    a. social-evaluative threats can provide support.
    b. the general adaptation syndrome ends.
    c. stressors are related to health problems.
    d. an acculturative stress response occurs.

12. _____ refers to the cognitive, behavioral, and emotional abilities used to manage a challenging or difficult situation.
    a. Stress   c. Altruism
    b. Coping   d. Eustress

13. A college you are applying to provides two essay prompts: an essay about a childhood friend or an essay about a favorite relative. These two options sound equally boring to you. You are faced with an:
    a. avoidance–approach conflict.
    b. approach–approach conflict.
    c. approach–avoidance conflict.
    d. avoidance–avoidance conflict.

14. Someone who is competitive, aggressive, and hostile would likely have a _____, which indicates he is more inclined to develop cardiovascular disease than someone who is more relaxed, patient, and nonaggressive.
    a. Type A personality   c. Type C personality
    b. Type B personality   d. Type D personality

15. Last week, you met an exchange student who began to tell you about her life back home. She described times when she had to deal with hunger, war, and living in an orphanage. Yet, she seems so optimistic and resilient. Psychologists would likely suggest her personality includes a characteristic known as:
    a. Type A.   c. responsibility.
    b. hardiness.   d. locus of control.

16. When moving to a new country, how might someone use assimilation, separation, or integration to deal with the acculturative stress of this transition?

17. List the many hassles you have had to deal with during the past week. Also list any life events you have experienced in the past 12 months. Consider how all these stressors may have influenced your health and explain what you can do to reduce their impact.

18. Describe an example from a movie or television show of someone who seemed to be responding to a threat with the fight-or-flight response. What evidence suggests this is the case?

19. Give examples of an approach–approach conflict, an approach–avoidance conflict, and an avoidance–avoidance conflict that you have encountered in your own life.

20. Describe someone you know who has an internal locus of control, in particular regarding his or her health-related behaviors. Now describe someone you know who has an external locus of control, and focus on his or her health-related behaviors.

✓ CHECK YOUR ANSWERS IN APPENDIX C.

YOUR SCIENTIFIC WORLD

Apply psychology to the real world! Go to LaunchPad for access.

Halil Fidan/Anadolu Agency/Getty Images.

Ascent Xmedia/Getty Images.

AFP/Getty Images.

Heidi Pendergast/Ross Szabo.

Dan Pearson Photography /Alamy Stock Photo.

HARISH TYAGI/EPA/Newscom.

13 psychological disorders

Comstock/Getty Images.

An Introduction to Psychological Disorders

WINTER NIGHT It was a clear, cold night in January when 17-year-old Ross Szabo decided to end his life. Nothing bad had happened that day. Ross had woken up, gone to school, played in a basketball game (a victory for his team), and then gone with his buddies to Friendly's restaurant for mozzarella sticks and a sundae. But for some reason, on that winter night, Ross decided he could no longer take it. Riding home in the car, he gazed out the window at Pennsylvania's snow-blanketed cornfields. An overwhelming sense of calm descended on him.

For the 4 months leading to that moment, Ross had been free-falling into an abyss of sadness. No one knew—not his parents, his brothers, or his friends—because Ross was a good actor. Around other people, he was smiling, joking, acting like a normal teenager. But every time he was alone, he was crying. As he puts it, "I had been thinking about suicide 24 hours a day by that point."

Some people say suicide is a selfish act; a person ends his own suffering and destroys the lives of those left behind. Ross truly believed his friends and family would be happier without him. *Maybe you're the problem; maybe you'd be doing them a favor by removing the problem,* Ross remembers thinking to himself. "I didn't think I would have a funeral," he says. "I didn't think anyone should care about me."

When Ross got home, he tried calling a friend but was too upset to speak. So he walked into the bathroom and prepared to kill himself. Fortunately, his father was home and could tell Ross was in distress. He convinced his son to come downstairs and talk. "If you don't take me to the hospital right now, I'm going to kill myself," Ross said as he walked into the kitchen. Instead of returning to school the next day, Ross was admitted to the hospital. ●

Looks Can Be Deceiving
Ross Szabo appears happy in his senior class photo, but beneath his smile is profound pain. This was the year Ross began to have persistent thoughts of death and suicide that nearly drove him to take his own life.
Martin Fella/Fella Studios.

What's Normal, What's Not

LO 1 Define psychological disorders and the criteria used to identify abnormal behavior.

A year-and-a-half earlier, Ross had been diagnosed with **bipolar disorder**, a condition marked by dramatic mood swings. We all have our ups and downs—periods of feeling happy, sad, anxious, or irritable—but the emotional roller coaster of bipolar disorder is

bipolar disorder
A psychological disorder marked by dramatic swings in mood, ranging from manic episodes to depressive episodes.

Note: Ross Szabo's story is based on personal communications with Ross Szabo and various passages from the book he coauthored with Melanie Hall: *Behind Happy Faces* (Szabo & Hall, 2007). Unless otherwise specified, quotations attributed to Ross Szabo and Melissa Hopely are personal communications.

535

Ross, in His Own Words

http://qrs.ly/8z5a5fr

CONNECTIONS

In **Chapter 1,** we described various mental health professions, and the training they require. The current chapter focuses on abnormal psychology, a subfield many people associate with the word "psychology." The field of abnormal psychology encompasses the study of psychological disorders as well as their treatment.

something quite different. We will soon explore bipolar disorder in greater detail, but first let's familiarize ourselves with the broader focus of this chapter: psychological disorders.

A **psychological disorder** is a set of behavioral, emotional, and cognitive symptoms that are significantly distressing and disabling in terms of social functioning, work endeavors, and other aspects of life. These symptoms are not the result of religious or spiritual experiences; nor are they mere departures from cultural norms. And although stressors can trigger symptoms of psychological disorders, these conditions primarily result from disturbances in psychological, biological, and developmental processes (American Psychiatric Association, 2013).

The behaviors and symptoms associated with psychological disorders are not typical in the general population; in other words, they are abnormal. The academic field devoted to the study of psychological disorders is generally referred to as abnormal psychology. Researchers and scholars in this field have a variety of backgrounds, including clinical psychology, neuroscience, and psychiatry.

DEFINING ABNORMAL BEHAVIOR Psychologists and other mental health professionals determine if a behavior is *abnormal* using a variety of criteria (**TABLE 13.1**). Perhaps the most straightforward criterion is *typicality* (or lack thereof). An atypical behavior is one that is rarely seen, or infrequent. The profound sadness Ross experienced is relatively rare. Most people experience sadness, even deep sadness at times, but suicidal thoughts are unusual. Although the typicality criterion is useful, it is not enough to confirm the existence of a psychological disorder. A child prodigy who learns to play the piano like a virtuoso by age 5 is atypical, but his rare talent does not indicate a psychological disorder.

We should also consider **maladaptive behaviors,** or actions that run counter to one's best interests. The degree of risk or danger associated with these maladaptive behaviors (both to oneself and others) is often used by professionals to determine if a person needs to be admitted to a hospital. In Chapter 14, you will see how Dr. Dan Foster uses this criterion in deciding whether to seek hospital care for a client with schizophrenia. We should point out, however, that maladaptive behavior is not always a sign of abnormality. People without disorders may exhibit maladaptive behaviors; just think of a child who has tantrums from time to time, or an adult who drowns his sorrows in alcohol one night.

To arrive at a more definitive determination of **abnormal behavior,** mental health professionals typically rely on three criteria (in addition to typicality): *dysfunction, distress,* and *deviance,* or the "3 Ds" (American Psychiatric Association, 2013; Wakefield, 1992).

The first D, *dysfunction,* indicates the degree to which a behavior interferes with daily life and relationships. Ross' depression sometimes rendered him unable to get out of bed; this type of behavior certainly has the potential to interfere with daily life. But dysfunction alone does not confirm the presence of a psychological disorder. If you stay up all night to meet a deadline, you might experience temporary dysfunction in memory and attention, but that doesn't mean you have a disorder.

TABLE 13.1	DEFINING ABNORMAL BEHAVIOR
Criteria	**What does it mean?**
Typicality	Degree to which behavior is atypical, meaning rarely seen or statistically abnormal
Dysfunction	Degree to which behavior interferes with daily life and relationships
Distress	Degree to which behavior or emotions cause an individual to feel upset or uncomfortable
Deviance	Degree to which behavior is considered outside the standards or rules of society

Psychologists typically identify abnormal behavior using the criteria above.

The second D is personal *distress.* Feeling regularly upset or uncomfortable because of unwanted behaviors or emotions is another feature of abnormality, and it's not always evident from the outside. Prior to his suicide attempt, Ross appeared to be happy and healthy, but inside he was suffering. There are times, however, when distress does not accompany a disorder. When Ross experienced the euphoric highs of bipolar disorder, he may not have been distressed at all. People with psychological disorders do not always have the insight to recognize that a problem exists.

The third D is *deviance,* or the degree to which a behavior is considered to be outside the standards or rules of a society. Behaving in a way that does not conform to social expectations might be indicative of a psychological disorder. Individuals who are euphoric might talk too loudly in a library or church where people are expected to be quiet, or become so disinhibited that they walk around naked in a public place. Yet, the presence of deviance alone does not necessarily indicate a psychological disorder. Political protesters, for example, may deliberately break social norms to make a statement—lying on sidewalks, or setting up camp and sleeping in public places. Their behavior is deviant but not necessarily suggestive of a psychological disorder.

We should note that conceptions of abnormality and definitions of psychological disorders have changed over the course of history. During the 18th century, some women were said to exhibit a psychological disorder called *hysteria,* linked to "wandering movements of the womb" and characterized by "excessive emotion, irrational speech, paralysis, and convulsions" (Wickens, 2015, p. 245). No such diagnosis exists in today's world. Always remember that the meaning of "abnormal" is relative to time.

IT'S A CONTINUUM It's important to understand that anyone can have experiences that resemble symptoms of psychological disorders. This is because there is a continuum for many behaviors and feelings: Those at the ends are generally viewed as abnormal, and those in the middle more normal. Consider the vastly different degrees of sadness. Ross' profound sadness would likely fall at the *abnormal* end of the continuum; a teary farewell to a close friend who is moving away would be considered a *normal* reaction in the middle; and someone with limited emotions would be at the other end of the continuum. Bear in mind that notions of normality are not the same throughout the world. As the biopsychosocial model reminds us, we must consider culture and other social influences when trying to understand psychological disorders.

Deviant, but Not Disordered
Demonstrators in New Delhi, India, mourn the death of a young woman who was viciously raped and beaten by a group of men on a bus. The behavior of these protestors defies social norms and is therefore considered deviant. Yet in this case, deviance is not linked to a mental disorder. HARISH TYAGI/EPA/Newscom.

Consider the Culture

Many disorders are universal, meaning they occur throughout the world and have a strong biological foundation. An example is schizophrenia, which has been documented across cultures. There are also *cultural syndromes* whose symptoms and attributions (explanations for those symptoms) appear to be unique to particular societies. *Koro,* for example, is an episode of intense anxiety observed mainly in Southeast Asia, although similar conditions have been documented in China. The main feature of *koro* is the unrealistic and intense fear that sexual organs will be pulled into the body, perhaps resulting in death (American Psychiatric Association, 2013; Roy et al., 2011). A man with *koro* might be exceedingly anxious about the idea of his penis disappearing into his abdomen, whereas a woman might fear that her nipples will be pulled into her chest. Another example is *susto,* most evident in Mexico, Central America, South America, and Latino populations of the United States. People with *susto* have extreme reactions to frightening situations; they believe their soul has left their body, which results in illness, sadness, lack of motivation, and other symptoms (American Psychiatric Association, 2013). Later in the chapter, we will discuss eating disorders, which have a strong cultural component as well.

Even with universal disorders such as schizophrenia, culture plays an important role in determining how symptoms are interpreted. For example, people living in South Asia are more likely than those in the United States and Canada to attribute symptoms of

Synonyms

psychological disorder mental disorder, mental illness, psychiatric illness, mental disability, mental disease

abnormal psychology experimental psychopathology, clinical psychology

psychological disorder A set of behavioral, emotional, and cognitive symptoms that are significantly distressing or disabling in terms of social functioning, work endeavors, and other aspects of life.

maladaptive behaviors Behaviors or actions that run counter to what is in one's best interests.

abnormal behavior Behavior that is atypical, dysfunctional, distressful, and/or deviant.

psychological disorders to supernatural powers—"hexes and curses" or "punishment from God," for example (Knettel, 2016, p. 134). Even within the United States, we see evidence of culture shaping people's attitudes and beliefs about psychological disorders. Some research suggests that African Americans have a tendency to view these disorders as a sign of weakness, and may be "very concerned about stigma associated with mental illness" (Ward, Wiltshire, Detry, & Brown, 2013, p. 2). Meanwhile, Asian Americans and Hispanics appear more inclined than other groups to *normalize* the symptoms of psychological disorders, for example, believing that "mental health problems" are a "normal part of life" (Bignall, Jacquez, & Vaughn, 2015, p. 542). How do you think such attitudes affect people's willingness to seek mental health services?

Keep in mind that these are only cultural generalizations, not rules that apply to every member of the group. Within each category is immense diversity; for example, "Asian American" could refer to people who have roots in countries as different as China, India, and the Philippines, while "Hispanic" encompasses the distinct cultures of Mexico, Argentina, and many other parts of the world.

In Class: Collaborate and Report

In groups, **A)** identify examples of abnormal behaviors you've seen reported in the news; **B)** show how these behaviors fit the criteria for abnormality listed in Table 13.1; **C)** give examples of some behaviors that might appear deviant, but do not fit the criteria; and **D)** identify a behavior that might be considered abnormal in one cultural context, but not another.

We have learned how psychologists use three main criteria (in addition to typicality) to identify abnormality—*dysfunction, distress,* and *deviance.* Now let's explore abnormality in the context of the judicial system.

THINK IT THROUGH
The Insanity Plea

Perhaps you have heard the term "insanity" used in a legal context. "The defendant got off on an insanity plea," or "The defense failed to demonstrate insanity." What do these statements mean? **Insanity** is a legal determination of the degree to which a person is responsible for his criminal behaviors. Those deemed legally insane are thought to have little or no control over or understanding of their behaviors at the time they committed their crimes. Therefore, they are given psychological treatment in a locked psychiatric facility rather than criminal punishment such as imprisonment or the death penalty. In America, 46 states offer a form of the insanity defense; only Idaho, Kansas, Montana, and Utah do not (Cevallos, 2015, July 17; Lilienfeld & Arkowitz, 2011, January/February). Many people believe that the insanity defense is frequently used, but it's invoked in only about 1% of cases. Of those cases, just 10–25% of insanity defenses are successful (Torry & Billick, 2010). Among those who avoided prison after entering an insanity plea was John Hinckley Jr., the man who attempted to assassinate President Ronald Reagan in 1981 (PBS, 2014). The insanity plea did not work so well for the man who murdered Kris Kyle, the Navy SEAL whose memoir served as the basis for the Oscar-winning movie *American Sniper.* Kyle's killer, Eddie Ray Routh, is serving life in prison without parole (Payne, Ford, & Morris, 2015, February 25).

IT'S INVOKED IN ONLY ABOUT 1% OF CASES.

Now that we have explored the meaning of abnormality, let's explore how it might feel to face a psychological disorder—and the negative judgments that sometimes accompany it.

Insanity?

In the summer of 2012, James Holmes walked into a movie theater in Aurora, Colorado, and opened fire on the audience, killing 12 people. Holmes' attorneys entered a plea of insanity; they claimed that he committed the murders while in a psychotic state (Ingold, 2013, September 30). Refusing to accept the insanity plea, jurors determined he should spend the rest of his life in prison (Associated Press, 2015, August 26). REUTERS/RJ Sangosti.

CONNECTIONS

In **Chapter 7,** we discussed the availability heuristic; we often predict the probability of something happening in the future based on how easily we can recall a similar type of event from the past. Here, the vividness of a crime and the ensuing trial make the insanity plea more available in our memories, so we tend to overestimate its likelihood in the future.

insanity A legal determination of the degree to which a person is responsible for criminal behaviors.

stigma A negative attitude or opinion about a group of people based on certain traits or characteristics.

DISPELLING STIGMA: ROSS FINDS HIS VOICE

After being discharged from the hospital, Ross returned to school, where he was greeted with rumors and stares. A couple of his friends stopped spending time with him, perhaps because they were afraid of what they didn't understand. Or maybe it was because people in the farmlands of Pennsylvania didn't talk much about emotions and mental health.

Not long after the hospital stay, a psychologist came to Ross' school to give his annual presentation about helping people with psychological disorders. Most of the students thought the topic was funny and laughed throughout the presentation (perhaps out of discomfort). But Ross did not find it one bit amusing. After class, he told his teacher that he wanted to give his own presentation. Before long, Ross was standing before his peers, heart pounding and knees wobbling, talking about life with bipolar disorder. The students listened intently, and some approached Ross after class to talk about their own struggles with psychological disorders. By coming forward to share his experiences, Ross dispelled some of his classmates' misconceptions and fears about psychological disorders. He was a real person they knew and liked, and he had a disorder. ●

Hollywood Stereotypes
The late Heath Ledger plays the "Joker" in *The Dark Knight* (2008). Ledger described the Joker as a "psychopathic, mass-murdering, schizophrenic clown with zero empathy" (Lyall, 2007, November 4, para. 13). Such characterizations tend to perpetuate stereotypes about people with psychological disorders, most of whom are not violent (Arkowitz & Lilienfeld, 2011, July/August; Fazel et al., 2009). Warner Bros./Photofest.

WHAT IS STIGMA? Watching his classmates laugh about people with psychological disorders, Ross bore witness to the *stigma* attached to mental illness. **Stigma** is a negative attitude or opinion about groups of individuals based on certain traits or characteristics they have. Being the target of stigma may lower self-esteem, impair social functioning, and make a person less likely to seek treatment. Stigma can also lead to discrimination, stereotypes, and negative characterizations in general, although researchers are actively exploring strategies to counteract it (Corrigan, 2005, Corrigan & Penn, 2015). Surely, you have heard people equate psychological disorders with violence and aggression, or perhaps you have seen TV shows portraying people with mental illness as wild and aggressive. Reality check: People with psychological disorders are usually *not* violent. Other factors, such as lower socioeconomic status, male gender, and substance abuse, may be better predictors of violence (McAra & McVie, 2016; Stuart, 2003). The criterion of being a danger to oneself or others does determine the necessity of treatment, but given the degree of violence in our society, violent behavior is actually *atypical* of people with serious psychological disorders, and more commonly associated with substance abuse (Arkowitz & Lilienfeld, 2011, July/August; Fazel, Gulati, Linsell, Geddes, & Grann, 2009).

What can we do to combat stigma? One suggestion is to use "people-first language"; that is, refer to the individual affected by the disorder ("She has been diagnosed with schizophrenia"), rather than defining the person by her disorder ("She is *schizophrenic*"; American Psychological Association, 2010; Granello & Gibbs, 2016). We should also be cautious about using terms such as "crazy" and "insane." When used to describe people, these words are inappropriate, derogatory, and sure indicators of stigma.

Thus far, our discussion has focused on overarching concepts like abnormal behavior and stigma, which have relevance for all psychological disorders. Now it's time to shift to a discussion of more practical matters. How do psychologists and psychiatrists go about identifying and classifying disorders?

○✓○○ **show what you know**

1. Which of the following is a criterion used to define abnormal behavior?
   a. dysfunction
   b. psychopathology
   c. developmental processes
   d. stigma

2. A _____ is a set of behavioral, emotional, and cognitive symptoms that are significantly distressing and disabling in terms of social functioning, work endeavors, and other aspects of life.

3. Using Table 13.1 as your guide, think of behaviors that are (1) atypical but not dysfunctional; (2) dysfunctional but not distressful; and (3) deviant but not dysfunctional.

✓ CHECK YOUR ANSWERS IN APPENDIX C.

You Asked, Ross Answers

http://qrs.ly/f45a5fw

How do you explain
your ability to hide what
was going on with your
bipolar disorder?

scan this →

Classifying and Explaining Psychological Disorders

How was Ross diagnosed with bipolar disorder? He consulted with a psychiatrist. But how did this mental health professional come to the conclusion that Ross suffered from bipolar disorder, and not something else? Given the complexity of determining abnormal behavior, it probably comes as no surprise that clinicians have not always agreed on what qualifies as a psychological disorder. Over the years, however, they have developed common criteria and procedures for making reliable diagnoses. These criteria and decision-making procedures are presented in manuals, which are shared across mental health professions, and are based on research findings and clinical observations.

The *Diagnostic and Statistical Manual of Mental Disorders*

Think about the last time you were ill and went to a doctor. You probably answered a series of questions about your symptoms. The nurse took your blood pressure and temperature, and the doctor performed a physical exam. Based on these subjective and objective findings, the doctor formulated a diagnosis. Mental health professionals must do the same—make diagnoses based on evidence. In addition to gathering information from interviews and other clinical assessments, psychologists typically rely on manuals to guide their diagnoses. Most mental health professionals in North America use the *Diagnostic and Statistical Manual of Mental Disorders* (*DSM–5;* American Psychiatric Association, 2013). The *DSM–5* is an evidence-based classification system of mental disorders first developed and published by the American Psychiatric Association (www. psych.org) in 1952. This manual was conceived and designed to help ensure accurate and consistent diagnoses based on the observation of symptoms. Although the *DSM* is published by the American Psychiatric Association—different from the American Psychological Association—it is used by psychiatrists, psychologists, social workers, and a variety of other clinicians. The most recent edition of the manual, the *DSM–5,* lists 157 disorders (American Psychiatric Association Division of Research, personal communication, July 26, 2013) and presents some new ideas on how to think about them (**INFOGRAPHIC 13.1** on page 542).

LO 2   Recognize limitations in the classification of psychological disorders.

CRITICISMS OF CLASSIFICATION Why is the *DSM* important? Classifying psychological disorders helps therapists develop treatment plans, enables clients to obtain reimbursement from their insurance companies, and facilitates research and communication among professions. But there is a downside to this *atheoretical approach,* which de-emphasizes theories and focuses on checklists of observable signs and symptoms. Relying on checklists rather than theory tends to limit clinicians' understanding of their patients, and the overlapping of criteria across disorders may result in some individuals being over-diagnosed (McHugh & Slavney, 2012). Once a person is diagnosed, he runs the risk of being labeled, and this affects how others perceive his behaviors—it changes their expectations. Few studies illustrate this phenomenon more starkly than David Rosenhan's classic 1973 study "On Being Sane in Insane Places."

THINK IT THROUGH
"On Being Sane in Insane Places"

What do you think would happen if you secretly planted eight completely "sane" people (no history of psychological disorders) in American psychiatric hospitals? The hospital employees would immediately identify them as "normal" and send them home . . . right?

NO HOSPITAL STAFF MEMBER IDENTIFIED THE PSEUDOPATIENTS AS FRAUDS. In the early 1970s, psychologist David Rosenhan and seven other mentally healthy people managed to get themselves admitted to various psychiatric hospitals by faking auditory hallucinations ("I am hearing voices"), a common symptom of schizophrenia. (Such a feat would be close to impossible today, as psychiatric facilities are too stretched to accommodate the scores of Americans with documented psychological disorders; Sisti, Segal, & Emanuel, 2015.) Upon admission, each of these pretend patients, or "pseudopatients," immediately stopped putting on an act and began behaving like their normal selves. But within the walls of a psychiatric hospital, their ordinary behavior assumed a whole new meaning. Staff members who spotted the pseudopatients taking notes concluded it must be a symptom of their psychological disorder. "Patient engaged in writing behavior," nurses wrote of one pseudo-patient. "Nervous, Mr. X?" a nurse asked a pseudo-patient who had been walking the halls out of sheer boredom (Rosenhan, 1973, p. 253).

No hospital staff member identified the pseudopatients as frauds. If anyone had them figured out, it was the other patients in the hospital. "You're not crazy," they would say to the pseudopatients. "You're a journalist, or a professor. You're checking up on the hospital" (Rosenhan, 1973, p. 252). After an average stay of 19 days (the range being 7 to 52 days), the pseudopatients were discharged, but not because doctors recognized their diagnostic errors. The pseudopatients, they determined, had gone into "remission" from their fake disorders. They were released back into society—but not without their labels.

Some critics raised legitimate concerns about the methodology, results, and conclusions of Rosenhan's study (Lando, 1976; Spitzer, 1975). Nevertheless, it shed light on the persistence of labels and stigma.

If eight "sane" people could be diagnosed with serious disorders like schizophrenia, you might be wondering if psychological diagnoses are **reliable or valid**. We've come a long way since 1973, but the diagnosis of psychological disorders remains a challenge, in part because it often relies on self-reports. Evaluating complex behaviors will never be as straightforward as measuring blood pressure or running a test for strep throat.

Movie with a Message

Silver Linings Playbook is one of the few movies that has received praise from mental health advocates. Directed by David O. Russell, whose own son has bipolar disorder, the movie focuses on the personal journey of a bipolar sufferer "Pat Solitano" (played by Bradley Cooper). "Making a film about mental illness is tricky: It can sensationalize, trivialize or exploit it," National Alliance on Mental Illness (NAMI) spokesperson Katrina Gay told *USA Today.* "But *Silver Linings Playbook* not only entertains us, it shows us how alike we all really are" (Lopez, 2013, February 12, para. 7).
© Weinstein Company/Courtesy Everett Collection.

CONNECTIONS

In **Chapter 11,** we discussed reliability and validity in the context of personality assessment. These concepts are also relevant to classification systems for psychological disorders. We must determine if diagnoses are reliable (providing consistent, reproducible results) and valid (measuring what they intend to measure).

In Class: Collaborate and Report

In your group, discuss the following: **A)** How does being labeled with a psychological disorder affect a person's interactions with family and friends? **B)** Once a label is assigned, can it ever be fully removed? **C)** How does using words like "crazy," "insane," and "nuts" impact perceptions of psychological disorders? **D)** How can using "people-first language" counteract the damaging effects of labels?

"Abnormal," but Not Uncommon

You probably know someone with bipolar disorder, major depressive disorder, or attention-deficit/hyperactivity disorder (ADHD). Perhaps you have experienced a disorder yourself. Psychological disorders are not uncommon (**TABLE 13.2**). Findings from a large study of approximately 9,000 individuals indicate that around 50% of the population in the United States, at some point in life, experience symptoms that meet the criteria for a psychological disorder

TABLE 13.2 YEARLY RATES OF PSYCHOLOGICAL DISORDERS

Psychological Disorder	Annual Prevalence
Anxiety disorders	18.1%
Specific phobia	8.7%
Social phobia	6.8%
Disruptive behavior disorders	8.9%
Mood disorders	9.5%
Major depression	6.7%
Substance disorders	3.8%
Any disorder	26.2%

In any given year, many people are diagnosed with a psychological disorder. The numbers here represent annual prevalence: the percentage of the U.S. population affected by a disorder over a year. (Elsewhere, we have referred to lifetime prevalence, which means the percentage of the population affected by a disorder any time in life.)
Information from Kessler (2010).

The *DSM-5*

Revising the *Diagnostic and Statistical Manual of Mental Disorders* was no small task. The process took over 10 years and involved hundreds of experts poring over the most relevant and current research. The final product helps researchers conduct studies and clinicians develop treatment plans and work with other professionals.

Where does the *DSM-5* come from?

PREPARATION Nearly 400 scientists from around the world evaluate research on psychological disorders for 10 years prior to publication of the *DSM-5*.

DRAFTING 160 scientists participating in the American Psychiatric Association's *DSM-5* Task Force and Work Groups review the research regarding disorders. Working with other researchers and clinicians, they gather as much information as possible about the current understanding of disorders. Then they compose and revise diagnostic criteria.

APPROVAL Following approval of the diagnostic criteria by the APA Board of Trustees, the prepublication *DSM-5* goes through two more rounds of review. The Scientific Review Committee examines the evidence informing the proposed changes to the *DSM*, and the Clinical and Public Health committee provides feedback on the criteria from a clinical and public health standpoint.

Some disorders included in the *DSM-5*

Each chapter of the *DSM-5* describes disorders that share common features and/or symptoms. Here we list six chapters, along with a sample disorder that you can read more about in your textbook.

Schizophrenia Spectrum and Other Psychotic Disorders
Dysfunction resulting from delusions, hallucinations, disorganized thinking, abnormal motor behavior, and negative symptoms.

> **READ ABOUT**
> *Schizophrenia, page 560*

Bipolar and Related Disorders
Manic and depressive behavior characterized by changes in mood and activity levels.

> **READ ABOUT**
> *Bipolar I Disorder, page 558*

Depressive Disorders
Dysfunction relating to profound sadness, feelings of emptiness, and irritable mood.

> **READ ABOUT**
> *Major Depressive Disorder, page 553*

Obsessive-Compulsive and Related Disorders
Dysfunction relating to obsessions and/or compulsions that cause distress and disrupt day-to-day functioning.

> **READ ABOUT**
> *Obsessive-Compulsive Disorder, page 550*

Trauma- and Stressor-Related Disorders
Distress resulting from exposure to traumatic or stressful incidents.

> **READ ABOUT**
> *Posttraumatic Stress Disorder, page 503*

Dissociative Disorders
Problems with memory, identity, consciousness, perception, and motor control that disrupt psychological functioning.

> **READ ABOUT**
> *Dissociative Amnesia, page 568*

How are disorders of childhood covered in the *DSM-5*?

The *DSM-5* does not include a separate chapter dedicated to disorders diagnosed in childhood, but diagnoses within chapters are presented in chronological order. The *DSM-5* also includes age-related factors in its descriptions and criteria. Here are two disorders commonly diagnosed in childhood:

Autism Spectrum Disorder
This spectrum of disorders recognizes a continuum of symptoms associated with social communication and interaction, repetitive behaviors or speech, and intellectual ability.

Attention-deficit/hyperactivity disorder (ADHD)
This disorder begins in childhood, and must be recognized in more than one situation (for example, school and home). A child may have difficulty paying attention, and may easily get off task, fidget, or act impulsively. The manual also recognizes that this disorder does not necessarily end in childhood, and may continue into adulthood.

Who uses the *DSM-5*, and how is it used?

Trained mental health professionals use the *DSM-5* to diagnose psychological disorders. The manual is designed to summarize the signs and symptoms of disorders for the clinician to use as an evaluative tool. The presence of specified signs and symptoms may indicate an underlying psychological disorder, and the *DSM-5* criteria can help guide clinicians to accurate diagnoses and appropriate treatment.

American Psychiatric Association, 2013.

(Kessler, Berglund, et al., 2005; Kessler & Wang, 2008). Yes, you read that correctly; "Nearly half the population meet criteria for a mental disorder in their life. . . ." (Kessler, 2010, p. 60). The majority of these disorders begin before the age of 14. Longitudinal studies monitoring children through young adulthood indicate that psychological disorders are "very common," with more than 70% being diagnosed by age 30 (Copeland, Shanahan, Costello, & Angold, 2011; Farmer, Kosty, Seeley, Olino, & Lewinsohn, 2013). Psychological disorders are observed throughout the world. Results from surveys conducted in 59 countries indicated that 1 in 5 people had a psychological disorder within a 12-month period. The lifetime prevalence of disorders varied based on geographic region, with "countries of North and South East Asia in particular returning lower prevalence estimates than countries in other regional groupings" (Steel et al., 2014, p. 490).

A TOUGH ROAD With such high rates of disorders, you can be sure there are many people around you dealing with tough issues. In some cases, psychological disorders lead to greater impairment than chronic medical conditions, yet people with mental ailments are *less* likely to get treatment (Druss et al., 2009). Further complicating the picture is the fact that many people suffer from more than one psychological disorder at a time, a phenomenon called **comorbidity** (koh-mawr-BID-i-tee). The Kessler studies mentioned above found that nearly a quarter of participants with disorders had received two diagnoses in the course of a year (Kessler, Chiu, Demler, & Walters, 2005). You already know that one psychological disorder can lead to significant impairment; now just imagine how these problems compound for a person coping with more than one disorder. Also keep in mind that various psychological disorders are chronic (a person suffers from them continuously), others have a regular pattern (symptoms appear every winter, for example), and some are temporary.

What Causes Psychological Disorders?

LO 3 Summarize the etiology of psychological disorders.

As we describe psychological disorders throughout this chapter, we will highlight some of the major theories of their *etiology*, or causal factors. Let's familiarize ourselves with the models commonly used to explain the causes of psychological disorders.

IT'S IN YOUR BIOLOGY: THE MEDICAL MODEL The **medical model** explains psychological disorders from a biological standpoint, focusing on genes, neurochemical imbalances, and problems in the brain. This medical approach has had a long and uninterrupted history, as our culture continues to view psychological disorders as illnesses. It is evident in the language used to discuss disorders and their treatment: *mental illness, therapy, remission, symptoms, patients,* and *doctors.* Some scholars criticize this approach (Szasz, 2011), in part because it fails to acknowledge how concepts of mental health and illness have changed over time and across cultures (Kawa & Giordano, 2012).

IT'S IN YOUR MIND: PSYCHOLOGICAL FACTORS Another way to understand the etiology of disorders is to focus on psychological factors. Some theories propose that cognitive factors or personality characteristics contribute

Stress Can Be a Trigger
A mother and her daughters rest after crossing the border from Syria to Turkey. Refugees face a host of stressors that may increase their risk for developing symptoms of psychological disorders. Among them are loss of home, exposure to violence and death, lack of employment and educational opportunities, and crowded living conditions in refugee camps (Gary & Rubin, 2014; Leigh, 2014, August 1). According to one psychiatrist who has worked in the refugee settlements, "Depression, anxiety, and hopelessness pervade the camps with suicidal ideation rates reaching at least 70 percent" (Soudi, 2016, August 1, para. 4). Halil Fidan/Anadolu Agency/ Getty Images.

Synonyms
medical model biological model

comorbidity The occurrence of two or more disorders at the same time.
medical model An approach suggesting that psychological disorders are illnesses that have underlying biological causes.

CONNECTIONS

In **Chapter 5,** we discussed a variety of theories that explain how behaviors are learned. In this chapter, we see how learning theories help us understand the development of psychological disorders.

to the development and maintenance of disorders. Others focus on the ways learning or childhood experiences might lay their foundation.

IT'S IN YOUR ENVIRONMENT: SOCIOCULTURAL FACTORS Earlier, we mentioned that culture can shape definitions of "abnormal" and influence the development of psychological disorders. Social factors, like poverty and community support systems, can also play a role in the development and course of these conditions (Lund et al., 2011; Mills, 2015).

THE BIOPSYCHOSOCIAL PERSPECTIVE As we have suggested in previous chapters, the best way to understand human behavior is to examine it from a variety of perspectives. The *biopsychosocial perspective* provides an excellent model for explaining psychological disorders, suggesting they result from a complex interaction of biological, psychological, and sociocultural factors (**FIGURE 13.1**). For example, some disorders appear to have a genetic basis, but their symptoms may not be evident until social or psychological factors come into play. We will discuss this again in the section on schizophrenia, when we take a look at the *diathesis–stress model.*

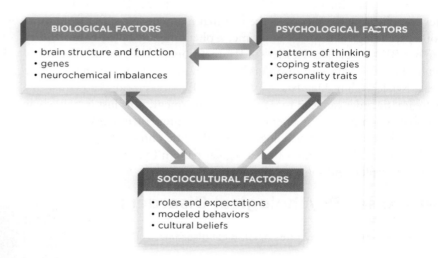

FIGURE 13.1

The Biopsychosocial Perspective
The biopsychosocial perspective considers the complex interaction of biological, psychological, and sociocultural factors that may contribute to a specific disorder

Now that we have a general understanding of how psychologists conceptualize psychological disorders, let's delve into specifics. We cannot cover every disorder identified in the DSM–5, but we can offer an overview of those commonly discussed in an introductory psychology course.

CONNECTIONS

Psychological disorders are presented in other chapters as well. For example, in **Chapter 4** we discussed sleep disorders, and **Chapter 12** explored the relationship between stressors and posttraumatic stress disorder (PTSD).

Photodisc/
Getty Images.

UNWELCOME THOUGHTS: MELISSA'S STORY

Melissa Hopely was about 5 years old when she began doing "weird things" to combat anxiety: flipping light switches on and off, touching the corners of tables, and running to the kitchen to make sure the oven was turned off. Taken at face value, these behaviors may not seem too strange, but for Melissa they were the first signs of a psychological disorder that eventually pushed her to the edge.

Anxiety is a normal part of growing up. Children get nervous for an untold number of reasons: doctors' appointments, the first day of school, or the neighbor's German shepherd. But Melissa was not suffering from common childhood jitters. Her anxiety overpowered her physically, gripping her arms and legs in pain and twisting her stomach into a knot. It affected her emotionally, bringing on a vague feeling that something awful was about to occur—unless she did something to stop it. *If I just touch all the corners of this table like so, nothing bad will happen,* she would think to herself.

From Girl to Woman
Melissa Hopely was about 3 years old when the photo on the left was taken. Within a couple of years, she would begin to experience the symptoms of a serious mental disorder that would carry into adulthood. Melissa Hopely.

As Melissa grew older, her behaviors became increasingly regimented. She felt compelled to do everything an even number of times. Instead of entering a room once, she would enter or leave twice, four times, perhaps even 20 times—as long as the number was a multiple of 2. Some days she would sit in her bedroom for hours, methodically touching all of her possessions twice, then repeating the process again, and again. By performing these rituals, Melissa felt she could prevent her worst fears from becoming reality.

What was she so afraid of? Dying, losing all her friends, and growing up to be jobless, homeless, and living in a dumpster. She also feared striking out in her next softball game and making the whole team lose. Something dreadful was about to happen, though she couldn't quite put her finger on what it was. In reality, Melissa had little reason to worry. She had health, smarts, beauty, and a loving circle of friends and family.

We all experience irrational worries from time to time, but Melissa's anxiety had become overwhelming. Where do we draw the line between anxiety that is normal and anxiety that is abnormal? ●

  show what you know

1. The classification and diagnosis of psychological disorders have been criticized for:
   a. having specific criteria to identify disorders.
   b. the creation of labeling and expectations.
   c. placing too much emphasis on sociocultural factors.
   d. their research base.

2. One common approach to explaining the etiology of psychological disorders is the _____, which implies that psychological disorders have underlying biological causes, such as genes, neurochemical imbalances, and problems in the brain.

3. Melissa has indicated her worries began early in her life. Using the biopsychosocial perspective, speculate about the factors that may have caused and reinforced these worries.

✓ CHECK YOUR ANSWERS IN APPENDIX C.

Anxiety Disorders

LO 4 Define anxiety disorders and demonstrate an understanding of their causes.

Think about the objects or situations that cause you to feel afraid or uneasy. Maybe you fear creepy crawly insects, slithery snakes, or crowded public spaces. A mild fear of spiders or overcrowded subways is normal, but if you become highly disturbed

TABLE 13.3 ANXIETY DISORDERS

Disorder	Annual Prevalence	Description	Cultural Impact
Separation anxiety disorder	0.9–1.9% in adults; 1.6% in adolescents; 4% in children	Anxiety or fear related to "separation from home or attachment figures" (p. 191)	Cultures vary with respect to age at which it is appropriate to move from parental home.
Specific phobia	7–9%	Anxiety about, or fear of, a specific object or situation	Specific phobias vary across cultures.
Social anxiety disorder (social phobia)	7%	Anxiety about, or fear of being in, a social situation that could result in scrutiny by other people	*Taijin kyofusho* (Japan and Korea)
Panic disorder	2–3%	Reoccurring panic attacks that are unexpected and for which there is no apparent cue or trigger	*Trúng gió* (Vietnam); *ataque de nervios* (Latin America); *khyâl* (Cambodia)
Agoraphobia	1.7%	Anxiety or fear regarding "using public transportation; being in open spaces; being in enclosed places; standing in line or being in a crowd; or being outside of the home" (p. 217)	None listed in *DSM-5*
Generalized anxiety disorder	0.9% in adolescents; 2.9% in adults	Anxiety and worry that are out of proportion to the actual event or situation	Varies by culture

Anxiety disorders are relatively common among both sexes, but they are more apparent in women by an approximate 2:1 ratio. Information from *DSM-5* (American Psychiatric Association, 2013).

Combatting Anxiety

Basketball pro Royce White suffers from panic attacks and generalized anxiety disorder (discussed later in the chapter; Golliver, 2013, January 19). White has become an outspoken advocate for creating new policies to address mental health issues facing players in the National Basketball Association (NBA). Currently, the NBA provides players with access to therapists and treatment, but there is no "separate and distinct mental health policy enumerated in the Collective Bargaining Agreement" (Aldridge, 2016, June 13, para. 46). Howard Smith-USA TODAY Sports.

by the mere thought of them, or if the fear interferes with your everyday functioning, then a problem may exist. People who suffer from **anxiety disorders** have extreme anxiety and/or irrational fears that are debilitating (**TABLE 13.3**). Let's take a look at some of the anxiety disorders identified in the *DSM–5:* panic disorder, specific phobia, agoraphobia, social anxiety disorder, and generalized anxiety disorder.

Panic Disorder

What should you do if you see somebody trembling and sweating, gasping for breath, or complaining of heart palpitations? If you are concerned it's a heart attack, you may be correct; call 911 immediately if you are not sure. However, a person experiencing a **panic attack** may behave very similarly to someone having a heart attack. A panic attack is a sudden, extreme fear or discomfort that escalates quickly, often with no evident cause, and includes symptoms such as increased heart rate, sweating, shortness of breath, chest pain, nausea, lightheadedness, and fear of dying. A diagnosis of **panic disorder** requires such attacks to recur unexpectedly and have no obvious trigger. In addition, the person worries about having more panic attacks, or feels she may be losing control. People with panic disorder often make decisions that are maladaptive, like purposefully avoiding exercise or unfamiliar places in hope of preventing a panic attack.

THE BIOLOGY OF PANIC DISORDER Panic disorder does appear to have a biological cause (American Psychiatric Association, 2013). Researchers have identified specific parts of the brain thought to be involved in panic attacks, including regions of the hypothalamus, which is involved in the fight-or-flight response, and its associated structures (Johnson et al., 2010; Wintermann, Kirschbaum, & Petrowski, 2016). Irregularities in the size and shape of the amygdala may help explain dysfunction in the fight-or-flight response, which could be associated with the physical and behavioral symptoms of panic attacks (Yoon et al., 2016).

GENETICS, GENDER, AND PANIC DISORDER Panic disorder affects about 2–3% of the population (American Psychiatric Association, 2013). Research indicates this disorder runs in families, with heritability estimates around 40–48% (Maron, Hettema, & Shlik, 2010; Weber et al., 2012). This means that over 40% of the variation of the disorder in the *population* can be attributed to genetic factors, while the remaining 60% results from environmental factors. In other words, the frequency and distribution of panic disorder across people result from a combination of factors, 40% of which are genetic, and 60% nongenetic. People often assume heritability refers to an individual's risk for a disorder. ("Her panic disorder is 40% the result of her genes, and 60% due to her environment.") This is incorrect. Remember, heritability explains the variation and risk among individuals in a population. Researchers continue to explore how panic disorder is inherited, identifying some specific genes that might be involved in the process (Hohoff et al., 2015; Smoller et al., 2014).

Women are twice as likely as men to be diagnosed with panic disorder, and this disparity is already apparent by the age of 14 (American Psychiatric Association, 2013; Craske et al., 2010; Weber et al., 2012). Such gender differences may have a biological basis, but we must also consider psychological and social factors.

LEARNING AND PANIC DISORDER Some researchers propose that learning —particularly classical conditioning—can play a role in the development of panic disorder (Bouton, Mineka, & Barlow, 2001; Duits et al., 2015). In a panic disorder scenario, the neutral stimulus might be something like a location (a shopping mall), the unconditioned stimulus an unexpected panic attack, and the unconditioned response the fear resulting from the panic attack. The panic attack location (the shopping mall) would become the conditioned stimulus, such that every time the person thinks of the shopping mall, she responds with fear (now the conditioned response).

Specific Phobias and Agoraphobia

Panic attacks can occur without apparent triggers. This is not the case with a **specific phobia**, which centers on a particular object or situation, such as rats or airplane travel (TABLE 13.4 on the next page). Most people who have a phobia do their best to avoid the feared object or situation. If avoidance is not possible, they withstand it, but only with extreme fear and anxiousness.

LEARNING AND SPECIFIC PHOBIAS As with panic disorder, phobias can be explained using the principles of learning (LeBeau et al., 2010; Rofé & Rofé, 2015). Classical conditioning may lead to the acquisition of a fear, through the pairing of stimuli. Operant conditioning could maintain the phobia, through negative reinforcement; if anxiety (the unpleasant stimulus) is reduced by avoiding a feared object or situation, the avoidance behavior is negatively reinforced and thus more likely to recur. Observational learning can also help explain the development of a phobia. Simply watching someone else experience its symptoms could create fear in an observer (Reynolds, Field, & Askew, 2015). Some research demonstrates that even rhesus monkeys become afraid of snakes if they observe other monkeys reacting fearfully to real or toy snakes (Heyes, 2012; Mineka, Davidson, Cook, & Keir, 1984).

CONNECTIONS

In **Chapter 2,** we described how the sympathetic division of the autonomic nervous system directs the body's stress response. When a stressful situation arises, the sympathetic nervous system prepares the body to react, causing the heart to beat faster, respiration to increase, and the pupils to dilate.

CONNECTIONS

In **Chapter 5,** we described how Little Albert acquired a conditioned emotional response: An originally neutral stimulus (a rat) was paired with an unconditioned stimulus (a loud sound), which led to an unconditioned response (fear). With repeated pairings, the conditioned stimulus (the rat) led to a conditioned response (fear).

CONNECTIONS

In **Chapter 5,** we discussed negative reinforcement; behaviors increase when they are followed by the removal of something unpleasant. Here, the avoidance behavior takes away the anxious feeling, increasing the likelihood of avoiding the object in the future.

anxiety disorders A group of psychological disorders associated with extreme anxiety and/or debilitating, irrational fears.

panic attack Sudden, extreme fear or discomfort that escalates quickly, often with no obvious trigger, and includes symptoms such as increased heart rate, sweating, shortness of breath, chest pain, nausea, lightheadedness, and fear of dying.

panic disorder A psychological disorder that includes recurrent, unexpected panic attacks and fear that can cause significant changes in behavior.

specific phobia A psychological disorder that includes a distinct fear or anxiety in relation to an object or situation.

skydie/Shutterstock.

TABLE 13.4 ARE YOU AFRAID?

Scientific Name	Fear of . . .	Scientific Name	Fear of . . .
Acrophobia	Heights	Epistemophobia	Knowledge
Astraphobia or keraunophobia	Lightning	Gamophobia	Marriage
Brontophobia	Thunder	Ophidiophobia	Snakes
Claustrophobia	Closed spaces	Odontophobia	Dental procedures
Cynophobia	Dogs	Xenophobia	Strangers

The phobias listed above are not specifically included in the *DSM-5*, but they are all associated with the same general response. A person with a specific phobia feels extreme anxiety about a particular object or situation. Fears center on anything from dogs to dental procedures. Information from Reber, Allen, and Reber (2009).

Whoa!
Emotional responses, such as fear of heights, snakes, and spiders, may have evolved to protect us from danger (Plomin, DeFries, Knopik, & Neiderhiser 2013). Avoiding precarious drop-offs and harmful creatures would tend to increase the chances of survival, particularly for our primitive ancestors living in the wild. But when such fears become excessive and irrational, a specific phobia might be present. Ascent Xmedia/Getty Images.

agoraphobia Extreme fear of situations involving public transportation, open spaces, or other public settings.

BIOLOGY, CULTURE, AND SPECIFIC PHOBIAS Phobias can also be understood through the lens of evolutionary psychology. Humans seem to be biologically predisposed to fear certain threats such as spiders, snakes, and bitter foods (Shackelford & Liddle, 2014; Van Strien, Franken, & Huijding, 2014). Spiders, in particular, may inspire fear or disgust because they can be dangerous, but such reactions can also be influenced by culture (Gerdes, Uhl, & Alpers, 2009). From an evolutionary standpoint, these types of fears would tend to protect us from true danger (a poisonous spider bite). But the link between anxiety and evolution is not always so apparent. It's hard to imagine how an intense fear of being in public, for example, would promote survival.

AGORAPHOBIA Do you ever feel a little anxious when you are out in public, in a new city, or at a crowded amusement park? A person with **agoraphobia** (ag-o-ruh-FOH-bee-uh) feels extremely anxious in these types of settings. This disorder is characterized by a distinct fear or anxiety related to public transportation, open spaces, retail stores, crowds, or being alone and away from home in general. Agoraphobia may also result in "panic-like symptoms," which can be difficult to handle. Typically, people with agoraphobia need another person to accompany them on outings, because they feel they may not be able to cope on their own. They may avoid situations that frighten them, or be overwhelmed with fear when avoidance or escape is not possible. As with other anxiety disorders, the fear felt by someone with agoraphobia is beyond what is commonly expected in a particular cultural context (American Psychiatric Association, 2013).

Social Anxiety Disorder

According to the *DSM–5,* a person with *social anxiety disorder* (*social phobia*) has an "intense" fear of social situations and scrutiny by others. The extreme fear could arise during a speech or presentation, while eating a meal, or simply in an intimate conversation. Social anxiety often stems from a preoccupation with offending someone or behaving in a way that reveals one's anxiety, and frequently includes an overestimation of the potential undesirable consequences of behaviors. This intense fear is not warranted, however. Being evaluated or even mocked by others is not necessarily dangerous and should not cause debilitating stress. This type of social anxiety, where one fears the judgment and scrutiny of others, is what psychologists often observe in Western societies. In other parts of the world, social anxiety may take a different form.

ACROSS THE WORLD
The Many Faces of Social Anxiety

Every society has its own collection of social rules, so it's not surprising that social anxiety presents itself in distinct ways across the world. People in East Asian cultures, for example, tend to avoid anxiety-provoking situations that might cause them to blush, sweat, or shake. Some individuals in Japan and Korea suffer from *taijin kyofusho,* a cultural syndrome characterized by an intense fear of offending or embarrassing other people with one's body odor, stomach rumblings, or facial expressions. Note that with *taijin kyofusho,* the fear is associated with causing distress in others. In the United States and other Western countries, social anxiety manifests as worry about humiliating oneself (Hofmann & Hinton, 2014; Hofmann, Asnaani, & Hinton, 2010). This distinction may stem from cultural differences; East Asian societies are more collectivist than those of the Western world. Collectivist cultures value social harmony over individual needs, so causing discomfort in others is worse than personal humiliation.

It's important to note that nobody completely fits the collectivist or individualist mold of their cultures: "There is always a degree of individualistic and collectivistic value orientation in us" (Tse & Ng, 2014, p. 11). A person from Japan (a collectivist society) might be highly focused on herself and her own goals, and thus be classified as more individualistic than collectivist. What kind of social anxiety would you expect this type of person to experience?

The anxiety disorders we have discussed thus far relate to specific objects and scenarios. You can predict that a person with agoraphobia will feel distressed walking through an enormous shopping mall, and there is a good chance that someone with social phobia will feel very uncomfortable at a cocktail party. But what about anxiety that is more pervasive, affecting many aspects of life?

Generalized Anxiety Disorder

A person with **generalized anxiety disorder** experiences an excessive amount of worry and anxiety about many activities relating to family, health, school, and other aspects of daily life (American Psychiatric Association, 2013). The psychological distress is accompanied by physical symptoms such as muscle tension and restlessness. Individuals with generalized anxiety disorder may avoid activities they believe will not go smoothly, spend a great deal of time getting ready for such events, or wait until the very last minute to engage in the anxiety-producing activity. Like other disorders, the anxiety must cause substantial distress in social settings or work environments to merit a diagnosis.

The development of generalized anxiety disorder is influenced by both nature and nurture. Some affected individuals appear to have a genetic predisposition to developing irregularities in parts of the brain associated with fear, such as the amygdala and hippocampus (Hettema et al., 2012; Hettema, Neale, & Kendler, 2001). Environmental factors such as adversity in childhood and overprotective parents may also play a role (American Psychiatric Association, 2013).

BODY ODOR AND OTHER CULTURAL AFFRONTS

"Social Anxiety?"
In Japan, social anxiety is sometimes manifested through *taijin kyofusho,* "a cultural syndrome characterized by anxiety about and avoidance of interpersonal situations due to the thought, feeling, or conviction that one's appearance and actions in social interactions are inadequate or offensive to others" (American Psychiatric Association, 2013, p. 837). *Taijin kyofusho* is more likely to affect men than women, and has been observed in Korea and other countries outside of Japan (Hofmann & Hinton, 2014). Tokyo Space Club/Corbis/VCG/Getty Images.

Synonyms

taijin kyofusho *taijin kyofu*

generalized anxiety disorder A psychological disorder characterized by an excessive amount of worry and anxiety about activities relating to family, health, school, and other aspects of daily life.

 **MELISSA'S STRUGGLE** We introduced this section with the story of Melissa Hopely, a girl who struggled with anxiety and performed elaborate rituals to alleviate it. Melissa's behavior caused significant distress and dysfunction, which suggests that it was abnormal, but does it match any of the anxiety disorders described above? Her anxiety was not attached to a specific object or situation, so it doesn't appear to be a phobia. Nor was her anxiety widespread and nonspecific, as might be the case with generalized anxiety disorder. Melissa's fears emanated from nagging, dreadful thoughts generated by her own mind. She may not have been struggling with an anxiety disorder per se, but she certainly was experiencing anxiety as a result of some disorder. So what was it? ●

◯✓◯◯ show what you know

1. Someone with a diagnosis of panic disorder will experience unexpected and recurrent:
   a. comorbidity.
   c. panic attacks.
   b. medical illnesses.
   d. dramatic mood swings.

2. A behaviorist might propose that you acquire a phobia through _____, but the maintenance of that phobia could be the result of _____.

3. People suffering from *taijin kyofusho* tend to worry more about embarrassing others than they do about being embarrassed themselves. Yet in Western cultures, the opposite is generally true. What cultural characteristics might lead to these differences in the expression of anxiety?

✓ CHECK YOUR ANSWERS IN APPENDIX C.

Fear of Germs
Comedian and television personality Howie Mandel participates in the *America's Got Talent* panel at the NBC Universal Summer Press Day in Westlake Village, California. Mandel, who has spoken publicly about his struggle with obsessive-compulsive disorder (OCD), is known for his signature "fist bump." Receiving people with a fist bump (as opposed to a handshake) allays his worries about catching germs (Hines, 2015, May 27).
Frederick M. Brown/Getty Images.

Obsessive-Compulsive Disorder

At age 12, Melissa was diagnosed with **obsessive-compulsive disorder (OCD)**, a psychological disorder characterized by unwanted thoughts, or obsessions, and repetitive, ritualistic behaviors known as compulsions.

LO 5 Summarize the symptoms and causes of obsessive-compulsive disorder.

Troubling Thoughts, Troubling Behaviors

An **obsession** is a thought, urge, or image that recurs repeatedly, is intrusive and unwelcome, and often causes feelings of intense anxiety and distress. Melissa's recurrent, all-consuming thoughts of disaster and death are examples of obsessions. People with OCD attempt to stop, or at least ignore, their obsessions by engaging in a replacement thought or activity. This isn't always helpful, though, because the replacement can become a **compulsion**, which is a behavior or "mental act" repeated over and over.

Those who suffer from OCD experience various types of obsessions and compulsions. In many cases, obsessions focus on fears of contamination with germs or dirt, and compulsions revolve around cleaning and sterilizing (Cisler, Brady, Olatunji, & Lohr, 2010). Some OCD sufferers report that they repeatedly wash their hands even after abrasions have formed (Gillan & Robbins, 2014). Other common compulsions include repetitive rituals and checking behaviors. Melissa, for example, developed a compulsion about locking her car. Unlike most people, who lock their cars once and walk away, Melissa felt compelled to lock it twice. Then she would begin to wonder whether the car was really locked, so she would lock it a third time—just in case. But 3 is an odd number, and odd numbers don't sit well with Melissa, so she would lock it a fourth time. When Melissa finally felt comfortable enough to walk away, she had locked her car eight times. And sometimes that was still not enough.

How do you explain this type of behavior? OCD compulsions often aim to thwart unwanted situations, and thereby reduce anxiety and distress. Melissa was tormented by multiple obsessions ranging from catastrophic (the death of her mother) to minor (someone stealing her iPod). But the compulsive behaviors of OCD are either "clearly excessive" or not logically related to the event or situation the person is trying to prevent (American Psychiatric Association, 2013).

Where do we draw the line between obsessive or compulsive behavior and the diagnosis of a disorder? Remember, behaviors or symptoms must be significantly distressing or disabling in order to be considered abnormal and qualify as a disorder. This is certainly the case with OCD, in which obsessions and/or compulsions are very time-consuming (taking more than 1 hour a day) and cause a great deal of distress and disruption in daily life. Everyone has odd thoughts and quirky routines, but they don't eat up multiple hours of the day and interfere with school, work, and relationships. That's the key distinction between normal preoccupations and OCD (American Psychiatric Association, 2013). The 12-month prevalence of OCD is estimated to be 1.2% in the United States (American Psychiatric Association, 2013; Ruscio, Stein, Chiu, & Kessler, 2010).

The Biology of OCD

Evidence suggests that the symptoms of OCD are related to abnormal activity of neurotransmitters. Reduced activity of serotonin is thought to play a role, and additional neurotransmitters are being studied (Bloch, McGuire, Landeros-Weisenberger, Leckman, & Pittenger, 2010; Pittenger et al., 2016). Certain areas of the brain have been implicated, including locations in the basal ganglia, cingulate gyri, and orbital frontal cortex (American Psychiatric Association, 2013; Radua & Mataix-Cols, 2009). Normally, these regions play a role in planning and regulating movement (Rotge et al., 2009).

Why do these biological differences arise? There appears to be a genetic basis for OCD. If a first-degree relative (parent, sibling, or offspring who shares about 50% of one's DNA) has an OCD diagnosis, the risk of developing OCD is twice as high as someone whose first-degree relatives do not have the disorder (American Psychiatric Association, 2013). However, genes do not tell the whole story. The heritability for OCD is around 40%, suggesting that environmental factors also play a substantial role in the development of this disorder (Pauls, Abramovitch, Rauch, & Geller, 2014).

The Role of Learning

To ease her anxiety, Melissa turned to compulsions—repetitive, ritualistic behaviors aimed at relieving or offsetting her obsessions. Because her greatest fears never came to pass, Melissa assumed that her actions had prevented them. *I didn't die because I touched all the things in my room just the right way,* she would think to herself. The more she followed through on her compulsions and saw that her fears never played out, the more convinced she became that her behaviors prevented them. As Melissa put it, "When you feed it, feed it, feed it, it gets stronger."

Melissa's case illustrates how learning can play a role in OCD. Her compulsions were negatively reinforced by the reduction in her fear. Negative reinforcement leads to more compulsive behaviors, those compulsions are negatively reinforced, and the "negative reinforcement cycle" continues (Pauls et al., 2014, p. 420). Here, we can draw a parallel with drug addiction. Taking a drug can remove unpleasant withdrawal symptoms, just like carrying out compulsions reduces unpleasant feelings of fear. In both cases, the behavior increases when an unpleasant experience is removed (Abramovitch

---

CONNECTIONS

Negative reinforcement (**Chapter 5**) promotes the maladaptive behavior here. The compulsions are not actually preventing unwanted occurrences, but they do lead to a decrease in anxiety, and thus negatively reinforce the behavior. Repeatedly locking the car temporarily reduced Melissa's anxiety, making her more likely to perform this behavior in the future.

obsessive-compulsive disorder (OCD) A psychological disorder characterized by obsessions and/or compulsions that are time-consuming and cause a great deal of distress.

obsession A thought, an urge, or an image that happens repeatedly, is intrusive and unwelcome, and often causes anxiety and distress.

compulsion A behavior or "mental act" that a person repeats over and over in an effort to reduce anxiety.

& McKay, 2016). This learning process is ongoing and potentially very powerful. In one study, researchers monitored 144 people with OCD diagnoses for more than 40 years. The participants' OCD symptoms improved, in some cases with the help of treatment, but almost half continued to show "clinically relevant" symptoms after four decades (Skoog & Skoog, 1999).

We should note that not all compulsive behaviors stem from OCD. Do you ever bite your nails or pick at your skin?

from the pages of

SCIENTIFIC AMERICAN

Nail Biting May Arise from Perfectionism

Body-focused repetitive behaviors may be a reaction to boredom or frustration.

Many people think of nail biting as a nervous habit, but the driving force may not be anxiety. Mounting evidence shows that people who compulsively bite their nails, pick their skin or pull their hair are often perfectionists, and their actions may help soothe boredom, irritation and dissatisfaction.

As many as one in 20 people suffer from body-focused repetitive disorders, engaging in behaviors such as biting their nails or plucking out hair until they damage their appearance or cause themselves pain. These disorders are related to tic disorders and, more distantly, obsessive-compulsive disorder. As such, the repetitive behavior is extremely difficult to quit—yet many people continue to think they simply have a nervous habit and are too weak-willed to overcome it.

A new study adds evidence to a theory that perfectionism rather than anxiety is at the root of these behaviors. The researchers first surveyed 48 participants, half of whom had these disorders and half of whom did not, on their organizational behavior and ability to regulate their emotions. Those with the disorders scored as organizational perfectionists, indicating a tendency to overplan, overwork themselves and get frustrated quickly without high levels of activity.

Researchers then put the subjects in situations designed to provoke four different emotions: to incite stress, they showed a movie of a plane crash; to promote relaxation, they showed a movie of waves; to elicit frustration, they presented a difficult puzzle but said it was easy; and to evoke boredom, they made participants sit in a room alone. People who had the disorders engaged in the body-focused behaviors during all the situations except the relaxing movie.

The work, which was published earlier this year in the *Journal of Behavior Therapy and Experimental Psychiatry,* jibes with a recent theory that stress is far from the sole cause of these compulsions. Boredom and frustration, easily elicited by an underlying perfectionist personality, may be more important triggers. Past research suggests that the biting or scratching indeed makes people feel better temporarily—perhaps satisfying the perfectionist urge to be doing something rather than nothing. After the initial relief, however, comes pain, shame and embarrassment.

The findings could help therapists treat patients who suffer from the disorders; studies have shown that these types of perfectionist beliefs and behaviors can be eased with cognitive-behavior therapy. If patients can learn to think and act differently when tension builds, they may be able to stop the urge before it starts. **Susan Cosier. Reproduced with permission. Copyright © 2015 Scientific American, a division of Nature America, Inc. All rights reserved.**

  show what you know

1. Melissa has demonstrated recurrent all-consuming thoughts and feelings of worry. She tries to stop unwanted thoughts through a variety of behaviors that she repeats over and over again. These behaviors are known as:
   a. obsessions.
   b. classical conditioning.
   c. panic attacks.
   d. compulsions.

2. Evidence points to a _____ basis for OCD. If a first-degree relative has an OCD diagnosis, a person's risk of developing the same disorder is twice as high as someone whose first-degree relatives do not have the disorder.

3. Melissa's therapist helped reduce the negative reinforcement of her compulsions by not allowing her to repeatedly check that her car was locked. Explain why such a technique would work.

✓ CHECK YOUR ANSWERS IN APPENDIX C.

Depressive Disorders

MELISSA'S SECOND DIAGNOSIS Unfortunately for Melissa, receiving a diagnosis and treatment did not solve her problems. She hated herself for having OCD, and her parents and some friends had a hard time accepting her diagnosis. "Every day I woke up, I wanted to die," says Melissa, who reached a breaking point during her sophomore year in high school. After a particularly difficult day at school, Melissa returned home with the intention of taking her own life. Luckily, a friend recognized that she was in distress and notified Melissa's family members, who rushed home to find Melissa curled up in a ball in the corner of her room, rocking back and forth and mumbling nonsense. They took Melissa to the hospital, where she would be safe and begin treatment. During her 3-day stay in the psychiatric unit, Melissa finally met people who didn't think she was "crazy" or define her by the disorder. For the first time, she explains, "I realized I wasn't my disorder."

During that hospital stay, doctors gave Melissa a new diagnosis in addition to OCD. They told her that she was suffering from *depression*. Apparently, the profound sadness and helplessness she had been feeling were symptoms of **major depressive disorder**, one of the depressive disorders described in the *DSM–5* (**TABLE 13.5** on the next page). ●

The Importance of Friends
Melissa (right) poses with childhood friend Mary Beth, whom she credits for helping to save her life. The day that Melissa arrived home intending to attempt suicide, Mary Beth recognized her friend's distress and called for help. Thanks to the intervention of friends and family, Melissa received the treatment she needed. Melissa Hopely.

DSM–5 and Major Depressive Disorder

LO 6 Summarize the symptoms and causes of major depressive disorder.

A *major depressive episode* is evident if five or more of the symptoms listed below (1) occur for at least 2 consecutive weeks and represent a change from prior functioning, (2) cause significant distress or impairment, and (3) are not due to a medical or drug-related condition:

- depressed mood, which might result in feeling sad or hopeless;
- reduced pleasure in activities almost all of the time;
- substantial loss or gain in weight, without conscious effort, or changes in appetite;
- sleeping excessively or not sleeping enough;
- feeling tired, drained of energy;
- feeling worthless or extremely guilt-ridden;
- difficulty thinking or concentrating;
- persistent thoughts about death or suicide.

As you can imagine, someone with five or more of these symptoms would feel distraught and experience problems in social interactions and at work.

In order to be diagnosed with major depressive disorder, a person must have experienced at least one major depressive episode. Some people suffer a single episode, while others battle *recurrent* episodes. In some instances, the disorder is triggered by the birth of a baby. Approximately 3–6% of women experience depression starting in pregnancy or within weeks or months of giving birth; this is known as *peripartum onset* (American Psychiatric Association, 2013).

Talking About Depression
Rapper Kendrick Lamar performs at the 2016 British Summer Time Festival in London, England. Lamar has touched upon the topic of depression in some of his song lyrics. In a 2015 interview with MTV, he described some of the emotional trauma he experienced as a young person in Compton, California: "Three of my homeboys [one] summertime was murdered, close ones too, not just somebody that I hear about. These [are] people I grew up with. It all, psychologically, it messes your brain up" (Boardman, 2015, April 3, para. 8). If you or someone you know appears to be experiencing depression or suicidal thoughts, do not hesitate to seek help. Call the National Suicide Prevention Line: 1-800-273-TALK or 1-800-273-8255. Samir Hussein/Redferns/Getty Images.

major depressive disorder
A psychological disorder that includes at least one major depressive episode, with symptoms such as depressed mood, problems with sleep, and loss of energy.

TABLE 13.5 DEPRESSIVE DISORDERS

Depressive Disorder	Description	Annual Prevalence
Disruptive mood dysregulation disorder	Persistent irritability that typically results in "temper outbursts' and "angry mood that is present between the severe temper outbursts" (p. 156)	2–5% in children
Major depressive disorder	Feeling depressed (sad, empty, hopeless) almost every day for 2 weeks, or "a loss of interest or pleasure in" almost all activities (p. 163)	7% in the 18-29 age bracket, and 3 times higher among those age 60 and older
Persistent depressive disorder (dysthymia)	Feeling depressed the majority of the time: at least 2 years in adults and 1 year in children and adolescents	0.05%

As you can see from these descriptions, the word "depression" can mean many things. Listed above are various types of depression and their annual prevalence. Information from *DSM-5* (American Psychiatric Association, 2013).

Diagnosing major depressive disorder can be challenging. The clinician must be able to distinguish the symptoms from normal reactions to a "significant loss," such as the death of a loved one. This is not always easy because responses to death often resemble depression. A key distinction is that grief generally decreases with time, and comes in waves associated with memories or reminders of the loss; the sadness associated with a major depressive episode tends to remain steady (American Psychiatric Association, 2013).

Major depressive disorder is one of the most common and devastating psychological disorders. In the United States, the lifetime prevalence of major depressive disorder is almost 17% (Kessler, Berglund, et al., 2005; Kessler, Petukhova, Sampson, Zaslavsky, & Wittchen, 2012); this means that nearly 1 in 5 Americans experience a major depressive episode at least once in life. Beginning in adolescence, rates of this disorder are already 1.5 to 3 times higher for females (American Psychiatric Association, 2013). This gender difference persists after puberty when rates of depression "dramatically" rise (Hankin et al., 2015). In adulthood, women continue to be affected more than men (Kessler et al., 2003).

The effects of major depressive disorder extend far beyond the individual. For Americans ages 15 to 44, this condition is a "leading cause" of disability (Greenberg, Fournier, Sisitky, Pike, & Kessler, 2015)—and this means it impacts the productivity of the workforce. In a comprehensive study of major depressive disorder, respondents reported that their symptoms prevented them from going to work or performing day-to-day activities for an average of 35 days a year (Kessler et al., 2003). Stop and think about this statistic—we are talking about a loss of 7 work weeks!

CULTURE Depression is one of the most common disorders in the world, yet the symptoms experienced, the course of treatment, and the words used to describe it vary from culture to culture. For example, people in China rarely report feeling "sad," but instead focus on physical symptoms, such as dizziness, fatigue, or inner pressure (Kleinman, 2004). In Thailand, depression is commonly expressed through mental and physical symptoms such as headaches, fatigue, daydreaming, social withdrawal, irritation, and forgetfulness (Chirawatkul, Prakhaw, & Chomnirat, 2011). Culture affects the way people experience emotion, and it may even impact rates of depression (Chan, Zhang, Fung, & Hagger, 2015).

SUICIDE The recurrent nature of major depressive disorder increases one's risk for suicide and health complications (Knorr et al., 2016; Monroe & Harkness, 2011).

Around 9% of adults in 21 countries confirm they have harbored "serious thoughts of suicide" at least once (**INFOGRAPHIC 13.2** on the next page), and around 3% have attempted suicide (Borges et al., 2010). According to the National Institute of Mental Health (NIMH; 2013, October 1), approximately 90% of people who commit suicide have a psychological disorder, usually depressive disorder and/or substance abuse disorder.

The Biology of Depression

Nearly 7% of Americans battle depression in any given year (American Psychiatric Association, 2013; Kessler, Chiu, et al., 2005). What underlies this staggering statistic? There appears to be something biological at work.

GENETIC FACTORS Studies of twins, family pedigrees, and adoptions tell us that major depressive disorder runs in families, with heritability estimates between 37% and 50% (American Psychiatric Association, 2013; Levinson, 2006; Wray et al., 2012). This means that about 37–50% of the variability of major depressive disorder in the population can be attributed to genetic factors. People who have a first-degree relative with this disorder are 2 to 4 times more likely to develop it than those whose first-degree relatives are unaffected (American Psychiatric Association, 2013).

DEPRESSION AND THE BRAIN Three neurotransmitters appear to be associated with the cause and course of major depressive disorder: *norepinephrine, serotonin,* and *dopamine.* The relationships among these neurotransmitters are complicated and research is ongoing (El Mansari et al., 2010; Torrente, Gelenberg, & Vrana, 2012), but the findings are intriguing. For example, serotonin deficiency has been associated with major depressive disorder (Kambeitz & Howes, 2015; Torrente et al., 2012), and genes may be responsible for some of this irregular activity, particularly in the amygdala and other brain areas involved in processing depression-related emotions (Northoff, 2012).

Depression also seems to be correlated with specific structural features in the brain (Andrus et al., 2012). Studies have zeroed in on a variety of factors, such as increased structure size, decreased volume, and changes in neural activity (Kempton et al., 2011; Sacher et al., 2012; Singh et al., 2013). Functional magnetic resonance imaging (fMRI) research points to irregularities in neural pathways involved in processing emotions and rewards for people with major depressive disorder (American Psychiatric Association, 2013). There is also evidence that some of those affected have irregularities in the amygdala, the prefrontal cortex, and the hippocampus. For example, some regions of the right cortex show significant thinning in people who face a high risk of developing major depressive disorder (Peterson et al., 2009).

Major depressive disorder most likely results from a complex interplay of many neural factors. What's difficult to determine is the causal direction: Do changes in the brain precede the disorder, or does the disorder lead to changes in the brain?

HORMONES There is also evidence that hormones play a role in depression. People with depressive disorders may have high levels of cortisol, a hormone secreted by the adrenal glands (Belmaker & Agam, 2008; Dougherty, Klein, Olino, Dyson, & Rose, 2009). Women sufferers, in particular, appear to be affected by stress-induced brain activity and hormonal fluctuations (Holsen et al., 2011), particularly those associated with pregnancy and childbirth (Schiller, Meltzer-Brody, & Rubinow, 2015). For both women and men, depressive symptoms may link to abnormal activity of the hypothalamic-pituitary-adrenal (HPA) system, which plays an important role in the stress response (American Psychiatric Association, 2013).

Baby Blues
Actor Hayden Panettiere smiles for photographers at the 66th Annual Primetime Emmy Awards in Los Angeles. The *Nashville* star has been open about her struggle with postpartum depression (Abrahamson, 2016, May 13). Having a baby is a stressful, life-changing event, and a time of dramatic hormonal shifts. These changes may contribute to the major depressive episodes some women experience before and after the birth of a baby. Jon Kopaloff/FilmMagic/Getty Images.

CONNECTIONS

In **Chapter 2,** we described the endocrine system, which uses glands to convey messages via hormones. These chemicals released into the bloodstream can cause aggression and mood swings, as well as influence growth and alertness. Hormones may also play a role in major depressive disorder.

CONNECTIONS

In **Chapter 12,** we discussed the HPA system, which helps maintain balance in the body by overseeing the sympathetic nervous system, the neuroendocrine system, and the immune system. The HPA system is also associated with depressive episodes.

Suicide in the United States

In 2009, suicide emerged as the leading cause of death from injury in the United States, surpassing rates for homicide and traffic accidents (Rockett et al., 2012). Researchers examine suicide rates across gender, age, and ethnicity in order to better understand risk factors and to help develop suicide prevention strategies. Let's take a look at what this means—and what you can do if a friend or family member might be contemplating suicide.

Among adults aged 18 and older, **8.7 million reported having serious thoughts about suicide** in the past year.

1,100,000 attempted suicide.

(SUBSTANCE ABUSE AND MENTAL HEALTH SERVICES ADMINISTRATION, 2011)

In 2010, someone died as a result of suicide almost every **14 minutes**.
(AMERICAN FOUNDATION FOR SUICIDE PREVENTION, 2013)

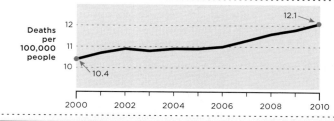

Deaths per 100,000 people

12 — 12.1
11
10 — 10.4

2000 2002 2004 2006 2008 2010

From 2000 to 2010, suicide rates **increased by nearly 20%.**
(AMERICAN FOUNDATION FOR SUICIDE PREVENTION, 2013)

Suicide is the second leading cause of death for people aged 25 to 34, and the third leading cause of death for people aged 15 to 24.

(CENTERS FOR DISEASE CONTROL AND PREVENTION, NATIONAL CENTER FOR INJURY PREVENTION AND CONTROL, 2010)

Until 2006, people aged 85 and older had the highest rate of suicide. Now people 45 to 64 years old have the highest rate.

The suicide rate for males is nearly 4 times higher than females.

(AMERICAN FOUNDATION FOR SUICIDE PREVENTION, 2013)

WHITE — 14.1
AMERICAN INDIAN AND ALASKAN NATIVE — 11.0
ASIAN AND PACIFIC ISLANDER — 6.2
HISPANIC — 5.9
BLACK — 5.1

White Americans have the highest rate of suicide: In 2010, 14.1 out of every 100,000 died by suicide.
(AMERICAN FOUNDATION FOR SUICIDE PREVENTION, 2013)

Risk factors for suicide include:

✔ Previous suicide attempt(s)
✔ Family history of suicide or violence
✔ Alcohol or drug abuse
✔ Physical illness
✔ History of depression or other mental illness
✔ Feeling alone

(CENTERS FOR DISEASE CONTROL AND PREVENTION, 2012i)

If you believe a friend may be thinking about suicide:

- Encourage your friend to contact a responsible person who can help. This may be a counselor, teacher, or health-care professional. Or call a suicide prevention hotline.
- Don't be afraid to be wrong. Talking about suicide will not put the idea in your friend's head. Be direct and ask your friend if he is thinking about hurting himself.
- Just talking with your friend can help. Listen without being judgmental.
- If your friend admits that she has made a detailed plan or obtained a means of hurting herself, stay with her until help arrives or until she is willing to go talk with someone who can help.
- Never agree to keep someone's thoughts about suicide a secret.

(MAINE SUICIDE PREVENTION PROGRAM, 2006; YOUTH SUICIDE PREVENTION PROGRAM, 2011)

Ninety percent of those who commit suicide had a psychological disorder. Of these, 60% involved major depressive disorder. More than 80% of those people with disorders had not been receiving treatment at the time (Mann et al., 2005).

NATIONAL SUICIDE PREVENTION LIFELINE: 1-800-273-TALK (8255)
suicidepreventionlifeline.org

Photo is being used for illustrative purposes only; persons depicted in the photos are models.

Psychological Roots of Depression

Earlier, we mentioned heritability rates of 37–50% for depression. But what about the other 50–63% of the variability? Clearly, biology is not everything. Psychological factors also play a role in the onset and course of major depressive disorder.

LEARNED HELPLESSNESS According to American psychologist Martin Seligman (1942–), people often become depressed because they believe they have no control over the consequences of their behaviors (Overmier & Seligman, 1967; Seligman, 1975; Seligman & Maier, 1967). To demonstrate this **learned helplessness**, Seligman restrained dogs in a hammock and then randomly administered inescapable painful electric shocks to their paws (**FIGURE 13.2**). The next day, the same dogs were put into another cage. Although unrestrained, they did not try to escape shocks administered through a floor grid (even though they could have, by jumping over a low barrier in the cage). Seligman concluded the dogs had learned they couldn't control painful experiences during the prior training; they were acting in a depressed manner. He translated this finding to people with major depressive disorder, suggesting that they, too, feel powerless to change things for the better, and therefore become passive and depressed.

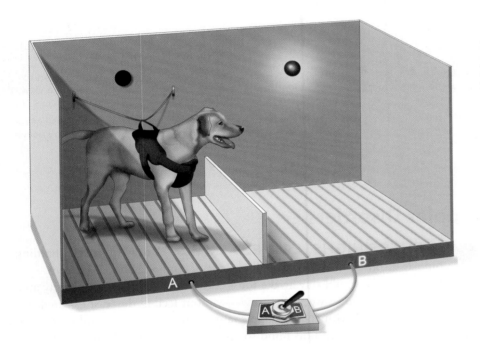

FIGURE 13.2

Seligman's Research on Learned Helplessness

Dogs restrained in a hammock were unable to escape painful shocks administered through an electrical grid on the floor of a specially designed cage called a shuttle box. The dogs soon learned that they were helpless and couldn't control these painful experiences. They did not try to escape by jumping over the barrier even when they were not restrained. The figure here shows the electrical grid activated on side B.

NEGATIVE THINKING American psychiatrist Aaron Beck (1921–) suggests that depression is connected with negative thinking. Depression, according to Beck (1976), is the product of a "cognitive triad"—a negative view of experiences, self, and the future. Here's an example: A student receives a failing grade on an exam, so she begins to think she is a poor student, and that belief leads her to the conclusion that she will fail the course. This self-defeating attitude may actually lead to her failing the course, reinforcing her belief that she is a poor student, and perhaps evolving into a broader belief that her life is a failure. People with this negative thinking style are thought to be at risk for developing a deep sense of hopelessness when they experience "negative life events." This "hopelessness depression" can include symptoms such as sadness, suicidal behavior, self-blame, and a low sense of belonging (Fisher, Overholser, Ridley, Braden, & Rosoff, 2015; Liu, Kleiman, Nestor, & Cheek, 2015).

learned helplessness A tendency for people to believe they have no control over the consequences of their behaviors, resulting in passive behavior.

If you aren't convinced that beliefs contribute to depression, consider this: The way people respond to their experience of depression may impact the severity of the disorder. People who repeatedly focus on this experience are much more likely to remain depressed and perhaps even descend into deeper depression (Eaton et al., 2012; Nolen-Hoeksema, 1991). Women tend to *ruminate* or constantly think about their negative emotions more than men, rather than using "active problem solving" (Eaton et al., 2012). Yet changing negative thoughts and moods during major depressive episodes is difficult to do without help. We should also note that a correlation between rumination and depression is not the same as a cause-and-effect relationship. Not every negative thinker develops depression, and depression can lead to negative thoughts.

 In Class: Collaborate and Report

Team up and **A)** consider the psychological roots of depression, such as learned helplessness and negative thinking, **B)** brainstorm some scenarios in which a person falls prey to the "cognitive triad" of negative thinking, and **C)** discuss how your understanding of this perspective might influence your interactions with someone who is depressed.

Now that we have explored the darkest, saddest realm of human emotion, it's time to venture to another extreme.

 ◯⊘◯◯ show what you know

1. Melissa is sleeping too much, feeling tired all the time, and avoiding activities she once enjoyed. Which of the following best describes the disorder Melissa may be experiencing?
   a. obsessive-compulsive disorder
   c. agoraphobia
   b. major depressive disorder
   d. panic attacks

2. Aaron Beck proposed that _____ is connected to negative thinking, and is the product of a negative view of experiences, self, and future.

3. Many factors contribute to the etiology and course of major depressive disorder. Prepare notes for a 5-minute speech you might give on this topic.

√ CHECK YOUR ANSWERS IN APPENDIX C.

Bipolar Disorders

HIGHEST HIGHS, LOWEST LOWS When Ross began battling bipolar disorder, he went through periods of euphoria and excitement. Sometimes he would stay awake for 4 consecutive days, or sleep barely an hour per night for 2 weeks in a row—without feeling the least bit tired. In fact, he was exploding with energy, supercharged with confidence, and feeling high on life. Ideas flashed through his mind so fast that it was difficult to focus on any one of them. "My brain was a television," Ross says, "and someone was just constantly flipping channels." The only way he could ease his mind was by drinking—and we're not talking about a couple of beers or a few shots of vodka, but an entire case or a whole bottle. Ross was using alcohol to drown out his symptoms. ●

DSM-5 and Bipolar Disorders

LO 7   Compare and contrast bipolar disorders and major depressive disorder.

manic episodes States of continuous elation that is out of proportion to the setting, and can include irritability, very high and sustained levels of energy, and an "expansive" mood.

The extreme energy, euphoria, and confidence Ross felt were most likely the result of **manic episodes**, also known as *mania*. Manic episodes are often characterized by continuous elation that is out of proportion to the situation. For example, a person might show up to work wearing inappropriate, extravagant clothing, talking too fast, and acting like an authority on topics outside his area of expertise. Other features include irritability, very high and sustained levels of energy, and an "expansive" mood, meaning the person feels more powerful than he really is and behaves in a showy or overly confident way. During one of these manic episodes, a person exhibits three or more of the symptoms listed below, which represent deviations from normal behavior (American Psychiatric Association, 2013):

- grandiose or extremely high self-esteem;
- reduced sleep;
- increased talkativeness;
- a "flight of ideas" or the feeling of "racing" thoughts;
- being easily distracted;
- heightened activity at school or work;
- physical agitation;
- displaying poor judgment and engaging in activities that could have serious consequences (risky sexual behavior, or excessive shopping sprees, for example).

It is not unusual for a person experiencing a severe manic episode to be hospitalized. Mania is difficult to hide and can be dangerous. One may act out of character, doing things that damage important relationships or jeopardize work. A person may become violent, posing a risk to himself and others. Seeking help is unlikely, because mania leads to impaired judgment, feelings of grandiosity, and euphoria. (Why would you seek help if you feel on top of the world?) At these times, the support of others is essential.

There are various types of bipolar disorder. To be diagnosed with *bipolar I disorder,* a person must experience at least one *manic episode,* substantial distress, and great impairment. *Bipolar II disorder* requires at least one major depressive episode, as well as a *hypomanic episode. Hypomania* is associated with some of the same symptoms as a manic episode, but the manic behavior does not last as long and generally does not impair one's ability to function (American Psychiatric Association, 2013; **TABLE 13.6**).

BIPOLAR CYCLING Some people with bipolar disorder cycle between extreme highs and lows of emotion and energy that last for days, weeks, or even months. As

Battling Bipolar
Demi Lovato takes the stage at the 93.3 FLZ Jingle Ball 2014 in Tampa, Florida. This singer/songwriter is one of millions of Americans living with bipolar disorder, and she has encouraging words for those who share her struggle: "It's possible to live well, feel well, and also find happiness with bipolar disorder or any other mental illness" (Heiser, 2015, May 28, para. 2). Alexander Tamargo/Getty Images for iHeartMedia.

You Asked, Ross Answers

qrs.ly/1v5duf1

What was the hardest part of having your disorder when you were younger, and what's the hardest part now?

scan this ➜

TABLE 13.6	BIPOLAR DISORDERS	
Bipolar Disorder	**Description**	**Annual**
Bipolar I disorder	Episodes of mania that include an "abnormally, persistently elevated, expansive, or irritable mood and persistently increased activity or energy that is present for most of the day, nearly every day, for a period of at least 1 week" (p. 127). This may be preceded by hypomania or depression.	0.6%
Bipolar II disorder	Repeated major depressive episodes (lasting at least 2 weeks) and "at least one hypomanic episode," which must last for a minimum of 4 days (p. 135).	0.8%

Bipolar I disorder and bipolar II disorder have distinct patterns of highs and lows. Looking at the annual prevalence (yearly occurrence) of these disorders, you can see that they are relatively rare. Information from *DSM–5* (American Psychiatric Association, 2013).

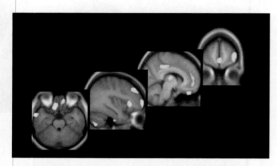

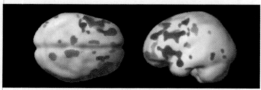

Bipolar in the Brain
Using imaging techniques, researchers have identified certain brain irregularities that appear to be linked to bipolar disorder. These MRI images highlight areas of decreased gray matter volume in prefrontal and temporal areas associated with high-level cognitive functioning and emotional regulation (Rietschel, Maier, & Schulze, 2013). Dr. Marcella Rietschel.

mentioned earlier, bouts of *mania* are often characterized by unusually elevated, irritable, or expansive moods. At the other extreme are feelings of deep sadness, emptiness, and helplessness—the depression pole of bipolar disorder can be as severe as the major depressive episodes described earlier. Periods of mania and depression may be brought on by life changes and stressors, though some research suggests it is only the *first* episode that tends to be triggered by some sort of life event, such as a first love. Subsequent episodes may not be as closely linked to such events (Belmaker, 2004; Malkoff-Schwartz et al., 1998; Weiss et al., 2015).

Bipolar disorder is uncommon. Over the course of a lifetime, about 0.8% of the American population will receive a diagnosis of bipolar I disorder, and 1.1% bipolar II disorder (Merikangas et al., 2007). Men and women have an equal chance of being affected, but men tend to experience earlier onset of symptoms, while the incidence for women seems to be higher later in life (Altshuler et al., 2010; Kennedy et al., 2005).

WHO GETS BIPOLAR DISORDER? Although researchers have not determined the cause of bipolar disorder, evidence from twin and adoption studies underscores the importance of genes. If one identical twin is diagnosed with bipolar disorder, there is a 40–70% chance the other twin will have the disorder as well. Among fraternal twins, there is only a 5% chance that the second twin will develop the disorder (Craddock, O'Donovan, & Owen, 2005). The heritability estimates of bipolar disorder are high, falling somewhere between 79% and 90% (Hanford, Nazarov, Hall, & Sassi, 2016). According to the American Psychiatric Association (2013), "A family history of bipolar disorder is one of the strongest and most consistent risk factors for bipolar disorders" (p. 130). Adults with a family member who has bipolar disorder, on average, have a "10-fold increased risk" for developing the disorder themselves. When parents or grandparents have "psychiatric difficulties," an individual with bipolar disorder is at risk for a "more complex and difficult course of bipolar illness" (Post et al., 2015, p. 304).

But nature is not the only force at work in bipolar disorder; nurture plays a role, too. The fact that there is a higher rate of bipolar disorder in high-income countries (1.4%) than in low-income countries (0.7%; American Psychiatric Association, 2013) suggests that environment may act as a catalyst for its development. Additionally, some researchers hypothesize that exposure to viruses, poor nutrition, and stress during fetal development sparks a cascade of biological events that leads to the development of bipolar disorder. The same has been said of another serious disorder: schizophrenia (Carter, 2007; Yolken & Torrey, 1995).

  show what you know

1. Ross described going for 4 days straight without sleeping at all, or 2 weeks in a row sleeping only 1 hour per night. He was exploding with energy, supercharged with confidence, and feeling on top of the world. It is likely that Ross was experiencing periods of euphoria and excitement, which can best be described as:
   a. depression.
   b. manic episodes.
   c. panic attacks.
   d. anxiety.

2. What is the difference between bipolar I disorder and bipolar II disorder?

3. Compare the symptoms of bipolar disorder with those of major depressive disorder.

✓ CHECK YOUR ANSWERS IN APPENDIX C.

Schizophrenia

DSM-5 and Schizophrenia

LO 8 Recognize the symptoms of schizophrenia.

schizophrenia A disabling psychological disorder that can include delusions, hallucinations, disorganized speech, and abnormal motor behavior.

psychosis Loss of contact with reality that is severe and chronic.

How would it feel to have voices following you throughout the day, commenting on your behaviors, attacking your character, and taunting you with hurtful remarks:

"You're ugly, you're worthless, you deserve to die" (Halpern, 2013, April, p. 102)? Meanwhile, your perception of the world is grossly distorted. Nickels, dimes, and pennies all look the same, and the subway you take to class is really on its way to a Nazi concentration camp—or so you believe. These are actual symptoms reported by Lisa Halpern, who suffers from a disabling psychological disorder called **schizophrenia** (skit-suh-FREH-nee-uh). People with schizophrenia experience **psychosis**, a loss of contact with reality that is severe and chronic.

The hallmark features of schizophrenia are disturbances in thinking, perception, and language (**TABLE 13.7**). Psychotic symptoms include **delusions**, which are strange or false beliefs that a person maintains even when presented with evidence to the contrary. Common delusional themes are being persecuted by others, spied upon, or ridiculed. Some people have grandiose delusions; they may believe they are extraordinarily talented or famous, for example. Others are convinced that radio reports, newspaper headlines, or public announcements are about them. Delusions appear very real to those experiencing them.

People with schizophrenia may also hear voices or see things that are not actually present. This psychotic symptom is known as a **hallucination**—a "perception-like experience" that the individual believes is real, but that is not evident to others. Hallucinations can occur with any of the senses, but auditory hallucinations are most common. Often they manifest as voices commenting on what is happening in the environment, or voices using threatening or judgmental language (American Psychiatric Association, 2013).

The symptoms of schizophrenia are often classified as positive and negative (**TABLE 13.8**). **Positive symptoms** are excesses or distortions of normal behavior, and include delusions, hallucinations, and disorganized speech—all of which are generally not observed in people without psychosis. In other words, positive symptoms indicate the *presence* of abnormal behaviors. **Negative symptoms**, on the other hand, refer to the reduction or *absence* of expected behaviors. Common negative symptoms include social withdrawal, diminished speech or speech content, limited emotions, and loss of energy and follow-up (Fusar-Poli et al., 2015; Tandon, Nasrallah, & Keshavan, 2009).

To be diagnosed with schizophrenia, a person must display symptoms for the majority of days in a 1-month period and experience significant dysfunction in work, school, relationships, or personal care for at least 6 months. (And it must be

TABLE 13.7 **IDENTIFYING SCHIZOPHRENIA**
• Delusions
• Hallucinations
• Disorganized speech
• Grossly disorganized or catatonic behavior
• Decreased emotional expression
• Decreased functioning at work, in social situations, or in self-care
• Continuous disturbance lasting at least 6 months
• Symptoms not related to substance use
• Symptoms not related to another medical condition
• Lack of motivation

Many people have heard of schizophrenia but don't really understand what it is. Listed above are some common features of this frequently misunderstood disorder. Information from *DSM–5* (American Psychiatric Association, 2013).

CONNECTIONS

In **Chapter 5,** we noted that the term positive does not always mean "good." Positive punishment means the addition of an aversive stimulus. Positive symptoms refer to additions or excesses, not an evaluation of how "good" the symptoms are. Negative refers to the reduction or absence of behaviors, not an evaluation of how "bad" the symptoms are.

TABLE 13.8	**SYMPTOMS OF SCHIZOPHRENIA**
Positive Symptoms of Schizophrenia	**Negative Symptoms of Schizophrenia**
Delusions	Decreased emotional expression
Hallucinations	Lack of motivation
Disorganized speech	Decreased speech production
Grossly disorganized behavior	Reduced pleasure
Abnormal motor behavior	Lack of interest in interacting with others

Schizophrenia symptoms can be grouped into two main categories: Positive symptoms indicate the presence of excesses or distortions of normal behavior; negative symptoms refer to a reduction in normal behaviors and mental processes. Information from *DSM–5* (American Psychiatric Association, 2013).

delusions Strange or false beliefs that a person firmly maintains even when presented with evidence to the contrary.

hallucinations Perception-like experiences that an individual believes are real, but that are not evident to others.

positive symptoms Excesses or distortions of normal behavior; examples are delusions, hallucinations, and disorganized speech.

negative symptoms Behaviors or characteristics that are limited or absent; examples are social withdrawal, diminished speech, limited or no emotions, and loss of energy and follow-up.

determined that these problems do not result from substance abuse or a serious medical condition.) Using the *DSM-5,* clinicians can rate the presence and severity of symptoms (hallucinations, delusions, disorganized speech, unusual psychomotor behaviors, and negative symptoms).

With estimates ranging from a 0.3–1% lifetime risk, schizophrenia is uncommon (American Psychiatric Association, 2013; Saha, Chant, Welham, & McGrath, 2005). Although men and women appear to face an equal risk (Abel, Drake, & Goldstein, 2010; Saha et al., 2005), the onset of the disorder tends to occur earlier in men, by an average of 3–5 years (Mendrek & Mancini-Marïe, 2016). Males are typically diagnosed during their late teens or early twenties, whereas the peak age for women is the late twenties (American Psychiatric Association, 2013; Gogtay, Vyas, Testa, Wood, & Pantelis, 2011). In most cases, schizophrenia is a lifelong disorder that causes significant disability and a high risk of suicide. The prognosis is worse for earlier onset schizophrenia, but this may be related to the fact that men, who tend to develop symptoms earlier in life, are in poorer condition when first diagnosed (American Psychiatric Association, 2013). Schizophrenia disproportionately affects people of lower socioeconomic classes, but the causal relationship remains unclear (Tandon, Keshavan, & Nasrallah, 2008a, 2008b). Having the disorder makes it hard to hold down a job; up to 90% of those affected are unemployed (Evensen et al., 2016).

Untangling the Roots of Schizophrenia

LO 9   **Analyze the biopsychosocial factors that contribute to schizophrenia.**

Schizophrenia is a complex psychological disorder that results from an interaction of biological, psychological, and social factors, making it difficult to predict who will be affected. For many years, various experts focused the blame on environmental factors, such as unhealthy family dynamics and bad parenting. A common scapegoat was the "schizophrenogenic mother," whose poor parenting style was believed to cause the disorder in her child (Harrington, 2012). Thankfully, this belief has been shattered by our new understanding of the brain. Research on schizophrenia, particularly in the area of genetics, has made great leaps. A large body of evidence now confirms that schizophrenia runs in families (Makin, 2014; Schizophrenia Working Group of the Psychiatric Genomics Consortium, 2014). Few cases illustrate this principle better than that of the Genain sisters.

NATURE AND NURTURE
Four Sisters

Nora, Iris, Myra, and Hester Genain were identical quadruplets born in 1930. Their mother went to great lengths to treat them equally, and in many ways the children were equals (Mirsky & Quinn, 1988). As babies, they cried in unison and teethed at the same times. As toddlers, they played with the same toys, wore the same dresses, and rode the same tricycles. The little girls were said to be so mentally in sync that they never argued (Quinn, 1963).

Mr. and Mrs. Genain kept the girls isolated. Spending most of their time at home, the quads cultivated few friendships and didn't go out with boys. The Genains may have protected their daughters from the world outside, but they could not shield them from the trouble brewing inside their brains.

At age 22, one of the sisters, Nora, was hospitalized for a psychiatric disorder characterized by hallucinations, delusions, altered speech, and other symptoms. Within

> LIKE ANY PSYCHOLOGICAL PHENOMENON, SCHIZOPHRENIA IS A PRODUCT OF BOTH NATURE AND NURTURE.

months, a second sister, Iris, was admitted to a psychiatric ward as well. She, too, had the symptoms of psychosis. Both Nora and Iris were diagnosed with schizophrenia, and it was only a matter of years before Myra and Hester were as well (Mirsky & Quinn, 1988). As you can imagine, the case of the Genain quads has drawn the attention of many scientists. David Rosenthal and his colleagues at the National Institute of Mental Health studied the women when they were in their late twenties and again when they were 51. To protect the quads' identities, Rosenthal assigned them the pseudonyms Nora, Iris, Myra, and Hester, which spell out NIMH, the acronym for the National Institute of Mental Health. *Genain* is also an alias, meaning "dreadful gene" in Greek (Mirsky & Quinn, 1988).

Identical quads have nearly all the same genes, so the Genain case suggests that there is some heritable component to schizophrenia. Yet, each woman experienced the disorder in her own way, highlighting the importance of environmental factors, or nurture. Hester did not receive a diagnosis of schizophrenia until she was in her twenties, but she started to show signs of psychological impairment much earlier than her sisters and was never able to hold down a job or live alone. Myra, however, was employed for the majority of her life and has a family of her own (Mirsky et al., 2000; Mirsky & Quinn, 1988). When researchers interviewed Myra at age 81, she was still living on her own, with some assistance from her son (Mirsky, Bieliauskas, Duncan, & French, 2013). Like any psychological phenomenon, schizophrenia is a product of both nature and nurture. ◊🏠

GENETIC FACTORS Overall, researchers agree that schizophrenia is "highly heritable," with genetic factors accounting for 60–80% of the population-wide risk for developing this disorder (Edwards et al., 2016; Tandon et al., 2008a, 2008b). Much of the evidence derives from twin, family, and adoption studies (**FIGURE 13.3**). If one identical twin has schizophrenia, the risk of the other twin developing the disorder is approximately 41–65% (Petronis, 2004). Compare that to a mere 2% risk for those whose first cousins have schizophrenia (Tsuang, Stone, & Faraone, 2001). The risk for an offspring developing schizophrenia when one parent has the disorder is 10–15%

The Quads

Identical quadruplets (known under the fictitious surname Genain), each of whom developed symptoms of schizophrenia between the ages of 22 and 24. Schizophrenia is a highly heritable disorder that has been linked to 108 gene areas (Dhindsa & Goldstein, 2016; Schizophrenia Working Group of the Psychiatric Genomics Consortium, 2014).
© AP Images

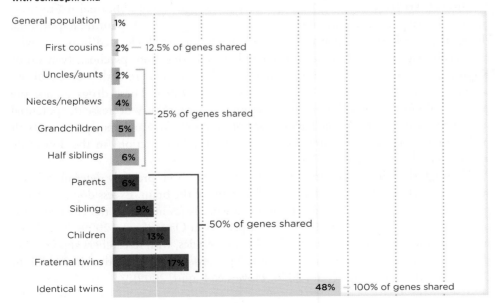

Relationship to person with schizophrenia

Risk of developing schizophrenia

General population	1%
First cousins	2% — 12.5% of genes shared
Uncles/aunts	2%
Nieces/nephews	4% — 25% of genes shared
Grandchildren	5%
Half siblings	6%
Parents	6%
Siblings	9% — 50% of genes shared
Children	13%
Fraternal twins	17%
Identical twins	48% — 100% of genes shared

Risk of developing schizophrenia

FIGURE 13.3

The Role of Genetics in Schizophrenia

The average lifetime risk of developing schizophrenia for the general population is 1% or lower. However, for someone with a sibling diagnosed with schizophrenia, the lifetime risk increases to 9%. If that sibling is an identical twin, someone with nearly 100% of the same genes, the risk rockets to 48%. This suggests a significant role for genetic factors in the development of schizophrenia (Gottesman, 2001).

(Svrakic, Zorumksi, Svrakic, Zwir, & Cloninger, 2013). If both parents have schizophrenia, the risk of their children being diagnosed with this disorder is 27% (Gottesman, Laursen, Bertelsen, & Mortensen, 2010). Keep in mind that schizophrenia is not caused by a single gene, but by a combination of many genes interacting with the environment (Ripke et al., 2014; Svrakic et al., 2013).

DIATHESIS-STRESS MODEL Like other disorders, schizophrenia is best understood from the biopsychosocial perspective. One model that takes this perspective into account is the _diathesis–stress model_, where _diathesis_ refers to the inherited disposition (to schizophrenia, for example), and _stress_ refers to the stressors and other factors in the environment (internal and external). Identical twins share 100% of their genetic make-up at conception (diathesis), yet the environment produces different stressors for the twins (only one of them loses a spouse, for example). This helps explain why one twin may develop the disorder, but the other does not. The diathesis–stress model suggests that developing schizophrenia involves a genetic predisposition _and_ environmental triggers. Researchers are realizing that "research and treatment of people with schizophrenia must become more person-centered, that is, informed by their biology, psychology, environmental and life event history" (Svrakic et al., 2013, p. 193).

THE BRAIN People with schizophrenia generally experience a thinning of the cortex, leading to enlarged ventricles, the cavities in the brain that are filled with cerebrospinal fluid. Research also shows that the total volume of the brain is reduced in schizophrenia (Haijma et al., 2013; Tandon et al., 2008a). People with schizophrenia have been found to have a smaller hippocampus, amygdala, and thalamus (van Erp et al., 2016). In general, these types of abnormalities are thought to be related to problems with cognitive functioning, psychotic symptoms, and sensory changes (Fusar-Poli et al., 2013; Glahn et al., 2008; Matheson, Shepherd, & Carr, 2014). A word of caution when interpreting these findings, however: It is possible that differences in brain structures are not just due to schizophrenia, but may also result from long-term use of medications to control its symptoms (Fusar-Poli et al., 2013; Jaaro-Peled, Ayhan, Pletnikov, & Sawa, 2010).

NEUROTRANSMITTER THEORIES Evidence suggests that abnormal neurotransmitter activity plays a role in schizophrenia. According to the **dopamine hypothesis,** the synthesis, release, and concentrations of dopamine are all elevated in people who have been diagnosed with schizophrenia and are suffering from psychosis (van Os & Kapur, 2009). Support for the dopamine hypothesis comes from the successful use of medications that block the receptor sites for dopamine. These drugs reduce the psychotic symptoms of schizophrenia, presumably because they decrease the potential impact of the excess dopamine (van Os & Kapur, 2009). Researchers report that both positive and negative symptoms are associated with "dysfunction" in the dopamine system (Kirschner, Aleman, & Kaiser, 2016).

Although the effect of increased dopamine has not been precisely determined, one suggestion is that it influences the "reward system" of the brain. Excess dopamine may make it hard for a person to pay attention to what is rewarding in the environment, or pick out its most salient, or important, aspects (van Os & Kapur, 2009). The dopamine hypothesis has evolved over the last several decades, with researchers appreciating the ongoing dynamic between neurochemical processes of the individual in relation to the environment (Edwards et al., 2016; Howes & Kapur, 2009).

ENVIRONMENTAL TRIGGERS AND SCHIZOPHRENIA Some experts suspect that schizophrenia is associated with exposure to a virus in utero, such as human

CONNECTIONS

In **Chapter 2,** we discussed activity at the synapse. Neurotransmitters released by the sending neuron must bind to receptor sites on the receiving neuron to relay their message ("fire" or "don't fire"). Medications that block or inhibit the receptor sites on the receiving neuron are referred to as antagonists, and some of these are used to reduce symptoms of schizophrenia.

Synonyms

diathesis-stress model stress-vulnerability model, constitutional vulnerability

dopamine hypothesis A theory suggesting that the synthesis, release, and concentrations of the neurotransmitter dopamine play a role in schizophrenia.

papilloma virus (HPV). Several illnesses a woman can contract while pregnant, including genital or reproductive infections, influenza, and some parasites, may increase her baby's risk of developing schizophrenia later in life, as can pregnancy and birth complications (Brown & Patterson, 2011; Matheson et al., 2014). Retrospective evidence (that is, information collected much later) suggests that the offspring of mothers who were exposed to viruses while pregnant are more likely to develop schizophrenia as adolescents. However, research exploring this theory is still ongoing and must be replicated.

Finally, sociocultural and environmental factors may play a minor role in one's risk for developing schizophrenia and the severity of its symptoms. Social stress, childhood adversities, and cannabis abuse have been associated with a slightly increased risk of schizophrenia onset, for example (Matheson et al., 2014; Tandon et al., 2008a, 2008b).

As you can see, schizophrenia is a highly complex disorder with a strong genetic component and many possible environmental causes. The same could be said of autism, a neurodevelopmental disorder that may share some genetic risk factors with schizophrenia and bipolar disorder (Goes et al., 2016).

Autism

Autism spectrum disorder (ASD) affects 1 in 68 American children (Centers for Disease Control and Prevention, 2016c). This disorder, which is 4 times more common in boys than girls, "is characterized by persistent deficits in social communication and social interaction across multiple contexts" and "restricted, repetitive patterns of behavior, interests, or activities" (American Psychiatric Association, 2013, p. 31). As the name implies, ASD refers to a vast spectrum of symptoms ranging from very mild to debilitating. With proper support, some people with ASD can communicate and function with few obvious deficiencies; others appear to be severely impaired and need a great deal of assistance carrying out daily activities.

The causes of ASD are still under investigation, but research demonstrates that the disorder runs in families. One large study estimated the heritability of ASD to be about 50% (Sandin et al., 2014), the implication being that half of the variability in ASD in the population can be attributed to genes. If these findings are accurate, that leaves a lot of room for environment. Some research suggests that infections during pregnancy (those requiring hospitalization of the mother) may heighten a baby's risk for developing ASD by as much as 30% (Lee at al., 2015). Other studies have focused on teratogens, or prenatal exposure to environmental toxins such as pesticides, lead, and methanol (a chemical released into the body during the breakdown of the artificial sweetener aspartame); however, these results are somewhat inconclusive (Dickerson, Pearson, Loveland, Rahbar, & Filipek, 2014; Nevison, 2014; Walton & Monte, 2015). The etiology of this disorder remains a puzzle, and "many cases of ASD are likely to involve complex interactions between genetic and environmental risk factors" (LaSalle, 2013, p. 2).

We now turn our focus to another type of disorder that is intimately connected to one of psychology's core areas of study: personality.

 **show what you know**

1. A loss of contact with reality is referred to as _____.

2. A woman with schizophrenia reports hearing voices that tell her she is ugly and worthless. This is an example of a:
   a. hallucination.
   b. delusion.
   c. negative symptom.
   d. diathesis.

3. What are some biopsychosocial factors that contribute to the development of schizophrenia?

✓ CHECK YOUR ANSWERS IN APPENDIX C.

Personality, Dissociative, and Eating Disorders

Before reading this chapter, you probably knew something about depression, bipolar disorder, and schizophrenia. But you may have been less familiar with a somewhat common group of disorders relating to personality, which can be very debilitating with regard to work and interpersonal relationships. Almost 11% of adults in the United States have a *personality disorder* (Clarkin, Meehan, & Lenzenweger, 2015).

Personality Disorders

People with **personality disorders** exhibit "an enduring pattern of inner experience and behavior that deviates markedly from the expectations of the individual's culture, is pervasive and inflexible, has an onset in adolescence or early adulthood, is stable over time, and leads to distress or impairment" (American Psychiatric Association, 2013, p. 645). Specifically, someone with a personality disorder behaves in a way that deviates substantially in the following areas: (1) cognition, including perceptions of self, others, and events; (2) emotional responses; (3) interpersonal functioning; and (4) impulse control. In order to be diagnosed with a personality disorder, one must struggle in at least two of these four categories. In addition, these problems must be resistant to change and have far-reaching consequences for interpersonal relationships.

Like personality traits in general, the core qualities of people with personality disorders (as well as the problems that result) are fairly stable over a lifetime and across situations. When diagnosing this type of disorder, the clinician must focus on troublesome personality traits—and be very careful not to confuse them with problems resulting from developmental changes, culture, drug use, or medical conditions.

The *DSM–5* includes 10 personality disorder types (**TABLE 13.9**). Here, we direct the spotlight onto two that have received considerable research attention: *antisocial personality disorder* and *borderline personality disorder*.

LO 10   Differentiate between antisocial and borderline personality disorders.

ANTISOCIAL PERSONALITY DISORDER Many films, including *The Last King of Scotland* and *There Will Be Blood,* feature characters who behave in ways most people find incomprehensible. The qualities of these characters often parallel a diagnosis of **antisocial personality disorder.**

People with antisocial personality disorder may seek personal gratification even when it means violating ethical standards and breaking laws. They sometimes lie or con others, and exhibit aggressive, impulsive, or irritable behaviors. These individuals have difficulty feeling empathy, and may not show concern for others or feel remorse upon hurting them. Other common behavior patterns include carelessness in sexual relationships, and the use of intimidation to control others (American Psychiatric Association, 2013). Around 1–4% of American adults are diagnosed with antisocial personality disorder, which is more common in men than women (Lenzenweger, Lane, Loranger, & Kessler, 2007; Werner, Few, & Bucholz, 2015). Moreover, some studies have shown that as many as 80% of prison inmates have been diagnosed with antisocial personality disorder (Edens, Kelley, Lilienfeld, Skeem, & Douglas, 2015).

How does antisocial personality disorder develop? Heredity does appear to play a role, as first-degree biological relatives of people with antisocial personality disorder are more likely to be affected than those in the general population (American Psychiatric Association, 2013). There is some evidence for family risk factors, but it is unclear how much of this risk is transmitted through genes, and how much results from learning. No single gene has been implicated in the development of antisocial behavior patterns. Like most mental health problems, antisocial personality disorder seems to result from

Synonyms

antisocial personality disorder
psychopathy, sociopathy

personality disorders A group of psychological disorders that can include impairments in cognition, emotional responses, interpersonal functioning, and impulse control.

antisocial personality disorder A psychological disorder distinguished by unethical behavior, deceitfulness, impulsivity, irritability, aggressiveness, disregard for others, and lack of remorse.

borderline personality disorder A psychological disorder distinguished by an incomplete sense of self, extreme self-criticism, unstable emotions, and feelings of emptiness.

TABLE 13.9   PERSONALITY DISORDERS

Personality Disorder	Description
Paranoid	Widespread distrust of others without basis
Schizoid	Detachment from relationships and a limited range of emotional expression
Schizotypal	Difficulty in establishing relationships, limited ability to maintain close relationships, and eccentric or strange behavior
Antisocial	Unethical behavior, deceitfulness, impulsivity, irritability, aggressiveness, disregard for others, and lack of remorse
Borderline	Incomplete sense of self, extreme self-criticism, unstable emotions, and feelings of emptiness
Histrionic	Extreme emotions used to gain attention
Narcissistic	Self-absorbed, needs to be admired, lack of empathy
Avoidant	Social self-consciousness, hypersensitive to negative feedback
Dependent	Clingy, needs to be cared for by others
Obsessive-compulsive	Fixation with order, perfection, and control

Listed here are the 10 personality disorders identified by the *DSM–5*. Information from *DSM-5* (American Psychiatric Association, 2013).

a complex interaction of genes and environment (Ferguson, 2010; Werner et al., 2015).

You may be wondering what is unique about the brain of a person with antisocial personality disorder. Some studies point to irregularities in the frontal lobes. For example, reduced tissue volume in the prefrontal cortex (11% less than expected) is apparent in some men with antisocial personality disorder. This deficit might be linked to reduced morality, and problems with decision making, planning, and learning in relation to fear, all potentially associated with antisocial behavior. The fact that the prefrontal cortex plays a role in controlling arousal may explain why people with this disorder tend to seek out stimulation, including aggressive and antisocial activities (Raine, Lencz, Bihrle, LaCasse, & Colletti, 2000). That being said, not everyone with this diagnosis has frontal lobe abnormalities, and the development of this disorder likely involves biological, psychological, and social factors (Paris, 2015).

BORDERLINE PERSONALITY DISORDER **Borderline personality disorder** is distinguished by an incomplete sense of self and feelings of emptiness. People with this disorder tend to be emotionally unstable and extremely needy. They may exhibit intense anger, have difficulty controlling their temper, and get into physical fights. When it comes to sexual activity, substance abuse, and spending money, they tend to be impulsive. Recurrent suicide threats or attempts are not uncommon. Developing intimacy may be a struggle, as relationships tend to be unstable, tainted with feelings of mistrust and fear of abandonment. Those with borderline personality disorder may see the world in terms of black and white, rather than different shades of gray. This tendency to perceive extremes may lead a person to become overinvolved or totally withdrawn in relationships (American Psychiatric Association, 2013).

Antisocial Personality Disorder?
Actor Michael C. Hall plays "Dexter Morgan" in the Showtime series *Dexter*. Some might argue that Dexter offers a good example of antisocial personality disorder, but most individuals with this diagnosis are not serial killers. As one person with the disorder writes, "A sociopath can have a wide range of symptoms, meaning that not every sociopath is like Dexter" (Anonymous, 2014, April 16, para. 2). SHOWTIME/THE KOBAL COLLECTION at Art Resource, NY.

Mozart's Mystery
Did the great composer suffer from a psychological disorder? Some scholars believe his mood swings were indicative of depression or bipolar disorder, while others speculate he had a personality disorder. Mozart's symptoms included "efforts to avoid real or imagined abandonment, impulsiveness, affective instability due to a marked reactivity of mood . . . . a feeling of emptiness, and identity disturbance" (Huguelet & Perroud, 2005, p. 137). What disorder do these symptoms suggest? DEA/A. DAGLI ORTI/ Getty Images.

According to the *DSM–5,* individuals with borderline personality disorder experience emotions that are unstable, intense, and inappropriate for the situation at hand. They may feel extreme anxiety and insecurity, concern about being rejected one moment, worry about being too dependent the next. Depressed moods are common, along with feelings of hopelessness, pessimism, and shame. The person may act without thinking and frequently change plans.

Seventy-five percent of people diagnosed with borderline personality disorder are female, and research suggests that some traits associated with this disorder have a genetic component (American Psychiatric Association, 2013). There is also evidence that childhood trauma sets the stage for the development of this condition. A biosocial developmental model has been proposed, indicating an early vulnerability that includes impulsive behavior and increased "emotional sensitivity." If the environment is right, this susceptibility can lead to problems with emotions, behaviors, and cognitive processes (Crowell, Beauchaine, & Linehan, 2009). In addition to the potential contributions of childhood trauma and temperament, overprotective parenting may inhibit a developing child's ability to independently handle "her own emotions" (Sharp & Kim, 2015, p. 3).

As you now know, personality disorders stem from well-established personality characteristics. People suffering from these disorders have traits that are relatively easy to characterize. This is *not* the case for those with dissociative disorders, whose personal identities may be very difficult to pin down.

Dissociative Disorders

LO 11 **Identify differences among dissociative disorders.**

Dissociative disorders are disturbances in normal psychological functioning that can include problems with memory, identity, consciousness, emotion, perception, and motor control (American Psychiatric Association, 2013). The main feature of these disorders is **dissociation**, or a disturbance in the normally unified experience of psychological functions involved in memory, consciousness, perception, or identity (Spiegel et al., 2011). Dissociation may lead to difficulty recalling personal information (for example, where I live, who I am), or the feeling of being detached from one's body. Here, we focus our discussion on two dissociative disorders: *dissociative amnesia* and *dissociative identity disorder.*

dissociative disorders Psychological disorders distinguished by disturbances in normal psychological functioning; may include problems with memory, identity, consciousness, perception, and motor control.

dissociation A disturbance in the normally integrated experience of psychological functions involved in memory, consciousness, perception, or identity.

dissociative amnesia A psychological disorder marked by difficulty remembering important personal information and life events.

dissociative fugue A condition in which a person with dissociative amnesia wanders about in a confused and unexpected manner.

DISSOCIATIVE AMNESIA People suffering from **dissociative amnesia** have difficulty remembering important personal information. Often the lost memories center on traumatic or stressful experiences. In some cases, the amnesia is localized, or fixed around a certain event; other times, it may span a lifetime. Those with dissociative amnesia typically report a great deal of distress or impairment in relationships, work, and other important areas of life, and put a lot of effort into managing the mundane details of daily existence (Staniloiu & Markowitsch, 2012).

A person with dissociative amnesia who wanders in a confused and unexpected manner may also be experiencing **dissociative fugue** (fyoog; Spiegel et al., 2011). Consider this example from a case study: A 62-year-old woman was found in a city many miles from home. She had no understanding of her whereabouts or activities since leaving home. After a medical evaluation, physicians determined there was no neurological or physical explanation for her memory loss. Over time, she was able to recall some events from the "preceding weeks," including an argument with her husband that had left her in despair (Rajah, Kumar, Somasundaram, & Kumar, 2009). As often occurs with dissociative disorders, this woman's memory loss seemed to be associated with distressing events.

DISSOCIATIVE IDENTITY DISORDER   Perhaps the most commonly known dissociative disorder is **dissociative identity disorder** (once referred to as multiple personality disorder). This extremely rare condition is characterized by the presence of two or more distinct personalities within the same person (American Psychiatric Association, 2013). Dissociative identity disorder is considered the most complicated and persistent of the dissociative disorders (Sar, 2011). One of its key features is a lack of connection among behavior, awareness, memory, and cognition. There is often a reported gap in remembering day-to-day events and personal information. One may feel significant distress in relationships, work, and other areas. And this experience cannot be related to substance use or medical issues.

Dissociative identity disorder has been observed all over the world and in many cultures (Dorahy et al., 2014). But clinicians must be mindful of cross-cultural and religious differences in relation to dissociative states. For example, some characteristics associated with dissociative identity disorder seem to occur in Brazilian spiritist mediums, and it is important to distinguish between a culturally accepted religious practice and disordered behavior (Delmonte, Lucchetti, Moreira-Almeida, & Farias, 2016; Moreira-Almeida, Neto, & Cardeña, 2008).

WHAT CAUSES DISSOCIATIVE DISORDERS?   Historically, a great deal of controversy surrounded the apparent increase in diagnoses of dissociative identity disorder in the United States. One possible explanation was that clinicians were reinforcing the development of these dissociations. In other words, by suggesting the possibility of alternate personalities or using hypnosis to "recover" lost memories, the clinician "cues" the individual to believe an alternate personality is responsible for behaviors (Lynn, Lilienfeld, Merckelbach, Giesbrecht, & van der Kloet, 2012). However, there is now general agreement that trauma plays a causal role in experiences of dissociation, as do factors like fantasy proneness, suggestibility, and neurological deficits (Dalenberg et al., 2014; Lynn et al., 2014). We should also note that these disorders are often linked to childhood abuse and neglect, war, and terrorism in regions throughout the world (American Psychiatric Association, 2013).

Before reading this chapter, you may not have known much about dissociative disorders; however, this is probably not the case with eating disorders, which have received considerable media attention.

Trance Dance
A young man in São Paulo, Brazil, dances in a trance state during a religious ceremony. Behaviors observed in this type of context may resemble those of dissociative identity disorder, but it is important to differentiate between religious practices and disordered behaviors (Moreira-Almeida, Neto, & Cardeña, 2008). AFP/Getty Images.

Eating Disorders

LO 12   Outline the characteristics of the major eating disorders.

Eating disorders are serious dysfunctions in eating behavior that can involve restricting food consumption, obsessing over weight or body shape, eating too much, and purging (American Psychiatric Association, 2013). These disorders usually begin in the early teens and typically affect girls, though boys make up a substantial proportion of eating disorder cases, specifically anorexia nervosa, bulimia nervosa, and binge-eating disorder (Raevuori, Keski-Rahkonen, & Hoek, 2014). Let's take a closer look at these three disorders.

ANOREXIA NERVOSA   One of the most commonly known eating disorders is **anorexia nervosa**, which is characterized by self-imposed restrictions on calories needed to maintain a healthy weight. These restrictions lead to extremely low body weight in relation to age, sex, development, and physical health. A person with anorexia nervosa has an extreme fear of gaining weight and getting fat, even though her body weight is extremely low. Often there is an altered and distorted sense of body weight and figure, and no realization of the "seriousness" of one's low body weight

dissociative identity disorder
A psychological disorder that involves the occurrence of two or more distinct personalities within an individual.

anorexia nervosa   An eating disorder identified by significant weight loss, an intense fear of being overweight, a false sense of body image, and a refusal to eat the proper amount of calories to achieve a healthy weight.

Making Weight
Wrestlers in the 120-kilogram (265-pound) weight class weigh in before a tournament. For some athletes, this pressure to maintain a certain body weight may set the stage for the development of eating disorders. AP Photo/Craig Ruttle.

Distorted Perceptions
People with anorexia nervosa may look in the mirror and behold a version of themselves that others never see. Altered perceptions of body size and shape are common features of this disorder (American Psychiatric Association, 2013). Dan Pearson Photography /Alamy Stock Photo.

bulimia nervosa An eating disorder characterized by extreme overeating followed by purging, with serious health risks.

binge-eating disorder An eating disorder characterized by episodes of extreme overeating, during which a larger amount of food is consumed than most people would eat in a similar amount of time under similar circumstances.

(American Psychiatric Association, 2013). In some cases, women experience an absence of menstrual periods, a condition called *amenorrhea* (Mehler & Brown, 2015). Other severe symptoms may include brain damage, multi-organ failure, infertility, and thinning of the bones (NIMH, n.d.-b; Mehler & Brown, 2015). Anorexia is associated with the highest death rates of all psychological disorders (Darcy et al., 2012; Smink, van Hoeken, & Hoek, 2012). Over half of the deaths associated with anorexia are due to medical complications (Mehler & Brown, 2015), while approximately 20% occur through suicide (Joy, Kussman, & Nattiv, 2016; Smink et al., 2012). Although anorexia nervosa affects mostly women and adolescent girls, males can also be affected, particularly those involved in wrestling, running, or dancing, who are required to maintain a certain weight.

BULIMIA NERVOSA   Another eating disorder is **bulimia nervosa**, which involves recurrent episodes of binge eating, or consuming large amounts of food in short periods of time (with that amount being greater than most people would eat in the same time frame). While bingeing, the person feels a lack of control and thus engages in purging behaviors to prevent weight gain—for example, self-induced vomiting, misuse of laxatives, fasting, or excessive exercise (American Psychiatric Association, 2013). Like anorexia, bulimia more often affects women and girls, but it can also impact males (Peschel et al., 2016). Bulimia has serious health risks, such as high blood pressure, heart disease, and Type 2 diabetes (Haedt-Matt & Keel, 2011). Other symptoms include decaying teeth, damage to the throat, gastrointestinal disorders, and electrolyte imbalance, which can lead to a heart attack (Joy et al., 2016; NIMH, n.d.-b). Research indicates that 23% of deaths associated with bulimia nervosa result from suicide (Joy et al., 2016; Smink et al., 2012).

BINGE-EATING DISORDER   Less commonly known, **binge-eating disorder** is characterized by episodes of excessive food consumption—eating more than most people would in the same amount of time and under similar circumstances (American Psychiatric Association, 2013). As in bulimia, the individual feels unable to control her eating during that period of time, but the difference is that she does not engage in excessive weight control or purging behaviors. Psychological effects could include feelings of embarrassment about the quantity of food consumed, depression, and guilt after overeating.

We know that eating disorders occur in America—we see evidence of them on television, in magazines, and in everyday life. But are these disorders also observed in India, South Africa, Egypt, and other parts of the world?

ACROSS THE WORLD
A Cross-Cultural Look at Eating Disorders

Close your eyes and imagine the stereotypical beauty queen. Is she curvy like a Coke bottle or long and lean like a Barbie doll? For many of us, the image that popped into mind looked more like the famed plastic doll. Let's face it: Western concepts of beauty, particularly female beauty, often go hand-in-hand with *thinness*.

With all this pressure to be slender, it's no wonder eating disorders like anorexia and bulimia are most commonly diagnosed and treated in Western societies such as the United States (TABLE 13.10; Keel & Klump, 2003; Littlewood, 2004). Psychologists once believed these conditions were mainly seen in "wealthy, white, educated, young women in industrialized Western nations" (Pike & Dunne, 2015, p. 1). But evidence

EATING DISORDERS AFFECT MEN AND WOMEN OF ALL COLORS LIVING IN COUNTRIES AROUND THE WORLD.

TABLE 13.10 TREATMENT OF EATING DISORDERS

Treatment Option	Description
Counseling and psychotherapy	Treatment may involve individual, group, or family counseling, which may focus on nutrition, psychological issues, or thoughts and behaviors surrounding the eating disorder.
Health care and medical monitoring	Many eating disorders result in medical crises. Medical monitoring and care are critical.
Drug therapies	While drugs will not prevent, cure, or restore normal weight, drug therapies may be useful in treating the mood issues (often anxiety and depression) that can accompany eating disorders.

Effective treatment of eating disorders often involves a combination of approaches tailored to the individual. This tends to be more effective than using only one treatment option. Information from NIMH (n.d.-b).

suggests that eating disorders affect men and women of all colors living in countries around the world, from Fiji to Malaysia to Pakistan (Gerbasi et al., 2014; Marques et al., 2011; Pike & Dunne, 2015).

In recent decades, eating disorders have become increasingly common in non-Western countries. This trend often coincides with industrialization, urbanization, and "media-exposure promoting the Western beauty-ideal" (Smink et al., 2012, p. 412). For women, this Western beauty ideal implies thinness; for men, a muscular physique (Pike & Dunne, 2015). As researchers studying teens in Arab countries explain, "The Western standard of beauty has contributed to the preoccupation with thinness and body image dissatisfaction" (Musaiger et al., 2013, p. 165). This influence may be important, but researchers caution against viewing eating disorders as an "export of Western culture"; every society has its own experience with eating disorders (Pike & Dunne, 2015, p. 11).

In Class: Collaborate and Report

The content presented in this chapter has the potential to raise personal issues for students—as we've noted, psychological disorders touch many of our lives. In your group, discuss **A)** the most surprising things you learned about abnormal behaviors and psychological disorders, and **B)** describe how your perspective on mental illness has changed as a result of what you have learned in your psychology class this term.

 show what you know

1. Individuals with _____ are likely to feel a sense of emptiness, anger easily, and maintain intense but unstable relationships.

2. Two identifiers of abnormal behavior are distress and impairment. How would the personality disorders fit these criteria for abnormal behavior?

3. _____ involves two or more distinct personalities within an individual. This experience is characterized by

a lack of connection among behavior, awareness, memory, cognition, and other functioning.

4. Bulimia nervosa is an eating disorder characterized by:
   a. restrictions of energy intake.
   b. extreme fear of gaining weight, although one's body weight is extremely low.
   c. a distorted sense of body weight and figure.
   d. extreme overeating followed by purging.

✓ CHECK YOUR ANSWERS IN APPENDIX C.

DEFYING STIGMA: ROSS LEARNS TO THRIVE

After graduating from high school, Ross started college at American University in Washington, D.C. Within 2 months, he experienced a major relapse with bipolar disorder and returned to Pennsylvania, where he was hospitalized. Ross eventually returned to American University to finish what he had started, but drinking alcohol was still a big part of his life. One night, after downing multiple shots of liquor, Ross passed out cold. He awoke 22 hours later, looked in the mirror, and started to weep. "Okay. ENOUGH. You are either going to continue this pattern and DIE, or you are going to make a change," Ross remembers thinking to himself (Szabo & Hall, 2007, p. 102).

What followed were years of hard work. Ross quit using alcohol, caffeine, nicotine, and marijuana. He imposed structure on his life, waking up and going to sleep at the same time each day, eating regular meals, and exercising. He started being open and honest in his relationships with friends, family, and his therapist. And most important, he confronted his self-hatred, working hard to identify and appreciate things he liked about himself. "What was missing was me being an active member in my treatment," Ross says, "and doing things outside of treatment [to get better]."

After graduating cum laude from American University, Ross picked up where he left off that day he spoke to his high school class about his experience with bipolar disorder. He became a mental health advocate, giving presentations at high schools and colleges across America. Today, Ross is busy running his own consulting group, Human Power Project, that designs cutting-edge mental health curricula for middle and high schools. His battle with bipolar disorder is ongoing ("I'm not cured," says Ross), but he continues learning better ways to cope. ●

Making a Difference
Ross celebrates graduation day at a center for people with disabilities in Botswana, Africa, where he served in the Peace Corps. After completing his work with the Peace Corps, Ross returned to the United States and founded a consulting group that designs mental health curricula for middle and high schools. Heidi Pendergast/Ross Szabo.

Voice of Inspiration
As a presenter for the mental health organization Minding Your Mind, Melissa travels across the country, educating students about mental health issues. She has also published *The People You Meet in Real Life,* which provides first-person accounts of resilient individuals facing a variety of trials and tribulations. The book addresses issues related to mental health, bullying, suicide, cancer, and HIV, sending a message of hope and inspiration. Photo by Ken Alexander.

OUTSMARTING OCD: MELISSA FINDS A THERAPY THAT WORKS

Shortly after leaving the hospital, Melissa found out about a study on OCD treatments at the University of Pennsylvania. She decided to participate and got acquainted with the lead investigator, who became her therapist. "He taught me how to live with OCD," says Melissa. "He basically saved my life." Melissa had been taking medications since she was 12, but she only experienced a dramatic improvement when she combined her medication with cognitive behavioral therapy (CBT), an approach you can learn about in Chapter 14 on psychological therapies.

Like Ross, Melissa discovered she had a gift for public speaking. She started a mental health awareness group on her college campus, opening a chapter of the national organization Active Minds, and later joined a speakers' bureau led by Ross Szabo. Today, Melissa is a speaker for Minding Your Mind, an organization devoted to educating school communities and families about mental health issues. She still has OCD, but it's under control. Instead of walking through a doorway 20 times, she now passes through it twice. And the time she once spent sitting alone in her room meticulously touching objects in sets of 2s, she now spends talking to classrooms full of students, shattering the stigma surrounding psychological disorders. ●

Improve your grade! Use LearningCurve adaptive quizzing to create your personalized study plan, which will direct you to the resources that will help you most in LaunchPad

13

summary of concepts

LO 1 Define psychological disorders and the criteria used to identify abnormal behavior. (p. 535)

A psychological disorder is a set of behavioral, emotional, and cognitive symptoms that are significantly distressing in terms of social functioning, work endeavors, and other aspects of life. Abnormal behavior falls along a continuum and is based on typicality and the 3 Ds: dysfunction, distress, and deviance. This continuum includes what we would consider normal at one end and abnormal at the other end, and is determined in part by one's culture.

LO 2 Recognize limitations in the classification of psychological disorders. (p. 540)

Although a classification system is important for communication and treatment planning among professionals, it can lead to labeling and expectations. Because of the stigma associated with psychological disorders, the effects of a diagnosis can be long lasting. Some critics suggest there is too much emphasis on the medical model, which may ignore the importance of psychological and sociocultural factors.

LO 3 Summarize the etiology of psychological disorders. (p. 543)

The biopsychosocial perspective provides a model for explaining the causes of psychological disorders, which are complicated and often result from interactions among biological, psychological, and sociocultural factors. Important biological factors include neurochemical imbalances and genetic predispositions. Psychological influences include cognitive factors, personality, and childhood experiences. Sociocultural factors, such as poverty and support systems, may also impact the development and course of psychological disorders.

LO 4 Define anxiety disorders and demonstrate an understanding of their causes. (p. 545)

Anxiety disorders are a group of psychological disorders associated with extreme anxiety and/or irrational and debilitating fears. People with panic disorder worry about losing control and having unexpected panic attacks; those with specific

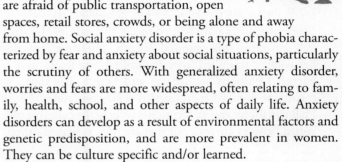

phobias fear specific objects or situations; and individuals with agoraphobia are afraid of public transportation, open spaces, retail stores, crowds, or being alone and away from home. Social anxiety disorder is a type of phobia characterized by fear and anxiety about social situations, particularly the scrutiny of others. With generalized anxiety disorder, worries and fears are more widespread, often relating to family, health, school, and other aspects of daily life. Anxiety disorders can develop as a result of environmental factors and genetic predisposition, and are more prevalent in women. They can be culture specific and/or learned.

LO 5 Summarize the symptoms and causes of obsessive-compulsive disorder. (p. 550)

Obsessive-compulsive disorder (OCD) includes obsessions and/or compulsions that are very time-consuming (taking more than 1 hour a day) and cause a great deal of distress and disruptions in everyday life. An obsession is a thought, urge, or image that occurs repeatedly, is intrusive and unwelcome, and often causes feelings of intense anxiety and distress. Compulsions are behaviors or "mental acts" that a person repeats over and over in an attempt to neutralize obsessions. Sociocultural factors, learning, and biological causes are all involved in the course and maintenance of OCD.

LO 6 Summarize the symptoms and causes of major depressive disorder. (p. 553)

Symptoms of major depressive disorder include feelings of sadness or hopelessness, reduced pleasure, sleeping excessively or not at all, loss of energy, feelings of worthlessness, or difficulties thinking or concentrating. Symptoms are severe and accompanied by impairment in the ability to perform expected roles. Biological theories suggest the disorder results from a genetic predisposition, and irregular activity of neurotransmitters and hormones. Psychological theories suggest that feelings of learned helplessness and negative thinking play a role. Major depressive disorder results from a combination of several factors.

LO 7 Compare and contrast bipolar disorders and major depressive disorder. (p. 558)

A diagnosis of bipolar I disorder requires that a person experience at least one manic episode, substantial distress, and great impairment. Bipolar II disorder involves at least one major depressive episode as well as a hypomanic episode, which is associated with some of the same symptoms as a manic episode, but is not as severe and does not impair functioning. People with bipolar disorder cycle between extreme highs and lows of emotion and energy that last for days, weeks, or even months. Individuals with major depressive disorder, on the other hand, tend to experience a persistent low mood, loss of energy, and feelings of worthlessness.

LO 8 Recognize the symptoms of schizophrenia. (p. 560)

Schizophrenia is a disabling disorder that can involve delusions, hallucinations, disorganized speech, abnormal psychomotor behavior, diminished speech, limited emotions, and loss of energy. Delusions are strange and false beliefs that a person maintains even when presented with contradictory evidence. Hallucinations are "perception-like experiences" that the individual believes are real, but that are not evident to others.

LO 9 Analyze the biopsychosocial factors that contribute to schizophrenia. (p. 562)

Schizophrenia is a complex psychological disorder that results from biological, psychological, and social factors. Because this disorder springs from an interaction of genes and environment, researchers have a hard time predicting who will be affected. The diathesis–stress model takes these factors into account, with diathesis referring to the inherited disposition, and stress referring to the stressors in the environment (internal and external). Genes, neurotransmitter activity, differences in the brain, and exposure to a virus in utero are all possible biopsychosocial influences in the development of schizophrenia.

LO 10 Differentiate between antisocial and borderline personality disorders. (p. 566)

People with antisocial personality disorder may seek personal gratification even when it means violating ethics and breaking laws. They sometimes deceive people, and exhibit aggressive, impulsive, or irritable behavior. These individuals lack empathy, and may not show concern for others or feel remorse upon hurting someone. Borderline personality disorder is distinguished by an incomplete sense of self and feelings of emptiness. Those affected may exhibit intense anger, have difficulty controlling their temper, and get into physical fights. They can be impulsive, especially where sexual activity, substance abuse, and spending money are concerned. Suicide threats and attempts may occur repeatedly. Both disorders may result in issues with intimacy and trust

LO 11 Identify differences among dissociative disorders. (p. 568)

People suffering from dissociative amnesia seem unable to remember important information about their lives. If a person with dissociative amnesia also wanders in a confused and unexpected manner, this is considered dissociative amnesia with dissociative fugue. Dissociative identity disorder occurs when an individual experiences two or more distinct personalities. This disorder is considered the most complicated and persistent of the dissociative disorders. The commonality in this group of disorders is dissociation, or a disturbance in the normally unified experience of psychological functions involved in memory, consciousness, perception, or identity.

LO 12 Outline the characteristics of the major eating disorders. (p. 569)

Anorexia nervosa is a serious, life-threatening eating disorder characterized by a significantly low body weight in relation to age, sex, development, and physical health; an extreme fear of gaining weight or getting fat; an altered and distorted sense of body weight and figure; and self-imposed restrictions on "energy intake" (calories) needed to maintain a healthy weight. Bulimia nervosa is characterized by recurrent episodes of binge eating followed by purging (self-induced vomiting, misuse of laxatives, fasting, or excessive exercise). Binge-eating disorder is characterized by episodes during which a larger amount of food is consumed than most people would eat in a similar amount of time under similar circumstances. As in bulimia, the individual feels unable to control eating during that period of time, but the difference is that there are no excessive weight control or purging behaviors.

key terms

insanity, p. 538
learned helplessness, p. 557
major depressive disorder, p. 553
maladaptive behaviors, p. 536
manic episodes, p. 558

medical model, p. 543
negative symptoms, p. 561
obsession, p. 550
obsessive-compulsive disorder (OCD), p. 550

panic attack, p. 546
panic disorder, p. 546
personality disorders, p. 566
positive symptoms, p. 561

psychological disorder, p. 536
psychosis, p. 561
schizophrenia, p. 561
specific phobia, p. 547
stigma, p. 539

test prep *are you ready?*

1. Which of the 3 Ds used to distinguish abnormal behavior indicates the degree to which a behavior interferes with daily life and relationships?
   a. distress
   b. deviance
   c. depression
   d. dysfunction

2. A researcher studying psychological disorders from a biological standpoint, focusing on genes, neurochemical imbalances, and problems in the brain, is using an approach known as:
   a. comorbidity.
   b. the medical model.
   c. the diathesis–stress model.
   d. heritability.

3. Melissa experienced recurrent, all-consuming thoughts of disaster and death. These _____ were accompanied by her _____, which included repeating certain behaviors, such as locking her car and entering a room, an even number of times.
   a. obsessions; compulsions
   b. compulsions; obsessions
   c. compulsions; contamination
   d. negative reinforcers; obsessions

4. To help explain the causes of psychological disorders, researchers often use the _____ perspective, which examines the complex interaction of biological, psychological, and sociocultural factors.
   a. medical model
   b. biopsychosocial
   c. etiological
   d. learning

5. A woman is extremely anxious when she is unaccompanied in public. She no longer uses public transportation, refuses to go to the mall, and does not like being away from home. Perhaps she should get evaluated to see if she has which of the following diagnoses?
   a. panic disorder
   b. agoraphobia
   c. social anxiety disorder
   d. specific phobia

6. A man with a diagnosis of _____ exhibits a distinct fear or anxiety related to social situations, particularly the idea of being scrutinized by others.
   a. generalized anxiety disorder
   b. panic attack
   c. social anxiety disorder
   d. panic disorder

7. While walking to class one day, you notice a woman who is short of breath, clutches her chest, and appears lightheaded. You are concerned she may be experiencing a heart attack. She tells you she knows it is not her heart, but that she suffers from _____, which involve sudden, extreme bouts of fear that escalate quickly.
   a. psychotic episodes
   b. manic episodes
   c. panic attacks
   d. hallucinations

8. A neighbor describes a newspaper article she read last night about a man in his twenties who has been known to lie and con others, be aggressive and impulsive, and show little empathy or remorse. These are long-standing traits of his, so it is possible that he has:
   a. borderline personality disorder.
   b. antisocial personality disorder.
   c. dissociative identity disorder.
   d. dissociative amnesia.

9. Which of the following plays a role in the etiology of major depressive disorder?
   a. manic episodes
   b. virus contracted by the mother
   c. classical conditioning
   d. serotonin

10. Rhonda routinely eats large amounts of food that most people could not eat in similar situations or in a similar amount of time. Rhonda often feels an inability to control her eating and frequently eats alone because she is embarrassed by how much she eats. It is likely that Rhonda has a diagnosis of:
    a. anorexia nervosa.
    b. bulimia nervosa.
    c. amenorrhea.
    d. binge-eating disorder.

11. One symptom that both major depressive disorder and bipolar disorder share is:
    a. hypomania.
    b. manic episodes.
    c. problems associated with sleep.
    d. extremely high self-esteem.

12. Which of the following is a symptom of a manic episode?
    a. low energy level
    b. need for more sleep
    c. quiet or shy personality
    d. irritability

13. A man with schizophrenia has hallucinations and delusions, and seems to be out of touch with reality. A psychologist explains to his mother that her son is experiencing:
    a. mania.
    b. psychosis.
    c. dissociative identity disorder.
    d. hypomania.

14. A woman in your neighborhood develops a reputation for being emotionally unstable, intense, and extremely needy. She also doesn't seem to have a sense of herself and complains of feeling empty. She struggles with intimacy and her relationships are unstable. If these are long-standing traits, which of the following might she be evaluated for?
    a. borderline personality disorder
    b. antisocial personality disorder
    c. bipolar II disorder
    d. major depressive disorder

15. Dissociative identity disorder involves two or more distinct _____ within an individual.
    a. hypomanic episodes
    b. personalities
    c. panic disorders
    d. psychotic episodes

16. Describe the 3 Ds and give an example of each in relation to a psychological disorder.

17. What is wrong with the following statement: "My friend is anorexic"?

18. How can classical conditioning be used to explain the development of panic disorder?

19. How does negative thinking lead to depression?

20. Briefly summarize the theories of schizophrenia's etiology.

✓ CHECK YOUR ANSWERS IN APPENDIX C.

YOUR SCIENTIFIC WORLD

Apply psychology to the real world!
Go to LaunchPad for access.

Thierry Falise/LightRocket via Getty Images.

Macmillan Learning.

Hunter Hoffman.

CHAPTER OUTLINE AND LEARNING OBJECTIVES

An Introduction to Treatment

LO 1   Outline the history of the treatment of psychological disorders.

LO 2   Explain how the main approaches to therapy differ and identify their common goal.

Insight Therapies

LO 3   Describe how psychoanalysis differs from psychodynamic therapy.

LO 4   Outline the principles and characteristics of humanistic therapy.

LO 5   Describe person-centered therapy.

Behavior Therapies

LO 6   Outline the principles and characteristics of behavior therapy.

Cognitive Therapies

LO 7   Outline the principles and characteristics of cognitive therapy.

Biomedical Therapies

LO 8   Summarize the biomedical interventions and identify their common goal.

Psychotherapy: Who's in the Mix?

LO 9   Describe how culture interacts with the therapy process.

LO 10   Identify the benefits and challenges of group therapy.

Psychotherapy Today

LO 11   Evaluate the effectiveness of psychotherapy.

LO 12   Summarize the strengths and weaknesses of online psychotherapy.

Robert VAN DER HILST/Gamma-Rapho via Getty Images.

Dan Penn.

Bjanka Kadic/Alamy Stock Photo.

14 treatment of psychological disorders

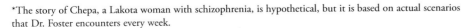

Glow Asia/Superstock.

An Introduction to Treatment

VOICES It's a beautiful evening on the Rosebud Indian Reservation in south-central South Dakota. The sun, low in the sky, casts a warm glow over pine-covered hills. Oceans of prairie grass roll in the wind. The scene could not be more tranquil. But for Chepa,* a young Lakota woman living in this Northern Plains sanctuary, life has been anything but tranquil. For days, Chepa has been tormented by the voice of a deceased uncle. Hearing voices is nothing unusual in the Lakota spiritual tradition; ancestors visit the living often. But in the case of this young woman, the voice is telling her to kill herself. Chepa has tried to make peace with her uncle's spirit using prayer, pipe ceremony, and other forms of traditional medicine, but he will not be appeased. Increasingly paranoid and withdrawn, Chepa is making her relatives uneasy, so they take her to the home of a trusted neighbor, Dr. Dan Foster. A sun dancer and pipe carrier, Dr. Foster is a respected member of the community. He also happens to be the reservation's lead clinical psychologist.

Breathtaking
The Rosebud Indian Reservation is a vast and beautiful land, but its residents struggle with severe poverty—and all the problems that come with it. Poverty-related stressors can interfere with work, strain personal relationships, and trigger the symptoms of psychological disorders. Robert VAN DER HILST/Gamma-Rapho via Getty Images.

Upon meeting with Chepa and her family, Dr. Foster realizes that she is having *hallucinations,* **perception-like experiences** she thinks are real, but that are not evident to anyone else. Chepa is also experiencing *delusions,* which are strange or false beliefs that a person firmly maintains even when presented with evidence to the contrary. And because she is vulnerable to acting on these hallucinations and delusions, she poses a risk to herself, and possibly others. Chepa needs to go to the hospital, and it is Dr. Foster's responsibility

*The story of Chepa, a Lakota woman with schizophrenia, is hypothetical, but it is based on actual scenarios that Dr. Foster encounters every week.

CONNECTIONS

In **Chapter 3,** we described sensation as the detection of stimuli by sensory organs. Stimuli are transduced into neural signals and sent to various parts of the brain. Perception turns sensory data into something meaningful. With hallucinations, the first step does not occur (no apparent physical stimuli).

Dr. Foster, in His Own Words

http://qrs.ly/m65a5fy

Photo: Macmillan Learning.

The Sun Dancer
Dr. Dan Foster is the lead clinical psychologist on the Rosebud Reservation. He frequently works with clients suffering from severe emotional trauma, but he maintains a positive outlook. "I feel like the crucible of poverty and pain also is the crucible for transformation," says Dr. Foster, who is a respected member of the Lakota community he serves. Macmillan Learning.

CONNECTIONS

In **Chapter 13,** we reported that schizophrenia is a persistent and debilitating disorder that affects approximately 0.3% to 1% of the population. In this chapter, we will present some approaches to treating people with this diagnosis.

to make sure she gets there, even if it requires going to a judge and getting a court order. "I'm going to make an intervention," Dr. Foster says, "and I'm going to have to do it in a way that's respectful to that person and to the culture, but still respectful to the body of literature and training that I come from as a psychologist."

Chepa's grandmother protests: "I don't want her going to the hospital. I want to use Indian medicine." Trying to remain as clear and neutral as possible, Dr. Foster explains that if the voice were that of a spirit, it would have responded to prayer, pipe ceremony, and other traditional approaches. "I believe you're hearing voices," he says to Chepa. "But that voice is not coming from your uncle. . . . I think it's coming from your own mind." He goes on to describe how the brain has a region that specializes in hearing, and areas that store memories of people and their voices. It is possible, he explains, that the brain is calling forth a voice from the past, making it seem like it is here at this moment.

Chepa may not agree with Dr. Foster, but she trusts him. He is, after all, a relative. In Lakota culture, *relatives* are not necessarily linked by blood. One can be adopted into a family or community through a formal ceremony known as *hunka*. At Rosebud, all of the therapists and medical providers are linked to the community through *hunka*— a great honor and also a great responsibility.

An ambulance arrives and transports Chepa to the emergency room, where she finds Dr. Foster waiting. He is there to make a diagnosis and develop a treatment plan, but also to provide her with a sense of security, and to do so in the context of a nurturing relationship. "First of all my concern is safety, and secondly my concern is that you realize I am concerned about you," Dr. Foster says. "We're going to form a relationship, you and I," he says. "Whatever it is that we're facing, we are going to make it so that it comes out better than it is right now."

The blood and urine screens come back negative, indicating that the hallucinations and delusions do not result from a drug, such as PCP or methamphetamine, and doctors find no evidence of a medical condition that could be driving the symptoms. Dr. Foster's observations and assessments point to a complex psychological disorder known as schizophrenia.

Because Chepa poses an imminent risk to herself, Dr. Foster and his colleagues arrange a transfer to a psychiatric hospital, where she may stay for several days. The medical staff will stabilize her with a drug to help reduce her symptoms, the first of many doses likely to be administered in years to come. When she returns to the reservation, Dr. Foster and his colleagues will offer Chepa treatment designed with her specific needs in mind. ●

Who Gets Treatment?

Therapists working on the Rosebud Reservation tend to see clients in crises, often related to the conditions of extreme poverty that exist on Northern Plains Indian reservations. The average household income among American Indians

Note: Quotations attributed to Dr. Dan Foster and Laura Lichti are personal communications.

and Alaskan Natives is $37,277, compared to a national average of $53,657 (United States Census Bureau, 2015, November 2). Affordable housing is scarce, and it's not unusual to have 14 or 15 relatives packed into living quarters the size of a two-bedroom apartment. "Here we are in this beautiful, pastoral Northern Plains setting with the kind of crowding [you might] experience in New York City," Dr. Foster says. "We're a rural ghetto." Squeezed into their homes without employment, entertainment, or access to transportation, people tend to feel strained, and **stress** can play a role in psychological disorders. Some seek relief in alcohol, drugs, risky sex, gambling, or as Dr. Foster puts it, "outlets that [temporarily] feel good in the midst of a painful life." Young people may turn to gangs, which can provide a sense of self-worth and belonging. Dr. Foster believes and hopes that Indian language, spiritual ceremony, and culture can act somewhat like a shield, protecting people from self-destructive behaviors. But centuries of assaults by Western society have eroded American Indian cultures.

As we learn more about Dr. Foster's work on Rosebud Reservation, be mindful that therapists work with a broad spectrum of psychological issues. Dr. Foster tends to work with people in severe distress. Some of his clients do not seek therapy, but end up in his care only because friends and relatives intervene. Other therapists spend much of their time serving people who seek help with issues such as shyness, low self-esteem, and unresolved childhood conflicts. Therapy is not just for those with psychological disorders and life catastrophes, but for anyone wishing to live a more fulfilling existence.

Psychologists use various **models** to explain abnormal behavior and psychological disorders. As our understanding of psychological disorders has changed over time, so have treatments. While reading the brief history that follows, try to identify connections between the perceived causes of disorders and the treatments designed to resolve them.

CONNECTIONS

In **Chapter 13,** we noted that stressors can impact the course of some psychological disorders. Periods of mania and depression, for example, can be brought on by life changes and stressors. And as the diathesis–stress model suggests, both a genetic predisposition and environmental triggers play a role in the development of schizophrenia and other disorders.

The Power of Culture
Residents of the Rosebud Reservation gather for a cultural event. Participating in ceremony and prayer may help people deal with stressors that could otherwise impact psychological problems. Robert VAN DER HILST/Gamma-Rapho.

CONNECTIONS

In **Chapter 13**, we discussed the etiology of psychological disorders. The medical model implies that disorders have biological causes. The biopsychosocial perspective suggests disorders result from an interaction of biological, psychological, and sociocultural factors.

A Primitive Past: The History of Treatment

LO 1   Outline the history of the treatment of psychological disorders.

Psychological disorders are as old as recorded history, and some of the early attempts to cure and treat them were inhumane and unproven. According to one theory, Stone Age people believed psychological disorders were caused by possession with demons and evil spirits. They may have practiced *trephination,* or drilling of holes in the skull, perhaps to create exit routes for evil spirits (Maher & Maher, 2003). Trephination was used beyond the Stone Age, and some have speculated this "earliest known" surgical procedure was intended to treat "madness, idiocy, moral degeneration, headache, the removal of foreign bodies, and the release of pressures, airs, vapours, and humours" (Wickens, 2015, p. 8).

ASYLUMS OR PRISONS? A major shift came in the 16th century. Religious groups began creating *asylums,* special places to house and treat people with psychological disorders. However, these asylums were overcrowded and resembled prisons, with inmates chained in dungeonlike cells, starved, and subjected to sweltering heat and frigid cold. One early hospital for the "mentally disturbed," London's St. Mary

The Reformer
American schoolteacher Dorothea Dix led the nation's "mental hygiene movement," an effort to improve the treatment of people living in institutions. Her advocacy began in the mid-1800s, when people in some mental hospitals were chained, beaten, and locked in cages (Parry, 2006). National Portrait Gallery, Smithsonian Institution/Art Resource, NY.

CONNECTIONS

In **Chapter 13,** we noted that most mental health professionals in the United States use the *DSM–5.* The *DSM–5* is a classification system designed to help clinicians ensure accurate and consistent diagnoses based on the observation of symptoms. This manual does not include information on treatment.

FIGURE 14.1

Deinstitutionalization
Since the 1950s, the rate of institutionalization has declined dramatically (Torrey, Fuller, Geller, Jacobs, & Rogasta, 2012). Copyright © 2011 by the University of Chicago Press from Harcourt (2011).

of Bethlehem (also known as Bedlam), exploited its patients in a most degrading way, making them "a constant source of entertainment for the rich, who visited on Sundays, bought tickets, and amused themselves by observing the behavior of the psychotic" (Dimitrijevic, 2015, p. 3). During the French Revolution (the late 1700s), Philippe Pinel (1745–1826), a French physician, began working in Paris asylums. Horrified by the conditions he observed, Pinel removed the inmates' chains and insisted they be treated more humanely (Frances, 2016; Maher & Maher, 2003). The idea of using "moral treatment," or respect and kindness instead of harsh methods, spread throughout Europe and America (Frances, 2016; Routh & Reisman, 2003). Moral treatment "prescriptions" might include exercise, dance, music, and time outdoors (Sussman, 2015).

During the mid- to late-1800s, an American schoolteacher named Dorothea Dix (1802–1887) vigorously championed the "mental hygiene movement," a campaign to reform asylums in the United States. Appalled by what she witnessed in American prisons and institutions housing the poor, including the caging of naked inmates, Dix helped establish and upgrade dozens of state mental hospitals (Parry, 2006; Whitaker, 2015). Despite the good intentions of reformers like Pinel and Dix, many institutions eventually deteriorated into warehouses for people with psychological disorders: overcrowded, understaffed, and underfunded.

In the early 1900s, psychiatrists began to realize that mental health problems existed outside asylums, among ordinary people who were capable of functioning in society. Rather than drawing a line between the sane and insane, psychiatrists began to view mental health as a continuum. They started developing a system to classify psychological disorders based on symptoms and progression, and this effort ultimately led to the creation of the first *Diagnostic and Statistical Manual of Mental Disorders* in 1952 (*DSM;* American Psychiatric Association, 1952; Pierre, 2012; Shorter, 2015).

RETURN TO THE COMMUNITY In the 1950s and 1960s, the United States saw a mass exodus of American patients out of institutions and back into the community (**FIGURE 14.1**). This **deinstitutionalization** was partly the result of a movement to reduce the social isolation of people with psychological disorders and integrate them into society. Deinstitutionalization was also made possible by the introduction of medications that

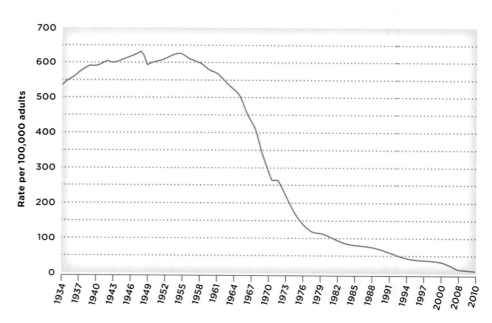

Inspiring Psychologist
Dr. Nneka Jones Tapia stands in a cell in Chicago's Cook County Jail. Unlike most jail wardens, who have a background in criminal justice, Tapia is a clinical psychologist (Decker, 2016b). Her psychology training is invaluable to the jail's residents, a third of whom are said to suffer from psychological disorders. Tapia has ensured that all incoming inmates receive mental health evaluations and treatment if necessary (Williams, 2015, July 30). JOSHUA LOTT/The New York Times/Redux.

reduced some symptoms of severe psychological disorders (Sisti, Segal, & Emanuel, 2015). Thanks to these new drugs, many people who had previously needed constant care and supervision began caring for themselves and managing their own medications —an arrangement that worked for some but not all, as many former patients ended up living on the streets or incarcerated (Harrington, 2012).

Today, approximately 4% of American adults (around 10 million people) suffer from serious and "treatment-resistant psychotic disorders" (often severe schizophrenia or bipolar disorder). These individuals lack insight, often suffer from psychotic symptoms, and can pose a risk to themselves and others, yet the great majority lack access to long-term care (Sisti et al., 2015). In fact, 250,000 "severely ill" people are "living on the street," and many others are incarcerated (Frances, 2016, p. 59). As of 2007, approximately 2.2 million inmates in American jails and prisons were suffering from mental health problems, representing more than one half of the inmate population (Hawthorne et al., 2012). Thus we see how history repeats itself: "We began with the mad in jail and the noble intent to ease their suffering by providing appropriate asylum care. But jail is precisely where hundreds of thousands of the mentally ill find themselves today, especially in the United States." While this issue has received some attention, it has not "been received with the true horror it deserves" (Decker, 2016a, p. 53).

In spite of the deinstitutionalization movement, psychiatric hospitals and institutions continue to play an important role in the treatment of psychological disorders. The scenario involving Dr. Foster and his client Chepa may be unusual in some respects, but not when it comes to the initiation of treatment. For someone experiencing a dangerous **psychotic episode**, the standard approach includes a stay in a psychiatric facility. Some of these admissions are voluntary; others are not.

Typically, a person is ready to leave the hospital after a few days or weeks, but many people in crisis are released after just a few hours, due to the high cost of treatment and financial pressures on hospitals. As some critics contend, patients are being "held hostage" by the financial needs of insurance companies and physicians (Decker, 2016a). The length of a hospital stay is often determined by what insurance will cover, rather than what a patient needs, and restricted by the severe shortage of available beds. Many psychiatric facilities simply cannot accommodate

CONNECTIONS

In **Chapter 13,** we described psychotic symptoms, such as hallucinations and delusions. Psychotic episodes can be risky for the person experiencing them—as well as those around him. In these cases, a person may be admitted to a hospital against his will. Hospitals have procedures in place to ensure that involuntary admissions are ethical.

deinstitutionalization The mass movement of patients with psychological disorders out of institutions, and the attempt to reintegrate them into the community.

the scores of people seeking treatment (Frances, 2016; Honberg, Diehl, Kimball, Gruttadaro, & Fitzpatrick, 2011; Interlandi, 2012, June 22). We have come a long way in the treatment of psychological disorders, but there is still considerable progress to be made.

Treatment Today: An Overview of Major Approaches

LO 2 Explain how the main approaches to therapy differ and identify their common goal.

Today, people receive treatment for a variety of reasons, not just mental disorders. Psychotherapy can help clients resolve work problems, cope with chronic illness, and adjust to major life changes like immigration and divorce. Some people seek psychotherapy to work on a specific issue or to improve their relationships.

The word "psychotherapy" derives from the Ancient Greek *psyche*, meaning "soul," and *therapeuo*, meaning "to heal" (Brownell, 2010), and there are many ways to go about this healing of the soul. Some therapies promote increased awareness of situations and the self: You need to understand the origins of your problems in order to deal with them. Others focus on active steps toward behavioral change: The key to resolving issues is not so much understanding their origins, but changing the thoughts and behaviors directly preceding them. Finally, there are interventions aimed at correcting disorders from a physical standpoint. Such treatments often take the form of medication, and may be combined with other therapies.

These approaches share many common features: The relationship between the client and the treatment provider is of utmost importance, as is a sense of hope that things will get better (Feinstein, Heiman, & Yager, 2015; Snyder et al., 2000). They also share a common goal, that is, to reduce symptoms and increase the quality of life.

Psychological therapies can be categorized along three major dimensions (**INFO-GRAPHIC 14.1**). The first dimension is the manner of delivery—whether therapy is administered to an *individual* (one therapist working with one person) or a *group* (therapists working with multiple people). The second dimension is the treatment approach, which can be biomedical or psychological. **Biomedical therapy** refers to drugs and other medical interventions that target the biological basis of a disorder. **Psychotherapy**, or "talk therapy," homes in on psychological factors. The third dimension of therapy is the theoretical perspective, or approach. We can group the various approaches into two broad categories: **insight therapies**, which aim to increase awareness of self and the environment, and **behavior therapies**, which focus on behavioral change. As you learn about the many forms of therapy, keep in mind that they are not mutually exclusive; therapists often incorporate various perspectives (Frances, 2016). Around 25% to 50% of today's therapists use this type of combined approach (Norcross & Beutler, 2014). Even those who are trained in one discipline may integrate multiple methods, tailoring treatment for each client with an **eclectic approach to therapy**. Guidelines provided by the American Psychological Association (APA) highlight the importance of using **evidence-based practice**, that is, making treatment decisions that integrate the "best available" research findings, "clinical expertise," and knowledge of a patient's culture, values, and preferences (APA Presidential Task Force on Evidence-Based Practice, 2006; Bufka & Halfond, 2016).

In addition to describing the various approaches to psychological treatment, we will examine how well they work. *Outcome research,* which evaluates the success of therapies, is a complicated endeavor. First, it is not always easy to pinpoint the

Synonyms

eclectic approach to therapy
integrative approach to therapy

biomedical therapy Drugs and other physical interventions that target the biological processes underlying psychological disorders; primary goal is to reduce symptoms.

psychotherapy "Talk therapy"; a treatment approach in which a client works with a mental health professional to reduce psychological symptoms and improve quality of life.

insight therapies A type of psychotherapy aimed at increasing awareness of self and the environment.

behavior therapies A type of therapy that focuses on behavioral change.

eclectic approach to therapy Drawing on multiple theories and approaches to tailor treatment for a client.

evidence-based practice Making decisions about treatment that integrate valuable research findings, clinical expertise, and knowledge of a patient's culture, values and preferences.

According to some estimates, there exist at least 500 specific types of psychotherapy (Lilienfeld & Arkowitz, 2012, September 1). Many approaches to therapy share common features, and it can be helpful to use these broad dimensions as a means of organizing our discussion. However, keep in mind that divisions between therapeutic approaches are much less rigid than it may appear in this diagram. As many as half of therapists today combine approaches, either in terms of specific techniques associated with theoretical perspectives, or in terms of the perspectives themselves (Norcross & Beutler, 2014). But for every approach the goal remains the same: to reduce symptoms and increase the quality of life.

Major Approaches to Therapy

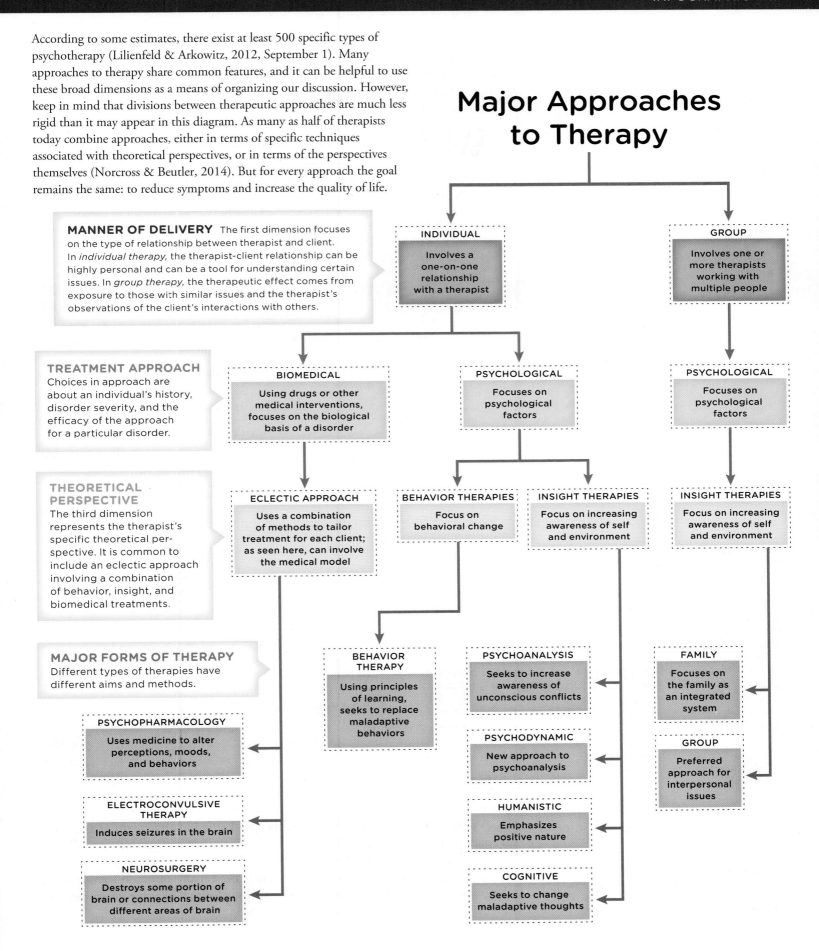

CONNECTIONS

In **Chapter 1,** we described the importance of operational definitions. An operational definition is the precise manner in which we define and measure a characteristic of interest. Here, it is important to create an operational definition of success, which allows for the comparison of different treatment approaches.

meaning of success, or operationalize it. Should we measure self-esteem, happiness, or some other benchmark? Second, it can be difficult for clinicians to remain free of bias (both positive and negative) when reporting on the successes and failures of clients (see Chapter 15 on the self-serving bias). **TABLE 14.1** describes some of the variables that may impact the success of psychotherapy.

 **In Class: Collaborate and Report**

Before you team up, **A)** outline the major approaches to therapy discussed in this section (including those described in Infographic 14.1). Then in your group, **B)** imagine a man who is terrified of flying, and consider the obstacles he faces getting over his fear. **C)** Provide explicit examples to illustrate how the various approaches to therapy might be used for this individual. **D)** Decide on the best approach, as well as one you would never use, and give reasons for both choices.

TABLE 14.1 VARIABLES AFFECTING OUTCOMES OF PSYCHOTHERAPY

Variables That *Will* Improve Outcomes	Variables *Likely* to Improve Outcomes	Variables That *Could* Improve Outcomes
Hope	Therapist and client agreement on goals	Genuineness of therapist
Optimistic expectations	Teamwork	Emotional intelligence of therapist
Positive partnerships		Therapist's ability to mend alliance "ruptures"
Unity (group setting)		Therapist's ability to manage his or her own emotional reactions toward a client
Therapist empathy		

What determines the outcome of psychotherapy? Listed here are several factors that come into play. As you can see, some are more critical than others. Information from Feinstein, Heiman, and Yager (2015).

 show what you know

1. A therapist writes a letter to the editor of a local newspaper in support of more funding for mental health facilities, stating that regardless of therapists' training, all therapy shares the same goal of reducing _____ and increasing the quality of life.
   a. symptoms
   b. combined approaches
   c. biomedical therapy
   d. the number of asylums

2. Philippe Pinel was horrified by the conditions in Parisian asylums in the late 1700s. He insisted that the inmates' chains be removed and that they be treated with respect and kindness. This _____ then spread throughout Europe and America.

3. What were some of the consequences of deinstitutionalization?

✓ CHECK YOUR ANSWERS IN APPENDIX C.

Insight Therapies

AWARENESS EQUALS POWER Laura Lichti grew up in a picturesque town high in the clouds of the Rocky Mountains. Her family was, in her words, "very, very conservative," and her church community tight-knit and isolated. As an adolescent, Laura experienced many common teenage feelings (*Who am I? No one understands me*), and she longed for someone to listen

Blue Jean Images/ SuperStock.

and understand. Fortunately, she found that safe spot in a former Sunday school teacher, a twenty-something woman with children of her own, who had a wise "old soul," according to Laura. "The role she played for me was just like a life line," Laura recalls. "What I appreciated is that she really didn't direct me." If Laura felt distressed, her mentor would never say, "I told you so." Instead, she would listen without judgment. Then she would respond with an empathetic statement such as, "I can see that you're having a really hard time. . . ."

With her gentle line of inquiry, the mentor encouraged Laura to search within herself for answers. Thoughtfully, empathically, she taught Laura how to find her voice, create her own solutions, and direct her life in a way that was true to herself. "[She] took it back to me," Laura says. "It was beautiful."

Inspired to give others what her mentor had given her, Laura resolved to become a psychotherapist for children and teens. She paid her way through community college, went on to a 4-year university, and eventually received her master's degree in psychology, gaining experience in various internships along the way. After logging in hundreds of hours of supervised training and passing the state licensing exam, Laura finally became a licensed professional counselor. The process was 10 years in the making.

Today, Laura empowers clients much in the same way her mentor empowered her—by developing their self-awareness. She knows that therapy is working when clients become aware enough to anticipate a problem and use coping skills without her prompting. "I got into an argument and started getting really angry," a client might say, "but instead of flying off the handle I took a walk and calmed down." Developing self-awareness is one of the unifying goals of the insight therapies, which we will now explore. ●

On Her Way
Laura Lichti had many reasons to feel proud the day she received her master's degree in counseling. After working full-time to put herself through college, earning an associate's degree from a community college and then a bachelor's degree from a 4-year institution, Laura was one of 16 people admitted to a highly competitive master's program in counseling. Dan Penn.

Taking It to the Couch, Freudian Style: Psychoanalysis

LO 3 Describe how psychoanalysis differs from psychodynamic therapy.

When imagining the stereotypical therapy session, many people picture a person reclining on a couch and talking about dreams and childhood memories. Modern-day therapy generally does not resemble this image. But if we could travel back in time to 1930s Vienna, Austria, and sit on the sofa of Sigmund Freud, we just might see this stereotype come to life.

FREUD AND THE UNCONSCIOUS Sigmund Freud (1900/1953), the father of *psychoanalysis,* proposed that humans are motivated by two animal-like drives: aggression and sex. But acting on these drives is not always compatible with social norms, so they create conflict and get pushed beneath the surface, or repressed. These drives do not just go away, though; they continue simmering beneath our conscious awareness, affecting our moods and behaviors. And when we can no longer keep them at bay, the result may be disordered behavior, such as that seen with phobias, obsessions, and panic attacks (Solms, 2006, April/May). To help patients deal with these drives, Freud created psychoanalysis, the first formal system of psychotherapy. Psychoanalysis attempts to increase awareness of unconscious conflicts, thus making it possible to address and work through them.

Dreams, according to Freud, are a pathway to unconscious thoughts and desires (Freud, 1900/1953). The overt material of a dream (what we remember upon waking) is called its *manifest content,* and it can disguise a deeper meaning, or *latent content*. Because this latent content often consists of uncomfortable issues

CONNECTIONS

In **Chapter 11,** we introduced the concept of repression, a defense mechanism through which the ego moves anxiety-provoking thoughts, memories, or feelings from consciousness to unconsciousness. Here, we will see how psychoanalysis helps uncover some of these unconscious processes.

CONNECTIONS

In **Chapter 4,** we introduced Freud's theory of dreams. Freud suggested manifest content is the dream's apparent meaning, or reported storyline. Latent content contains the dream's hidden meaning, and represents unconscious urges. To expose the latent content, we must look deeper than the manifest content.

"It's that same dream, where I'm drowning in a bowl of noodles."

CONNECTIONS

In **Chapter 11,** we presented projective personality tests. The assumption is that the test taker's unconscious conflicts are projected onto the test material. It is up to the therapist to try to uncover these underlying issues. In the context of therapy, a patient projects conflicts onto the therapist.

The Famous Couch

Freud's psychoanalytic couch appears on display at the Freud Museum in London. All of Freud's patients reclined on this piece of furniture, which is reportedly quite comfortable with its soft cushions and Iranian rug cover (Freud Museum, n.d., para. 4). Freud sat in the chair at the head of the couch, close to but not within view of his patient.
Bjanka Kadic/Alamy Stock Photo.

and desires, it is hidden from awareness. But with the help of a therapist, it can be unearthed. Freud would often use dreams as a launching pad for **free association**, a therapy technique in which a patient says anything and everything that comes to mind, regardless of how silly, bizarre, or inappropriate it may seem.

Freud believed this seemingly directionless train of thought would lead to clues about the patient's unconscious. Piecing together the hints he gathered from dreams, free association, and other parts of therapy sessions, Freud would identify and make inferences about the unconscious conflicts driving the patient's behavior. He called this investigative work **interpretation**. When the time seemed right, Freud would share his interpretations, increasing the patient's self-awareness and helping her come to terms with conflicts, with the aim of moving forward (Freud, 1900/1953).

You might be wondering what behaviors psychoanalysts consider signs of unconscious conflict. One indicator is **resistance**, a patient's unwillingness to cooperate in therapy. Examples of resistance might include arriving late or "forgetting" appointments, or becoming angry or agitated when certain topics arise. Resistance is a crucial step in psychoanalysis because it means the discussion might be veering close to something that makes the patient feel uncomfortable and threatened, like a critical memory or conflict causing distress. If resistance occurs, the job of the therapist is to help the patient identify its unconscious roots.

Another sign of unconscious conflict is **transference**, which occurs when a patient reacts to the therapist as if she were dealing with her parents or other important people from childhood. Suppose Chepa relates to Dr. Foster as if he were a favorite uncle. She never liked letting her uncle down, so she resists telling Dr. Foster things she suspects would disappoint him. Transference can be a good thing, especially when it illuminates the unconscious conflicts fueling a patient's behaviors (Hoffman, 2009). One of the reasons Freud sat off to the side and out of a patient's line of vision was to encourage transference. With Freud in this neutral position, patients would have an easier time projecting their unconscious conflicts and feelings onto him.

TAKING STOCK: AN APPRAISAL OF PSYCHOANALYSIS The oldest form of talk therapy, psychoanalysis is still alive and well today. But Freud's theories have come under sharp criticism. For one thing, they are not evidence-based, or backed up by scientific data. How can you effectively evaluate the subjective interpretations of psychoanalysts? Neither therapists nor patients actually know if they are tapping the patients' unconscious because it is made up of thoughts, memories, and desires that are often beyond awareness and hard to operationalize (Parth & Loeffler-Stastka, 2015). How then can we know if their conflicts are being resolved? What's more, not every person is a good candidate for psychoanalysis; one must be an effective communicator, available for multiple sessions each week, and able to pay for this often expensive therapy.

Although Freud's theories have been criticized, the impact of his work is extensive (just note how often it is cited in this textbook). Freud helped us appreciate how childhood experiences and unconscious processes can shape personality and behavior. Even Laura, who does not identify herself as a psychoanalyst, says that Freudian notions sometimes come into play with her clients. If a person has a traumatic experience in childhood, for example, it may resurface both in therapy and real life, she notes. Like Laura, many contemporary psychologists do not identify themselves as psychoanalysts. But that doesn't mean Freud has left the picture. Far from it.

Goodbye, Couch; Hello, Chairs: Psychodynamic Therapy

Psychodynamic therapy is an updated take on psychoanalysis. This newer approach to insight therapy has been evolving over the last 30 to 40 years, incorporating many of Freud's core themes, including the idea that personality and behaviors frequently can be traced to unconscious conflicts and experiences from the past.

However, psychodynamic therapy breaks from traditional psychoanalysis in important ways. Therapists tend to see clients once a week for several months rather than many times a week for years. And instead of sitting quietly off to the side as the client reclines on a couch, the therapist sits face-to-face with the client, engaging in a two-way dialogue. The therapist may use a direct approach, guiding the discussion and providing feedback and advice. Frequently, the goal of psychodynamic therapy is to understand and resolve a specific, current problem. Suppose a client finds herself in a pattern of dating abusive men. Her therapist might help her see how unconscious conflicts from the past creep into the present, influencing her feelings and behaviors. (*My father was abusive. Maybe I'm drawn to what feels familiar, even if it's bad for me.*)

For many years, psychodynamic therapists treated clients without much evidence to back up their approach (Levy & Ablon, 2010, February 23). But recently, researchers have begun testing the effects of psychodynamic therapy with rigorous scientific methods, and their results are encouraging (Leichsenring, Abbass, et al., 2016; Leichsenring, Luyten, et al., 2015; Levy, Hilsenroth, & Owen, 2015). Randomized controlled trials suggest psychodynamic psychotherapy is effective for treating an array of disorders, including depression, panic disorder, and eating disorders (Driessen et al., 2015; Leichsenring & Rabung, 2008; Milrod et al., 2007; Shedler, 2010), and the benefits may last long after treatment has ended. People with borderline personality disorder, for example, appear to experience fewer and less severe symptoms (such as a reduction in suicide attempts) for several years following psychodynamic therapy (Bateman & Fonagy, 2008; Shedler, 2010). Yet, this approach is not ideal for everyone. It requires high levels of verbal expression and awareness of self and the environment. Symptoms like hallucinations or delusions might interfere with these requirements.

You Can Do It! Humanistic Therapy

LO 4　Outline the principles and characteristics of humanistic therapy.

For the first half of the 20th century, most psychotherapists leaned on the theoretical framework established by Freud. But in the 1950s, some psychologists began to question Freud's dark view of human nature and his approach to treating clients. A new perspective began to take shape, one that focused on the positive aspects of human nature; this *humanism* would have a powerful influence on generations of psychologists, including Laura Lichti.

THE CLIENT KNOWS During college, Laura worked as an adult supervisor at a residential treatment facility for children and teens struggling with mental health issues. The experience was eye-opening. "I hadn't really been exposed to the level of intensity, and severe needs . . . of that population," Laura says. "I really had never been with people who constantly wanted to kill themselves, or had a severe eating disorder, or [who] were extreme

CONNECTIONS

In **Chapter 11,** we introduced the neo-Freudians, who disagreed with Freud's main ideas, including his singular focus on sex and aggression, his negative view of human nature, and his idea that personality is set by the end of childhood. Here, we can see that psychodynamic therapy grew out of discontent with Freud's ideas concerning treatment.

CONNECTIONS

In **Chapter 1,** we described the experimental method, a research design that can uncover cause-and-effect relationships. Here we see how this method is used to study the outcome of therapy. In randomized controlled trials, participants are randomly assigned to treatment and control groups. The independent variable is the type of treatment, and the dependent variables are measures of their effectiveness.

free association A psychoanalytic technique in which a patient says anything that comes to mind.

interpretation A psychoanalytic technique used to explore unconscious conflicts driving behavior.

resistance A patient's unwillingness to cooperate in therapy; a sign of unconscious conflict.

transference A type of resistance that occurs when a patient reacts to a therapist as if dealing with parents or other caregivers from childhood.

psychodynamic therapy A type of insight therapy that incorporates core psychoanalytic themes, including the importance of unconscious conflicts and experiences from the past.

cutters." Laura was not a therapist at the time, so she could not offer them professional help. To connect with the residents, she relied on the relational skills she had learned from her mentor. Her message was, *I'm here. I'll meet you where you are, and I really care about you.*

Laura continues to use this approach in her work as a therapist, allowing each client to steer the course of his therapy. For example, Laura might begin a session by asking a client to experiment with art therapy. Some people are enthusiastic about art therapy; others resist, but Laura makes it a rule never to coerce a client with statements such as, "Well, you need to do it because I am your therapist." Instead, she might say, "Okay, what do you think would work? If art is not going to work, what is interesting to you?" Maybe the client likes writing song lyrics; if so, Laura will follow his lead. "Okay, then why don't you write a song for me?" ●

CONNECTIONS

In **Chapter 1,** we introduced the field of positive psychology, which draws attention to human strengths and potential for growth. The humanistic perspective was a forerunner to positive psychology. Humanistic therapy emphasizes the positive nature of humans and strives to harness this in treatment.

This approach to therapy is very much a part of the humanistic movement, which was championed by American psychotherapist Carl Rogers. Rogers believed that human beings are inherently good and inclined toward growth. "It has been my experience that persons have a basically positive direction," he wrote in his widely popular book *On Becoming a Person* (Rogers, 1961, p. 26). Rogers recognized that people have basic biological "demands" for food and sex, but he also saw that we have powerful desires to form close relationships, treat others with warmth and tenderness, and grow and mature as individuals (Rogers, 1961).

Drawing to Feel Better
A child refugee injured during the conflict in Syria participates in an art therapy session organized by the nonprofit Doctors Without Borders. Art therapy is an approach that uses art to help people understand, express, and deal with their emotions in a constructive way (American Art Therapy Association, 2016). REUTERS/Ali Jarekji.

With this optimistic spirit, Rogers and others pioneered several types of insight therapy collectively known as **humanistic therapy**, which emphasizes the positive nature of humankind. Unlike psychoanalysis, which tends to focus on the distant past, humanistic therapy concentrates on the present, seeking to identify and address current problems. And rather than digging up unconscious thoughts and feelings, humanistic therapy emphasizes the conscious experience: what's going on in your mind right now?

LO 5 Describe person-centered therapy.

PERSON-CENTERED THERAPY Rogers' distinct form of humanistic therapy is known as **person-centered therapy**, and it closely follows his theory of personality. According to Rogers, each person has a natural tendency toward growth and *self-actualization,* or achieving one's full potential. But expectations from family and society can stifle the process. He suggested these types of external factors often cause an *incongruence,* or a mismatch, between the client's *ideal self* (often involving unrealistic expectations of who she should be) and *real self* (the way the client views herself). The main goal of treatment is to reduce the incongruence between these two selves.

Suppose Laura has a male client who is drawn toward artistic endeavors. He loves dancing, singing, and acting, but his parents believe that boys should be tough and play sports. The client has spent his life trying to become the person others expect him to be, meanwhile denying the person he is deep down, which leaves him feeling unfulfilled and empty. Using a person-centered approach, Laura would take this client on a journey toward self-actualization. She would be supportive and involved throughout the process, but she would not tell him where to go, because as Rogers stated, "It is the *client* who knows what hurts, what directions to go, what problems

Synonyms

person-centered therapy client-centered therapy

humanistic therapy A type of insight therapy that emphasizes the positive nature of humankind.

person-centered therapy A form of humanistic therapy developed by Rogers; aimed at helping clients achieve their full potential.

nondirective A technique used in person-centered therapy whereby the therapist follows the lead of the client during treatment sessions.

therapeutic alliance A warm and accepting client–therapist relationship that serves as a safe place for self-exploration.

empathy The ability to feel what a person is experiencing by attempting to observe the world through his or her eyes.

TABLE 14.2 BUILDING A THERAPEUTIC ALLIANCE

Components	Description
Empathy	The ability to feel what a client is experiencing; seeing the world through the client's eyes (Rogers, 1951); therapist perceives feelings and experiences from "inside" the client (Rogers, 1961)
Unconditional positive regard	Total acceptance of a client no matter how distasteful the client's behaviors, beliefs, and words may be (see Chapter 11)
Genuineness	Being authentic, responding to a client in a way that is real rather than hiding behind a polite or professional mask; knowing exactly where the therapist stands, allowing the client to feel secure enough to open up (Rogers, 1961)
Active listening	Picking up on the content and emotions behind words in order to understand a client's point of view; reflection, or echoing the main point of what a client says

Humanist Carl Rogers believed it was critical to establish a strong and trusting therapist–client relationship. Above are the key elements of a therapeutic alliance.

I Believe in You
Carl Rogers leads a group therapy session in 1966. One of the founders of humanism, Rogers firmly believed that every person is fundamentally good and capable of self-actualization, or becoming all that she can be. The LIFE Picture Collection/Getty Images.

are crucial, what experiences have been deeply buried" (Rogers, 1961, pp. 11–12). This type of therapy is **nondirective**, meaning the therapist follows the lead of the client. The goal is to help clients see they have the power to make changes in their lives and continue along a path of positive growth. The assumption is that all humans have an innate drive to become fully functioning.

Part of Rogers' philosophy was his refusal to identify the people he worked with as "patients" (Rogers, 1951). Patients depend on doctors to make decisions for them, or at least give them instructions. In Rogers' mind, it was the patient who had the answers, not the therapist. So he began using the term *client* and eventually settled on the term *person*.

The focus in person-centered therapy is not therapeutic techniques; the goal is to create a warm and accepting relationship between therapist and client. This **therapeutic alliance** is based on mutual respect and caring between the therapist and the client, and it provides a safe place for self-exploration.

At this point, you may be wondering what exactly the therapist does during sessions. If a client has all the answers, why does he need a therapist at all? Sitting face-to-face with a client, the therapist's main job is to "be there" for that person through **empathy**, *unconditional positive regard*, **genuineness**, and **active listening**—all essential components of the therapeutic alliance (**TABLE 14.2**).

TAKING STOCK: AN APPRAISAL OF HUMANISTIC THERAPY The humanistic perspective has had a profound impact on our understanding of personality development and on the practice of psychotherapy. Therapists of all different theoretical orientations draw on humanistic techniques to build stronger relationships with clients and create positive therapeutic environments. This type of therapy is useful for an array of people dealing with complex and diverse problems, and in many cases its success rivals that of other methods (Angus, Watson, Elliott, Schneider, & Timulak, 2015; Corey, 2017). Studying humanistic therapy is difficult because its methodology has not been operationalized and its use varies from one therapist to the next. Like other insight therapies, humanistic therapy is not ideal for everyone; it requires a high level of verbal ability and self-awareness. Clients play an important role in determining its

CONNECTIONS

In **Chapter 11,** we discussed unconditional positive regard, or total acceptance of a person regardless of his or her behavior. Rogers believed unconditional positive regard is not only a crucial part of the caregiver–child relationship, but also the therapist–client relationship.

genuineness The ability to respond to a client in an authentic way rather than hiding behind a polite or professional mask.

active listening The ability to pick up on the content and emotions behind words in order to understand a client's perspective, often by echoing the main point of what the client says.

success; they need to be receptive, open, and actively involved in the therapeutic process, and collaboration with the therapist is optimal (Cain, 2016).

The insight therapies we have explored—psychoanalysis, psychodynamic therapy, and humanistic therapy—help clients develop a deeper understanding of self. By exploring events of the past, clients in psychoanalysis or psychodynamic therapy may discover how prior experiences affect their current thoughts and behaviors. Those working with humanistic therapists may become more aware of what they want in life—and how their desires conflict with the expectations of others. These insights are invaluable, and they often lead to positive changes in behavior. But is it also possible to alter behavior directly? This is the goal of behavior therapy, the subject of the next section.

 show what you know

1. Suzanne is late for her therapy appointment yet again. Her therapist suggests this might be due to _____, which refers to a patient's unwillingness to cooperate in therapy.

2. The group of therapies known as _____ therapy focus on the positive nature of human beings and on the here and now.
   a. humanistic
   b. psychoanalytic
   c. psychodynamic
   d. free association

3. Seeing the world through a client's eyes and understanding how it feels to be that person is referred to as
   a. interpretation.
   b. genuineness.
   c. empathy.
   d. self-actualization.

4. What are the differences between psychoanalytic and psychodynamic therapy?

✓ CHECK YOUR ANSWERS IN APPENDIX C.

White Terror
A classic in the history of psychology, the case study of Little Albert showed that emotional responses such as fear can be classically conditioned. Researchers John B. Watson and Rosalie Rayner (1920) repeatedly exposed Albert to a frightening "bang!" every time he reached for a white rat, which led him to develop an intense fear of these animals. Vasiliy Koval/Shutterstock.

CONNECTIONS

In **Chapter 5,** we learned about negative reinforcement; behaviors followed by a reduction in something unpleasant are likely to recur. If anxiety is reduced as a result of avoiding a feared object, the avoidance will be repeated.

Behavior Therapies

The most famous baby in the history of psychology is probably Little Albert. At the age of 11 months, Albert developed an intense fear of rats while participating in a classic study conducted by John B. Watson and Rosalie Rayner (1920). You would hope the researchers did something to reverse the effects of their ethically questionable experiment, that is, help Albert overcome his fear of rats. As far as we know, they did not. Is it possible Albert could have benefited from some form of *behavior therapy?*

Get to Work! Behavior Therapy

LO 6   **Outline the principles and characteristics of behavior therapy.**

Using the learning principles of classical conditioning, operant conditioning, and observational learning (Chapter 5), behavior therapy aims to replace maladaptive behaviors with those that are more adaptive. If behaviors are learned, who says they can't be changed through the same mechanisms? Little Albert learned to fear rats, so perhaps he could have learned to be comfortable around them, too.

EXPOSURE AND RESPONSE PREVENTION To help a person overcome a fear or phobia, a behavior therapist might use **exposure**, a technique of placing clients in the situations they fear—without any actual risks involved. Take, for example, a client struggling with a rat phobia. Rats cause this person extreme anxiety; the mere thought of seeing one scamper beneath a dumpster causes considerable distress. The client usually goes to great lengths to avoid the rodents, and this makes his anxiety drop. The reduced anxiety (and the satisfaction associated with it) will **negatively reinforce** his avoidance behavior. With exposure therapy, the therapist might arrange for the client to be in a room with a very friendly pet rat. After a positive experience with the animal, the client's anxiety diminishes (along with his efforts to avoid it), and he learns the situation does not have to be anxiety-provoking. Ideally, both the anxiety and the avoidance behavior are extinguished. This process of stamping out learned associations is called *extinction*. The theory behind this *response prevention* technique is that if you encourage someone to confront a feared object or situation, and prevent him from responding the way he normally does, the fear response eventually diminishes or disappears.

A particularly intense form of exposure is to *flood* a client with an anxiety-provoking stimulus that she cannot escape, causing a high degree of arousal. In one study, for example, women with snake phobias sat very close to a garter snake in a glass aquarium for 30 minutes without a break (Girodo & Henry, 1976). Flooding is potentially stressful for some therapists, which may be one reason this technique is not commonly used (Schumacher et al., 2015). Just imagine being a therapist and watching your client become extremely anxious or frightened during a flooding session you orchestrated.

For some clients, it's better to approach a feared scenario with "baby steps," upping the exposure with each movement forward (Prochaska & Norcross, 2014). This can be accomplished with an *anxiety hierarchy*, which is essentially a list of activities or experiences ordered from least to most anxiety-provoking (**INFOGRAPHIC 14.2** on the next page). For example, Step 1: Think about a caged rat; Step 2: Look at a caged rat from across the room; Step 3: Walk two steps toward the cage, and so on.

But take note: Working up the anxiety hierarchy needn't involve actual rodents. With technologies available today, you could put on some fancy goggles and travel into a virtual "rat world," where it is possible to reach out and "touch" that creepy crawly animal with the simple click of a rat, er . . . mouse. Virtual reality exposure therapy has become a popular way of reducing anxiety associated with various disorders, including specific phobias. Let's see how it works.

DIDN'T SEE THAT COMING
Virtual Reality Exposure Therapy

SOUNDS LIKE A GREAT IDEA, BUT DOES IT WORK?

Imagine you suffer from a specific phobia (you may not have to imagine anything at all, as this disorder is quite common, affecting about 12% of the U.S. population ages 13 and older; Kessler, Petukhova, Sampson, Zaslavsky, & Wittchen, 2012). The object of your phobia does not happen to be rats, snakes, or anything with a heartbeat, but a huge machine that zooms through the clouds at 500 miles per hour. You have an intense and irrational fear of airplane travel (aviaphobia). The idea of flying makes you so anxious that you haven't stepped on a plane in years. In fact, your phobia has prevented you from taking your dream trip to Mexico, and you are tired of being afraid. So you consult a therapist who develops a treatment plan incorporating virtual reality exposure therapy. Are you ready to fly the virtual skies?

Wearing a head-mounted display (HMD) or a headset like Google Cardboard, you are suddenly transported into the virtual interior of a jumbo jet (Powers & Carlbring, 2016; Rothbaum, Hodges, Smith, Lee, & Price, 2000). The rows of blue seats, the luggage compartments overhead, and the tray table on the seat in front of you—all of it seems so real. So, too, do the sound of the flight attendant's voice and the rumble of the engine, thanks to the woofer situated beneath your seat. Turn your head to the side or look toward the ceiling, and the computer creating this experience automatically adjusts to show you the part of the "plane" you are viewing (Rothbaum et al., 2000). The surroundings are so realistic that you almost forget you're sitting on a chair in a therapist's office.

Face the Spider
A woman with arachnophobia (spider phobia) confronts the dreaded creature in a virtual environment called SpiderWorld. The goal of exposure therapy (virtual or otherwise) is to reduce the fear response by exposing clients to situations they fear. When nothing bad happens, their anxiety diminishes and they are less likely to avoid the feared situations in the future. Hunter Hoffman.

exposure A therapeutic technique that brings a person into contact with a feared object or situation while in a safe environment, with the goal of extinguishing or eliminating the fear response.

Classical Conditioning in Behavior Therapies

Behavior therapists believe that most behaviors—either desirable or undesirable—are learned. When a behavior is maladaptive, a new, more adaptive behavior can be learned to replace it. Behavior therapists use learning principles to help clients eliminate unwanted behaviors. The two behavior therapies highlighted here rely upon classical conditioning techniques. In exposure therapy, a therapist might use an approach known as *systematic desensitization* to reduce an unwanted response, such as a fear of needles, by pairing it with relaxation. In *aversion therapy,* an unwanted behavior such as excessive drinking is paired with unpleasant reactions, creating an association that prompts avoidance of that behavior.

SYSTEMATIC DESENSITIZATION

A client practices relaxation techniques while engaging in situations listed on her anxiety hierarchy, beginning with the least anxiety-provoking situation. After repeated pairings, the client learns to associate the anxiety-provoking situation with the desirable, conditioned response (calm), which is incompatible with fear or anxiety. The process is repeated for every step on the hierarchy.

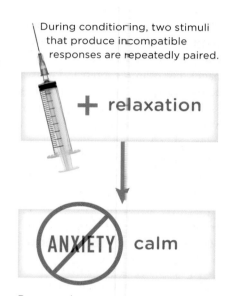

During conditioning, two stimuli that produce incompatible responses are repeatedly paired.

+ relaxation

ANXIETY | calm

Because the responses are incompatible, one response will eventually be extinguished. Starting at the bottom of the hierarchy with the least anxiety-provoking situation enables the desired response (calm) to prevail.

MOST ANXIETY PROVOKING

LEAST ANXIETY PROVOKING

Anxiety Hierarchy for Fear of Needles

8 Getting a flu shot.

7 Allowing someone to prep your arm for a shot.

6 Visiting a health clinic to discuss getting a shot.

5 Watching someone get a shot.

4 Holding a hypodermic needle.

3 Touching a hypodermic needle in its packaging.

2 Looking at an actual hypodermic needle.

1 Looking at a photo of a hypodermic needle.

Before conditioning

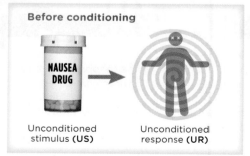

Unconditioned stimulus (US)

Unconditioned response (UR)

During conditioning

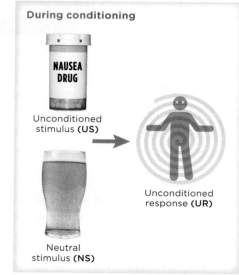

Unconditioned stimulus (US)

Unconditioned response (UR)

Neutral stimulus (NS)

After conditioning

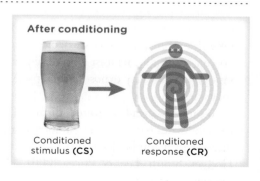

Conditioned stimulus (CS)

Conditioned response (CR)

AVERSION THERAPY

Aversion therapy seeks to diminish a behavior by linking it with an unpleasant reaction. To reduce alcohol consumption, alcohol is consumed with a drug that causes feelings of nausea. Eventually, alcohol becomes a conditioned stimulus, prompting the unpleasant physical reaction all on its own.

A few feet away, your therapist sits at her desk clicking away at a keyboard or swiping and typing on a phone screen; she is moving you through the virtual airplane and monitoring your reports of anxiety every step of the way (Krijn, Emmelkamp, Olafsson, & Biemond, 2004). Now it's time for you to buckle your seatbelt. Once that is accomplished, prepare yourself for takeoff. If you're really feeling comfortable, your therapist might simulate some turbulence or a bumpy landing. With enough virtual reality trials and your regular therapy, you just might be ready for that flight to Mexico.

Virtual reality exposure therapy sounds like a great idea, but does it work? Studies suggest this method is effective for treating various phobias, including fear of airplane travel, spiders, and heights (Krijn et al., 2004; Seinfeld et al., 2016; Shiban, Schelhorn, Pauli, & Mühlberger, 2015). More randomized controlled trials are needed to determine how this approach compares to other interventions (McCann et al., 2014), but researchers seem optimistic: "[Virtual reality exposure therapy] can produce significant behavior change in real-life situations," and it may be as effective as real-world exposure therapy (Morina, Ijntema, Meyerbröker, & Emmelkamp, 2015, p. 18). It's certainly a lot more practical than using a real plane! ☻!

SYSTEMATIC DESENSITIZATION Therapists often combine anxiety hierarchies with relaxation techniques in an approach called **systematic desensitization**, which takes advantage of the fact that we can't be relaxed and anxious at the same time. The therapist begins by teaching clients how to relax their muscles. One technique for doing this is progressive muscle relaxation, which is the process of tensing and then relaxing muscle groups, starting at the head and ending at the toes. Using this method, a client can learn to release all the tension in his body. It's very simple—want to try it?

CONNECTIONS

In **Chapter 12,** we described progressive muscle relaxation for relieving stress and reducing anxiety. Here, we see it can also be used to help with the treatment of phobias.

> Sit in a comfortable chair in a quiet room. Start by tensing the muscles controlling your scalp: Hold that position for about 10 seconds and then release, focusing on the tension leaving your scalp. Next follow the same procedure for the muscles in your face, tensing and releasing. Continue all the way down to your toes and see what happens.

← try this

Once a client has learned how to relax, it's time to face the anxiety hierarchy (either in the real world or via imagination) while trying to maintain a sense of calm. Imagine a client who fears flying, moving through an anxiety hierarchy with her therapist. Starting with the least-feared scenario at the bottom of her hierarchy, she imagines purchasing a ticket online. If she can stay relaxed through the first step, then she moves to the second item in the hierarchy, thinking about boarding a plane. At some point in the process, she might start to feel jittery or unable to take the next step. If this happens, the therapist guides her back a step or two in the hierarchy, or as many steps as she needs to feel calm again, using the relaxation technique described above. Then it's back up the hierarchy she goes. It's important to note that this process does not happen in one session, but over the course of many.

AVERSION THERAPY Exposure therapy focuses on *extinguishing* or eliminating associations, but there is another behavior therapy aimed at producing them. It's called **aversion therapy**. Seizing on the power of classical conditioning, aversion therapy seeks to link problematic behaviors, such as drug use or fetishes, to unpleasant physical reactions like sickness and pain (Infographic 14.2). The goal of

systematic desensitization
A treatment that combines anxiety hierarchies with relaxation techniques.

aversion therapy Therapeutic approach that uses the principles of classical conditioning to link problematic behaviors to unpleasant physical reactions.

CONNECTIONS

In **Chapter 5,** we described classical conditioning. Here, we see how this type of learning could reduce the use of alcohol. The neutral stimulus is drinking alcohol; the unconditioned stimulus is the nausea-inducing drug; and the unconditioned response is nausea. After repeated pairings with the drug, alcohol becomes the conditioned stimulus, and nausea the conditioned response.

CONNECTIONS

In **Chapter 5,** we described how positive reinforcement (supplying something desirable) increases the likelihood of a behavior being repeated. With behavior modification, therapists use reinforcers to shape behaviors, thereby making them more adaptive.

Coveted Coins

In a token economy, target behaviors are reinforced with tokens, which can be used to purchase food, obtain privileges, and secure other desirable things. Token economies are typically used in institutions such as schools and mental health facilities. Jon Schulte/Getty Images.

CONNECTIONS

Tokens are an excellent example of secondary reinforcers. In **Chapter 5,** we reported that secondary reinforcers derive their power from their connection with primary reinforcers, which satisfy biological needs.

Synonyms

behavior modification applied behavior analysis

behavior modification Therapeutic approach in which behaviors are shaped through reinforcement and punishment.

token economy A treatment approach that uses behavior modification, harnessing the power of positive reinforcement to encourage good behavior.

aversion therapy is to prompt a person to experience an involuntary—and unpleasant—physical reaction to an undesirable behavior so that the behavior eventually becomes associated with feeling bad. One type of aversion therapy incorporates the drug Antabuse, which has helped some people with alcoholism stop drinking, at least temporarily (Cannon, Baker, Gino, & Nathan, 1986; Gaval-Cruz & Weinshenker, 2009). Antabuse interferes with the body's ability to break down alcohol, so combining it with even a small amount of alcohol brings on an immediate unpleasant reaction (vomiting, throbbing headache, and so on). With repeated pairings of alcohol consumption and physical misery, drinkers are less inclined to drink in the future. But aversion therapies like this are only effective if the client is motivated to change and comply with treatment (Newton-Howes, Levack, McBride, Gilmor, & Tester, 2016).

LEARNING, REINFORCEMENT, AND THERAPY Another form of behavior therapy is **behavior modification**, which draws on the principles of operant conditioning, shaping behaviors through reinforcement. Therapists practicing behavior modification use positive and negative reinforcement, as well as punishment, to help clients increase adaptive behaviors and reduce those that are maladaptive. For behaviors that resist modification, therapists might reinforce behaviors through successive approximations, or incremental changes. Some will incorporate observational learning (that is, learning by watching and imitating others) to help clients change their behaviors.

One approach using behavior modification is the **token economy** which harnesses the power of positive reinforcement to encourage good behavior. Token economies

have proven successful for a variety of populations, including psychiatric patients in residential treatment facilities and hospitals, children in classrooms, and convicts in prisons (Dickerson, Tenhula, & Green-Paden, 2005; Kazdin, 1982; Walker, Pann, Shapiro, & Van Hasselt, 2016). In a residential treatment facility, for example, patients with schizophrenia may earn tokens for socializing with each other, cleaning up after themselves, and eating meals. Tokens can be exchanged for candy, outings, privileges, and other perks. They can also be taken away as a punishment to reduce undesirable behaviors. Critics contend that token economies manipulate and humiliate the people they intend to help (you might agree that giving grown men and women play money for good behavior is degrading). We also have to consider what happens to those residents who move on to less structured settings—do the changes in their behavior persist? Nonetheless, from a practical standpoint, these systems can help people adopt healthier behaviors.

TAKING STOCK: AN APPRAISAL OF BEHAVIOR THERAPY Because they focus on observable behaviors occurring in the present moment, behavior therapies offer a few key advantages over insight therapies. Behavior therapies tend to work fast, producing quick resolutions to stressful situations, sometimes in a single session (Oar, Farrell, & Ollendick, 2015; Öst, 1989). And reduced time in therapy typically translates to a lower cost. What's more, the procedures used in behavior therapy are often easy to operationalize (remember, the focus is on modifying observable behavior), so evaluating the outcome is more straightforward.

Behavior therapy has its drawbacks, of course. The goal is to change learned behaviors, but not all behaviors and symptoms are learned (for example, you can't "learn" to have hallucinations). And because the reinforcement comes from an external source, newly learned behaviors may disappear when reinforcement stops. Finally, the emphasis on observable behavior may downplay the social, biological, and cognitive roots of psychological disorders. This narrow approach works well for treating phobias and other clear-cut behavior problems, but not as well for addressing far-reaching, complex issues arising from disorders such as schizophrenia.

 **show what you know**

1. The goal of _____ therapy is to replace maladaptive behaviors with more adaptive ones.
   a. behavior
   b. exposure
   c. humanistic
   d. psychodynamic

2. Therapists often help a client develop a(n) _____, which includes a list of anxiety-producing stimuli ordered from least to most anxiety-provoking.

3. The goal of _____ is to get people to have an involuntary and unpleasant physical reaction to an undesirable behavior.

4. Imagine you are working in a treatment facility with a child who acts out by throwing objects at other residents during quiet time. Using the principles of operant conditioning and observational learning, how might you use behavior modification to change the child's bad behavior?

✓ CHECK YOUR ANSWERS IN APPENDIX C.

Cognitive Therapies

FOLLOW-UP After being discharged from the psychiatric hospital, Chepa returns to the reservation, where Dr. Foster and his colleagues from Indian Health Service follow her progress. Every month, she goes to the medical clinic for an injection of medication to quell her psychosis (more on these antipsychotic drugs later in the chapter). This is also when she is most likely to have a therapy session with Dr. Foster.

Psychologists on the reservation typically don't have the luxury of holding more than two or three sessions with a client, so Dr. Foster has to make the most of every minute. For someone who has just received a new diagnosis, a good portion of the session is spent on *psychoeducation,* or learning more about a disorder: *What is schizophrenia, and how will it affect my life?* Dr. Foster and the client might go over some of the user-friendly literature on schizophrenia published by the National Alliance on Mental Illness (NAMI; www.nami.org).

Another main goal is to help clients restructure cognitive processes, or turn negative thought patterns into healthier ones. To help clients recognize the irrational nature of their thoughts, Dr. Foster might provide an analogy as he does here:

Dr. Foster: If we had a blizzard in February and it's 20 degrees below for 4 days in a row, would you consider that a strange winter?

Chepa: No.

Dr. Foster: If we had a day that's 105 degrees in August, would you consider that an odd summer?

Chepa: Well, no.

Dr. Foster: Yet you're talking about a difference of 125 degrees, and we're in the same place and we're saying this is normal weather.... We're part of nature. You and I are part of this natural world, and so you might have a day today where you're very distressed, very upset, and a week from now where you're very calm and very at peace, and both of those are normal. Both of those are appropriate.

Dr. Foster might also remind Chepa that her symptoms result from her psychological condition. "Your response is a normal response [for] a human being with this [psychological disorder]," he says, "and so of course you're scared, of course you're upset." Here, Dr. Foster is helping his client see the situation differently; he is normalizing her response by placing it in context. ●

Beck's Cognitive Approach
The father of cognitive therapy, Aaron Beck, believes that distorted thought processes lie at the heart of psychological problems. Macmillan Learning.

You Are What You Think: Cognitive Therapies

LO 7 Outline the principles and characteristics of cognitive therapy.

Dr. Foster has identified his client's maladaptive thoughts and is beginning to help her change the way she views her world and her relationships. This is the basic goal of **cognitive therapy**, an approach advanced by psychiatrist Aaron Beck.

BECK'S COGNITIVE THERAPY Beck was trained in psychoanalysis, but he opted to develop his own approach after trying (without luck) to produce scientific evidence showing that Freud's methods worked (Beck & Weishaar, 2014). Beck believes that patterns of *automatic thoughts* lie at the root of psychological disturbances. These distortions in thinking cause individuals to misinterpret events in their lives (**TABLE 14.3**).

Beck identified a collection of common *cognitive distortions* or *errors* associated with psychological problems such as depression (Beck, Rush, Shaw, & Emory, 1979). One such distortion is **overgeneralization**, or thinking that self-contained events will have major repercussions in life (Prochaska & Norcross, 2014). For example, a person may assume that just because something is true under one set of circumstances, it will be true in all others (*I have had difficulty working for a male boss, so I will never be able to work effectively under a male supervisor*). Another cognitive distortion is *dichotomous thinking*, or seeing things in extremes (*I can either be a good student, or I can have a social life*). One goal of cognitive therapy is to help clients recognize and challenge these cognitive errors.

Beck suggests that cognitive schemas underlie such patterns of automatic thoughts, directing the way we interpret events. Beck's cognitive therapy aims to dismantle or take apart the schemas harboring these errors and replace them with beliefs that nurture more positive, realistic thoughts. Dr. Foster calls these mental frameworks "paradigms," and he also tries to create a more holistic change in thinking. "I tell people that thoughts, behaviors, and words come from beliefs, and when

CONNECTIONS

In **Chapter 8,** we presented Piaget's concept of the schema, a collection of ideas or notions representing a basic unit of understanding. Young children form schemas based on functional relationships they observe in the environment. Beck suggests that schemas can also direct the way we interpret events, not always in a realistic or rational manner.

TABLE 14.3 COGNITIVE DISTORTIONS

Cognitive Distortion	Explanation	Example of Distorted Thinking
Arbitrary inference	Coming to a conclusion even when there is no evidence to support it	*I am a horrible student.*
Selective abstraction	Ignoring information and assuming something has happened based on details taken out of context	*I know he is cheating because he is e-mailing a woman at work.*
Overgeneralizing	Belief that something may always occur because it has occurred before	*My boss doesn't like me; I will never be liked.*
Magnification/minimization	Belief that something is more or less critical than it really is	*If I don't pass this first quiz, I will fail the course.*
Dichotomous thinking	Viewing experiences in extremes	*I can either be at the top of my class, or I can get married and have a family.*
Personalizing	Taking other people's behaviors too personally	*I waved at her, but she didn't even acknowledge me. I must have upset her.*

Aaron Beck contends that psychological problems stem from distorted patterns of thought. Cognitive therapy aims to replace these cognitive distortions with more realistic and constructive ways of thinking. Information from Beck and Weishaar (2014).

a belief is not working for you, let's change it," he says. "To modify a belief doesn't mean all or none," he adds, "but when we outgrow a belief, that's a wonderful time for transformation."

The restructuring of schemas can be facilitated by client homework. For example, the therapist may challenge a client to test a "hypothesis" related to her dysfunctional thinking. ("If it's true you don't work effectively under male bosses, then why did your previous boss give you a promotion?") Client homework is an important component of cognitive therapy. So, too, is psychoeducation, which might include providing resources that help clients understand their disorders and thus adopt more realistic attitudes and expectations.

ELLIS' RATIONAL EMOTIVE BEHAVIOR THERAPY The other major figure in cognitive therapy is psychologist Albert Ellis (1913–2007). Like Beck, Ellis was trained in psychoanalysis but was disappointed by its results, so he created his own treatment approach: **rational emotive behavior therapy (REBT)**. The goal of REBT is to help people identify their irrational or illogical thoughts and convert them into rational ones. An REBT therapist uses the ABC model to understand a client's problems. Point A represents an *Activating event* in the client's life ("My boss fired me."); point B stands for the *irrational Beliefs* that follow ("I will never be able to hold a steady job."); and point C represents the *emotional Consequences* ("I feel hopeless and depressed."). Therapy focuses on addressing point B, the irrational beliefs causing distress. If all goes well, the client successfully reaches point D: *Disputing flawed beliefs* ("Losing one job does not spell the end of my career."). That leads to point E: an *Effective new philosophy* ("I am capable of being successful in another job.") (Ellis & Dryden, 1997; **FIGURE 14.2**).

FIGURE 14.2
The ABCs of REBT
A rational-emotive behavior therapist uses the ABC model to understand a client's problems. This part of the model is depicted in blue. Therapy, shown in green, helps a client identify and address irrational beliefs—and ultimately develop a mature and realistic perspective.

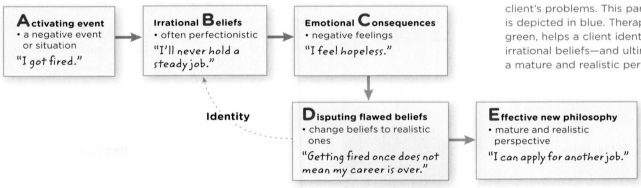

According to Ellis, people tend to have unrealistic beliefs, often perfectionist in nature, about how they and others should think and act. This inevitably leads to disappointment, as no one is perfect. The ultimate goal of REBT is to arrive at self-acceptance, that is, to change these irrational thoughts to realistic ones. This often involves letting go of the "I shoulds" and "I musts," what Ellis called "musturbatory thinking" (Prochaska & Norcross, 2014, p. 266). Through REBT, one develops a rational way of thinking that helps reduce suffering and amplify enjoyment: "The purpose of life," as Ellis was known to say, "is to have a $&%#@ good time" (p. 263). Ellis took a hard line with clients, forcefully challenging them to provide evidence for their irrational ideas and often shocking people with his direct manner (Kaufman, 2007, July 25; Prochaska & Norcross, 2014).

As Ellis developed his therapy throughout the years, he realized it was important to focus on cognitive processing as well as behavior. Thus, REBT therapists focus on changing both cognitions and behaviors, assigning homework to implement the

cognitive therapy A type of therapy aimed at addressing the maladaptive thinking that leads to maladaptive behaviors and feelings.

overgeneralization A cognitive distortion that assumes self-contained events will have major repercussions.

rational emotive behavior therapy (REBT) A type of cognitive therapy, developed by Ellis, that identifies illogical thoughts and attempts to convert them into rational ones.

insights clients gain during therapy. Because Ellis and Beck incorporated both cognitive and behavior therapy methods, their approaches are commonly referred to as **cognitive behavioral therapy (CBT)**. Both are action-oriented, as they require clients to confront and resist their illogical thinking.

TAKING STOCK: AN APPRAISAL OF COGNITIVE THERAPY There is considerable overlap between the approaches of Ellis and Beck. Both are short-term (usually no more than about 20 one-hour sessions), action-oriented, and homework-intensive. Some research suggests that cognitive therapy is more effective than relaxation and exposure therapy for treating certain disorders, such as social phobia and generalized anxiety disorder (Clark et al., 2006; Dugas et al., 2010). If you compare the effectiveness of Beck's and Ellis' approaches, you will find some studies showing greater support for Beck's cognitive therapy. But this advantage is only apparent with certain client characteristics and problems, such as pathological gambling and chronic pain (Prochaska & Norcross, 2014).

In some cases, cognitive models that focus on flawed assumptions and attitudes present a chicken-and-egg problem. People experiencing depression often have distorted beliefs, but are distorted beliefs causing their depression or is depression causing their distorted beliefs? Perhaps it is a combination of both.

All the therapies we have discussed thus far involve interactions among people. But in many cases, psychotherapy is not enough. The problem is rooted in the brain, and a biological solution may also be necessary.

 show what you know

1. The basic goal of _____ is to help clients identify maladaptive thoughts and change the way they view the world and their relationships.

2. Describe the similarities and differences between cognitive and behavior therapy.

3. _____ therapy uses the ABC model to help people identify their illogical thoughts and convert them into logical ones.
   a. Behavior
   b. Psychodynamic
   c. Exposure
   d. Rational-emotive behavior

✓ CHECK YOUR ANSWERS IN APPENDIX C.

Psychologists Who Prescribe
Psychotropic medications are typically prescribed by psychiatrists, but a small number of psychologists have prescription privileges as well. New Mexico, Louisiana, Iowa, and Illinois have passed laws giving psychologists the green light to prescribe, provided they have certain qualifications, such as a master's degree in psychopharmacology. The same is true for psychologists working in the Defense Department or Indian Health Service.
Wavebreakmedia Ltd/Getty Images.

Biomedical Therapies

Earlier in the chapter, we described Dr. Foster's work with Chepa, a young woman facing schizophrenia. In addition to receiving psychotherapy, Chepa goes to the medical clinic for monthly injections of drugs to control her psychosis. Prescribing medications for psychological disorders is generally the domain of *psychiatrists,* physicians who specialize in treating people with psychological disorders (psychiatrists are medical doctors, whereas clinical psychologists have PhDs and generally cannot prescribe medication).

LO 8 **Summarize the biomedical interventions and identify their common goal.**

People with severe disorders like depression, schizophrenia, and bipolar disorder often benefit from biomedical therapy, a type of treatment that targets the biological processes underlying psychological

TABLE 14.4   MEDICATIONS FOR PSYCHOLOGICAL DISORDERS

Category	Commonly Used Medication		Target of Treatment
Antidepressant	Fluoxetine (Prozac) Citalopram (Celexa) Sertraline (Zoloft) Paroxetine (Paxil)	Escitalopram (Lexapro) Venlafaxine (Effexor) Duloxetine (Cymbalta) Bupropion (Wellbutrin)	Depression
Mood-stabilizing	Lithium Valproic acid (Valproic)	Carbamazepine (Tegretol) Lamotrignine (Lamictal) Oxcarbazepine (Trileptal)	Mania and depression
Traditional antipsychotics	Chlorpromazine (Thorazine, Largactil) Haloperidol (Haldol)	Perphenazine (Trilafon) Fluphenazine (Prolixin)	Psychosis
Atypical antipsychotics	Risperidone (Risperdal) Olanzapine (Zyprexa) Quetiapine (Seroquel) Ziprasidon (Geodon)	Aripiprazole (Abilify) Paliperidone (Invega) Lurasidone (Latuda)	Psychosis
Anti-anxiety	Clonazepam (Klonopin) Alprazolam (Xanax) Lorazapam (Ativan)	Diazepam (Valium) Buspirone (Buspar)	Anxiety

Listed here are some of the medications commonly used for treating psychological disorders. Research has shown that psychotropic drugs are most effective for some disorders when used alongside psychotherapy (Cuijpers, De Wit, Weitz, Andersson, & Huibers, 2015; Manber et al., 2008).

disorders. There are three basic biological approaches to treating psychological disorders: (1) drugs, or *psychotropic* medications; (2) electroconvulsive therapy; and (3) surgery.

Medicines That Help: Psychopharmacology

Psychotropic medications are used to treat psychological disorders and their symptoms. *Psychopharmacology* is the scientific study of how these medications alter perceptions, moods, behaviors, and other aspects of psychological functioning. These drugs can be divided into four categories: *antidepressant, mood-stabilizing, antipsychotic,* and *anti-anxiety* (TABLE 14.4).

ANTIDEPRESSANT DRUGS The most common mental health problem plaguing Dr. Foster's clients is major depressive disorder. *Depression,* as it is often called, is one of the most prevalent psychological disorders in America and a frequent cause of disability in young adults (National Institute of Mental Health, 2013, October 1). Major depressive disorder affects around 7% of the population in any given year (American Psychiatric Association, 2013), resulting in a high demand for treatment to alleviate its symptoms.

Major depressive disorder is commonly treated with **antidepressant drugs**, a category of psychotropic medication used to improve mood (and to treat anxiety and eating disorders in certain individuals). Essentially, there are three classes of antidepressant drugs: monoamine oxidase inhibitors (MAOIs), such as Nardil; tricyclic antidepressants, such as Elavil; and selective serotonin reuptake inhibitors (SSRIs),

cognitive behavioral therapy (CBT) An action-oriented type of therapy that requires clients to confront and resist their illogical thinking.

antidepressant drugs Psychotropic medications used for the treatment of depression.

CONNECTIONS ────────

In **Chapter 2,** we described how sending neurons release neurotransmitters into the synapse, where they bind to receptors on the receiving neuron. Neurotransmitters that do not immediately attach are reabsorbed by the sending neuron (reuptake) or are broken down in the synapse. Here, we see how medications can influence this process.

such as Prozac. All these antidepressants are thought to work by influencing the activity of neurotransmitters hypothesized to be involved in depression and other disorders (**INFOGRAPHIC 14.3**). (Keep in mind, no one has pinpointed the exact neurological mechanisms underlying depression.)

The monoamine oxidase inhibitors (MAOIs), developed in the 1950s, help people with major depressive disorder by slowing the breakdown of certain neurotransmitters known as monoamines: norepinephrine, serotonin, and dopamine. MAOIs extend the amount of time these neurotransmitters remain in the synapse by hindering the normal activity of monoamine oxidase, whose natural role is to break down the monoamines. Again, the cause of depression is not entirely clear, but low levels of norepinephrine and serotonin could play a role. By making these neurotransmitters more available (that is, allowing them more time in the synapse), MAOIs might lessen symptoms of depression. Even so, this class of drugs has fallen out of use due to safety concerns and side effects, as they require great attention to diet. MAOIs can trigger a life-threatening jump in blood pressure when ingested alongside tyramine, a substance found in many everyday foods, including cheddar cheese, salami, and wine (Anastasio et al., 2010; Horwitz, Lovenberg, Engelman, & Sjoerdsma, 1964; Larsen, Krogh-Nielsen, & Brøsen, 2016).

The tricyclic antidepressants, named as such because of their three-ringed molecular structure, inhibit the reuptake of serotonin and norepinephrine in the synaptic gap. This allows these neurotransmitters more time to be active, which appears to reduce symptoms. The tricyclic drugs are not always well tolerated by patients and can cause a host of problematic side effects, including sexual dysfunction, confusion, and increased risk of heart attack (Cohen, Gibson, & Alderman, 2000; Coupland et al., 2016; Higgins, Nash, & Lynch, 2010). Overdoses can be fatal.

Doctors relied heavily on monoamine oxidase inhibitors and tricyclics until newer, more popular pharmaceutical interventions were introduced in the 1980s. These selective serotonin reuptake inhibitors (SSRIs)—brands such as Prozac, Paxil, and Zoloft—inhibit the reuptake of serotonin specifically. SSRIs may reduce the potentially devastating symptoms of depression, and improvement is typically noticed within 3–5 weeks of starting treatment. These drugs are generally safer and have fewer negative effects than the older generation of antidepressants, but they are far from perfect. Weight gain, fatigue, hot flashes, chills, insomnia, nausea, and sexual dysfunction are all possible side effects. Some research suggests that SSRIs are not better than a placebo when it comes to treating mild to moderate depression (Fournier et al., 2010; Khan & Brown, 2015). They may also be harmful to children and teens—you'll find out why when you turn the page.

CONNECTIONS ────────

In **Chapter 1,** we stated that a placebo is a "pretend" treatment used to explore the effectiveness of a "true" treatment. The placebo effect is the tendency to feel better if we believe we are being treated with a medication. Expectations about getting better can change treatment outcomes.

Black Box
A growing number of children and teenagers are taking SSRIs to combat depression, but these medications may increase the risk of suicidal behaviors and thoughts for a small percentage of youth. For this reason, the U.S. Food and Drug Administration (FDA) requires manufacturers to include a "black box" warning on the packaging of these drugs (National Institute of Mental Health, n.d.-a, para. 3). Todor Tsvetkov/Getty Images.

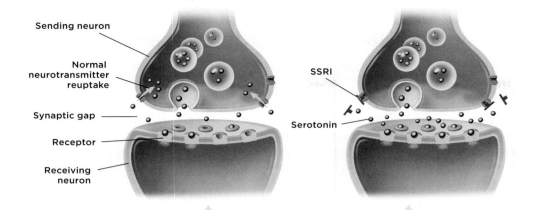

Sending neuron

Normal neurotransmitter reuptake

Synaptic gap

Receptor

Receiving neuron

SSRI

Serotonin

CHEMICAL:
Psychotropic Medications

Drug therapies, which alter the brain's chemistry, are the most commonly prescribed biomedical treatment. Each works to influence neurotransmitters thought to be associated with certain disorders. This illustration shows the action of a class of antidepressants known as selective serotonin reuptake inhibitors (SSRIs).

In normal communication between neurons, neurotransmitters released into the synaptic gap bind to the receiving neuron, sending a message. Excess neurotransmitters are reabsorbed.

As indicated by their name, SSRIs inhibit the reuptake of the neurotransmitter serotonin. Allowed to remain longer in the synapse, serotonin can achieve a greater effect.

Biomedical Therapies

Biomedical therapies use physical interventions to treat psychological disorders. These therapies can be categorized according to the method by which they influence the brain's functioning: chemical, electrical, or structural.

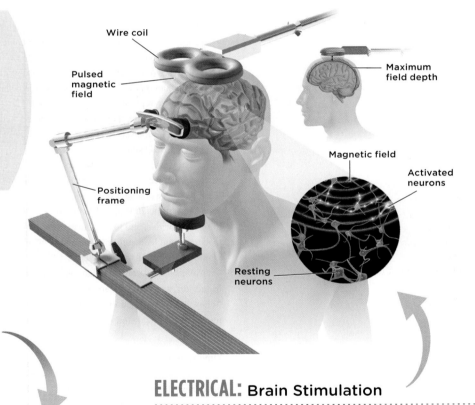

Wire coil

Pulsed magnetic field

Positioning frame

Maximum field depth

Magnetic field

Activated neurons

Resting neurons

STRUCTURAL: Neurosurgery

Modern surgical techniques are able to target a very precise area of the brain known to be directly involved in the condition being treated. For example, the black circles on these scans mark areas typically targeted for a form of surgery known as anterior cingulotomy, which has been shown to reduce symptoms in patients suffering severe cases of major depression (Steele, Christmas, Elijamel, & Matthews, 2008). Using radio frequencies emitted from a 6-millimeter probe, the surgeon destroys part of the anterior cingulate cortex, an area known to be associated with emotions (Faria, 2013).

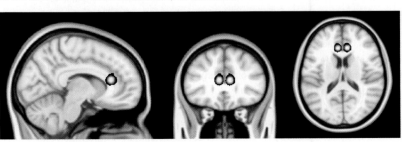

ELECTRICAL: Brain Stimulation

Brain stimulation techniques can be used to relieve symptoms by affecting the electrical activity of the brain. Research on electroconvulsive therapy found an 86% remission rate for those with severe major depression (Kellner et al., 2006). Repetitive transcranial magnetic stimulation (rTMS), shown here, is a noninvasive procedure. A coil pulses a magnetic field that passes painlessly through scalp and bone, penetrating just to the outer cortex. The field induces electric current in nearby neurons, activating targeted regions in the brain (George, 2003).

Credits: (Illustration) Graphic by Bryan Christie Design. Stimulating the Brain by Mark S. George. *Scientific American,* September 2003, page 69; (Brain photo) Reprinted by permission from Macmillan Publishers Ltd: Tractographic analysis of historical lesion surgery for depression. Schoene-Bake JC, Parpaley Y, Weber B, Panksepp J, Hurwitz TA, Coenen VA. *Neuropsychopharmacology.* 2010 December; 35(13): 2553–2563.

from the pages of
SCIENTIFIC
AMERICAN

The Hidden Harm of Antidepressants

An in-depth analysis of clinical trials reveals widespread under-reporting of negative side effects, including suicide attempts and aggressive behavior.

Antidepressants are some of the most commonly prescribed medications out there. More than one out of 10 Americans over age 12—roughly 11 percent—take these drugs, according to a 2011 report by the National Center for Health Statistics. And yet, recent reports have revealed that important data about the safety of these drugs—especially their risks for children and adolescents—has been withheld from the medical community and the public.

In the latest and most comprehensive analysis, published . . . in *BMJ* (the *British Medical Journal*), a group of researchers at the Nordic Cochrane Center in Copenhagen showed that pharmaceutical companies were not presenting the full extent of serious harm in clinical study reports, which are detailed documents sent to regulatory authorities such as the U.S. Food and Drug Administration and the European Medicines Agency (EMA) when applying for approval of a new drug. The researchers examined documents from 70 double-blind, placebo-controlled trials of two common types of antidepressants—selective serotonin reuptake inhibitors (SSRI) and serotonin and norepinephrine reuptake inhibitors (SNRI)—and found that the occurrence of suicidal thoughts and aggressive behavior doubled in children and adolescents who used these medications.

Riddled with conflicts

This paper comes on the heels of disturbing charges about conflicts of interest in reports on antidepressant trials. Last September a study published in the *Journal of Clinical Epidemiology* revealed that a third of meta-analyses of antidepressant studies were written by pharma employees and that these were 22 times less likely than other meta-studies to include negative statements about the drug. That same month another research group reported that after reanalyzing the data from Study 329, a 2001 clinical trial of Paxil funded by GlaxoSmithKline, they uncovered exaggerated efficacy and undisclosed harm to adolescents.

Because of the selective reporting of negative outcomes in journal articles, the researchers in the most recent *BMJ* study turned to clinical trial reports, which include more detailed information about the trials. They discovered that some of most the useful information was in individual patient listings buried in the appendices. For example, they uncovered suicide attempts that were passed off as "emotional liability" or "worsening depression" in the report itself. This information, however, was only available for 32 out of the 70 trials. "We found that a lot of the appendices were often only available upon request to the authorities, and the authorities had never requested them," says Tarang Sharma, a PhD student at Cochrane and lead author of the study. "I'm actually kind of scared about how bad the actual situation would be if we had the complete data."

"[This study] confirms that the full degree of harm of antidepressants is not reported," says Joanna Moncrieff, a psychiatrist and researcher at University College London who was not involved in the study. "They are not reported in the published literature, we know that—and it appears that they are not properly reported in clinical study reports that go to the regulators and form the basis of decisions about licensing."

....

Time to reassess?

Because many prior studies found increased suicidal ideation with antidepressant use, in 2004 the FDA gave these drugs a black box warning—a label reserved for the most serious hazards—and the EMA issued similar alerts. There are no labels about risks for aggression, however. Although hints about hostile behavior existed in the past, including in published case studies, last week's *BMJ* study was the first large-scale work to document an increase in aggressive behavior in children and adolescents. "This is obviously important in the debate about school shootings in the States and in other places where the perpetrators are frequently taking antidepressants," Moncrieff says.

Taken together with other research that raises questions about the pros and cons of this class of drugs—including studies that suggest antidepressants are only marginally better than placebos—some experts say it is time to reevaluate. "My view is that we really don't have good enough evidence that antidepressants are effective and we have increasing evidence that they can be harmful," Moncrieff says. "So we need to go into reverse and stop this increasing trend of prescribing [them]." Diana Kwon.

MOOD-STABILIZING DRUGS In Chapter 13, we introduced Ross Szabo, a man who suffers from bipolar disorder. At various points in life, Ross has battled extreme mood swings—the highest highs and the lowest lows. Many people suffering from bipolar disorder find some degree of relief in **mood-stabilizing drugs**, which can minimize the lows of depression and the highs of mania. Lithium, for instance, helps smooth the mood swings of people with bipolar disorder, leveling out the dramatic peaks (mania) and valleys (depression) (Song et al., 2016). For this reason, it is sometimes called a "mood normalizer" (Bech, 2006), and it has been widely used to treat bipolar disorder for decades. Unlike many standard drugs that chemists cobble together in laboratories, lithium is a mineral salt, in other words, a naturally occurring substance. (You can find lithium in the Periodic Table of the Elements—just look for the symbol Li.)

Scientists have yet to determine the cause of bipolar disorder and how its symptoms might be lessened with lithium. But numerous theories exist, some pointing to imbalances in neurotransmitters such as glutamate and serotonin (Cho et al., 2005; Dixon & Hokin, 1998; Song et al., 2015). Lithium also seems to be effective in lowering suicide risk among people with bipolar disorder (Angst, Angst, Gerber-Werder, & Gamma, 2005; Hayes et al., 2016), who are 20 times more likely than people in the general population to die by suicide (Inder et al., 2016; Tondo, Isacsson, & Baldessarini, 2003). Doctors must be very careful when prescribing lithium, monitoring the blood levels of patients who use it. Too small a dose will fall short of controlling bipolar symptoms, while too large a dose can be lethal. Even when the amount is just right, mild side effects such as hand tremors, thirst, and loss of appetite may occur (National Library of Medicine, 2014).

Anticonvulsant medications are also used to treat bipolar disorder. These drugs were originally created to alleviate symptoms of seizure disorders, but scientists discovered they might also function as mood stabilizers, and some research suggests that they can reduce the symptoms of mania (Bowden et al., 2000). Unfortunately, certain anticonvulsants may increase the risk of suicide or of possible suicide masked as violent death through injury or accident (Muller et al., 2015; Patorno et al., 2010). For this reason, the U.S. Food and Drug Administration (FDA, 2008) requires drug companies to place warnings on their labels.

ANTIPSYCHOTIC DRUGS The hallucinations and delusions of people with disorders like schizophrenia can be subdued with antipsychotics. **Antipsychotic drugs** are designed to block neurotransmitter receptors. Although it is not entirely clear how neurotransmitter activity causes the symptoms of schizophrenia, blocking their receptor sites reduces the firing of neurons presumably associated with psychotic symptoms.

Two kinds of medications can be used in these cases: *traditional antipsychotics* and *atypical antipsychotics* (each with about a half-dozen generic drug offshoots). Both types seek to reduce dopamine activity in certain areas of the brain, as abnormal activity of this neurotransmitter is believed to contribute to the psychotic symptoms of schizophrenia and other disorders (Blasi et al., 2015; Schnider, Guggisberg, Nahum, Gabriel, & Morand, 2010). Antipsychotics accomplish this by acting as dopamine antagonists, meaning they "pose" as dopamine, binding to receptors normally reserved for dopamine (sort of like stealing someone's parking space). By blocking dopamine's receptors, antipsychotic drugs reduce dopamine's excitatory effect on neurons. The main difference between atypical antipsychotics and the traditional variety is that the atypical antipsychotics *also* interfere with neural pathways involving other neurotransmitters, such as serotonin (also associated with psychotic symptoms).

First rolled out in the 1950s, traditional antipsychotics, such as Haldol, made it possible for scores of people to transition out of psychiatric institutions and into society. These new drugs reduced hallucinations and delusions for many patients, but doctors

CONNECTIONS

In **Chapter 2,** we described how drugs influence behavior by changing what is happening in the synapse. Agonists increase the normal activity of a neurotransmitter, and antagonists block normal neurotransmitter activity. Here, we see how antipsychotics can act as antagonists.

Synonyms

mood-stabilizing drugs antimanic drugs

traditional antipsychotics first-generation antipsychotic medications, typical antipsychotic medications

atypical antipsychotics second-generation antipsychotic medications

mood-stabilizing drugs Psychotropic medications that minimize the lows of depression and the highs of mania.

antipsychotic drugs Psychotropic medication used in the treatment of psychotic symptoms, such as hallucinations and delusions.

soon realized that they had other, not-so-desirable effects. After taking the drugs for about a year, some patients developed a neurological condition called *tardive dyskinesia,* the symptoms of which include shaking, restlessness, and bizarre facial grimaces.

These problems were partially solved with the development of the atypical antipsychotics, such as Risperdal (risperidone), which reduce psychotic symptoms and usually do not cause tardive dyskinesia (Correll, Leucht, & Kane, 2004; Jacobsen, 2015). But there are other potential side effects, such as weight gain, increased risk for Type 2 diabetes, sexual dysfunction, and heart disease (Üçok & Gaebel, 2008). And although these drugs reduce symptoms in 60–85% of patients, they are not a cure for the disorder.

Community in Pain
A young man stands among the graves of relatives on the Pine Ridge Indian Reservation in South Dakota. Pine Ridge, which lies about 100 miles west of Rosebud, has witnessed a tragic epidemic of suicides in recent years. During one 6-month period in 2014–2015, nine residents between the ages of 12 and 24 took their own lives (Bosman, 2015, May 1). This is a shocking statistic for a population of approximately 38,000 (Pine Ridge Indian Reservation, 2016). Matthew Ryan Williams/Redux.

CONNECTIONS

In **Chapter 4,** we discussed psychoactive drugs. Repeated use of certain drugs can lead to physiological dependence, indicated by tolerance and withdrawal symptoms. Psychological dependence is apparent when a strong desire or need to continue using a substance occurs, but without tolerance or withdrawal symptoms.

ANTI-ANXIETY DRUGS Anxiety disorders are the second most common class of conditions Dr. Foster encounters on the reservation. Like many impoverished areas, Rosebud has a high rate of trauma (for example, alcohol-associated accidents and homicides). In the United States, the suicide rate among American Indian and Alaska Native youth (ages 10 to 24) exceeds that of all other racial groups. Youth suicides have increased substantially over the last two decades (Dorgan, 2010; Willis, DeLeon, Haldane, & Heldring, 2014). Researchers have tried to untangle the complex web of factors responsible for these deeply troubling statistics, but few would question its connection to the centuries of psychological and cultural damage wrought by colonization and ongoing marginalization and discrimination. Traumatic incidents like suicides inevitably have witnesses, and those witnesses suffer from what they see and hear. Their pain often manifests itself in the form of anxiety.

Anti-anxiety drugs are used to treat the symptoms of anxiety and anxiety disorders, including panic disorder, social phobia, and generalized anxiety disorder. Most of today's anti-anxiety medications are *benzodiazepines,* such as Xanax and Ativan, also called "minor tranquilizers." These drugs are used for a continuum of anxiety, from fear of flying to extreme panic attacks. And since they promote sleep in high doses, they can also be used to treat insomnia. Doctors often prescribe benzodiazepines in combination with other psychotropic medications.

Valium is one of the most commonly used minor tranquilizers, and it was the first psychotropic drug to be used by people who were not necessarily suffering from serious disorders. For most of the 1970s, Valium was so popular among white collar businessmen and women that it came to be called "Executive Excedrin." But then people began to realize how dependent they had become on Valium, both physically and psychologically, and its popularity diminished (Barber, 2008). Nevertheless, the benzodiazepines Valium and Xanax are still the most commonly abused anti-anxiety drugs (Phillips, 2013).

A key benefit of benzodiazepines is that they are fast-acting. But they are also dangerously addictive, and mixing them with alcohol can produce a lethal cocktail. Between 1996 and 2013, there has been a 67% increase in the number of people filling prescriptions for benzodiazepines, and the rate of deaths from overdosing on these drugs has nearly quadrupled (Bachhuber, Hennessy, Cunningham, & Starrels, 2016). Benzodiazepines ease anxiety by enhancing the effect of the neurotransmitter GABA. An inhibitory neurotransmitter, GABA works by decreasing or stopping some types of neural activity. By giving GABA a boost, these drugs inhibit the firing of neurons that normally induce anxiety reactions.

PSYCHOTROPIC MEDICATION PLUS PSYCHOTHERAPY Psychotropic medications have helped countless people get back on their feet and enjoy life, but drugs alone don't produce the best long-term outcomes. Ideally, medications should be taken in conjunction with psychotherapy. With therapy, Dr. Foster says, "The person feels greater self-efficacy. They're not relying on a pill to manage depression."

Indeed, studies suggest that psychotropic drugs are most effective when used alongside psychotherapy. For example, combining medication with an integrative approach to psychotherapy, including cognitive, behavioral, and psychodynamic perspectives, may reduce major depressive symptoms faster than either approach alone (Cuijpers, De Wit, Weitz, Andersson, & Huibers, 2015; Manber et al., 2008).

Another key point to remember: Medications affect people in different ways. An antidepressant that works for one person may have no effect on another; this is also the case for side effects. We metabolize (break down) drugs at different rates, which means dosages must be assessed on a case-by-case basis. To complicate matters further, many people take multiple medications at once, and some drugs interact in harmful ways.

When Drugs Aren't Enough: The Other Biomedical Therapies

As you may already realize, psychotropic drugs are not a cure-all. Sometimes symptoms of psychological disorders do not improve with medication. In these extreme cases, there are other biomedical options. For example, repetitive transcranial magnetic stimulation (rTMS) appears to be effective in treating symptoms of depression and some types of hallucinations (Sommer & Neggers, 2014). With rTMS, electromagnetic coils are put on (or above) a person's head, directing brief electrical current into a particular area of the brain (Slotema, Blom, Hoek, & Sommer, 2010). Another technique under investigation is deep brain stimulation, which involves implanting a device that supplies weak electrical stimulation to specific areas of the brain thought to be linked to depression (Kennedy et al., 2011; Schlaepfer, Bewernick, Kayser, Mädler, & Coenen, 2013). These technologies show great promise, but more research is required to determine their long-term impact.

ELECTROCONVULSIVE THERAPY One biomedical approach that essentially causes seizures in the brain is **electroconvulsive therapy (ECT)**, which is used to treat severely depressed people who have not responded to psychotropic medications or psychotherapy. If you've ever seen ECT, or "shock therapy," portrayed in movies, you might think it's a barbaric form of abuse. Truth be told, ECT was a brutal and overly used treatment in the mid-20th century (Glass, 2001; Smith, 2001). Doctors jolted patients (in some cases, a dozen times a day) with powerful electric currents, creating seizures violent enough to break bones and erase weeks or months of memories (Smith, 2001). Today, ECT is much more humane, administered according to guidelines developed by the American Psychiatric Association (2001). Patients take painkillers and muscle relaxants before the treatment, and general anesthesia can be used during the procedure. Furthermore, the electrical currents are weaker, inducing seizures only in the brain. Patients in the United States typically get three treatments per week for up to a month (Glass, 2001; National Institute of Mental Health, 2016).

Scientists don't know exactly how ECT reduces the symptoms of depression, although a variety of theories have been proposed (Cyrzyk, 2013; Pirnia et al., 2016). And despite its enduring "bad rap," ECT can be an effective treatment for depression, bipolar disorder, and schizophrenia in people who haven't responded well to psychotherapy or drugs (Glass, 2001; Oremus et al., 2015). Yet in the United States, the number of patients admitted to a hospital for ECT treatment in 2009 was 7.2 per 100,000 adults, which represents a substantial decline from previous years (Case et al.,

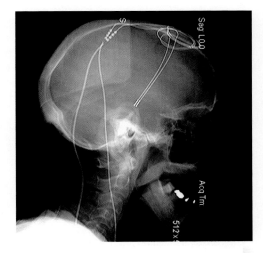

Stimulate the Brain
An X-ray image of a person undergoing deep brain stimulation reveals two electrodes—one implanted in each hemisphere. These electrodes send electrical impulses through certain neural networks, inducing changes that may lead to reduced symptoms. This treatment has produced promising results in patients with depression, but further research is needed to identify its long-term effects (Kennedy et al., 2011; Schlaepfer et al., 2013). Medical Body Scans/Science Source.

anti-anxiety drugs Psychotropic medications used for treating the symptoms of anxiety.

electroconvulsive therapy (ECT) A biomedical treatment for severe depression that induces seizures in the brain through electrical currents.

CONNECTIONS

In **Chapter 6,** we discussed amnesia, which is memory loss due to physical or psychological conditions. Retrograde amnesia is the inability to access old memories; anterograde amnesia is the inability to make new memories. ECT can cause these types of amnesia, which is one reason the American Psychiatric Association developed guidelines for its use.

CONNECTIONS

Chapter 2 describes the split-brain operation, a treatment for drug-resistant seizures. When the hemispheres are disconnected, researchers can study them separately to explore their unique capabilities. People who undergo this operation have fewer seizures, and can have normal cognitive abilities and no obvious changes in temperament or personality.

2013). The major downside of ECT is its tendency to induce confusion and memory loss, including anterograde and retrograde amnesia (American Psychiatric Association, 2001; Fink & Taylor, 2007; Read & Bentall, 2010).

NEUROSURGERY One extreme option for patients who don't show substantial improvement with psychotherapy or psychotropic drugs is **neurosurgery**, which destroys some portion of the brain or connections between different areas of the brain. Like ECT, neurosurgery is tarnished by an unethical past. During the 1930s, 1940s, and 1950s, doctors performed *prefrontal lobotomies,* destroying part of the frontal lobes or disconnecting them from lower areas of the brain (Kucharski, 1984; Wickens, 2015). But lobotomies may have severe side effects, including permanent impairments to everyday functioning. In the past, this procedure lacked precision, frequently resulting in personality changes and diminished function. The consequences of lobotomy were often worse than the disorders they aimed to fix. The popularity of this surgery plummeted in the 1950s when the first-generation antipsychotics were introduced, offering a safer alternative to psychosurgery (Mashour, Walker, & Martuza, 2005; Schlich, 2015, May).

Today, brain surgeries are a last-resort treatment for psychological disorders, and they are far more precise than the archaic lobotomy. Surgeons home in on a small target, destroying only tiny tracts of tissue. One of these surgeries has been a lifesaver for a select few suffering from a severe, drug-resistant form of obsessive-compulsive disorder (OCD), but the precise effects have yet to be determined (Castle, Bosanac, & Rossell, 2015; Mashour et al., 2005). People struggling with severe seizure disorders (as opposed to psychological disorders) sometimes undergo split-brain operations—the surgical separation of the right and left hemispheres. With the corpus callosum severed, the two hemispheres are disconnected, preventing the spread of electrical storms responsible for seizures. These more invasive biomedical therapies are seldom used, but they can make a difference in the quality of life for some individuals.

TAKING STOCK: AN APPRAISAL OF BIOMEDICAL THERAPY Medications and other biomedical treatments can reduce the symptoms of major psychological disorders. In fact, psychotropic drugs work so well that their introduction led to the deinstitutionalization of thousands of people. But it would be a mistake to think of these biological interventions as a cure-all, as this deemphasizes the importance of the other two components of the biopsychosocial model: psychological and social factors. Furthermore, research on the long-term outcomes of many of these treatments remains inconclusive.

 *In Class: Collaborate and Report*

In your group, **A)** identify the pros and cons of using psychotropic medication, **B)** discuss why people in the United States are so quick to use medications as the first line of treatment for psychological disorders, and **C)** consider how this approach to treating psychological disorders differs across cultures.

 show what you know

1. A young man is taking psychotropic medications for major depression, but the drugs do not seem to be alleviating his symptoms. Which of the following biomedical approaches might his psychiatrist try next?
   a. split-brain operation
   b. tardive dyskinesia
   c. prefrontal lobotomy
   d. electroconvulsive therapy

2. Psychotropic drugs can be divided into four categories, including mood-stabilizing, antipsychotic, anti-anxiety, and:
   a. mood normalizer.
   b. antidepressant.
   c. antagonist.
   d. atypical antipsychotic.

3. One treatment option sometimes used for patients who don't show substantial improvement with psychotherapy or psychotropic drugs is _____, which destroys some portion of the brain or connections between different areas of the brain.

4. How do biomedical interventions differ from psychotherapy? Compare their goals.

✓ CHECK YOUR ANSWERS IN APPENDIX C.

Psychotherapy: Who's in the Mix?

LO 9 Describe how culture interacts with the therapy process.

allindiaimages/Superstock.

WHEN TO LISTEN, WHEN TO TALK One of the challenges of providing therapy in a country like the United States, where ethnic minorities comprise over a third of the population (SAMHSA, 2016), is meeting the needs of clients from vastly different cultures. A therapist living in a diverse city like San Francisco or Houston may serve clients from multiple cultures in a single week, and each of those cultures has its own set of social norms dictating when to be quiet, when to speak, and how to express oneself.

For Dr. Foster, this part of the job is relatively straightforward. All of his clients are Northern Plains Indians, which means they follow similar social rules. And because Dr. Foster belongs to this culture, its norms are second nature to him. He has come to expect, for example, that a young Lakota client will not begin talking until he, the therapist, has spoken first. Dr. Foster is an elder, and elders are shown respect. Thus, to make a younger client feel more comfortable, he might begin a session by talking for 3 or 4 minutes. Once the client does open up, he limits his verbal and nonverbal feedback, sitting quietly and avoiding eye contact. In mainstream American culture, people continuously respond to each other with facial animation and filler words like "wow" and "uh-huh," but the Lakota find this ongoing feedback intrusive. "I might even shut my eyes so they're not feeling influenced by my responses," Dr. Foster says. "I'm not going to respond to what they're telling me, out of respect to their story."

Another facet of Lakota communication—one that often eludes therapists from outside the culture—is the tendency to pause for long periods in the middle of a conversation. If Dr. Foster poses the question, "How are you doing?" a client might take 20 to 30 seconds to respond. "They are not going to answer me on a superficial social level," he explains. "They're going to go inside"—meaning really take the time to consider the question and formulate an answer. These long pauses make some non-Indians very uncomfortable, according to Dr. Foster. "I've found that an outside provider will feel awkward, will start talking within 3 to 5 seconds," he adds. "The client will feel that they never have a chance to speak, and they'll leave frustrated because the person wouldn't be quiet [and] listen." ●

Culture-Conscious
A psychologist meets with two young Muslim women at the Centre for Needy Orphans and Poor Children in Thailand. Psychologists must always be mindful of cultural factors that may come into play during therapy. Thierry Falise/LightRocket via Getty Images.

You Asked, Dr. Foster Answers

http://qrs.ly/765a5g6

What are the risks if a psychologist fails to pay appropriate attention to both therapy methods and cultural tradition?

scan this →

ACROSS THE WORLD
Know Thy Client

Clearly, it is important for a therapist to know the cultural context in which he works. But does that mean therapists and clients should be matched according to ethnicity? Some clients prefer to discuss private thoughts and feelings

SHOULD THERAPISTS AND CLIENTS BE MATCHED ACCORDING TO ETHNICITY?

with a therapist who shares their experience—someone who knows firsthand how it feels to be, say, African American or Hispanic (Cabral & Smith, 2011). For clients with certain disorders (severe PTSD), treatment outcomes may be better when the therapist and client belong to the same ethnicity. However, it's important to remember that a common ethnic background does not always translate to shared experiences and perspectives. People of the same ethnicity may belong to different religions and socioeconomic groups, and their views on psychotherapy may conflict (Ruglass et al., 2014).

Synonyms

neurosurgery psychosurgery, brain surgery

neurosurgery A biomedical therapy that involves the destruction of some portion of the brain or connections between different areas of the brain.

Working with a therapist of the same background may be helpful in some instances, but it is not essential.

When the therapist and client do come from different worlds, it is the therapist's job to get in touch with the client's unique perspective. That includes being respectful of cultural norms. Western therapists working in Sri Lanka, for example, should be aware that mental illness is highly stigmatized in this cultural setting, and that intense emotional displays (crying in group therapy, for example) are taboo (Christopher, Wendt, Marecek, & Goodman, 2014). Therapists must also be cognizant of their own cultural biases and sensitive to the many forms of prejudice and discrimination people experience.

Within any group, there is vast variation from one individual to the next, but cultural themes do emerge. The Sioux and Blackfeet Indians, for example, are very relationship-oriented. "What kind of car you drive or how nice your home is, and so forth, is not even important," Dr. Foster says. "Relationships matter." Some therapists working with American Indian groups report that entire families may show up at sessions to express support for the client (Prochaska & Norcross, 2014). Similarly, Latino and Polynesian cultures place a high value on family, often prioritizing relationships with relatives over individual needs (Allen & Smith, 2015; Greenfield & Quiroz, 2013). These groups are generally more collectivist, or community-minded, whereas European American cultures tend to place a high premium on individualism (Greenfield & Quiroz, 2013).

Immigrant populations face their own set of challenges. Men often have a difficult time adjusting to the declining social status and income that comes with moving to a new country. Women tend to fare better, adapting to the new culture and finding jobs more quickly, which can lead to tension between spouses (Prochaska & Norcross, 2014). Keep in mind that these are only general trends; assuming they apply to an entire population promotes stereotyping.

This brings us to one of the key themes of the chapter: When it comes to psychological treatment, there is no "one-size-fits-all." Every client has a unique story and a singular set of psychological needs. Responding to the needs of the person—her culture, religious beliefs, and unique personal qualities—is essential for successful therapy (Lakes, Lopez, & Garro, 2006; Norcross & Wampold, 2011). 🌐

Let's Get Through This Together

For some people, group therapy is a better fit than individual therapy. First developed in the 1940s, group therapy has adapted to the ever-changing demands of clinical work (Yalom & Leszcz, 2005). Usually, group therapy is led by one or two therapists trained in any of the various approaches (for example, psychoanalytic or cognitive). Sessions can include as few as 3 clients, or upwards of 10, and members share their problems as openly as possible. There are groups to help people cope with shyness, panic disorder, chronic pain, compulsive gambling, divorce, grief, and sexual identity issues, just to name a few. These group settings often provide clients with the valuable realization that they are not alone in their struggles to improve. It is not always a psychological disorder that brings people to group therapy, but instead a desire to work on a specific issue.

LO 10 Identify the benefits and challenges of group therapy.

GROUP THERAPY Research typically shows that group therapy is as effective as individual therapy for addressing many problems. In fact, it is the preferred approach for interpersonal issues, because it allows therapists to observe clients interacting with others. The therapist's skills play an important role in the success of group sessions, and the dynamics between clients and therapists may be similar to those that arise in individual therapy. (Clients may demonstrate resistance or transference, for example.)

SELF-HELP GROUPS* Another type of group that offers opportunities for personal growth is the *self-help group*. Among the most commonly known are Alcoholics Anonymous (AA), Al-Anon, Parents without Partners, and Weight Watchers. Members of self-help groups support each other while facing bereavement, divorce, infertility, HIV/AIDS, cancer, and other issues. Some evidence suggests that self-help groups can even benefit people who struggle with psychosis (Scott, Webb, & Rowse, 2015).

Finding Strength in Others
Self-help groups provide valuable support for people facing similar struggles, but they usually are not led by mental health professionals. Steve Debenport/Getty Images.

With over 2 million active members, AA is the most widely used self-help group in the world (Alcoholics Anonymous, 2016a). Group meetings are open to anyone who wants help overcoming an alcohol problem. AA does not provide counseling, but one-on-one support called "sponsorship" (Alcoholics Anonymous, 2016b). Known as a "twelve-step group," AA bases its model on 12 steps the members must follow to take control of their drinking problems. Groups like Al-Anon and Alateen are based on the 12 steps of AA, but provide support for friends and family of people with alcohol problems. Other 12-step programs include Debtors Anonymous, Narcotics Anonymous, Overeaters Anonymous, and Sex Addicts Anonymous. These groups strive to ensure a high level of confidentiality for all participants.

Self-help groups are *not* typically run by a psychiatrist, licensed psychologist, or other mental health professional, but by a mental health advisor or *paraprofessional* trained to run the groups. The typical AA leader, for example, is a "recovering alcoholic" who grasps the complexities of alcoholism and recovery, but is not necessarily a mental health professional. How effective are 12-step programs like AA? The answer to that question is still under investigation (Glaser, 2015, April). One large review concluded that "no experimental studies unequivocally demonstrated the effectiveness of AA or [12-step] approaches for reducing alcohol dependence or problems" (Ferri, Amato, & Davoli, 2006, p. 2). Even so, many people claim that AA has helped them turn their life around (Alcoholics Anonymous Australia, 2016; Alcoholics Anonymous Great Britain, 2016; David, 2015, August 13).

FAMILY THERAPY Introduced in North America in the 1940s, **family therapy** focuses on the family as an *integrated system,* recognizing how the interactions within can create instability or lead to collapse of the family unit (Corey, 2017). Family therapy explores relationship problems rather than the symptoms of particular disorders, teaching communication skills in the process. The family is viewed as a dynamic, holistic entity, and the goal is to understand each person's role in the system, not to root out troublemakers, assign blame, or identify one member who must be "fixed." Because families typically seek the resolution of a specific problem, the course of therapy tends to be brief (Corey, 2017). Suppose a teenage girl has become withdrawn at home and is acting out in school, and the whole family decides to participate in therapy. The therapist begins by helping the parents identify ways they encourage her behaviors (not following through with consequences, for example), and may examine how their marital dynamics affect their children. If it becomes evident that the marriage is in trouble, the parents might seek therapy without the rest of the family, which brings us to the next topic: couples therapy.

Synonyms

self-help groups mutual help groups, support groups

family therapy family counseling

family therapy A type of therapy that focuses on the family as an integrated system, recognizing that the interactions within it can create instability or lead to the breakdown of the family unit.

* You can learn more about self-help groups in your area from the National Mental Health Consumers' Self-Help Clearinghouse, at www.mhselfhelp.org.

TABLE 14.5 BENEFITS AND DRAWBACKS OF GROUP THERAPY

Strengths of Group Therapy	Weaknesses of Group Therapy
Sessions generally cost about half as much as individual therapy (Helliker, 2009, March 24).	Not everyone feels at ease discussing personal troubles in a room full of people.
People find relief and comfort knowing that others face similar struggles.	Group members may not always get along. This friction can inhibit the therapeutic process.
Group members offer support and encouragement. They also challenge one another to think and behave in new ways.	Groups may include members who show resistance to group therapy, resulting in poor attendance, tardiness, or dropouts (Yalom & Leszcz, 2005).
Seeing others improve offers hope and inspiration.	Some group therapy participants have had negative family experiences, and thus maintain negative expectations of the group setting (Yalom & Leszcz, 2005).

Listed above are some of the pros and cons of group therapy.

CONNECTIONS

In **Chapter 10,** sex therapist Dr. Stephanie Buehler reports that low desire is the number one sexual problem reported by her clients. We also note gender differences regarding how much men and women think about sex, as well as how often they masturbate. This information can be used to help couples in treatment.

COUPLES THERAPY Let's face it, most couples have issues. High on the list are conflicts about money ("You are so stingy!"), failures to communicate ("You never listen!"), languishing physical bonds ("Sorry, I'm not in the mood tonight"), along with disputes about children and jealousy (Jackson et al., 2016; Storaasli & Markman, 1990). But when these problems begin to cause significant distress, *couples therapy* is a smart choice. Couples therapists are trained in many of the therapeutic approaches described earlier, and they tend to focus on conflict management and communication. One goal of couples therapy and relationship education programs is to provide guidance on how to communicate within relationships (Doherty, Harris, & Wilde, 2015; Scott, Rhoades, Stanley, Allen, & Markman, 2013).

Couples therapy can yield positive results for many couples—they stay together, and feel more satisfied with the relationship—but some seem to benefit more than others. This is especially true for those who are committed to saving their relationships (Baucom, Atkins, Rowe, Doss, & Christensen, 2015; Greenberg, Warwar, & Malcolm, 2010). Partners attending couples therapy with "mixed-agendas" (one partner wants to preserve the relationship and the other wants a divorce) can still benefit from couples therapy by addressing issues such as responsibility, differentiation, and next steps (Doherty et al., 2015). Relationship education programs before marriage are also beneficial because they may help couples identify some of the situations that could lead to divorce, including infidelity, aggression, and substance abuse.

TAKING STOCK: AN APPRAISAL OF GROUP, FAMILY, AND COUPLES THERAPY Like any treatment, group therapy has its strengths and limitations (TABLE 14.5). Group members may not get along, or they may feel uncomfortable discussing sensitive issues. But conflict and discomfort are not necessarily bad when it comes to therapy (group or otherwise), because such feelings often motivate people to reevaluate how they interact with others, and perhaps try new approaches.

Evaluating group therapies can be difficult because there is so much variation in approaches (psychodynamic, cognitive behavioral, and so on). However, there is strong evidence that couples therapy is effective for treating a wide range of problems, particularly when couples exhibit "higher levels of commitment" and have been "married for a longer period of time" (Baucom et al., 2015, p. 108; Shadish & Baldwin, 2003). The outcomes of group therapy rival those of individual therapy for many types of clients and problems (Barrera, Mott, Hofstein, & Teng, 2013;

Synonyms

couples therapy marital therapy

Burlingame & Baldwin, 2011; Yalom & Leszcz, 2005). As with individual therapies, the role of the therapist is of critical importance: Empathy, good facilitation skills, listening, and careful observation are important predictors of successful outcomes. So, too, are the preparation of the group members, the therapist's verbal style, and the "climate" and cohesion of the group (Burlingame & Baldwin, 2011).

 **In Class: Collaborate and Report**

Team up and **A)** discuss the advantages and disadvantages of group therapy. **B)** Looking back at Chapter 13, identify which psychological disorders would be best addressed through group therapy, and explain your reasoning. **C)** Identify disorders that would be best addressed in private sessions, again explaining your reasoning.

 show what you know

1. A single man has had trouble dealing with his co-workers and has not been on a second date in over a year because of his poor interpersonal skills. His therapist decides the best course of treatment is _____, which is led by one or two mental health professionals, involves three or more clients, and allows the therapists to observe the client interacting with others.

2. _____ bring(s) together people with common disorders, addictions, or other problems. Sessions typically are not run

by psychiatrists, psychologists, or other mental health professionals.
   a. Self-help groups   c. Couples therapy
   b. Family therapy   d. Group therapies

3. Under what conditions might group therapy fail or be inappropriate?

✓ CHECK YOUR ANSWERS IN APPENDIX C.

Psychotherapy Today

Now that you have learned about the various approaches to therapy, you may be wondering how it applies to your life. What if you or someone you care about needs psychological help—is psychotherapy effective? Do you need to consult a professional, or can you get the same results from self-help books and online resources?

Does Psychotherapy Work?

LO 11   Evaluate the effectiveness of psychotherapy.

So far, we have familiarized ourselves with the strengths and weaknesses of various therapeutic approaches, but now let's direct our attention to overall outcomes. How effective is psychotherapy in general? This question is not easily answered, partly because therapeutic "success" is so difficult to quantify. What constitutes success in one context may not be the same in another. And for therapists trying to measure the efficacy of methods they use, eliminating bias can be very challenging.

That being said, decades worth of research has established that psychotherapy is effective (Campbell, Norcross, Vasquez, & Kaslow, 2013). For many disorders, the benefits derived from psychotherapy may actually surpass those provided by medication (Decker, 2016a). In one large study investigating the effects of psychotherapy, all therapeutic approaches performed equally well across all disorders. But there is one caveat: Individuals who were limited by their insurance companies in terms of therapist choice and duration of treatment did not see the same improvement as those who were less restricted by insurance (Seligman, 1995). Perhaps this is not surprising, since people who start therapy but then quit prematurely tend to experience less successful outcomes (Swift & Greenberg, 2012).

How much therapy is enough? The answer to this question depends on the specific needs of the client and the ability of the therapist to help reduce "symptom distress" and improve "life functioning" (Owen, Adelson, Budge, Kopta, & Reese, 2016). Around 50% of clients show "clinically significant improvement" after 21 psychotherapy sessions, whereas some 75% show the same degree of improvement after twice that many sessions (Lambert, Hansen, & Finch, 2001). Given the many types of therapeutic approaches, the unique qualities of each client, and the variety of therapists, identifying the best type of therapy can be challenging (Pope & Wedding, 2014). But we can say this with relative confidence: Psychotherapy is "cost-effective, reduces disability, morbidity, and mortality, improves work functioning, decreases uses of psychiatric hospitalization, and . . . leads to reduction in unnecessary use of medical and surgical services" (American Psychological Association [APA], 2012c, para. 19).

I Think I Need Help: What Should I Do?

If you suspect you or someone you care about is suffering from a psychological disorder or needs support coping with a divorce, death, or major life change, do not hesitate to seek professional help. The first step is figuring out what kind of therapy best fits the person and the situation (individual, family, group, and so on). Then there is the issue of cost: Therapy can be expensive. These days, one 60-minute therapy session can cost anywhere from $80 to $250 (or more). If you attend a college or university, however, your student fees may cover services at a student counseling center.

Many people have health insurance that helps pay for medication and psychotherapy. In 2010 the Mental Health Parity and Addiction Equity Act (MHPAEA) took effect, requiring all group health insurance plans (with 50 employees or more) to provide mental health treatment benefits as part of their plan—with benefits equal to those provided for medical treatment. Essentially, this means that mental health problems merit the same treatment benefits as physical health problems. Co-payments must be the same, limits on treatment must be the same, and so on. If your insurance plan does not restrict the number of times you can see your family physician, it also cannot limit the number of visits you have with a psychologist (American Psychological Association, 2014, May). For those without insurance, community-based mental health centers provide quality care to all in need, often with a sliding scale for fees.

The next step is finding the right therapist, that is, the right *qualified* therapist. Helping others manage their mental health issues is a tremendous responsibility that only licensed professionals should take on. But who exactly meets the criteria for a "qualified professional"? It depends on where you live. Different states have different licensing requirements, so we encourage you to verify the standing of a therapist's license with your state's Department of Regulatory Agencies. The pool of potential therapists might include clinical psychologists with PhDs or PsyDs, counseling psychologists, psychiatrists, psychiatric nurses, social workers, marriage and family therapists, pastoral counselors, people with EdDs (doctorates in education), and more. (See Appendix B for more information about education and careers in psychology.) If you don't seek psychological help from a trained and certified professional in person, you should be very cautious about seeking assistance online.

Nonstandard Treatment: Self-Help and E-Therapy

Type "psychology" or "self-help" into the search engine of Amazon.com, and you will come across thousands of books promising to eliminate your stress, boost your self-esteem, and help you beat depression. Although some self-help books contain valuable information, others are packed with claims that have little or no scientific basis. Keep an open mind, but approach these resources with skepticism, especially when it comes to the research their authors cite. As you have learned, determining the effect of therapy is a difficult business, even when studies are impeccably designed. Reader beware.

LO 12 Summarize the strengths and weaknesses of online psychotherapy.

With more people gaining access to the Internet and more therapists trying to specialize and make themselves marketable, online therapies are multiplying. A relative newcomer to the treatment world, **e-therapy** can mean anything from e-mail communication between client and therapist to real-time sessions via webcam. Some approaches include a hybrid version of online and face-to-face sessions, whereas others offer virtual support through chat rooms. These digital tools are valuable for serving rural areas and providing services to those who would otherwise have no access. Video-conferencing is a useful supplement to regular therapy, particularly for consultation and supervision. But online psychotherapy and telehealth raise many concerns about licensing and privacy, and difficulties with "nonverbal communication" and the development of therapeutic relationships (Barak, Hen, Boniel-Nissim, & Shapira, 2008; de Bitencourt Machada et al., 2016; Maheu, Pulier, McMenamin, & Posen, 2012; Sucala et al., 2012).

While we are on the topic of the Internet, we cannot resist a tie-in to social media. What role do Facebook, LinkedIn, and other types of social media play in the lives of therapists and their clients?

SOCIAL MEDIA AND PSYCHOLOGY
Therapist or Friend?

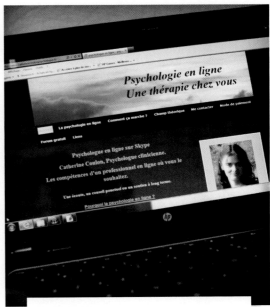

Imagine that you are the psychotherapist serving a small community college. You talk to students about their deepest fears and conflicts. They tell you about their mothers, fathers, lovers, and enemies. In some respects, you know these students better than their closest friends do. But your clients are not your buddies. They are your clients. So what do you say when a client asks you to become a friend on Facebook, a contact on LinkedIn, or a follower on Instagram?

DOES FACEBOOK HAVE A PLACE IN THERAPY?

Our answer to that question is a definitive no. Psychotherapy is a private affair, social media is very public, and "when psychologists interact in both spheres, they do risk violating clients' confidentiality or crossing boundaries" (Lannin & Scott, 2014, February, p. 56). However, that does not mean social media has no place in the mental health field. Like other health professionals, psychologists use social media to connect with colleagues, distribute credible information, and market their services (Gagnon & Sabus, 2015; Moorhead et al., 2013). These platforms may even come in handy during therapy; imagine a client with public speaking anxiety who shows his therapist a video of himself giving a speech (Kolmes, 2012).

But psychologists who use social media must be adept at distinguishing between acceptable and unacceptable online activity. Discussing the details of a clinical case is risky, if not reckless. Imagine a therapist posting this message for colleagues on social media: "Need referral for a 30-year-old bisexual male living in Greenwich Village, New York, who has substance abuse issues with cocaine and alcohol and is engaging in unsafe sexual practices" (Kolmes, 2012, p. 3). Even if no names are mentioned, this type of communication threatens confidentiality, which can harm the client, create legal problems for the therapist, and damage the reputation of the profession (Lannin & Scott, 2014).

As you can see, the emergence of social media presents new opportunities and risks for mental health professionals. Therapists who use social media would be wise to create two separate profiles (one personal, and the other professional) and establish a formal policy outlining the parameters of their social media use that would be shared with clients (Lannin & Scott, 2014). As technology and online culture evolve, therapists should periodically reevaluate their relationship with social media. It's an exciting area of research, so stay tuned for future developments.... 💬

Online Therapy

A clinical psychologist conducts an online consultation with a client. With digital communication technologies such as Skype and Google Hangouts, therapists can conduct sessions with clients on the opposite side of the globe. But problems may arise when therapy occurs online; for example, certain types of "non-verbal communication" may be difficult to detect (de Bitencourt Machada et al., 2016). HAMILTON/REA/Redux.

e-therapy A category of treatment that utilizes the Internet to provide support and therapy.

In Class: Collaborate and Report

Team up and decide which of the approaches presented in this chapter would most likely be successful in online therapy. Which approaches should never be used online? Explain your reasoning.

PASSIONATE PROVIDERS Before wrapping up, we thought you might like to know what Dr. Dan Foster and Laura Lichti are doing these days. Dr. Foster is as busy as ever, working with one other psychologist and a mental health technician to provide mental health services to Rosebud's 13,000 residents. In addition to working up to 70 hours per week, he and his wife Becky (also a doctorate-level psychologist) have seven adopted children, five of whom are affected by fetal alcohol spectrum disorders (FASDs). Dr. Foster doesn't get more than 5 or 6 hours of sleep at night, but he seems to have a limitless supply of energy and optimism.

It's been a time of growth for Laura, who is now working as a behavior therapist for people with intellectual and developmental disabilities. She also opened her own private practice, which focuses on grief counseling for people of all ages, and began teaching psychology at a community college. "I love the variety," Laura says. "It keeps me very busy!" ●

Dr. Dan Foster with his wife, Dr. Becky Foster. Macmillan Learning.

Laura Lichti. Laura Lichti/Lee Bernhard.

 show what you know

1. E-therapy is a relatively new approach to helping people with psychological problems or disorders. It varies in terms of how much and what type of contact the "client" has with a "therapist." Concerns regarding online psychotherapy include _____.

2. If you were trying to convince a friend that treatment for psychological disorders works for many people, how would you summarize the effectiveness of psychotherapy?

3. Studies investigating the effects of psychotherapy indicate that, in general, psychotherapy is effective. But which of the following factors has been linked to less successful outcomes?
   a. type of therapeutic approach
   b. client's disorder
   c. limits placed by insurance company
   d. Mental Health Parity and Addiction Equity Act

✓ CHECK YOUR ANSWERS IN APPENDIX C.

Improve your grade! Use 📖 **LearningCurve** macmillan learning adaptive quizzing to create your personalized study plan, which will direct you to the resources that will help you most in 📖 **LaunchPad** macmillan learning

summary of concepts

14

LO 1 Outline the history of the treatment of psychological disorders. (p. 579)

Early "treatments" for psychological disorders were often inhumane. According to one theory, Stone Age people believed psychological disorders were caused by possession with demons and evil spirits; they may have used trephination (drilling holes through the skull) to let them escape. In the late 1700s, Philippe Pinel advanced the notion that people in mental institutions should be treated with kindness and respect; the idea of using "moral treatment" eventually spread throughout Europe and America. In the mid- to late 1800s, Dorothea Dix supported the "mental hygiene movement," a campaign to reform asylums in America. She helped establish and upgrade many state mental hospitals. The mid-1900s witnessed deinstitutionalization, a mass movement of patients with psychological disorders out of America's mental institutions and into the community.

LO 2 Explain how the main approaches to therapy differ and identify their common goal. (p. 582)

Insight therapies include psychoanalysis, psychodynamic therapy, and humanistic therapy, which aim to increase awareness of self and the environment. Behavior therapies focus on behavioral change. Biomedical therapy targets the biological basis of disorders, often using medications. All these approaches share a common goal: They aim to reduce symptoms and increase quality of life, whether the person suffers from a debilitating psychological disorder or simply wants to lead a happier existence.

LO 3 Describe how psychoanalysis differs from psychodynamic therapy. (p. 585)

Psychoanalysis, the first formal system of psychotherapy, attempts to uncover unconscious conflicts, making it possible to address and work through them. Psychodynamic therapy is an updated form of psychoanalysis that incorporates many of Freud's core themes, including the notion that personality characteristics and behavior problems often can be traced to unconscious conflicts. With psychodynamic therapy, therapists see clients once a week for several months rather than many times a week for years. And instead of sitting quietly off to the side, therapists sit facing clients and engage in a two-way dialogue.

LO 4 Outline the principles and characteristics of humanistic therapy. (p. 587)

Humanistic therapy concentrates on the positive aspects of human nature: our powerful desires to form close relationships, treat others with warmth and empathy, and grow as individuals. Instead of digging up unconscious thoughts and feelings, humanistic therapy emphasizes conscious experience and problems in the present.

LO 5 Describe person-centered therapy. (p. 588)

Person-centered therapy focuses on achieving one's full potential, creating a warm and accepting client–therapist relationship using a nondirective approach. Sitting face-to-face with the client, the therapist's main job is to "be there" for the client through empathy, unconditional positive regard, genuineness, and active listening, all important components of building a therapeutic alliance. The main goal of treatment is to reduce the incongruence between the ideal self and the real self.

LO 6 Outline the principles and characteristics of behavior therapy. (p. 590)

Using the learning principles of classical conditioning, operant conditioning, and observational learning, behavior therapy aims to replace maladaptive behaviors with more adaptive behaviors. It incorporates a variety of techniques, including exposure therapy, aversion therapy, systematic desensitization, and behavior modification. Behavior therapy covers a broad range of treatment approaches, and focuses on observable behaviors in the present.

LO 7 Outline the principles and characteristics of cognitive therapy. (p. 596)

The goal of cognitive therapy is to identify maladaptive thinking and help individuals change the way they view the world and relationships. Aaron Beck believed patterns of automatic thoughts and cognitive distortions, such as overgeneralization (thinking that self-contained events will have major repercussions in life), lie at the root of psychological disturbances. The aim of cognitive therapy is to help clients recognize and challenge cognitive distortions and illogical thought in short-term, action-oriented, and homework-intensive therapy sessions. Albert Ellis created rational-emotive behavior therapy (REBT), another form of cognitive therapy, to help people identify and correct irrational or illogical ways of thinking.

LO 8 Summarize the biomedical interventions and identify their common goal. (p. 598)

Psychopharmacology is the scientific study of how psychotropic medications alter perception, mood, behavior, and other aspects of psychological functioning. Psychotropic drugs include antidepressant, mood-stabilizing, antipsychotic, and anti-anxiety medications. When severe symptoms do not improve with medication and psychotherapy, other biomedical options are available: electroconvulsive therapy (ECT), which causes seizures in the brain, for cases of severe depression; and neurosurgery, which destroys some portion of the brain or connections between different areas of the brain, only as a last resort. Biomedical interventions target the biological roots of psychological disorders.

LO 9 Describe how culture interacts with the therapy process. (p. 607)

Therapists work with clients from a vast array of cultures. Every client has a unique story and a singular set of psychological needs, but therapists should know the cultural context in which they work and be mindful of the client's unique experience. This includes being respectful of cultural norms and sensitive to the many forms of prejudice and discrimination that people can experience.

LO 10 Identify the benefits and challenges of group therapy. (p. 608)

The benefits of group therapy include cost-effectiveness, identification with others, accountability, support, encouragement, and a sense of hope. Challenges include potential conflict among group members and discomfort expressing feelings in the presence of others.

LO 11 Evaluate the effectiveness of psychotherapy. (p. 611)

In general, psychotherapy "works," especially if it is long-term. All approaches perform equally well across all disorders. But clients with insurance plans that limit their choice of therapists and the duration of therapy do not see the same improvement as those with less restrictive insurance. In addition, people who start therapy but then quit prematurely experience less successful outcomes. The Mental Health Parity and Addiction Equity Act of 2010 requires group health insurance plans to provide mental health treatment benefits equal to those provided for medical treatment.

LO 12 Summarize the strengths and weaknesses of online psychotherapy. (p. 613)

As more people gain access to the Internet and as more therapists try to specialize and make themselves marketable, online therapies have multiplied. E-therapy can mean anything from an e-mail communication between client and therapist to real-time sessions via webcam. These digital tools are valuable for serving rural areas and providing services to those who would otherwise have no access. Videoconferencing is useful for consultation and supervision. However, online psychotherapy raises many concerns about licensing, privacy, communication with nonverbal cues, and the development of therapeutic relationships.

key terms

active listening, p. 589
anti-anxiety drugs, p. 604
antidepressant drugs, p. 599
antipsychotic drugs, p. 603
aversion therapy, p. 593
behavior modification, p. 594
behavior therapies, p. 582
biomedical therapy, p. 582
cognitive therapy, p. 596
cognitive behavioral therapy (CBT), p. 598

deinstitutionalization, p. 580
eclectic approach to therapy, p. 582
electroconvulsive therapy (ECT), p. 605
empathy, p. 589
e-therapy, p. 613
evidence-based practice, p. 582
exposure, p. 590
family therapy, p. 609
free association, p. 586

genuineness, p. 589
humanistic therapy, p. 588
insight therapies, p. 582
interpretation, p. 586
mood-stabilizing drugs, p. 603
neurosurgery, p. 606
nondirective, p. 589
overgeneralization, p. 596
person-centered therapy, p. 588

psychodynamic therapy, p. 587
psychotherapy, p. 582
rational emotive behavior therapy (REBT), p. 597
resistance, p. 586
systematic desensitization, p. 593
therapeutic alliance, p. 589
token economy, p. 594
transference, p. 586

test prep *are you ready?*

1. Philippe Pinel was horrified by what he observed in the asylums of Paris. He worked to improve the living conditions of people with psychological disorders, removing inmates' chains and showing them respect and care. This _____ eventually spread throughout Europe and America.
   a. trephination
   b. moral treatment
   c. psychoanalysis
   d. deinstitutionalization

2. The American Psychological Association highlights the importance of clinical expertise and knowledge of a patient's culture, values, and preferences; in other words, using _____ when making decisions about which treatment is best for a client.
   a. biomedical therapy
   b. behavior therapy
   c. evidence-based practice
   d. moral treatment

3. Free association and interpretation are used by _____ in their treatment of patients.
   a. psychoanalysts
   b. humanists
   c. behaviorists
   d. cognitive therapists

4. Which of the following is a weakness of Freud's theory?
   a. It is evidence-based.
   b. It is difficult to test through experimentation.
   c. It is client-directed.
   d. It focuses on the present.

5. A friend told you about his therapist, who is nondirective, uses active listening, and shows empathy and unconditional positive regard. It sounds as if your friend's therapist is conducting:
   a. cognitive therapy.
   b. behavior therapy.
   c. psychoanalysis.
   d. person-centered therapy.

6. Systematic desensitization uses _____ that represent(s) a gradual increase in a client's anxiety.
   a. hierarchies
   b. token economies
   c. behavior modification
   d. free association

7. Which of the following statements would not be among Beck's collection of cognitive errors?
   a. My friend stole from me; therefore, everyone will steal from me.
   b. Getting fired once does not mean my career is over.
   c. I forgot to vote; that's why the president lost.
   d. My hairdresser added $20 to my Visa charge. You can't trust salons.

8. The key advantage of behavior therapy is that it:
   a. tends to work quickly.
   b. focuses on changing innate behaviors.
   c. addresses global issues arising from personality disorders.
   d. brings about changes on the inside.

9. Which of the following claims about group therapy is true?
   a. It generally costs twice as much as one-on-one therapy.
   b. Everyone feels comfortable sharing their troubles with a group.
   c. Group members avoid pushing others to own up to their mistakes.
   d. Seeing others improve offers hope and inspiration.

10. Family therapy focuses on all of the following except:
    a. communication skills.
    b. the family as a holistic entity.
    c. resolution of specific problems.
    d. symptoms of particular disorders.

11. Humanistic therapy emphasizes the positive nature of humans, with a focus on:
    a. the unconscious.
    b. rational emotive behavior.
    c. past problems.
    d. the present.

12. _____ is the scientific study of how medication alters perceptions, moods, behaviors, and other aspects of psychological functioning.
    a. Biomedical therapy
    b. Psychoeducation
    c. Therapeutic alliance
    d. Psychopharmacology

13. Overall, psychotherapy is cost-effective and helps to decrease disability, hospitalization, and problems at work. Which of the following factors seems to reduce its effectiveness?
    a. unlimited number of sessions
    b. limitations on choice of therapist as mandated by a health insurance policy
    c. number of people in a therapy session
    d. gender of therapist

14. Electroconvulsive therapy (ECT) is a technique that essentially causes _____ in the brain.
    a. increased activity of neurotransmitters
    b. tardive dyskinesia
    c. seizures
    d. MAO inhibitors

15. One factor a therapist needs to consider is how _____ may interact with the therapy process: for example, whether a client is from a group that is collectivist or one that values individualism.
    a. culture
    b. biomedical interventions
    c. repression
    d. unconscious conflicts

16. Compare cognitive behavioral therapy to insight therapies.

17. Beck identified a collection of common cognitive distortions. Describe two of these distortions and give examples of each.

18. How would a behavior therapist help someone overcome a fear of spiders?

19. How does culture influence and interact with the therapeutic process?

20. Describe several strengths and weaknesses of online psychotherapy.

✔ CHECK YOUR ANSWERS IN APPENDIX C.

YOUR SCIENTIFIC WORLD
Apply psychology to the real world!
Go to LaunchPad for access.

Joseph Maggio.

RIZWAN TABASSUM/AFP/Getty Images.

SAMSON OPUS.

CHAPTER OUTLINE AND LEARNING OBJECTIVES

An Introduction to Social Psychology

LO 1 Define social psychology and identify how it is different from sociology.

Social Cognition

LO 2 Describe social cognition and how we use attributions to explain behavior.

LO 3 Outline how attributions lead to mistakes in our explanations for behaviors.

Social Influence

LO 4 Explain the meaning of social influence and recognize factors associated with persuasion.

LO 5 Define compliance and explain some of the techniques used to gain it.

LO 6 Identify the factors that influence the likelihood of someone conforming.

LO 7 Describe obedience and explain how Stanley Milgram studied it.

Groups and Relationships

LO 8 Recognize the circumstances that influence the occurrence of the bystander effect.

Aggression

LO 9 Demonstrate an understanding of aggression and identify some of its causes.

LO 10 Recognize how group affiliation influences the development of stereotypes.

LO 11 Describe prosocial behavior and altruism.

Attraction and Love

LO 12 Identify the three major factors contributing to interpersonal attraction.

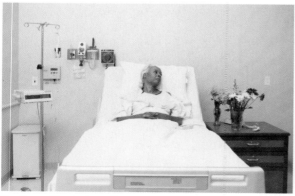

Blend Images–ERproductions Ltd/Getty Images.

Image of Sport/Newscom/Image of Sport Photos/Stanford California United States.

Courtesy Dr. Julie Gralow.

15 social psychology

An Introduction to Social Psychology

LOVE STORY Prior to 2006, Joe Maggio did not have a fulfilling love life. While serving overseas in the military, he had a relationship with a local woman that didn't work out. But something beautiful came out of their failed union: a baby girl named Kristina. Joe was awarded full custody, and he returned to Long Island, New York, to begin his life as a single dad. In between work and taking care of his daughter, there was little time for dating. Joe was not the type to frequent bars and nightclubs, and his work as an ice cream truck driver provided few opportunities for meeting other singles. It never seemed to work out with the girlfriends he did manage to date. As Joe admits, "I had my share of doozies [extraordinarily bad experiences]."

Loving Dad
Before joining Match.com, Joe Maggio was a single father to daughter Kristina. Dating was a challenge, as most of the women Joe met lacked the qualities he desired. Then, with a few clicks and keystrokes, along came Susanne. . . .
Joseph Maggio.

Everything abruptly changed when Susanne entered the picture. Their first face-to-face meeting was at a Chili's restaurant. Joe and Kristina, then 7 years old, were chatting at a table when Susanne appeared. "The minute she walked in the door on our first date, I honestly felt like I was actually waiting for my wife to have dinner with me and my daughter," Joe says. He remembers exactly how she looked: straight hair, a pink blouse with a butterfly necklace, a black vest, and a pair of blue jeans. As Joe puts it, "Very, very cute."

Instantly at ease, Susanne sat down and began to talk with Joe and Kristina. "It was just kind of relaxed . . . like we had known each other forever," says Susanne, who at 32 was finished playing games and exploring dead-end relationships. "At this point in my life I was really just looking for somebody that wanted to settle down," she offers. Joe seemed so kind, it was hard to believe he was authentic.

The next morning, Joe called Susanne and invited her for a cup of coffee. "We did not leave the local Starbucks until almost seven, eight hours later," he recalls. During that marathon date, Joe and Susanne shared stories about their families and talked about their hopes and dreams. "I didn't want the day to end," says Joe, who then invited Susanne home and made her a dinner of sautéed pork chops, roasted peppers, and potatoes. "I think I kind of won her heart that night."

Joe and Susanne's initial impressions of one another were right on. They were extremely compatible people with similar backgrounds and family values. Both were big fans of cooking, baseball (the Mets), and spending Friday night curled up on the couch watching a movie. Susanne found it attractive that Joe was a single father. And Joe came to love how Susanne treated Kristina like her own daughter, and how Kristina loved her back. You might say Joe and Susanne were perfectly matched. How did they find one another? ●

What Is Social Psychology?

Joe and Susanne did not meet at a church, a library, or a bar. They did not work in the same office, nor were they introduced by mutual friends. Like a growing number of couples, Joe and Susanne first encountered one another online. They met through Match.com, the popular dating website.

Since the early 2000s, online dating sites have become increasingly popular (**FIGURE 15.1**). Research suggests that the Internet is the second most common way to connect with a potential partner, the first being an introduction by mutual friends (Finkel, Eastwick, Karney, Reis, & Sprecher, 2012). Joe and Susanne met through one of the mainstream dating services, but there are also highly specialized sites and mobile apps to accommodate particular interests. Looking for a vegetarian mate? Try VeggieDate.org. Searching for a farmer to love? Visit FarmersOnly.com. There are even digital services designed to match people with the same book preferences and food allergies.

Online dating has forever changed the singles' landscape. What other medium allows you to scan and research a database of thousands, if not millions, of potential partners from the comfort of your sofa, or filter potential mates with the ease of a finger swipe? Digital dating has also created a new laboratory for psychologists to study the way people's thoughts, emotions, and behaviors are influenced by others. Put differently, it is an emerging topic of research in many areas of psychology, especially *social psychology*.

LO 1 **Define social psychology and identify how it is different from sociology.**

In every chapter of this book, we have touched on issues relevant to **social psychology,** the study of human cognition, emotion, and behavior in relation to others. In Chapter 3, we journeyed into the world of Zoe, Emma, and Sophie, identical triplets who are deaf and blind. How might the triplets' social behaviors differ from those of children with normal hearing and vision? Then there was Clive Wearing from Chapter 6. How do you suppose Clive's devastating memory loss affects his relationships? Social psychologists strive to answer these types of questions.

Throughout this text, we have emphasized the importance of the biopsycho*social* perspective, which recognizes the biological, psychological, and social factors underlying human behavior. This chapter focuses on the third aspect of that triad: social forces.

WHAT'S THE DIFFERENCE? SOCIAL PSYCHOLOGY VERSUS SOCIOLOGY
Students often ask how social psychology differs from the field of *sociology*. The

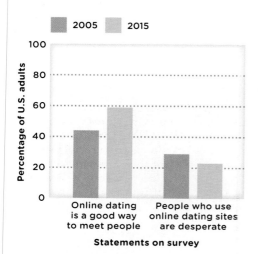

FIGURE 15.1

Online Dating Goes Mainstream
Attitudes toward online dating have shifted significantly in the last decade, with more Americans viewing it as a valuable resource for regular people seeking romance (Pew Research Center, 2016, February 29).

social psychology The study of human cognition, emotion, and behavior in relation to others.

Note: Quotations attributed to Julius Achon and Joe and Susanne Maggio are personal communications.

answer is simple: Social psychology explores the way individuals behave in relation to others and groups, while sociology examines the groups themselves—their cultures, societies, and subcultures. A social psychologist studying religion might focus on the relationship between individual congregants and their spiritual leaders. A sociologist would more likely investigate religious practices, rituals, and organizations.

RESEARCH METHODS IN SOCIAL PSYCHOLOGY Social psychologists use the same general research methods as other psychologists, but often with an added twist of deception. Deception is sometimes necessary because people do not always behave naturally when they know they are being observed. Some participants try to conform to expectations; others do just the opposite, behaving in ways they believe will contradict the researchers' predictions. Suppose a team of researchers is studying facial expressions in social settings. If participants know that every glance and grimace are being analyzed, they may feel self-conscious and display atypical facial expressions. Instead of telling participants the real focus of the study, researchers might lead them to believe they are participating in a study on, say, problem solving. That way, they can study the behavior of interest (facial expressions in social settings) more naturally.

Social psychology studies often involve *confederates,* or people secretly working for the researchers. Playing the role of participants, experimenters, or simply bystanders, confederates say what the researchers tell them to say and do what the researchers tell them to do. They are, unknown to the participants, just part of the researchers' experimental manipulation.

In most cases, the deception is not kept secret forever. Researchers debrief their participants at the end of a study, or review aspects of the research initially kept under wraps. Even after learning they were deceived, many participants report they are willing to take part in subsequent psychology experiments (Blatchley & O'Brien, 2007). In one survey concerning medical research, respondents said deception is appropriate as long as there isn't "outright lying" (Pugh, Kahane, Maslen, & Savulescu, 2016). Debriefing is also a time when researchers make sure that participants were not harmed or upset by their involvement in a study. We should note that all psychology research affiliated with colleges and universities must be approved by an Institutional Review Board (IRB) to ensure that no harm will come from participation. This requirement is partly a reaction to early studies involving extreme deception and manipulation—studies that many viewed as dehumanizing and unethical. Psychologists agree that deception is only acceptable if there is no other way to study the topic of interest. We will describe many examples of such research in the upcoming pages, but first let's familiarize ourselves with some basic concepts in social psychology.

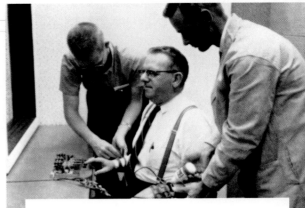

In the Name of Science
A research confederate in Stanley Milgram's classic experiment is strapped to a table and hooked up to electrodes. Participants in this study were led to believe they were administering electrical shocks to the confederate when in reality the confederate was just pretending to be shocked. This allowed the researchers to study how far participants would go in applying shocks—without anyone actually being hurt. From the film *Obedience* © 1968 by Stanley Milgram, © renewed 1993 by Alexandra Milgram, and distributed by Alexander Street Press.

CONNECTIONS

In **Chapter 1,** we discussed deception in the context of the experimental method. In a double-blind study, neither participants nor researchers administering the treatment know who is getting the placebo and who is receiving the real treatment. Participants are told ahead of time they might receive a placebo.

CONNECTIONS

In **Chapter 1,** we discussed debriefing, which occurs after the participant's involvement in the study has ended. In a debriefing session, researchers provide participants with useful information about the study. Sometimes this means informing participants of deception or manipulation that was used in the study—information that couldn't be shared beforehand.

 show what you know

1. When a participant has completed his involvement in a research project, generally the researcher will _____ him by discussing aspects of the study previously kept secret and making sure he was not upset or harmed by his involvement.

2. Social psychology research occasionally employs some form of deception involving confederates. How is this type of deception different from that used in a double-blind study?

3. _____ studies individuals in relation to others and groups, whereas _____ studies the groups themselves, including cultures and societies.
   a. Sociology; social psychology
   b. Social psychology; sociology
   c. Sociology; a confederate
   d. A confederate; social psychology

✓ CHECK YOUR ANSWERS IN APPENDIX C.

Social Cognition

THE DATING GAME Joe and Susanne's story begins right around Valentine's Day 2006, when Joe decided to sign up for a full membership to Match.com. A couple of days after Joe joined the site, Susanne came across his page. "I thought he was cute," she says. "That was obviously the reason why I originally opened it." Joe was a burly guy with a dynamite smile, and Susanne was drawn to big, teddy bear types. Reading his profile, she was immediately intrigued. "The fact that he was a single parent, you know, kind of piqued my interest," she says. Before long, Joe was checking out Susanne's page, liking what he saw, and initiating the e-mail exchange that ultimately led to that first date at Chili's. ●

Attributions

LO 2   Describe social cognition and how we use attributions to explain behavior.

Put yourself in Joe or Susanne's position. There you are on Match.com, looking at the profile page of someone you find attractive. On a conscious level, you are tallying up all the interests you have in common and scrutinizing every self-descriptive adjective this person has chosen. There is also some information processing happening outside of your awareness. You might not even realize that this person reminds you of someone you know, like your mother or father, and that sense of familiarity makes you more inclined to reach out. Will you contact this person?

Whatever your decision may be, it is very much reliant on **social cognition**—the way you think about others, attend to social information, and use this information in your life, both consciously and unconsciously. Joe and Susanne used social cognition in forming first impressions of one another. You use social cognition anytime you try to interpret or respond to another person's behavior. Let's take a closer look at a critical facet of social cognition: *attributions*.

CONNECTIONS

In **Chapter 14,** we described psychoanalysis, which aims to increase awareness of unconscious conflicts. Here, we discuss how unconscious processes can drive social behaviors. Therapists can help clients become aware of these unconscious influences.

CONNECTIONS

In **Chapter 7,** we defined cognition as the mental activity associated with obtaining, storing, converting, and using knowledge. Thinking is a type of cognition that involves coming to a decision, forming a belief, or developing an attitude. In this section, we examine how cognition and thinking affect the way we use social information.

Which Face Do You Trust?

One aspect of social cognition is forming "first impressions" of people, and that includes ultra-fast judgments about trustworthiness. Research suggests we gage the trustworthiness of a face before consciously perceiving it. This subliminal processing is evident on an fMRI scan, with both sides of the amygdala becoming more excited in response to a low-trustworthy face (left), compared to an average- or high-trustworthy face (Freeman, Stolier, Ingbretsen, & Hehman, 2014).
Republished with permission from Freeman, J. B., Stolier, R. M., Ingbretsen, Z. A., & Hehman, E. A. (2014). Amygdala responsivity to high-level social information from unseen faces. *The Journal of Neuroscience, 34(32),* 10573–10581; permission conveyed through Copyright Clearance Center, Inc..

Low	Neutral	High

WHAT ARE ATTRIBUTIONS? Joe and Susanne's relationship has always been fairly open, with Joe rarely having to wonder what Susanne is thinking and vice versa. This is usually *not* the case with online dating, or any kind of dating for that matter. The "dating game" typically involves a lot of guesswork about the other person's behavior: *Why didn't he call back? What did she mean by that 😕 yesterday?* These kinds of questions have relevance for all human relationships, not just the romantic kind. Just think about how much time you spend wondering why people do the things they do. The "answers" you come up with to resolve these questions are called *attributions*.

Attributions are beliefs we develop to explain human behaviors and characteristics, as well as situations. "Why is my friend in such a bad mood?" you ask yourself. Your attribution might be, "Maybe he just got some bad news" or "Perhaps he is hungry." When psychologists characterize attributions, they use the term *observer* to identify the

Emoji credit: Maxi_m/Shutterstock.

person making the attribution, and *actor* to identify the person exhibiting a behavior of interest. If Joe was trying to explain why Susanne had checked out his profile page, then Joe is the observer and Susanne is the actor.

ATTRIBUTIONAL DIMENSIONS There are many types of attributions, and differentiating among them is quite a task. To make things more manageable, psychologists often describe attributions along three dimensions: controllable–uncontrollable, stable–unstable, and internal–external. Let's see how these might apply to attributions relating to Joe and Susanne:

> *Controllable–uncontrollable dimension:* Suppose Susanne had been 15 minutes late to meet Joe at Starbucks. If Joe assumed it happened because she got stuck in unavoidable traffic, we would say he was making an uncontrollable attribution. (As far as he knows, Susanne has no control over the traffic.) If, however, Joe assumed that Susanne's lateness resulted from factors within her control, such as how fast she drove or what time she left her house, then the attribution would be controllable.

> *Stable–unstable dimension:* Why did Joe cook Susanne a delicious dinner of pork chops? Susanne could infer his behavior stemmed from a longtime interest in cooking. This would be an example of a stable attribution. With stable attributions, the cause is long-lasting. If Susanne thought Joe's behavior resulted from a short-lived inspiration after watching a really good cooking show, then her attribution would be unstable. With unstable attributions, the cause is temporary.

> *Internal–external dimension:* Why did Joe have trouble meeting suitable single women before Susanne entered his life? If Susanne thought it was because few single women lived in his immediate area, this would be an external attribution, because the cause of the problem resides outside of Joe. However, if she believed Joe had trouble meeting women because he was reluctant to attend singles events, this would be an internal attribution—the cause lies within Joe. With internal attributions, the cause is located inside the person, such as a skill, belief system, or attitude.

 **In Class: Collaborate and Report**

Imagine you have a classmate who is frequently absent from class. In your group, **A)** generate several attributions for the frequent absences that are external, uncontrollable, and unstable. **B)** Generate several attributions that are internal, controllable and stable. **C)** Consider how your emotional reactions might be different if you think the cause of your classmate's absenteeism is more like **A)** than **B)**.

LO 3 Outline how attributions lead to mistakes in our explanations for behaviors.

When people make attributions, they are often guessing about the causes of events or behaviors, which of course leaves plenty of room for error. Let's take a look at four of the most common mistakes (**INFOGRAPHIC 15.1** on the next page).

FUNDAMENTAL ATTRIBUTION ERROR Suppose you are hosting a party tomorrow night. You sent out the invitations a month ago, and everyone responded except your friend Julia. If you automatically assume Julia failed to reply because she is a little snooty and thinks she's too good for your party, rather than considering situational factors (like the fact that your invitation may have gone straight into her spam folder), then you might be falling prey to the **fundamental attribution error**. Here, the tendency is to favor *dispositional attributions* over

Synonyms

fundamental attribution error
correspondence bias

social cognition The way people think about others, attend to social information, and use this information in their lives, both consciously and unconsciously.

attributions Beliefs one develops to explain human behaviors and characteristics, as well as situations.

fundamental attribution error The tendency to overestimate the degree to which the characteristics of an individual are the cause of an event, and to underestimate the involvement of situational factors.

Errors in Attribution

Attributions are beliefs we develop to explain human behaviors and characteristics, as well as situations. We can explain behaviors in many ways, but social psychologists often compare explanations based on traits or personality characteristics (dispositional attributions) to explanations based on external situations (situational attributions). But as we seek to explain events and behaviors, we tend to make predictable errors, making the wrong assumption about why someone is behaving in a certain way. Let's look at four of the most common types of errors in attribution.

Fundamental attribution error

Observer tends to think actor's behavior is caused by internal characteristics, ignoring the role of the situation.

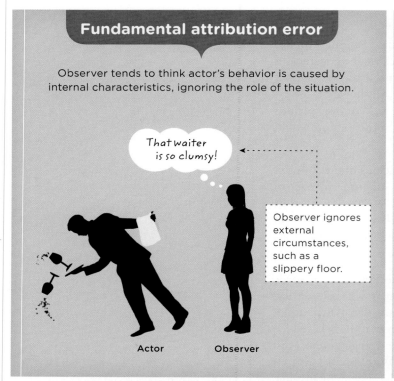

That waiter is so clumsy!

Observer ignores external circumstances, such as a slippery floor.

Actor   Observer

Just-world hypothesis

Observer tends to think people get what they deserve.

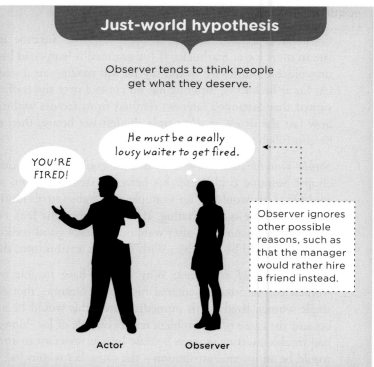

YOU'RE FIRED!

He must be a really lousy waiter to get fired.

Observer ignores other possible reasons, such as that the manager would rather hire a friend instead.

Actor   Observer

Self-serving bias

We tend to attribute our successes to internal characteristics and our failures to external circumstances.

Success! I got a lot of tips tonight.

I'm an excellent waiter so I earn good tips.

TIPS

Failure! I hardly earned any tips.

Diners were really stingy tonight, so I wasn't tipped well.

TIPS

False consensus effect

Observer tends to assume the actor is behaving similarly to how she would act in that situation.

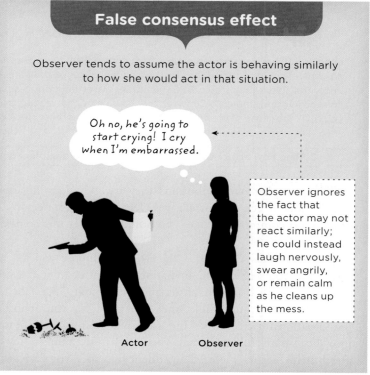

Oh no, he's going to start crying! I cry when I'm embarrassed.

Observer ignores the fact that the actor may not react similarly; he could instead laugh nervously, swear angrily, or remain calm as he cleans up the mess.

Actor   Observer

situational attributions. A **dispositional attribution** is a particular type of internal attribution in which the presumed causes are traits or personality characteristics. Here, we are referring to deep-seated, enduring characteristics, as opposed to those that are more transient, like feeling tired and cranky. A **situational attribution** is an external attribution whereby behaviors are assumed to result from situational factors.

The fundamental attribution error is common; we often think that the cause of other people's behaviors is a characteristic of them (a dispositional attribution) as opposed to the environment (a situational attribution) (Ross, 1977; Ross, Amabile, & Steinmetz, 1977). When thinking about what causes or controls behavior, we "underestimate the impact of situational factors and . . . overestimate the role of dispositional factors" (Ross, 1977, p. 183). Why does this happen?

When trying to understand the intentions of others, we speculate about the "contents" of their minds. This mental exercise, and the errors it can produce, may be influenced by activity in a region of the frontal cortex that is part of the "social brain." We are more likely to make dispositional attributions when these brain regions are spontaneously activated in social settings, but these attributions "are not always warranted" (Moran, Jolly, & Mitchell, 2014, p. 575).

Let's reinforce this concept of the fundamental attribution error with two more examples: Imagine you observe actor Michael J. Fox's irregular movements and immediately assume he has an alcohol problem (a dispositional attribution). You fail to consider these behaviors might be a symptom of Parkinson's disease (situational attribution). Now suppose you're stopped at a red light and the car behind you starts to honk. You jump to the conclusion that the driver is impatient and rude (dispositional attribution) rather than considering the situational factors that may prompt such behavior, such as the appearance of thick black smoke coming out of your tailpipe (situational attribution).

Why do we make the fundamental attribution error? Perhaps it has something to do with our tendency to make quick decisions about others based on the labels we assign to them. Imagine how dangerous this could be in a medical setting, when doctors and nurses need to make quick choices about treatment. A nurse seeing a patient who has slurred speech, can't walk, and is aggressive might assume he is a drunk "alcoholic," ignoring other situational factors that might be involved, such as homelessness and severe dehydration (Levett-Jones et al., 2010). Similarly, a doctor might take one look at a patient and decide he is uncooperative, dirty, and just "another homeless hippie," when in fact the patient is on the verge of a diabetic coma (Groopman, 2008, p. 55). Doctors must be careful not to let negative stereotypes color their diagnoses, and patients and their families should recognize that doctors are not immune to these types of attribution errors (Groopman, 2008). The good news is that we may be able to reduce biases associated with the fundamental attribution error. In one study, researchers showed that single training sessions with educational videos and games can have "significant debiasing effects" on participants (Morewedge et al., 2015).

Errors may happen, but we must make do with the information we have—even if that information is biased and based on our own values and belief systems (Callan, Ferguson, & Bindemann, 2013). These values and belief systems are apparent in the *just-world hypothesis.*

JUST-WORLD HYPOTHESIS People who believe the world is a fair place tend to expect that "bad things" happen for a reason. Their thinking is that when someone is "bad," it should be no surprise when things don't go well for him (Riggio & Garcia, 2009). Many people blame the actor by applying the **just-world hypothesis**, which

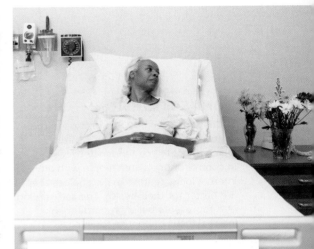

Unfair Health Care?
Research suggests that African American patients generally receive lower-quality medical care than their white counterparts. Even doctors with the best intentions may harbor unconscious racial stereotypes that affect how they deliver care (Ansell & McDonald, 2015). Could such mistakes be related to the fundamental attribution error? Blend Images-ERproductions Ltd/Getty Images.

dispositional attribution A belief that some characteristic of an individual is involved in the cause of an event or activity.

situational attribution A belief that some environmental factor is involved in the cause of an event or activity.

just-world hypothesis The tendency to believe the world is a fair place and individuals get what they deserve.

assumes that if someone is suffering, he must have done something to deserve it (Rubin & Peplau, 1975). In one study, researchers told a group of participants about a man who was violent toward his wife, slapping and yelling at her. Another group heard about a loving man who gave his wife flowers and frequently made her dinner. Participants who heard about the "bad person" were more likely to predict a bad outcome for him (he will have a "terrible car accident") than those who heard about the "good person" (he will win a "hugely successful business contract"; Callan et al., 2013, p. 35).

This belief in a just world, to some degree, may result from cultural teachings. Children in Western cultures are taught this concept so that they learn how to behave properly, show respect for authority figures, and delay gratification (Rubin & Peplau, 1975). For example, in the original tale of *Cinderella* (Grimm & Grimm, 1884), doves rest on Cinderella's shoulders prior to her wedding to the Prince. As the bridal party enters and leaves the church, the doves poke out her evil stepsisters' eyes—a punishment for being cruel to Cinderella. Through this tale, children learn that the stepsisters got what they deserved. We see this perspective at work in other scenarios, sometimes to the detriment of innocent people. In cases of assault, people may blame the victim (rather than the perpetrator), suggesting that the victim somehow deserved the abuse (*If she hadn't been wearing those clothes, maybe that wouldn't have happened*.) (Correia, Alves, Morais, & Ramos, 2015).

SELF-SERVING BIAS The tendency to attribute one's successes to internal characteristics and one's failures to environmental factors is known as the **self-serving bias**. Before meeting Joe, Susanne dated a guy who tended to blame his failures on external circumstances. If he lost his job, it was because the boss never liked him—not because his performance fell short. This "woe is me" attitude annoyed Susanne, who had learned to take responsibility for what happened in her life. As her mother often told her, "You can be a survivor, or you can be a victim." Susanne's ex-boyfriend appears to have been influenced by self-serving bias.

CONNECTIONS

In **Chapters 11** and **12,** we discussed the concept of internal locus of control, which refers to the tendency to feel in control of one's life. People with an internal locus tend to make choices that are better for their health. The self-serving bias represents beliefs regarding an internal locus of control for successes

Don't Look at Me
There are many reasons the bathroom is messy, but none of them have to do with the little boy Calvin. Here, we have an example of self-serving bias, the tendency to attribute mistakes and failures to factors outside ourselves (or to assume personal credit for our successes).

self-serving bias The tendency to attribute our successes to personal characteristics and our failures to environmental factors.

FALSE CONSENSUS EFFECT When trying to decipher the causes of other people's behaviors, we over-rely on knowledge about ourselves. This can lead to the

false consensus effect, which is the tendency to overestimate the degree to which people think or act like we do (Ross, Greene, & House, 1977). And when others do not share our thoughts and behaviors, we tend to believe they are acting abnormally or inappropriately. This false consensus effect is evident in our beliefs about everything from celebrities—*Since I love Katy Perry, you should, too*—to childhood vaccines—*I don't vaccinate my child, so you shouldn't either* (Bui, 2012; Rabinowitz, Latella, Stern, & Jost, 2016). We seem to make this mistake because we have an overabundance of information about ourselves, and often limited information about others. Struggling to understand those around us, we fill in the gaps with what we know about ourselves.

In Class: Collaborate and Report

A man is eating a messy sandwich while driving. If he hits another car while reaching for a napkin, how might an observer explain his actions? In your group, generate examples of explanations that illustrate the fundamental attribution error, just-world hypothesis, self-serving bias, and false consensus effect.

Attribution errors may lead us astray, but we can minimize their impact by being aware of our tendency to fall back on them. Now it's time to explore another facet of social cognition. Where did you get that attitude?

Attitudes

For many people, including Joe and Susanne, the purpose of online dating is to find someone who shares common values, interests, and lifestyle choices—all variables that are strongly influenced by *attitudes*. **Attitudes** are the relatively stable thoughts, feelings, and responses we have toward people, situations, ideas, and things (Ajzen, 2001; Wicker, 1969).

Psychologists suggest that attitudes are composed of cognitive, affective, and behavioral components (**FIGURE 15.2**). The *cognitive* aspect of an attitude refers to our beliefs or ideas about an object, person, or situation. Generally, our attitudes include an emotional evaluation, which is the *affective* component relating to mood or emotion. We often have positive or negative feelings about objects, people, or situations (Ajzen, 2001). Feelings and beliefs guide the *behavioral* aspect of attitudes, or the way we respond.

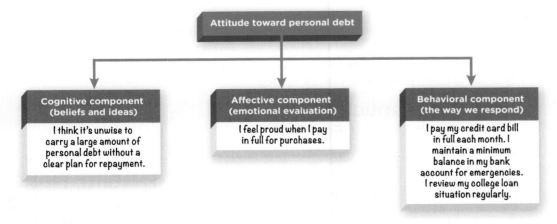

FIGURE 15.2

Attitudes

Attitudes are composed of cognitive, affective, and behavioral components. Cognitive and affective components usually guide the behavioral aspect of an attitude.

WHERE DO ATTITUDES COME FROM? The attitudes you hold are strongly influenced by nurture, or forces in your environment. They develop through experiences, interactions with others, and exposure to social media, television, and other

In **Chapter 7,** we described how the availability heuristic predicts the probability of something happening in the future based on how easily we can recall a similar event from the past. With the false consensus effect, judgments about the degree to which others think or act like we do seem to be based on an availability heuristic; we rely on information about ourselves that is easy to recall.

CONNECTIONS

false consensus effect The tendency to overestimate the degree to which others think or act like we do.

attitudes The relatively stable thoughts, feelings, and responses one has toward people, situations, ideas, and things.

CONNECTIONS

In **Chapter 5,** we described classical conditioning and how it might instill emotions and attitudes toward product brands. Observational learning can lead children to imitate others, including their attitudes.

CONNECTIONS

In **Chapter 7,** we explored the heritability of intelligence. Heritability is the degree to which hereditary factors are responsible for differences across a variety of physical and psychological characteristics. Heritability research often involves comparing identical and fraternal twins, as seen here with the study of attitudes.

All in the Family?
Children and parents frequently have the same attitudes about politics and social issues. To a certain degree, these similarities can be traced to common personality traits, which are partly inherited (Kandler, Bleidorn, & Riemann, 2012). But attitudes are more strongly influenced by life experiences (Huppertz et al., 2014; Olson, Vernon, Harris, & Jang, 2001). Adina Tovy-Amsel /Eye Ubiquitous/Getty Images.

cognitive dissonance A state of tension that results when behaviors are inconsistent with attitudes.

communication outlets. We adopt attitudes through learning processes such as classical conditioning and observational learning. Nurture appears to dominate in this particular arena, but genetic factors play a role in shaping attitudes, too.

NATURE AND NURTURE
Why the Attitude?

One of the best ways to gauge the relative weights of nature and nurture is through the study of twins. If nature has a substantive effect on attitudes, then the following should be true: Identical twins (who have the same genetic make-up at conception) should have more similar attitudes than fraternal twins (who share about 50% of their genes). Research suggests this is the case for attitudes about politics, divorce, voluntary exercise, reading books, and many other topics (Hatemi et al., 2014; Hatemi, McDermott, & Eaves, 2015; Huppertz et al., 2014; Olson, Vernon, Harris, & Jang, 2001).

DOES THIS MEAN . . . EACH OF US IS BORN WITH A "PRO-LIFE" OR "PRO-CHOICE" GENE?

Do such findings imply that each of us is born with a "pro-life" or "pro-choice" gene, and yet another gene that determines how we feel about sports? Highly unlikely. As researchers explain, "A single gene or small group of genes does not directly influence ideological preferences" (Hatemi et al., 2014, p. 292). In all probability, attitudes result from an interaction between a large number of genes (perhaps thousands) and a variety of environmental factors (Hatemi et al., 2014). Our genetic predispositions can influence the environments we create for ourselves, which in turn impact our attitudes (Hatemi et al., 2015). Attitudes result from an ongoing interplay between nature and nurture.

CAN ATTITUDES PREDICT BEHAVIOR? There are many factors determining whether an attitude can predict a behavior (Ajzen, 2001). The strength of an attitude is important, with stronger, more enduring attitudes having a greater impact (Armitage & Christian, 2003; Holland, Verplanken, & Van Knippenberg, 2002; Luttrell, Petty, & Briñol, 2016). Specificity is also key; the more specific an attitude, the more likely it will sway behavior (Armitage & Christian, 2003).

Not surprisingly, people are more likely to act on their attitudes when something important is at stake—like money. Imagine your college is holding a meeting to discuss the possibility of increasing student parking fees. What are the chances of your showing up to that meeting if you don't own a car? The greater personal investment you have in an issue, the more likely you are to act (Sivacek & Crano, 1982; Steindl & Jonas, 2015).

We now know that attitudes can influence behaviors, but is the opposite true—that is, can behaviors shape attitudes? Absolutely.

THINK IT THROUGH
Something Doesn't Feel Right

Most people would agree that cheating on a girlfriend, boyfriend, or spouse is not right. Even so, some people contradict their beliefs by seeking sexual gratification outside their primary relationships. How do you think cheating makes a person feel—relaxed and at peace? Probably not. The tension that results when a behavior (in this case, cheating) clashes with an attitude (cheating is wrong) is known as **cognitive dissonance** (Aronson & Festinger, 1958; Festinger, 1957). One way to reduce cognitive dissonance is to adjust the behavior (stop fooling around). Another approach

APPARENTLY, THE BIG BUCKS MADE IT EASIER TO JUSTIFY THEIR LIES.

is to change the attitude to better match the behavior (*Cheating is actually good for our relationship, because it makes me a better partner*). Such attitude shifts often occur without our awareness.

The phenomenon of cognitive dissonance was elegantly brought to light in a study by Leon Festinger and J. Merrill Carlsmith (1959). Imagine, for a moment, that you are a participant in this classic study. The researchers have assigned you to a very boring task—placing 12 objects on a tray and then putting them back on a shelf, over and over again for a half-hour. Upon finishing, you spend an additional half-hour twisting 48 pegs ever so slightly, one peg at a time, again and again and again. How would you feel at the end of the hour—pretty bored, right?

Regardless of how you may feel about these activities, you have been paid money to convince someone else that they are a blast: "I had a lot of fun [doing] this task," you say. "It was intriguing, it was exciting . . ." (Festinger & Carlsmith, 1959, p. 205). Unless you like performing repetitive behaviors like a robot, we assume you would feel some degree of *cognitive dissonance,* or tension resulting from this mismatch between your attitude (*Ugh, this activity is so boring*) and your behavior (saying, "I had so much fun!"). What could you do to reduce the cognitive dissonance? If you're like participants in Festinger and Carlsmith's study, you would probably adjust your attitude to better fit your claims. In other words, you would rate the task as more interesting than it actually was.

But here's the really fascinating part: The participants who were paid more money ($20 versus $1) were less inclined to change their attitudes to match their claim—a sign that they felt less cognitive dissonance. Apparently, the big bucks made it easier to justify their lies. *I said I liked the boring task because I got paid $20, not because I actually liked it.*

And now, one more example to drive home the concept of cognitive dissonance. Imagine you are a doctor who specializes in treating concussions in children, many of whom sustain their injuries playing football. You know this sport poses a neurological risk, yet you are a devoted fan of the NFL. One Sunday afternoon, you're watching an intense game between the Dallas Cowboys and Minnesota Vikings. Just as you leap from the couch to celebrate a touchdown, the phone rings; it's the hospital calling to inform you that your 14-year-old patient just had a seizure on the football field. At this moment, you may experience a great degree of cognitive dissonance. Your behavior (patronizing the NFL) clashes with your attitude (playing football is dangerous). Reducing the conflict between the attitude and behavior could be accomplished in one of two ways: by changing the attitude or by changing the behavior. Which path would you take?

Promises, Promises
Political campaigns are all about making promises. "Vote for me if you want to see your taxes decrease," says one candidate. "When I get into office, I will fix the health-care system," says the next. Despite good intentions, many politicians do not follow through on their promises once they assume office. How do you think this conflict between beliefs and behaviors affects them? We suspect they experience a bit of cognitive dissonance. Susana Gonzalez/Bloomberg via Getty Images.

We have now learned about cognitive processes that form the foundation of our social existence. Attributions help us make sense of events and behaviors, and attitudes provide continuity in the way we think and feel about the surrounding world. It's time to shift our attention to behavior. How do other people influence the way we act? Are you ready to meet runner extraordinaire Julius Achon?

 **show what you know**

1. _____ are beliefs used to explain events, situations, and characteristics.
   a. Attributions
   b. Confederates
   c. Dispositions
   d. Attitudes

2. Describe the three components of an attitude.

3. Because of the fundamental attribution error, we tend to attribute causes of behaviors to the:
   a. characteristics of the situation.
   b. factors involved in the event.
   c. length of the activity.
   d. disposition of the person.

✓ CHECK YOUR ANSWERS IN APPENDIX C.

Social Influence

11 ORPHANS In 1983 a 7-year-old boy in northern Uganda came down with the measles. The child was feverish and coughing, and his skin was covered in a blotchy rash. He appeared to be dying. In fact, he did die—or so the local villagers believed. They dug his grave, wrapped him in a burial cloth, and sang him a farewell song. Then, just as they were about to lower the body into the ground, someone heard a sneeze. A few moments later, another sneeze. Could it be? The body inside the burial cloth started to writhe. Hastily unwrapping the cloth, the mourners found the child frantically kicking and crying. It's a good thing the boy sneezed that day at his funeral, as the world is a much happier place because he survived. His name is Julius Achon, and he would grow up to become an Olympic athlete and, perhaps more important, a world-class humanitarian.

Julius was born on December 12, 1976, in Awake, a village that had no electricity or running water. "Life in Uganda is very tough," says Julius, who spent his childhood sleeping between eight brothers and sisters on the floor of a one-room hut. Julius grew up during a period when a government opposition group known as the Lord's Resistance Army (LRA) began its campaign of terror in northern Uganda. At age 12, Julius was kidnapped by the LRA and forced to become a child soldier, but his spirit would not be broken. After 3 months with the rebels, he escaped from their camp and, running much of the distance, returned to his village some 100 miles away.

Home in Uganda
A group of women sit together in Awake, Uganda, the village where Julius Achon was born and raised. Day-to-day life was difficult, and young Julius dreamed of leaving the village and pursuing a better life in the city. Inspired by the accomplishments of Uganda's Olympic hurdler John Akii-Bua, he decided to start running. Courtesy Dr. Julie Gralow.

After coming home, Julius began to run competitively. Running made him feel free, and running was his great gift. He ran 42 miles barefoot to his first major track meet in the city of Lira. Hours after arriving, Julius was racing—and winning—the 800 meters, the 1,500 meters, and the 3,000 meters (Kahn, 2012, January). From that point on, it was one success after another: a stunning victory at the national championships, a track scholarship at a prestigious high school in the capital city of Kampala, a gold medal at the World Junior Championships, a college scholarship from George Mason University in the United States, a collegiate record in 1996, and participation in the 1996 and 2000 Olympics (Kahn, 2012, January).

As awe-inspiring as these accomplishments may be, the greatest achievement in Julius Achon's life was yet to come, and it had little to do with running. In 2003, while training back home in Uganda, he came upon a bus station in Lira. "I stopped, and then I saw children lying under the bus," Julius says. They had been sleeping there for warmth. One of them stood up and started to beg for money—a 13- or 14-year-old girl clad in a tattered skirt and torn blouse. Then more children emerged, 11 of them in all, some teenagers and others as young as 3. They were terribly thin and dirty, and the little ones wore nothing more than long T-shirts and underwear.

"Where are your parents?" Julius remembers asking. One of the children said their parents had been shot and killed. "Can I walk you to my home, you know, to go eat?" Julius asked. The children eagerly agreed and followed him home for a meal of rice, beans, and porridge. What happened next may seem unbelievable, but Julius and his family are extraordinary people. Julius asked his father to shelter the 11 orphans, provided that he, Julius, would send money home to cover their living expenses. Julius had been running with a professional team in Portugal,

Photodisc/ Getty Images.

making about $5,000 a year, not even enough to cover his own expenses. His parents already had six people living in their one-room home. How did his father respond?

"Ah, it's no problem," said Julius' father. And just like that, Julius and his family adopted 11 children. ●

Power of Others

Throughout the years Julius was trotting the globe and winning medals, he never forgot about Uganda. He remembered the people back home with empty stomachs and no access to lifesaving medicine, living in constant fear of the LRA. Julius was raised in a family that had always reached out to neighbors in need. "You will get help from other people when you do good," his parents used to say. Julius also felt blessed by all the support that people outside the family had given him. "I feel I was so loved [by] others," says Julius, referring to the mentors and coaches who had provided him with places to stay, clothes to wear, and family away from home.

So when Julius encountered those 11 orphans lying under the bus, he didn't think twice about coming to their rescue. His decision to bring them into his life probably had something to do with the positive interactions he had experienced with people in his past.

LO 4   **Explain the meaning of social influence and recognize factors associated with persuasion.**

SOCIAL INFLUENCE DEFINED Rarely a day goes by that we do not come into contact with other human beings. This contact may be up close and personal, in a family or a tight-knit work group. Other times it's more superficial, like the "Hello, how are you?" type of exchange you might have with a cashier at the store. Sometimes the interaction is so superficial that you never see the person face to face, like the online banker who helps you figure out why you were charged that mysterious fee. All these interactions impact you in ways you may not realize. Psychologists refer to this as **social influence**—how a person is affected by others as evidenced in behaviors, emotions, and cognition. We begin our discussion with a powerful, yet often unspoken, form of social influence: expectations.

EXPECTATIONS Think back to your days in elementary school. What kind of student were you—an overachiever, a kid who struggled, or perhaps the class clown? The answer to this question may depend somewhat on the way your teachers perceived you. In a classic study, Rosenthal and Jacobson (1966, 1968) administered a nonverbal intelligence test to students in a San Francisco elementary school. Then all the teachers were provided with a list of students who were likely to "show surprising gains in intellectual competence" during the next year (Rosenthal, 2002, p. 841). But the list was fake; the "intellectually competent" kids were just a group selected at random (a good example of how deception is used in social psychology research). About 8 months later, the students were given a second intelligence test. Children whom the teachers expected to "show surprising gains" achieved greater increases in their test scores than their peers. Mind you, the only difference between these two groups was in teacher expectations and their resulting behaviors. The students who were expected to be superior actually became superior. Why do you think this happened?

Expectations can have a powerful impact on behaviors. Here, we have a case in which teachers' expectations (based on false information) seemed to transform students' aptitudes and facilitate substantial gains. Let's consider the types of teacher

Fast and Free
Julius wins the 1,500 meters at the 2005 Payton Jordan U.S. Open at Stanford University. With two Olympics under his belt, the young runner had enjoyed an extremely successful athletic career, but his focus was beginning to shift onto something bigger—the task of providing for 11 orphans back home in Uganda. Image of Sport/Newscom/Image of Sport Photos/Stanford California United States.

Julius, in His Own Words

http://qrs.ly/ea5a5ga

Photo: Macmillan Learning.

social influence How a person is affected by others as evidenced in behaviors, emotions, and cognition.

Great Expectations
Children tend to perform better in school when teachers expect them to succeed (Rosenthal, 2002). This is especially true for students who are young and socioeconomically disadvantaged (Sorhagen, 2013).
Steve Debenport/Getty Images.

CONNECTIONS

In **Chapter 12,** we discussed how poverty and its associated stressors can have a lasting impact on the development of the brain and subsequent cognitive abilities. Some factors that influence children's brain development are nutrition toxins, and abuse. Here, we see that the expectations of others can impact cognitive functioning as well.

You Asked, Julius Answers

http://qrs.ly/dm5a5gh

How did you persuade your father to take in 11 orphans?

scan this ➔

behaviors that could explain this effect. The teachers may have inadvertently communicated expectations by demonstrating "warmer socioemotional" attitudes toward the "surprising gain" students; they may have provided them with more material and opportunities to respond to high expectations; and they may have given them more complex and personalized feedback (Rosenthal, 2002, 2003). From the student's perspective, teacher behaviors can create a desire to work hard, or they can result in a decline in interest and confidence (Kassin, Fein, & Markus, 2017).

Since this classic study was conducted some 50 years ago, researchers have studied expectations in a variety of classroom settings. Their results demonstrate that teacher expectations do not have the same effect or degree of impact on all students (Jussim & Harber, 2005). They appear to have greater influence on younger children (first and second graders) and those of lower socioeconomic status (Sorhagen, 2013). Expectations also may have a significant impact on second-language students. When teachers consider "language-minority" students to be hard workers, these students "advance in math at the same rates" as their native English-speaking peers (Blanchard & Muller, 2015, p. 262).

Expectations are powerful, but they are just one form of social influence. Let's return to the story of Julius and learn about more targeted types of influence.

Persuasion

When Julius asked his father to shelter and feed the 11 orphans, he was using a form of social influence called **persuasion.** With persuasion, one intentionally tries to make other people change their attitudes and beliefs, which may (or may not) lead to changes in their behaviors. The person doing the persuading does not necessarily have control over those he seeks to persuade. Julius could not force his father to feel sympathy for the orphans.

The important elements of persuasion were first described by Carl Hovland, a social psychologist who studied the morale of soldiers fighting in World War II. According to Hovland, three factors determine persuasive power: the source, the message, and the audience (Hovland, Janis, & Kelley, 1953).

THE SOURCE The credibility of the person or organization sending a message is critical, and credibility can be dependent on perceived expertise and trustworthiness (Hovland & Weiss, 1951). Suppose you are searching for information about the risks associated with vaccines—whom do you trust to furnish reliable information? In one study, German adults deemed vaccine information provided by government agencies to be more credible than that supplied by pharmaceutical companies (Betsch & Sachse, 2013). Of course, this assessment of government credibility depends on whether citizens consider the government trustworthy. Persuasive ability also hinges on the attractiveness of the source. More attractive people tend to be more persuasive (Bekk & Spörrle, 2010).

THE MESSAGE The content of the message also determines persuasive power. One important factor is the degree to which the message is logical and to the point (Chaiken & Eagly, 1976). Fear-inducing information can increase persuasion, but it can also backfire. Imagine someone uses this message to encourage teeth-flossing: "If you don't floss daily, you can end up with infected gums, and that infection can spread to your eyes and create total blindness!" If the audience is overly frightened by a message (imagine small children being told to floss . . . or else!), the tension they feel may actually interfere with their ability to process the message (Janis & Feshbach, 1953). If fear is used for the purpose of persuasion, those being persuaded must be provided with information about how to cope with any negative outcomes (Leventhal, Watts, & Pagano, 1967). Being as "gruesome as possible" is not effective; a better approach is to provide clear information about the negative consequences of not being persuaded (de Hoog, Stroebe, & de Wit, 2007, p. 280).

THE AUDIENCE Finally, we turn to the characteristics of the audience. One important factor is age. For example, middle-age adults (40 to 60 years old) are unlikely to be persuaded, whereas children are relatively susceptible (Roberts & DelVecchio, 2000). Another factor is emotional state; when people are happy (and eating tasty food, interestingly enough), they are more likely to be persuaded (Aronson, 2012; Janis, Kaye, & Kirschner, 1965). Mental focus is also key: If your mind is somewhere else, you are less likely to be affected by message content (Petty & Cacioppo, 1986).

ELABORATION LIKELIHOOD MODEL The *elaboration likelihood model* proposes that persuasion hinges on the way people think about an argument, and it can occur via one of two pathways. With the *central route* to persuasion, the focus is on the content of the message, and thinking critically about it. With the *peripheral route,* the focus is not on the content but on "extramessage factors" such as the credibility or attractiveness of the source (Petty & Cacioppo, 1986). Little critical thinking is involved, and the commitment to the outcome is low. How do we know which route the message will take? If the person receiving the message is knowledgeable and invested in its outcome, the central route to persuasion is used. If the person is distracted, lacks knowledge about the topic, or does not feel invested in the outcome, the peripheral route is typically taken (O'Keefe, 2008).

Following the tragic Newtown, Connecticut, massacre of 2012, in which 20 elementary school children and 6 adults lost their lives in less than 5 minutes, the United States has seen an upsurge in calls for tighter gun control (Hussey & Foderaro, 2016, June 14; Barron, 2012, December 14). A person with strong feelings about gun control (either for or against it) would likely take advantage of central processing when trying to develop a persuasive argument. Consider this statement, written by a group of physicians and public health experts in response to a wave of mass shootings in the United States: "Commentators once again marveled at the vast gap between U.S. rates of gun deaths and those in other developed countries. . . . If any other public health menace were consistently killing and maiming so many Americans, without research, recommendations, and action by the CDC, the public would be outraged" (Malina, Morrissey, Campion, Hamel, & Drazen, 2016, p. 175). Such a message would be more persuasive to a person who is knowledgeable and invested in the issue, and thus uses the central processing route. Someone unfamiliar with or indifferent to gun-control policy would more likely be persuaded by the credibility of the source, appearance of the speaker, and so on.

The take-home message: If you want to persuade as many people as possible, make sure your arguments are logical *and* you present yourself as credible and attractive. That way you can take advantage of both routes.

Credible Source
Astrophysicist Neil deGrasse Tyson understands the science of climate change. Because he is a credible source, people are likely to be persuaded by his arguments: "The experimental consensus is there" (Wei, 2014, May 1, 0:48), Tyson explains. As humans continue burning fossil fuels, more carbon is being put into the atmosphere. "A greenhouse gas is warming the earth," he says. "We are changing the climate faster than our culture may be able to respond" (1:05–1:23). Richard Shotwell/Invision/AP.

persuasion Intentionally trying to make people change their attitudes and beliefs, which may lead to changes in their behaviors.

Compliance

LO 5   Define compliance and explain some of the techniques used to gain it.

The results of persuasion are internal and related to a change in *attitude* (Key, Edlund, Sagarin, & Bizer, 2009). **Compliance**, on the other hand, occurs when someone voluntarily changes her *behavior* at the request or direction of another person or group, who in general does not have any true authority over her. Compliance is evident in changes to "overt behavior" (Key et al., 2009; **TABLE 15.1**). Suppose you want someone to help clean up after a party. You could try to get him to comply with your request, perhaps through some mild form of guilt ("Remember the last party we had, when I helped you?").

TABLE 15.1   METHODS OF COMPLIANCE

Compliance Technique	What Is It?	Why It Works	Example
Foot-in-the-door technique	Making a small request followed by a larger request	If you have already said yes to a small request, chances are you will agree to a bigger request to remain consistent in your involvement.	Ask a parent for $5 and then $20.
Door-in-the-face technique	Making a large, sometimes unreasonable request followed by a smaller request	*Reciprocal concessions* suggest that if the solicitor is willing to give up the large request, the person being solicited tends to give in and satisfy the smaller request.	Ask a parent for $100 and then $5.

Here are two effective approaches for getting people to comply with your requests.

compliance Changes in behavior at the request or direction of another person or group, who in general do not have any true authority.

foot-in-the-door technique A compliance technique that involves making a small request, followed by a larger request.

door-in-the-face technique A compliance technique that involves making a large request, followed by a smaller request.

Surprisingly, compliance often occurs outside of our awareness. Think of an everyday situation in which you mindlessly comply with another person's request. You're waiting in line at the copy machine, and a man asks if he can cut in front of you. Do you allow it? Your response may depend on the wording of the request. Researchers studying this very scenario—a person asking for permission to cut in line—have found that compliance is much more likely to result when the request is accompanied by a reason. Saying, "Excuse me, I have five pages. May I use the [copy] machine?" will not work as well as "Excuse me, I have five pages. May I use the [copy] machine, *because I am in a rush?*" People are more likely to comply with a request that includes a "because" phrase, even if the reasoning is not logical. For example, stating that you need to use the copy machine "*because I am in a rush*" achieves about the same compliance as "*because I have to make copies*" (Langer, Blank, & Chanowitz, 1978). Kind of astonishing, right?

Salespeople and marketing experts use a variety of techniques to get consumers to comply with their requests. One way to achieve compliance is the **foot-in-the-door technique**, which occurs when someone makes a small request, followed by a larger request (Freedman & Fraser, 1966). If a college club is trying to persuade students to help with a large service project (such as raising money for packages to be sent to soldiers overseas), its members might first stop students in the hallway and ask them if they could help with a smaller task (labeling a couple of donated boxes lying close by). If a student responds positively to this small request, then the club members might make a bigger request (to sponsor packages), with the expectation that the student will comply with the second request on the grounds of having said yes to the first request. Why would this technique work?

The reasoning is that if you have already said yes to a small request, chances are you will agree to a bigger request in order to remain consistent in your involvement.

Your prior participation leads you to believe you are the type of person who gets involved; in other words, your attitude has shifted (Cialdini & Goldstein, 2004; Freedman & Fraser, 1966). So why is such a strategy called *foot-in-the-door?* In the past, salespeople went door to door trying to sell their goods and services, and they would often be successful if they could physically get a "foot in the door," thereby keeping it open, which allowed them to continue with their sales pitch.

Another method for gaining compliance is the **door-in-the-face technique**, which involves making a large, sometimes unreasonable request followed by a smaller request. With this technique, the expectation is that the person will not go along with the large request, but because the smaller request may seem so minor by comparison, she will comply with it. There are numerous reasons people comply under these circumstances, but the main reason seems to be one of *reciprocal concessions.* If the solicitor (the person trying to obtain something) is willing to give up something (the large request), the person being solicited tends to feel that he, too, should give in and satisfy the smaller request (Cialdini & Goldstein, 2004).

Let's review these concepts using Julius as an example. After meeting the 11 orphans, Julius brought them home and asked his parents to provide them with a meal. Once his parents *complied* with this initial request, Julius made a much larger request—he asked them to shelter the children indefinitely. This is an example of the *foot-in-the-door technique* because Julius first made a modest request ("Will you feed these children?") and then followed up with a larger one ("Will you shelter these children?"). Had these requests been flip-flopped, that is, had Julius only wanted to get the children a meal but first asked his parents to house them, we would call it the *door-in-the-face technique.*

Compliance generally occurs in response to specific requests or instructions: Will you pick up the kids after school? Can you chop these onions? Please collect your sweaty socks from the bathroom floor! But social influence needn't be explicit. Sometimes we adapt our behaviors and beliefs simply to fit in with the crowd.

Foot in the Door
Looks like this petitioner has gotten her "foot in the door," so to speak. With the foot-in-the-door approach, the solicitor makes a small request ("Would you take a moment to sign this petition?") followed by a larger request ("Will you donate money to this cause?"). ebstock/Getty Images.

Conformity

When Julius came to the United States on a college scholarship in 1995, he was struck by some of the cultural differences he observed between the United States and Uganda—the way people dressed, for example. Women wore considerably less clothing, and men could be seen wearing jeans halfway down their posteriors (the "sagging" pants style). There were other differences, like the way people addressed authority figures. In Africa, explains Julius, students speak to their teachers with a certain kind of respect, using a low voice and standing still with their legs close together. Americans tend to use a more casual tone, he notes; they stand with their legs farther apart and shift around during conversation.

During the decade Julius lived in the United States, he never stopped acting like a Ugandan. Before going out in the evening, he would tuck in his shirt, check his hair, and make sure his clothes were ironed—and never would he wear sagging pants. You might say Julius refused to *conform* to certain aspects of American culture—and resisting conformity is not always easy to do.

Courageous Non-Conformist
In 2014, 17-year-old Malala Yousafzai (photo held by girl) became the youngest recipient of the Nobel Peace Prize. Yousafzai began her activism at age 11, blogging for the BBC about life under the Taliban in her native Pakistan. Over the next few years, she became an outspoken advocate for girls' education, but her nonconformist stance was not welcomed by the Taliban. When Yousafzai was 15, a Taliban gunman entered her school bus and shot her in the head. She recovered from her injuries and has continued her campaign for women's rights, earning the respect and admiration of people around the world (NobelPrize.org, 2014, Kantor, 2014, October 10). RIZWAN TABASSUM/AFP/Getty Images.

LO 6 **Identify the factors that influence the likelihood of someone conforming.**

FOLLOWING THE CROWD Have you ever found yourself turning to look in the same direction as other people who are staring at something, just because you see them doing so? During the Waldo Canyon Fires in Colorado Springs in the summer of 2012, a day did not pass without people pointing to the mountain range. It was next to impossible to avoid looking in the direction they were pointing, and not just because of the smoke coming from the mountains. We seem to have a commanding urge to do what others are doing, even if it means changing our normal behavior. This tendency to modify our behaviors, attitudes, beliefs, and opinions to match those of others is known as **conformity**. Sometimes we conform to the **norms** or standards of the social environment, such as the group to which we are connected. Unlike compliance, which occurs in response to an explicit and direct request, conformity is generally unspoken. We often conform because we feel compelled to fit in and belong.

It is important to note that conformity is not always a bad thing. We rely on conformity in many cases to ensure the smooth running of day-to-day activities involving groups of people. Imagine how a third-grade classroom would run if it weren't for the human urge to do what others are doing. And what would it be like to check out at Target if none of the customers conformed to common social rules?

STUDYING CONFORMITY Social psychologists have studied conformity in a variety of settings, including American colleges. In a classic experiment by Solomon Asch (1907–1996), college-student participants were asked to sit at a table with six other people, all of whom were confederates working for the researcher (Asch, 1955). The participants were told to look at two cards; the first card had one vertical line on it, the standard line, and the second card had three vertical lines of different lengths, marked 1, 2, and 3 (**FIGURE 15.3**). The group was instructed to look at the two cards and then announce, one at a time going around the table, which of the three lines was closest in length to the standard line, thus making a "visual judgment." The first two rounds of this task went smoothly, with everybody in agreement about which of the three lines matched the standard. But then, in the third round, the first five people (all confederates) offered what was clearly

CONNECTIONS

In **Chapter 9,** we described Maslow's hierarchy of needs, which includes the need to belong. If physiological and safety needs are met, an individual will be motivated by the need for love and belongingness. This need can drive us to conform.

try this ↓

The next time you are outside in a fairly crowded area, look up and keep your eyes toward the sky. You will find that some people change their gazes to match yours, even though there is no other indication that something is happening above.

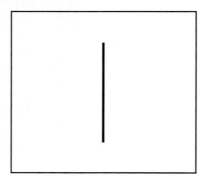
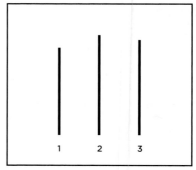

Standard line   Comparison lines

FIGURE 15.3
Asch's Conformity Experiment
Participants in this experiment were asked to look at the lines on two cards, announcing which of the comparison lines was closest in length to the standard line. Imagine you are a participant, like the man wearing glasses in this photo, and everyone else at the table chooses Line 3. Would that influence your answer? If you are like many participants, it would. Seventy-six percent conformed to the incorrect answer at least once. Photo by William Vandivert/Solomon E. Asch, Opinions and Social Pressure, *Scientific American,* Nov. 1955, Vol. 193, No. 5, 31–35.

the wrong answer, one after the other. (Prior to the experiment, the researchers had given the confederates instructions about which line to choose in each trial.)

Would the real participant (the sixth person to answer) follow suit and conform to the wrong answer, or would he stand his ground and report the correct answer? In roughly 37% of these trials, participants went along with the group and provided the incorrect answer. What's more, 76% of the participants conformed and gave the wrong answer at least once (Asch, 1955, 1956). When members of the control group made the same judgments alone in a room, they were correct 99% of the time, confirming that the differences between the standard line and the comparison lines were substantial, and generally not difficult to assess. It is worth noting that most participants (95%) refused to conform on at least one occasion, choosing an answer that conflicted with that of the group (Asch, 1956; Griggs, 2015b). Thus, they were capable of thinking and behaving independently. This type of study was later replicated in a variety of cultures, with mostly similar results (Bond & Smith, 1996).

WHY CONFORM? People do not always conform to the behavior of others, but what factors come into play when they do? There are three major reasons for conformity. Most of us want the approval of others, to be liked and accepted. This desire influences our behavior and is known as *normative social influence.* Just think back to middle school—do you remember feeling pressure to be like some of your classmates or friends? This might have been due to a normative social influence. A second reason we conform is to behave correctly; we look to others for confirmation when we are uncertain about something, and then do as they do. This is known as *informational social influence.* Perhaps you have a friend who is particularly well read in politics, or extremely knowledgeable about psychology. Your tendency is to defer to her expert knowledge. Third, we sometimes conform to others because they belong to a certain *reference group* we respect, admire, or long to join.

Listed below are certain conditions that increase the likelihood of conforming (Aronson, 2012; Asch, 1955):

1. The group includes at least three other people who are unanimous.

2. You have to report your decision in front of others and give your reasons.

3. You are faced with a task you think is difficult.

4. You are unsure of your ability to perform a task.

And here are some conditions that decrease the likelihood of conforming:

1. At least one other person is going against the group with you (Asch, 1955).

2. Group members come from individualist, or "me-centered" cultures, as opposed to collectivistic, or community-centered, cultures (Bond & Smith, 1996).

 *In Class: Collaborate and Report*

You are running a fund-raising drive for public television. How would you get people to donate money? Team up and discuss how you could **A)** manipulate attitudes (cognitive, affective, and behavioral components), **B)** use persuasion to get compliance (foot-in-the-door and door-in-the-face), and **C)** encourage conformity.

When you conform, no one is specifically telling you to do so. But this is not the case with all types of social influence (**TABLE 15.2** on the next page). Let's take a trip to the darker side and explore the frightening phenomenon of obedience.

CONNECTIONS

In **Chapter 1,** we explained that a control group in an experiment is not exposed to the treatment variable. In this case, the control group is not exposed to the confederates giving incorrect answers.

conformity The urge to modify behaviors, attitudes, beliefs, and opinions to match those of others.

norms Standards of the social environment.

TABLE 15.2 CONCEPTS OF SOCIAL INFLUENCE

Concept	Definition	Example
Persuasion	Intentionally trying to make people change their attitudes and beliefs, which may or may not lead to their behavior changing	Trust our product because it is the best on the market.
Compliance	Voluntarily changing behavior at the request or direction of another person or group, who in general does not have any authority over you	Remove your shoes before you walk into the house because you have been asked.
Conformity	The urge to modify our behaviors, attitudes, beliefs, and opinions to match those of others	Remove your shoes before you walk into the house because everyone else who has entered did the same.
Obedience	Changing our behavior because we have been ordered to do so by someone in authority	Follow the detour sign.

Whether or not you realize it, other people constantly shape your thoughts, emotions, and behaviors. Above are some of the key types of social influence.

Child Exploitation

A young boy wields a Kalashnikov rifle near Kampala, Uganda. He is among the tens of thousands of children who have been exploited by military groups in Uganda. Julius was just 12 years old when he was abducted by the Lord's Resistance Army (LRA) and forced to fight and plunder on the group's behalf. Dominique Aubert/AFP/Getty Images.

CONNECTIONS

In **Chapter 14,** we introduced the concept of transference, a reaction some clients have to their therapists. A client demonstrating transference responds to the therapist as if dealing with a parent, or other important caregiver from childhood; this may include behaving more childlike and obedient.

BOY SOLDIERS During Uganda's two-decade civil war, the Lord's Resistance Army (LRA) is said to have kidnapped some 66,000 youths. Scholars have estimated that 20% of male victims did not make it home (Annan, Blattman, & Horton, 2006). Julius came dangerously close to losing his life during a village raid that he and other child soldiers were forced to conduct. His boss ordered him to shoot a man who refused to hand over a chicken, but Julius would not pull the trigger. Had the boss not come from Julius' home village, the punishment probably would have been death. Instead, Julius received a beating that rendered him incapable of sitting for a week.

While a captive of the LRA, Julius witnessed other boy soldiers assaulting innocent people and stealing property. Sometimes at the end of the day, they would laugh or brag about how many people they had beaten or killed. But these were just "normal" boys from the villages, children who never would have behaved this way under regular circumstances. And some showed clear signs of regret. Julius remembers seeing other child soldiers cry alone at night after returning to the camp when there was time to reflect on what they had done.

How do you explain this tragedy? What drives an ordinary child to commit senseless violence? A psychologist might tell you it has something to do with *obedience*. ●

Obedience

LO 7   Describe obedience and explain how Stanley Milgram studied it.

One of the most disconcerting types of social influence is **obedience**, which occurs when we change our behavior, or act in a way we might not normally act, because we have been ordered to do so by an authority figure. In these situations, an imbalance of power exists, and the person with more power (for example, a teacher, police officer, doctor, or boss) generally has an advantage over someone with less power, who is likely to be obedient out of respect, fear, or concern. In some cases, the person in charge demands obedience for the well-being of those less powerful (a father demanding obedience from a child running wildly through a crowded store). Other times, the person wielding power demands obedience for his own benefit (an adult who perpetrates sexual abuses against children).

THIS WILL *SHOCK* YOU: MILGRAM'S STUDY Back in the 1960s, psychologist Stanley Milgram (1933–1984) was interested in determining the extent to which obedience can lead to behaviors that most people would consider unethical. Milgram (1963, 1974) conducted a series of experiments examining how far people would go, particularly in terms of punishing others, when urged to do so by an authority figure. Participants were told the study was about memory and learning (another example of research deception). Overall he included 780 participants, although only 40 of those were women (Martin, 2016). The samples included teachers, salespeople, post office workers, engineers, and laborers, representing a wide range of educational backgrounds, from elementary school dropouts to people with graduate degrees. Milgram conducted 24 variations of his experimental method over the course of one year, starting in the summer of 1961 (Martin, 2016). Described here is a basic outline of the method he used.

Upon arriving at Milgram's Yale University laboratory, participants were informed they would be using punishment as part of a learning experiment. They were then asked to draw a slip of paper from a hat, and led to believe that the slips read either "teacher" or "learner," when in fact both slips read "teacher." Meanwhile, a confederate always played the role of the *learner.* To start, the teacher was asked to sit in the learner's chair so that he could experience a 45-volt shock, just to know what the learner might be feeling. Then the teacher sat at a table that held a control panel for the shock generator. The panel went from 15 volts to 450 volts, and as you can see in **INFOGRAPHIC 15.2** on the next page, this range of voltage was labeled from "slight shock" to "XXX." The goal, the teacher was told, was for the learner to memorize a set of paired words. Each time the learner made a mistake, the teacher was to administer a shock, and the shock was to increase by 15 volts for every mistake. The learner was located in a separate room, arms strapped to a table and electrodes attached to his wrists; the electrodes were reportedly attached to a shock generator.

Troubling Discoveries
A photo of psychologist Stanley Milgram appears on the cover of his biography, *The Man Who Shocked the World: The Life and Legacy of Stanley Milgram (2004),* by Thomas Blass. Milgram's research illuminated the dangers of human obedience. Feeling pressure from authority figures, participants in Milgram's studies were willing to administer what they believed to be painful and life-threatening electric shocks to other human beings (Milgram, 1963). Alexandra Milgram.

The learner (the confederate) did not receive actual shocks, but instead had a script of responses he was to make as the experiment continued. The learner's behaviors, including the mistakes he made with the word pairs and his responses to the increasing shock levels (including mild complaints, screaming, references to his heart condition, pleas for the experiment to stop, and total silence as if he were unconscious or even dead), were identical for all participants. A researcher in a white lab coat (also a confederate with scripted responses) always remained in the room with the teacher, and he was insistent that the experiment proceed if the teacher began to question going any further given the learner's responses (such as "Experimenter, get me out of here. . . . I refuse to go on" or "I can't stand the pain"; Milgram, 1965, p. 62). The researcher would say to the teacher, "Please continue" and "You have no other choice, you *must* go on" (Milgram, 1963, p. 374).

How many participants do you think obeyed the researcher and proceeded with the experiment in spite of the learner's desperate pleas? Before the experiment, Milgram asked a variety of people (including psychiatrists and students) to predict how many teachers would obey the researcher. Many believed that the participants would refuse to continue at some point in the experiment. Most of the psychiatrists, for example, predicted that only 0.125% of participants would continue to the highest voltage (Milgram, 1965). They also guessed that the majority of the participants would quit the experiment when the learner began his protests.

Here's what actually happened: 60% to 65% of participants continued to the highest voltage level (Martin, 2016). Most of these participants were obviously not

obedience Changing behavior because we have been ordered to do so by an authority figure.

Milgram's Shocking Obedience Study

Stanley Milgram's study on obedience and authority was one of the most ground-breaking and surprising experiments in all of social psychology. Milgram wanted to test the extent to which we will follow the orders of an authority figure. Would we follow orders to hurt someone else, even when that person was begging us to stop? Milgram's experiment also raises ethical issues about deception and informed consent.

Participants had to actually think they were shocking another person for the experiment to work. Creating this deception involved the use of confederates (people secretly working for the researchers) whose behaviors and spoken responses were carefully scripted. Milgram found high levels of obedience in his participants—much higher than he and others had predicted at the beginning of the study.

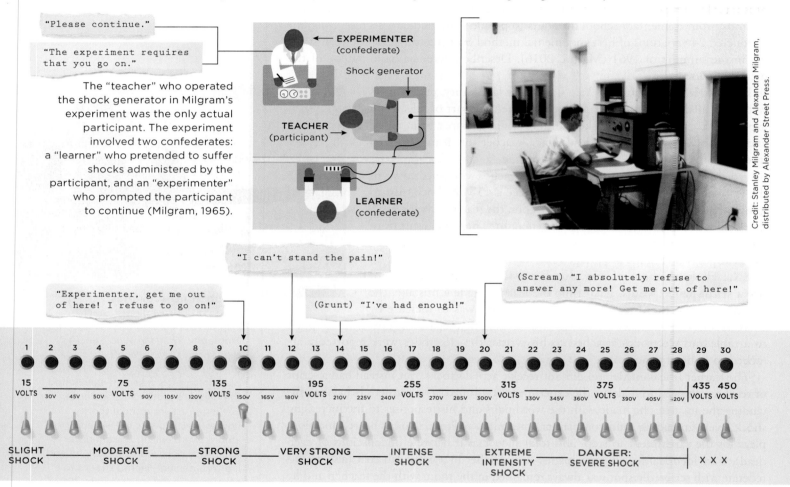

"Please continue."

"The experiment requires that you go on."

EXPERIMENTER (confederate)

Shock generator

The "teacher" who operated the shock generator in Milgram's experiment was the only actual participant. The experiment involved two confederates: a "learner" who pretended to suffer shocks administered by the participant, and an "experimenter" who prompted the participant to continue (Milgram, 1965).

TEACHER (participant)

LEARNER (confederate)

Credit: Stanley Milgram and Alexandra Milgram, distributed by Alexander Street Press.

"I can't stand the pain!"

(Scream) "I absolutely refuse to answer any more! Get me out of here!"

"Experimenter, get me out of here! I refuse to go on!"

(Grunt) "I've had enough!"

| 1 | 2 | 3 | 4 | 5 | 6 | 7 | 8 | 9 | 10 | 11 | 12 | 13 | 14 | 15 | 16 | 17 | 18 | 19 | 20 | 21 | 22 | 23 | 24 | 25 | 26 | 27 | 28 | 29 | 30 |

| 15 VOLTS | 30V | 45V | 50V | 75 VOLTS | 90V | 105V | 120V | 135 VOLTS | 150V | 165V | 180V | 195 VOLTS | 210V | 225V | 240V | 255 VOLTS | 270V | 285V | 300V | 315 VOLTS | 330V | 345V | 360V | 375 VOLTS | 390V | 405V | 420V | 435 VOLTS | 450 VOLTS |

SLIGHT SHOCK — MODERATE SHOCK — STRONG SHOCK — VERY STRONG SHOCK — INTENSE SHOCK — EXTREME INTENSITY SHOCK — DANGER: SEVERE SHOCK — X X X

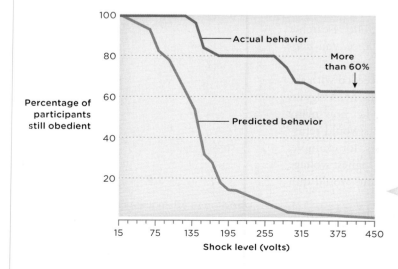

Percentage of participants still obedient

- 100
- 80
- 60
- 40
- 20

Actual behavior

More than 60%

Predicted behavior

15 75 135 195 255 315 375 450

Shock level (volts)

On the control panel of Milgram's shock generator, the participant would see 30 switches clearly labeled as delivering a range from "Slight shock" (15 volts) to "Danger: Severe shock" (375 volts) and beyond. The "learner" produced scripted responses at every level (Milgram, 1963).

Before the experiment, Milgram and a panel of experts predicted most participants would not proceed beyond 150 volts, when the "learner" explicitly demands to end the experiment. In fact, actual results show that most participants obeyed the experimenter's commands all the way to the highest shock level. (DATA FROM MILGRAM, 1965.)

comfortable with what they were doing (stuttering, sweating, trembling), yet they continued. Even those who eventually refused to proceed went much further than anyone (even Milgram himself) had predicted—they all used shocks up to at least 300 volts, labeled as "Intense Shock" (Milgram, 1963, 1964; Infographic 15.2).

We should emphasize that participants were not necessarily comfortable with their role as teachers. One person who witnessed the study reported the following: "I observed a mature and initially poised businessman enter the laboratory smiling and confident. Within 20 minutes he was reduced to a twitching, stuttering wreck, who was rapidly approaching a point of nervous collapse" (Milgram, 1963, p. 377).

REPLICATING MILGRAM This type of research has been replicated in the United States and in other countries, and the findings have remained fairly consistent, with 61–66% of participants continuing to the highest level of shock (Aronson, 2012; Blass, 1999). Not surprisingly, the criticisms of Milgram's studies were strong (Martin, 2016). Many were concerned that this research went too far with its deception (it would certainly not receive approval from an Institutional Review Board today), and some wondered if the participants were harmed by knowing that they theoretically could have killed someone with their choices during the study. Milgram (1964) spent time with participants following the study, and reported that 84% claimed they were "glad" they had participated, while only 1.3% reported they were "sorry" to have been involved. The participants were seen for psychiatric evaluations a year later, and reports indicate that none of them "show[ed] signs of having been harmed by his experiences" (Milgram, 1964, p. 850). Criticisms of Milgram's research remain strong today, with some questioning his representation of the "seriously inadequate debriefing process," "extended prodding of participants" to continue the experiment, and "selective nonreporting" of several of his 23 studies (Griggs & Whitehead, 2015, p. 315).

Milgram and others have followed up on the original study, to determine if there were specific factors or characteristics that made it more likely someone would be obedient in this type of scenario (Blass, 1991; Burger, 2009; Martin, 2016; Milgram, 1965). Several key factors determined whether participants were obedient in these studies: (1) the legitimacy of the authority figure (the more legitimate, the more obedience demonstrated by participants); (2) the physical proximity of the authority figure (the closer the experimenter was to participants, the higher their level of obedience); (3) the proximity of the learner (the closer the learner, the less obedient the participant); and (4) the presence of other teachers (if another confederate was acting as an obedient teacher, the participant was more likely to obey as well).

 **In Class: Collaborate and Report**

The experiments conducted by Asch and Milgram show how difficult it is to resist conforming and obeying authority. Team up and identify four people who have successfully resisted the urge to conform and/or be obedient.

Milgram's initial motivation for studying obedience came from learning about the horrific events of World War II and the Holocaust, which "could only have been carried out on a massive scale if a very large number of people obeyed orders" (Milgram, 1974, p. 1). And his experiments seem to support this suggestion. One ray of hope did shine through in his later experiments; participants responded differently when they saw others refuse to obey. In one follow-up experiment, two more confederates were included in the study as additional teachers. If these confederates showed signs of refusing to obey the authority figure, the research participant was far less likely to cooperate. In fact, Milgram (1974) reported that in this type of setting, only 10% of

CONNECTIONS

In **Chapter 1,** we reported that professional organizations have specific guidelines to ensure ethical treatment of research participants. They include doing no harm, safeguarding welfare, and respecting human dignity. An Institutional Review Board also ensures the well-being of participants.

the research participants were willing to carry on with the learning experiment. What this suggests is that one person can make a difference, and when someone stands up for what is right, others will follow that lead.

show what you know

1. Match each definition below with its corresponding term:
   a. how a person is affected by others
   b. intentionally trying to make people change their attitudes
   c. a person voluntarily changes behavior at the request of someone without authority
   d. someone asks for a small request, followed by a larger request
   e. the urge to modify behaviors, attitudes, and beliefs to match those of others

   _____ conformity   _____ persuasion

   _____ compliance   _____ foot-in-the-door technique

   _____ social influence

2. _____ occurs when we change our behavior, or act in a way we might not normally, because we have been ordered to do so by an authority figure.
   a. Persuasion   c. Conformity
   b. Compliance   d. Obedience

3. Can you think of an everyday example in which someone successfully resisted the urge to conform?

   ✓ CHECK YOUR ANSWERS IN APPENDIX C.

Groups and Relationships

Thus far, the primary focus of this chapter has been individuals in social situations. We learned, for example, how people process information about others (social cognition) and how behavior is shaped by social interactions (social influence). But human beings do not exist solely as isolated units. When striving toward a common goal, we often come together in groups, and these groups have their own fascinating social dynamics.

LET'S DO THIS TOGETHER The most important competition of Julius Achon's career was probably the 1994 World Junior Championships in Portugal. Julius was 17 at the time, and he represented Uganda in the 1,500 meters. It was his first time flying on an airplane, wearing running shoes, and racing on a rubber track. No one expected an unknown boy from Uganda to win, but Julius surprised everyone, including himself. Crossing the finish line strides ahead of the others, he almost looked uncertain as he raised his arms in celebration.

Julius ran the 1,500 meters (the equivalent of 0.93 miles) in approximately 3 minutes and 40 seconds. Do you suppose he would have run this fast if he had been alone? Research suggests the answer is no (Worringham & Messick, 1983). In some situations, people perform better in the presence of others. This is particularly true when the task at hand is uncomplicated (running) and the individual is well prepared (runners may spend months training for races). Thus, **social facilitation** can improve personal performance when the activity is fairly straightforward and the person is adequately prepped.

Sometimes other "people" don't have to be present and watching for social facilitation to work. In one study, researchers demonstrated that the presence of

Faster Together?
Athletes compete in the 5,000-meter T54 event of the 2016 Paralympics in Rio. Through social facilitation, competitive athletes may help each other perform better. Some research suggests that racers may actually synchronize their body movements at various points in time, without even being aware of it (Varlet & Richardson, 2015). Do you think this synchronization would help or hinder a racer's performance? Kyodo via AP Images.

competitive avatars (graphical representations of people) made some participants put forth a greater effort in a cycling activity (Anderson-Hanley, Snyder, Nimon, & Arciero, 2011). ●

When Two Heads Are Not Better Than One

Being around other people does not always provide a performance boost, however. Learning or performing difficult tasks may actually be harder in the presence of others (Aiello & Douthitt, 2001), and group members may not put forth their best effort. When individual contributions to the group aren't easy to ascertain, **social loafing** may occur (Latané, Williams, & Harkins, 1979). Social loafing is the tendency for people to make less than their best effort when individual contributions are too complicated to measure. Many students will shy away from working in groups because of the negative experiences they have had with other group members' social loafing. What types of attributions do you think most people make about others who seem to be social loafers? (*Hint:* Remember the fundamental attribution error.)

Social loafing often goes hand-in-hand with **diffusion of responsibility**, or the sharing of duties and responsibilities among all group members. Diffusion of responsibility can lead to feelings of decreased accountability and motivation. If we suspect other group members are slacking, we tend to follow suit in order to keep things equal.

CUT THE LOAFING Want some advice on how to reduce social loafing? Even if an instructor doesn't require it, you should try to get other students in your group to designate and take responsibility for specific tasks, have group members submit their part of the work to the group before the assignment is due, and specify their contributions to the end product (Jones, 2013; Maiden & Perry, 2011). If possible, use video conferencing technologies such as Skype or Google Hangouts to work together, as this type of collaboration may encourage group members to do their part. Keep in mind that social loafing is less likely to occur when the assignment is challenging and group members feel they have something special to contribute (Simms & Nichols, 2014). If you do have some "free riders" in your group, don't automatically assume they are lazy or apathetic. Some group members fail to pull their weight because they feel incompetent (perhaps a result of language difficulties), or they are not "team players" (Barr, Dixon, & Gassenheimer, 2005; Hall & Buzwell, 2012). Communicate with these individuals early in the process, and work with your group to identify a task that each person can perform with confidence and success.

ACROSS THE WORLD
Slackers of the West

 It turns out that social loafing is more likely to occur in societies where people place a high premium on individuality and autonomy. These *individualistic* societies include the United States, Western Europe, and other parts of the Western world. In the *collectivistic* cultures of China and other parts of East Asia, people tend to prioritize community over the individual, and social loafing is less likely to occur. Group members from these more community-oriented societies actually show evidence of working harder (Kerr & Tindale, 2004; Smrt & Karau, 2011). And unlike their individualistic counterparts, they are less interested in outshining their comrades. Preserving group harmony is more important (Tsaw, Murphy, & Detgen, 2011).

TRAVELING TO EAST ASIA? YOU MAY WANT TO LEAVE YOUR EGO AT HOME.

social facilitation The tendency for the presence of others to improve personal performance when the task or event is fairly uncomplicated and a person is adequately prepared.

social loafing The tendency for group members to put forth less than their best effort when individual contributions are too complicated to measure.

diffusion of responsibility The sharing of duties and responsibilities among all group members that can lead to feelings of decreased accountability and motivation.

Mine for the Taking

A classic study by Diener and colleagues found that children were most likely to swipe Halloween candy and coins when they were anonymous group members. The condition of being anonymous and part of a group seemed to create a state of deindividuation (Diener, Fraser, Beaman, & Kelem, 1976). samantha grandy/ Shutterstock.

CONNECTIONS

In **Chapter 1,** we discussed a type of descriptive research that involves studying participants in their natural environments. Naturalistic observation requires that the researcher not disturb the participants or their environment. Would Diener's study be considered naturalistic observation?

CONNECTIONS

What motivated the children who were alone? In **Chapter 9,** we discussed various sources of motivation, ranging from instincts to the need for power. These sources of motivation might help explain why some children took more than their fair share of candy when they thought no one was watching.

Nothing in psychology is ever that simple, however. Social loafing may be less common in collectivist cultures, but it certainly happens (Hong, Wyer, & Fong, 2008). And within every "individualistic" or "collectivistic" society are individuals who do not behave according to these generalities (Marcus & Le, 2013). We should also point out that many group tasks require both individual and shared efforts; in these situations, a combination of individualism and collectivism may lead to more successful outcomes (Wagner, Humphrey, Meyer, & Hollenbeck, 2012). 🌐➤

DEINDIVIDUATION In the last section, we discussed how obedience played a role in the senseless violence carried out by boy soldiers in Uganda. We suspect that the actions of these children also had something to do with *deindividuation.* People in groups sometimes feel a diminished sense of personal responsibility, inhibition, or adherence to social norms. This state of **deindividuation** can occur when group members are not treated as individuals, and thus begin to exhibit a "lack of self-aware-ness" (Diener, 1979). As members of a group, the boy soldiers may have felt a loss of personal identity, social responsibility, and ability to discriminate right from wrong.

Research suggests that children are indeed vulnerable to deindividuation. In a classic study of trick-or-treaters, psychologist Ed Diener (1946–) and his colleagues set up a study in 27 homes throughout Seattle, Washington. Children arriving at these houses to trick-or-treat were ushered in by a woman (who was a confederate, of course). She told them they could take *one* piece of candy, which was on a table in a bowl. Next to the bowl of candy (about 2 feet away) was a second bowl full of small coins (pennies and nickels). The woman then excused herself, saying she had to get back to work in another room. What the children didn't know was that an experimenter was observing their behavior through a peephole, tallying up the amount of candy and/or money they took. The other variable being recorded was the number of children and adults in the hallway; remember, the experimenters never knew how many people would show up when the doorbell rang!

The findings were fascinating. If a parent was present, the children were well be-haved (only 8% took more than their allotted one piece of candy). But with no adult present, children acted quite differently. Of the children who came through the door alone and anonymous (the confederate did not ask for names or other identifying information), 21% took more than they should have. By comparison, 80% of the children who were in a group and anonymous took extra candy and/or money. The researchers suggested that the condition of being in a group combined with anonymity created a sense of deindividuation (Diener, Fraser, Beaman, & Kelem, 1976). Are you wondering how much money and candy the kids took? It seems that the children who took more than their fair share of candy grabbed as much as their hands could hold (between 1.6 and 2.3 extra candy bars, on average). As for the money, around 14% of the children stole coins (and ignored the candy), while nearly 21% took both money and extra candy.

We have shown how deindividuation occurs in groups of children, but what about adults? Perhaps you have heard about "Bedlam," a football game between archrival teams from the University of Oklahoma (OU) and Oklahoma State University (OSU). Most years, OU has won, but in 2011, OSU beat OU 44–10. This was the first time in the university's history it captured a Big 12 championship, and the first time it had beaten OU in 9 years. With just a few seconds left, thousands of OSU fans stormed the field, tearing down the goalposts and injuring several people in the celebration. Even after an announcement instructing fans to stay off the field, hordes of people charged forward, some of them laughing. They showed virtually no regard for the safety of oth-ers. The fans' impulsive behavior seemed to be a result of deindividuation. This type of behavior has been repeated in many settings and with many groups of people. Why can't we learn to make better decisions when we find ourselves in groups? Unfortunately, people have a tendency to act in rash and extreme ways when surrounded by others.

RISKY SHIFT Imagine you have $250,000 to spend for your company. Will you spend more if you're making decisions alone or working as part of a committee? Researcher James A. F. Stoner (1961, 1968) set out to find the answer to this question, and here's what he discovered: When group members were asked to make a unanimous decision on how to spend the money, they were more likely to recommend uncertain and risky options than individuals working alone, a phenomenon known as the **risky shift.**

GROUP POLARIZATION AND GROUP-THINK When people with similar beliefs are assembled in a group, they tend to reinforce each other's positions. **Group polarization** is the tendency for a group to take a more extreme stance after deliberations and discussion (Myers & Lamm, 1976). Suppose you bring together several individuals who strongly support the legalization of marijuana. As they hear their opinions echoed by other members of the group, the conversation tends to become more extreme, as the new information reinforces and strengthens their original positions. So is group deliberation actually useful? Perhaps not when the members are initially in agreement.

Thinking Inside the Box
When group members become increasingly unified, frequently reaching agreement but seldom questioning each other, groupthink has probably taken hold. S. Harris/ Cartoonstock.

deindividuation The diminished sense of personal responsibility, inhibition, or adherence to social norms that occurs when group members are not treated as individuals.

risky shift The tendency for groups to recommend uncertain and risky options.

group polarization The tendency for a group to take a more extreme stance than originally held after deliberations and discussion.

groupthink The tendency for group members to maintain cohesiveness and agreement in their decision making, failing to consider possible alternatives and related viewpoints.

As a group becomes increasingly united, another group process known as **groupthink** can occur. This is the tendency for group members to maintain cohesiveness and agreement in their decision making, failing to consider possible alternatives and related viewpoints (Janis, 1972; Rose, 2011). Groupthink is thought to have played a role in a variety of disasters, including the 1912 Titanic disaster, the Challenger space shuttle explosion in 1986, the Mount Everest climbing tragedy in 1996, and the U.S. decision to invade Iraq in 2003 (Badie, 2010; Burnette, Pollack, & Forsyth, 2011).

As you can see, groupthink can have life-or-death consequences. So, too, can the bystander effect, another alarming phenomenon that occurs among people in groups.

Casualties of the Bystander Effect
Kitty Genovese (top) and Hugo Tale-Yax (bottom) lived in different eras, but both were victims of brutal assaults and the cold indifference of bystanders in New York City. Genovese and Tale-Yax might have survived if those who saw them in distress had done more to help. (Top) NY Daily News Archive via Getty Images; (bottom) Christopher Sadowski/Splash News/Newscom.

bystander effect The tendency for people to avoid getting involved in an emergency they witness because they assume someone else will help.

THE BYSTANDER WHO REFUSED TO STAND BY

Before meeting Julius in 2003, the orphans spent their days begging for money and searching for food. Usually, they ate food scraps that hotels had poured onto side roads for dogs and cats. Every morning, it was the same routine: Wake up, split apart, and search for something to eat, with no time for teamwork or group strategizing. But the orphans did help each other when possible, explains Samuel ("Sam") Mugisha, one of the older kids in the original 11. At night, they kept each other warm coiled beneath the bus, and they shared food when there was enough to go around. The older children looked after the little ones, making sure they had something to eat. The orphans leaned on one another, but they didn't get much assistance from the outside world.

Day after day, they encountered hundreds of passersby. But of all those people, only three or four would typically offer food or money, nothing more—until a thin, muscular man in his mid-twenties appeared wearing the most unusual outfit. Dressed in a sleeveless top (a runner's singlet), short shorts, and fancy sneakers, Julius Achon looked different from any person the orphans had seen before. And he was, of course, different. This man would ultimately ensure the orphans had everything they needed for a chance at a better life—food, clothing, a place to sleep, an education, and a family. ●

LO 8 Recognize the circumstances that influence the occurrence of the bystander effect.

THE BYSTANDER EFFECT Before meeting Julius, the orphans had been homeless for several months. Why didn't anyone try to rescue them? "Everybody was fearing responsibility," Julius says. In northern Uganda, many people cannot even afford to feed themselves, so they are reluctant to lend a helping hand.

But perhaps there was another factor at work, one that psychologists call the **bystander effect.** When a person is in trouble, bystanders have the tendency to assume (and perhaps wish) that someone else will help—and therefore they stand by and do nothing, partly a result of the *diffusion of responsibility.* This is particularly true when there are many other people present. Strange as it seems, we are more likely to aid a person in distress if no one else is around (Darley & Latané, 1968; Eagly & Crowley, 1986; Latané & Darley, 1968). So when people encountered the 11 orphans begging on the street, they probably assumed and hoped somebody else would take care of the problem. *These children must belong to someone; their parents will come back for them.*

Perhaps the most famous illustration of the bystander effect is the often-told story of the Kitty Genovese attack. It was March 13, 1964, around 3:15 A.M. when Catherine "Kitty" Genovese arrived home from work in her Queens, New York, neighborhood. As she approached her apartment building, an attacker brutally stabbed her. Kitty screamed for help, but initial reports suggested that no one came to her rescue. The attacker ran away, and Kitty stumbled to her apartment building. But he soon returned, raping and stabbing her to death. *The New York Times* originally reported that 38 neighbors heard her cries for help, witnessed the attack, and did nothing to assist. But the evidence suggests that there were far fewer eyewitnesses (perhaps only a half dozen), and that several people did respond (by screaming out their windows, with at least one person calling the police). What's more, the second attack occurred inside her building, where few people could have witnessed it (Griggs, 2015c; Manning, Levine, & Collins, 2007). The attacker Winston Moseley was a serial killer and necrophiliac (sexually attracted to corpses). After spending approximately 52 years behind bars, he died March 28, 2016, in prison (McFadden, 2016, April 4).

TABLE 15.3 WHY LEND A HAND?

Why People Help	Explanation
Kin selection	We are more likely to help those who are close relatives, as it might promote the survival of our genes (Alexander, 1974; Hamilton, 1964).
Empathy	We assist others to reduce their distress (Batson & Powell, 2003).
Social exchange theory	We help when the benefits of our good deeds outweigh the costs (Thibaut & Kelly, 1959).
Reciprocal altruism	We help those whom we believe can return the favor in the future (Trivers, 1971).
Mood	We tend to help others when our mood is good, but we also help when our spirits are low, knowing that this behavior can improve our mood (Batson & Powell, 2003; Schnall, Roper, & Fessler, 2010).

There are many reasons people assist each other in times of need. Above are some common explanations.

More recently, in April 2010, a homeless man (also in Queens) was left to die after several people walked by him and decided to do nothing. The man, Hugo Tale-Yax, had been trying to help a woman under assault, but the attacker stabbed him in the chest (Livingston, Doyle, & Mangan, 2010, April 25). As many as 25 people walked past Mr. Tale-Yax as he lay on the ground dying, and one even took a cell phone picture of him before walking away. Can you think of any reason they wouldn't help? Would you help someone in such a situation? The bystander effect can even happen online. In one study, only one-third of students surveyed reported that they came to the aid of cyberbullying victims (Olenik-Shemesh, Heiman, & Eden, 2015).

A review of the research suggests that things might not be as "bleak" as these events suggest. In extremely dangerous situations, bystanders are actually *more* likely to help even if there is more than one person watching. More dangerous situations are recognized and interpreted quickly as being such, leading to faster intervention and help (Fischer et al., 2011). If we want to increase the likelihood of bystanders getting involved in stopping violence, the community needs to educate its members about their responsibilities as neighbors and help them become more confident in their ability to help (Banyard & Moynihan, 2011). Take a look at **TABLE 15.3** to learn about factors that increase helping behavior.

 show what you know

1. _____ is the tendency for people to not react in an emergency, often thinking that someone else will step in to help.
   a. Group polarization
   c. The bystander effect
   b. The risky shift
   d. Deindividuation

2. In an experiment studying _____, trick-or-treating children were more likely to take extra candy and/or money if they were anonymous members of a group.

3. Group polarization is the tendency for a group to take a more extreme stance after deliberations and discussion. If you were part of a group making an important decision, what would you tell the other members about group polarization and how to guard against it?

✓ CHECK YOUR ANSWERS IN APPENDIX C.

Aggression

THE ULTIMATE INSULT When Julius attended high school in Uganda's capital city of Kampala, he never told his classmates that he had been kidnapped by the LRA. "I would not tell them, or anybody, that I was a child soldier," he says. Had the other students known, they might have called him a *rebel*—one of the most derogatory terms you can use to describe a person in Uganda. Calling someone a rebel is like saying that individual is worthless. "You're poor; you do not know anything; you're a killer," Julius says. "It's the same pain as in America [when] they used to call Black people 'nigger.' You feel that kind of pain inside you . . . when they call you a 'rebel' within your country." ●

LO 9 **Demonstrate an understanding of aggression and identify some of its causes.**

Using racial slurs and hurling threatening insults is a form of *aggression*. Psychologists define **aggression** as intimidating or threatening behavior or attitudes intended to hurt someone. Like any phenomenon studied in psychology, aggression results from an interplay of biology and environment. According to the **frustration–aggression hypothesis**, we can all exhibit aggressive behavior when placed in a frustrating situation (Dollard, Miller, Doob, Mowrer, & Sears, 1939). But aggressive tendencies also seem to be rooted in our genes. Studies comparing identical and fraternal twins suggest that aggression may run in families. Identical twins, who have nearly all the same genes, are more likely than fraternal twins to share aggressive traits (Bezdjian, Tuvblad, Raine, & Baker, 2011; Porsch et al., 2016; Rowe, Almeida, & Jacobson, 1999). Some research on identical twins suggests that approximately 50% of aggressive behavior can be explained by genetic factors (DiLalla, 2002; Tackett, Waldman, & Lahey, 2009). Hormones and neurotransmitters also appear to play a role, with high levels of testosterone and low levels of serotonin correlating with aggression (Glenn, Raine, Schug, Gao, & Granger, 2011; Montoya, Terburg, Bos, & van Honk, 2012).

The way we express our aggression may be influenced by our gender. Men tend to show more *direct aggression* (physical displays of aggression such as hitting), while women are more likely to engage in *relational aggression*—behaviors such as gossip, exclusion, and ignoring, which are indirect and aimed at relationships (Ainsworth & Maner, 2012; Archer, 2004; Archer & Coyne, 2005; Crick & Grotpeter, 1995). Why would women show a tendency toward relational aggression as opposed to direct aggression? One reason, according to the evolutionary perspective, is that females run a greater risk of bodily injury resulting from a physical confrontation (Campbell, 1999).

Gender disparities in aggressive behavior typically appear early in life (Card, Stucky, Sawalani, & Little, 2008; Hanish, Sallquist, DiDonato, Fabes, & Martin, 2012, September), and result from a complex interaction of genetics and environmental factors (Brendgen et al., 2005; Rowe, Maughan, Worthman, Costello, & Angold, 2004). As mentioned, high levels of testosterone have been linked to aggression, and men have more testosterone than women. Social and cultural factors also play a role. Boys tend to be more aggressive when raised in nonindustrial societies; patriarchal societies, in which women have less power and are considered inferior to men; and polygamous societies, in which men can have more than one wife. Evolutionary psychology would suggest that competition for resources (including females) increases the likelihood of aggression (Wood & Eagly, 2002).

Stereotypes and Discrimination

Typically, we associate aggression with behavior, but it can also exist in the mind, coloring our *attitudes* about people and things. This is evidenced by the existence of **stereotypes**—the conclusions or inferences we make about people who are different from us, based on their group membership (race, religion, age, or gender, for example).

CONNECTIONS

In previous chapters, we noted that identical twins share 100% of their genetic material at conception, whereas fraternal twins share approximately 50%. Here, we see that identical twins are more likely than fraternal twins to share aggressive traits.

CONNECTIONS

In **Chapter 10,** we described gender differences in aggression, including a variety of causes (such as differences in testosterone levels). Here, we note that environmental factors play a role as well.

Stereotypes are often negative (*Blonde girls are airheads*), but they can also be positive (*Asians are good at math*). It's important to understand that both positive and negative stereotypes can be harmful.

Stereotypes are often associated with a set of perceived characteristics that we think describe members of a group. The stereotypical college instructor is absentminded, absorbed in thought, and unapproachable. The quintessential motorcycle rider is covered in tattoos, and the teenager with the tongue ring is rebelling against her parents. What do all these stereotypes have in common? They are not objective or based on empirical research. In other words, they are like bad theories of personality that characterize people based on isolated behaviors and traits. Stereotypes typically include a variety of predicted behaviors and traits that are rooted in subjective observations and value judgments.

When Julius was living in Louisiana, a man once approached him and said, "Is it true in Africa people still walk [around] naked?" We can only imagine where this man had gathered his knowledge of Africa (perhaps he had spent a bit too much time flipping through dated issues of *National Geographic*), but one thing seems certain: He was relying on an inaccurate stereotype of African people. The underlying message was clearly aggressive; he judged African people to be primitive and not as advanced as he was.

Running Hero
Julius runs by the Lira bus station where he discovered 11 orphans lying under a bus. Despite all the personal struggles Julius faced—living abroad, struggling financially, and battling foreign stereotypes of African people—Julius made a most selfless decision. He and his family adopted all 11 children. Charlie Shoemaker.

LO 10 Recognize how group affiliation influences the development of stereotypes.

GROUPS AND SOCIAL IDENTITY Evolutionary psychologists would suggest that stereotypes allowed human beings to quickly identify the group to which they belonged (Liddle, Shackelford, & Weekes-Shackelford, 2012)—an adaptive trait, given that groups provide safety. But because we tend to think our group is superior, we may draw incorrect conclusions about members of other groups, or outsiders in general. We tend to see the world in terms of the **in-group** (the group to which we belong, or *us*) and the **out-group** (those outside our group, or *them*). For better or worse, our affiliation with an in-group helps us form our **social identity**, or view of ourselves within a social group, and this process begins at a very young age. Those in your in-group may influence your behaviors and thoughts more than you realize.

PREJUDICE People who harbor stereotypes are more likely to feel **prejudice**, hostile or negative attitudes toward individuals or groups (**INFOGRAPHIC 15.3** on the next page). While some would argue racial prejudice has declined in the United States over the last half-century, there is still considerable evidence that negative attitudes persist. The same is true when it comes to sexual orientation, disabilities, and religious beliefs (Carr, Dweck, & Pauker, 2012; Dovidio, Kawakami, & Gaertner, 2002). The causes of prejudice are complex and varied. Cognitive aspects of prejudice include the just-world hypothesis, which assumes that a person has done something to deserve the bad things happening to him, and that he should be able to control the events in his life. Prejudice may also result from conformity, as when a person seeks approval from others with strong prejudicial views.

Researchers have concluded that prejudice can be reduced when people are forced to work together toward a common goal. In the early 1970s, American psychologist Eliot Aronson (1932–) and colleagues developed the notion of a jigsaw classroom. The teachers created exercises that required all students to complete individual tasks, the results of which would fit together like a jigsaw puzzle. The students began to realize the importance of working cooperatively to reach the desired goal. Ultimately, every

aggression Intimidating or threatening behavior or attitudes intended to hurt someone.

frustration–aggression hypothesis Suggests that aggression may occur in response to frustration.

stereotypes Conclusions or inferences we make about people who are different from us based on their group membership, such as race, religion, age, or gender.

in-group The group to which we belong.

out-group People outside the group to which we belong.

social identity How we view ourselves within our social group.

prejudice Holding hostile or negative attitudes toward an individual or group.

Thinking About Other People
Stereotypes, Discrimination, and Prejudice

Attitudes are complex and only sometimes related to our behaviors. Like most attitudes, prejudicial attitudes can be connected with our *cognitions* about groups of people (also known as stereotypes), our negative *attitudes* and *feelings* about others (also referred to as prejudice), and our *behaviors* (discriminating against others). Understanding how and when these pieces connect to each other is an important goal of social psychology. Jane Elliott's classic "Blue Eyes/Brown Eyes" exercise helps demonstrate how stereotypes, discrimination, and prejudice may be connected.

Prejudicial attitude toward others

Cognitive component (beliefs and ideas)

We tend to categorize people in terms of the *in-group* (the group to which we belong) and the *out-group* (people different from us in some way). **Stereotypes** are beliefs or assumptions we hold about people, based on perceived differences we think describe members of their group.

Affective component (emotional evaluation)

Prejudice, or feelings of hostility, anger, or discomfort toward members of out-groups.

Social psychologists often use prejudice to refer to both these negative attitudes and the negative feelings tied to them.

Behavioral component (the way we respond)

Discrimination, or treating others differently because of their affiliation with a group. Can include showing hostility or anger to others, or can be more subtle, such as different body language or tone of voice.

Stereotype

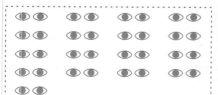

"cleaner, more civilized, smarter"

When Dr. Martin Luther King, Jr., was assassinated in 1968, a teacher named Jane Elliott gave her students a lesson about discrimination. Because no African Americans lived in their Iowa town, she knew students would have trouble understanding what motivated the terrible act. Elliott invited the class to join her in an exercise in which one set of students was segregated into a negatively stereotyped out-group: "Suppose we divided the class into blue-eyed people and brown-eyed people.... [B]rown-eyed people are better than blue-eyed people. They are cleaner . . . more civilized . . . smarter" (Peters, 1971, pp. 20–21).

Prejudice

Prejudice

Discrimination

Brown-eyes dislike blue-eyes, but have to be nice while in class.

Brown-eyes dislike blue-eyes and exclude them from games at recess.

Brown-eyes, who are required to sit at the front of the room, do not sit with blue-eyes, who must sit at the back.

In her exercise, Elliott created a situation in which discrimination initially existed without the presence of actual feelings of hostility or anger. Although prejudice and discrimination often go hand in hand, either condition can exist independently.

Discrimination

Credits: Vintage school desk, Eurobanks,/Shutterstock; B/W photo of students in discrimination lesson, Charlotte Button, Courtesy Jane & Mary Elliott.

During the exercise, a list of rules governed behavior for both groups. For example, only children with brown eyes were allowed to sit at the front of the room near the teacher. The effect of this manufactured discrimination surprised even Elliott. The brown-eyed children quickly became openly hostile toward the blue-eyed children. And "[t]he blue-eyed children were miserable.... [T]heir entire attitudes were those of defeat. Their classroom work regressed sharply from that of the day before" (Peters, 1971, p. 25).

Was Race a Factor?
Retired tennis star James Blake (left) and his "look-alike" (right), both of whom were mistakenly identified as suspects in a fraud case ("CBS2 Exclusive," 2015). In September 2015 Blake was tackled and arrested by a New York City police officer, then released shortly afterward when officers discovered their error (Goodman, 2015, October 7). Did the officer's display of "excessive force" have anything to do with racial prejudice? And why was Blake falsely identified in the first place? Research suggests that we have a harder time recognizing (and thus distinguishing among) faces of people whose race differs from our own; for example, a White person may find it more difficult to differentiate between similar-looking men who are Black, as opposed to White (Wan, Crookes, Reynolds, Irons, & McKone, 2015). (Left) Noam Galai/WireImage/Getty Images.

contribution was an essential piece of the puzzle, and this resulted in all the students feeling valuable (Aronson, 2015).

DISCRIMINATION Seeing the world from the narrow perspective of our own group may lead to **ethnocentrism.** This term is often used in reference to cultural groups, yet it can apply to any group (think of football teams, glee clubs, college rivals, or nations). We tend to see our own country or group as the one that is worthy of emulation, the superior group. This type of group identification can lead to stereotyping, discussed earlier, and **discrimination**, which involves showing favoritism or hostility to others because of their group affiliation.

Those in the out-group are particularly vulnerable to becoming scapegoats. A **scapegoat** is the target of negative emotions, beliefs, and behaviors. During periods of major stress (such as an economic crisis), scapegoats are often blamed for undesirable social situations (high unemployment).

STEREOTYPE THREAT Stereotypes, prejudice, and discrimination are conceptually related to **stereotype threat,** a "situational threat" in which a person is aware of others' negative expectations. This leads to a fear of being judged or treated as inferior, and it can actually undermine performance in a specific area associated with the stereotype (Steele, 1997).

African American college students are often the targets of racial stereotypes about poor academic abilities. These threatening stereotypes can lead to lowered performance on tests designed to measure ability, and to a *disidentification* with the role of a student (in other words, taking on the attitude that *I am not a student*). Interestingly, a person does not have to believe the stereotype is accurate in order for it to have an impact (Steele, 1997, 2010).

There is a great deal of variation in how people react to stereotype threats (Block, Koch, Liberman, Merriweather, & Roberson, 2011). Some people simply "fend off" the stereotype, by working harder to disprove it. Others feel discouraged and respond by getting angry, either overtly or quietly. Still others seem to ignore the threats. These

ethnocentrism Seeing the world only from the perspective of one's own group.

discrimination Showing favoritism or hostility to others because of their affiliation with a group.

scapegoat A target of negative emotions, beliefs, and behaviors; typically, a member of the out-group who receives blame for an upsetting social situation.

stereotype threat A "situational threat" in which individuals are aware of others' negative expectations, which leads to a fear of being judged or treated as inferior.

resilient types appear to "bounce back" and grow from the negative experience. When confronted with a stereotype, they redirect their responses to create an environment that is more inclusive and less conducive to stereotyping.

Unfortunately, stereotypes are pervasive in our society. Just contemplate all the positive and negative stereotypes associated with certain lines of work. Lawyers are greedy, truck drivers are overweight, and (dare we say) psychologists are manipulative. Can you think of any negative stereotypes associated with prison guards? As you read the next feature, think about how stereotypes can come to life when people fail to stop and think about their behaviors.

CONTROVERSIES

The Stanford "Prison"

➤◄ August 1971: Philip Zimbardo (1933–) of Stanford University launched what would become one of the most controversial experiments in the history of psychology. Zimbardo and his colleagues carefully selected 24 male college students to play the roles of prisoners and guards in a simulated "prison" setup in the basement of Stanford University's psychology building. (Three of the selected students did not end up participating, so the final number of participants included 10 prisoners and 11 guards.) The young men chosen for the experiment were deemed "normal-average" by the researchers, who administered several psychological tests (Haney, Banks, & Zimbardo, 1973, p. 90).

> ## "LOOKING BACK, I'M IMPRESSED HOW LITTLE I FELT FOR THEM."

After being "arrested" in their homes by Palo Alto Police officers, the prisoners were searched and booked at a local police station, and then sent to the "prison" at Stanford. The experiment was supposed to last for 2 weeks, but the behavior of some guards and prisoners was so disturbing the researchers abandoned the study after just 6 days (Haney & Zimbardo, 1998). Certain guards became abusive, punishing the prisoners, stripping them naked, and confiscating their mattresses. It seemed as if they had lost sight of the prisoners' humanity, as they ruthlessly wielded their newfound power. As one guard stated, "Looking back, I'm impressed how little I felt for them" (Haney et al., 1973, p. 88). Some prisoners became passive and obedient, accepting the guards' cruel treatment; others were released early due to "extreme emotional depression, crying, rage, and acute anxiety" (p. 81).

How can we explain this fiasco? The guards and prisoners, it seemed, took their assigned **social roles** and ran way too far with them. Social roles represent the positions we hold in social groups, and the responsibilities and expectations associated with those roles. The social roles we adopt guide our behavior.

The prison experiment may have shed light on the power of social roles, but its validity has come under fire. Critics suggest that the participants were merely "acting out their stereotypic images" of guards and prisoners, and behaving in accordance with the researchers' expectations (Banuazizi & Movahedi, 1975, p. 159). As one guard explained decades later, "[Zimbardo] knew what he wanted and then tried to shape the experiment . . . to fit the conclusion that he had already worked out. He wanted to be able to say that . . . people will turn on each other just because they're given a role and given power" (Ratnesar, 2011, July/August, para. 35). Apparently, Zimbardo made his expectations quite clear, instructing the guards to deny the prisoners their "privacy," "freedom," and "individuality" (Zimbardo, 2007). Without this type of guidance from Zimbardo, do you think the study outcome would have been the same? Perhaps not, as "guards" in other prison studies exhibited very different behaviors (Griggs & Whitehead, 2014; Haslam & Reicher, 2012). In the BBC Prison study, for instance, guards were "reluctant to impose their authority"; meanwhile, "prisoners began to mock, challenge, and undermine the guards," and some of them orchestrated a breakout (Haslam & Reicher, 2012, p. 159).

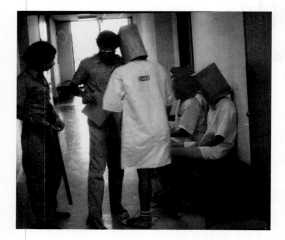

Prison Horrors
(Top) Prisoners in Zimbardo's 1971 prison experiment are forced to wear bags over their heads. In 2003 an Abu Ghraib detainee (bottom) lies on the floor attached to a leash. The dehumanization and cruel treatment of prisoners in the "Stanford Prison" and the Abu Ghraib facility were disturbingly similar. (Top) Philip G. Zimbardo, Inc.; (bottom) AP Photo.

social roles The positions we hold in social groups, and the responsibilities and expectations associated with those roles.

The Stanford Prison Experiment has been criticized for many reasons, including questionable ethics, bias in selecting participants, and failure to adequately explain why participants responded differently to their assigned roles (Griggs, 2014b). Nevertheless, this study continues to be relevant. In 2004 news broke that American soldiers and intelligence officials at Iraq's Abu Ghraib prison had beaten, sodomized, and forced detainees to commit degrading sexual acts (Hersh, 2004, May 10). The similarities between Abu Ghraib and the Stanford Prison are noteworthy (Zimbardo, 2007). In both cases, authority figures threatened, abused, and forced inmates to be naked. Those in charge seemed to derive pleasure from violating and humiliating other human beings (Haney et al., 1973; Hersh, 2004, May 10).

Much of this chapter has focused on the negative aspects of human behavior, such as obedience, stereotyping, and discrimination. While we cannot deny the existence of these phenomena, we believe they are overshadowed by the goodness that lies within every one of us. This positive side of human nature is apparent everywhere in our society, from preschools to prisons.

from the pages of **SCIENTIFIC AMERICAN**

Prisoner's Escape

Yoga practice reduces anxiety and impulsivity in prison populations.

Incarcerated thieves, drug dealers and murderers may not be the typical group you imagine doing yoga, but recent studies show that the ancient discipline might be able to play an important role in reducing prison violence. Several studies have shown that yoga helps to improve symptoms of anxiety and depression in prisoners, and now a study at the University of Oxford has found that it also increases focus and, crucially, decreases impulsivity—a known factor in much prison violence.

The Oxford researchers studied 100 prisoners from seven U.K. prisons. About half the prisoners practiced yoga once a week for 10 weeks; the other half were told they were on a waitlist for the yoga class and encouraged to go about their regular exercise routines. Prisoners in the yoga program—two women and 43 men—became less aggressive toward their fellow inmates and felt less stress, as measured by standard questionnaires. The yogis also performed better than the waitlisted group on a computerized test of executive control, suggesting they had become more attentive to their surroundings and more thoughtful about their actions.

"Attention and impulsivity are very important for this population, which has problems dealing with aggressive impulses," says Oxford psychologist Miguel Farias, one of the study's authors. With less anxiety and aggression, he notes, prisoners should be better able to reintegrate into society when they are released. **Georgia Pike. Reproduced with permission. Copyright © 2014 Scientific American, a division of Nature America, Inc. All rights reserved.**

Prosocial Behavior

LO 11 Describe prosocial behavior and altruism.

We like to believe that all human beings are capable of *prosocial behavior,* or behavior aimed at benefiting others. An exemplar of this ability is Julius Achon. After meeting the orphans in 2003, Julius kept his promise to assist them, wiring his family $150 a month to cover the cost of food, clothing, school uniforms, tuition, and other necessities—even when he and his wife were struggling to stay afloat. For 3 years, Julius was the children's sole source of financial support. Then in 2006, when Julius was living in Portland and working for Nike, a friend helped him gather additional support from others. The following year, Julius formalized his efforts by creating the Achon Uganda Children's Fund (AUCF), a nonprofit organization dedicated to improving the living conditions of children in the rural areas of northern Uganda. One of the AUCF's most important projects is the Kristina Acuma Achon Health Center in Julius' home county

You Asked, Julius Answers

http://qrs.ly/hz5a5gm

What advice would you give to someone interested in charitable work?

scan this →

Beautiful Children
Julius runs alongside boys and girls from the Orum primary school in Uganda's Otuke district. Julius' charitable work and other life experiences are detailed in *The Boy Who Runs*, a new book by John Brant. SAMSON OPUS.

of Otuke. The medical clinic is named after Julius' mother, who was shot by the LRA in 2004 and died from her wounds because she lacked access to proper medical care. It serves approximately 500 people per month and recently began offering pre- and post-natal care, dental services, and HIV treatment. Julius currently lives in Uganda, where he oversees the work of the AUCF and represents his home district in the Ugandan Parliament (similar to the Senate in the United States). For more information about Julius and the AUCF, please go to http://achonugandachildren.org.

As for the 11 orphans, all of them are flourishing. The teenage girl in tattered clothing—the first to emerge from under the bus that morning in 2003—is now a nurse at the Kristina Acuma Achon Health Center. Many of the older children attend a boarding school in Kampala, and Sam Mugisha (mentioned earlier in the chapter) has become a competitive runner like Julius. The other children attend school and remain in the care of Julius and his family.

On the Up Side

It feels good to give to others, even when you receive nothing in return. The satisfaction derived from knowing you made someone feel happier, more secure, or appreciated is enough of a reward. The desire or motivation to help others with no expectations of payback is called **altruism**. *Empathy,* or the ability to understand and recognize another's emotional point of view, is a major component of altruism.

ALTRUISM AND TODDLERS The seeds of altruism appear to be planted very early in life. Children as young as 18 months have been observed demonstrating helping behavior. One study found that the vast majority of 18-month-olds would help a researcher obtain an out-of-reach object, assist him in a book-stacking exercise, and open a door for him when his hands were full. It is important to note the babies did not lend a hand when the researcher intentionally put the object out of reach, or if he appeared satisfied with the stack of books. They only helped when it appeared assistance was needed (Warneken & Tomasello, 2006). What was happening in the brains of these young children? Research demonstrates that particular areas of the brain (such as the medial prefrontal cortex) show increased activity in association with feelings of empathy and helping behaviors (Rameson, Morelli, & Lieberman, 2012). Given that altruism shows up so early in life, perhaps you are wondering if it is innate. Researchers are trying to determine if this characteristic has a genetic component, and the findings from twin studies identify "considerable heritability" of altruistic tendencies and other prosocial behaviors (Jiang, Chew, & Ebstein, 2013). But as always, we must consider the biopsychosocial perspective, recognizing the interaction of genetics, environment, and culture (Knafo & Israel, 2010).

REDUCING STRESS AND INCREASING HAPPINESS Research suggests that helping and showing care for others reduce stress and increase happiness (Cohen, Janicki-Deverts, Turner, & Doyle, 2015; Schwartz, Keyl, Marcum, & Bode, 2009; Schwartz, Meisenhelder, Yunsheng, & Reed, 2003). One's gestures don't have to be grand in order to be altruistic or prosocial. Consider the last time you bought coffee for a colleague without being asked, or gave a stranger a quarter to fill his parking meter. Do you recycle, conserve electricity, and take public transportation? These behaviors

CONNECTIONS

In **Chapter 12,** we discussed how altruistic behaviors can reduce stress. When helping someone else, we generally don't have time to focus on our own problems; we also see that some people deal with issues more troubling than our own.

altruism A desire or motivation to help others with no expectation of anything in return.

indicate an awareness of the need to conserve resources for the benefit of all. Promoting sustainability is an indirect, yet very impactful, prosocial endeavor. Perhaps you haven't opened your home to 11 orphaned children, but you may perform acts of kindness more regularly than you realize.

Even if you're not the type to reach out to strangers, you probably demonstrate prosocial behavior toward your family and close friends. This giving of yourself allows you to experience the most magical element of human existence: love.

 show what you know

1. According to research, which of the following plays a role in aggressive behavior?
   a. low social identity
   b. low levels of the hormone testosterone
   c. low levels of the neurotransmitter serotonin
   d. low levels of ethnocentrism

2. Julius sent money home every month to help cover the cost of food, clothing, and schooling for his 11 adopted children. This is a good example of:
   a. the just-world hypothesis.
   b. deindividuation.
   c. individualistic behavior.
   d. prosocial behavior.

3. Name and describe the different displays of aggression exhibited by males and females.

4. Students often have difficulty identifying how the concepts of stereotype, discrimination, and prejudice are related. If you were conversing with a sixth-grade student, how would you explain their similarities and differences?

✓ CHECK YOUR ANSWERS IN APPENDIX C.

Attraction and Love

You may be wondering why we chose to include Joe and Susanne Maggio in the same chapter as Julius Achon. What do these people have in common, and why are they featured together in a chapter on social psychology? We selected these individuals because their stories send a positive message, illuminating what is best about human relationships, such as the capacity to love and feel empathy. They epitomize the positive side of social psychology.

Interpersonal Attraction

TO HAVE AND TO HOLD Less than a year after meeting Susanne, Joe purchased an engagement ring. He carried it around in his pocket for 3 months, and then proposed to her one morning over breakfast. They have now been happily married for over 8 years. Some things have changed since that rendezvous at Chili's in 2006. Joe left the ice cream business for a corporate career, *little* Kristina is now a teenager, and Susanne gave birth to TRIPLETS in February 2013—two boys and a girl.

Other things remain the same, like Joe's goofy sense of humor. He still strolls into the supermarket singing at the top of his lungs and tells people "good morning" when it's 11 o'clock at night. "I'm a big kid," Joe says, "but you know when it comes to my family, it's all about making sure that they are happy and making sure that they are taken care of, and that's my only priority in life." ●

Love Grows
Joe, Kristina, and Susanne celebrate the arrival of their new family members: Joseph Jr., Michael Charles Frank, and Sophia Elizabeth. The triplets came into the world on February 11, 2013. Joe Maggio.

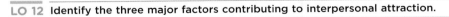

LO 12 **Identify the three major factors contributing to interpersonal attraction.**

It seems Joe and Susanne have made a very happy life for themselves. Things can get hectic with triplet toddlers and a teen, but they appear to be content and able to cope with whatever challenges may arise. Joe and Susanne make a great team. How do you explain their compatibility? We suspect it has something to do with **interpersonal attraction**, the factors that lead us to form friendships or romantic relationships with others. What are these mysterious attraction factors? Let's focus our attention on the three most important: proximity, similarity, and physical attractiveness.

WE'RE CLOSE: PROXIMITY We would guess that the majority of people in your social circle live nearby. **Proximity**, or nearness, plays a significant role in the formation of our relationships. The closer two people live geographically, the greater the odds that they will meet and spend time together, and the more likely they are to establish a bond (Festinger, Schachter, & Back, 1950; Nahemow & Lawton, 1975). One study looking at the development of friendships in a college classroom concluded that sitting in nearby seats and being assigned to the same work groups correlated with the development of friendships (Back, Schmukle, & Egloff, 2008). In other words, sitting next to someone in class, or even in the same row, increases the chances that you will become friends. Would you agree?

Notions of proximity have changed since the introduction of cell phones and the Internet. Thanks to applications like Skype and FaceTime, we can now have face-to-face conversations with people who are thousands of miles away. Dating sites and mobile apps offer similar capabilities through chats, instant messaging, and photo sharing. They also provide the option of geographic filtering, allowing users to narrow their searches to people who live in a certain zip code or city. But do all these new tools really improve the way people relate to one another? For Joe and Susanne, the answer seems to be "yes." If it weren't for Match.com, their paths probably would not have crossed. As for the rest of humanity, the answer is not so straightforward.

SOCIAL MEDIA AND PSYCHOLOGY
Relationships Online

There are several drawbacks to online dating. Browsing through a seemingly endless pool of candidates can be time-consuming and exhausting, and it may not even pay off (Ansari & Klinenberg, 2015, June 13; Finkel, Eastwick, Karney, Reis, & Sprecher, 2016, March 1). You reach out to that interesting woman, but she doesn't respond; or perhaps you finally meet that guy with the dynamite profile, only to find there is no spark in real life. Having a large number of options is not always an advantage. In fact, it might compromise our ability to make sound decisions, because we tend to direct our attention toward superficial features (Finkel et al., 2016, March 1). One of these superficial features—the profile photo—is a major focus of Tinder, a popular mobile dating app. Users swipe right when they see a person they find attractive, left if they are not interested, and those who display mutual approval are given the opportunity to connect. Yet profile photos may not provide reliable clues about someone's personality (Sheikh, 2016, July 1).

Despite these shortcomings, online dating has enabled some people, including Joe and Susanne, to find their soul mates. According to one estimate, a third of American couples that married between 2005 and 2012 met online. Perhaps more interesting, these marriages were slightly less likely than other marriages to end in divorce (Cacioppo, Cacioppo, Gonzaga, Ogburn, & VanderWeele, 2013). Given these successes, it's no surprise that 15% of U.S. adults have tried their luck at online dating (Smith, 2016, February 11).

Relationships that begin online may continue to have an online presence. A first step may be announcing the new relationship on Facebook, but note that "Facebook official" has various interpretations. Women may be more inclined to view it as a sign of "commitment and exclusivity," while some men take it less seriously and continue

LOOKING FOR LOVE IN ELECTRONIC PLACES

When the Swipe Is Right
Chris and SaraJane George are among the many married couples who first met on Tinder. This mobile dating app has a reputation for facilitating casual hookups, but social psychologist Eli J. Finkel of Northwestern University believes it has more potential: "As a psychological researcher who studies online dating, I believe that Tinder's approach is terrific for pursuing casual sex and for meeting a serious relationship partner" (Finkel, 2015, February 6, para. 4). Trent Nelson/ The Salt Lake Tribune via AP.

playing the field (Fox & Warber, 2013, p. 6). Assuming no misunderstandings have occurred, communicating through social media may facilitate bonding, as research suggests that Facebook can serve as "a tool for nurturing relationships" (Burke & Kraut, 2014, p. 8). 🗨

MERE-EXPOSURE EFFECT Repeated interactions with partners, whether online or offline, may bring us closer together through the **mere-exposure effect**. This suggests that the more we are exposed to people, food, jingles, songs, politics, or music, the more positive our reactions to them become. More time spent connecting online can strengthen relationships, *merely* through exposure.

The mere-exposure effect may, to a certain extent, explain why Joe and Susanne are more in love today than they were a decade past. After years of positive exposure to one another (living under the same roof, raising children together, and sharing new experiences), their connection has deepened.

Believe it or not, the mere-exposure effect also appears to affect your perception of your own face. Think of how many times you have looked in the mirror. How do you think that repeated exposure effects your estimation of your attractiveness? In one study, researchers showed students pictures of themselves and the reversed, or mirror image, versions of those pictures. Amazingly, students preferred the reversed image— the one they see every time they look in the mirror—to the "normal" photo. Yet, the opposite was true when the pictures were shown to their friends; they, too, preferred the image they repeatedly see—the normal photo (Mita, Dermer, & Knight, 1977).

But here's the flip side. Repeated *negative* exposures may lead to stronger distaste. If a person you frequently encounter has annoying habits or uncouth behavior, negative feelings might develop, even if your initial impression was positive (Cunningham, Shamblen, Barbee, & Ault, 2005). This can be problematic for romantic partners. All those minor irritations you overlooked early in the relationship can evolve into major headaches.

SIMILARITY Perhaps you have heard the saying "birds of a feather flock together." This statement alludes to the concept of *similarity,* another factor that contributes to interpersonal attraction (Moreland & Zajonc, 1982; Morry, Kito, & Ortiz, 2011). We tend to prefer those who share our interests, viewpoints, race, values, and other characteristics. Even age, education, and occupation tend to be similar among those who are close (Brooks & Neville, 2016; Lott & Lott, 1965). But similarity may have a different impact with speed-dating encounters, as "perceived similarity" seems to be a better predictor of romantic attraction than "actual similarity" in this setting. However, actual similarity may be a better predictor of the longevity of relationships (Tidwell, Eastwick, & Finkel, 2013).

PHYSICAL ATTRACTIVENESS We probably don't need to tell you that *physical attractiveness* plays a major role in interpersonal attraction (Eastwick, Eagly, Finkel, & Johnson, 2011; Lou & Zhang, 2009). Even online, men are more likely to reach out to women they find attractive. Research suggests that profile pictures play a more important role for men when it comes to making initial contact through an online dating site (Eastwick, Luchies, Finkel, & Hunt, 2014). But here is the question: Is beauty really in the eye of the beholder? In other words, do people from different cultures and historical periods have different concepts of beauty? There is some degree of consistency in the way people rate facial attractiveness (Langlois et al., 2000), with facial symmetry generally considered an attractive trait (Boothroyd, Meins, Vukovic, & Burt, 2014; Grammer & Thornhill, 1994). But certain aspects of beauty do appear to be culturally distinct (Gangestad & Scheyd, 2005). In some parts of the world, people go to great lengths to elongate their necks, increase height, pierce their bodies,

interpersonal attraction The factors that lead us to form friendships or romantic relationships with others.

proximity Nearness; plays an important role in the formation of relationships.

mere-exposure effect The more we are exposed to someone or something, the more positive our reaction to it becomes.

Sexy Stubble
Brothers Liam (left) and Chris Hemsworth sport some facial hair at a film premiere in Hollywood. What look do women find most attractive—a face that is cleanly shaven, fully bearded, or somewhere in between? According to research, "heavy stubble" wins the sexiness prize. Full beards, on the other hand, tend to be associated with "parenting ability and healthiness" (Dixson & Brooks, 2013, p. 236). GABRIEL BOUYS/AFP/Getty Images.

augment their breasts, enlarge or reduce the size of their waists, and paint themselves—just so others within their culture will find them attractive. In America, the ideal body shape for women has changed over the years (think of Marilyn Monroe versus Gisele Bündchen), suggesting that cultural concepts of beauty can morph over time.

LOOKING GOOD IN THOSE GENES: THE EVOLUTIONARY PERSPECTIVE Why is physical attractiveness so important? Beauty is a sign of health, and healthy people have greater potential for longevity and successful breeding (Gangestad & Scheyd, 2005). Consider this evidence: Women are more likely to seek out men with healthy-looking physical characteristics when they are experiencing peak fertility and therefore likely to conceive. Ovulating women tend to look for masculine characteristics that suggest a genetic advantage, such as facial symmetry and social dominance, in order to provide the greatest benefit to offspring. Although this type of man can provide good genes, meaning the offspring have a greater chance of being healthy, attractive, and living longer, he might be less likely to stick around and help raise the child.

One group of researchers used this "evolutionary explanation" to explore why women might seek out "sexy cads," or men who are unlikely to take care of their children. Female undergraduate students were asked to participate in what they thought was a study on how their health might influence their mate selection. The women were asked to provide several urine samples to determine when they were ovulating. In one of the research settings, women viewed pictures of men who were physically attractive or average-looking. The physically attractive men were charismatic and adventurous, and the average looking men were reliable, stable, and good providers—or so the women were told. When the women were ovulating, they tended to believe that the "sexy cads" (physically attractive and charismatic men) would actually be more devoted fathers and partners than the "nice," reliable men (Durante, Griskevicius, Simpson, Cantú, & Li, 2012). The implication is that women may choose these "sexy cads" even when it is not in their best interest.

In Class: Collaborate and Report

In your groups, **A)** identify some films that portray women who easily fall for "sexy cads." **B)** Do these stories usually have happy endings? **C)** Would you say Hollywood is accurate in its portrayal of these relationships and their outcomes?

BEAUTY PERKS We have discussed beauty in the context of romantic relationships, but how does physical appearance affect other aspects of social existence? Generally speaking, physically attractive people seem to have more opportunities. Beauty is correlated with how much money someone makes, the type of job she holds, and overall success (Pfeifer, 2012). Good-looking children and adults are viewed as more intelligent and popular, and are treated better in general (Langlois et al., 2000). Why would this be? From the perspective of evolutionary psychology, these characteristics would be good indicators of reproductive potential. And many people fall prey to the *halo effect,* or the tendency to assign excessive importance to one dimension of a person. Early psychologist Edward Thorndike described this concept in 1920 as it related to the evaluation of others. People tend to form these general impressions early on and then cling to them, even in the absence of supporting evidence, or the presence of contradictory evidence (Aronson, 2012). The way we respond to beautiful people is one example of the halo effect; our initial impression of their beauty may lead us to assume they have other positive characteristics like superior intelligence, popularity, and desirability.

romantic love Love that is a combination of connection, concern, care, and intimacy.

passionate love Love that is based on zealous emotion, leading to intense longing and sexual attraction.

companionate love Love that consists of profound fondness, camaraderie, understanding, and emotional closeness.

consummate love Love that combines intimacy, commitment, and passion.

Beauty may captivate you in the beginning stages of a relationship, but other characteristics and qualities gain importance as time goes along. Think about the type of person you want for a life partner. Whom would you want to hold your hand when you're sick in the hospital—the underwear model or the person you most respect and trust?

What Is Love?

In America, we are taught to believe that love is the foundation of marriage. People in Western cultures do tend to marry for love, but this is not the case everywhere. In Harare, Zimbabwe, for example, people might also marry for reasons associated with the needs of the family, such as maintaining alliances and social status (Wojcicki, van der Straten, & Padian, 2010). Similarly, many marriages in India and other parts of South Asia are arranged by family members. Love may not be present in the beginning stages of such unions, but it can blossom.

STERNBERG'S THEORY OF LOVE In a pivotal study published in 1986, Robert Sternberg proposed that love is made up of three elements: passion (feelings leading to romance and physical attraction); intimacy (feeling close); and commitment (the recognition of love). He conceptualized these elements as the corners of a triangle (FIGURE 15.4). Love takes many forms, according to Sternberg, and can include any combination of the three elements.

Many relationships begin with exhilaration and intense physical attraction, and then evolve into more intimate connections. This is the type of love we often see portrayed in the movies. The combination of connection, concern, care, and intimacy is what Sternberg called **romantic love**. Romantic love is similar to what some psychologists refer to as **passionate love** (also known as "love at first sight"), which is based on zealous emotion, leading to intense longing and sexual attraction (Hatfield, Bensman, & Rapson, 2012). As a relationship grows, intimacy and commitment develop into **companionate love**, or love that consists of profound fondness, camaraderie, understanding, and emotional closeness. Companionate love is typical of a couple that has been together for many years. They become comfortable with each other, routines set in, and passion often fizzles (Aronson, 2012). Although the passion may wane, the friendship is strong. **Consummate love** (KON-suh-mit) is evident when intimacy and commitment are accompanied by passion. The ultimate goal is to maintain all three components of the triangle.

Research and life experiences tell us that relationships inevitably change. Romantic love is generally what drives people to commit to one another (Berscheid, 2010). But the passion associated with this stage generally decreases over time. That does not mean it cannot reemerge, however. Can you think of ways this passion might be rekindled—a romantic night out, some sexy new underwear, a trip to fantasyland? Companionate love, in contrast, tends to grow over time. As we experience life with a partner, it is companionate love that seems to endear us to one another (Berscheid, 2010).

What type of love do you think online dating sites tend to select for? Is it companionate love (SF loves to garden, looking for someone who . . .)? Or is it passionate love (SM looking for a good time with no strings attached . . .)? As Joe can attest, passionate love was present from the beginning of his relationship with Susanne (he jokes about taking a few cold showers before anything happened). Although their passion is still strong and steady, the love and respect they have for one another have grown much deeper.

Have you ever wondered about the long-term stability of your relationships? Couples stay together for many reasons, some better than others. Caryl Rusbult's

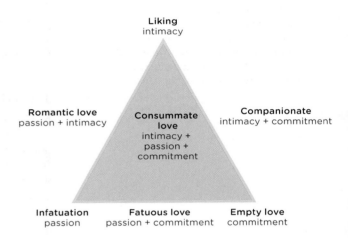

FIGURE 15.4
Sternberg's Triangular Model of Love
Sternberg proposed that there are different kinds of love resulting from a combination of three elements: passion, intimacy, and commitment. The ideal form, consummate love, combines all three elements. Sternberg (1986).

CONNECTIONS

In **Chapter 3,** we discussed sensory adaptation, which refers to the way in which sensory receptors become less sensitive to constant stimuli. In **Chapter 5,** we presented the concept of habituation, which occurs when an organism becomes less responsive to repeated stimuli. Humans seem to be attracted to novelty, which might underlie our desire for passion.

The Honeymoon Continues
After several years of marriage and three more children, the love between Joe and Susanne Maggio is stronger than ever. They have what you might call consummate love, a type of love characterized by intimacy, commitment, and passion. Joseph Maggio.

investment model of commitment focuses on the resources at stake in relationships, including finances, possessions, time spent together, and perhaps even children (Rusbult, 1983). According to this model, decisions to stay together or separate are based on how happy people are in their relationship, their notion of what life would be like without it, and their investment. Sometimes people stay in unsatisfying or unhealthy relationships because they feel they have too much to lose or no better alternatives (Rusbult & Martz, 1995). This helps explain why some people remain in destructive relationships.

The ability to deal with relationship conflicts may depend somewhat on perceptions of what the relationship represents: Do you view your relationship as something that was written in the stars (destined to happen), or more like a long journey you embark upon together (North, 2014, August 1). "It may be romantic for lovers to think they were made for each other, but it backfires when conflicts arise and reality pokes the bubble of perfect unity" (Lee & Schwarz, 2014, p. 64). A better approach may be to consider your love a journey—one that may have "twists and turns but ultimately [is] moving toward a destination" (p. 64).

THINK POSITIVE

Making Psychology Work for You

At last, we reach the end of our journey through social psychology. Hopefully what you have learned in this chapter will come in handy in your everyday social interactions. Be conscious of the attributions you use to explain the behavior of others—are you being objective or falling prey to self-serving bias? Bear in mind that attitudes have a powerful impact on behavior—what types of attitudes do you harbor and how do they impact your everyday decisions? Know that your behaviors are constantly being shaped by your social interactions—both as an individual and as a member of groups. Understand the dangers of prejudice, discrimination, and stereotyping, and know the human suffering caused by aggression. But perhaps most of all, be kind and helpful to others, and allow yourself to experience love.

Now step back and consider how you might benefit from the study of psychology in general. As instructors and authors, it is our goal to help you develop critical thinking skills, understand the scientific process used by psychologists, and connect their findings to events in the news and everyday experiences. But most important, we hope the lessons of psychology enable you to become a more tolerant and compassionate person. The key to self-improvement, we believe, is a deep understanding of thoughts, emotions, and behaviors—not only your own, but those of other people. If you know that memories are malleable, you may be less inclined to accuse another person of deceit; if you understand that psychological disorders are tied to chemical imbalances in the brain, you may be less likely to pass judgment on those who suffer from them; and if you are aware that human perception is prone to errors and distortions, you realize that the world is not always as you discern it.

Knowledge of psychology can also be harnessed for your own well-being. As you journey beyond this course, earning degrees and pursuing career goals, remember what you have learned about managing stress and maximizing happiness. If the stressors of work, family, and money are accumulating, take a minute and direct your attention to the here and now. Sometimes being fully present in the moment helps reduce stress and put life in perspective.

Above all, remember that showing kindness to other people is one of the best ways to boost your own happiness.

○◉○○ **show what you know**

1. What are the three major factors that play a role in interpersonal attraction?

a. social influence; obedience; physical attractiveness

b. proximity; similarity; physical attractiveness

c. obedience; proximity; social influence

d. proximity; love; social influence

2. Research has shown that most people prefer looking at pictures of their own faces when reversed, but friends prefer normal, nonreversed photos. This finding supports the _____.

3. We described how the investment model of commitment can be used to predict the long-term stability of a romantic relationship. How can you use this same model to predict the long-term stability of friendships, positions at work, or loyalty to institutions?

✓ CHECK YOUR ANSWERS IN APPENDIX C.

Improve your grade! Use 📖 **LearningCurve** macmillan learning adaptive quizzing to create your personalized study plan, which will direct you to the resources that will help you most in 📖 **LaunchPad** macmillan learning

summary of concepts

15

LO 1 Define social psychology and identify how it is different from sociology. (p. 620)

Social psychology is the study of human cognition, emotion, and behavior in relation to others. This includes how we perceive and react to others, and how we behave in social settings. Social psychology focuses on studying individuals in relation to others and groups, whereas sociology studies the groups themselves—their cultures, societies, and subcultures. Using the same general research methods as other psychologists, social psychologists often conduct studies involving confederates, or people who are secretly working for them. At the end of a study, researchers debrief participants, or review aspects of the research they had previously concealed.

LO 2 Describe social cognition and how we use attributions to explain behavior. (p. 622)

Social cognition refers to the way we think about others, attend to social information, and use this information in our lives, both consciously and unconsciously. Attributions are the beliefs we develop to explain human behaviors and characteristics, as well as situations. Because attributions rely on whatever information happens to be available (our observations of what people say and do, for example), they are vulnerable to personal bias and inaccuracies.

LO 3 Outline how attributions lead to mistakes in our explanations for behaviors. (p. 623)

Situational attributions are a type of external attribution in which the assumed causes of behaviors exist in the environment. Dispositional attributions are a

type of internal attribution in which the causes of behaviors are thought to be traits or characteristics. Making attributions involves a certain amount of guesswork concerning the causes of events or behaviors, and thus plenty of room for error. Three common errors are (1) the fundamental attribution error, which assumes the causes of behaviors are in the person (dispositional) as opposed to the environment (situational); (2) the just-world hypothesis, which assumes that if someone is suffering, he must have done something to deserve it; and (3) the self-serving bias, which attributes one's successes to internal characteristics and one's failures to environmental factors.

LO 4 Explain the meaning of social influence and recognize factors associated with persuasion. (p. 631)

Social influence refers to the way a person is affected by others, as apparent in behavior, emotion, and cognition. Expectations are an often overlooked form of social influence. Research suggests that student performance is impacted by teacher expectations. Persuasion is intentionally trying to make people change their attitudes and beliefs, which may (or may not) lead to changes in their behavior. There are three factors that determine persuasive power: the source, the message, and the audience.

LO 5 Define compliance and explain some of the techniques used to gain it. (p. 634)

Compliance occurs when someone voluntarily changes her behavior at the request or direction of another person or group, who in general does not have any true authority over her. A common method to gain compliance is the foot-in-the-door technique, which occurs when a small request is followed by a larger one. Another method is the door-in-the-face technique, which involves making a large request, followed by a smaller one.

LO 6 Identify the factors that influence the likelihood of someone conforming. (p. 636)

The urge to modify behaviors, attitudes, beliefs, and opinions to match those of others is known as conformity. There are three major reasons we conform. Most people want approval, to be liked and accepted by others. This desire, known as normative social influence, can have a significant impact on behaviors. A second reason to conform is that we want to be correct. We look to others for confirmation when we are uncertain about something, and then do as they do. This is known as informational social influence. Finally, we may conform to others because they belong to a certain reference group we respect, admire, or long to join.

LO 7 Describe obedience and explain how Stanley Milgram studied it. (p. 638)

Obedience occurs when we change our behavior, or act in a way that we might not normally act, because we have been ordered to do so by an authority figure. Milgram conducted a series of studies examining how far people would go when urged by an authority figure to inflict punishment on others. During an early experiment, the goal was for the confederate (*learner*) to memorize a set of paired words. The participant (*teacher*) sat at a table, which held a control panel for administering electrical "shocks." The teacher was told to administer a shock each time the learner made a mistake, and the shock was to increase by 15 volts for every mistake. Milgram was surprised that so many people obeyed the experimenter and continued to administer "shocks," even when they hesitated or were uncomfortable, simply because an authority figure had instructed them to do so.

LO 8 Recognize the circumstances that influence the occurrence of the bystander effect. (p. 646)

When a person is in trouble, bystanders have the tendency to assume that someone else will help—and therefore stand by and do nothing, partly because there is a diffusion of responsibility. This bystander effect is more likely to occur when there are many other people present. By contrast, individuals are more inclined to aid a person in distress if no one else is around.

LO 9 Demonstrate an understanding of aggression and identify some of its causes. (p. 648)

Aggression is defined as intimidating or threatening behavior or attitudes intended to hurt someone. Research on aggression suggests that it has a biological basis (for instance, high levels of testosterone and low levels of serotonin). In addition, the frustration–aggression hypothesis suggests that in a frustrating situation, we can all show aggressive behavior.

LO 10 Recognize how group affiliation influences the development of stereotypes. (p. 649)

We tend to see the world in terms of the in-group (the group to which we belong) and the out-group (those outside our group). Seeing the world from the narrow perspective of our own group may lead to ethnocentrism, which sets the stage for stereotyping and discrimination. Stereotypes are the conclusions or inferences we make about people based on their group membership. Discrimination means showing favoritism or hostility to others because of their affiliation with a group. People who harbor stereotypes are more likely to feel prejudice, that is, hostile or negative attitudes toward individuals or groups.

LO 11 Describe prosocial behavior and altruism. (p. 653)

Behavior aimed at benefiting others is known as prosocial behavior. Altruism is a desire or motivation to help others with no expectation of anything in return. Empathy, or the ability to understand and recognize another's emotional perspective, is a major component of altruism.

LO 12 Identify the three major factors contributing to interpersonal attraction. (p. 655)

Interpersonal attraction leads us to form friendships or romantic relationships with others. The three major factors of interpersonal attraction are proximity, similarity, and physical attractiveness. Many relationships begin with exhilaration and intense physical attraction, and then evolve into more intimate connections. The combination of connection, concern, care, and intimacy is romantic love. This is similar to passionate love, or love that is based on zealous emotion, leading to intense longing and sexual attraction. As a relationship grows, intimacy and commitment develop into companionate love, which consists of fondness, camaraderie, understanding, and emotional closeness. Consummate love is evident when intimacy and commitment are accompanied by passion.

key terms

aggression, p. 648
altruism, p. 654
attitudes, p. 627
attributions, p. 622
bystander effect, p. 646
cognitive dissonance, p. 628
companionate love, p. 659
compliance, p. 634
conformity, p. 636
consummate love, p. 659
deindividuation, p. 644
diffusion of responsibility,
  p. 643

discrimination, p. 651
dispositional attribution, p. 625
door-in-the-face technique, p. 635
ethnocentrism, p. 651
false consensus effect, p. 627
foot-in-the-door technique,
  p. 634
frustration–aggression hypothesis,
  p. 648
fundamental attribution error,
  p. 625
group polarization, p. 645
groupthink, p. 645

in-group, p. 649
interpersonal attraction,
  p. 656
just-world hypothesis, p. 625
mere-exposure effect, p. 657
norms, p. 636
obedience, p. 638
out-group, p. 649
passionate love, p. 659
persuasion, p. 632
prejudice, p. 649
proximity, p. 656
risky shift, p. 645

romantic love, p. 659
scapegoat, p. 651
self-serving bias, p. 626
situational attribution, p. 625
social cognition, p. 622
social facilitation, p. 642
social identity, p. 649
social influence, p. 631
social loafing, p. 643
social psychology, p. 620
social roles, p. 652
stereotypes, p. 648
stereotype threat, p. 651

test prep *are you ready?*

1. Which of the following topics is LEAST likely to be studied by a social psychologist?
   a. children's written responses to people with disabilities
   b. teachers' reactions to children with disabilities
   c. the impact of deafness on social behaviors
   d. school board policies regarding support for children with disabilities

2. _____ refers to the way we think about others, attend to social information, and use this information in our lives.
   a. Sociology
   b. Social cognition
   c. The internal–external dimension
   d. The false consensus effect

3. _____ is an uneasy feeling that occurs with the recognition that a mismatch exists between an attitude and a behavior.
   a. Cognitive dissonance
   b. A confederate
   c. An attitude
   d. Altruism

4. Sometimes we attribute behaviors to a person's traits or personality characteristics rather than situational factors, thus underestimating the powerful influence of the environment on behavior. This is known as:
   a. the just-world hypothesis.
   b. the false consensus effect.
   c. a dispositional attribution.
   d. the fundamental attribution error.

5. Which of the following provides a biological explanation for aggression?
   a. the tendency of boys in nonindustrial societies to be more aggressive
   b. the frustration–aggression hypothesis
   c. group polarization
   d. high levels of testosterone and low levels of serotonin

6. The desire to help others with no expectations of payback is called:
   a. groupthink.
   b. deindividuation.
   c. altruism.
   d. conformity.

7. Your neighbor seems to follow the lead in terms of decorating his house. If he sees others hanging lights, he immediately does the same. His urge to modify his behaviors to match those of others in the neighborhood is known as:
   a. conformity.
   b. informational social influence.
   c. obedience.
   d. cognitive dissonance.

8. When someone changes his behavior at the request or direction of another person who does not have authority over him, this is known as:
   a. obedience.
   b. conformity.
   c. compliance.
   d. normative social influence.

9. _____ occurs when the sharing of duties among all members of the group leads to feelings of decreased accountability.
   a. Obedience to authority
   b. Diffusion of responsibility
   c. A risky shift
   d. Groupthink

10. One study found that 80% of trick-or-treaters in a group who were anonymous took more candy or money than they were supposed to. The children's sense of anonymity as well as inclusion in a group likely led to their sense of:
    a. deindividuation.
    b. obedience.
    c. authority.
    d. a risky shift.

11. A friend of yours believes that suburban teenagers with tongue rings are often troublemakers who are rebelling against their parents. These _____ are conclusions he has drawn based on his subjective observations and value judgments.
    a. norms
    b. external attributions
    c. situational attributions
    d. stereotypes

12. Psychologists define _____ as intimidating or threatening behavior, or as attitudes intended to hurt someone.
    a. prejudice
    b. discrimination
    c. aggression
    d. stereotypes

13. When teachers in an elementary school in San Francisco were given a list of students who were likely to "show surprising gains in intellectual competence" during the coming year, the students on that list achieved greater increases in test scores than students not included. This example demonstrates the power of _____, a form of social influence.
    a. cognitive dissonance
    b. expectations
    c. altruism
    d. the mere-exposure effect

14. Proximity, similarity, and physical attractiveness all play a role in:
    a. interpersonal attraction.
    b. aggression.
    c. social identity.
    d. disidentification.

15. According to Sternberg, the three elements that make up love are:
    a. passion, mere exposure, and proximity.
    b. proximity, similarity, and passion.
    c. romantic love, mere exposure, and similarity.
    d. passion, intimacy, and commitment.

16. Social psychology explores the way individuals behave in relation to others and groups, while sociology examines the groups themselves. Give several examples of how these two fields might approach the same overall topic (for example, prosocial behavior of college students versus the impact of social support structures in higher education).

17. The findings from Milgram's experiment on obedience seemed surprising when they were first published, but they remain relevant today. Why is it important to pay attention to the way you behave when under the influence of an authority figure?

18. Knowledge about the bystander effect provides a lesson for all of us, particularly with respect to crisis situations in a group setting. How would you describe this lesson to others?

19. Identify stereotypes you might harbor about certain groups of people. How did your association with specific groups impact the development of these stereotypes?

20. Think about a close friend or partner and try to determine if—and how—proximity, similarity, and physical attractiveness played a role in your attraction to each other.

✓ CHECK YOUR ANSWERS IN APPENDIX C.

YOUR SCIENTIFIC WORLD

Apply psychology to the real world! Go to LaunchPad for access.

introduction to statistics

The vast knowledge base that defines the field of psychology is the result of rigorous and meticulous scientific research, most of which entails the careful collection of data. In Chapter 1, we presented various methods used to gather this data, but we only touched upon statistical approaches for analyzing it. Here, we will discover how we can use data meaningfully: Welcome to **statistics**, the science of collecting, organizing, analyzing, displaying, and interpreting data.

Statistics are everywhere—not just in the academic materials published by psychologists. Newspapers, websites, and television shows report on statistical findings everyday, though they sometimes make mistakes, exaggerate, or leave out important information. You can detect these types of errors if you understand statistics. It is important for everyone (not just psychology students) to think critically about how statistics are presented.

Descriptive and Inferential Statistics

There are two basic types of statistics: descriptive and inferential. With *descriptive statistics,* researchers summarize information they have gleaned from their studies. The raw data can be organized and presented through tables, graphs, and charts, examples of which we provide in this appendix. We can also use descriptive statistics to represent the average and the spread of the data (how dispersed the values are), a topic we will explore later. The goal of descriptive statistics is to describe data, or provide a snapshot of what is observed in a study. *Inferential statistics,* on the other hand, go beyond simple data presentation. With inferential statistics, for example, we can determine the probability of events and make predictions about general trends. The goals are to generalize findings from studies, make predictions based on relationships among variables, and test hypotheses. Inferential statistics also can be used to make statements about how confident we are in our findings based on the data collected.

In Chapter 1, we defined a *hypothesis* as a statement used to test a prediction. Once a researcher develops a hypothesis, she gathers data and uses statistics to test it. **Hypothesis testing** involves mathematical procedures to determine whether data support a hypothesis or simply result from chance. Let's look at an example to see how this works. (And you might find it useful to review Chapter 1 if your knowledge of research methods is a little rusty.)

Suppose a researcher wants to determine whether taking vitamin D supplements can boost cognitive function. The researcher designs an experiment to test if giving participants vitamin D pills (the independent variable) leads to better performance on some sort of cognitive task, such as a memory test (the test score is the dependent variable). Participants in the treatment group receive doses of vitamin D and participants in the control group receive a placebo. Neither the participants nor the researchers working directly with those participants

CONNECTIONS

In **Chapter 1,** we presented a study examining the impact of fast-paced cartoons on executive functioning. The researchers tested the following hypothesis: Children who watch 9 minutes of *SpongeBob Square Pants* will be more likely to show a decrease in cognitive function than children who watch an educational program or simply draw. The researchers used inferential statistics to determine that the children in the *SpongeBob* group did show a lapse in cognitive functioning in comparison to the other two groups in the study.

statistics A science that focuses on how to collect, organize, analyze, display, and interpret data; numbers that describe characteristics of a sample.

hypothesis testing Mathematical procedures used to determine the likelihood that a researcher's predictions are supported by the data collected.

CONNECTIONS

In **Chapter 14,** we presented the biomedical approach to treating psychological disorders. Many researchers use a double-blind procedure to determine whether psychotropic drugs reduce the symptoms of psychological disorders. For example, Schnider and colleagues (2010) used a randomized double-blind procedure to determine the impact of L-dopa, risperdone, and a placebo on participants' ability to "rapidly adapt thinking to ongoing reality" (p. 586). The researchers used a double-blind procedure to ensure that neither the participants' nor the researchers' expectations unduly influenced the results.

CONNECTIONS

In **Chapter 5,** we presented Bandura's work on observational learning and aggressive models. Bandura and colleagues (1961) divided participants into treatment and control groups and found that the average "expression of aggression" for children who viewed aggressive models was statistically significantly greater than for the control group children who did not observe an aggressive model. The difference in the amount of expressed aggression for the two groups was large enough to be attributed to the experimenters' manipulation as opposed to chance (for example, simply based on the children who were assigned randomly to each group).

statistical significance The probability that the findings of a study were due to chance.

know who is getting the vitamin D and who is getting the placebo, so we call it a **double-blind procedure**. After the data have been collected, the researcher needs to compare the memory scores for the two groups to see if the treatment worked. In all likelihood, the average test scores of the two groups will differ simply because they include two different groups of people. So how does the researcher know whether the difference is sufficient to conclude that vitamin D had an effect? Using statistical procedures, the researcher can state with a chosen level of certainty (for example, with 95% confidence) that the disparity in average scores resulted from the vitamin D treatment. In other words, there is a slight possibility (in this case, 5%) that the difference was merely due to chance.

With the use of statistical methods, researchers can establish **statistical significance**, indicating that differences between groups in a study (for example, the average scores for treatment and control groups) are so great that they are likely due to the researcher's manipulations; the mathematical analyses suggest a minimal probability the findings were due to chance. When we use the experimental method (that is, randomly assign individuals, manipulate an independent variable, and control extraneous variables) and find *statistically* significant differences between our experimental and control groups, we can be assured that these differences are very likely due to how we treated the participants (for example, administering vitamin D treatment versus a placebo).

In addition to determining statistical significance, we also have to consider the *practical importance* of findings, meaning the degree to which the results of a study can be used in a meaningful way. In other words, do the findings have any relevance to real life? If the vitamin D regimen produces statistically significant results (with a performance gap between the treatment and control groups most likely not due to chance), the researcher still must determine its practical importance. Suppose the two groups differ by only a few points on the cognitive test; then the question is whether vitamin D supplementation is really worth the trouble. We should note that big samples are more likely to result in *statistically* significant results (small differences between groups can be amplified by a large sample) even though the results might not provide much practical information.

Sampling Techniques

Long before data are collected and analyzed, researchers must select people to participate in their studies. Depending on what a psychologist is interested in studying, the probability of being able to include all members of a *population* is not likely, so generally a *sample,* or subset of the population, is chosen. The characteristics of the sample members must closely reflect those of the population of interest so that the researcher can generalize, or apply, her findings to the population at large.

In an effort to ensure that the sample accurately reflects the larger population, a researcher may use *random sampling,* which means that all members of the population have an equal chance of being invited to participate in the study. If the researcher has a numbered list of the population members, she could generate random numbers on a computer and then contact the individuals with those numbers. Because the numbers are randomly picked, everyone on the list has an equal chance of being selected. Another approach is *stratified sampling.* A researcher chooses this method if she wants a certain variable to be well represented—car ownership in urban areas, for example. She divides the population into four groups or *strata* (no car, one car, two cars, more than two cars), and then picks randomly from within each group or *stratum,* ensuring that all of the different types of car ownership are included in the sample. Researchers use strata such as ethnicity, gender, and age group to ensure a sample has appropriate representation of these important factors.

Some researchers use a method called *convenience sampling,* which involves choosing a sample from a group that is readily available or convenient. If a student researcher is interested in collecting data on coffee drinking behavior from people who frequent coffee shops, he might be tempted to go to the Starbucks and Peet's Coffee shops in his neighborhood. But this approach does not use random sampling (just think of all the Dunkin' Donuts and Caribou coffee drinkers who would be excluded), so the likelihood that it results in a *representative sample* is very slim. In other words, a randomly picked sample is more likely than a convenience sample to include members with characteristics similar to the population. Only if a sample is representative can a researcher use his findings to make accurate *inferences* or valid generalizations about the characteristics of the population. But it's important to note that even a randomly selected sample is not foolproof. There is always the possibility that the chosen participants have characteristics that are not typical for the population. The smaller the sample, the less likely it will be representative and the less reliable the results. Larger samples tend to provide more accurate reflections of the population being studied.

The ultimate goal of most studies is to provide results that can be used to make inferences about a population. We can describe a population using various **parameters,** or numbers that delineate its characteristics (for example, the average number of cars owned by *all* households in urban areas in the United States). When the same characteristics are determined for a sample, they are referred to as *statistics* (the average number of cars owned by households in the sample). (Recall that the word "statistics" can also refer to the scientific discipline of collecting, organizing, analyzing, displaying, and interpreting data.) We will introduce you to some of these numerical characteristics later when we discuss *measures of central tendency* and *measures of variation.*

Understanding sampling techniques can help you become a more critical consumer of scientific information. When reading or watching media reports on scientific studies, ask yourself whether the samples are truly representative. If not, the use of statistics to make inferences about parameters is suspect; the findings might only be true for the sample, not the population.

Variables

Once a study sample is selected, researchers can begin studying and manipulating the variables of interest. Variables are measurable characteristics that vary over time or across people, situations, or objects. In psychology, variables may include cognitive abilities, social behaviors, or even the font size in books. Statisticians often refer to two types of variables. *Quantitative variables* are numerical, meaning they have values that can be represented by numbered units or ranks. Midterm exam scores, age at graduation, and number of students in a class are all quantitative variables. *Qualitative variables* are characteristics that enable us to place participants in categories, but they cannot be assigned numbered units or ranks. An example might be college major; you can ask all of the students in the library to line up under signs for psychology, biology, chemistry, undeclared, and so on, and thereby categorize them by their majors. We can rank how much we like the majors based on the courses associated with them, but the majors cannot be ordered or ranked in and of themselves. We can alphabetize them, but that is a ranking based on their labels. We can even order the majors in terms of how many students are pursuing them, but that is a different variable (number of students). Other examples of qualitative variables include gender, ethnicity, and religious faith.

Variables are the focal point of experiments in psychology. Typically, the goal is to determine how one variable (the dependent variable) is affected by changes in another (the independent variable). Many studies focus on similar topics, so you might

try this ↓

Throughout this textbook, we have identified multiple characteristics and traits that can be used as variables in studies. Pick two chapters and see if you can identify five variables that are quantitative and five that are qualitative.

Synonyms
qualitative variables categorical variables

parameters Numbers that describe characteristics of a population.

imagine it's easy to compare their results. But this is not necessarily the case. Sometimes psychologists define variables in different ways, or study the same variables with vastly different samples, methods of measurement, and experimental designs. How do we reconcile all their findings? We rely on a **meta-analysis,** a statistical approach that allows researchers to combine the findings of different studies and draw general conclusions. A meta-analysis is an objective, quantitative (measurable) mechanism for gathering and analyzing findings from a set of studies on the same topic (Braver, Thoemmes, & Rosenthal, 2014; Lakens, Hilgard, & Stakks, 2016).

The Presentation of Data

Conducting an experiment is a major accomplishment, but it has little impact if researchers cannot devise an effective way to present their data. If they just display raw data in a table, others will find it difficult to draw any useful conclusions. Imagine you have collected the data presented in **TABLE A.I**, which represents the number of minutes of REM sleep (the dependent variable) each of your 44 participants ($n = 44$; n is the symbol for sample size) had during one night spent in your sleep lab. Looking at this table, you can barely tell what variable is being studied.

TABLE A.1 RAW DATA FROM REM SLEEP STUDY										
77	114	40	18	68	96	81	142	62	80	117
81	98	76	22	71	35	85	49	105	99	49
20	70	35	83	150	57	112	131	104	121	47
31	47	39	92	73	122	68	58	100	52	101

Quantitative Data Displays

A common and simple way to display data is to use a **frequency distribution,** which shows how often the various values in a data set are present. In **TABLE A.2,** we have displayed the data in seven *classes,* or groups, of equal width. The frequency for each class is tallied up and appears in the middle column. The first class goes from 4 to 24 minutes, and in our sample of 44 participants, only 3

meta-analysis A type of statistical analysis that combines findings from many studies on a single topic; statistics used to merge the outcomes of many studies.

frequency distribution A simple way to portray data that displays how often various values in a data set are present.

histogram Displays the classes of a variable on the *x*-axis and the frequency of the data on the *y*-axis; frequency is indicated by the height of the vertical bars.

frequency polygon A type of graphic display that uses lines to represent the frequency of data values.

stem-and-leaf plot A type of graphical display that uses the actual data values in the form of leading digits and trailing digits.

distribution shape How the frequencies of the values are shaped along the *x*-axis.

TABLE A.2 FREQUENCY DISTRIBUTION FOR REM SLEEP STUDY		
No. of Minutes in REM (Class Limits)	**Raw Frequency**	**Relative Frequency**
4 to 24	3	.068
25 to 45	5	.114
46 to 66	8	.182
67 to 87	12	.273
88 to 108	8	.182
109 to 129	5	.114
130 to 150	3	.068

had a total amount of REM in this class (18, 20, 22 minutes). The greatest number of participants experienced between 67 and 87 minutes of REM sleep. By looking at the frequency for each class, you begin to see patterns. In this case, the greatest number of participants had REM sleep within the middle of the distribution, and fewer appear on the ends. We will come back to this pattern shortly.

Frequency distributions can also be presented with a **histogram**, which displays the classes of a variable on the *x-axis* and the frequency of the data on the *y-axis* (portrayed by the height of the vertical bars). The values on the *y*-axis can be either the raw frequency (actual number) or the relative frequency (proportion of the whole set; see Table A.2, right column). The example portrayed in **FIGURE A.1** is a histogram of the minutes of REM sleep, with the classes representing the number of minutes in REM on the *x*-axis and the raw frequency on the *y*-axis. Looking at a histogram makes it easier to see how the data are distributed across classes. In this case, you can see that the most frequent duration of REM is in the middle of the distribution (the 67- to 87-minute class), and that the frequency tapers off toward both ends. Histograms are often used to display quantitative variables that have a wide range of values that would be difficult to interpret if they weren't grouped in classes.

Similar to a histogram is a **frequency polygon**, which uses lines instead of bars to represent the frequency of the data values, and shows midpoints of the classes (rather than class boundaries) along the *x*-axis. The same data displayed in the histogram (Figure A.1) appear in the frequency polygon in **FIGURE A.2** We see the same general shape in the frequency polygon, but instead of raw frequency, we have used the relative frequency to represent the proportion of participants in each of the classes (see Table A.2, right column). Thus, rather than saying 12 participants had 67 to 87 minutes of REM sleep, we can state that the proportion of participants in this class was approximately .27, or 27%. Relative frequencies are especially useful when comparing data sets with different sample sizes. Imagine we wanted to compare two different studies examining REM sleep: one with a sample size of 500, and the other with a sample size of 44. The larger sample might have a greater number of participants in the 67- to 87-minute group (let's say 50 participants out of 500 [.10] versus the 12 out of the 44 participants [.27] in the smaller sample), making the raw frequency of this group (50) in the larger sample greater than the raw frequency of this group (12) in the smaller sample. But the proportion for the smaller sample would still be greater (smaller sample = .27 versus larger sample = .10). The relative frequency makes it easier to detect these differences in proportion.

Another common way to display quantitative data is through a **stem-and-leaf plot,** which uses the actual data values in its display. The *stem* is made up of the first digits in a number, and the *leaf* is made up of the last digit in each number. This allows us to group numbers by 10s, 20s, 30s, and so on. In **FIGURE A.3**, we display the REM sleep data in a stem-and-leaf plot using the first part of the number (either the 10s and/or the 100s) as the stem, and the ones column as the leaf. In the top row, for example, 8 is from the ones column of the smallest number in the data set, 18; 0 and 2 in the second row represent the ones column from the numbers 20 and 22; the 0 in the bottom row comes from 150.

Distribution Shapes

Once the data have been displayed on a graph, researchers look very closely at the **distribution shape,** which is just what it sounds like—how the data are spread along the *x*-axis (that is, the shape is based on the variable represented along the *x*-axis and

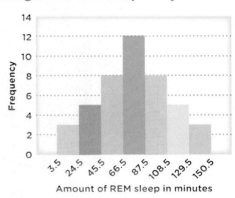

FIGURE A.1
Histogram of REM sleep study

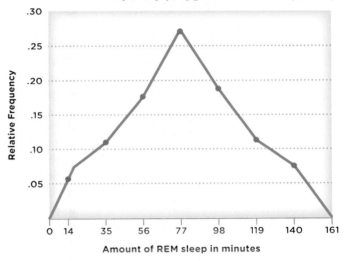

FIGURE A.2
Frequency polygon of REM sleep study

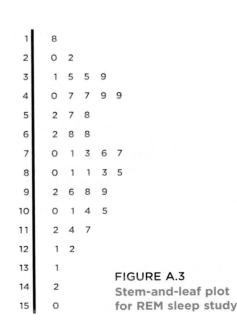

FIGURE A.3
Stem-and-leaf plot for REM sleep study

FIGURE A.4
Symmetrically shaped distributions

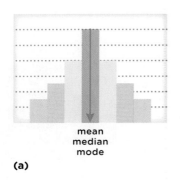

mean
median
mode

(a)

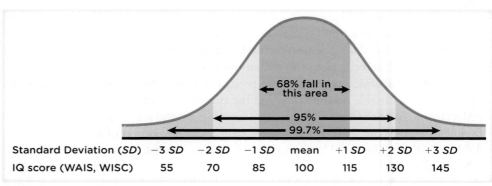

Standard Deviation (*SD*)	−3 *SD*	−2 *SD*	−1 *SD*	mean	+1 *SD*	+2 *SD*	+3 *SD*
IQ score (WAIS, WISC)	55	70	85	100	115	130	145

(b)

the frequency of its values portrayed on the *y*-axis). A symmetric shape is apparent in the histogram in **FIGURE A.4a,** which shows a distribution for a sample that is high in the middle, but tapers off at the same rate on each end. The bell-shaped or normal curve on the right (b) also has a symmetric shape, and this type of curve is fairly typical in psychology (curves generally represent the distribution of the entire population). Many human characteristics have this type of distribution, including cognitive abilities, personality characteristics, and a variety of physical characteristics such as height and weight. Through many years of study, we have found that measurements for the great majority of people fall in the middle of the distribution, and a smaller proportion have characteristics represented on the ends (tails) of the distribution. For example, if you look at the IQ scores displayed in **FIGURE A.4b,** you can see that 68% of people have scores between 85 and 115, about 95% have scores between 70 and 130, around 99.7% fall between 55 and 145, and only a tiny percentage (0.3%) are below 55 or above 145. These percentages are true for many other characteristics.

Some data have a **skewed distribution,** which is not symmetrical. As you can see in **FIGURE A.5a,** a **negatively skewed** or *left-skewed* distribution has a longer tail to the left side of the distribution. A **positively skewed** or *right-skewed* distribution (**FIGURE A.5b**) has a longer tail to the right side of the distribution. Determining whether a distribution is skewed is particularly important because it informs our decision about what type of statistical analysis to conduct. Later, we will see how certain types of data values can play a role in *skewing* a distribution.

FIGURE A.5
Skewed distributions

skewed distribution Nonsymmetrical frequency distribution.

negatively skewed A nonsymmetric distribution with a longer tail to the left side of the distribution; left-skewed distribution.

positively skewed A nonsymmetric distribution with a longer tail to the right side of the distribution; right-skewed distribution.

bar graph Displays qualitative data with categories of interest on the *x*-axis and frequency on the *y*-axis.

pie chart Displays qualitative data with categories of interest represented by slices of the pie.

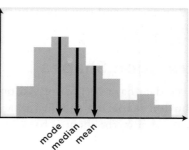

Qualitative Data Displays

Thus far, we have discussed several ways to represent quantitative data. With qualitative data, a frequency distribution lists the various categories and the number of members in each. For example, if we wanted to display the college major data on 44 students interviewed at the library, we could use a frequency distribution (**TABLE A.3**).

Another common way to display qualitative data is through a **bar graph,** which displays the categories of interest on the x-axis and their frequencies on the y-axis. **FIGURE A.6** shows how the data collected in the library can be presented in a bar graph. Bar graphs are useful for comparing several different populations on the same variable (for example, comparing college majors by gender or ethnicity).

College Major	Raw Frequency	Percent
Biology	3	7
Chemistry	5	11.5
Culinary Arts	8	18
English	5	11.5
Nursing	12	27
Psychology	3	7
Undecided	8	18

TABLE A.3 FREQUENCY DISTRIBUTION OF COLLEGE MAJORS

FIGURE A.6
Bar graph for college majors

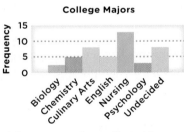

(a) Data on majors collected from library interviews

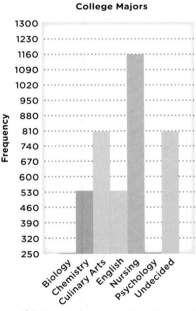

(b) Data on majors collected campus-wide

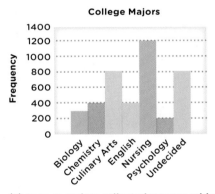

(c) Data on majors collected campus-wide

Pie charts can also be used to display qualitative data, with pie slices representing the proportion of the data set belonging to each category (**FIGURE A.7**). As you can see, the biggest percentage is nursing (27%), followed by culinary arts (18%), and undecided (18%). The smallest percentage is shared by biology and psychology (both 7%). Often researchers use pie charts to display data when it is important to know the relative proportion of each category (for example, a psychology department trying to gain support for funding its courses might want to display the relative number of psychologists in particular subfields; see Figure 1.1, page 3).

With any type of data display, one must be on the lookout for misleading portrayals. In Figure A.6a, we display data for the 44 students interviewed in the library. Notice that, while Figures A.6b and A.6c look different, they display the same data for the same campus of 4,400 students. Quickly look at (**b**) and (**c**) of the figure and decide, if you were head of the psychology department, which bar chart you would use to demonstrate the popularity of the psychology major. In (**b**), the size of the department (as measured by number of students) looks fairly small compared to that of other departments,

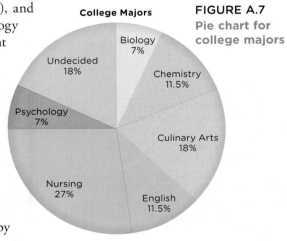

FIGURE A.7
Pie chart for college majors

particularly the nursing program. But notice that the scale on the y-axis starts at 250 in (**b**), whereas it begins at 0 in (**c**). In this third bar chart, it appears that the student count for the psychology program is not far behind that for other programs like chemistry and English. An important aspect of *critical thinking* is being able to evaluate the source of evidence, something one must consider when reading graphs and charts. (For example, does the author of the bar chart in Figure A.6b have a particular agenda to reduce funding for the psychology and biology departments?) It is important to recognize that manipulating the presentation of data can lead to faulty interpretations (the data on the 4,400 students are valid, but the way they are presented is not).

The Description of Data

In addition to using graphs and charts, psychologists can describe their data sets using numbers that express important characteristics: measures of central tendency, measures of variation, and measures of position. These numbers are an important component of descriptive statistics, as they provide a current snapshot of a data set.

Measures of Central Tendency

If you want to understand human behaviors and mental processes, it helps to know what is typical, or standard, for the population. What is the average level of intelligence? At what age do most people experience first love? To answer these types of questions, psychologists can describe their data sets by calculating **measures of central tendency,** which are numbers representing the "middle" of data sets. There are several ways of doing this. The **mean** is the arithmetic average of a data set. Most students learn how to calculate a mean, or "average," early in their schooling, using the following formula:

$$\bar{X} = \frac{\Sigma X}{n}$$ where $\bar{X}$ is the sample mean; X is a value in the data set; Σ, or sigma, tells us to take the sum of the values; and n represents the sample size

or

$$\text{Sample mean} = \frac{\text{Sum of all of the values in the data set}}{\text{Number of values}}$$

To calculate the sample mean ($\bar{X}$) for minutes of REM sleep, you would plug the numbers into the formula:

$$\bar{X} = (18 + 20 + 22 + 31 + 35 + 35 + 39 + \cdots + 131 + 142 + 150) \div 44$$
$$= 76.8 \text{ minutes}$$

Another measure of central tendency is the **median**—the number representing the position in the middle of a data set. In other words, 50% of the data values are greater than the median, and 50% are smaller. To find the median for a small set of numbers, start by ordering the values, and then determine which number lies exactly in the center. This is relatively simple when the data set is odd-numbered; all you have to do is find the value that has the same number of values above and below it. For a data set that has an even number of values, however, there is one additional step: You must take the average of the two middle numbers (add them together and divide by 2). With an odd number of values in a data set, the median will always be a member of the set. With an even number of values, the median may or may not be a member of the data set.

measures of central tendency Numbers that represent the middle of a data set.

mean The arithmetic average of a data set; a measure of central tendency.

median A number that represents the position in the data set for which 50% of the values are above it, and 50% are below it; a measure of central tendency.

Here is how you would determine the median (*Mdn*) for the minutes of REM sleep:

1. Order the numbers in the data set from smallest to largest. We can use the stem-and-leaf plot for this purpose. (See Figure A.3 on page A-5.)

2. Find the value in the data set that has 50% of the other values below it and 50% above it. Because we have an even number for our sample size (*n* = 44), we will have to find the middle two data values and calculate their average. We divide our sample size of 44 by 2, which is 22, indicating that the median is midway between the 22nd and 23rd values in our set. We count (starting at 18 in the stem-and-leaf plot) to the 22nd and 23rd numbers in our ordered list (76 and 77; there are 21 values below 76 and 21 values above 77).

3. $Mdn = \dfrac{(76 + 77)}{2}$

    = 76.5 minutes

A third measure of central tendency is the **mode,** which is the most frequently occurring value in a data set. If there is only one such value, we call it a *unimodal* distribution. With a symmetric distribution, the mean, median, and mode are the same (see Figure A.4a on page A-6). Sometimes there are two modes, indicating a **bimodal distribution,** and the shape of the distribution exhibits two vertical bars of equal height (**FIGURE A.8**). In our example of REM sleep data, we cannot see a clear mode, as there are several values that occur twice (35, 47, 49, 68, and 81 minutes). In bimodal distributions, the mode is often a better representation of the central tendency, because neither the mean nor median will indicate that there are in essence two "centers" for the data set.

Under other circumstances, the median is better than the mean for representing the middle of the data set. This is especially true when the data set includes one or more *outliers,* or values that are very different from the rest of the set. We can see why this is true by replacing just one value in our data set on REM sleep. See what happens to the mean and median when you swap 150 for 400. First calculate the mean:

1. $\bar{X}$ = (18 + 20 + 22 + 31 + 35 + 35 + 39 + $\cdots$ + 131 + 142 + 400) ÷ 44

    = 82.5 minutes (greater than the original mean of 76.8)

2. And now calculate the median. The numbers in the data set are ordered from smallest to largest. The middle two values have not changed (76 and 77).

    Mdn = 76.5 minutes (identical to the original median of 76.5).

No matter how large (or small) a single value is, it does not change the median, but it can have a great influence on the mean. When this occurs, psychologists often present both of these statistics, and discuss the possibility that an outlier is pulling the mean toward it. Look again at the skewed distributions in Figure A.5 on page A-6 and see how the mean is "pulled" toward the side of the distribution that has a possible outlier in its tail. When data are skewed, it is often a good idea to use the median as a measure of central tendency, particularly if a problem exists with outliers.

Measures of Variation

In addition to information on the central tendency, psychologists are interested in **measures of variation,** which describe how much variation or dispersion there is in a

FIGURE A.8
Bimodal distribution

mode The value of the data set that is most frequent; a measure of central tendency.

bimodal distribution A distribution with two modes, which are the two most frequently occurring values.

measures of variation Numbers that describe the variation or dispersion in a data set.

FIGURE A.9

Same mean, different variability for Sample A and Sample B
Data Values from Sample A (daily commute to school in miles) (9, 10, 15, 23, 25, 32, 35, 45, 48, 58). Data Values from Sample B (daily commute to school) (19, 27, 27, 28, 28, 30, 30, 32, 35, 44).

Data Values from Sample A

0	9
1	0 5
2	3 5
3	2 5
4	5 8
5	8

$\bar{X}$ = 30.0 miles, *Mdn* = 28.5 miles

Data Values from Sample B

1	9
2	7 7 8 8
3	0 0 2 5
4	4

$\bar{X}$ = 30.0 miles, *Mdn* = 29.0 miles

data set. If you look at the two data sets in **FIGURE A.9** (number of miles commuting to school), you can see that they have the same central tendency (identical means: the mean commute for both samples is 30 miles; $\bar{X}$ is 30.0), yet their dispersion is very different: One data set looks spread out (Sample A), and the other closely packed (Sample B).

There are several measures we can use to characterize the *variability*, or variation, of a data set. The **range** represents the length of a data set and is calculated by taking the highest value minus the lowest value. The range is a rough depiction of variability, but it's useful for comparing data on the same variable measured in two samples. For the data sets presented in Figure A.9, we can compare the ranges of the two samples and see that Sample A has a range of 49 miles and Sample B has a smaller range of 25 miles.

TABLE A.4 STANDARD DEVIATION FOR SAMPLE A

X	$X - \bar{X}$	$(X - \bar{X})^2$
9	9 − 30 = −21	$-21^2 = 441$
10	10 − 30 = − 20	$-20^2 = 400$
15	15 − 30 = −15	$-15^2 = 225$
23	23 − 30 = −7	$-7^2 = 49$
25	25 − 30 = −5	$-5^2 = 25$
32	32 − 30 = 2	$2^2 = 4$
35	35 − 30 = 5	$5^2 = 25$
45	45 − 30 = 15	$15^2 = 225$
48	48 − 30 = 18	$18^2 = 324$
58	58 − 30 = 28	$28^2 = 784$

$\sum(X - \bar{X})^2$ = 441 + 400 + 225 + 49 + 25 + 4 + 25 + 225 + 324 + 784 = 2,502

$n - 1 = (10 - 1) = 9$

$s = \sqrt{\dfrac{2,502}{9}}$

$s = 16.7$

	Sample A	Sample B
	Range = 58 − 9	Range = 44 − 19
	Range = 49 miles	Range = 25 miles

A more precise measure of variation is the **standard deviation** (referred to by the symbol *s* when describing samples), which essentially represents the average distance the data points are from their mean. Think about it like this: If the values in a data set are very close to each other, they will also be very close to their mean, and the dispersion will be small. Their average distance from the mean is small. If the values are widely spread, they will not all be clustered around the mean, and their dispersion will be great. Their average distance from the mean is large. One way we can calculate the standard deviation of a sample is by using the following formula:

$$s = \sqrt{\frac{\sum(X - \bar{X})^2}{(n - 1)}}$$

This formula does the following: (1) Subtract the mean from a value in the data set, then square the result. Do this for every value in the set and calculate the sum of the results. (2) Divide this sum by the sample size minus 1. (3) Take the square root of the result. In **TABLE A.4**, we have gone through each of these steps for Sample A.

The standard deviation for Sample A is 16.7 miles and the standard deviation for Sample B is 6.4 miles (the calculation is not shown here). These standard deviations are consistent with what we expect from looking at the stem-and-leaf plots in Figure A.9. Sample A is more variable, or spread out, than Sample B.

The standard deviation is useful for making predictions about the probability of a particular value occurring (Figure A.4b on page A-6). The *empirical rule* tells us that we can expect approximately 68% of all values to fall within 1 standard deviation below or above their mean on a normal curve. We can expect approximately 95% of all values to fall within 2 standard deviations below or above their mean. And we can expect approximately 99.7% of all values to fall within 3 standard deviations below or above their mean. Only 0.3% of the values will fall above or below 3 standard deviations—these values are extremely rare, as you can see in Figure A.4b.

range A number that represents the length of the data set and is a rough depiction of dispersion; a measure of variation.

standard deviation A number that represents the average distance the values in a data set are from their mean; a measure of variation.

Measures of Position

Another way to describe data is by looking at **measures of position,** which represent where particular data values fall in relation to other values in a set. You have probably heard of *percentiles,* which indicate the percentage of values occurring above and below a certain point in a data set. A value at the 50th percentile is at the median, which indicates that 50% of the values fall above it, and 50% fall below it. A value at the 10th percentile indicates that 90% fall above it, and 10% fall below it. Often you will see percentiles in reports from standardized tests, weight charts, height charts, and so on.

Statistics Is a Language

This introduction to statistics was created to provide you with an overview of the "language" of statistics that psychologists use to collect, organize, analyze, display, and interpret data. Like any foreign language, statistics is not something you master by reading a brief overview. To become proficient in statistical methods, you must study and practice them. And the best way to become fluent in this language is to immerse yourself in it. For starters, we recommend taking a course in elementary statistics and reading articles published in psychology journals (see **TABLE A.5** for some commonly used symbols). If you find statistics is your forte, keep taking classes, and consider the possibility of becoming a researcher. Perhaps your work will be published in a scientific journal one day—and cited in an introductory psychology textbook!

try this ↓

Using the data below, calculate the mean, median, range, and standard deviation. Also create a stem-and-leaf plot to display the data and then describe the shape of the distribution.

10 10 11 16 18 18 20 20 24 24 25 25 26 29 29 39 40 41 41 42 43 46 48 49 50 50 51 52 53 56 36 37 38 66 71 75 31 34 34 35 57 59 61 61 38

✓ CHECK YOUR ANSWERS IN APPENDIX C.

TABLE A.5 SYMBOLS COMMONLY USED IN STATISTICS

Concept	Symbol	Description
Sample correlation coefficient	*r*	Represents the strength and direction of the relationship between two variables
F-test value	*F*	Used to measure the statistical significance of the differences among 3 or more means
t-test value	*t*	Used to measure the statistical significance of the difference between 2 means
p-value	*p*	An indication of the probability of getting a test statistic of a certain size by chance
Population mean		The mean of a population (pronounced "mew")
Sample mean	M (or $\overline{X}$)	The mean of a sample (pronounced "X-bar")
Population standard deviation	σ	The standard deviation of the population (pronounced "sigma")
Sample standard deviation	*s*	The standard deviation of a sample
Population size	*N*	Indicates the size of a population
Sample size	*n*	Indicates the size of a sample
z-score	*z*	Indicates a standard score; number of standard deviations from the mean

measures of position Numbers that represent where particular data values fall in relation to other values in the data set.

key terms

bar graph, p. A-7

bimodal distribution,
 p. A-9

distribution shape, p. A-5

frequency distribution,
 p. A-4

frequency polygon, p. A-5

histogram, p. A-5

hypothesis testing, p. A-1

mean, p. A-8

measures of central tendency,
 p. A-8

measures of position, p. A-11

measures of variation, p. A-9

median, p. A-8

meta-analysis, p. A-4

mode, p. A-9

negatively skewed, p. A-6

parameters, p. A-3

pie chart, p. A-7

positively skewed, p. A-6

range, p. A-10

skewed distribution, p. A-6

standard deviation, p. A-10

statistical significance,
 p. A-2

statistics, p. A-1

stem-and-leaf plot, p. A-5

test prep *are you ready?*

1. _____ is the science of collecting, organizing, analyzing, displaying, and interpreting data.

2. With descriptive statistics, researchers use tables, graphs, and charts to:
   a. summarize data.
   b. make inferences about data.
   c. make predictions.
   d. test hypotheses.

3. A classmate is collecting data for a research project incorporating a treatment group and a control group. When the data collection is complete, she will check for _____ to see if the differences between the two groups are due to the researcher's manipulations.
   a. random sampling
   b. descriptive statistics
   c. standard deviations
   d. statistical significance

4. In the following, identify the variable as quantitative (1) or qualitative (2):
   a. political affiliation
   b. hair color
   c. yearly income
   d. weight in pounds

5. One common way to present data is to use a _____, which displays how often various values in a data set are present.
   a. qualitative variable
   b. meta-analysis
   c. frequency distribution
   d. measure of variation

6. A researcher is looking to measure cognitive ability in a large representative sample. She can expect that the distribution will be symmetric and have a bell shape. This type of distribution is also known as a:
   a. normal curve.
   b. stem-and-leaf plot.
   c. qualitative variable.
   d. parameter.

7. Some data will have a skewed distribution, which is not symmetrical. A _____ distribution has a longer tail to the left side and a _____ distribution has a longer tail to the right side.

8. Numbers that represent the "middle" of data sets are known as:
   a. standard deviations.
   b. measures of central tendency.
   c. measures of variability.
   d. misleading.

9. What is the mean for a sample that includes the following values: 4, 4, 6, 3, 8?
   a. 4
   b. 5
   c. 6
   d. 7

10. What is the median for a sample that includes the following values: 4, 4, 6, 3, 8?
   a. 4
   b. 5
   c. 6
   d. 7

11. What is the mode for a sample that includes the following values: 4, 4, 6, 3, 8?
   a. 4
   b. 5
   c. 6
   d. 7

12. A value that is very different from the rest of the data set is called a(n) _____, and it can have a great influence on the _____.
   a. mode; median
   b. variable; mode
   c. outlier; mean
   d. outlier; median

13. A classmate is trying to calculate a measure of variability. He takes the highest value in the data set and subtracts the lowest value from it. This is considered the _____ of the data set.
   a. range
   b. central tendency
   c. median
   d. standard deviation

14. What is the standard deviation for a sample that includes the following values: 4, 4, 6, 3, 8?
   a. 2
   b. 3
   c. 4
   d. 5

15. When you look at a graph in a newspaper, online, or elsewhere, you need to determine if it is a valid representation of the data being described. Graphic representations can be misleading; it depends on the values chosen for the y-axis. Find two examples of graphs in the media and examine their y-axes to see how the units are portrayed.

16. A positively skewed distribution is commonly found for data collected on income. Think of one other example of a positively skewed variable.

✓ CHECK YOUR ANSWERS IN APPENDIX C.

Improve your grade! Use 🐿 **LearningCurve** macmillan learning adaptive quizzing to create your personalized study plan, which will direct you to the resources that will help you most in 🐿 **LaunchPad** macmillan learning

careers in psychology

Most people hear the word "psychologist" and automatically think of therapy, counseling, and Freud, but as we noted in Chapter 1, psychologists perform a variety of roles in our society. Psychology is a vast field, and there is no shortage of career paths. If you are considering psychology, or even if you have already chosen psychology as your major, it is important to determine if this is the right career choice for you, and to figure out which subfield matches your interests, skills, and abilities. Then there is the issue of money. Will the career you choose allow you to reach your financial goals? Psychologists' salaries are highly variable and depend on many factors, including education level, specialty, and type of employer.

Any career in psychology will require some degree of specialized education. The question is, how much are you willing and able to attain? For many students, the answer depends on age, family responsibilities, financial concerns, and life experiences. In psychology, there are three types of degrees you can consider at the undergraduate and graduate level: bachelor's, master's, and doctoral.

What Can I Do with a Bachelor's Degree in Psychology?

Many students begin their journey by obtaining a 2-year associate's degree, and then go on to earn a bachelor's degree from a 4-year institution. A bachelor's degree in psychology is a great step toward understanding the scientific study of behavior and mental processes. It can prepare you to enter a graduate program, or it may serve as the foundation for your career. The psychology bachelor's degree is exceptionally popular, with 114,000 awarded in 2012–2013 (Snyder, de Bray, & Dillow, 2016), which could mean substantial competition in the job market. This is where the decision between entering the workforce or attending graduate school becomes important. **TABLE B.1** on the next page gives you a sense of the types of jobs you can obtain with a bachelor's degree in psychology.

When it comes to earning potential, education level matters. People with bachelor's degrees in psychology can expect to earn an annual starting salary of $30,000–$35,000. Those with master's degrees typically start at $40,000, while doctorate-level (PhD) professionals generally begin around $70,000. As you can see, advanced degrees have more lifetime earning potential (Morgan & Korschgen, 2014).

What Can I Do with a Master's Degree in Psychology?

Choosing to pursue a graduate degree in psychology requires a great deal of research. There are many types of degrees, and a multitude of colleges and universities that offer them. The American Psychological Association (APA) publishes a valuable resource for students thinking about this next step, *Graduate Study in Psychology* (2016a).

TABLE B.1 BACHELOR'S DEGREES AND CAREERS IN PSYCHOLOGY

Psychology Focus	Median Annual Salary	Business Focus	Median Annual Salary	Other Focus	Median Annual Salary
Correctional treatment specialist	$49,300	Administrative assistant	$36,500	Child-care employee	$20,300
Probation officer	$49,300	Customer relations	$31,700	Health services manager	$34,500
Social services worker	$45,000	Insurance agent	$48,200	High school teacher	$37,200
Social and community service manager	$63,500	Human resources	$58,300	Law enforcement	$60,200
Substance abuse counselor	$39,900	Public relations	$56,700	Recreation	$23,300

A bachelor's degree in psychology prepares you for many types of employment opportunities. Here, we see how this type of degree is not limited to the field of psychology. For more up-to-date information, log onto LaunchPad.

Information from Landrum (2001) and Lloyd (1997, July 16). Salary information from Bureau of Labor Statistics (2016–2017).

This guide, which is routinely updated, includes information on approximately 600 psychology graduate programs offered in the United States and Canada. In it you can find application deadlines, tuition costs, graduate employment data, and other useful information.

A master's degree in psychology is flexible and can prepare you to work in areas outside the field of psychology, including government, health care, business, marketing, and education. Many master's-level psychologists devote their careers to research, working under PhD-level researchers at universities and other institutions. Others become therapists. Typically, this means earning a master's degree, with an emphasis on counseling, and securing a state license to practice.

TABLE B.2 provides some general information about the types of degrees and training required of various mental health professions. In most states, master's-level clinicians must obtain a license to practice and share details about their education, training, and licensing status with their clients. One can also earn a master's degree in nonclinical specialties such as industrial/organizational psychology, engineering psychology, and leadership psychology. Some of these applied fields offer lucrative careers in business and industry. Finally, many students earning a master's degree in psychology go on to complete their doctorate degrees.

Doctorate Degrees: PhD and PsyD

Whether you need a degree at the doctoral level really depends on your interests. A PhD (doctor of philosophy) psychologist typically focuses on research, though some may provide therapy (American Psychological Association [APA], n.d.-b; Norcross & Castle, 2002). Earning a PhD requires graduate-level course work: 3 to 6 years of advanced college courses and training in addition to a bachelor's degree. PhD course work and research culminate in a dissertation, which you might think

TABLE B.2 MENTAL HEALTH PROFESSIONALS

Degree	Occupation	Training	Focus	Approximate Years of Study After Bachelor's Degree
Medical doctor, MD	Psychiatrist	Medical school and residency training	Treatment of psychological disorders; may include research focus	8 (including residency)
Doctor of philosophy, PhD	Clinical or counseling psychologist	Graduate school; includes dissertation and internship	Research-oriented and clinical practice	3–6
Doctor of psychology, PsyD	Clinical or counseling psychologist	Graduate school; includes internship; may include dissertation	Focus on professional practice	2–5
Master's degree, MA or MS	Mental health counselor	Graduate school; includes internship	Focus on professional practice	2

Mental health professionals have a variety of backgrounds. Here, we present a handful of these, including general information on training, focus, and the length of education.

of as a huge research paper in your field of study. PhD programs are highly competitive; it is not unusual for an applicant to apply to multiple schools, but only gain acceptance to one or two. The good news is that programs typically provide 70–80% of students with tuition assistance (American Psychological Association [APA], n.d.-b; Norcross & Castle, 2002). For some helpful tips on applying to PhD programs, you can visit the APA website at www.apa.org/education/grad/applying.aspx or log onto LaunchPad.

If your interest is more clinically focused, then you may consider the other doctoral-level degree in psychology, a PsyD (doctor of psychology). It emphasizes clinical practice rather than research, and typically requires 1 to 1.5 fewer years than a PhD program. This is not to say that PsyD programs do not require course work in statistics and research methods; it is just not the primary focus. PsyD programs traditionally emphasize clinical study, practice, and experience (Norcross & Castle, 2002). Because most PsyD degrees are offered by professional schools of psychology or private colleges and universities, students in these programs graduate with an average debt of $173,000 (Doran, Kraha, Marks, Ameen, & El-Ghoroury, 2016). There also tends to be less financial aid available for PsyD students.

Subfields of Psychology

Psychologists provide treatment for people with mental disorders, examine cognitive processes, study changes across the life span, work with children in schools, help corporations develop marketing strategies, and much more. Let's explore careers in some of the subfields of psychology.

Doctor of Psychology
David Brantley III celebrates with his daughter after receiving a doctor of psychology degree (PsyD) from Rutgers Graduate School of Applied and Professional Psychology. Unlike PhD programs, which are highly research focused, PsyD programs emphasize the clinical side of things—that is, the diagnosis and treatment of psychological disorders. MIKE DERER/AP Images.

Changing the World
With a budget of only $3,000, Dr. Tamara Russell launched an innovative mental health program at Washington State Penitentiary in Walla Walla, WA. Her treatment program provided inmates with opportunities to help others—by mentoring fellow inmates, tutoring students for the General Educational Development (GED) tests, and caring for orphaned kittens, among other things ("Walla Walla penitentiary," 2013). GREG LEHMAN/AP Images.

Clinical Psychology

Clinical psychologists focus on the diagnosis and treatment of people with psychological disorders. In addition to providing therapy, many of these professionals also conduct research. They may, for example, use brain scanning technologies to better understand the causes of depression, or design studies to compare the effects of different treatments. Some work as professors in colleges or universities, others as clinicians in medical facilities, schools, counseling centers, or private practice (APA, 2011b, 2014c).

Cognitive Psychology

Cognitive psychologists examine thinking, memory, intelligence, language, attention, and problem solving. Using the scientific method, these psychologists study how people "perceive, interpret and store information" (APA, 1998b, p. 14). Cognitive psychologists generally work in college and university settings, but many are employed as business consultants (APA, 1998b, 2011b, 2014c).

Counseling Psychology

Like clinical psychologists, counseling psychologists provide treatment for people with psychological disorders. But instead of helping people with severe disorders, they often work with those needing support concerning day-to-day problems. These psychologists tend to focus on relationship issues, career exploration, and stress management. They can be found in academic settings, clinical practice, and hospitals (APA, 1998b, 2011b). The work of clinical and counseling psychologists overlaps to some degree, although differences may result from their specific training programs. In some cases, counseling programs are located in a psychology department, which is also the case for most clinical programs. However, many counseling psychology programs are affiliated with education departments, which might conduct different types of research and training than psychology departments. Counseling psychologists may work in community mental health centers, hospitals, rehabilitation facilities, and business sectors (APA, 2014d).

Developmental Psychology

Developmental psychologists are primarily concerned with physical, cognitive, and socioemotional changes that occur over the life span (APA, 1998b, 2011b). Research in this field provides information about people from conception to death, impacting, for example, how children are treated in day-care settings, students are educated in classrooms, and elderly people are advised to manage their health. In the past, this field focused primarily on children from birth to adolescence, but developmental psychologists have become increasingly aware of the need to study adults as they age. They are especially concerned with helping people remain independent throughout life (APA, 2011b, 2014e).

Educational and School Psychology

Educational psychologists examine methods of learning and how memory relates to learning. These specialists play a key role in developing teaching strategies and curricula. School psychologists working in the classroom often apply lessons gleaned by educational psychologists. Research findings may inform decisions about how to classify students academically, for example. Educational and school psychologists work at colleges and universities, in school districts, and in private practice. Some educational psychologists are employed in industry, helping to create and evaluate standardized tests (APA, 1998b, 2011b). Psychologists specializing in teaching and learning may collaborate with school administrators, teachers, and parents to provide an effective and safe learning environment. They may assist students who are having learning difficulties, students identified as gifted, or teachers dealing with classroom management and student behavior problems (APA, 2014k).

Environmental Psychology

Environmental psychologists study the connection between behavior and the physical environment. "Physical environment" refers to anywhere that humans spend time, be it at home, in a college dorm, or on a city block. Environmental psychologists explore ways to promote "positive human behavior" in governmental agencies, businesses, and other types of settings, such as zoos or parks (APA, 1998b, 2011b, 2014b).

Experimental Psychology

Experimental psychologists are science enthusiasts. They spend their days conducting basic and applied research on people, animals, and data. These researchers typically focus on a particular area of study, such as cognitive psychology, neuroscience, or animal behavior. Experimental psychologists may teach at colleges and universities, or conduct research for government and industry (APA, 1998b, 2011b, 2014f).

Forensic Psychology

Forensic psychologists apply the principles of psychology to the legal system, working in diverse environments including criminal, family, and civil courts. These experts often are called upon in legal cases involving decisions about child custody, or situations in which a person's "mental competence to stand trial" is in question (APA, 2011b, p. 2). Some forensic psychologists are trained in law as well as in psychology, and they may conduct research on topics such as jury behavior or eyewitness testimony. Forensic psychologists may be employed in prisons, police departments, law offices, and government agencies (APA, 2014g).

Health Psychology

Health psychologists focus their efforts on promoting positive health behaviors and preventing illness. They research questions such as *Why do people smoke?* and *What drives people to overeat?* and their findings are used to promote good health practices. Health psychologists examine how individuals deal with sickness, pain, and medical treatment. They look at the interaction of biological, psychological, and social factors in relation to health and well-being. Health psychologists may be employed by hospitals, clinics, and rehabilitation centers, or they might work in private practice (APA, 1998b, 2011b, 2014h).

Human Factors and Engineering Psychology

Human factors and engineering psychologists use research to improve work environments by optimizing processes, systems, and equipment. These specialists observe on-the-job activities, conduct surveys, and recommend changes to facilitate optimal work environments with high productivity and safety. They may recommend changes in equipment, workload, personnel, or training (APA, 2011b, 2014i).

Industrial and Organizational (I/O) Psychology

Industrial and organizational psychologists examine the relationships of people working in organizations. They are particularly interested in employee job satisfaction, productivity, organizational structure and change, and the interface between humans and machines. In addition, I/O psychologists work with administrators to assist in hiring, training, and educating employees. These specialists are often employed in industry, government, business, and academic settings (APA, 1998b, 2011b, 2014j).

Media Psychology

Media psychologists examine human responses to the interactions among graphics, images, and sound. They study psychology and the development, production, and use of technology. Media psychologists investigate all forms of media (print, radio, television, social media) through different formats (mobile, interactive, virtual; APA, n.d.-d). They are particularly interested in how social media, text messaging, and other digital technologies shape the way we spend our time and relate to one another. Media psychologists might also examine the way reality TV shows can elevate ordinary people to celebrity status.

Neuropsychology and Psychobiology

Neuropsychologists and psychobiologists are interested in the link between human behavior and the body (neural activity, hormonal changes, and so on; APA, 1998b, 2011b). These psychologists work with people recovering from strokes and brain traumas, or struggling with learning disabilities and developmental delays. They investigate how the structure and function of the brain relate to behavior, cognition, and emotion. Neuropsychologists and psychobiologists often conduct research at colleges or universities, but they may also be employed by hospitals or other medical facilities (APA, 1998b, 2011b).

Rehabilitation Psychology

Rehabilitation psychologists either study or work with patients who have lost functioning as a result of stroke, epilepsy, autism, depression, chronic pain, or accidents, for example. These psychologists are particularly concerned with helping people adjust to work, relationships, and day-to-day living. Their research may impact the development of public programs (APA, 2011b, 2014l).

Social Psychology

Social psychologists examine the behaviors, thoughts, and emotions of people in groups. They may study attitudes, bullying, persuasion, discrimination, conformity, or group behavior. Social psychologists are interested in the many factors that influence interpersonal relationships, including those associated with attraction and love. While often employed by colleges and universities, these psychologists may also work for businesses and corporations (APA, 1998b, 2011b, 2014m).

Sport Psychology

Sport psychologists help athletes and their coaches set constructive goals, increase motivation, facilitate communication and conflict resolution among teammates or with leadership, as well as cope with anxiety related to athletic performance (APA, 2011b, 2014n). As any sport psychologist can testify, being physically fit is not the only requirement for athletic excellence; mental fitness is also critical. Sport psychologists also work in many corporations, helping to build their "teams" and supporting efforts to manage stress, build confidence, and improve job performance (APA, 2015).

Psychological Fitness
BMX rider Brooke Crain (left) meets with sport psychologist Jason Richardson (middle) and coach Tony Hoffman a couple weeks before the 2016 Olympics in Rio. Sport psychologists help athletes and coaches contend with the psychological challenges of their sport. Kris Arciaga/KPBS Public Broadcasting.

The science of psychology is relatively young compared to other sciences, and it is growing and changing with the advancement of technology and interdisciplinary research. If you are considering a career in psychology, keep up with the exciting developments in the field. A good way to stay abreast is by visiting the websites of the field's professional organizations (the Association for Psychological Science and the American Psychological Association) and logging onto LaunchPad.

1 introduction to the science of psychology

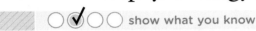 ○ ✓ ○ ○ show what you know

Presenting Psychology

1. behavior; mental processes

2. d. control

3. Answers will vary. *Common sense* is a collection of knowledge that any reasonably smart person can pick up through everyday experiences and casual observations. Findings from psychology, however, are based on meticulous and methodical observations of behaviors and mental processes, as well as data analysis. Many people respond to psychological findings with *hindsight bias,* or the feeling as if they knew it all along. If the results of a study seem obvious, someone may feel as if she "knew it all along," when in reality she wouldn't have predicted the outcome ahead of time.

Roots, Schools, and Perspectives of Psychology

1. d. introspection

2. b. behavioral

3. Answers will vary. *Sociocultural* and *biopsychosocial* perspectives are similar in that both examine how interactions with other people influence behaviors and mental processes. *Cognitive* and *biological* perspectives differ in that the *cognitive* perspective focuses on the thought processes underlying behavior, while the *biological* perspective emphasizes physiological processes.

Science and Psychology

1. b. critical thinking.

2. Pseudopsychology

3. Astrology is a great example of a *pseudopsychology,* an approach to explaining and predicting behavior and events that appears to be psychology but lacks scientific support. If you search the scientific literature for empirical, objective studies supporting astrological claims, you will have a very difficult time finding any. Another sign astrology is a pseudoscience is that its predictions are often too broad to refute. Let's say an astrologer predicts that a friend or close family member will soon need your kind words and support. Such a prediction would likely apply to the great majority of people, as family members and friends often look to each other for strength. Such a prediction would always seem to come true, because the probability of its occurrence is almost 100%.

The Scientific Method

1. An *opinion* is a belief or attitude formed through personal experience, and often lacking in scientific support. *Theories* synthesize research observations and can be used to explain phenomena and make predictions that are testable with the scientific method. Theories are often well-established bodies of principles that rest on a solid foundation of evidence.

2. d. operational definition

3. a. theory

Research Basics

1. c. representative sample

2. variables

3. Answers will vary. If the population is large, the researcher will need to select a sample. A random sample is a subset of the population chosen through a procedure that ensures all members have an equal chance of being selected. Random sampling increases the likelihood of achieving a representative sample, or subgroup, whose characteristics are similar to the population of interest. The researcher might be able to use a list of all currently enrolled students, and then randomly select potential participants from that list.

Descriptive Research

1. c. Descriptive research

2. a. naturalistic observation.

3. The correlational method is useful for illuminating links between variables, and it helps researchers make predictions, but it cannot determine cause and effect. Even if variables X and Y are strongly correlated, we cannot assume that changes in X are driving changes in Y (or vice versa); there may be some third variable influencing both X and Y. It is a valuable tool for uncovering links between variables when an experiment would be unethical or dangerous.

4. positive correlation

Experimental Research

1. d. cause-and-effect relationship

2. dependent

3. b. whether the child was alone or with others.

4. In a *double-blind study,* neither the participants nor the researchers working directly with those participants know who is getting the

treatment and who is getting the placebo. This type of study is designed to reduce expectations and biases that can arise when either participants or experimenters know what they've received or distributed. This use of deception is necessary so that neither experimenter nor participant consciously or unconsciously alters their behaviors, that is, unknowingly changes the outcome of the experiment.

Research Ethics

1. a. Informed consent
2. b. debriefing.
3. Answers will vary: "Pacifiers and Emotional Health"; "Pacifiers and Empathy"; "Binkie Psychology"

test prep *are you ready?*

1. b. applied research.
2. a. Common sense
3. c. the nature side of the nature–nurture issue.
4. d. functionalism.
5. d. Humanistic psychology
6. b. critical thinking
7. c. the scientific method
8. a. Inferential statistics
9. c. variables.
10. d. an equal chance of being picked to participate.
11. c. relationships among variables.
12. b. case study
13. d. independent; dependent
14. a. double-blind
15. d. random sample
16. Answers will vary. The goals of psychology are to describe, predict, explain, and control behavior. These goals lay the foundation for the scientific approach and the research designs used to carry out experiments. A researcher might conduct a study to describe differences in children's food preferences. She might conduct a study that predicted children's food preferences based on other close family members. If the researcher saw a pattern of food preferences among children within families, she might explain it by considering the children's home environment. The researcher might apply the findings to help experts create a campaign for healthy eating.
17. Answers will vary. Read through other studies on aggression and exposure to media violence to see how they ensured ethical treatment. She will also need to read through the ethical guidelines of the professional organizations and submit her proposal to the Institutional Review Board.
18. Answers will vary. See Table 1.4.

19. Answers will vary. Look for studies on topics that would be very hard for researchers to manipulate in an ethical manner (for example, breast feeding, amount of television watched, attitudes).
20. Answers will vary. The researchers used the experimental method to establish a cause-and-effect relationship between watching the cartoons and changes in cognitive function. The children were randomly assigned to the groups, and the researchers manipulated the activities they were involved in. Other variables were held constant. One way to change the study is to use a different age group.

2 biology and behavior

 show what you know

Introducing the Brain

1. neuroscience
2. d: using X-rays creates cross-sectional images
   b: records electrical activity from cortical area
   a: tracks changes of radioactive substances
   e: tracks changes in blood–oxygen levels
   c: with magnet creates cross-sectional images
3. Answers will vary. Building blocks can include items ranging from flour and butter in culinary training to numbers in mathematics. Atoms, chemical compounds, mechanical parts, and many other basic components may be building blocks in other fields of study.

Neurons and Neural Communication

1. myelin sheath
2. a. glial cells
3. b. Neurotransmitters; synaptic gap
4. Answers will vary. See Table 2.1 for examples.

The Supporting Systems

1. d. Motor neurons
2. b. spinal cord
3. pituitary
4. Both types of responses tend to increase the likelihood of survival and reproduction. The *fight-or-flight* strategy centers on self-preservation: By confronting or fleeing a threating situation, the individual is acting to ensure her own survival and ability to reproduce. *Tend and befriend* is perhaps a less direct approach. Forging social bonds and tending to the young strengthen the community as a whole, which can support the survival and reproduction of its members.

The Hemispheres

1. d. lateralization.
2. b. Broca's area.

3. The *corpus callosum* is a bundle of nerve fibers that allows the two halves of the brain to communicate and work together to process information. For example, with visual information each eye receives visual sensations, but that information is sent to the opposite hemisphere, and shared between the hemispheres via the corpus callosum. Specifically, information presented in the right visual field is processed in the left hemisphere, and information presented in the left visual field is processed in the right hemisphere. Because the hemispheres are disconnected through the surgery, researchers can study each hemisphere separately to explore its own unique capabilities (or specializations). In a split-brain individual, communication between the hemispheres is limited.

The Amazing Brain

1. a. neuroplasticity.

2. b. frontal lobes

3. association areas

4. The frontal lobes organize information among the other lobes of the brain. They are responsible for higher-level cognitive functions, such as thinking, perception, and impulse control. The occipital lobes process visual information, and help us see. The parietal lobes receive and process sensory information, and orient the body in space. The temporal lobes are instrumental in the comprehension of hearing and language. They process auditory stimuli, recognize visual objects, and play a key role in language comprehension and memory.

Digging Below the Cortex

1. b. limbic system

2. amygdala

3. a. relay sensory information.

4. cerebellum

test prep *are you ready?*

1. c. Neurons

2. a. an action potential

3. a. myelin sheath

4. 1. acetylcholine: c. movement; 2. glutamate: b. learning, memory; 3. endorphins: a. reduction of pain; 4. serotonin: d. mood, aggression, appetite

5. a. central nervous system.

6. b. spinal cord

7. d. peripheral nervous system

8. d. "rest-and-digest" process.

9. b. endocrine system; glands

10. b. The right hemisphere is more competent handling visual tasks.

11. a. locations in the brain are responsible for certain activities.

12. d. Wernicke's area

13. 1. association areas; b. integration of information from all over the brain; 2. temporal lobes: c. hearing and language comprehension; 3. meninges: a. three thin membranes protect brain; 4. occipital lobes: e. process visual information; 5. parietal lobes: d. receive sensory information, such as touch

14. 1. amygdala: b. processes basic emotions; 2. hippocampus: a. responsible for making new memories; 3. hypothalamus: d. keeps body systems in a steady state; 4. thalamus: c. relays sensory information

15. d. reticular formation

16. Neuroplasticity is the brain's ability to heal, grow new connections, and reorganize in order to adapt to the environment. Examples of neuroplasticity will vary, but Brandon Burns and Christina Santhouse provide compelling examples.

17. Diagrams will vary; see Figure 2.3. A *reflex* is an involuntary reaction that often protects us from bodily harm. For example, we automatically pull away when we touch a hot surface. Sensory neurons are activated and carry information from the environment to interneurons in the spinal cord, which activates motor neurons. The motor neurons excite the muscle and initiate the motion of pulling away.

18. *Neurotransmitters* are chemical messengers produced by neurons, which enable those neurons to communicate with each other. *Hormones* are chemical messengers produced by the endocrine system and released into the bloodstream. The effects of neurotransmitters are almost instantaneous, whereas those of hormones are usually delayed and longer lasting. Both influence thoughts, emotions, and behaviors. Neurotransmitters and hormones can work together, for example, directing the fight-or-flight response to stress.

19. Sperry and Gazzaniga's research demonstrated that the hemispheres of the human brain, while strikingly similar in appearance, specialize in different functions. The left hemisphere excels in language processing, and the right hemisphere excels at visuospatial tasks. The corpus callosum normally allows the two hemispheres to share and integrate information.

20. The *EEG* detects electrical impulses in the brain. The *CAT* uses X-rays to create many cross-sectional images of the brain. The *MRI* uses powerful magnets to produce more detailed cross-sectional images than those of a CAT scan, but both MRI and CAT are used to study the structure of the brain. The *PET* uses radioactivity to track glucose consumption and construct a map of brain activity. The *fMRI* also captures changes in brain activity, but instead of tracking glucose consumption, it reveals patterns of blood flow in the brain, which is a good indicator of how much oxygen is being used. All of these tools have strengths and limitations (see Infographic 2.1).

try this ↓ page 65

ANSWER: Yes, Brandon would display a reflex. Remember that the knee jerk is an involuntary reaction carried out by neurons outside of the brain.

3 sensation and perception

 ✓ show what you know

An Introduction to Sensation and Perception

1. a. Perception

2. Answers will vary, but can include examples such as hearing the honking of a car outside, or smelling food cooking in the kitchen, or the lamp illuminating the book that enables you to see the words on the page.

3. d. sensory adaptation.

4. difference thresholds

Vision

1. wavelength

2. b. photoreceptors.

3. The *trichromatic theory of color vision* suggests there are three types of cones, each sensitive to particular wavelengths in the red, green, and blue spectrums. The brain identifies a precise hue by calculating patterns of excitement among the three types of cones, that is, the relative activity of the three types.

   The *opponent-process theory of color vision* suggests that in addition to the color-sensitive cones, we also have neurons that respond to opponent colors (for example, red–green, blue–yellow). One neuron in an opponent pair fires in response to red but not green, for example. Both the trichromatic and opponent-process theories clarify different aspects of color vision, as color perception occurs in the light-sensing cones in the retina and in the opponent cells serving the brain.

4. d. rods.

Hearing

1. a. frequency

2. b. transduction.

3. place

Smell, Taste, Touch: The Chemical and Skin Senses

1. olfaction

2. b. transduction.

3. Answers will vary, but may include examples such as typing on my keyboard, holding my head upright, moving my head to watch the time, sitting upright in my chair, moving my hand to scratch my head.

4. c. the gate-control theory

Perception

1. Gestalt

2. a. convergence

3. *ESP* is the purported ability to obtain information about the world in the absence of sensory stimuli. There is a lack of scientific evidence to support the existence of ESP, and most so-called evidence comes in the form of personal anecdotes. Subjective information can be biased. Using critical thinking, we must determine the credibility of the source and validity of the evidence. Despite ESP's lack of scientific credibility, many people still believe in its existence in part because of illusory correlations, which appear to be links between variables that are not closely related at all.

4. b. perceptual constancy

test prep *are you ready?*

1. c. sensation.

2. a. transduction.

3. b. fatigue and motivation

4. d. cornea

5. b. wavelength

6. a. afterimage effect; trichromatic

7. d. audition

8. c. neural impulses firing

9. c. chemical sense.

10. a. thalamus

11. a. Feature detectors

12. a. proprioceptors

13. a. tension of the muscles focusing the eyes

14. d. proximity.

15. c. relative size.

16. Answers will vary. Tastes push us toward foods we need and away from those that could harm us. We gravitate toward sweet, calorie-rich foods for their life-sustaining energy. We are also drawn to salty foods, which tend to contain valuable minerals, and to umami, which signals the presence of proteins essential for cellular health and growth. Bitter and sour tastes we tend to avoid. This also gives us an evolutionary edge because poisonous plants or rancid foods are often bitter or sour.

17. Answers will vary. Subliminal stimuli are well beneath our absolute thresholds (such as light too dim to see and sounds too faint to hear). Extrasensory perception (ESP) is the purported ability to obtain information about the world without any sensory stimuli (absolutely no measurable sensory data).

18. Diagrams will vary; see Infographic 3.2. The pinna funnels sound waves into the auditory canal, focusing them toward the eardrum. Vibrations in the eardrum cause the hammer to push the anvil, which moves the stirrup, which presses on the oval window, amplifying waves. Pressure on the oval window causes fluid in the cochlea to vibrate and bend the hair cells on the basilar membrane. If the vibration is sufficiently strong, the hair cells bend enough to initiate the firing of nearby nerve cells. The auditory nerve carries signals to the auditory cortex in the brain, where sounds are given meaning.

19. The *gate-control theory of pain* suggests that the perception of pain can either increase or decrease through the interaction of biopsychosocial factors. Signals are sent to open or close the "gates" that control the neurological pathways for pain. When large myelinated fibers are active, the gates are more likely to close, which then inhibits pain messages from being sent on. With

a sore shoulder, applying ice to the injured area can stimulate the temperature and pressure receptors of the large fibers. This activity closes the gates, temporarily interfering with the pain message that would have been sent to the brain.

20. An absolute threshold is the weakest stimuli that can be detected 50% of the time. Difference thresholds indicate the minimum difference between two stimuli noticed 50% of the time. Weber's law states the ratios that determine these difference thresholds. The ability to detect weak signals in the environment is based on many factors.

4 consciousness

 show what you know

An Introduction to Consciousness

1. Consciousness

2. b. automatic processing

3. Answers will vary. The ability to focus awareness on a small segment of information that is available through our sensory systems is called *selective attention*. Although we are exposed to many different stimuli at once, we tend to pay particular attention to abrupt or unexpected changes in the environment. Such events may pose a danger and we need to be aware of them. However, selective attention can cause us to be blind to objects directly in our line of vision. This "looking without seeing" can have serious consequences, as we fail to see important occurrences in our surroundings. Our advice would be to try to remain aware of the possibility of inattentional blindness, in particular when you are in situations that could involve serious injury.

Sleep

1. d. retinal ganglion cells.

2. b. Stage N2

3. cataplexy

4. Drawings will vary; see Infographic 4.2. A normal adult sleeper begins in non-rapid eye movement sleep. Stage N1, the lightest sleep, is associated with theta waves. Stage N2 includes evidence of sleep spindles. Stage N3 is associated with delta waves and deep sleep. Sleep then becomes less deep as the sleeper works back from Stages N3 to N1. But instead of waking up, the sleeper enters rapid eye movement sleep (REM). Each cycle lasts about 90 minutes, with the average adult sleeper looping through five cycles per night.

Dreams

1. manifest content; latent content

2. c. activation–synthesis model

3. Electroencephalogram (EEG) and PET scan technologies can demonstrate neural activity of the sleeping brain. During REM sleep, the motor areas of the brain are inhibited, but a great deal of neural activity is occurring in the sensory areas of the brain. The *activation–synthesis model* suggests dreams result when the brain responds to this random neural activity as if it has meaning. The creative human mind makes up stories to match the neural activity. The vestibular system is also active during REM sleep, resulting in sensations of floating or flying. The *neurocognitive theory of dreams*

proposes that a network of neurons in the brain (including some areas in the limbic system and forebrain) is necessary for dreaming to occur.

4. a. until children are around 13 to 15 years old, their reported dreams are less vivid.

Altered States of Consciousness

1. 1. depressant: b. slows down activity in the CNS; 2. opioid: a. blocks pain; 3. alcohol: d. cirrhosis of the liver; 4. cocaine: c. increases neural activity in the CNS

2. c. LSD

3. psychoactive drugs

4. To determine if behaviors should be considered problematic, one could evaluate the presence of tolerance or withdrawal, both signs of physiological dependence. With *tolerance,* one's system adapts to a drug over time and therefore needs more and more of the substance to re-create the original effect. *Withdrawal* can occur with constant use of some psychoactive drugs, when the body has become dependent and then reacts when the drug is withheld. In some cases, with *psychological dependence,* behaviors may be problematic when there is a strong desire or need to continue the behavior, but with no evidence of tolerance or withdrawal symptoms. If an individual harms himself or others around him as a result of his behaviors, it is a problem. Overuse is maladaptive and causes significant impairment or distress to the user and/or his family. This might include difficulties at work or school, neglect of children and household duties, and physically dangerous behaviors.

test prep *are you ready?*

1. d. consciousness

2. b. selective attention.

3. a. the cocktail party effect.

4. d. circadian rhythm.

5. c. hypothalamus; reticular formation

6. a. insomnia

7. b. alpha

8. d. REM sleep

9. a. REM rebound.

10. b. wish fulfillment.

11. d. the neurocognitive theory

12. c. Psychoactive drugs

13. a. dopamine

14. b. tobacco

15. c. Physiological; withdrawal

16. Answers will vary. If someone walks into your room while you are asleep, you wake up immediately if there is a noise. You hear a text message come in during the night and immediately wake up to answer the message.

17. Without one's awareness, the brain determines what is important, what requires immediate attention, and what can be processed and stored for later use if necessary. This *automatic processing* happens involuntarily, with little or no conscious effort, and is important because our sensory systems absorb large amounts of information

that need to be processed. But it would not be possible to be consciously aware of all of it. Automatic processing also enables *sensory adaption,* which is the tendency to become less sensitive to and less aware of constant stimuli after a period of time.

18. We might not want a doctor with such a schedule to care for us because staying up for 48 hours can result in problems with memory, attention, reaction time, and decision making, all important processes that doctors use in caring for patients. Sleep deprivation impairs the ability to focus attention on a single activity, such as delivering medical care.

19. Answers will vary. See Table 4.2 for information on sleep disturbances and their defining characteristics.

20. Answers will vary. There are many different drugs that people use legally on an everyday basis. Caffeine is a psychoactive drug found in coffee, soda, tea, and some medicines. Over-the-counter painkillers are legal drugs used to treat minor aches and pains. Nicotine is a highly addictive drug found in cigarettes or cigars. Alcohol is a legal psychoactive drug used on a daily basis by many people, as they drink a glass of wine or beer with an evening meal.

5 learning

 show what you know

An Introduction to Learning

1. behavior or thinking; experiences

2. c. associations

Classical Conditioning

1. Classical conditioning

2. biological preparedness

3. a. salmonella

4. When Little Albert heard the loud bang, it was an unconditioned stimulus (US) that elicited fear, the unconditioned response (UR). Through conditioning, the sight of the rat became paired with the loud noise, and thus the rat went from being a *neutral stimulus* to a conditioned stimulus (CS). Little Albert's fear of the rat became a conditioned response (CR). Little Albert showed stimulus generalization, as he not only began to fear rats, but he generalized this fear to other furry objects, including a sealskin coat and a rabbit.

Operant Conditioning

1. law of effect

2. d. stimulus generalization.

3. a. positive punishment

4. Answers will vary, but can be based on the following definitions. *Reinforcers* are consequences that increase the likelihood of a behavior reoccurring. *Positive reinforcement* is the process by which pleasant reinforcers are presented following a target behavior. *Negative reinforcement* occurs with the removal of an unpleasant stimulus following a target behavior. *Successive approximation* is a method that uses reinforcers to condition a series of small steps that gradually approach the target behavior. We could consider using food as a primary reinforcer (meeting a biological need). Good grades, or money, are examples of secondary reinforcers.

5. *Continuous reinforcement* is a schedule of reinforcement in which every target behavior is reinforced. *Partial reinforcement* is a schedule of reinforcement in which target behaviors are reinforced intermittently, not continuously. Continuous reinforcement is generally more effective for establishing a behavior, whereas learning through partial reinforcement is more resistant to extinction and useful for maintaining behavior.

Observational Learning and Cognition

1. a. observational learning.

2. Answers will vary, but can be based on the following definitions. A *model* is an individual or character whose behavior is being imitated. *Observational learning* occurs as a result of watching the behavior of others.

3. c. latent learning.

test prep *are you ready?*

1. b. habituation

2. c. ability to learn through positive reinforcement.

3. a. involuntary; voluntary

4. b. conditioned response.

5. b. conditioned stimulus.

6. a. adaptive value

7. c. conditioned emotional response.

8. d. The law of effect

9. c. a dog whining in the morning, leading an owner to wake up and take it outside

10. a. positive reinforcement.

11. b. positive reinforcement.

12. a. were more likely to display aggressive behavior

13. a. cause-and-effect relationship

14. a. latent learning.

15. b. insight.

16. With stimulus generalization, once an association is forged between a conditioned stimulus and a conditioned response, the learner often responds to similar stimuli as if they were the conditioned stimulus. Stimulus discrimination is the ability to differentiate between the conditioned stimulus and other sufficiently different stimuli.

17. Answers will vary. See Infographics 5.2 through 5.4, and Table 5.2.

18. Answers will vary, but can be based on the following definitions. *Primary reinforcers* are reinforcers that satisfy biological needs, such as food, water, or physical contact. *Secondary reinforcers* do not satisfy biological needs, but often gain their power through their association with primary reinforcers. A primary reinforcer used to change behavior might be food. A college tries to increase student participation by providing food at important school functions. Money can be used as a secondary reinforcer. Employees are paid money, which increases attendance at work.

19. Answers will vary, but can be based on the following. *Punishment decreases* the likelihood of a behavior recurring. On the other

hand, *negative reinforcement increases* the likelihood of a behavior recurring. See Table 5.2 for examples.

20. Answers can vary. A conditioned taste aversion is a form of classical conditioning that occurs when an organism learns to associate the taste of a particular food or drink with illness. Avoiding foods that induce sickness increases the odds the organism will survive and reproduce, passing its genes along to the next generation. Imagine a grizzly bear that avoids poisonous berries after vomiting from eating them. In this case, the unconditioned stimulus (US) is the poison in the berries; the unconditioned response (UR) is the vomiting. After acquisition, the conditioned stimulus (CS) would be the sight of the berries, and the conditioned response (CR) would be a nauseous feeling.

try this ↓ page 199

ANSWER: The neutral stimulus (NS) is the sight of a hot dog, the unconditioned stimulus (US) is the virus, the unconditioned response (UR) is the upset stomach, the conditioned stimulus (CS) is the sight or thought of a hot dog, and the conditioned response (CR) is the sick feeling you get even after you have recovered.

try this ↓ page 224

ANSWER: Independent variable: exposure to an adult displaying aggressive or nonaggressive behavior. Dependent variable: child's level of aggression.
  Ideas for altering the study: Conducting the same study with older or younger children; exposing the children to other children (as opposed to adults) behaving aggressively; pairing children with adults of the same and different ethnicities to determine the impact of ethnic background.

6 memory

 show what you know

An Introduction to Memory

1. Memory
2. b. Encoding
3. Paying little attention to data entering our sensory system results in *shallow processing*. For example, you remember seeing a word that has been boldfaced in the text while studying. You might even be able to recall the page that it appears on, and where on the page it is located. *Deeper-level processing* relies on characteristics related to patterns and meaning, and generally results in longer-lasting and easier to retrieve memories. As we study, if we contemplate incoming information and relate it to memories we already have, deeper processing occurs and the new memories are more likely to persist.

Flow With It: Stages of Memory

1. b. 30 seconds
2. b. working memory.
3. chunking

4. Answers will vary. **Ex**quisitely **Se**rious **Ep**isodes **Fl**ashed **Im**possible **Pr**oteins **L**ightning **S**tyle.
  Explicit memory, **Se**mantic memory, **Ep**isodic memory, **Fl**ashbulb memory, **Im**plicit memory, **Pr**ocedural memory, **L**ong-term memory, **S**ensory memory.

Retrieval and Forgetting

1. a. encoding specificity principle
2. a. context-dependent memory.
3. b. curve of forgetting.
4. Answers will vary. See Infographic 6.1. You can create your own retrieval cues to memorize important information. When taking notes, don't copy everything you are reading; write down enough information (the cue) to help you later retrieve what you are trying to learn. Or name photo files in your computer so you can remember when each photo was taken.

The Reliability of Memory

1. d. rich false memory.
2. misinformation effect
3. A *reconstructionist model* of memory suggests that memories are a combination of "fact and fiction." Over time, memories can fade, and because they are permeable, they become more vulnerable to the invasion of new information. In other words, memory of an event might include revisions to what really happened, based on knowledge, opinions, and information you have gained since the event occurred. The Loftus and Palmer experiment indicates that the wording of questions can significantly influence recall, demonstrating that memories can change in response to new information (that is, they are malleable).

The Biology of Memory

1. a. Anterograde amnesia
2. c. hippocampus
3. b. Memory consolidation
4. Answers will vary, but can be based on the following information. *Infantile amnesia* is the inability to remember events from one's earliest years. Most adults cannot remember events that occurred before the age of 3.

test prep *are you ready?*

1. d. retrieval
2. a. hierarchy of processing
3. c. iconic memory.
4. d. chunking
5. b. working memory
6. a. the encoding specificity principle.
7. c. recognition
8. c. Proactive interference; retroactive interference
9. d. a reconstructionist model of memory
10. b. rich false memory
11. a. the misinformation effect.
12. c. repressed

13. b. access memories of events created before the trauma.

14. b. Long-term potentiation

15. d. hippocampus

16. Information enters sensory memory, which includes an overwhelming array of sensory stimuli. If it is not lost in sensory memory, it enters the short-term memory stage. The amount of time information is maintained and processed in short-term memory can be about 30 seconds. And short-term memory has a limited capacity. Because short-term memories cannot last for a couple of hours, it is more likely his grandmother is having difficulty encoding, storing, and/or recalling information that would normally be held in long-term memory.

17. *Iconic memories* are visual impressions that are photograph-like in their accuracy but dissolve in less than a second. *Echoic memories* are exact copies of the sounds we hear, lasting about 1–10 seconds. Iconic memory uses our visual system, whereas echoic memory uses our auditory system.

18. *Short-term memory* is a stage of memory that temporarily maintains and processes a limited amount of information. *Working memory* is the active processing of information in short-term memory. Working memory refers to what is going on in short-term memory.

19. Answers will vary. **E**very **S**tudent **R**emembers

20. The teacher should list the most important rules first and last in the list. The *serial position effect* suggests items at the beginning and at the end of a list are more likely to be recalled. The *primacy effect* suggests we are more likely to remember items at the beginning of a list, because they have a better chance of moving into long-term memory. The *recency effect* suggests we are more likely to remember items at the end of a list because they linger in short-term memory. Students are likely to remember rules at the beginning of the list, as these would be encoded into long-term memory.

7 cognition, language, and intelligence

 show what you know

An Introduction to Cognition

1. Cognition

2. b. concept

3. c. formal concept

4. Answers will vary. Structures in the brain are associated with cognition. For example, the association areas integrate information from all over the brain. Broca's and Wernicke's areas work with other parts of the brain to generate and understand language.

   The biology of cognition can be found at the neural level as well. For example, changes at the level of neurons make it possible to store and retrieve information. It is also at the neuronal level where we see the plasticity of the brain at work.

Problem Solving

1. c. trial and error.

2. Answers will vary. A *means–ends analysis* is a heuristic used to determine how to decrease the distance between a goal and the current state. The goal in this example is to complete an assignment in a timely manner. The means could be to break the problem into two subproblems: (1) choosing a topic (for example, by reading the textbook for interesting ideas, discussing ideas with your instructor); and (2) conducting a literature review (for example, identifying appropriate databases, finding a library to obtain and read articles).

3. a. functional fixedness

Decision Making

1. Decision making

2. d. availability heuristic.

3. Answers will vary. A *heuristic* uses a "rule of thumb" or a broad application of a strategy to solve a problem, but it can also be used to help predict the probability of an event occurring. However, heuristics can lead us astray in our assessment of situations or predictions of outcomes. In the current example, you can present information to your friend that indicates flying is the safest form of travel. But you can also describe how the *availability heuristic* might lead him to believe that air travel is not safe. The vividness of airplane crashes can influence his recall; even though they are rare events, he is likely to overestimate the probability of them happening again due to the ease with which he recalls similar events. Highly detailed media reports of an airplane crash are likely to linger in his memory.

Head Trauma and Cognition

1. chronic traumatic encephalopathy (CTE)

2. Answers will vary. Chronic traumatic encephalopathy (CTE) is a neurodegenerative disease caused by repeated head trauma. The telltale sign of CTE is abnormal accumulation of the protein tau in the brain. This disease has been identified in deceased boxers, football players, and others who sustained traumatic head injuries.

Language

1. Phonemes

2. b. thinking and perception.

3. Answers will vary. Bilingualism is associated with enhanced creativity, abstract thought, and working memory. And knowing more than one language has been found to be associated with more efficient executive functioning, including abilities related to planning ahead and solving problems. In summary, bilingualism has been correlated with certain cognitive benefits.

Intelligence

1. c. analytic, creative, practical.

2. aptitude; achievement

3. The *intelligence quotient (IQ)* is a score from an intelligence assessment, which provides a way to compare levels of intelligence across ages. Originally, an IQ score was derived by dividing mental age by chronological age and multiplying that number by 100. Modern intelligence tests still assign a numerical score, although they no longer use the actual quotient score.

4. originality

test prep *are you ready?*

1. d. Cognition; thinking
2. a. Concepts
3. c. natural concepts
4. b. the plasticity
5. d. an algorithm
6. d. linguistic relativity hypothesis
7. b. availability heuristic.
8. d. confirmation bias.
9. c. the framing effect.
10. b. phonemes
11. b. tau
12. c. morphemes
13. d. Intelligence
14. b. validity
15. c. genetic hypothesis

16. *Formal concepts* are created through rigid and logical rules, or features of a concept. *Natural concepts* are acquired through everyday experience, and they do not have the same types of rigid rules for identification that formal concepts have.

    Examples will vary. An example of a formal concept is an isosceles triangle, which refers to a three-sided polygon with at least two equal-length sides. The concept of family is an example of a natural concept. Is a family a group of people who just live together, or do they have to be related genetically? Family is a natural concept that can change based on individual experiences.

17. See Table 7.2. Charles Spearman speculated that intelligence consists of a *general intelligence* (or *g* factor), which refers to a singular underlying aptitude or intellectual ability. Howard Gardner suggested we have *multiple intelligences,* proposing eight different types of intelligences or "frames of mind": linguistic (verbal), logical-mathematical, spatial, bodily-kinesthetic, musical, intrapersonal, interpersonal, and naturalist. Robert Sternberg proposed three kinds of intelligences. His *triarchic theory of intelligence* suggests that humans have varying degrees of analytical, creative, and practical abilities.

18. Using the *availability heuristic,* we predict the probability of something happening in the future based on how easily we can recall a similar type of event from the past. The availability heuristic is essentially a decision-making strategy that relies on memory. They remembered a recent storm in which they did not have to leave their homes, and so they decided it was safe to stay.

19. *Reliability* is the ability of an assessment to provide consistent, reproducible results. *Validity* is the degree to which an assessment measures what it intends to measure. An unreliable IQ test might result in getting different scores for the IQ test taken now and again in a few months; it would not be consistent across time, which is counter to what you would expect (we expect level of intelligence to remain fairly stable over time). An IQ test that is not valid would not be able to predict future performance on tasks related to intellectual ability.

20. Answers will vary. *Divergent thinking* is the ability to devise many solutions to a problem.

Possible solutions: As a door stop, icebreaker, paper weight, shovel, or axe; for putting out cigarettes; for breaking glass; for crushing ingredients for a recipe; for putting out a candle; and so on.

8 human development

 show what you know

The Study of Human Development

1. development
2. Developmental psychologists' longstanding discussions have centered on three major themes: stages and continuity; nature and nurture; and stability and change. Each of these themes relates to a basic question: (1) Does development occur in separate or discrete stages, or is it a steady, continuous process? (2) What are the relative roles of heredity and environment in human development? (3) How stable is one's personality over a lifetime and across situations?
3. c. cross-sectional

Genetics, Conception, and Prenatal Development

1. d. Chromosomes
2. Genotype; phenotype
3. a. embryonic period

Infancy and Child Development

1. rooting; sucking
2. a. theories of behaviorism
3. d. assimilation.
4. scaffolding
5. c. developmental tasks or emotional crises.
6. There is a universal sequence of language development. At around 2–3 months, infants typically start to produce vowel-like sounds known as *cooing.* At 4–6 months, in the *babbling stage,* infants combine consonants with vowels. Around their first birthday, many babies utter their first word, and at about 18 months, many are using two-word phrases (*telegraphic speech*). As children mature, they start to use more complete sentences. Infants pay more attention to adults who use infant-directed speech and are more likely to provide them with chances to learn and interact, thus allowing more exposure to language. Parents and caregivers should talk with their infants and children as much as possible, as babies benefit from a lot of chatter.

Adolescence

1. b. secondary sex characteristics.
2. a. formal operational stage.
3. Preconventional
4. Answers will vary. During the stage of *ego identity versus role confusion,* an adolescent seeks to define himself through his values, beliefs, and goals. If a helicopter parent has been troubleshooting all of her child's problems, the child has never had to learn to take care of things for himself. Thus, he may feel helpless and unsure of how to handle a problem that arises. The parent might also have ensured the child was successful in every endeavor, but this, too,

could cause the child to be unable to identify his true strengths, again interfering with the creation of an adult identity.

Adulthood

1. a. physical exercise
2. fluid; crystallized
3. d. acceptance
4. integrity; despair

test prep *are you ready?*

1. b. longitudinal research.
2. d. nature and nurture
3. d. genes
4. a. epigenetics.
5. c. synaptic pruning
6. d. Teratogens
7. b. language acquisition device
8. c. trust versus mistrust
9. b. scaffolding
10. c. Primary sex characteristics
11. a. formal operational stage.
12. b. socioemotional
13. d. menopause
14. c. coo; babble; first words
15. a. denial
16. Answers will vary. A specific type of egocentrism emerges in adolescence. Before this age, children can only imagine the world from their own perspective; children may appear to act "spoiled" or "entitled" at this age, but their behavior may simply be a function of where they are in their cognitive development. During adolescence they begin to become aware of others' perspectives. Egocentrism is still apparent, however, as they believe others share their preoccupations. These types of egocentrism refer to their cognitive abilities to understand other people's points of view, which is not the same as a child being selfish or spoiled.
17. Answers will vary. See Infographic 8.3, Tables 8.3 and 8.4.
18. Answers will vary, but can be based on the following definitions. Crystallized intelligence refers to the knowledge we gain through experience, and fluid intelligence refers to the ability to think in the abstract and create associations among concepts. As we age, the speed with which we learn new material and create associations decreases, but crystallized intelligence increases.
19. Answers will vary. According to Erikson, young adults face the crisis of intimacy versus isolation, and failure to create meaningful, deep relationships may lead to a life of isolation. During middle adulthood, people face the crisis of generativity versus stagnation. Positive resolution at this stage includes feeling that one has made a valuable impact on the next generation. Late adulthood is characterized by the crisis of integrity versus despair; people look back on life and evaluate how they have done.
20. Practical abilities seem to increase. Experiences allow people to develop a more balanced understanding of the world surrounding

them. What's more, aging may be accompanied by increases in *crystallized intelligence,* or knowledge gained through learning and experience.

9 motivation and emotion

 show what you know

Motivation

1. Motivation
2. b. intrinsic motivation.
3. Answers will vary. *Extrinsic motivation* is the drive or urge to continue a behavior because of external reinforcers. *Intrinsic motivation* is the drive or urge to continue a behavior because of internal reinforcers. A teacher wants to encourage intrinsic motivation because the reinforcers originate inside of the students, through personal satisfaction, interest in a subject matter, and so on. There are some potential disadvantages to extrinsic motivation. For example, using rewards, such as money and candy, to reinforce already interesting activities can lead to a decrease in what was intrinsically motivating. Thus, the teacher would want students to respond to intrinsic motivation because the tasks themselves are motivating.

   When activities are not novel, challenging, or do not have aesthetically pleasing characteristics, intrinsic motivation might not be useful. Thus, using rewards might be the best way to motivate these types of activities.

Theories of Motivation

1. c. instinct theory
2. d. drive-reduction
3. hierarchy of needs
4. Answers will vary, but can be based on the following definitions. *Competence* means being able to reach goals through the mastery of everyday functioning (such as fixing meals, getting ready for work and school). *Relatedness* is the need to create relationships with others (for example, to make and keep friends, develop families). *Autonomy* means managing one's behavior to reach personal goals (such as finishing one's college degree).
5. The *drive-reduction theory* of motivation suggests that biological needs and homeostasis motivate us to meet needs. If a need is not fulfilled, this creates a drive, or state of tension, that pushes us or motivates behaviors to meet the need. Once a need is met, the drive is reduced, at least temporarily, because this is an ongoing process, as the need inevitably returns. *Arousal theory* suggests that humans seek an optimal level of arousal, and what is optimal is based on individual differences. Behaviors can arise out of the simple desire for stimulation, or arousal, which is a level of alertness and engagement in the world, and people are motivated to seek out activities that fulfill this need. Drive-reduction theory suggests that the motivation is to reduce tension, but arousal theory suggests that in some cases the motivation is to increase tension.

Back to Basics: Hunger

1. a. stomach was contracting.
2. When glucose levels dip, the stomach and liver send signals to the brain that something must be done about this reduced energy

source. The brain, in turn, initiates a sense of hunger. When the lateral hypothalamus is activated, appetite increases. On the other hand, if the ventromedial hypothalamus becomes activated, appetite declines, causing an animal to stop eating.

3. Answers will vary. Physical factors include the complex system of hormones and activity of the lateral and ventromedial hypothalamus. Cultural and social factors may include gender, the presence (or absence) of others, and exposure to large portion sizes.

Emotion

1. d. Emotion

2. arousal level

3. Answers will vary, but can be based on the following definitions. *Emotion* is a psychological state that includes a subjective or inner experience. It also has a physiological component and entails a behavioral expression. Emotions are quite strong, but they don't generally last as long as moods. In addition, emotions are more likely to have an identifiable cause (that is, a reaction to a stimulus that provoked it), which has a greater probability of motivating a person to take some sort of action. *Moods* are longer-term emotional states that are less intense than emotions and do not appear to have distinct beginnings or ends. It is very likely that on your way to a wedding you are in a happy mood, and you have been that way for quite a while. If you were to get mud on your clothing, it is likely that you would experience an emotion such as anger, which might have been triggered by someone jumping in a large mud puddle and splashing you. Your anger would have a subjective experience (your feeling of anger), a physiological component (you felt your face flush with heat), and a behavioral expression (you glared angrily at the person who splashed you).

Theories of Emotion

1. James–Lange

2. b. Display rules

3. d. facial feedback hypothesis

4. Answers may vary. See Infographic 9.3. The *Cannon–Bard* theory of emotion suggests that environmental stimuli are the starting point for emotions, and that body changes and emotions happen together. The *Schachter–Singer* theory of emotion suggests there is a general pattern of physiological arousal caused by the sympathetic nervous system, and this pattern is common to a variety of emotions. Unlike the Cannon–Bard theory, the Schachter–Singer theory suggests our thoughts about our body changes can lead to emotions. The experience of emotion is the result of two factors: physiological arousal and a cognitive label for this physiological state (the arousal). Cannon–Bard did not suggest that a cognitive label is necessary for emotions to be experienced.

5. Darwin suggested that interpreting facial expressions is not something we learn but rather is an innate ability that evolved because it promotes survival. Sharing the same facial expressions allows for communication. Research on an isolated group of indigenous peoples in New Guinea suggests that the same facial expressions represent the same basic emotions across cultures. In addition, the fact that children born deaf and blind have the same types of emotional expressions as children with normal sensory abilities indicates that these displays, and the emotions behind them, may be universal.

Types of Emotion

1. amygdala

2. *Heritability* is the degree to which heredity is responsible for a particular characteristic in a population. In this case, the heritability for happiness is as high as 80%, indicating that around 80% of the variation in happiness can be attributed to genes, and 20% to environmental influences. In other words, we can explain a high proportion of the variation in happiness, life satisfaction, and well-being by considering genetic make-up, as opposed to environmental factors.

3. c. the sympathetic nervous system.

test prep *are you ready?*

1. d. an incentive

2. a. extrinsic motivation

3. c. Instincts

4. b. drive-reduction

5. a. sensation seekers

6. d. ventromedial hypothalamus

7. b. competence, relatedness, autonomy.

8. c. flow

9. c. behavioral expression.

10. b. could identify the facial expressions common across the world

11. c. physiological arousal and cognitive labeling.

12. b. cognitive–appraisal approach

13. a. physiological arousal.

14. a. cortex; amygdala

15. d. be better able to identify what emotion is being felt than men.

16. Answers will vary, but can be based on the following. Happiness has heritability estimates between 35% and 50%, and as high as 80% in longitudinal studies. There may be a set point for happiness, suggesting that we all have a degree of happiness around which our happiness levels will hover. Our set point is strong, and directed by our genes and temperament.

17. Answers will vary, but can be based on the following. Maslow's hierarchy of needs is considered universal. Needs are ordered according to the strength of their associated drives, with more critical needs at the base of the hierarchy and non-essential, higher-level needs at the top: physiological needs; safety needs; love and belongingness needs; esteem needs; self-actualization; self-transcendence. Maslow suggested that one's most basic needs must be met before higher-level needs motivate behavior. An example of someone not following the prescribed order of needs might be a martyr who is motivated by self-transcendence needs, ignoring safety needs altogether.

18. Answers will vary. Stomach contractions accompany feelings of hunger, and the stomach (and liver) send signals to the brain when glucose levels in the blood decrease. The brain, in turn, initiates a sense of hunger. When the lateral hypothalamus is activated, appetite increases. If the ventromedial hypothalamus becomes activated, appetite declines, causing an animal to stop eating. A variety of social and cultural factors, including exposure to large portion sizes and the presence of eating companions, may impact eating behaviors.

19. Answers will vary, but can be based on the following definition. *Display rules* provide a framework or guidelines for when, how, and where an emotion is expressed. Display rules are a product of cultures.

20. Answers will vary but may be based on the following. There is relatively little fluctuation in adult weight over time. The communication between the brain and the appetite hormones helps regulate the body's set point, or stable weight that we tend to maintain despite variability in day-to-day exercise and intake of food. The set point helps to maintain a consistent weight in part through changes in metabolism. Research suggests that the biological basis of happiness may include a "set point," similar to the set point for body weight. Happiness tends to fluctuate around a fixed level, which is influenced by genes and related to temperament. We may experience periodic ups and downs, but ultimately we move back toward that fixed level of happiness. However, the set points for body weight and happiness may not be as powerful as researchers once suspected. To some degree, they depend on our conscious choices and behaviors.

10 sexuality and gender

 show what you know

Sex and Sexuality

1. c. Sexuality

2. b. into a male.

3. Answers may vary. Differences of sex development can be traced to irregularities in the 23rd pair of chromosomes, also referred to as the sex chromosomes. The 23rd pair provides the specific instructions for the zygote to develop into a female or male (the biological sex of the individual). However, the creation of the 23rd pair does not always follow the expected pattern of *XX* or *XY*. In some cases, genetic abnormalities will lead to differences of sex development (for example, too many sex chromosomes, or one is missing). In other cases, the sex chromosomes are normal, but the developing fetus does not respond to hormones in a typical way. See Infographic 10.1.

Gender

1. c. gender role

2. gender schemas

3. Transgender refers to the mismatch between a person's gender identity and expression and the gender assignment he/she was given at birth. Some transgender people try to resolve this conflict through medical interventions. A transsexual person seeks or undergoes a social transition to an alternative gender, often through sex reassignment surgery and/or medical treatment.

The Birds and the Bees

1. a. excitement, plateau, orgasm, and resolution.

2. evolutionary

3. Because monozygotic twins share nearly 100% of their genetic make-up, we expect them to share more genetically influenced characteristics than dizygotic twins, who only share about 50% of their genes. Using twins, researchers explored the impact of genes and environment on same-sex sexual behavior. Monozygotic twins were moderately more likely than dizygotic twins to have the same sexual orientation. They found men and women differ in terms of the heritability of same-sex sexual behavior. These studies highlight that the influence of the environment is substantial with regard to same-sex sexual behavior.

The Trouble with Sex

1. c. desire, arousal, orgasm, and pain.

2. Answers may vary, but could include *biological factors* (for example, age-related changes to physiology, hormonal changes, physical exhaustion), *psychological factors* (for example, balancing the stressors related to raising a family and working, raising young children), and *social factors* (for example, finding alone time to be together, feeling slightly jealous of friends who do not have small children at home, media influences).

Sex, Its Consequences, and Culture

1. a. Syphilis; gonorrhea

2. sexual scripts

3. Human immunodeficiency virus (HIV) is spread through the transfer of bodily fluids (blood, semen, vaginal fluid, or breast milk) and eventually causes the breakdown of the immune system. Although HIV often does not show up on blood tests for up to 6 months after infection occurs, it eventually progresses to acquired immune deficiency syndrome (AIDS), which generally results in a severely compromised immune system. A weakened immune system makes the body much more susceptible to opportunistic infections caused by bacteria, viruses, or fungi, and this vulnerability increases as the disease progresses.

test prep *are you ready?*

1. b. Sex; Gender

2. a. 23rd pair of chromosomes

3. d. hormones

4. a. sex; sexuality

5. d. gender roles.

6. c. observational learning

7. a. excitement

8. c. transsexual

9. b. mothers develop an anti-male antibody while pregnant.

10. d. men and women experience a similar pattern or cycle.

11. b. erectile disorder.

12. a. Human immunodeficiency virus; acquired immune deficiency syndrome

13. c. have a lower risk of acquiring an STI than those who don't know of this activity.

14. a. sexual scripts

15. d. Paraphilia

16. Answers will vary, but might include the following. Explain to potential participants that they will remain anonymous and their responses will be confidential. You might also explain that

the study has been approved by an Institutional Review Board, which ensures ethical studies. To help convince them that their participation is worthwhile and that they should be honest, you could remind them that because our knowledge of sexual behavior is often limited to self-reporting, their answers will be analyzed as reflective of the population.

17. *Gender* refers to the dimension of masculinity and femininity based on social, cultural, and psychological characteristics. It is often used in reference to the cultural roles that distinguish males and females. We generally learn gender roles by observing other people's behavior and by internalizing cultural beliefs about what is appropriate for men and women. This process also involves operant conditioning (reinforcement and punishment for behaviors deemed gender appropriate or inappropriate, respectively) and observational learning (observing and imitating role models).

18. In general, the purpose of sex is to reproduce and ensure the survival of the species. To a certain extent, the more children we have, the higher the probability that our genes will outlast us. Evolutionary psychologists might suggest that extramarital sex could support these goals. Men will want to be with a woman (or women) who can bear many children, so men might be motivated to accomplish this through extramarital activities. For a female, involvement in extramarital sex might be more likely if her mate is not fertile. Or, she might seek out an extramarital experience with someone who has more material resources than her mate.

19. Difficulties related to sexual activity can be divided into four, sometimes overlapping categories: desire, arousal, orgasm, and pain. Problems associated with desire must be persistent to be considered a dysfunction. When an individual has the desire to engage in sexual behavior, but the body does not cooperate, an arousal problem exists. Difficulties with orgasm may include reduced orgasmic intensity and the inability to reach orgasm. Problems associated with pain are more frequently reported by women, and may also be associated with reduced desire and arousal.

20. Answers will vary. See Table 10.5.

try this ↓ page 436

ANSWER: Answers will vary. However, the majority of people will not be able to answer questions #1 and #2, because they feel extremely uncomfortable imagining that they chose a different sexual orientation (this was never a conscious decision in the first place). This probably has something to do with the fact that sexual orientation exists on a continuum. Some people lie at one extreme or another, and have great difficulty changing the focus of their attraction. Others are closer to the middle and have more flexibility in their orientation.

11 personality

 show what you know

An Introduction to Personality

1. Personality

2. Answers will vary (see Table 11.1).

Psychoanalytic Theories

1. psychosexual; fixation

2. d. topographical model of the mind

3. b. collective unconscious.

4. Answers will vary, but could include the following. Some of *Freud's followers* branched out on their own due to disagreements about certain issues, such as his focus on the instincts of sex and aggression, his idea that personality is determined by the end of childhood, and his somewhat negative view of human nature. *Adler* proposed that humans are conscious and intentional in their behaviors. *Jung* suggested that we are driven by a psychological energy (as opposed to sexual energy), which encourages positive growth, self-understanding, and balance. *Horney* emphasized the role of relationships between children and their caregivers, not erogenous zones and psychosexual stages.

Humanistic Theories

1. Abraham Maslow; Carl Rogers

2. d. unconditional positive regard.

3. Answers will vary, but could include the following. The *psychoanalytic perspective* assumes that personality development begins early in life and is heavily influenced by processes of which we are unaware (like conflict, aggression, sexual urges) and the way caregivers respond. The *humanistic perspective* suggests that we have capabilities we can and should take advantage of as we strive for personal growth, the choices we make in life influence our personalities, and we are innately good and control our own destinies. The psychoanalytic perspective states that we have little control over our development and personality, while the humanistic perspective states that we can influence our growth.

Learning and Social-Cognitive Theories

1. learning theory

2. b. locus of control

3. Answers will vary, but can be based on the following definition (also see Infographic 11.2). *Reciprocal determinism* refers to the multidirectional interactions among cognition, behaviors, and the environment guiding our behavior patterns and personality.

Trait Theories and Their Biological Basis

1. a. traits.

2. surface traits

3. Answers will vary (also see Table 11.4). The *Big Five* traits include openness, conscientiousness, extraversion, agreeableness, and neuroticism. Three decades of twin and adoption studies point to a genetic (and therefore biological) basis of these five factors. The proportion of variation in the Big Five traits attributed to genetic make-up is substantial (ranging from .41 to .61), suggesting that the remainder can be attributed to environmental influences.

Personality Assessment

1. b. Projective

2. Answers will vary, but can be based on the following definitions. A *valid measure* is one that can be shown to measure what it

intends to measure. If a measure is not valid, a client might be given information that is not meaningful because the findings have not been shown to measure their intended topic. A *reliable measure* provides consistent results across time as well as across raters or people scoring the measure. If findings from a personality test are not reliable, a client may be given information that will not reflect a consistent pattern, or may be questionable due to problems with scoring.

3. a. standardization

test prep *are you ready?*

1. d. behavioral
2. c. psychoanalytic
3. d. mental processes that occur at three levels of consciousness.
4. c. id, ego, superego
5. a. psychosexual stages; fixation
6. c. Self-actualization
7. a. incongruent
8. c. self-efficacy
9. a. Personality
10. a. source traits
11. a. three dimensions of traits.
12. b. the stability of personality characteristics over time.
13. c. Reliability
14. a. projective personality tests
15. c. his intense emphasis on sex and aggression
16. Answers will vary, but can be based on the following information. According to behaviorists and learning theory, the *environment* shapes personality through *classical* and *operant* conditioning. *Observation* and *modeling* also play a role in personality development.
17. Answers will vary. The *humanistic perspective* suggests that we are innately good and that we have capabilities we can and should take advantage of as we strive for personal growth. The choices we make in life influence our personalities. The *social-cognitive perspective* focuses on relationships, environmental influences, cognitive activity, and individual behavior as they come together to form personality. The humanistic perspective views personality as what we are able to do, whereas the social-cognitive perspective views personality, in part, as how we react to the environment.
18. Both the Oedipus (for boys) and the Electra (for girls) complex represent an important conflict that occurs during the phallic stage. For both boys and girls, the conflict can be resolved through the process of identification. Although basic urges and developmental processes underlie both of these complexes, there are several important differences. The *Oedipus complex* is the attraction a boy feels toward his mother, along with resentment or envy directed toward his father. When a little boy becomes aware of his attraction to his mother, he realizes his father is a formidable rival and experiences jealousy and anger toward him. With the *Electra complex,* a little girl feels an attraction to her father and becomes jealous and angry toward her mother. Realizing she

doesn't have a penis, she may respond with anger, blaming her mother for her missing penis.

19. Answers will vary, but can be based on the following definitions. An *internal locus of control* suggests that the causes of life events reside within an individual, and that one has some control over them. An *external locus of control* suggests that causes for outcomes reside outside of an individual, and there is little control over them.

20. *Objective assessments* of personality are based on a standardized procedure in which the scoring is free of opinions, beliefs, expectations, and values. Critics of objective assessments contend they do not allow flexibility or fully appreciate individual differences in experiences. Findings from *subjective assessments* of personality are based, in part, on personal intuition, opinions, and interpretations. Critics of the subjective assessments suggest there is not enough consistency across findings because of nonstandard scoring procedures.

12 stress and health

 show what you know

An Introduction to Stress

1. Stress
2. d. illness
3. b. Acculturative stress
4. Answers will vary, but can be based on the following definitions. *Daily hassles* are the minor problems or irritants we deal with on a regular basis (for example, heavy traffic, financial worries, messy roommates). *Uplifts* are positive experiences that have the potential to make us happy (for example, a humorous text message, small gift).

Responding to Stressors

1. general adaptation syndrome (GAS)
2. a. alarm stage
3. c. The hypothalamic–pituitary–adrenal system
4. The *general adaptation syndrome (GAS)* suggests that the body passes through three stages. The first is the alarm stage, or initial response to a threatening situation. This stage includes an increase in arousal, during which the body prepares to deal with a threat. Next is the resistance stage, during which the body maintains a high level of arousal as it deals with a threatening situation; at this point, there is a decreased response to new stress. During the resistance stage, some people start to show signs of diseases of adaptation. Finally, there is the exhaustion stage. During this phase, the body's resources become depleted, resulting in vulnerability to illnesses, physical exhaustion, and even death.

Stress and Your Health

1. self-medication hypothesis
2. c. cortisol
3. When the body is expending its resources to deal with an ongoing stressor, the immune system is less powerful, and the work of the lymphocytes is compromised. During times of stress, people tend to sleep poorly, eat erratically, and may increase their drug

and alcohol use, along with other poor behavioral choices. These tendencies can lead to health problems.

Can You Deal?

1. approach–approach

2. d. Problem-focused coping

3. b. Type B personality.

4. Answers may vary. *Stress management* incorporates tools to lower the impact of possible stressors. Exercise, meditation, progressive muscle relaxation, biofeedback, and social support all have positive physical and psychological effects on the response to stressors. In addition, looking out for the well-being of others by caring and giving of yourself is an effective way to reduce the impact of stress.

test prep *are you ready?*

1. d. stressors.

2. a. eustress.

3. d. life-changing events

4. b. sympathetic nervous system

5. a. parasympathetic nervous system

6. c. exhaustion stage

7. d. sympathetic nervous system

8. a. the immune system

9. b. endorphins

10. d. progressive muscle relaxation

11. c. stressors are related to health problems.

12. b. Coping

13. d. avoidance–avoidance conflict.

14. a. Type A personality

15. b. hardiness.

16. Answers will vary, but can be based on the following explanation. There are various ways people respond to acculturative stress. Some try to assimilate into the culture, letting go of old ways and adopting those of the new culture. Another approach is to cling to one's roots and remain separated from the new culture. Such an approach can be very problematic if the new culture does not support this type of separation and requires assimilation. A combination of these two approaches is integration, or holding onto some elements of the old culture, but also adopting aspects of the new one.

17. Answers will vary, but can be based on the following definitions. *Daily hassles* are the minor problems or irritants we deal with on a regular basis. *Life-changing events* are occurrences that require a life adjustment (for example, marriage, change in school status). During times of stress, people tend to sleep poorly, eat erratically, and may increase their drug and alcohol use, along with other poor behavioral choices. These tendencies can lead to health problems. Exercise, meditation, progressive muscle relaxation, biofeedback, and social support all have positive physical and psychological effects on the response to stressors.

18. Answers will vary, but can be based on the following information. Reactions associated with the fight-or-flight response include

increased pulse, breathing rate, and mental alertness. A coordinated effort of the sympathetic nervous system and the endocrine system, the fight-or-flight reaction primes the body to respond to danger, either by escaping or confronting the threat head-on.

19. Answers will vary, but can be based on the following definitions. One major source of stress is conflict, which can be defined as the discomfort felt when making tough choices. Often two choices presented are both attractive to you (*approach–approach conflict*); at times a choice or situation has favorable and unfavorable characteristics (*approach–avoidance conflict*); and at other times the two alternatives are both unattractive (*avoidance–avoidance conflict*).

20. Answers will vary, but can be based on the following definitions. Someone with an *internal locus of control* generally feels as if she is in control of life and its circumstances; she probably believes it is important to take charge and make changes when problems occur. A person with an *external locus of control* generally feels as if chance, luck, or fate is responsible for her circumstances; there is no need to try to change things or make them better. Any decisions related to healthy choices can be influenced by locus of control.

13 psychological disorders

 show what you know

An Introduction to Psychological Disorders

1. a. dysfunction

2. psychological disorder

3. Answers will vary (see Table 13.1). An *atypical* behavior that is not dysfunctional might be an adolescent who dyes his hair in many different shades of green. A *dysfunctional* behavior that is not distressful might be someone having difficulty getting out of bed in the morning because she stayed up late to meet a deadline for the next day. *Deviant* but not dysfunctional behaviors are often demonstrated by political protesters. For example, demonstrators have been known to lie down on sidewalks and streets, or camp out in public places.

Classifying and Explaining Psychological Disorders

1. b. the creation of labeling and expectations.

2. medical model

3. Answers will vary, but can be based on the following information (see Figure 13.1). The *biopsychosocial perspective* suggests that psychological disorders result from a complex interaction of factors: *biological* (for example, neurotransmitters, hormones), *psychological* (for example, thinking, coping, personality traits), and *sociocultural* (for example, media, cultural beliefs).

Anxiety Disorders

1. c. panic attacks.

2. classical conditioning; operant conditioning

3. *Taijin kyofusho* tends to occur in collectivist societies, where great emphasis is placed on the surrounding people, which might lead

individuals from these societies to become overly concerned about making someone else feel uncomfortable. *Collectivist* societies value social harmony over individual needs; in this cultural context, embarrassing others is worse than humiliating oneself. Western cultures are more *individualistic*. People from these societies are much more afraid of embarrassing themselves than they are of embarrassing someone else. They tend to value their own feelings over those of others.

Obsessive-Compulsive Disorder

1. d. compulsions.

2. genetic

3. Repeatedly locking the car temporarily reduced Melissa's anxiety, making her more likely to perform this behavior in the future; thus, negative reinforcement promoted this maladaptive behavior. The therapist probably expected that if Melissa was not able to repeatedly check the locks and nothing bad happened, eventually Melissa would not need to continue locking her car repeatedly.

Depressive Disorders

1. b. major depressive disorder

2. depression

3. Answers will vary, but can be based on the following information. The symptoms of major depressive disorder can include feelings of sadness or hopelessness, reduced pleasure, sleeping excessively or not at all, loss of energy, feelings of worthlessness, or difficulties thinking or concentrating. The hallmarks of major depressive disorder are the "substantial" severity of symptoms and impairment in the ability to perform expected roles. *Biological theories* suggest the disorder results from a genetic predisposition, neurotransmitters, and hormones. *Psychological theories* suggest that feelings of learned helplessness and negative thinking may play a role. Not just one factor is involved in major depressive disorder, but rather the interplay of several.

Bipolar Disorders

1. b. manic episodes.

2. In order to be diagnosed with *bipolar I disorder,* a person must experience at least one manic episode spanning a week or more. These periods of mania are characterized by increased energy and activity and unusual excitement and/or irritability. Depression and hypomania may also occur.

   To be diagnosed with *bipolar II disorder,* a person must experience recurrent episodes of major depression lasting 2 or more weeks and at least one episode of hypomania spanning 4 or more days. *Hypomania* is a mild version of mania; the symptoms are similar, but not disabling.

3. A diagnosis of *bipolar I disorder* requires that a person experience at least one manic episode, substantial distress, and great impairment. *Bipolar II disorder* requires at least one major depressive episode as well as a hypomanic episode, which is associated with some of the same symptoms as a manic episode, but is not as severe and does not impair one's ability to function. People with bipolar disorder cycle between extreme highs and lows of emotion and energy that last for days, weeks, or even months. Individuals with *major depressive disorder,* on the other hand, tend to experience a persistent low mood, loss of energy, and feelings of worthlessness.

Schizophrenia

1. psychosis

2. a. hallucination.

3. Answers will vary, but can be based on the following information. Schizophrenia is a complex psychological disorder that results from a combination of biological, psychological, and social factors. This disorder springs from a complex interaction of genes and environment. The diathesis–stress model takes these factors into account, with *diathesis* referring to an inherited disposition (for example, to schizophrenia) and *stress* referring to the stressors in the environment (internal and external). Genes, neurotransmitters, differences in the brain, and exposure to a virus in utero are all possible influences in the development of schizophrenia. There are some sociocultural and environmental factors that may play a minor role in one's risk for developing the disorder, as well as the severity of symptoms. Evidence exists, for instance, that complications at birth, social stress, and cannabis abuse are related to a slightly increased risk of schizophrenia onset.

Personality, Dissociative, and Eating Disorders

1. borderline personality disorder

2. Answers will vary, but can be based on the following information (see Table 13.1). *Distress* is the degree to which behavior or emotions cause an individual to feel upset or uncomfortable. *Impairment* or *dysfunction* is the degree to which behavior interferes with daily life and relationships. *Deviance* means violating the norms, or rules, of society. Personality disorders are a group of psychological disorders that can include impairments in cognition, emotional responses, interpersonal functioning, and impulse control. Thus, they involve issues that can meet three of the criteria of abnormal behavior: dysfunction (they interfere with daily life and relationships), distress (from problems in interpersonal relationships, anxiety), and deviance (behaviors often considered outside the standards of society).

3. Dissociative identity disorder

4. d. extreme overeating followed by purging.

test prep *are you ready?*

1. d. dysfunction

2. b. the medical model.

3. a. obsessions; compulsions

4. b. biopsychosocial

5. b. agoraphobia

6. c. social anxiety disorder.

7. c. panic attacks

8. b. antisocial personality disorder.

9. d. serotonin

10. d. binge-eating disorder.

11. c. problems associated with sleep.

12. d. irritability

13. b. psychosis.

14. a. borderline personality disorder

15. b. personalities

16. Answers will vary, but can be based on the following information. *Dysfunction* is the degree to which a behavior interferes with one's life or ability to function (for example, washing one's hands to the point of making them raw). *Distress* is feeling regularly upset or uncomfortable because of unwanted behaviors or emotions (for example, continually feeling sad and hopeless). *Deviance* is the degree to which a behavior is considered to be outside of the standards or rules of a society (for example, removing one's clothes in inappropriate settings).

17. Answers will vary. This statement does not follow the suggestion of using "people-first language." Instead, it is defining an individual by her disorder. People are much more than their diagnoses. The diagnosis does not describe who your friend is, but only what is causing her distress or discomfort.

18. Classical conditioning can play a role in the development of a panic disorder by pairing an initially neutral stimulus (for example, a mall) with an unexpected panic attack (the unconditioned stimulus). The panic attack location then becomes a conditioned stimulus. When the location is visited or even considered, a panic attack can ensue (now the conditioned response).

19. Cognitive therapist Aaron Beck suggested that depression is a product of a cognitive triad, which includes a negative view of experiences, self, and the future. Negative thinking may lead to self-defeating behaviors, which, in turn, reinforce the beliefs.

20. Answers will vary, but can be based on the following information. Schizophrenia is a complex psychological disorder that results from biological, psychological, and social factors. Because this disorder springs from a complex interaction of genes and environment, researchers have a hard time predicting who will be affected. The diathesis–stress model takes these factors into account, with *diathesis* referring to an inherited disposition (for example, to schizophrenia) and *stress* referring to the stressors in the environment (internal and external). Genes, neurotransmitters, differences in the brain, and exposure to a virus in utero are all possible biological factors. Neurotransmitters are also thought to play a role in schizophrenia. The *dopamine hypothesis,* for example, suggests that the synthesis, release, and concentrations of dopamine are all elevated in people who have been diagnosed with schizophrenia and are suffering from psychosis. There are several environmental triggers thought to be involved in one's risk for developing the disorder as well as the severity of symptoms (for example, complications at birth, social stress, and cannabis abuse are related to a slightly increased risk of schizophrenia onset).

14 treatment of psychological disorders

 show what you know

An Introduction to Treatment

1. a. symptoms

2. moral treatment

3. *Deinstitutionalization* was the mass movement of patients with psychological disorders out of mental institutions, in an attempt to reintegrate them into the community. Deinstitutionalization was partially the result of a movement to reduce the social isolation of people with psychological disorders. This movement marked the beginning of new treatment modalities that allowed individuals to better care for themselves and function in society. However, many former patients ended up living on the streets or behind bars. Many people locked up in American jails and prisons are suffering from mental health problems.

Insight Therapies

1. resistance

2. a. humanistic

3. c. empathy.

4. *Psychoanalysis,* the first formal system of psychotherapy, attempts to increase awareness of unconscious conflicts, making it possible to address and work through them. The therapist's goal is to uncover these unconscious conflicts. *Psychodynamic therapy* is an updated form of psychoanalysis; it incorporates many of Freud's core themes, including the notion that personality characteristics and behavior problems often can be traced to unconscious conflicts. In psychodynamic therapy, therapists see clients once a week for several months rather than many times a week for years. And instead of sitting quietly off to the side, therapists and clients sit face-to-face and engage in a two-way dialogue.

Behavior Therapies

1. a. behavior

2. anxiety hierarchy

3. aversion therapy

4. Answers will vary, but may be based on the following information. In *behavior modification,* one uses positive and negative reinforcement, as well as punishment, to help a child increase adaptive behaviors and reduce those that are maladaptive. For behaviors that resist modification, therapists might use successive approximations by reinforcing incremental changes. Some therapists will incorporate observational learning (that is, learning by imitating and watching others) to help clients change their behaviors.

Cognitive Therapies

1. cognitive therapy

2. Answers will vary, but may be based on the following information. *Behavior therapies* focus on behavioral change, with the belief that the key to resolving problems is not understanding their origins. Using the learning principles of classical conditioning, operant conditioning, and observational learning, behavior therapy aims to replace maladaptive behaviors with more adaptive behaviors. It incorporates a variety of techniques, including exposure therapy, aversion therapy, systematic desensitization, and behavior modification. Behavior therapy covers a broad range of treatment approaches, and focuses on observable behaviors in the present. *Cognitive therapy* is a type of therapy aimed at addressing the maladaptive thinking that leads to negative behaviors and feelings. The aim of cognitive therapy is

to help clients recognize and resist their own cognitive distortions and illogical thoughts in short-term, action-oriented, and homework-intensive therapy sessions. The goal of both approaches is to change the way an individual works or functions in the world. One major difference is that behavioral therapy focuses on behaviors, whereas cognitive therapy focuses on thinking—the way an individual views the world, and views herself in the world.

3. d. Rational-emotive behavior

Biomedical Therapies

1. d. electroconvulsive therapy

2. b. antidepressant.

3. neurosurgery

4. Answers will vary. *Biomedical therapies* use physical interventions to treat psychological disorders. These therapies can be categorized according to the method by which they influence the brain's functioning: chemical, electrical, or structural. *Psychotherapy* is a treatment approach in which a client works with a mental health professional to reduce psychological symptoms and increase his or her quality of life. These approaches share common features: The relationship between the client and the treatment provider is of utmost importance, as is a sense of hope that things will get better. And these approaches generally seek to reduce symptoms and increase the quality of life, whether a person is struggling with a psychological disorder or simply wants to be more fulfilled.

Psychotherapy: Who's in the Mix?

1. group therapy

2. a. Self-help groups

3. Answers will vary (see Table 14.5). Group therapy would be inappropriate for an individual who is not comfortable talking or interacting with others and is unwilling to share his or her own thoughts, feelings, or problems. A group may fail if group members do not get along, are continually late for meetings, or drop out. The skills of the group therapist also play a role in the success of treatment (for example, empathy, facilitation skills, observation skills).

Psychotherapy Today

1. licensing issues; privacy issues; limited empirical support

2. Answers will vary, but may be based on the following information. In general, therapy "works," especially if it is long-term. All approaches to psychotherapy perform equally well across all disorders. But individuals whose insurance companies limit their choice of therapists and how long they can receive treatment do not experience the same improvement as those who are less restricted. In addition, people who start therapy but then decide to stop it experience less successful outcomes. The client's cultural experience is important to keep in mind. Within any group, there is vast variation from one individual to the next, but it is still necessary for therapists to understand the cultural context in which they work. This includes being respectful of cultural norms and sensitive to the many forms of prejudice and discrimination that people can experience.

3. c. limits placed by insurance company

test prep *are you ready?*

1. b. moral treatment
2. c. evidence-based practice
3. a. psychoanalysts
4. b. It is difficult to test through experimentation
5. d. person-centered therapy.
6. a. hierarchies
7. b. Getting fired once does not mean my career is over.
8. a. tends to work quickly.
9. d. Seeing others improve offers hope and inspiration.
10. d. symptoms of particular disorders.
11. d. the present.
12. d. Psychopharmacology
13. b. limitations on choice of therapist as mandated by a health insurance policy
14. c. seizures
15. a. culture
16. Answers will vary, but may be based on the following information. *Cognitive behavior therapy* is an action-oriented type of therapy that requires clients to confront and resist their illogical thinking. *Insight therapies* aim to increase awareness of self and the environment. These approaches share common features: The relationship between the client and the treatment provider is of utmost importance, as is a sense of hope that things will get better. And these approaches generally seek to reduce symptoms and increase the quality of life, whether a person is struggling with a psychological disorder or simply wants to be more fulfilled.
17. Answers will vary (see Table 14.3).
18. Answers will vary, but may be based on the following information. *Exposure* is a therapeutic technique that brings a person into contact with a feared object or situation while in a safe environment, with the goal of extinguishing or eliminating the fear response. An anxiety hierarchy (a list of activities ordered from least to most anxiety-provoking) can be used to help with exposure. *Aversion therapy* is an approach that uses principles of classical conditioning to link problematic behaviors to unpleasant physical reactions.
19. Answers will vary, but may be based on the following information. One challenge of providing therapy is to meet the needs of clients from vastly different cultures. Within any group, there is great variation from one individual to the next, but it is still necessary for the therapist to keep in mind the client's cultural experience. This includes being respectful of cultural norms and sensitive to the many forms of prejudice and discrimination that people can experience. Every client has a unique story and a singular set of psychological needs. Responding to those needs and determining which approach will be most effective are key to successful therapy.
20. Answers will vary, but may be based on the following information. As more people gain access to the Internet and as more therapists try to specialize and market their services, online therapies have multiplied. *E-therapy* can mean anything from e-mail communications between client and therapist to

real-time sessions via a webcam. These digital tools are valuable for serving rural areas and providing treatment to those who would otherwise have no access. Videoconferencing is also useful for consultation and supervision. But online psychotherapy raises many concerns, including licensing and privacy issues, lack of nonverbal cues, and potential problems with developing therapeutic relationships.

15 social psychology

 show what you know

An Introduction to Social Psychology

1. debrief

2. Social psychology studies often involve confederates, who are working for the researchers. Playing the role of participants, confederates say what the researchers tell them to say and do what the researchers tell them to do. They are, unknown to the other participants, just part of the researchers' experimental manipulation. In a double-blind study, neither participants nor researchers administering a treatment know who is getting the real treatment. Participants are told ahead of time that they might receive a placebo, but do not necessarily know about confederates until after the study is complete.

3. b. Social psychology; sociology

Social Cognition

1. a. Attributions

2. Answers will vary, but may be based on the following information. *Attitudes* are the relatively stable thoughts, feelings, and responses one has toward people, situations, ideas, and things. Attitudes are composed of three elements: cognitive (beliefs or ideas), affective (mood or emotion), and behavioral (response).

3. d. disposition of the person.

Social Influence

1. a. social influence; b. persuasion; c. compliance; d. foot-in-the-door technique; e. conformity

2. d. Obedience

3. Answers will vary. Examples may include resisting the urge to eat dessert when others at the table are doing so, saying no to a cigarette when others offer one, and so forth.

Groups and Relationships

1. c. The bystander effect

2. deindividuation

3. Group members should know that when people hear their own opinions echoed by other members of a group, new information tends to reinforce and strengthen the group members' original positions. And, as the members of the group listen to each other make arguments, their original positions become more entrenched. Thus, group deliberation may not be helpful when the members of the group are initially in agreement.

Aggression

1. c. low levels of the neurotransmitter serotonin

2. d. prosocial behavior.

3. Males tend to show more direct aggression (physical displays of aggression), whereas females are more likely to engage in relational aggression (gossip, exclusion, ignoring), perhaps because females have a higher risk for physical or bodily harm than males do.

4. Answers will vary, but may be based on the following information. *Discrimination* is showing favoritism or hostility to others because of their affiliation with a group. *Prejudice* is holding hostile or negative attitudes toward an individual or group. *Stereotypes* are conclusions or inferences we make about people who are different from us based on their group membership, such as their race, religion, age, or gender. Discrimination, prejudice, and stereotypes involve making assumptions about others we may not know. They often lead to unfair treatment of others.

Attraction and Love

1. b. proximity; similarity; physical attractiveness

2. mere-exposure effect

3. According to this model, decisions to stay together or part ways are based on how happy people are in their relationship, their notion of what life would be like without it, and their investment in the relationship. People may stay in unsatisfying or unhealthy relationships if they feel there are no better alternatives or believe they have too much to lose. This model helps us understand why people remain in destructive relationships. These principles also apply to friendships, positions at work, or loyalty to institutions.

test prep *are you ready?*

1. d. school board policies regarding support for children with disabilities

2. b. Social cognition

3. a. Cognitive dissonance

4. d. the fundamental attribution error.

5. d. high levels of testosterone and low levels of serotonin

6. c. altruism.

7. a. conformity.

8. c. compliance.

9. b. Diffusion of responsibility

10. a. deindividuation.

11. d. stereotypes

12. c. aggression

13. b. expectations

14. a. interpersonal attraction.

15. d. passion, intimacy, and commitment.

16. Answers will vary, but may be based on the following information. Social psychology is the study of human cognition, emotion, and behavior in relation to others. This includes how we perceive

and react to others, and how we behave in social settings. Social psychology focuses on studying individuals in relation to others and groups, whereas sociology studies the groups themselves—their cultures, societies, and subcultures.

17. Answers will vary. *Obedience* occurs when we change our behavior, or act in a way that we might not normally, because we have been ordered to do so by an authority figure. An imbalance of power exists, and the person with more power generally has an advantage over a person with less power. It is important for us to pay attention to how we react when under the influence of an authority figure as we could inflict harm on others. One person can make a difference when he or she stands up for what is right.

18. Answers will vary. When a person is in trouble, bystanders have the tendency to assume that someone else will help—and therefore they stand by and do nothing, a phenomenon that is partly due to the diffusion of responsibility. This bystander effect is particularly common when there are many other people present. Individuals are more likely to aid a person in distress if no one else is present.

19. Answers will vary, but can be based on the following. *Stereotypes* are the conclusions or inferences we make about people who are different from us, based on their group membership (such as race, religion, age, or gender). We tend to see the world in terms of *in-groups* (the group to which we belong) and *out-groups* (people who are outside the group to which we belong), which can impact the stereotypes we hold.

20. Answers will vary, but can be based on the following definitions. *Proximity* means nearness, which may play an important role in the formation of relationships. *Similarity* has to do with how much you have in common with someone else. We tend to prefer those who share our interests, viewpoints, ethnicity, values, and other characteristics.

appendix A

introduction to statistics

test prep *are you ready?*

1. Statistics
2. a. summarize data.
3. d. statistical significance
4. a. 2; b. 2; c. 1; d. 1.
5. c. frequency distribution
6. a. normal curve.
7. negatively skewed; positively skewed
8. b. measures of central tendency.
9. b. 5
10. a. 4
11. a. 4
12. c. outlier; mean
13. a. range
14. a. 2
15. Answers will vary, but it is important to consider what is being measured, how that measurement is actually being depicted, where the data come from, and the purpose of gathering the data.
16. Answers will vary, but can be based on the following information. A *positively skewed distribution* has a longer tail to the right side of the distribution. Sometimes the mean is "pulled" toward the side of distribution that has a possible outlier in the tail of the distribution. Examples of positively skewed distributions are housing prices, prices of cars (used and new), and so on.

try this ↓ page A-3

Answers will vary, but here are examples from Chapter 3:

quantitative variables: frequency of sound waves, pitch of sound, number of hair cells, weight of paper, color wavelength

qualitative variables: gender, religious affiliation, marital status, supertaster status, carpentered worlds versus traditional settings

try this ↓ page A-11

The mean for the sample is 38.6, the median is 38, the range is 65, and the standard deviation is 16.5. A stem-and-leaf plot would look like the following, and it appears it might be positively skewed.

1	001688
2	004455699
3	01123689
4	01123689
5	00123679
6	116
7	15

Glossary

abnormal behavior Behavior that is atypical, dysfunctional, distressful, and/or deviant. (p. 536)

absolute thresholds The weakest stimuli that can be detected 50% of the time. (p. 98)

accommodation The process by which the lens changes shape in order to focus on objects near and far. (p. 104)

accommodation A restructuring of old ideas to make a place for new information. (p. 346)

acculturation The process of cultural adjustment and adaptation, including changes to one's language, values, cultural behaviors, and sometimes national identity. (p. 505)

acculturative stress Stress that occurs when people move to new countries or cultures and must adjust to a new way of life. (p. 505)

achievement Acquired knowledge, or what has been learned. (p. 312)

acquired immune deficiency syndrome (AIDS) This condition, caused by HIV, generally results in a severely compromised immune system, which makes the body vulnerable to other infections. (p. 446)

acquisition The initial learning phase in both classical and operant conditioning. (p. 195)

action potential The spike in voltage that passes through the axon of a neuron, the purpose of which is to convey information. (p. 57)

activation–synthesis model Theory proposing that humans respond to random neural activity while in REM sleep as if it has meaning. (p. 166)

active listening The ability to pick up on the content and emotions behind words in order to understand a client's perspective, often by echoing the main point of what the client says. (p. 589)

adaptive value The degree to which a trait or behavior helps an organism survive. (p. 199)

adolescence The transition period between late childhood and early adulthood. (p. 355)

adrenal glands Endocrine glands involved in the stress response and the regulation of salt balance. (p. 70)

afterimage An image that appears to linger in the visual field after its stimulus, or source, is removed. (p. 109)

aggression Intimidating or threatening behavior or attitudes intended to hurt someone. (p. 648)

agoraphobia Extreme fear of situations involving public transportation, open spaces, or other public settings. (p. 548)

algorithm An approach to problem solving using a formula or set of rules that, if followed, ensures a solution. (p. 290)

all-or-none A neuron either fires or does not fire; action potentials are always the same strength. (p. 57)

alpha waves Brain waves that indicate a relaxed, drowsy state. (p. 154)

altruism A desire or motivation to help others with no expectation of anything in return. (p. 654)

amphetamines Stimulant drugs; methamphetamine falls in this class of drugs. (p. 174)

amplitude The height of a wave; distance from midpoint to peak, or from midpoint to trough. (p. 103)

amygdala A pair of almond-shaped structures in the limbic system that processes aggression and basic emotions such as fear, as well as associated memories. (p. 84)

androgens The male hormones secreted by the testes in males and by the adrenal glands in both males and females. (p. 420)

androgyny The tendency to cross gender-role boundaries, exhibiting behaviors associated with both genders. (p. 429)

anorexia nervosa An eating disorder identified by significant weight loss, an intense fear of being overweight, a false sense of body image, and a refusal to eat the proper amount of calories to achieve a healthy weight. (p. 569)

anterograde amnesia A type of memory loss; an inability to create new memories following damage or injury to the brain. (p. 265)

anti-anxiety drugs Psychotropic medications used for treating the symptoms of anxiety. (p. 604)

antidepressant drugs Psychotropic medications used for the treatment of depression. (p. 599)

antipsychotic drugs Psychotropic medication used in the treatment of psychotic symptoms, such as hallucinations and delusions. (p. 603)

antisocial personality disorder A psychological disorder distinguished by unethical behavior, deceitfulness, impulsivity, irritability, aggressiveness, disregard for others, and lack of remorse. (p. 566)

anxiety disorders A group of psychological disorders associated with extreme anxiety and/or debilitating, irrational fears. (p. 546)

approach–approach conflict A type of conflict in which one must choose between two or more options that are attractive. (p. 508)

approach–avoidance conflict A type of conflict that occurs when one is faced with a choice or situation that has favorable and unfavorable characteristics. (p. 508)

aptitude An individual's potential for learning. (p. 312)

archetypes Primal images, patterns of thoughts, and storylines stored in the collective unconscious, with themes that may be found in art, literature, music, dreams, and religions. (p. 470)

arousal theory Suggests that humans are motivated to seek an optimal level of arousal, or alertness and engagement in the world. (p. 385)

assimilation Using existing information and ideas to understand new knowledge and experiences. (p. 346)

association areas Regions of the cortex that integrate information from all over the brain, allowing us to learn, think in abstract terms, and carry out other intellectual tasks. (p. 81)

attachment The degree to which an infant feels an emotional connection with primary caregivers. (p. 352)

attitudes The relatively stable thoughts, feelings, and responses one has toward people, situations, ideas, and things. (p. 627)

attributions Beliefs one develops to explain human behaviors and characteristics, as well as situations. (p. 622)

audition The sense of hearing. (p. 111)

authoritarian parenting A rigid parenting style characterized by strict rules and poor communication skills. (p. 367)

authoritative parenting A parenting style characterized by high expectations, strong support, and respect for children. (p. 367)

automatic processing Collection and sometimes storage of information without conscious effort or awareness. (p. 147)

autonomic nervous system The branch of the peripheral nervous system that controls involuntary processes within the body, such as contractions in the digestive tract and activity of glands. (p. 66)

availability heuristic A decision-making strategy that predicts the likelihood of something happening based on how easily a similar type of event from the past can be recalled. (p. 296)

aversion therapy Therapeutic approach that uses the principles of classical conditioning to link problematic behaviors to unpleasant physical reactions. (p. 593)

avoidance–avoidance conflict A type of conflict in which one is faced with two or more options that are unattractive. (p. 508)

axon Skinny tube-like structure of a neuron that extends from the cell body, and which sends messages to other neurons through its terminal buds. (p. 53)

barbiturates Depressant drugs that decrease neural activity and reduce anxiety; a type of sedative. (p. 169)

bar graph Displays qualitative data with categories of interest on the x-axis and frequency on the y-axis. (p. A-7)

behavioral perspective An approach suggesting that behavior is primarily learned through associations, reinforcers, and observation. (p. 12)

behaviorism The scientific study of observable behavior. (p. 11)

behavior modification Therapeutic approach in which behaviors are shaped through reinforcement and punishment. (p. 594)

behavior therapies A type of therapy that focuses on behavioral change. (p. 582)

beta waves Brain waves that indicate an alert, awake state. (p. 154)

bimodal distribution A distribution with two modes, which are the two most frequently occurring values. (p. A-9)

binge-eating disorder An eating disorder characterized by episodes of extreme overeating, during which a larger amount of food is consumed than most people would eat in a similar amount of time under similar circumstances. (p. 570)

binocular cues Information gathered from both eyes to help judge depth and distance. (p. 132)

biofeedback A technique that involves providing visual or auditory information about biological processes, allowing a person to control physiological activity (for example, heart rate, blood pressure, and skin temperature). (p. 528)

biological perspective An approach that uses knowledge about underlying physiology to explain behavior and mental processes. (p. 13)

biological preparedness The tendency for animals to be predisposed or inclined to form certain kinds of associations through classical conditioning. (p. 200)

biological psychology The branch of psychology that focuses on how the brain and other biological systems influence human behavior. (p. 50)

biomedical therapy Drugs and other physical interventions that target the biological processes underlying psychological disorders; primary goal is to reduce symptoms. (p. 582)

biopsychosocial perspective Explains behavior through the interaction of biological, psychological, and sociocultural factors. (p. 13)

bipolar disorder A psychological disorder marked by dramatic swings in mood, ranging from manic episodes to depressive episodes. (p. 535)

bisexual Attraction to members of both the same and opposite sex. (p. 433)

blind spot A hole in the visual field caused by the optic disc (the location where the optic nerve exits the retina). (p. 106)

borderline personality disorder A psychological disorder distinguished by an incomplete sense of self, extreme self-criticism, unstable emotions, and feelings of emptiness. (p. 567)

bottom-up processing Taking basic information about incoming sensory stimuli and processing it for further interpretation. (p. 96)

Broca's area A region of the cortex that is critical for speech production. (p. 75)

bulimia nervosa An eating disorder characterized by extreme overeating followed by purging, with serious health risks. (p. 570)

burnout Emotional, mental, and physical fatigue that results in reduced motivation, enthusiasm, and performance. (p. 520)

bystander effect The tendency for people to avoid getting involved in an emergency they witness because they assume someone else will help. (p. 646)

Cannon–Bard theory of emotion Suggests that environmental stimuli are the starting point for emotions, and physiological or behavioral responses occur at the same time emotions are felt. (p. 398)

case study A type of descriptive research that closely examines an individual or small group. (p. 28)

cell body The region of the neuron that includes structures that nourish the cell, and a nucleus containing DNA. (p. 53)

central nervous system (CNS) A major component of the human nervous system that includes the brain and spinal cord. (p. 63)

cerebellum Structure located behind the brainstem that is responsible for muscle coordination and balance; Latin for "little brain." (p. 87)

cerebral cortex The wrinkled outermost layer of the cerebrum, responsible for higher mental functions, such as decision making, language, and processing visual information. (p. 77)

cerebrum The largest part of the brain, includes virtually all parts of the brain except brainstem structures; has two distinct hemispheres. (p. 71)

chromosomes Inherited threadlike structures composed of deoxyribonucleic acid (DNA). (p. 333)

chunking Grouping numbers, letters, or other items into meaningful subsets as a strategy for increasing the quantity of information that can be maintained in short-term memory. (p. 242)

circadian rhythm The daily patterns roughly following the 24-hour cycle of daylight and darkness; a 24-hour cycle of physiological and behavioral functioning. (p. 151)

classical conditioning Learning process in which two stimuli become associated with each other; when an originally neutral stimulus is conditioned to elicit an involuntary response. (p. 195)

cochlea Fluid-filled, snail-shaped organ of the inner ear lined with the basilar membrane. (p. 114)

cognition The mental activity associated with obtaining, converting, and using knowledge. (p. 281)

cognitive appraisal approach Suggests that the appraisal or interpretation of interactions with surroundings causes an emotional reaction. (p. 401)

cognitive behavioral therapy (CBT) An action-oriented type of therapy that requires clients to confront and resist their illogical thinking. (p. 598)

cognitive dissonance A state of tension that results when behaviors are inconsistent with attitudes. (p. 628)

cognitive map The mental representation of a physical space. (p. 226)

cognitive perspective An approach examining the mental processes that direct behavior. (p. 12)

cognitive psychology The scientific study of conscious processes such as thinking, problem solving, and language. (p. 146)

cognitive therapy A type of therapy aimed at addressing the maladaptive thinking that leads to maladaptive behaviors and feelings. (p. 596)

cohort effect The differences across groups that result from common experiences within the groups. (p. 330)

collective unconscious According to Jung, the universal experiences of humankind passed from generation to generation, including memories. (p. 470)

color constancy Objects are perceived as maintaining their color, even with changing sensory data. (p. 134)

comorbidity The occurrence of two or more disorders at the same time. (p. 543)

companionate love Love that consists of profound fondness, camaraderie, understanding, and emotional closeness. (p. 659)

compliance Changes in behavior at the request or direction of another person or group, who in general do not have any true authority. (p. 634)

compulsion A behavior or "mental act" that a person repeats over and over in an effort to reduce anxiety. (p. 550)

concepts Mental representations of categories of objects, situations, and ideas that belong together based on their central features or characteristics. (p. 282)

concrete operational stage Piaget's stage of cognitive development during which children begin to think more logically, but mainly in reference to concrete objects and circumstances. (p. 348)

conditioned emotional response An emotional reaction acquired through classical conditioning; process by which an emotional reaction becomes associated with a previously neutral stimulus. (p. 201)

conditioned response (CR) A learned response to a conditioned stimulus. (p. 195)

conditioned stimulus (CS) A previously neutral stimulus that an organism learns to associate with an unconditioned stimulus. (p. 195)

conditioned taste aversion A form of classical conditioning that occurs when an organism learns to associate the taste of a particular food or drink with illness. (p. 199)

cones Photoreceptors that enable us to sense color and minute details. (p. 106)

confirmation bias The tendency to look for evidence that upholds our beliefs and to overlook evidence that runs counter to them. (p. 298)

conformity The urge to modify behaviors, attitudes, beliefs, and opinions to match those of others. (p. 636)

confounding variable A type of extraneous variable that changes in sync with the independent variable, making it difficult to discern which one is causing changes in the dependent variable. (p. 37)

consciousness The state of being aware of oneself, one's thoughts, and/or the environment; includes various levels of conscious awareness. (p. 144)

conservation Refers to the unchanging properties of volume, mass, or amount in relation to appearance. (p. 348)

consummate love Love that combines intimacy, commitment, and passion. (p. 659)

continuous reinforcement A schedule of reinforcement in which every target behavior is reinforced. (p. 212)

control group The participants in an experiment who are not exposed to the treatment variable; this is the comparison group. (p. 35)

conventional moral reasoning Kohlberg's stage of moral development that determines right and wrong from the expectations of society and important others. (p. 360)

convergence A binocular cue used to judge distance and depth based on the tension of the muscles that direct where the eyes are focusing. (p. 132)

convergent thinking A conventional approach to problem solving that focuses on finding a single best solution to a problem by using previous experience and knowledge. (p. 321)

coping The cognitive, behavioral, and emotional abilities used to manage something that is perceived as difficult or challenging. (p. 521)

cornea The clear, outer layer of the eye that shields it from damage and focuses incoming light waves. (p. 104)

corpus callosum The thick band of nerve fibers connecting the right and left cerebral hemispheres; principal structure for information shared between the two hemispheres. (p. 71)

correlation An association or relationship between two (or more) variables. (p. 30)

correlational method A type of descriptive research examining the relationships among variables. (p. 30)

correlation coefficient The statistical measure (symbolized as r) that indicates the strength and direction of the relationship between two variables. (p. 30)

creativity In problem solving, the ability to construct valuable results in innovative ways; the ability to generate original ideas. (p. 320)

critical period Specific time frame in which an organism is sensitive to environmental factors, and certain behaviors and abilities are readily shaped or altered by events or experiences. (p. 329)

critical thinking The process of weighing various pieces of evidence, synthesizing them, and determining the contributions of each; disciplined thinking that is clear, rational, open-minded, and informed by evidence. (p. 17)

cross-sectional method A research design that examines people of different ages at a single point in time. (p. 330)

cross-sequential method A research design that examines groups of people of different ages, following them across time. (p. 332)

crystallized intelligence Knowledge gained through learning and experience. (p. 365)

culture-fair intelligence tests Assessments designed to minimize cultural bias. (p. 317)

daily hassles Minor and regularly occurring problems that can act as stressors. (p. 506)

dark adaptation Ability of the eyes to adjust to dark after exposure to bright light. (p. 107)

debriefing Sharing information with participants after their involvement in a study has ended, including the purpose of the research and any deception used. (p. 41)

decision making The cognitive process of choosing from alternatives that might be used to reach a goal. (p. 295)

deindividuation The diminished sense of personal responsibility, inhibition, or adherence to social norms that occurs when group members are not treated as individuals. (p. 644)

deinstitutionalization The mass movement of patients with psychological disorders out of institutions, and the attempt to reintegrate them into the community. (p. 580)

delirium tremens (DTs) Withdrawal symptoms that can occur when a person who is physiologically dependent on alcohol suddenly stops drinking; can include sweating, restlessness, hallucinations, severe tremors, and seizures. (p. 180)

delta waves Brain waves that indicate a deep sleep. (p. 155)

delusions Strange or false beliefs that a person firmly maintains even when presented with evidence to the contrary. (p. 561)

dendrites Tiny, branchlike fibers extending from the cell body that receive messages from other neurons and send information in the direction of the cell body. (p. 53)

deoxyribonucleic acid (DNA) A molecule that provides instructions for the development of an organism. (p. 333)

dependent variable (DV) In the experimental method, the characteristic or response that is measured to determine the effect of the researcher's manipulation. (p. 35)

depressants A class of psychoactive drugs that *depress* or slow down activity in the central nervous system. (p. 169)

depth perception The ability to perceive three-dimensional objects and judge distances. (p. 132)

descriptive research Research methods that describe and explore behaviors, but with findings that cannot definitively state cause-and-effect relationships. (p. 26)

developmental psychology A field of psychology that examines physical, cognitive, and socioemotional changes across the life span. (p. 328)

difference threshold The minimum difference between two stimuli that can be noticed 50% of the time. (p. 99)

diffusion of responsibility The sharing of duties and responsibilities among all group members that can lead to feelings of decreased accountability and motivation. (p. 643)

discrimination Showing favoritism or hostility to others because of their affiliation with a group. (p. 651)

display rules Framework or guidelines for when, how, and where an emotion is expressed. (p. 404)

dispositional attribution A belief that some characteristic of an individual is involved in the cause of an event or activity. (p. 625)

dissociation A disturbance in the normally integrated experience of psychological functions involved in memory, consciousness, perception, or identity. (p. 568)

dissociative amnesia A psychological disorder marked by difficulty remembering important personal information and life events. (p. 568)

dissociative disorders Psychological disorders distinguished by disturbances in normal psychological functioning; may include problems with memory, identity, consciousness, perception, and motor control. (p. 568)

dissociative fugue A condition in which a person with dissociative amnesia wanders about in a confused and unexpected manner. (p. 568)

dissociative identity disorder A psychological disorder that involves the occurrence of two or more distinct personalities within an individual. (p. 569)

distress The stress response to unpleasant or undesirable stressors. (p. 501)

distributed practice Spreading out study sessions over time with breaks in between. (p. 250)

distribution shape How the frequencies of the values are shaped along the x-axis. (p. A-5)

divergent thinking The ability to devise many solutions to a problem; a component of creativity. (p. 320)

dizygotic twins Fraternal twins who develop from two eggs inseminated by two sperm, and are as genetically similar as any sibling pair. (p. 336)

dominant gene One of a pair of genes that has power over the expression of an inherited characteristic. (p. 335)

door-in-the-face technique A compliance technique that involves making a large request first, followed by a smaller request. (p. 635)

dopamine hypothesis A theory suggesting that the synthesis, release, and concentrations of the neurotransmitter dopamine play a role in schizophrenia. (p. 564)

double-blind study Type of study in which neither the researchers who are administering the independent variable nor the participants know what type of treatment is being given. (p. 37)

drive A state of tension that pushes us or motivates behaviors to meet a need. (p. 383)

drive-reduction theory Suggests that homeostasis motivates us to meet biological needs. (p. 383)

echoic memory Exact copies of the sounds we hear; a form of sensory memory. (p. 241)

eclectic approach to therapy Drawing on multiple theories and approaches to tailor treatment for a client. (p. 582)

effortful processing The encoding and storage of information with conscious effort, or awareness. (p. 249)

ego According to Freud, the structure of the mind that uses the reality principle to manipulate situations, plan for the future, solve problems, and make decisions. (p. 461)

egocentrism When a person is only able to imagine the world from his or her own perspective. (p. 348)

ego defense mechanisms Distortions of perceptions and memories of the real world, without one's awareness, to reduce the anxiety created by the conflict among the id, ego, and superego. (p. 462)

elaborative rehearsal The method of connecting incoming information to knowledge in long-term memory; a deep level of encoding. (p. 249)

electroconvulsive therapy (ECT) A biomedical treatment for severe depression that induces seizures in the brain through electrical currents. (p. 605)

embryo The unborn human from the beginning of the 3rd week of pregnancy, lasting through the 8th week of prenatal development. (p. 336)

emerging adulthood A phase of life between 18 and 25 years that includes exploration and opportunity. (p. 361)

emotion A psychological state that includes a subjective or inner experience, a physiological component, and a behavioral expression. (p. 395)

emotional intelligence The capacity to perceive, understand, regulate, and use emotions to adapt to social situations. (p. 318)

emotion-focused coping A coping strategy in which a person addresses the emotions that surround a problem, as opposed to trying to solve it. (p. 521)

empathy The ability to feel what a person is experiencing by attempting to observe the world through his or her eyes. (p. 589)

encoding The process through which information enters our memory system. (p. 236)

encoding specificity principle Memories are more easily recalled when the context and cues at the time of encoding are similar to those at the time of retrieval. (p. 255)

endocrine system The communication system that uses glands to convey messages by releasing hormones into the bloodstream. (p. 69)

epigenetics A field of study that examines the processes involved in the development of phenotypes. (p. 334)

episodic memory The record of memorable experiences or "episodes" including when and where an experience occurred; a type of explicit memory. (p. 246)

estrogen The female hormone secreted primarily by the ovaries and by the adrenal glands in both males and females. (p. 420)

e-therapy A category of treatment that utilizes the Internet to provide support and therapy. (p. 613)

ethnocentrism Seeing the world only from the perspective of one's own group. (p. 651)

eustress The stress response to agreeable or positive stressors. (p. 501)

evidence-based practice Making decisions about treatment that integrate valuable research findings, clinical expertise, and knowledge of a patient's culture, values, and preferences. (p. 582)

evolutionary perspective An approach that uses knowledge about evolutionary forces, such as natural selection, to understand behavior. (p. 12)

expectancy A person's predictions about the consequences or outcomes of behavior. (p. 477)

experiment A controlled procedure that involves careful examination through the use of scientific observation and/or manipulation of variables (measurable characteristics). (p. 19)

experimental group The members of an experiment who are exposed to the treatment variable or manipulation by the researcher; represents the treatment group. (p. 35)

experimental method A type of research that manipulates a variable of interest (independent variable) to uncover cause-and-effect relationships. (p. 34)

experimenter bias Researchers' expectations that influence the outcome of a study. (p. 38)

explicit memory A type of memory you are aware of having and can consciously express in words or declare, including memories of facts and experiences. (p. 245)

exposure A therapeutic technique that brings a person into contact with a feared object or situation while in a safe environment, with the goal of extinguishing or eliminating the fear response. (p. 590)

extinction In classical conditioning, the process by which the conditioned response decreases after repeated exposure to the conditioned stimulus in the absence of the unconditioned stimulus; in operant conditioning, the disappearance of a learned behavior through the removal of its reinforcer. (p. 196)

extraneous variable A characteristic of participants or the environment that could unexpectedly influence the outcome of a study. (p. 37)

extrasensory perception (ESP) The purported ability to obtain information about the world without any sensory stimuli. (p. 136)

extrinsic motivation The drive or urge to continue a behavior because of external reinforcers. (p. 379)

facial feedback hypothesis The facial expression of an emotion can affect the experience of that emotion. (p. 405)

false consensus effect The tendency to overestimate the degree to which others think or act like we do. (p. 627)

family therapy A type of therapy that focuses on the family as an integrated system, recognizing that the interactions within it can create instability or lead to the breakdown of the family unit. (p. 609)

feature detectors Neurons in the visual cortex specialized in detecting specific features of the visual experience, such as angles, lines, and movements. (p. 108)

fetal alcohol syndrome (FAS) Delays in development that result from moderate to heavy alcohol use during pregnancy. (p. 337)

fetus The unborn human from 2 months following conception to birth. (p. 338)

figure–ground A central principle of Gestalt psychology, involving the shifting of focus; as attention is focused on one object, all other features drop or recede into the background. (p. 132)

five-factor model of personality A trait approach to explaining personality, including dimensions of openness to experience, conscientiousness, extraversion, agreeableness, and neuroticism; also known as "the Big Five." (p. 481)

fixation Being stuck in a particular psychosexual stage of development as a result of unsuccessfully dealing with the conflict characteristic of that stage. (p. 465)

fixed-interval schedule A schedule in which the reinforcer comes after a preestablished interval of time; the behavior is only reinforced after the given interval is over. (p. 215)

fixed-ratio schedule A schedule in which the subject must exhibit a predetermined number of desired behaviors before a reinforcer is given. (p. 213)

flashbulb memory A detailed account of circumstances surrounding an emotionally significant or shocking, sometimes historic, event. (p. 246)

fluid intelligence The ability to think in the abstract and create associations among concepts. (p. 365)

foot-in-the-door technique A compliance technique that involves making a small request first, followed by a larger request. (p. 634)

forebrain Largest part of the brain; includes the cerebral cortex and the limbic system. (p. 86)

formal concepts The mental representations of categories that are created through rigid and logical rules or features. (p. 283)

formal operational stage Piaget's stage of cognitive development during which children begin to think more logically and systematically. (p. 349)

framing effect Occurs when the wording of questions or the context of a problem influences the outcome of a decision. (p. 298)

free association A psychoanalytic technique in which a patient says anything that comes to mind. (p. 586)

frequency The number of sound waves passing a given point per unit of time; higher frequency is perceived as higher pitch, and lower frequency is perceived as lower pitch. (p. 112)

frequency distribution A simple way to portray data that displays how often various values in a data set are present. (p. A-4)

frequency polygon A type of graphic display that uses lines to represent the frequency of data values. (p. A-5)

frequency theory States that pitch is determined by the vibrating frequency of the sound wave, basilar membrane, and associated neural impulses. (p. 115)

frontal lobes The area of the cortex that organizes information among the other lobes of the brain and is responsible for cognitive functions, such as thinking, perception, and impulse control. (p. 77)

frustration–aggression hypothesis Suggests that aggression may occur in response to frustration. (p. 648)

functional fixedness A barrier to problem solving that occurs when familiar objects can only be imagined to function in their normal or usual way. (p. 293)

functionalism An early school of psychology that focused on the function of thought processes, feelings, and behaviors and how they help us adapt to the environment. (p. 10)

fundamental attribution error The tendency to overestimate the degree to which the characteristics of an individual are the cause of an event, and to underestimate the involvement of situational factors. (p. 625)

gate-control theory Suggests that the perception of pain will either increase or decrease through the interaction of biopsychosocial factors; signals are sent to open or close "gates" that control the neurological pathways for pain. (p. 125)

gender The dimension of masculinity and femininity based on social, cultural, and psychological characteristics. (p. 418)

gender identity The feeling or sense of being either male or female, and compatibility, contentment, and conformity with one's gender. (p. 427)

gender roles The collection of actions, beliefs, and characteristics that a culture associates with masculinity and femininity. (p. 426)

gender schemas The psychological or mental guidelines that dictate how to be masculine and feminine. (p. 427)

gene Specified segment of a DNA molecule. (p. 333)

general adaptation syndrome (GAS) A specific pattern of physiological reactions to stressors that includes the alarm stage, resistance stage, and exhaustion stage. (p. 509)

general intelligence (g-factor) A singular underlying aptitude or intellectual competence that drives abilities in many areas, including verbal, spatial, and reasoning. (p. 310)

generalized anxiety disorder A psychological disorder characterized by an excessive amount of worry and anxiety about activities relating to family, health, school, and other aspects of daily life. (p. 549)

genotype An individual's complete collection of genes. (p. 334)

genuineness The ability to respond to a client in an authentic way rather than hiding behind a polite or professional mask. (p. 589)

gestalt The natural tendency for the brain to organize stimuli into a whole, rather than perceiving the parts and pieces. (p. 130)

gifted Highly intelligent; defined as having an IQ score of 130 or above. (p. 318)

glial cells Cells that support, nourish, and protect neurons; some produce myelin that covers axons. (p. 54)

grammar The rules associated with word and sentence structure. (p. 304)

group polarization The tendency for a group to take a more extreme stance than originally held after deliberations and discussion. (p. 645)

groupthink The tendency for group members to maintain cohesiveness and agreement in their decision making, failing to consider possible alternatives and related viewpoints. (p. 645)

gustation The sense of taste. (p. 121)

habituation A basic form of learning evident when an organism does not respond as strongly or as often to an event following multiple exposures to it. (p. 191)

hallucinations Perception-like experiences that an individual believes are real, but that are not evident to others. (p. 561)

hallucinogens A group of psychoactive drugs that can produce hallucinations (auditory, visual, or kinesthetic), distorted sensory experiences, alterations of mood, and distorted thinking. (p. 176)

hardiness A personality characteristic indicating an ability to remain resilient and optimistic despite enduring intensely stressful situations. (p. 524)

health psychology The study of the biological, psychological, and social factors that contribute to health and illness. (p. 510)

heritability The degree to which hereditary factors (genes) are responsible for a particular characteristic observed within a population; the proportion of variation in a characteristic attributed to genetic factors. (p. 319)

heterosexual Attraction to members of the opposite sex. (p. 433)

heuristics Problem-solving approaches that incorporate a rule of thumb or broad application of a strategy. (p. 290)

hierarchy of needs A continuum of needs that are universal and ordered in terms of the strength of their associated drives. (p. 385)

higher order conditioning With repeated pairings of a conditioned stimulus and a neutral stimulus, that second neutral stimulus becomes a conditioned stimulus as well. (p. 197)

hindbrain Includes areas of the brain responsible for fundamental life-sustaining processes. (p. 87)

hippocampus A pair of structures located in the limbic system; primarily responsible for creating new memories. (p. 85)

histogram Displays the classes of a variable on the x-axis and the frequency of the data on the y-axis; frequency is indicated by the height of the vertical bars. (p. A-5)

homeostasis The tendency for bodies to maintain constant states through internal controls. (p. 383)

homosexual Attraction to members of the same sex. (p. 433)

hormones Chemical messengers released into the bloodstream that influence mood, cognition, appetite, and many other processes and behaviors. (p. 69)

hue The color of an object, determined by the wavelength of light it reflects. (p. 103)

human immunodeficiency virus (HIV) A virus transferred via bodily fluids (blood, semen, vaginal fluid, or breast milk) that causes the breakdown of the immune system, eventually resulting in AIDS. (p. 446)

humanistic psychology An approach suggesting that human nature is by and large positive, and the human direction is toward growth. (p. 12)

humanistic therapy A type of insight therapy that emphasizes the positive nature of humankind. (p. 588)

hypnosis An altered state of consciousness allowing for changes in perceptions and behaviors, which result from suggestions made by a hypnotist. (p. 182)

hypothalamus A small structure located below the thalamus that maintains a constant internal environment within a healthy range; helps regulate sleep–wake cycles, sexual behavior, and appetite (p. 84)

hypothesis A statement that can be used to test a prediction. (p. 19)

hypothesis testing Mathematical procedures used to determine the likelihood that a researcher's predictions are supported by the data collected. (p. A-1)

iconic memory Visual impressions that are photograph-like in their accuracy but dissolve in less than a second; a form of sensory memory. (p. 241)

id According to Freud, the most primitive structure of the mind, the activities of which occur at the unconscious level and are guided by the pleasure principle. (p. 461)

ideal self The self-concept a person strives for and fervently wishes to achieve. (p. 474)

identity A sense of self based on values, beliefs, and goals. (p. 357)

illusion A perception that is inconsistent with sensory data. (p. 128)

implicit memory A memory of something you know or know how to do, which may be automatic, unconscious, and difficult to bring to awareness and express. (p. 246)

incentive An association established between a behavior and its consequences, which then motivates that behavior. (p. 379)

independent variable (IV) In the experimental method, the variable manipulated by the researcher to determine its effect on the dependent variable. (p. 35)

informed consent Acknowledgment from study participants that they understand what their participation will entail. (p. 41)

in-group The group to which we belong. (p. 649)

insanity A legal determination of the degree to which a person is responsible for criminal behaviors. (p. 538)

insight An understanding or solution that occurs in a sudden stroke of clarity (the feeling of "aha!"). (p. 292)

insight therapies A type of psychotherapy aimed at increasing awareness of self and the environment. (p. 582)

insomnia Sleep disturbance characterized by an inability to fall asleep or stay asleep, impacting both the quality and quantity of sleep. (p. 160)

instinctive drift The tendency for animals to revert to instinctual behaviors after a behavior pattern has been learned. (p. 208)

instincts Complex behaviors that are fixed, unlearned, and consistent within a species. (p. 382)

Institutional Review Board (IRB) A committee that reviews research proposals to protect the rights and welfare of all participants. (p. 42)

intelligence Innate ability to solve problems, adapt to the environment, and learn from experiences. (p. 309)

intelligence quotient (IQ) A score from an intelligence assessment; originally based on mental age divided by chronological age, multiplied by 100. (p. 313)

interneurons Neurons that reside exclusively in the brain and spinal cord; act as a bridge connecting sensory and motor neurons. (p. 64)

interpersonal attraction The factors that lead us to form friendships or romantic relationships with others. (p. 656)

interpretation A psychoanalytic technique used to explore unconscious conflicts driving behavior. (p. 586)

intersexual Having ambiguous or inconsistent biological indicators of male or female in the sexual structures and organs. (p. 423)

intrinsic motivation The drive or urge to continue a behavior because of internal reinforcers. (p. 380)

introspection The examination of one's own conscious activities. (p. 9)

iris The muscle responsible for changing the size of the pupil. (p. 104)

James–Lange theory of emotion Suggests that a stimulus initiates the experience of a physiological and/or behavioral reaction, and this reaction leads to the feeling of an emotion. (p. 398)

just-world hypothesis The tendency to believe the world is a fair place and individuals generally get what they deserve. (p. 625)

kinesthesia Sensory system that conveys information about body position and movement. (p. 126)

language A system for using symbols to think and communicate. (p. 303)

latent content The hidden meaning of a dream, often concealed by the manifest content of the dream. (p. 166)

latent learning Learning that occurs without awareness and regardless of reinforcement, and is not evident until needed. (p. 225)

lateralization The idea that each cerebral hemisphere processes certain types of information and excels in certain activities. (p. 73)

law of effect Thorndike's principle stating that behaviors are more likely to be repeated when followed by pleasurable outcomes, and less likely to be repeated when followed by unpleasant outcomes. (p. 205)

learned helplessness A tendency for people to believe they have no control over the consequences of their behaviors, resulting in passive behavior. (p. 557)

learning A relatively enduring change in behavior or thinking that results from experiences. (p. 190)

light adaptation Ability of the eyes to adjust to light after being in the dark. (p. 107)

limbic system A collection of structures that regulates emotions and basic drives like hunger, and aids in the creation of memories. (p. 83)

longitudinal method A research design that examines one sample of people over a period of time to determine age-related changes. (p. 330)

long-term memory A stage of memory with essentially unlimited capacity that stores enduring information about facts and experiences. (p. 239)

long-term potentiation The increased efficiency of neural communication over time, resulting in learning and the formation of memories. (p. 270)

lymphocyte Type of white blood cell produced in the bone marrow whose job is to battle enemies such as viruses and bacteria. (p. 513)

lysergic acid diethylamide (LSD) A synthetically produced, odorless, tasteless, and colorless hallucinogen that is very potent; produces extreme changes in sensations and perceptions. (p. 176)

maintenance rehearsal Technique of repeating information to be remembered, increasing the length of time it can be held in short-term memory. (p. 242)

major depressive disorder A psychological disorder that includes at least one major depressive episode, with symptoms such as depressed mood, problems with sleep, and loss of energy. (p. 553)

maladaptive behaviors Behaviors or actions that run counter to what is in one's best interest. (p. 536)

manic episodes States of continuous elation that is out of proportion to the setting, and can include irritability, very high and sustained levels of energy, and an "expansive" mood. (p. 558)

manifest content The apparent meaning of a dream; the remembered story line of a dream. (p. 166)

massed practice Studying for long periods of time without breaks. (p. 250)

maturation Physical growth beginning with conception and ending when the body stops growing. (p. 328)

mean The arithmetic average of a data set; a measure of central tendency. (p. A-8)

means–ends analysis Heuristic used to determine how to decrease the distance between a goal and the current status (the means), leading to the solution of a problem (the end). (p. 292)

measures of central tendency Numbers that represent the middle of a data set. (p. A-8)

measures of position Numbers that represent where particular data values fall in relation to other values in the data set. (p. A-11)

measures of variation Numbers that describe the variation or dispersion in a data set. (p. A-9)

median A number that represents the position in the data set for which 50% of the values are above it, and 50% are below it; a measure of central tendency. (p. A-8)

medical model An approach suggesting that psychological disorders are illnesses that have underlying biological causes. (p. 543)

medulla A structure that oversees vital functions, including breathing, digestion, and heart rate. (p. 87)

memory Brain processes involved in the encoding, storage, and retrieval of information. (p. 235)

memory trace The location where memories are etched in the brain via physiological changes. (p. 267)

menarche The point at which menstruation begins. (p. 356)

menopause The time when a woman no longer ovulates, her menstrual cycle stops, and she is no longer capable of reproduction. (p. 363)

mental age (MA) A score representing the mental abilities of an individual in relation to others of a similar chronological age. (p. 313)

mere-exposure effect The more we are exposed to someone or something, the more positive our reaction to it becomes. (p. 657)

meta-analysis A type of statistical analysis that combines findings from many studies on a single topic; statistics used to merge the outcomes of many studies. (p. A-4)

methylenedioxymethamphetamine (MDMA) A synthetic drug chemically similar to the stimulant methamphetamine and the hallucinogen mescaline; produces a combination of stimulant and hallucinogenic effects. (p. 177)

midbrain The part of the brainstem involved in levels of arousal; responsible for generating movement patterns in response to sensory input. (p. 86)

mindfulness meditation Being fully present in the moment; focusing attention on the here-and-now without passing judgment. (p. 529)

misinformation effect The tendency for new and misleading information obtained after an incident to distort one's memory of it. (p. 261)

mnemonic Technique to improve memory. (p. 247)

mode The value of the data set that is most frequent; a measure of central tendency. (p. A-9)

model The individual or character whose behavior is being imitated. (p. 223)

monocular cues Depth and distance cues that require the use of only one eye. (p. 133)

monozygotic twins Identical twins who develop from one egg inseminated at conception, which then splits into two separate cells. (p. 336)

mood-stabilizing drugs Psychotropic medications that minimize the lows of depression and the highs of mania. (p. 603)

morphemes The fundamental units that bring meaning to language. (p. 304)

motivation A stimulus that can direct behavior, thinking, and feeling. (p. 379)

motor cortex A band of tissue toward the rear of the frontal lobes that works with other brain regions to plan and execute voluntary movements. (p. 79)

motor neurons Neurons that transmit information from the central nervous system to the muscles and glands. (p. 64)

myelin sheath Fatty substance that insulates the axon and speeds the transmission of neural messages. (p. 53)

narcolepsy A neurological disorder characterized by excessive daytime sleepiness, which includes lapses into sleep and napping. (p. 156)

natural concepts The mental representations of categories resulting from experiences in daily life. (p. 283)

naturalistic observation A type of descriptive research that studies participants in their natural environment through systematic observation. (p. 27)

natural selection The process through which inherited traits in a given population either increase in frequency because they are adaptive or decrease in frequency because they are maladaptive. (p. 12)

nature The inherited biological factors that shape behaviors, personality, and other characteristics. (p. 2)

need for achievement (n-Ach) A drive to reach attainable and challenging goals, especially in the face of competition. (p. 387)

need for power (n-Pow) A drive to control and influence others. (p. 388)

needs Physiological or psychological requirements that must be maintained at some baseline or constant state. (p. 383)

negatively skewed A nonsymmetric distribution with a longer tail to the left side of the distribution; left-skewed distribution. (p. A-6)

negative punishment The removal of something desirable following an unwanted behavior, with the intention of decreasing that behavior. (p. 218)

negative reinforcement The removal of an unpleasant stimulus following a target behavior, which increases the likelihood of it occurring again. (p. 210)

negative symptoms Behaviors or characteristics that are limited or absent; examples are social withdrawal, diminished speech, limited or no emotions, and loss of energy and follow-up. (p. 561)

nerves Bundles of neurons that carry information to and from the central nervous system; provide communication between the central nervous system and the muscles, glands, and sensory receptors. (p. 66)

neurogenesis The generation of new neurons in the brain. (p. 77)

neurons Specialized cells of the nervous system that transmit electrical and chemical signals in the body; nerve cells. (p. 51)

neuroplasticity The brain's ability to heal, grow new connections, and reorganize in order to adapt to the environment. (p. 76)

neuroscience The study of the brain and nervous system. (p. 50)

neurosurgery A biomedical therapy that involves the destruction of some portion of the brain or connections between different areas of the brain. (p. 606)

neurotransmitters Chemical messengers that neurons use to communicate at the synapse. (p. 58)

neutral stimulus (NS) A stimulus that does not cause a relevant automatic or reflexive response. (p. 193)

nightmares Frightening dreams that occur during REM sleep. (p. 161)

nondirective A technique used in person-centered therapy whereby the therapist follows the lead of the client during treatment sessions. (p. 589)

non–rapid eye movement (non-REM or NREM) The nondreaming sleep that occurs during sleep Stages N1 to N3. (p. 155)

normal curve Depicts the frequency of values of a variable along a continuum; bell-shaped symmetrical distribution, with the highest point reflecting the average score. (p. 315)

norms Standards of the social environment. (p. 636)

nurture The environmental factors that shape behaviors, personality, and other characteristics. (p. 2)

obedience Changing behavior because we have been ordered to do so by an authority figure. (p. 638)

object permanence A milestone of the sensorimotor stage of cognitive development; an infant's realization that objects and people still exist even when out of sight or touch. (p. 348)

observational learning Learning that occurs as a result of watching the behavior of others. (p. 223)

observer bias Errors in the recording of observations, the result of a researcher's value system, expectations, or attitudes. (p. 28)

obsession A thought, an urge, or an image that happens repeatedly, is intrusive and unwelcome, and often causes anxiety and distress. (p. 550)

obsessive-compulsive disorder (OCD) A psychological disorder characterized by obsessions and/or compulsions that are time-consuming and cause a great deal of distress. (p. 550)

obstructive sleep apnea hypopnea A serious disturbance of non-REM sleep characterized by complete absence of air flow (apnea) or reduced air flow (hypopnea). (p. 159)

occipital lobes The area of the cortex in the back of the head that processes visual information. (p. 79)

Oedipus complex According to Freud, the attraction a child feels toward the opposite-sex parent, along with the resentment or envy directed toward the same-sex parent. (p. 466)

olfaction The sense of smell. (p. 117)

operant conditioning Learning that occurs when voluntary actions become associated with their consequences. (p. 204)

operational definition The precise manner in which a variable of interest is defined and measured. (p. 20)

opiates A class of psychoactive drugs that cause a sense of euphoria; a drug that imitates the endorphins naturally produced in the brain. (p. 171)

opioids A class of psychoactive drugs that minimize perceptions of pain. (p. 169)

opponent-process theory Perception of color derives from a special group of neurons that respond to opponent colors (red–green, blue–yellow). (p. 110)

optic nerve The bundle of axons from ganglion cells leading to the visual cortex. (p. 106)

orgasm A powerful combination of extremely gratifying sensations and a series of rhythmic muscular contractions. (p. 432)

out-group People outside the group to which we belong. (p. 649)

overgeneralization A cognitive distortion that assumes self-contained events will have major repercussions. (p. 596)

panic attack Sudden, extreme fear or discomfort that escalates quickly, often with no obvious trigger, and includes symptoms such as increased heart rate, sweating, shortness of breath, chest pain, nausea, lightheadedness, and fear of dying. (p. 546)

panic disorder A psychological disorder that includes recurrent, unexpected panic attacks and fear that can cause significant changes in behavior. (p. 546)

parameters Numbers that describe characteristics of a population. (p. A-3)

paraphilia Uncommon sexual acts. (p. 447)

parapsychology The study of extrasensory perception. (p. 136)

parasympathetic nervous system The division of the autonomic nervous system that orchestrates the "rest-and-digest" response to bring the body back to a noncrisis mode. (p. 66)

parietal lobes The area of the cortex that receives and processes sensory information such as touch, pressure, temperature, and spatial orientation. (p. 79)

partial reinforcement A schedule of reinforcement in which target behaviors are reinforced intermittently, not continuously. (p. 212)

partial reinforcement effect The tendency for behaviors acquired through intermittent reinforcement to be more resistant to extinction than those acquired through continuous reinforcement. (p. 213)

passionate love Love that is based on zealous emotion, leading to intense longing and sexual attraction. (p. 659)

perception The organization and interpretation of sensory stimuli by the brain. (p. 96)

perceptual constancy The tendency to perceive objects in our environment as stable in terms of shape, size, and color, regardless of changes in the sensory data received. (p. 134)

perceptual set The tendency to perceive stimuli in a specific manner based on past experiences and expectations. (p. 135)

peripheral nervous system (PNS) The part of the nervous system that connects the central nervous system to the rest of the body. (p. 63)

permissive parenting A parenting style characterized by low demands of children and few limitations. (p. 367)

personality The unique, core set of characteristics that influence the way one thinks, acts, and feels, and that are relatively consistent and enduring throughout the life span. (p. 456)

personality disorders A group of psychological disorders that can include impairments in cognition, emotional responses, interpersonal functioning, and impulse control. (p. 566)

person-centered therapy A form of humanistic therapy developed by Rogers; aimed at helping clients achieve their full potential. (p. 588)

persuasion Intentionally trying to make people change their attitudes and beliefs, which may lead to changes in their behaviors. (p. 632)

phenotype The observable expression or characteristics of one's genetic inheritance. (p. 334)

phonemes The basic building blocks of spoken language. (p. 303)

photoreceptors Specialized cells in the retina that absorb light energy and turn it into electrical and chemical signals for the brain to process. (p. 106)

phrenology An early approach to explaining the functions of the brain by trying to link the physical structure of the skull with a variety of characteristics. (p. 51)

physiological dependence With constant use of some psychoactive drugs, the body no longer functions normally without the drug. (p. 179)

pie chart Displays qualitative data with categories of interest represented by slices of the pie. (p. A-7)

pitch The degree to which a sound is high or low, determined by the frequency of its sound wave. (p. 112)

pituitary gland The pea-sized gland located in the center of the brain just under the hypothalamus; known as the master gland. (p. 69)

placebo An inert substance given to members of the control group; the fake treatment that has no benefit, but is administered as if it does. (p. 38)

place theory States that pitch corresponds to the location of the vibrating hair cells along the cochlea. (p. 115)

pleasure principle Collection of rules that guide the id resulting in behavior to achieve instant gratification without thought to consequences. (p. 461)

pons A hindbrain structure that helps regulate sleep–wake cycles and coordinate movement between the right and left sides of the body. (p. 87)

population All members of an identified group about which a researcher is interested. (p. 25)

positively skewed A nonsymmetric distribution with a longer tail to the right side of the distribution; right-skewed distribution. (p. A-6)

positive psychology An approach that focuses on the positive aspects of human beings, seeking to understand their strengths and uncover the roots of happiness, creativity, humor, and so on. (p. 44)

positive punishment The addition of something unpleasant following an unwanted behavior, with the intention of decreasing that behavior. (p. 216)

positive reinforcement The process by which reinforcers are added or presented following a targeted behavior, increasing the likelihood of it occurring again. (p. 209)

positive symptoms Excesses or distortions of normal behavior; examples are delusions, hallucinations, and disorganized speech. (p. 561)

postconventional moral reasoning Kohlberg's stage of moral development in which right and wrong are determined by the individual's beliefs about morality, which sometimes do not coincide with society's rules and regulations. (p. 360)

posttraumatic stress disorder (PTSD) A psychological disorder characterized by exposure to or being threatened by an event involving death, serious injury, or sexual violence; can include disturbing memories, nightmares, flashbacks, and other distressing symptoms. (p. 503)

pragmatics The social rules that help to organize language. (p. 305)

preconventional moral reasoning Kohlberg's stage of moral development in which a person, usually a child, focuses on the consequences of behaviors, good or bad, and is concerned with avoiding punishment. (p 360)

prejudice Holding hostile or negative attitudes toward an individual or group. (p. 649)

preoperational stage Piaget's stage of cognitive development during which children can start to use language to explore and understand their worlds. (p. 348)

primacy effect The tendency to remember items at the beginning of a list. (p. 254)

primary appraisal One's initial assessment of a situation to determine its personal impact and whether it is irrelevant, positive, challenging, or harmful. (p. 521)

primary reinforcer A reinforcer that satisfies a biological need, such as food, water, physical contact; innate reinforcer. (p. 211)

primary sex characteristics Organs associated with reproduction, including the ovaries, uterus, vagina, penis, scrotum, and testes. (p. 356)

priming The stimulation of memories as a result of retrieval cues in the environment. (p. 253)

proactive interference The tendency for information learned in the past to interfere with the retrieval of new material. (p. 259)

problem-focused coping A coping strategy in which a person deals directly with a problem by attempting to solve and address it head-on. (p. 521)

problem solving The variety of approaches that can be used to achieve a goal. (p. 289)

procedural memory The unconscious memory of how to carry out a variety of skills and activities; a type of implicit memory. (p. 247)

projective personality tests Assessments that present stimuli without a specified meaning to test takers, whose responses can then be interpreted to uncover underlying personality characteristics. (p. 487)

proprioceptors Specialized nerve endings primarily located in the muscles and joints that provide information about body location and orientation. (p. 126)

prosocial behaviors Actions that are kind, generous, and beneficial to others. (p. 225)

prototype The ideal or most representative example of a natural concept; helps us categorize or identify specific members of a concept. (p. 285)

proximity Nearness; plays an important role in the formation of relationships. (p. 656)

pseudopsychology An approach to explaining and predicting behavior and events that appears to be psychology, but has no empirical or objective evidence to support it. (p. 17)

psychoactive drugs Substances that can cause changes in psychological activities such as sensation, perception, attention, judgment, memory, self-control, emotion, thinking, and behavior; substances that cause changes in conscious experiences. (p. 168)

psychoanalysis Freud's views regarding personality as well as his system of psychotherapy and tools for the exploration of the unconscious. (p. 459)

psychoanalytic perspective An approach developed by Freud suggesting that behavior and personality are shaped by unconscious conflicts. (p. 11)

psychodynamic therapy A type of insight therapy that incorporates core psychoanalytic themes, including the importance of unconscious conflicts and experiences from the past. (p. 587)

psychological dependence With constant use of some psychoactive drugs, a strong desire or need to continue using the substance occurs without the evidence of tolerance or withdrawal symptoms. (p. 180)

psychological disorder A set of behavioral, emotional, and cognitive symptoms that are significantly distressing or disabling in terms of social functioning, work endeavors, and other aspects of life. (p. 536)

psychologists Scientists who study behavior and mental processes. (p. 3)

psychology The scientific study of behavior and mental processes. (p. 2)

psychoneuroimmunology The field that studies the relationships among psychological factors, the nervous system, and immune system functioning. (p. 520)

psychosexual stages According to Freud, the stages of development, from birth to adulthood, each of which has an erogenous zone as well as a conflict that must be dealt with. (p. 464)

psychosis Loss of contact with reality that is severe and chronic. (p. 561)

psychotherapy "Talk therapy"; a treatment approach in which a client works with a mental health professional to reduce psychological symptoms and improve quality of life. (p. 582)

puberty The period of development during which the body changes and becomes sexually mature and capable of reproduction. (p. 356)

punishment The application of a consequence that decreases the likelihood of a behavior recurring. (p. 216)

random assignment The process of appointing study participants to the experimental or control groups, ensuring that every person has an equal chance of being assigned to either. (p. 35)

random sample A subset of the population chosen through a procedure that ensures all members of the population have an equal chance of being selected to participate in the study. (p. 25)

range A number that represents the length of the data set and is a rough depiction of dispersion; a measure of variation. (p. A-10)

rapid eye movement (REM) The stage of sleep associated with dreaming; sleep characterized by bursts of eye movements, with brain activity similar to that of a waking state, but with a lack of muscle tone. (p. 155)

rational emotive behavior therapy (REBT) A type of cognitive therapy, developed by Ellis, that identifies illogical thoughts and attempts to convert them into rational ones. (p. 597)

reality principle Collection of rules that guide the ego as it negotiates between the id and the environment. (p. 461)

recall The process of retrieving information held in long-term memory without the help of explicit retrieval cues. (p. 253)

recency effect The tendency to remember items at the end of a list. (p. 254)

receptor sites Locations on the receiving neuron's dendrites where neurotransmitters attach. (p. 58)

recessive gene One of a pair of genes that is overpowered by a dominant gene. (p. 335)

reciprocal determinism According to Bandura, multidirectional interactions among cognition, behaviors, and the environment. (p. 479)

recognition The process of matching incoming data to information stored in long-term memory. (p. 253)

reflex arc An automatic response to a sensory stimulus, such as the "knee-jerk" reaction; a simple pathway of communication from sensory neurons through interneurons in the spinal cord back out through motor neurons. (p. 64)

refractory period An interval of time during which a man cannot attain another orgasm. (p. 432)

reinforcement Process by which an organism learns to associate a voluntary behavior with its consequences. (p. 205)

reinforcers Consequences, such as events or objects, that increase the likelihood of a behavior reoccurring. (p. 205)

relearning Material learned previously is acquired more quickly in subsequent exposures. (p. 256)

reliability The ability of an assessment to provide consistent, reproducible results. (p. 314)

REM rebound An increased amount of time spent in REM after sleep deprivation. (p. 162)

REM sleep behavior disorder A sleep disturbance in which the mechanism responsible for paralyzing the body during REM sleep is not functioning, resulting in the acting out of dreams. (p. 159)

replicate To repeat an experiment, generally with a new sample and/or other changes to the procedures, the goal of which is to provide further support for the findings of the first study. (p. 23)

representativeness heuristic A decision-making strategy that evaluates the degree to which the primary characteristics of a person or situation are similar to our prototype of that type of person or situation. (p. 297)

representative sample A subgroup of a population selected so that its members have characteristics similar to those of the population of interest. (p. 25)

repression The way the ego moves uncomfortable thoughts, memories, or feelings from the conscious level to the unconscious. (p. 464)

resistance A patient's unwillingness to cooperate in therapy; a sign of unconscious conflict. (p. 586)

resting potential The electrical potential of a cell "at rest"; the state of a cell when it is not activated. (p. 55)

reticular formation A network of neurons running through the midbrain that controls levels of arousal and quickly analyzes sensory information on its way to the cortex. (p. 86)

retina The layer of the eye containing photoreceptor cells, which transduce light energy into neural activity. (p. 104)

retinal disparity A binocular cue that uses the difference between the images the two eyes see to determine the distance of objects. (p. 133)

retrieval The process of accessing information encoded and stored in memory. (p. 236)

retrieval cues Stimuli that help in the retrieval of stored information that is difficult to access. (p. 253)

retroactive interference The tendency for recently learned information to interfere with the retrieval of things learned in the past. (p. 259)

retrograde amnesia A type of memory loss; an inability to access memories formed prior to damage or injury to the brain, or difficulty retrieving them. (p. 266)

reuptake Process by which neurotransmitters are reabsorbed by the sending terminal bud. (p. 58)

rich false memories Recollections of an event that never occurred, which are expressed with emotions and confidence and include details. (p. 262)

risky shift The tendency for groups to recommend uncertain and risky options. (p. 645)

rods Photoreceptors that enable us to see in dim lighting; not sensitive to color, but useful for night vision. (p. 106)

romantic love Love that is a combination of connection, concern, care, and intimacy. (p. 659)

sample A subset of a population chosen for inclusion in an experiment. (p. 25)

saturation Color purity. (p. 103)

scaffolding Pushing children to go just beyond what they are competent and comfortable doing, while providing help in a decreasing manner. (p. 349)

scapegoat A target of negative emotions, beliefs, and behaviors; typically, a member of the out-group who receives blame for an upsetting social situation. (p. 651)

Schachter–Singer theory of emotion Suggests that the experience of emotion is the result of physiological arousal and a cognitive label for this physiological state. (p. 400)

schema A collection of ideas that represents a basic unit of understanding. (p. 346)

schizophrenia A disabling psychological disorder that can include delusions, hallucinations, disorganized speech, and abnormal motor behavior. (p. 561)

scientific method The process scientists use to conduct research, which includes a continuing cycle of exploration, critical thinking, and systematic observation. (p. 19)

secondary appraisal An assessment to determine how to respond to a challenging or threatening situation. (p. 521)

secondary reinforcer Reinforcers that do not satisfy biological needs but often gain power through their association with primary reinforcers. (p. 211)

secondary sex characteristics Body characteristics, such as pubic hair, underarm hair, and enlarged breasts, that develop in puberty but are not associated with reproduction. (p. 356)

selective attention The ability to focus awareness on a small segment of information that is available through our sensory systems. (p. 147)

self-actualization The need to be one's best and strive for one's fullest potential. (p. 386)

self-concept The knowledge an individual has about his strengths, abilities, behavior patterns, and temperament. (p. 474)

self-determination theory (SDT) Suggests that humans are born with the needs for competence, relatedness, and autonomy, which are always driving us in the direction of growth and optimal functioning. (p. 387)

self-efficacy Beliefs one has regarding how effective he or she will be in reaching a goal. (p. 477)

self-serving bias The tendency to attribute our successes to personal characteristics and our failures to environmental factors. (p. 626)

semantic memory The memory of information theoretically available to anyone, which pertains to general facts about the world; a type of explicit memory. (p. 246)

semantics The rules used to bring meaning to words and sentences. (p. 304)

sensation The process by which sensory organs in the eyes, ears, nose, mouth, skin, and other tissues receive and detect stimuli. (p. 96)

sensorimotor stage Piaget's stage of cognitive development during which infants use their sensory capabilities and motor skills to learn about the surrounding world. (p. 348)

sensory adaptation The process through which sensory receptors become less sensitive to constant stimuli. (p. 98)

sensory memory A stage of memory that captures near-exact copies of vast amounts of sensory stimuli for a very brief period of time. (p. 239)

sensory neurons Neurons that receive information from the sensory systems and convey it to the brain for further processing. (p. 64)

serial position effect The ability to recall items in a list depends on where they are in the series. (p. 254)

set point The stable weight that is maintained despite variability in exercise and food intake. (p. 392)

sex The classification of someone as male or female based on biological characteristics; a sexual act such as intercourse. (p. 418)

sexual dysfunction A significant disturbance in the ability to respond sexually or to gain pleasure from sex. (p. 443)

sexuality A dimension of human nature encompassing everything that makes us sexual beings; sexual activities, attitudes, and behaviors. (p. 418)

sexually transmitted infections (STIs) Diseases or illnesses transmitted through sexual activity. (p. 445)

sexual orientation A person's enduring sexual attraction to individuals of the same sex, opposite sex, or both sexes; a continuum that includes dimensions of sexuality, attraction, desire, and emotions. (p. 432)

shape constancy An object is perceived as maintaining its shape, regardless of the image projected on the retina. (p. 134)

shaping Process by which a person observes the behaviors of another organism, providing reinforcers if the organism performs at a required level. (p. 206)

short-term memory A stage of memory that temporarily maintains and processes a limited amount of information. (p. 239)

signal detection theory A theory explaining how internal and external factors influence our ability to detect weak signals in the environment. (p. 101)

situational attribution A belief that some environmental factor is involved in the cause of an event or activity. (p. 625)

size constancy An object is perceived as maintaining its size, regardless of the image projected on the retina. (p. 134)

skewed distribution Nonsymmetrical frequency distribution. (p. A-6)

sleep terrors A disturbance of non-REM sleep, generally occurring in children; characterized by screaming, staring fearfully, and usually no memory of the episode the following morning. (p. 161)

social cognition The way people think about others, attend to social information, and use this information in their lives, both consciously and unconsciously. (p. 622)

social-cognitive perspective Suggests that personality results from patterns of thinking (cognitive) as well as relationships and other environmental factors (social). (p. 477)

social facilitation The tendency for the presence of others to improve personal performance when the task or event is fairly uncomplicated and a person is adequately prepared. (p. 642)

social identity How we view ourselves within our social group. (p. 649)

social influence How a person is affected by others as evidenced in behaviors, emotions, and cognition. (p. 631)

social loafing The tendency for people to make less than their best effort when individual contributions are too complicated to measure. (p. 643)

social psychology The study of human cognition, emotion, and behavior in relation to others. (p. 620)

social roles The positions we hold in social groups, and the responsibilities and expectations associated with those roles. (p. 652)

social support The assistance we acquire from others. (p. 506)

sociocultural perspective An approach examining how social interactions and culture influence behavior and mental processes. (p. 13)

somatic nervous system The branch of the peripheral nervous system that includes sensory nerves and motor nerves; gathers information from sensory receptors and controls the skeletal muscles responsible for voluntary movement. (p. 66)

somatosensory cortex A band of tissue running parallel to the motor cortex that receives and integrates sensory information from all over the body. (p. 80)

source traits Basic underlying or foundational characteristics of personality. (p. 480)

specific phobia A psychological disorder that includes a distinct fear or anxiety in relation to an object or situation. (p. 547)

spermarche A boy's first ejaculation. (p. 356)

spinal cord The bundle of neurons that allows communication between the brain and the peripheral nervous system. (p. 63)

split-brain operation A rare procedure used to disconnect the right and left hemispheres by cutting the corpus callosum. (p. 72)

spontaneous recovery The reappearance of a conditioned response following its extinction. (p. 196)

standard deviation A number that represents the average distance the values in a data set are from their mean; a measure of variation. (p. A-10)

standardization Occurs when test developers administer a test to a large sample and then publish the average scores for specified groups. (p. 314)

statistical significance The probability that the findings of a study were due to chance. (p. A-2)

statistics A science that focuses on how to collect, organize, analyze, display, and interpret data; numbers that describe characteristics of a sample. (p. A-1)

stem-and-leaf plot A type of graphical display that uses the actual data values in the form of leading digits and trailing digits. (p. A-5)

stem cells Cells responsible for producing new neurons. (p. 77)

stereotypes Conclusions or inferences we make about people who are different from us based on their group membership, such as race, religion, age, or gender. (p. 648)

stereotype threat A "situational threat" in which individuals are aware of others' negative expectations, which leads to a fear of being judged or treated as inferior. (p. 651)

stigma A negative attitude or opinion about a group of people based on certain traits or characteristics. (p. 539)

stimulants A class of drugs that increase neural activity in the central nervous system. (p. 173)

stimulus An event or occurrence that generally leads to a response. (p. 191)

stimulus discrimination The ability to differentiate between a conditioned stimulus and other stimuli sufficiently different from it. (p. 196)

stimulus generalization The tendency for stimuli similar to the conditioned stimulus to elicit the conditioned response. (p. 196)

storage The process of preserving information for possible recollection in the future. (p. 236)

stress The response to perceived threats or challenges resulting from stimuli or events that cause strain. (p. 498)

stressors Stimuli that cause psychological, physiological, and emotional reactions. (p. 500)

structuralism An early school of psychology that used introspection to determine the structure and most basic elements of the mind. (p. 10)

successive approximations A method that uses reinforcers to condition a series of small steps that gradually approach the target behavior. (p. 206)

superego According to Freud, the structure of the mind that guides behavior to follow the rules of society, parents, or other authority figures. (p. 461)

surface traits Easily observable characteristics that derive from source traits. (p. 480)

survey method A type of descriptive research that uses questionnaires or interviews to gather data. (p. 29)

sympathetic nervous system The division of the autonomic nervous system that mobilizes the "fight-or-flight" response to stressful or crisis situations. (p. 66)

synapse Tiny gap between a terminal bud of one axon and a dendrite of a neighboring neuron; junction between neurons where communication occurs. (p. 53)

syntax The collection of rules concerning where to place words or phrases. (p. 304)

systematic desensitization A treatment that combines anxiety hierarchies with relaxation techniques. (p. 593)

telegraphic speech Two-word phrases typically used by infants around the age of 18 months. (p. 344)

temperament Characteristic differences in behavioral patterns and emotional reactions that are evident from birth. (p. 350)

temporal lobes The area of the cortex that processes auditory stimuli and language. (p. 79)

teratogens Environmental agents that can damage the growing zygote, embryo, or fetus. (p. 337)

testosterone An androgen produced by the testes. (p. 420)

tetrahydrocannabinol (THC) The active ingredient of marijuana. (p. 178)

thalamus A structure in the limbic system that processes and relays sensory information to the appropriate areas of the cortex. (p. 83)

theory Synthesizes observations in order to explain phenomena and guide predictions to be tested through research. (p. 20)

therapeutic alliance A warm and accepting client–therapist relationship that serves as a safe place for self-exploration. (p. 589)

theta waves Brain waves that indicate light sleep. (p. 155)

thinking Mental activity associated with coming to a decision, reaching a solution, or forming a belief. (p. 281)

third variable An unaccounted for characteristic of participants or the environment that explains changes in the variables of interest. (p. 32)

thyroid gland Endocrine gland that regulates metabolic rate by secreting thyroxin. (p. 70)

token economy A treatment approach that uses behavior modification, harnessing the power of positive reinforcement to encourage good behavior. (p. 594)

tolerance With constant use of some psychoactive drugs, a condition in which the body requires more and more of the drug to create the original effect; a sign of physiological dependence. (p. 180)

top-down processing Drawing on past experiences and knowledge to understand and interpret sensory information. (p. 96)

traits The relatively stable properties that describe elements of personality. (p. 479)

trait theories Theories that focus on personality dimensions and their influence on behavior; can be used to predict behaviors. (p. 479)

transduction The process of transforming stimuli into neural signals. (p. 97)

transference A type of resistance that occurs when a patient reacts to a therapist as if dealing with parents or other caregivers from childhood. (p. 586)

transgender Refers to people whose gender identity and expression do not match the gender assigned to them at birth. (p. 430)

transsexual An individual who seeks or undergoes a social transition to the other gender, and who may make changes to his or her body through surgery and medical treatment. (p. 430)

trial and error An approach to problem solving that involves finding a solution through a series of attempts and eliminating those that do not work. (p. 289)

triarchic theory of intelligence Sternberg's theory suggesting that humans have varying degrees of analytical, creative, and practical abilities. (p. 310)

trichromatic theory The perception of color is the result of three types of cones, each sensitive to wavelengths in the red, green, and blue spectrums. (p. 108)

Type A personality A person who exhibits a competitive, aggressive, impatient, and often hostile pattern of behaviors. (p. 523)

Type B personality A person who exhibits a relaxed, patient, and nonaggressive pattern of behaviors. (p. 523)

unconditional positive regard According to Rogers, the total acceptance or valuing of a person, regardless of behavior. (p. 475)

unconditioned response (UR) A reflexive, involuntary response to an unconditioned stimulus. (p. 195)

unconditioned stimulus (US) A stimulus that automatically triggers an involuntary response without any learning needed. (p. 195)

unconscious According to Freud, the level of consciousness outside of awareness, which is difficult to access without effort or therapy. (p. 460)

uninvolved parenting A parenting style characterized by a parent's indifference to a child, including a lack of emotional involvement. (p. 367)

uplifts Experiences that are positive and have the potential to make one happy. (p. 506)

validity The degree to which an assessment measures what it intends to measure. (p. 314)

variable-interval schedule A schedule in which the reinforcer comes after an interval of time, but the length of the interval changes from trial to trial. (p. 215)

variable-ratio schedule A schedule in which the number of desired behaviors that must occur before a reinforcer is given changes across trials and is based on an average number of behaviors to be reinforced. (p. 215)

variables Measurable characteristics that can vary over time or across people. (p. 25)

vestibular sense The sense of balance and equilibrium. (p. 126)

volley principle States that the perception of pitches between 400 Hz and 4,000 Hz is made possible by neurons working together to fire in volleys. (p. 115)

wavelength The distance between wave peaks (or troughs). (p. 102)

Weber's law The law stating that each of the five senses has its own constant ratio determining difference thresholds. (p. 99)

Wernicke's area A region of the cortex that plays a pivotal role in language comprehension. (p. 75)

withdrawal With constant use of some psychoactive drugs, a condition in which the body becomes dependent and then reacts when the drug is withheld; a sign of physiological dependence. (p. 180)

working memory The active processing of information in short-term memory; the maintenance and manipulation of information in the memory system. (p. 243)

zone of proximal development The range of cognitive tasks that can be accomplished alone and those that require the guidance and help of others. (p. 350)

zygote A single cell formed by the union of a sperm cell and egg. (p. 334)

References

Abdellaoui, A., Ehli, E. A., Hottenga, J. J., Weber, Z., Mbarek, H., Willemsen, G., … De Geus, E. J. (2015). CNV concordance in 1,097 MZ twin pairs. *Twin Research and Human Genetics, 18*(01), 1–12.

Abel, A., Hayes, A. M., Henley, W., & Kuyken, W. (2016). Sudden gains in cognitive–behavior therapy for treatment-resistant depression: Processes of change. *Journal of Consulting and Clinical Psychology, 84,* 726–737.

Abel, K. M., Drake, R., & Goldstein, J. M. (2010). Sex differences in schizophrenia. *International Review of Psychiatry, 22,* 417–428.

Abou-Khalil, B. W. (2010). When should corpus callosotomy be offered as palliative therapy? *Epilepsy Currents, 10,* 9–10.

About Sean Saifa Wall. (2016). Retrieved from http://saifaemerges.com/saifa/

Abrahamson, R. P. (2016, May 13). Hayden Panettiere seeks treatment: Experts explain postpartum depression. *US Weekly.* Retrieved from http://www.usmagazine.com/celebrity-moms/news/hayden-panettiere-seeks-treatment-experts-explain-postpartum-depression-w206472

Abramovitch, A., & McKay, D. (2016). Behavioral impulsivity in obsessive–compulsive disorder. *Journal of Behavioral Addictions, 5,* 1–3.

Ackerman, P. L., Kanfer, R., & Calderwood, C. (2010). Use it or lose it? Wii brain exercise practice and reading for domain knowledge. *Psychology and Aging, 25,* 753–766.

Adams, T. D., Davidson, L. E., Litwin, S. E., Kolotkin, R. L., LaMonte, M. J., Pendleton, R. C., … Hunt, S. C. (2012). Health benefits of gastric bypass surgery after 6 years. *Journal of the American Medical Association, 308,* 1122–1131.

Adinolfi, B., & Gava, N. (2013). Controlled outcome studies of child clinical hypnosis. *Acta Bio Medica Atenei Parmensis, 84,* 94–97.

Adler, A. (1927/1994). *Understanding human nature.* Oxford, UK: Oneworld.

Adolphs, R. (2008). Fear, faces, and the human amygdala. *Current Opinion in Neurobiology, 18,* 166–172.

Adolphs, R. (2013). The biology of fear. *Current Biology, 23,* R79–R93.

Advocates for Youth. (2009) *Adolescent sexual health in Europe and the U.S.—Why the difference?* (3rd ed.). Retrieved from www.advocatesforyouth.org/storage/advfy/documents/fsest.pdf

Afifi, T. O., Mota, N. P., Dasiewicz, P., MacMillan, H. L., & Sareen, J. (2012). Physical punishment and mental disorders: Results from a nationally representative US sample. *Pediatrics, 130,* 184–192.

Aiello, J. R., & Douthitt, E. A. (2001). Social facilitation from Triplett to electronic performance monitoring. *Group Dynamics: Theory, Research, and Practice, 5,* 163–180.

Ailshire, J. A., & Clarke, P. (2014). Fine particulate matter air pollution and cognitive function among U.S. older adults. *Journals of Gerontology, Series B: Psychological Sciences and Social Sciences, 70,* 322–328.

Ainsworth, M. D. (1979). Infant–mother attachment. *American Psychologist, 34,* 932–937.

Ainsworth, M. D. (1985). Patterns of attachment. *Clinical Psychologist, 38,* 27–29.

Ainsworth, M. D. S., & Bell, S. M. (1970). Attachment, exploration, and separation: Illustrated by the behavior of one-year-olds in a strange situation. *Child Development, 41,* 49–67.

Ainsworth, M. D. S., Blehar, M. C., Waters, E., & Wall, S. (1978). *Patterns of attachment: A psychological study of the strange situation.* Hillsdale, NJ: Lawrence Erlbaum Associates.

Ainsworth, S. E., & Baumeister, R. F. (2012). Changes in sexuality: How sexuality changes across time, across relationships, and across sociocultural contexts. *Clinical Neuropsychiatry, 9,* 32–38.

Ainsworth, S. E., & Maner, J. K. (2012). Sex begets violence: Mating motives, social dominance, and physical aggression in men. *Journal of Personality and Social Psychology, 103,* 819–829. doi:10.1037/a0029428

Ajzen, I. (2001). Nature and operation of attitudes. *Annual Review of Psychology, 52,* 27–58.

Akcay, O., Dalgin, M. H., & Bhatnagar, S. (2011). Perception of color in product choice among college students: A cross-national analysis of USA, India, China and Turkey. *International Journal of Business and Social Science, 2,* 42–48.

Akinola, M., & Mendes, W. B. (2012). Stress-induced cortisol facilitates threat-related decision making among police officers. *Behavioral Neuroscience, 126,* 167–174.

Albert, D., Chein, J., & Steinberg, L. (2013). The teenage brain: Peer influences on adolescent decision making. *Current Directions in Psychological Science, 22,* 114–120.

Albuquerque, D., Stice, E., Rodríguez-López, R., Manco, L., & Nóbrega, C. (2015). Current review of genetics of human obesity: From molecular mechanisms to an evolutionary perspective. *Molecular Genetics and Genomics, 290,* 1191–1221.

Alcoholics Anonymous. (2016a). *Estimated worldwide A.A. individual and group membership.* Service Material from the General Service Office. Retrieved from http://www.aa.org/assets/en_US/smf-132_en.pdf

Alcoholics Anonymous. (2016b). *Information on Alcoholics Anonymous.* Retrieved from http://www.aa.org/assets/en_US/f-2_InfoonAA.pdf

Alcoholics Anonymous Australia. (2016). *Members' stories.* Retrieved from http://www.aa.org.au/new-to-aa/personal-stories.php

Alcoholics Anonymous Great Britain. (2016). *Personal stories.* Retrieved from http://www.alcoholics-anonymous.org.uk/About-AA/Newcomers/Members'-Stories

Aldrete, J. A., Marron, G. M., & Wright, A. J. (1984). The first administration of anesthesia in military surgery: On occasion of the Mexican-American War. *Anesthesiology, 61,* 585–588.

Aldridge, D. (2016, June 13). Does NBA have right plan for mental health going forward? *NBA.com.* Retrieved from http://www.nba.com/2016/news/features/david_aldridge/06/13/morning-tip-royce-white-mental-health-in-nba-segment-nobody-asked-me-but-hack-a-strategy-solutions/

Alexander, D. A., & Klein, S. (2001). Ambulance personnel and critical incidents: Impact of accident and emergency work on mental health and emotional well-being. *British Journal of Psychiatry, 178,* 76–81.

Alexander, G. M., & Hines, M. (2002). Sex differences in response to children's toys in nonhuman primates (*Cercopithecus aethiops sabaeus*). *Evolution and Human Behavior, 23,* 467–479.

Alexander, G. M., Wilcox, T., & Woods, R. (2009). Sex differences in infants' visual interest in toys. *Archives of Sexual Behavior, 38,* 427–433.

Alexander, R. D. (1974). The evolution of social behavior. *Annual Review of Ecology and Systematics, 5,* 325–383.

Alexander, S. A., Frohlich, K. L., & Fusco, C. (2014). Playing for health? Revisiting health promotion to examine the emerging public health position on children's play. *Health Promotion International, 29*(1), 155–164.

Al Firdaus, M. M. (2012). SQ3R strategy for increasing students' retention of reading and written information. *Majalah Ilmiah Dinamika, 31,* 49–63.

Alho, J., Salminen, N., Sams, M., Hietanen, J. K., & Nummenmaa, L. (2015). Facilitated early cortical processing of nude human bodies. *Biological Psychology, 109,* 103–110.

Allegood, J. (2011, July 27). Durham girl in good spirits after Ocracoke shark attack. *News & Observer.* Copy in possession of author.

Allemand, M., Steiger, A. E., & Hill, P. L. (2013). Stability of personality traits in adulthood: Mechanisms and implications. *GeroPsych: The Journal of Gerontopsychology and Geriatric Psychiatry, 26*(1), 5–13.

Allen, G. E., & Smith, T. B. (2015). Collectivistic coping strategies for distress among Polynesian Americans. *Psychological Services, 12,* 322–329.

Allen, K. (2003). Are pets a healthy pleasure? The influence of pets on blood pressure. *Current Directions in Psychological Science, 12,* 236–239.

Allen, M. S., & McCarthy, P. J. (2016). Be happy in your work: The role of positive psychology in working with change and performance. *Journal of Change Management, 16,* 55–74.

Allik, J., & McCrae, R. R. (2004). Toward a geography of personality traits. Patterns of profiles across 36 cultures. *Journal of Cross-Cultural Psychology, 35,* 13–28.

Allport, G. W., & Odbert, H. S. (1936). Trait-names: A psycho-lexical study. *Psychological Monographs, 47*(211), i–171.

Alpert, P. T. (2012). The health lowdown on caffeine. *Home Health Care Management Practice, 24,* 156–158.

Altman, D., & Beyrer, C. (2014). The global battle for sexual rights. *Journal of the International AIDS Society, 17,* 19243–19244.

Altshuler, L. L., Kuaka, R. W., Hellemann, G., Frye, M. A., Sugar, C. A., McElroy, S. L., … Suppes, T. (2010). Bipolar disorder evaluated prospectively in the Stanley Foundation Bipolar Treatment Outcome Network. *American Journal of Psychiatry, 167,* 708–715.

Alzheimer's Association. (2013a). *Alzheimer's and dementia testing for earlier diagnosis.* Retrieved from http://www.alz.org/research/science/earlier_alzheimers_diagnosis.asp#Brain

Alzheimer's Association. (2013b) Alzheimer's disease facts and figures. *Alzheimer's & Dementia, 9,* 208–245.

American Academy of Ophthalmology. (2014a). *EyeSmart: Preventing eye injuries.* Retrieved from http://www.geteyesmart.org/eyesmart/living/eye-injuries/preventing.cfm

American Academy of Ophthalmology. (2014b). *EyeSmart: Smoking and eye health.* Retrieved from http://www.geteyesmart.org/eyesmart/living/smokers.cfm

American Academy of Ophthalmology. (2014c). *EyeSmart: The sun, UV radiation and your eyes.* Retrieved from http://www.geteyesmart.org/eyesmart/living/sun.cfm

American Academy of Pediatrics. (1998). Guidance for effective discipline. *Pediatrics, 101,* 723–728.

American Academy of Pediatrics. (2009). Policy statement—Media violence. *Pediatrics, 124,* 1495–1503.

American Academy of Pediatrics. (2014, August 25). *Let them sleep: AAP recommends delaying start times of middle and high schools to combat teen sleep.* Retrieved from https://www.aap.org/en-us/about-the-aap/aap-press-room/Pages/Let-Them-Sleep-AAP-Recommends-Delaying-Start-Times-of-Middle-and-High-Schools-to-Combat-Teen-Sleep-Deprivation.aspx

American Academy of Pediatrics. (2016a). Media and young minds. *Pediatrics, 138,* e20162399. doi: 10.1542/peds.2016–2591

American Academy of Pediatrics. (2016b). Media use in school-aged children and adolescents. *Pediatrics, 138,* e20162592. doi: 10.1542/peds.2016–2592

American Academy of Pediatrics. (n.d.). *Media and children.* Retrieved from https://www.aap.org/en-us/advocacy-and-policy/aap-health-initiatives/pages/media-and-children.aspx

American Art Therapy Association. (2016). *About art therapy.* Retrieved from http://arttherapy.org/aata-aboutus/

American Cancer Society. (2013, November 15). *Child and teen tobacco use.* Retrieved from http://whyquit.com/Youth/2013_ACS_Child_and_Teen_Tobacco-Use.pdf

American Heart Association. (2014a). *Atherosclerosis.* Retrieved from http://www.heart.org/HEARTORG/Conditions/Cholesterol/WhyCholesterolMatters/Atherosclerosis_UCM_305564_Article.jsp

American Heart Association. (2014b). *Overweight in children.* Retrieved from http://www.heart.org/HEARTORG/GettingHealthy/Overweight-in-Children_UCM_304054_Article.jsp

American Heart Association. (2015). Alcohol and heart health. Retrieved from http://www.heart.org/HEARTORG/HealthyLiving/HealthyEating/Nutrition/Alcohol-and-Heart-Health_UCM_305173_Article.jsp#.V1mI7mQrI34

American Lung Association. (2014). *Smoking.* Retrieved from http://www.lung.org/stop-smoking/about-smoking/health-effects/smoking.html

American Psychiatric Association. (1952). *Diagnostic and statistical manual of mental disorders.* Arlington, VA: Author.

American Psychiatric Association. (2001). *The practice of ECT: A task force report* (2nd ed.). Washington, DC: Author.

American Psychiatric Association. (2013). *Diagnostic and statistical manual of mental disorders* (5th ed., DSM-5). Arlington, VA: Author.

American Psychological Association [APA]. (1998a). Final conclusions of the American Psychological Association's working group on investigation of memories of childhood abuse. *Psychology, Public Policy, and Law, 4,* 933–940.

American Psychological Association [APA]. (1998b). *Psychology education & careers guidebook for college students of color: Subfields in psychology* [Brochure]. Retrieved from http://www.apa.org/careers/resources/guides/college-students.aspx

American Psychological Associatio [APA]. (2004). *The truth about lie detectors (aka polygraph tests).* Retrieved from http://www.apa.org/research/action/polygraph.aspx

American Psychological Association [APA]. (2006). *Answers to your questions about individuals with intersex conditions.* Retrieved from http://www.apa.org/topics/lgbt/intersex.aspx

American Psychological Association [APA]. (2008). *Answers to your questions: For a better understanding of sexual orientation and homosexuality.* Retrieved from www.apa.org/topics/sorientation.pdf

American Psychological Association [APA]. (2010a). *Ethical principles of psychologists and code of conduct,* 1–18. Retrieved from http://www.apa.org/ethics/code/principles.pdf

American Psychological Association [APA]. (2010b). *Publication manual of the American Psychological Association* (6th ed.). Washington, DC: Author.

American Psychological Association [APA]. (2011). *Careers in psychology: Some of the subfields in psychology* [Brochure]. Retrieved from http://www.apa.org/careers/resources/guides/careers.aspx–item=3#

American Psychological Association [APA]. (2012a). *Guidelines for ethical conduct in the care and use of nonhuman animals in research developed by the American Psychological Association Committee on Animal Research and Ethics in 2010–11.* Washington, DC: Author.

American Psychological Association [APA]. (2012b). Guidelines for psychological practice with lesbian, gay, and bisexual clients. *American Psychologist, 67,* 10–42.

American Psychological Association [APA]. (2012c). *Resolution on the recognition of psychotherapy effectiveness.* Retrieved from http://www.apa.org/about/policy/resolution-psychotherapy.aspx

American Psychological Association [APA]. (2012, March). *Understanding alcohol use disorders and their treatment.* Retrieved from www.http://www.apa.org/helpcenter/alcohol-disorders.aspx

American Psychological Association [APA]. (2013a). *APA guidelines for the undergraduate psychology major: Version 2.0.* Retrieved from http://www.apa.org/ed/precollege/about/undergraduate-major.aspx

American Psychological Association [APA]. (2013b). *Margaret Floy Washburn, PhD: 1921 APA President.* Retrieved from http://www.apa.org/about/governance/president/bio-margaret-washburn.aspx

American Psychological Association [APA]. (2013c). *Violence in the media: Psychologists study potential harmful effects.* Retrieved from http://www.apa.org/action/resources/research-in-action/protect.aspx

American Psychological Association [APA]. (2013d). *Roper v. Simmons.* Retrieved from http://www.apa.org/about/offices/ogc/amicus/roper.aspx

American Psychological Association [APA]. (2013e). *Stress in America: Missing the health care connection.* Retrieved from http://www.apa.org/news/press/releases/stress/2012/full-report.pdf

American Psychological Association [APA]. (2014a). *Answers to your questions about transgender people, gender identity, and gender expression.* Retrieved from http://www.apa.org/topics/lgbt/transgender.aspx

American Psychological Association [APA]. (2014b). *Psychology: Science in action. Pursuing a career in climate and environmental psychology.* Retrieved from http://www.apa.org/action/science/environment/education-training.pdf

American Psychological Association [APA]. (2014c). *Psychology: Science in action. Pursuing a career in clinical or counseling psychology.* Retrieved from http://www.apa.org/action/science/clinical/education-training.pdf

American Psychological Association [APA]. (2014d). *Psychology: Science in action. Pursuing a career in counseling psychology.* Retrieved from http://www.apa.org/action/science/counseling/education-training.pdf

American Psychological Association [APA]. (2014e). *Psychology: Science in action. Pursuing a career in developmental psychology.* Retrieved from http://www.apa.org/action/science/developmental/education-training.pdf

American Psychological Association [APA]. (2014f). *Psychology: Science in action. Pursuing a career in experimental psychology.* Retrieved from http://www.apa.org/action/science/experimental/education-training.pdf

American Psychological Association [APA]. (2014g). *Psychology: Science in action. Pursuing a career in forensic and public service psychology.* Retrieved from http://www.apa.org/action/science/forensic/education-training.pdf

American Psychological Association [APA]. (2014h). *Psychology: Science in action. Pursuing a career in health psychology.* Retrieved from http://www.apa.org/action/science/health/education-training.pdf

American Psychological Association [APA]. (2014i). *Psychology: Science in action. Pursuing a career in human factors and engineering psychology.* Retrieved from http://www.apa.org/action/science/human-factors/education-training.pdf

American Psychological Association [APA]. (2014j). *Psychology: Science in action. Pursuing a career in industrial and organizational psychology.* Retrieved from http://www.apa.org/action/science/organizational/education-training.pdf

American Psychological Association [APA]. (2014k). *Psychology: Science in action. Pursuing a career in the psychology of teaching and learning.* Retrieved from http://www.apa.org/action/science/teaching-learning/education-training.pdf

American Psychological Association [APA]. (2014l). *Psychology: Science in action. Pursuing a career in rehabilitation psychology.* Retrieved from http://www.apa.org/action/science/rehabilitation/education-training.pdf

American Psychological Association [APA]. (2014m). *Psychology: Science in action. Pursuing a career in social psychology.* Retrieved from http://www.apa.org/action/science/social/education-training.pdf

American Psychological Association [APA]. (2014n). *Psychology: Science in action. Pursuing a career in sport and performance psychology.* Retrieved from http://www.apa.org/action/science/performance/education-training.pdf

American Psychological Association [APA]. (2014, May). *Resources on Mental Health Parity Law.* Retrieved from http://www.apa.org/helpcenter/parity-law-resources.aspx

American Psychological Association [APA]. (2015a). *Demographics of the U.S. psychology workforce: Findings from the American Community Survey.* Washington, DC: Author.

American Psychological Association [APA]. (2015b). *Key terms and concepts in understanding gender diversity and sexual orientation among students.* Retrieved from http://dx.doi.org/10.1037/e527502015-001

American Psychological Association [APA]. (2015c). Proceedings of the American Psychological Association for the legislative year 2014. Minutes of the annual meeting of the Council of Representatives and minutes of the meetings of the Board of Directors. *American Psychologist, 70,* 386–430.

American Psychological Association [APA]. (2015d). Psychology & global climate change: Addressing a multifaceted phenomenon and set of challenges. *Task Force on the Interface Between Psychology and Global Climate Change.* Retrieved from http://www.apa.org/science/about/publications/climate-change.aspx

American Psychological Association [APA]. (2016a). *Graduate study in psychology, 2017 edition.* Washington, DC: Author.

American Psychological Association [APA]. (2016b). *Psychology: Science in action.* David Strayer, PhD, cognitive neuroscientist. Retrieved from https://www.apa.org/action/careers/improve-lives/david-strayer.aspx

American Psychological Association [APA]. (2016c). *Stress in America: The impact of discrimination.* Retrieved from http://www.apa.org/news/press/releases/stress/2015/impact-of-discrimination.pdf.

American Psychological Association [APA]. (n.d.-a). *Divisions of the APA.* Retrieved from http://www.apa.org/about/division/index.aspx

American Psychological Association [APA]. (n.d.-b). *Frequently asked questions about graduate school.* Retrieved from http://www.apa.org/education/grad/faqs.aspx

American Psychological Association [APA]. (n.d.-c). *Questions and answers about memories of childhood abuse.* Retrieved from http://apa.org/topics/trauma/memories.aspx

American Psychological Association [APA]. (n.d.-d). *What is media psychology?* Retrieved from http://www.apadivisions.org/division-46/about/what-is.aspx

American Speech-Language-Hearing Association. (n.d.). *Noise.* Retrieved from http://www.asha.org/public/hearing/Noise/

American Stroke Association. (2012). *What is an arteriovenous malformation (AVM)?* Retrieved from http://www.strokeassociation.org/STROKEORG/AboutStroke/TypesofStroke/HemorrhagicBleeds/What-Is-an-Arteriovenous-Malformation-AVM_UCM_310099_Article.jsp

Amesbury, E. C., & Schallhorn, S. C. (2003). Contrast sensitivity and limits of vision. *International Ophthalmology Clinics, 43,* 31–42.

Anastasi, A., & Urbina, S. (1997). *Psychological testing* (7th ed.). Upper Saddle River, NJ: Prentice Hall.

Anastasio, A., Draisci, R., Pepe, T., Mercogliano, R., Quadri, F. D., Luppi, G., & Cortesi, M. L. (2010). Development of biogenic amines during the ripening of Italian dry sausages. *Journal of Food Protection, 73,* 114–118.

Anderson, G. S., Litzenberger, R., & Plecas, D. (2002). Physical evidence of police officer stress. *Policing: An International Journal of Police Strategies & Management, 25,* 399–420.

Anderson, R. C. (1971). Encoding processes in the storage and retrieval of sentences. *Journal of Experimental Psychology, 91,* 338–340.

Anderson-Hanley, C., Snyder, A. L., Nimon, J. P., & Arciero, P. J. (2011). Social facilitation in virtual reality-enhanced exercise: Competitiveness moderates exercise effort of older adults. *Clinical Interventions in Aging, 6,* 275–280.

André, M. A. E., Güntürkün, O., & Manahan-Vaughan, D. (2015). The metabotropic glutamate receptor, mGlu5, is required for extinction learning that occurs in the absence of a context change. *Hippocampus, 25,* 149–158.

Andreotti, C., Root, J. C., Ahles, T. A., McEwen, B. S., & Compas, B. E. (2015). Cancer, coping, and cognition: A model for the role of stress reactivity in cancer-related cognitive decline. *Psycho-Oncology, 24,* 617–623.

Andrus, B. M., Blizinsky, K., Vedell, P. T., Dennis, K., Shukla, P. K., Schaffer, D. J., … Redei, E. E. (2012). Gene expression patterns in the hippocampus and amygdala of endogenous depression and chronic stress models. *Molecular Psychiatry, 17,* 49–61.

Angst, J., Angst, F., Gerber-Werder, R., & Gamma, A. (2005). Suicide in 406 mood-disorder patients with and without long-term medication: A 40 to 44 years' follow-up. *Archives of Suicide Research, 9,* 279–300.

Angus, L., Watson, J. C., Elliott, R., Schneider, K., & Timulak, L. (2015). Humanistic psychotherapy research 1990–2015: From methodological innovation to evidence-supported treatment outcomes and beyond. *Psychotherapy Research, 25,* 330–347.

Annan, J., Blattman, C., & Horton, R. (2006). *The state of youth and youth protection in northern Uganda: Findings from the Survey for War Affected Youth* (Report for UNICEF Uganda), ii–89. Retrieved from http://chrisblattman.com/documents/policy/sway/SWAY.Phase1.FinalReport.pdf

Annese, J., Schenker-Ahmed, N. M., Bartsch, H., Maechler, P., Sheh, C., Thomas, N., … Corkin, S. (2014). Postmortem examination of patient H.M.'s brain based on histological sectioning and digital 3D reconstruction. *Nature Communications, 5,* 3122. doi: 10.1038/ncomms4122

Anokhin, A. P., Grant, J. D., Mulligan, R. C., & Heath, A. C. (2015). The genetics of impulsivity: Evidence for the heritability of delay discounting. *Biological Psychiatry, 77*(10), 887–894.

Anonymous. (2014, April 16). Here's what it's like to have the mental illness associated with psychopaths. *Business Insider.* Retrieved from http://mobile.businessinsider.com/what-its-like-to-have-antisocial-personality-disorder-2014-4

Ansari, A., & Klinenberg, E. (2015, June 13). How to make online dating work. *The New York Times.* Retrieved from http://www.nytimes.com/2015/06/14/opinion/sunday/how-to-make-online-dating-work.html?_r=0

Ansbacher, H. L., & Ansbacher, R. R. (Eds.). (1956). *The individual psychology of Alfred Adler.* New York, NY: Harper & Row.

Ansell, D. A., & McDonald, E. K. (2015). Bias, black lives, and academic medicine. *The New England Journal of Medicine, 372,* 1087–1089.

Anton, M. T., Jones, D. J., & Youngstrom, E. A. (2015). Socioeconomic status, parenting, and externalizing problems in African American single-mother homes: A person-oriented approach. *Journal of Family Psychology, 29,* 405–415.

Anusic, I., Yap, S. C., & Lucas, R. E. (2014). Testing set-point theory in a Swiss national sample: Reaction and adaptation to major life events. *Social Indicators Research, 119,* 1265–1288.

APA Center for Workforce Studies. (2015). Table 3: Current major field of APA members by membership status. *APA Directory.* Retrieved from http://www.apa.org/workforce/publications/15-member/table-3.pdf

APA Presidential Task Force on Evidence-Based Practice. (2006). Evidence-based practice in psychology. *American Psychologist, 61,* 271–285.

Arab, L., & Ang. A. (2015). A cross sectional study of the association between walnut consumption and cognitive function among adult US populations represented in NHANES. *The Journal of Nutrition, Health & Aging, 19*(3), 284–290.

Aranake, A., Mashour, G. A., & Avidan, M. S. (2013). Minimum alveolar concentration: ongoing relevance and clinical utility. *Anaesthesia, 68,* 512–522.

Araque, A., & Navarrete, M. (2010). Glial cells in neuronal network function. *Philosophical Transactions of the Royal Society of Biological Sciences, 365,* 2375–2381.

Archer, J. (2004). Sex differences in aggression in real-world settings: A meta-analytic review. *Review of General Psychology, 8,* 291–322.

Archer, J., & Coyne, S. M. (2005). An integrated review of indirect, relational, and social aggression. *Personality and Social Psychology Review, 9,* 212–230.

Ardila, A., Rosselli, M., Matute, E., & Inozemtseva, O. (2011). Gender differences in cognitive development. *Developmental Psychology, 47,* 984–990.

Arganini, C., & Sinesio, F. (2015). Chemosensory impairment does not diminish eating pleasure and appetite in independently living older adults. *Maturitas, 82,* 241–244.

Arkes, H. R. (2013). The consequences of the hindsight bias in medical decision making. *Current Directions in Psychological Science, 22,* 356–360.

Arkowitz, H., & Lilienfeld, S. O. (2011, July/August). Deranged and dangerous? *Scientific American Mind, 22,* 64–65.

Arlin, P. K. (1975). Cognitive development in adulthood: A fifth stage? *Developmental Psychology, 11,* 602–606.

Armitage, C. J., & Christian, J. (2003). From attitudes to behaviour: Basic and applied research on the theory of planned behaviour. *Current Psychology, 22,* 187–195.

Arnal L., H., Flinker, A., Kleinschmidt, A., Giraud A. L., & Poeppel, D. (2015). Human screams occupy a privileged niche in the communication soundscape. *Current Biology, 25,* 2051–2056. doi:10.1016/j.cub.2015.06.043

Arnett, J. J. (2000). Emerging adulthood: A theory of development from the late teens through the twenties. *American Psychologist, 55,* 469–480.

Arnold, A. P., Chen, X., & Itoh, Y. (2012). What a difference an X or Y makes: Sex chromosomes, gene dose, and epigenetics in sexual differentiation. In V. Regitz-Zagrosek (Ed.), *Sex and gender differences in pharmacology* (pp. 67–88). Berlin, Germany: Springer-Verlag.

Aronson, E. (2012). *The social animal* (11th ed.). New York, NY: Worth.

Aronson, E. (2015). *Jigsaw classroom.* Retrieved from http://www.jigsaw.org

Aronson, E., & Festinger, L. (1958). *Some attempts to measure tolerance for dissonance* (WADC.TR-58.492ASTIA Document No. AD 207 337). San Antonio, TX: Lackland Air Force Base.

Asch, S. E. (1955). Opinions and social pressure. *Scientific American, 193,* 31–35.

Asch, S. E. (1956). Studies of independence and conformity: I. A minority of one against a unanimous majority. *Psychological Monographs: General and Applied, 70,* 1–70.

Assefa, S. Z., Diaz-Abad, M., Wickwire, E. M., & Scharf, S. M. (2015). The functions of sleep. *AIMS Neuroscience, 2*(3), 155–171.

Assmann, K. E., Touvier, M., Andreeva, V. A., Deschasaux, M., Constans, T., Hercberg, S., … Kesse-Guyot, E. (2015). Midlife plasma vitamin D concentrations and performance in different cognitive domains assessed 13 years later. *British Journal of Nutrition, 113,* 1628–1637.

Associated Press. (2014, May 8). Therapy dogs help troops deal with postwar stress. *CBS News.* Retrieved from http://www.cbsnews.com/news/therapy-dog-helps-troops-deal-with-postwar-stress/

Associated Press. (2015, August 26). James Holmes trial: Judge formally sentences Aurora gunman to life in prison. *NBC News.* Retrieved from http://www.nbcnews.com/news/us-news/james-holmes-trial-judge-formally-sentences-aurora-gunman-life-prison-n416396

Association for Psychological Science. (n.d.). *Psychology links.* Retrieved from http://www.psychologicalscience.org/index.php/about/psychology-links

Atkinson, R. C., & Shiffrin, R. M. (1968, January 31–February 2). *Some speculations on storage and retrieval processes in long-term memory* (Technical Report No. 127). Paper presented at Conference on Research on Human Decision Making sponsored by NASA-Ames Research Center, Moffett Field, CA.

Attarian, H. P., Schenck, C. H., & Mahowald, M. W. (2000). Presumed REM sleep behavior disorder arising from cataplexy and wakeful dreaming. *Sleep Medicine, 1,* 131–133.

Attrill, M. J., Gresty, K. A., Hill, R. A., & Barton, R. A. (2008). Red shirt colour is associated with long-term team success in English football. *Journal of Sports Sciences, 26,* 577–582.

Aurora, R. N., Zak, R. S., Maganti, R. K., Auerbach, S. H., Casey, K. R., Chowdhuri, S., … American Academy of Sleep Medicine. (2010). Best practice guide for the treatment of REM sleep behavior disorder (RBD). *Journal of Clinical Sleep Medicine, 15,* 85–95.

Auster, C. J., & Mansbach, C. S. (2012). The gender marketing of toys: An analysis of color and type of toy on the Disney store website. *Sex Roles, 67,* 375–388.

Australian Department of Health. (2016, May 27). *Tobacco control key facts and figures.* Retrieved from http://www.health.gov.au/internet/main/publishing.nsf/Content/tobacco-kff

Awikunprasert, C., & Sittiprapapom, W. (2012). Sleep pattern and efficiency in Thai children aged 3–6. *Research Journal of Pharmaceutical, Biological and Chemical Sciences, 3,* 1208–1217.

Axelrod, V., Bar, M., Rees, G., & Yovel, G. (2015). Neural correlates of subliminal language processing. *Cerebral Cortex, 25,* 2160–2169.

Bachhuber, M. A., Hennessy, S., Cunningham, C. O., & Starrels, J. L. (2016). Increasing benzodiazepine prescriptions and overdose mortality in the United States, 1996–2013. *American Journal of Public Health, 106,* 686–688.

Back, M. D., Schmukle, S. C., & Egloff, B. (2008). Becoming friends by chance. *Psychological Science, 19,* 439–440.

Back, M. D., Stopfer, J. M., Vazire, S., Gaddis, S., Schmukle, S. C., Egloff, B., & Gosling, S. D. (2010). Facebook profiles reflect actual personality, not self-idealization. *Psychological Science, 21,* 372–374.

Baddeley, A. (1995). Working memory. In M. S. Gazzaniga (Ed.), *The cognitive neurosciences* (pp. 755–764). Cambridge, MA: MIT Press.

Baddeley, A. (1999). *Essentials of human memory.* East Sussex, UK: Psychology Press.

Baddeley, A. (2000). The episodic buffer: A new component of working memory? *Trends in Cognitive Sciences, 4,* 417–423.

Baddeley, A. (2002). Is working memory still working? *European Psychologist, 7,* 85–97.

Baddeley, A. (2006). Working memory: An overview. In S. J. Pickering (Ed.), *Working memory in education* (pp. 3–31). Burlington, MA: Elsevier.

Baddeley, A. (2012). Working memory: Theories, models, and controversies. *Annual Review of Psychology, 63,* 1–29.

Baddeley, A. D., & Hitch, G. J. (1974). Working memory. In G. Bower (Ed.), *Recent advances in learning and memory* (Vol. 8, pp. 47–90). New York, NY: Academic Press.

Badie, D. (2010). Groupthink, Iraq, and the war on terror: Explaining US policy shift toward Iraq. *Foreign Policy Analysis, 6,* 277–296.

Baer, J. M. (1993). *Creativity and divergent thinking.* Hillsdale, NJ: Lawrence Erlbaum Associates.

Baggetto, M. (2010). Meet the women of the administration: Claudia Gordon [Web log post]. Retrieved from https://www.whitehouse.gov/blog/2010/08/30/meet-women-administration-claudia-gordon

Bahrick, H. P., Hall, L. K., & Da Costa, L. A. (2008). Fifty years of memory of college grades: Accuracy and distortions. *Emotion, 8,* 13–22.

Bahrick, L. E., Gogate, L. J., & Ruiz, I. (2002). Attention and memory for faces and actions in infancy: The salience of actions over faces in dynamic events. *Child Development, 73,* 1629–1643.

Bahrick, L. E., & Newell, L. C. (2008). Infant discrimination of faces in naturalistic events: Actions are more salient than faces. *Developmental Psychology, 44,* 983–996.

Baibazarova, E., van de Beek, C., Cohen-Kettenis, P. T., Buitelaar, J., Shelton, K. H., & van Goozen, S. H. M. (2013). Influence of prenatal maternal stress, maternal plasma cortisol and cortisol in the amniotic fluid on birth outcomes and child temperament at 3 months. *Psychoneuroendocrinology, 38,* 907–915.

Baik, J.-H. (2013). Dopamine signaling in food addiction: Role of dopamine D2 receptors. *BMB Reports, 46,* 519–526.

Bailey, S. J., & Covell, K. (2011). Pathways among abuse, daily hassles, depression and substance use in adolescents. *The New School Psychology Bulletin, 8,* 4–14.

Baillargeon, R., Spelke, E. S., & Wasserman, S. (1985). Object permanence in five-month-old infants. *Cognition, 20,* 191–208.

Bakalar, N. (2015, October 28). Don't blame it on birth order [Web log post]. Retrieved from http://well.blogs.nytimes.com/2015/10/28/dont-blame-it-on-birth-order/?_r=0

Balliet, D., & Ferris, D. L. (2013). Ostracism and prosocial behavior: A social dilemma perspective. *Organizational Behavior and Human Decision Processes, 120,* 298–308.

Bandell, M., Macpherson, L. J., & Patapoutian, A. (2007). From chills to chilis: Mechanisms for thermosensation and chemesthesis via thermoTRPs. *Current Opinion in Neurobiology, 17,* 490–497.

Bandura, A. (1977a). Self-efficacy: Toward a unifying theory of behavioral change. *Psychological Review, 84,* 191–215.

Bandura, A. (1977b). *Social learning theory.* Englewood Cliffs, NJ: Prentice Hall.

Bandura, A. (1978). The self system in reciprocal determinism. *American Psychologist, 33,* 344–358.

Bandura, A. (1986). *Social foundations of thought and action: A social cognitive theory.* Englewood Cliffs, NJ: Prentice Hall.

Bandura, A. (2001). Social cognitive theory: An agentic perspective. *Annual Review of Psychology, 52,* 1–26.

Bandura, A. (2006). Toward a psychology of human agency. *Perspectives on Psychological Science, 1,* 164–180.

Bandura, A., Ross, D., & Ross, S. A. (1961). Transmission of aggression through imitation of aggressive models. *Journal of Abnormal and Social Psychology, 63,* 575–582.

Banissy, M. J., Jonas, C., & Kadosh, R. C. (2014). Synesthesia: An introduction. *Frontiers in Psychology, 5,* 1414. doi:10.3389/fpsyg.2014.01414

Banks, M. S., & Salapatek, P. (1978). Acuity and contrast sensitivity in 1-, 2-, and 3-month-old human infants. *Investigative Ophthalmology & Visual Science, 17,* 361–365.

Banks, S., & Dinges, D. F. (2007). Behavioral and physiological consequences of sleep restriction. *Journal of Clinical Sleep Medicine, 3,* 519–528.

Banuazizi, A., & Movahedi, S. (1975). Interpersonal dynamics in a simulated prison: A methodological analysis. *American Psychologist, 30,* 152–160.

Banyard, V. L., & Moynihan, M. M. (2011). Variation in bystander behavior related to sexual and intimate partner violence prevention: Correlates in a sample of college students. *Psychology of Violence, 1,* 287–301.

Barak, A., Hen, L., Boniel-Nissim, M., & Shapira, N. A. (2008). A comprehensive review and a meta-analysis of the effectiveness of Internet-based psychotherapeutic interventions. *Journal of Technology in Human Services, 26,* 109–160.

Barash, P. G., Cullen, B. F., Stoelting, R. K., & Cahalan, M. (2009). *Clinical anesthesia* (6th ed.). Philadelphia, PA: Lippincott Williams & Wilkins.

Barber, C. (2008). *Comfortably numb.* New York, NY: Pantheon Books.

Barber, R. (2012, October 27). Yes, I give dogs electric shocks and use spike chokers … but I'm NOT cruel, says Hollywood's favourite pet guru. *Daily Mail.* Retrieved from http://www.dailymail.co.uk/news/article-2224252/Yes-I-dogs-electric-shocks-use-spike-chokers--Im-NOT-cruel-says-Hollywoods-favourite-pet-guru-Cesar-Millan.html

Barberá, E. (2003). Gender schemas: Configuration and activation processes. *Canadian Journal of Behavioural Science, 35,* 176–184.

Bard, P. (1934). Emotion I: The neuro-humoral basis of emotional reactions. In C. Murchison (Ed.), *International University series in psychology: Handbook of general experimental psychology* (pp. 264–311). Worcester, MA: University Press.

Bar-Hillel, M. (2015). Position effects in choice from simultaneous displays: A conundrum solved. *Perspectives on Psychological Science, 10,* 419–433.

Barker, E. T., Greenberg, J. S., Seltzer, M. M., & Almeida, D. M. (2012). Daily stress and cortisol patterns in parents of adult children with serious mental illness. *Health Psychology, 31,* 130–134.

Barlé, N., Wortman, C. B., & Latack, J. A. (2016). Traumatic bereavement: Basic research and clinical implications. *Journal of Psychotherapy Integration.* http://dx.doi.org/10.1037/int0000013

Barnes, A. J., De Martinis, B. S., Gorelick, D. A., Goodwin, R. S., Kolbrich, E. A., & Huestis, M. A. (2009). Disposition of MDMA and metabolites in human sweat following controlled MDMA administration. *Clinical Chemistry, 55,* 454–462.

Barnes, S. K. (2010). Sign language with babies: What difference does it make? *Dimensions of Early Childhood, 38,* 21–30.

Baron, K. G., & Reid, K. J. (2014). Circadian misalignment and health. *International Review of Psychiatry, 26,* 139–154.

Barr, T. F., Dixon, A. L., & Gassenheimer, J. B. (2005). Exploring the "lone wolf" phenomenon in student teams. *Journal of Marketing Education, 27,* 81–90.

Barredo, J. L., & Deeg, K. E. (2009, February 24). Could living in a mentally enriching environment change your genes? *Scientific American.* Retrieved from http://www.scientificamerican.com/article.cfm–id=enriched-environments-memory

Barrera, T. L., Mott, J. M., Hofstein, R. F., & Teng, E. J. (2013). A meta-analytic review of exposure in group cognitive behavioral therapy for posttraumatic stress disorder. *Clinical Psychology Review, 33,* 24–32.

Barrett, L. F., & Bliss-Moreau, E. (2009). She's emotional. He's having a bad day: Attributional explanations for emotion stereotypes. *Emotion, 9,* 649–658.

Barron, J. (2012, December 14). Nation reels after gunman massacres 20 children at school in Connecticut. *The New York Times.* Retrieved from http://www.nytimes.com/2012/12/15/nyregion/shooting-reported-at-connecticut-elementary-school.html

Barss, T. S., Pearcey, G. E., & Zehr, E. P. (2016). Cross-education of strength and skill: An old idea with applications in the aging nervous system. *The Yale Journal of Biology and Medicine, 89,* 81–86.

Bartels, M., Saviouk, V., De Moor, M. H. M., Willemsen, G., van Beijsterveldt, T. C. E. M., Hottenga, J-J., … Boomsma, D. I. (2010). Heritability and genome-wide linkage scan of subjective happiness. *Twin Research and Human Genetics, 13,* 135–142.

Bartlett, T. (2014). The search for psychology's lost boy. *Chronicle of Higher Education, 60* (38). Retrieved from http://chronicle.com/interactives/littlealbert

Barton, R. A., & Capellini, I. (2016). Sleep, evolution and brains. *Brain, Behavior and Evolution, 87,* 65–68. doi:10.1159/000443716

Bateman, A., & Fonagy, P. (2008). 8-year follow-up of patients treated for borderline personality disorder: Mentalization-based treatment versus treatment as usual. *American Journal of Psychiatry, 165,* 631–638.

Batson, C. D., & Powell, A. A. (2003). Altruism and prosocial behavior. In I. B. Weiner, T. Millon, & M. J. Lerner (Eds.), *Handbook of psychology: Vol. 5. Personality and social psychology* (pp. 463–484). Hoboken, NJ: John Wiley & Sons.

Baucom, B. R., Atkins, D. C., Rowe, L. S., Doss, B. D., & Christensen, A. (2015). Prediction of treatment response at 5-year follow-up in a randomized clinical trial of behaviorally based couple therapies. *Journal of Consulting and Clinical Psychology, 83,* 103–114.

Bauer, M., Haesler, E., & Fetherstonhaugh, D. (2015). Let's talk about sex: Older people's views on the recognition of sexuality and sexual health in the health-care setting. *Health Expectations.* doi:10.1111/hex.12418

Bauer, P. J. (2006). Constructing a past in infancy: A neuro-developmental account. *Trends in Cognitive Sciences, 10,* 175–181.

Bauer, P. J. (2015). A complementary processes account of the development of childhood amnesia and a personal past. *Psychological Review, 122,* 204–231.

Bauer, P. J., & Larkina, M. (2014). The onset of childhood amnesia in childhood: A prospective investigation of the course and determinants of forgetting of early-life events. *Memory, 22,* 907–924.

Baughman, H. M., Giammarco, E. A., Veselka, L., Schermer, J. A., Martin, N. G., Lynskey, M., & Vernon, P. A. (2012). A behavioral genetic study of humor styles in an Australian sample. *Twin Research and Human Genetics, 15,* 663–667.

Baumrind, D. (1966). Effects of authoritative parental control on child behavior. *Child Development, 37,* 887–907.

Baumrind, D. (1971). Current patterns of parental authority. *Developmental Psychology Monograph, 4,* 1–103.

Baumrind, D. (1991). The influence of parenting style on adolescent competence and substance use. *Journal of Early Adolescence, 11,* 56–95.

Baumrind, D. (1996). Personal statements. *Pediatrics, 98,* 857–860.

Baumrind, D., Larzelere, R. E., & Cowan, P. A. (2002). Ordinary physical punishment: Is it harmful? [Peer commentary on the paper "Corporal Punishment by Parents and Associated Child Behaviors and Experiences: A Meta-Analytic and Theoretical Review" by E. T. Gershoff]. *Psychological Bulletin, 128,* 580–589.

Bayley, N. (1993). *The Bayley Scales of Infant Development* (2nd ed.). San Antonio, TX: Psychological Test Corporation.

BBC. (2005, September). *Dr. Money and the boy with no penis—programme transcript.* Retrieved from http://www.bbc.co.uk/sn/tvradio/programmes/horizon/dr_money_trans.shtml

BBC News. (2001, November 16). *Rise of the blockbuster.* Retrieved from http://news.bbc.co.uk/2/hi/entertainment/1653733.stm

BBC News. (2010, November 20). *Global health officials target tobacco additives.* Retrieved from http://www.bbc.co.uk/news/world-latin-america-11804767–print=true

BBC News. (2011, June 28). *Somalia fleeing to Kenya in large numbers.* Retrieved from http://www.bbc.co.uk/news/world-africa-13937486

BBC News. (2011, July 22). *EU must do more on East Africa famine—David Cameron.* Retrieved from http://www.bbc.co.uk/news/uk-politics-14253766

BBC News. (2014, October 16). *Ebola crisis: WHO says major outbreak in West "unlikely."* Retrieved from http://www.bbc.com/news/world-us-canada-29640470

BBC News. (2016, September 20). *Somalia food crisis: 300,000 children need help, says UN.* Retrieved from http://www.bbc.com/news/world-africa-37423792

Beauchamp, M. H., & Anderson, V. (2010). Social: An integrative framework for the development of social skills. *Psychological Bulletin, 136,* 39–64.

Bech, P. (2006). The full story of lithium. *Psychotherapy and Psychosomatics, 75,* 265–269.

Beck, A. T. (1976). *Cognitive therapy and the emotional disorders.* New York, NY: International Universities Press.

Beck, A. T., Rush, A. J., Shaw, B. F., & Emory, G. (1979). *Cognitive therapy of depression.* New York, NY: Guilford Press.

Beck, A. T., & Weishaar, M. E. (2014). Cognitive therapy. In R. J. Corsini & D. Wedding (Eds.), *Current psychotherapies* (10th ed., pp. 231–264). Belmont, CA: Brooks/Cole, Cengage Learning.

Beck, H. P., & Irons, G. (2011). Finding Little Albert: A seven-year search for psychology's lost boy. *The Psychologist, 24,* 392–395.

Beck, H. P., Levinson, S., & Irons, G. (2009). Finding Little Albert: A journey to John B. Watson's infant laboratory. *American Psychologist, 64,* 605–614.

Becker, K. A. (2003). History of the Stanford-Binet intelligence scales: Content and psychometrics. In *Stanford-Binet intelligence scales,* Fifth Edition Assessment Service Bulletin (No. 1). Itasca, IL: Riverside Publishing.

Bedrosian, T. A., Fonken, L. K., & Nelson, R. J. (2016). Endocrine effects of circadian disruption. *Annual Review of Physiology, 78,* 1.1–1.23.

Beebe-Center, J. G. (1951). Feeling and emotion. In H. Helson (Ed.), *Theoretical foundations of psychology* (pp. 254–317). Princeton, NJ: D. Van Nostrand.

Bekk, M., & Spörrle, M. (2010). The influence of perceived personality characteristics on positive attitude towards and suitability of a celebrity as a marketing campaign endorser. *Open Psychology Journal, 3,* 54–66.

Belizaire, L. S., & Fuertes, J. N. (2011). Attachment, coping, acculturative stress, and quality of life among Haitian immigrants. *Journal of Counseling & Development, 89,* 89–97.

Belmaker, R. H. (2004). Bipolar disorder. *New England Journal of Medicine, 351,* 476–486.

Belmaker, R. H., & Agam, G. (2008). Major depressive disorder. *New England Journal of Medicine, 358,* 55–68.

Bem, D. J. (2011). Feeling the future: Experimental evidence for anomalous retroactive influences on cognition and affect. *Journal of Personality and Social Psychology, 100,* 407–425.

Bem, D. J., Utts, J., & Johnson, W. O. (2011). Must psychologists change the way they analyze their data? *Journal of Personality and Social Psychology, 101,* 716–719.

Bem, S. L. (1981). Gender schema theory: A cognitive account of sex typing. *Psychological Review, 88,* 354–364.

Bench, S. W., Lench, H. C., Liew, J., Miner, K., & Flores, S. A. (2015). Gender gaps in overestimation of math performance. *Sex Roles, 72,* 536–546.

Benedek, M., Franz, F., Heene, M., & Neubauer, A. C. (2012). Differential effects of cognitive inhibition and intelligence on creativity. *Personality and Individual Differences, 53,* 480–485.

Benestad, R. E., Nuccitelli, D., Lewandowsky, S., Hayhoe, K., Hygen, H. O., van Dorland, R., & Cook, J. (2016). Learning from mistakes in climate research. *Theoretical and Applied Climatology, 126,* 699–703.

Benham, G. (2010). Sleep: An important factor in stress-health models. *Stress and Health, 26,* 201–214.

Benjamin, L. T. (2007). *A brief history of modern psychology.* Malden, MA: Blackwell.

Bennett, A. T. D., Cuthill, I. C., Partridge, J. C., & Maier, E. J. (1996). Ultraviolet vision and mate choice in zebra finches. *Nature, 380,* 433–435.

Ben-Porath, Y. S. (2012). *Interpreting the MMPI 2 RF.* Minneapolis, MN: University of Minnesota Press.

Bensky, M. K., Gosling, S. D., & Sinn, D. L. (2013). The world from a dog's point of view: A review and synthesis of dog cognition research. *Advances in the Study of Behavior, 45,* 209–406.

Benson, H. (2000). *The relaxation response.* New York, NY: Avon Books.

Ben-Zvi A., Vernon S. D., & Broderick G. (2009). Model-based therapeutic correction of hypothalamic-pituitary-adrenal axis dysfunction. *PLOS Computational Biology, 5,* e1000273. doi:10.1371/journal.pcbi.1000273

Berenbaum, S. A., & Beltz, A. M. (2016). How early hormones shape gender development. *Current Opinion in Behavioral Sciences, 7,* 53–60.

Berenbaum, S. A., Blakemore, J. E. O., & Beltz, A. M. (2011). A role for biology in gender-related behavior. *Sex Roles, 64,* 804–825.

Beresin, E. V. (2015). The impact of media violence on children and adolescents: Opportunities for clinical interventions. *American Academy of Child and Adolescent Psychiatry.* Retrieved from https://www.aacap.org/aacap/Medical_Students_and_Residents/Mentorship_Matters/DevelopMentor/The_Impact_of_Media_Violence_on_Children_and_Adolescents_Opportunities_for_Clinical_Interventions.aspx

Berg, K. S., Delgado, S., Cortopassi, K. A., Beissinger, S. R., & Bradbury, J. W. (2012). Vertical transmission of learned signatures in a wild parrot. *Proceedings of the Royal Society of London B, 279,* 585–591.

Berger, W., Coutinho, E. S. F., Figueira, I., Marques-Portella, C., Luz, M. P., Neylan, T. C., … Mendlowicz, M. V. (2011). Rescuers at risk: A systematic review and meta-regression analysis of the worldwide current prevalence and correlates of PTSD in rescue workers. *Social Psychiatry and Psychiatric Epidemiology, 47,* 1001–1011.

Bergh, C., Sjöstedt, S., Hellers, G., Zandian, M., & Södersten, P. (2003). Meal size, satiety and cholecystokinin in gastrectomized humans. *Physiology & Behavior, 78,* 143–147.

Bernard, L. L. (1926). *An introduction to social psychology.* New York, NY: Henry Holt.

Bernier, A., Carlson, S. M., & Whipple, N. (2010). From external regulation to self-regulation: Early parenting precursors of young children's executive functioning. *Child Development, 81,* 326–229.

Berry, J. W. (1997). Immigration, acculturation, and adaptation. *Applied Psychology: An International Review, 46,* 5–34.

Berry, R. B., Brooks, R., Gamald, C. E., Harding, S. M., Lloyd, R. M., Marcus, C. L., & Vaughn, B. V. for the American Academy of Sleep Medicine. (2016). *The AASM manual for the scoring of sleep and associated events: Rules, terminology, and technical specifications, Version 2.3.* Darien, IL: American Academy of Sleep Medicine.

Berry, R. B., & Wagner, M. H. (2015). *Sleep medicine pearls* (3rd ed.). Philadelphia, PA: Elsevier Saunders.

Berscheid, E. (2010). Love in the fourth dimension. *Annual Review of Psychology, 61,* 1–25.

Berthoz, S., Blair, R. J. R., Le Clec'h, G., & Martinot, J.-L. (2002). Emotions: From neuropsychology to functional imaging. *International Journal of Psychology, 37,* 193–203.

Berwick, R. C., Friederici, A. D., Chomsky, N., & Bolhuis, J. J. (2013). Evolution, brain, and the nature of language. *Trends in Cognitive Sciences, 17*(2), 89–98.

Besedovsky, L., Lange, T., & Born, J. (2012). Sleep and immune function. *Pflügers Archiv-European Journal of Physiology, 463,* 1–17.

Best, P., Manktelow, R., & Taylor, B. (2014). Online communication, social media and adolescent well-being: A systematic narrative review. *Children and Youth Services Review, 41,* 27–36.

Betsch, C., & Sachse, K. (2013). Debunking vaccination myths: Strong risk negations can increase perceived vaccination risks. *Health Psychology, 32,* 145–155.

Bezdjian, S., Baker, L. A., & Tuvblad, C. (2011). Genetic and environmental influences on impulsivity: A meta-analysis of twin, family and adoption studies. *Clinical Psychology Review, 31,* 1209–1223.

Bezdjian, S., Tuvblad, C., Raine, A., & Baker, L. A. (2011). The genetic and environmental covariation among psychopathic personality traits, and reactive and proactive aggression in childhood. *Child Development, 82,* 1267–1281.

Bialystok, E. (2011). Reshaping the mind: The benefits of bilingualism. *Canadian Journal of Experimental Psychology, 65,* 229–235.

Bialystok, E., Poarch, G., Luo, L., & Craik, F. I. (2014). Effects of bilingualism and aging on executive function and working memory. *Psychology and Aging, 29,* 696–705.

Bieniek, K. F., Ross, O. A., Cormier, K. A., Walton, R. L., Soto-Ortolaza, A., Johnston, A. E., … Rademakers, R. (2015). Chronic traumatic encephalopathy pathology in a neurodegenerative disorders brain bank. *Acta Neuropathologica, 130,* 877–889.

Bignall, W. J. R., Jacquez, F., & Vaughn, L. M. (2015). Attributions of mental illness: An ethnically diverse community perspective. *Community Mental Health Journal, 51,* 540–545.

Bihm, E. M., Gillaspy, J. A., Lammers, W. J., & Huffman, S. P. (2010). IQ Zoo and teaching operant concepts. *Psychological Record, 60,* 523–526.

Bikle, D. D. (2004). Vitamin D and skin cancer. *Journal of Nutrition, 134,* 3472S–3478S.

Binda, P., Pereverzeva, M., & Murray, S. O. (2013). Pupil constrictions to photographs of the sun. *Journal of Vision, 13*(6):8, 1–9.

Birch, J. (2012). Worldwide prevalence of red-green color deficiency. *Journal of the Optical Society of America A, 29,* 313–320.

Bishara, D., Sauer, J., & Taylor, D. (2015). The pharmacological management of Alzheimer's disease. *Progress in Neurology and Psychiatry, 19*(4), 9–16.

Blackmore, S. J. (2005). *Consciousness: A very short introduction.* New York, NY: Oxford University Press.

Blair, C., & Raver, C. C. (2012). Child development in the context of adversity: Experiential canalization of brain and behavior. *American Psychologist, 67,* 309–318.

Blair, C., & Raver, C. C. (2015). School readiness and self-regulation: A developmental psychobiological approach. *Annual Review of Psychology, 66,* 711–731.

Blake, A. B., Nazarian, M., & Castel, A. D. (2015). The Apple of the mind's eye: Everyday attention, metamemory, and reconstructive memory for the Apple logo. *The Quarterly Journal of Experimental Psychology, 68,* 858–865.

Blakemore, E. (2016, June 9). The world's "ugliest" color could help people quit smoking. *Smithsonian.com.* Retrieved from http://www.smithsonianmag.com/smart-news/worlds-ugliest-color-could-help-people-quit-smoking-180959364/?no-ist

Blanchard, R. (2008). Review and theory of handedness, birth order, and homosexuality in men. *Laterality, 13,* 51–70.

Blanchard, S., & Muller, C. (2015). Gatekeepers of the American dream: How teachers' perceptions shape the academic outcomes of immigrant and language-minority students. *Social Science Research, 51,* 262–275.

Blasi, A. (1980). Bridging moral cognition and moral action: A critical review of the literature. *Psychological Bulletin, 88,* 1–45.

Blasi, G., Selvaggi, P., Fazio, L., Antonucci, L. A., Taurisano, P., Masellis, R., … Popolizio, T. (2015). Variation in dopamine D2 and serotonin 5-HT2A receptor genes is associated with working memory processing and response to treatment with antipsychotics. *Neuropsychopharmacology, 40,* 1600–1608.

Blass, T. (1991). Understanding behavior in the Milgram obedience experiment: The role of personality, situations, and their interactions. *Journal of Personality and Social Psychology, 60,* 398–413.

Blass, T. (1999). The Milgram paradigm after 35 years: Some things we now know about obedience to authority. *Journal of Applied Social Psychology, 25,* 955–978.

Blatchley, B., & O'Brien, K. R. (2007). Deceiving the participant: Are we creating the reputational spillover effect? *North American Journal of Psychology, 9,* 519–534.

Blecher, S. R., & Erickson, R. P. (2007). Genetics of sexual development: A new paradigm. *American Journal of Medical Genetics Part A, 143A,* 3054–3068.

BlinkNow. (n.d.). *Women's Center.* Retrieved from http://www.blinknow.org/pages/womens-center

Bliss-Moreau, E., Bauman, M. D., & Amaral, D. G. (2011). Neonatal amygdala lesions result in globally blunted affect in adult Rhesus Macaques. *Behavioral Neuroscience, 125,* 848–858.

Bloch, M. H., McGuire, J., Landeros-Weisenberger, A., Leckman, J. F., & Pittenger, C. (2010). Meta-analysis of the dose-response relationship of SSRI in obsessive-compulsive disorder. *Molecular Psychiatry, 15,* 850–855.

Block, C. J., Koch, S. M., Liberman, B. E., Merriweather, T. J., & Roberson, L. (2011). Contending with stereotype threat at work: A model of long-term responses. *Counseling Psychologist, 39,* 570–600.

Blumenthal, H., Leen-Feldner, E. W., Babson, K. A., Gahr, J. L., Trainor, C. D., & Frala, J. L. (2011). Elevated social anxiety among early maturing girls. *Developmental Psychology, 47,* 1133–1140.

Boardman, M. (2015, April 3). Kendrick Lamar opens up about depression, suicidal thoughts: Watch. *US Weekly.* Retrieved from http://www.usmagazine.com/celebrity-news/news/kendrick-lamar-opens-up-about-depression-suicidal-thoughts-watch-201534

Bodenmann, G., Meuwly, N., Germann, J., Nussbeck, F. W., Heinrichs, M., & Bradbury, T. N. (2015). Effects of stress on the social support provided by men and women in intimate relationships. *Psychological Science, 26,* 1584–1594.

Boeve, B. F., Silber, M. H., Saper, C. B., Ferman, T. J., Dickson, D. W., Parisi, J. E., … Braak, H. (2007). Pathophysiology of REM sleep behaviour disorder and relevance to neurodegenerative disease. *Brain, 130,* 2770–2788.

Bogaert, A. F. (2007). Extreme right-handedness, older brothers, and sexual orientation in men. *Neuropsychology, 21,* 141–148.

Bogaert, A. F., & Skorska, M. (2011). Sexual orientation, fraternal birth order, and the maternal immune hypothesis: A review. *Frontiers in Neuroendocrinology, 32,* 247–254.

Bold, K. W., Yoon, H., Chapman, G. B., & McCarthy, D. E. (2013). Factors predicting smoking in a laboratory-based smoking-choice task. *Experimental and Clinical Psychopharmacology, 21,* 133–143. doi:10.1037/a0031559

Bonanno, G. A., Westphal, M., & Mancini, A. D. (2011). Resilience to loss and potential trauma. *Annual Review of Clinical Psychology, 7,* 1.1–1.25.

Bond, R., & Smith, P. B. (1996). Culture and conformity: A meta-analysis of studies using Asch's (1952b, 1956) line judgment task. *Psychological Bulletin, 119,* 111–137.

Bongers, P., van den Akker, K., Havermans, R., & Jansen, A. (2015). Emotional eating and Pavlovian learning: Does negative mood facilitate appetitive conditioning? *Appetite, 89,* 226–236.

Bonnet, L., Comte, A., Tatu, L., Millot, J. L., Moulin, T., & de Bustos, E. M. (2015). The role of the amygdala in the perception of positive emotions: An "intensity detector." *Frontiers in Behavioral Neuroscience, 9.* doi: 10.3389/fnbeh.2015.00178.

Bonnie, R. J., & Scott, E. S. (2013). The teenage brain: Adolescent brain research and the law. *Current Directions in Psychological Science, 22,* 158–161.

Boothroyd, L. G., Meins, E., Vukovic, J., & Burt, D. M. (2014). Developmental changes in children's facial preferences. *Evolution and Human Behavior, 35,* 376–383.

Borbély, A. A., Daan, S., Wirz-Justice, A., & Deboer, T. (2016). The two-process model of sleep regulation: A reappraisal. *Journal of Sleep Research, 25,* 131–143.

Borges, G., Nock, M. K., Abad, J. M. H., Hwang, I., Sampson, N. A., Alonso, J., … Kessler, R. C. (2010). Twelve month prevalence of and risk factors for suicide attempts in the WHO world mental health surveys. *Journal of Clinical Psychiatry, 71,* 1617–1628.

Boring, E. G. (1953). A history of introspection. *Psychological Bulletin, 50,* 169–189.

Bornstein, R. F. (2005). Reconnecting psychoanalysis to mainstream psychology: Challenges and opportunities. *Psychoanalytic Psychology, 22,* 323–340.

Borota, D., Murray, E., Keceli, G., Chang, A., Watabe, J. M., Ly, M., … Yassa, M. A. (2014). Post-study caffeine administration enhances memory consolidation in humans. *Nature Neuroscience, 17,* 201–203.

Borra, J. E. (2005). Roper v. Simmons. *Journal of Gender, Social Policy, & the Law, 13,* 707–715.

Bos, H., van Gelderen, L., & Gartrell, N. (2015). Lesbian and heterosexual two-parent families: Adolescent–parent relationship quality and adolescent well-being. *Journal of Child and Family Studies, 24,* 1031–1046.

Bosman, J. (2016, March 23). Flint water crisis inquiry finds state ignored warning signs. Retrieved from http://www.nytimes.com/2016/03/24/us/flint-water-crisis.html?_r=0

Botta, P., Demmou, L., Kasugai, Y., Markovic, M., Xu, C., Fadok, J. P., … Lüthi, A. (2015). Regulating anxiety with extrasynaptic inhibition. *Nature Neuroscience, 18,* 1493–1500.

Bouchard, T. J. (2004). Genetic influence on human psychological traits: A survey. *Current Directions in Psychological Science, 13, 148–151.*

Bouchard, T. J., Jr., Lykken, D. T., McGue, M., Segal, N. L., & Tellegen, A. (1990). Sources of human psychological differences: The Minnesota Study of Twins Reared Apart. *Science, 250*(4978), 223–228.

Boureau, Y. L., Sokol-Hessner, P., & Daw, N. D. (2015). Deciding how to decide: Self-control and meta-decision making. *Trends in Cognitive Sciences, 19,* 700–710.

Bouton, M. E., Mineka, S., & Barlow, D. H. (2001). A modern learning theory perspective on the etiology of panic disorder. *Psychological Review, 108,* 4–32.

Bowden, C. L., Calabrese, J. R., McElroy, S. L., Gyulai, L., Wassef, A., Petty, F., … Wozniak, P. J. (2000). A randomized, placebo-controlled 12-month trial of divalproex and lithium in treatment of outpatients with bipolar I disorder. *Archives of General Psychiatry, 57,* 481–489.

Bower, B. (2013, May 21). Dog sniffs out grammar. *ScienceNews.* Retrieved from https://www.sciencenews.org/article/dog-sniffs-out-grammar

Bower, G. H., Clark, M. C., Lesgold, A. M., & Winzenz, D. (1969). Hierarchical retrieval schemes and recall of categorized word lists. *Journal of Verbal Learning and Verbal Behavior, 8,* 323–343.

Bower, G. H., Gilligan, S. G., & Menteiro, K. P. (1981). Selectivity of learning caused by affective states. *Journal of Experimental Psychology: General, 110,* 451–473.

Bower, J. M., & Parsons, L. M. (2003, July 14). Rethinking "the lesser brain." *Scientific American, 289,* 51–57.

Bowers, J. S., Mattys, S. L., & Gage, S. H. (2009). Preserved implicit knowledge of a forgotten childhood language. *Psychological Science, 20,* 1064–1069.

Boyd, R. (2008, February 7). Do people only use 10 percent of their brains? *Scientific American.* Retrieved from http://www.scientificamerican.com/article/do-people-only-use-10-percent-of-their-brains/

Bradley, L. A. (2011). Culture, gender and clothing. *Paideusis-Journal for Interdisciplinary and Cross-Cultural Studies, 5,* A1–A6.

Brady, S. T., Reeves, S. L., Garcia, J., Purdie-Vaughns, V., Cook, J. E., Taborsky-Barba, S., … Cohen, G. L. (2016). The psychology of the affirmed learner: Spontaneous self-affirmation in the face of stress. *Journal of Educational Psychology, 108*(3), 353–373.

Bragard, I., Dupuis, G., & Fleet, R. (2015). Quality of work life, burnout, and stress in emergency department physicians: A qualitative review. *European Journal of Emergency Medicine, 22,* 227–234.

Branch, J. (2016, March 3). Brandi Chastain to donate her brain for C.T.E. research. *The New York Times.* Retrieved from http://www.nytimes.com/2016/03/04/sports/soccer/brandi-chastain-to-donate-her-brain-for-cte-research.html?_r=0

Brandone, A. C., Salkind, S. J., Golinkoff, R. M., & Hirsh-Pasek, K. (2006). Language development. In G. G. Bear & K. M. Minke (Eds.), *Children's needs III: Development, prevention, and intervention* (pp. 499–514). Washington, DC: National Association of School Psychologists.

Brandt, J., & Benedict, R. H. B. (1993). Assessment of retrograde amnesia: Findings with a new public events procedure. *Neuropsychology, 7,* 217–227.

Brann, J. H., & Firestein, S. J. (2014). A lifetime of neurogenesis in the olfactory system. *Frontiers in Neuroscience, 8.* http://dx.doi.org/10.3389/fnins.2014.00182

Brascamp, J. W., Blake, R., & Kristjánsson, A. (2011). Deciding where to attend: Priming of pop-out drives target selection. *Journal of Experimental Psychology: Human Perception and Performance, 37,* 1700–1707.

Braver, S. L., Thoemmes, F. J., & Rosenthal, R. (2014). Continuously cumulating meta-analysis and replicability. *Perspectives on Psychological Science, 9,* 333–342.

Breland, K., & Breland, M. (1951). A field of applied animal psychology. *American Psychologist, 6,* 202–204.

Breland, K., & Breland, M. (1961). The misbehavior of organisms. *American Psychologist, 16,* 681–684.

Bremner, J. G., Slater, A., & Johnson, S. (2015). Perception of object persistence: The origins of object permanence in infancy. *Child Development Perspectives, 9,* 7–13.

Brendgen, M., Dionne, G., Girard, A., Boivin, M., Vitaro, F., & Pérusse, D. (2005). Examining genetic and environmental effects on social aggression: A study of 6-year-old twins. *Child Development, 76,* 930–946.

Brent, R. L. (2004). Environmental causes of human congenital malformations: The pediatrician's role in dealing with these complex clinical problems caused by a multiplicity of environmental and genetic factors. *Pediatrics, 113,* 957–968.

Breus, M. J. (2009, May 6). Are you fooling yourself? *Huffington Post.* Retrieved from http://www.huffingtonpost.com/dr-michael-j-breus/are-you-fooling-yourself_b_198525.html

Brewin, C. R., & Andrews, B. (2014). Why it is scientifically respectable to believe in repression: A response to Patihis, Ho, Tingen, Lilienfeld, and Loftus (2014). *Psychological Science, 25,* 1964–1966.

Brewster, K. L., & Tillman, K. H. (2008). Who's doing it? Patterns and predictors of youths' oral sexual experiences. *Journal of Adolescent Health, 42,* 73–80.

Brickman, A. M., Khan, U. A., Provenzano, F. A., Yeung, L. K., Suzuki, W., Schroeter, H., … Small, S. A. (2014). Enhancing dentate gyrus function with dietary flavanols improves cognition in older adults. *Nature Neuroscience, 17*(12), 1798–1803.

Bridge, H., Harrold, S., Holmes, E. A., Stokes, M., & Kennard, C. (2012). Vivid visual mental imagery in the absence of the primary visual cortex. *Journal of Neurology, 259,* 1062–1070.

Briere, J., Agee, E., & Dietrich, A. (2016). Cumulative trauma and current post-traumatic stress disorder status in general population and inmate samples. *Psychological Trauma: Theory, Research, Practice, and Policy, 8,* 439–446.

Briggs, K. C., & Myers, I. B. (1998). *Myers–Briggs type indicator.* Palo Alto, CA: Consulting Psychologists Press.

Briley, D. A., & Tucker-Drob, E. M. (2014). Genetic and environmental continuity in personality development: A meta-analysis. *Psychological Bulletin, 140,* 1303–1331.

Broadbelt, K. G., Paterson, D. S., Rivera, K. D., Trachtenberg, F. L., & Kinney, H. C. (2010). Neuroanatomic relationships between the GABAergic and serotonergic systems in the developing human medulla. *Autonomic Neuroscience: Basic & Clinical, 154,* 30–41.

Brody, S. (2010). The relative health benefits of different sexual activities. *The Journal of Sexual Medicine, 7,* 1336–1361.

Brody, S., & Costa, R. M. (2009). Satisfaction (sexual, life, relationship, and mental health) is associated directly with penile-vaginal intercourse, but inversely with other sexual behavior frequencies. *The Journal of Sexual Medicine, 6,* 1947–1954.

Brogaard, P., & Marlow, K. (2012, December 11). Kim Peek, the real rain man [Web log post]. Retrieved from http://www.psychologytoday.com/blog/the-superhuman-mind/201212/kim-peek-the-real-rain-man

Brooks, J. E., & Neville, H. A. (2016). Interracial attraction among college men: The influence of ideologies, familiarity, and similarity. *Journal of Social and Personal Relationships.* doi:10.1177/0265407515627508

Brothers, J. R., & Lohmann, K. J. (2015). Evidence for geomagnetic imprinting and magnetic navigation in the natal homing of sea turtles. *Current Biology, 25,* 392–396.

Brotto, L. A. (2010). The DSM diagnostic criteria for hypoactive sexual desire disorder in men. *The Journal of Sexual Medicine, 7,* 2015–2030.

Brouwer, R. M., Koenis, M. M. G., Schnack, H. G., van Baal, G. C., van Soelen, I. L., Boomsma, D. I., & Pol, H. E. H. (2015). Longitudinal development of hormone levels and grey matter density in 9- and 12-year-old twins. *Behavior Genetics, 45,* 313–323.

Brown, A. S., & Nix, L. A. (1996). Age-related changes in the tip-of-the-tongue experience. *American Journal of Psychology, 109,* 79–91.

Brown, A. S., & Patterson, P. H. (2011). Maternal infection and schizophrenia: Implications for prevention. *Schizophrenia Bulletin, 37,* 284–290.

Brown, P. K., & Wald, G. (1964). Visual pigments in single rods and cones of the human retina. *Science, 144,* 45–52.

Brown, R., & Kulik, J. (1977). Flashbulb memories. *Cognition, 5,* 73–99.

Brown, S. L, Nesse, R. M., Vinokur, A. D., & Smith, D. M. (2003). Providing social support may be more beneficial than receiving it: Results from a prospective study of mortality. *Psychological Science, 14,* 320–327.

Brown, T. T., & Dobs, A. S. (2002). Endocrine effects of marijuana. *Journal of Clinical Pharmacology, 42,* 90S–96S.

Brownell, P. (2010). *Gestalt therapy: A guide to contemporary practice.* New York, NY: Springer.

Brunstein, J. C. (1993). Personal goals and subjective well-being: A longitudinal study. *Journal of Personality and Social Psychology, 65,* 1061–1070.

Brusewitz, G., Cherkas, L., Harris, J., & Parker, A. (2013). Exceptional experiences amongst twins. *Journal of the Society for Psychical Research, 77*(913), 220–235.

Bryan, A., Hutchison, K. E., Seals, D. R., & Allen, D. L. (2007). A transdisciplinary model integrating genetic, physiological, and psychological correlates of voluntary exercise. *Health Psychology, 26,* 30–39.

Buchanan, L. R., Rooks-Peck, C. R., Finnie, R. K., Wethington, H. R., Jacob, V., Fulton, J. E., … Glanz, K. Reducing recreational sedentary screen time: A community guide systematic review. *American Journal of Preventive Medicine, 50,* 402–415.

Buchanan, T. W., Tranel, D., & Adolphs, R. (2004). Anteromedial temporal lobe damage blocks startle modulation by fear and disgust. *Behavioral Neuroscience, 188,* 429–437.

Buck, R. (1980). Nonverbal behavior and the theory of emotion: The facial feedback hypothesis. *Journal of Personality and Social Psychology, 38,* 811–824.

Buckle, C. E., Udawatta, V., & Straus, C. M. (2013). Now you see it, now you don't: Visual illusions in radiology. *Radiographics, 33,* 2037–2102.

Budden, J. S., Zhong, E. H., Moulton, P., & Cimiotti, J. P. (2013). Highlights of the National Workforce Survey of Registered Nurses. *Journal of Nursing Regulation, 4,* 5–14.

Buettner D. (2015). *The Blue Zones solution.* Washington, DC: National Geographic.

Buffardi, L. E., & Campbell, W. K. (2008). Narcissism and social networking web sites. *Personality and Social Psychology Bulletin, 34,* 1303–1314.

Bufka, L. F., & Halfond, R. (2016) Professional standards and guidelines. In J. C. Norcross, G. R. VandenBos, D. K. Freedheim, & L. E. Campbell (Eds.), *APA handbook of clinical psychology: Education and profession* (Vol. 5, pp. 355–373). Washington, DC: American Psychological Association.

Bui, N. H. (2012). False consensus in attitudes toward celebrities. *Psychology of Popular Media Culture, 1,* 236–243. doi:10.1037/a0028569

Bulpitt, C. J., Markowe, H. L. J., & Shipley, M. J. (2001). Why do some people look older than they should? *Postgraduate Medical Journal, 77,* 578–581.

Burda, J. E., Bernstein, A. M., & Sofroniew, M. V. (2016). Astrocyte roles in traumatic brain injury. *Experimental Neurology, 275,* 305–315.

Bureau of Labor Statistics, U.S. Department of Labor. (2014). Employment Projections Program. *Employment by industry, occupation, and percent distribution, 2014 and projected 2024: 19-3030 Psychologists.* Retrieved from http://www.bls.gov/emp/ind-occ-matrix/occ_xlsx/occ_19-3030.xlsx

Bureau of Labor Statistics, U.S. Department of Labor. (2016–2017). *Occupational outlook handbook.* Retrieved from http://www.bls.gov/ooh

Burgaleta, M., Head, K., Álvarez-Linera, J., Martínez, K., Escorial, S., Haier, R., & Colom, R. (2012). Sex differences in brain volume are related to specific skills, not to general intelligence. *Intelligence, 40,* 60–68.

Burge, J., Fowlkes, C. C., & Banks, M. S. (2010). Natural-scene statistics predict how the figure-ground cue of convexity affects human depth perception. *Journal of Neuroscience, 30,* 7269–7280.

Burger, J. M. (2009). Replicating Milgram: Would people still obey today? *American Psychologist, 64,* 1–11.

Burger, J. M. (2015). *Personality* (9th ed.). Belmont, CA: Wadsworth, Cengage Learning.

Burke, M., & Kraut, R. E. (2014). Growing closer on Facebook: Changes in tie strength through social network site use. In *Proceedings of the SIGCHI Conference on Human Factors in Computing Systems* (pp. 4187–4196). New York, NY: Association for Computing Machinery.

Burlingame, G. M., & Baldwin, S. (2011). Group therapy. In J. C. Norcross, G. R. VandenBos, & D. K. Freedheim (Eds.), *History of psychotherapy: Continuity and change* (2nd ed., pp. 505–515). Washington, DC: American Psychological Association.

Burnette, J. L., Pollack, J. M., & Forsyth, D. R. (2011). Leadership in extreme contexts: A groupthink analysis of the May 1996 Mount Everest disaster. *Journal of Leadership Studies, 4,* 29–40.

Burstein, A. G., & Loucks, S. (1989). *Rorschach's test: Scoring and interpretation.* New York, NY: Hemisphere.

Burton, H. (2003). Visual cortex activity in early and late blind people. *Journal of Neuroscience, 23,* 4005–4011.

Bushdid, C., Magnasco, M. O., Vosshall, L. B., & Keller, A. (2014). Humans can discriminate more than 1 trillion olfactory stimuli. *Science, 343,* 1370–1372.

Bushman, B. J., Newman, K., Calvert, S. L., Downey, G., Dredze, M., Gottfredson, M., … Romer, D. (2016). Youth violence: What we know and what we need to know. *American Psychologist, 71,* 17–39.

Buss, D. M. (1989). Sex differences in human mate preferences: Evolutionary hypotheses tested in 37 cultures. *Behavioral and Brain Sciences, 12,* 1–14.

Buss, D. M. (1995). Psychological sex differences: Origins through sexual selection. *American Psychologist, 50,* 164–168.

Buss, D. M., & Penke, L. (2015). Evolutionary personality psychology. In M. Mikulincer, P. R. Shaver, M. L. Cooper, & R. J. Larsen (Eds.), *APA handbook of personality and social psychology* (Vol. 4, pp. 3–29). Washington, DC: American Psychological Association.

Buss, D. M., Shackelford, T. K., Kirkpatrick, L. A., & Larsen, R. J. (2001). A half century of mate preferences: The cultural evolution of values. *Journal of Marriage and Family, 63,* 491–503.

Buss, L., Tolstrup, J., Munk, C., Bergholt, T., Ottensen, B., Grønbæk, M., & Kjaer, S. K. (2006). Spontaneous abortion: A prospective cohort study of younger women from the general population in Denmark. Validation, occurrence and risk determinants. *Acta Obstetricia et Gynecologic, 85,* 467–475.

Bussey, K., & Bandura, A. (1999). Social cognitive theory of gender development and differentiation. *Psychological Review, 106,* 676–713.

Bustin, G. M., Jones, D. N., Hansenne, M., & Quoidbach, J. (2015). Who does Red Bull give wings to? Sensation seeking moderates sensitivity to subliminal advertisement. *Frontiers in Psychology, 6.* doi: 10.3389/fpsyg.2015.00825

Butcher, J. N., & Rouse, S. V. (1996). Personality: Individual differences and clinical assessment. *Annual Review of Psychology, 47,* 87–111.

Butler, A. C., Zaromb, F. M., Lyle, K. B., & Roediger, H. L. (2009). Using popular films to enhance classroom learning. *Psychological Science, 20*(9), 1161–1168.

Butler, J. (2015). Hypnosis for dental professionals. *BDJ Team, 1.* doi:10.1038/bdjteam.2015.28

Butler, R. A. (1960). Acquired drives and the curiosity-investigative motives. In R. H. Waters, D. A. Rethlingshafer, & W. E. Caldwell (Eds.), *McGraw-Hill Series in Psychology: Principles of comparative psychology* (pp. 144–176). New York, NY: McGraw-Hill.

Byers, E. S. (2011). Beyond the birds and the bees and was it good for you? Thirty years of research on sexual communication. *Canadian Psychology, 52,* 20–28.

Bynum, H. (2007). Anesthesia and the practice of medicine: Historical perspectives. *Journal of the American Medical Association, 298,* 2551–2552.

Cabanatuan, M., & Sebastian, S. (2005, October 19). Surfer fights off shark, escapes with bitten leg. *SFGate.com.* Retrieved from http://www.sfgate.com/news/article/Surfer-fights-off-shark-escapes-with-bitten-leg-2601443.php

Cabral, R. R., & Smith, T. B. (2011). Racial/ethnic matching of clients and therapists in mental health services: A meta-analytic review of preferences, perceptions, and outcomes. *Journal of Counseling Psychology, 58,* 537–554.

Cacioppo, J. T., Cacioppo, S., Gonzaga, G. C., Ogburn, E. L., & VanderWeele, T. J. (2013). Marital satisfaction and break-ups differ across on-line and off-line meeting venues. *Proceedings of the National Academy of Sciences, 110,* 10135–10140.

Cahill, L. (2012). His brain, her brain. *Scientific American Classics Mind, 1,* 40–47.

Cain, D. J. (2016). Toward a research-based integration of optimal practices of humanistic psychotherapies. In D. J. Cain, K. Keenan, & S. Rubin (Eds.), *Humanistic psychotherapies: Handbook of research and practice* (2nd ed., pp. 485–535). Washington, DC: American Psychological Association.

Cain, M. S., Leonard, J. A., Gabrieli, J. D., & Finn, A. S. (2016). Media multitasking in adolescence. *Psychonomic Bulletin & Review,* 1–10. doi:10.3758/s13423-016-1036-3

Calabrese, M., Magliozzi, R., Ciccarelli, O., Geurts, J. J., Reynolds, R., & Martin, R. (2015). Exploring the origins of grey matter damage in multiple sclerosis. *Nature Reviews Neuroscience, 16,* 147–158.

Caldicott, D. G., Mahajani R., & Kuhn M. (2001). The anatomy of a shark attack: A case report and review of the literature. *Injury, 32,* 445–453.

Callan, M. J., Ferguson, H. J., & Bindemann, M. (2013). Eye movements to audiovisual scenes reveal expectations of a just world. *Journal of Experimental Psychology: General, 142,* 34–40. doi:10.1037/a0028261

Campbell, A. (1999). Staying alive: Evolution, culture, and women's intrasexual aggression. *Behavioral and Brain Sciences, 22,* 203–252.

Campbell, G. A., & Rosner, M. H. (2008). The agony of Ecstasy: MDMA (3,4-Methylenedioxymethamphetamine) and the kidney. *Clinical Journal of the American Society of Nephrology, 3,* 1852–1860.

Campbell, L. F., Norcross, J. C., Vasquez, M. J. T., & Kaslow, N. J. (2013). Recognition of psychotherapy effectiveness: The APA resolution. *Psychotherapy, 50,* 98–101.

Campos, F., Sobrino, T., Ramos-Cabrer, P., Argibay, B., Agulla, J., Pérez-Mato, M., … Castillo, J. (2011). Neuroprotection by glutamate oxaloacetate transaminase in ischemic stroke: An experimental study. *Journal of Cerebral Blood Flow & Metabolism, 31,* 1378–1386.

Cannon, D. S., Baker, T. B., Gino, A., & Nathan, P. E. (1986). Alcohol-aversion therapy: Relation between strength of aversion and abstinence. *Journal of Consulting and Clinical Psychology, 54,* 825–830.

Cannon, W. B. (1927). The James-Lange theory of emotions: A critical examination and an alternative theory. *The American Journal of Psychology, 39,* 106–124.

Cannon, W. B., & Washburn, A. L. (1912). An explanation of hunger. *American Journal of Physiology, 29,* 441–454.

Cantero, J. L., Atienza, M., Salas, R. M., & Gómez, C. M. (1999). Alpha EEG coherence in different brain states: An electrophysiological index of the arousal level in human subjects. *Neuroscience Letters, 271,* 167–170.

Caporro, M., Haneef, Z., Yeh, H. J., Lenartowicz, A., Buttinelli, C., Parvizi, J., & Stern, J. M. (2012). Functional MRI of sleep spindles and K-complexes. *Clinical Neurophysiology, 123*(2), 303–309.

Carbon, C. C. (2014). Understanding human perception by human-made illusions. *Frontiers in Human Neuroscience, 8.* http://dx.doi.org/10.3389/fnhum.2014.00566.

Card, N. A., Stucky, B. D., Sawalani, G. M., & Little, T. D. (2008). Direct and indirect aggression during childhood and adolescence: A meta-analytic review of gender differences, intercorrelations, and relations to maladjustment. *Child Development, 79,* 1185–1229.

Cardno, A. G., & Owen, M. J. (2014). Genetic relationships between schizophrenia, bipolar disorder, and schizoaffective disorder. *Schizophrenia Bulletin, 40*(3), 504–515.

Carey, B. (2008, December 4). H.M., an unforgettable amnesiac, dies at 82. *The New York Times.* Retrieved from http://www.nytimes.com/2008/12/05/us/05hm.html–pagewanted=all&_r=0

Carlsson, K., Petersson, K. M., Lundqvist, D., Karlsson, A., Ingvar, M., & Öhman, A. (2004). Fear and the amygdala: Manipulation of awareness generates differential cerebral responses to phobic and fear-relevant (but nonfeared) stimuli. *Emotion, 4,* 340–353.

Carr, K., Kendal, R. L., & Flynn, E. G. (2015). Imitate or innovate? Children's innovation is influenced by the efficacy of observed behaviour. *Cognition, 142,* 322–332.

Carr, P. B., Dweck, C. S., & Pauker, K. (2012). "Prejudiced" behavior without prejudice? Beliefs about the malleability of prejudice affect interracial interactions. *Journal of Personality and Social Psychology, 103,* 452–471.

Carrier, L. M., Rosen, L. D., Cheever, N. A., & Lim, A. F. (2015). Causes, effects, and practicalities of everyday multitasking. *Developmental Review, 35,* 64–78.

Carson, H. (2011). *Captain for life: My story as a hall of fame linebacker.* New York, NY: St. Martin's Press.

Carstensen, L. L., Turan, B., Scheibe, S., Ram, N., Ersner-Hershfield, H., Samanez-Larkin, G. R., … Nesselroade, J. R. (2011). Emotional experience improves with age: Evidence based on over 10 years of experience sampling. *Psychology and Aging, 26,* 21–33.

Carter, C. J. (2007). eIF2B and oligodendrocyte survival: Where nature and nurture meet in bipolar disorder and schizophrenia? *Schizophrenia Bulletin, 33,* 1343–1353.

Caruso, R. (2007, August 13). Why does it take so long for our vision to adjust to a darkened theater after we come in from bright sunlight? *Scientific American Online.* Retrieved from http://www.scientificamerican.com/article.cfm–id=experts-eyes-adjust-to-darkness

Case, B. G., Bertollo, D. N., Laska, E. M., Price, L. H., Siegel, C. E., Olfson, M., & Marcus, S. C. (2013). Declining use of electroconvulsive therapy in United States general hospitals. *Biological Psychiatry, 73,* 119–126.

Caspi, A., Roberts, B. W., & Shiner, R. L. (2005). Personality development: Stability and change. *Annual Review of Psychology, 56,* 453–484.

Cassidy, J. (2001). Truth, lies, and intimacy: An attachment perspective. *Attachment & Human Development, 3,* 121–155.

Castel, A. D., Humphreys, K. L., Lee, S. S., Galván, A., Balota, D. A., & McCabe, D. P. (2011). The development of memory efficiency and value-directed remembering across the life span: A cross-sectional study of memory and selectivity. *Developmental Psychology, 47,* 1553–1564.

Castillo, M. (2014). The ins and outs of sexual imaging. *American Journal of Neuroradiology, 35,* 1847–1848.

Castle, D. J., Bosanac, P., & Rossell, S. (2015). Treating OCD: What to do when first-line therapies fail. *Australasian Psychiatry, 23,* 350–353.

Catalino, L. I., & Fredrickson, B. L. (2011). A Tuesday in the life of a flourisher: The role of positive emotional reactivity in optimal mental health. *Emotion, 11,* 938–950.

Catanzaro, D., Chesbro, E. C., & Velkey, A. J. (2013). Relationship between food preferences and PROP taster status of college students. *Appetite, 68,* 124–131.

Cattell, R. B. (1950). *Personality: A systematic theoretical and factual study.* New York, NY: McGraw-Hill.

Cattell, R. B. (1973a). *Personality and mood by questionnaire.* San Francisco, CA: Jossey-Bass.

Cattell, R. B. (1973b). Personality pinned down. *Psychology Today, 7,* 40–46.

Cattell, R. B., Eber, H. W., & Tatsuoka, M. M. (1970). *Handbook for the sixteen personality factor questionnaire (16PF).* Champaign, IL: Institute for Personality and Ability Testing.

Catts, V. S., Lai, Y. L., Weickert, C. S., Weickert, T. W., & Catts, S. V. (2016). A quantitative review of the postmortem evidence for decreased cortical N-methyl-d-aspartate receptor expression levels in schizophrenia: How can we link molecular abnormalities to mismatch negativity deficits? *Biological Psychology, 116,* 57–67.

Cavallini, A., Fazzi, E., Viviani, V., Astori, M. G., Zaverio, S., Bianchi, P. E., & Lanzi, G. (2002). Visual acuity in the first two years of life in healthy term newborns: An experience with the teller acuity cards. *Functional Neurology, 17,* 87–92.

CBC News. (2004, May 10). *David Reimer: The boy who lived as a girl.* Copy in possession of author.

CBS News. (2011, July 26). *Shark survivor girl: "I like dolphins way better."* Retrieved from http://www.cbsnews.com/news/shark-survivor-girl-i-like-dophins-way-better/

CBS2. (2015, September 15). *Exclusive: Sean Satha, man James Blake was mistaken for in arrest, was wrong man too.* Retrieved from http://newyork.cbslocal.com/2015/09/15/cbs2-exclusive-sean-satha-james-blake/

Ceci, S. J., Ginther, D. K., Kahn, S., & Williams, W. M. (2014). Women in academic science: A changing landscape. *Psychological Science in the Public Interest, 15*(3), 75–141.

Ceci, S. J., & Williams, W. M. (2009). Yes: The scientific truth must be pursued. *Nature, 457,* 788–789.

Celizic, M. (2010, June 7). Al's fit club: Roker on 115-pound loss. *Today Health.* Retrieved from http://www.today.com/id/37550535/ns/today-today_health/t/als-fit-club-roker--pound-loss/#.V7XCDpMrKkt

Center for Sexual Health Promotion. (2010). *National survey of sexual health and behavior.* Retrieved from http://www.nationalsexstudy.indiana.edu

Centers for Disease Control and Prevention. (2010). Vital signs: Current cigarette smoking among adults aged ≥18 Years—United States, 2009. *Morbidity and Mortality Weekly Report, 59,* 1135–1140.

Centers for Disease Control and Prevention. (2011, February 11). *Effects of blood alcohol concentration (BAC).* Retrieved from http://www.cdc.gov/Motorvehiclesafety/Impaired_Driving/bac.html

Centers for Disease Control and Prevention. (2013). *Incidence, prevalence, and cost of sexually transmitted infections in the United State.* Retrieved from http://www.cdc.gov/std/stats/STI-Estimates-Fact-Sheet-Feb-2013.pdf

Centers for Disease Control and Prevention. (2014a). *Health effects of secondhand smoke* [Fact sheet]. Retrieved from http://www.cdc.gov/tobacco/data_statistics/fact_sheets/secondhand_smoke/health_effects/

Centers for Disease Control and Prevention. (2014b). *Nursing home care.* Retrieved from http://www.cdc.gov/nchs/fastats/nursing-home-care.htm

Centers for Disease Control and Prevention. (2015a). *Genital herpes.* Retrieved from http://www.cdc.gov/std/Herpes/STDFact-Herpes.htm

Centers for Disease Control and Prevention. (2015b). *Gonorrhea.* Retrieved from http://www.cdc.gov/std/gonorrhea/STDFact-gonorrhea.htm

Centers for Disease Control and Prevention. (2015c). *HIV in the United States: At a glance.* Retrieved from http://www.cdc.gov/hiv/statistics/overview/ataglance.html

Centers for Disease Control and Prevention. (2015d). *Sexually transmitted disease surveillance 2014.* Atlanta: U.S. Department of Health and Human Services.

Centers for Disease Control and Prevention. (2015e). *Sexually transmitted diseases: Adolescents and young adults.* Retrieved from http://www.cdc.gov/std/life-stages-populations/adolescents-youngadults.htm

Centers for Disease Control and Prevention. (2015f). *Tobacco-related mortality* [Fact sheet]. Retrieved from http://www.cdc.gov/tobacco/data_statistics/fact_sheets/health_effects/tobacco_related_mortality/index.htm

Centers for Disease Control and Prevention. (2015, November 13). Current cigarette smoking among adults—United States, 2005–2014. *Morbidity and Mortality Weekly Report, 64*(44). Retrieved from http://www.cdc.gov/mmwr/pdf/wk/mm6444.pdf

Centers for Disease Control and Prevention. (2016a) *About teen pregnancy.* Retrieved from http://www.cdc.gov/teenpregnancy/about/index.htm

Centers for Disease Control and Prevention. (2016b). *Alcohol use and your health* [Fact sheet]. Retrieved from http://www.cdc.gov/alcohol/fact-sheets/alcohol-use.htm

Centers for Disease Control and Prevention. (2016c) *Autism spectrum disorder: Data and statistics.* Retrieved from http://www.cdc.gov/ncbddd/autism/data.html

Centers for Disease Control and Prevention. (2016d). *Chlamydia.* Retrieved from http://www.cdc.gov/std/chlamydia/STDFact-chlamydia-detailed.htm

Centers for Disease Control and Prevention. (2016e). *Genital HPV infection.* Retrieved from http://www.cdc.gov/std/HPV/STDFact-HPV.htm

Centers for Disease Control and Prevention. (2016f). *Important milestones: Your baby at six months.* Retrieved from http://www.cdc.gov/ncbddd/actearly/milestones/milestones-6mo.html

Centers for Disease Control and Prevention. (2016g). *Questions and answers: 2014 Ebola outbreak.* Retrieved from http://www.cdc.gov/vhf/ebola/outbreaks/2014-west-africa/qa.html

Centers for Disease Control and Prevention. (2016h). *Syphilis.* Retrieved from http://www.cdc.gov/std/syphilis/STDFact-Syphilis.htm

Centola, D. (2010). The spread of behavior in an online social network experiment. *Science, 329,* 1194–1197.

Centre for Addiction and Mental Health. (2010). *LSD: What's LSD?* Retrieved from http://www.camh.ca/en/hospital/health_information/a_z_mental_health and _addiction_information/LSD/Pages/default.aspx

Cerasoli, C. P., Nicklin, J. M., & Ford, M. T. (2014). Intrinsic motivation and extrinsic incentives jointly predict performance: A 40-year meta-analysis. *Psychological Bulletin, 140,* 980–1008. http://dx.doi.org/10.1037/a0035661

Cerda-Molina, A. L., Hernández-López, L., de la O, C. E., Chavira-Ramírez, R., & Mondragón-Ceballos, R. (2013). Changes in men's salivary testosterone and cortisol levels, and in sexual desire after smelling female axillary and vulvar scents. *Frontiers in Endocrinology, 28* (4), Article 159. doi:10.3389/fendo.2013.00159

Cerny, J. A., & Janssen, E. (2011). Patterns of sexual arousal in homosexual, bisexual, and heterosexual men. *Archives of Sexual Behavior, 40,* 687–697.

Cesar Millan PACK Project. (n.d.). *Mission vision values.* Retrieved from http://millanpackproject.org/who-we-are/mission-vision-values/#

Cevallos, D. (2015, July 17). Don't rely on insanity defense. *CNN.* Retrieved from http://www.cnn.com/2015/02/11/opinion/cevallos-insanity-defense/

Chaiken, S., & Eagly, A. H. (1976). Communication modality as a determinant of message persuasiveness and message comprehensibility. *Journal of Personality and Social Psychology, 34,* 605–614.

Chaimay, B. (2011). Influence of breastfeeding practices on children's cognitive development—systematic review. *Asia Journal of Public Health, 2,* 40–44.

Chan, D. K., Zhang, X., Fung, H. H., & Hagger, M. S. (2015). Does emotion and its daily fluctuation correlate with depression? A cross-cultural analysis among six developing countries. *Journal of Epidemiology and Global Health, 5,* 65–74.

Chan, W., McCrae, R. R., De Fruyt, F., Jussim, L., Löckenhoff, C. E., De Bolle, M., … Nakazato, K. (2012). Stereotypes of age differences in personality traits: Universal and accurate? *Journal of Personality and Social Psychology, 103,* 1050–1066.

Chander, D., Garcia, P. S., MacColl, J. N., Illing, S., & Sleigh, J. W. (2014). Electroencephalographic variation during end maintenance and emergence from surgical anesthesia. *PLOS ONE, 9*(9), e106291. doi:10.1371/journal.pone.0106291

Chandrashekar, J., Hoon, M. A., Ryba, N. J., & Zuker, C. S. (2006). The receptors and cells for mammalian taste. *Nature, 444,* 288–294.

Chaplin, T. M. (2015). Gender and emotion expression: A developmental contextual perspective. *Emotion Review, 7,* 14–21.

Charlton, B., & Verghese, A. (2010). Caring for Ivan Ilyich. *Journal of General Internal Medicine, 25,* 93–95.

Chatterjee, R. (2015). Out of the darkness. *Science, 350*(6259), 372–375.

Chawla, J. (2013). Neurologic effects of caffeine. *Medscape.* Retrieved from http://emedicine.medscape.com/article/1182710-overview

Chechik, G., Meilijson, I., & Ruppin, E. (1998). Synaptic pruning in development: A computational account. *Neural Computation, 10,* 1759–1777.

Chen, C.-P., Wu, C.-C., Chang, L.-R., & Lin, Y.-H. (2014). Possible association between phantom vibration syndrome and occupational burnout. *Neuropsychiatric Disease and Treatment, 10,* 2307–2314.

Chen, C.-Y., Lin, Y.-H., & Hsaio, C.-L. (2012). Celebrity endorsement for sporting events using classical conditioning. *International Journal of Sports Marketing and Sponsorship, 13,* 209–219.

Chen, H., Chen, S., Zeng, L., Zhou, L., & Hou, S. (2014). Revisiting Einstein's brain in Brain Awareness Week. *Bioscience Trends, 8*(5), 286–289.

Chen, P. W. (2014, June 26). Putting us all at risk for measles [Web log post]. Retrieved from http://well.blogs.nytimes.com/2014/06/26/putting-us-all-at-risk-for-measles/?_r=0

Cheng, C., Cheung, S.-f., Chio, J. H.-m., & Chan, M.-p. S. (2013). Cultural meaning of perceived control: A meta-analysis of locus of control and psychological symptoms across 18 cultural regions. *Psychological Bulletin, 139,* 152–188.

Cheng, D. T., Knight, D. C., Smith, C. N., & Helmstetter, F. J. (2006). Human amygdala activity during the expression of fear responses. *Behavioral Neuroscience, 120,* 1187–1195.

Cheng, H. L., McDermott, R. C., Wong, Y. J., & La, S. (2016). Drive for muscularity in Asian American men: Sociocultural and racial/ethnic factors as correlates. *Psychology of Men and Masculinity, 17,* 215–227.

Cheng, S. Y., Suh, S. Y., Morita, T., Oyama, Y., Chiu, T. Y., Koh, S. J., … Tsuneto, S. (2015). A cross-cultural study on behaviors when death is approaching in East Asian countries: What are the physician-perceived common beliefs and practices? *Medicine, 94,* e1573.

Cherney, I. D. (2008). Mom, let me play more computer games: They improve my mental rotation skills. *Sex Roles, 59,* 776–786.

Cheyne, J. A. (2002). Situational factors affecting sleep paralysis and associated hallucinations: Position and timing effects. *Journal of Sleep Research, 11,* 169–177.

Chiao, J. Y., Iidka, T., Gordon, H. L., Nogawa, J., Bar, M., Aminoff, E., … Ambady, N. (2008). Cultural specificity in amygdala response to fear faces. *Journal of Cognitive Neuroscience, 20,* 2167–2174.

Child Trends Databank. (2015). *Attitudes toward spanking.* Retrieved from http://www.childtrends.org/?indicators=attitudes-toward-spanking

Chin, H. B., Sipe, T. A., Elder, R., Mercer, S. L., Chattopadhyay, S. K., Jacob, V., … Santelli, J. (2012). The effectiveness of group-based comprehensive risk-reduction and abstinence education interventions to prevent or reduce the risk of adolescent pregnancy, human immunodeficiency virus, and sexually transmitted infections: Two systematic reviews for the Guide to Community Preventive Services. *American Journal of Preventive Medicine, 42,* 272–294.

Chiras, D. D. (2015). *Human biology* (8th ed.). Burlington, MA: Jones & Bartlett Learning.

Chirawatkul, S., Prakhaw, P., & Chomnirat, W. (2011). Perceptions of depression among people of Khon Kaen City: A gender perspective. *Journal of Nursing Science & Health, 34,* 66–75.

Chivers, M. L., Seto, M. C., Lalumiere, M. L., Laan, E., & Grimbos, T. (2010). Agreement of self-reported and genital measures of sexual arousal in men and women: A meta-analysis. *Archives of Sexual Behavior, 39,* 5–56.

Cho, H. J., Meira-Lima, I., Cordeiro, Q., Michelon, L., Sham, P., Vallada, H., & Collie, D. A. (2005). Population-based and family-based studies on the serotonin transporter gene polymorphisms and bipolar disorder: A systematic review and meta-analysis. *Molecular Psychiatry, 10,* 771–781.

Choi, C. (2007, May 24). Strange but true: When half a brain is better than a whole one. *Scientific American Online.* Retrieved from http://www.scientificamerican.com/article/strange-but-true-when-half-brain-better-than-whole/

Choi, C. Q. (2008, March). Do you need only half your brain? *Scientific American, 298,* 104.

Chomsky, N. (1959). Verbal behavior. *Language, 35,* 26–58.

Chomsky, N. (2000). *New horizons in the study of language and mind.* Cambridge, UK: Cambridge University Press.

Chouchou, F., Khoury, S., Chauny, J. M., Denis, R., & Lavigne, G. J. (2014). Postoperative sleep disruptions: A potential catalyst of acute pain? *Sleep Medicine Reviews, 18,* 273–282.

Christakis, D. A., Garrison, M. M., Herrenkohl, T., Haggerty, K., Rivara, F. P., Zhou, C., & Liekweg, K. (2013). Modifying media content for preschool children: A randomized controlled trial. *Pediatrics, 131,* 431–438.

Christakos, S., Hewison, M., Gardner, D. G., Wagner, C. L., Sergeev, I. N., Rutten, E., … Bikle, D. D. (2013). Vitamin D: Beyond bone. *Annals of the New York Academy of Sciences, 1287*(1), 45–58.

Christopher, J. C., Wendt, D. C., Marecek, J., & Goodman, D. M. (2014). Critical cultural awareness: Contributions to a globalizing psychology. *American Psychologist, 69,* 645–655.

Chung, F., & Elsaid, H. (2009). Screening for obstructive sleep apnea before surgery: Why is it important? *Current Opinion in Anesthesiology, 22,* 405–411.

Cialdini, R. B., & Goldstein, N. J. (2004). Social influence: Compliance and conformity. *Annual Review of Psychology, 55,* 591–621.

Cicero, T. J., Ellis, M. S., Surratt, H. L., & Kurtz, S. P. (2014). The changing face of heroin use in the United States: A retrospective analysis of the past 50 years. *JAMA Psychiatry, 71,* 821–826.

Cirelli, C. (2012). Brain plasticity, sleep and aging. *Gerontology, 58*(5), 441–445.

Cisler, J. M., Brady, R. E., Olatunji, B. O., & Lohr, J. M. (2010). Disgust and obsessive beliefs in contamination-related OCD. *Cognitive Therapy Research, 34,* 439–448.

City of New York. (2012). *Mayor Bloomberg and Police Commissioner Kelly announce 2012 sets all-time record for fewest murders and fewest shootings in New York City history* [Press release]. Retrieved from http://www.nyc.gov/html/nypd/html/pr/pr_2012_all_time_records_lows_for_murders_and_shootings.shtml

Clark, A. M., DesMeules, M., Luo, W., Duncan, A. S., & Wielgosz, A. (2009). Socioeconomic status and cardiovascular disease: Risk and implications for care. *Nature Reviews Cardiology, 6,* 712–722.

Clark, D. M., Ehlers, A., Hackmann, A., McManus, F., Fennell, M., Grey, N., … Wild, J. (2006). Cognitive therapy versus exposure and applied relaxation in social phobia: A randomized controlled trial. *Journal of Consulting and Clinical Psychology, 74,* 568–578.

Clarkin, J. F., Meehan, K. B., & Lenzenweger, M. F. (2015). Emerging approaches to the conceptualization and treatment of personality disorder. *Canadian Psychology/Psychologie Canadienne, 56,* 155–167.

Clay, Z., & Zuberbühler, K. (2012). Communication during sex among female bonobos: Effects of dominance, solicitation and audience. *Scientific Reports, 2,* Article 291.

Coan, J. A. (2010). Emergent ghosts of the emotion machine. *Emotion Review, 2,* 274–285.

Cochrane, R. E., Tett, R. P., & Vandecreek, L. (2003). Psychological testing and the selection of police officers: A national survey. In Curt R. Bartol and Anne M. Bartol (Eds.), *Current perspectives in forensic psychology and criminal justice* (pp. 25–34). Thousand Oaks, CA: SAGE.

Cohen, D. A., Wang, W., Wyatt, J. K., Kronauer, R. E., Dijk, D. J., Czeisler, C. A., & Klerman, E. B. (2010). Uncovering residual effects of chronic sleep loss on human performance. *Science Translational Medicine, 13,* 14ra3.

Cohen, D. J., & Jones, H. E. (2008). How shape constancy relates to drawing accuracy. *Psychology of Aesthetics, Creativity, and the Arts, 2,* 8–19.

Cohen, H. W., Gibson, G., & Alderman, M. H. (2000). Excess risk of myocardial infarction in patients treated with antidepressant medications: Association with use of tricyclic agents. *American Journal of Medicine, 108,* 2–8.

Cohen, S., Doyle, W., Frank, E., Gwaltney, J. M. Jr., Rabin, B. S., & Skoner, D. P. (1998). Types of stressors that increase susceptibility to the common cold in healthy adults. *Health Psychology, 17,* 214–223.

Cohen, S., Janicki-Deverts, D., Turner, R. B., & Doyle, W. J. (2015). Does hugging provide stress-buffering social support? A study of susceptibility to upper respiratory infection and illness. *Psychological Science, 26,* 135–147.

Cohen, S., Kamarck, T., & Mermelstein, R. (1983). A global measure of perceived stress. *Journal of Health and Social Behavior, 24,* 385–396.

Cohen, S., Miller, G. E., & Rabin, B. S. (2001). Psychological stress and antibody response to immunization: A critical review of the human literature. *Psychosomatic Medicine, 63,* 7–18.

Coker, T. R., Elliott, M. N., Schwebel, D. C., Windle, M., Toomey, S. L., Tortolero, S. R., … Schuster, M. A. (2015, January/February). Media violence exposure and physical aggression in fifth-grade children. *Academic Pediatrics, 15* (1), 82–88.

Colapinto, J. (2000). *As nature made him: The boy who was raised as a girl.* New York, NY: HarperCollins.

Cole, C. F., Labin, D. B., & del Rocio Galarza, M. (2008). Begin with the children: What research on Sesame Street's international coproductions reveals about using media to promote a new more peaceful world. *International Journal of Behavioral Development, 32*(4), 359–365.

Coleman-Jensen, A., Rabbitt, M., Gregory, C., & Singh, A. (2015). *Household food security in the United States in 2014* (ERR-194). Washington, DC: United States Department of Agriculture. Retrieved from http://www.ers.usda.gov/publications/err-economic-research-report/err194.aspx

Collins, P. A., & Gibbs, A. C. C. (2003). Stress in police officers: A study of the origins, prevalence and severity of stress–related symptoms within a county police force. *Occupational Medicine, 53,* 256–264.

Colrain, I. M. (2005). The k-complex: A 7-decade history. *SLEEP, 28,* 255–273.

Compton, W. M., Grant, B. F., Colliver, J. D., Glantz, M. D., & Stinson, F. S. (2004). Prevalence of marijuana use disorders in the United States: 1991–1992 and 2001–2002. *Journal of the American Medical Association, 291,* 2114–2121.

Cone, B. K., Wake, M., Tobin, S., Poulakis, Z., & Rickards, F. W. (2010). Slight–mild sensorineural hearing loss in children: Audiometric, clinical, and risk factor profiles. *Ear and Hearing, 31,* 202–212.

Congdon, E., Service, S., Wessman, J., Seppänen, J. K., Schönauer, S., Miettunen, J., … Nelson B. (2012). Early environment and neurobehavioral development predict adult temperament clusters. *PLOS ONE, 7,* e38065. doi:10.1371/journal.pone.0038065

Conley, A. M. (2012). Patterns of motivation beliefs: Combining achievement goal and expectancy-value perspectives. *Journal of Educational Psychology, 104,* 32–47.

Conley, T. D., Ziegler, A., Moors, A. C., Matsick, J. L., & Valentine, B. (2013). A critical examination of popular assumptions about the benefits and outcomes of monogamous relationships. *Personality and Social Psychology Review, 17,* 124–141.

Contie, V., Defibaugh, A., Steinberg, D., & Wein, H. (2013, April). Sleep on it. How snoozing strengthens memories. *NIH News in Health.* Retrieved from https://newsinhealth.nih.gov/issue/apr2013/feature2

Convento, S., Russo, C., Zigiotto, L., & Bolognini, N. (2016). Transcranial electrical stimulation in post-stroke cognitive rehabilitation. *European Psychologist, 21,* 55–64.

Conway, M. A., Cohen, G., & Stanhope, N. (1991). On the very long-term retention of knowledge acquired through formal education: Twelve years of cognitive psychology. *Journal of Experimental Psychology: General, 120,* 395–409.

Cook, T. M., Andrade, J., Bogod, D. G., Hitchman, J. M., Jonker, W. R., Lucas, N., … Pandit, J. J. (2014). The 5th National Audit Project (NAP5) on accidental awareness during general anaesthesia: Patient experiences, human factors, sedation, consent and medicolegal issues. *Anaesthesia, 69,* 1102–1116.

Copeland, W., Shanahan, L., Costello, J., & Angold, A. (2011). Cumulative prevalence of psychiatric disorders by young adulthood: A prospective cohort analysis from the Great Smoky Mountain Study. *Journal of the American Academy of Child & Adolescent Psychiatry, 50,* 252–261.

Copen, C. E., Chandra, A., & Febo-Vazquez, I. (2016). Sexual behavior, sexual attraction, and sexual orientation among adults aged 18–44 in the United States: Data from the 2011–2013 National Survey of Family Growth. *National Health Statistics Reports, 88,* 1–14.

Copen, C. E., Daniels, K., Vespa, J., & Mosher, W. D. (2012). *First marriages in the United States: Data from the 2006–2010 National Survey of Family Growth.* Washington, DC: National Center for Health Statistics, Centers for Disease Control and Prevention, Department of Health and Human Services.

Corballis, M. C. (2014). Left brain, right brain: Facts and fantasies. *PLOS Biology, 12*(1), e1001767. doi:10.1371/journal.pbio.1001767

Coren, S. (2008, October 20). Can dogs see colors? [Web log post]. Retrieved from https://www.psychologytoday.com/blog/canine-corner/200810/can-dogs-see-colors

Corey, G. (2017). *Theory and practice of counseling and psychotherapy* (10th ed.). Belmont, CA: Brooks/Cole, Cengage Learning.

Corkin, S. (2002). What's new with the amnesic patient H.M.? *Nature Reviews Neuroscience, 3,* 153–160.

Cornelius, S. W., & Caspi, A. (1987). Everyday problem solving in adulthood and old age. *Psychology and Aging, 2,* 144–153.

Correia, I., Alves, H., Morais, R., & Ramos, M. (2015). The legitimation of wife abuse among women: The impact of belief in a just world and gender identification. *Personality and Individual Differences, 76,* 7–12.

Correll, C. U., Leucht, S., & Kane, J. M. (2004). Lower risk for tardive dyskinesia associated with second-generation antipsychotics: A systematic review of 1-year studies. *American Journal of Psychiatry, 161,* 414–425.

Corrigan, P. (2005). How stigma interferes with mental health care. *American Psychologist, 59,* 614–625.

Corrigan, P. W., & Penn, D. L. (2015). Lessons from social psychology on discrediting psychiatric stigma. *Stigma and Health, 1*(S), 2–15.

Corti, R., Binggeli, C., Sudano, I., Spieker, L., Hänseler, E., Ruschitzka, F., … Noll, G. (2002). Coffee acutely increases sympathetic nerve activity and blood pressure independently of caffeine content: Role of habitual versus nonhabitual drinking. *Circulation, 106*(23), 2935–2940.

Cosier, S. (2015, July/August). Nail biting may arise from perfectionism. *Scientific American Mind, 26,* 15.

Costa, G. (2003). Shift work and occupational medicine: An overview. *Occupational Medicine, 53,* 83–88.

Costa, P. T. Jr., Terracciano, A., & McCrae, R. R. (2001). Gender differences in personality traits across cultures: Robust and surprising findings. *Journal of Personality and Social Psychology, 81,* 322–331.

Costandi, M. (2009, February 10). Where are old memories stored in the brain? *Scientific American Online.* Retrieved from http://www.scientificamerican.com/article/the-memory-trace/

Costanzo, E. S., Lutgendorf, S. K., & Roeder, S. L. (2011). Common-sense beliefs about cancer and health practices among women completing treatment for breast cancer. *Psycho-Oncology, 20,* 53–61.

Cotman, C. W., & Berchtold, N. C. (2002). Exercise: A behavioral intervention to enhance brain health and plasticity. *Trends in Neurosciences, 25,* 295–301.

Cottrell, J. M., Newman, D. A., & Roisman, G. I. (2015). Explaining the Black–White gap in cognitive test scores: Toward a theory of adverse impact. *Journal of Applied Psychology, 100,* 1713–1736.

Coulson, S., & Van Petten, C. (2007). A special role for the right hemisphere in metaphor comprehension? ERP evidence from hemifield presentation. *Brain Research, 1146,* 128–145.

Couperus, J. W. (2011). Perceptual load influences selective attention across development. *Developmental Psychology, 47,* 1431–1439.

Coupland, C., Hill, T., Morriss, R., Moore, M., Arthur, A., & Hippisley-Cox, J. (2016). Antidepressant use and risk of cardiovascular outcomes in people aged 20 to 64: Cohort study using primary care database. *BMJ Open, 352,* i1350.

Courage, M. L., Bakhtiar, A., Fitzpatrick, C., Kenny, S., & Brandeau, K. (2015). Growing up multitasking: The costs and benefits for cognitive development. *Developmental Review, 35,* 5–41.

Cowan, N. (1988). Evolving conceptions of memory storage, selective attention, and their mutual constraints within the human information-processing system. *Psychological Bulletin, 104,* 163–191.

Cowan, N. (2015). George Miller's magical number of immediate memory in retrospect: Observations on the faltering progression of science. *Psychological Review, 122,* 536–541.

Cowan, N., Chen, Z., & Rouder, J. N. R. (2004). Constant capacity in an immediate serial-recall task: A logical sequel to Miller (1956). *Psychological Science, 15,* 634–640.

Cowan, N., Nugent, L. D., & Elliott, E. M. (2000). Memory-search and rehearsal processes and the word length effect in immediate recall: A synthesis in reply to service. *Quarterly Journal of Experimental Psychology, 53,* 666–670.

Coyne, S. M. (2016). Effects of viewing relational aggression on television on aggressive behavior in adolescents: A three-year longitudinal study. *Developmental Psychology, 52,* 284–295.

Crabtree, A. (2012). Hypnosis reconsidered, resituated, and redefined. *Journal of Scientific Exploration, 26,* 297–327.

Craddock, N., O'Donovan, M. C., & Owen, M. J. (2005). The genetics of schizophrenia and bipolar disorder: Dissecting psychosis. *Journal of Medical Genetics, 42,* 193–204.

Craik, F. I. M., & Lockhart, R. S. (1972). Levels of processing: A framework for memory research. *Journal of Verbal Learning and Verbal Behavior, 11,* 671–684.

Craik, F. I. M., & Tulving, E. (1975). Depth of processing and the retention of words in episodic memory. *Journal of Experimental Psychology, 104,* 268–294.

Cramer, P. (2000). Defense mechanisms in psychology today: Further processes for adaptation. *American Psychologist, 55,* 637–646.

Cramer, P. (2008). Identification and the development of competence: A 44-year longitudinal study from late adolescence to late middle age. *Psychology and Aging, 23,* 410–421.

Craske, M. G., Kircanski, K., Epstein, A., Wittchen, H.-U., Pine, D. S., Lewis-Fernández, … DSM-V Anxiety, OC Spectrum, Posttraumatic and Dissociative Disorder Work Group. (2010). Panic disorder: A review of *DSM-IV* panic disorder and proposals for *DSM-V. Depression and Anxiety, 27,* 93–112.

Crick, N. R., & Grotpeter, J. K. (1995). Relational aggression, gender, and social-psychological adjustment. *Child Development, 66,* 710–722.

Crisco, J. J., Fiore, R., Beckwith, J. G., Chu, J. J., Brolinson, P. G., Duma, S., … Greenwald, R. M. (2010). Frequency and location of head impact exposures in individual collegiate football players. *Journal of Athletic Training, 45,* 549–559.

Croce, P. J. (2010). Reaching beyond Uncle William: A century of William James in theory and in life. *History of Psychology, 13,* 351–377.

Crooks, R., & Baur, K. (2017). *Our sexuality* (13th ed.). Boston, MA: Cengage Learning.

Crosby, L. E., Quinn, C. T., & Kalinyak, K. A. (2015). A biopsychosocial model for the management of patients with sickle-cell disease transitioning to adult medical care. *Advances in Therapy, 32,* 293–305.

Crowell, S. E., Beauchaine, T. P., & Linehan, M. M. (2009). A biosocial developmental model of borderline personality: Elaborating and extending Linehan's theory. *Psychological Bulletin, 135,* 495–510.

Csikszentmihalyi, M. (1975). Play and intrinsic rewards. *Journal of Humanistic Psychology, 15,* 41–63.

Csikszentmihalyi, M. (1990). *Flow: The psychology of optimal experience.* New York, NY: Harper Perennial.

Csikszentmihalyi, M. (1999). If we are so rich, why aren't we happy? *American Psychologist, 54,* 821–827.

Cuijpers, P., De Wit, L., Weitz, E., Andersson, G., & Huibers, M. J. H. (2015). The combination of psychotherapy and pharmacotherapy in the treatment of adult depression: A comprehensive meta-analysis. *Journal of Evidence-Based Psychotherapies, 15,* 147–168.

Culbertson, S. S., Fullagar, C. J., Simmons, M. J., & Zhu, M. (2015). Contagious flow antecedents and consequences of optimal experience in the classroom. *Journal of Management Education, 39,* 319–349.

Cunha, J. P., & Stöppler, M. C. (Eds.) (2016, June 6). Jetlag. *Medicine.net.com.* Retrieved from http://www.medicinenet.com/jet_lag/article.htm

Cunningham, J. H., & Edelman, A. (2012, December 17). Comfort dogs help ease the pain of mourning Newtown community. *New York Daily News.* Retrieved from http://www.nydailynews.com/news/national/comfort-dogs-helping-ease-pain-sandy-hook-tragedy-article-1.1222295

Cunningham, M., & Cox, E. O. (2003). Hearing assessment in infants and children: Recommendations beyond neonatal screening. *Pediatrics, 111,* 436–440.

Cunningham, M. R., Shamblen, S. R., Barbee, A. P., & Ault, L. K. (2005). Social allergies in romantic relationships: Behavioral repetition, emotional sensitization, and dissatisfaction in dating couples. *Personal Relationships, 12,* 273–295.

Curtiss, S., Fromkin, V., Krashen, S., Rigler, D., & Rigler, M. (1974). The linguistic development of Genie. *Language, 50,* 528–554.

Cyna, A., Crowther, C., Robinson, J., Andrew, M., Antoniou, G., & Baghurst, P. (2013). Hypnosis antenatal training for childbirth: A randomized controlled trial. *BJOG: An International Journal of Obstetrics & Gynaecology, 120,* 1248–1259.

Cyna, A. M., McAuliffe, G. L., & Andrew, M. I. (2004). Hypnosis for pain relief in labour and childbirth: A systematic review. *British Journal of Anesthesia, 93,* 505–511.

Cynkar, A. (2007). The changing gender composition of psychology. *Monitor on Psychology, 38,* 46. Retrieved from http://www.apa.org/monitor/jun07/changing.aspx

Cyrzyk, T. (2013). Electroconvulsive therapy: Why it is still controversial. *Mental Health Practice, 16,* 22–27.

Czarnowski, C., Bailey, J., & Bal, S. (2007). Curare and a Canadian connection. *Canadian Family Physician, 53,* 1531–1532.

Daenen, L., Varkey, E., Kellmann, M., & Nijs, J. (2015). Exercise, not to exercise, or how to exercise in patients with chronic pain? Applying science to practice. *The Clinical Journal of Pain, 31,* 108–114.

Daffner, K. R., Chong, H., Riis, J., Rentz, D. M., Wolk, D. A., Budson, A. E., & Holcomb, P. J. (2007). Cognitive status impacts age-related changes in attention to novel and target events. *Neuropsychology, 21,* 291–300.

Daily News Staff. (2015, May 4). Ahead of Mother's Day, celebs share lessons from their moms. *Daily News.* Retrieved from http://www.nydailynews.com/entertainment/gossip/advice-mom-article-1.2205932

Dalenberg, C. J., Brand, B. L., Loewenstein, R. J., Gleaves, D. H., Dorahy, M. J., Cardeña, E., … Spiegel, D. (2014). Reality versus fantasy: Reply to Lynn et al. (2014). *Psychological Bulletin, 140,* 911–920.

Dalton, P. H., Opiekun, R. E., Gould, M., McDermott, R., Wilson, T., Maute, C., … Moline, J. (2010, May 18). Chemosensory loss: Functional consequences of the World Trade Center disaster. *Environmental Health Perspectives, 118,* 1251–1256. doi:10.1289/ehp.1001924

Damasio, A. R., Grabowski, T. J., Bechara, A., Damasio, H., Ponto, L. L. B., Parvizi, J., & Hichwa, R. D. (2000). Subcortical and cortical brain activity during the feeling of self-generated emotions. *Nature Neuroscience, 3,* 1049–1056.

Damasio, H., Grabowski, T., Frank, R., Galaburda, A. M., & Damasio, A. R. (1994). The return of Phineas Gage: Clues about the brain from the skull of a famous patient. *Science, 264,* 1102–1105.

Damian, R. I., & Roberts, B. W. (2015). Settling the debate on birth order and personality. *Proceedings of the National Academy of Sciences, 112,* 14119–14120.

Danker, J. F., & Anderson, J. R. (2010). The ghosts of brain states past: Remembering reactivates the brain regions engaged during encoding. *Psychological Bulletin, 136,* 87–102.

Dapretto, M., Lee, S. S., & Caplan, R. (2005). A functional magnetic resonance imaging study of discourse coherence in typically developing children. *NeuroReport, 16,* 1661–1665.

Darcy, A. M., Doyle, A. C., Lock, J., Peebles, R., Doyle, P., & Le Grange, D. (2012). The eating disorders examination in adolescent males with anorexia nervosa: How does it compare to adolescent females? *International Journal of Eating Disorders, 45,* 110–114.

Darley, J. M., & Latané, B. (1968). Bystander intervention in emergencies: Diffusion of responsibility. *Journal of Personality and Social Psychology, 8*, 377–383.

Dar-Nimrod, I., & Heine, S. J. (2011). Genetic essentialism: On the deceptive determinism of DNA. *Psychological Bulletin, 137*, 800–818.

Darwin, C. (1872/2002). *The expression of the emotions in man and animals.* New York, NY: Oxford University Press.

David, A. (2015, August 13). AA saved my life (and I get why you hate it). *Huffington Post.* Retrieved from http://www.huffingtonpost.com/anna-david/aa-saved-my-life-and-i-get-why-you-hate-it_b_7978690.html

Davidson, R. J., Scherer, K. R., & Goldsmith, H. H. (Eds.). (2002). *Handbook of affective sciences.* New York, NY: Oxford University Press.

Davies, G., Tenesa, A., Payton, A., Yang, J., Harris, S. E., Liewald, D., … McGhee, K. (2011). Genome-wide association studies establish that human intelligence is highly heritable and polygenic. *Molecular Psychiatry, 16*, 996–1005.

Davies, M. (2015). A model of critical thinking in higher education. In M. B. Paulsen (Ed.), *Higher education: Handbook of theory and research* (Vol. 30, pp. 41–92). Cham, Switzerland: Springer International.

d'Avila, J., Lam, T., Bingham, D., Shi, J., Won, S., Kauppinen, T., … Swanson, R. (2012). Microglial activation induced by brain trauma is suppressed by post-injury treatment with a PARP inhibitor. *Journal of Neuroinflammation, 9*, 31–42.

Davis, E. P., & Sandman, C. A. (2010). The timing of prenatal exposure to maternal cortisol and psychosocial stress is associated with human infant cognitive development. *Child Development, 81*, 131–148.

Davis, K. (2015, October 20). Federal judge says neuroscience is not ready for the courtroom—yet. *ABA Journal.* Retrieved from http://www.abajournal.com/news/article/federal_judge_says_neuroscience_is_not_ready_for_the_courtroom_yet

Davis, M., & Whalen, P. J. (2001). The amygdala: Vigilance and emotion. *Molecular Psychiatry, 6*, 13–34.

DeafPeople.com (n.d.). *Deaf person of the year: Claudia Gordon Federal anti-discrimination advocate.* Retrieved from http://www.deafpeople.com/dp_of_month/GordonYear.html

Deary, I. J., Penke, L., & Johnson, W. (2010). The neuroscience of human intelligence differences. *Nature Reviews Neuroscience, 11*, 201–211.

de Bitencourt Machado, D., Braga Laskoski, P., Trelles Severo, C., Margareth Bassols, A., Sfoggia, A., Kowacs, C. (2016). A psychodynamic perspective on a systematic review of online psychotherapy for adults. *British Journal of Psychotherapy, 32*, 79–108.

de Boysson-Bardies, B., Halle, P., Sagart, L., & Durand, C. (1989). A cross-linguistic investigation of vowel formats in babbling. *Journal of Child Language, 16*, 1–17.

DeCaro, M. S., Van Stockum Jr., C. A., & Wieth, M. B. (2015). When higher working memory capacity hinders insight. *Journal of Experimental Psychology: Learning, Memory, and Cognition, 42*, 39–49.

DeCasper, A. J., & Fifer, W. P. (1980). Of human bonding: Newborns prefer their mothers' voices. *Science, 208*, 1174–1176.

Deci, E. L., Koestner, R., & Ryan, R. M. (1999). A meta-analytic review of experiments examining the effects of extrinsic rewards on intrinsic motivation. *Psychological Bulletin, 125*, 627–668.

Deci, E. L., Koestner, R., & Ryan, R. M. (2001). Extrinsic rewards and intrinsic motivation in education: Reconsidered once again. *Review of Educational Research, 71*, 1–27.

Deci, E. L., & Ryan, R. M. (2008). Self-determination theory: A macrotheory of human motivation, development, and health. *Canadian Psychology, 49*, 182–185.

Decker, H. S. (2016a). Cyclical swings: The bête noire of psychiatry. *History of Psychology, 19*, 52–56.

Decker, H. S. (2016b). Professor Decker replies. *History of Psychology, 19*, 66–67.

Deeb, S. S. (2005). The molecular basis of variation in human color vision. *Clinical Genetics, 67*, 369–377.

Deer, B. (2011). How the case against the MMR vaccine was fixed. *BMJ, 342*, c5347.

Deese, J., & Kaufman, R. A. (1957). Serial effects in recall of unorganized and sequentially organized verbal material. *Journal of Experimental Psychology, 54*, 180–187.

de Fockert, J. W. (2013). Beyond perceptual load and dilution: A review of the role of working memory in selective attention. *Frontiers in Psychology, 4.* Article 287. doi: 10.3389/fpsyg.2013.00287

de Gelder, D. B., Hortensius, R., & Tamietto, M. (2012). Attention and awareness each influence amygdala activity for dynamic bodily expressions—a short review. *Frontiers in Integrative Neuroscience, 6.* doi: 10.3389/fnint.2012.00054

Degenhardt, L., & Hall, W. (2012). Extent of illicit drug use and dependence, and their contribution to the global burden of disease. *Lancet, 379*, 55–70.

Degnan, K. A., Hane, A. A., Henderson, H. A., Moas, O. L., Reeb-Sutherland, B. C., & Fox, N. A. (2011). Longitudinal stability of temperamental exuberance and social-emotional outcomes in early childhood. *Developmental Psychology, 47*, 765–780.

DeGregory, L. (2008, July 31). The girl in the window. *Tampa Bay Times.* Retrieved from http://www.tampabay.com/specials/2008/reports/danielle/

de Hoog, N., Strobe, W., & de Wit, J. B. F. (2007). The impact of vulnerability to and severity of a health risk on processing and acceptance of fear-arousing communications: A meta-analysis. *Review of General Psychology, 11*, 258–285.

Deisseroth, K. (2015). Optogenetics: 10 years of microbial opsins in neuroscience. *Nature Neuroscience, 18*(9), 1213–1225.

de Lauzon-Guillain, B., Wijndaele, K., Clark, M., Acerini, C. L., Hughes, I. A., Dunger, D. B., … Ong, K. K. (2012). Breastfeeding and infant temperament at age three months. *PLOS ONE, 7*(1), e29326. doi:10.1371/journal.pone.0029326

Del Giudice, M., Booth, T., & Irwing, P. (2012) The distance between Mars and Venus: Measuring global sex differences in personality. *PLOS ONE, 7*(1), e29265. doi:10.1371/journal.pone.0029265

Delmonte, R., Lucchetti, G., Moreira-Almeida, A., & Farias, M. (2016). Can the *DSM-5* differentiate between nonpathological possession and dissociative identity disorder? A case study from an Afro-Brazilian religion. *Journal of Trauma & Dissociation, 17*, 322–337.

DeLongis, A., Coyne, J. C., Dakof, G., Folkman, S., & Lazarus, R. S. (1982). Relationship of daily hassles, uplifts, and major life events to health status. *Health Psychology, 1*, 119–136.

DeLongis, A., Folkman, S., & Lazarus, R. S. (1988). The impact of daily stress on health and mood: Psychological and social resources as mediators. *Journal of Personality and Social Psychology, 54*, 486–495.

Demartini, D. R., Schilling, L. P., da Costa, J. C., & Carlini, C. R. (2014). Alzheimer's and Parkinson's diseases: An environmental proteomic point of view. *Journal of Proteomics, 104*, 24–36.

Dement, W., & Kleitman, N. (1957). The relation of eye movements during sleep to dream activity: An objective method for the study of dreaming. *Journal of Experimental Psychology, 53*, 339–346.

Dement, W.C., & Vaughan, C. (1999). *The promise of sleep.* New York, NY: Delacorte Press.

Demir, M. (2015). Effects of laughter therapy on anxiety, stress, depression and quality of life in cancer patients. *Journal of Cancer Science & Therapy, 9*, 272–273.

DeNavas-Walt, C., & Proctor, B. D. (2015). *Income and poverty in the United States: 2014* (U.S. Census Bureau, Current Population Reports, P60-252). Washington, DC: U.S. Government Printing Office.

Dennis, C. (2004). The most important sexual organ. *Nature, 427*, 390–392.

Denollet, J., & Conraads, V. M. (2011). Type D personality and vulnerability to adverse outcomes in heart disease. *Cleveland Clinic Journal of Medicine, 78*, S13–S19.

Denworth, L. (2014, April 25). Science gave my son the gift of sound. *TIME Magazine.* Retrieved from http://time.com/76154/deaf-culture-cochlear-implants/

Department of Justice. (2006). *Use of polygraph examinations in the Department of Justice* (I-2006-008). Washington, DC: Office of the Inspector General, Evaluation and Inspections Division.

DeRobertis, E. M. (2016). On framing the future of humanistic psychology. *The Humanistic Psychologist, 44*, 18–41.

Desco, M., Navas-Sanchez, F. J., Sanchez-González, J., Reig, S., Robles, O., Franco, C., … Arango, C. (2011). Mathematically gifted adolescents use more extensive and more bilateral areas of the fronto-parietal network than controls during executive functioning and fluid reasoning tasks. *NeuroImage, 57*, 281–292.

deShazo, R. D., Hall, J. E., & Skipworth, L. B. (2015). Obesity bias, medical technology, and the hormonal hypothesis: Should we stop demonizing fat people? *The American Journal of Medicine, 128*, 456–460.

Deslandes, A., Moraes, H., Ferreira, C., Veiga, H., Silverira, H., Mouta, R., … Laks, J. (2009). Exercise and mental health: Many reasons to move. *Neuropsychobiology, 59*, 191–198.

Despins, L. A., Scott-Cawiezell, J., & Rouder, J. N. (2010). Detection of patient risk by nurses: A theoretical framework. *Journal of Advanced Nursing, 66,* 465–474.

Dessens, A. B., Slijper, F. M., & Drop, S. L. (2005). Gender dysphoria and gender change in chromosomal females with congenital adrenal hyperplasia. *Archives of Sexual Behavior, 34,* 389–397.

Detrick, P., & Chibnall, J. T. (2014). Underreporting on the MMPI—2-RF in a high-demand police officer selection context: An illustration. *Psychological Assessment, 26,* 1044–1049.

DeValois, R. L., & DeValois, K. K. (1975). Neural coding of color. In E. C. Carterette, & M.P. Friedman (Eds.), *Handbook of Perception:* Vol. 5, (pp. 117–166). New York, NY: Academic Press.

Devaney, S. A., Palomaki, G. E., Scott, J. A., & Bianchi, D. W. (2011). Non-invasive fetal sex determination using cell-free fetal DNA. *JAMA, 306,* 627–636.

Devore, E. E., Grodstein, F., Duffy, J. F., Stampfer, M. J., Czeisler, C. A., & Schernhammer, E. S. (2014). Sleep duration in midlife and later life in relation to cognition. *Journal of American Geriatric Society, 62,* 1073–1081.

Devore, E. E., Kang, J. H., Breteler, M. M., & Grodstein, F. (2012). Dietary intake of berries and flavonoids in relation to cognitive decline. *Annals of Neurology, 72*(1), 135–143.

De Waal, F. B. M. (2009). Bonobo sex and society. *Scientific American, 20,* 4–11.

DeWall, C. N., Baumeister, R. F., & Vohs, K. D. (2008). Satiated with belongingness? Effects of acceptance, rejection, and task framing on self-regulatory performance. *Journal of Personality and Social Psychology, 95,* 1367–1382.

Dewar, M., Alber, J., Butler, C., Cowan, N., & Della Sala, S. (2012). Brief wakeful resting boosts new memories over the long term. *Psychological Science, 23,* 955–960.

De Winter, F. L., Zhu, Q., Van den Stock, J., Nelissen, K., Peeters, R., de Gelder, B., ... Vandenbulcke, M. (2015). Lateralization for dynamic facial expressions in human superior temporal sulcus. *NeuroImage, 106,* 340–352.

DeYoung, C. G., Carey, B. E., Krueger, R. F., & Ross, S. R. (2016). Ten aspects of the Big Five in the Personality Inventory for *DSM–5. Personality Disorders: Theory, Research, and Treatment, 7,* 113–123.

Dhabhar, F. S. (2014). Effects of stress on immune function: The good, the bad, and the beautiful. *Immunologic Research, 58,* 193–210.

Dhindsa, R. S., & Goldstein, D. B. (2016). Schizophrenia: From genetics to physiology at last. *Nature, 530,* 162–163.

Diamond, E. L. (1982). The role of anger and hostility in essential hypertension and coronary heart disease. *Psychological Bulletin, 92,* 410–433.

Diamond, L. M., & Dickenson, J. A. (2012). The neuroimaging of love and desire: Review and future directions. *Clinical Neuropsychiatry, 9,* 39–46.

Diamond, M. (2004). Sex, gender, and identity over the years: A changing perspective. *Child and Adolescent Psychiatric Clinics of North America, 13,* 591–607.

Diamond, M., & Sigmundson, H. K. (1997). Sex reassignment at birth: Long-term review and clinical implications. *Archives of Pediatric & Adolescent Medicine, 151,* 298–304.

Dickens, W. T., & Flynn, J. R. (2001). Heritability estimates vs. large environmental effects: The IQ paradox resolved. *Psychological Review, 108,* 346–369.

Dickens, W. T., & Flynn, J. R. (2006). Black Americans reduce the racial IQ gap: Evidence from standardization samples. *Psychological Science, 17,* 913–920.

Dickerson, A. S., Pearson, D. A., Loveland, K. A., Rahbar, M. H., & Filipek P. A. (2014). Role of parental occupation in autism spectrum disorder diagnosis and severity. *Research in Autism Spectrum Disorders, 8,* 997–1007.

Dickerson, F. B., Tenhula, W. N., & Green-Paden, L. D. (2005). The token economy for schizophrenia: Review of the literature and recommendations for future research. *Schizophrenia Research, 75,* 405–416.

Diekelmann, S., & Born, J. (2010). The memory function of sleep. *Nature Reviews Neuroscience, 11,* 114–126.

Diener, E. (1979). Deindividuation, self-awareness, and disinhibition. *Journal of Personality and Social Psychology, 3,* 1160–1171.

Diener, E., Fraser, S. C., Beaman, A. L., & Kelem, R. T. (1976). Effects of deindividuation variables on stealing among Halloween trick-or-treaters. *Journal of Personality and Social Psychology, 33,* 178–183.

Diener, E., Lucas, R. E., & Scollon, C. N. (2006). Beyond the hedonic treadmill. *American Psychologist, 6,* 305–314.

Digdon, N., Powell R. A., & Harris, B. (2014). Little Albert's alleged neurological impairment: Watson, Rayner, and historical revision. *History of Psychology, 17*(4), 4, 312–324.

DiLalla, L. F. (2002). Behavior genetics of aggression in children: Review and future directions. *Developmental Review, 22,* 593–622.

Di Lorenzo, L., De Pergola, G., Zocchetti, C., L'Abbate, N., Basso, A., Pannacciulli, N., ... Soleo, L. (2003). Effect of shift work on body mass index: Results of a study performed in 319 glucose-tolerant men working in a Southern Italian industry. *International Journal of Obesity, 21,* 1353–1358.

Dimberg, U., Thunberg, M., & Elmehed, K. (2000). Unconscious facial reactions to emotional facial expressions. *Psychological Science, 11,* 86–89.

Dimidjian, S., Goodman, S. H., Felder, J. N., Gallop, R., Brown, A. P., & Beck, A. (2016). Staying well during pregnancy and the postpartum: A pilot randomized trial of mindfulness-based cognitive therapy for the prevention of depressive relapse/recurrence. *Journal of Consulting and Clinical Psychology, 84,* 134–145.

Dimitrijevic, A. (2015). Being mad in early modern England. *Frontiers in Psychology, 6,* 1740. http://dx.doi.org/10.3389/fpsyg.2015.01740

Dimsdale, J. E. (2008). Psychological stress and cardiovascular disease. *Journal of the American College of Cardiology, 51,* 1237–1247.

Ding, M., Bhupathiraju, S. N., Chen, M., van Dam, R. M., & Hu, F. B. (2014). Caffeinated and decaffeinated coffee consumption and risk of type 2 diabetes: A systematic review and a dose-response meta-analysis. *Diabetes Care, 37*(2), 569–586.

DiSalvo, D. (2010). Are social networks messing with your head? *Scientific American Mind, 20,* 48–55.

Dissel, S., Melnattur, K., & Shaw, P. J. (2015). Sleep, performance, and memory in flies. *Current Sleep Medicine Reports, 1*(1), 47–54.

Dixon, J. F., & Hokin, L. E. (1998). Lithium acutely inhibits and chronically up-regulates and stabilizes glutamate uptake by presynaptic nerve endings in mouse cerebral cortex. *Proceedings of the National Academy of Sciences, 95,* 8363–8368.

Dixson, B. J., & Brooks, R. C. (2013). The role of facial hair in women's perceptions of men's attractiveness, health, masculinity and parenting abilities. *Evolution and Human Behavior, 34,* 236–241.

Dobkin, B. H. (2005). Rehabilitation after stroke. *New England Journal of Medicine, 352,* 1677–1684.

Doherty, W. J., Harris, S. M., & Wilde, J. L. (2015). Discernment counseling for "mixed-agenda" couples. *Journal of Marital and Family Therapy, 42,* 246–255.

Doherty-Sneddon, G. (2008). The great baby signing debate. *Psychologist, 21,* 300–303.

Dolbier, C. L., & Rush, T. E. (2012). Efficacy of abbreviated progressive muscle relaxation in a high-stress college sample. *International Journal of Stress Management, 19,* 48–68.

Dollard, J., Miller, N. E., Doob, L. W., Mowrer, O. H., & Sears, R. R. (1939). *Frustration and aggression.* New Haven, CT: Yale University Press.

Domhoff, G. W. (2001). A new neurocognitive theory of dreams. *Dreaming, 11,* 13–33.

Domhoff, G. W., & Fox, K. C. (2015). Dreaming and the default network: A review, synthesis, and counterintuitive research proposal. *Consciousness and Cognition, 33,* 342–353.

Donaldson, S. I., Dollwet, M., & Rao, M. A. (2015) Happiness, excellence, and optimal human functioning revisited: Examining the peer-reviewed literature linked to positive psychology. *The Journal of Positive Psychology, 10,* 185–195.

Donovan, N. J., Amariglio, R. E., Zoller, A. S., Rudel, R. K., Gomez-Isla, T., Blacker, D., ... Rentz, D. M. (2014). Subjective cognitive concerns and neuropsychiatric predictors of progression to the early clinical stages of Alzheimer's disease. *The American Journal of Geriatric Psychiatry, 22,* 1642–1651.

Dorahy, M. J., Brand, B. L., Şar, V., Krüger, C., Stavropoulos, P., Martínez-Taboas, A., ... Middleton, W. (2014). Dissociative identity disorder: An empirical overview. *Australian & New Zealand Journal of Psychiatry, 48,* 402–417.

Doran, J. M., Kraha, A., Marks, L. R., Ameen, E. J., & El-Ghoroury, N. H. (2016). Graduate debt in psychology: A quantitative analysis. *Training and Education in Professional Psychology, 10,* 3–13.

Dorgan, B. L. (2010). The tragedy of Native American youth suicide. *Psychological Services, 7,* 213–218.

Doty, R. L., & Kamath, V. (2014). The influences of age on olfaction: A review. *Frontiers in Psychology, 5.* doi: 10.3389/fpsyg.2014.00020

Doucleff, M. (2014, October 23). What's my risk of catching Ebola? *NPR*. Retrieved from http://www.npr.org/sections/goatsandsoda/2014/10/23/358349882/an-answer-for-americans-who-ask-whats-my-risk-of-catching-ebola

Dougherty, L. R., Klein, D. N., Olino, T. M., Dyson, M., & Rose, S. (2009). Increased waking salivary cortisol and depression risk in preschoolers: The role of maternal history of melancholic depression and early child temperament. *Journal of Child Psychology and Psychiatry, 50,* 1495–1503.

Dovidio, J. F., Kawakami, K., & Gaertner, S. L. (2002). Implicit and explicit prejudice and interracial interaction. *Journal of Personality and Social Psychology, 82,* 62–68.

Drace, S., Ric, F., & Desrichard, O. (2010). Affective biases in likelihood perception: A possible role of experimental demand in mood-congruence effects. *International Review of Social Psychology, 23,* 93–109.

Drake, C., Roehrs T., Shambroom, J., & Roth, T. (2013). Caffeine effects on sleep taken 0, 3, or 6 hours before going to bed. *Journal of Clinical Sleep Medicine, 9,* 1195–1200.

Drew, T., Vo, M. L. H., & Wolfe, J. M. (2013). The invisible gorilla strikes again: Sustained inattentional blindness in expert observers. *Psychological Science, 24,* 1848–1853.

Drewnowski, A., & Rehm, C. D. (2016). Sources of caffeine in diets of U.S. children and adults: Trends by beverage type and purchase location. *Nutrients, 8.* doi:10.3390/nu8030154

Drexler, B., Zinser, S., Huang, S., Poe, M. M., Rudolph, U., Cook, J. M., & Antkowiak, B. (2013). Enhancing the function of alpha5-subunit-containing GABA_A receptors promotes action potential firing of neocortical neurons during up-states. *European Journal of Pharmacology, 702,* 18–24.

Driessen, E., Van, H. L., Peen, J., Don, F. J., Kool, S., Westra, D., … Dekker, J. J. (2015). Therapist-rated outcomes in a randomized clinical trial comparing cognitive behavioral therapy and psychodynamic therapy for major depression. *Journal of Affective Disorders, 170,* 112–118.

Driver, H. S., & Taylor, S. R. (2000). Exercise and sleep. *Sleep Medicine Reviews, 4,* 387–402.

drjilltaylor.com. (2015). *Dr. Jill Bolte Taylor.* Retrieved from http://drjilltaylor.com/about.html

Drolsbaugh, M. (1996). *What is deaf pride?* Retrieved from http://www.ldpride.net/deafpride.htm

Drougard, A., Fournel, A., Valet, P., & Knauf, C. (2015). Impact of hypothalamic reactive oxygen species in the regulation of energy metabolism and food intake. *Frontiers in Neuroscience, 9,* 1–12. doi: 10.3389/fnins.2015.00056

Druckman, D., & Bjork, R. A. (Eds.). (1994). *Learning, remembering, believing: Enhancing human performance* [Study conducted by the National Research Council]. Washington, DC: National Academies Press.

Drug Abuse Warning Network. (2011). *Drug Abuse Warning Network, 2011: National estimates of drug-related emergency department visits.* Retrieved from http://www.samhsa.gov/data/2k13/DAWN2k11ED/DAWN2k11ED.htm#high

Drug Enforcement Administration. (2012). *Rohypnol* [Fact sheet]. Retrieved from http://www.justice.gov/dea/druginfo/drug_data_sheets/Rohypnol.pdf

Druss, B. G., Hwang, I., Petukhova, M., Sampson, N. A., Wang, P. S., & Keller, R. C. (2009). Impairment in role functioning in mental and chronic medical disorders in the United States: Results from the National Comorbidity Survey Replication. *Molecular Psychiatry, 14,* 728–737.

D'Souza, J., & Gurin, M. (2016). The universal significance of Maslow's concept of self-actualization. *The Humanistic Psychologist, 44,* 210–214.

Duckworth, A. L., Gendler, T. S., & Gross, J. J. (2016). Situational strategies for self-control. *Perspectives on Psychological Science, 11,* 35–55.

Duckworth, A. L., & Seligman, M. E. P. (2005). Self-discipline outdoes IQ in predicting academic performance of adolescents. *Psychological Science, 16,* 939–944.

Duckworth, A. L., Weir, D., Tsukayama, E., & Kwok, D. (2012). Who does well in life? Conscientious adults excel in both objective and subjective success. *Frontiers in Psychology, 3.* http://dx.doi.org/10.3389/fpsyg.2012.00356

Duff, J., Rubenstein, C., & Prilleltensky, I. (2016). Wellness and fairness: Two core values for humanistic psychology. *The Humanistic Psychologist, 44,* 127–141.

Dugas, M. J., Brillon, P., Savard, P., Turcotte, J., Gaudet, A., Ladouceur, R., … Gervais, N. J. (2010). A randomized clinical trial of cognitive-behavioral therapy and applied relaxation for adults with generalized anxiety disorder. *Behavioral Therapies, 41,* 46–58.

Duits, P., Cath, D. C., Lissek, S., Hox, J. J., Hamm, A. O., Engelhard, I. M., … Baas, J. M. (2015). Updated meta-analysis of classical fear conditioning in the anxiety disorders. *Depression and Anxiety, 32,* 239–253.

Dumfart, B., & Neubauer, A. C. (2016). Conscientiousness is the most powerful noncognitive predictor of school achievement in adolescents. *Journal of Individual Differences, 37,* 8–15.

Dunlosky, J., Rawson, K. A., Marsh, E. J., Nathan, M. J., & Willingham, D. T. (2013). Improving students' learning with effective learning techniques: Promising directions from cognitive and educational psychology. *Psychological Science in the Public Interest, 14,* 4–58.

Durante, K. M., Griskevicius, V., Simpson, J. A., Cantú, S. M., & Li, N. P. (2012). Ovulation leads women to perceive sexy cads as good dads. *Journal of Personality and Social Psychology, 103,* 292–305.

Duregotti, E., Zanetti, G., Scorzeto, M., Megighian, A., Montecucco, C., Pirazzini, M., & Rigoni, M. (2015). Snake and spider toxins induce a rapid recovery of function of botulinum neurotoxin paralysed neuromuscular junction. *Toxins, 7*(12), 5322–5336.

Durrant, J., & Ensom, R. (2012). Physical punishment of children: Lessons from 20 years of research. *Canadian Medical Association Journal, 184*(12), 1373–1377.

Dusek, J. A., Out, H. H., Wohlhueter, A. L., Bhasin, M., Zerbini, L. F., Joseph, M. G., … Libermann, T. A. (2008) Genomic counter-stress changes induced by the relaxation response. *PLOS ONE, 3,* e2576. doi:10.1371/journal.pone.0002576

Eagly, A. H., & Crowley, M. (1986). Gender and helping behavior: A meta-analytic review of the social psychological literature. *Psychological Bulletin, 100,* 283–308.

Eastwick, P. W., Eagly, A. H., Finkel, E. J., & Johnson, S. E. (2011). Implicit and explicit preferences for physical attractiveness in a romantic partner: A double dissociation in predictive validity. *Journal of Personality and Social Psychology, 101,* 993–1011.

Eastwick, P. W., Luchies, L. B., Finkel, E. J., & Hunt, L. L. (2014). The predictive validity of ideal partner preferences: A review and meta-analysis. *Psychological Bulletin, 140,* 623–665.

Eaton, N. R., Keyes, K. M., Krueger, R. F., Balsis, S., Skodol, A. E., Markon, K. E., … Hasin, D. S. (2012). An invariant dimensional liability model of gender differences in mental disorder prevalence: Evidence from a national sample. *Journal of Abnormal Psychology, 121,* 282–288.

Ebbinghaus, H. (1885/1913). *Memory: A contribution to experimental psychology.* H. A. Ruger & C. E. Bussenius (Trans.). New York, NY: Teachers College, Columbia University.

Ebrahim, I. O., Shapiro, C. M., Williams, A. J., & Fenwick, P. B. (2013). Alcohol and sleep I: Effects on normal sleep. *Alcoholism: Clinical and Experimental Research, 37,* 539–549.

Eckert, M. A., Keren, N. I., Roberts, D. R., Calhoun, V. D., & Harris, K. C. (2010). Age-related changes in processing speed: Unique contributions of cerebellar and prefrontal cortex. *Frontiers in Human Neuroscience, 4,* 1–14. http://dx.doi.org/10.3389/neuro.09.010.2010

Eckstein, D., Aycock, K. J., Sperber, M. A., McDonald, J., Van Wiesner, V. III, Watts, R. E., & Ginsburg, P. (2010). A review of 200 birth-order studies: Lifestyle characteristics. *Journal of Individual Psychology, 6,* 408–434.

Edens, J. F., Kelley, S. E., Lilienfeld, S. O., Skeem, J. L., & Douglas, K. S. (2015). *DSM-5* antisocial personality disorder: Predictive validity in a prison sample. *Law and Human Behavior, 39,* 123–129.

Editors of The Lancet. (2010). Retraction—Ileal-lymphoid-nodular hyperplasia, non-specific colitis, and pervasive developmental disorder in children. *Lancet, 375,* 445.

Edwards, A. C., Bigdeli, T. B., Docherty, A. R., Bacanu, S., Lee, D., De Candia, T. R., … Walsh, D. (2016). Meta-analysis of positive and negative symptoms reveals schizophrenia modifier genes. *Schizophrenia Bulletin, 42,* 279–287.

Egan, S. K., & Perry, D. G. (2001). Gender identity: A multidimensional analysis with implications for psychosocial adjustment. *Developmental Psychology, 37,* 451–463.

Eichenbaum, H. (2004). Hippocampus: Cognitive processes and neural representations that underlie declarative memory. *Neuron, 44,* 109–120.

Ekman, P. (1992). Are there basic emotions? *Psychological Review, 99,* 550–553.

Ekman, P. (2003). *Emotions revealed* (2nd ed.). New York, NY: Henry Holt.

Ekman, P. (2016). What scientists who study emotion agree about. *Perspectives on Psychological Science, 11,* 31–34.

Ekman, P., & Friesen, W. V. (1971). Constants across cultures in the face and emotion. *Journal of Personality and Social Psychology, 17,* 124–129.

Ekman, P., & Keltner, D. (2014, April 10). Darwin's claim of universals in facial expressions not challenged. *Huffington Post*. Retrieved from http://www.huffingtonpost.com/paul-ekman/darwins-claim-of-universals-in-facial-expression-not-challenged_b_5121383.html

Ekman, P., Levenson, R. W., & Friesen, W. V. (1983). Autonomic nervous system activity distinguishes among emotions. *Science, 221,* 1208–1210.

El Ansary, M., Steigerwald, I., & Esser, S. (2003). Egypt: Over 5000 years of pain management—Cultural and historic aspects. *Pain Practice, 3,* 84–87.

Elder, B. L., Ammar, E. M., & Pile, D. (2015). Sleep duration, activity levels, and measures of obesity in adults. *Public Health Nursing, 33,* 200–205.

Elder, C. R., Gullion, C. M., Funk, K. L., DeBar, L. L., Lindberg, N. M., & Stevens, V. J. (2012). Impact of sleep, screen time, depression and stress on weight change in the intensive weight loss phase of the LIFE Study. *International Journal of Obesity, 36,* 86–92.

Elkind, D. (1967). Egocentrism in adolescence. *Child Development, 38,* 1025–1034.

Elliot, A. J., & Niesta, D. (2008). Romantic red: Red enhances men's attraction to women. *Journal of Personality and Social Psychology, 95,* 1150–1164.

Elliott, D. B., Krivickas, K., Brault, M. W., & Kreider, R. M. (2012). *Historical marriage trends from 1890–2010: A focus on race differences.* Paper presented at Annual Meeting of the Population Association of America, San Francisco, CA, May 3–5, 2012.

Ellis, A., & Dryden, W. (1997). *The practice of rational emotive behavior therapy* (2nd ed.). New York, NY: Springer.

El Mansari, M., Guiard, B. P., Chernoloz, O., Ghanbari, R., Katz, N., & Blier, P. (2010). Relevance of norepinephrine-dopamine interactions in the treatment of major depressive disorder. *CNS Neuroscience & Therapeutics, 16,* e1–e17. doi: 10.1111/j.1755-5949.2010.00146.x

Else-Quest, N. M., Higgins, A., Allison, C., & Morton, L. C. (2012). Gender differences in self-conscious emotional experience: A meta-analysis. *Psychological Bulletin, 138,* 947–981.

Emmons, R. A., & McCullough, M. E. (2003). Counting blessings versus burdens: An experimental investigation of gratitude and subjective well-being in daily life. *Journal of Personality and Social Psychology, 84,* 377–389.

Emmorey, K. (2015). The neurobiology of sign language. *Brain Mapping: An Encyclopedic Reference, 3,* 475–479.

Endicott, L., Bock, T., & Narvaez, D. (2003). Moral reasoning, intercultural development, and multicultural experiences: Relations and cognitive underpinnings. *International Journal of Intercultural Relations, 27,* 403–419.

Enea, V., & Dafinoiu, I. (2009). Motivational/solution-focused intervention for reducing school truancy among adolescents. *Journal of Cognitive and Behavioral Psychotherapies, 9,* 185–198.

Engel de Abreu, P. M., Cruz-Santos, A., Tourinho, C. J., Martin, R., & Bialystok, E. (2012). Bilingualism enriches the poor: Enhanced cognitive control in low-income minority children. *Psychological Science, 23,* 1364–1371.

Epstein, L., & Mardon, S. (2007). *The Harvard Medical School guide to a good night's sleep.* New York, NY: McGraw-Hill.

Epstein, R. (2016). Do gays have a choice? *Scientific American, 25,* 56–63.

Epstein, R., McKinney, P., Fox, S., & Garcia, C. (2012). Support for a fluid-continuum model of sexual orientation: A large-scale Internet study. *Journal of Homosexuality, 59,* 1356–1381.

Erdberg, P. (1990). Rorschach assessment. In G. Goldstein & M. Hersen (Eds.), *Handbook of psychological assessment* (2nd ed.). New York, NY: Pergamon.

Erickson, K. I., Voss, M. W., Prakash, R. S., Basak, C., Szabo, A., Chaddock, L., ... Kramer, A. F. (2011). Exercise training increases size of hippocampus and improves memory. *Proceedings of the National Academy of Sciences, 108*(7), 3017–3022.

Erickson-Schroth, L. (2010). The neurobiology of sex/gender-based attraction. *Journal of Gay & Lesbian Mental Health, 14,* 56–69.

Ericsson, K. A. (2003). The acquisition of expert performance as problem solving. In J. E. Davidson & R. J. Sternberg (Eds.), *The psychology of problem solving* (pp. 31–83). Cambridge, UK: Cambridge University Press.

Erikson, E. H. (1993). *Childhood and society.* New York, NY: W.W. Norton.

Erikson, E. H., & Erikson, J. M. (1997). *The life cycle completed.* New York, NY: W. W. Norton.

Eriksson, P. S., Perfilieva, E., Bjork-Eriksson, T., Alborn, A. M., Nordborg, C., Peterson, D. A., & Gage, F. H. (1998). Neurogenesis in the adult human hippocampus. *Nature Medicine, 4,* 1313–1317.

Ernst, A., & Frisén, J. (2015). Adult neurogenesis in humans—Common and unique traits in mammals. *PLOS Biology, 13,* e1002045. doi:10.1371/journal.pbio.1002045

Etaugh, C. (2008). Women in the middle and later years. In F. L. Denmark and M. Paludi (Eds.), *Psychology of women handbook of issues and theories* (2nd ed., pp. 271–302). Westport, CT: Praeger.

Evans, J. S. B., & Stanovich, K. E. (2013). Dual-process theories of higher cognition: Advancing the debate. *Perspectives on Psychological Science, 8,* 223–241.

Evans, V., & Green, M. (2006). *Cognitive linguistics: An introduction.* Mahwah, NJ: Lawrence Erlbaum Associates.

Evensen, S., Wisløff, T., Lystad, J. U., Bull, H., Ueland, T., & Falkum, E. (2016). Prevalence, employment rate, and cost of schizophrenia in a high-income welfare society: A population-based study using comprehensive health and welfare registers. *Schizophrenia Bulletin, 42,* 476–483.

Exner, J. E. (1980). But it's only an inkblot. *Journal of Personality Assessment, 44,* 562–577.

Exner, J. E. (1986). *The Rorschach: A comprehensive system* (Vol. 1, 2nd ed.). New York, NY: John Wiley & Sons.

Eysenck, H. J. (1967). *The biological basis of personality.* Springfield, IL: C.C. Thomas.

Eysenck, H. J. (1990). *Biological dimensions of personality.* In L. A. Pervin (Ed.), *Handbook of personality: Theory of research* (pp. 244–276). New York, NY: Guilford Press.

Eysenck, H. J., & Eysenck, B. G. (1968). *Manual for the Eysenck Personality Inventory.* San Diego, CA: Educational Industrial Testing Service.

Facebook Help Center. (2015). What is the maximum number of friends that we can add on Facebook? Retrieved April 2, 2015, from https://www.facebook.com/help/community/question/?id=567604083305019

Facer-Childs, E., & Brandstaetter, R. (2015). The impact of circadian phenotype and time since awakening on diurnal performance in athletes. *Current Biology, 25*(4), 518–522.

Fainaru, S. (2016, March 15). NFL acknowledges, for first time, link between football, brain disease. *ESPN.* Retrieved from http://espn.go.com/espn/otl/story/_/id/14972296/top-nfl-official-acknowledges-link-football-related-head-trauma-cte-first

Falk, D., Lepore, F. E., & Noe, A. (2013). The cerebral cortex of Albert Einstein: A description and preliminary analysis of unpublished photographs. *Brain. 136,* 1304–1327.

Fan, S. P., Liberman, Z., Keysar, B., & Kinzler, K. D. (2015). The exposure advantage: Early exposure to a multilingual environment promotes effective communication. *Psychological Science, 26,* 1090–1097.

Fancher, R. E., & Rutherford, A. (2012). *Pioneers of psychology: A history* (4th ed.). New York, NY: W. W. Norton.

Fantini, M. L., Corona, A., Clerici, S., & Ferini-Strambi, L. (2005). Aggressive dream content without daytime aggressiveness in REM sleep behavior disorder. *Neurology, 65,* 1010–1015.

Farah, M. J., Hutchinson, J., Phelps, E. A., & Wagner, A. D. (2014). Functional MRI-based lie detection: Scientific and societal challenges. *Nature Reviews Neuroscience, 15,* 123–131.

Farb, N. A., Chapman, H. A., & Anderson, A. K. (2013). Emotions: Form follows function. *Current Opinion in Neurobiology, 23,* 393–398.

Farha, B. (2007). *Paranormal claims: A critical analysis.* Lanham, MD: University Press of America.

Faria, M. A. (2013). Violence, mental illness, and the brain. A brief history of psychosurgery: Part 2–From the limbic system and cingulotomy to deep brain stimulation. *Surgical Neurology International, 4.* http://doi.org/10.4103/2152-7806.112825

Farmer, R. F., Kosty, D. B., Seeley, J. R., Olino, T. M., & Lewinsohn, P. M. (2013). Aggregation of lifetime axis I psychiatric disorders through age 30: Incidence, predictors, and associated psychosocial outcomes. *Journal of Abnormal Psychology, 122,* 573–586.

Farthing, G. W. (1992). *The psychology of consciousness.* Upper Saddle River, NJ: Prentice Hall.

Fawal, J. (2015, November 23). After an 11-mile journey, a lost dog finds his way back to his foster mom. *Woman's Day.* Retrieved from http://www.womansday.com/life/pet-care/a52822/dog-walks-11-miles-back-to-foster-mom/

Faymonville, M. E., Laureys, S., Degueldre, C., DelFiore, G., Luxen, A., Franck, G., … Maquet, P. (2000). Neural mechanisms of antinociceptive effects of hypnosis. *Anesthesiology, 2,* 1257–1267.

Fazel, S., Gulati, G., Linsell, L., Geddes, J. R., & Grann, M. (2009). Schizophrenia and violence: Systematic review and meta-analysis. *PLOS Medicine, 6,* e1000120. doi:10.1371/journal.pmed.1000120

Federal Bureau of Investigation. (n.d.). *Special agent selection process candidate information packet.* Retrieved from https://www.fbijobs.gov/sites/default/files/Special_Agent_Candidate_Information_Packet.pdf

Feigelman, S. (2011). The first year. In R. M. Kliegman, R. E. Behrman, H. B. Jenson, & B. F. Stanton (Eds.), *Nelson textbook of pediatrics* (19th ed., pp. 26–30). Philadelphia, PA: Saunders Elsevier.

Feinstein, A., Freeman, J., & Lo, A. C. (2015). Treatment of progressive multiple sclerosis: What works, what does not, and what is needed. *The Lancet Neurology, 14*(2), 194–207.

Feinstein, J. S., Adolphs, R., Damasio, A., & Tranel, D. (2011). The human amygdala and the induction and experience of fear. *Current Biology, 21,* 34–38.

Feinstein, R., Heiman, N., & Yager, J. (2015). Common factors affecting psychotherapy outcomes: Some implications for teaching psychotherapy. *Journal of Psychiatric Practice, 21,* 180–189.

Feis, D. L., Brodersen, K. H., von Cramon, D. Y., Luders, E., & Tittgemeyer, M. (2013). Decoding gender dimorphism of the human brain using multimodal anatomical and diffusion MRI data. *NeuroImage, 70,* 250–257.

Feist, G. J. (2004). Creativity and the frontal lobes. *Bulletin of Psychology and the Arts, 5,* 21–28.

Feltman, R., & Elliot, A. J. (2011). The influence of red on perceptions of relative dominance and threat in a competitive context. *Journal of Sport & Exercise Psychology, 33,* 308–314.

Feng, P., Huang, L., & Wang, H. (2013). Taste bud homeostasis in health, disease, and aging. *Chemical Senses, 39,* 3–16.

Fenko, A., & Loock, C. (2014). The influence of ambient scent and music on patients' anxiety in a waiting room of a plastic surgeon. *HERD: Health Environments Research & Design Journal, 7,* 38–59.

Fennell, A. B., Benau, E. M., & Atchley, R. A. (2016). A single session of meditation reduces of physiological indices of anger in both experienced and novice meditators. *Consciousness and Cognition, 40,* 54–66.

Ferguson, C. J. (2010). Genetic contributions to antisocial personality and behavior: A meta-analytic review from an evolutionary perspective. *Journal of Social Psychology, 150,* 160–180.

Ferguson, C. J. (2013). Spanking, corporal punishment and negative long-term outcomes: A meta-analytic review of longitudinal studies. *Clinical Psychology Review, 33,* 196–208.

Ferland, G. (2012). Vitamin K, an emerging nutrient in brain function. *Biofactors, 38*(2), 151–157.

Fernald, A., Marchman, V. A., & Weisleder, A. (2014). SES differences in language processing skill and vocabulary are evident at 18 months. *Developmental Science, 16,* 234–248.

Ferrante, A., Gellerman, D., Ay, A., Woods, K. P., Filipowica, A. M., Jain, K., … Ingram, K. K. (2015). Diurnal preference predicts phase differences in expression of human peripheral circadian clock genes. *Journal of Circadian Rhythms, 13,* 1–7.

Ferrante, G., Simoni, M., Cibella, F., Ferrara, F., Liotta, G., Malizia, V., … La Grutta, S. (2015). Third-hand smoke exposure and health hazards in children. *Monaldi Archives for Chest Disease, 79,* 38–43.

Ferri, M., Amato, L., & Davoli, M. (2006). Alcoholics Anonymous and other 12-step programmes for alcohol dependence. *Cochrane Database of Systematic Reviews.* doi:10.1002/14651858.CD005032.pub2

Ferris, P. A., Kline, T. J. B., & Bourdage, J. S. (2012). He said, she said: Work, biopsychosocial, and lifestyle contributions to coronary heart disease risk. *Health Psychology, 31,* 503–511.

Fessler, D. M. T., & Abrams, E. T. (2004). Infant mouthing behavior: The immunocalibration hypothesis. *Medical Hypotheses, 63,* 925–932.

Festinger, L. (1957). *A theory of cognitive dissonance.* New York, NY: Harper & Row.

Festinger, L., & Carlsmith, J. M. (1959). Cognitive consequences of forced compliance. *Journal of Abnormal and Social Psychology, 58,* 203–210.

Festinger, L., Schachter, S., & Back, K. (1950). *Social pressures in informal groups: A study of human factors in housing.* Stanford, CA: Stanford University Press.

Fiegl, A. (2012, December 12). The healing power of dogs. *National Geographic News.* Retrieved from http://news.nationalgeographic.com/news/2012/12/121221-comfort-dogs-newtown-tragedy-animal-therapy/

Field, T. (1996). Attachment and separation in young children. *Annual Review of Psychology, 47,* 541–561.

Field, T., & Diego, M. (2008). Cortisol: The culprit prenatal stress variable. *International Journal of Neuroscience, 118,* 1181–1205.

Filkins, D. (2004, November 21). In Falluja, young Marines saw the savagery of an urban war. *The New York Times.* Retrieved from http://www.nytimes.com/2004/11/21/international/middleeast/21battle.html?_r=0

Fine, E. J., Ionita, C. C., & Lohr, L. (2002). The history of the development of the cerebellar examination. *Seminars in Neurology, 22,* 375–384.

Fine, J. (2013, February 7). Rescuing Cesar Millan. *Men's Journal.* Retrieved from http://www.mensjournal.com/magazine/rescuing-dog-whisperer-cesar-millan-20130207

Finer, L. B. (2007). Trends in premarital sex in the United States, 1954–2003. *Public Health Reports, 122,* 73–78.

Finger, S. (2001). *Origins of neuroscience: A history of explorations into brain function.* New York, NY: Oxford University Press.

Fink, G. (2011). Stress controversies: Post-traumatic stress disorder, hippocampal volume, gastroduodenal ulceration. *Journal of Neuroendocrinology, 23,* 107–117.

Fink, M., & Taylor, M. A. (2007). Electroconvulsive therapy: Evidence and challenges. *Journal of the American Medical Association, 298,* 330–332.

Finkel, E. J. (2015, February 6). In defense of Tinder. *The New York Times.* Retrieved from http://www.nytimes.com/2015/02/08/opinion/sunday/in-defense-of-tinder.html

Finkel, E. J., Eastwick, P. W., Karney, B. R., Reis, H. T., & Sprecher, S. (2012). Online dating: A critical analysis from the perspective of psychological science. *Psychological Science in the Public Interest, 13,* 3–66.

Finkel, E. J., Eastwick, P. W., Karney, B. R., Reis, H. T., & Sprecher, S. (2016, March 1). Tips for successful dating in a digital world. *Scientific American.* Retrieved from http://www.scientificamerican.com/article/tips-for-successful-dating-in-a-digital-world/

Finucane, A. M. (2011). The effect of fear and anger on selective attention. *Emotion, 11,* 970–974.

Firestein, S. (2001). How the olfactory system makes sense of scents. *Nature, 413,* 211–218.

Firth, S. (2005). End-of-life: A Hindu view. *Lancet, 366,* 682–686.

Fischer, B., & Rehm, J. (2007). Illicit opioid use in the 21st century: Witnessing a paradigm shift? *Addiction, 102,* 499–501.

Fischer, J. A. (2009). *Happiness and age cycles—Return to start…? On the functional relationship between subjective well-being and age* (OECD Social, Employment and Migration Working Paper No. 99). Retrieved from http://dx.doi.org/10.1787/220573570724

Fischer, P., Krueger, J. I., Greitemeyer, T., Vogrincic, C., Kastenmüller, A., Frey, D., … Kainbacher, M. (2011). The bystander-effect: A meta-analytic review on bystander intervention in dangerous and non-dangerous emergencies. *Psychological Bulletin, 137,* 517–537.

Fisher, L. B., Overholser, J. C., Ridley, J., Braden, A., & Rosoff, C. (2015). From the outside looking in: Sense of belonging, depression, and suicide risk. *Psychiatry, 78,* 29–41.

Fisher, T. D., & Brunell, A. B. (2014). A bogus pipeline approach to studying gender differences in cheating behavior. *Personality and Individual Differences, 61,* 91–96.

Fitzpatrick, M. J., & McPherson, B. J. (2010). Coloring within the lines: Gender stereotypes in contemporary coloring books. *Sex Roles, 62,* 127–137.

Flor, H., & Birbaumer, N. (1993). Comparison of the efficacy of electromyographic biofeedback, cognitive-behavioral therapy, and conservative medical interventions in the treatment of chronic musculoskeletal pain. *Journal of Consulting and Clinical Psychology, 61,* 653–658.

Flor, H., Nikolajsen, L., & Jensen, T. S. (2006). Phantom limb pain: A case of maladaptive CNS plasticity? *Nature Reviews Neuroscience, 7,* 873–881.

Florida Museum of Natural History. (2014). *Ichthyology: Sharks.* Retrieved from http://www.flmnh.ufl.edu/fish/sharks/isaf/isaf.htm

Flynn, J. R. (2009). *What is intelligence? Beyond the Flynn effect.* Cambridge, UK: Cambridge University Press.

Flynn, J. R. (2012). *Are we getting smarter? Rising IQ in the twenty-first century.* Cambridge, UK: Cambridge University Press.

Foell, J., Bekrater-Bodmann, R., Diers, M., & Flor, H. (2014). Mirror therapy for phantom limb pain: Brain changes and the role of body representation. *European Journal of Pain, 18,* 729–739.

Fogel, S. M., & Smith, C. T. (2011). The function of the sleep spindle: A psychological index of intelligence and a mechanism for sleep-dependent memory consolidation. *Neuroscience & Biobehavioral Reviews, 35,* 1154–1165.

Folkman, S., & Lazarus, R. S. (1985). If it changes it must be a process: Study of emotion and coping during three stages of a college examination. *Journal of Personality and Social Psychology, 48,* 150–170.

Fonagy, P. (2015). The effectiveness of psychodynamic psychotherapies: An update. *World Psychiatry, 14,* 137–150.

Foos, P. W., & Goolkasian, P. (2008). Presentation format effects in a levels-of-processing task. *Experimental Psychology, 55,* 215–227.

Forbes, C. E., Poore, J. C., Krueger, F., Barbey, A. K., Solomon, J., & Grafman, J. (2014). The role of executive function and the dorsolateral prefrontal cortex in the expression of neuroticism and conscientiousness. *Social Neuroscience, 9*(2), 139–151.

Ford, M., Acosta, A., & Sutcliffe, T. J. (2013). Beyond terminology: The policy impact of a grassroots movement. *Intellectual and Developmental Disabilities, 51,* 108–112.

Forgas, J. P. (2008). Affect and cognition. *Perspectives on Psychological Science, 3,* 94–101.

Forger, D. B., & Peskin, C. S. (2003). A detailed predictive model of the mammalian circadian clock. *Proceedings of the National Academy of Sciences, 100,* 14806–14811.

Foroni, F., & Semin, G. R. (2011). When does mimicry affect evaluative judgment? *Emotion, 11,* 687–690.

Fournier, J. C., DeRubeis, R. J., Hollon, S. D., Dimidjian, S., Amsterdam, J. D., Shelton, R. C., & Fawcett, J. (2010). Antidepressant drug effects and depression severity. *Journal of the American Medical Association, 303,* 47–53.

Fowlkes, C. C., Martin, D. R., & Malik, J. (2007). Local figure–ground cues are valid for natural images. *Journal of Vision, 7,* 1–9.

Fox, J., & Warber, K. M. (2013). Romantic relationship development in the age of Facebook: An exploratory study of emerging adults' perceptions, motives, and behaviors. *Cyberpsychology, Behavior, and Social Networking, 16,* 3–7.

Fox, M. (2013, July 25). Virginia Johnson, Masters' collaborator in sex research, dies at 88. *The New York Times.* Retrieved from http://www.nytimes.com/2013/07/26/us/virginia-johnson-masterss-collaborator-in-sex-research-dies-at-88.html–pagewanted=all&_r=0

Fox News. (2012, September 19). *Pacifier use can lead to emotional problems in boys, study finds.* Retrieved from http://www.foxnews.com/health/2012/09/19/pacifier-use-can-lead-to-emotional-problems-in-boys-study-finds/

Fozard, J. L. (1990). Vision and hearing in aging. *Handbook of the Psychology of Aging, 3,* 143–156.

Frances, A. (2016). Entrenched reductionisms: The bete noire of psychiatry. *History of Psychology, 19,* 57–59.

Francis, W. S., & Gutiérrez, M. (2012). Bilingual recognition memory: Stronger performance but weaker levels-of-processing effects in the less fluent language. *Memory Cognition, 40,* 496–503.

Frankenburg, W. K., Dodds, J., Archer, P., Shapiro, H., & Bresnick, B. (1992). The Denver II: A major revision and restandardization of the Denver Developmental Screening Test. *Pediatrics, 89,* 91–97.

Fratiglioni, L., Paillard-Borg, S., & Winblad, B. (2004). An active and socially integrated lifestyle in late life might protect against dementia. *Lancet Neurology, 3,* 343–353.

Frawley, T. J. (2008). Gender schema and prejudicial recall: How children misremember, fabricate, and distort gendered picture book information. *Journal of Research in Childhood Education, 22,* 291–303.

Fredrickson, B. L. (1998). What good are positive emotions? *Review of General Psychology, 2,* 300–319.

Fredrickson, B. L. (2000). Cultivating positive emotions to optimize health and well-being. *Prevention & Treatment, 3.* http://dx.doi.org/10.1037/1522-3736.3.1.31a

Fredrickson, B. L. (2004). The broaden-and-build theory of positive emotions. *Philosophical Transactions of the Royal Society of London B, 359,* 1367–1378.

Fredrickson, B. L. (2013). Updated thinking on positivity ratios. *American Psychologist, 68,* 814–822.

Freedman, J. L., & Fraser, S. C. (1966). Compliance without pressures: The foot-in-the-door technique. *Journal of Personality and Social Psychology, 4,* 195–202.

Freeman, J. B., Stolier, R. M., Ingbretsen, Z. A., & Hehman, E. A. (2014). Amygdala responsivity to high-level social information from unseen faces. *The Journal of Neuroscience, 34,* 10573–10581.

Frequently Asked Questions About Chronic Traumatic Encephalopathy. (n.d.). Retrieved from http://www.bu.edu/cte/about/what-is-cte/

Freud Museum. (n.d.). *About the museum.* Retrieved from http://www.freud.org.uk/about/

Freud, S. (1953). The interpretation of dreams. In J. Strachey (Ed. & Trans.), *The standard edition of the complete psychological works of Sigmund Freud* (Vol. 4, pp. 1–338; Vol. 5, pp. 339–621). London, UK: Hogarth Press. (Original work published 1900)

Freud, S. (1953). Three essays on the theory of sexuality. In J. Strachey (Ed. & Trans.), *The standard edition of the complete psychological works of Sigmund Freud* (Vol. 7, pp. 123–245). London, UK: Hogarth Press. (Original work published 1905)

Freud, S. (1966). *Introductory lectures on psycho-analysis: The standard edition.* New York, NY: W. W. Norton. (Original work published 1917)

Freud, S. (1960). *The ego and the id* (J. Riviere, Trans., & J. Strachey, Ed.). New York, NY: W. W. Norton. (Original work published 1923)

Freud, S. (1961). The ego and the id. In J. Strachey (Ed. & Trans.), *The standard edition of the complete psychological works of Sigmund Freud* (Vol. 19, pp. 1–66). London, UK: Hogarth Press. (Original work published 1923)

Freud, S. (1964). New introductory lectures on psycho-analysis. In J. Strachey (Ed. & Trans.), Vol. 22 (pp. 1–182). London, UK: Hogarth Press. (Original work published 1933)

Freud, S. (1949). *An outline of psychoanalysis* (J. Strachey, Trans.). New York, NY: W. W. Norton. (Original work published 1940)

Fridlund, A. J., Beck, H. P., Goldie, W. D., & Irons, G. (2012). Little Albert: A neurologically impaired child. *History of Psychology, 15*(4), 302–327.

Friedman, B. H., Stephens, C. L., & Thayer, J. F. (2014). Redundancy analysis of autonomic and self-reported, responses to induced emotions. *Biological Psychology, 98,* 19–28.

Friedman, H. (2014). Are humanistic and positive psychology really incommensurate? *American Psychologist, 69,* 89–90. http://dx.doi.org/10.1037/a0034865

Friedman, M., & Rosenman, R. H. (1974). *Type A behavior and your heart.* New York, NY: Alfred A. Knopf.

Friedman, N. P., Miyake, A., Altamirano, L. J., Corley, R. P., Young, S. E., Rhea, S. A., & Hewitt, J. K. (2016). Stability and change in executive function abilities from late adolescence to early adulthood: A longitudinal twin study. *Developmental Psychology, 52,* 326–340.

Friedmann, N., & Rusou, D. (2015). Critical period for first language: The crucial role of language input during the first year of life. *Current Opinion in Neurobiology, 35,* 27–34.

Fry, R. (2015, November 11). Record share of young women are living with their parents, relatives. *Pew Research Center.* Retrieved from http://www.pewresearch.org/fact-tank/2015/11/11/record-share-of-young-women-are-living-with-their-parents-relatives/

Fukada, M., Kano, E., Miyoshi, M., Komaki, R., & Watanabe, T. (2012). Effect of "rose essential oil" inhalation on stress-induced skin-barrier disruption in rats and humans. *Chemical Senses, 37,* 347–356.

Fully Present: The Book. (2010, August 3). *Fully present: The book- meditation* [Video file]. Retrieved from https://www.youtube.com/watch?v=k8ARntepT6g

Furtado, A. (Writer). (2014). Boss with a bark [Television series episode]. In D. Leepson & C. Millan (Producers), *Cesar 911.* Washington, DC: Nat Geo Wild.

Fusar-Poli, P., Papanastasiou, E., Stahl, D., Rocchetti, M., Carpenter, W., Shergill, S., & McGuire, P. (2015). Treatments of negative symptoms in schizophrenia: Meta-analysis of 168 randomized placebo-controlled trials. *Schizophrenia Bulletin, 41,* 892–899.

Fusar-Poli, P., Smieskova, R., Kempton, M. J., Ho, B. C., Andreasen, N. C., & Borgwardt, S. (2013). Progressive brain changes in schizophrenia related to antipsychotic treatment? A meta-analysis of longitudinal MRI studies. *Neuroscience & Biobehavioral Reviews, 37*, 1680–1691.

Füzesi, T., & Bains, J. S. (2015). A tonic for anxiety. *Nature Neuroscience, 18*, 1434–1435.

Gabrieli, J. D. E., Corkin, S., Mickel, S. F., & Growdon, J. H. (1993). Intact acquisition and long-term retention of mirror-tracing skill in Alzheimer's disease and in global amnesia. *Behavioral Neuroscience, 107*, 899–910.

Gackenbach, J., & LaBerge, S. (Eds.). (1988). *Conscious mind, sleeping brain: Perspectives on lucid dreaming.* New York, NY: Plenum Press.

Gagnon, K., & Sabus, C. (2015). Professionalism in a digital age: Opportunities and considerations for using social media in health care. *Physical Therapy, 95*, 406–414.

Galanter, E. (1962). Contemporary psychophysics. In R. Brown, E. Galanter, E. H. Hess, & G. Mandler (Eds.), *New directions in psychology* (pp. 87–156). New York, NY: Holt, Rinehart & Winston.

Galati, D., Scherer, K. R., & Ricci-Bitti, P. E. (1997). Voluntary facial expression of emotion: Comparing congenitally blind with normally sighted encoders. *Journal of Personality and Social Psychology, 73*, 1363–1379.

Galbraith, K. (2015, April 7). Can orange glasses help you sleep better? [Web log post]. Retrieved from http://well.blogs.nytimes.com/2015/04/07/can-orange-glasses-help-you-sleep-better/?_r=1

Gale, C. R., Batty, G. D., & Deary, I. J. (2008) Locus of control at age 10 years and health outcomes and behaviors at age 30 years: The 1970 British Cohort Study. *Psychosomatic Medicine, 70*, 397–403.

Gamer, M. (2009). Portrait of a lie. *Scientific American Mind, 20*, 50–55.

Gandhi, T., Kalia, A., Ganesh, S., & Sinha, P. (2015). Immediate susceptibility to visual illusions after sight onset. *Current Biology, 25*(9), R358–R359.

Gangestad, S. W., & Haselton, M. G. (2015). Human estrus: Implications for relationship science. *Current Opinion in Psychology, 1*, 45–51.

Gangestad, S. W., & Scheyd, G. J. (2005). The evolution of human physical attractiveness. *Annual Review of Anthropology, 34*, 523–548.

Ganis, G., Thompson, W. L., & Kosslyn, S. M. (2004). Brain areas underlying visual mental imagery and visual perception: An fMRI study. *Cognitive Brain Research, 20*, 226–241.

Ganzel, B. L., Morris, P. A., & Wethington, E. (2010). Allostasis and the human brain: Integrating models of stress from the social and life sciences. *Psychological Review, 117*, 134–174.

Garcia, J., Ervin, F. R., & Koelling, R. A. (1966). Learning with prolonged delay of reinforcement. *Psychonomic Science, 5*, 121–122.

Garcia, J. R., Reiber, C., Massey, S. G., & Merriwether, A. M. (2012). Sexual hookup culture: A review. *Review of General Psychology, 16*, 161–176.

García-Lázaro, H., Ramirez-Carmona, R., Lara-Romero, R., & Roldan-Valadez, E. (2012). Neuroanatomy of episodic and semantic memory in humans: A brief review of neuroimaging studies. *Neurology India, 60*, 613–617.

Gardner, H. (1999). *Intelligence reframed: Multiple intelligences for the 21st century.* New York, NY: Basic Books.

Gardner, H. (2011). *Frames of mind: The theory of multiple intelligences.* New York, NY: Basic Books.

Gardner, H., & Hatch, T. (1989). Educational implications of the theory of multiple intelligences. *Educational Researcher, 18*, 4–10.

Garry, M., & Gerrie, M. P. (2005). When photographs create false memories. *Current Directions in Psychological Science, 14*, 321–325.

Gary, J., & Rubin, N.S. (2014, December). A first person account of the refugee experience: Identifying psychosocial stressors and formulating psychological responses. *Psychology International.* Retrieved from http://www.apa.org/international/pi/2014/12/global-violence.aspx

Gassmann, P. (1991, December 21). Somalia: The agony of a dying nation. *The New York Times.* Retrieved from http://www.nytimes.com/1991/12/21/opinion/21iht-edga.html-scp=2&sq=somalia%201991&st=cse

Gastil, J. (1990). Generic pronouns and sexist language: The oxymoronic character of masculine generics. *Sex Roles, 23*, 629–643.

Gatchel, R. J., Haggard, R., Thomas, C., & Howard, K. J. (2013). Biopsychosocial approaches to understanding chronic pain and disability. In R. J. Moore (Ed.), *Handbook of pain and palliative care* (pp. 1–16). New York, NY: Springer.

Gatchel, R. J., & Maddrey, A. M. (2004). The biopsychosocial perspective of pain. In J. M. Raczynski & L. C. Leviton (Eds.), *Handbook of clinical health psychology: Vol 2. Disorders of behavior and health* (pp. 357–378). Washington, DC: American Psychological Association.

Gatchel, R. J., Peng, Y. B., Peters, M. L., Fuchs, P. N., & Turk, D. C. (2007). The biopsychosocial approach to chronic pain: Scientific advances and future directions. *Psychological Bulletin, 133*, 581–624.

Gates, G. J. (2011). How many people are lesbian, gay, bisexual, and transgendered? Los Angeles, CA: The Williams Institute, UCLA School of Law.

Gates, G., Ewing, J., Russell, K., & Watkins, D. (2016, September 12). How Volkswagen is grappling with its diesel scandal. *The New York Times.* Retrieved from http://www.nytimes.com/interactive/2015/business/international/vw-diesel-emissions-scandal-explained.html

Gatto, N. M., Henderson, V. W., Hodis, H. N., St John, J., Lurmann, F., Chen, J. C., & Mack, W. J. (2014). Components of air pollution and cognitive function in middle-aged and older adults in Los Angeles. *Neurotoxicology, 40*, 1–7.

Gaval-Cruz, M., & Weinshenker, D. (2009). Mechanisms of disulfiram-induced cocaine abstinence: Antabuse and cocaine relapse. *Molecular Interventions, 9*, 175–187.

Gavie, J., & Revonsuo, A. (2010). The future of lucid dreaming treatment [Commentary on "The Neurobiology of Consciousness: Lucid Dreaming Wakes Up" by J. Allan Hobson]. *International Journal of Dream Research, 3*, 13–15.

Gay, P. (1988). *Freud: A life for our time.* New York, NY: W. W. Norton.

Gayton, S. D., & Lovell, G. P. (2012). Resilience in ambulance service paramedics and its relationships with well-being and general health. *Traumatology, 18*, 58–64.

Gazzaniga, M. S. (1967). The split brain in man. *Scientific American, 217*, 24–29.

Gazzaniga, M. S. (1998). The split brain revisited. *Scientific American, 279*, 50–55.

Gazzaniga, M. S. (2005). Forty-five years of split-brain research and still going strong. *Nature Reviews Neuroscience, 6*, 653–659.

Gazzaniga, M. S., Bogen, J. E., & Sperry, R. W. (1965). Observations on visual perception after disconnection of the cerebral hemispheres in man. *Brain, 88*, 221–236.

Geake, J. (2008). Neuromythologies in education. *Educational Research, 50*, 123–133.

Geary, D. C., Vigil, J, & Byrd-Craven, J. (2004). Evolution of human mate choice. *The Journal of Sex Research, 41*, 27–42.

Geer, E. B., Lalazar, Y., Couto, L. M., Cohen, V., Lipton, L. R., Shi, W., ... Post, K. D. (2016). A prospective study of appetite and food craving in 30 patients with Cushing's disease. *Pituitary, 19*, 117–126.

Geier, A., Wansink, B., & Rozin, P. (2012). Red potato chips: Segmentation cues can substantially decrease food intake. *Health Psychology, 31*, 398–401.

Gentile, D. A., Reimer, R. A., Nathanson, A. I., Walsh, D. A., & Eisenmann, J. C. (2014). Protective effects of parental monitoring of children's media use: A prospective study. *JAMA Pediatrics, 168*(5), 479–484.

George, M. S. (2003). Stimulating the brain. *Scientific American, 289*, 68–73.

Georgiadis, J. R., Reinders, A. A. T., Paans, A. M., Renken, R., & Kortekaas, R. (2009). Men versus women on sexual brain function: Prominent differences during tactile genital stimulation, but not during orgasm. *Human Brain Mapping, 30*, 3089–3101.

Gerbasi, M. E., Richards, L. K., Thomas, J. J., Agnew-Blais, J. C., Thompson-Brenner, H., Gilman, S. E., & Becker, A.E. (2014). Globalization and eating disorder risk: Peer influence, perceived social norms, and adolescent disordered eating in Fiji. *International Journal of Eating Disorders, 47*, 727–737.

Gerdes, A. B. M., Uhl, G., & Alpers, G. W. (2009). Spiders are special: Fear and disgust evoked by pictures of arthropods. *Evolution and Human Behavior, 30*, 66–73.

Gerhart, B., & Fang, M. (2015). Pay, intrinsic motivation, extrinsic motivation, performance, and creativity in the workplace: Revisiting long-held beliefs. *Annual Reviews of Organizational Psychology and Organizational Behavior, 2*, 489–521.

German, T. P., & Defeyter, M. A. (2000). Immunity to functional fixedness in young children. *Psychonomic Bulletin & Review, 7*, 707–712.

Gerressu, M., Mercer, C. H., Graham, C. A., Wellings, K., & Johnson, A. M. (2008). Prevalence of masturbation and associated factors in a British National Probability Survey. *Archives of Sexual Behavior, 37*, 266–278.

Gershoff, E. T. (2013). Spanking and child development: We know enough now to stop hitting our children. *Child Development Perspectives, 7*(3), 133–137.

Gerstorf, D., Ram, N., Hoppmann, C., Willis, S. L., & Schaie, K. W. (2011). Cohort differences in cognitive aging and terminal decline in the Seattle Longitudinal Study. *Developmental Psychology, 47,* 1026–1041.

Gettleman, J. (2011, July 15). Misery follows as Somalis try to flee hunger. *The New York Times.* Retrieved from http://www.nytimes.com/2011/07/16/world/africa/16somalia.html

Ghose, T. (2014, August 18). Botox: Uses and side effects. *LiveScience.* Retrieved from http://www.livescience.com/44222-botox-uses-side-effects.html

Gibson, B., Thompson, J., Hou, B., & Bushman, B. J. (2016). Just "harmless entertainment"? Effects of surveillance reality TV on physical aggression. *Psychology of Popular Media Culture, 5,* 66–73.

Gibson, E. J., & Walk, R. D. (1960). The "visual cliff." *Scientific American, 202,* 80–92.

Giedd, J. N., Lalonde, F. M., Celano, M. J., White, S. L., Wallace, G. L., Lee, N. R., & Lenroot, R. K. (2009). Anatomical brain magnetic resonance imaging of typically developing children and adolescents. *Journal of the American Academy of Child and Adolescent Psychiatry, 48*(5), 465–470.

Gifford, K. (2013, March 22). Meditation saved my job and changed my life. *The Huffington Post.* Retrieved from http://www.huffingtonpost.com/karen-gifford/meditation-saved-my-job_b_2932819.html

Gigerenzer, G. (2004). Dread risk, September 11, and fatal traffic accidents. *Psychological Science, 15,* 286–287.

Gillan, C. M., & Robbins, T. W. (2014). Goal-directed learning and obsessive–compulsive disorder. *Philosophical Transactions of the Royal Society B, 369,* 1–11.

Gilligan, C. (1982). *In a different voice: Psychological theory and women's development.* Cambridge, MA: Harvard University Press.

Gillin, J. C. (2002, March 25). How long can humans stay awake? *Scientific American.* Retrieved from http://www.scientificamerican.com/article.cfm–id=how-long-can-humans-stay

Girodo, M., & Henry, D. R. (1976). Cognitive, physiological and behavioural components of anxiety in flooding. *Canadian Journal of Behavioural Science/Revue canadienne des sciences du comportement, 8,* 224–231.

Glahn, D. C., Laird, A. R., Ellison-Wright, I., Thelen, S. M., Robinson, J. L., Lancaster, J. L., … Fox, P. (2008). Meta-analysis of gray matter anomalies in schizophrenia: Application of anatomic likelihood estimation and network analysis. *Biological Psychiatry, 64,* 774–781.

Glaser, G. (2015, April). The irrationality of alcoholics anonymous. *The Atlantic.* Retrieved from http://www.theatlantic.com/magazine/archive/2015/04/the-irrationality-of-alcoholics-anonymous/386255/

Glaser, R., & Kiecolt-Glaser, J. K. (2005). Stress-induced immune dysfunction: Implications for health. *Nature Reviews Immunology, 5,* 243–251.

Glass, R. M. (2001). Electroconvulsive therapy: Time to bring it out of the shadows. *Journal of the American Medical Association, 285,* 1346–1348.

Glass, S. T., Lingg, E., & Heuberger, E. (2015). Do ambient urban odors evoke basic emotions? *Frontiers in Psychology, 5.* doi:10.3389/fpsyg.2014.00340

Glenn, A. L., Raine, A., Schug, R. A., Gao, Y., & Granger, D. A. (2011). Increased testosterone-to-cortisol ratio in psychopathy. *Journal of Abnormal Psychology, 120,* 389–399.

Global Sex Survey. (2005). Retrieved from http://www.data360.org/pdf/20070416064139.Global%20Sex%20Survey.pdf

Gnambs, T., Appel, M., & Oeberst, A. (2015). Red color and risk-taking behavior in online environments. *PLOS ONE, 10* (7), e0134033. doi:10.1371/journal.pone.0134033

Go, A. S., Mozaffarian, D., Roger, V. L., Benjamin, E. J., Berry, J. D., Borden, W. B., … Turner, M. B. (2013). Heart disease and stroke statistics—2013 update: A report from the American Heart Association. *Circulation, 127,* e6–e245.

Godden, D. R., & Baddeley, A. D. (1975). Context-dependent memory in two natural environments: On land and underwater. *British Journal of Psychology, 66,* 325–331.

Godlee, F., Smith, J., & Marcovitch, H. (2011). Wakefield's article linking MMR vaccine and autism was fraudulent. *BMJ, 342,* c7452.

Goel, N., Rao, H., Durmer, J. S., & Dinges, D. F. (2009, September). Neurocognitive consequences of sleep deprivation. *Seminars in Neurology, 29,* 320–339.

Goes, F. S., Pirooznia, M., Parla, J. S., Kramer, M., Ghiban, E., Mavruk, S., … Potash, J. B. (2016). Exome sequencing of familial bipolar disorder. *JAMA Psychiatry, 73,* 590–597.

Goforth, A. N., Oka, E. R., Leong, F. T. L., & Denis, D. J. (2014). Acculturation, acculturative stress, religiosity and psychological adjustment among Muslim Arab American adolescents. *Journal of Muslim Mental Health, 8,* 3–19.

Gogtay, N., Vyas, N. S., Testa, R., Wood, S. J., & Pantelis, C. (2011). Age of onset of schizophrenia: Perspectives from neural structural neuroimaging studies. *Schizophrenia Bulletin, 37,* 504–513.

Gold, R. B. (2005). The implications of defining when a woman is pregnant. *Guttmacher Report on Public Policy, 8*(2), 7–10.

Goldin, P. R., Morrison, A., Jazaieri, H., Brozovich, F., Heimberg, R., & Gross, J. J. (2016). Group CBT versus MBSR for social anxiety disorder: A randomized controlled trial. *Journal of Consulting and Clinical Psychology, 84,* 427–437.

Goldin-Meadow, S. (1978). Review: A study in human capacities. *Science, 200,* 649–651.

Goldman, J. G. (2012, December 13). What is operant conditioning? (and how does it explain driving dogs?) [Web log post]. Retrieved from http://blogs.scientificamerican.com/thoughtful-animal/what-is-operant-conditioning-and-how-does-it-explain-driving-dogs/

Goldsmith, H. H., Buss, A. H., Plomin, R., Rothbart, M. K., Chess, S., Hinde, R. A., & McCall, R. B. (1987). What is temperament? Four approaches. *Child Development, 58,* 505–529.

Goldstein, A. N., & Walker, M. P. (2014). The role of sleep in emotional brain function. *Annual Review of Clinical Psychology, 10,* 678–708.

Goldstein, E. B. (2011). *Cognitive psychology: Connecting mind, research, and everyday experience* (3rd ed.). Belmont, CA: Wadsworth, Cengage Learning.

Goleman, D. (1995). *Emotional intelligence.* New York, NY: Bantam Books.

Golinkoff, R. M., Can, D. D., Soderstrom, M., & Hirsh-Pasek, K. (2015). (Baby) Talk to me: The social context of infant-directed speech and its effects on early language acquisition. *Current Directions in Psychological Science, 24,* 339–344.

Golliver, B. (2013, January 19). Royce White: I would be "risking my life" by playing without health protocol. *Sports Illustrated.* Retrieved from http://www.si.com/nba/point-forward/2013/01/19/rockets-royce-white-mental-health-protocol-hbo

Golumbic, E. M. Z., Ding, N., Bickel, S., Lakatos, P., Schevon, C. A., McKhann, G. M., … Poeppel, D. (2013). Mechanisms underlying selective neuronal tracking of attended speech at a "cocktail party." *Neuron, 77*(5), 980–991.

Goodman, D. (2015, October 7). Officer in James Blake arrest used excessive force, panel says. *The New York Times.* Retrieved from http://www.nytimes.com/2015/10/08/nyregion/officer-in-james-blake-arrest-used-excessive-force-panel-says.html

Gooriah, R., & Ahmed, F. (2015). Therapeutic uses of botulinum toxin. *Journal of Clinical Toxicology, 5*(225). doi:10.4172/2161-0495.1000225

Gordon, B. (2013, January 1). Does photographic memory exist? *Scientific American Mind, 23.* Retrieved from http://www.scientificamerican.com/article/i-developed-what-appears-to-be-a-ph/

Gordon, S. M. (2001, July 5). What are the effects of the drug Ecstasy? *Scientific American Online.* Retrieved from http://www.scientificamerican.com/article/what-are-the-effects-of-t/

Gordon-Messer, D., Bauermeister, J. A., Grodzinski, A., & Zimmerman, M. A. (2013). Sexting among young adults. *Journal of Adolescent Health, 52,* 301–306.

Goshtasebi, A., Gandevani, S. B., & Foroushani, A. R. (2011). Prevalence of sexual dysfunctions: A systemic approach. *Sexual Dysfunctions* [Special issues]. Retrieved from http://www.intechopen.com/books/sexual-dysfunctions-specialissues/prevalence-of-sexual-dysfunctions-a-systemic-approach

Gottesman, I. I. (2001). Psychopathology through a life span—genetic prism. *American Psychologist, 56,* 867–878.

Gottesman, I. I., Laursen, T. M., Bertelsen, A., & Mortensen, P. B. (2010). Severe mental disorders in offspring with 2 psychiatrically ill parents. *Archives of General Psychiatry, 67,* 252–257.

Gottfried, J. A., Smith, A. P. R., Rugg, M. D., & Dolan, R. J. (2004) Remembrance of odors past: Human olfactory cortex in cross-modal recognition memory. *Neuron, 42,* 687–695.

Gottlieb, B., Beitel, L. K., & Trifiro, M. A. (2014). Androgen insensitivity syndrome. In R. A. Pagon, M. P. Adam, H. H. Ardinger, et al. (Eds.), *GeneReviews* [Internet]. Seattle, WA: University of Washington. Retrieved from http://www.ncbi.nlm.nih.gov/books/NBK1429/

Gould, E., Beylin, A., Tanapat, P., Reeves, A., & Shors, T. J. (1999). Learning enhances adult neurogenesis in the hippocampal formation. *Nature Neuroscience, 2,* 260–265.

Govindaraju, D., Atzmon, G., & Barzilai, N. (2015). Genetics, lifestyle and longevity: Lessons from centenarians. *Applied & Translational Genomics, 4*, 23–32.

Goyal, M., Singh, S., Sibinga, E. M. S., Gould, N. F., Rowland-Seymour, A., Sharma, R., ... Haythornthwaite, J. A. (2014). Meditation programs for psychological stress and well-being. *JAMA Internal Medicine, 174*, 357–368.

Grabner, R. H., Ansari, D., Reishofer, G., Stern, E., Ebner, F., & Neuper, C. (2007). Individual differences in mathematical competence predict parietal brain activation during mental calculation. *NeuroImage, 38*, 346–356.

Gracheva, E. O., Ingolia, N. T., Kelly, Y. M., Cordero-Morales, J. F., Hollopeter, G., Chesler, A. T., ... Julius, D. (2010). Molecular basis of infrared detection by snakes. *Nature, 464*, 1006–1011.

Gradin, M., & Eriksson, M. (2011). Neonatal pain assessment in Sweden—a fifteen-year follow up. *Acta Pædiatrica, 100*, 204–208.

Grady, J. S., Ale, C. M., & Morris, T. L. (2012). A naturalistic observation of social behaviours during preschool drop-off. *Early Child Development and Cue, 182*, 1683–1694.

Graham, L. C., Harder, J. M., Soto, I., de Vries, W. N., John, S. W., & Howell, G. R. (2016). Chronic consumption of a western diet induces robust glial activation in aging mice and in a mouse model of Alzheimer's disease. *Scientific Reports, 6*, 1–13.

Grammer, K., & Thornhill, R. (1994). Human (Homo sapiens) facial attractiveness and sexual selection: The role of symmetry and averageness. *Journal of Comparative Psychology, 108*, 233–242.

Granello, D. H., & Gibbs, T. A. (2016). The power of language and labels: "The mentally ill" versus "people with mental illnesses." *Journal of Counseling & Development, 94*, 31–40.

Granrud, C. E. (2009). Development of size constancy in children: A test of the metacognitive theory. *Perception & Psychophysics, 71*, 644–654.

Grant, B. F., Stinson, F. S., Dawson, D. A., Chou, S. P., Dufour, M. C., Compton, W., ... Kaplan, K. (2004). Prevalence and co-occurrence of substance use disorders and independent mood and anxiety disorders: Results from the National Epidemiologic Survey on Alcohol and Related Conditions. *Archives of General Psychiatry, 61*, 807–816.

Grant, P. R. (1991). Natural selection and Darwin's finches. *Scientific American, 265*, 82–87.

Green, J. P. (1999). Hypnosis and the treatment of smoking cessation and weight loss. In I. Kirsch, A. Capafons, E. Cardeña-Buelna, & S. Amigó (Eds.), *Dissociation, Trauma, Memory, and Hypnosis Book Series: Clinical hypnosis and self-regulation: Cognitive-behavioral perspectives* (pp. 249–276). Washington, DC: American Psychological Association.

Green, M., & Elliott, M. (2010). Religion, health, and psychological well-being. *Journal of Religious Health, 49*, 149–163.

Greenberg, L., Warwar, S., & Malcolm, W. (2010) Emotion-focused couples therapy and the facilitation of forgiveness. *Journal of Marital and Family Therapy, 36*, 28–42.

Greenberg, P. E., Fournier, A. A., Sisitsky, T., Pike, C. T., & Kessler, R. C. (2015). The economic burden of adults with major depressive disorder in the United States (2005 and 2010). *The Journal of Clinical Psychiatry, 76*, 155–162.

Greenblatt, S. H., Dagi, T. F., & Epstein, M. H. (1997). *A history of neurosurgery.* Park Ridge, IL: American Association of Neurological Surgeons.

Greenfield, P. M., & Quiroz, B. (2013). Context and culture in the socialization and development of personal achievement values: Comparing Latino immigrant families, European American families, and elementary schoolteachers. *Journal of Applied Developmental Psychology, 34*, 108–118.

Greitemeyer, T. (2009). Effects of songs with prosocial lyrics on prosocial thoughts, affect, and behavior. *Journal of Experimental Social Psychology, 45*, 186–190.

Griebe, M., Nees, F., Gerber, B., Ebert, A., Flor, H., Wolf, O. T., ... Szabo, K. (2015). Stronger pharmacological cortisol suppression and anticipatory cortisol stress response in transient global amnesia. *Frontiers in Behavioral Neuroscience, 9.* doi:10.3389/fnbeh.2015.00063

Grigalavicius, M., Moan, J., Dahlback, A., & Juzeniene, A. (2015). Daily, seasonal, and latitudinal variations in solar ultraviolet A and B radiation in relation to vitamin D production and risk for skin cancer. *International Journal of Dermatology, 55*, e23–e28.

Griggs, R. A. (2014a). The continuing saga of Little Albert in introductory psychology textbooks. *Teaching of Psychology, 41*, 309–317.

Griggs, R. A. (2014b). Coverage of the Stanford Prison experiment in introductory psychology textbooks. *Teaching of Psychology, 41*, 195–203.

Griggs, R. A. (2015a). Coverage of the Phineas Gage story in introductory psychology textbooks: Was Gage no longer Gage? *Teaching of Psychology, 42*, 195–202.

Griggs, R. A. (2015b). The disappearance of independence in textbook coverage of Asch's social pressure experiments. *Teaching of Psychology, 42*, 137–142.

Griggs, R. A. (2015c). The Kitty Genovese story in introductory psychology textbooks fifty years later. *Teaching of Psychology, 42*, 149–152.

Griggs, R. A. (2015d). Psychology's lost boy. Will the real Little Albert please stand up? *Teaching of Psychology, 42*, 14–18.

Griggs, R. A., & Whitehead, G. I. III. (2014). Coverage of the Stanford Prison experiment in introductory social psychology textbooks. *Teaching of Psychology, 41*, 318–324.

Griggs, R. A., & Whitehead, G. I. III (2015). Coverage of Milgram's obedience experiments in social psychology textbooks: Where have all the criticisms gone? *Teaching of Psychology, 42*, 315–322.

Grimm, J., & W. Grimm. (1884). *Grimm's household tales* [Vol. 1, Margaret Hunt (Trans. & Ed.)]. London, UK: George Bell and Sons.

Grisham, L. (2016, July 22). What does the Q in LGBTQ stand for? *USA Today.* Retrieved from http://www.usatoday.com/story/news/nation-now/2015/06/01/lgbtq-questioning-queer-meaning/26925563/

Griskevicius, V., Haselton, M, G., & Ackerman, J. M. (2015). Evolution and close relationships. In M. Mikulincer, P. R. Shaver, J. A. Simpson, & J. F. Dovidio (Eds.), *APA handbook of personality and social psychology: Vol. 3. Interpersonal relation* (pp. 3–32). Washington, DC: American Psychological Association.

Griswold, A. (2013, December 27). 20 low-paying jobs that workers love. *Business Insider.* Retrieved from http://www.businessinsider.com/happy-low-paying-jobs-2013-12

Groopman, J. (2008). *How doctors think.* Boston, MA: Houghton Mifflin.

Gross, C. G. (2007). The discovery of motor cortex and its background. *Journal of the History of the Neurosciences, 16*, 320–331.

Grossman, A. J. (2012, June 9). The science of Cesar Millan's dog training: Good timing and hard kicks in the stomach. *The Huffington Post.* Retrieved from http://www.huffingtonpost.com/anna-jane-grossman/the-dog-whisperer-technique_b_1406337.html

Grossman, R. P., & Till, B. D. (1998). The persistence of classically conditioned brand attitudes. *Journal of Advertising, 21*, 23–31.

Grotenhermen, F., & Müller-Vahl, K. (2012). The therapeutic potential of cannabis and cannabinoids. *Deutsches Ärzteblatt International, 109*, 495–501.

Gruber, D. F. (2009). Three's company. *Nature Medicine, 15*, 232–235.

Grusec, J. E., & Goodnow, J. J. (1994). Impact of parental discipline methods on the child's internalization of values: A reconceptualization of current points of view. *Developmental Psychology, 30*, 4–19.

Grusec, J. E., Goodnow, J. J., & Kuczynski, L. (2000). New directions in analyses of parenting contributions to children's acquisition of values. *Child Development, 71*, 205–211.

Guéguen, N. (2012). Does red lipstick really attract men? An evaluation in a bar. *International Journal of Psychological Studies, 4*, 206–209.

Guéguen, N., & Jacob, C. (2012). Clothing color and tipping: Gentlemen patrons give more tips to waitresses with red clothes. *Journal of Hospitality & Tourism Research, 38*, 275–280.

Guilford, J. P. (1967). *The nature of human intelligence.* New York, NY: McGraw-Hill.

Guilford, J. P., Christensen, P. R., Merrifield, P. R., & Wilson, R. C. (1960). *Alternate uses.* Beverly Hills, CA: Sheridan Psychological Services.

Guillot, C. (2007). Is recreational Ecstasy (MDMA) use associated with higher levels of depressive symptoms? *Journal of Psychoactive Drugs, 39*, 31–39.

Guiney, H., & Machado, L. (2013). Benefits of regular aerobic exercise for executive functioning in healthy populations. *Psychonomic Bulletin & Review, 20*, 73–86.

Gulevich, G., Dement, W., & Johnson, L. (1966). Psychiatric and EEG observations on a case of prolonged (264 hours) wakefulness. *Archives of General Psychiatry, 15*, 29–35.

Gundel, J. (2003). The migration-development nexus: Somalia case study. *International Migration, 40*, 255–281.

Gunderson, E. A., Ramirez, G., Levine, S. C., & Beilock, S. L. (2012). The role of parents and teachers in the development of gender-related math attitudes. *Sex Roles, 66,* 153–166.

Gurpegui, M., Aguilar, M. C., Martínez-Ortega, J. M., Diaz, F. J., & de Leon, J. (2004). Caffeine intake in outpatients with schizophrenia. *Schizophrenia Bulletin, 30,* 935–945.

Gurven, M., von Rueden, C., Massenkoff, M., Kaplan, H., & Lero Vie, M. (2013). How universal is the Big Five? Testing the five-factor model of personality variation among forager-farmers in the Bolivian Amazon. *Journal of Personality and Social Psychology, 104,* 354–370.

Gushanas, T. (2015, April 14). Twins study—About. *NASA.* Retrieved from https://www.nasa.gov/twins-study/about

Güss, C. D. (2004). Decision making in individualistic and collectivistic cultures. *Online Readings in Psychology and Culture, 4.* http://dx.doi.org/10.9707/2307-0919.1032

Güss, C. D., & Robinson, B. (2014). Predicted causality in decision making: The role of culture. *Frontiers in Psychology, 5.* http://dx.doi.org/10.3389/fpsyg.2014.00479

Güss, D. (2011). Fire and ice: Testing a model on culture and complex problem solving. *Journal of Cross-Cultural Psychology, 42,* 1279–1298.

Habersaat, S. A., Geiger, A. M., Abdellaoui, S., & Wolf, J. M. (2015). Health in police officers: Role of risk factor clusters and police divisions. *Social Science & Medicine, 14,* 213–222.

Haedt-Matt, A. A., & Keel, P. K. (2011). Revisiting the affect regulation model of binge eating: A meta-analysis of studies using ecological momentary assessment. *Psychological Bulletin, 137,* 660–681.

Haijma, S. V., Van Haren, N., Cahn, W., Koolschijn, P. C. M., Pol, H. E. H., & Kahn, R. S. (2013). Brain volumes in schizophrenia: A meta-analysis in over 18,000 subjects. *Schizophrenia Bulletin, 39,* 1129–1138.

Halim, M. L., Ruble, D. N., Tamis-LeMonda, C. S., Zosuls, K. M., Lurye, L. E., & Greulich, F. K. (2014). Pink frilly dresses and the avoidance of all things "girly": Children's appearance rigidity and cognitive theories of gender development. *Developmental Psychology, 50,* 1091–1101. doi:10.1037/a0034906

Hall, D., & Buzwell, S. (2012). The problem of free-riding in group projects: Looking beyond social loafing as reason for non-contribution. *Active Learning in Higher Education, 14,* 37–49.

Hall, J. A., & Matsumoto, D. (2004). Gender differences in judgments of multiple emotions from facial expressions. *Emotion, 4,* 201–206.

Hall, J. K., Hutton, S. B., & Morgan, M. J. (2010). Sex differences in scanning faces: Does attention to the eyes explain female superiority in facial expression recognition? *Cognition and Emotion, 24,* 629–637.

Hall, J. W., Smith, S. D., & Popelka, G. R. (2004). Newborn hearing screening with combined otoacoustic emissions and auditory brainstem responses. *Journal of the American Academy of Audiology, 15,* 414–425.

Halpern, D. F. (2014). It's complicated—in fact, it's complex: Explaining the gender gap in academic achievement in science and mathematics. *Psychological Science in the Public Interest, 15*(3), 72–74.

Halpern, D. F., Benbow, C. P., Geary, D. C., Gur, R. C., Hyde, J. S., & Gernsbacher, M. A. (2007). The science of sex differences in science and mathematics. *Psychological Science in the Public Interest, 8,* 1–51.

Halpern, L. (2013, April). Let me tell you what it's like to have schizophrenia. *Ladies Home Journal,* 101–104.

Hameed, M. A., & Lewis, A. J. (2016). Offspring of parents with schizophrenia: A systematic review of developmental features across childhood. *Harvard Review of Psychiatry, 24*(2), 104–117.

Hamer, D. H., Hu, S., Magnuson, V. L., Hu, N., & Pattatucci, A. M. (1993). A linkage between DNA markers on the X chromosome and male sexual orientation. *Science, 261,* 321–327.

Hamilton, W. D. (1964). The genetical evolution of social behavior. *Journal of Theoretical Biology, 12,* 12–45.

Hammond, S. I., Müller, U., Carpendale, J. I. M., Bibok, M. B., & Liebermann-Finestone, D. P. (2012). The effects of parental scaffolding on preschoolers' executive function. *Developmental Psychology, 48,* 271–281.

Hampton, J. A. (1998). Similarity-based categorization and fuzziness of natural categories. *Cognition, 65,* 137–165.

Hamzelou, J. (2015, January 26). Is MSG a silent killer or useful flavour booster? *NewScientist.* Retrieved from https://www.newscientist.com/article/dn26854-is-msg-a-silent-killer-or-useful-flavour-booster/

Haney, C., Banks, C., & Zimbardo, P. (1973). Interpersonal dynamics in a simulated prison. *International Journal of Criminology and Penology, 1,* 69–97.

Haney, C., & Zimbardo, P. (1998). The past and future of U.S. prison policy: Twenty-five years after the Stanford prison experiment. *American Psychologist, 53,* 709–727.

Hanford, L. C., Nazarov, A., Hall, G. B., & Sassi, R. B. (2016). Cortical thickness in bipolar disorder: A systematic review. *Bipolar Disorders, 18,* 4–18.

Hanish, L. D., Sallquist, J., DiDonato, M., Fabes, R. A., & Martin, C. L. (2012). Aggression by whom—aggression toward whom: Behavioral predictors of same- and other-gender aggression in early childhood. *Developmental Psychology, 48,* 1450–1462. doi:10.1037/a0027510

Hankin, B. L., Young, J. F., Abela, J. R. Z., Smolen, A., Jenness, J. L., Gulley, L. D., … Oppenheimer, C. W. (2015). Depression from childhood into late adolescence: Influence of gender, development, genetic susceptibility, and peer stress. *Journal of Abnormal Psychology, 124,* 803–816.

Hanley, A. W., Warner, A. R., Dehili, V. M., Canto, A. I., & Garland, E. L. (2015). Washing dishes to wash the dishes: Brief instruction in an informal mindfulness practice. *Mindfulness, 6,* 1095–1103.

Hanley, J. R., & Chapman, E. (2008). Partial knowledge in a tip-of-the-tongue state about two- and three-word proper names. *Psychonomic Bulletin & Review, 15,* 156–160.

Hanna, C. (2012, October 27). Dog Whisperer Cesar Millan accused of punching dogs and using shock collars. *Examiner.com.* Retrieved from https://web.archive.org/web/20160422035235/http://www.examiner.com/article/dog-whisperer-cesar-milan-accused-of-punching-dogs-and-using-shock-collars

Hanna-Pladdy, B., & MacKay, A. (2011). The relation between instrumental musical activity and cognitive aging. *Neuropsychology, 25,* 378–386.

Hans, J. D., Gillen, M., & Akande, K. (2010). Sex redefined: The reclassification of oral–genital contact. *Perspectives on Sexual and Reproductive Health, 42,* 74–78.

Hanscombe, K. B., Trzaskowski, M., Haworth, C. M. A., Davis, O. S. P., Dale, P. S., & Plomin, R. (2012). Socioeconomic status (SES) and children's intelligence (IQ): In a UK-representative sample SES moderates the environmental, not genetic, effect on IQ. *PLOS ONE, 7,* e30320. doi:10.1371/journal.pone.0030320

Hansen, C. J., Stevens, L. C., & Coast, J. R. (2001). Exercise duration and mood state: How much is enough to feel better? *Health Psychology, 20,* 267–275.

Happiness Research Institute. (2015). *The Facebook experiment.* Retrieved from http://www.happinessresearchinstitute.com/publications/4579836749

Harcourt, B. E. (2011). An institutionalization effect: The impact of mental hospitalization and imprisonment on homicide in the United States, 1934–2001. *Journal of Legal Studies, 40,* 39–83.

Harden, K. P., & Mendle, J. (2012). Gene-environment interplay in the association between pubertal timing and delinquency in adolescent girls. *Journal of Abnormal Psychology, 121,* 73–87.

Hareli, S., Kafetsios, K., & Hess, U. (2015). A cross-cultural study on emotion expression and the learning of social norms. *Frontiers in Psychology, 6.* doi:10.3389/fpsyg.2015.01501

Hariri, A. R., Tessitore, A., Mattay, V. S., Fera, F., & Weinberger, D. R. (2002). The amygdala response to emotional stimuli: A comparison of faces and scenes. *NeuroImage, 17,* 317–323.

Harlow, H. F. (1958). The nature of love. *American Psychologist, 13,* 673–685.

Harlow, H. F., Harlow, M. K., & Meyer, D. R. (1950). Learning motivated by a manipulation drive. *Journal of Experimental Psychology, 40,* 228–234.

Harlow, H. F., Harlow, M. K., & Suomi, S. J. (1971). From thought to therapy: Lessons from a primate laboratory. *American Scientist, 59,* 538–549.

Harlow, H. F., & Zimmerman, R. R. (1959). Affectional responses in the infant monkey. *Science, 130,* 421–432.

Harmon, D. K., Masuda, M., & Holmes, T. H. (1970). The social readjustment rating scale: A cross-cultural study of Western Europeans and Americans. *Journal of Psychosomatic Research, 14,* 391–400.

Harmon, K. G., Drezner, J., Gammons, M., Guskiewicz, K., Halstead, M., Herring, S., … Roberts, W. (2013). American Medical Society for Sports Medicine position statement: Concussion in sport. *Clinical Journal of Sports Medicine, 23,* 1–18.

Harrington, A. (2012). The fall of the schizophrenogenic mother. *Lancet, 379,* 1292–1293.

Harrington, A., & Dunne, J. D. (2015). When mindfulness is therapy: Ethical qualms, historical perspectives. *American Psychologist, 70,* 621–631.

Harrington, J. M. (2001). Health effects of shift work and extended hours of work. *Occupational and Environmental Medicine, 58,* 68–72.

Harrington, R. (2013). *Stress, health & well-being: Thriving in the 21st century.* Belmont, CA: Wadsworth, Cengage Learning.

Harris, B. (1979). Whatever happened to Little Albert? *American Psychologist, 34,* 151–160.

Harris, J. A., Petersen, R. S., & Diamond, M. E. (2001). The cortical distribution of sensory memories. *Neuron, 30,* 315–318.

Hart, B., & Risley, T. R. (1995). *Meaningful differences in the everyday experience of young American children.* Baltimore, MD: Paul H. Brookes.

Hartnett, M. E. (2015). Pathophysiology and mechanisms of severe retinopathy of prematurity. *Ophthalmology, 122,* 200–210.

Harvard Medical School. (2007). *Healthy sleep: Jet lag and shift work.* Retrieved from http://healthysleep.med.harvard.edu/healthy/science/variations/jet-lag-and-shift-work

Harvey, M. A., Sellman, J. D., Porter, R. J., & Frampton, C. M. (2007). The relationship between non-acute adolescent cannabis use and cognition. *Drug and Alcohol Review, 26,* 309–319.

Hasher, L., & Zacks, R. T. (1979). Automatic and effortful processes in memory. *Journal of Experimental Psychology: General, 108,* 356–388.

Haslam, S. A., & Reicher, S. D. (2012). When prisoners take over the prison: A social psychology of resistance. *Personality and Social Psychology Review, 16,* 154–179.

Hassett, J. .M., Siebert, E. R., & Wallen, K. (2008). Sex differences in rhesus monkey toy preferences parallel those of children. *Hormones and Behavior, 54,* 359–364.

Hassin, R. R., Bargh, J. A., & Zimerman, S. (2009). Automatic and flexible: The case of non-conscious goal pursuit. *Social Cognition, 27,* 20–36.

Hasson, U., Andric, M., Atilgan, H., & Collignon, O. (2016). Congenital blindness is associated with large-scale reorganization of anatomical networks. *NeuroImage, 128,* 362–372.

Hatch, S. L., & Dohrenwend, B. P. (2007). Distribution of traumatic and other stressful life events by race/ethnicity, gender, SES and age: A review of the research. *American Journal of Community Psychology, 40,* 313–332.

Hatemi, P. K., McDermott, R., & Eaves, L. (2015). Genetic and environmental contributions to relationships and divorce attitudes. *Personality and Individual Differences, 72,* 135–140.

Hatemi, P. K., Medland, S. E., Klemmensen, R., Oskarsson, S., Littvay, L., Dawes, C. T., ... Martin, N. G. (2014). Genetic influences on political ideologies: Twin analyses of 19 measures of political ideologies from five democracies and genome-wide findings from three populations. *Behavior Genetics, 44,* 282–294.

Hatfield, E., Bensman, L., & Rapson, R. L. (2012). A brief history of social scientists' attempts to measure passionate love. *Journal of Social and Personal Relationships, 29,* 143–164.

Hatfield, E., Luckhurst, C., & Rapson, R. L. (2010). Sexual motives: Cultural, evolutionary, and social psychological perspectives. *Sexuality & Culture, 14,* 173–190.

Havelka, M., Luçanin, J. D., & Luçanin, D. (2009). Biopsychosocial model—the integrated approach to health and disease. *Collegium Antropologicum, 33,* 303–310.

Hawthorne, W. B., Folsom, D. P., Sommerfeld, D. H., Lanouette, N. M., Lewis, M., Aarons, G. A., ... Jeste, D. V. (2012). Incarceration among adults who are in the public mental health system: Rates, risk factors, and short-term outcomes. *Psychiatric Services, 63,* 26–32.

Hay, J., Johnson, V. E., Smith, D. H., & Stewart, W. (2016). Chronic traumatic encephalopathy: The neuropathological legacy of traumatic brain injury. *Annual Review of Pathology: Mechanisms of Disease, 11,* 21–45.

Hayes, J. E., & Keast, R. E. (2011). Two decades of supertasting: Where do we stand? *Physiology & Behavior, 104,* 1072–1074.

Hayes, J. F., Pitman, A., Marston, L., Walters, K., Geddes, J. R., King, M., & Osborn, D. P. (2016). Self-harm, unintentional injury, and suicide in bipolar disorder during maintenance mood stabilizer treatment: A UK population-based electronic health records study. *JAMA Psychiatry, 73,* 630–637.

Hecht, S., & Mandelbaum, J. (1938). Rod-cone dark adaptation and vitamin A. *Science, 88,* 219–221.

Hedström, A. K., Mowry, E. M., Gianfrancesco, M. A., Shao, X., Schaefer, C. A., Shen, L., ... Alfredsson, L. (2016). High consumption of coffee is associated with decreased multiple sclerosis risk; results from two independent studies. *Journal of Neurology, Neurosurgery & Psychiatry, 87,* 454–460. doi:10.1136/jnnp-2015-312176

Hegarty, P. (2012). Beyond Kinsey: The committee for research on problems of sex and American psychology. *History of Psychology, 15,* 197–200.

Hegarty, P., & Buechel, C. (2006). Androcentric reporting of gender differences in APA journals: 1965–2004. *Review of General Psychology, 10,* 377–389.

Heijnen, S., Hommel, B., Kibele, A., & Colzato, L. S. (2015). Neuromodulation of aerobic exercise—a review. *Frontiers in Psychology, 6.* http://doi.org/10.3389/fpsyg.2015.0189.

Heiman, J. R. (2002). Sexual dysfunction: Overview of prevalence, etiological factors, and treatments. *The Journal of Sex Research, 39,* 73–78.

Heiser, C. (2015, May 28). Demi Lovato speaks up about living with bipolar disorder. *Women's Health.* Retrieved from http://www.womenshealthmag.com/health/demi-lovato-be-vocal-campaign

Helliker, K. (2009, March 24). No joke: Group therapy offers savings in numbers. *The Wall Street Journal.* Retrieved from http://www.wsj.com/articles/SB123785686766020551

Helliwell, J. F., Layard, R., & Sachs, J. (Eds.) (2015). *World happiness report 2015.* New York, NY: Sustainable Development Solutions Network.

Henderson, S. N., Van Hasselt, V. B., LeDuc, T. J., & Couwels, J. (2016). Firefighter suicide: Understanding cultural challenges for mental health professionals. *Professional Psychology: Research and Practice, 47,* 224–230.

Hendricks, M. L., & Testa, R. J. (2012). A conceptual framework for clinical work with transgender and gender nonconforming clients: An adaptation of the minority stress model. *Professional Psychology: Research and Practice, 43,* 460–467.

Henneman, W. J., Sluimer, J. D., Barnes, J., van der Flier, W. M., Sluimer, I. C., Fox, N. C., ... Barkhof, F. (2009). Hippocampal atrophy rates in Alzheimer disease: Added value over whole brain volume measures. *Neurology, 72,* 999–1007.

Hensch, T. K. (2004). Critical period regulation. *Annual Review of Neuroscience, 27,* 549–579.

Herbenick, D., Reece, M., Schick, V., Sanders, S. A., Dodge, B., & Fortenberry, J. D. (2010). Sexual behavior in the United States: Results from a national probability sample of men and women ages 14–94. *The Journal of Sexual Medicine, 7* (Suppl. 5), 255–265.

Herculano-Houzel, S. (2012). The remarkable, yet not extraordinary, human brain as a scaled-up primate brain and its associated cost. *Proceedings of the National Academy of Sciences, 109* (Suppl. 1), 10661–10668.

Herman, C. P., Roth, D. A., & Polivy, J. (2003). Effects of the presence of others on food intake: A normative interpretation. *Psychological Bulletin, 129,* 873–886.

Hersh, S. M. (2004, May 10). Torture at Abu Ghraib. *The New Yorker.* Retrieved from http://www.newyorker.com/archive/2004/05/10/040510fa_fact—printable=true&currentPage=all

Hertenstein, M. J., & McCullough, M. A. (2005). Separation anxiety. In N. J. Salkind (Ed.), *Encyclopedia of human development* (Vol. 3, pp. 1146–1147). Thousand Oaks, CA: SAGE.

Hertzog, C., Kramer, A. F., Wilson, R. S., & Lindenberger, U. (2009, July/August). Fit body, fit mind? *Scientific American Mind, 20,* 24–31.

Herz, D. M., Haagensen, B. N., Christensen, M. S., Madsen, K. H., Rowe, J. B., Løkkegaard, A., & Siebner, H. R. (2015). Abnormal dopaminergic modulation of striato-cortical networks underlies levodopa-induced dyskinesias in humans. *Brain, 138,* 1658–1666.

Herz, R. (2007). *The scent of desire: Discovering our enigmatic sense of smell.* New York, NY: William Morrow/HarperCollins.

Herzog, T. K., Hill-Chapman, C., Hardy, T. K., Wrighten, S. A., & El-Khabbaz, R. (2015). Trait emotion, emotional regulation, and parenting styles. *Journal of Educational and Developmental Psychology, 5,* 119–135.

Hess, U., & Thibault, P. (2009). Darwin and emotion expression. *American Psychologist, 64,* 120–128.

Hettema, J. M., Kettenmann, B., Ahluwalia, V., McCarthy, C., Kates, W. R., Schmitt, J. E., ... Fatouros, P. (2012). Pilot multimodal twin imaging study of generalized anxiety disorder. *Depression and Anxiety, 29,* 202–209.

Hettema, J. M., Neale, M. C., & Kendler, K. S. (2001). A review and meta-analysis of the genetic epidemiology of anxiety disorders. *American Journal of Psychiatry, 158,* 1568–1578.

Hetzel, L., & Smith, A. (2001). The 65 years and over populations: 2000. *Census 2000 Brief.* Retrieved from http://www.census.gov/prod/2001pubs/c2kbr01-10.pdf

Heyes, C. (2012). What's social about social learning? *Journal of Comparative Psychology, 126,* 193–202.

Hickok, G., & Poeppel, D. (2000). Towards a functional neuroanatomy of speech perception. *Trends in Cognitive Sciences, 4,* 131–138.

Higgins, A., Nash, M., & Lynch, A. M. (2010). Antidepressant-associated sexual dysfunction: Impact, effects, and treatment. *Drug, Healthcare and Patient Safety, 2,* 141–150.

Hilgard, E. R. (1977). *Divided consciousness.* New York, NY: John Wiley & Sons.

Hilgard, E. R. (1987). *Psychology in America: A historical survey.* Orlando, FL: Harcourt Brace Jovanovich.

Hilgard, E. R. (1994). Neodissociation theory. In S. J. Lynn & J. W. Rhue (Eds.), *Dissociation: Clinical, theoretical and research perspectives* (pp. 32–51). New York, NY: Guilford Press.

Hilgard, E. R., Morgan, A. H., & Macdonald, H. (1975). Pain and dissociation in the cold pressor test: A study of hypnotic analgesia with "hidden reports" through automatic key pressing and automatic talking. *Journal of Abnormal Psychology, 84,* 280–289.

Hill, B. J., Sanders, S. A., & Reinisch, J. M. (2016). Variability in sex attitudes and sexual histories across age groups of bisexual women and men in the United States. *Journal of Bisexuality, 16,* 20–40.

Hill, R. A., & Barton, R. A. (2005). Red enhances human performance in contests. *Nature, 435,* 293.

Hines, M. (2011a). Gender development and the human brain. *Annual Review of Neuroscience, 34,* 69–88.

Hines, M. (2011b). Prenatal endocrine influences on sexual orientation and on sexually differentiated childhood behavior. *Frontiers in Neuroendocrinology, 32,* 170–182.

Hines, M., Constantinescu, M., & Spencer, D. (2015). Early androgen exposure and human gender development. *Biology of Sex Differences, 6,* 3. doi:10.1186/s13293-015-0022-1

Hines, R. (2015, May 27). Howie Mandel says "AGT" hypnotism didn't cure him, it sent him to therapy. *Today.* Retrieved from http://www.today.com/popculture/howie-mandel-says-agt-hypnotism-act-didnt-cure-him-t23106

Hingson, R. W., Zha, W., & Weitzman, E. R. (2009). Magnitude of and trends in alcohol-related mortality among U.S. college students ages 18–24, 1998–2005. *Journal of Studies on Alcohol and Drugs, 16,* 12–20.

Hirshkowitz, M., Whiton, K., Albert, S. M., Alessi, C., Bruni, O., DonCarols, L., …Ware, J. C. (2015). National Sleep Foundation's updated sleep duration recommendations: Final report. *Sleep Health, 1,* 233–243.

Hirsh-Pasek, K., Adamson, L. B., Bakeman, R., Owen, M. T., Golinkoff, R. M., Pace, A., … Suma, K. (2015). The contribution of early communication quality to low-income children's language success. *Psychological Science, 26,* 1071–1083.

Hirst, W., & Phelps, E. A. (2016). Flashbulb memories. *Current Directions in Psychological Science, 25,* 36–41.

Hirst, W., Phelps, E. A., Meksin, R., Vaidya, C. J., Johnson, M. K., Mitchell, K. J., … Mather, M. (2015). A ten-year follow-up of a study of memory for the attack of September 11, 2001: Flashbulb memories and memories for flashbulb events. *Journal of Experimental Psychology: General, 144,* 604–623.

Hjerrild, B. E., Mortensen, K. H., & Gravholt, C. H. (2008). Turner syndrome and clinical treatment. *British Medical Bulletin, 86,* 77–93.

Hobson, J. A. (1989). *Sleep.* New York, NY: Scientific American Library.

Hobson, J. A. (2006, April/May). Freud returns? Like a bad dream. *Scientific American Mind, 17,* 35.

Hobson, J. A. (2009). REM sleep and dreaming: Towards a theory of protoconsciousness. *Nature Reviews Neuroscience, 10,* 803–813.

Hobson, J. A., & Friston, K. J. (2012). Waking and dreaming consciousness: Neurobiological and functional considerations. *Progress in Neurobiology, 98,* 82–98.

Hobson, J. A., & McCarley, R. W. (1977). The brain as a dream state generator: An activation-synthesis hypothesis of the dream process. *American Journal of Psychiatry, 134,* 1335–1348.

Hobson, J. A., & Pace-Schott, E. F. (2002). The cognitive neuroscience of sleep: Neuronal systems, consciousness and learning. *Nature Reviews Neuroscience, 3,* 679–693.

Hochard, K. D., Heym, N., & Townsend, E. (2016). The behavioral effects of frequent nightmares on objective stress tolerance. *Dreaming, 26,* 42–49.

Hock, R. R. (2016). *Human sexuality* (4th ed.). Upper Saddle River, NJ: Pearson Education.

Hodgson, A. B., Randell, R. K., & Jeukendrup, A. E. (2013). The metabolic and performance effects of caffeine compared to coffee during endurance exercise. *PLOS ONE, 8*(4), e59561. doi:10.1371/journal.pone.0059561

Hodis, F. A., Meyer, L. H., McClure, J., Weir, K. F., & Walkey, F. H. (2011). A longitudinal investigation of motivation and secondary school achievement using growth mixture modeling. *Journal of Educational Psychology, 103,* 312–323.

Hoeft, F., Gabrieli, J. D., Whitfield-Gabrieli, S., Haas, B. W., Bammer, R., Menon, V., & Spiegel, D. (2012). Functional brain basis of hypnotizability. *Archives of General Psychiatry, 69,* 1064–1072.

Hoff, E. (2003). The specificity of environmental influence: Socioeconomic status affects early vocabulary development via maternal speech. *Child Development, 74,* 1368–1378.

Hoff, E. (2013). Interpreting the early language trajectories of children from low-SES and language minority homes: Implications for closing achievement gaps. *Developmental Psychology, 49,* 4–14.

Hoffman, I. Z. (2009). Therapeutic passion in the countertransference. *Psychoanalytic Dialogues, 19,* 617–636.

Hoffman, S. (2006). *By the numbers: The public costs of teen childbearing.* Washington, DC: National Campaign to Prevent Teen Pregnancy.

Hoffman, S. J., & Tan, C. (2013). Following celebrities' medical advice: Meta-narrative analysis. *BMJ, 347,* f7151.

Hofmann, L., & Palczewski, K. (2015) . Advances in understanding the molecular basis of the first steps in color vision. *Progress in Retinal and Eye Research, 49,* 46–66.

Hofmann, S. G., Asnaani, M. A., & Hinton, D. E. (2010). Cultural aspects in social anxiety and social anxiety disorder. *Depression and Anxiety, 27,* 1117–1127.

Hofmann, S. G., & Hinton, D. E. (2014). Cross-cultural aspects of anxiety disorders. *Current Psychiatry Reports, 16,* 1–5. doi:10.1007/s11920-014-0450-3

Hofmann, W., Vohs, K. D., & Baumeister, R. F. (2012). What people desire, feel conflicted about, and try to resist in everyday life. *Psychological Science, 23,* 582–588.

Hogan, C. L., Mata, J., & Carstensen, L. L. (2013). Exercise holds immediate benefits for affect and cognition in younger and older adults. *Psychology and Aging, 28,* 587–594. doi:10.1037/a0032634

Hoge, C. W., & Warner, C. H. (2014). Estimating PTSD prevalence in US veterans: Considering combat exposure, PTSD checklist cutpoints, and *DSM-5.* The *Journal of Clinical Psychiatry, 75,* 1439–1441.

Hohoff, C., Weber, H., Richter, J., Domschke, K., Zwanzger, P. M., Ohrmann, P., … Klauke, B. (2015). RGS2 genetic variation: Association analysis with panic disorder and dimensional as well as intermediate phenotypes of anxiety. *American Journal of Medical Genetics Part B: Neuropsychiatric Genetics, 168,* 211–222.

Holahan, C. K., & Sears, R. R. (1995). *The gifted group in later maturity.* Stanford, CA: Stanford University Press.

Holland, R. W., Verplanken, B., & Van Knippenberg, A. (2002). On the nature of attitude-behavior relations: The strong guide, the weak follow. *European Journal of Social Psychology, 32,* 869–876.

Holmes, T. H., & Rahe, R. H. (1967). The Social Readjustment Rating Scale. *Journal of Psychosomatic Research, 11,* 213–318.

Holowka, S., & Petitto, L. A. (2002). Left hemisphere cerebral specialization for babies while babbling. *Science, 297,* 1515.

Holsen, L. M., Spaeth, S. B., Lee, J.-H., Ogden, L. A., Klibanski, A., Whitfield-Gabrieli, S., & Goldstein, J. M. (2011). Stress response circuitry hypoactivation related to hormonal dysfunction in women with major depression. *Journal of Affective Disorders, 131,* 379–387.

Holtgraves, T. (2015). I think I am doing great but I feel pretty bad about it: Affective versus cognitive verbs and self-reports. *Personality & Social Psychology Bulletin, 41,* 677–686.

Honberg, R., Diehl, S., Kimball, A., Gruttadaro, D., & Fitzpatrick, M. (2011). *State mental health cuts: A national crisis* (Report by the National Alliance on Mental Illness). Retrieved from https://www.nami.org/getattachment/About-NAMI/Publications/Reports/NAMIStateBudgetCrisis2011.pdf

Honda, H., Shimizu, Y., & Rutter, M. (2005). No effect of MMR withdrawal on the incidence of autism: A total population study. *Journal of Child Psychology and Psychiatry, 46,* 572–579.

Hong, Y.-Y., Wyer, R. S. Jr., & Fong, C. P. S. (2008). Chinese working in groups: Effort dispensability versus normative influence. *Asian Journal of Social Psychology, 11*, 187–195.

Hoogland, T. M., & Parpura, V. (2015). Editorial: The role of glia in plasticity and behavior. *Frontiers in Cellular Neuroscience, 9*, doi:10.3389/fncel.2015.00356

Hook, J. (2015, March 9). Support for gay marriage hits all-time high—WSJ/NBC News Poll [Web log post]. Retrieved from http://blogs.wsj.com/washwire/2015/03/09/support-for-gay-marriage-hits-all-time-high-wsjnbc-news-poll/

Hooper, J., Sharpe, D., & Roberts, S. G. B. (2016). Are men funnier than women, or do we just think they are? *Translational Issues in Psychological Science, 2*, 54–62.

Horikawa, T., Tamaki, M., Miyawaki, Y., & Kamitani, Y. (2013). Neural decoding of visual imagery during sleep. *Science, 340*, 639–642.

Horne, J. (2006). *Sleepfaring*. Oxford, UK: Oxford University Press.

Horney, K. (1926/1967). The flight from womanhood: The masculinity-complex in women as viewed by men and by women. In H. Kelmam (Ed.), *Feminine psychology* (pp. 54–70). New York, NY: W.W. Norton.

Horney, K. (1945). *Our inner conflicts: A constructive theory of neurosis*. New York, NY: W. W. Norton.

Horoscope.com. (2014). *Monthly horoscope: Gemini*. Retrieved September 14, 2014 from http://my.horoscope.com/astrology/free-monthly-horoscope-gemini.html

Horsley, R. R., Osborne, M., Norman, C., & Wells, T. (2012). High-frequency gamblers show increased resistance to extinction following partial reinforcement. *Behavioural Brain Research, 229*, 438–442.

Horwitz, B., Amunts, K., Bhattacharyya R., Patkin, D., Jeffries, K., Zilles, K., & Braun, A. R. (2003). Activation of Broca's area during the production of spoken and signed language: A combined cytoarchitectonic mapping and PET analysis. *Neuropsychologia, 41*, 1868–1876.

Horwitz, D., Lovenberg, W., Engelman, K., & Sjoerdsma, A. (1964). Monoamine oxidase inhibitors, tyramine, and cheese. *Journal of the American Medical Association, 188*, 1108–1110.

Horwood, L. J., & Fergusson, D. M. (1998). Breastfeeding and later cognitive and academic outcomes. *Pediatrics, 101*, 1–7.

Hothersall, D. (2004). *History of psychology* (4th ed.). New York, NY: McGraw-Hill.

House, J. S., Landis, K. R., & Umberson, D. (1988). Social relationships and health. *Science, 241*, 540–545.

Hovland, C. I., Janis, I. L., & Kelley, H. H. (1953). *Communication and persuasion: Psychological studies of opinion change*. New Haven, CT: Yale University Press.

Hovland, C. I., & Weiss, W. (1951). The influence of source credibility on communication effectiveness. *Public Opinion Quarterly, 15*, 635–650.

Howard, C., & Inverso, E. (2016). *Forbes 30 under 30*. Retrieved from http://www.forbes.com/30-under-30-2016/#113bdc6e64fe

Howard-Jones, P. A. (2014). Neuroscience and education: Myths and messages. *Nature Reviews Neuroscience, 15*, 817–824.

Howes, O. D., & Kapur, S. (2009). The dopamine hypothesis of schizophrenia: Version III—the final common pathway. *Schizophrenia Bulletin, 35*, 549–562.

Howland, J., Rohsenow, D. J., Greece, J. A., Littlefield, C. A., Almeida, A., Heeren, T., ... Hermos, J. (2010). The effects of binge drinking on college students' next-day academic test-taking performance and mood state. *Addiction, 105*, 655–665.

Hoyert, D., & Xu, J. (2012). Deaths: Preliminary data for 2011. *National Vital Statistics Reports, 61*, 1–64.

Hsu, C.-T., Jacobs, A. M., Altmann, U., & Conrad, M. (2015). The magical activation of left amygdala when reading Harry Potter: An fMRI study on how descriptions of supra-natural events entertain and enchant. *PLOS ONE, 10*(2), e0118179. doi:10.1371/journal.pone.0118179

Hsu, P. J., Shoud, H., Benzinger, T., Marcus, D., Durbin, T., Morris, J. C., & Sheline, Y. I. (2015). Amyloid burden in cognitively normal elderly is associated with preferential hippocampal subfield volume loss. *Journal of Alzheimer's Diseases, 45*, 27–33.

Huang, Z. J., & Luo, L. (2015). It takes the world to understand the brain. *Science, 350*(6256), 42–44.

Hubbard, T. L. (2010). Auditory imagery: Empirical findings. *Psychological Bulletin, 136*, 302–329.

Hubel, D. H., & Wiesel, T. N. (1979, September). Brain mechanisms of vision. *Scientific American, 241*, 150–162.

Hudson, C., & Paul, J. (Producers). (2007). *Through your eyes*. [DVD]. Los Angeles, CA: Global Universal Film Group.

Huesmann, L. R., Moise-Titus, J., Podolski, C., & Eron, L. D. (2003). Longitudinal relations between children's exposure to TV violence and their aggressive and violent behavior in young adulthood: 1977–1992. *Developmental Psychology, 33*, 201–221.

Hughes, S., Lyddy, F., Kaplan, R., Nichols, A. L., Miller, H., Saad, C. G., ... Lynch, A. J. (2015) Highly prevalent but not always persistent: Undergraduate and graduate student's misconceptions about psychology. *Teaching of Psychology, 42*, 34–42.

Huguelet, P., & Perroud, N. (2005). Wolfgang Amadeus Mozart's psychopathology in light of the current conceptualization of psychiatric disorders. *Psychiatry, 68*, 130–139.

Huizink, A. C. (2014). Prenatal cannabis exposure and infant outcomes: Overview of studies. *Progress in Neuro-Psychopharmacology and Biological Psychiatry, 52*, 45–52.

Hull, C. L. (1952). *A behavior system: An introduction to behavior theory concerning the individual organism*. New Haven, CT: Yale University Press.

Hulsegge, G., Looman, M., Smit, H. A., Daviglus, M. L., van der Schouw, Y. T., & Verschuren, W. M. (2016). Lifestyle changes in young adulthood and middle age and risk of cardiovascular disease and all-cause mortality: The Doetinchem Cohort Study. *Journal of the American Heart Association, 5*. http://dx.doi.org/10.1161/JAHA.115.002432

Humane Society. (2015, June 26). July fourth fireworks: Awesome for humans, terrifying for pets. Retrieved from http://www.humanesociety.org/animals/resources/tips/pets_fireworks.html

Humphrey, E. K. (2011). Laughter leads to insight: Happy moods facilitate aha! moments. *Scientific American Mind, 22*, 5.

Humphries, T., Kushalnagar, P., Mathur, G., Napoli, D. J., Padden, C., Rathmann, C., & Smith, S. R. (2012). Language acquisition for deaf children: Reducing the harms of zero tolerance to the use of alternative approaches. *Harm Reduction Journal, 3*, 1–9.

Hunsley, J., Lee, C. M., & Wood, J. M. (2003). Controversial and questionable assessment techniques. In S. O. Lilienfeld, J. M. Lohr, & S. J. Lynn (Eds.), *Science and pseudoscience in clinical psychology* (pp. 39–76). New York, NY: Guilford Press.

Hunt, J. (2012). A state-by-state examination of nondiscrimination laws and policies: State nondiscrimination policies fill the void but federal protections are still needed. *Center for American Progress*. Retrieved from https://www.americanprogress.org/wp-content/uploads/issues/2012/06/pdf/state_nondiscrimination.pdf

Hunt, W. A. (1939). A critical review of current approaches to affectivity. *Psychological Bulletin, 36*, 807–828.

Hunter, S. C., Fox, C. L., & Jones, S. E. (2016). Humor style similarity and difference in friendship dyads. *Journal of Adolescence, 46*, 30–37.

Hupp, J. M., Smith, J. L, Coleman, J. M., & Brunell, A. B. (2010). That's a boys' toy: Gender-typed knowledge in toddlers as a function of mother's marital status. *The Journal of Genetic Psychology, 171*, 389–401.

Huppertz, C., Bartels, M., Jansen, I. E., Boomsma, D. I., Willemsen, G., de Moor, M. H. M., & de Geus, E. J. C. (2014). A twin-sibling study on the relationship between exercise attitudes and exercise behavior. *Behavior Genetics, 44*, 45–55.

Hurley, S. W., & Johnson, A. K. (2014). The role of the lateral hypothalamus and orexin in ingestive behavior: A model for the translation of past experience and sensed deficits into motivated behaviors. *Frontiers in Systems Neuroscience, 8*, http://dx.doi.org/10.3389/fnsys.2014.00216

Hurst, L. C. (1982). What was wrong with Anna O? *Journal of the Royal Society of Medicine, 75*, 129–131.

Hussey, K., & Foderaro, L. W. (2016, June 14). Surprising progress in Newtown families' suit against maker of the AR-15 rifle. *The New York Times*. Retrieved from http://www.nytimes.com/2016/06/15/nyregion/in-newtown-families-suit-against-maker-of-the-ar-15-rifle-surprising-progress.html?_r=0

Hutson, M. (2016, March/April). Keeping up with the Joneses—in bed. *Scientific American Mind, 27*, 13.

Hyde, J. S. (2005). The gender similarities hypothesis. *American Psychologist, 60*, 581–592.

Hyde, J. S. (2007). New directions in the study of gender similarities and differences. *Current Directions in Psychological Science, 16*, 259–263.

Hyde, J. S., & Linn, M. C. (1988). Gender differences in verbal ability: A meta-analysis. *Psychological Bulletin, 104*, 53–69.

Hyman, I. E. Jr., Husband, T. H., & Billings, F. J. (1995). False memories of childhood experiences. *Applied Cognitive Psychology, 3,* 181–197.

Ilias, I., Tayeh, L. S., & Pachoundakis, I. (2016). Diversity in endocrinology practice: The case of Ramadan. *Hormones, 15,* 147–148.

IMDB. (2015). *My stroke of insight.* Retrieved from http://www.imdb.com/title/tt1738297/?ref_=nm_flmg_wr_1

Impey, C., Buxner, S., & Antonellis, J. (2012). Non-scientific beliefs among undergraduate students. *Astronomy Education Review, 11.* doi:10.3847/AER2012016

Inder, M. L., Crowe, M. T., Luty, S. E., Carter, J. D., Moor, S., Frampton, C. M., & Joyce, P. R. (2016). Prospective rates of suicide attempts and nonsuicidal self-injury by young people with bipolar disorder participating in a psychotherapy study. *Australian and New Zealand Journal of Psychiatry, 50,* 167–173.

Ingold, J. (2013, September 30). Sides debate lengthy witness lists for James Holmes trial. *The Denver Post.* Retrieved from http://www.denverpost.com/breakingnews/ci_24205468/psychiatric-exam-up-debate-new-aurora-theater-shooting#

Institute of Medicine and National Research Council. (2014). *Sports-related concussions in youth: Improving the science, changing the culture.* Washington, DC: National Academies Press.

Interlandi, J. (2012, June 22). When my crazy father actually lost his mind. *The New York Times.* Retrieved from http://www.nytimes.com/2012/06/24/magazine/when-my-crazy-father-actually-lost-his-mind.html?_r=0

Inui, K., Urakawa, T., Yamahiro, K., Otsuru, N., Takeshima, Y., Nishihara, M., … Kakigi, R. (2010). Echoic memory of a single pure tone by change-related brain activity. *BMS Neuroscience, 11,* 135–145.

Ireland, T. (2014, June 12). What does mindfulness meditation do to your brain? [Web log post]. Retrieved from http://blogs.scientificamerican.com/guest-blog/what-does-mindfulness-meditation-do-to-your-brain/

Isen, A. (2008). Some ways in which positive affect influences decision making and problem solving. In M. Lewis, J. M. Haviland-Jones, & L. F. Barrett (Eds.), *Handbook of emotions* (3rd ed., pp. 548–573). New York, NY: Guilford Press.

Ismail, Z., Smith, E. E., Geda, Y., Sultzer, D., Brodaty, H., Smith, G., … Lyketsos, C. G. (2016). Neuropsychiatric symptoms as early manifestations of emergent dementia: Provisional diagnostic criteria for mild behavioral impairment. *Alzheimer's & Dementia, 12,* 195–202.

Iversen, L. (2003). Cannabis and the brain. *Brain, 126,* 1252–1270.

Izard, C. E. (1992). Basic emotions, relations among emotions, and emotion-cognition relations. *Psychological Review, 99,* 561–565.

Izard, C. E. (2007). Basic emotions, natural kinds, emotion schemas, and a new paradigm. *Perspectives on Psychological Science, 2,* 260–280.

Jaaro-Peled, H., Ayhan, Y., Pletnikov, M. V., & Sawa, A. (2010). Review of pathological hallmarks of schizophrenia: Comparison of genetic models with patients and nongenetic models. *Schizophrenia Bulletin, 36,* 301–313.

Jaarsveld, S., Fink, A., Rinner, M., Schwab, D., Benedek, M., & Lachmann, T. (2015). Intelligence in creative processes: An EEG study. *Intelligence, 49,* 171–178.

Jack, R. E., Sun, W., Delis, I., Garrod, O. G., & Schyns, P. G. (2016). Four not six: Revealing culturally common facial expressions of emotion. *Journal of Experimental Psychology, 145,* 708–730.

Jackson, G. L., Trail, T. E., Kennedy, D. P., Williamson, H. C., Bradbury, T. N., & Karney, B. R. (2016). The salience and severity of relationship problems among low-income couples. *Journal of Family Psychology, 30,* 2–11.

Jacobs, H. (2012). Don't ask, don't tell, don't publish. *EMBO Reports, 13.* doi: 10.1038/embor.2012.48

Jacobsen, F. M. (2015). Second-generation antipsychotics and tardive syndromes in affective illness: A public health problem with neuropsychiatric consequences. *American Journal of Public Health, 105,* e10–e16.

Jacobson, E. (1938). *Progressive relaxation.* Chicago, IL: University of Chicago Press.

Jain, A., Marshall, J., Buikema, A., Bancroft, T., Kelly J. P., & Newschaffer, C. J. (2015). Autism occurrence by MMR vaccine status among US children with older siblings with and without autism. *Journal of the American Medical Association, 313,* 1534–1540.

Jalal, B., & Ramachandran, V. S. (2014). Sleep paralysis and "the bedroom intruder": The role of the right superior parietal, phantom pain and body image projection. *Medical Hypotheses, 83,* 755–757.

Jalal, B., Taylor, C. T., & Hinton, D. E. (2014). A comparison of self-report and interview methods for assessing sleep paralysis: Pilot investigations in Denmark and the United States. *Journal of Sleep Disorders: Treatment & Care, 3,* doi:http://dx.doi.org/10.4172/2325-9639.1000131

James, J. E. (2014). Dietary caffeine: "Unnatural" exposure requiring precaution? *Journal of Substance Use, 19,* 394–397.

James, L. E., & Burke, D. M. (2000). Phonological priming effects on word retrieval and tip-of-the-tongue experiences in young and older adults. *Journal of Experimental Psychology: Learning, Memory, and Cognition, 26,* 1378–1391.

James, S. D. (2008, May 7). Wild child speechless after tortured life. *ABC News.* Retrieved from http://abcnews.go.com/Health/story-id=4804490&page=1#.UW4DxHApsVs

James, W. J. (1890/1983). *The principles of psychology.* Cambridge, MA: Harvard University Press.

Jameson, D., & Hurvich, L. M. (1989). Essay concerning color constancy. *Annual Review of Psychology, 40,* 1–24.

Jamkhande, P. G., Chintawar, K. D., & Chandak, P. G. (2014). Teratogenicity: A mechanism based short review on common teratogenic agents. *Asian Pacific Journal of Tropical Disease, 4,* 421–432.

Janak, P. H., & Tye, K. M. (2015). From circuits to behaviour in the amygdala. *Nature, 517,* 284–292.

Janata, P., & Paroo, K. (2006). Acuity of auditory images in pitch and time. *Perception & Psychophysics, 68,* 829–844.

Jang, K. L., Livesley, W. J., & Vernon, P. A. (1996). Heritability of the Big Five personality dimensions and their facets: A twin study. *Journal of Personality, 64,* 577–592.

Janis, I. J., Kaye, D., & Kirschner, P. (1965). Facilitating effects of "eating-while-reading" on responsiveness to persuasive communication. *Journal of Personality and Social Psychology, 1,* 181–186.

Janis, I. L. (1972). *Victims of groupthink: A psychological study of foreign-policy decisions and fiascoes.* Oxford, UK: Houghton Mifflin.

Janis, I. L., & Feshbach, S. (1953). Effects of fear-arousing communications. *Journal of Abnormal and Social Psychology, 48,* 78–92.

Jankovic, N., Geelen, A., Streppel, M. T., de Groot, L. C., Orfanos, P., van den Hooven, E. H., … Feskens, E. J. (2014). Adherence to a healthy diet according to the World Health Organization guidelines and all-cause mortality in elderly adults from Europe and the United States. *American Journal of Epidemology, 180,* 978–988.

Javanbakht, A., King, A. P., Evans, G. W., Swain, J. E., Angstadt, M., Phan, K. L., & Liberzon, I. (2015). Childhood poverty predicts adult amygdala and frontal activity and connectivity in response to emotional faces. *Frontiers in Behavioral Neuroscience, 9,* 1–8.

Javitt, D. C., & Sweet, R. A. (2015). Auditory dysfunction in schizophrenia: Integrating clinical and basic features. *Nature Reviews Neuroscience, 16*(9), 535–550.

Jenaro, C., Flores, N., & Arias, B. (2007). Burnout and coping in human service practitioners. *Professional Psychology: Research and Practice, 38,* 80–87.

Jensen, M. P., Adachi, T., Tomé-Pires, C., Lee, J., Osman, Z. J., & Miró, J. (2015). Mechanisms of hypnosis: Toward the development of a biopsychosocial model. *International Journal of Clinical and Experimental Hypnosis, 63*(1), 34–75.

Jessberger, S., & Gage, F. H. (2014). Adult neurogenesis: Bridging the gap between mice and humans. *Trends in Cell Biology, 24,* 558–563.

Jeste, D. V., Savla, G. N., Thompson, W. K., Vahia, I. V., Glorioso, D. K., Palmer, B. W., … Depp, C. A. (2013). Association between older age and more successful aging: Critical role of resilience and depression. *American Journal of Psychiatry, 170,* 188–196.

Jiang, W., Liu, H., Zeng, L., Liao, J., Shen, H., Luo, A., … Wang, W. (2015). Decoding the processing of lying using functional connectivity MRI. *Behavioral and Brain Functions, 11*(1). doi:10.1186/s12993-014-0046-4

Jiang, Y., Chew, S. H., & Ebstein, R. P. (2013). The role of D4 receptor gene exon III polymorphisms in shaping human altruism and prosocial behavior. *Frontiers in Human Neuroscience, 7.* http://dx.doi.org/10.3389/fnhum.2013.00195

Johannsson, M., Snaedal, J., Johannesson, G. H., Gudmundsson, T. E., & Johnsen, K. (2015). The acetylcholine index: An electroencephalographic marker of cholinergic activity in the living human brain applied to Alzheimer's disease and other dementias. *Dementia and Geriatric Cognitive Disorders, 39*(3–4), 132–142.

John, O. P., Naumann, L. P., & Soto, C. J. (2008). Paradigm shift to the integrative Big-Five Trait taxonomy: History, measurement, and conceptual issues. In O. P. John, R. W. Robins, & L. A. Pervin (Eds.), *Handbook of personality: Theory and research* (pp. 114–158). New York, NY: Guilford Press.

John-Henderson, N. A., Stellar, J. E., Mendoza-Denton, R., & Francis, D. D. (2015). Socioeconomic status and social support: Social support reduces inflammatory reactivity for individuals whose early-life socioeconomic status was low. *Psychological Science, 26,* 1620–1629.

Johnson, D. M. (2005). *Introduction to and review of simulator sickness research* (Research Report 1832, Army Project No. 2O262785A790). Arlington, VA: U.S. Army Research Institute for the Behavioral and Social Sciences. Retrieved from http://www.dtic.mil/dtic/tr/fulltext/u2/a434495.pdf

Johnson, H. D., McNair, R., Vojick, A., Congdon, D., Monacelli, J., & Lamont, J. (2006). Categorical and continuous measurement of sex-role orientation: Differences in associations with young adults' reports of well-being. *Social Behavior and Personality, 34,* 59–76.

Johnson, H. D., Sholcosky, D., Gabello, K., Ragni, R., & Ogonosky, N. (2003). Sex differences in public restroom handwashing behavior associated with visual behavior prompts. *Perceptual and Motor Skills, 97,* 805–810.

Johnson, L. R., LeDoux, J. E., & Doyère, V. (2009). Hebbian reverberations in emotional memory micro circuits. *Frontiers in Neuroscience, 3,* http://dx.doi.org/10.3389/neuro.01.027.2009

Johnson, P. L., Truitt, W., Fitz, S. D., Minick, P. E., Dietrich, A., Sanghani, S., … Shekhar, A. (2010). A key role for orexin in panic anxiety. *Nature Medicine, 16,* 111–115.

Johnson, R. D. (1987). Making judgments when information is missing: Inferences, biases, and framing effects. *Acta Psychologica, 66,* 69–72.

Johnson, W., & Bouchard, T. J. (2011). The MISTRA data: Forty-two mental ability tests in three batteries. *Intelligence, 39,* 82–88.

Johnston, L. D., O'Malley, P. M., Bachman, J. G., & Schulenberg, J. E. (2012). *Monitoring the future national results on adolescent drug use: Overview of key findings, 2011.* Ann Arbor, MI: Institute for Social Research, University of Michigan.

Johnston, M. V. (2009). Plasticity in the developing brain: Implications for rehabilitation. *Developmental Disabilities Research Reviews, 15,* 94–101.

Jones, K. (2013). Discouraging social loafing during team-based assessments. *Teaching Innovation Projects, 3,* http://ir.lib.uwo.ca/tips/vol3/iss1/13

Jordan, J. (2009, May 13). Wanda Sykes becomes mom of twins! *People.* Retrieved from http://www.people.com/people/article/0,,20278746,00.html

Jordan-Young, R. M. (2012). Hormones, context, and "Brain Gender": A review of evidence from congenital adrenal hyperplasia. *Social Science & Medicine, 74,* 1738–1744.

Joseph, D. L., Jin, J., Newman, D. A., & O'Boyle, E. H. (2015). Why does self-reported emotional intelligence predict job performance? A meta-analytic investigation of mixed EI. *Journal of Applied Psychology, 100,* 298–342.

Joseph, N. T., Matthews, K. A., & Myers, H. F. (2014). Conceptualizing health consequences of Hurricane Katrina from the perspective of socioeconomic status decline. *Health Psychology, 33,* 139–146.

Jouvet, M. (1979). What does a cat dream about? *Trends in Neurosciences, 2,* 280–282.

Joy, E., Kussman, A., & Nattiv, A. (2016). 2016 Update on eating disorders in athletes: A comprehensive narrative review with a focus on clinical assessment and management. *British Journal of Sports Medicine, 50,* 154–162.

Juberg, D. R., Alfano, K., Coughlin, R. J., & Thompson, K. M. (2001). An observational study of object mouthing behavior by young children. *Pediatrics, 107,* 135–142.

Judge, T. A., Piccolo, R. F., Podsakoff, N. P., Shaw, J. C., & Rich, B. L. (2010). The relationship between pay and job satisfaction: A meta-analysis of the literature. *Journal of Vocational Behavior, 77,* 157–167.

Julien, R. M., Advokat, C. D., & Comaty, J. E. (2014). *A primer of drug action* (13th ed.). New York, NY: Worth.

Junco, R. (2015). Student class standing, Facebook use, and academic performance. *Journal of Applied Developmental Psychology, 36,* 18–29.

Junco, R., & Cotten, S. R. (2012). No A 4 U: The relationship between multitasking and academic performance. *Computers and Education, 59,* 505–514.

Jung, C. G. (1969). *Collected works: Vol. 8. The structure and dynamics of the psyche* (R. F. C. Hull, Ed., 2nd ed.). Princeton, NJ: Princeton University Press.

Jussim, L., & Harber, K. D. (2005). Teacher expectations and self-fulfilling prophecies: Knowns and unknowns, resolved and unresolved controversies. *Personality and Social Psychology Review, 9,* 131–155.

Juul, A., Main, K. M., & Skakkebaek, N. E. (2011). Disorders of sex development—the tip of the iceberg? *Nature, 7,* 504–505.

Kaczmarek, M. (2015). On the doorstep to senility: Physical changes, health status and well-being in midlife. *Anthropological Review, 78,* 269–287.

Kadohisa, M. (2013). Effects of odor on emotion, with implications. *Frontiers in Systems Neuroscience, 7.* doi:10.3389/fnsys.2013.00066

Kaduvettoor-Davidson, A., & Inman, A. G. (2013). South Asian Americans: Perceived discrimination, stress, and well-being. *Asian American Journal of Psychology, 4,* 155–165. doi:10.1037/a0030634

Kafka, M. P. (2009). The *DSM* diagnostic criteria for paraphilia not otherwise specified. *Archives of Sexual Behavior, 39,* 373–376.

Kagan, J. (1985). The human infant. In A. M. Rogers & C. J. Scheirer (Eds.), *The G. Stanley Hall Lecture Series: Vol. 5* (pp. 55–86). Washington, DC: American Psychological Association.

Kagan, J. (2003). Biology, context, and developmental inquiry. *Annual Review of Psychology, 54,* 1–23.

Kagan, J. (2016). An overly permissive extension. *Perspectives on Psychological Science, 11,* 442–450.

Kagan, J., & Snidman, N. (1991). Temperamental factors in human development. *American Psychologist, 46,* 856–862.

Kahlenberg, S. G., & Hein, M. M. (2010). Progression on Nickelodeon? Gender-role stereotypes in toy commercials. *Sex Roles, 62,* 830–847.

Kahn, J. (2012, January). Born to run back. *Runner's World,* Retrieved from http://rw.runnersworld.com/selects/born-to-run-back.html

Kahneman, D., & Tversky, A. (1973). On the psychology of prediction. *Psychological Review, 80,* 238–251.

Kahneman, D., & Tversky, A. (1984). Choices, values, and frames. *American Psychologist, 39,* 341–350.

Kahneman, D., & Tversky, A. (1996). On the reality of cognitive illusions. *Psychological Review, 103,* 582–591.

Kaiser, D. (2015, January 9). Why you should care that *Selma* gets LBJ wrong. *TIME Magazine.* Retrieved from http://time.com/3658593/selma-lbj-history/

Kalant, H. (2015). Cannabis in the treatment of rheumatic diseases: Suggestions for a reasoned approach. *The Journal of Rheumatology, 42*(2), 146–148.

Kambeitz, J. P., & Howes, O. D. (2015). The serotonin transporter in depression: Meta-analysis of in vivo and post mortem findings and implications for understanding and treating depression. *Journal of Affective Disorders, 186,* 358–366.

Kamilar-Britt, P., & Bedi, G. (2015). The prosocial effects of 3, 4-methylenedioxymethamphetamine (MDMA): Controlled studies in humans and laboratory animals. *Neuroscience & Biobehavioral Reviews, 57,* 433–446.

Kamimori, G. H., McLellan, T. M., Tate, C. M., Voss, D. M., Niro, P., & Lieberman, H. R. (2015). Caffeine improves reaction time, vigilance and logical reasoning during extended periods with restricted opportunities for sleep. *Psychopharmacology, 232*(12), 2031–2042.

Kaminski, J., Call, J., & Fischer, J. (2004). Word learning in a domestic dog: Evidence for "fast mapping." *Science, 304,* 1682–1683.

Kanai, R., Bahrami, B., Roylance, R., & Rees, G. (2012). Online social network size is reflected in human brain structure. *Proceedings of the Royal Society B, 279,* 1327–1334.

Kandel, E. R. (2009). The biology of memory: A forty-year perspective. *Journal of Neuroscience, 29,* 12748–12756.

Kandel, E. R., & Pittenger, C. (1999). The past, the future and the biology of memory storage. *Philosophical Transactions: Biological Sciences, 354,* 2027–2052.

Kandler, C., Bleidorn, W., & Riemann, R. (2012). Left or right? Sources of political orientation: The roles of genetic factors, cultural transmission, assortative mating, and personality. *Journal of Personality and Social Psychology, 102,* 633–645.

Kandler, C., Bleidorn, W., Riemann, R., Spinath, F. M., Thiel, W., & Angleitner, A. (2010). Sources of cumulative continuity in personality: A longitudinal multiple-rater twin study. *Journal of Personality and Social Psychology, 98,* 995–1008.

Kandler, C., Kornadt, A. E., Hagemeyer, B., & Neyer, F. J. (2015). Patterns and sources of personality development in old age. *Journal of Personality and Social Psychology, 109,* 175–191.

Kaneda, H., Maeshima, K., Goto, N., Kobayakawa, T., Ayabe-Kanamura, S., & Saito, S. (2000). Decline in taste and odor discrimination abilities with age, and relationship between gustation and olfaction. *Chemical Senses, 25,* 331–337.

Kantor, J. (2014, October 10). Malala Yousafzai, youngest Nobel Peace Prize winner, adds to her achievements and expectations. *The New York Times.* Retrieved from http://www.nytimes.com/2014/10/11/world/asia/malala-yousafzai-youngest-nobel-peace-prize-winner-adds-to-her-achievements-and-expectations.html

Kanwisher, N., McDermott, J., & Chun, M. M. (1997). The fusiform face area: A module in human extrastriate cortex specialized for face perception. *Journal of Neuroscience, 17,* 4302–4311.

Kapler, I. V., Weston, T., & Wiseheart, M. (2015). Spacing in a simulated undergraduate classroom: Long-term benefits for factual and higher-level learning. *Learning and Instruction, 36,* 38–45.

Kaptchuk, T. J., & Miller, F. G. (2015). Placebo effects in medicine. *New England Journal of Medicine, 373*(1), 8–9.

Karanicolas, P. J., Graham, D., Gönen, M., Strong, V. E., Brennan, M. F., & Coit, D. G. (2013). Quality of life after gastrectomy for adenocarcinoma: A prospective cohort study. *Annals of Surgery, 257,* 1039–1046.

Karlen, S. J., Kahn, D. M., & Krubitzer, L. (2006). Early blindness results in abnormal cortico-cortical and thalamocortical connections. *Neuroscience, 142,* 843–858.

Karpinski, A. C., Kirschner, P. A., Ozer, I., Mellott, J. A., & Ochwo, P. (2013). An exploration of social networking site use, multitasking, and academic performance among United States and European university students. *Computers in Human Behavior, 29,* 1182–1192.

Karremans, J. C., Stroebe, W., & Claus, J. (2006). Beyond Vicary's fantasies: The impact of subliminal priming and brand choice. *Journal of Experimental Social Psychology, 42,* 792–798.

Karwowski, M., & Lebuda, I. (2016). The Big Five, the Huge Two, and creative self-beliefs: A meta-analysis. *Psychology of Aesthetics, Creativity, and the Arts, 10,* 214–232.

Kasparson, A. A., Badridze, J., & Maximov, V. V. (2013). Colour cues proved to be more informative for dogs than brightness. *Proceedings of the Royal Society of London B: Biological Sciences, 280.* doi:10.1098/rspb.2013.1356

Kassin, S., Fein, S., & Markus, H. R. (2017). *Social psychology* (10th ed.). Boston, MA: Cengage Learning.

Kastenbaum, R., & Costa, P. T. Jr. (1977). Psychological perspectives on death. *Annual Review of Psychology, 28,* 225–249.

Katotomichelakis, M., Balatsouras, D., Tripsianis, G., Davris, S., Maroudias, N., Danielides, V., & Simopoulos, C. (2007). The effect of smoking on the olfactory function. *Rhinology, 45,* 273–280.

Katz, E. S., Mitchell, R. B., & D'Ambrosio, C. M. (2012). Obstructive sleep apnea in infants. *American Journal of Respiratory and Critical Care Medicine, 185,* 805–816.

Kaufman, M. T. (2007, July 25). Albert Ellis, 93, influential psychotherapist, dies. *The New York Times.* Retrieved from http://www.nytimes.com/2007/07/25/nyregion/25ellis.html—pagewanted=all&_r=0

Kauten, R. L., Lui, J. H., Stary, A. K., & Barry, C. T. (2015). "Purging my friends list. Good luck making the cut": Perceptions of narcissism on Facebook. *Computers in Human Behavior, 51,* 244–254.

Kavšek, M., & Granrud, C. E. (2012). Children's and adults' size estimates at near and far distances: A test of the perceptual learning theory of size constancy development. *i-Perception, 3*(7), 459–466.

Kawa, S., & Giordano, J. (2012). A brief historicity of the *Diagnostic and Statistical Manual of Mental Disorders:* Issues and implications for the future of psychiatric canon and practice. *Philosophy, Ethics, and Humanities in Medicine, 7.* doi:10.1186/1747-5341-7-2

Kay, L. M., & Sherman, S. M. (2007). An argument for an olfactory thalamus. *Trends in Neurosciences, 30,* 47–53.

Kazdin, A. E. (1982). The token economy: A decade later. *Journal of Applied Behavior Analysis, 15,* 431–445.

Keefe, P. R. (2012, July 13). The uncannily accurate depiction of the meth trade in "Breaking Bad." *The New Yorker.* Retrieved from http://www.newyorker.com/culture/culture-desk/the-uncannily-accurate-depiction-of-the-meth-trade-in-breaking-bad

Keel, P. K., & Klump, K. L. (2003). Are eating disorders culture-bound syndromes? Implications for conceptualizing their etiology. *Psychological Bulletin, 129,* 747–769.

Keesey, R. E., & Hirvonen, M. D. (1997). Body weight set-points: Determination and adjustment. *The Journal of Nutrition, 127,* 1875S–1883S.

Keirstead, H. S., Nistor, G., Bernal, G., Totoiu, M., Cloutier, F., Sharp, K., & Oswald, S. (2005). Human embryonic stem cell-derived oligodendrocyte progenitor cell transplants remyelinate and restore locomotion after spinal cord injury. *Journal of Neuroscience, 25,* 4694–4705.

Keith, S. E., Michaud, D. S., & Chiu, V. (2008). Evaluating the maximum playback sound levels from portable digital audio players. *Journal of the Acoustical Society of America, 123,* 4227–4237.

Keller, A., & Malaspina, D. (2013). Hidden consequences of olfactory dysfunction: A patient report series. *BMC Ear, Nose and Throat Disorders, 13*(8). doi:10.1186/1472-6815-13-8

Kelley, M. R., Neath, I., & Surprenant, A. M. (2015). Serial position functions in general knowledge. *Journal of Experimental Psychology: Learning, Memory, and Cognition, 41,* 1715–1727.

Kellner, C. H., Knapp, R. G., Petrides, G., Rummans, T. A., Husain, M. M., Rasmussen, K., … Fink, M. (2006). Continuation electroconvulsive therapy vs. pharmacotherapy for relapse prevention in major depression: A multisite study from the Consortium for Research Electroconvulsive Therapy (CORE). *Archives of General Psychiatry, 63,* 1337–1344.

Kelly, M. L., Peters, R. A., Tisdale, R. K., & Lesku, J. A. (2015). Unihemispheric sleep in crocodilians? *Journal of Experimental Biology, 218,* 3175–3178.

Kemeny, M. E., & Shestyuk, A. (2008). Emotions, the neuroendocrine and immune systems, and health. In M. Lewis, J. M. Haviland-Jones, & L. F. Barrett (Eds.), *Handbook of emotions* (3rd ed., pp. 661–675). New York, NY: Guilford Press.

Kempton, M. J., Salvador, Z., Munafò, M. R., Geddes, J. R., Simmons, A., Frangou, S., & Williams, S. C. R. (2011). Structural neuroimaging studies in major depressive disorder. *Archives of General Psychiatry, 68,* 675–690.

Kendall, A. E. (2012). U.S. response to the global threat of HIV/AIDS: Basic facts. *Congressional Research Service,* 1–13.

Kennedy, M., Kreppner, J., Knights, N., Kumsta, R., Maughan, B., Golm, D., … Sonuga-Barke, E. J. (2016). Early severe institutional deprivation is associated with a persistent variant of adult attention-deficit/hyperactivity disorder: Clinical presentation, developmental continuities and life circumstances in the English and Romanian adoptees study. *Journal of Child Psychology and Psychiatry. 57,* 1113–1125.

Kennedy, N., Boydell, J., Kalidindi, S., Fearon, P., Jones, P. B., van Os, J., & Murray, R. M. (2005). Gender differences in incidence and age at onset of mania and bipolar disorder over a 35-year period in Camberwell, England. *American Journal of Psychiatry, 162,* 257–262.

Kennedy, P. G. E., & Chaudhuri, A. (2002). Herpes simplex encephalitis. *Journal of Neurology, Neurosurgery & Psychiatry, 13,* 237–238.

Kennedy, S. H., Giacobbe, P., Rizvi, S. J., Placenza, F. M., Nishikawa, Y., Mayberg, H. S., & Lozano, A. M. (2011). Deep brain stimulation for treatment-resistant depression: Follow-up after 3 to 6 years. *American Journal of Psychiatry, 168,* 502–510.

Kerr, N. L., & Tindale, R. S. (2004). Group performance and decision making. *Annual Review of Psychology, 55,* 623–655.

Kersten, A. W., Meissner, C. A., Lechuga, J., Schwartz, B. L., Albrechtsen, J. S., & Iglesias, A. (2010). English speakers attend more strongly than Spanish speakers to manner of motion when classifying novel objects and events. *Journal of Experimental Psychology: General, 139,* 638–653.

Kessler, R. C. (2010). The prevalence of mental illness. In T. L. Scheid & T. N. Brown (Eds.), *A handbook for the study of mental health: Social contexts, theories, and systems* (2nd ed., pp. 46–63). Cambridge, UK: Cambridge University Press.

Kessler, R. C., Berglund, P. A., Coulouvrat, C., Fitzgerald, T., Hajak, G., Roth, T., … Walsh, J. K. (2012). Insomnia, comorbidity, and risk of injury among insured Americans: Results from the America Insomnia Survey. *SLEEP, 35,* 825–834.

Kessler, R. C., Berglund, P., Demler, O., Jin, R., Koretz, D., Merikangas, K. R., … Wang, P. S. (2003). The epidemiology of major depressive disorder: Results from the National Comorbidity Survey Replication (NCS-R). *Journal of the American Medical Association, 289,* 3095–3105.

Kessler, R. C., Berglund, P., Delmer, O., Jin, R., Merikangas, K. R., & Walters, E. E. (2005). Lifetime prevalence and age-of-onset distributions of *DSM-IV* disorders in the National Comorbidity Survey Replication. *Archives of General Psychiatry, 62,* 593–602.

Kessler, R. C., Chiu, W. T., Demler, O., & Walters, E. E. (2005). Prevalence, severity, and comorbidity of 12-month *DSM-IV* disorders in the National Comorbidity Survey Replication. *Archives of General Psychiatry, 62,* 617–627.

Kessler, R. C., Petukhova, M., Sampson, N. A., Zaslavsky, A. M., & Wittchen, H. U. (2012). Twelve-month and lifetime prevalence and lifetime morbid risk of anxiety and mood disorders in the United States. *International Journal of Methods in Psychiatric Research, 21,* 169–184.

Kessler, R. C., & Wang, P. S. (2008). The descriptive epidemiology of commonly occurring mental disorders in the United States. *Annual Review of Public Health, 29,* 115–129.

Key, M. S., Edlund, J. E., Sagarin, B. J., & Bizer, G. Y. (2009). Individual differences in susceptibility to mindlessness. *Personality and Individual Differences, 46,* 261–264.

Keys, T. E. (1945). *The history of surgical anesthesia.* New York, NY: Schuman's.

Khan, A., & Brown, W. A. (2015). Antidepressants versus placebo in major depression: An overview. *World Psychiatry, 14,* 294–300.

Khan, N. A., & Hillman, C. H. (2014). The relation of childhood physical activity and aerobic fitness to brain function and cognition: A review. *Pediatric Exercise Science, 26,* 138–146.

Khanna, S., Briggs, Z., & Rink, C. (2015). Inducible glutamate oxaloacetate transaminase as a therapeutic target against ischemic stroke. *Antioxidants & Redox Signaling, 22*(2), 175–186.

Kidd, S. A., Eskenazi, B., & Wyrobek, A. J. (2001). Effects of male age on semen quality and fertility: A review of the literature. *Fertility and Sterility, 75,* 237–248.

Kihlstrom, J. F. (1985). Hypnosis. *Annual Review of Psychology, 36,* 385–418.

Kihlstrom, J. F. (2014). Hypnosis and cognition. *Psychology of Consciousness: Theory, Research, and Practice, 1,* 139–152.

Kilmartin, C. T., & Dervin, D. (1997). Inaccurate representation of the Electra complex in psychology textbooks. *Teaching of Psychology, 24,* 269–270.

Kim, P., Strathearn, L., & Swain, J. E. (2016). The maternal brain and its plasticity in humans. *Hormones and Behavior, 77,* 113–123.

King, B. M. (2006). The rise, fall, and resurrection of the ventromedial hypothalamus in the regulation of feeding behavior and body weight [Invited review]. *Physiology & Behavior, 87,* 221–244.

King, C., & Laurent, O. (2016, February 6). Meet the photographer who found how to balance a life of love and war. *TIME Magazine.* Retrieved from http://time.com/3699030/lynsey-addario-war-photographer/

King, R. D., George, A. T., Jeon, T., Hynan, L. S, Youn, T. S., Kennedy, D. N., & Dickerson, B. (2009). Characterization of atrophic changes in the cerebral cortex using fractal dimensional analysis. *Brain Imaging and Behavior, 3*(2), 154–166.

Kingsbury, M. K., & Coplan, R. J. (2012). Mothers' gender-role attitudes and their responses to young children's hypothetical display of shy and aggressive behaviors. *Sex Roles, 66,* 506–517.

Kinsella, E. L., Ritchie, T. D., & Igou, E. R. (2015). Zeroing in on heroes: A prototype analysis of hero features. *Journal of Personality and Social Psychology, 108,* 114–127.

Kinsey, A. C., Pomeroy, W. B., & Martin, C. E. (1948). *Sexual behavior in the human male.* Philadelphia, PA: W. B. Saunders.

Kinsey, A. C., Pomeroy, W. B., Martin, C. E., & Gebhard, P. H. (1953). *Sexual behavior in the human female.* Philadelphia, PA: W. B. Saunders.

Kirk, M. (Interviewer) & Carson, H. (Interviewee). (2013, September 4). Harry Carson [Interview transcript]. Retrieved from PBS *Frontline* website: http://www.pbs.org/wgbh/pages/frontline/sports/league-of-denial/the-frontline-interview-harry-carson/#seg10

Kirk, M. (Producer & Director), Gilmore, J. (Producer), & Wiser, M. (Producer). (2013). *League of Denial: The NFL's Concussion Crisis* [Documentary movie]. Boston, MA: WGBH. Retrieved from http://www.pbs.org/wgbh/frontline/film/league-of-denial/

Kirschner, M., Aleman, A., & Kaiser, S. (2016). Secondary negative symptoms—A review of mechanisms, assessment and treatment. *Schizophrenia Research.* doi: http://dx.doi.org/10.1016/j.schres.2016.05.003

Kisilevsky, B. S., Hains, S. M. J., Lee, K., Xie, X., Huang, H., Ye, H. H., … Wang, Z. (2003). Effects of experience on fetal voice recognition. *Psychological Science, 14,* 220–224.

Kite, M. E., & Bryant-Lees, K. B. (2016). Historical and contemporary attitudes toward homosexuality. *Teaching of Psychology, 43,* 164–170.

Klass, P. (2011, October 10). Hearing bilingual: How babies sort out language. *The New York Times.* Retrieved from http://www.nytimes.com/2011/10/11/health/views/11klass.html?_r=1

Klaver, C. C., Wolfs, R. C., Vingerling, J. R., Hoffman, A., & de Jong, P. T. (1998). Age-specific prevalence and causes of blindness and visual impairment in an older population: The Rotterdam Study. *Archives Opthamology, 116,* 653–658.

Kleber, H. D., & DuPont, R. (2012). Physicians and medical marijuana. *American Journal of Psychiatry, 169,* 564–568.

Klein, S. (2014, November 6). 8 Celebrities with sleep problems. *The Huffington Post.* Retrieved from http://www.huffingtonpost.com/2014/11/06/celebrity-sleep-problems_n_1322186.html

Kleinman, A. (2004). Culture and depression. *New England Journal of Medicine, 351,* 951–953.

Klepper, D. (2016, July 19). Lawsuits: VW employees tried to cover up emissions cheating. *Salon.* Retrieved from http://www.salon.com/2016/07/20/lawsuits_vw_employees_tried_to_cover_up_emissions_cheating/

Klettke, B., Hallford, D., & Mellor, D. J. (2014). Sexting prevalence and correlates: A systematic literature review. *Clinical Psychology Review, 34,* 44–53.

Klimstra, T. A., Luyckx, K., Hale III, W. W., Frijns, T., van Lier, P. A. C., & Meeus, W. H. J. (2010). Short-term fluctuations in identity: Introducing a micro-level approach to identity formation. *Journal of Personality and Social Psychology, 99,* 191–202.

Klugman, A., & Gruzelier, J. (2003). Chronic cognitive impairment in users of "Ecstasy" and cannabis. *World Psychiatry, 2,* 184–190.

Kluver, H., & Bucy, P. (1939). Preliminary analysis of function of the temporal lobe in monkeys. *Archives of Neurology, 42,* 979–1000.

Knafo, A. (2014, September/October). Are people inclined to act cooperatively or selfishly? Is such behavior genetic? *Scientific American Mind, 25,* 78.

Knafo, A., & Israel, S. (2010). Genetic and environmental influences on prosocial behavior. In M. Mikulincer & P. R. Shaver (Eds.), *Prosocial motives, emotions, and behavior: The better angels of our nature* (pp. 149–167). Washington, DC: American Psychological Association.

Knapp, S., & VandeCreek, L. (2000). Recovered memories of childhood abuse: Is there an underlying professional consensus? *Professional Psychology: Research and Practice, 31,* 365–371.

Knecht, S., Dräger, B., Deppe, M., Bobe, L., Lohmann, H., Flöel, A., … Henningsen, H. (2000). Handedness and hemispheric language dominance in healthy humans. *Brain, 123,* 74–81.

Knettel, B. A. (2016). Exploring diverse mental illness attributions in a multi-national sample: A mixed-methods survey of scholars in international psychology. *International Perspectives in Psychology: Research, Practice, Consultation, 5,* 128–140.

Knorr, A. C., Tull, M. T., Anestis, M. D., Dixon-Gordon, K. L., Bennett, M. F., & Gratz, K. L. (2016). The interactive effect of major depression and nonsuicidal self-injury on current suicide risk and lifetime suicide attempts. *Archives of Suicide Research, 20,* 539–552.

Knudsen, E. I. (2004). Sensitive periods in the development of the brain and behavior. *Journal of Cognitive Neuroscience, 16,* 1412–1425.

Ko, H. J., & Youn, C. H. (2011). Effects of laughter therapy on depression, cognition and sleep among the community-dwelling elderly. *Geriatrics & Gerontology International, 3,* 267–274.

Ko, K. H. (2015). Brain reorganization allowed for the development of human language: Lunate sulcus. *International Journal of Biology, 7,* 55–65.

Kobasa, S. C. (1979). Stressful life events, personality, and health: An inquiry into hardiness. *Journal of Personality and Social Psychology, 37,* 1–11.

Koch, C. (2016, January 1). Does size matter—for brains? *Scientific American.* Retrieved from http://www.scientificamerican.com/article/does-size-matter-mdash-for-brains/

Koch, I., Lawo, V., Fels, J., & Vorländer, M. (2011). Switching in the cocktail party: Exploring intentional control of auditory selective attention. *Journal of Experimental Psychology: Human Perception and Performance, 37,* 1140–1147.

Kochanek, K. D., Xu, J., Murphy, S. L., Miniño, A. M., & Kung., H.-C. (2011). *Deaths: Final data for 2009* (National Vital Statistics Reports, Vol. 60, No. 3). Hyattsville, MD: National Center for Health Statistics. Retrieved from http://www.cdc.gov/nchs/data/nvsr/nvsr59/nvsr59_04.pdf

Kochanska, G., Kim, S., & Boldt, L. J. (2015). (Positive) power to the child: The role of children's willing stance toward parents in developmental cascades from toddler age to early preadolescence. *Development and Psychopathology, 27,* 987–1005.

Koenig, B. A., & Gates-Williams, J. (1995). Understanding cultural difference in caring for dying patients. *Western Journal of Medicine, 163,* 244–249.

Kogan, S. M., Cho, J., Simons, L. G., Allen, K. A., Beach, S. R., Simons, R. L., & Gibbons, F. X. (2015). Pubertal timing and sexual risk behaviors among rural African American male youth: Testing a model based on life history theory. *Archives of Sexual Behavior, 44,* 609–618.

Kohl, S., Jägle, H., & Wissinger, B. (2013) Achromatopsia. In R. A. Pagon, M. P. Adam, H. H. Ardinger, T. D. Bird, C. R. Dolan, C. T. Fong, … B. Wissinger (Eds.), *GeneReviews* [Internet]. Seattle, WA: University of Washington. Retrieved from http://www.ncbi.nlm.nih.gov/books/NBK1418/

Kohlberg, L. (1981). *The philosophy of moral development: Vol. 1. Essays on moral development.* San Francisco, CA: Harper & Row.

Kohlberg, L., & Hersh, R. H. (1977). Moral development: A review of the theory. *Theory into Practice, 16,* 53–59.

Kohler, P. K., Manhart, L. E., & Lafferty, W. E. (2008). Abstinence-only and comprehensive sex education in the initiation of sexual activity and teen pregnancy. *Journal of Adolescent Health, 42,* 344–351.

Köhler, W. (1925). *The mentality of apes.* New York, NY: Harcourt Brace Jovanovich.

Kolb, B., & Gibb, R. (2011). Brain plasticity and behaviour in the developing brain. *Journal of the Canadian Academy of Child and Adolescent Psychiatry, 20,* 265–276.

Kolb, B., & Gibb, R. (2015). Childhood poverty and brain development. *Human Development, 58,* 215–217.

Kolb, B., & Whishaw, I. P. (2015). *Fundamentals of human neuropsychology* (7th ed.). New York, NY: Worth.

Kolb, B., & Whishaw, I. Q. (1998). Brain plasticity and behavior. *Annual Review of Psychology, 49,* 43–64.

Kolb, B., Whishaw, I. Q., & G. C. Teskey (2016). *An introduction to brain and behavior* (5th ed.). New York, NY: Worth.

Kolmes, K. (2012). Social media in the future of professional psychology. *Professional Psychology: Research and Practice, 43,* 606–612.

Koltko-Rivera, M. E. (2006). Rediscovering the later version of Maslow's hierarchy of needs: Self-transcendence and opportunities for theory, research, and unification. *Review of General Psychology, 10,* 302–317.

Kong, C. W., Tong, L. Y., Lam, W. C., Chan, L. W., & To, W. W. K. (2016). Learning curve in determining fetal sex by first trimester ultrasound scan. *Journal of Medical Ultrasound, 24,* 54–59. http://dx.doi.org/10.1016/j.jmu.2015.12.002

Koopman, P., Sinclair, A., & Lovell-Badge, R. (2016). Of sex and determination: Marking 25 years of Randy, the sex-reversed mouse. *Development, 143,* 1633–1637.

Koopmann-Holm, B., & Matsumoto, D. (2011). Values and display rules for specific emotions. *Journal of Cross-Cultural Psychology, 42,* 355–371.

Koopmann-Holm, B., & Tsai, J. L. (2014). Focusing on the negative: Cultural differences in expressions of sympathy. *Journal of Personality and Social Psychology, 107,* 1092–1115.

Kornheiser, A. S. (1976). Adaptation to laterally displaced vision: A review. *Psychological Bulletin, 5,* 783–816.

Kosslyn, S. M. (1978). Measuring the visual angle of the mind's eye. *Cognitive Psychology, 10,* 356–389.

Kosslyn, S. M., Ball, T. M., & Reiser, B. J. (1978). Visual images preserve metric spatial information: Evidence from studies of image scanning. *Journal of Experimental Psychology: Human Perception and Performance, 4,* 47–60.

Kosslyn, S. M., Thompson, W. L., Costantini-Ferrando, M. F., Alpert, N. M., & Spiegel, D. (2000). Hypnotic visual illusion alters color processing in the brain. *American Journal of Psychiatry, 157,* 1279–1284.

Kossoff, E. H., Vining, E. P. G., Pillas, D. J., Pyzik, P. L., Avellino, A. M., Carson, B. S., & Freeman, J. M. (2003). Hemispherectomy for intractable unihemispheric epilepsy: Epilepsy vs. outcome. *Neurology, 61,* 887–890.

Kostora, N. (2012, May 16). 25 Craziest football terms and where they come from. *Bleacher Report.* Retrieved from http://bleacherreport.com/articles/1184750-25-craziest-football-terms-and-where-they-come-from

Kothadia, J. P., Chhabra, S., Marcus, A., May, M., Saraiya, B., & Jabbour, S. K. (2012). Anterior mediastinal mass in a young marijuana smoker: A rare case of small-cell lung cancer. *Case Reports in Medicine, 2012.* http://dx.doi.org/10.1155/2012/754231

Kouider, S., & Dehaene, S. (2007). Levels of processing during non-conscious perception: A critical review of visual masking. *Philosophical Transactions of the Royal Society B: Biological Sciences, 362,* 857–875.

Kounios, J., & Beeman, M. (2009). The Aha! moment: The cognitive neuroscience of insight. *Current Directions in Psychological Science, 18,* 210–216.

Kovács, A. M., & Mehler, J. (2009). Cognitive gains in 7-month-old bilingual infants. *Proceedings of the National Academy of Sciences, 106,* 6556–6560.

Kowalski, R. M., Giumetti, G. W., Schroeder, A. N., & Lattanner, M. R. (2014). Bullying in the digital age: A critical review and meta-analysis of cyberbullying research among youth. *Psychological Bulletin, 140,* 1073–1137.

Kozusznik, M. W., Rodríguez, I., & Peiró, J. M. (2015). Eustress and distress climates in teams: Patterns and outcomes. *International Journal of Stress Management, 22,* 1–23.

Kraft, D. (2012). Successful treatment of heavy smoker in one hour using split screen imagery, aversion, and suggestions to eliminate cravings. *Contemporary Hypnosis and Integrative Therapy, 29,* 175–188.

Kramer, A. F., Erickson, K. I., & Colcombe, S. J. (2006). Exercise, cognition, and the aging brain. *Journal of Applied Physiology, 101,* 1237–1242.

Krapohl, E., Rimfeld, K., Shakeshaft, N. G., Trzaskowski, M., McMillan, A., Pingault, J. B., … Plomin, R. (2014). The high heritability of educational achievement reflects many genetically influenced traits, not just intelligence. *Proceedings of the National Academy of Sciences, 111,* 15273–15278.

Krasnova, I. N., & Cadet, J. L. (2009). Methamphetamine toxicity and messengers of death. *Brain Research Reviews, 60,* 379–407.

Krebs, D. L., & Denton, K. (2005). Toward a more pragmatic approach to morality: A critical evaluation of Kohlberg's model. *Psychological Review, 112,* 629–649.

Krech, D., & Crutchfield, R. S. (1958). *Elements of psychology.* New York, NY: Alfred A. Knopf.

Kreiman, G., Koch, C., & Fried, I. (2000). Imagery neurons in the human brain. *Nature, 408,* 357–361.

Kremen, W. S., Panizzon, M. S., & Cannon, T. D. (2016). Genetics and neuropsychology: A merger whose time has come. *Neuropsychology, 30*(1), 1–5.

Krijn, M., Emmelkamp, P. M. G., Olafsson, R. P., & Biemond, R. (2004). Virtual reality exposure therapy of anxiety disorders: A review. *Clinical Psychology Review, 24,* 259–281.

Krikorian, R., Shidler, M. D., Nash, T. A., Kalt, W., Vinqvist-Tymchuk, M. R., Shukitt-Hale, B., & Joseph, J. A. (2010). Blueberry supplementation improves memory in older adults. *Journal of Agricultural and Food Chemistry, 58*(7), 3996–4000.

Kripke, D. F., Langer, R. D., & Kline, L. E. (2012). Hypnotics' association with mortality or cancer: A matched cohort study. *BMJ Open, 2.* doi:10.1136/bmjopen-2012-000850

Krizan, Z., & Windschitl, P. D. (2007). The influence of outcome desirability on optimism. *Psychological Bulletin, 133,* 95–121.

Krosnick, J. A., Betz, A. L., Jussim, L. J., & Lynn, A. R. (1992). Subliminal conditioning of attitudes. *Personality and Social Psychology Bulletin, 18,* 152–162.

Krueger, E. T., & Reckless, W. C. (1931). The theory of human motivation. In *Longmans' Social Science Series: Social psychology* (pp. 142–170). New York, NY: Longmans, Green and Co.

Kruger, J., Blanck, H. M., & Gillespie, C. (2006). Dietary and physical activity behaviors among adults successful at weight loss maintenance. *International Journal of Behavioral Nutrition and Physical Activity, 3,* 17–27.

Kübler-Ross, E. (2009). *On death and dying. What the dying have to teach doctors, nurses, clergy, and their own families* (40th Anniversary Ed.). London, UK: Routledge.

Kucharski, A. (1984). History of frontal lobotomy in the United States, 1935–1955. *Neurosurgery, 14,* 765–772.

Kuhl, P. K. (2015). Baby talk. *Scientific American, 313,* 64–69.

Kuhl, P. K., Conboy, B. T., Padden, D., Nelson, T., & Pruitt, J. (2005). Early speech perception and later language development: Implications for the "critical period." *Language Learning and Development, 1,* 237–264.

Kujawa, S. G., & Liberman, M. C. (2006). Acceleration of age-related hearing loss by early noise exposure: Evidence of a misspent youth. *Journal of Neuroscience, 26,* 2115–2123.

Kumsta, R., Marzi, S. J., Viana, J., Dempster, E. L., Crawford, B., Rutter, M., … Sonuga-Barke, E. J. S. (2016). Severe psychosocial deprivation in early childhood is associated with increased DNA methylation across a region spanning the transcription start site of CYP2E1. *Translational Psychiatry, 6,* e830. doi:10.1038/tp.2016.95

Kuo, Z. Y. (1921). Giving up instincts in psychology. *The Journal of Philosophy, 18,* 654–664.

Kuppens, S., Laurent, L., Heyvaert, M., & Onghena, P. (2013). Associations between parental psychological control and relational aggression in children and adolescents: A multilevel and sequential meta-analysis. *Developmental Psychology, 49,* 1697–1712.

Kwon, D. (2016, February 3). The hidden harm of antidepressants. *Scientific American.* Retrieved from http://www.scientificamerican.com/article/the-hidden-harm-of-antidepressants/

LaBerge, S. (2014). Lucid dreaming: Paradoxes of dreaming consciousness. In C. Etzel, S. J. Lynn, & S. Krippner (Eds.), *Dissociation, Trauma, Memory, and Hypnosis Series: Varieties of anomalous experience: Examining the scientific evidence* (2nd ed., pp. 145–173). Washington, DC: American Psychological Association.

Lackner, J. R. (2014). Motion sickness: More than nausea and vomiting. *Experimental Brain Research, 232,* 2493–2510.

Lacourse, E., Boivin, M., Brendgen, M., Petitclerc, A., Girard, A., Vitaro, F., … Tremblay, R. E. (2014). A longitudinal twin study of physical aggression during early childhood: Evidence for a developmentally dynamic genome. *Psychological Medicine, 44*(12), 2617–2627.

Ladouceur, C. D. (2012). Neural systems supporting cognitive-affective interactions in adolescence: The role of puberty and implications for affective disorders. *Frontiers in Integrative Neuroscience, 6.* http://dx.doi.org/10.3389/fnint.2012.00065

Laeng, B., & Falkenberg, L. (2007). Women's pupillary responses to sexually significant others during the hormonal cycle. *Hormones and Behavior, 52,* 520–530.

Laeng, B., Profeti, I., Sæther, L., Adolfsdottir, S., Lundervold, A. J., Vangberg, T., … Waterloo, K. (2010). Invisible expressions evoke core impressions. *Emotion, 10,* 573–586.

Lafer-Sousa, R., Hermann, K. L., & Conway, B. R. (2015). Striking individual differences in color perception uncovered by "the dress" photograph. *Current Biology, 25* (13), R545–R546.

Lahav, O., & Mioduser, D. (2008). Construction of cognitive maps of unknown spaces using a multi-sensory virtual environment for people who are blind. *Computers in Human Behavior, 24,* 1139–1155.

Laird, J. D., & Lacasse, K. (2014). Bodily influences on emotional feelings: Accumulating evidence and extensions of William James's theory of emotion. *Emotion Review, 6,* 27–34.

Lakens, D., Hilgard, J., & Staaks, J. (2016). On the reproducibility of meta-analyses: Six practical recommendations. *BMC Psychology, 4.* doi:10.1186/s40359-016-0126-3

Lakes, K., Lopez, S. R., & Garro, L. C. (2006). Cultural competence and psychotherapy: Applying anthropologically informed conceptions of culture. *Psychotherapy: Theory, Research, Practice, Training, 43,* 380–396.

Lambert, M. J., Hansen, N. B., & Finch, A. E. (2001). Patient-focused research: Using patient outcome data to enhance treatment effects. *Journal of Consulting and Clinical Psychology, 69,* 159–172.

Lanagan-Leitzel, L. K. (2012). Identification of critical events by lifeguards, instructors, and non-lifeguards. *International Journal of Aquatic Research and Education, 6,* 203–214.

Lanagan-Leitzel, L. K., Skow, E., & Moore, C. M. (2015). Great expectations: Perceptual challenges of visual surveillance in lifeguarding. *Applied Cognitive Psychology, 29,* 425–435.

Lando, H. A. (1976). On being sane in insane places: A supplemental report. *Professional Psychology, 7,* 47–52.

Landolt, H. P. (2015). Caffeine, the circadian clock, and sleep. *Science, 349*(6254), 1289.

Landrum, R. E. (2001). I'm getting my bachelor's degree in psychology—What can I do with it? *Eye on Psi Chi, 6,* 22–24.

Lange, C. G., & James, W. (1922). In K. Dunlap (Ed.), *Psychology Classics: A Series of Reprints and Translations: The emotions.* Baltimore, MD: Williams & Wilkins.

Langer, E., Blank, A., & Chanowitz, B. (1978). The mindlessness of ostensibly thoughtful action: The role of "placebic" information in interpersonal interaction. *Journal of Personality and Social Psychology, 36,* 635–642.

Langer, E. J., & Rodin, J. (1976). The effects of choice and enhanced personal responsibility for the aged: A field experiment in an institutional setting. *Journal of Personality and Social Psychology, 34,* 191–198.

Langlois, J. H., Kalakanis, L., Rubenstein, A. J., Larson, A., Hallam, M., & Smoot, M. (2000). Maxims or myths of beauty? A meta-analytic and theoretical review. *Psychological Bulletin, 126,* 390–423.

Långström, N., Rahman, Q., Carlström, E., & Lichtenstein, P. (2010). Genetic and environmental effects on same-sex sexual behavior: A population study of twins in Sweden. *Archives of Sexual Behavior, 39,* 75–80.

Lannin, D. G., & Scott, N. A. (2014, February). Best practices for an online world. *Monitor on Psychology, 45,* 56–61.

Lara, D. R. (2010). Caffeine, mental health, and psychiatric disorders. *Journal of Alzheimer's Disease, 20,* S239–S248.

Larsen, J. K., Krogh-Nielsen, L., & Brøsen, K. (2016). The monoamine oxidase inhibitor isocarboxazid is a relevant treatment option in treatment-resistant depression-experience-based strategies in Danish psychiatry. *Health Care: Current Reviews, 4.* doi:10.4172/2375-4273.1000168

Larsen, L., Hartmann, P., & Nyborg, H. (2008). The stability of general intelligence from early adulthood to middle-age. *Intelligence, 36,* 29–34.

Larsson, G., Berglund, A. K., & Ohlsson, A. (2016). Daily hassles, their antecedents and outcomes among professional first responders: A systematic literature review. *Scandinavian Journal of Psychology, 57,* 359–367.

Larsson, M., Finkel, D., & Pedersen, N. L. (2000). Odor identification: Influences of age, gender, cognition, and personality. *Journal of Gerontology: Psychological Sciences, 55,* P304–P310.

Larsson, M., & Willander, J. (2009). Autobiographical odor memory. *Annals of the New York Academy of Sciences, 1170,* 318–323.

Larzelere, R. E., & Baumrind, D. (2010). Are spanking injunctions scientifically supported? *Law and Contemporary Problems, 73,* 57–87.

Larzelere, R. E., Cox, R. B., & Swindle, T. M. (2015). Many replications do not causal inferences make: The need for critical replications to test competing explanations of nonrandomized studies. *Perspectives on Psychological Science, 10*(3), 380–389.

LaSalle, J. M. (2013). Epigenomic strategies at the interface of genetic and environmental risk factors for autism. *Journal of Human Genetics, 58,* 396–401.

Lashley, K. D. (1950). In search of the engram. *Symposia of the Society for Experimental Biology, 4,* 454–482.

Latané, B., & Darley, J. M. (1968). Group inhibition of bystander intervention in emergencies. *Journal of Personality and Social Psychology, 10,* 215–221.

Latané, B., Williams, K., & Harkins, S. (1979). Many hands make light the work: The causes and consequences of social loafing. *Journal of Personality and Social Psychology, 37,* 822–832.

Lauer, J. E., Udelson, H. B., Jeon, S. O., & Lourenco, S. F. (2015). An early sex difference in the relation between mental rotation and object preference. *Frontiers in Psychology, 6.* http://dx.doi.org/10.3389/fpsyg.2015.00553

Laumann, E. O., Gagnon, J. H., Michael, R. T., & Michaels, S. (1994). *The social organization of sexuality: Sexual practices in the United States.* Chicago, IL: University of Chicago Press.

Laumann, E. O., Paik, A., & Rosen, R. C. (1999). Sexual dysfunction in the United States: Prevalence and predictors. *JAMA, 281,* 537–544.

Lauriola, M., Panno, A., Levin, I. P., & Lejuez, C. W. (2014). Individual differences in risky decision making: A meta-analysis of sensation seeking and impulsivity with the Balloon Analogue Risk Task. *Journal of Behavioral Decision Making, 27,* 20–26.

Lavee, Y., & Ben-Ari, A. (2008). The association of daily hassles and uplifts with family and life satisfaction: Does cultural orientation make a difference? *American Journal of Community Psychology, 41,* 89–98.

Laventure, S., Fogel, S., Lungu, O., Albouy, G., Sévigny-Dupont, P., Vien, C., … Doyon, J. (2016). NREM2 and sleep spindles are instrumental to the consolidation of motor sequence memories. *PLOS Biology, 14.* http://dx.doi.org/10.1371/journal.pbio.1002429

Lawler-Row, K. A., & Elliott, J. (2009). The role of religious activity and spirituality in the health and well-being of older adults. *Journal of Health Psychology, 14,* 43–52.

Lazarus, R. S. (1984). On the primacy of cognition. *American Psychologist, 39,* 124–129.

Lazarus, R. S. (1991a). Cognition and motivation in emotion. *American Psychologist, 46,* 352–367.

Lazarus, R. S. (1991b). Progress on a cognitive-motivational-relational theory of emotion. *American Psychologist, 46,* 819–834.

Lazarus, R. S. (1993). From psychological stress to the emotions: A history of changing outlooks. *Annual Review of Psychology, 44,* 1–21.

Lazarus, R. S., & Folkman, S. (1984). *Stress, appraisal, and coping.* New York, NY: Springer.

Lazzouni, L., & Lepore, F. (2014). Compensatory plasticity: Time matters. *Frontiers in Human Neuroscience 8.* http://dx.doi.org/10.3389/fnhum.2014.00340

LeBeau, R. T., Glenn, D., Liao, B., Wittchen, H.-U., Beesdo-Baum, K., Ollendick, T., & Craske, M. G. (2010). Specific phobia: A review of *DSM-IV* specific phobia and preliminary recommendations for *DSM-V. Depression and Anxiety, 27,* 148–167.

LeDoux, J. (2012). Rethinking the emotional brain. *Neuron, 73,* 653–676.

LeDoux, J. E. (1996). *The emotional brain: The mysterious underpinnings of emotional life.* New York, NY: Simon & Schuster.

LeDoux, J. E. (2000). Emotion circuits in the brain. *Annual Review of Neuroscience, 23,* 155–184.

LeDoux, J. E. (2002). Emotion, memory and the brain. *Scientific American, 12,* 62–71.

Lee, B. K., Magnusson, C., Gardner, R. M., Blomström, Å., Newschaffer, C. J., Burstyn I., … Dalman, C. (2015). Maternal hospitalization with infection during pregnancy and risk of autism spectrum disorders. *Brain, Behavior, and Immunity, 44,* 100–105.

Lee, J. H., Chang, Y. S., Yoo, H. S., Ahn, S. Y., Seo, H. J., Choi, S. H., … Park, W. S. (2011). Swallowing dysfunction in very low birth weight infants with oral feeding desaturation. *World Journal of Pediatrics, 7,* 337–343.

Lee, J. H., O'Keefe, J. H., Bell, D., Hensrud, D. D., & Holick, M. F. (2008). Vitamin D deficiency: An important, common, and easily treatable cardiovascular risk factor? *Journal of the American College of Cardiology, 52,* 1949–1956.

Lee, K. W., Im, J. Y., Woo, J. M., Grosso, H., Kim, Y. S., Cristovao, A. C., … Mouradian, M. M. (2013). Neuroprotective and anti-inflammatory properties of a coffee component in the MPTP model of Parkinson's disease. *Neurotherapeutics, 10*(1), 143–153.

Lee, P. A., Houk, C. P., Ahmed, S. F., & Hughes, I. A. (2006) Consensus statement on management of intersex disorders. *Pediatrics, 118,* e488–e500.

Lee, S. J., Altschul, I., & Gershoff, E. T. (2013). Does warmth moderate longitudinal associations between maternal spanking and child aggression in early childhood? *Developmental Psychology, 49*(11), 2017–2028.

Lee, S. W. S., & Schwarz, N. (2014). Framing love: When it hurts to think we were made for each other. *Journal of Experimental Social Psychology, 54,* 61–67.

Lee, V. E., & Burkan, D. T. (2002). *Inequality at the starting gate.* Washington, DC: Economic Policy Institute.

Lee, W., Reeve, J., Xue, Y., & Xiong, J. (2012). Neural differences between intrinsic reasons for doing versus extrinsic reasons for doing: An fMRI study. *Neuroscience Research, 73,* 68–72.

Lehrner, J., Eckersberger, C., Walla, P., Pötsch, G., & Deecke, L. (2000). Ambient odor of orange in a dental office reduces anxiety and improves mood in female patients. *Physiology & Behavior, 71,* 83–86.

Leichsenring, F., Abbass, A., Gottdiener, W., Hilsenroth, M., Keefe, J. R., Luyten, P., … Steinert, C. (2016). Psychodynamic therapy: A well-defined concept with increasing evidence. *Evidence Based Mental Health, 19.* doi: 10.1136/eb-2016-102372.

Leichsenring, F., Luyten, P., Hilsenroth, M. J., Abbass, A., Barber, J. P., Keefe, J. R., … Steinert, C. (2015). Psychodynamic therapy meets evidence-based medicine: A systematic review using updated criteria. *The Lancet Psychiatry, 2,* 648–660.

Leichsenring, F., & Rabung, S. (2008). Effectiveness of long-term psychodynamic psychotherapy. *Journal of the American Medical Association, 300,* 1551–1565.

Leigh, K. (2014, August 1). Syria's mental health crisis [Web log post]. Retrieved from http://kristof.blogs.nytimes.com/2014/08/01/syrias-mental-health-crisis/

Leighty, K. A., Grand, A. P., Pittman Courte, V. L., Maloney, M. A., & Bettinger, T. L. (2013). Relational responding by eastern box turtles (Terrapene carolina) in a series of color discrimination tasks. *Journal of Comparative Psychology, 127,* 256–264. doi:10.1037/a0030942

Leininger, G. (2011). Lateral thinking about leptin: A review of leptin action via the lateral hypothalamus. *Physiology & Behavior, 104,* 572–581.

Lenaert, B., van de Ven, V., Kaas, A. L., & Vlaeyen, J. W. (2016). Generalization on the basis of prior experience is predicted by individual differences in working memory. *Behavior Therapy, 47*(1), 130–140.

Lenhart, A. (2015, April 9). Teens, social media & technology overview 2015. *Pew Research Center.* Retrieved from http://www.pewinternet.org/2015/04/09/teens-social-media-technology-2015/

Lenhart, A., Madden, M., Smith, A., Purcell, K., Zickuhr, K., & Rainie, L. (2011). *Teens, kindness and cruelty on social network sites.* Washington, DC: Pew Internet & American Life Project.

Lenzenweger, M. F., Lane, M. C., Loranger, A. W., & Kessler, R. C. (2007). *DSM-IV* personality disorders in the national comorbidity survey replication. *Biological Psychiatry, 62,* 553–564.

Leo, J. (1987, January 12). Behavior: Exploring the traits of twins. *TIME Magazine.* Retrieved from http://content.time.com/time/magazine/article/0,9171,963211,00.html

Leontopoulou, S., Jimerson, S. R., & Anderson, G. E. (2011). An international exploratory investigation of students' perceptions of stressful life events: Results from Greece, Cyprus, and the United States. *School Psychology International, 32,* 632–644.

LePort, A. K., Mattfeld, A. T., Dickinson-Anson, H., Fallon, J. H., Stark, C. E., Kruggel, F., … McGaugh, J. L. (2012). Behavioral and neuroanatomical investigation of highly superior autobiographical memory (HSAM). *Neurobiology of Learning and Memory, 98,* 78–92.

Lerman, C., & Audrain-McGovern, J. (2010). Reinforcing effects of smoking: More than a feeling. *Biological Psychiatry, 67,* 699–701.

Lerner, J. S., Li, Y., Valdesolo, P., & Kassam, K. S. (2015). Emotion and decision making: Online supplement. *Annual Review of Psychology, 66,* 799–823.

Lessmoellmann, A. (2006, October 4). Can we talk? *Scientific American Mind, 17,* 44–49.

Levänen, S., Uutela, K., Salenius, S., & Hari, R. (2001). Cortical representations of sign language: Comparison of deaf signers and hearing non-signers. *Cerebral Cortex, 11,* 506–512.

LeVay, S. (1991). A difference in hypothalamic structure between heterosexual and homosexual men. *Science, 253,* 1034–1037.

Levenson, R. W. (1992). Autonomic nervous system differences among emotions. *Psychological Science, 3,* 23–27.

Levenson, R. W., Carstensen, L. L., Friesen, W. V., & Ekman, P. (1991). Emotion, physiology, and expression in old age. *Psychology and Aging, 6,* 28–35.

Leventhal, H., Watts, J. C., & Pagano, F. (1967). Effects of fear and instructions on how to cope with danger. *Journal of Personality and Social Psychology, 6,* 313–321.

Levett-Jones, T., Sundin, D., Bagnall, M., Hague, K., Schuman, W., Taylor, C., & Wink, J. (2010). Learning to think like a nurse. *HNE Handover: For Nurses and Midwives, 3,* 15–20.

Levin, R. J. (2008). Critically revisiting aspects of the human sexual response cycle of Masters and Johnson: Correcting errors and suggesting modifications. *Sexual and Relationship Therapy, 23,* 393–399.

Levine, B. (2002, September 25). Redeeming Rover. *Los Angeles Times.* Retrieved from http://articles.latimes.com/2002/sep/25/news/lv-dogtherapy25

Levine, M. P., & Troiden, R. R. (1988). The myth of sexual compulsivity. *The Journal of Sex Research, 25,* 347–363.

Levinson, D. F. (2006). The genetics of depression: A review. *Biological Psychiatry, 60,* 84–92.

Levy, B. R., Pilver, C., Chung, P. H., & Slade, M. D. (2014). Subliminal strengthening: Improving older individuals' physical function over time with an implicit-age-stereotype intervention. *Psychological Science, 25,* 2127–2135.

Levy, R. A., & Ablon, S. J. (2010, February 23). Talk therapy: Off the couch and into the lab. *Scientific American.* Retrieved from http://www.scientificamerican.com/article/talk-therapy-off-couch-into-lab/

Levy, S. R., Hilsenroth, M. J., & Owen, J. J. (2015). Relationship between interpretation, alliance, and outcome in psychodynamic psychotherapy: Control of therapist effects and assessment of moderator variable impact. *The Journal of Nervous and Mental Disease, 203,* 418–424.

Lew, S. M. (2014). Hemispherectomy in the treatment of seizures: A review. *Translational Pediatrics, 3,* 208–217.

LeWine, H. (2014, May 2). Too little sleep, and too much, affect memory [Web log post]. Retrieved from http://www.health.harvard.edu/blog/little-sleep-much-affect-memory-201405027136

Lewis, D. (2014). Small mammals vanish in northern Australia. *Science, 345*(6201), 1109–1110.

Lewis, D. J., & Duncan, C. P. (1956). Effect of different percentages of money reward on extinction of a lever-pulling response. *Journal of Experimental Psychology, 52,* 23–27.

Lewis, T. (2016, August 11). 7 Things you didn't know about Uzo Aduba. *Essence.* Retrieved from http://www.essence.com/2016/08/11/uzo-aduba-essence-magazine-facts

Ley, J., Bennett, P., & Coleman, G. (2008). Personality dimensions that emerge in companion canines. *Applied Animal Behaviour Science, 110,* 305–317.

Li, A., Montaño, Z., Chen, V. J., & Gold, J. I. (2011). Virtual reality and pain management: Current trends and future directions. *Pain Management, 1,* 147–157.

Li, J. (2005). Mind or virtue: Western and Chinese beliefs about learning. *Current Directions in Psychological Science, 14,* 190–194.

Liberles, S. B. (2015). Mammalian pheromones. *Annual Review of Physiology, 76,* 151–175.

Liberman, M. C. (2015). Hidden hearing loss. *Scientific American, 313,* 48–53.

Lichtwarck-Aschoff, A., Kunnen, S. E., & van Geert, P. L. C. (2009). Here we go again: A dynamic systems perspective on emotional rigidity across parent-adolescent conflicts. *Developmental Psychology, 45,* 1364–1375.

Licis, A. K., Desruisseau, D. M., Yamada, K. A., Duntley, S. P., & Gurnett, C. A. (2011). Novel findings in an extended family pedigree with sleepwalking. *Neurology, 76,* 49–52.

Liddle, J. R., Shackelford, T. K., & Weekes-Shackelford, V. A. (2012). Why can't we all just get along? Evolutionary perspectives on violence, homicide, and war. *Review of General Psychology, 16,* 24–36.

Likhtik, E., Stujenske, J. M., Topiwala, M. A., Harris, A. Z., & Gordon, J. A. (2014). Prefrontal entrainment of amygdala activity signals safety in learned fear and innate anxiety. *Nature Neuroscience, 17*(1), 106–113.

Lilienfeld, S. O. (2012). Public skepticism of psychology: Why many people perceive the study of human behavior as unscientific. *American Psychologist, 67,* 111–129.

Lilienfeld, S. O., & Arkowitz, H. (2011, January/February). The insanity verdict on trial. *Scientific American Mind,* 64–65.

Lilienfeld, S. O., & Arkowitz, H. (2012, September 1). Are all psychotherapies created equal? *Scientific American.* Retrieved from http://www.scientificamerican.com/article/are-all-psychotherapies-created-equal/

Lilienfeld, S. O., Lynn, S. J., Ruscio, J., & Beyerstein, B. L. (2010). Busting big myths in popular psychology. *Scientific American Mind, 21,* 42–49.

Lilienfeld, S. O., Lynn, S. J., Ruscio, J., & Beyerstein, B. L. (2011). *50 Great myths of popular psychology: Shattering widespread misconceptions about human behavior.* Hoboken, NJ: Wiley-Blackwell.

Lilienfeld, S. O., Wood, J. M., & Garb, H. N. (2005). What's wrong with this picture? *Scientific American Mind, 16,* 50–57.

Lillard, A. S., Drell, M. B., Richey, E. M., Boguszewski, K., & Smith, E. D. (2015). Further examination of the immediate impact of television on children's executive function. *Developmental Psychology, 51,* 792–805. doi:10.1037/a0039097

Lillard, A. S., & Peterson, J. (2011). The immediate impact of different types of television on young children's executive function. *Pediatrics, 128,* 644–649.

Lim, J., & Dinges, D. F. (2010). A meta-analysis of the impact of short-term sleep deprivation on cognitive variables. *Psychological Bulletin, 136,* 375–389.

Lim, L., Radua, J., & Rubia, K. (2014). Gray matter abnormalities in childhood maltreatment: A voxel-wise meta-analysis. *American Journal of Psychiatry, 171*(8), 854–863.

Lin, Y. H., Chen, C. Y., Li, P., & Lin, S. H. (2013). A dimensional approach to the phantom vibration and ringing syndrome during medical internship. *Journal of Psychiatric Research, 47,* 1254–1258.

Lin, Y.-H., Lin, S.-H., Li, P., Huang, W.-L., & Chen, C.-Y. (2013). Prevalent hallucinations during medical internships: Phantom vibration and ringing syndromes. *PLOS ONE, 8,* e65152. http://dx.doi.org/10.1371/journal.pone.0065152

Lind, O., & Delhey, K. (2015). Visual modelling suggests a weak relationship between the evolution of ultraviolet vision and plumage coloration in birds. *Journal of Evolutionary Biology, 28,* 715–722.

Lindau, S. T., Schumm, L. P., Laumann, E. O., Levenson, W., O'Muircheartaigh, C. A., & Waite, L. J. (2007). A study of sexuality and health among older adults in the United States. *New England Journal of Medicine, 357,* 762–774.

Lindberg, S. M., Hyde, J. S., Petersen, J. L., & Linn, M. C. (2010). New trends in gender and mathematics performance: A meta-analysis. *Psychological Bulletin, 136,* 1123–1135.

Lindquist, K. A., Satpute, A. B., & Gendron, M. (2015). Does language do more than communicate emotion? *Current Directions in Psychological Science, 24,* 99–108.

Lineberry, T. W., & Bostwick, J. M. (2006). Methamphetamine abuse: A perfect storm of complications. *Mayo Clinic Proceedings, 81,* 77–84.

Linhares, J. M., Pinto, P. D., & Nascimento, S. M. (2008). The number of discernible colors in natural scenes. *Journal of the Optical Society of America, 25,* 2918–2924.

Linnenbrink, E. A., & Pintrich, P. R. (2002). Motivation as an enabler for academic success. *School Psychology Review, 31,* 313–327.

Linneroth, P. J., Mrdjenovich, A. J., & Moore, B. A. (2011). Professional burnout in clinical military psychologists: Recommendations before, during, and after deployment. *Professional Psychology: Research and Practice, 42,* 87–93.

Lisman, J. (2015). The challenge of understanding the brain: Where we stand in 2015. *Neuron, 86,* 864–882.

Littlewood, R. (2004). Commentary: Globalization, culture, body image, and eating disorders. *Culture, Medicine and Psychiatry, 28,* 597–602.

Liu, C. C., Kanekiyo, T., Xu, H., & Bu, G. (2013). Apolipoprotein E and Alzheimer disease: Risk, mechanisms and therapy. *Nature Reviews Neurology, 9,* 106–118.

Liu, K., Daviglus, M. L., Loria, C. M., Colangelo, L. A., Spring, B., Moller, A. C., & Lloyd-Jones, D. M. (2012). Healthy lifestyle through young adulthood and the presence of low cardiovascular disease risk profile in middle age: The coronary artery risk development in (young) adults (cardia) study. *Circulation, 125,* 996–1004.

Liu, R. T., Kleiman, E. M., Nestor, B. A., & Cheek, S. M. (2015). The hopelessness theory of depression: A quarter-century in review. *Clinical Psychology: Science and Practice, 22,* 345–365.

Liu, Y., Wheaton, A. G., Chapman, D. P., Cunningham, T. J., Lu, H., & Croft, J. B. (2016). Prevalence of healthy sleep duration among adults—United States, 2014. *Morbidity and Mortality Weekly Report* (MMWR), 65, 137–141.

Liu, Y., Yu, C., Liang, M., Li, J., Tian, L., Zhou, Y., … Jiang, T. (2007). Whole brain functional connectivity in the early blind. *Brain, 130,* 2085–2096.

Livingston, I., Doyle, J., & Mangan, D. (2010, April 25). Stabbed hero dies as more than 20 people stroll past him. *New York Post.* Retrieved from http://www.nypost.com/p/news/local/queens/passers_by_let_good_sam_die_5SGkf5XDP5ooudVuEd8fbI

Loftus, E., & Ketcham, K. (1994). *The myth of repressed memory.* New York, NY: St. Martin's Griffin.

Loftus, E. F. (1994). The repressed memory controversy. *American Psychologist, 49,* 443–445.

Loftus, E. F. (1997). Creating false memories. *Scientific American, 277,* 70–75.

Loftus, E. F. (2005). Planting misinformation in the human mind: A 30-year investigation of the malleability of memory. *Learning and Memory, 12,* 361–366.

Loftus, E. F., & Bernstein, D. M. (2005). Rich false memories. In A. F. Healy (Ed.), *Experimental cognitive psychology and its applications* (pp. 101–113). Washington, DC: American Psychological Association Press.

Loftus, E. F., Miller, D. G., & Burns, H. J. (1978). Semantic integration of verbal information into a visual memory. *Journal of Experimental Psychology: Human Learning and Memory, 4,* 19–31.

Loftus, E. F., & Palmer, J. C. (1974). Reconstruction of automobile destruction. *Journal of Verbal Learning and Verbal Behavior, 13,* 585–589.

Loftus, E. F., & Pickrell, J. E. (1995). The formation of false memories. *Psychiatric Annals, 25,* 720–725.

Lohr, J. (2015, September/October). Does napping really help cognitive function? *Scientific American Mind, 26,* 70.

Lois, C., & Kelsch, W. (2014). Adult neurogenesis and its promise as a hope for brain repair. *Frontiers in Neuroscience, 8.* http://dx.doi.org/10.3389/fnins.2014.00165

Looker, K. J., Garnett, G. P., & Schmid, G. P. (2008). An estimate of the global prevalence and incidence of herpes simplex virus type 2 infection. *Bulletin of the World Health Organization, 86*(10), 805–812.

Lopez, K. (2013, February 12). "Silver Linings" hits close to home for director Russell. *USA Today.* Retrieved from http://www.usatoday.com/story/news/nation/2013/02/08/silver-lining-playbook-mental-illness/1891065/

Lopez, R. (2012, March 18). "Dog Whisperer" Cesar Millan grooms his canine–training empire. *Los Angeles Times.* Retrieved from http://articles.latimes.com/2012/mar/18/business/la-fi-himi-millan-20120318

Lopez-Garcia, E., Rodriguez-Artalejo, F., Rexrode, K. M., Logroscino, G., Hu, F. B., & van Dam, R. M. (2009). Coffee consumption and risk of stroke in women. *Circulation, 119,* 1116–1123.

Lorang, M. R., McNiel, D. E., & Binder, R. L. (2016). Minors and sexting: Legal implications. *Journal of the American Academy of Psychiatry and the Law Online, 44,* 73–81.

Lorenz, K. Z. (1937). The companion in the bird's world. *Auk, 54,* 245–273.

Lott, A. J., & Lott, B. E. (1965). Group cohesiveness as interpersonal attraction: A review of relationships with antecedent and consequent variables. *Psychological Bulletin, 64,* 259–309.

Lou, S., & Zhang, G. (2009). What leads to romantic attractions: Similarity, reciprocity, security, or beauty? Evidence from a speed-dating study. *Journal of Personality, 77,* 933–964.

Louie, J. Y., Oh, B. J., & Lau, A. S. (2013). Cultural differences in the links between parental control and children's emotional expressivity. *Cultural Diversity and Ethnic Minority Psychology, 19,* 424–434.

Lourida, I., Soni, M., Thompson-Coon, J., Purandare, N., Lang, I. A., Ukoumunne, O. C., & Llewellyn, D. J. (2013). Mediterranean diet, cognitive function, and dementia: A systematic review. *Epidemiology, 24,* 479–489.

Lowenstein, J. A., Blank, H., & Sauer, J. D. (2010). Uniforms affect the accuracy of children's eyewitness identification and decisions. *Journal of Investigative Psychology and Offender Profiling, 7,* 59–73.

Lu, Z.-L., Williamson, S. J., & Kaufman, L. (1992). Behavioral lifetime of human auditory sensory memory predicted by physiological measures. *Science, 258,* 1668–1670.

Ludel, J. (1978). *Introduction to sensory processes.* San Francisco, CA: W. H. Freeman.

Luders, E., Gaser, C., Narr, K. L., & Toga, A. W. (2009). Why sex matters: Brain size independent differences in gray matter distributions between men and women. *The Journal of Neuroscience, 29*(45), 14265–14270.

Lukaszewski, A. W., Larson, C. M., Gildersleeve, K. A., Roney, J. R., & Haselton, M. G. (2014). Condition-dependent calibration of men's uncommitted mating orientation: Evidence from multiple samples. *Evolution and Human Behavior, 35,* 319–326.

Lund, C., De Silva, M., Plagerson, S., Cooper, S., Chisholm, D., Das, J., … Patel, V. (2011). Poverty and mental disorders: Breaking the cycle in low-income and middle-income countries. *Lancet, 78,* 1502–1514.

Lundin, R. W. (1963). Personality theory in behavioristic psychology. In J. M. Wepman, & R. W. Heine (Eds.), *Concepts of personality* (pp. 257–290). Hawthorne, NY: Aldine.

Luo, Y. H.-L., & da Cruz, L. (2014). A review and update on the current status of retinal prostheses (bionic eye). *British Medical Bulletin, 109,* 31–44.

Lupo, M., Troisi, E., Chiricozzi, F. R., Clausi, S., Molinari, M., & Leggio, M. (2015). Inability to process negative emotions in cerebellar damage: A functional transcranial Doppler sonographic study. *The Cerebellum, 14,* 663–669.

Luttrell, A., Petty, R. E., & Briñol, P. (2016). Ambivalence and certainty can interact to predict attitude stability over time. *Journal of Experimental Social Psychology, 63,* 56–68.

Luyster, F. S., Strollo Jr., P. J., Zee, P. C., & Walsh, J. K. (2012). Sleep: A health imperative. *SLEEP, 35,* 727–734.

Lyall, S. (2007, November 4). In Stetson or wig, he's hard to pin down. *The New York Times.* Retrieved from http://www.nytimes.com/2007/11/04/movies/moviesspecial/04lyal.html

Lyckholm, L. J. (2004). Thirty years later: An oncologist reflects on Kübler-Ross's work. *American Journal of Bioethics, 4,* 29–31.

Lynch, G. (2002). Memory enhancement: The search for mechanism-based drugs. *Nature Neuroscience, 5* (Suppl.), 1035–1038.

Lynch, K. (1960). *The image of the city.* Cambridge, MA: MIT Press.

Lynn, S. J., Lilienfeld, S. O., Merckelbach, H., Giesbrecht, T., McNally, R. J., Loftus, E. F., … Malaktaris, A. (2014). The trauma model of dissociation: Inconvenient truths and stubborn fictions: Comment on Dalenberg et al. (2012). *Psychological Bulletin, 140,* 896–910.

Lynn, S. J., Lilienfeld, S. O., Merckelbach, H., Giesbrecht, T., & van der Kloet, D. (2012). Dissociation and dissociative disorders: Challenging conventional wisdom. *Current Directions in Psychological Science, 21,* 48–53.

Lynn, S. J., Rhue, J. W., & Weekes, J. R. (1990). Hypnotic involuntariness: A social cognitive analysis. *Psychological Review, 97,* 169–184.

Lyubomirsky, S., Dickerhoof, R., Boehm, J. K., & Sheldon, K. M. (2011). Becoming happier takes both a will and a proper way: An experimental longitudinal intervention to boost well-being. *Emotion, 11,* 391–402.

Lyubomirsky, S., & Layous, K. (2013). How do simple positive activities increase well-being? *Current Directions in Psychological Science, 22,* 57–62.

Lyubomirsky, S., Sheldon, S. M., & Schkade, D. (2005). Pursuing happiness: The architecture of sustainable change. *Review of General Psychology, 9,* 111–131.

MacCann, C., Fogarty, G. J., Zeidner, M., & Roberts, R. D. (2011). Coping mediates the relationship between emotional intelligence (EI) and academic achievement. *Contemporary Educational Psychology, 36,* 60–70.

Maccoby, E. E., & Martin, J. A. (1983). Socialization in the context of the family: Parent–child interaction. In P. Mussen & E. M. Hetherington (Eds.), *Handbook of child psychology: Vol. IV. Socialization, personality and social development* (pp. 1–101). New York, NY: John Wiley & Sons.

Mack, A. (2003). Inattentional blindness: Looking without seeing. *Current Directions in Psychological Science, 12,* 180–184.

MacKenzie, M. J., Nicklas, E., Waldfogel, J., & Brooks-Gunn, J. (2013). Spanking and child development across the first decade of life. *Pediatrics, 132,* e1118–e1125.

Macknik, S. L., Martinez-Conde, S., & Conway, B. R. (2015). Unraveling "The Dress." *Scientific American Mind, 26,* 19–21.

MacLean, E. L., & Hare, B. (2015). Dogs hijack the human bonding pathway. *Science, 348*(6232), 280–281.

MacLeod, C. M., Jonker, T. R., & James, G. (2013). Individual differences in remembering. In T. J. Perfect & D. S. Lindsay (Eds.), *The SAGE handbook of applied memory* (pp. 385–403). Thousand Oaks, CA: SAGE.

Macmillan, M. (2000). Restoring Phineas Gage: A 150th retrospective. *Journal of the History of the Neurosciences, 9,* 46–66.

Madsen, K. M., Hviid, A., Vestergaard, M., Schendel, D., Wohlfahrt, J., Thorsen, P., … Melbye, M. (2002). A population-based study of measles, mumps, and rubella vaccination and autism. *New England Journal of Medicine, 347,* 1477–1482.

Maeda, Y., & Yoon, S. Y. (2013). A meta-analysis on gender differences in mental rotation ability measured by the Purdue spatial visualization tests: Visualization of rotations (PSVT: R). *Educational Psychology Review, 25*(1), 69–94.

Maeda, Y., & Yoon, S. Y. (2016). Are gender differences in spatial ability real or an artifact? Evaluation of measurement invariance on the revised PSVT: R. *Journal of Psychoeducational Assessment, 34,* 397–403.

Maguen, S., Metzler, T. J., McCaslin, S. E., Inslicht, S. S., Henn-Haase, C., Neylan, T. C., & Marmar, C. R. (2009). Routine work environment stress and PTSD symptoms in police officers. *Journal of Nervous and Mental Disease, 197,* 754–760.

Maguire, E . A ., Valentine, E . R ., Wilding, J. M., & Kapur, N. (2003). Routes to remembering: The brains behind superior memory. *Nature Neuroscience, 6,* 90–95.

Maguire, E. A., Woollett, K., & Spiers, H. J. (2006). London taxi drivers and bus drivers: A structural MRI and neuropsychological analysis. *Hippocampus, 16,* 1091–1101.

Mah, K., & Binik, Y. M. (2001). Do all orgasms feel alike? Evaluating a two-dimensional model of orgasm experience across gender and sexual context. *The Journal of Sex Research, 39,* 104–113.

Maher, C. A., Lewis, L. K., Ferrar, K., Marshall, S., De Bourdeaudhuij, I., & Vandelanotte, C. (2014). Are health behavior change interventions that use online social networks effective? A systematic review. *Journal of Medical Internet Research, 16,* e40. doi:10.2196/jmir.2952

Maher, W. B., & Maher, B. A. (2003). Abnormal psychology. In D. K. Freedheim (Ed.), *Handbook of psychology: History of psychology* (Vol. 1, pp. 303–336). New York, NY: John Wiley & Sons.

Maheu, M. M., Pulier, M. L., McMenamin, J. P., & Posen, L. (2012). Future of telepsychology, telehealth, and various technologies in psychological research and practice. *Professional Psychology: Research and Practice, 43,* 613–621.

Mahmood, N. (2010, March 31). Here's how easily a hacker can crack your weak passwords. *Tech Journal.* Retrieved from http://thetechjournal.com/electronics/computer/security-computer-electronics/heres-how-easily-a-hacker-can-crack-your-weak-passwords.xhtml#ixzz1F7chbAEr

Mahoney, J. (2010). Strategic communication and anti-smoking campaigns. *Public Communication Review, 1,* 33–48.

Mai, E., & Buysse, D. J. (2008). Insomnia: Prevalence, impact, pathogenesis, differential diagnosis, and evaluation. *Sleep Medicine Clinics, 3,* 167–174.

Maiden, B., & Perry, B. (2011). Dealing with free-riders in assessed group work: Results from a study at a UK university. *Assessment & Evaluation in Higher Education, 36,* 451–464.

Majid, A. (2012). Current emotion research in the language sciences. *Emotion Review, 4,* 432–443.

Ma-Kellams, C., & Blascovich, J. (2012). Enjoying life in the face of death: East–West differences in responses to mortality salience. *Journal of Personality and Social Psychology, 103,* 773–386.

Makin, J. W., & Porter, R. H. (1989). Attractiveness of lactating females' breast odors to neonates. *Child Development, 60,* 803–810.

Makin, S. (2014). Schizophrenia's genetic roots. *Scientific American Mind, 25,* 13.

Makin, T. R., Scholz, J., Slater, D. H., Johansen-Berg, H., & Tracey, I. (2015). Reassessing cortical reorganization in the primary sensorimotor cortex following arm amputation. *Brain, 138,* 2140–2146.

Malenka, R. C., & Nicoll, R. A. (1999). Long-term potentiation—A decade of progress? *Science, 285,* 1870–1874.

Malina, D., Morrissey, S., Campion, E. W., Hamel, M. B., & Drazen, J. M. (2016). Rooting out gun violence. *The New England Journal of Medicine, 374,* 175–176.

Malinowski, J., & Horton, C. L. (2014). Evidence for the preferential incorporation of emotional waking-life experiences into dreams. *Dreaming, 24,* 18–31.

Malkemus, S. A. (2015). Reclaiming instinct: Exploring the phylogenetic unfolding of animate being. *Journal of Humanistic Psychology, 55,* 3–29.

Malkoff-Schwartz, S., Frank, E., Anderson, B, Sherrill, J. T., Siegel, L., Patterson, D., & Kupfer, D. J. (1998). Stressful life events and social rhythm disruption in the onset of manic and depressive bipolar episodes. *Archives of General Psychiatry, 55,* 702–707.

Mallow, J., Bernarding, J., Luchtmann, M., Bethmann, A., & Brechmann, A. (2015). Superior memorizers employ different neural networks for encoding and recall. *Frontiers in Systems Neuroscience, 9.* http://doi.org/10.3389/fnsys.2015.00128

Maloney, E. A., Ramirez, G., Gunderson, E. A., Levine, S. C., & Beilock, S. L. (2015). Intergenerational effects of parents' math anxiety on children's math achievement and anxiety. *Psychological Science, 26,* 1480–1488.

Manber, R., Kraemer, H. C., Arnow, B. A., Trivedi, M. H., Rush, A. J., Thase, M. E., … Keller, M. E. (2008). Faster remission of chronic depression with combined psychotherapy and medication than with each therapy alone. *Journal of Consulting and Clinical Psychology, 76,* 459–467.

Mancini, A. D., Bonanno, G. A., & Clark, A. E. (2011). Stepping off the hedonic treadmill: Individual differences in response to major life events. *Journal of Individual Differences, 32,* 144–152.

Mandler, J. M. (2008). On the birth and growth of concepts. *Philosophical Psychology, 21,* 207–230.

Mandoki, M.W., Sumner, G. S., Hoffman, R. P., & Riconda, D. L. (1991). A review of Klinefelter's syndrome in children and adolescents. *Psychiatry, 30,* 167–172.

Mann, J. J., Apter, A., Bertolote, J., Beautrais, A., Currier, D., Haas, A., … Hendin, H. (2005). Suicide prevention strategies. *Journal of the American Medical Association, 294,* 2064–2074.

Manninen, B. A. (2011). Parental, medical, and sociological responsibilities: "Octomom" as a case study in the ethics of fertility treatments. *Journal of Clinical Research & Bioethics, S1,* 1–11.

Manning, J. T., Kilduff, L. P., & Trivers, R. (2013). Digit ratio (2D:4D) in Klinefelter's syndrome. *Andrology, 1,* 1–6.

Manning, R., Levine, M., & Collins, A. (2007). The Kitty Genovese murder and the social psychology of helping: The parable of the 38 witnesses. *American Psychologist, 62,* 555–562.

Manns, J. R., Hopkins, R. O., & Squire, L. R. (2003). Semantic memory and the human hippocampus. *Neuron, 38,* 127–133.

Maquet, P. (2000). Functional neuroimaging of normal human sleep by positron emission tomography. *Journal of Sleep Research, 3,* 208–231.

Marceau, K., Ram, N., Houts, R. M., Grimm, K. J., & Susman, E. J. (2011). Individual differences in boys' and girls' timing and tempo of puberty: Modeling development with nonlinear growth models. *Developmental Psychology, 47,* 1389–1409.

March of Dimes. (2013). *Premature babies.* Retrieved from http://www.marchofdimes.org/baby/premature-babies.aspx#

Marcus, A., & Oransky, I. (2015, May 22). What's behind big science frauds? *The New York Times.* Retrieved from http://www.nytimes.com/2015/05/23/opinion/whats-behind-big-science-frauds.html?_r=0

Marcus, J., & Le, H. (2013). Interactive effects of levels of individualism–collectivism on cooperation: A meta-analysis. *Journal of Organizational Behavior, 34,* 813–834.

Mariën, P., Ackermann, H., Adamaszek, M., Barwood, C. H., Beaton, A., Desmond, J., … Ziegler, W. (2014). Consensus paper: Language and the cerebellum: An ongoing enigma. *The Cerebellum, 13*(3), 386–410.

Marin, M. M., Rapisardi, G., & Tani, F. (2015). Two-day-old newborn infants recognise their mother by her axillary odour. *Acta Paediatrica, 104,* 237–240.

Marinsek, N., Turner, B. O., Gazzaniga, M., & Miller, M. B. (2014). Divergent hemispheric reasoning strategies: Reducing uncertainty versus resolving inconsistency. *Frontiers in Human Neuroscience, 8.* http://dx.doi.org/10.3389/fnhum.2014.00839

Marmurek, H. C., & Grant, R. D. (1990). Savings in a recognition test. *Canadian Journal of Psychology, 44,* 414–419.

Maron, D. F. (2015, November). Fake weed, real crisis. *Scientific American, 313,* 23.

Maron, E., Hettema, J. M., & Shlik, J. (2010). Advances in molecular genetics of panic disorder. *Molecular Psychiatry, 15,* 681–701.

Maroon, J. C., Winkelman, R., Bost, J., Amos, A., Mathyssek, C., & Miele, V. (2015). Chronic traumatic encephalopathy in contact sports: A systematic review of all reported pathological cases. *PLOS ONE, 10,* e0117338.

Marques, L., Alegria, M., Becker, A. E., Chen, C. N., Fang, A., Chosak, A., & Diniz, J. B. (2011). Comparative prevalence, correlates of impairment, and service utilization for eating disorders across US ethnic groups: Implications for reducing ethnic disparities in health care access for eating disorders. *International Journal of Eating Disorders, 44,* 412–420.

Marsh, H. W., Nagengast, B., & Morin, A. J. (2013). Measurement invariance of Big-Five factors over the life span: ESEM tests of gender, age, plasticity, maturity, and La Dolce Vita effects. *Developmental Psychology, 49,* 1194–1218.

Marshall, L., & Born, L. (2007). The contribution of sleep to hippocampus-dependent memory consolidation. *Trends in Cognitive Sciences, 10,* 442–450.

Martin, C. (2013). Memorable outliers. *Current Biology, 23* (17), R731–R733.

Martin, C. L., & Halverson, C. F. (1983). The effects of sex-typing schemas on young children's memory. *Child Development, 54,* 563–574.

Martin, C. L., & Ruble, D. N. (2010). Patterns of gender development. *Annual Review of Psychology, 61,* 353–381.

Martin, C. L., Ruble, D. N., & Szkrybalo, J. (2002). Cognitive theories of early gender development. *Psychological Bulletin, 128,* 903–933.

Martin, J. (2016). Ernest Becker and Stanley Milgram: Twentieth-century students of evil. *History of Psychology, 19,* 3–21.

Martin, L. A., Doster, J. A., Critelli, J. W., Purdum, M., Powers, C., Lambert, P. L., & Miranda, V. (2011). The "distressed" personality, coping and cardiovascular risk. *Stress and Health, 27,* 64–72.

Martin, R. A., Puhlik-Doris, P., Larsen, G., Gray, J., & Weir, K. (2003). Individual differences in uses of humor and their relation to psychological well-being: Development of the Humor Styles Questionnaire. *Journal of Research in Personality, 37,* 48–75.

Martin, R. C., & Allen, C. (2012). Case studies in neuropsychology. In H. Cooper, P. M. Camic, D. L. Long, A. T. Panter, D. Rindskopf, & K. J. Sher (Eds.), *APA handbook of research methods in psychology: Vol. 2. Research designs: Quantitative, qualitative, neuropsychological, and biological* (pp. 633–645). Washington, DC: American Psychological Association.

Martín, R., Bajo-Grañeras, R., Moratalla, R., Perea, G., & Araque, A. (2015). Circuit-specific signaling in astrocyte-neuron networks in basal ganglia pathways. *Science, 349*(6249), 730–734.

Marx, V., & Nagy, E. (2015). Fetal behavioural responses to maternal voice and touch. *PLOS ONE, 10*, e0129118.

Masaoka, K., Berns, R. S., Fairchild, M. D., & Moghareh Abed, F. (2013). Number of discernible object colors is a conundrum. *Journal of the Optical Society of America A, 30*, 264–277.

Mashour, G. A., & Avidan, M. S. (2015). Intraoperative awareness: Controversies and non-controversies. *British Journal of Anesthesia, 115* (Suppl.), i20–i26.

Mashour, G. A., Walker, E. E., & Martuza, R. L. (2005). Psychosurgery: Past, present, and future. *Brain Research Reviews, 48*, 409–419.

Maslow, A. H. (1943). A theory of human motivation. *Psychological Review, 50*, 370–396.

Massen, J. J., Dusch, K., Eldakar, O. T., & Gallup, A. C. (2014). A thermal window for yawning in humans: Yawning as a brain cooling mechanism. *Physiology & Behavior, 130*, 145–148.

Masters, W., & Johnson, V. (1966). *Human sexual response*. Boston, MA: Little, Brown.

Masters, W., & Johnson, V. (1979). *Homosexuality in perspective*. Boston, MA: Little, Brown.

Mather, V. (2016, May 24). The BMX rider Dave Mirra, who died in a suicide, had C.T.E. *The New York Times*. Retrieved from http://www.nytimes.com/2016/05/25/sports/dave-mirra-cte-bmx.html?_r=0

Mathes, J., Schredl, M., & Göritz, A. S. (2014). Frequency of typical dream themes in most recent dreams: An online study. *Dreaming, 24*, 57–66.

Matheson, S. L., Shepherd, A. M., & Carr, V. J. (2014). How much do we know about schizophrenia and how well do we know it? Evidence from the schizophrenia library. *Psychological Medicine, 44*, 3387–3405.

Matlin, M. W., & Farmer, T. A. (2016). *Cognition* (9th ed.). Hoboken, NJ: John Wiley & Sons.

Matloubian, M., Lo, C. G., Cinamon, G., Lesneski, M. J., Xu, Y., Brinkmann, V., ... Cyster, J. G. (2004). Lymphocyte egress from thymus and peripheral lymphoid organs is dependent on S1P receptor 1. *Nature, 427*, 355–360.

Matsumoto, D., & Willingham, B. (2009). Spontaneous facial expressions of emotion of congenitally and noncongenitally blind individuals. *Journal of Personality and Social Psychology, 96*, 1–10.

Matsumura, S., Bito, S., Liu, H., Kahn, K., Fukuhara, S., Kagawa-Singer, M., & Wenger, N. (2002). Acculturation of attitudes toward end-of-life care: A cross-cultural survey of Japanese Americans and Japanese. *Journal of General Internal Medicine, 17*, 531–539.

Mattarella-Micke, A., Mateo, J., Kozak, M. N., Foster, K., & Beilock, S. L. (2011). Choke or thrive? The relation between salivary cortisol and math performance depends on individual differences in working memory and math-anxiety. *Emotion, 11*, 1000–1005.

Maulia, E. (2013, February 15). Social media addiction a new "pathological" disorder. *The Jakarta Globe*. Retrieved from http://jakartaglobe.id/health/social-media-addiction-a-new-pathological-disorder/

Maxmen, A. (2012). Generic HIV drugs will widen US treatment net. *Nature, 488*, 267.

Max-Planck-Gesellschaft. (2015). *Optogenetics*. Retrieved from https://www.mpg.de/18011/Optogenetics.

Mayo Clinic. (2014, June 2). *Fetal alcohol syndrome: Symptoms*. Retrieved from http://www.mayoclinic.com/health/fetal-alcohol-syndrome/DS00184/DSECTION=symptoms

Mayo Clinic. (2014, October 17). *Presbyopia*. Retrieved from http://www.mayoclinic.org/diseases-conditions/presbyopia/basics/definition/con-20032261

Mayo Clinic. (2015, September 3). *Hearing loss*. Retrieved from http://www.mayoclinic.org/diseases-conditions/hearing-loss/basics/definition/con-20027684

Mayo Clinic. (2014, July 18). *Transient global amnesia*. Retrieved from http://www.mayoclinic.org/diseases-conditions/transient-global-amnesia/basics/definition/con-20032746

McAdams, D. P., & Olson, B. D. (2010). Personality development: Continuity and change over the life course. *Annual Review of Psychology, 61*, 5.1–5.26.

McAnulty, R. D., Dillon, J., & Adams, H. E. (2002). Sexual deviation: Paraphilias. In P. B. Sutker & H. E. Adams (Eds.), *Comprehensive handbook of psychopathology* (3rd ed., pp. 749–773). New York, NY: Springer.

McAra, L., & McVie, S. (2016). Understanding youth violence: The mediating effects of gender, poverty and vulnerability. *Journal of Criminal Justice, 45*, 71–77.

McCaffrey, J., & Machery, E. (2012). Philosophical issues about concepts. *Wiley Interdisciplinary Reviews: Cognitive Science, 3*, 265–279.

McCann, R. A., Armstrong, C. M., Skopp, N. A., Edwards-Stewart, A., Smolenski, D. J., June, J. D., ... Reger, G. M. (2014). Virtual reality exposure therapy for the treatment of anxiety disorders: An evaluation of research quality. *Journal of Anxiety Disorders, 28*, 625–631.

McCarthy, C. (2013). Pediatricians and television: It's time to rethink our messaging and our efforts. *Pediatrics, 131*, 589–590.

McCarthy, J. R., & Skowronski, J. J. (2011). The interplay of controlled and automatic processing in the expression of spontaneously inferred traits: A PDP analysis. *Journal of Personality and Social Psychology, 100*, 229–240.

McCarty, W. P., Schuck, A., Skogan, W., & Rosenbaum, D. (2011, January 7). Stress, burnout, and health. *National Police Research Platform*. Retrieved from http://static1.1.sqspcdn.com/static/f/733761/10444483/1296183365827/Stress+Burnout++and+Health+FINAL.pdf?token=yHjV0T0%2BrgsT6n45ITGmtQN1DAo%3D

McCauley, E., & Sybert, V. (2006). Social and behavioral development of girls and women with Turner syndrome. *International Congress Series, 1298*, 93–99.

McClelland, D. C., Atkinson, J. W., Clark, R. W., & Lowell, E. L. (1976). *The achievement motive*. New York, NY: Irvington.

McClintock, M. K. (1971) Menstrual synchrony and suppression. *Nature, 229*, 244–245.

McCosker, B., & Moran, C. C. (2012). Differential effects of self-esteem and interpersonal competence on humor styles. *Psychology Research and Behavior Management, 5*, 143–150.

McCrae, R. R. (2011). Personality theories for the 21st century. *Teaching of Psychology, 38*, 209–214.

McCrae, R. R., Chan, W., Jussim, L., De Fruyt, F., Löckenhoff, C. E., De Bolle, M., ... Allik, J. (2013). The inaccuracy of national character stereotypes. *Journal of Research in Personality, 47*, 831–842.

McCrae, R. R., & Costa, P. T. Jr. (1987). Validation of the five-factor model of personality across instruments and observers. *Journal of Personality and Social Psychology, 49*, 81–90.

McCrae, R. R., & Costa, P. T. Jr. (1990). *Personality in adulthood*. New York, NY: Guilford Press.

McCrae, R. R., Costa, P. T. Jr., Ostendorf, F., Angleitner, A., Hřebíčková, M., Avia, M. D., ... Smith, P. B. (2000). Nature over nurture: Temperament, personality, and life span development. *Journal of Personality and Social Psychology, 78*, 173–186.

McCrae, R. R., Scally, M., Terracciano, A., Abecasis, G. R., & Costa, P. T. Jr. (2010). An alternative to the search for single polymorphisms: Toward molecular personality scales for the five-factor model. *Journal of Personality and Social Psychology, 99*, 1014–1024.

McCrae, R. R., Terracciano, A., & 78 Members of the Personality Profiles of Cultures Project. (2005). Universal features of personality traits from the observer's perspective: Data from 50 cultures. *Journal of Personality and Social Psychology, 88*, 547–561.

McDermott, R. C., Schwartz, J. P., & Rislin, J. L. (2016). Men's mental health: A biopsychosocial critique. In Y. J. Wong & S. R. Wester (Eds.), *APA Handbooks in Psychology Series: APA handbook of men and masculinities* (pp. 731–751). Washington, DC: American Psychological Association.

McDougall, W. (1912). *An introduction to social psychology* (rev. 4th ed.). Boston, MA: John W. Luce.

McEwen, B. S. (2000). The neurobiology of stress: From serendipity to clinical relevance. *Brain Research, 886*, 172–189.

McFadden, R. D. (2016, April 4). Winston Moseley, who killed Kitty Genovese, dies in prison at 81. *The New York Times*. Retrieved from http://www.nytimes.com/2016/04/05/nyregion/winston-moseley-81-killer-of-kitty-genovese-dies-in-prison.html?_r=0

McGaugh, J. L., & LePort, A. (2014). Remembrance of all things past. *Scientific American, 310*, 40–45.

McGue, M., Bouchard, T. J. Jr., Iacono, W. G., & Lykken, D. T. (1993). Behavioral genetics of cognitive ability: A life-span perspective. In R. Plomin & G. E. McClearn (Eds.), *Nature, nurture & psychology* (pp. 59–76). Washington, DC: American Psychological Association.

McHugh, P. R., & Slavney, P. R. (2012). Mental illness—Comprehensive evaluation or checklist? *New England Journal of Medicine, 366*, 1853–1855.

McKee, A. C., Cairns, N. J., Dickson, D. W., Folkerth, R. D., Keene, C. D., Litvan, I., … Tripodis, Y. (2016). The first NINDS/NIBIB consensus meeting to define neuropathological criteria for the diagnosis of chronic traumatic encephalopathy. *Acta Neuropathologica, 131,* 75–86.

McKee, A. C., Cantu, R. C., Nowinski, C. J., Hedley-Whyte, E. T., Gavett, B. E., Budson, A. E., … Stern, R. A. (2009). Chronic traumatic encephalopathy in athletes: Progressive tauopathy after repetitive head injury. *Journal of Neuropathology & Experimental Neurology, 68*(7), 709–735.

McKee, A. C., Stein, T. D., Nowinski, C. J., Stern, R. A., Daneshvar, D. H., Alvarez, V. E., … Riley, D. O. (2013). The spectrum of disease in chronic traumatic encephalopathy. *Brain, 136,* 43–64.

McKinney, A., & Coyle, K. (2006). Alcohol hangover effects on measures of affect the morning after a normal night's drinking. *Alcohol & Alcoholism, 41,* 54–60.

McMurray, B. (2007). Defusing the childhood vocabulary explosion. *Science, 317,* 631.

McNally, R. J., & Clancy, S. A. (2005). Sleep paralysis, sexual abuse, and space alien abduction. *Transcultural Psychiatry, 42,* 113–122.

McPherson, M., Smith-Lovin, L., & Cook, J. M. (2001). Birds of a feather: Homophily in social networks. *Annual Review of Sociology, 27,* 415–444.

McRae, A. F., Visscher, P. M., Montgomery, G. W., & Martin, N. G. (2015). Large autosomal copy-number differences within unselected monozygotic twin pairs are rare. *Twin Research and Human Genetics, 18*(1), 13–18.

Medeiros-Ward, N., Watson, J. M., & Strayer, D. L. (2015). On supertaskers and the neural basis of efficient multitasking. *Psychonomic Bulletin & Review, 22,* 876–883.

MedicineNet. (2015, June 1). *Cocaine hydrochloride.* Retrieved from http://www.medicinenet.com/cocaine_hydrochloride-topical/article.htm

Medline Plus. (2015, April 25). *Caffeine in the diet.* Retrieved from https://www.nlm.nih.gov/medlineplus/ency/article/002445.htm.

Medline Plus. (2015, March 31). *Gastric bypass surgery.* Retrieved from https://medlineplus.gov/ency/article/007199.htm

Mehler, P. S., & Brown, C. (2015). Anorexia nervosa—Medical complications. *Journal of Eating Disorders, 3.* doi: 10.1186/s40337-015-0040-8

Mehta, C. M., & Strough, J. (2010). Gender segregation and gender-typing in adolescence. *Sex Roles, 63,* 251–263.

Mekawi, Y., & Bresin, K. (2015). Is the evidence from racial bias shooting task studies a smoking gun? Results from a meta-analysis. *Journal of Experimental Social Psychology, 61,* 120–130.

Melin, A. D., Hiramatsu, C., Parr, N. A., Matsushita, Y., Kawamura, S., & Fedigan, L. M. (2014). The behavioral ecology of color vision: Considering fruit conspicuity, detection distance and dietary importance. *International Journal of Primatology, 35,* 258–287.

Melnikova, N., Welles, W. L., Wilburn, R. E., Rice, N., Wu, J., & Stanbury, M. (2011). Hazards of illicit methamphetamine production and efforts at reduction: Data from the hazardous substances emergency events surveillance system. *Public Health Reports, 126,* 116–123.

Melzack, R. (1993). Pain: Past present and future. *Canadian Journal of Experimental Psychology, 47,* 615–629.

Melzack, R. (2008). The future of pain. *Nature Reviews, 7,* 629.

Melzack, R., & Wall, P. D. (1965). Pain mechanisms: A new theory. *Science, 150,* 971–979.

Méndez-Bértolo, C., Moratti, S., Toledano, R., Lopez-Sosa, F., Martínez-Alvarez, R., Mah, Y. H., … Strange, B. A. (2016). A fast pathway for fear in human amygdala. *Nature Neuroscience, 19,* 1041–1049.

Mendle, J., & Ferrero, J. (2012). Detrimental psychological outcomes associated with pubertal timing in adolescent boys. *Developmental Review, 32,* 49–66.

Mendle, J., Harden, K. P., Brooks-Gunn, J., & Graber, J. A. (2010). Development's tortoise and hare: Pubertal timing, pubertal tempo, and depressive symptoms in boys and girls. *Developmental Psychology, 46,* 1341–1353.

Mendrek, A., & Mancini-Marïe, A. (2016). Sex/gender differences in the brain and cognition in schizophrenia. *Neuroscience & Biobehavioral Reviews, 67,* 57–78.

Menken, J., Trussell, J., & Larsen, U. (1986). Age and infertility. *Science, 233,* 1389–1394.

Mennella, J. A., Coren P., Jagnow, M. S., & Beauchamp, G. K. (2001). Prenatal and postnatal flavor learning by human infants. *Pediatrics, 107,* e88.

Merikangas, K. R., Akiskal, H. S., Angst, J., Greenberg, P. E., Hirschfeld, R. M., Petukhova, M., & Kessler, R. C. (2007). Lifetime and 12-month prevalence of bipolar spectrum disorder in the national comorbidity survey replication. *Archives of General Psychiatry, 64,* 543–552.

Mervis, C. B., & Rosch, E. (1981). Categorization of natural objects. *Annual Review of Psychology, 32,* 89–115.

Meshi, D., Tamir, D. I., & Heekeren, H. R. (2015). The emerging neuroscience of social media. *Trends in Cognitive Sciences, 19,* 771–782.

Michael, R. T., Laumann, E. O., Kolata, G. B., & Gagnon, J. H. (1994). *Sex in America: A definitive survey.* Boston, MA: Little, Brown.

Michaels, B. M., Csank, G. A., Ryb, G. E., Eko, F. N., & Rubin, A. (2012). Prospective randomized comparison of onabotulinumtoxinA (Botox) and abobotulinumtoxinA (Dysport) in the treatment of forehead, glabellar, and periorbital wrinkles. *Aesthetic Surgery Journal, 32,* 96–102.

Michals, D. (2015). *Harriet Tubman.* Retrieved from https://www.nwhm.org/education-resources/biography/biographies/harriet-tubman/

Michalski, D., Kohout, J., Wicherski, M., & Hart, B. (2011). 2009 Doctorate Employment Survey. *APA Center for Workforce Studies.* Retrieved from http://www.apa.org/workforce/publications/09-doc-empl/index.aspx

Michely, J., Volz, L. J., Barbe, M. T., Hoffstaedter, F., Viswanathan, S., Timmermann, L., … Grefkes, C. (2015). Dopaminergic modulation of motor network dynamics in Parkinson's disease. *Brain, 138,* 664–678.

Michikyan, M., Subrahmanyam, K., & Dennis, J. (2015). Facebook use and academic performance among college students: A mixed-methods study with a multi-ethnic sample. *Computers in Human Behavior, 45,* 265–272.

Milani, R. V., & Lavie, C. J. (2009). Reducing psychosocial stress: A novel mechanism of improving survival from exercise training. *The American Journal of Medicine, 122,* 931–938. doi:10.1016/j.amjmed.2009.03.028

Milgram, S. (1963). Behavioral study of obedience. *Journal of Abnormal and Social Psychology, 67,* 371–378.

Milgram, S. (1964). Issues in the study of obedience: A reply to Baumrind. *American Psychologist, 19,* 848–852.

Milgram, S. (1965). Some conditions of obedience and disobedience to authority. *Human Relations, 18*(1), 57–76.

Milgram, S. (1974). *Obedience to authority: An experimental view.* New York, NY: Harper & Row.

Millan, C. (2013). *Cesar Millan's short guide to a happy dog.* Washington, DC: National Geographic Society.

Millan, C. (2013, March 26). It isn't always about the dog. *The Huffington Post.* Retrieved from http://www.huffingtonpost.com/cesar-millan/it-isnt-always-about-the-_b_2541801.html

Millan, C. (n.d.). The Dog Psychology Center: Evolution of a dream. [Web log comment]. Retrieved from https://www.cesarsway.com/cesar-millan/cesars-blog/dog-psychology-center-evolution-of-a-dream

Millan, C., & Peltier, M. J. (2006). *Cesar's way: The natural, everyday guide to understanding & correcting common dog problems.* New York, NY: Random House.

Millan, C., & Peltier, M. J. (2010). *Cesar's rules: Your way to train a well-behaved dog.* New York, NY: Three Rivers Press.

Miller, G. (1956). The magical number seven, plus or minus two: Some limits on our capacity for processing information. *Psychological Review, 63,* 81–97.

Miller, G. E., Chen, E., & Parker, K. J. (2011). Psychological stress in childhood and susceptibility to the chronic diseases of aging: Moving toward a model of behavioral and biological mechanisms. *Psychological Bulletin, 137,* 959–997.

Miller, S. L., & Maner, J. K. (2010). Scent of a woman: Men's testosterone responses to olfactory ovulation cues. *Psychological Science, 21,* 276–283.

Mills, C. (2015). The psychiatrization of poverty: Rethinking the mental health-poverty nexus. *Social and Personality Psychology Compass, 9,* 213–222.

Milrod, B., Leon, A. C., Busch, F., Rudden, M., Schwalberg, M., Clarkin, J., … Shear, M. K. (2007). A randomized control trial of psychoanalytic psychotherapy for panic disorder. *American Journal of Psychiatry, 164,* 265–272.

Mineka, S., Davidson, M., Cook, M., & Keir, R. (1984). Observational conditioning of snake fear in rhesus monkeys. *Journal of Abnormal Psychology, 93,* 355–372.

Mirsky, A. F., Bieliauskas, L. A., Duncan, C. C., & French, L. M. (2013). Letter to the editor. *Schizophrenia Research, 148,* 186–187.

Mirsky, A. F., Bieliauskas L. A., French, L. M., Van Kammen, D. P., Jönsson, E., & Sedvall G. A. (2000). A 39-year followup of the Genain quadruplets. *Schizophrenia Bulletin, 26,* 699–708.

Mirsky, A. F., & Quinn, O. W. (1988). The Genain triplets. *Schizophrenia Bulletin, 14,* 595–612.

Mischel, W., & Shoda, Y. (1995). A cognitive-affective system theory of personality: Reconceptualizing the invariances in personality and the role of situations. *Psychological Review, 102,* 229–258.

Mistry, R. S., & Wadsworth, M. E. (2011). Family functioning and child development in the context of poverty. *Prevention Researcher, 18,* 11–15.

Mita, T. H., Dermer, M., & Knight, J. (1977). Reversed facial images and the mere-exposure hypothesis. *Journal of Personality and Social Psychology, 35,* 597–601.

Mitchell, H. A., & Weinshenker, D. (2010). Good night and good luck: Norepinephrine in sleep pharmacology. *Biochemical Pharmacology, 79,* 801–809.

Moed, A., Gershoff, E. T., Eisenberg, N., Hofer, C., Losoya, S., Spinrad, T. L., & Liew, J. (2015). Parent–adolescent conflict as sequences of reciprocal negative emotion: Links with conflict resolution and adolescents' behavior problems. *Journal of Youth and Adolescence, 44,* 1607–1622.

Moisse, K. (2011, September 20). Drug deaths exceed traffic deaths. *ABC News.* Retrieved from http://abcnews.go.com/Health/Drugs/drug-deaths-exceed-traffic-deaths/story-id=14554903

Mokdad, A. H., Marks, J. S., Stroup, D. F., & Gerberding, J. L. (2004). Actual causes of deaths in the United States, 2000. *Journal of the American Medical Association, 291,* 1238–1245.

Mollon, J. D. (1982). Color vision. *Annual Review of Psychology, 33,* 41–85.

Monk, T. H., & Buysse, D. J. (2013). Exposure to shift work as a risk factor for diabetes. *Journal of Biological Rhythms, 28,* 356–359.

Monroe, S. M., & Harkness, K. L. (2011). Recurrence in major depression: A conceptual analysis. *Psychological Review, 118,* 655–674.

Monteleone, G. T., Phan, L., Nusbaum, H. C., Gitzgerald, D., Irick, J. -S., Fienberg, S. E., & Cacioppo, J. T. (2009). Detection of deception using fMRI: Better than chance, but well below perfection. *Social Neuroscience, 4,* 528–538.

Montemayor, R. (1983). Parents and adolescents in conflict: All families some of the time and some families most of the time. *Journal of Early Adolescence, 3,* 83–103.

Montenigro, P. H., Bernick, C., & Cantu, R. C. (2015). Clinical features of repetitive traumatic brain injury and chronic traumatic encephalopathy. *Brain Pathology, 25,* 304–317.

Montoya, E. R., Terburg, D., Bos, P. A., & van Honk, J. (2012). Testosterone, cortisol, and serotonin as key regulators of social aggression: A review and theoretical perspective. *Motivation and Emotion, 36,* 65–73.

Moon, C., Lagercrantz, H., & Kuhl, P. K. (2013). Language experienced in utero affects vowel perception after birth: A two-country study. *Acta Paediatrica, 102*(2), 156–160.

Moon, C., Zernzach, R. C., & Kuhl, P. K. (2015). Mothers say "baby" and their newborns do not choose to listen: A behavioral preference study to compare with ERP results. *Frontiers in Human Neuroscience, 9.* http://journal.frontiersin.org/article/10.3389/fnhum.2015.00153/full

Moore, D. S. (2013). Current thinking about nature and nurture. In K. Kampourakis (Ed.), *The philosophy of biology: A companion for educators* (pp. 629–652). Dordrecht, The Netherlands: Springer Science.

Moore, S. R., & Depue, R. A. (2016). Neurobehavioral foundation of environmental reactivity. *Psychological Bulletin, 142*(2), 107–164.

Moorhead, S. A., Hazlett, D. E., Harrison, L., Carroll, J. K., Irwin, A., & Hoving, C. (2013). A new dimension of health care: Systematic review of the uses, benefits, and limitations of social media for health communication. *Journal of Medical Internet Research, 15.* doi:10.2196/jmir.1933

Moosa, A. N., Jehi, L., Marashly, A., Cosmo, G., Lachhwani, D., Wyllie, E., … Gupta, A. (2013). Long-term functional outcomes and their predictors after hemispherectomy in 115 children. *Epilepsia, 54,* 1771–1779.

Morales, A., Heaton, J. P. W., & Carson III, C. C. (2000). Andropause: A misnomer for a true clinical entity. *Journal of Urology, 163,* 705–712.

Moran, J. M., Jolly, E., & Mitchell, J. P. (2014). Spontaneous mentalizing predicts the fundamental attribution error. *Journal of Cognitive Neuroscience, 26,* 569–576.

Mora-Rodriguez, R., & Pallarés, J. G. (2014). Performance outcomes and unwanted side effects associated with energy drinks. *Nutrition Reviews, 72* (Suppl. 1), 108–120.

Moreira-Almeida, A., Neto, F. L., & Cardeña, E. (2008). Comparison of Brazilian spiritist mediumship and dissociative identity disorder. *Journal of Nervous and Mental Disease, 196,* 420–424.

Moreland, R. L., & Zajonc, R. B. (1982). Exposure effects in person perception: Familiarity, similarity, and attraction. *Journal of Experimental Social Psychology, 18,* 395–415.

Morewedge, C. K., Yoon, H., Scopelliti, I., Symborski, C. W., Korris, J. H., & Kassam, K. S. (2015). Debiasing decisions improved decision making with a single training intervention. *Policy Insights from the Behavioral and Brain Sciences, 2,* 129–140.

Morgan, B. L., & Korschgen, A. J. (2014). *Majoring in psych? Career options for psychology undergaduates* (5th ed.). Boston, MA: Pearson.

Morina, N., Ijntema, H., Meyerbröker, K., & Emmelkamp, P. M. (2015). Can virtual reality exposure therapy gains be generalized to real-life? A meta-analysis of studies applying behavioral assessments. *Behaviour Research and Therapy, 74,* 18–24.

Morita, T., Oyama, Y., Cheng, S. Y., Suh, S. Y., Koh, S. J., Kim, H. S., … Tsuneto, S. (2015). Palliative care physicians' attitudes toward patient autonomy and a good death in East Asian countries. *Journal of Pain and Symptom Management, 50,* 190–199.

Morone, N. E., & Greco, C. M. (2007). Mind–body interventions for chronic pain in older adults: A structured review. *Pain Medicine, 8,* 359–375.

Morrison, P. (2016, February 3). Patt Morrison asks: "Concussion" doctor Bennet Omalu. *Los Angeles Times.* Retrieved from http://www.latimes.com/opinion/op-ed/la-ol-concussion-doctor-bennet-omalu-on-racism-in-football-o-j-and-why-he-won-t-be-watching-the-super-bowl-20160202-story.html

Morrot, G., Brochet, F., & Dubourdieu, D. (2001). The color of odors. *Brain and Language, 79,* 309–320.

Morry, M. M., Kito, M., & Ortiz, L. (2011). The attraction-similarity model and dating couples: Projection, perceived similarity, and psychological benefits. *Personal Relationships, 18,* 125–143.

Moshagen, M., Hilbig, B. E., Erdfelder, E., & Moritz, A. (2014). An experimental validation method for questioning techniques that assess sensitive issues. *Experimental Psychology, 61,* 48–54.

Mosher, W. D., Chandra, A., & Jones, J. (2005, September 15). *Sexual behavior and selected health measures: Men and women 15–44 years of age, United States, 2002* (Advance Data from Vital and Health Statistics No. 362). Washington, DC: National Center for Health Statistics, Centers for Disease Control and Prevention, Department of Health and Human Services.

Moss, D. (2015). The roots and genealogy of humanistic psychology. In K. J. Schneider, J. F. Pierson, & J. F. T. Bugental (Eds.), *The handbook of humanistic psychology: Theory, research, and practice* (2nd ed., pp. 5–20). Thousand Oaks, CA: SAGE.

Most, S. B., Simons, D. J., Scholl, B. J., Jimenez, R., Clifford, E., & Chabris, C. F. (2001). How not to be seen: The contribution of similarity and selective ignoring to sustained inattentional blindness. *Psychological Science, 12,* 9–17.

Mrug, S., Tyson, A., Turan, B., & Granger, D. A. (2016). Sleep problems predict cortisol reactivity to stress in urban adolescents. *Physiology & Behavior, 155,* 95–101.

MSNBC.com. (2011, July 26). *Girl, 6, on shark that bit her: "I forgive him"* [Video file]. Retrieved from http://today.msnbc.msn.com/id/43892097/ns/today-today_people/t/girl-shark-bit-her-i-forgive-him/#.TqR3Sc33LjQ

Mueller, P. A., & Oppenheimer, D. M. (2014). The pen is mightier than the keyboard: Advantages of longhand over laptop note taking. *Psychological Science, 25,* 1159–1168.

Mukherjee, S., & Manahan-Vaughan, D. (2013). Role of metabotropic glutamate receptors in persistent forms of hippocampal plasticity and learning. *Neuropharmacology, 66,* 65–81.

Mulkerrins, J. (2016, June 10). Laverne Cox: On growing up trans, *Orange is the New Black* and Caitlyn Jenner. *The Telegraph.* Retrieved from http://www.telegraph.co.uk/on-demand/2016/06/10/laverne-cox-on-growing-up-trans-orange-is-the-new-black-and-cait/

Muller, P. Y., Dambach, D., Gemzik, B., Hartmann, A., Ratcliffe, S., Trendelenburg, C., & Urban, L. (2015). Integrated risk assessment of suicidal ideation and behavior in drug development. *Drug Discovery Today, 20,* 1135–1142.

Müllerová, J., Hansen, M., Contractor, A. A., Elhai, J. D., & Armour, C. (2016). Dissociative features in posttraumatic stress disorder: A latent profile analysis. *Psychological Trauma: Theory, Research, Practice, and Policy, 8*(5), 601–608.

Mulvey, S. (2006, May 15). Cakes and jokes at Cafe d'Europe. *BBC News*. Retrieved from http://news.bbc.co.uk/2/hi/europe/4755659.stm

Murdock, B. (1962). The serial position effect of free recall. *Journal of Experimental Psychology, 64*, 482–488.

Murkar, A., Smith, C., Dale, A., & Miller, N. (2014). A neuro-cognitive model of sleep mentation and memory consolidation. *International Journal of Dream Research, 7*, 85–89.

Murphy, D., & Joseph, S. (2016). Person-centered therapy: Past, present, and future orientations. In D. J. Cain, K. Keenan, & S. Rubin (Eds.) *Humanistic psychotherapies: Handbook of research and practice* (2nd ed., pp. 185–218). Washington, DC: American Psychological Association.

Murray, R. M., Morrison, P. D., Henquet, C., & Di Forti, M. (2007). Cannabis, the mind and society: The hash realities. *Nature Reviews Neuroscience, 8*, 885–895.

Murre, J. M., & Dros, J. (2015). Replication and analysis of Ebbinghaus' forgetting curve. *PLOS ONE, 10*, e0120644. doi:10.1371/journal.pone.0120644

Musaiger, A. O., Al-Mannai, M., Tayyem, R., Al-Lalla, O., Ali, E. Y., Kalam, F., … Chirane, M. (2013). Risk of disordered eating attitudes among adolescents in seven Arab countries by gender and obesity: A cross-cultural study. *Appetite, 60*, 162–167.

Mustanski, B. S., Chivers, M. L., & Bailey, J. M. (2002). A critical review of recent biological research on human sexual orientation. *Annual Review of Sex Research, 13*, 89–140.

Musto, D. F. (1991). Opium, cocaine and marijuana in American history. *Scientific American, 265*, 41–47.

Myers, B. J. (1987/2014). Mother–infant boding as a critical period. In M. H. Bornstein (Ed.), *Sensitive periods in development: Interdisciplinary perspectives* (pp. 223–245). New York, NY: Psychology Press.

Myers, D. G., & Lamm, H. (1976). The group polarization phenomenon. *Psychological Bulletin, 83*, 602–627.

Mysterud, I. (2003). Long live nature via nurture! *Evolutionary Psychology, 1*, 188–191.

Nadorff, M. R., Nadorff, D. K., & Germain, A. (2015). Nightmares: Underreported, undetected, and therefore untreated. *Journal of Clinical Sleep Medicine, 11*(7), 747–750.

Nagasawa, M., Mitsui, S., En, S., Ohtani, N., Ohta, M., Sakuma, Y., … Kikusui, T. (2015). Oxytocin-gaze positive loop and the coevolution of human–dog bonds. *Science, 348*(6232), 333–336.

Nagel, I. E., Chicherio, C., Li, S., von Oertzen, T., Sander, T., Villringer, A., … Lindenberger, U. (2008). Human aging magnifies genetic effects on executive functioning and working memory. *Frontiers in Human Neuroscience, 2.* http://dx.doi.org/10.3389/neuro.09.001.2008

Nahemow, L., & Lawton, M. P. (1975). Similarity and propinquity in friendship formation. *Journal of Personality and Social Psychology, 32*, 205–213.

Naimi, T. S., Brewer, R. D., Mokdad, A., Denny, C., Serdula, M. K., & Marks, J. S. (2003). Binge drinking among US adults. *Journal of the American Medical Association, 289*, 70–75.

Narula, K. (2014, April 29). The 5 U.S. counties where racial diversity is highest—and lowest. *The Atlantic*. Retrieved from http://www.theatlantic.com/national/archive/2014/04/mapping-racial-diversity-by-county/361388/

Nash, M. R. (2001). The truth and the hype of hypnosis. *Scientific American, 285*, 44–55.

National Association of the Deaf. (2013). *NAD applauds appointment of Claudia Gordon as Public Engagement Advisor at the White House.* Retrieved from http://nad.org/news/2013/7/nad-applauds-appointment-claudia-gordon-public-engagement-advisor-white-house

National Eye Institute. (n.d.-a). *Facts about the cornea and corneal disease.* Retrieved from https://nei.nih.gov/health/cornealdisease

National Eye Institute. (n.d.-b). *Facts about retinopathy of prematurity (ROP).* Retrieved from https://nei.nih.gov/health/rop/rop

National Geographic. (n.d.). *Dia de los Muertos.* Retrieved from http://education.nationalgeographic.com/education/media/dia-de-los-muertos/?ar_a=1

National Institute of Mental Health. (2013, October 1). *The numbers count: Mental disorders in America.* Retrieved from http://www.lb7.uscourts.gov/documents/12-cv-1072url2.pdf

National Institute of Mental Health. (2016). *Brain stimulation therapies.* Retrieved from https://www.nimh.nih.gov/health/topics/brain-stimulation-therapies/brain-stimulation-therapies.shtml

National Institute of Mental Health. (n.d.-a). *Antidepressant medications for children and adolescents: Information for parents and caregivers.* Retrieved from http://www.nimh.nih.gov/health/topics/child-and-adolescent-mental-health/antidepressant-medications-for-children-and-adolescents-information-for-parents-and-caregivers.shtml

National Institute of Mental Health. (n.d.-b). *Eating disorders.* http://www.nimh.nih.gov/health/topics/eating-disorders/index.shtml

National Institute of Neurological Disorders and Stroke. (2013, September). *Narcolepsy* [Fact sheet]. Retrieved from http://www.ninds.nih.gov/disorders/narcolepsy/detail_narcolepsy.htm

National Institute of Neurological Disorders and Stroke (2013, January 10). *NIH statement.* Retrieved from http://espn.go.com/pdf/2013/0110/espn_otl_NIH_Statement.pdf

National Institute of Neurological Disorders and Stroke. (n.d.-a). *Arteriovenous malformations and other vascular lesions of the central nervous system* [Fact sheet]. Retrieved from http://www.ninds.nih.gov/disorders/avms/detail_avms.htm

National Institute of Neurological Disorders and Stroke. (n.d.-b). *NINDS Rasmussen's encephalitis information page.* Retrieved from http://www.ninds.nih.gov/disorders/rasmussen/rasmussen.htm

National Institute on Aging. (n.d.). *About Alzheimer's disease: Alzheimer's basics.* Retrieved from http://www.nia.nih.gov/alzheimers/topics/alzheimers-basics

National Institute on Alcohol Abuse and Alcoholism. (2015). *Women and alcohol.* Retrieved from http://pubs.niaaa.nih.gov/publications/womensfact/womensFact.pdf

National Institute on Alcohol Abuse and Alcoholism (n.d.). *Alcohol facts and statistics.* Retrieved from https://www.niaaa.nih.gov/alcohol-health/overview-alcohol-consumption/alcohol-facts-and-statistics

National Institute on Drug Abuse. (2012, July). *Nationwide trends.* Retrieved from http://www.drugabuse.gov/sites/default/files/drugfactsnationtrends_1.pdf

National Institute on Drug Abuse. (2013a). *Cocaine.* Retrieved from http://www.drugabuse.gov/drugs-abuse/cocaine

National Institute on Drug Abuse. (2013b). *DrugFacts: Heroin.* Retrieved from http://www.drugabuse.gov/publications/drugfacts/heroin

National Institute on Drug Abuse. (2013c). *MDMA (Ecstasy or Molly).* Retrieved from http://www.drugabuse.gov/publications/drugfacts/mdma-ecstasy-or-molly

National Institute on Drug Abuse. (2013d). *Methamphetamine.* Retrieved from http://d14rmgtrwzf5a.cloudfront.net/sites/default/files/methrrs.pdf

National Institute on Drug Abuse. (2014a). *DrugFacts: Prescription and over-the-counter medications.* Retrieved from http://www.drugabuse.gov/publications/drugfacts/prescription-over-counter-medications

National Institute on Drug Abuse. (2014b). *Marijuana.* Retrieved from http://www.drugabuse.gov/drugs-abuse/marijuana

National Institute on Drug Abuse. (2014c). *Media guide: The science of drug abuse and addiction: The Basics.* Retrieved from http://www.drugabuse.gov/publications/media-guide/science-drug-abuse-addiction-basics

National Institute on Drug Abuse. (2015a). *Marijuana.* Retrieved from http://d14rmgtrwzf5a.cloudfront.net/sites/default/files/mjrrs_4_15.pdf

National Institute on Drug Abuse. (2015b). *Synthetic cannabinoids.* Retrieved from https://www.drugabuse.gov/publications/drugfacts/synthetic-cannabinoids

National Institutes of Health. (2012). Tips for getting a good night's sleep. *Medline Plus, 7*, 20.

National Institutes of Health, National Institute on Alcohol Abuse and Alcoholism. (2013). *Alcohol use disorders.* Retrieved from http://www.niaaa.nih.gove/alcohol-health/overview-alcohol-consumption/alcohol-use-disorders

National Library of Medicine. (2014). *Lithium.* Retrieved from https://medlineplus.gov/druginfo/meds/a681039.html

National Library of Medicine. (2016, February 22). *Natal teeth.* Retrieved from https://www.nlm.nih.gov/medlineplus/ency/article/003268.htm

National Safety Council. (2015). *Annual estimate of cell phone crashes 2013.* Retrieved from http://www.nsc.org/DistractedDrivingDocuments/Attributable-Risk-Estimate.pdf

National Safety Council. (2016). *Injury facts 2016 edition.* Itasca, IL: Author.

National Science Foundation, Division of Science Resources Statistics. (2011). *Women, minorities, and persons with disabilities in science and engineering: 2011* (Special Report No. NSF 11-309). Arlington, VA: Author. Retrieved from http://www.nsf.gov/statistics/wmpd/

National Sleep Foundation. (2009). *Sleep in America poll: Highlights and key findings.* Retrieved from http://sleepfoundation.org/sites/default/files/2009%20POLL%20HIGHLIGHTS.pdf

National Sleep Foundation. (2015a). *Children and sleep.* Retrieved from http://www.sleepfoundation.org/article/sleep-topics/children-and-sleep

National Sleep Foundation. (2015b). *Healthy sleep tips.* Retrieved from http://sleepfoundation.org/sleep-tools-tips/healthy-sleep-tips

National Sleep Foundation. (2015c). *Teens and sleep.* Retrieved from http://www.sleepfoundation.org/article/sleep-topics/teens-and-sleep

National Sleep Foundation. (2016). *See: A great night's sleep can depend on the visual conditions in your bedroom environment.* Retrieved from https://sleepfoundation.org/bedroom/see.php

NBC Universal. (2013, February 12). UK clinics treating patients for social-media addiction. *9 News.* Retrieved from http://www.9news.com/story/news/local/4-pm-show/2014/02/24/1839802/

Ndubaku, U., & de Bellard, M. (2008). Glial cells: Old cells with new twists. *Acta Histochemica, 110,* 182–195.

Nehlig, A. (2012). The neuroprotective effects of cocoa flavanol and its influence on cognitive performance. *British Journal of Clinical Pharmacology, 75*(3), 716–727.

Neisser, U. (1979). The control of information pickup in selective looking. In A. D. Pick (Ed.), *Perception and its development: A tribute to Eleanor J. Gibson* (pp. 201–219). Hillsdale, NJ: Lawrence Erlbaum Associates.

Neisser, U. (1991). A place of misplaced nostalgia. *American Psychologist, 46,* 34–36.

Neisser, U., & Becklen, R. (1975). Selective looking: Attending to visually specified events. *Cognitive Psychology, 7,* 480–494.

Neligan, A. (2014). Temporal trends in epilepsy surgery. *European Journal of Neurology, 21,* 814–815.

Nelson, R. (2014). Scientific basis for polygraph testing. *Polygraph, 44,* 28–61.

Nelson, R., & Handler, M. (2013). A brief history of scientific reviews of polygraph accuracy research. *APA Magazine, 46,* 22–28.

Nelson, S. K., Layous, K., Cole, S. W., & Lyubomirsky, S. (2016). Do unto others or treat yourself? The effects of prosocial and self-focused behavior on psychological flourishing. *Emotion, 16* (6), 850–861. doi:10.1037/emo0000178

Nelson, S. M., Telfer, E. E., & Anderson, R. A. (2013). The ageing ovary and uterus: New biological insights. *Human Reproduction Update, 19,* 67–83.

Nes, R. B., Czajkowski, N., & Tambs, K. (2010). Family matters: Happiness in nuclear families and twins. *Behavioral Genetics, 40,* 577–590.

Nevison, C. D. (2014). A comparison of temporal trends in United States autism prevalence to trends in suspected environmental factors. *Environmental Health, 13,* 73. doi:10.1186/1476-069X-13-73

The New York Times. (2016, February 13). The N.F.L.'s tragic C.T.E. roll call. Retrieved from http://www.nytimes.com/interactive/2016/02/03/sports/football/nfl-brain-disease-cte-concussions.html

Newell, A., Shaw, J. C., & Simon, H. A. (1958). Elements of a theory of human problem solving. *Psychological Review, 65,* 151–166.

Newell, B. R., & Andrews, S. (2004). Levels of processing effects on implicit and explicit memory tasks: Using question position to investigate the lexical-processing hypothesis. *Experimental Psychology, 51,* 132–144.

Newman, A. A. (2015, July 14). Women who dye their (armpit) hair. *The New York Times.* Retrieved from http://www.nytimes.com/2015/07/16/fashion/women-who-dye-their-armpit-hair.html

Newsweek. (2004, June 20). He's one smart puppy. Retrieved from http://www.newsweek.com/hes-one-smart-puppy-128631

Newton, K. M., Reed, S. D., LaCroix, A. Z., Grothaus, L. C., Ehrlich, K., & Guiltinan, J. (2006). Treatment of vasomotor symptoms of menopause with black cohosh, multibotanicals, soy, hormone therapy, or placebo. *Annals of Internal Medicine, 145,* 869–879.

Newton-Howes, G., Levack, W. M., McBride, S., Gilmor, M., & Tester, R. (2016). Non-physiological mechanisms influencing disulfiram treatment of al-cohol use disorder: A grounded theory study. *Drug and Alcohol Dependence, 165,* 126–131.

Neylan, T. C. (1999). Frontal lobe function: Mr. Phineas Gage's famous injury. *Journal of Neuropsychiatry and Clinical Neurosciences, 11,* 280–281.

Ng, C. (2016, August 18). Andre De Grasse, Usain Bolt set to clash in 200 final. *CBC News.* Retrieved from http://feed.cbc.ca/sports/olympics/rio2016/track-field/de-grasse-bolt-semis-1.3725866

Ng, D. M., & Jeffery, R. W. (2003). Relationships between perceived stress and health behaviors in a sample of working adults. *Health Psychology, 22,* 638–642.

Ngun, T. C., Ghahramani, N., Sánchez, F. J., Bocklandt, S., & Vilain, E. (2011). The genetics of sex differences in brain and behavior. *Frontiers in Neuroendocrinology, 32,* 227–248.

Nichols, A. L., & Edlund, J. E. (2015). Practicing what we preach (and sometimes study): Methodological issues in experimental laboratory research. *Review of General Psychology, 19,* 191–202. http://dx.doi.org/10.1037/gpr0000027

Niedenthal, P. M., Augustinova, M., Rychlowska, M., Droit-Volet, S., Zinner, L., Knafo, A., & Brauer, M. (2012). Negative relations between pacifier use and emotional competence. *Basic and Applied Social Psychology, 34,* 387–394.

Nielsen, N. R., Kristensen, T. S., Strandberg-Larsen, K., Zhang, Z.-F., Schnohr, P., & Grønbæk, M. (2008). Perceived stress and risk of colorectal cancer in men and women: A prospective cohort study. *Journal of Internal Medicine, 263,* 192–202.

Nile, S. H., & Park, S. W. P. (2014). Edible berries: Bioactive components and their effect on human health. *Nutrition, 30,* 134–144.

Nir, S. M. (2016, February 23). Woman exonerated after serving 10 years for manslaughter conviction. *The New York Times.* Retrieved from http://www.nytimes.com/2016/02/24/nyregion/womans-manslaughter-conviction-in-1991-death-to-be-vacated.html?_r=0

Nisbett, R. E., Aronson, J., Blair, C., Dickens, W., Flynn, J., Halpern, D. F., & Turkehimer, E. (2012). Intelligence: New findings and theoretical developments. *American Psychologist, 67,* 130–159.

Nishitani, S., Miyamura, T., Tagawa, M., Sumi, M., Takase, R., Doi, H., … Shinohara, K. (2009). The calming effect of a maternal breast milk odor on the human newborn infant. *Neuroscience Research, 63,* 66–71.

Niskar, A. S., Kieszak, S. M., Holmes, A. E., Esteban, E., Rubin, C., & Brody, D. J. (2001). Estimated prevalence of noise-induced hearing threshold shifts among children 6 to 19 years of age: The Third National Health and Nutrition Examination Survey, 1988–1994, United States. *Pediatrics, 108,* 40–43.

Niven, K. (2015). Can music with prosocial lyrics heal the working world? A field intervention in a call center. *Journal of Applied Social Psychology, 45*(3), 132–138.

NobelPrize.org. (2014). Malala Yousafzai—biographical. Retrieved from https://www.nobelprize.org/nobel_prizes/peace/laureates/2014/yousafzai-bio.html

Nolen-Hoeksema, S. (1991). Responses to depression and their effects on the duration of depressive episodes. *Journal of Abnormal Psychology, 100,* 569–582.

Noller, G. (2009). *Literature review and assessment report on MDMA/Ecstasy.* Wellington, New Zealand: Ministry of Health. Retrieved from http://www.moh.govt.nz/notebook/nbbooks.nsf/0/EE5BDDAA39721D6ACC257B8000708A11/$file/July2010Literature-Review-Assessment-Report-MDMA-Ecstasy.pdf

Nonnemaker, J., Hersey, J., Homsi, G., Busey, A., Hyland, A., Juster, H., & Farrelly, M. (2011). Self-reported exposure to policy and environmental influences on smoking cessation and relapse: A 2-year longitudinal population-based study. *International Journal of Environmental Research and Public Health, 8,* 3591–3608.

Norbury, A., & Husain, M. (2015). Sensation-seeking: Dopaminergic modulation and risk for psychopathology. *Behavioural Brain Research, 288,* 79–93.

Norcross, J. C., & Beutler, L. E. (2014). Integrative psychotherapies. In R. J. Corsini & D. Wedding (Eds.), *Current psychotherapies* (10th ed., pp. 499–532). Belmont, CA: Brooks/Cole, Cengage Learning.

Norcross, J. C., & Wampold, B. E. (2011). What works for whom: Tailoring psychotherapy to the person. *Journal of Clinical Psychology, 67,* 127–132.

North, A. (2014, August 1). Here's the thing that "lasting love" is really about [Web log post]. Retrieved from http://op-talk.blogs.nytimes.com/2014/08/01/heres-the-thing-that-lasting-love-is-really-about/?_r=0

Northoff, G. (2012). Genes, brains, and environment—genetic neuroimaging of depression. *Current Opinion in Neurobiology, 23,* 1–10.

Northoff, G., Schneider, F., Rotte, M., Matthiae, C., Tempelmann, C., Wiebking, C., ... Panksepp, J. (2009). Differential parametric modulation of self-relatedness and emotions in different brain regions. *Human Brain Mapping, 30*, 369–382.

Nour, N. M. (2009). Child marriage: A silent health and human rights issue. *Reviews in Obstetrics & Gynecology, 2*, 51–56.

NPR. (2013, December 31). *Pharrell Williams on juxtaposition and seeing sounds.* Retrieved from http://www.npr.org/sections/therecord/2013/12/31/258406317/pharrell-williams-on-juxtaposition-and-seeing-sounds

NPR. (2014, March 30). *Cesar Millan's long walk to becoming the "Dog Whisperer."* Retrieved from http://www.npr.org/2014/03/30/295796786/cesar-millans-long-walk-to-becoming-the-dog-whisperer

Nusbaum, E. C., & Silvia, P. J. (2011). Are intelligence and creativity really so different? Fluid intelligence, executive processes, and strategy use in divergent thinking. *Intelligence, 39*, 36–45.

Nutt, D. J. Lingford-Hughes, A., Erritzoe, D., & Stokes, P. R. A. (2015). The dopamine theory of addiction: 40 years of highs and lows. *Nature Reviews Neuroscience, 16*, 305–312.

O'Brien, D. (2013). *How to develop a brilliant memory week by week: 50 Proven ways to enhance your memory skills.* London, UK: Watkins Publishing.

O'Brien, P. (2007). Is it all right for women to drink small amounts of alcohol in pregnancy? Yes. *British Journal of Medicine, 335*, 856.

O'Donnell, S., Webb, J. K., & Shine, R. (2010). Conditioned taste aversion enhances the survival of an endangered predator imperiled by a toxic invader. *Journal of Applied Ecology, 47*, 558–565.

O'Keefe, D. J. (2008). Elaboration likelihood model. In W. Donsbach (Ed.), *International encyclopedia of communication* (Vol. IV, pp. 1475–1480). Malden, MA: Blackwell.

O'Keeffe, G. S., Clarke-Pearson, K., & Council on Communications and Media. (2011). The impact of social media on children, adolescents, and families. *Pediatrics, 127*, 800–804.

O'Riordan, K. (2012). The life of the gay gene: From hypothetical genetic marker to social reality. *Journal of Sex Research, 49*, 362–368.

Oakley, S. (2012, May 30). Mayo Clinic medical edge: Cochlear implants a good next step when hearing aids are no longer effective. *The Chicago Tribune.* Retrieved from http://articles.chicagotribune.com/2012-05-30/lifestyle/sns-201205291800--tms--premhnstr--k-b20120530-20120530_1_cochlear-auditory-nerve-implant-device

Oar, E. L., Farrell, L. J., & Ollendick, T. H. (2015). One session treatment for specific phobias: An adaptation for paediatric blood-injection-injury phobia in youth. *Clinical Child and Family Psychology Review, 18*, 370–394.

Oatley, K., Keltner, D., & Jenkins, J. (2006). *Understanding emotions.* Malden, MA: Blackwell.

Öberg, M., Jaakkola, M. S., Woodward, A., Peruga, A., & Prüss-Ustün, A. (2011). Worldwide burden of disease from exposure to second-hand smoke: A retrospective analysis of data from 192 countries. *Lancet, 311*, 139–146.

Occupational Safety & Health Administration. (n.d.). *Occupational noise exposure.* Retrieved from https://www.osha.gov/SLTC/noisehearingconservation/

Oda, R., Matsumoto-Oda, A., & Kurashima, O. (2005). Effects of belief in genetic relatedness on resemblance judgments by Japanese raters. *Evolution of Human Behavior, 26*, 441–450.

Oerlemans, W. G. M., Bakker, A. B., & Veenhoven, R. (2011). Finding the key to happy aging: A day reconstruction study of happiness. *Journal of Gerontology: Psychological Sciences, 6*(6), 665–674. doi:10.1093/geronb/gbr040

Oexman, R. (2013, May 5). Better sleep month: Top 10 sleep myths debunked. *Huffpost Healthy Living.* Retrieved from http://www.huffingtonpost.com/dr-robert-oexman/sleep-myths_b_3177375.html

Ohayon, M. (2011). Epidemiological overview of sleep disorders in the general population. *Sleep Medicine Reviews, 2*, 1–9.

Ohayon, M., Carskadon, M. A., Guilleminault, C., & Vitiello, M. V. (2004). Meta-analysis of quantitative sleep parameters from childhood to old age in healthy individuals: Developing normative sleep values across the human lifespan. *SLEEP, 21*, 1255–1273.

Ohbuchi, K., Fukushima, O., & Tedeschi, J. T. (1999). Cultural values in conflict management: Goal orientation, goal attainment, and tactical decision. *Journal of Cross-Cultural Psychology, 30*, 51–70.

Oishi, S., Talhelm, T., & Lee, M. (2015). Personality and geography: Introverts prefer mountains. *Journal of Research in Personality, 58*, 55–68.

Olenik-Shemesh, D., Heiman, T., & Eden, S. (2015). Bystanders' behavior in cyberbullying episodes: Active and passive patterns in the context of personal-socio-emotional factors. *Journal of Interpersonal Violence.* doi:10.1177/0886260515585531

Olson, J. M., Vernon, P. A., Harris, J. A., & Jang, K. L. (2001). The heritability of attitudes: A study of twins. *Journal of Personality and Social Psychology, 80*, 845–860.

Omalu, B. I., DeKosky, S. T., Minster, R. L., Kamboh, M. I., Hamilton, R. L., & Wecht, C. H. (2005). Chronic traumatic encephalopathy in a National Football League player. *Neurosurgery, 57*, 128–134.

Oremus, C., Oremus, M., McNeely, H., Losier, B., Parlar, M., King, M., ... Hanford, L. (2015). Effects of electroconvulsive therapy on cognitive functioning in patients with depression: Protocol for a systematic review and meta-analysis. *BMJ Open, 5*, e006966.

Orzeł-Gryglewska, J. (2010). Consequences of sleep deprivation. *International Journal of Occupational Medicine & Environmental Health, 23*, 94–114.

Oskin, B. (2013, May 17). Fighting to save an endangered bird—with vomit. *LiveScience.* Retrieved from http://www.livescience.com/32092-saving-marbled-murrelet-with-vomit-eggs.html

Öst, L. G. (1989). One-session treatment for specific phobias. *Behaviour Research and Therapy, 27*, 1–7.

Ostrofsky, J., Kozbelt, A., & Seidel, A. (2012). Perceptual constancies and visual selection as predictors of realistic drawing skill. *Psychology of Aesthetics, Creativity, and the Arts, 6*, 124–136.

Overmier, J. B., & Seligman, M. E. P. (1967). Effects of inescapable shock upon subsequent escape and avoidance responding. *Journal of Comparative and Physiological Psychology, 63*, 28–33.

Owen, E. (2016, June 22). Girl endures childhood neglect, makes amazing progress with adoptive family. *The San Francisco Globe.* Retrieved from http://sfglobe.com/2015/09/20/girl-endures-childhood-neglect-makes-amazing-progress-with-adoptive-family/

Owen, J. J., Adelson, J., Budge, S., Kopta, S. M., & Reese, R. J. (2016). Good-enough level and dose-effect models: Variation among outcomes and therapists. *Psychotherapy Research, 26*, 22–30.

Owen, P. R., & Padron, M. (2016). The language of toys: Gendered language in toy advertisements. *Journal of Research on Women and Gender, 6*, 67–80.

Oxford Royale Academy (2014, October 15). 11 *Great jokes to help you remember English grammar rules.* Retrieved from https://www.oxford-royale.co.uk/articles/11-great-jokes-remember-english-grammar-rules.html

Pachana, N. A., Brilleman, S. L., & Dobson, A. J. (2011). Reporting of life events over time: Methodological issues in a longitudinal sample of women. *Psychological Assessment, 23*, 277–281.

Padden, C., & Humphries, T. (1988). *Deaf in America: Voices from a culture.* Cambridge, MA: Harvard University Press.

Pagnini, F., Bercovitz, K., & Langer, E. (2016). Perceived control and mindfulness: Implications for clinical practice. *Journal of Psychotherapy Integration, 26*, 91–102.

Paikoff, R. L., & Brooks-Gunn, J. (1991). Do parent–child relationships change during puberty? *Psychological Bulletin, 110*, 47–66.

Palermo, T. M., Eccleston, C., Lewandowski, A. S., Williams, A. C., & Morley, S. (2010). Randomized controlled trials of psychological therapies for management of chronic pain in children and adolescents: An updated meta-analytic review. *Pain, 148*, 387–397.

Pallister, T., Sharafi, M., Lachance, G., Pirastu, N., Mohney, R. P., MacGregor, A., ... Menni, C. (2015). Food preference patterns in a UK twin cohort. *Twin Research and Human Genetics, 18*(6), 793–805.

Palmatier, J. J., & Rovner, L. (2015). Credibility assessment: Preliminary process theory, the polygraph process, and construct validity. *International Journal of Psychophysiology, 95*, 3–13.

Palmer, K. M. (2015, January 26). Why did vaccinated people get measles at Disneyland? Blame the unvaccinated. *Wired.* Retrieved from http://www.wired.com/2015/01/vaccinated-people-get-measles-disneyland-blame-unvaccinated/

Pan, J.-Y., & Wong, D. F. K. (2011). Acculturative stressors and acculturative strategies as predictors of negative affect among Chinese international students in

Australia and Hong Kong: A cross-cultural comparative study. *Academic Psychiatry, 35,* 376–381.

Pape, H-C., & Pare, D. (2010). Plastic synaptic networks of the amygdala for the acquisition, expression, and extinction of conditioned fear. *Physiological Review, 90,* 419–463.

Paris, J. (2014). Modernity and narcissistic personality disorder. *Personality Disorders: Theory, Research, and Treatment, 5,* 220–226.

Paris, J. (2015). Antisocial personality disorder. In J. Paris, *A concise guide to personality disorders* (pp. 65–71). Washington, DC: American Psychological Association.

Parker, K. N., & Ragsdale, J. M. (2015). Effects of distress and eustress on changes in fatigue from waking to working. *Applied Psychology: Health and Well-Being, 7,* 293–315.

Parmentier, F. B. R., & Andrés, P. (2010). The involuntary capture of attention by sound: Novelty and postnovelty distraction in young and older adults. *Experimental Psychology, 57,* 68–76.

Parrott, A. C. (2004). MDMA (3,4-Methylenedioxymethamphetamine) or Ecstasy: The neuropsychobiological implications of taking it at dances and raves. *Neuropsychobiology, 50,* 329–335.

Parrott, A. C. (2015). Why all stimulant drugs are damaging to recreational users: An empirical overview and psychobiological explanation. *Human Psychopharmacology: Clinical and Experimental, 30*(4), 213–224.

Parry, M. S. (2006). Dorothea Dix (1802–1887). *American Journal of Public Health, 96,* 624–625.

Partanen, E., Kujala, T., Näätänen, R., Liitola, A., Sambeth, A., & Huotilainen, M. (2013). Learning-induced neural plasticity of speech processing before birth. *Proceedings of the National Academy of Sciences, 110*(37), 15145–15150.

Parth, K., & Loeffler-Stastka, H. (2015). Psychoanalytic core competence. *Frontiers in Psychology, 6.* doi:10.3389/fpsyg.2015.00356

Partisan Pictures (Producer). (2012). *Cesar Millan: The Real Story* [DVD]. Available from https://www.amazon.com/Cesar-Millan-Real-Story-Milan/dp/B00A4Y61SC

Pasanen, T. P., Tyrväinen, L., & Korpela, K. M. (2014). The relationship between perceived health and physical activity indoors, outdoors in built environments, and outdoors in nature. *Applied Psychology: Health and Well-Being, 6,* 324–346.

Pashler, H., Rohrer, D., Cepeda, N. J., & Carpenter, S. K. (2007). Enhancing learning and retarding forgetting: Choices and consequences. *Psychonomic Bulletin & Review, 14,* 187–193.

Patihis, L. (2016). Individual differences and correlates of highly superior autobiographical memory. *Memory, 24,* 961–978.

Patihis, L., Frenda, S. J., LePort, A. K., Petersen, N., Nichols, R. M., Stark, C. E., … Loftus, E. F. (2013). False memories in highly superior autobiographical memory individuals. *Proceedings of the National Academy of Sciences, 110,* 20947–20952.

Patihis, L., Ho, L. Y., Lilienfeld, S. O., & Loftus, E. F. (2014). Unconscious repressed memory is scientifically questionable. *Psychological Science, 25,* 1967–1968.

Patihis, L., Ho, L. Y., Tingen, I. W., Lilienfeld, S. O., & Loftus, E. F. (2014). Are the "Memory Wars" over? A scientist-practitioner gap in beliefs about repressed memory. *Psychological Science, 25,* 519–530.

Patil, K., Pressnitzer, D., Shamma, S., & Elhilali, M. (2012) Music in our ears: The biological bases of musical timbre perception. *PLOS Computational Biology, 8*(11): e1002759. doi:10.1371/journal.pcbi.1002759

Patorno, E., Bohn, R. L., Wahl, P. M., Avorn, J., Patrick, A. R., Liu, J., & Schneeweiss, S. (2010). Anticonvulsant medications and the risk of suicide, attempted suicide, or violent death. *Journal of the American Medical Association, 303,* 1401–1409.

Pauls, D. L., Abramovitch, A., Rauch, S. L., & Geller, D. A. (2014). Obsessive-compulsive disorder: An integrative genetic and neurobiological perspective. *Nature Reviews Neuroscience, 15,* 410–424.

Pavličev, M., & Wagner, G. (2016).The evolutionary origin of female orgasm. *Journal of Experimental Zoology B: Molecular and Developmental Evolution, 326*(6), 326–327.

Pavlos, P., Vasilios, N., Antonia, A., Dimitrios, K., Georgios, K., & Georgios, A. (2009). Evaluation of young smokers and non-smokers with electrogustometry and contact endoscopy. *BMC Ear, Nose and Throat Disorders, 9*(9). doi:10.1186/1472-6815-9-9

Pavlov, I. (1906). The scientific investigation of the psychical faculties or processes in the higher animals. *Science, 24,* 613–619.

Pavlov, I. (1927/1960). *Conditioned reflexes.* New York, NY: Dover.

Pavlovich-Danis, S. J., & Patterson, K. (2006, January 9). For a good night's sleep. *Nurseweek News.*

Payne, E. Ford, D., & Morris, J. (2015, February 25). Jury finds Eddie Ray Routh guilty in "American Sniper" case. *CNN.* Retrieved from http://www.cnn.com/2015/02/24/us/american-sniper-chris-kyle-trial/

Pazda, A. D., Elliot, A. J., & Greitemeyer, T. (2012). Sexy red: Perceived sexual receptivity mediates the red-attraction relation in men viewing women. *Journal of Experimental Social Psychology, 48,* 787–790.

Pazda, A. D., Prokop, P., & Elliot, A. J. (2014). Red and romantic rivalry: Viewing another woman in red increases perceptions of sexual receptivity, derogation, and intentions to mate-guard. *Personality and Social Psychology Bulletin, 40,* 1260–1269.

Pazzaglia, M. (2015). Body and odors not just molecules, after all. *Current Directions in Psychological Science, 24,* 329–333.

PBS. (1997, March 4). Secret of the wild child. *NOVA.* Retrieved from http://www.pbs.org/wgbh/nova/transcripts/2112gchild.html

PBS. (2005, January 27). Kinsey. *American Experience.* Retrieved from http://www.pbs.org/wgbh/amex/kinsey/peopleevents/p_kinsey.html

PBS. (2014). Other notorious insanity cases. *Frontline.* Retrieved from http://www.pbs.org/wgbh/pages/frontline/shows/crime/trial/other.html

Pearce, J. M. (2009). Marie-Jean-Pierre Flourens (1794–1867) and cortical localization. *European Journal of Neurology, 61,* 311–314.

Penfield, W., & Boldrey E. (1937). Somatic motor and sensory representation in the cerebral cortex of man as studied by electrical stimulation. *Brain, 60,* 389–443.

Pennisi, E. (2012, September 5). Human genome is much more than just genes. *Science NOW.* Retrieved from http://www.sciencemag.org/news/2012/09/human-genome-much-more-just-genes

Peplau, L. A. (2003). Human sexuality: How do men and women differ? *Current Directions in Psychological Science, 12,* 37–40.

Perkins, K. A., Karelitz, J. L., Conklin, C. A., Sayette, M. A., & Giedgowd, G. E. (2010). Acute negative affect relief from smoking depends on the affect measure and situation, but not on nicotine. *Biological Psychiatry, 67,* 707–714.

Perlman, L. M., & Segal, N. L. (2005). Memories of the Child Development Center study of adopted monozygotic twins reared apart: An unfulfilled promise. *Twin Research and Human Genetics, 8*(3), 271–381.

Perrin, A. J., Cohen, P. N., & Caren, N. (2013). Are children of parents who had same-sex relationships disadvantaged? A scientific evaluation of the no-differences hypothesis. *Journal of Gay & Lesbian Mental Health, 17,* 327–336.

Peschel, S. K., Feeling, N. R., Vögele, C., Kaess, M., Thayer, J. F., & Koenig, J. (2016). A systematic review on heart rate variability in bulimia nervosa. *Neuroscience & Biobehavioral Reviews, 63,* 78–97.

Peters, W. (1971). *A class divided: Then and now.* New Haven, CT: Yale University Press.

Peterson, B. S., Warner, V., Bansal, R., Zhu, H., Hao, X., Liu, J., … Weissman, M. M. (2009). Cortical thinning in persons at increased familial risk for major depression. *Proceedings of the National Academy of Sciences, 106,* 6273–6278.

Peterson, G. B. (2000). The discovery of shaping: B. F. Skinner's big surprise. *The Clicker Journal: The Magazine for Animal Trainers, 43,* 6–13.

Peterson, G. B. (2004). A day of great illumination: B. F. Skinner's discovery of shaping. *Journal of the Experimental Analysis of Behavior, 82,* 317–328.

Peterson, L. R., & Peterson, M. J. (1959). Short-term retention of individual verbal items. *Journal of Experimental Psychology, 58,* 193–198.

Peterson, M. J., Meagher, R. B. Jr., & Ellsbury, S. W. (1970). Repetition effects in sensory memory. *Journal of Experimental Psychology, 84,* 15–23.

Petit, D., Pennestri, M. H., Paquet, J., Desautels, A., Zadra, A., Vitaro, F., … Montplaisir, J. (2015). Childhood sleepwalking and sleep terrors: A longitudinal study of prevalence and familial aggregation. *JAMA Pediatrics, 169,* 653–658.

Petitto, L. A. (1994). Are signed languages "real" languages? *International Quarterly of the Sign Linguistics Association, 7,* 1–10.

Petitto, L. A., & Marentette, P. F. (1991). Babbling in the manual mode: Evidence for the ontogeny of language. *Science, 251,* 1493–1496.

Petronis, A. (2004). The origin of schizophrenia: Genetic thesis, epigenetic antithesis, and resolving synthesis. *Biological Psychiatry, 55,* 965–970.

Pettit, M. (2012). The queer life of a lab rat. *History of Psychology, 15*(3), 217–222.

Petty, R. E., & Cacioppo, J. T. (1986). The elaboration likelihood model of persuasion. *Advances in Experimental Social Psychology, 19,* 123–205.

Pew Research Center. (2013, June 4). *The global divide on homosexuality.* Retrieved from http://www.pewglobal.org/2013/06/04/the-global-divide-on-homosexuality/

Pew Research Center. (2014, February 3). *6 New facts about Facebook.* Retrieved from http://www.pewresearch.org/fact-tank/2014/02/03/6-new-facts-about-facebook/

Pew Research Center. (2014, October 6). *Most are confident in government's ability to prevent major Ebola outbreak in U.S.* Retrieved from http://www.people-press.org/files/2014/10/10-6-14-Ebola-Release.pdf

Pew Research Center. (2016, November 3). *U.S. unauthorized immigration population estimates.* Retrieved from http://www.pewhispanic.org/interactives/unauthorized-immigrants/

Pew Research Center. (2015, September 28). *Modern immigration wave brings 59 million to U.S., driving population growth and change through 2065: Views of immigration's impact on U.S. society mixed.* Retrieved from http://www.pewhispanic.org/2015/09/28/chapter-5-u-s-foreign-born-population-trends/

Pew Research Center. (2015, October 8). *Social media usage: 2005–2015.* Retrieved from http://www.pewinternet.org/2015/10/08/social-networking-usage-2005-2015/

Pfeifer, C. (2012). Physical attractiveness, employment and earnings. *Applied Economics Letters, 19,* 505–510.

Phillips, J. (2013). Prescription drug abuse: Problem, policies, and implications. *Nursing Outlook, 61,* 78–84.

Phillips, R. G., & LeDoux, J. E. (1992). Differential contribution of amygdala and hippocampus to cued and contextual fear conditioning. *Behavioral Neuroscience, 106,* 274–285.

Piaget, J. (1936/1952). *The origins of intelligence in children.* New York, NY: W. W. Norton.

Pich, E. M., Pagliusi, S. R., Tessari, M., Talabot-Ayer, D., Van Huijsduijnen, R. H., & Chiamulera, C. (1997). Common neural substrates for the addictive properties of nicotine and cocaine. *Science, 275,* 83–86.

Pickren, W. E., & Burchett, C. (2014). Making psychology inclusive: A history of education and training for diversity in American psychology. In W. E. Pickren, C. Burchett, F. T. L. Leong, L. Comas-Díaz, G. C. Nagayama Hall, C. Gordon, … J. E. Trimble (Eds.), *APA handbook of multicultural psychology: Vol. 2. Applications and training* (pp. 3–18). Washington, DC: American Psychological Association.

Pierre, J. M. (2012). Mental illness and mental health: Is the glass half empty or half full? *Canadian Journal of Psychiatry, 57,* 651–658.

Pike, G. (2014, March/April). Prisoner's escape. *Scientific American Mind, 25,* 16.

Pike, K. M., & Dunne, P. E. (2015). The rise of eating disorders in Asia: A review. *Journal of Eating Disorders, 3,* 33. doi:10.1186/s40337-015-0070-2

Pilley, J. W., & Reid, A. K. (2011). Border collie comprehends object names as verbal referents. *Behavioural Processes, 86,* 184–195.

Pine Ridge Indian Reservation. (2016). Retrieved from http://www.re-member.org/pine-ridge-reservation.aspx

Pines, A. (2011). Male menopause: Is it a real clinical syndrome? *Climacteric, 14,* 15–17.

Pinker, S. (1994). *The language instinct.* New York, NY: Harper Perennial.

Pinker, S. (2003). Language as an adaptation to the cognitive niche. In M. H. Christiansen & S. Kirby (Eds.), *Language evolution: The states of the art* (pp. 16–37). New York, NY: Oxford University Press.

Piper, A., Lillevik, L., & Kritzer, R. (2008). What's wrong with believing in repression?: A review for legal professionals. *Psychology, Public Policy, and Law, 14,* 223–242.

Pirnia, T., Joshi, S. H., Leaver, A. M., Vasavada, M., Njau, S., Woods, R. P., Espinoza, R., & Narr, K. L. (2016). Electroconvulsive therapy and structural neuroplasticity in neocortical, limbic and paralimbic cortex. *Translational Psychiatry, 6,* e832. doi:10.1038/tp.2016.102

Pison, G., Monden, C., & Smits, J. (2015). Twinning rates in developed countries: Trends and explanations. *Population and Development Review, 41*(4), 629–649.

Pittenger, C., Adams, T. G., Gallezot, J. D., Crowley, M. J., Nabulsi, N., Ropchan, J., … Hannestad, J. (2016). OCD is associated with an altered association between sensorimotor gating and cortical and subcortical 5-HT1b receptor binding. *Journal of Affective Disorders, 196,* 87–96.

Pittenger, D. J. (1993, November). Measuring the MBTI and coming up short. *Journal of Career Planning & Placement, 54,* 48–52.

Pittenger, D. J. (2005). Cautionary comments regarding the Myers-Briggs Type Indicator. *Consulting Psychology Journal: Practice and Research, 57,* 210–221.

Platt, J. R. (2011, December 27). Lions vs. cattle: Taste aversion could solve African predator problem [Web log post]. Retrieved from http://blogs.scientificamerican.com/extinction-countdown/lions-vs-cattle-taste-aversion/

Platt, J. R. (2015, June 24). African lion populations drop 42 percent in past 21 years [Web log post]. Retrieved from http://blogs.scientificamerican.com/extinction-countdown/african-lion-populations-drop-42-percent-in-past-21-years/

Pletcher, M. J., Vittinghoff, E., Kalhan, R., Richman, J., Safford, M., Sidney, S., … Kertesz, S. (2012). Association between marijuana exposure and pulmonary function over 20 years. *Journal of the American Medical Association, 307,* 173–181.

Plomin, R., & DeFries, J. C. (1998). Genetics of cognitive abilities and disabilities. *Scientific American, 218,* 62–69.

Plomin, R., DeFries, J. C., Knopik, V. S., & Neiderhiser, J. M. (2013). *Behavioral genetics* (6th ed.). New York, NY: Worth.

Plomin, R., DeFries, J. C., Knopik, V. S., & Neiderhiser, J. M. (2016). Top 10 replicated findings from behavioral genetics. *Perspectives on Psychological Science, 11,* 3–23.

Poisson, J. (2013, November 5). Remember Storm? We check in on the baby being raised gender-neutral. *thestar.com.* Retrieved from https://www.thestar.com/life/parent/2013/11/15/remember_storm_we_check_in_on_the_baby_being_raised_genderneutral.html

Polderman, T. J., Benyamin, B., de Leeuw, C. A., Sullivan, P. F., van Bochoven, A., Visscher, P. M., & Posthuma, D. (2015). Meta-analysis of the heritability of human traits based on fifty years of twin studies. *Nature Genetics, 47*(7), 702–709.

Polidori, M. C., Nelles, G., & Pientka, L. (2010). Prevention of dementia: Focus on lifestyle. *International Journal of Alzheimer's Disease, 2010,* 1–9. http://dx.doi.org/10.4061/2010/393579

Poly, C., Massaro, J. M., Seshadri, S., Wolf, P. A., Cho, E., Krall, E., … Au, R. (2011). The relation of dietary choline to cognitive performance and white-matter hyperintensity in the Framingham Offspring Cohort. *American Journal of Clinical Nutrition, 94*(6), 1584–1591.

Poole, S. (2016, April 20). 20 Things you probably didn't know about Harriet Tubman. *The Atlanta Journal-Constitution.* Retrieved from http://www.ajc.com/news/lifestyles/think-you-know-everything-about-harriet-tubman-thi/nq8Xd/

Pope, K. S., & Wedding, D. (2014). Contemporary challenges and controversies. In R. J. Corsini & D. Wedding (Eds.), *Current psychotherapies* (10th ed., pp. 569–604). Belmont, CA: Brooks/Cole, Cengage Learning.

Porsch, R. M., Middeldorp, C. M., Cherny, S. S., Krapohl, E., Van Beijsterveldt, C. E., Loukola, A., … Kaprio, J. (2016). Longitudinal heritability of childhood aggression. *American Journal of Medical Genetics Part B: Neuropsychiatric Genetics, 171B,* 697–707.

Porter, J. S., Stern, M., & Zak-Place, J. (2009). Prematurity, stereotyping, and perceived vulnerability at 5 months: Relations with mothers and their premature and full-term infants at 9 months. *Journal of Reproductive and Infant Psychology, 27,* 168–181.

Porter, R. H., & Winberg, J. (1999). Unique salience of maternal breast odors for newborn infants. *Neuroscience & Biobehavioral Reviews, 23,* 439–449.

Porter, S. B., & Baker, A. T. (2015). CSI (Crime Scene Induction): Creating false memories of committing crime. *Trends in Cognitive Sciences, 19,* 716–718.

Portnuff, C. D. (2016). Reducing the risk of music-induced hearing loss from overuse of portable listening devices: Understanding the problems and establishing strategies for improving awareness in adolescents. *Adolescent Health, Medicine and Therapeutics, 7,* 27–35.

Post, R. M., Altshuler, L., Kupka, R., McElroy, S. L., Frye, M. A., Rowe, M., … Nolen, W. A. (2015). Multigenerational positive family history of psychiatric disorders is associated with a poor prognosis in bipolar disorder. *The Journal of Neuropsychiatry and Clinical Neurosciences, 27,* 304–310.

Postuma, R. B., Gagnon, J. F., Vendette, M., Fantini, M. L., Massicotte-Marquez, J., & Montplaisir, J. (2009). Quantifying the risk of neurodegenerative disease in idiopathic REM sleep behavior disorder. *Neurology, 72,* 1296–1300.

Pottala, J. V., Yaffe, K., Robinson, J. G., Espeland, M. A., Wallace, R., & Harris, W. S. (2014). Higher RBC EPA + DHA corresponds with larger total brain and hippocampal volumes: WHIMS-MRI Study. *Neurology, 82*(5), 435–442.

Potter, R. H. (2006). "As firecrackers to atom bombs": Kinsey, science, and authority. *Sexuality & Culture, 10,* 29–38.

Poulain, M., Herm, A., & Pes, G. (2013). The Blue Zones: Areas of exceptional longevity around the world. *Vienna Yearbook of Population Research, 11,* 87–108.

Poulose, S. M., Miller, M. G., & Shukitt-Hale, B. (2014). Role of walnuts in maintaining brain health with age. *The Journal of Nutrition, 144* (Suppl. 4), 561S–566S.

Poulton, E. C. (1967). Population norms of top sensory magnitudes and SS Stevens' exponents. *Perception & Psychophysics, 2,* 312–316.

Powell, L. H., Shahabi, L., & Thoresen, C. E. (2003). Religion and spirituality: Linkages to physical health. *American Psychologist, 58,* 36–52.

Powell, R. A. (2010). Little Albert still missing. *American Psychologist, 65,* 299–300.

Powell, R. A., Digdon, N., Harris, B., & Smithson, C. (2014). Correcting the record on Watson, Rayner and Little Albert: Albert Barger as "Psychology's Lost Boy." *American Psychologist, 69,* 600–611.

Power, R. A., & Pluess, M. (2015). Heritability estimates of the Big Five personality traits based on common genetic variants. *Translational Psychiatry, 5,* e604. doi:10.1038/tp.2015.96

Powers, A., Cross, D., Fani, N., & Bradley, B. (2015). PTSD, emotion dysregulation, and dissociative symptoms in a highly traumatized sample. *Journal of Psychiatric Research, 61,* 174–179.

Powers, M. B., & Carlbring, P. (2016). Technology: Bridging the gap from research to practice. *Cognitive Behaviour Therapy, 45,* 1–4.

Premack, A. J., & Premack, D. (1972). Teaching language to an ape. *Scientific American, 227,* 92–99.

Presse, N., Belleville, S., Gaudreau, P., Greenwood, C. E., Kergoat, M. J., Morais, J. A., … Ferland, G. (2013). Vitamin K status and cognitive function in healthy older adults. *Neurobiology of Aging, 34*(12), 2777–2783.

Pribis, P., Bailey, R. N., Russell, A. A., Kilsby, M. A., Hernandez, M., Craig, W. J., … Sabatè, J. (2012). Effects of walnut consumption on cognitive performance in young adults. *British Journal of Nutrition, 107*(9), 1393–1401.

Pribis, P., & Shukitt-Hale, B. (2014). Cognition: The new frontier for nuts and berries. *The American Journal of Clinical Nutrition, 100* (Suppl. 1), 3475–3525.

Prinstein, M. J., Meade, C. S., & Cohen, G. L. (2003). Adolescent oral sex, peer popularity, and perceptions of best friends' sexual behavior. *Journal of Pediatric Psychology, 28,* 243–249.

Pro Football Hall of Fame. (n.d.). *Harry Carson enshrinement speech.* Retrieved from http://www.profootballhof.com/players/harry-carson/enshrinement/

Prochaska, J. J., Velicer, W. F., Prochaska, J. O., Delucchi, K., & Hall, S. M. (2006). Comparing intervention outcomes in smokers treated for single versus multiple behavioral risks. *Health Psychology, 25,* 380–388.

Prochaska, J. O., & Norcross, J. C. (2014). *Systems of psychotherapy* (8th ed.). Pacific Grove, CA: Brooks/Cole, Cengage Learning.

Prüfer, K., Munch, K., Hellmann, I., Akagi, K., Miller, J. R., Walenz, B., … Pääbo, S. (2012). The bonobo genome compared with the chimpanzee and human genomes. *Nature, 486,* 527–531.

Pryor, K. (2002). *Don't shoot the dog!* Dorking, UK: Ringpress Books.

Przybelski, R. J., & Binkley, N. C. (2007). Is vitamin D important for preserving cognition? A positive correlation of serum 25-hydroxyvitamin D concentration with cognitive function. *Archives of Biochemistry and Biophysics, 460,* 202–205.

Przybylski, A. K., & Weinstein, N. (2012). Can you connect with me now? How the presence of mobile communication technology influences face-to-face conversation quality. *Journal of Social and Personal Relationships, 30,* 237–246.

Puce, A., & Carey, L. (2010). Somatosensory function. In I. B. Weiner & W. E. Craighead (Eds.), *The Corsini encyclopedia of psychology* (4th ed., Vol. 4, pp. 1678–1680). Hoboken, NJ: John Wiley & Sons.

Pugh, J., Kahane, G., Maslen, H., & Savulescu, J. (2016). Lay attitudes toward deception in medicine: Theoretical considerations and empirical evidence. *AJOB Empirical Bioethics, 7,* 31–38.

Puig, J., Englund, M. M., Simpson, J. A., & Collins, W. A. (2013). Predicting adult physical illness from infant attachment: A prospective longitudinal study. *Health Psychology, 32,* 409–417.

Pullum, G. K. (1991). *The great Eskimo vocabulary hoax and other irreverent essays on the study of language.* Chicago, IL: University of Chicago Press.

Punjabi, N. M. (2008). The epidemiology of adult obstructive sleep apnea. *Proceedings of the American Thoracic Society, 5,* 136–143.

Qin, S., Ge, S., Yin, H., Xia, J., & Heynderickx, I. (2010). Just noticeable difference in black level, white level and chroma for natural images measured in two different countries. *Displays, 31,* 25–34.

Quinn, O. W. (1963). The public image of the family. In David Rosenthal (Ed.), *The Genain quadruplets: A case study and theoretical analysis of heredity and environment in schizophrenia* (pp. 355–372). New York, NY: Basic Books.

Rabinowitz, M., Latella, L., Stern, C., & Jost, J. T. (2016). Beliefs about childhood vaccination in the United States: Political ideology, false consensus, and the illusion of uniqueness. *PLOS ONE, 11,* e0158382.

Rabkin, J. G., & Struening, E. L. (1976). Life events, stress, and illness. *Science, 194,* 1013–1020.

Radak, Z., Hart, N., Sarga, L., Koltai, E., Atalay, M., Ohno, H., & Boldough, I. (2010). Exercise plays a preventive role against Alzheimer's disease. *Journal of Alzheimer's Disease, 20,* 777–783.

Radua, J., & Mataix-Cols, D. (2009). Voxel-wise meta-analysis of grey matter changes in obsessive-compulsive disorder. *British Journal of Psychiatry, 195,* 393–402.

Raevuori, A., Keski-Rahkonen, A., & Hoek, H. W. (2014). A review of eating disorders in males. *Current Opinion in Psychiatry, 27,* 426–430.

Raichle, K. A., Hanley, M., Jensen, M. P., & Cardenas, D. D. (2007). Cognitions, coping, and social environment predict adjustment to pain in spinal cord injury. *Journal of Pain, 8,* 718–729.

Raine, A., Lencz, T., Bihrle, S., LaCasse, L., & Colletti, P. (2000). Reduced prefrontal gray matter volume and reduced autonomic activity in antisocial personality disorder. *Archives of General Psychiatry, 57,* 119–127.

Rainville, P., Duncan, G. H., Price, D. D., Carrier, B., & Bushnell, M. C. (1997, August 15). Pain affect encoded in human anterior cingulate but not somatosensory cortex. *Science, 277* (5328), 968–971.

Rajah, A., Kumar, R. S., Somasundaram, C. P., & Kumar, A. A. (2009). Dissociative fugue in the elderly. *Indian Journal of Psychiatry, 51,* 305–307.

Ramachandran, V. S., & Brang, D. (2009). Sensations evoked in patients with amputation from watching an individual whose corresponding intact limb is being touched. *Archives of Neurology, 66,* 1281–1284.

Ramachandran, V. S., & Rogers-Ramachandran, D. (2008). Right side up. *Scientific American, 18,* 22–25.

Ramachandran, V. S., & Rogers-Ramachandran, D. (2009). I see, but I don't know. Patients with unusual visual deficits provide insights into how we normally see. *Scientific American Mind, 19,* 20–22.

Ramchandran, K., & Hauser, J. (2010). Phantom limb pain #212. *Journal of Palliative Medicine, 13,* 1285–1287.

Rameson, L. T., Morelli, S. A., & Lieberman, M. D. (2012). The neural correlates of empathy: Experience, automaticity, and prosocial behavior. *Journal of Cognitive Neuroscience, 24,* 235–245.

Randall, D. K. (2012, September 22). Rethinking sleep. *The New York Times.* Retrieved from http://www.nytimes.com/2012/09/23/opinion/sunday/rethinking-sleep.html

Rasch, B., & Born, J. (2013). About sleep's role in memory. *Physiological Reviews, 93,* 681–766.

Rasmussen, S. C. (2007). The history of science as a tool to identify and confront pseudoscience. *Journal of Chemical Education, 84,* 949–951.

Ratiu, P., Talos, I. F., Haker, S., Lieberman, D., & Everett, P. (2004). The tale of Phineas Gage, digitally remastered. *Journal of Neurotrauma, 21,* 637–643.

Ratnesar, R. (2011, July/August). The menace within. *Stanford Magazine.* Retrieved from http://alumni.stanford.edu/get/page/magazine/article/?article_id=40741

Rawson, R. (1979, May 7). Two Ohio strangers find they're twins at 39—and a dream to psychologists. *People.* Retrieved from http://www.people.com/people/archive/article/0,,20073583,00.html

Read, J., & Bentall, R. (2010). The effectiveness of electroconvulsive therapy: A literature review. *Epidemiologia e Psichiatria Sociale, 19,* 333–347.

Reas, E. (2014). Exercise counteracts genetic risk for Alzheimer's. *Scientific American Mind, 25,* 12.

Reas, E. (2014, July/August). Sugar may harm brain health. *Scientific American Mind, 25,* 14.

Reber, P. (2010, May/June). Ask the brains: What is the memory capacity of the human brain? Is there a physical limit to the amount of information it can store? *Scientific American Mind, 21,* 70.

Reber, S., Allen, R., & Reber, E. S. (2009). Appendix A: Simple phobias. In S. Reber, R. Allen, & E. S. Reber (Eds.). *The Penguin dictionary of psychology* (4th ed.). London, UK: Penguin.

Reby, D., Levréro, F., Gustafsson, E., & Mathevon, N. (2016). Sex stereotypes influence adults' perception of babies' cries. *BioMed Central Psychology, 4*(19). doi: 10.1186/s40359-016-0123-6

Rechtschaffen, A., & Bergmann, B. M. (1995). Sleep deprivation in the rat by the disk-over-water method. *Behavioural Brain Research, 69,* 55–63.

Reece, A. S. (2009). Chronic toxicology of cannabis. *Clinical Toxicology, 47,* 517–524.

Rees, J. L. (2003). Genetics of hair and skin color. *Annual Review of Genetics, 37,* 67–90.

Reese, H. W. (2010). Regarding Little Albert. *American Psychologist, 65,* 300–301.

Regnerus, M., & Gordon, D. (2013). *Social, emotional, and relational distinctions in patterns of recent masturbation among young adults.* Austin, TX: Austin Institute for the Study of Family and Culture. Retrieved from http://www.austin-institute.org/wp-content/uploads/2014/02/M-word-manuscript-for-website-working-paper-v2.pdf

Rehm, J., Shield, K. D., Roerecke, M., & Gmel, G. (2016). Modelling the impact of alcohol consumption on cardiovascular disease mortality for comparative risk assessments: An overview. *BMC Public Health, 16,* 363–372. doi:10.1186/s12889-016-3026-9

Reiche, E. M. V., Nunes, S. O. V., & Morimoto, H. K. (2004). Stress, depression, the immune system, and cancer. *Lancet Oncology, 5,* 617–625.

Reichert, C., Fendrich, R., Bernarding, J., Tempelmann, C., Hinrichs, H., & Rieger, J. W. (2014). Online tracking of the contents of conscious perception using real-time fMRI. *Probing Auditory Scene Analysis, 69.* http://dx.doi.org/10.3389/fnins.2014.00116.

Reisenzein, R. (1983). The Schachter theory of emotion: Two decades later. *Psychological Bulletin, 94,* 239–264.

Ren, J., Wu, Y. D., Chan, J. S., & Yan, J. H. (2013). Cognitive aging affects motor performance and learning. *Geriatrics & Gerontology International, 13,* 19–27. doi:10.1111/j.1447-0594.2012.00914.x

Reneman, L., Booij, J., de Bruin, K., Reitsma, J. B., de Wolff, F. A., Gunning, W. B., … van den Brink, W. (2001). Effects of dose, sex, and long-term abstention from use on toxic effects of MDMA (Ecstasy) on brain serotonin neurons. *Lancet, 358,* 1864–1869.

Renner, M. J., & Mackin, R. S. (1998). A life stress instrument for classroom use. *Teaching of Psychology, 25,* 46–48.

Renner, W., Laireiter, A.-R., & Maier, M. (2012). Social support as a moderator of acculturative stress among refugees and asylum seekers. *Social Behavior and Personality, 40,* 129–146.

Rentzeperis, I., Nikolaev, A. R., Kiper, D. C., & van Leeuwen, C. (2014). Distributed processing of color and form in the visual cortex. *Frontiers in Psychology, 5.* doi:10.3389/fpsyg.2014.00932

Reuter-Lorenz, P. A. (2013). Aging and cognitive neuroimaging: A fertile union. *Perspectives on Psychological Science, 8,* 68–71.

Reynard, J., Brewster, S., & Biers, S. (2013). *Oxford handbook of urology* (3rd ed.). Oxford, UK: Oxford University Press.

Reynolds, B. A., & Weiss, S. (1992). Generation of neurons and astrocytes from isolated cells of the adult mammalian central nervous system. *Science, 255,* 1707–1710.

Reynolds, G., Field, A. P., & Askew, C. (2015). Learning to fear a second-order stimulus following vicarious learning. *Cognition and Emotion.* doi: 1080/02699931.2015.1116978

Rhudy, J. L., & Meagher, M. W. (2000). Fear and anxiety: Divergent effects on human pain thresholds. *Pain, 84,* 65–75.

Rice, E., Rhoades, H., Winetrobe, H., Sanchez, M., Montoya, J., Plant, A., & Kordic, T. (2012). Sexually explicit cell phone messaging associated with sexual risk among adolescents. *Pediatrics, 130,* 667–673.

Richtel, M. (2016, April 27). Texting and driving? Watch out for the textalyzer. *The New York Times.* Retrieved from http://www.nytimes.com/2016/04/28/science/driving-texting-safety-textalyzer.html

Ridout, K. K., Carpenter, L. L., & Tyrka, A. R. (2016). The cellular sequelae of early stress: Focus on aging and mitochondria. *Neuropsychopharmacology, 41,* 388–389.

Rieger, G., Cash, B. M., Merrill, S. M., Jones-Rounds, J., Dharmavaram, S. M., & Savin-Williams, R. C. (2015). Sexual arousal: The correspondence of eyes and genitals. *Biological Psychology, 104,* 56–64.

Rieger, G., & Savin-Williams, R. C. (2012). The eyes have it: Sex and sexual orientation differences in pupil dilation patterns. *PLOS ONE, 7.* doi:10.1371/journal.pone.0040256

Rieke, F., & Baylor, D. A. (1998). Single-photon detection by rod cells of the retina. *Reviews of Modern Physics, 70,* 1027–1036.

Riener, C. (2010/2011). Learning styles: Separating fact and fiction. *Psychology Teacher Network, 20*(4), 1–4.

Rietschel, M., Maier, W., & Schulze, T. G. (2013). *Phenotype refinement in bipolar affective disorder as a prerequisite for the identification of disease genes.* Federal Ministry of Education and Research, Disease-Oriented Genome Networks. Retrieved from http://www.science.ngfn.de/6_148.htm

Riggio, H. R., & Garcia, A. L. (2009). The power of situations: Jonestown and the fundamental attribution error. *Teaching of Psychology, 36,* 108–112.

Rihanna. [rihanna]. (2012, January 4). Waited all yr+Finally I have time off, time 4 rest n quiet. Suddenly all the silence is being drowned by my thoughts! No sleep #HEAVY #SCARY [Tweet]. Retrieved from https://twitter.com/rihanna/status/154801966898364417

Ringo, A. (2013, August 9). Understanding deafness: Not everyone wants to be "fixed." *The Atlantic.* Retrieved from http://www.theatlantic.com/health/archive/2013/08/understanding-deafness-not-everyone-wants-to-be-fixed/278527/

Ripke, S., Neale, B. M., Corvin, A., Walters, J. T., Farh, K. H., Holmans, P. A., … Pers, T. H. (2014). Biological insights from 108 schizophrenia-associated genetic loci. *Nature, 511,* 421–427.

Ritchie, J. (2009, January 12). Fact or fiction: Elephants never forget. *Scientific American Online.* Retrieved from http://www.scientificamerican.com/article.cfm—id=elephants-never-forget

Ritchie, S. J., Wiseman, R., & French, C. C. (2012). Replication, replication, replication. *Psychologist, 25,* 346–348.

Robbins, B. D. (2008). What is the good life? Positive psychology and the renaissance of humanistic psychology. *The Humanistic Psychologist, 36,* 96–112.

Robbins, R. N., & Bryan, A. (2004). Relationships between future orientation, impulsive sensation seeking, and risk behavior among adjudicated adolescents. *Journal of Adolescent Research, 19,* 428–445.

Roberti, J. W. (2004). A review of behavioral and biological correlates of sensation seeking. *Journal of Research in Personality, 38,* 256–279.

Roberts, B. W., & DelVecchio, W. F. (2000). The rank-order consistency of personality traits from childhood to old age: A quantitative review of longitudinal studies. *Psychological Bulletin, 126,* 3–25.

Roberts, C. A., Jones, A., & Montgomery, C. (2016). Meta-analysis of molecular imaging of serotonin transporters in Ecstasy/polydrug users. *Neuroscience & Biobehavioral Reviews, 63,* 158–167.

Roberts, J. A., & David, M. E. (2016). My life has become a major distraction from my cell phone: Partner phubbing and relationship satisfaction among romantic partners. *Computers in Human Behavior, 54,* 134–141.

Robertson, L. A., McAnally, H. M., & Hancox, R. J. (2013). Childhood and adolescent television viewing and antisocial behavior in early adulthood. *Pediatrics, 131,* 439–446.

Robinson, D. K. (2010). Gustav Fechner: 150 Years of *Elemente der Psychophysik. History of Psychology, 13,* 409–410.

Robinson, E., Oldham, M., Cuckson, I., Brunstrom, J. M., Rogers, P. J., & Hardman, C. A. (2016). Visual exposure to large and small portion sizes and perceptions of portion size normality: Three experimental studies. *Appetite, 98,* 28–34.

Rockett, I. R., Regier, M. D., Kapusta, N. D., Coben, J. H. Miller, T. R., Hanzlick, R. L., … & Smith, G. S. (2012) Leading causes of unintentional and intentional injury mortality: United States, 2000–2009. *American Journal of Public Health, 102,* e-84-392. doi: 10.2105/AJPH.2012.300960

Rodin, J. (1986). Aging and health: Effects of the sense of control. *Science, 233,* 1271–1276. doi:10.1126/science.3749877

Rockett, I. R., Regier, M. D., Kapusta, N. D., Coben, J. H., Miller, T. R., Hanzlick, R. L., … & Smith, G. S. (2012). Leading causes of unintentional and intentional injury mortality: United States, 2000–2009. *American Journal of Public Health, 102,* e84-e92. doi:10.2105/AJPH.2012.300960

Rodin, J., & Langer, E. J. (1977). Long-term effects of a control-relevant intervention with the institutionalized aged. *Journal of Personality and Social Psychology, 12,* 897–902.

Rodkey, E. N. (2015). The visual cliff's forgotten menagerie: Rats, goats, babies, and myth-making in the history of psychology. *Journal of the History of the Behavioral Sciences, 51,* 113–140.

Rodriguez, T. (2012). Open mind, longer life. *Scientific American Mind, 23,* 18.

Rodriguez, T. (2014). Food tastes bland while multitasking. *Scientific American Mind, 25,* 11.

Rodriguez, T. (2015, January/February). Performance anxiety. *Scientific American Mind, 26,* 9.

Rodriguez, T. (2015, May/June). Wait for it: Delayed feedback enhances learning—but only if you're curious. *Scientific American Mind, 26,* 8–9.

Roediger, H. L., & Bergman, E. T. (1998). The controversy over recovered memories. *Psychology, Public Policy, and Law, 4,* 1091–1109.

Roediger, H. L., III, Putnam, A. L., & Smith, M. A. (2011). Ten benefits of testing and their applications to educational practice. *Psychology of Learning and Motivation: Advances in Research and Theory, 55,* 1–36.

Roenigk, A. (2016, May 24). Doctors say late BMX legend Dave Mirra had CTE. *ESPN.* Retrieved from http://espn.go.com/action/story/_/id/15614274/bmx-legend-dave-mirra-diagnosed-cte

Rofé, Y., & Rofé, Y. (2015). Fear and phobia: A critical review and the rational-choice theory of neurosis. *International Journal of Psychological Studies, 7,* 37–73.

Rogers, C. R. (1951). *Client-centered therapy: Its current practice, implications, and theory.* Boston, MA: Houghton Mifflin.

Rogers, C. R. (1959). A theory of therapy, personality, and interpersonal relationships as developed in the client-centered framework. In S. Koch (Ed.), *Psychology: A study of a science: Vol. 3. Formulations of the person and the social context* (pp. 184–256). New York, NY: McGraw-Hill.

Rogers, C. R. (1961). *On becoming a person.* New York, NY: Houghton Mifflin.

Rogers, C. R. (1979). The foundations of the person-centered approach. *Education, 100,* 98–107.

Rohrer, D., & Taylor, K. (2006). The effects of overlearning and distributed practice on the retention of mathematics knowledge. *Applied Cognitive Psychology, 20,* 1209–1224.

Rohrer, J. M., Egloff, B., & Schmukle, S. C. (2015). Examining the effects of birth order on personality. *Proceedings of the National Academy of Sciences, 112,* 14224–14229.

Rohwedder, S., & Willis, R. J. (2010). Mental retirement. *Journal of Economic Perspective, 24,* 119–138.

Roid, G. H. (2003). *Stanford-Binet Intelligence Scales* (5th ed.). Itasca, IL: Riverside.

Romero, J. R., Mercado, M., Beiser, A. S., Pikula, A., Seshadri, S., Kelly-Hayes, M., … Kase, C. S. (2013). Transient global amnesia and neurological events: The Framingham Heart Study. *Frontiers in Neurology, 4,* 1–2.

Rosales-Lagarde, A., Armony, J. L., del Rio-Portilla, Y., Trejo-Mardnez, D., Conde, R., & Corsi-Cabrera, M. (2012). Enhanced emotional reactivity after selective REM sleep deprivation in humans: An fMRI study. *Frontiers in Behavioral Neuroscience, 6.* http://dx.doi.org/10.3389/fnbeh.2012.00025

Rosch, E. (1973). Natural categories. *Cognitive Psychology, 4,* 328–350.

Rosch, E., & Mervis, C. B. (1975). Family resemblances: Studies in the internal structure of categories. *Cognitive Psychology, 7,* 573–605.

Rosch, E., Mervis, C. B., Gray, W. D., Johnson, D. M., & Boyes-Braem, P. (1976). Basic objects in natural categories. *Cognitive Psychology, 8,* 382–439.

Rose, J. D. (2011). Diverse perspectives on the groupthink theory—A literary review. *Emerging Leadership Journeys, 4,* 37–57.

Rosen, J. (2014, November 10). The knowledge, London's legendary taxi-driver test, puts up a fight in the age of GPS. *The New York Times.* Retrieved from http://www.nytimes.com/2014/11/10/t-magazine/london-taxi-test-knowledge.html

Rosenblum, L. D. (2010). *See what I'm saying: The extraordinary powers of our five senses.* New York, NY: W. W. Norton.

Rosenhan, D. L. (1973). On being sane in insane places. *Science, 179,* 250–258.

Rosenkranz, M. A. (2007). Substance P at the nexus of mind and body in chronic inflammation and affective disorders. *Psychological Bulletin, 133,* 1007–1037.

Rosenman, R. H., Brand, R. J., Jenkins, D., Friedman, M., Straus, R., & Wurm, M. (1975). Coronary heart disease in the Western Collaborative Group Study: Final follow-up experience of 8 1/2 years. *Journal of the American Medical Association, 233,* 872–877.

Rosenthal, R. (2002a). Covert communication in classrooms, clinics, courtrooms, and cubicles. *American Psychologist, 57,* 839–849.

Rosenthal, R. (2002b). Experimenter and clinician effects in scientific inquiry and clinical practice. *Prevention & Treatment, 5,* 1–12.

Rosenthal, R. (2003). Covert communication in laboratories, classrooms, and the truly real world. *Current Directions in Psychological Science, 12,* 151–154.

Rosenthal, R., & Jacobson, L. (1966). Teachers' expectancies: Determinants of pupils' IQ gains. *Psychological Reports, 19,* 115–118.

Rosenthal, R., & Jacobson, L. (1968). *Pygmalion in the classroom: Teacher expectation and pupils' intellectual development.* New York, NY: Holt, Rinehart, & Winston.

Rosenzweig, M. R. (1984). Experience, memory, and the brain. *American Psychologist, 39,* 365–376.

Roseth, C. J., Johnson, D. W., & Johnson, R. T. (2008). Promoting early adolescents' achievement and peer relationships: The effects of cooperative, competitive, and individualistic goal structures. *Psychological Bulletin, 134,* 223–246.

Rosky, J. W. (2013). The (f)utility of post-conviction polygraph testing. *Sexual Abuse, 25,* 259–281.

Ross, L. (1977). The intuitive psychologist and his shortcomings: Distortions in the attribution process. In L. Berkowitz (Ed.), *Advances in experimental social psychology* (Vol. 10, pp. 173–220). New York, NY: Academic Press.

Ross, L., Greene, D., & House, P. (1977). The "false consensus effect": An egocentric bias in social perception and attribution processes. *Journal of Experimental Social Psychology, 13,* 279–301.

Ross, L. D., Amabile, T. M., & Steinmetz, J. L. (1977). Social roles, social control, and biases in social-perception processes. *Journal of Personality and Social Psychology, 33,* 485–494.

Rossion, B. (2014). Understanding face perception by means of prosopagnosia and neuroimaging. *Frontiers in Bioscience* (Elite edition), *6,* 258–307.

Rosso, A., Mossey, J., & Lippa, C. F. (2008). Review: Caffeine: Neuroprotective functions in cognition and Alzheimer's disease. *American Journal of Alzheimer's Disease and Other Dementias, 23,* 417–422.

Rostgaard, T. (2014). *Family policies in Scandinavia.* Berlin: Friedrich-Ebert-Stiftung. Retrieved from http://vbn.aau.dk/ws/files/216735568/Rostgaard_Family_policies_in_Scandinavia.pdf

Rotge, J.-Y., Guehl, D., Dilharreguy, B., Tignol, J., Bioulac, B., Allard, M., … Aouizerate, B. (2009). Meta-analysis of brain volume changes in obsessive-compulsive disorder. *Biological Psychiatry, 65,* 75–83.

Roth, T. (2007). Insomnia: Definition, prevalence, etiology, and consequences. *Journal of Clinical Sleep Medicine, 3,* 7–10.

Rothbaum, B. O., Hodges, L., Smith, S., Lee, J. H., & Price, L. (2000). A controlled study of virtual reality exposure therapy for the fear of flying. *Journal of Consulting and Clinical Psychology, 68,* 1020–1026.

Rothbaum, F., Weisz, J., Pott, M., Miyake, K., & Morelli, G. (2000). Attachment and culture: Security in the United States and Japan. *American Psychologist, 55,* 1093–1104.

Rotter, J. B. (1966). Generalized expectancies for internal versus external control of reinforcement. *Psychological Monographs: General and Applied, 80,* 1–28.

Rotter, J. B. (1990). Internal versus external control of reinforcement: A case history of a variable. *American Psychologist, 45,* 489–493.

Rouder, J. N., & Morey, R. D. (2011). A Bayes factor meta-analysis of Bem's ESP claim. *Psychonomic Bulletin and Review, 18,* 682–689.

Routh, D. K., & Reisman, J. M. (2003). Clinical psychology. In D. K. Freedheim (Ed.), *Handbook of psychology: Vol. 1. History of psychology* (pp. 337–355). Hoboken, NJ: John Wiley & Sons.

Rowe, D. C., Almeida, D. M., & Jacobson, K. C. (1999). School context and genetic influences on aggression in adolescence. *Psychological Science, 10,* 277–280.

Rowe, M. L. (2012). A longitudinal investigation of the role of quantity and quality of child-directed speech in vocabulary development. *Child Development, 83,* 1762–1774.

Rowe, R., Maughan, B., Worthman, C. M., Costello, E. J., & Angold, A. (2004). Testosterone, antisocial behavior, and social dominance in boys: Pubertal development and biosocial interaction. *Biological Psychiatry, 55,* 546–552.

Roy, D., Hazarika, S., Bhattacharya, A., Das, S., Nath, K., & Saddichha, S. (2011). Koro: Culture bound or mass hysteria? *Royal Australian & New Zealand Journal of Psychiatry, 45,* 683.

Rubin, Z., & Peplau, L. A. (1975). Who believes in a just world? *Journal of Social Issues, 31,* 65–89.

Rudd, R. A., Aleshire, N., Zibbell, J. E., & Gladden, R. M. (2016, January). Increases in drug and opioid overdose deaths—United States, 2000–2014. *Morbidity and Mortality Weekly Report (MMWR), 64,* 1378–1382.

Rugg, D. (1941). Experiments in wording questions: II. *Public Opinion Quarterly, 5*(1), 91–92.

Ruglass, L. M., Hien, D. A., Hu, M. C., Campbell, A. N., Caldeira, N. A., Miele, G. M., & Chang, D. F. (2014). Racial/ethnic match and treatment outcomes for women with PTSD and substance use disorders receiving community-based treatment. *Community Mental Health Journal, 50,* 811–822.

Running, C. A., Craig B. A., & Mattes, R. D. (2015). Oleogustus: The unique taste of fat. *Chemical Senses, 40,* 507–516. doi:10.1093/chemse/bjv036

Rupert, P. A., Stevanovic, P., & Hunley, H. A. (2009). Work-family conflict and burnout among practicing psychologists. *Professional Psychology: Research and Practice, 40,* 54–61.

Rupp, R. (2014, September 30). Are you a supertaster? *National Geographic.* Retrieved from http://theplate.nationalgeographic.com/2014/09/30/are-you-a-supertaster/

Rusbult, C. E. (1983). A longitudinal test of the investment model: The development (and deterioration) of satisfaction and commitment in heterosexual involvements. *Journal of Personality and Social Psychology, 45,* 101–117.

Rusbult, C. E., & Martz, J. M. (1995). Remaining in an abusive relationship: An investment model analysis of nonvoluntary dependence. *Personality and Social Psychology Bulletin, 21,* 558–571.

Ruscio, A. M., Stein, D. J., Chiu, W. T., & Kessler, R. C. (2010). The epidemiology of obsessive-compulsive disorder in the National Comorbidity Survey Replication. *Molecular Psychiatry, 15,* 53–63.

Rushton, J. P., & Jensen, A. R. (2010). Race and IQ: A theory-based review of the research in Richard Nisbett's *Intelligence and How to Get It. Open Psychology Journal, 3,* 9–35.

Russell, J. A. (1980). A circumplex model of affect. *Journal of Personality and Social Psychology, 39,* 1161–1178.

Rutherford, A. (2012). Mamie Phipps Clark: Developmental psychologist, starting from strengths. In W. E. Pickren, D. A. Dewsbury, & M. Wertheimer (Eds.), *Portraits of pioneers in developmental psychology* (pp. 261–275). New York, NY: Psychology Press.

Ruxton, C. H. S. (2008). The impact of caffeine on mood, cognitive function, performance and hydration: A review of benefits and risks. *Nutrition Bulletin, 33,* 15–25.

Ryan, R. M., & Deci, E. L. (2000). Intrinsic and extrinsic motivations: Classic definitions and new directions. *Contemporary Educational Psychology, 25,* 54–67.

Sabah, M., Mulcahy, J., & Zeman, A. (2012). Herpes simplex encephalitis. *BMJ, 344,* e3166. doi:10.1136/British Medical Journal.e3166

Sable, P., & Akcay, O. (2011). Response to color: Literature review with cross-cultural marketing perspective. *International Bulletin of Business Administration, 11,* 34–41.

Sachdeva, A., Choudhary, M., & Chandra, M. (2015). Alcohol withdrawal syndrome: Benzodiazepines and beyond. *Journal of Clinical and Diagnostic Research, 9*(9), VE01–VE07.

Sacher, J., Neumann, J., Fünfstück, T., Soliman, A., Villringer, A., & Schroeter, M. L. (2012). Mapping the depressed brain: A meta-analysis of structural and functional alterations in major depressive disorder. *Journal of Affective Disorders, 140,* 142–148.

Sacks, O. (2007, September 24). The abyss. *The New Yorker.* Retrieved from http://www.newyorker.com/reporting/2007/09/24/070924fa_fact_sacks

Sagiv, M., Vogelaere, P. P., Soudry, M., & Ehrsam, R. (2000). Role of physical activity training in attenuation of height loss through aging. *Gerontology, 46,* 266–270.

Saha, S., Chant, D., Welham, J., & McGrath, J. (2005). A systematic review of the prevalence of schizophrenia. *PLOS Medicine, 2,* e141.

Saini, R., Saini, S., & Sharma, S. (2010). Oral sex, oral health and orogenital infections. *Journal of Global Infection Diseases, 2,* 57–62.

Salimpoor, V. N., Benovoy, M., Larcher, K., Dagher, A., & Zatorre, R. J. (2011). Anatomically distinct dopamine release during anticipation and experience of peak emotion to music. *Nature Neuroscience, 14,* 257–264.

Salmon, C., Cuthbertson, A. M., & Figueredo, A. J. (2016). The relationship between birth order and prosociality: An evolutionary perspective. *Personality and Individual Differences, 96,* 18–22.

Salmon, P. (2001). Effects of physical exercise on anxiety, depression, and sensitivity to stress: A unifying theory. *Clinical Psychology Review, 21,* 33–61.

Salovey, P., Mayer, J. D., & Caruso, D. (2002). The positive psychology of emotional intelligence. In C. R. Snyder & S. J. Lopez, *Handbook of positive psychology* (pp. 159–171). New York, NY: Oxford University Press.

Salthouse, T. A. (2006). Mental exercise and mental aging: Evaluating the validity of the "use it or lose it" hypothesis. *Perspectives on Psychological Science, 1,* 68–87.

Salva, O. R., Farroni, T., Regolin, L., Vallortigara, G. & Johnson, M. H. (2011). The evolution of social orienting: Evidence from chicks (*gallus gallus*) and human newborns. *PLOS ONE, 6,* e18802. doi:10.1371/journal.pone.0018802

Sanbonmatsu, D. M., Strayer, D. L., Medeiros-Ward, N., & Watson, J. M. (2013). Who multi-tasks and why? Multi-tasking ability, perceived multi-tasking ability, impulsivity, and sensation seeking. *PLOS ONE, 8*(1), e54402.

Sanders, G., Sjodin, M., & de Chastelaine, M. (2002). On the elusive nature of sex differences in cognition: Hormonal influences contributing to within-sex variation. *Archives of Sexual Behavior, 31,* 145–152.

Sandin, S., Lichtenstein, P., Kuja-Halkola, R., Larsson, H., Hultman C. M., & Reichenberg, A. (2014). The familial risk of autism. *Journal of the American Medical Association, 311,* 1770–1777.

Sansom-Daly, U. M., Peate, M., Wakefield, C. E., Bryant, R. A., & Cohn, R. (2012). A systematic review of psychological interventions for adolescents and young adults living with chronic illness. *Health Psychology, 31,* 380–393.

Santa Maria, C. (2012, February 14). Bonobo love: Valentine's advice from Christopher Ryan. *Huffington Post.* Retrieved from http://www.huffingtonpost.com/2012/02/14/bonobo-love_n_1275381.html—ref=science

Santye, L. (2013, July 14). Heroin use rising at alarming rate among teens. *The Trentonian.* Retrieved from http://www.trentonian.com/article/TT/20130714/NEWS01/130719794

Saper, C. B., Scammell, T. E., & Lu, J. (2005). Hypothalamic regulation of sleep and circadian rhythms. *Nature, 437,* 1257–1263.

Sar, V. (2011). Epidemiology of dissociative disorders: An overview. *Epidemiology Research International, 2011.* http://dx.doi.org/10.1155/2011/404538

Sastre, J. P., & Jouvet, M. (1979). Le comportement onirique du chat [Oneiric behavior in cats]. *Physiology & Behavior, 22,* 979–989.

Sattler, J. M. (1990). *Assessment of children* (3rd ed.). San Diego, CA: Author.

Savin-Williams, R. C. (2009). How many gays are there? It depends. In D. A. Hope (Ed.), *Contemporary perspectives on lesbian, gay, and identities* (pp. 5–41). New York, NY: Springer Science + Business Media.

Scarr, S., & McCartney, K. (1983). How people make their own environments: A theory of genotype-environment effects. *Child Development, 54,* 424–435.

Schachner, A., & Hannon, E. E. (2011). Infant-directed speech drives social preferences in 5-month-old infants. *Developmental Psychology, 47,* 19–25.

Schachter, S., & Singer, J. E. (1962). Cognitive, social, and physiological determinants of emotional state. *Psychological Review, 69,* 379–399.

Schaie, K. W. (1993). The Seattle longitudinal studies of adult intelligence. *Current Directions in Psychological Science, 2,* 171–175.

Schaie, K. W. (2008). Historical processes and patterns of cognitive aging. In S. M. Hofer and D. F. Alwin (Eds.), *Handbook of cognitive aging: Interdisciplinary perspectives* (pp. 368–383). Thousand Oaks, CA: SAGE.

Schalock, R. L., Borthwick-Duffy, S., Bradley, V. J., Bunting, W. H. E., Coulter, D. L., & Craig, E. M. (2010). *Intellectual disability: Definition classification, and systems of supports* (11th ed.). Washington, DC: American Association on Intellectual and Developmental Disabilities.

Schellenberg, E. G. (2011). Music lessons, emotional intelligence, and IQ. *Music Perception, 29,* 185–194.

Schellenberg, E. G., & Winner, E. (2011). Music training and nonmusical abilities. *Music Perception, 29,* 129–132.

Schenck, C. H., & Mahowald, M. W. (2002). REM sleep behavior disorder: Clinical, developmental, and neuroscience perspectives 16 years after its formal identification in SLEEP. *SLEEP, 25,* 120–138.

Scherer, A. M., Windschitl, P. D., O'Rourke, J., & Smith, A. R. (2012). Hoping for more: The influence of outcome desirability on information seeking and predictions about relative quantities. *Cognition, 125,* 113–117.

Schickedanz, A., Dreyer, B. P., & Halfon, N. (2015). Childhood poverty: Understanding and preventing the adverse impacts of a most-prevalent risk to pediatric health and well-being. *Pediatric Clinics of North America, 62,* 1111–1135.

Schiffman, S. S. (1997). Taste and smell losses in normal aging and disease. *JAMA, 278,* 1357–1362.

Schiller, C. E., Meltzer-Brody, S., & Rubinow, D. R. (2015). The role of reproductive hormones in postpartum depression. *CNS Spectrums, 20,* 48–59.

Schilling, O. K., Wahl, H. W., Boerner, K., Horowitz, A., Reinhardt, J. P., Cimarolli, V. R., … Heckhausen, J. (2016). Developmental regulation with progressive vision loss: Use of control strategies and affective well-being. *Developmental Psychology, 52,* 679–694.

Schizophrenia Working Group of the Psychiatric Genomics Consortium. (2014). Biological insights from 108 schizophrenia-associated genetic loci. *Nature, 511,* 421–427.

Schlaepfer, T. E., Bewernick, B. H., Kayser, S., Mädler, B., & Coenen, V. A. (2013). Rapid effects of deep brain stimulation for treatment-resistant major depression. *Biological Psychiatry, 73,* 1204–1212.

Schlaug, G. (2015). Musicians and music making as a model for the study of brain plasticity. *Progress in Brain Research, 217,* 37–55.

Schleppenbach, M., Flevares, L. M., Sims, L. M., & Perry, M. (2007). Teachers' responses to student mistakes in Chinese and U.S. mathematics classrooms. *The Elementary School Journal, 108,* 131–147.

Schlich, T. (2015, May). Cutting the body to cure the mind. *The Lancet, 2,* 390–392.

Schmaltz, R., & Lilienfeld, S. O. (2014). Hauntings, homeopathy, and the Hopkinsville Goblins: Using pseudoscience to teach scientific thinking. *Frontiers in Psychology, 5.* http://dx.doi.org/10.3389/fpsyg.2014.00336

Schmidt, H. G., Peeck, V. H., Paas, F., & van Breukelen, G. J. P. (2000). Remembering the street names of one's childhood neighbourhood: A study of very long-term retention. *Memory, 8,* 37–49.

Schmidt-Daffy, M. (2011). Modeling automatic threat detection: Development of a face-in-the-crowd task. *Emotion, 11,* 153–168.

Schmitt, D. P., Realo, A., Voracek, M., & Allik, J. (2008). Why can't a man be more like a woman? Sex differences in big five personality traits across 55 cultures. *Journal of Personality and Social Psychology, 94,* 168–182.

Schnall, S., Roper, J., & Fessler, D. M. (2010). Elevation leads to altruistic behavior. *Psychological Science, 21,* 315–320.

Schneidman, E. S. (1973). *Deaths of man.* New York, NY: Quadrangle/The New York Times Book Co.

Schnider, A., Guggisberg, A., Nahum, L., Gabriel, D., & Morand, S. (2010). Dopaminergic modulation of rapid reality adaptation in thinking. *Neuroscience, 167,* 583–587.

Schocker, L. (2012, September 25). Celebrities with sleep apnea: Rick Perry and 7 others with the condition. *Huffington Post.* Retrieved from http://www.huffingtonpost.com/2012/09/25/http/www.huffingtonpost.com/2012/09/25/celebrities-sleep-apnea_n_1911549.html

Schoenborn, C. A., Adams, P. F., & Peregoy, J. A. (2013). Health behaviors of adults: United States, 2008–2010. *Vital Health Stat, 10*(257), 1–184.

Schommer-Aikins, M., & Easter, M. (2008). Epistemological beliefs' contributions to study strategies of Asian Americans and European Americans. *Journal of Educational Psychology, 100,* 920–929.

Schreiner, A. M., & Dunn, M. E. (2012). Residual effects of cannabis use on neurocognitive performance after prolonged abstinence: A meta-analysis. *Experimental and Clinical Psychopharmacology, 20,* 420–429.

Schroeder, K. (2013). History of regional anesthesia. In L. Campoy and M. R. Read (Eds.). *Small animal regional anesthesia and analgesia.* Hoboken, NJ: John Wiley & Sons. doi: 10.1002/9781118783382.ch1

Schultz, D. P., & Schultz, S. E. (2016). *A history of modern psychology* (11th ed.). Boston, MA: Cengage Learning.

Schultz, D. P., & Schultz, S. E. (2017). *Theories of personality* (11th ed.). Boston, MA: Cengage Learning.

Schumacher, S., Miller, R., Fehm, L., Kirschbaum, C., Fydrich, T., & Ströhle, A. (2015). Therapists' and patients' stress responses during graduated versus flooding in vivo exposure in the treatment of specific phobia: A preliminary observational study. *Psychiatry Research, 230,* 668–675.

Schutte, N. M., Nederend, I., Hudziak, J. J., de Geus, E. J., & Bartels, M. (2016). Differences in adolescent physical fitness: A multivariate approach and meta-analysis. *Behavior Genetics, 46,* 217–227.

Schwartz, B. L. (2012). *Tip-of-the-tongue states: Phenomenology, mechanism, and lexical retrieval.* Mahwah, NJ: Psychology Press.

Schwartz, C., Meisenhelder, J. B., Yunsheng, M., & Reed, G. (2003). Altruistic social interest behaviors are associated with better mental health. *Psychosomatic Medicine, 65,* 778–785.

Schwartz, C. E., Keyl, P. M., Marcum, J. P., & Bode, R. (2009). Helping others shows differential benefits on health and well-being for male and female teens. *Journal of Happiness Studies, 10,* 431–448.

Schwartz, S. J. (2001). The evolution of Eriksonian and neo-Eriksonian identity theory and research: A review and integration. *Identity: An International Journal of Theory and Research, 1,* 7–58.

Schwartz, S. J., Benet-Martínez, V., Knight, G. P., Unger, J. B., Zamboanga, B. L., Des Rosiers, S. E., … Szapocznik, J. (2014). Effects of language of assessment on the measurement of acculturation: Measurement equivalence and cultural frame switching. *Psychological Assessment, 26,* 100–114.

Schwarz, S., & Hassebrauck, M. (2012). Sex and age differences in mate-selection preferences. *Human Nature, 23,* 447–466.

Schwarz, S., Hassebrauck, M., & Dörfler, R. (2010). Let us talk about sex: Prototype and personal templates. *Personal Relationships, 17,* 533–555.

Schweinsburg, A. D., Brown, S. A., & Tapert, S. F. (2008). The influence of marijuana use on neurocognitive functioning in adolescents. *Current Drug Abuse Reviews, 1,* 99–111.

Schweizer, A., Brunner, F., Handford, C., & Richter-Appelt, H. (2014). Gender experience and satisfaction with gender allocation in adults with diverse intersex conditions (divergences of sex development, DSD). *Psychology & Sexuality, 5,* 56–82.

Scott, A. J., Webb, T. L., & Rowse, G. (2015). Self-help interventions for psychosis: A meta-analysis. *Clinical Psychology Review, 39,* 96–112.

Scott, S. B., Rhoades, G. K., Stanley, S. M., Allen, E. S., & Markman, H. J. (2013). Reasons for divorce and recollections of premarital intervention: Implications for improving relationship education. *Couple and Family Psychology: Research and Practice, 2,* 131–145.

Scott, S. K., Blank, C. C., Rosen, S., & Wise, R. J. S. (2000). Identification of a pathway for intelligible speech in the left temporal lobe. *Brain, 123,* 2400–2406.

Scoville, W. B., & Milner, B. (1957). Loss of recent memory after bilateral hippocampal lesions. *Journal of Neurology, Neurosurgery, & Psychiatry, 20,* 11–21.

Scullin, M. K., & Bliwise, D. L. (2015). Sleep, cognition, and normal aging: Integrating a half century of multidisciplinary research. *Perspectives on Psychological Science, 10,* 97–137.

Scully, J. A., Tosi, H., & Banning, K. (2000). Life event checklists: Revisiting the Social Readjustment Rating Scale after 30 years. *Educational and Psychological Measurement, 60,* 864–876.

Searight, H. R., & Gafford, J. (2005). Cultural diversity at the end of life: Issues and guidelines for family physicians. *American Family Physician, 71,* 515–522.

Searleman, A. (2007, March 12). Is there such a thing as a photographic memory? And if so, can it be learned? *Scientific American Online.* Retrieved from http://www.scientificamerican.com/article/is-there-such-a-thing-as/

Seely, R. (2012, September 19). *UW study says boys' pacifier use limits social development. Wisconsin State Journal.* Retrieved from http://host.madison.com/news/local/education/university/uw-study-says-boys-pacifier-use-limits-social-development/article_c44e3998-01f9-11e2-9b69-0019bb2963f4.html

Seery, M. D. (2011). Resilience: A silver lining to experiencing adverse life events? *Current Directions in Psychological Science, 20,* 390–394.

Segal, D. L., Coolidge, F. L., & Mizuno, H. (2007). Defense mechanism differences between younger and older adults: A cross-sectional investigation. *Aging and Mental Health, 11,* 415–422.

Segal, N. (1984). Cooperation, competition, and altruism within twin sets: A reappraisal. *Ethology and Sociobiology, 5*(3), 163–177.

Segal, N. L. (1999). *Entwined lives: Twins and what they tell us about human behavior.* New York, NY: Dutton/Penguin Books.

Segal, N. L. (2012). *Born together—reared apart: The landmark Minnesota Twin Study.* Cambridge, MA: Harvard University Press.

Segal, N. L., & Cortez, F. A. (2014). Born in Korea-adopted apart: Behavioral development of monozygotic twins raised in the United States and France. *Personality and Individual Differences, 70,* 97–104.

Segall, M. H., Campbell, D. T., & Herskovits, M. J. (1968). The influence of culture on visual perception. In H. Toch and C. Smith (Eds.), *Social perception* (pp. 1–5). Oxford, UK: Bobbs-Merrill.

Segerstrom, S. C., & Miller, G. E. (2004). Psychological stress and the human immune system: A meta-analytic study of 30 years of inquiry. *Psychological Bulletin, 130,* 601–630.

Segraves, R. T. (2010). Considerations for a better definition of male orgasmic disorder in *DSM V. Journal of Sexual Medicine, 7,* 690–699.

Seinfeld, S., Bergstrom, I., Pomes, A., Arroyo-Palacios, J., Vico, F., Slater, M., & Sanchez-Vives, M. V. (2016). Influence of music on anxiety induced by fear of heights in virtual reality. *Frontiers in Psychology, 6.* doi:10.3389/fpsyg.2015.01969

Seligman, M. E. P. (1975). *Helplessness: On depression, development, and death.* San Francisco, CA: W. H. Freeman.

Seligman, M. E. P. (1995). The effectiveness of psychotherapy: The *Consumer Reports* study. *American Psychologist, 50,* 965–974.

Seligman, M. E. P., & Csikszentmihalyi, M. (2000). Positive psychology: An introduction. *American Psychologist, 55,* 5–14.

Seligman, M. E. P., & Maier, S. F. (1967). Failure to escape traumatic shock. *Journal of Experimental Psychology, 74,* 1–9.

Seligman, M. E. P., & Steen, T. A. (2005). Positive psychology progress. *American Psychologist, 60,* 410–421.

Seltenrich, N. (2015, October). POPs and pubertal timing: Evidence of delayed development. *Environmental Health Perspectives, 123,* A266.

Selye, H. (1936). A syndrome produced by diverse nocuous agents. *Nature, 138,* 32.

Selye, H. (1953). The General-Adaptation-Syndrome in its relationships to neurology, psychology, and psychopathology. In A. Weider (Ed.)., *Contributions toward medical psychology: Vol. 1. Theory and psychodiagnostic methods* (pp. 234–274). New York, NY: Ronald Press.

Selye, H. (1956). *The stress of life.* New York, NY: McGraw-Hill.

Selye, H. (1976). Forty years of stress research: Principal remaining problems and misconceptions. *Canadian Medical Association Journal, 115,* 53–56.

Selye, H., & Fortier, C. (1950). Adaptive reaction to stress. *Psychosomatic Medicine, 12,* 149–157.

Seri, I., & Evans, J. (2008). Limits of viability: Definition of the gray zone. *Journal of Perinatology, 28,* S4–S8.

Seubert, J., Freiherr, J., Djordjevic, J., & Lundström, J. N. (2013). Statistical localization of human olfactory cortex. *Neuroimage, 66,* 333–342.

Shackelford, T. K., & Liddle, J. R. (2014). Understanding the mind from an evolutionary perspective: An overview of evolutionary psychology. *Wiley Interdisciplinary Reviews: Cognitive Science, 5,* 247–260.

Shackelford, T. K., Schmitt, D. P., & Buss, D. M. (2005). Mate preferences of married persons in the newlywed year and three years later. *Cognition and Emotion, 19,* 1262–1270.

Shadish, W. R., & Baldwin, S. A. (2003). Meta-analysis of MFT interventions. *Journal of Marital and Family Therapy, 29,* 547–570.

Shah, A. K., & Oppenheimer, D. M. (2008). Heuristics made easy: An effort-reduction framework. *Psychological Bulletin, 134,* 207–222.

Shahkhase, M. S., Gharaei, A., Fathi, M., Yaghoobi, H., & Bayazi, M. H. (2014). The study of hypnosis effectiveness in the treatment of headaches. *Reef Resources Assessment and Management Technical Paper, 40,* 426–432.

Shakeshaft, N. G., Trzaskowski, M., McMillan, A., Krapohl, E., Simpson, M. A., Reichenberg, A., … Plomin, R. (2015). Thinking positively: The genetics of high intelligence. *Intelligence, 48,* 123–132.

Shapiro, D. H. Jr., Schwartz, C. E., & Astin, J. A. (1996). Controlling ourselves, controlling our world: Psychology's role in understanding positive and negative consequences of seeking and gaining control. *American Psychologist, 51,* 1213–1230.

Shargorodsky, J., Curhan, S. G., Curhan, G. C., & Eavey, R. (2010). Change in prevalence of hearing loss in US adolescents. *Journal of the American Medical Association, 304,* 772–778.

Sharp, C., & Kim, S. (2015). Recent advances in the developmental aspects of borderline personality disorder. *Current Psychiatry Reports, 17.* doi:10.1007/s11920-015-0556-2

Sharpless, B. A., & Barber, J. P. (2011). Lifetime prevalence rates of sleep paralysis: A systematic review. *Sleep Medicine Reviews, 15,* 311–315.

Shaw, J., & Porter, S. (2015). Constructing rich false memories of committing crime. *Psychological Science, 26,* 291–301.

Shaywitz, S. E. (1996). Dyslexia. *Scientific American, 275,* 98–104.

Shaywitz, S. E. (2003). *Overcoming dyslexia: A new and complete science-based program for reading problems at any level.* New York, NY: Vintage Books.

Shearer, A., Hunt, M., Chowdhury, M., & Nicol, L. (2016). Effects of a brief mindfulness meditation intervention on student stress and heart rate variability. *International Journal of Stress Management, 23,* 232–254.

Shedler, J. (2010). The efficacy of psychodynamic psychotherapy. *American Psychologist, 63,* 98–109.

Sheikh, K. (2016, July 1). Why your profile picture doesn't reveal the true you. *Scientific American.* Retrieved from http://www.scientificamerican.com/article/why-your-profile-picture-doesn-t-reveal-the-true-you/#

Sheldon, P., & Bryant, K. (2016). Instagram: Motives for its use and relationship to narcissism and contextual age. *Computers in Human Behavior, 58,* 89–97.

Shelton, K. H., & van den Bree, M. B. M. (2010). The moderating effects of pubertal timing on the longitudinal associations between parent–child relationships' quality and adolescent substance use. *Journal of Research on Adolescence, 20,* 1044–1064.

Shen, C., Vasilyeva, M., & Laski, E. V. (2016). Here, but not there: Cross-national variability of gender effects in arithmetic. *Journal of Experimental Child Psychology, 146,* 50–65.

Shepard, R. N., & Metzler, J. (1971). Mental rotation of three-dimensional objects. *Science, 171,* 701–703.

Shernoff, D. J., Csikszentmihalyi, M., Shneider, B., & Shernoff, E. S. (2003). Student engagement in high school classrooms from the perspective of flow theory. *School Psychology Quarterly, 18,* 158–176.

Sherwood, L. (2016). *Human physiology: From cells to systems* (9th ed.). Boston, MA: Cengage Learning.

Shi, F., Yap, P.-T., Wu, G., Jia, H., Gilmore, J. H., Lin, W., & Shen, D. (2011). Infant brain atlases from neonates to 1- and 2-year-olds. *PLOS ONE, 6.* doi:10.1371/journal.pone.0018746

Shi, J., Zhang, C., & Jiang, F. (2014). Does red undermine individuals' intellectual performance? A test in China. *International Journal of Psychology, 50*(1), 81–84.

Shiban, Y., Schelhorn, I., Pauli, P., & Mühlberger, A. (2015). Effect of combined multiple contexts and multiple stimuli exposure in spider phobia: A randomized clinical trial in virtual reality. *Behaviour Research and Therapy, 71,* 45–53.

Shiota, M. N., Neufeld, S. L., Yeung, W. H., Moser, S. E., & Perea, E. F. (2011). Feeling good: Autonomic nervous system responding in five positive emotions. *Emotion, 11,* 1368–1378.

Shonkoff, J. P., Garner, A. S., the Committee on Psychosocial Aspects of Child and Family Health, Committee on Early Childhood, Adoption, and Dependent Care, and Section on Developmental and Behavioral Pediatrics, Siegel, B. S., Dobbins, M. I., Earls, M. F., … Wood, D. L. (2012). The lifelong effects of early childhood adversity and toxic stress. *Pediatrics, 129,* e232–e246.

Shors, T. J. (2016). A trip down memory lane about sex differences in the brain. *Philosophical Transactions of the Royal Society B, 371.* doi: 10.1098/rstb.2015.0124

Shorter, E. (2015). The history of nosology and the rise of the *Diagnostic and Statistical Manual of Mental Disorders. Dialogues in Clinical Neuroscience, 17,* 59–67.

Shutts, K., Kinzler, K. D., & DeJesus, J. M. (2013). Understanding infants' and children's social learning about foods: Previous research and new prospects. *Developmental Psychology, 49,* 419–425.

Siegel, J. M. (2005). Clues to the functions of mammalian sleep. *Nature, 437,* 1264–1271.

Siegel, J. M. (2008). Do all animals sleep? *Trends in Neurosciences, 31,* 208–213.

Silber, M. H., Ancoli-Israel, S., Bonnet, M. H., Chokroverty, S., Grigg-Damberger, M. M., Hirshkowitz, M., … Pressman, M. R. (2007). The visual scoring of sleep in adults. *Journal of Clinical Sleep Medicine, 3*(2), 121–131.

Sili, U., Kaya, A., Mert, A., & HSV Encephalitis Study Group. (2014). Herpes simplex virus encephalitis: Clinical manifestations, diagnosis and outcome in 106 adult patients. *Journal of Clinical Virology, 60,* 112–118.

Silva, C. E., & Kirsch, I. (1992). Interpretive sets, expectancy, fantasy proneness, and dissociation as predictors of hypnotic response. *Journal of Personality and Social Psychology, 63,* 847–856.

Simion, F., & Di Giorgio, E. (2015). Face perception and processing in early infancy: Inborn predispositions and developmental changes. *Frontiers in Psychology, 6.* doi:10.3389/fpsyg.2015.00969

Simms, A., & Nichols, T. (2014). Social loafing: A review of the literature. *Journal of Management Policy and Practice, 15,* 58–67.

Simon, S. (2015, January 16). 6 Steps to help lower your cancer risk. *American Cancer Society.* Retrieved from http://www.cancer.org/cancer/news/features/6-steps-to-help-lower-your-cancer-risk

Simons, D. J. (2010). Monkeying around with the gorillas in our midst: Familiarity with an inattentional-blindness task does not improve the detection of unexpected events. *i-Perception, 1,* 3–6.

Simonton, D. K. (2000). Creativity: Cognitive, personal, developmental, and social aspects. *American Psychologist, 55,* 151–158.

Simonton, D. K. (2012, November/December). The science of genius. *Scientific American Mind, 23,* 35–41.

Simpson, J. A., & Rholes, W. S. (2010). Attachment and relationships: Milestones and future directions. *Journal of Social and Personal Relationships, 27,* 173–180.

Singh, L., Nestor, S., Parikh, C., & Yull, A. (2009). Influences of infant-directed speech on early word recognition. *Infancy, 14,* 654–666.

Singh, M. K., Kesler, S. R., Hosseini, S. M. H., Kelley, R. G., Amatya, D., Hamilton, J. P., ... Gotlib, I. H. (2013). Anomalous gray matter structural networks in major depressive disorder. *Biological Psychiatry, 74,* 777–785.

Singh, P. B., Hummel, T., Gerber, J. C., Landis, B. N., & Iannilli, E. (2015). Cerebral processing of umami: A pilot study on the effects of familiarity. *Brain Research, 1614,* 67–74.

Singh-Manoux, A., Kivimaki, M., Glymour, M. M., Elbaz, A., Berr, C., Ebmeier, K. P., ... Harville, E. W. (2015). Use of a resiliency framework to examine pregnancy and birth outcomes among adolescents: A qualitative study. *Families, Systems, & Health, 33*(4), 349–355.

Sinha, A., Hurakadli, M., & Yadav, P. (2015). Botox and derma fillers: The twin-face of cosmetic dentistry. *International Journal of Contemporary Dental and Medical Reviews, 2015.* doi: 10.15713/ins.ijcdmr.27

Sinn, D. L., & Moltschaniwskyj, N. A. (2005). Personality traits in dumpling squid (*Euprymna Tasmania*): Context-specific traits and their correlation with biological characteristics. *Journal of Comparative Psychology, 119,* 99–110.

Sio, U. N., & Ormerod, T. C. (2009). Does incubation enhance problem solving? A meta-analytic review. *Psychological Bulletin, 135,* 94–120.

Sisario, B. (2015, April 24). Shawn Mendes and the 6-second path to stardom. *The New York Times.* Retrieved from http://www.nytimes.com/2015/04/25/arts/music/a-rapid-rise-for-shawn-mendes-in-tune-with-social-media.html?_r=0

Sisti, D. A., Segal, A. G., & Emanuel, E. J. (2015). Improving long-term psychiatric care: Bring back the asylum. *Journal of the American Medical Association, 313,* 243–244.

Sivacek, J., & Crano, W. D. (1982). Vested interest as a moderator of attitude-behavior consistency. *Journal of Personality and Social Psychology, 43,* 210–221.

Skeldon, A. C., Derks, G., & Dijk, D. J. (2016). Modelling changes in sleep timing and duration across the lifespan: Changes in circadian rhythmicity or sleep homeostasis? *Sleep Medicine Reviews, 28,* 92–103.

Skinner, B. F. (1953). *Science and human behavior.* New York, NY: Macmillan.

Skinner, B. F. (1956). A case history in scientific method. *American Psychologist, 11,* 221–233.

Skinner, B. F. (1957). *Verbal behavior.* New York, NY: Macmillan.

Skinner, B. F. (1976). *Particulars of my life.* New York, NY: Alfred A. Knopf.

Skinner, N. F. (2009). Academic folk wisdom: Fact, fiction and falderal. *Psychology Learning and Teaching, 8,* 46–50.

Skirbekk, V., Loichinger, E., & Weber, D. (2012). Variation in cognitive functioning as a refined approach to comparing aging across countries. *Proceedings of the National Academy of Sciences, 109,* 770–774.

Skoog, G., & Skoog, I. (1999). A 20-year follow-up of patients with obsessive-compulsive disorder. *Archives of General Psychiatry, 56,* 121–127.

Slaney, K. L., & Racine, T. P. (2011). On the ambiguity of concept use in psychology: Is the concept "concept" a useful concept? *Journal of Theoretical and Philosophical Psychology, 31,* 73–89.

Slatcher, R. B., & Robles, T. F. (2012). Preschoolers' everyday conflict at home and diurnal cortisol patterns. *Health Psychology, 31,* 834–838. doi:10.1037/a0026774

Slavich, G. M. (2016). Life stress and health: A review of conceptual issues and recent findings. *Teaching of Psychology, 43,* 346–355.

Slewa-Younan, S., Uribe Guajardo, M. G., Heriseanu, A., & Hasan T. (2015). A systematic review of post-traumatic stress disorder and depression amongst Iraqi refugees located in Western countries. *Journal of Immigrant and Minority Health, 17,* 1231–1239.

Slife, B. D. (1990). Introduction and overview of the special issue on Aristotle. *Theoretical & Philosophical Psychology, 10,* 3–6.

Slotema, C. W., Blom, J. D., Hoek, H. W., & Sommer, I. E. C. (2010). Should we expand the toolbox of psychiatric treatment methods to include Repetitive Transcranial Magnetic Stimulation (rTMS)? A meta-analysis of the efficacy of rTMS in psychiatric disorders. *Journal of Clinical Psychiatry, 71,* 873–884.

Sloter, E., Schmid, T. E., Marchetti, F., Eskenazi, B., Nath, J., & Wyrobek, A. J. (2006). Quantitative effects of male age on sperm motion. *Human Reproduction, 21,* 2868–2875.

Slovic, P., & Weber, E. U. (2002, April). *Perception of risk posed by extreme events.* Paper presented at Conference on Risk Management Strategies in an Uncertain World, Palisades, NY.

Small, B. J., Dixon, R. A., & McArdle, J. J. (2011). Tracking cognition–health changes from 55 to 95 years of age. *Journals of Gerontology Series B: Psychological Sciences and Social Sciences, 66,* i153–i161.

Small, B. J., Dixon, R. A., McArdle, J. J., & Grimm, K. J. (2012). Do changes in lifestyle engagement moderate cognitive decline in normal aging? Evidence from the Victoria Longitudinal Study. *Neuropsychology, 26,* 144–155. doi:10.1037/a0026579

Smiley, M. (2014) . The smell of money: How marketers sell with scent. *Advertising Age, 85,* 34–34.

Smink, F. R., van Hoeken, D., & Hoek, H. W. (2012). Epidemiology of eating disorders: Incidence, prevalence and mortality rates. *Current Psychiatry Reports, 14,* 406–414.

Smith, A. (2016, February 11). 15% of American adults have used online dating sites or mobile dating apps. *Pew Research Center.* Retrieved from http://www.pewinternet.org/2016/02/11/15-percent-of-american-adults-have-used-online-dating-sites-or-mobile-dating-apps/

Smith, B. L. (2012, April). The case against spanking. *Monitor on Psychology, 43,* 60–63.

Smith, C. N., & Squire, L. R. (2009). Medial temporal lobe activity during retrieval of semantic memory is related to the age of the memory. *Journal of Neuroscience, 29,* 930–938.

Smith, D. (2001). Shock and disbelief. *Atlantic Monthly, 287,* 79–90.

Smith, S. M., Glenberg, A. M., & Bjork, R. A. (1978). Environmental context and human memory. *Memory and Cognition, 6,* 342–353.

Smith, T. W., Birmingham, W., & Uchino, B. N. (2012). Evaluative threat and ambulatory blood pressure: Cardiovascular effects of social stress in daily experience. *Health Psychology, 31,* 763–766.

Smith, T. W., & MacKenzie, J. (2006). Personality and risk of physical illness. *Annual Review of Clinical Psychology, 2,* 435–467.

Smith, T. W., & Ruiz, J. M. (2002). Psychosocial influences on the development and course of coronary heart disease: Current status and implications for research and practice. *Journal of Consulting and Clinical Psychology, 70,* 548–568.

Smoller, J. W., Gallagher, P. J., Duncan, L. E., McGrath, L. M., Haddad, S. A., Holmes, A. J., ... Young, S. (2014). The human ortholog of acid-sensing ion channel gene ASIC1a is associated with panic disorder and amygdala structure and function. *Biological Psychiatry, 76,* 902–910.

Smrt, D. L., & Karau, S. J. (2011). Protestant work ethic moderates social loafing. *Group Dynamics: Theory, Research, and Practice, 15,* 267–274.

Snyder, C. R., Ilardi, S. S., Cheavens, J., Michael, S. T., Yamhure, L., & Sympson, S. (2000). The role of hope in cognitive-behavior therapies. *Cognitive Therapy and Research, 24,* 747–762.

Snyder, T. D., de Brey, C., and Dillow, S. A. (2016). *Digest of education statistics 2014* (NCES 2016-006). Washington, DC: National Center for Education Statistics, Institute of Education Sciences, U.S. Department of Education. Retrieved from http://nces.ed.gov/pubs2016/2016006.pdf

Society for Neuroscience. (2012). Sensation and perception. In M. Miller (Ed.), *Brain facts* (6th ed., pp. 15–21). Washington, DC: Author.

Solms, M. (2006, April/May). Freud returns. *Scientific American, 17,* 28–35.

Solomon, B. C., & Jackson, J. J. (2014). The long reach of one's spouse: Spouses' personality influences occupational success. *Psychological Science, 25,* 2189–2198.

Solomon, S. G., & Lennie, P. (2007). The machinery of color vision. *Nature Reviews Neuroscience, 8,* 276–286.

Sommer, I. E., & Neggers, S. F. W. (2014). Repetitive transcranial magnetic stimulation as a treatment for auditory hallucinations. *Neuropsychopharmacology Reviews, 39,* 239–240.

Song, C., & Knöpfel, T. (2016). Optogenetics enlightens neuroscience drug discovery. *Nature Reviews Drug Discovery, 15,* 97–109.

Song, H., Zmyslinski-Seelig, A., Kim, J., Drent, A., Victor, A., Omori, K., & Allen, M. (2014). Does Facebook make you lonely? A meta analysis. *Computers in Human Behavior, 36,* 446–452.

Song, J., Bergen, S. E., Di Florio, A., Karlsson, R., Charney, A., Ruderfer, D. M., … Forty, L. (2016). Genome-wide association study identifies SESTD1 as a novel risk gene for lithium-responsive bipolar disorder. *Molecular Psychiatry, 21,* 1290–1297.

Sørensen, K., Aksglaede, L., Petersen, J. H., & Juul, A. (2010). Recent changes in pubertal timing in healthy Danish boys: Associations with Body Mass Index. *Journal of Clinical Endocrinology & Metabolism, 95,* 263–270.

Sorhagen, N. S. (2013). Early teacher expectations disproportionately affect poor children's high school performance. *Journal of Educational Psychology, 105,* 465–477.

Sorokowski, P., Sorokowska, A., & Witzel, C. (2014). Sex differences in color preferences transcend extreme differences in culture and ecology. *Psychonomic Bulletin & Review, 21(5),* 1195–1201.

Soto, C. J. (2016). The Little Six personality dimensions from early childhood to early adulthood: Mean-level age and gender differences in parents' reports. *Journal of Personality, 84,* 409–422.

Soto, C. J., & Tackett, J. L. (2015). Personality traits in childhood and adolescence structure, development, and outcomes. *Current Directions in Psychological Science, 24,* 358–362.

Soudi, L. (2016, August 1). A first-hand look at refugee camps in Greece [Web log post]. Retrieved from http://scopeblog.stanford.edu/2016/08/01/a-first-hand-look-at-refugee-camps-in-greece/

Southworth, M. R., Kortepeter, C., & Hughes, A. (2008). Nonbenzodiazepine hypnotic use and cases of sleep driving. *Annals of Internal Medicine, 148,* 486–487.

Spalding, K. L., Bergmann, O., Alkass, K., Bernard, S., Salehpour, M., Huttner, H. B., … Frisén, J. (2013). Dynamics of hippocampal neurogenesis in adult humans. *Cell, 153(6),* 1219–1227.

Spangenberg, E. R., Sprott, D. E., Grohmann, B., & Tracy, D. L. (2006). Gender-congruent ambient scent influences on approach and avoidance behaviors in a retail store. *Journal of Business Research, 59,* 1281–1287.

Sparling, J., Wilder, D. A., Kondash, J., Boyle, M., & Compton, M. (2011). Effects of interviewer behavior on accuracy of children's responses. *Journal of Applied Behavior Analysis, 44,* 587–592.

Sparrow, B., & Chatman, L. (2013a). Social cognition in the Internet Age: Same as it ever was? *Psychological Inquiry: An International Journal for the Advancement of Psychological Theory, 24,* 273–292.

Sparrow, B., & Chatman, L. (2013b). We're not burning down the house: Synthesizing pre-Internet, current findings, and future research on social cognition and being online. *Psychological Inquiry: An International Journal for the Advancement of Psychological Theory, 24,* 349–355.

Sparrow, B., Liu, J., & Wegner, D. W. (2011). Google effects on memory: Cognitive consequences of having information at our fingertips. *Science, 333,* 776–778.

Sparrow, R. (2005). Defending deaf culture: The case of cochlear implants. *Journal of Political Philosophy, 13,* 135–152.

Speakman, J. R., Levitsky, D. A., Allison, D. B., Bray, M. S., de Castro, J. M., Clegg, D. J., … Westerterp-Plantenga, M. S. (2011). Set points, settling points and some alternative models: Theoretical options to understand how genes and environments combine to regulate body adiposity. *Disease Models & Mechanisms, 4,* 733–745.

Spear, L. P. (2013). Adolescent neurodevelopment. *Journal of Adolescent Health, 52,* S7–S13.

Specht, J., Egloff, B., & Schmukle, S. C. (2011). Stability and change of personality across the life course: The impact of age and major life events on mean-level and rank-order stability of the Big Five. *Journal of Personality and Social Psychology, 101,* 862–882.

Spencer, S. J., Emmerzaal, T. L., Kozicz, T., & Andrews, Z. B. (2015). Ghrelin's role in the hypothalamic-pituitary-adrenal axis stress response: Implications for mood disorders. *Biological Psychiatry, 78,* 19–27.

Sperling, G. (1960). The information available in brief visual presentations. *Psychological Monographs: General and Applied, 74,* 1–29.

Spiegel, D., Loewenstein, R. J., Lewis-Fernández, R., Sar, V., Simeon, D., Vermetten, E., … Dell, P. F. (2011). Dissociative disorders in *DSM-5. Depression and Anxiety, 28,* 824–852.

Spitz, E. H. (2016). Anna, Gregor, and Ajax: Translation and transference. *Psychoanalytic Psychology, 33(S1),* S8–S18.

Spitzer, R. L. (1975). On pseudoscience in science, logic in remission, and psychiatric diagnosis: A critique of Rosenhan's "On Being Sane in Insane Places." *Journal of Abnormal Psychology, 84,* 442–451.

Spong, C. Y. (2013). Defining "term" pregnancy: Recommendations from the Defining "Term" Pregnancy Workgroup. *Journal of the American Medical Association, 309(23),* 2445–2446.

Squire, L. R., & Bayley, P. J. (2007). The neuroscience of remote memory. *Current Opinion in Neurobiology, 17,* 185–196.

Squire, L. R., Stark, C. E. L., & Clark, R. E. (2004). The medial temporal lobe. *Annual Review of Neuroscience, 27,* 279–306.

Squire, L. R., & Wixted, J. T. (2011). The cognitive neuroscience of human memory since HM. *Annual Review of Neuroscience, 34,* 259–288.

St. John, K. (2003, August 19). Yosemite landmark falls/Sentinel Dome's oft-photographed Jeffrey pine topples. *San Francisco Chronicle.* Retrieved from http://www.sfgate.com/news/article/Yosemite-landmark-falls-Sentinel-Domes-2574496.php#ixzz2HLMo2N31

Stahre, M., Roeber, J., Kanny, D., Brewer, R. D., & Zhang, X. (2014). Contribution of excessive alcohol consumption to deaths and years of potential life lost in the United States. *Preventing Chronic Disease, 11.* http://dx.doi.org/10.5888/pcd11.130293

Stamatakis, A. M., Van Swieten, M., Basiri, M. L., Blair, G. A., Kantak, P., & Stuber, G. D. (2016). Lateral hypothalamic area glutamatergic neurons and their projections to the lateral habenula regulate feeding and reward. *The Journal of Neuroscience, 36,* 302–311.

Stanford School of Medicine. (n.d.). *About narcolepsy.* Center for Narcolepsy. Retrieved from http://med.stanford.edu/narcolepsy/symptoms.html

Stanger, S., Abaied, J., & Wagner, C. (2016). Predicting heavy alcohol use in college students: Interactions among socialization of coping, alcohol use onset, and physiological reactivity. *Journal of Studies on Alcohol and Drugs, 77,* 483–494.

Stanger-Hall, K., & Hall, D. W. (2011). Abstinence-only education and teen pregnancy rates: Why we need comprehensive sex education in the U.S. *PLOS ONE, 6,* e24658. doi:10.1371/journal.pone.0024658

Staniloiu, A., & Markowitsch, H. J. (2012). The remains of the day in dissociative amnesia. *Brain Sciences, 2,* 101–129.

Stanovich, K. E. (2013). *How to think straight about psychology* (10th ed.). Upper Saddle River, NJ: Pearson.

Staub, M. E. (2016). The other side of the brain: The politics of split-brain research in the 1970s–1980s. *History of Psychology, 19,* 259–273.

Steel, E. (2015, June 19). Brian Williams says fabrications came from "bad urge inside of me." *The New York Times.* Retrieved from http://www.nytimes.com/2015/06/20/business/media/brian-williams-apologizes-matt-lauer-nbc-interview.html?_r=0

Steel, Z., Marnane, C., Iranpour, C., Chey, T., Jackson, J. W., Patel, V., & Silove, D. (2014). The global prevalence of common mental disorders: A systematic review and meta-analysis 1980–2013. *International Journal of Epidemiology, 43,* 476–493.

Steele, C. M. (1997). A threat in the air: How stereotypes shape intellectual identity and performance. *American Psychologist, 52,* 613–629.

Steele, C. M. (2010). *Whistling Vivaldi: How stereotypes affect us and what we can do.* New York, NY: W. W. Norton.

Steele, J. D., Christmas, D., Elijamel, M. S., & Matthews, K. (2008). Anterior cingulotomy for major depression: Clinical outcome and relationship to lesion characteristics. *Biological Psychology, 63,* 670–677.

Stein, B. E., Stanford, T. R., & Rowland, B. A. (2009). The neural basis of multisensory integration in the midbrain: Its organization and maturation. *Hearing Research, 258,* 4–15.

Steinberg, L. (2010). Commentary: A behavioral scientist looks at the science of adolescent brain development. *Brain and Cognition, 72,* 160–164.

Steinberg, L. (2012). Should the science of adolescent brain development inform public policy? *Issues in Science & Technology, 28,* 76–78.

Steindl, C., & Jonas, E. (2015). The dynamic reactance interaction–How vested interests affect people's experience, behavior, and cognition in social interactions. *Frontiers in Psychology, 6.* doi:10.3389/fpsyg.2015.01752

Steiner, M. (2012, September 4). The importance of pragmatic communication. *Monocracy Neurodevelopmental Center.* Retrieved from http://monocacycenter.com/the-importance-of-pragmatic-communication/

Stemwedel, J. D. (2011, October 4). Drawing the line between science and pseudoscience [Web log post]. Retrieved from http://blogs.scientificamerican.com/doing-good-science/2011/10/04/drawing-the-line-between-science-and-pseudo-science/

Stenseng, F., Belsky, J., Skalicka, V., & Wichstrøm, L. (2014). Preschool social exclusion, aggression, and cooperation: A longitudinal evaluation of the need-to-belong and the social-reconnection hypotheses. *Personality and Social Psychology Bulletin, 40,* 1637–1647.

Stern, E. M. (2016). Foreword to the second edition. In K. J. Schneider, J. F. Pierson, & J. F. T. Bugental (Eds.), *The handbook of humanistic psychology: Theory, research, and practice* (2nd ed., p. xi). Thousand Oaks, CA: SAGE.

Stern, K., & Karraker, K. H. (1989). Sex stereotyping of infants: A review of gender labeling studies. *Sex Roles, 20,* 501–522.

Stern, K., & McClintock, M. K. (1998). Regulation of ovulation by human pheromones. *Nature, 392,* 177–179.

Sternberg, R. J. (1986). A triangular theory of love. *Psychological Review, 93,* 119–135.

Sternberg, R. J. (1988). *The triarchic mind: A new theory of human intelligence.* New York, NY: Viking.

Sternberg, R. J. (2004). Culture and intelligence. *American Psychologist, 59,* 325–338.

Sternberg, R. J. (2006a). Creating a vision of creativity: The first 25 years. *Psychology of Aesthetics, Creativity, and the Arts, S,* 2–12.

Sternberg, R. J. (2006b). The nature of creativity. *Creativity Research Journal, 18,* 87–98.

Sternberg, R. J., & Grigorenko, E. L. (2005). Intelligence and wisdom. In M. L. Johnson (Ed.), *The Cambridge handbook of age and ageing* (pp. 209–213). Cambridge, UK: Cambridge University Press.

Stix, G. (2014, May/June). My brain made me pull the trigger. *Scientific American Mind, 25,* 14.

Stolarski, M., Jasielska, D., & Zajenkowski, M. (2015). Are all smart nations happier? Country aggregate IQ predicts happiness, but the relationship is moderated by individualism–collectivism. *Intelligence, 50,* 153–158.

Stoltenborgh, M., Bakermans-Kranenburg, M. J., Alink, L. R. A., & van IJzendoorn, M. H. (2015). The prevalence of child maltreatment across the globe: Review of a series of meta-analyses. *Child Abuse Review, 24,* 37–50.

Stone, A. A., Schwartz, J. E., Broderick, J. E., & Deaton, A. (2010). A snapshot of the age distribution of psychological well-being in the United States. *Proceedings of the National Academy of Sciences, 107,* 9985–9990.

Stone, D. (2009). Brainy Bonnie. *Smithsonian Zoogoer.* Retrieved from https://web.archive.org/web/20160403031716/http://nationalzoo.si.edu/Publications/ZooGoer/2009/1/BrainyBonnie.cfm

Stone, D. N., Deci, E. L., & Ryan, R. M. (2009). Beyond talk: Creating autonomous motivation through self-determination theory. *Journal of General Management, 34,* 75–102.

Stoner, J. A. F. (1961). *A comparison of individual and group decisions involving risk* (Unpublished master's thesis). Alfred P. Sloan School of Management, Massachusetts Institute of Technology, Cambridge, MA. Retrieved from http://dspace.mit.edu/bitstream/handle/1721.1/11330/33120544-MIT.pdf–sequence=2

Stoner, J. A. F. (1968). Risky and cautious shifts in group decisions: The influence of widely held values. *Journal of Experimental Social Psychology, 4,* 442–459.

Storaasli, R. D., & Markman, H. J. (1990). Relationship problems in the early stages of marriage: A longitudinal investigation. *Journal of Family Psychology, 4,* 80–98.

Storm, B. C., Bjork, E. L., & Bjork, R. A. (2008). Accelerated relearning after retrieval-induced forgetting: The benefit of being forgotten. *Journal of Experimental Psychology: Learning, Memory, and Cognition, 34,* 230–236.

Strack, F., Martin, L. L., & Stepper, S. (1988). Inhibiting and facilitating conditions of the human smile: A nonobtrusive test of the facial feedback hypothesis. *Journal of Personality and Social Psychology, 54,* 768–777.

Strain, G. M. (2003). *How well do dogs and other animals hear?* Department of Comparative Biomedical Sciences, School of Veterinary Medicine, Louisiana State University. Retrieved from http://www.lsu.edu/deafness/HearingRange.html

Strassberg, D. S., McKinnon, R. K., Sustaíta, M. A., & Rullo J. (2013). Sexting by high school students: An exploratory and descriptive study. *Archives of Sexual Behavior, 42,* 15–21.

Stratton, G. (1896, August). *Some preliminary experiments on vision without inversion of the retinal image.* Paper presented at the Third International Congress for Psychology, Munich.

Straub, R. O. (2014). *Health psychology: A biopsychosocial approach* (4th ed.). New York, NY: Worth.

Straus, M. A., & Paschall, M. J. (2009). Corporal punishment by mothers and development of children's cognitive ability: A longitudinal study of two nationally representative age cohorts. *Journal of Aggression, Maltreatment & Trauma, 18,* 459–483.

Strayer, D. L. (2015). Is the technology in your car driving you to distraction? *Policy Insights from the Behavioral and Brain Sciences, 2,* 157–165.

Strayer, D. L., & Watson, J. M. (2012, March). Top multitaskers help explain how brain juggles thoughts. *Scientific American Mind, 23,* 22–29.

Streit, W. J. (2000). Microglial response to brain injury: A brief synopsis. *Toxicologic Pathology, 28,* 28–30.

Strenger, C. (2015). Can psychoanalysis reclaim the public sphere? *Psychoanalytic Psychology, 32,* 293–306.

Stroebe, W., van Koningsbruggen, G. M., Papies, E. K., & Aarts, H. (2013). Why most dieters fail but some succeed: A goal conflict model of eating behavior. *Psychological Review, 120,* 110–138.

Stroud, M. (2015, February 2). Will lie detectors ever get their day in court again? *Bloomberg.* Retrieved from http://www.bloomberg.com/news/articles/2015-02-02/will-lie-detectors-ever-get-their-day-in-court-again-

Stuart, H. (2003). Violence and mental illness: An overview. *World Psychiatry, 2,* 121–124.

Stull, A. T., & Hegarty, M. (2016). Model manipulation and learning: Fostering representational competence with virtual and concrete models. *Journal of Educational Psychology, 108,* 509–527.

Stump, S. (2011, July 26). Girl, 6, on shark that bit her: "I forgive him." *Today.com.* Retrieved from http://today.msnbc.msn.com/id/43892097/ns/today-today_people/t/girl-shark-bit-her-i-forgive-him/#.Tpnf6s1lYjw

Stuss, D. T., & Alexander, M. P. (2000). Executive functions and the frontal lobes: A conceptual view. *Psychological Research, 63,* 289–298.

Su, K. G., Banker, G., Bourdette, D., & Forte, M. (2009). Axonal degeneration in multiple sclerosis: The mitochondrial hypothesis. *Current Neurological Neuroscience, 9,* 411–417.

Substance Abuse and Mental Health Services Administration. (2011). *Results from the 2010 National Survey on Drug Use and Health: Summary of national findings* [NSDUH Series H-41, HHS Publication No. (SMA) 11-4658]. Retrieved from http://www.samhsa.gov/data/nsduh/2k10nsduh/2k10results.htm

Substance Abuse and Mental Health Services Administration. (2012). *Results from the 2011 National Survey on Drug Use and Health: Summary of national findings* [NSDUH Series H-44, HHS Publication No. (SMA) 12-4713]. Retrieved from http://www.samhsa.gov/data/nsduh/2k11results/nsduhresults2011.htm

Substance Abuse and Mental Health Services Administration. (2014). *The NSDUH Report: Substance use and mental health estimates from the 2013 National Survey on Drug Use and Health: Overview of findings.* Rockville, MD: Author.

Substance Abuse and Mental Health Services Administration. (2016). *Racial and ethnic minority populations.* Retrieved from http://www.samhsa.gov/specific-populations/racial-ethnic-minority

Sucala, M., Schnur, J. B., Constantino, M. J., Miller, S. J., Brackman, E. H., & Montgomery, G. H. (2012). The therapeutic relationship in e-therapy for mental health: A systematic review. *Journal of Medical Internet Research, 14,* e110. doi:10.2196/jmir.2084

Summa, K. C., & Turek, F. W. (2015, February). The clocks within us. *Scientific American, 312,* 50–55.

Sun-Edelstein, C., & Mauskop, A. (2011). Alternative headache treatments: Nutraceuticals, behavioral, and physical treatments. *Headache, 25,* 469–483.

Sussman, S. (2015). A historical sketch of mental health services in Canada from the nineteenth century to community care. *International Journal of Behavioral Research & Psychology, 3,* 121–133.

Susuki, K. (2010). Myelin: A specialized membrane for cell communication. *Nature Education, 3,* 59–63.

Sutherland, S. (2012). Brain freeze explained. *Scientific American Mind, 23,* 7.

Suwanrath, C., & Suntharasaj, T. (2010). Sleep–wake cycles in normal fetuses. *Archives of Gynecology and Obstetrics, 281,* 449–454.

Svrakic, D. M., Zorumski, C. F., Svrakic, N. M., Zwir, I., & Cloninger, C. R. (2013). Risk architecture of schizophrenia: The role of epigenetics. *Current Opinion in Psychiatry, 26,* 188–195.

Swan, S. H., Liu, F., Hines, M., Kruse, R. L., Wang, C., Redmon, … Weiss, B. (2010). Prenatal phthalate exposure and reduced masculine play in boys. *International Journal of Andrology, 3,* 259–269.

Swanson, L. (1997). Cochlear implants: The head-on collision between medical technology and the right to be deaf. *Canadian Medical Association Journal, 157,* 929–932.

Swendsen, J. D., Tennen, H., Carney, M. A., Affleck, G., Willard, A., & Hromi, A. (2000). Mood and alcohol consumption: An experience sampling test of the self-medication hypothesis. *Journal of Abnormal Psychology, 109,* 198–204.

Swift, J. K., & Greenberg, R. P. (2012). Premature discontinuation in adult psychotherapy: A meta-analysis. *Journal of Consulting and Clinical Psychology, 80,* 547–559.

Szabo, R., & Hall, M. (2007). *Behind happy faces.* Los Angeles, CA: Volt Press.

Szalavitz, M. (2011, May 13). Q&A: Positive psychologist Martin Seligman on the good life. *TIME Magazine.* Retrieved from http://healthland.time.com/2011/05/13/mind-reading-positive-psychologist-martin-seligman-on-the-good-life/print/

Szasz, T. (2011). The myth of mental illness: 50 years later. *Psychiatrist Online, 35,* 179–182.

Tackett, J. L., Waldman, I. D., & Lahey, B. B. (2009). Etiology and measurement of relational aggression: A multi-informant behavior genetic investigation. *Journal of Abnormal Psychology, 118,* 722–733.

Tallandini, M. A., & Caudek, C. (2010). Defense mechanisms development in typical children. *Psychotherapy Research, 20,* 535–545.

Tan, R., & Goldman, M. S. (2015). Exposure to female fertility pheromones influences men's drinking. *Experimental and Clinical Psychopharmacology, 23*(3), 139–146.

Tandon, R., Keshavan, M. S., & Nasrallah, H. A. (2008a). Schizophrenia, "just the facts": What we know in 2008. Part 1: Overview. *Schizophrenia Research, 100,* 4–19.

Tandon, R., Keshavan, M. S., & Nasrallah, H. A. (2008b). Schizophrenia, "just the facts": What we know in 2008. 2. Epidemiology and etiology. *Schizophrenia Research, 102,* 1–18.

Tandon, R., Nasrallah, H. A., & Keshavan, M. S. (2009). Schizophrenia, "just the facts." 4. Clinical features and conceptualization. *Schizophrenia Research, 110,* 1–23.

Tang, Y. Y., Hölzel, B. K., & Posner, M. I. (2015). The neuroscience of mindfulness meditation. *Nature Reviews Neuroscience, 16,* 213–225.

Tanis, M., Beukeboom, C. J., Hartmann, T., & Vermeulen, I. E. (2015). Phantom phone signals: An investigation into the prevalence and predictors of imagined cell phone signals. *Computers in Human Behavior, 51,* 356–362.

Tate, M. C., Herbet, G., Moritz-Gasser, S., Tate, J. E., & Duffau, H. (2014). Probabilistic map of critical functional regions of the human cerebral cortex: Broca's area revisited. *Brain, 137,* 2773–2782.

Tauer, J. (2009). Monday morning quarterbacking: The case of the hindsight bias [Web log post]. Retrieved from https://www.psychologytoday.com/blog/goal-posts/200911/monday-morning-quarterbacking-the-case-the-hindsight-bias

Taverniers, J., Smeets, T., Van Ruysseveldt, J., Syroit, J., & von Grumbkow, J. (2011). The risk of being shot at: Stress, cortisol secretion, and their impact on memory and perceived learning during reality-based practice for armed officers. *International Journal of Stress Management, 18,* 113–132.

Taylor, A., & Gosney, M. A. (2011). Sexuality in older age: Essential considerations for healthcare professionals. *Age and Ageing, 40,* 538–543.

Taylor, C., Clifford, A., & Franklin, A. (2013). Color preferences are not universal. *Journal of Experimental Psychology: General, 142,* 1015–1027.

Taylor, C. A., Manganello, J. A., Lee, S. J., & Rice, J. (2010). Mothers' spanking of 3-year-old children and subsequent risk of children's aggressive behavior. *Pediatrics, 125,* e1057–e1065.

Taylor, J. B. (2006). *My stroke of insight.* New York, NY: Plume.

Taylor, J. B. (2008, February). *Jill Bolte Taylor: My stroke of insight* [Video file]. Retrieved from http://www.ted.com/talks/jill_bolte_taylor_s_powerful_stroke_of_insight

Taylor, S. E., Klein, L. C., Lewis, B. P., Gruenewald, T. L., Gurung, R. A., & Updegraff, J. A. (2000). Biobehavioral responses to stress in females: Tend-and-befriend, not fight-or-flight. *Psychological Review, 107,* 411–429.

Taylor, S. E., & Master, S. L. (2011). Social responses to stress: The tend-and-befriend model. In R. J. Contrada & A. Baum (Eds.), *The handbook of stress science: Biology, psychology, and health* (pp. 101–109). New York: NY: Springer.

Teghtsoonian, R. (1971). On the exponents in Stevers' law and the constant in Ekman's law. *Psychological Review, 78,* 71–80.

Tellegen, A., Lykken, D. T., Bouchard, T. J., Jr., Wilcox, K. J., Segal, N. L., & Rich, S. (1988). Personality similarity in twins reared apart and together. *Journal of Personality and Social Psychology, 54,* 1031–1039.

Temmel, A. F., Quint, C., Schickinger-Fischer, B., Klimek, L., Stoller, E., & Hummel, T. (2002). Characteristics of olfactory disorders in relation to major causes of olfactory loss. *Archives of Otolaryngology—Head & Neck Surgery, 128,* 635–641.

Ten Velden, F. S., Baas, M., Shalvi, S., Preenen, P. T. Y., & De Dreu, C. K. W. (2012). In competitive interaction, displays of red increase actors' competitive approach and perceivers' withdrawal. *Journal of Experimental Social Psychology, 48,* 1205–1208.

Tenenbaum, H. R., & Leaper, C. (2002). Are parents' gender schemas related to their children's gender-related cognitions? A meta-analysis. *Developmental Psychology, 38,* 615–630.

Teodorescu, M., Barnet, J. H., Hagen, E. W., Palta, M., Young, T. B., & Peppard, P. E. (2015). Association between asthma and risk of developing obstructive sleep apnea. *Journal of the American Medical Association, 313,* 156–164.

Terman, L. M. (1916). *The measurement of intelligence.* Boston, MA: Houghton Mifflin.

Terman, L. M. (1925). *Genetic studies of genius: Mental and physical traits of a thousand gifted children.* Palo Alto, CA: Stanford University Press.

Terman, L. M., & Oden, M. H. (1947). *The gifted child grows up: Twenty-five years' follow-up of a superior group.* Palo Alto, CA: Stanford University Press.

Terracciano, A., Abdel-Khalek, A. M., Ádám, N., Adamovová, L., Ahn, C. K., Ahn, H. N., … McCrae, R. R. (2005). National character does not reflect mean personality trait levels in 49 cultures. *Science, 310,* 96–100

Terracciano, A., Costa, P. T., & McCrae, R. R. (2006). Personality plasticity after age 30. *Personality and Social Psychology Bulletin, 32,* 999–1009.

Thelen, E., & Fisher, D. M. (1982). Newborn stepping: An explanation for a "disappearing" reflex. *Developmental Psychology, 18,* 760–775.

Thibaut, J., & Kelly, H. (1959). *The social psychology of groups.* New York, NY: John Wiley & Sons.

Thomas, A., & Chess, S. (1986). The New York Longitudinal Study: From infancy to early adult life. In R. Plomin & J. Dunn (Eds.), *The study of temperament: Changes, continuities, and challenges* (pp. 39–52). Hillsdale, NJ: Lawrence Erlbaum Associates.

Thomas, I., & Bruck, D. (2010). Awakening of sleeping people: A decade of research. *Fire Technology, 46*(3), 743–761.

Thompson, P. M., Giedd, J. N., Woods, R. P., MacDonald, D., Evans, A. C., & Toga, A. W. (2000). Growth patterns in the developing brain detected by using continuum mechanical tensor maps. *Nature, 404,* 190–193.

Thompson, R. F., & Kim, J. J. (1996). Memory systems in the brain and localization of a memory. *Proceedings of the National Academy of Sciences, USA, 93,* 13438–13444.

Thompson, R. F., & Steinmetz, J. E. (2009). The role of the cerebellum in classical conditioning of discrete behavioral responses. *Neuroscience, 162,* 732–755.

Thorndike, E. L. (1898). Animal intelligence: An experimental study of the associative process in animals. *Psychological Review Monograph Supplement,* Vol. II, No. 4. London: Macmillan.

Thorndike, E. L. (1936). Edward Lee Thorndike. In C. Murchison (Ed.), *The International University Series in Psychology: A history of psychology in autobiography* (Vol. 3, pp. 263–270). Worcester, MA: Clark University Press.

Thorne, B. (1993). *Gender play: Girls and boys in school.* Buckingham, UK: Open University Press.

Thorne, M., & Henley, T. B. (2005). *Connections in the history and systems of psychology* (3rd ed.). Boston, MA: Houghton Mifflin.

Thurlow, H. J., & Girvin, J. P. (1971). Use of anti-epileptic medication in treating "flashbacks" from hallucinogenic drugs. *Canadian Medical Association Journal, 105,* 947–948.

Tian, L., Wang, J., Yan, C., & He, Y. (2011). Hemisphere-and gender-related differences in small-world brain networks: A resting-state functional MRI study. *NeuroImage, 54,* 191–202.

Tidwell, N. D., Eastwick, P. W., & Finkel, E. J. (2013). Perceived, not actual, similarity predicts initial attraction in a live romantic context: Evidence from the speed-dating paradigm. *Personal Relationships, 20,* 199–215.

Times Staff Writer. (2014, June 18). Now 15, the "Girl in the Window" is featured on Oprah show (w/video). *Tampa Bay Times.* Retrieved from http://www.tampabay.com/features/humaninterest/now-15-the-girl-in-the-window-is-featured-on-oprah-show/2184949

Tirindelli, R., Dibattista, M., Pifferi, S., & Menini, A. (2009). From pheromones to behavior. *Physiological Reviews, 89*(3), 921–956.

Tobin, D. D., Menon, M., Menon, M., Spatta, B. C., Hodges, E. V., & Perry, D. G. (2010). The intrapsychics of gender: A model of self-socialization. *Psychological Review, 117,* 601–622.

Todes, D. P. (2014). *Ivan Pavlov: A Russian life in science.* New York, NY: Oxford University Press.

Toga, A. W., Thompson, P. M., & Sowell, E. R. (2006). Mapping brain maturation. *Trends in Neuroscience, 29,* 148–159.

Tollenaar, M. S., Beijers, R., Jansen, J., Riksen-Walraven, J. M. A., & De Weerth, C. (2011). Maternal prenatal stress and cortisol reactivity to stressors in human infants. *Stress, 14,* 53–65.

Tolman, E. C. (1948). Cognitive maps in rats and men. *Psychological Review, 55*(4), 189–208.

Tolman, E. C., & Honzik, C. H. (1930). Introduction and removal of reward, and maze performance in rats. *University of California Publications in Psychology, 4,* 257–275.

Tomoda, A., Suzuki, H., Rabi, K., Sheu, Y., Polcari, A., & Teicher, M. H. (2009). Reduced prefrontal cortical gray matter volume in young adults exposed to harsh corporal punishment. *NeuroImage, 47,* T66 –T71.

Tondo, L., Isacsson, G., & Baldessarini, R. J. (2003). Suicidal behaviour in bipolar disorder: Risk and prevention. *CNS Drugs, 17,* 491–511.

Tononi, G., & Cirelli, C. (2014). Sleep and the price of plasticity: From synaptic and cellular homeostasis to memory consolidation and integration. *Neuron, 81*(1), 12–34.

Topp, S. S. (2013). Against the quiet revolution: The rhetorical construction of intersex individuals as disordered. *Sexualities 16,* 180–194.

Torrente, M. P., Gelenberg, A. J., & Vrana, K. E. (2012). Boosting serotonin in the brain: Is it time to revamp the treatment of depression? *Journal of Psychopharmacology, 26,* 629–635.

Torrey, E., F., Fuller, D. A., Geller, J., Jacobs, C., & Rogasta, K. (2012). *No room at the inn: Trends and consequences of closing public psychiatric hospitals.* Arlington, VA: Treatment Advocacy Center.

Torry, Z. D., & Billick, S. B. (2010). Overlapping universe: Understanding legal insanity and psychosis. *Psychiatric Quarterly, 81,* 253–262.

Toufexis, A. (2001, June 24). Why men can outdrink women. *TIME Magazine.* Retrieved from http://content.time.com/time/magazine/article/0,9171,153672,00.html

Tourangeau, R., & Yan, T. (2007). Sensitive questions in surveys. *Psychological Bulletin, 133,* 859–883.

Tränkner, D., Jagle, H., Kohl, S., Apfelstedt-Sylla, E., Sharpe, L. T., Kaupp, U. B., … Wissinger, B. (2004). Molecular basis of an inherited form of incomplete achromatopsia. *Journal of Neuroscience, 24,* 138–147.

Treffers-Daller, J., & Milton, J. (2013) Vocabulary size revisited: The link between vocabulary size and academic achievement. *Applied Linguistics Review, 4,* 151–172.

Treffert, D. A. (2015). Accidental genius. *Scientific American, 23,* 54–59.

Trivers, R. L. (1971). The evolution of reciprocal altruism. *Quarterly Review of Biology, 46,* 35–57.

True lies. (2004, April 15). *Nature.* Retrieved from http://www.nature.com/nature/journal/v428/n6984/full/428679a.html

Tsaw, D., Murphy, S., & Detgen, J. (2011). Social loafing and culture: Does gender matter? *International Review of Business Research, 7,* 1–8.

Tse, S., & Ng, R. M. K. (2014). Applying a mental health recovery approach for people from diverse backgrounds: The case of collectivism and individualism paradigms. *Journal of Psychosocial Rehabilitation and Mental Health, 1,* 7–13.

Tsuang, M. T., Stone, W. S., & Faraone, S. V. (2001). Genes, environment and schizophrenia. *British Journal of Psychiatry, 178,* s18–s24.

Tullis, J. G., & Benjamin, A. S. (2015). Cue generation: How learners flexibly support future retrieval. *Memory & Cognition, 43,* 922–938.

Tulving, E. (1972). Episodic and semantic memory. In E. Tulving & W. Donaldson (Eds.), *Organization of memory* (pp. 381–403). New York, NY: Academic Press.

Tulving, E. (1985). Memory and consciousness. *Canadian Psychology/Psychologice Canadienne, 26,* 1–11.

Tulving, E., & Osler, S. (1968). Effectiveness of retrieval cues in memory for words. *Journal of Experimental Psychology, 77,* 593–601.

Tulving, E., & Thomson, D. M. (1973). Encoding specificity and retrieval processes in episodic memory. *Psychological Review, 80,* 352–373.

Tummala-Narra, P. (2016). A historical overview and critique of the psychoanalytic approach to culture and context. In P. Tummala-Narra, *Psychoanalytic theory and cultural competence in psychotherapy* (pp. 7–29). Washington, DC: American Psychological Association. http://dx.doi.org/10.1037/14800-002

Tummala-Narra, P., Alegria, M., & Chen, C.-N. (2012). Perceived discrimination, acculturative stress, and depression among South Asians: Mixed findings. *Asian American Journal of Psychology, 3,* 3–16.

Turiano, N. A., Spiro, A. III, & Mroczek, D. K. (2012). Openness to experience and mortality in men: Analysis of trait and facets. *Journal of Aging and Health, 24,* 654–672.

Turner, P. L., & Mainster, M. A. (2008). Circadian photoreception: Ageing and the eye's important role in systemic health. *British Journal of Ophthalmology, 92,* 1439–1444.

Turner, R. C., Lucke-Wold, B. P., Robson, M. J., Omalu, B. I., Petraglia, A. L., & Bailes, J. E. (2013). Repetitive traumatic brain injury and development of chronic traumatic encephalopathy: A potential role for biomarkers in diagnosis, prognosis, and treatment? *Frontiers in Neurology, 3* (186). doi:10.3389/fneur.2012.00186

Tversky, A., & Kahneman, D. (1981). The framing of decisions and the psychology of choice. *Science, 211,* 453–458.

Tversky, A., & Kahneman, D. (1982). Judgment under uncertainty: Heuristics and biases. In D. Kahneman, P. Slovic, & A. Tversky (Eds.), *Judgment under uncertainty: Heuristics and biases* (pp. 3–20). New York, NY: Cambridge University Press.

Twenge, J. M., Baumeister, R. F., DeWall, C. N., Ciarocco, N. J., & Bartels, J. M. (2007). Social exclusion decreases prosocial behavior. *Journal of Personality and Social Psychology, 92,* 56–66.

Uchida, S., Shioda, K., Morita, Y., Kubota, C., Ganeko, M., & Takeda, N. (2012). Exercise effects on sleep physiology. *Frontiers in Neurology, 3.* http://dx.doi.org/10.3389/fneur.2012.00048

Uchino, B. N., Berg, C. A., Smith, T. W., Pearce, G., & Skinner, M. (2006). Age-related differences in ambulatory blood pressures during daily stress: Evidence for greater blood pressure reactivity with age. *Psychology and Aging, 21,* 231–239.

Ücok, A., & Gaebel, W. (2008). Side effects of atypical antipsychotics: A brief overview. *World Psychiatry, 7,* 58–62.

UCSF Medical Center. (n.d.). *FAQ: Cochlear implants.* Retrieved from http://www.ucsfhealth.org/education/cochlear_implants/index.html

UNAIDS. (2015). *South Africa: HIV and AIDS estimates.* Retrieved from http://www.unaids.org/en/regionscountries/countries/southafrica

Uncapher, M. R., Thieu, M. K., & Wagner, A. D. (2016) Media multitasking and memory: Differences in working memory and long-term memory. *Psychonomic Bulletin & Review, 23,* 483–490.

Underwood, E. (2014). The taste of things to come. *Science, 345*(6198), 750–751.

United Nations. (2012). *World drug report 2012* (No. E.12.XI.1). Vienna, Austria: Office on Drugs and Crime.

United Nations, General Assembly. (1987, August 4). *Report of the World Commission on Environment and Development: Our common future* (A/42/427). Retrieved from http://www.un-documents.net/our-common-future.pdf

United Nations Office for the Coordination of Humanitarian Affairs. (2011, September 5). *Key facts on Somalia.* Retrieved from http://reliefweb.int/report/somalia/key-figures-somalia-05-september-2011

United Nations Population Fund. (n.d.). *Migration.* Retrieved from http://www.unfpa.org/migration

Urso, A. M. (2007). The reality of neonatal pain and the resulting effects. *Journal of Neonatal Nursing, 13,* 236–238.

U.S. Census Bureau. (2011 and earlier). *Current Population Survey (CPS) data on educational attainment* [Annual Social and Economic (ASEC) or March Supplements]. Retrieved from http://www.census.gov/hhes/socdemo/education/data/cps/

U.S. Census Bureau. (2015). Figure MS-2. Median age at first marriage: 1890 to present. Retrieved from https://www.census.gov/hhes/families/files/graphics/MS-2.pdf

U.S. Census Bureau. (2015, November 2). *Facts for features: American Indian and Alaska Native heritage month* [Press release]. Retrieved from http://www.census.gov/newsroom/facts-for-features/2015/cb15-ff22.html

U.S. Department of Defense. (2015, July 23). *National security implications of climate-related risks and a changing climate* (Report No. 8-6475571). Retrieved from http://archive.defense.gov/pubs/150724-congressional-report-on-national-implications-of-climate-change.pdf?source=govdelivery

U.S. Fish & Wildlife Service. (2006). *Laysan Albatross Phoebastria immutabilis conservation status* (Alaska Seabird Information Series, 3–4). Retrieved from http://www.fws.gov/alaska/mbsp/mbm/seabirds/pdf/laal.pdf

U.S. Food and Drug Administration. (2008). *Drugs: Information for healthcare professionals: Suicidal behavior and ideation and antiepileptic drugs.* Retrieved from http://www.fda.gov/Drugs/DrugSafety/PostmarketDrugSafetyInformationforPatientsandProviders/ucm100192.htm

U.S. Food and Drug Administration. (n.d.). *For consumers: Side effects of sleep drugs.* Retrieved from http://www.fda.gov/forconsumers/consumerupdates/ucm107757.htm

Uttal, D. H., Meadow, N. G., Tipton, E., Hand, L. L., Alden, A. R., Warren, C., & Newcombe, N. S. (2013). The malleability of spatial skills: A meta-analysis of training studies. *Psychological Bulletin, 139,* 352–402.

Vadeboncoeur, C., Townsend, N., & Foster, C. (2015). A meta-analysis of weight gain in first year university students: Is freshman 15 a myth? *BMC Obesity, 2.* doi:10.1186/s40608-015-0051-7

Vaillancourt, T. (2013). Do human females use indirect aggression as an intrasexual competition strategy? *Philosophical Transactions of the Royal Society of London B: Biological Sciences, 368*(1631), 20130080.

Vaillant, G. E. (1992). *Ego mechanisms of defense: A guide for clinicians and researchers.* Arlington, VA: American Psychiatric Association.

Vaillant, G. E. (2000). Adaptive mental mechanisms: Their role in a positive psychology. *American Psychologist, 55,* 89–98.

Valenza, E., Leo, I., Gava, L., & Simion, F. (2006). Perceptual completion in newborn human infants. *Child Development, 77,* 1810–1821.

Vall, O., Salat-Batlle, J., & Garcia-Algar, O. (2015). Alcohol consumption during pregnancy and adverse neurodevelopmental outcomes. *Journal of Epidemiology and Community Health, 69*(10), 927–929.

van der Lely, S., Frey, S., Garbazza, C., Wirz-Justice, A., Jenni, O. G., Steiner, R., … Schmidt, C. (2015). Blue blocker glasses as a countermeasure for alerting effects of evening light-emitting diode screen exposure in male teenagers. *Journal of Adolescent Health, 56,* 113–119.

Van Doorn, M. D., Branje, S. J. T., & Meeus, W. H. (2011). Developmental changes in conflict resolution styles in parent-adolescent relationships: A four-wave longitudinal study. *Journal of Youth and Adolescence, 40,* 97–107.

van Erp, T. G. M., Hibar, D. P., Rasmussen, J. M., Glahn, D. C., Pearlson, G. D., Andreassen, O. A., … Melle, I. (2016). Subcortical brain volume abnormalities in 2028 individuals with schizophrenia and 2540 healthy controls via the ENIGMA consortium. *Molecular Psychiatry, 21,* 547–553.

van Geel, M., Vedder, P., & Tanilon, J. (2014). Relationship between peer victimization, cyberbullying, and suicide in children and adolescents: A meta-analysis. *JAMA Pediatrics, 168,* 435–442.

Van Horn, J. D., Irimia, A., Torgerson, C. M., Chambers, M. C., Kikinis, R., & Toga, A. W. (2012). Mapping connectivity damage in the case of Phineas Gage. *PLOS ONE, 7*(5), e37454.

van Os, J., & Kapur, S. (2009). Schizophrenia. *Lancet, 374,* 635–645.

Van Petegem, S., Soenens, B., Vansteenkiste, M., & Beyers, W. (2015). Rebels with a cause? Adolescent defiance from the perspective of reactance theory and self-determination theory. *Child Development, 86,* 903–918.

van Praag, H., Kempermann, G., & Gage, F. H. (2000). Neural consequences of environmental enrichment. *Nature Reviews Neuroscience, 1,* 191–198.

Van Someren, E. J. W., Cirelli, C., Dijk, D. J., Van Cauter, E., Schwartz, S., & Chee, M. W. (2015). Disrupted sleep: From molecules to cognition. *The Journal of Neuroscience, 35,* 13889–13895.

Van Strien, J. W., Franken, I. H., & Huijding, J. (2014). Testing the snake-detection hypothesis: Larger early posterior negativity in humans to pictures of snakes than to pictures of other reptiles, spiders and slugs. *Frontiers in Human Neuroscience, 8.* doi: 10.3389/fnhum.2014.00691

Vanini, G., Lydic, R., & Baghdoyan, H. A. (2012). GABA-to-ACh ratio in basal forebrain and cerebral cortex varies significantly during sleep. *SLEEP, 35,* 1325–1334.

Vaquero, L., Hartmann, K., Ripollés, P., Rojo, N., Sierpowska, J., François, C., … Münte, T. F. (2016). Structural neuroplasticity in expert pianists depends on the age of musical training onset. *NeuroImage, 126,* 106–119.

Varlet, M., & Richardson, M. J. (2015, January 5). What would be Usain Bolt's 100-meter sprint world record without Tyson Gay? Unintentional interpersonal synchronization between the two sprinters. *Journal of Experimental Psychology: Human Perception and Performance, 41,* 36–41.

Vartanian, L. R. (2015). Impression management and food intake. Current directions in research. *Appetite, 86,* 74–80.

Vartanian, L. R., Herman, C. P., & Polivy, J. (2016). What does it mean to eat an appropriate amount of food? *Eating Behaviors, 23,* 24–27.

Vartanian, L. R., Spanos, S., Herman, C. P., & Polivy, J. (2015). Modeling of food intake: A meta-analytic review. *Social Influence, 10,* 119–136.

Vas, A. K., Chapman, S. B., & Cook, L. G. (2015). Language impairments in traumatic brain injury: A window into complex cognitive performance. In J. Grafman & A. M. Salazar (Eds.), *Handbook of clinical neurology: Traumatic brain injury, part II* (pp. 497–510). Amsterdam: Elsevier B.V.

Vassos, E., Collier, D. A., & Fazel, S. (2014). Systematic meta-analyses and field synopsis of genetic association studies of violence and aggression. *Molecular Psychiatry, 19,* 471–477.

Velagaleti, G. V. N., & Moore, C. M. (2011). Role of array comparative genomic hybridization of cytogenetic causes of pregnancy loss. *Pathology Case Reviews, 16,* 214–221.

Vennard, M. (2011, November 21). How can musicians keep playing despite amnesia? *BBC World Service.* Retrieved from http://www.bbc.co.uk/news/magazine-15791973

Verduyn, P., Lee, D. S., Park, J., Shablack, H., Orvell, A., Bayer, J., … Kross, E. (2015). Passive Facebook usage undermines affective well-being: Experimental and longitudinal evidence. *Journal of Experimental Psychology: General, 144,* 480–488.

Vernon, P. A., Martin, R. A., Schermer, J. A., Cherkas, L. F., & Spector, T. D. (2008). Genetic and environmental contributions to humor styles: A replication study. *Twin Research and Human Genetics, 11,* 44–47.

Vervecken, D., & Hannover, B. (2015). Effects of gender fair job descriptions on children's perceptions of job status, job difficulty, and vocational self-efficacy. *Social Psychology, 46*(2), 76–92.

Verwijmeren, T., Karremans, J. C., Bernritter, S. F., Stroebe, W., & Wigboldus, D. H. (2013). Warning: You are being primed! The effect of a warning on the impact of subliminal ads. *Journal of Experimental Social Psychology, 49,* 1124–1129.

Vilain, E. J. N. (2008). Genetics of sexual development and differentiation. In D. L. Rowland & L. Incrocci (Eds.), *Handbook of sexual and gender identity disorders* (pp. 329–353). Hoboken, NJ: John Wiley & Sons.

Vingtdeux, V., Davies, P., Dickson, D. W., & Marambaud, P. (2011). AMPK is abnormally activated in tangle- and pre-tangle-bearing neurons in Alzheimer's disease and other tauopathies. *Acta Neuropathologica, 121,* 337–349.

Violanti, J. M. (1992). Coping strategies among police recruits in a high-stress training environment. *Journal of Social Psychology, 132,* 717–729.

Visser, B. A., Ashton, M. C., & Vernon, P. A. (2006). Beyond g: Putting multiple intelligences theory to the test. *Intelligence, 34,* 487–502.

Visser, P. L., & Hirsch, J. K. (2014). Health behaviors among college students: The influence of future time perspective and basic psychological need satisfaction. *Health Psychology and Behavioral Medicine, 2,* 88–99.

Vlahos, J. (2007, September 9). Scent and sensibility. *The New York Times.* Retrieved from http://query.nytimes.com/gst/fullpage.html–res=9D07EFDC1E3AF9 3AA3575AC0A9619C8B63&pagewanted=all

Vogel, G. (2014, October 6). Updated: Brain's GPS earns three neuroscientists a Nobel Prize. *Science.* Retrieved from http://www.sciencemag.org/news/2014/10/ updated-brains-gps-earns-three-neuroscientists-nobel-prize

Volkow, N. D., Chang, L., Wang, G. J., Fowler, J. S., Leonido-Yee, M., Franceschi, D., … Miller, E. N. (2001). Association of dopamine transporter reduction with psychomotor impairment in methamphetamine abusers. *American Journal of Psychiatry, 158,* 377–382.

Volkow, N. D., Frieden, T. R., Hyde, P. S., & Cha, S. S. (2014). Medication-assisted therapies—tackling the opioid-overdose epidemic. *New England Journal of Medicine, 370*(22), 2063–2066.

von Dawans, B., Fischbacher, U., Kirschbaum, C., Fehr, E., & Heinrichs, M. (2012). The social dimension of stress reactivity: Acute stress increases prosocial behavior in humans. *Psychological Science, 23,* 829–839.

von Stumm, S., & Deary, I. J. (2012). Typical intellectual engagement and cognition in the ninth decade of life: The Lothian Birth Cohort 1921. *Psychology and Aging, 27,* 761–767.

von Stumm, S., & Plomin, R. (2015). Socioeconomic status and the growth of intelligence from infancy through adolescence. *Intelligence, 48,* 30–36.

Vorster, A. P., & Born, J. (2015). Sleep and memory in mammals, birds and invertebrates. *Neuroscience & Biobehavioral Reviews, 50,* 103–119.

Vredeveldt, A., Baddeley, A. D., & Hitch, G. J. (2014). The effectiveness of eye-closure in repeated interviews. *Legal and Criminological Psychology, 19,* 282–295.

Vreeman, R. C., & Carroll, A. E. (2008). Festive medical myths. *BMJ, 337,* a2769. http://dx.doi.org/10.1136/bmj.a2769

Vygotsky, L. S. (1934/1962). *Thought and language* (Eugenia Hanfmann & Gertrude Vakar, Eds. & Trans.). Cambridge, MA: Massachusetts Institute of Technology.

Wagenmakers, E. J., Wetzels, R., Borsboom, D., & van der Maas, H. L. (2011). Why psychologists must change the way they analyze their data: The case of psi [Peer commentary on the paper "Feeling the Future: Experimental Evidence for Anomalous Retroactive Influences on Cognition and Affect" by D. J. Bem]. *Journal of Personality and Social Psychology, 100,* 426–432.

Wagner, J. A. III, Humphrey, S. E., Meyer, C. J., & Hollenbeck, J. R. (2012). Individualism–collectivism and team member performance: Another look. *Journal of Organizational Behavior, 33,* 946–963.

Wahlstrom, K., Dretzke, B., Gordon, M., Peterson, K., Edwards, K., & Gdula, J. (2014). Examining the impact of later high school start times on the health and academic performance of high school students: A multi-site study. Retrieved from http://hdl.handle.net/11299/162769

Wai, J., Cacchio, M., Putallaz, M., & Makel, M. C. (2010). Sex differences in the right tail of cognitive abilities: A 30 year examination. *Intelligence, 38,* 412–423.

Wakefield, A. J., Murch, S. H., Anthony, A., Linnell, J., Casson, D. M., Malik, M., … Walker-Smith, J. A. (1998). Ileal-lymphoid-nodular hyperplasia, non-specific colitis, and pervasive developmental disorder in children. *Lancet, 28,* 637–641.

Wakefield, J. C. (1992). The concept of mental disorder: On the boundary between biological facts and social values. *American Psychologist, 47,* 373–388.

Walker, L. E., Pann, J. M., Shapiro, D. L., & Van Hasselt, V. B. (2016). A review of best practices for the treatment of persons with mental illness in jail. In *Best practices for the mentally ill in the criminal justice system* (pp. 57–69). Cham, Switzerland: Springer International.

Wall, S. S. (2015). Standing at the intersections: Navigating life as a black intersex man. *Narrative Inquiry in Bioethics, 5,* 117–119.

Walla Walla penitentiary psychologist honored nationally. (2013, September 20). Retrieved from http://www.columbian.com/news/2013/sep/20/walla-walla-penitentiary-psychologist-honored-nati/

Wallentin, M. (2009). Putative sex differences in verbal abilities and language cortex: A critical review. *Brain and Language, 108,* 175–183.

Wallin, P. (1949). An appraisal of some methodological aspects of the Kinsey Report. *American Sociological Review, 14,* 197–210.

Walma van der Molen, J. H., & van der Voort, T. H. A. (2000). The impact of television, print, and audio on children's recall of the news: A study of three alternative explanations for the dual-coding hypothesis. *Human Communication Research, 26,* 3–26.

Walsh, R. (2011). Lifestyle and mental health. *American Psychologist, 66,* 579–592.

Walton, R. G., & Monte, W. C. (2015). Dietary methanol and autism. *Medical Hypotheses, 85,* 441–446.

Wan, L., Crookes, K., Reynolds, K. J., Irons, J. L., & McKone, E. (2015). A cultural setting where the other-race effect on face recognition has no social-motivational component and derives entirely from lifetime perceptual experience. *Cognition, 144,* 91–115.

Wang, H.-X., Karp, A., Winblad, B., & Fratiglioni, L. (2002). Late-life engagement in social and leisure activities is associated with a decreased risk of dementia: A longitudinal study from the Kungsholmen Project. *American Journal of Epidemiology, 155,* 1081–1087.

Wang, Q., & Conway, M. A. (2004). The stories we keep: Autobiographical memory in American and Chinese middle-aged adults. *Journal of Personality, 72,* 911–938.

Wansink, B., Cao, Y., Saini, P., Shimizu, M., & Just, D. R. (2013). College cafeteria snack food purchases become less healthy with each passing week of the semester. *Public Health Nutrition, 16,* 1291–1295.

Wansink, B., & Kim, J. (2005). Bad popcorn in big buckets: Portion size can influence intake as much as taste. *Journal of Nutrition Education and Behavior, 37,* 242–245.

Warburton, D. E. R., Charlesworth, S., Ivey, A., Nettlefold, L., & Bredin, S. S. D. (2010). A systematic review of the evidence for Canada's physical activity guidelines for adults. *International Journal of Behavioral Nutrition and Physical Activity, 7,* 1–220.

Ward, E., Wiltshire, J. C., Detry, M. A., & Brown, R. L. (2013). African American men and women's attitude toward mental illness, perceptions of stigma, and preferred coping behaviors. *Nursing Research, 62,* 185–194.

Warneken, F., & Tomasello, M. (2006). Altruistic helping in human infants and young chimpanzees. *Science, 311,* 1301–1303.

Washburn, D. A. (2010). Book reviews: The animal mind at 100. *Psychological Record, 60,* 369–376.

Wasserstein, R. L. (2013, May 16). A statistician's view: What are your chances of winning the Powerball lottery? *The Huffington Post.* Retrieved from http:// www.huffingtonpost.com/ronald-l-wasserstein/chances-of-winning-powerball-lottery_b_3288129.html

Waterhouse, L. (2006). Multiple intelligences, the Mozart effect, and emotional intelligence: A critical review. *Educational Psychologist, 41,* 207–225.

Watson, J. B., & Rayner, R. (1920). Conditioned emotional reactions. *Journal of Experimental Psychology, 3,* 1–14. (Reprinted in *American Psychologist, 55,* 313–317.)

Watson, J. M., & Strayer, D. L. (2010). Supertaskers: Profiles in extraordinary multi-tasking ability. *Psychonomic Bulletin and Review, 17,* 479–485.

Watson, N. F., Morgenthaler, T., Chervin, R., Carden, K., Kirsch, D., Kristo, D., … Weaver, T. (2015). Confronting drowsy driving: The American Academy of Sleep Medicine perspective. *Journal of Clinical Sleep Medicine, 11*(11), 1335–1336.

Watson, R. I. (1968). *The great psychologists* (2nd ed.). Philadelphia, PA: J.B. Lippincott.

Waugh, N. C., & Norman, D. A. (1965). Primary memory. *Psychological Review, 72,* 89–104.

Wearing, D. (2005). *Forever today: A memoir of love and amnesia.* London: Corgi Books.

Webb, S. J., Monk, C. S., & Nelson, C. A. (2001). Mechanisms of postnatal neurobiological development: Implications for human development. *Developmental Neuropsychology, 19,* 147–171.

Weber, H., Scholz, C. J., Domschke, K., Baumann, C., Klauke, B., Jacob, C. P., … Reif, A. (2012). Gender differences in associations of glutamate decarboxylase 1 gene (GAD1) variants with panic disorder. *PLOS ONE, 7,* e37651.

Weber, L. (2015, April 15). Today's personality tests raise the bar for job seekers. *The Wall Street Journal.* Retrieved from http://www.wsj.com/articles/a-personality-test-could-stand-in-the-way-of-your-next-job-1429065001

Webster's New International Dictionary of the English Language. (1925). W. T. Harris & F. Sturges Allen (Eds.). Springfield, MA: G.&C. Merriam.

Wei, W. (2014, May 1). Neil deGrasse Tyson: Don't worry, Earth will survive climate change — we won't [Video file]. *Business Insider.* Retrieved from http://www.businessinsider.com/neil-degrasse-tyson-climate-change-greenhouse-gas-2014-4

Weidner, R., Plewan, T., Chen, Q., Buchner, A., Weiss, P. H., & Fink, G. R. (2014). The moon illusion and size–distance scaling—evidence for shared neural patterns. *Journal of Cognitive Neuroscience, 26,* 1871–1882.

Weingarten, J. A., & Collop, N. A. (2013). Air travel: Effects of sleep deprivation and jet lag. *Chest, 144,* 1394–1401.

Weisberg, S. M., & Newcombe, N. S. (2016). How do (some) people make a cognitive map? Routes, places, and working memory. *Journal of Experimental Psychology: Learning, Memory, and Cognition, 42*(5), 768–785.

Weisel, O., & Shalvi, S. (2015). The collaborative roots of corruption. *Proceedings of the National Academy of Sciences, 112,* 10651–10656.

Weisgram, E. S., Fulcher, M., & Dinella, L. M. (2014). Pink gives girls permission: Exploring the roles of explicit gender labels and gender-typed colors on preschool children's toy preferences. *Journal of Applied Developmental Psychology, 35*(5), 401–409.

Weiss, A., King, J. E., & Perkins, L. (2006). Personality and subjective well-being in orangutans (*Pongo pygmaeus* and *Pongo abelii*). *Journal of Personality and Social Psychology, 90,* 501–511.

Weiss, R. B., Stange, J. P., Boland, E. M., Black, S. K., LaBelle, D. R., Abramson, L. Y., & Alloy, L. B. (2015). Kindling of life stress in bipolar disorder: Comparison of sensitization and autonomy models. *Journal of Abnormal Psychology, 124,* 4–16.

Weisskirch, R. S., & Delevi, R. (2011). "Sexting" and adult romantic attachment. *Computers in Human Behavior, 27,* 1697–1701.

Wemer, A., Uldbjerg, N., Zachariae, R., Rosen, G., & Nohr, E. (2013). Self-hypnosis for coping with labour pain: A randomised controlled trial. *BJOG, 120,* 346–353.

Wen, C. P., Wai, J. P., Tsai, M. K., Yang, Y. C., Cheng, T. Y., Lee, M. C., … Wu, X. (2011). Minimum amount of physical activity for reduced mortality and extended life expectancy: A prospective cohort study. *Lancet, 378,* 1244–1253.

Wen, X. J., Kanny, D., Thompson, W. W., Okoro, C. A., Town, M., & Balluz, L. S. (2012). Binge drinking intensity and health-related quality of life among US adult binge drinkers. *Preventing Chronic Disease, 9.* doi: http://dx.doi.org/10.5888/pcd9.110204.

Wendell, C. R., Waldstein, S. R., & Zonderman, A. B. (2014). Nonlinear longitudinal trajectories of cholesterol and neuropsychological function. *Neuropsychology, 28,* 106–112.

Wentzel, K. R., McNamara Barry, C., & Caldwell, K. A. (2004). Friendships in middle school: Influences on motivation and school adjustment. *Journal of Educational Psychology, 96,* 195–203.

Werker, J. F., & Tees, R. C. (1984). Cross-language speech perception: Evidence for perceptual reorganization during the first year of life. *Infant Behavior and Development, 7,* 49–63.

Werner, K. B., Few, L. R., & Bucholz, K. K. (2015). Epidemiology, comorbidity, and behavioral genetics of antisocial personality disorder and psychopathy. *Psychiatric Annals, 45,* 195–199.

Wernig, M., Zhao, J. P., Pruszak, J., Hedlund, E., Fu, D., Soldner, F., … Jaenisch, R. (2008). Neurons derived from reprogrammed fibroblasts functionally integrate into the fetal brain and improve symptoms of rats with Parkinson's disease. *Proceedings of the National Academy of Sciences, 105*(15), 5856–5861.

Wertheimer, M. (2012). *A brief history of psychology* (5th ed.). New York, NY: Taylor & Francis.

Wertheimer, M. (2014). Music, thinking, perceived motion: The emergence of Gestalt theory. *History of Psychology, 17,* 131–133.

Westbrook, A., & Braver, T. S. (2015). Cognitive effort: A neuroeconomic approach. *Cognitive, Affective, & Behavioral Neuroscience, 15,* 395–415.

Westen, D. (1990). Psychoanalytic approaches to personality. In L. A. Pervin (Ed.), *Handbook of personality* (pp. 21–65). New York, NY: Guilford Press.

Westen, D., Gabbard, G. O., & Ortigo, K. M. (2008). Psychoanalytic approaches to personality. In O. P. John, R. W. Robins, & L. A. Pervin (Eds.), *Handbook of personality: Theory of research* (pp. 61–113). New York, NY: Guilford Press.

Westly, E. (2011, July/August). The bilingual advantage. *Scientific American Mind, 22,* 38–41.

Westly, E. (2015). Join a club, stay sharp. *Scientific American Mind, 26,* 19.

Weuve, J., Puett, R. C., Schwartz, J., Yanosky, J. D., Laden, F., & Grodstein, F. (2012). Exposure to particulate air pollution and cognitive decline in older women. *Archives of Internal Medicine, 172,* 219–227.

Whisman, M. A., & Snyder, D. K. (2007). Sexual infidelity in a national survey of American women: Differences in prevalence and correlates as a function of method of assessment. *Journal of Family Psychology, 21,* 147–154.

Whitaker, R. (2015). The triumph of American psychiatry: How it created the modern therapeutic state. *European Journal of Psychotherapy & Counselling, 17,* 326–341.

Whitlock, J. R., Heynen, A. J., Shuler, M. G., & Bear, M. F. (2006). Learning induces long-term potentiation in the hippocampus. *Science, 313,* 1093–1097.

Whorf, B. L. (1956). *Language, thought, and reality.* Cambridge, MA: MIT Press.

Wich, S. A., Swartz, K. B., Hardus, M. E., Lameira, A. R., Stromberg, E., & Shumaker, R. W. (2009). Case of spontaneous acquisition of a human sound by an orangutan. *Primates, 50,* 56–64.

Wickens, A. P. (2015). *A history of the brain: From stone age surgery to modern neuroscience.* New York, NY: Psychology Press.

Wicker, A. W. (1969). Attitudes versus actions: The relationship of verbal and overt behavioral responses to attitude objects. *Journal of Social Issues, 24,* 41–78.

Wickman, F. (2013, September 26). 10 things *Breaking Bad* has actually gotten wrong [Web log post]. Retrieved from http://www.slate.com/blogs/browbeat/2013/09/26/breaking_bad_accuracy_the_show_s_biggest_errors_and_mistakes_from_blue_meth.html

Widmer, E. D., Treas, J., & Newcomb, R. (1998). Attitudes toward nonmarital sex in 24 countries. *Journal of Sex Research, 35,* 349–358.

Wijnands, J. M. A., & Kingwell, E. (2016). Time to wake up and smell the coffee? Coffee consumption and multiple sclerosis. *Journal of Neurology, Neurosurgery & Psychiatry, 87,* 453.

Wilkowski, B. M., Hartung, C. M., Crowe, S. E., & Chai, C. A. (2012). Men don't just get mad; they get even: Revenge but not anger mediates gender differences in physical aggression. *Journal of Research in Personality, 46*(5), 546–555.

Williams, D. R., & Mohammed, S. A. (2009). Discrimination and racial disparities in health: Evidence and needed research. *Journal of Behavioral Medicine, 32,* 20–47. doi:10.1007/s10865-008-9185-0

Williams, P. G., Suchy, Y., & Kraybill, M. L. (2010). Five-factor model personality traits and executive functioning among older adults. *Journal of Research in Personality, 44,* 485–491.

Williams, S. C. P. (2015, July 16). Why screams are so scary. *Science News.* Retrieved from http://news.sciencemag.org/biology/2015/07/why-screams-are-so-scary

Williams, T. (2015, July 30). A psychologist as warden? Jail and mental illness intersect in Chicago. *The New York Times.* Retrieved from http://www.nytimes.com/2015/07/31/us/a-psychologist-as-warden-jail-and-mental-illness-intersect-in-chicago.html?_r=0

Williams, T. R., Alam, S., & Gaffney, M. (2015). Progress in identifying infants with hearing loss—United States, 2006–2012. *Morbidity and Mortality Weekly Report, 64*(13), 351–356.

Williamson, A. M., & Feyer, A. M. (2000). Moderate sleep deprivation produces impairments in cognitive and motor performance equivalent to legally prescribed levels of alcohol intoxication. *Occupational and Environmental Medicine, 57,* 649–655.

Willis, D. J., DeLeon, P. H., Haldane, S., & Heldring, M. B. (2014). A policy article—personal perspectives on the public policy process: Making a difference. *Professional Psychology: Research and Practice, 45,* 143–151.

Willoughby, K. A., Desrocher, M., Levine, B., & Rovet, J. F. (2012). Episodic and semantic autobiographical memory and everyday memory during late childhood and early adolescence. *Frontiers in Psychology, 3.* http://dx.doi.org/10.3389/fpsyg.2012.00053

Willyard, C. (2008). Hungry for sleep. *Nature Medicine, 14,* 477–480.

Willyard, C. (2011). Men: A growing minority. *gradPSYCH Magazine, 9,* 40–44.

Wilson, B. A., Baddeley, A. D., & Kapur, N. (1995). Dense amnesia in a professional musician following herpes simplex virus encephalitis. *Journal of Clinical and Experimental Neuropsychology, 17,* 668–681.

Wilson, B. A., Kopelman, M., & Kapur, N. (2008). Prominent and persistent loss of past awareness in amnesia: Delusion, impaired consciousness or coping strategy. *Neuropsychological Rehabilitation, 18,* 527–540.

Wilson, B. A., & Wearing, D. (1995). Prisoner of consciousness: A state of just awakening following herpes simplex encephalitis. In R. Campbell & M. Conway (Eds.), *Broken memories: Case studies in memory impairment* (pp. 14–30). Oxford, UK: Blackwell.

Wilson, R. S., & Bennett, D. A. (2003). Cognitive activity and risk of Alzheimer's disease. *Current Directions in Psychological Science, 12,* 87–91.

Wimber, M., Alink, A., Charest, I., Kriegeskorte, N., & Anderson, M. C. (2015). Retrieval induces adaptive forgetting of competing memories via cortical pattern suppression. *Nature Neuroscience, 18,* 582–589.

Windham, G. C., Pinney, S. M., Voss, R. W., Sjödin, A., Biro, F. M., Greenspan, L. C., … Kushi, L. H. (2015). Brominated flame retardants and other persistent organohalogenated compounds in relation to timing of puberty in a longitudinal study of girls. *Environmental Health Perspectives, 123,* 1046–1052.

Winerman, L. (2015). A double life. *Monitor on Psychology, 46*(1), 30.

Winickoff, J. P., Friebely, J., Tanski, S. E., Sherrod, C., Matt, G. E., Hovell, M. F., & McMillen, R. C. (2009). Beliefs about the health effects of "thirdhand" smoke and home smoking bans. *Pediatrics, 123,* e74–e79.

Wintermann, G.-B., Kirschbaum, C., & Petrowski, K. (2016). Predisposition or side effect of the duration: The reactivity of the HPA-axis under psychosocial stress in panic disorder. *International Journal of Psychophysiology, 107,* 9–15.

Wipfli, B., Landers, D., Nagoshi, C., & Ringenbach, S. (2011). An examination of serotonin and psychological variables in the relationship between exercise and mental health. *Scandinavian Journal of Medicine and Science in Sports, 21*(3), 474–481.

Wisniewski, P., Jia, H., Xu, H., Rossen, M. B., & Carrroll, J. M. (2015). "Preventative" vs. "reactive": How parental mediation influences teens' social media privacy behaviors. In *Proceedings of the 18th ACM Conference on Computer Supported Cooperative Work & Social Computing* (pp. 302–316). New York, NY: Association for Computing Machinery.

Witelson S., Kigar, D., & Harvey, T. (1999). The exceptional brain of Albert Einstein. *Lancet, 353,* 2149–2153.

Witelson, S. F., Kigar, D. L., Scamvougeras, A., Kideckel, D. M., Buck, B., Stanchev, P. L., … Black, S. (2008). Corpus callosum anatomy in right-handed homosexual and heterosexual men. *Archives of Sexual Behavior, 37,* 857–863.

Witte, A. V., Kerti, L., Hermannstädter, H. M., Fiebach, J. B., Schreiber, S. J., Schuchardt, J. P., … Flöel, A. (2014). Long-chain omega-3 fatty acids improve brain function and structure in older adults. *Cerebral Cortex, 24*(11), 3059–3068.

Wixted, J. T., Mickes, L., Clark, S. E., Gronlund, S. D., & Roediger, H. L. III. (2015). Initial eyewitness confidence reliably predicts eyewitness identification accuracy. *American Psychologist, 70,* 515–526.

Wobst, A. H. K. (2007). Hypnosis and surgery: Past, present, and future. *Anesthesia & Analgesia, 104,* 1199–1208.

Wodrich, D. L., & Tarbox, J. (2008). Psychoeducational implications of sex chromosome anomalies. *School Psychology Quarterly, 23,* 301–311.

Wohlfahrt-Veje, C., Korsholm Mouritsen, A., Hagen, C. P., Tinggaard, J., Grunnet Mieritz, M., Boas, M., … Main, K. M. (2016). Pubertal onset in boys and girls is influenced by pubertal timing of both parents. *The Journal of Clinical Endocrinology & Metabolism.* http://dx.doi.org/10.1210/jc.2016-1073#sthash.6PNVCAkZ.dpuf

Wojcicki, J. M., van der Straten, A., & Padian, N. (2010). Bridewealth and sexual and reproductive practices among women in Harare, Zimbabwe. *AIDS Care, 22,* 705–710.

Wolfe, U., & Ali, N. (2015). Dark adaptation and Purkinje shift: A laboratory exercise in perceptual neuroscience. *The Journal of Undergraduate Neuroscience Education, 13*(2), A59–A63.

Wolman, D. (2012, March 15). The split brain: A tale of two halves. *Nature, 483,* 260–263.

Wolpert, D. M., Goodbody, S. J., & Husain, M. (1998). Maintaining internal representations: The role of the human superior parietal lobe. *Nature Neuroscience, 1,* 529–533.

Wong, B. (2011). Point of view: Color blindness. *Nature Methods, 8,* 441.

Wood, B., Rea, M. S., Plitnick, B., & Figueiro, M. G. (2013). Light level and duration of exposure determine the impact of self-luminous tablets on melatonin suppression. *Applied Ergonomics, 44,* 237–240.

Wood, E., Zivcakova, L., Gentile, P., Archer, K., De Pasquale, D., & Nosko, A. (2011). Examining the impact of off-task multi-tasking with technology on real-time classroom learning. *Computers & Education, 58,* 365–374.

Wood, G., & Pennington, J. (1973). Encoding and retrieval from long-term storage. *Journal of Experimental Psychology, 99,* 243–254.

Wood, W., & Eagly, A. H. (2002). A cross-cultural analysis of the behavior of women and men: Implications for the origins of sex differences. *Psychological Bulletin, 128,* 699–727.

Wood, W., & Eagly, A. H. (2015). Two traditions of research on gender identity. *Sex Roles, 73,* 461–473.

Woon, T.-H., Masuda, M., Wagner, N. N., & Holmes, T. H. (1971). The social readjustment rating scale: A cross-cultural study of Malaysians and Americans. *Journal of Cross-Cultural Psychology, 2,* 373–386.

Workowski, K. A., & Bolan, G. A. (2015). Sexually transmitted diseases treatment guidelines, 2015. *Centers for Disease Control and Prevention MMWR Recommendations and Reports, 64,* 1–138.

World Health Organization. (2008). Table A2, Burden of disease in DALYs by cause, sex and income group in WHO regions, estimates for 2004. In *The global burden of disease: 2004 update.* Retrieved from http://www.who.int/healthinfo/global_burden_disease/GBD_report_2004update_AnnexA.pdf

World Health Organization. (2015). *Hearing loss due to recreational exposure to loud sounds: A review.* Retrieved from http://apps.who.int/iris/bitstream/10665/154589/1/9789241508513_eng.pdf

World Health Organization. (2016a). *Obesity and overweight.* Retrieved from http://www.who.int/mediacentre/factsheets/fs311/en/#dx.doi.org/10.1037/tra0000148

World Health Organization. (2016b). *UNAIDS: Global facts & figures.* Retrieved from http://www.unaids.org/sites/default/files/media_asset/UNAIDS_FactSheet_en.pdf

World Memory Sports Council. (2016a). *World memory statistics: Discipline: 5 minute random words.* Retrieved June 28, 2016, from http://www.world-memory-statistics.com/discipline.php–id=WORDS5

World Memory Sports Council. (2016b). *World memory statistics: Official world records.* Retrieved June 28, 2016, from http://www.world-memory-statistics.com/disciplines.php

Worringham, C. J., & Messick, D. M. (1983). Social facilitation of running: An unobtrusive study. *Journal of Social Psychology, 121,* 23–29.

Wray, N. R., Pergadia, M. L., Blackwood, D. H. R., Penninx, B. W. J. H., Gordon, S. D., Nyholt, D. R., … Smit, J. H. (2012). Genome-wide association study of major depressive disorder: New results, meta-analysis, and lessons learned. *Molecular Psychiatry, 17,* 36–48.

Wright, K. (2002). The times of our lives. *Scientific American, 287,* 59–65.

Wright, K. P., Bogan, R. K., & Wyatt, J. K. (2013). Shift work and the assessment and management of shift work disorder (SWD). *Sleep Medicine Reviews, 17,* 41–54.

Wyatt, T. D. (2015). The search for human pheromones: The lost decades and the necessity of returning to first principles. *Proceedings of the Royal Society B, 282,* 20142994. doi:10.1098/rspb.2014.2994

Xu, H., Wen, L. M., Hardy, L. L., & Rissel, C. (2016). Associations of outdoor play and screen time with nocturnal sleep duration and pattern among young children. *Acta Paediatrica, 105,* 297–303.

Xu, J., Gannon, P. J., Emmorey, K., Smith, J. F., & Braun, A. R. (2009). Symbolic gestures and spoken language are processed by a common neural system. *Proceedings of the National Academy of Sciences, USA, 106,* 20664–20669.

Xu, M., Chung, S., Zhang, S., Zhong, P., Ma, C., Chang, W.-C., … Dan, Y. (2015). Basal forebrain circuit for sleep–wake control. *Nature Neuroscience, 18,* 1641–1647.

Yalom, I. D., & Leszcz, M. (2005). *The theory and practice of group psychotherapy* (5th ed.). New York, NY: Basic Books.

Yamagata, S., Suzuki, A., Ando, J., Ono, Y., Kijima, N., Yoshimura, K., ... Jang, K. (2006). Is the genetic structure of human personality universal? A cross-cultural twin study from North America, Europe, and Asia. *Journal of Personality and Social Psychology, 90,* 987–998.

Yanchar, S. C., Slife, B. D., & Warne, R. (2003). Critical thinking as disciplinary practice. *Review of General Psychology, 12,* 265–281.

Yee, E., & Thompson-Schill, S. L. (2016). Putting concepts into context. *Psychonomic Bulletin & Review, 23,* 1015–1027.

Yee, M., & Brown, R. (1994). The development of gender differentiation in young children. *British Journal of Social Psychology, 33,* 183–196.

Yetish, G., Kaplan, H., Gurven, M., Wood, B., Pontzer, H., Manger, P. R., ... Siegel, J. M. (2015). Natural sleep and its seasonal variations in three pre-industrial societies. *Current Biology, 25*(21), 2862–2868.

Yolken, R. H., & Torrey, E. F. (1995). Viruses, schizophrenia, and bipolar disorder. *Clinical Microbiology Reviews, 8,* 131–145.

Yoon, S., Kim, J. E., Kim, G. H., Kang, H. J., Kim, B. R., Jeon, S., ... Lyoo, I. K. (2016). Subregional shape alterations in the amygdala in patients with panic disorder. *PLOS ONE, 11,* e0157856.

Young, M. E., Mizzau, M., Mai, N. T., Sirisegaram, A., & Wilson, M. (2009). Food for thought. What you eat depends on your sex and eating companions. *Appetite, 53,* 268–271.

Young-Bruehl, E. (2009). Women and children first! *Modern Psychoanalysis, 34,* 52–74.

Youngstedt, S. D., & Kline, C. E. (2006). Epidemiology of exercise and sleep. *Sleep and Biological Rhythms, 4,* 215–221.

Yu, C. K. C. (2015). One hundred typical themes in most recent dreams, diary dreams, and dreams spontaneously recollected from last night. *Dreaming, 25,* 206–219.

Yu, C. K. C., & Fu, W. (2011). Sex dreams, wet creams, and nocturnal emissions. *Dreaming, 21,* 197–212.

Yu, D., Ponomarev, A., & Davis, R. L. (2004). Altered representation of the spatial code for odors after olfactory classical conditioning: Memory trace formation by synaptic recruitment. *Neuron, 42,* 437–449.

Yuhas, D. (2013, March/April). Is cocoa the brain drug of the future? *Scientific American Mind, 24,* 16–17.

Yuhas, D., & Jabr, F. (2012, June 13). Know your neurons: What is the ratio of glia to neurons in the brain? [Web log post]. Retrieved from http://blogs.scientificamerican.com/brainwaves/2012/06/13/know-your-neurons-what-is-the-ratio-of-glia-to-neurons-in-the-brain/

Yule, G. (1996). *Pragmatics.* Oxford, UK: Oxford University Press.

Zacks, J. M. (2015, February 13). Why movie "facts" prevail. *The New York Times.* Retrieved from http://www.nytimes.com/2015/02/15/opinion/sunday/why-movie-facts-prevail.html?_r=0

Zafeiriou, D. I. (2004). Primitive reflexes and postural reactions in the neurodevelopmental examination. *Pediatric Neurology, 31,* 1–8.

Zajonc, R. B. (1980). Feeling and thinking: Preferences need no inferences. *American Psychologist, 35,* 151–175.

Zajonc, R. B. (1984). On the primacy of affect. *American Psychologist, 39,* 117–123.

Zaretskii, V. K. (2009). The zone of proximal development: What Vygotsky did not have time to write. *Journal of Russian and East European Psychology, 47,* 70–93.

Zell, E., Krizan, Z., & Teeter, S. R. (2015). Evaluating gender similarities and differences using metasynthesis. *American Psychologist, 70,* 10–20.

Zhang, J., Brackbill, D., Yang, S., & Centola, D. (2015). Efficacy and causal mechanism of an online social media intervention to increase physical activity: Results of a randomized controlled trial. *Preventive Medicine Reports, 2,* 651–657.

Zhang, L., Dong, Y., Doyon, W. M, & Dani, J. A. (2012). Withdrawal from chronic nicotine exposure alters dopamine signaling dynamics in the nucleus accumbens. *Biological Psychiatry, 71,* 184–191.

Zhang, T.-Y., & Meaney, M. J. (2010). Epigenetics and the environmental regulation of the genome and its function. *Annual Review of Psychology, 61,* 439–466.

Zhang, Y., Picetti, R., Butelman, E. R., Schlussman, S. D., Ho, A., & Kreek, J. (2009). Behavioral and neurochemical changes induced by oxycodone differ between adolescent and adult mice. *Neuropsychopharmacology, 34,* 912–922.

Zimbardo, P. (2007). *The Lucifer effect: Understanding how good people turn evil.* New York, NY: Random House.

Zimmerman, A., Bai, L., & Ginty, D. D. (2014). The gentle touch receptors of mammalian skin. *Science, 346*(6212), 950–954.

Zolotor, A. J., Theodore, A. D., Runyan, D. K., Chang, J. J., & Laskey, A. L. (2011). Corporal punishment and physical abuse: population-based trends for three-to-11-year-old children in the United States. *Child Abuse Review, 20,* 57–66.

Zosuls, K. M., Miller, C. F., Ruble, D. N., Martin, C. L., & Fabes, R. A. (2011). Gender development research in *Sex Roles:* Historical trends and future directions. *Sex Roles, 64,* 826–842.

Zuckerman, M. (1979). *Sensation seeking: Beyond the optimal level of arousal.* Hillsdale, NJ: Lawrence Erlbaum Associates.

Zuckerman, M. (1994). *Behavioral expressions and biosocial bases of sensation seeking.* Cambridge, UK: Cambridge University Press.

Zuckerman, M. (2015). Behavior and biology: Research on sensation seeking and reactions to the media. In L. Donohew, H. Sypher & E. T. Higgins (Eds.), *Communication, social cognition and affect* (pp. 173–194). Hillsdale, NJ: Psychology Press.

Name Index

Note: Page numbers followed by f indicate figures; t indicates tables; i indicates Infographics; c indicates Connections

Subject Index

Note: **Boldface** type indicates key terms; *italics* indicates features; f indicates figures; t indicates tables; i indicates Infographics; c indicates Connections.

Ablation, 51
Abnormal behavior, 536–537, 536t
  and culture, 537–538
Abnormal psychology, 536, 536c, B-4
Absolute thresholds, 98, 98f
  of hearing, 113i
  of vision, 106
Abstraction, 282, 306i, 307
Abu Ghraib prison, 652f, 653
Accommodation [cognitive
  development], **346**
Accommodation [eye], **104**
Acculturation, 505
  and assimilation, 505, 505c
Acculturative stress, 505–506, 505f
Acetylcholine, 59i, 60, 60t
Achievement, 312
**Acquired immune deficiency syndrome
  (AIDS), 446**–447, 447f, 448i
Acquisition, 195, 220, 221t
Acronyms
  and memory improvement, 247,
    248f, 251i
Acrophobia, 548t
Across the World...
  acculturation, 505–506, 505f
  "blue zones" of health, 512
  death and dying, 370, 370f
  eating disorders, 570–571
  emotion display rules, 404–405
  happiness, 32–33, 33f
  homosexuality, 436
  personality, 484
  personality stereotypes, 484
  problem solving, 294, 294f
  sexual activity, 440–441, 441f
  social anxiety, 549, 549f
  social loafing, 643–644
  therapy, 607–608
Action potential, 55, 56i, **57**
  and neural communication, 58,
    59i
Activation–synthesis model, 166, 167f
Active listening, 589, 589t
Adaptive value, 199
Addiction. *See also* Physiological
  dependence; Psychological
  dependence
  and genes, 181
  and nature–nurture, 181
  to psychoactive drugs, 179–181
  to social media, 179
Additive model, 295–296
Adenosine, 62

ADHD. *See* Attention-deficit/
  hyperactivity disorder (ADHD)
Adler, Alfred
  and individual psychology, 469, 469f,
    471
Adolescence, 355–361. *See also*
  Developmental psychology
  and antidepressants, 602
  cognitive development in, 357, 357f
  hearing loss in, 363c
  physical development in, 356, 356f
  socioemotional development in,
    357–358
Adrenal glands, 69f, **70**
  and depression, 555
  and "fight-or-flight" response, 511i
  and sex hormones, 420
"Adrenaline junkies." *See* Sensation-
  seeking
Adulthood, 362–371. *See also*
  Developmental psychology
  cognitive development in, 364–366,
    365f
  emerging, 361
  physical development in, 363–364,
    363f, 364f
  socioemotional development in,
    366–369
Advertising. *See also* Media
  and classical conditioning, 202–203,
    202t, 203f
  and food portion size, 392
  and gaining compliance, 634–635,
    635f
  and scent marketing, 118–119
  and subliminal stimuli, 100
Affective aspect of attitudes, 627, 627f,
  650i
Affective well-being, 388, 388f
  and uplifts, 507c
Afferent neurons. *See* Sensory neurons
Afterimages, 109–110, 109f
Aggression, 647–**648**
  and amygdala, 83–84
  and antidepressants, 602
  and antisocial personality disorder,
    566, 567t
  and chronic traumatic
    encephalopathy (CTE), 273,
    301
  and culture, 422–423, 648, 648c
  direct, 648
  and endocrine system, 61, 69,
    177c

and gender, 422–423, 648, 648c
and genital stage, 465t, 466
heritability of, 422c
and limbic system, 83–84
and the media, 32, 223, 225
naturalistic observations of, 27–28
and observational learning,
  223–224
and polygenetic inheritance, 335
and poverty, 504
and psychoactive drugs, 169, 171
and psychoanalysis, 585, 587c
and psychological disorders, 539
and red, 128
relational *vs.* physical, 422, 648
and socioeconomic status, 504
and spanking, 218–219
and third variables, 32
and twin studies, 648, 648c
and Type A personality, 523
Aging, 368
  and sexual activity, 440
  and subliminal stimuli, 368c
Agonists, 59i, 62
Agoraphobia, 546t, **548**
Agreeableness dimension of personality,
  481, 481f, 482t
"Aha" moments. *See* Insight
AIDS. *See* Acquired immune deficiency
  syndrome (AIDS)
Ainsworth, Mary
  and attachment, 352–353
AIS. *See* Androgen insensitivity syndrome
  (AIS)
Alarm stage of stress response, 510,
  511i
Alcohol, 171–173, 172f, 173f, 181t
  abuse of, 171–173, 172f, 173f
  and aversion therapy, 592i, 594
  in combination with barbiturates,
    170i
  and gender, 172f
  and health, 172–173, 172f
  as psychoactive drug, 169
  and self-help groups, 609
  and sexual activity, 171
  and sleep, 163
  and stress, 516–517, 516f
  as teratogen, 337–338, 337t, 338f
Algorithms, 290, 291i
All-or-none, 57
Allport, Gordon
  and personality, 480, 481
Alpha waves, 154, 155i

Altered states of consciousness,
  149
Altruism, 24, 654–655
  kin, 436
  and nature–nurture, 25f
  and stress management, 528, 528f,
    654c
Alzheimer, Alois
  and neuropathology, 271
Alzheimer's disease, 271
  and acetylcholine, 60
  and diet, 85
  and exercise, 34f, 364
  and nature–nurture, 271–272
  and neuroimaging, 20f
Ambivalent attachment, 352
Amenorrhea, 570
American Psychiatric Association (APA)
  and DSM-5, 540, 542i
  and electroconvulsive therapy, 605,
    606c
  and overuse of drugs, 180
  and term "addiction," 179
  and term "gender," 418
  and term "intersexual," 418
  and term "transsexual," 430
American Psychological Association
  (APA), 4
  and citation style, 4f
  and critical thinking, 17
  and degrees in psychology, B-1–B-2
  and people-first language, 539
  and psychoanalysis, 11f, 582
  and repressed memories, 263
  and research ethics, 40, 41t
  and stress surveys, 499i
  and terminology related to sexuality,
    418, 430
  women in, 11
American Sign Language (ASL), 305,
  307, 307f
Ames Room illusion, 129i
Amnesia, 265–267, 266f. *See also*
  Alzheimer's disease; Chronic
  traumatic encephalopathy (CTE)
  and electroconvulsive therapy, 606,
    606c
  and hypnotism, 182
  infantile, 269
  and priming, 253
  transient global, 498, 501
Amniotic sac, 336
Amphetamines, 174
Amplitude, 103

INTRODUCING THE INFOGRAPHICS: Full-page visual presentations of each chapter's most challenging concepts